FILM NOIR

An Encyclopedic Reference
to the American Style

FILM NOIR

Revised & Expanded Edition

Edited by Alain Silver and Elizabeth Ward

Co-Editors: Carl Macek and Robert Porfirio

Co-Editor Third Edition: James Ursini

THE OVERLOOK PRESS
Woodstock, New York

ACKNOWLEDGMENTS

Numerous persons whose names do not appear here have contributed indirectly since the First Edition appeared, in many instances only through expressions of enthusiasm about this book which has helped those responsible for it to sustain their own interest over more than a decade. For their invaluable assistance in viewing additional files that were otherwise unavailable from the Classical Period, our thanks to the Mark Haggard Archives of Sherman Oaks, and to Lee Sanders and Glenn Erickson. For helping define Neo-Noir and offering numerous suggestions: Todd Erickson. For final proofing: Tina Harris-Rougette. Other helpful comments and assistance came from filmmakers, among them directors John Flynn, Kurt Voss, Robert Wise, Carl Colpaert, Walter Hill, and Mark Rutland; producers Zane Levitt, Lawrence Bender, Dan Hassid, Alexander W. Korgan, Jr., and Dan Ireland. For putting up with countless hours of videotape, all too often featuring screams and gunshots late into the night, a special thank you to Linda Brookover.

As before, the research on this edition would have been much harder to accomplish without the existence of the Margaret Herrick Library of the Academy of Motion Picture Arts and Sciences and its most helpful staff. Additional research was done at the Beverly Hills Public Library.

First published in 1979 by
The Overlook Press, Peter Mayer Publishers, Inc.

OVERLOOK • DUCKWORTH

NEW YORK:
141 Wooster Street
New York, NY 10012

WOODSTOCK:
One Overlook Drive
Woodstock, NY 12498
www.overlookpress.com
[for individual orders, bulk and special sales, contact our Woodstock office]
Third Edition first published in 1992

LONDON:
90-93 Cowcross Street
London, EC1M 6BF
inquiries@duckworth-publishers.co.uk
www.ducknet.co.uk

Library of Congress Cataloguing-in-Publication Data

Film Noir : Third Edition

Bibliography p.
Includes Index
Moving pictures — United States. 2. Moving picture plays — History and criticism. 3. Moving pictures — Plots, themes, etc.
I. Silver, Alain, 1947- II. Ward, Elizabeth, 1952-

PN1993.5.U6F5   791.43'0909'12   88-062182

Printed in the United States of America
ISBN-10: 0-87951-479-5 / ISBN 13: 978-0-87951-479-2

10 9 8 7 6

CONTENTS

CONTRIBUTORS

A.S.

ALAIN SILVER. Other books include *The Samurai Film* (2nd Edition, Overlook press, 1983); with James Ursini *David Lean and His Films* (2nd Edition, Silman-James, 1992), and *The Vampire Film* (Barnes, 1974); and with Elizabeth Ward *Raymond Chandler's Los Angeles* (Overlook, 1987), *The Film Director's Team* (2nd edition, Silman-James, 1992), and *Robert Aldrich* (G.K. Hall, 1979). Articles include contributions to *Film Comment, Movie (U.K.), Photon, Literature/Film Quarterly, Wide Angle* and the Los Angeles *Times*. Ph.D. in motion picture history and criticism, University of California, Los Angeles. Producer, production manager, and assistant director on numerous feature and television productions since 1977.

B.L.

BLAKE LUCAS. Freelance writer. Completing a critical study of the films of Vincente Minnelli, of which one chapter has been published by *Film Notebooks* (University of California at Santa Cruz, 1978). Contributor to the Los Angeles County Museum of Art film programs, notably the 1978 series of the films of Raoul Walsh.

B.P.

BOB PORFIRIO. Formerly Assistant Professor of American Studies at California State University, Fullerton. Ph.D from Yale University with a dissertation entitled, "The Dark Age of American Film: A Study of American Film Noir (1940-1960.)" Articles in contributions to *Continuum, Literature/Film Quarterly,* and *Sight and Sound,* most notably the oft-cited essay, "No Way Out: Existential Motifs in Film Noir."

C.M.

CARL MACEK. Books include *The Complete Star Wars* (Ballantine, 1978). Former Editor of *Mediascene* magazine, director of the Archive of Popular Culture, California State University, Fullerton, and supervising producer of several television series for Harmony Gold Productions. Currently free-lance writer and director of the motion picture distribution company, Streamline Pictures. Graduate, media department, C.S.U.F.

D.L.W.

DENNIS L. WHITE. Freelance writer, publisher, and hotel bellman. Oral history interview with W.R. Burnett (American Film Institute).

E.K.

ELLEN KENESHEA. Freelance film editor and writer. Published articles include contributions to *Women In Film*. M.J., University of California at Los Angeles, Journalism. M.A., University of California at Los Angeles, motion picture history and criticism.

E.M.

EILEEN McGARRY. Freelance writer. Completing a doctoral dissertation for University of California at Los Angeles on the films of Sergio Leone.

E.W.

ELIZABETH WARD. Other books include, with Alain Silver, *Raymond Chandler's Los Angeles* (Overlook, 1987), *The Film Director's Team* (2nd edition, Silman-James, 1992), and *Robert Aldrich* (G.K. Hall, 1979). Freelance writer and researcher, with articles for *Movie, Dialogue on Film,* and the Los Angeles *Times*, as well as director, assistant director, stage manager, production coordinator, and still photographer in motion picture, television, and music video productions since 1978. Graduate of the UCLA Motion Picture/Television department.

G.E.

GLENN ERICKSON Free-lance writer and trailer advertising editor with a background in feature film editorial and special effects. Co-author of *The Making of 1941* (Ballantine, 1980). Graduate of the University of California, Los Angeles.

J.B.

JONATHAN BENAIR. Freelance television writer, contributor to "America Tonight." Published articles include contributions to *Film Society* and *Phonograph Record*. Member of the programming staff, Los Angeles County Museum of Art, Film Department.

CONTRIBUTORS

J.C.

JOAN COHEN. Assistant Director of Film Programs, Los Angeles County Museum of Art. Formerly Library Assistant at the American Film Institute, Center for Advanced Film Studies. Published articles include contributions to *Mankind, Choice, AFI Report.* Freelance research includes contributions to *Child Stars* by Diana Carey. Graduate, University of California at Berkeley, English Department.

J.K.

JULIE KIRGO. Television story editor for "One Day at a Time." Television writing includes scripts for "Welcome Back, Kotter" and "Paper Chase." Formerly publicist at Universal Studios; assistant editor for *TV Guide.* Graduate, Harvard University, History and Literature Department.

J.P.

JAMES PARIS. Senior Partner of Desktop Marketing Corporation, Los Angeles. Numerous articles on information processing for trade periodicals, *Marketing News* and *American Demographics.* Graduate, Dartmouth College, English Department

J.U.

JAMES URSINI. Books include *Preston Sturges: An American Dreamer* (Curtis, 1972), and with Alain Silver *The Vampire Film* and *David Lean and His Films.* Researcher for the American Film Institute Life Achievement Award Programs (1981-1985) and the film Tango Bar. Articles include contributions to *Mediascene, Photon, Cinema* (U.S.). and *Cinefantastique.* Writer of educational and documentary films for school districts and public broadcasting. Oral Historian: John F. Seitz, Paramount Studios (American Film Institute). M.A. in Film History/Criticism, UCLA, 1971. Instructor in Theater Arts and English at university, community college, and secondary levels.

L.S.

LEE SANDERS. Motion picture projectionist. Freelance writer. Coordinator of several film series for colleges and clubs. Contributor to Los Angeles County Art Museum film programs.

M.B.

MEREDITH BRODY. Director of development for A-Team Productions. Formerly assistant to John Milius productions. Graduate, University of Southern California Film School.

T.T.

TRACEY THOMPSON. Senior cataloguer, Film Department, Museum of Modern Art, New York City. Research assistant for *Motion Pictures, Television and Radio: A Union Catalogue of Manuscript and Special Collections in the Western United States* (Boston: G.K. Hall, 1978). M.A., New York University, Cinema Studies.

W.R.E.

WILL R. EVANS. Freelance writer. M.A., U.C.L.A. Motion Picture History and Criticism.

Research Assistants

ROBERTA M. WARD. Freelance writer and researcher.

RICHARD PRINCE. Co-producer of several television episodes of "That's Hollywood." Assistant director of motion pictures and television. M.B.A., University of California at Los Angeles, Arts Management. Graduate, University of California at Los Angeles, Motion Picture and Television Production Department.

DEBRA BERGMAN. Freelance writer, researcher, and script supervisor. Research assistant at the Academy of Motion Picture Arts and Sciences. Graduate, Syracuse University Film Department.

INTRODUCTION

With the Western, film noir shares the distinction of being an indigenous American form. Unlike Westerns, noir films have no precise antecedents either in terms of a well-defined literary genre or a period in American history. As a result, what may be termed the noir cycle has a singular position in the brief history of American motion pictures: a body of films that not only presents a cohesive vision of America but that does so in a manner transcending the influences of *auteurism* or genre. Film noir is grounded neither in personal creation nor in translation of another tradition into film terms. Rather it is a self-contained reflection of American cultural preoccupations in film form. In short, it is the unique example of a wholly American film style.

That may seem a substantial claim to make for a group of films whose plots frequently turn on deadly violence or sexual obsession, whose catalogue of characters includes numbers of down-and-out private eyes, desperate women, and petty criminals. Nor does the visceral unease felt by a viewer who watches a shadowy form move across a lonely street or who hears the sound of car tires creeping over wet asphalt automatically translate into sociological assertions about paranoia or postwar guilt. At the same time, it is clear that the emergence of film noir coincides with these and other popular sentiments at large in America. "Film noir" is literally "black film," not just in the sense of being full of physically dark images, nor of reflecting a dark mood in American society, but equally, almost empirically, as a black slate on which the culture could inscribe its ills and in the process produce a catharsis to help relieve them.

This is not to claim that film noir is without antecedents of any sort. To begin with, it may seem strange for a group of films indigenously American to be identified by a French term. This is simply because French critics were the first to discern particular aspects in a number of American productions initially released in France after World War II. They also noticed a thematic resemblance between these motion pictures and certain novels published under the generic title of "Serie Noire." "Serie Noire" and its later publishing competitor, "Fleuve Noire" use the French word for "black" to designate a type of detective fiction. As it happens, the majority of the "Serie Noire" titles were translations of American novels and featured the work of such authors as Hammett, Chandler, James M. Cain, and Horace McCoy. The association between such films as *Double Indemnity, Murder My Sweet,* or *The Postman Always Rings Twice* and the "Serie Noire" novels—which was discussed in a typical article in 1946 under the title: "Americans also make 'noir' films"[1]—was all the more apparent because such films were adapted from, and occasionally by, authors who figured prominently in the "Serie Noire" catalogue.

Equally obvious was the fact that the narratives of these noir films possessed an economy of expression and a graphic impact substantially different from the hard-boiled novels or the pulp short stories of the *Black Mask* magazine from which they may have been derived. Certainly that genre of writing, as well as the social realism of the American theater in the 1920s and 1930s or the proletarian literature of the same period, reflects many of the stylistic and cultural preoccupations from which film noir ultimately emerged. But film noir is equally, if not more significantly, a product of other mediating influences, of social, economic, technical, and even aesthetic developments that preceded its inception.

[1]Jean Pierre Chartier, *La Revue du Cinema,* V. I, no. 3 (November 1946). The actual invention of the term "film noir" is attributed to cineaste Nino Frank earlier in 1946.

INTRODUCTION

The first two areas are powerful yet indirect in their influence on film noir. Both the social upheaval of World War II and the sociopathy on a smaller scale of American gangsterism in the decade preceding it created a class of individuals that would frequently be depicted in film noir. From the latter came the film stereotype of the ambitious criminal and his corrupt organizations; from the war, in considerably greater number, came the veteran and his burden of readjustment to civilian life.

The film industry began its exploitation of the gangster myth in the 1920s and developed it to its fullest extent as a genre in the following decade. By transmuting contemporary figures and events, the gangster films of the 1930s rapidly defined a genre that was grounded in social verisimilitude but elaborated through such violent icons as tommy guns and fast cars. The criminal archetype that emerged was romanticized in response to an undercurrent of social alienation: By ingenuity and daring the individual achieved power and success. Simplistically, the cause of such a figure's destruction was usually reduced to a megalomaniac loss of self-control. In short, the gangster most often perished from the consequences of his own excesses.

Such a figure, in its initial stages, antedates the noir sensibility to some extent. But whereas the gangster is a chaotic element ultimately eradicated by the forces of social order, the truly noir figure more often represents the perspective of normality assailed by the twists of fate of an irrational universe. The soldier returned from combat falls midway between these categories. In the underlying irony of film noir, the viewer realizes from convention that the war veterans depicted in such diverse films as *Somewhere in the Night, Ride the Pink Horse,* and *The Blue Dahlia* have undergone physical and emotional changes that alter their perceptions of civilian society. At the same time, the expressive components of film noir compel the viewer—in a manner the gangster film never could—to participate actively in that character's distorted point-of-view. Various background elements are recruited to mask this effect. In *Ride the Pink Horse* the unfamiliar Western locale and the ingenuous denizens of the carousel constantly reinforce the uneasiness of the urban man, Gagin. In *The Blue Dahlia,* the severely disturbed Buzz, with his shrapnel-damaged skull and psychotic aversion to "monkey music," makes the sexual estrangement and violence of Johnny Morrison seem normal in comparison. An even more obvious cipher for the difficulties of readjustment is the amnesiac ex-Marine, George Taylor, in *Somewhere in the Night.* His loss of memory and identity is an absolute metaphor for the inability of the noir hero to distinguish between benign and malign as he moves through the complex noir underworld.

Foremost in the list of socio-political developments that influences the post-World War II film industry are McCarthyism and nuclear weapons. The effect of the former has been well documented. The resultant blacklists altered or aborted careers in all phases of motion picture production; but of the actors, writers, directors, and producers associated primarily with film noir—such as Garfield, Polonsky,

Losey, and Dmytryk—an inordinately large number were affected. The potential hazards of the atomic bomb and, after 1949, the threat of nuclear war may have been depicted most explicitly in the scores of radioactive monsters raised from the depths or the visions of Armageddon produced in the science fiction genre; but such concepts also altered the narratives of film noir. In fact, McCarthyism and the specter of the Bomb became the unspoken inspirations for a leitmotif of fear or, more specifically, paranoia that resounded through the noir cycle after the war. *Pitfall, Night and the City, The Pretender, Out of the Past, Nightfall*—all are typical in their depiction of frightened, fugitive characters struggling to survive. While a manifest treatment of McCarthyism was for obvious reasons not possible, the parallels between congressional Red hunts and the actions of a frenzied lynch mob in films like *Try and Get Me* were underscored by film-makers like Cy Enfield, who susequently left the country under blacklist. Two motion pictures directed by Robert Aldrich most clearly invoke the portent of nuclear power. In *World for Ransom,* a nuclear physicist is kidnapped so that his knowledge may be sold to the highest bidder among various competing nations. In *Kiss Me Deadly* forces vie for a hot box containing a primordial mystery, the "great whatsit," which proves to be radioactive material that triggers a literally explosive conclusion. *Kiss Me Deadly* is unique in its direct identification of the unstable noir underworld with the elemental instability of fissionable matter. Such an association creates a powerful metaphoric statement in that particular film; but the converse is also true: The unstable universe depicted in so many noir films is a continual reflection of the tremendous cultural apprehension focused on both the "Red menace" and the chances of nuclear devastation.

Several other mediating forces within the film industry helped to perpetuate and enlarge the noir cycle after the war. The gradual demise of the B or program picture supported by block-booking compelled the major studios to produce less expensive films that would appeal to exhibitors on their own merits. In such a context, film noir with a record of favorable audience response and a potential for being profitably promoted on the basis of sensational and/or violent content became a preferred stock. A number of technical innovations further supported film noir's growing appeal. More sensitive, fine-grain negatives, high speed lenses, smaller camera dollies, and portable power supplies, all perfected during World War II, alleviated many of the logistical problems previously connected with location filming. The location work in such productions as *Thieves' Highway, T-Men, Naked City,* and *White Heat* demonstrated that noir films could be made not only with greater verisimilitude but also with greater economy. Novel location methods also permitted such striking sequences as the aerial shot that opens *They Live by Night* or the packing plant robbery in *Gun Crazy.*

Studio sets were still used, of course, but even within them film-makers could exploit the new technology for stylistic effect. Fritz Lang, in discussing the camera movement in *The Blue Gardenia,* asserted that the film's fluid tracking shots, which relentlessly pursue his guilt-ridden heroine, could not have been executed without the compact crab dolly. The detailed exterior night work in *Kiss Me Deadly*, repeatedly framing its protagonist against dark structures and flashing street lights, is a conspicuous example of expressive implementation of higher speed lenses and film stock. Handheld camerawork in that same film, or ten years earlier in the fight sequences of *Body and Soul*, underscore at yet another level that sense of instability so central to the noir vision.

In an industry where postwar economics dictated recycling of existing sets, exploiting stock film libraries, and generally minimizing shooting times, the flexibility of film noir made it a fiscally sounder proposition than many other types of motion picture. Film noir already had an established emphasis on low-key lighting. The influx of foreign directors and other craftsmen before and during World War II—most notably the German "refugees": Fritz Lang, Robert Siodmak, Max Ophuls, William Dieterle, Billy Wilder, Otto Preminger—had previously helped to refine film noir's distinctive visual style. That was not merely low-key photography, but the full heritage of German Expressionism: moving camera; oddly angled shots; a chiaroscuro frame inscribed with wedges of light or shadowy mazes, truncated by foreground objects, or punctuated with glinting headlights bounced off mirrors, wet surfaces, or the polished steel of a gun barrel. The years of production immediately after the war, with film more able to incorporate exterior locales, more mobile cameras, and more film-makers, both foreign and domestic, ready to test the limits of technical innovations, became the most visually homogeneous of the entire noir cycle. In a random selection of productions, such as *The Big Clock* (Paramount), *Cry of the City* (Fox), *Strangers on a Train* (Warners), *The People Against O'Hara* (MGM), *Out of the Past* (RKO), *Criss Cross* (Universal), and *Dead Reckoning* (Columbia), seven different directors and cinematographers, of great and small technical reputations, working at seven different studios, completed seven ostensibly unrelated motion pictures with one cohesive visual style.

Such a cohesion is clearly not totally coincidental; but there is no express chain of causality leading up to it. Visual experimentation in the gangster and horror genres at Warner Brothers and Universal respectively during the 1930s broadened the number of film-making personnel familiar with exterior and low-key photography. At RKO the seminal impact of the Welles/Toland collaboration on *Citizen Kane* (1941) gave later directors, cinematographers, and designers access to a wide range of previously unproven visual methods. But film noir's visual integrity ultimately puts more in question than the vestigial influences of German Expressionism or the earliest manifestations of technological advances, whether by individual film-makers or studio staffs. At the root of the issue is the simple consideration of what binds film noir together. Unlike any number of genres which antedate it, the noir cycle does not possess a ready catalogue of icons—it has none of the recurrent paraphernalia of the cowboy, the soldier, or the

supernatural being. At another level, the expressive conventions of film noir are not used to engender or fulfill a set of key genre expectations analogous to those in the Western, war, or horror film. To elaborate, there is nothing intrinsic in side-light or a moving camera that connotes such qualities as alienation, obsession, or paranoia in the manner that a tied-down pistol may imply a gunfight, a drone of planes, an air raid, or marks on the neck, a vampire. Film noir does exhibit certain relationships between elements of style—not icons—and narrative events or character sentiments. A side-lit close-up may reveal a face, half in shadow, half in light, at the precise narrative moment of indecision. A sustained moving camera may forge a visual link between characters or events simultaneously with a parallel narrative connection. But such relationships between image and narrative only lead to the same abstractions, which are basically generalizations of protagonists' mental states; and such generalizations do not evoke a generic milieu equivalent to the war, the West, or the supernatural.

If the relationship of film noir to genre is a tenuous one at best, how then is the cycle to be classified? Film noir could be termed a group movement like its contemporary, Italian Neorealism, or its antecedent, German Expressionism. Those film movements are normally defined as a group of film-makers who share political and/or aesthetic beliefs and demonstrate a common stylistic approach. The noir cycle evidently possesses the latter quality and, to an arguable extent, the former also; but it does not supersede generic constructs or display a narrative diversity in the manner of these other movements, which may encompass war films as well as psychological melodramas and may range from the horrific to the comic. While it may not be a genre nor wholly a movement in these traditional senses, the characteristics of film noir are fairly apparent and straightforward. It is contemporaneous, usually urban, and almost always American in setting. The few exceptions involve either urban men in a rural locale or Americans abroad. There is a narrative assumption that only natural forces are in play: extraordinary occurrences are either logically elucidated or left unexplained—no metaphysical values are adopted. Finally, the noir cycle's consistent visual style is keyed specifically to recurrent narrative patterns and character emotions. Because these patterns and emotions are repeatedly suggestive of certain abstractions, such as alienation or obsession, it may seem that film noir is overly dependent on external constructions, such as Existentialism or Freudianism, for its dramatic meanings. Irrefutably, film noir does recruit the ethical and philosophical values of the culture as freely as it recruits visual conventions, iconic notations, or character types from other extrinsic sources. The results of such a process are neither aesthetically invalid nor structurally amorphous. Such a process does, however, enrich and dislocate the noir cycle as a phenomenon and does so in a way that resists facile explication.

The most consistent aspect of film noir, apart from its visual style, is its protagonists. If a usable definition of the noir protagonist is to be formulated, it must encompass two key character motifs. Of the two, alienation is perhaps the more intrinsic. The examples are certainly multiform from the ostensibly ordinary people in *Side Street* and *The Big Night* to the driven war vets in *Thieves' Highway* and *Ride the Pink Horse* to the explicitly psychotic figures in *The Dark Mirror* and *The Dark Past*. The darkness that fills the mirror or the past, which lurks in a dark corner or obscures a dark passage out of the oppressively dark city, is not merely the key adjective of so many film noir titles but the obvious metaphor for the condition of the progatonist's mind. As these figures struggle through their particular dark night of the soul, alienation is the common factor, the narrative constant that binds together the policeman (*The Big Heat*) and the criminal (*This Gun for Hire*); the psychologist (*Woman in the Window*) and the mental patient (*The Night Runner*); the rich and famous (*Mr. Arkadin*) and the poor and unknown (*Try and Get Me*); the doctors (*Where Danger Lives*), lawyers (*Force of Evil; Party Girl*), sideshow performers (*Nightmare Alley; Gun Crazy*), private detectives (*Murder My Sweet; Kiss Me Deadly*), boxers (*Body and Soul; The Set-Up*), newspapermen (*Scandal Sheet; Call Northside 777*), salesmen (*Double Indemnity*), seers (*Night Has a Thousand Eyes*), and even screenwriters (*In a Lonely Place*). While the individual plots must dictate the particular events entrapping the protagonists, the anguished expression of Bradford Galt in *The Dark Corner* is prototypical: "I feel all dead inside. I'm backed up in a dark corner, and I don't know who's hitting me."

With its simple, graphic language, Galt's statement captures the basic emotion of the noir figure. The assailant is not a person but an unseen force. The pain is more often mental than physical: the plunge into spiritual darkness, the sense of being "dead inside." For Galt in his dark corner the mere fact of being outside the law is neither new nor terrifying. It is the loss of order, the inability either to discover or to control the underlying causes of his distress, that is mentally intolerable. The narrative position of Galt, the ex-con, like that of the returning veterans is made all the more ironic because of the scorn and egocentricity with which he initially confronts postwar society. As he senses the ground being cut from beneath him, Galt's cynicism quickly gives way to desperation. Many, if not most, noir figures from Eddie Taylor in *You Only Live Once* (1937) to Phil Gaines in *Hustle* (1975) may seem more acutely despondent or alienated because they have been idealistic or romantic. Even as fallen idealists or estranged romantics, their responses to being thrown into Galt's "dark corner" betray some residue of their initial positive social attitudes. If it also seems that events must conspire to crush these positive inclinations in men like Taylor or Gaines, their despair only becomes fully as ironic as Galt's when they are compelled to pause and assess their situations. While Galt ultimately penetrates the structure of his trap, others like the hapless Al Roberts in *Detour* are frustrated and finally destroyed by that structure. "Someday fate or some mysterious force can put the finger on you or me for no reason at all." Roberts' sober if somewhat self-pitying reflection

does not save him. For him or Taylor or Gaines, this moment of realization, this resignation to being annihilated by a relentless, deterministic abstraction, is the only, bitter solace that the noir vision permits.

Roberts's "mysterious force" is to some degree the film noir equivalent of an existential belief in the "benign indifference" of the material world. Camus illustrates his term for the absence of malice in the world's random causality with an observation that is very similar to Roberts's: "At any street corner, the absurd may strike a man in the face." As manifestations of the absurd, the quirks of fate that permit the hard-bitten Galt to survive while they slowly kill an equally innocent and more sympathetic figure like Frank Bigelow in *D.O.A.*—a man poisoned because he happened to notarize an incriminating bill of sale—could well exemplify a concept such as "benign indifference" at work in the noir universe. But while Camus's fictional characters experience an "existential despair" that is based on the consequences of choosing and the operation of free will, the choices of the noir protagonists are most often overwhelmed by an underlying determinism that is neither benign nor indifferent. The critical distinction is not between *Detour*'s image of a pointed finger and Camus's of a slap in the face, but between that film's dramatization of "fate" and Camus's notion of "the absurd." For absurdity in Camus's philosophy may occasionally prove perilous; but fate in the noir vision almost always becomes fatality. It could almost be said that film noir anticipates fatality. From its very titles the noir cycle uses boldface and continually points that deadly finger: Its figures are *The Accused, Abandoned, Cornered, Framed, Railroaded, Convicted, Caged,* and *Desperate*. A character who makes a *Journey into Fear* or lives *Between Midnight and Dawn, Somewhere in the Night* does so in isolation: *I Walk Alone, In a Lonely Place, On Dangerous Ground*. Ultimately, the fateful narrative patterns that precipitate the remarks of Bradford Galt and Al Roberts bring forth even simpler generalizations: Nick Blake mouthing the words of the title in *Nobody Lives Forever* or, even more direct, the Swede in *The Killers* saying, "Everybody dies. . . ." However predestined their alienation, and whether or not their awareness of their condition is truly existential, the reaction of its protagonists to these structural elements is the fundamental conflict in film noir.

There are certain characters, like Walter Neff in *Double Indemnity*, whose behavior is more classically existential because he understands from the beginning that he need not have chosen as he metaphorically puts it, to get on a "streetcar that only goes one way." Because he is subsequently enmeshed by the undesired aftereffects of his choice, Neff, unlike Galt, never escapes from his dark corner. Still as he sits in his darkened office at the film's conclusion dictating his personal narrative, Neff may begin to perceive that his choice was not so free as it seemed.

Neff is less a victim of alienation than of the second key emotion in the noir universe: obsession. To a certain extent—the extent to which it is neither rational nor predictable—obsessive behavior transcends such ordinary considerations as morality and causality. "I never cared about the money. All I wanted was you. I walked the streets of strange cities thinking about you." Steve Thompson's avowal of fidelity to his ex-wife in *Criss Cross* is indicative of the forlorn quality of the typical noir figure's obsession. In its sexuality, it may appear patently Freudian: Thompson is attached to Anna because she symbolizes not just sexual release but psychological reunion with a happier, less complicated life, i.e., a fantasy of escape from the present and its oppressive reality. The dialogue—his self-image of walking alone in strange places while lost in thoughts of her—reveals an underlying romanticism. Thompson's past with Anna seems neither metaphorically dark nor physically threatening, as are those of so many other noir figures; indeed, Thompson recalls it as the best part of his life. Nevertheless, his obsessive attachment to it does literally seal his doom from the narrative's beginning.

Certainly Thompson is not unique in the way he idealizes a particular woman. The same quasi-tragic flaw destoys other men in films as diverse as *Scarlet Street*, *Angel Face*, and *The Locket*. What these films do have in common are characters with the fatal inability to perceive the dishonesty of the women with whom they involve themselves. A different, perhaps more extreme, example would be the protagonists of *Laura* and *Woman in the Window*; for them such qualities as honesty and reciprocation of feeling cannot be important, as they are initially fascinated to the point of distraction not by actual women but by mere paintings of them. Another extreme is the male half of the fugitive couple in *Gun Crazy*, a man whose youthful fascination with firearms eventually leads into a relationship with a woman who not only shares his "gun craziness" but who also completes his initiation into the parallel worlds of eroticism and violence.

Again the overtly Freudian aspects of such relationships function as a foundation on which to construct a sequence of narrative events that typify the noir vision. Obsession, like Roberts's "mysterious force," erodes the sense of free will as it undermines the character's ability to make rational decisions. Not all the victims are entrapped by a purely sexual obsession. Unquestionably, Neff in *Double Indemnity* first considers whether he may be capable of committing murder because of his passion for Phyllis Dietrichson; but while she is mainly interested in money, Neff is clearly aware of the challenge in the act in itself, the possibility of beating the very system in which he works. Even more abstracted is a fixation like that of the detective in *Kiss Me Deadly*, who is caught up in his quest for a "great whatsit" without even knowing what it contains. Like inveterate gamblers, neither he nor Neff can resist the opportunity of "making a play" no matter how uncertain the prize. Like their alienated counterparts, the compulsive behavior of such figures can lead to sardonic, bitter, even existential, realizations. Of course, those who perish do not always do so alone. Thompson and his wife slump together in a final, lifeless union at the close of *Criss Cross*. Equally lethal is the last embrace of Neff and Phyllis in *Double Indemnity*, as they

first clasp their bodies together then shoot each other in a deadly parody of sexual climax.

The irony of Neff's position when he discovers that he must, as he himself predicted, "ride to the end of the line," resides less in the sexuality than in the self-destructive quality of his actions. To a certain extent all of the figures who act similarly in film noir, whether they are obsessed sexually or otherwise, concurrently know at some level that they need not act in that way. For a man or woman whom "the absurd may strike in the face," psychological trauma follows from being in a double bind: unable and unwilling to choose between equally bleak alternatives. For those whose illogical attachment to another person or thing imperils them, there is no double-faceted irony of this sort. As Neff winces from the bain of his wound at the conclusion of *Double Indemnity*, Keyes, who represents the system which Neff tried to outsmart, lights a match for him. With that gesture, a subtle nuance of the *noir* sensibility is invoked: the greatest failure is not succumbing to the temptation, or being caught in a double bind. The greatest failure is never accepting the possibility of redemption, however small.

If the full range of the noir vision is initially defined by such characterizations as Galt and Neff, it is sustained by its visual style. That style, rooted as it may be in other movements and however much it may borrow from various genres, is essentially a translation of both character emotions and narrative concepts into a pattern of visual usage. It might be asserted that there is considerable preconception involved when someone "detects" alienation lurking beyond the frame line in a panorama of dark, wet city streets or obsession in a point-of-view shot that picks a woman's face out of a crowd. On the other hand, to resist such a reading is to deny the full potential of figurative values not merely in film noir but in all film. Obviously none of the various elements of visual style—angle, composition, lighting, montage, depth, movement—which inform any given shot or sequence are unique to film noir. What sets the noir cycle apart is the unity of its formal vision. This unity goes beyond such bravura effects as the equation of a drug-induced breakdown with visual distortion in *Murder My Sweet* or the unbroken subjective cameras in *Dark Passage* or *Lady in the Lake*. If anything such displays run counter to the emphasis on naturalistic staging in most noir films. In fact, the most familiar or evocative images of the noir universe, from a general motif of street lights flashing off those damp, urban landscapes to a particular broken sign flashing its remaining neon letters—"kill . . . kill . . . kill . . ." outside a murderer's window in *The Unsuspected*, are arguably also the most naturalistic. A high angle long shot, cluttered with dark foreground masses and twisted shadows, entangles the private detective in a deterministic web in *Kiss Me Deadly*; a traveling camera traces a long, slow arc around an oversized mechanism to reveal a figure concealed behind its threatening bulk in *The Big Clock*; a succession of low, wide angle cuts awkwardly frames a fleeing man as he moves around corners and down steps against an unending array of backstreets and narrow alleys in *Night and the City*—

the key elements of each sequence differ radically, from static shot to moving one to montage, from high angle to low; but the result is the same. The viewer understands from convention that the characters are threatened, alienated, hemmed in. It is through this sort of direct, nonverbal association that film noir's visual substance is created, that relationships or situations established through narrative and characterization are refined or reassessed.

There is no grammar attached to this visual substance because its conventions of expression are not analogous to those of language. The side-lit close-up, the long take, the foreground object bisecting the frame may respectively imply a person's indecision, a building tension, a figurative separation; or they may not. The potential meaning is always there. The specific image may or may not participate in it. Again such an observation holds true for all film. It is the associations that film noir repeatedly elects to make that are telling: the dark streets become emblems of alienation; the character's unrelenting gaze becomes obsessive; the whole environment becomes deterministic, hostile, chaotic. Can such diverse, disruptive effects be truly unifying factors in a cycle of films? The ultimate demonstration of this unity resides with those films. The frequent use of flashback and other diffuse narrative techniques may endistance the audience. Leering villains like those in *Kiss of Death* and *The Garment Jungle* or other equally grotesque caricatures may threaten suspension of disbelief. But the underlying texture remains constant. The visualization brings the viewer back again and again into the fixed perspective of film noir.

As difficult as it may be to penetrate the screen of mediating influences which surrounds the inception of film noir, it would be much easier to designate an arbitrary point where the cycle began than a similar point where it ended. Given that the cycle did end and that this occurred sometime before 1960, several factors suggest themselves as causes. A change in exhibition patterns in the film industry, and a severe reduction in the total number of motion pictures produced began in the early 1950s. In response to this, there was a phasing out with rare exceptions of non-color, non-wide screen films and low-key lighting methods by the end of that decade. Perhaps most important of all was a sociological change, a shift in national preoccupations as an undirected, postwar malaise was replaced by legitimate if less apocalyptic concerns over economic recessions and foreign entanglements.

Whatever the reasons, it could be said that the cycle of noir films never did conclude, as such, but rather diminished gradually in scope and impact until it was lost in some vanishing point in film history. The few productions in the 1960s and 1970s from *Manchurian Candidate* to *Hustle* are not so much a part of that cycle as individual attempts to resurrect the noir sensibility. One thing is certain: in the "classic" period, the span of years from just before World War II to just after the Korean conflict, the major and minor studios put several hundred film noir into distribution. As the individual entries in this study reveal, those motion pictures vary considerably in many respects from plot to production value; but they all reflect a common ethos: they consistently evoke the dark side of the American *persona*. The central figures in these films, caught in their double binds, filled with existential bitterness, drowning outside the social mainstream, are America's stylized vision of itself, a true cultural reflection of the mental dysfunction of a nation in uncertain transition.

ABANDONED (1949)
[Original Release Title: ABANDONED WOMAN]

Director: Joseph M. Newman
Producer: Jerry Bresler (Universal-International)
Screenplay: Irwin Gielgud, with additional dialogue by William Bowers; from articles published in the *Los Angeles Mirror*
Director of Photography: William Daniels
Special Photography: David S. Horsley
Sound: Leslie I. Carey, Joe Lapis
Music: Walter Scharf
Art Directors: Bernard Herzbrun, Robert Boyle
Set Decoration: Russell A. Gausman, Ruby R. Levitt
Costumes: Yvonne Wood
Makeup: Bud Westmore, Emil LeVigne
Hairstyles: Joan St. Oegger, Emmy Eckhart
Production Manager: Howard Christie
Dialogue Director: Jack Daniels
Assistant Director: William Holland
Script Supervisor: Dorothy Hughes
Film Editor: Edward Curtiss

CAST: Dennis O'Keefe (Mark Sitko), Gale Storm (Paula Considine), Jeff Chandler (Chief McRae), Meg Randall (Dottie Jensen), Raymond Burr (Kerric), Marjorie Rambeau (Mrs. Donner), Jeanette Nolan (Major Ross), Mike Mazurki (Hoppe), Will Kuluva (Little Guy DeCola), David Clarke (Harry), William Page (Scoop), Sid Tomack (Mr. Humes), Perc Launders (Dowd), Steve Darrell (Brenn), Clifton Young (Eddie), Ruth Sanderson (Mrs. Spence). **BITS:** Bert Conway (Delaney), Bruce Hamilton (Doc Tilson), Francis McDonald (Wingy), Virginia Mullen (Nurse Sully), Edwin Max (Morrie), Isabel Withers (Mrs. Humes), Charles Jordan (Charlie), Frank Cady (City Editor), William Tannen (Taxi Driver), Marcella Cisney (Nurse Kay), Sally Corner (Head Nurse Tripp), Maudie Prickett (Nurse Ferris), Jerry Hausner (Orderly), Earl Smith (Sammy), Edward Clark (Clerk), Mary George (Nurse Ward), Beatrice Gray (Nurse), Franklin "Pinky" Parker, Dick Ryan, Stuart Wilson (Plainclothes Policemen), Billy Gray (Boy), Howard Mitchell (Judge), Felice Richmond (Telephone Operator).
Location: Los Angeles, California
Filming Completed: May 28, 1949
Released: Universal-International, October 28, 1949
Running Time: 78 minutes

A young woman, Paula Considine, comes to Los Angeles to find her missing sister. She is befriended and assisted by a newspaperman, Mark Sitko. Unfortunately, they soon discover that the sister died of an apparent suicide shortly after giving birth to a baby. All the evidence points to a baby-stealing racket. Impersonating the distraught mother, Considine infiltrates the racket in the hopes of breaking open the whole scandalous operation while rescuing her dead sister's child. Kerric, a mobster involved with the phony adoption scheme, decides to double-cross his partners. In the ensuing confusion the police, aided by the district attorney, raid the entire setup, rescuing Considine and ending the baby brokerage.

Abandoned is first and foremost a sensationalized melodrama. However, there are several elements that allow *Abandoned* to function as a noir film, most significantly William Daniels's photography. Daniels, who had worked with such directors as Von Stroheim in the 1920s and who had just prior to *Abandoned* received the Academy Award

Mark Sitko (Dennis O'Keefe) and Paula Considine (Gale Storm) in Abandoned.

for best black and white cinematography for Jules Dassin's New York based *Naked City*, imbued Los Angeles with a sinister, almost surreal, visual malevolence. This low-key vision of slick, rain-dampened streets and oblique vertical chiaroscuro lighting created an atmosphere that underscores the noir developments of the narrative. Placed into this environment are such classic noir heavies as Raymond Burr and Mike Mazurki. They lend a sense of grotesque identity to *Abandoned*'s plot. Yet it is the moralizing tone exposing the baby-stealing swindle that displaces the noir quality of the film. *Abandoned* is a film that has adopted the look and conventions of noir film making without surrendering itself to the hopelessness of film noir.

—C.M.

THE ACCUSED (1949)
[Working Title: STRANGE DECEPTION]

Director: William Dieterle
Producer: Hal B. Wallis (Paramount)
Screenplay: Ketti Frings; from the novel *Be Still, My love* by June Truesdell. [Uncredited Contributing Writers: Leonard Spigelgass, Barre Lyndon, Jonathan Latimer, Allen Rivkin, Charles Schnee]
Photography: Milton Krasner
Process Photography: Farciot Edouart

Special Photographic Effects: Gordon Jennings
Sound: Don McKay, Walter Oberst
Music: Victor Young
Art Directors: Hans Dreier, Earl Hedrick
Set Decoration: Sam Comer, Grace Gregory
Costumes: Edith Head
Makeup: Wally Westmore
Assistant Director: Richard McWhorter
Film Editor: Warren Low

CAST: Loretta Young (Wilma Tuttle), Robert Cummings (Warren Ford), Wendell Corey (Lt. Ted Dorgan), Sam Jaffe (Dr. Romley), Douglas Dick (Bill Perry), Suzanne Dalbert (Susan Duval), Sara Allgood (Mrs. Conner), Mickey Knox (Jack Hunter). **BITS:** George Spaulding (Dean Rhodes), Ann Doran (Miss Rice), Sally Shepherd (Tea Room Hostess), Frances Sandford (Waitress), Albin Robeling (Waiter), George Armstrong, Bill Perrott (Students), Carole Mathews (Waitress), Bill Mauch (Harry Brice), Nolan Leary (Coroner), Jacqueline Thomas (Miss Parker), Edward Clark (Professor), Rolland R. Morris, Jr. (Boy), Eric Alden, John Bishop, Douglas Carter (Detectives), Josephine Whittell (Dean's Secretary), Ralph Montgomery (Newsman), Joe Gray (Abe Comar), Dick Holland (Kid San Fran), John Indrisano (Referee), Frank Darien (Jerry), Miles Lally (Timekeeper), Evelynne Smith, Gladys Blake (Women), Joe McTurk (Man), Franz Roehn (Assistant to Dr. Romely), Al Ferguson (Judge), Richard Kipling (Bailiff), Jim Davies, Bess Flowers (Deputies), Bert Moorhouse (Prosecutor).

Location: Veterans Administration Hospital, Los Angeles, California
Filming Completed: May 28, 1948
Released: Paramount, January 12, 1949
Running Time: 101 minutes

A spinsterish young professor of psychology, Wilma Tuttle, accidentally kills one of her students, Bill Perry, when he attempts to seduce her. On the pretext of discussing his research on "psychothymia," which he implies is actually a description of Wilma, Perry takes her to a remote stretch of beach and attempts to break down Wilma's 'resistance to displaying emotion. Initially responding to his kiss, Wilma panics and hits him with a steel bar. Realizing he is dead, she draws water into Perry's lungs through "reverse" respiration and makes his death appear an accident. She hitches a ride home but is hospitalized after an overdose of sleeping pills. During the police investigation, Wilma meets Warren Ford, Perry's lawyer and guardian, and Lt. Ted Dorgan, both of whom are romantically drawn to her. A coroner's jury finds the death accidental but Wilma's distraught condition arouses the suspicions of both Ford and Lt. Dorgan; Furthermore, Perry's girl friend remembers that he was meeting with a "psychothymiac" the night he died.

With the aid of the clinical police scientist, Dr. Romley, Dorgan breaks Wilma down so that she incriminates herself. Put on trial for murder, Wilma is defended by Ford, who insists that her only crime was concealment of the accident, and he achieves her acquittal.

The Accused is reminiscent of Lang's *Woman In The Window*, but it eliminates the "framing" story of the latter and replaces the older man with a young woman as the shy, retiring professor of psychology. The opening night-for-night sequence (in which the disheveled and frightened Wilma leaves the beach to be picked up by a truck driver on the highway) and the revelation of the killing and attempted cover-up through a series of flashbacks (via Wilma's nightmares and hallucinations) are visually noir. *The Accused* is also a good example of Hollywood's postwar psychologizing and its postwar stereotypes of frustration: Sam Jaffe's brief but excellent portrayal of the callous scientist whose quest for knowledge demeans his empathy for others, and Loretta Young's portrayal of the prim and proper teacher whose frenetic responses suggest the sexual energies beneath her rigid persona. A good deal of the prevailing American attitude towards femininity is implicit in the fact that Wilma, in her role as an intellectual and teacher, must repress her sexuality; it is when she temporarily abandons this role that she is able, literally, to let her hair down and become a complete woman, responding in a normal fashion to a man's love.

In terms of the characters, however, Dorgan is much closer to the prototypical noir hero. His obsession with Wilma, despite her open preference for Ford, creates an emotional conflict with his investigation of her and tempts him to tamper with evidence. Although Dorgan convinces himself that he has done his job in spite of his feelings, he is afflicted by doubts that his ill-concealed desire for her may affect her prosecution. It is, in fact, a source of great relief to Wilma—and of equally great distress to Dorgan—when his constant questioning finally causes her to break down and reveal her actions. Repeated close-ups isolate Dorgan in the courtroom as he watches Wilma sitting confidently next to Ford; they reveal his bitter realization that his relationship with Wilma, however formal it has been, will soon be terminated; that she will be acquitted and marry Ford; and that he will have tormented her—possibly gained her hatred—for nothing.

—B.P. & A.S.

ACT OF VIOLENCE (1949)

Director: Fred Zinnemann
Producer: William H. Wright (MGM)
Screenplay: Robert L. Richards; from an unpublished story by Collier Young
Director of Photography: Robert Surtees
Sound: Douglas Shearer
Music Score: Bronislau Kaper
Conductor: Andre' Previn
Art Directors: Cedric Gibbons, Hans Peters
Set Decoration: Edwin B. Willis, Henry W. Grace
Costumes: Helen Rose
Hairstyles: Sydney Guilaroff
Makeup: Jack Dawn
Assistant Director: Marvin Stuart
Film Editor: Conrad A. Nervig
CAST: Van Heflin (Frank R. Enley), Robert Ryan (Joe Parkson), Janet Leigh (Edith Enley), Mary Astor (Pat), Phyllis Thaxter (Ann Sturges), Barry Kroeger (Johnny), Nicholas Joy (Mr. Gavery), Harry Antrim (Fred Finney), Connie Gilchrist (Martha Finney), Will Wright (Pop).
BITS: Tom Hanlon (Radio Voice), Phil Tead (Clerk), Eddie Waglin, Johnny Albright (Bellboys), William Phillips, Dick Simmons (Veterans), Larry and Leslie Holt (Georgie Enley), Garry Owen (Attendant), Fred Santley (Drunk), Dick Elliott (Pompous Man), Irene Seidner (Old Woman), Ralph Peters (Tim, Bartender), Douglas Carter (Heavy Jowled Man), Frank Scannell (Bell Captain), Rocco Lanzo, Rex Downing, Mickey Martin (Teenage Boys), Bill Cartledge (Newsboy), Don Haggerty, Paul Kruger, Wesley Hopper, Jim Drum, George Backus (Policemen), Nolan Leary, Barbara Billingsley (Voices), Harry Tenbrook (Man), Everett Glass (Night Clerk), Phil Dunham, William Bailey, Wilbur Mack (Ad Lib Drunks), Howard Mitchell (Bartender), Ralph Montgomery, Cameron Grant, Walter Merrill (Men), Roger Moore, Mahlon Hamilton (Winos), Candy Toxton (Veteran's Wife), Florita Romero (Girl), George Ovey, Jimmie Kelly,

AMONG THE LIVING

David Newell, Fred Datig, Jr., Margaret Bert, Mary Jo Ellis, Ann Lawrence (Bystanders), Andre' Pola, Rudolph Anders, Roland Varno (German Voices), Robert Skelton (Cab Driver).
Location: Big Bear Lake, California
Filming Completed: July 7, 1948
Released: MGM, January 23, 1949
Running Time: 81 minutes
[NOTE: *ACT OF VIOLENCE* was originally announced in 1947 as an independent production starring Howard Duff. Subsequently in 1948, Hellinger Productions-SRO Releasing announced the film was to star Gregory Peck and Humphrey Bogart.]

A disabled war veteran, Joe Parkson, has traveled from the East to find a man named Frank Enley. Enley is a respected contractor and civic-minded man, but in a prison camp during the war he was responsible for the death of his men by revealing their plans for escape. Actually, Enley informed his captors of the plan believing that the plan would not succeed and his men would be spared if he interceded; but all of the men were massacred except Parkson. No one knows of the incident except Parkson and the guilt-ridden Enley; and, as Parkson begins to create terror in Enley's mind, he first confesses to his wife and then flees into the night world of the city. Taking refuge with Pat, a woman of dubious reputation, Enley meets Johnny who offers to help by killing Parkson for money. Meanwhile, Ann Sturges, Parkson's girl friend, finds him and begs him not to go through with his plans for revenge; but he confronts Enley. Johnny appears and Enley intervenes, sacrificing himself to save Parkson.

Act of Violence is a film noir with a social theme. It is primarily involved with the torments of Enley's conscience: he cannot forget that his comrades were shot down, but his memory focuses on such marginal questions as the food with which the enemy had rewarded him. Parkson is not a complex character, and his desire for revenge is apparently more the result of his mind being unbalanced by his wounds than by any genuine moral decision. The entire film moves toward Enley's act of atonement but without suggesting an attitude to the incident that precipitated his guilt. Consequently, the social theme is not forceful and the whole tone of the film is dispassionate. This is often true of films directed by Fred Zinnemann.

Enley and Parkson are not among the more interesting characterizations of Heflin's and Ryan's careers, although the presence of these two actors does create interest. More importantly, there is a predictable visual schematization to the film. It begins in daylight in unthreatening surroundings and proceeds to a seamier environment as Enley journeys through the desperate night. These later scenes reveal the talent of photographer Robert Surtees, who contributes atmospheric night-for-night exteriors and evocatively lit interiors that are worthy of the best film noir.
—B.L.

AMONG THE LIVING (1941)

Director: Stuart Heisler
Producer: Sol C. Siegel (Paramount)
Associate Producer: Colbert Clark
Screenplay: Lester Cole and Garrett Fort; from an unpublished story by Brian Marlow and Lester Cole.
Director of Photography: Theodor Sparkuhl
Art Director: Haldane Douglas
Assistant Director: Arthur Black
Film Editor: Everett Douglas

CAST: Albert Dekker (John Raden/Paul Raden), Susan Hayward (Millie Pickens), Harry Carey (Dr. Ben Saunders), Frances Farmer (Elaine Raden), Gordon Jones (Bill Oakley), Jean Phillips (Peggy Nolan), Ernest Whitman (Pompey), Maude Eburne (Mrs. Pickens), Frank M. Thomas (Sheriff), Harlan Briggs (Judge), Archie Twitchell (Tom Reilly), Dorothy Sebastian (Woman in Café), William Stack (Minister). **BITS:** Ella Neal (1st Mill Girl), Catherine Craig (2nd Mill Girl), George Turner, Harry Tenbrook (Mill Workers), Patti Lacey, Roy Lester, Ray Hirsch, Jane Allen (Jitterbug Dancers), Delmar Watson (Newsboy), Eddy Chandler (Motorcycle Cop), Richard Webb (Hotel Clerk), Mimi Doyle (Telephone Operator), John Kellogg (Reporter), Blanche Payson (Woman at Trial), Ethan Laidlaw, Charles Hamilton (Guards), Frank S. Hagney, Lane Chandler (Neighbors), Lee Shumway (Scissors Grinder), Clarence Muse (Waiter), Len Hendry (Clerk), Besse Wade, Rod Cameron, Keith Richards, Abe Dinovitch, Jack Curtis, Chris Frank.
Filming Completed: June 6, 1941
Released: Paramount, September 1941
Running Time: 67 minutes

John Raden, with his wife, Elaine, returns to his hometown for his father's funeral. John is reputedly the sole survivor of a once proud and prosperous Southern family; but the family physician, Dr. Saunders, informs him that his identical twin brother, Paul, thought to have died as a child, is alive. Paul is hopelessly insane and lives in the abandoned family mansion, cared for by a faithful servant, Pompey. The insanity is a result of abuse by his father and Paul has never matured. He has fits in which he hears his dead mother cry out and holds his ears attempting to block out her screams. To conceal the family scandal, the doctor falsified Paul's death and received the money to build a badly needed town medical center. Saunders and John decide to visit Paul at the mansion, but they find that old Pompey has been killed and his hands placed carefully over his ears. Realizing Paul is responsible, the doctor believes Paul can be found and insitutionalized, convincing John to cover up Pompey's death. But a woman's body is found in an alley with her hands placed over her ears, and a reward is offered for her killer. John wishes to tell the truth to the police, but Doc Saunders threatens to accuse him of insanity. A group of the local men believe the killer is hiding at the old Raden mansion and they arrive just as Paul attacks a young woman, Millie, who befriended him. One of the men shoots Paul, but he escapes, knocking down John, who followed the men. Because John has been identified as the killer, no one believes his story that Paul is alive, and the enraged townspeople prepare to lynch John. But he escapes and runs to the cemetery where the dead body of Paul is draped over their mother's grave. Doc Saunders tells the sheriff the truth and the people realize John's innocence.

Among The Living was released in the fall of 1941, about the same time as *The Maltese Falcon,* and these films stand at the beginning of the film noir period, before many of the conventions of this type of film had been established. It is not surprising then that *Among the Living* wavers between the noir tradition and Southern Gothic, a literary tradition made quite respectable by writers like Poe and Faulkner and which can be seen sporadically in several postwar Hollywood films such as *Dark Waters, Night Of The Hunter,* and *Hush...Hush, Sweet Charlotte.* What makes *Among The Living* more than a curio, however, is the near brilliant photography of Theodor Sparkuhl, who worked on a number of classic German films in the 1920s and was Renoir's photographer for *La Chienne.* Sparkuhl's work is one indication of the American noir film's debt to German Expressionism and French poetic realism. The jazz sequence in a bar and the shot of Paul killing the B-girl in the alley (an extreme example of depth staging), are particularly important and set a stylistic precedent for expressing confusion and violence.

—B.P.

ANGEL FACE (1953)
[Working Titles: THE MURDER; THE BYSTANDER]

Director and Producer: Otto Preminger (Howard Hughes Productions)
Screenplay: Frank Nugent and Oscar Millard; from an unpublished story by Chester Erskine
Director of Photography: Harry Stradling
Sound: Earl Wolcott, Clem Portman
Music Score and Conductor: Dmitri Tiomkin
Music Director: Constantin Bakaleinikoff
Art Directors: Albert S. D'Agostino, Carroll Clark
Set Decoration: Darrell Silvera, Jack Mills
Costumes: Michael Woulfe
Makeup: Mel Berns
Hairstyles: Larry Germaine
Assistant Director: Fred A. Fleck
Film Editor: Frederic Knudtson

CAST: Robert Mitchum (Frank Jessup) Jean Simmons (Diane Tremayne), Mona Freeman (Mary), Herbert Marshall (Mr. Tremayne), Leon Ames (Fred Barrett), Barbara O'Neil (Mrs. Tremayne), Kenneth Tobey (Bill), Raymond Greenleaf (Arthur Vance), Griff Barnett (Judge), Robert Gist (Miller), Morgan Farley (Juror), Jim Backus (Judson). **BITS:** Morgan Brown (Harry), Frank Kumagai (Satsuma), Lucille Barkley (Waitress), Herbert Lytton (Doctor), Lewis Martin (Police Sergeant), Max Takasugi (Chiyo), Alex Gerry (Frank's Attorney), Bess Flowers (Barrett's Secretary), Buck Young, Roy D'Armour (Assistant District Attorneys), Mike Lally, Bob Peoples, Clark Curtiss (Reporters), Frank O'Connor (Bailiff), Bob Haines (Court Reporter), Jeffrey Sayre (Court Clerk), Gertrude Astor (Matron), Brick Sullivan (Deputy Sheriff), Grandon Rhodes (Prison Chaplain), Cora Shannon, Charlotte Portney, Mary Martin, Doreen Tryden (Patients), Theresa Harris (Nurse), Jack Ellis (Jury Foreman), Marvin Jones (Policeman), Charmienne Harker (Secretary), Larry Blake (Brady), Pete Kellett, Jim Hope (Detectives), George Sherwood, Jack Chefe, Sam Shack, Carl Sklover (Men), Mary Jane Carey (Woman), Ralph Volkie (Good Humor Man), Peggy Walker (TV Girl), Charles Tannen (TV Broadcaster).
Filming Completed: September 27, 1952
Released: RKO, February 2, 1953
Running Time: 91 minutes

Ambulance driver Frank Jessup is called to a hillside estate and saves the life of Mrs. Tremayne, who was almost asphyxiated by gas in her bedroom. When Frank tells Diane Tremayne that her stepmother has survived, Diane becomes hysterical. Despite this, he is attracted to Diane. She in turn, encourages her father to hire Frank as the family chauffeur. Frank suspects that Diane now desires to murder her stepmother by contriving a car accident; but he feels unable to leave her, even though she has broken up his engagement to Mary. Diane's tampering with the car is effective; but her father is also killed when he and Mrs. Tremayne careen off a cliff. Both Diane and Frank are indicted for the murder, so their lawyer, Fred Barrett, urges them to marry and play on the jury's sympathy. When Frank prepares to leave Diane after their acquittal, Diane offers to drive him to the bus station; but she shifts the car into reverse and backs it off a cliff, killing them both.

At its melodramatic extremes in Otto Preminger's work, sexuality may be either therapeutic (*Tell Me That You Love Me, Junie Moon*) or destructive (*Fallen Angel; Carmen Jones; Such Good Friends*). *Angel Face* epitomizes the latter quality. The fascination that Frank, the lower-class ambulance driver, develops for the spoiled but beautiful and wealthy Diane not only evokes the traditional noir motivations of sex and money but the danger of obsessive relationships as well. Although Preminger does not suggest that Frank is a hapless victim, his *mise-en-scène*—which repeatedly frames the figures in obliquely angled medium shots against the depth of field created by the expensive furnishings of the Tremayne mansion—and Mitchum's subdued portrayal engender an atmosphere of fatality that is generally understated. The climactic moments of murder and suicide, however, are not attenuated by the casting, against type, of Jean Simmons. Her more usual, heroic parts belie the barely repressed violence of her character for the viewer as well as for Frank. By encouraging the audience to empathize with Frank's uncontrollable attraction to Diane and by adding visual stability to her insular, mentally unbalanced world, Preminger compels them to coexperience both Frank's hopes for ultimate salvation and also, in the film's fundamental noir statement, the moral resolution of his death.

—A.S.

APPOINTMENT WITH DANGER(1951)
[Working Title: UNITED STATES MAIL]

Director: Lewis Allen
Producer: Robert Fellows (Paramount)
Screenplay: Richard Breen and Warren Duff
Director of Photography: John F. Seitz
Process Photography: Farciot Edouart
Sound: Harold Lewis, Gene Garvin
Music Score: Victor Young
Art Directors: Hans Dreier, Albert Nozaki
Set Decoration: Sam Comer, Bertram Granger
Costumes: Mary Kay Dodson
Makeup: Wally Westmore
Assistant Director: Francisco Day
Film Editor: LeRoy Stone

CAST: Alan Ladd (Al Goddard), Phyllis Calvert (Sister Augustine), Paul Stewart (Earl Boettiger), Jan Sterling (Dodie), Jack Webb (Joe Regas), Stacy Harris (Paul Ferrar), Henry Morgan (George Soderquist), David Wolfe (David Goodman), Dan Riss (Maury Ahearn), Harry Antrim (Taylor, Postmaster), Paul Lees (Gene Gunner). **BITS:** Geraldine Wall (Mother Ambrose), Leo Cronin (George J. Lewis), Sid Tomack (Trainman), Murray Alper (Driver), James Cornell (Gruber), Frank Hagney (Motorcycle Cop), Volta Boyer, Anitra Sparrow, Frances Sandford, Kathleen Freeman (Nuns), Harry Tyler (Brakeman), Sheldon Jett (Fat Man), Bruce Wong (Chop Suey Restaurant Proprietor), Erno Verebes, Fritz Feld (Window Dressers), Russell Saunders (Gary Policeman), Ralph Sanford (Wilder, Bartender), Maxie Thrower (Attendant), Hal Rand (Postal Truck Driver), Howard Gardiner (Hot Dog Man), John Whitney, Allan Douglas (Postal Inspectors), Bill Meader (Sharkey), Herb Vigran, Pat Lane, Jerry James, Byron Barr (Policemen), Patsy O'Byrne, Symona Boniface (Women), Ann Tyrell (Secretary), James Davies, Billy Engle (Men), William Tamara, Terry Goodman, Gerald Courtemarche, Wyatt Haupt (Boys), Jeanette Williams (Girl), Arnold Daly (Clerk).
Filming Completed: September 24, 1949

Released: Paramount, May 9, 1951
Running Time: 89 minutes

When a post office detective is killed in Gary, Indiana, a tough, cynical, postal inspector named Al Goddard is sent to investigate. The two killers, Joe Regas and George Soderquist, are strong-arm men for a local hoodlum, Earl Boettiger, who has conceived a neat plan to defraud the mail of one million dollars. Regas and Soderquist know they were observed near the murder and the vicious Regas wants to find the nun, Sister Augustine, who may be able to identify them, and kill her. Soderquist, the most humane of the trio, opposes hurting her and Boettiger does not think she could identify them anyway. Regas, on his own, unsuccessfully attempts to kill her, which convinces Goddard that he is on the right track in obtaining the nun's help. Posing as a criminal himself, Goddard is able to infiltrate Boettiger's gang and slowly learns of their robbery plan. Regas remains suspicious of Goddard and convinces Boettiger that Soderquist's personality is too weak to withstand questioning and should be eliminated, so Earl permits Regas to kill Soderquist. The criminals ultimately learn that Goddard is a government agent; and he unsuccessfully attempts to enlist the aid of Dodie, Earl's moll, in his cause. While Regas and Boettiger plan to get rid of both Goddard and the nun, whom they have abducted, Goddard gains added time by pretending to be open to bribery. The gang takes its hostages to a remote industrial section of town, but with the nun's aid, Goddard is able to fight it out with them until the police arrive. Surprisingly, Goddard's toughness and cynicism have been mollified through his association with Sister Augustine.

Appointment With Danger—an unsuccessful effort by many of the same crew to recapture the success of the earlier *Chicago Deadline*—represents the last of a series of film noir starring Alan Ladd. That it lacks the corrosiveness of such earlier efforts as *The Glass Key* and *Blue Dahlia* is due to the writer's insistence on peppering the dialogue with humorous asides; to the rather trite "conversion" of Ladd; and to the film's unfortunate wavering between the conventions of the romantic private eye and the semidocumentary thriller as the producers no doubt were attempting to update the stereotype of the Ladd vehicle. There are, however, two or three things that are memorable. It contains some of the crispest tough dialogue outside *The Big Sleep*. Ladd, for example, when told he doesn't know what love is, replies, "Sure I do, it's something that goes on between a man and a .45 that won't jam." Also, the film contains two scenes so charged with tension and brutality that they have seldom been surpassed: the testing of Ladd in a squash match with Webb and Stewart where the ball is a deadly missile; and the killing of Soderquist by his buddy Regas when he has been told to leave town. As he is packing, Regas picks up the bronzed booties that are a revered memento of Soderquist's departed son and beats him to death with them.

—B.P.

ARMORED CAR ROBBERY (1950)

Director: Richard Fleischer
Producer: Herman Schlom (RKO)
Screenplay: Earl Felton and Gerald Drayson Adams; from a story by Robert Angus and Robert Leeds
Director of Photography: Guy Roe
Sound: Frank Sarver, Clem Portman
Music: Roy Webb
Music Director: Constantin Bakaleinikoff
Art Directors: Albert S. D'Agostino, Ralph Berger
Set Decoration: Darrell Silvera, James Altwies
Makeup: Mel Burns, Burrows Grimwood
Hairstyles: Vera Peterson
Production Manager: John Burch
Assistant Director: John E. Pommer
Script Supervisor: Mercy Wireter
Film Editor: Desmond Marquette

CAST: Charles McGraw (Cordell), Adele Jergens (Yvonne), William Talman (Dave Purvis), Douglas Fowley (Benny), Steve Brodie (Al Mapes), Don McGuire (Ryan), Don Haggerty (Cuyler), James Flavin (Phillips), Gene Evans (Ace Foster). BITS: Anne O'Neal (Mrs. Page), Barry Brooks (Witwer), Linda Johnson (Girl Transmitter), Carl Saxe (Chandler), Charles Flynn (Rhodes), Dick Irving (Craig), James Bush (Control Tower Operator), Roger Creed (Operator), Anne Nagel (Mrs. Phillips), Mary Randall (Nurse Paxton), Frederick Howard (Dr. Leslie), Allen Mathews (2nd Detective), William Tannen (Johnson), Paul Bryar (Duncan), Jack Shea (Evans), Art Dupuis (Cashier), Paul E. Burns (Mr. Kelly), Mack Williams (Marshall), Frank Scannell (Kimball), Dick Dickenson (Newsboy), Max Hellinger (Mr. Bronson), Carey Loftin (Duff).
Filming Completed: January 27, 1950
Released: RKO, June 8, 1950
Running Time: 67 minutes

Dave Purvis is a cruel, intelligent criminal who maintains a clean police record by planning robberies that others carry out. He is introduced to strong-arm men, Al Mapes and Ace Foster, by a mutual friend, Benny, a down-and-out promoter whose wife, Yvonne, is a flashy stripper and is having an affair with Purvis. Benny convinces Mapes and Foster that although Purvis is unknown (he keeps his real identity a secret), he is indeed one of the best "brain men" in the business; and they agree to implement Purvis's plan to rob a local sports stadium. During the robbery a police car cruising the area arrives sooner than planned; and in the ensuing gun battle, Benny is shot. By disguising themselves as oil-field workers, the thieves get through a roadblock to a prearranged hideout near the waterfront, where Purvis kills the wounded Benny. When the police, led by Lt. Cordell, surround the hideout, Ace is killed, while Mapes and Purvis escape. Purvis feels secure in his motel room, since his identity is unknown to the police; but they locate him

through his phone number, which Benny had kept. Once again the mastermind escapes, but the police arrest Mapes and thereby learn the identities of Yvonne and Purvis. The fleeing couple are trapped at the airport when their small private plane is delayed from departure by the arrival of a commercial airliner. In the subsequent gun battle with the police, Purvis is run over by a plane and the stolen money is thrown up into the air only to fall and scatter about his body.

Armored Car Robbery, a conventional caper film, does not possess the budget or pretensions of such later productions as *The Asphalt Jungle* or *The Killing*. Yet the narrative substantially anticipates both films with the marked exception of Kubrick's restructuring of the chronological order. *Armored Car Robbery* does possess the noir visual style of many RKO crime and suspense films in the post-Welles era: high contrast photography integrating studio and location sequences by use of expressionistic lighting and deep focus and completed by the haunting music of Roy Webb.

—B.P.

THE ASPHALT JUNGLE (1950)

Director: John Huston
Producer: Arthur Hornblow, Jr. (MGM)
Screenplay: Ben Maddow and John Huston; from the novel by W.R. Burnett
Director of Photography: Harold Rosson
Sound: Douglas Shearer, Robert Lee
Music: Miklos Rozsa
Art Directors: Cedric Gibbons, Randall Duell
Set Decoration: Edwin B. Willis, Jack D. Moore
Makeup: Jack Dawn, Law Lacava
Hairstyles: Sydney Guilaroff, Elaine Ramsey
Production Manager: Lee Katz
Assistant Director: Jack Greenwood
Script Supervisor: John Banse
Film Editor: George Boemler

CAST: Sterling Hayden (Dix Handley), Louis Calhern (Alonzo D. Emmerich), Jean Hagen (Doll Conovan), James Whitmore (Gus Minissi), Sam Jaffe (Doc Riedenschneider), John McIntire (Police Commissioner Hardy), Marc Lawrence (Cobby), Barry Kelley (Lt. Ditrich), Anthony Caruso (Louis Ciavelli), Terese Calli (Maria Ciavelli), Marilyn Monroe (Angela Phinlay), William Davis (Timmons), Dorothy Tree (May Emmerich), Brad Dexter (Bob Brannom), Alex Gerry (Maxwell), Thomas Browne Henry (James X. Connery), James Seay (Janocek), Don Haggerty (Andrews), Henry Rowland (Franz Schurz), Helene Stanley (Jeannie), Raymond Roe (Tallboy), Charles Courtney (Red). BITS: Jean Carter, Constance Weiler, Judith Wood (Women), Ralph Dunn, Pat Flaherty, Jack Shea, Saul Gorss, John Cliff, Ray Teal (Policemen), Tim Ryan (Jack, Police

Doll Conovan (Jean Hagen) and Dix Handley (Sterling Hayden) in The Asphalt Jungle.

Left to right: Dix Handley (Sterling Hayden), Doc Riedenschneider (Sam Jaffe), and Alonzo D. Emmerich (Louis Calhern) in The Asphalt Jungle.

Clerk), Frank Cady (Night Clerk), Strother Martin (Karl Anton Smith), Henry Corden (William Doldy), Benny Burt (Driver), Fred Graham (Truck Driver), David Hydes (Evans), Joseph Darr Smith (Reporter), William Washington (Suspect), Leah Wakefield, Kerry O'Day, Patricia Miller (Girls), Eloise Hardt (Vivian), Albert Morin (Eddie Donato), Fred Marlow (Reporter), Howard Mitchell (Secretary), Wilson Wood (Man).

Filming Completed: December 21, 1949
Released: MGM, June 8, 1950
Running Time: 112 minutes

An elaborate jewel robbery is planned by a criminal mastermind, Doc Riedenschneider, with the financial backing of a corrupt lawyer, Alonzo D. Emmerich. Doc carefully assembles a small group of semiprofessional local criminals and proceeds with his robbery. However, from the very outset the robbery and the subsequent escape plans fail because of an ill-fated set of circumstances. Initially Emmerich plans to double-cross Doc and his associates while taking the money received for the stolen jewels. Dix Handley, the "hooligan" of the gang, catches wind of Emmerich's swindle and puts a stop to it. He kills a private detective hired by Emmerich to sabotage the fencing operation, but Dix is mortally wounded in the exchange. About this time the police move in, and the corrupt lawyer, unable to face up to his crimes, commits suicide. In a final gallant gesture, Dix persuades Doc to take some money and escape before the police arrive. Once sure that Doc is on his way, Dix collapses. He is taken to a doctor who calls the police. Once Dix recovers enough to understand that the police are coming after him, he escapes to the Kentucky farmland of his youth. Doc is captured when he stops to watch a young girl dance at a cafe. Dix dies in a farm field.

John Huston directed this naturalistic film noir, which is derived in part from a hard-boiled tradition and a tough code of social decay. Adapting W.R. Burnett's novel to the screen, Huston and Ben Maddow instilled *The Asphalt Jungle* with a feeling of authenticity unmatched in films of that period. The dialogue is gritty and the attitudes developed by the film point to distinctively sympathetic portraits of the small-time crooks who have elevated the ritual of Doc's meticulous robbery to an act of salvation, as they believe there is nothing criminal in what they do. This idealization quickly melts into a slush of wasted ambitions and petty obsessions. Surrounding the very human criminals is a society that is almost as corrupt as they are. Society's hypocrisy, illustrated by the crooked dealings of bad cops and the irresponsible judgments given by uninvolved onlookers, is a bitter comment on the brutal realities of the noir world. It is one of Ben Maddow's major concerns, which he explored elsewhere in such films as *Intruder in the Dust* and *The Unforgiven*. *The Asphalt Jungle* is a vivid contrast to Huston's other noir films. He has eliminated the claustrophobic quality found in both *The Maltese Falcon* and *Key Largo*, replacing it with a smooth, uncluttered style. However, grotesque characters are still present in *The Asphalt Jungle* although they exist on the periphery of the action rather than residing at the core like Gutman in *The Maltese Falcon* and the mobsters in *Key Largo*. The failure of Doc and his associates to transcend the common nature of criminals suggests the irony of many of Huston's films. *The Asphalt Jungle* is a classic noir film because of its elements of despair and alienation. It is also the film that serves as the dividing line between the old Huston and the new Huston. After *The Asphalt Jungle* Huston concerned himself with filmic adaptations of classic literary works such as *The Red Badge of Courage, Moby Dick,* and *Night of The Iguana*. He also experimented with color in *Moulin Rouge* and with structure in *Freud*. Following *The Asphalt Jungle,* Huston was able to put aside the noir world and concentrate on other goals.

—C.M.

BABY FACE NELSON (1957)

Director: Don Siegel
Producer: Al Zimbalist (Fryman-ZS)
Screenplay: Daniel Mainwaring; from an unpublished story by Robert Adler
Director of Photography: Hal Mohr
Sound: Harold Lewis

Music: Van Alexander
Art Director: David Milton
Set Decoration: Joseph Kish
Film Editor: Leon Barsche

CAST: Mickey Rooney (Lester Gillis/Nelson), Carolyn Jones (Sue), Sir Cedric Hardwicke (Doc Saunders), Leo Gordon (John Dillinger), Ted De Corsia (Rocco),

Anthony Caruso (Hamilton), Jack Elam (Fatso), Chris Dark (Jerry), Emile Meyer (Mac), Dan Terranova (Miller), Dabbs Greer (Bonner), Bob Osterloh (Johnson), Dick Crocett (Powell), Paul Baxley (Aldridge), Thayer David (Connelly), Ken Patterson (Vickman), Sol Gorse (Preston), Gil Perkins (Duncan), Tom Fadden (Harkins Postman), Lisa Davis (Ann Saper, the Lady in Red), John Hoytz (Parker, F.B.I. Agent), Elisha Cook, Jr., (Van Meter), Murray Alper (Bank Guard), George E. Stone (Mr. Hall), Hubie Kerns (Kearns), Paul and Richard Donnelly (Boys).

Location: Los Angeles, California
Filming Completed: August 1957
Released: United Artists, November 1957
Running Time: 85 minutes
[NOTE: Irving Shulman wrote the first draft of this screenplay. Through arbitration by the Screen Writers Guild, Siegel and Mainwaring proved that Mainwaring should receive sole screenplay credit. However, the film was released with Shulman's name on the credits. Al Zimbalist ran an announcement in the trade papers on June 23, 1958, apologizing for and correcting his mistake in the release credits.]

A cheap hood, Lester Gillis, is released from prison and begins a violent career, with Sue, his girl friend and eventual wife, at his side. Gillis goes to work for Rocco, who soon becomes afraid of Gillis and sets him up. Escaping with Sue, Gillis kills Rocco but is wounded and treated by Doc Saunders, who secretly desires Sue. Gillis, now the infamous Baby Face Nelson, joins with John Dillinger. Dillinger is subsequently killed in front of a movie theater and Nelson takes over, becoming Public Enemy Number One. The psychopathic Nelson kills everyone in his way, including Doc Saunders. Only a bank teller who happens to be smaller in stature than Nelson is spared. Finally, the F.B.I. catches up with Nelson who, looking for refuge in the countryside, is almost seen by two small boys. Sue claims that he would have shot the boys if they had recognized him, but he denies it. Later, mortally wounded and coughing blood, Nelson persuades Sue to kill him by convincing her he would have readily killed the two boys.

A harsh, raw, and occasionally ugly film, *Baby Face Nelson* possesses energy, ferocity, and crude but undeniable artistry. For the most part, it is a work without tenderness or pity, full of random and frequently offhanded violence that ultimately proves self-destructive. The casting of Mickey Rooney as Nelson gives the infamous figure a physical dimension that graphically supports his inferiority complex. Moreover, Nelson's self-conscious awareness of his own twisted values suggests an interior conflict between his need to merit Sue's affection and his uncontrollable rage against society; it is a response conditioned by years of being abused and looked down on by "big" people. Siegel organizes the formal elements of the film to support this conflict. Hal Mohr, responsible for the decorative cinematography of *A Midsummer Night's Dream* (which featured

Rooney in his most precocious role), contributes images devoid of any superficial beauty and expressively correct for the antisentimental tone of the dialogue. Van Alexander's jazz sound track aptly underscores Nelson's high level of nervous energy. In the most violent sequences, Siegel's cutting to reverse angles, holding Nelson in the foreground, reveals his psychological position of being momentarily in control, almost staging the action, a position that gives him more satisfaction than any monetary gain or notoriety. The most noir moment of *Baby Face Nelson* is clearly reserved for its final scene: Nelson estranges himself from Sue, the only person who had valued him, to find the death he had been seeking all along ironically at her hands. Thus he ends simultaneously not only his immediate physical pain but also his lifelong mental anguish.

—B.L. & A.S.

BEAST OF THE CITY (1932)
[Working Title: CITY SENTINEL]

Director: Charles Brabin
Producer: Hunt Stromberg (Cosmopolitan Productions)
Screenplay: John Lee Mahin; from an unpublished story by W.R. Burnett
Director of Photography: Norbert Brodine
Film Editor: Anne Bauchens

CAST: Walter Huston (Captain Jim Fitzpatrick), Jean Harlow (Daisy Stevens), Wallace Ford (Ed Fitzpatrick), Jean Hersholt (Sam Belmonte), Dorothy Peterson (Mary Fitzpatrick), Tully Marshall (Michaels, Defense Attorney), Mickey Rooney (Mickey Fitzpatrick), John Miljan (District Attorney), Emmett Corrigan (Bert, Police Chief), Warner Richmond (Tom), Sandy Roth (Mac), J. Carrol Naish (Pietro Cholo), **BITS:** Edward Coppo (Fingerprint Expert), George Chandler (Reporter), Clarence Wilson (Coroner), Morgan Wallace (Police Captain), Nat Pendleton (Abe), Arthur Hoyt (Witness), Robert Homans (Desk Sergeant), Ed Brophy (Police Announcer), Julie Haydon (Blond), Chuck Hamilton, Tom London, Charles Sullivan (Policemen).

Released: MGM, March 11, 1932
Running Time: 74 minutes

Police Captain, Jim Fitzpatrick sent to investigate the murder of four men, is so outraged that he personally arrests Sam Belmonte, the head of a politically influential gang. Belmonte and his men are quickly out of jail and Fitzpatrick is transferred to the suburbs. The crime problem in the city worsens and when Fitzpatrick thwarts a bank robbery and becomes a public hero, the city administration is forced to appoint him chief of police. Using tough quasi-legal methods, Fitzpatrick sets out to clean up the police department and destroy the gangs. Meanwhile, Ed, Fitzpatrick's ambitious brother, falls in love with Daisy, a gangland moll, and becomes involved with the Belmonte gang; he eventually goes so far as to set up a robbery in which a close friend on the police force is killed. Even when he finds out that his own brother is involved, Fitzpatrick takes the gang to trial. When Michaels, the corrupt defense lawyer, succeeds in obtaining acquittals for all the gang, including Ed, Fitzpatrick is convinced that the system will not work. He leads a group of police officers and a repentant Ed in a raid on Belmonte's victory party. The result is a cataclysmic shootout. All are killed, including Fitzpatrick, Ed, Belmonte, and Daisy.

That *Beast Of The City* is a noir film and an easily miscategorized one that raises some interesting questions: Perhaps the term "gangster film," particularly when applied to films of the early 1930s, is a misnomer; perhaps such films as *Little Caesar, Public Enemy,* and *Scarface* are best seen as part of a larger phenomenon; perhaps there is a mass of commercially and aesthetically significant films that use the subject matter of the gangster film, but not its central gangster character; and perhaps because of the over-emphasis on the gangster character, these films have been overlooked. What is needed is the more general concept of the underworld film. What is primary here is the existence of gangsterism and the unique political, social, and law enforcement problems that first surfaced with Prohibition and the Great Depression. The profession of the leading character in such an underworld film is secondary and can, for instance, include not only a variety of gangsters, but newsmen *(Five Star Final)*, private eyes (the 1931 *The Maltese Falcon)*, politicians *(Gabriel Over The White House)*, gamblers *(Street of Chance)*, doctors *(Dr. Socrates)*, lawyers *(Border Town)*, working girls *(Safe in Hell)* and, as in this film, policemen.

Beast Of The City was conceived in 1930 when Irving Thalberg decided that MGM should make a Warner's style underworld picture. W.R. Burnett, author of *Little Caesar,* was hired to write it. Burnett combined his experiences in Chicago in the 1920s with some material borrowed from his Western novel *St. Johnson* to produce a story in which the rise, fall, and death of a gangster became that of a cop. When MGM executives saw the finished film they were nonplused, and its release was badly handled. Its title was changed from *The City Sentinel* to *Beast Of The City* and its distribution held up for over a year and then restricted to second-run houses.

Although not in the MGM tradition, *Beast Of The City* is not to be mistaken for Warner's film of the period either. Its low-key visual imagery resembles the work of von Sternberg. Its sophisticated use of sound foreshadows that of Mamoulian. Its sordid yet romantic subplot is in the tradition of James M. Cain and the noir films adapted from his work in the 1940s. Most significantly, in the person of Fitzpatrick, *Beast Of The City* contains a character prototypically noir. Through Fitzpatrick, the film's treatment of the limits and perils of police power is less qualified and more critical than the recent trilogy of motion pictures—*Dirty Harry* 1971; *Magnum Force* 1973; and *The Enforcer*

1976—featuring Sgt. Harry Callahan. Moreover, Fitzpatrick's obsessive moral righteousness is of a destructive and ultimately suicidal nature, a fixation typical of the noir vision and as acute in *Beast Of The City* as in such later, psychologically overt narratives as *The Big Heat* and *Beat Generation.*

—D.L.W.

THE BEAT GENERATION (1959)

Director: Charles Haas
Producer: Albert Zugsmith (MGM)
Screenplay: Richard Matheson and Lewis Meltzer
Director of Photography: Walter H. Castle [CinemaScope]
Sound: Franklin Milton
Music: Lewis Meltzer and Albert Glasser
Songs: "Someday You'll Be Sorry" by Louis Armstrong; "The Beat Generation" by Tom Walton and Walter Kent
Music Conductor: Albert Glasser
Art Directors: William A. Horning, Addison Hehr
Set Decoration: Henry Grace, Jack Mills
Paintings: John Altoon
Costumes: Kitty Mager
Makeup: William Tuttle
Choreography: Hamil Petroff
Dialogue Coach: Jackie Coogan
Assistant Director: Ridgeway Callow
Film Editor: Ben Lewis

CAST: Steve Cochran (Dave Culloran), Mamie Van Doren (Georgia Altera), Ray Danton (Stan Hess), Fay Spain (Francee Culloran), Louis Armstrong and his All Stars (Band), Maggie Hayes (Joyce Greenfield), Jackie Coogan (Jake Baron), Jim Mitchum (Art Jester), Cathy Crosby (Singer), Ray Anthony (Harry Altera), Dick Contino (Singing Beatnik), Irish McCalla (Marie Baron), Vampira (Poetess), Billy Daniels (Dr. Elcott), Maxie Rosenbloom (Wrestling Beatnik), Charles Chaplin, Jr. (Lover Boy), Grabowski (Beat Beatnik), Anne Anderson (Meg), **BITS:** Nancy Kay (Anna Baron), Melody Gale (Angel Baron), Gerry Cohen (Joseph Baron), William Vaughn (Officer Crenshaw), Paul Cavanagh (Will Belmont), Carolyn Hughes (Jayne Belmont), Paul Genge (Capt. Wilson), Sid Melton, Guy Stockwell (Detectives), Gil Perkins (Lovers' Lane Bandit), Renata Vanni (Rosa Costa), Bobi Byrnes (Mrs. Gastro), Shirle Haven (Mrs. Grant), William Schallert (Father Dinelli), Darlene Hendricks (Nurse), Fred Hansen, Hamil Petroff, Fred Engleberg, John Melfi, Cole Simpson, Camille Williams, Kathy Reed, Phyllis Douglas, Phyllis Standish, Diane Fredrick, Larri Thomas, Regina Gelfan (Beatniks).
Filming Completed: November 13, 1958
Released: MGM, October 21, 1959
Running Time: 93 minutes
[NOTE: This film has been broadcast on television as *THIS REBEL AGE.*]

BEHIND LOCKED DOORS

Detectives Dave Culloran and Jake Baron are assigned to the case of a rapist-robber known as the Aspirin Kid, because his modus operandi involves arriving at a home and asking to use the telephone after a supposed car problem and then distracting the woman by feigning a headache and requesting aspirin. Culloran, an experienced street cop, doubts the story of the first victim whom they interview and suspects that she may have invited the sexual assault. The detectives arrest a suspect named Arthur Jester, but he has an alibi. While Culloran argues with Baron over continuing the investigation, Jester complains to the authentic Aspirin Kid, Stan Hess, about his using Jester's name and causing him to be arrested. Hess, who is supported by a wealthy, dissolute father, is unconcerned about Jester, whom he can blackmail into keeping silent; but he is infuriated that the investigation has come close to discovering him. Learning that Culloran is newly remarried, Hess makes Culloran's wife, Francee, his next victim. Outraged at the assault but also alienated because, under his puritanical standards, his wife has been "soiled," Culloran becomes monomaniacal in his pursuit of the Aspirin Kid. Worried, Hess persuades Jester to imitate his M.O. on Georgia Altera, and throw the police off the track. While Culloran spends his nights and days on the case, Francee turns to Baron and his wife for counsel, because she is pregnant and fears complete estrangement from her husband. Culloran refuses to give up, even when Francee is hospitalized with premature labor pains. Georgia Altera recognizes Jester, and Culloran follows him to a gathering of beatniks at Hess's beach house. Hess panics and attempts to flee but is caught in the surf and viciously beaten by Culloran, who is prevented from killing him only by Baron's arrival. Purged of his doubts, Culloran is reconciled with Francee and accepts their child.

Promoted at the time of its release as a quasi-satire of the contemporary youth cult, *Beat Generation*'s actual narrative structure is a parallel character study of an alienated criminal and equally alienated policeman. The most noir aspect of the film—the suggestion that a policeman under mental stress may become fully as sociopathic as those he is paid to subdue—is partially mitigated by Culloran's final reconciliation with his wife. Nonetheless, his compulsive and ruthless behavior following the attack on her, particularly his exploitation of Georgia Altera's sexual attraction to him—which ultimately imperils her life—draws criticism from all his peers and unalterably undercuts his pose of moral righteousness for the audience. In fact, as Hess and Culloran battle each other through intermediaries, the similarities between the two become all the more apparent. The few glimpses offered into their pasts—the scene between Hess and his father and Culloran's bitter remarks about the virtue of his first wife—not only develop a causality for their violence but reinforce the semblance in their respective psychological aberrations. Both are abusively misogynistic—Hess obviously so in his sexual assaults but Culloran equally vicious and demeaning in his inter-

action with women on a verbal level—and both have no qualms about manipulating others (Hess in his extortion of Jester; Culloran with Georgia Altera) to further their own needs.

The visual style of *The Beat Generation* is eclectic. Frequent close-ups of Hess and Culloran underscore the narrative focus. Their slight flattening effect simultaneously emphasizes both the physical resemblance and the behavioral contrast between the men, aided by Ray Danton's icy, self-assured portrayal of Hess and Steve Cochran's nervous and explosive rendering of Culloran. The *de rigeur* scenes of bearded bongo drummers and recitals of free verse in dimly lit coffee houses are reserved for Culloran and Altera's search for her assailant and effectively provide an almost surreal background for Culloran's growing sense of estrangement. Scenes such as these or the moment of comic relief when Culloran and Baron, who is dressed as a woman, stake out a lovers' lane in a parked car give *The Beat Generation* a staccato tempo that matches the sense of physical unease shared by its protagonist and antagonist. Typical of these shifts in mood is the fact that the film's only killing, when the lovers' lane bandit is shot, follows immediately after its most comic moment. The more Culloran begins to blame his environment for his difficulties—from the attack on his wife and home to something as simple as burning his hand on a coffee pot—the less he is able to cope with the natural instability of that environment.

—A.S.

BEHIND LOCKED DOORS (1948)

Director: Oscar [Budd] Boetticher, Jr.
Producer: Eugene Ling (ARC Productions)
Screenplay: Malvin Wald and Eugene Ling; from an unpublished story by Malvin Wald
Director of Photography: Guy Roe
Photographic Effects: George J. Teague
Sound: Leon S. Becker, Robert Pritchard
Music: Irving Friedman
Art Director: Edward L. Ilou
Set Decoration: Armor Marlowe, Alexander Orenbach
Costumes: Frances Ehren
Makeup: Ern Westmore, Del Armstrong
Hairstyles: Joan St. Oegger, Helen Turpin
Dialogue Director: Burk Symon
Production Supervisor: James T. Vaughn
Assistant Director: Emmett Emerson
Script Supervisor: Richard Walton
Film Editor: Norman Colbert

CAST: Lucille Bremer (Kathy Lawrence), Richard Carlson (Ross Stewart), Douglas Fowley (Larson), Thomas Browne Henry (Dr. Clifford Porter), Herbert Heyes (Judge Drake), Ralf Harolde (Fred Hopps), Gwen Donovan (Madge Bennett), Morgan Farley (Topper),

Trevor Bardette (Mr. Purvis), Dickie Moore (Jim). **BITS:** Wally Vernon (Sign Painter), John Hollans (State Psychiatrist), Thor Johnson (Butcher Blackmer), Kathleen Freeman (Nurse), Tony Horton (Sheriff).
Filming Completed: June 25, 1948
Released: Eagle Lion Films, November 1, 1948
Running Time: 62 minutes

An ambitious newspaper reporter, Ross Stewart, is eager to discover the whereabouts of a judge who suddenly vanished in the wake of charges filed against him. By following the judge's daughter, Kathy Lawrence, the reporter hopes to get a lead on the location of the missing official. Time after time, Kathy makes her way to a cheap and sinister looking mental hospital. Convinced that the asylum is a front for nefarious activities, which include harboring the judge, the reporter finagles his way into the mysterious hospital. Stewart's life in the strange asylum becomes an unending nightmare of induced paranoia and real fear of the unknown. The reporter is suspected of being too inquisitive by Larson, the sadistic mental ward intern. It is only after suffering an almost complete mental breakdown that the reporter finally solves the riddle of the asylum and reunites the judge with his daughter.

Behind Locked Doors is a predictable low-budget thriller. The basic flavor of the film rests in its melodramatic tenseness. However *Behind Locked Doors* does detail a claustrophobic atmosphere and delineates a paranoia that brings the film into the noir framework. There is little stylistic power in this film, so that what noir content exists arises out of the Woolrich-like situations and oppressive narrative atmosphere of perversion and oneirism, so common in a number of lesser quality noir films such as *Fall Guy, Whispering Footsteps,* and *Fear In The Night.*

—C.M.

BERLIN EXPRESS (1948)

Director: Jacques Tourneur
Executive Producer: Dore Schary (RKO)
Producer: Bert Granet
Screenplay: Harold Medford; from an unpublished story by Curt Siodmak
Director of Photography: Lucien Ballard
Special Effects: Harry Perry, Russell A. Cully, Harold Stine
Sound: Jack Grubb, Clem Portman
Music: Frederick Hollander
Music Director: Constantin Bakaleinikoff
Dance Director: Charles O'Curran
Art Directors: Albert S. D'Agostino, Alfred Herman
Set Decoration: Darrell Silvera, William Stevens
Costumes: Orry-Kelly for Merle Oberon
Makeup: Gordon Bau
Producer's Assistant: William Dorfman
Assistant Director: Nate Levinson

Script Supervisor: D. Ullman
Film Editor: Sherman Todd

CAST: Merle Oberon (Lucienne), Robert Ryan (Robert Lindley), Charles Korvin (Perrot), Paul Lukas (Dr. H. Bernhardt), Robert Coote (Sterling), Reinhold Schunzel (Walther), Roman Toporow (Lt. Maxim), Peter Von Zerneck (Hans Schmidt), Otto Waldis (Kessler), Fritz Kortner (Franzen), Michael Harvey (Sgt. Barnes), Richard Powers (Major). **BITS:** Jim Nolan (Train Captain), Arthur Dulac (Dining Car Steward), Ray Spiker (1st Husky), Bruce Cameron (2nd Husky), Charles McGraw (Col. Johns), Buddy Roosevelt (M.P. Sergeant), David Clarke (Army Technician), Roger Creed (M.P.), Gene Evans (Train Sergeant), Robert Shaw (Sergeant), Eric Wyland (Clown), Norbert Schiller (Saxophone Player), Marle Hayden (Maja), Bert Goodrich, George Redpath (Acrobatic Team), Richard Flato (Master of Ceremonies), Jack Serailian (Cigarette Maker), Lisl Valetti (German Waitress), Evan Hyde (Ticket Taker), Allan Ray (Corporal), Taylor Allen (Fraulein), David Wold, George Holt, Bill Raisch, Carl Ekberg, Hans Hopf (Germans), Willy Wickerhauser (Frederich), Will Allister (Richard), William Yetter, Jr. (1st German Youth), Robert Boon (2nd German Youth), Ernest Brengk (Artist), Hermine Sterler (Frau Borne), Rory Mallinson (M.P. Guard), Fernanda Eliscu (German Woman), Curt Furburg (German Bystander), Larry Nunn (1st G.I.), Jim Drum (2nd G.I.), Fred Spitz (German Civilian), Hans Moebus (Clerk), Jack G. Lee (Captain), Frank Alten (German Steward), Leonid Snegoff (Russian Colonel), James Craven (British Major), Fred Datig, Jr. (American Jeep Driver), William Stelling (American Sergeant), Al Winters (German Peasant).
Location: The Reichs chancellery, Reichstag, Brandenburg Gate, and Adlon Hotel, Berlin; Frankfurt, West Germany; Paris, France.
Filming Completed: November 21, 1947
Released: RKO, May 1, 1948
Running Time: 86 minutes
[NOTE: This was the first United States film unit to photograph in postwar Germany, and the production was in cooperation with the United States, British, and Soviet Armies of Occupation. The French sector was not involved.]

After an assassination attempt on a train traveling from Paris to Berlin fails to kill Dr. H. Bernhardt, a mysterious Nazi-underground group kidnaps the elder statesman in an attempt to thwart his plans for the reunification of postwar Germany. A group of Bernhardt's foreign colleagues who have accompanied him on his secret mission join forces in order to search through wartorn Frankfurt for their missing comrade. Realizing that one or more of the members of their group must be allied with the Nazi organization, their relationships become strained. Suspicion is leveled at everyone as they comb the rubble and hollowed office buildings for clues. As Bernhardt's secretary, Lucienne,

19

BETWEEN MIDNIGHT AND DAWN

wanders through the nightmarish landscape in the hope of finding him, she is accompanied by an American scientist, Robert Lindley. After almost all hope is lost, they stumble onto the Nazi hideout. The occupation forces are called in to mop up the nest of conspirators while Bernhardt is freed from his hellish abduction.

Much of the interest of *Berlin Express* rests in the location photography of Frankfurt. The backdrop of a once bustling society torn into a scattered mass of debris and pulverized dreams, brings an existential bias to the film. This futility is echoed in the sentiment of Bernhardt's Thomas Mann-like humanism. Frankfurt's compelling icons of a destroyed and decaying society are blended with a pervasive, yet muted, idealism into an exceedingly sinister atmosphere under Jacques Tourneur's direction. The ambivalence found in many of the characters populating the film is indicative of the disillusionment that followed World War II, while the grotesques contained in the plot are conventions of the black thriller and further emphasize the decay and corruption rooted in the film noir sensibility.

—C.M.

BETWEEN MIDNIGHT AND DAWN (1950)
[Working Title: PROWL CAR]

Director: Gordon Douglas
Producer: Hunt Stromberg (Columbia)
Screenplay: Eugene Ling; from an unpublished story by Gerald Drayson Adams and Leo Katcher
Director of Photography: George E. Diskant
Sound: Russell Malmgren
Music Score: George Duning
Music Director: Morris Stoloff
Art Director: George Brooks
Set Decoration: Frank Tuttle
Costumes: Jean Louis
Makeup: Clay Campbell
Hairstyles: Helen Hunt
Assistant Director: James Nicholson
Film Editor: Gene Havlick

CAST: Mark Stevens (Rocky Barnes), Edmond O'Brien (Dan Purvis), Gale Storm (Kate Mallory), Donald Buka (Richie Garris), Gale Robbins (Terry Romaine), Anthony Ross (Masterson), Roland Winters (Leo Cusick), Tito Vuolo (Romano), Grazia Narciso (Mrs. Romano), Madge Blake (Mrs. Mallory), Lora Lee Michel (Kathy), Jack Del Rio (Louis Franissi), Phillip Van Zandt (Joe Quist), Cliff Bailey (Sgt. Bailey), Tony Barr (Harry Yost), Peter Mamakos (Cootie Adams), Earl Brietbard (Rod Peters), Wheaton Chambers (Building Superintendent), Frances Morris (Superintendent's Wife). **BITS:** Lee Fredericks (Officer Zeigler), James Brown (Haynes), Ted Jordan (Carr), Douglas Evans (Detective Captain), Robert Bice, Gaylord Pendleton, Don Kohler, Harry Lauter (Detectives), Janey Fay, Mary Ellen Kay (Girls), Richard Karlan (Officer Nichols), John Butler (Drunk), Myron Healey (Officer Davis), Ruth Warren (Police-woman), Eric Mack (Booking Officer), Marc Krah (Rocco), Dudley Dickerson (Garbage Man), Paul Baxley (Cop), Charles Marsh (Husband), Maudie Prickett (Wife), Harry Harvey, Jr. (Driver), Mary Alan Hokanson (Broadcaster), Edwin Chandler (Supervisor), Billy Gray (Petey), Tony Taylor (Thurlow), Paul Palmer, Al Caruso, Fred Shellac, Ralph Brooks, Thomas F. Quinn, Jr., George Ford, Frank Pharr, Carle Tricoli, Richard La Marr, John Kascier (Men), Symona Boniface (Woman), Tommy Mann, Donald Fields (Boys), Robert Foulk (Fred, Jailor), Arnold Daly, Tomy Daly (Deputies), Gayne Whitman (Doctor), Joe Recht (Busboy), Mile Lally (Waiter), Ted Stanhope (Headwaiter), Alex Gerry (Oliver), Sydney Mason (Captain Evans), Nolan Leary (Foreman), William E. Green (Judge), Jack Gargan (Court Clerk), Louis Kane (Girl Broadcaster).

Filming Completed: March 20, 1950
Released: Columbia, October 2, 1950
Running Time: 89 minutes

Police officers Dan Purvis and Rocky Barnes, assigned to the same mobile unit, have been buddies since the war. Barnes is easygoing, while Purvis is intense and disillusioned by his experiences with "scum." The pair have fallen in love with the voice of Kate Mallory over their police radio, and they both court her. She is more charmed by the light-hearted Rocky. In the meantime Purvis is frustrated by witnesses who are too frightened to identify a despicable hoodlum, Richie Garris, as the bomber of an Italian grocery. Syndicate figure Leo Cusik moves into town and attempts to coerce Garris into his organization; but the recalcitrant Garris kills him. Dan and Rocky arrest Garris, but he escapes and later fatally shoots Rocky. Dan is now obsessed with Garris's capture and unsuccessfully' attempts intimidating Terry Romaine, Garris's girl friend, to deliver information. Later a stakeout spots Garris entering Terry's apartment; but Garris uses a small child as a shield and escapes. Climbing up to the apartment via the fire escape, Dan throws a tear-gas bomb and is about to be shot by Garris when Terry steps in front of the gun and is killed instead. Dan then kills Garris and decides that maybe Terry was not so bad after all.

Posing as a semidocumentary with its opening credits over the Los Angeles skyline while an impersonal narrator talks about the police, *Between Midnight and Dawn* was written for matinee crowd appeal. It has many weaknesses, but the director, Gordon Douglas, is efficient in handling sequences of action or brutality. He includes two grisly noir scenes: the brutal shooting of Rocky Barnes and the final gunfight in which Dan shoots Garris who, in grabbing the wall before falling, leaves the imprint of his hand in blood. Despite the film's didactic approach, Don Buka's stylish portrayal of Garris is compelling and contrasts effectively with Edmond O'Brien's stolid, embittered Dan.

—B.P.

BEWARE, MY LOVELY (1952)

[Working Titles: THE RAGGED EDGE; DAY WITHOUT END; ONE FALSE MOVE]

Director: Harry Horner
Producer: Collier Young (The Filmakers)
Associate Producer: Mel Dinelli
Screenplay: Mel Dinelli; from his play and short story *The Man*
Director of Photography: George E. Diskant
Sound: John Cass, Clem Portman
Music: Leith Stevens
Music Direction: Constantin Bakaleinikoff
Art Directors: Albert S. D'Agostino, Alfred Herman
Film Editor: Paul Weatherwax

CAST: Ida Lupino (Mrs. Gordon), Robert Ryan (Howard), Taylor Holmes (Mr. Armstrong), Barbara Whiting (Ruth Williams), James Williams (Mr. Stevens), O. Z. Whitehead (Mr. Franks), Dee Pollack (Grocery Boy). **BITS:** Brad Morrow, Jimmy Mobley, Shelly Lynn Anderson, Ronnie Patterson (Boys), Jeanne Eggenweiler (Girl).
Filming Completed: August 3, 1951
Released: RKO, August 7, 1952
Running Time: 76 minutes

Howard, an itinerant handyman, flees in terror when he finds his employer strangled but remains unaware that he has killed her in a moment of rage. He goes to another town, where he finds work at the home of a teacher and war widow, Mrs. Gordon. Howard, a morose and unhappy loner, begins to suspect Mrs. Gordon of secretly spying on him. When a teenager, Ruth Williams, taunts him for doing "women's work," it precipitates another breakdown. After Ruth departs, Howard locks himself in with Mrs. Gordon. All her frantic attempts to escape fail, until, in a moment of frenzy, Howard tries to strangle her, causing her to faint. When she comes to she sees Howard calmly going about his work, as if nothing has happened. He is once again unaware of his insane outburst. When a telephone repairman calls, Howard leaves peaceably with him and is turned over to the police.

Mel Dinelli's earlier success with screenplays grounded in suspenseful situations (*The Spiral Staircase, The Window*) was not repeated in *Beware, My Lovely.* by 1952 the noir cycle was going into decline, and many elements and devices previously original and emotionally affecting had become predictable through overuse. Despite better than average production values and photography and some excellent performances by the principals (particularly Ryan who

draws much pathos from an essentially negative character), much of the narrative is devoted to redeveloping stereotypes of Ida Lupino as a typically lonely and harassed young woman and Robert Ryan as the alienated man bordering on psychosis. Such expressionistic shots as the superimposition of a corpse in the water bucket into which the psychotic Ryan is staring or his distorted reflection in a Christmas ornament, (as in *They Live By Night*), become, in context, a complement of visual clichés. For all of its failings, *Beware, My Lovely* is an interesting film and a good example of how film noir could rapidly develop and exhaust the dramatic impact of its stylistic conventions.

—B.P.

BEYOND A REASONABLE DOUBT (1956)

Director: Fritz Lang
Producer: Bert Friedlob (Bert Friedlob Productions)
Screenplay: Douglas Morrow
Director of Photography: William Snyder (RKO-Scope)
Sound: Jimmy Thompson, Terry Kellum
Music: Herschel Burke Gilbert
Song: "Beyond a Reasonable Doubt," lyric by Alfred Perry, music by Herschel Burke Gilbert; sung by the Hi-Lo's
Art Director: Carroll Clark
Set Decoration: Darrell Silvera
Makeup: Lou LaCava
Hairstyles: Ruby Felker
Production Manager: Maurie Suess
Production Assistant: Leo Taub
Assistant Director: Maxwell Henry
Film Editor: Gene Fowler, Jr.

CAST: Dana Andrews (Tom Garrett), Joan Fontaine (Susan Spencer), Sidney Blackmer (Austin Spencer), Philip Bourneur (Thompson), Shepperd Strudwick (Wilson), Arthur Franz (Hale), Edward Binns (Lt. Kennedy), Robin Raymond (Terry), Barbara Nichols (Sally), William Leicester (Charlie Miller), Dan Seymour (Greco), Rusty Lane (Judge), Joyce Taylor (Joan), Carleton Young (Kirk), Trudy Wroe (Hatcheck Girl), Joe Kirk (Clerk), Charles Evans (Governor), Wendell Niles (Announcer). **BITS:** Dorothy Ford (Blond), Joey Ray (Eddie), Larry Barton (Customer), Frank Mitchell (Waiter), Billy Reed (Master of Ceremonies), Carl Sklover (Taxi Driver, Photographer), Phil Barnes (Policeman), Bayness Barron (Higgens), Jeffrey Sayre (Foreman of Jury), Bob Whitney (Bailiff), Hal Taggert (Court Clerk), Dorothy Gordon (Secretary), Bill Boyett, Joel Mondeaux (Staff), Eric Wilton (Clergyman), Dave Wiechman (Condemned Man), Harry Strang (Warden), Tony De Mario (Doctor), Benny Burt, Myron Cook (Reporters), Ralph Volkie (Photographer).
Filming Completed: August 7, 1956
Released: RKO, September 5, 1956
Running Time: 80 minutes

BEYOND THE FOREST

[NOTE: In 1954, Ida Lupino, Howard Duff, and Douglas Morrow formed an independent production company and announced their first film would be *Beyond A Reasonable Doubt*, starring Duff and Joseph Cotten from a script by Morrow and Lupino.]

Tom Garrett, a rising novelist, enters into an agreement with Austin Spencer, a wealthy publisher and also the father of Tom's fiancée, Susan. The two plan a journalistic coup: they will incriminate Tom in a local murder and allow him to be tried and sentenced to death so that they can discredit capital punishment by revealing Tom's innocence. Their plan goes amiss when, after Tom has been convicted, Spencer is accidentally killed and the evidence needed to exonerate Tom is destroyed. As the date of the execution approaches, Susan's increasingly frantic maneuvering produces additional evidence to save Tom. But in the critical moments before he is to be pardoned, Tom accidentally reveals to Susan that he is the killer, being the murder victim's long missing husband who took advantage of the scheme to rid himself of a threat to his forthcoming marriage and subsequent social advance. Susan reveals this to the authorities before Tom can be pardoned.

Beyond A Reasonable Doubt is Fritz Lang's last American film, made on a low budget, with poor production values and, on the surface, not strikingly directed. Nevertheless, the film has considerable impact, due not so much to visual style, as to the narrative structure and mood and to the expertly devised plot, in which the turnabout is both surprising and convincing. A subtle sense of narrative uneasiness, conveyed mainly through the acting and *mise-en-scène,* permeates the entire length of the film and subtly foreshadows the final plot twist. The film poses as a social statement about the plight of an innocent man, but it is filled with an array of submerged plot elements that belie a far more complex and sinister world than is otherwise suggested by the simple sets and washed-out images. First, there is the lurking possibility that the entire scheme is a trap engineered by Spencer to frame Tom. When this is suddenly dispelled by Spencer's death, his place is filled by the missing husband whom Susan believes to be the murderer. Both possibilities function to produce the suspicion that the crime is far more complex than the random sex murder it first appears to be. There is also a certain coldness and sterility in Tom himself; he witnesses an execution at the film's opening but does not seem particularly affected by it; and he jokes with Susan about marrying her for her money. There are a number of small, seemingly irrelevant incidents such as an unexplained phone call to Tom and the fact that, even before he knows of Spencer's scheme, he postpones his marriage to Susan. In addition, at Tom's trial there emerges certain, quite damaging evidence against him that was not planted by Spencer—evidence that, at the time, the viewer assumes to be coincidental. Finally and most unusual, there is an odd stylistic tendency evident throughout the film. First, Lang cuts repeatedly to seemingly insignificant actions such as picking up a drink or lighting a cigarette; and, second, he inexplicably focuses on such inanimate objects as matchbooks and ashtrays. Although most of these actions and objects turn out to be irrelevant to the plot, they put the viewer on edge with diorienting detail and create a subliminal uncertainty about surface reality. None of these elements is particularly intrusive and, until the final revelation, the dominant reality for the viewer is that Tom is innocent—indeed, the threat of Tom's death forces the viewer to accept this concept all the more. Yet on the subconscious level, these elements give the film a disturbing quality that prepares us for the sordid revelation. The plot elements have been cleverly devised so that the surprise ending is not much of a surprise; but it is a shock of insight, in which all the unsettling facts reassemble to create a new reality that is far more emotionally and logically convincing. Consistent with this revelation is Susan's decision to allow the execution of her fiancé to continue.

—D.L.W.

BEYOND THE FOREST (1949)
[Working Title: ROSA MOLINE]

Director: King Vidor
Producer: Henry Blanke (Warner Brothers)
Screenplay: Lenore Coffee; from the novel by Stuart Engstrand
Director of Photography: Robert Burks
Special Effects: William McGann, Edwin DuPar
Sound: Charles Lang
Music: Max Steiner
Orchestration: Murray Cutter
Art Director: Robert Haas
Set Decoration: William Kuehl
Costumes: Edith Head
Makeup: Perc Westmore
Production Manager: Eric Stacey
Assistant Director: Al Alleborn
Film Editor: Rudi Fehr

CAST: Bette Davis (Rosa Moline), Joseph Cotten (Dr. Lewis Moline), David Brian (Neil Latimer), Ruth Roman (Carol), Minor Watson (Moose), Dona Drake (Jenny), Regis Toomey (Sorren), Sarah Selby (Mildred Sorren), Mary Servoss (Mrs. Wetch), Frances Charles (Miss Elliott). **BITS:** Harry Tyler (Stationmaster), Ralph Littlefield (Driver), Creighton Hale (Old Man), Joel Allen (Minister), Ann Doran (Edith Williams), Buddy Roosevelt, Bobby Henshaw, James Craven (Men), Eve Miller (Switchboard Operator), Gail Bonney, Hallene Hill, June Evans (Women), Judith Wood (Waitress), Eileen Stevens (Operator), Hal Gerard (Waiter), Jim Haward (Bar Manager), Charles Jordan (Jury Foreman), Frank Pharr (Coroner).
Location: Lake Tahoe, Truckee River, Angeles Crest, California

Released: Warner Brothers, October 22, 1949
Running Time: 97 minutes

Rosa Moline, the dissatisfied wife of a small-town doctor is having an affair with Neil Latimer, a Chicago millionaire, while he vacations at his cabin near the Molines' hometown. When Latimer returns to Chicago, Rosa insists that her husband's patients pay their bills and then uses the money for a trip to that city ostensibly to buy a new wardrobe. Latimer avoids her but finally admits he is engaged to a wealthy society woman and breaks off with Rosa. Discouraged, she returns home and discovers she is pregnant. Dr. Moline is happy and feels confident that the baby will solidify their marriage. They attend a party given for their friend, Moose, who is caretaker for Latimer's cabin. Latimer is at the party and tells Rosa he has broken his engagement and wants her to come to Chicago with him. Excited, Rosa agrees but Moose threatens to tell Latimer about her pregnancy if she leaves Dr. Moline. The next day at a hunting party, Rosa shoots Moose. Claiming it was accidental, she is absolved of murder. Later, Dr. Moline intercepts a telephone call from Latimer urging Rosa to run away with him soon. Moline angrily tells Rosa she can be free after the baby is born. Rosa drives to see another doctor about an abortion but is discovered by her husband. On their way home, she makes him stop the car and then leaps into a ravine, hoping her injury will cause a miscarriage. The baby is lost, and Rosa's recovery is slow. She develops blood poisoning but insists on going to Chicago. Hysterically she prepares to leave and staggers out of the house. As she nears the boarding platform of the local train station, she falls and dies.

King Vidor's vision of melodrama in smalltown America is never darker than in *Beyond The Forest*. Unlike the rather random violence of *Ruby Gentry* or the aptly titled *Lightning Strikes Twice*, the arrangement of formal elements in *Beyond The Forest* possesses the rigor and occasionally the overstatement of a Euripidean tragedy. Even as a third-person narrator introduces the character of Rosa Moline as an "evil" person scandalizing the inhabitants of her small hometown, the visuals isolate the causes of Rosa's own sense of oppression: the gaunt faces of the villagers following her as she goes to trial, the glaring white-washed walls of their meager homes, and, in contrast, the constant aural assault from the blast furnace of the local mill. Vidor leaves no question that the fiery image of the furnace and its constant, barely controlled explosive rumbling are metaphors for Rosa's passion; and Bette Davis's interpretation of Rosa conveys the appropriate hysteria beneath the pulled-back hair and a swarthy complexion that makes her eyes seem to flash each time she widens them.

What is most interesting and most noir in Vidor's passion play is the manner in which Rosa Moline's "evil" becomes a role forced on her by her repressive environment. Because, as the narrator notes, she had ambitions beyond marriage and child rearing, because she "put on airs" in an unschooled attempt to be somebody, Rosa was ostracized long before her trial for killing Moose. By beginning with the trial and flashing back, Vidor initially delineates the context for Rosa's reputation as evil and then the chain of events leading to her literally criminal acts. This does not, of course, exculpate Rosa—as her peers must, for lack of evidence—but it does reveal the desperate alienation that motivates her frantic desire to escape her surroundings. Ultimately, Rosa's tragedy is personal, not social; and, in the final scenes, the visuals repeatedly capture her crazed behavior in sharp side-light or low-light to underscore her fever-induced madness. The climax uses montage for a restatement of the furnace metaphor and a traveling shot that moves back from Rosa over the train that promises freedom, so that when the cars have pulled away and the intermittent light from their windows has abated, Rosa's figure is visible, crumpled and alone in the roadway.

—A.S.

THE BIG CARNIVAL (1951)
[Working Title: THE HUMAN INTEREST STORY: Original Release Title: ACE IN THE HOLE]

Director and Producer: Billy Wilder (Paramount)
Assistant Producer: William Schorr
Screenplay: Billy Wilder, Lesser Samuels, and Walter Newman
Director of Photography: Charles B. Lang
Sound: Harold Lewis and John Cope
Music: Hugo Friedhofer
Song: "We're Coming, Leo" by Ray Evans and Jay Livingston
Art Directors: Hal Pereira, Earl Hedrick
Set Decoration: Sam Comer, Ray Moyer
Makeup: Wally Westmore
Assistant Director: C. C. Coleman, Jr.
Film Editor: Arthur Schmidt
Editorial Supervisor: Doane Harrison

CAST: Kirk Douglas (Charles Tatum), Jan Sterling (Lorraine), Robert Arthur (Herbie Cook), Porter Hall (Jacob Q. Boot), Frank Cady (Mr. Federber), Richard Benedict (Leo Minosa), Ray Teal (Sheriff), Lewis Martin (McCardle), John Berkes (Papa Minosa), Frances Dominguez (Mama Minosa), Gene Evans (Deputy Sheriff), Frank Jacquet (Smollett), Harry Harvey (Dr. Hilton), Bob Bumps (Radio Announcer), Geraldine Hall (Mrs. Federber), Richard Gaines (Nagel), Paul D. Merrill, Stewart Kirk Clawson (Federber Boys). BITS: John Stuart Fulton (Boy), Bob Kortman (Digger), Edith Evanson (Miss Deverich), Ralph Moody (Kusac, Miner), Claire Dubrey (Spinster), William Fawcett (Sad-Faced Man), Bill Sheehan (Man), Frank Keith (Fireman), Basil Chester (Indian), Joe J. Merrill (Digger), Bert Moorhouse (Morgan), Ken Christy (Jessop), Martha Maryman (Wo-

Outside the cave-in, The Big Carnival (Ace In The Hole).

man), Lester Dorr (Priest), Larry Hogan (Television Announcer), John "Bub" Sweeney, Stanley McKay, Bert Stevens, Frank Parker (Reporters), Iron Eyes Cody (Indian Copy Boy), Charles Griffin (Mr. Wendel), Jack Roberts (Newspaperman), Oscar Belinda, Martin Bendleton (Barkers), William N. Peters, Chico Day (Photographers).

Location: Gallup, New Mexico

Filming Completed: September 11, 1950

Released: Paramount, as *Ace In The Hole* on June 29, 1951; as *The Big Carnival* in July 1951

Running Time: 119 minutes (110 minutes press previews)

Charles Tatum, once an ace journalist, is now a ruthlessly ambitious, alcoholic reporter working in Albuquerque, New Mexico, and looking for a way back to the big time. He stumbles onto a seemingly minor story of a man trapped alive in a cave-in. By shoring up the cave's weakened tunnels, rescue workers could reach the entombed Leo Minosa in a matter of hours; but Tatum remembers the national sensation caused by the 1925 Floyd Collins story and has other plans for Leo. He recommends rescue by a lengthy drilling process, pointing out to Leo's faithless wife, Lorraine, the profits to be made selling refreshments to sensation seekers and convincing the local sheriff that his upcoming election campaign can be helped by prolonged publicity. Drilling begins, the story goes out, and hordes of eager onlookers, reporters, and radio and television personalities pour into the dingy little town. Tatum is on top again. But before the rescuers can reach him, Leo dies.

The Big Carnival is one of the most grimly cynical motion pictures ever to emerge from Hollywood. It was condemned as a compassionless and contemptuous distortion of human nature, while several newspaper film reviewers complained that American journalists had been slandered. However, although the film was reportedly banned in Malaya for portraying a facet of American life "that might be misunderstood," it received the Venice Film Festival award for the outstanding Hollywood film of that year. The controversy inspired Paramount executives to nickname the film "Ass In the Wringer," a take-off on its original title, *Ace in the Hole.*

None of this can detract from *The Big Carnival*'s evident

strengths. Its cynicism is so unrelenting that it becomes compelling; and the atmosphere in which that cynicism is presented is so painstakingly detailed, so richly realized, that its point of view defies repudiation. Audiences of the postwar, witch-hunt years were forced to turn their backs on such darkness; if *The Big Carnival* had been made today, in an age that makes a fetish of acknowledging errors, it might very well have been a success.

The film has two determinedly noir performances by Kirk Douglas and Jan Sterling. Douglas is all bluster and calculation; never has he made such significant use of his manic laugh, his egotistical ferocity, and the cheap, slick side of his personality. In contrast to Douglas's "big" peformance, Sterling's is quiet and subtle, conveyed by the obsequious look of her saucer eyes, in the twist of her pouting mouth, and in the brassy tone of her voice. Urged to pose praying for her husband in publicity photos, she snarls, "I don't pray. Kneeling bags my nylons." The highlight of Sterling's performance is that she reveals the fear and the emptiness beneath her tough broad facade.

Her emptiness is reflected also in the film's bleak locale: the tawdry roadside cafe and souvenir shop, typical of those that unremittingly punctuate the American landscape. Familiar, too, is what this emptiness becomes when inundated by gawkers, sensation-seekers, profiteers, and "gentlemen" of the press—all feeding off the misery and ultimately the death of another human being. The enthusiastic attempted rescue of Leo Minosa is shown to be a universally hypocritical, exploitative side-show and is presented by Wilder with exaggerated precision and detail. It includes an interview with the doomed man, a topical tune entitled, "We're Coming, Leo," sung by the spectators to cheer him, and then culminates as these people garner grisly souvenirs from around the death site. The major events of the film take place in glaring desert sunlight that relentlessly beats down on the crowd and gives a hard edge to every action of the characters and plot. In contrast to the literally bright and cheerful sympathizers, Leo is truly suffering in a dank cave. He ultimately dies of pneumonia—a disease associated with cold temperatures. In Wilder's noir vision, the individual is figuratively frozen by the neglect of his fellow human beings, even as they imitate concern. Leo, as a film noir protagonist, could not be more alienated as his world is supported by humanitarian ideals that are made of sand.

—J.K. & E.W.

THE BIG CLOCK (1948)

Director: John Farrow
Producer: Richard Maibaum (Paramount)
Screenplay: Jonathan Latimer, adapted by Harold Goldman; from the novel by Kenneth Fearing
Director of Photography: John F. Seitz
Special Photographic Effects: Gordon Jennings

Process Photography: Farciot Edouart
Sound: Hugo Grenzbach, Gene Garvin
Music: Victor Young
Song: "The Big Clock," by Jay Livingstone and Ray Evans; performed by the Ernie Filice Quartet
Art Directors: Hans Dreier, Roland Anderson, Albert Nozaki
Set Decoration: Sam Comer, Ross Dowd
Costumes: Edith Head
Makeup: Wally Westmore
Assistant Director: William H. Coleman
Film Editor: Gene Ruggiero
Editorial Supervisor: Eda Warren

CAST: Ray Milland (George Stroud), Charles Laughton (Earl Janoth), Maureen O'Sullivan (Georgette Stroud), George Macready (Steve Hagen), Rita Johnson (Pauline Delos), Elsa Lanchester (Louise Patterson), Harold Vermilyea (Don Klausmeyer), Dan Tobin (Roy Cordette), Henry Morgan (Bill Womack), Richard Webb (Nat Sperling), Tad Van Brunt (Tony Watson), Elaine Riley (Lily Gold), Luis Van Rooten(Edwin Orlin), Lloyd Corrigan (Mckinley), Margaret Field (Second Secretary), Philip Van Zandt (Sidney Kislav), Henri Letondal (Antique Dealer), Douglas Spencer (Bert Finch). **BITS:**

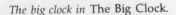

The big clock in The Big Clock.

Left to right: Earl Janoth (Charles Laughton) and George Stroud (Ray Milland) in The Big Clock.

George Stroud (Ray Milland) and Pauline Delos (Rita Johnson) in The Big Clock.

Bobby Watson (Morton Spaulding), B.G. Norman (George, Jr.), Frances Morris (Grace Adams), Erno Verebes (Waiter), Lucille Barkley (Hatcheck Girl), Frank Orth (Burt), Harland Tucker (Seymour Roberts), Gordon Richards (Warren Parks), Joe Whitehead (Fisher), James Burke (O'Brien), Joey Ray (Joe Talbot), Henry Guttman (Rufus Rowe), Len Hendry (Bill Morgan), Jim Davies (Bartender), Harry Rosenthal (Charlie), Noel Neill, Bea Allen, Kathy Young, Lee Emery, Wally Earl, Lillian Lindsco (Elevator Operators), Mary Currier (Ivy Temple), Earle Hodgins (Guide), Darlene Mohilef, Sheila Raven (Elevator Starters), Robert Coleman (Messenger), Norman Leavitt (Tourist), William Meader (Airways), Bill Burt (Sportsways), Jerry James (Man with Fish), Frances Conley, Lucy Knoch, Dorothy Barrett, Jean Marshall, Virginia Doffy, Robbie Franks, Julia Faye (Secretaries), Skippy Elliott (Miss Blanchard), Pepito Perez (Headwater at Van Barth's), Bill Burt (Bartender), Henry Guttman, Barry Norton (Men at Van Barth's), Frederick Howard (Baxter James), Theresa Harris (Daisy), Broderick O'Farrell (Flavin), James Carlisle (Van Spove), Bert Moorhouse (Editor), Don McGill (Kiska), Bess Flowers (Stylist in Conference Room), Mary Donovan (Girl in Conference Room), Bess Flowers (Woman at Van Barth's), Barry Norton (Man at Van Barth's), Sheila Raven (Girl at Van Barth's), John Farrell (Drunk), Helen Spring (Woman), Robert Riordan, Franklyn Farnum, John Sheehan, Stuart Holmes, Richard Gordon (Men), Frank Hagney (Iceman), Marlene Aames (Rosa), Judy Nugent (Penelope), Napoleon Whiting (Bootblack), Eric Alden, Harry Anderson, Pat Lane, Ralph Dunn, Mike Donovan, Al Ferguson, Chuck Hamilton, Jim Drum, Bob Kortman, Stuart Holmes (Guards), Diane Stewart (Girl), Bea Allen (Newsstand Operator), Dick Keene (Hamburger Cook), Cliff Heard, Lester Dorr, Robert Stephenson, Gary Owen (Cab Drivers), Nicholas Vehr (Doorman at Van Barth's), William Bloom (Third Avenue Bum), Lane Chandler (Doorman at Apartment House).

Filming Completed: April 11, 1947
Released: Paramount, April 9, 1948
Running Time: 93 minutes
[NOTE: A Paramount press release dated October 28, 1946, announced that Leslie Fenton would direct *The Big Clock*.]

George Stroud is the brilliant editor of *Crimeways Magazine,* one of the many publications of Earl Janoth, a monomaniacal tycoon with worldwide corporate holdings who treats his employees like slaves. *Crimeways'* biggest circulation feature is its staff's ability to track down criminals who elude the police by using George's "clueboard," a giant bulletin board on which all clues are posted and the personality of the criminal is reconstructed and from which George second guesses the culprit's moves and captures him. But George's wife, Georgette, complains that he is married to the magazine and, indeed, even on the eve of George's departure for his five-year overdue honeymoon, Janoth insists that he stay and "see this one story through to the end." Tired of Janoth's tactics, George quits the magazine

and relaxes in a bar before meeting his wife at the train station. But he meets a blond, Pauline Delos, and misses his train. Disgusted with his mistake, George spends a wild night on the town with Pauline. George is not aware that Pauline is Janoth's mistress. Leaving Pauline at her apartment, George does not see Janoth arrive, but the tycoon is aware that a man has just left her apartment. Janoth and Pauline argue viciously and he kills her in a fit of rage. Panicked, Janoth confesses the murder to a friend and assistant, Steve Hagen, and they plan to find and implicate as the murderer, the man Janoth saw leaving Pauline's apartment. Meanwhile, George arrives at the vacation resort and convinces Georgette of his misfortune in missing the train. The telephone rings, and Janoth demands that he return to New York to locate Pauline's murderer. Realizing his life is threatened, George returns despite his wife's claim that their marriage is finished. As *Crimeway's* staff pieces the clues together, George throws them off while attempting to find the murderer himself. Ultimately, he deduces Janoth was Pauline's lover and makes Hagen believe that the tycoon will double cross him. Janoth shoots Hagen and then chases George throughout the publishing offices with a gun, but George outwits him and Janoth plunges down an elevator shaft to his death. George reveals the whole problem to Georgette and they are reunited.

The opening of *The Big Clock* contains many classic noir elements: a pan across a dark city into a darkened corridor then to a dark figure hiding and running; a voice-over of the character bemoaning his fate; and a flashback to explain the origin of his current trouble. The body of the film, however, reveals fewer stylistic characteristics of film noir and the instances of low-key lighting, asymetric or dramatic compositions, and radical camera angles are rare.

The only visual device of note is the "slightly-too-wide-angle" lens, which is used for close-ups of Laughton during his vilest moments; it distorts his face just enough to be uglier than real, but not enough to break startlingly with naturalism. The use of this subtle distortion increases quite gradually during the film, until, when the flashback catches up with the opening of the film, the viewer may be convinced of the archvillain's both superhuman and subhuman capabilities. The performances are all adequate to the roles but Laughton and Lanchester are especially noteworthy. Laughton affects a rapid and nearly monotone speech pattern that equates Janoth's mechanical and compulsive behavior with that of the mammoth clock symbolizing his corporate power. The title refers to that giant clock in his building's lobby, which synchronizes and runs all other clocks in the global Janoth empire. When George momentarily takes refuge in the big clock, he accidentally stops and starts this symbol of Janoth's egomania, thus presaging his final victory over Janoth himself.

Elsa Lanchester gives a memorable rendition of an extremely talented but totally zany artist. Her home is filled with the clutter of four or five young children each of whom, she blithely announces, has a different father and provides a living history of her checkered marital career.

THE BIG COMBO

Her endearing eccentricity is the light side of the dark coin of insanity, which is carried to epitome by Laughton. It is the combination of Janoth's madness and the Frankensteinian horror of finding his own machine turned against him and closing in fast that provides the movement in this plot and the menace to George Stroud. In a more thoroughly noir film, the protagonist would generate much of his own miserable fate through misjudgment, stubborness, or greed; but since George's only folly is to dally too long in a bar with the wrong woman and the greatest threat to George's life comes from Janoth's madness, this is one of the lightest of the films that can be considered noir.

—E.M.

THE BIG COMBO (1955)

Director: Joseph Lewis
Producer: Sidney Harmon (Security-Theodora)
Screenplay: Philip Yordan
Director of Photography: John Alton
Special Effects: Jack Rabin, Louis DeWitt
Sound: Earl Snyder
Music: David Raksin

Music Editor: Robert Tracy
Piano Soloist: Jacob Gimpel
Production Designer: Rudi Feld
Set Decoration: Jack McConaghy
Costumes: Don Loper for Jean Wallace
Makeup: Larry Butterworth
Hairstyles: Carla Hadley
Production Manager: George Moskov
Assistant Directors: Mack Wright, Robert Justman
Continuity: Mary Chaffee
Film Editor: Robert Eisen

CAST: Cornel Wilde (Leonard Diamond), Richard Conte (Mr. Brown), Brian Donlevy (McClure), Jean Wallace (Susan Lowell), Robert Middleton (Peterson), Lee Van Cleef (Fante), Earl Holliman (Mingo), Helen Walker (Alicia), Jay Adler (Sam Hill), John Hoyt (Dreyer), Ted De Corsia (Bettini), Helene Stanton (Rita), Roy Gordon (Audubon), Whit Bissell (Doctor), Steve Mitchell (Bennie Smith), Baynes Barron (Young Detective), James McCallion (Lab Technician), Tony Michaels (Photo Technician), Brian O'Hara (Malloy), Rita Gould (Nurse), Bruce Sharpe (Detective), Michael Mark (Hotel Clerk), Philip Van Zandt (Mr. Jones), Donna Drew (Miss Hartleby).

The silhouettes of Susan Lowell (Jean Wallace) and Leonard Diamond (Cornel Wilde) in The Big Combo.

Filming Completed: September 21, 1954
Released: Allied Artists, February 13, 1955
Running Time: 89 minutes

The head of a local mob, Mr. Brown, has thoroughly captivated a young society woman, Susan Lowell. Brown's entire setup is scrutinized by a zealous detective, Leonard Diamond, who is obsessed with exposing Brown as a top mob financier while taking Susan away from him. Diamond's tactics range from mass false arrests to harassment and exploitation in order to get at Brown. Pushed too far by Diamond, Brown, whose philosophy is "first is first and second is nobody," reacts. A contract is put out, and Diamond is picked up by two hit men, Mingo and Fante, who appear to have a covert relationship as lovers. They torture Diamond, using the hearing aid of one-time top mobster, McClure, to amplify sounds past the point of normal tolerance. The detective, after recovering, is determined to see Brown imprisoned. He begins to link Brown with the murder of the racket boss whose place he has taken. Brown eliminates McClure and his henchmen before they discover his treacheries. But he is betrayed by his ex-wife, and, in a shoot-out in an isolated airplane hangar, Brown is trapped by Diamond.

There is a sense of fatalism and perverse sexuality found in *The Big Combo* that exists in few noir films. The relationship between Susan Lowell and Mr. Brown is a blending of fatalistic deference combined with a feeling of raw sexual abandon. Brown adores Susan's body. In one sequence, he brings her to the height of sexual excitement by worshipping her with lewd compliments and lavishing her entire body with kiss after kiss. Despite her sense of guilt, Susan resigns herself to this situation because of her own sexual dependence on Brown. Her eventual attempt at suicide and apparent rebirth at Diamond's insistence suggests no more than a weak effort to alter her amoral lifestyle. Beyond this obvious sexual exploitation, *The Big Combo* is filled with violence of a brutal and erotic nature. The homosexuality of Mingo and Fante is smothered in an atmosphere of murder and sadistic torture, as they refine the conventions of violence into a sexual ritual. Joseph H. Lewis's direction strongly points to a crude sexual bias throughout the film. Even Diamond appears to be sexually frustrated and compensating for impotence. Much in the same way as Lewis's classic *Gun Crazy*, there is an affinity between sex and violence; and the exploration of futility presents an ambience strangely reminiscent of an earlier period of noir films, such as *Scarlet Street* and *Woman in the Window*. These attitude combine with John Alton's photography to create a wholly defined film noir, as the striking contrasts between the black and white photography and Lewis's sexual overtones isolate *The Big Combo's* characters in a dark, insular universe of unspoken repression and graphic violence.

—C.M.

THE BIG HEAT (1953)

Director: Fritz Lang
Producer: Robert Arthur (Columbia)
Screenplay: Sydney Boehm; from the novel by William P. McGivern
Director of Photography: Charles Lang
Sound: George Cooper
Music: Daniele Amfiteatrof
Music Director: Mischa Bakaleinikoff
Art Director: Robert Peterson
Set Decoration: William Kiernan
Costumes: Jean Louis
Makeup: Clay Campbell
Hairstyles: Helen Hunt
Assistant Director: Milton Feldman
Film Editor: Charles Nelson

CAST: Glenn Ford (Dave Bannion), Gloria Grahame (Debby Marsh), Jocelyn Brando (Katie Bannion), Alexander Scourby (Mike Lagana), Lee Marvin (Vince Stone), Jeanette Nolan (Bertha Duncan), Peter Whitney (Tierney), Willis Bouchey (Lt. Wilkes), Robert Burton (Gus Burke), Adam Williams (Larry Gordon), Howard Wendell (Commissioner Higgins), Chris Alcaide (George Rose), Michael Granger (Hugo), Dorothy Green (Lucy Chapman), Carolyn Jones (Doris), Ric Roman (Baldy), Dan Seymour (Atkins), Edith Evanson (Selma Parker). **BITS:** Norma Randall (Jill), Sid Clute (Bartender), Joe Mell (Dr. Kane), Linda Bennett (Joyce), Herbert Lytton (Martin), Lyle Latell (Moving Man), Ezelle Poule (Mrs. Tucker), Byron Kane (Dr. Jones), Mike Ross (Segal), Ted Stanhope (Butler), Phil Arnold (Nick), Bill Murphy (Reds), Douglas Evans (Gillen), Mike Mahoney (Dixon), Paul Maxey (Fuller), Pat Miller (Intern), Charles Cane (Hopkins), John Merton (Man), Kathryn Eames (Marge), Al Eben (Harry Shoenstein), William Vedder (Janitor), Harry Lauter (Hank O'Connell), Robert Forrest (Bill Rutherford), Phil Chambers (Hettrick), Jimmy Gray (Man), John Close (Policeman), John Crawford (Al), John Doucette (Mark Reiner).
Filming Completed: April 18, 1953
Released: Columbia, October 14, 1953
Running Time: 90 minutes

Dave Bannion is a homicide sergeant investigating the sudden suicide of a police officer named Duncan. He is suddenly told by higher-ups to "lay off the case." But Bannion is aware of unsavory implications detailed to him by the suicide's girl friend, Lucy Chapman. Lucy believes that Duncan's widow is blackmailing gangster Mike Lagana with a hidden suicide confession note. When Lucy's tortured body is discovered by the side of the road, Bannion is convinced that he should pursue the forbidden investigation. The town and police force are in the grip of syndicate chief Lagana, and the sergeant confronts the hoodlum. Bannion accuses Lagana of stifling the investigation and threatens to tie him to the murder of Lucy. Lagana retaliates by planting a bomb in Bannion's car, which accidentally kills Bannion's wife instead. When he gets no answers from his lieutenant about the investigation of his wife's murder, Bannion accuses the commissioner of intentional foot-dragging and cooperation with Lagana's gang. Bannion loses his job and, hiding his threatened child with in-laws, he becomes a lone wolf whose single purpose is to wreak vengeance on Lagana. He uncovers Vince Stone, a sadistic Lagana aide, and his girl, Debby. Bannion is seen with Debby, possibly getting information from her, and the jealous Vince disfigures Debby's face with scalding coffee. Bannion nurses Debby and she tips him to Vince's and Lagana's guilt in the three deaths. Debby, realizing that Mrs. Duncan's death would release the incriminating suicide note and bring down the "big heat" to destroy Lagana, shoots and kills Bertha Duncan. Debby lures Vince into a trap, scalds him with coffee, and is fatally wounded by him. Bannion arrives and fights with Vince, who is taken into custody. Debby dies with the disfigured side of her face hidden in her mink coat; and Bannion, vindicated returns to his desk at homicide.

Sgt. Dave Bannion is squarely in the tradition of the crusading detective: honest, tough, unbought, and unbuyable; and with the dogged persistence to confront any situation, no matter how complex or dangerous. But something is wrong with this noble character—he lives in the real world where crooks do not fall down when good guys point a finger. Bannion is compulsively upright and thorough in his investigations in a city where not only does crime pay, but morality has a very low return. At one level of the film, Bannion is the avenging angel and must be admired: his vendetta puts in motion the elements that finally bring down the "big heat" on the citywide criminal syndicate. The cost of this heroic action is the lives of four women, the loss of Bannion's home, and the jeopardy of his daughter's life. While women are to be protected like cherished property, they are essentially expendable when power, moral principles, or male egos are at stake. Further, there are two classes of females in *The Big Heat*. In the one class are the women who have demonstrated legitimate pedigree by marriage, purity, and youth: Bannion's wife and daughter, and, to a certain extent, the innocent daughter of the gangster chief, Lagana. In the other category fall those women who through age, infirmity, or indications of independent sexuality are "things": Mrs. Duncan, Lucy Chapman, the crippled woman from the garage, and Debby. The differentiation of women is totally unconscious for Bannion, who slanders Lucy Chapman as a whore for loving Duncan and is enraged when a gangster uses insulting language to his wife. The sergeant does not mind exposing the crippled woman to possible harm, even while his own daughter is guarded from the same group of thugs by armed men. Debby is the most compelling link between the two groups of women, but she is a connection that Bannion does not comprehend clearly, as her faults are numerous and offensive to him. Sophisticated, sexy, and

gay in dress and deportment, Debby is consciously happy despite being involved with the sadistic Vince Stone. But she becomes useful to Bannion, and therefore sympathetic. Her deeply buried innocence surfaces with Bannion's ministrations. She is trying to cross the line into decency; but a woman like Debby, once sullied, can never be totally accepted. The only possible "salvation" for Debby is death, by which she approaches the status of Bannion's sainted wife. Her dual nature is illustrated by the pure and disfigured sides of her face. When she dies with her hideous scars hidden in the mink, she is transformed into a lovable object for Bannion. Leaving behind him a wake of death and destruction, Bannion is restored to good standing on the police force and in the community. On the human scale, however, the victory is pyrrhic; and the noir vision of the film is indeed nihilistic.

—E.M.

THE BIG KNIFE (1955)

Director and Producer: Robert Aldrich (Associates and Aldrich)
Screenplay: James Poe; from the play by Clifford Odets
Director of Photography: Ernest Laszlo
Sound: Jack Solomon
Music: Frank DeVol
Art Director: William Glasgow
Production Supervisor: Jack R. Berne
Assistant Directors: Nate Slott, Bob Justman
Film Editor: Michael Luciano

CAST: Jack Palance (Charlie Castle), Ida Lupino (Marion Castle), Wendell Corey (Smiley Coy), Jean Hagen (Connie Bliss), Rod Steiger (Stanley Hoff), Shelley Winters (Dixie Evans), Ilka Chase (Patty Benedict), Everett Sloane (Nat Danziger), Wesley Addy (Hank Teagle), Paul Langton (Buddy Bliss), Nick Dennis (Mickey Feeney), Bill Walker (Russell), Mike Winkelman (Billy Castle), Mel Welles (Bearded Man), Robert Sherman (Bongo Player), Strother Martin (Stillman), Ralph Volkie (Referee), Michael Fox (Announcer), Richard Boone (Narrator).
Filming Completed: May 14, 1955
Released: United Artists, November 8, 1955
Running Time: 111 minutes

Charlie Castle, a former Broadway actor and current star of Hoff International Pictures, does not want to renew his contract. Dissatisfied with the type of parts he has been given, he has told his agent, Nat Danziger, to inform producer Stanley Hoff of his decision. Additionally, Charlie's insecurity and alcoholism have estranged him from his wife, Marion, to whom he hopes to be reconciled after breaking with Hoff.

Through his aide, Smiley Coy, Hoff sends Charlie word of his displeasure and offers him more money if he reconsiders. Charlie refuses but lapses into depression, seeking solace in drink and dalliance with Connie Bliss, the wife of an associate. Not understanding Charlie's behavior, Marion makes plans to leave him. Hoff appears in person and, after histrionic appeals have failed, resorts to blackmail. He threatens to expose Charlie as the drunk driver of a car that killed a pedestrian, an accident for which Buddy Bliss had taken the blame. Under this threat, Charlie agrees to sign. In the aftermath of the confrontation, Charlie confides to Smiley Coy that he is concerned about Dixie Evans, a bit player who had been with him at the time of the accident. Smiley promises to take care of this problem.

Smiley's method is to get Dixie drunk and then push her in front of a car. Her violent death and his wife's departure throw Charlie into an even blacker depression. Charlie is visited on the set by Hank Teagle who confesses that he hopes to marry Marion after her divorce. Charlie returns home and makes one last appeal to Marion to stay with him. Just after she decides she will stay, Marion discovers that Charlie has slit his wrists in the bath and died.

Much of the invective of *The Big Knife* derives from the original Odets play. The film adds a quasi-satirical dimension: Rod Steiger's blubbering, imbalanced Stanley Hoff ("Charlie, Charlie...the pain of this moment!") Wendell Corey's unctuous press agentry as Smiley Coy; Jack Palance's leering, paranoiac Charlie Castle. The portrayals form an ensemble not only of Hollywood's clichés about itself but also of prototypical Robert Aldrich gargoyles. The unabashed theatrics, the drum rolls, the wildly expressive dialogue, such as "You came in here and threw this mess of naked pigeons in my face!," create the vulgarity and hysteria that are fundamental to Aldrich's stylized, personal interpretation of Hollywood.

For Charlie Castle, in specific, the Hollywood dream resolves itself into an oppressive, insane hell, largely of his own making. Insulated in the ranch-style home, assaulted by his parasites and demons, Aldrich's extreme angles and short lenses distort the perspectives of Charlie's world, externalize the frenzy of Charlie's own viewpoint. Charlie seeks shelter in the rear ground of his claustrophobic environment, behind lamps, sofas, and other furnishings, and in the romantic conception of himself as "the warrior minstrel with the forlorn hope." Such thoughts and actions are both psychologically telling and futile.

Visually, the framing shifts so that the foreground and background become constricting rather than concealing elements. The sequence shot of Charlie at the studio with Hank Teagle is most informative. Only at the studio, with its connotations of fictional existences and false settings, is there any visual (or figurative) continuity to Charlie's life; only among the painted flats and artificial daylight is he at ease. (The fluid motion that follows him at eye level captures the sense of barriers being removed.) Yet even then, there is an underlying tension (the sustained shot) that threatens both a visual and emotional breakdown.

When Charlie's noir melodrama is played out, the final craning shot, up out of the set into the heights of the soundstage, is a sardonic afterthought, a detached expression of the fact that a "Hollywood" life is not, figuratively or literally, a real life, is not lived but only acted out in an empty search for stage center with darkness surrounding.

—A.S.

THE BIG NIGHT (1951)

Director: Joseph Losey
Producer: Philip A. Waxman (Philip A. Waxman Productions)
Screenplay: Stanley Ellin and Joseph Losey; from the novel *Dreadful Summit* by Stanley Ellin
Director of Photography: Hal Mohr
Sound: Leon Becker
Music: Lynn Murray
Art Director: Nicholas Remisoff
Assistant Director: Ivan Volkman
Film Editor: Edward Mann

CAST: John Barrymore, Jr. (George La Main), Preston Foster (Andy La Main), Joan Lorring (Marion Rostina), Howard St. John (Al Judge), Dorothy Comingore (Julie Rostina), Philip Bourneuf (Dr. Lloyd Cooper), Howland Chamberlin (Flanagan), Emil Meyer (Packingpaugh), Myron Healey (Kennealy), Mauri Lynn (Terry Angeleus), Robert Aldrich (Ringside Fight Fan).
Filming Completed: August 1951
Released: United Artists, December 7, 1951
Running Time: 75 minutes

George La Main, a teenager who is tormented by his peers for being shy and inarticulate, is given a small birthday celebration by his widowed father, Andy, at the bar he owns. As George inquires about the absence of his father's longtime girl friend, Frances, and receives no answer, Al Judge, a local sportswriter enters the bar. Judge forces La Main to take off his shirt, kneel down, and submit to a vicious caning. Outraged by his father's lack of resistance to the invalid Judge, George runs from the bar taking with him his father's gun and the prize fight tickets that were part of his birthday present. While waiting outside the auditorium, George is asked to sell his extra ticket by Lloyd Cooper but is hustled out of the money by a small-time hood, Packingpaugh, posing as a policeman. Inside Cooper tells George he has been tricked. The prize fight ends quickly, but not before George has spotted Judge at ringside. George accompanies Cooper to a local bar that Judge frequents and tries to confront the sportwriter in the rest room, only to discover that Packingpaugh is also there. Frustrated at Judge's escape, George turns savagely on Packingpaugh and beats him.

George goes with Cooper, who buys him several drinks, to a nightclub and then to the apartment of the Rostina sisters, Julie and Marion. Although he is attracted to Marion

31

Left to right: Andy La Main (Preston Foster), Flanagan (Howland Chamberlain), and George La Main (John Barrymore, Jr.) in The Big Night.

and tempted to remain, George is told by Cooper how to find Judge and he leaves. The newspaper refers George to an address where Judge is working; but when George arrives, he discovers that it is Frances's apartment. Upstairs Judge is going through her things, when George confronts him. Judge explains that Frances was his siser and that he beat George's father because his refusal to marry her led to his sister's suicide. Shaken, George allows Judge to overpower him; but when Judge threatens to have him jailed as further revenge on his father, George wrestles for the gun and shoots Judge. Returning to the Rostina apartment, George is turned away by Cooper, who fears a scandal might get back to his wife in Northern California. When he goes home instead and tells his father of Judge's accusation, the elder La Main admits they are true but explains that he could not marry Frances because George's mother is probably still alive after deserting them. Disillusioned, George initially allows his father to take the blame for shooting Al Judge; but on seeing him in handcuffs, George confesses and learns that Judge was only wounded.

Although it is burdened with narrative structure that is at times self-consciosly allegorical, *The Big Night* functions basically as film noir because of the relationship it establishes between the protagonist and his mutable environment. George's half-Odyssey, half-vendetta, which takes him through a series of unfamiliar settings—and metaphorically acts as a rite of passage from adolescence to adulthood—can be viewed from the same proletarian perspectives as *Force Of Evil*. Judge's cane (as well as his very name) and Andy La Main's gun (which, in George's pocket, gives him the confidence to beat Packingpaugh) become easily read symbols of corrupting power; and Cooper, the alcoholic college professor, represents intellectual decadence. Unlike *Force Of Evil* and its rather theatricalized confrontations, *The Big Night* exploits for dramatic effect conventions that are more purely noir. Because the figures of Andy La Main and Al Judge both play against type—as the burly La Main meekly submits to Judge's beating and the older, lame journalist gives vent to a sadistic frenzy—the audience shares George's disturbance and inability to reconcile this visual anomaly. Already estranged from his peer group, who administer a ritual spanking to him in the first scene after the credits, George retreats into the security of his father's bar, only to have his reassuring birthday celebration viciously disrupted by Judge and his father, the emblem of George's own emerging manhood, humiliated. Without unnecessary psychologizing, the audience can again empathize from situation, as well as from visual convention, with George's extreme alienation and the fact that he focuses his discontent on the figure of Judge.

George's pursuit of Judge takes him out of the familiar

locus of the bar into those of boxing auditorium, after-hours joint, nightclub, and newspaper office. His humiliation by Packingpaugh, followed by the prize fight, drinking, and finally the deafening roar of the newspaper's presses constitute an unrelieved assault on George's senses, which culminate in his confrontation with Judge. All these scenes are underscored with a visual directness, punctuated by an occasional, side-lit close-up of George as his intentions vacillate. After Judge is shot, George suddenly discovers a noir cityscape that was hidden from him earlier by his anger and the night. His dwarfed figure moves past ominous buildings barely outlined by the dawn and goes in and out of shadows from such massive structures as oil tanks. The final ritual, after the denial of sanctuary at the Rostina apartment, is one of confirmation. In noir terms, that cannot be a simple and painless slap on the cheek but requires the exculpation of his father and surrender to the police.

—A.S.

THE BIG SLEEP (1946)

Director and Producer: Howard Hawks (Warner Brothers)
Screenplay: William Faulkner, Leigh Brackett, and Jules Furthman; from the novel by Raymond Chandler
Director of Photography: Sid Hickox
Special Effects: E. Roy Davidson, Warren E. Lynch
Sound: Robert B. Lee
Music: Max Steiner
Music Director: Leo F. Forbstein
Art Director: Carl Jules Weyl
Set Decoration: Fred M. MacLean
Costumes: Leah Rhodes
Assistant Directors: Chuck Hansen, Robert Vreeland
Film Editor: Christian Nyby

CAST: Humphrey Bogart (Philip Marlowe), Lauren Bacall (Vivian Sternwood), John Ridgeley (Eddie Mars), Martha Vickers (Carmen Sternwood), Dorothy Malone (Bookstore Proprietress), Patricia Clarke (Mona Mars), Regis Toomey (Bernie Ohls), Charles Waldron (Gen. Sternwood), Charles D. Brown (Norris), Louis Jean Heydt (Joe Brody), Elisha Cook, Jr. (Harry Jones), Sonia Darrin (Agnes), Bob Steele (Canino), James Flavin (Capt. Cronjager), Thomas Jackson (Wilde), Thomas Rafferty (Carol Lundgren), Theodore Von Eltz (Arthur Gwynne Geiger), Dan Wallace (Owen Taylor), Joy Barlowe (Taxi Driver). BITS: Forbes Murray (Furtive Man), Pete Kooy (Motorcycle Officer), Emmett Vogan (Deputy Sheriff), Joe Crehan (Medical Examiner), Carole Douglas (Librarian), Jack Chefe (Croupier), Tom Fadden (Sidney), Ben Weldon (Pete), Paul Weber, Jack Perry, Wally Walker (Eddie Mars's Thugs), Lorraine Miller (Hatcheck Girl), Shelby Payne (Cigarette Girl), Trevor Bardette (Art Huck), Tanis Chandler, Deannie Best (Waitresses).
Filming Completed: January 12, 1945

Released: Warner Brothers, August 31, 1946
Running Time: 118 minutes

Private detective Philip Marlowe is asked by the wealthy Gen. Sternwood to rid him of a blackmailer named Geiger who holds compromising photos of Sternwood's younger daughter, Carmen. After meeting Carmen and her older sister, Vivian, Marlowe accepts the case. He discovers that Geiger's Hollywood bookstore is a front for a blackmail racket; but before Marlowe can act, Geiger is murdered. Marlowe, who finds Carmen in Geiger's house, takes her home before the police arrive and learns from Vivian something about the tangled web of intrigue and murder surrounding the Sternwood family. There is a possible link with two missing persons, the wife of gambler Eddie Mars and Sternwood's former confidant, Sean Regan, which Vivian discourages Marlowe from pursuing. Ignoring Vivian's suggestion that he quit the case, Marlowe learns that a second man has made blackmail threats against Carmen. Ultimately, this leads to a confrontation between Marlowe, Vivian, and a drunken Carmen with a couple of Geiger's employees, Joe Brody and Agnes, who now have the blackmailer's files. Marlowe uses the blackmailer's own ploy and threatens Brody with implication in Geiger's death unless he talks; but before he can, Brody is shot by another of Geiger's former associates. When Marlowe can get no useful information from this killer, he turns to Eddie Mars. On a vist to Mars's gambling house, he discovers that Vivian is a patron there. Mars, who is the owner of Geiger's house and had already warned Marlowe off the case once, claims to have no information of use to Marlowe and refuses to discuss the sensitive subject of his wife and Sean Regan. Just as things seem to be at a dead end for Marlowe, he is visited by Harry Jones, a new boyfriend of Agnes's. Marlowe, who has just been beaten by thugs he suspects were sent by Eddie Mars, leaves Jones alone for a minute and returns through an outer office to find him with Canino, Mars's hired killer, who forces Jones to drink poison. Canino flees and Jones dies without betraying Agnes; but Marlowe is able to deduce her phone number.

The information he buys from Agnes leads Marlowe to a ranch house in an outlying stretch of the county. When Marlowe feigns car trouble at a nearby garage, he is overpowered by Mars's henchmen. When he comes to inside the ranch house, he discovers that both Mars's wife and Vivian are there. Realizing that her efforts to protect her sister may cost Marlowe his life, Vivian frees the detective. With her help, Marlowe gets a gun from his car and kills Canino. Then they return to Geiger's house and call Mars to arrange a meeting. Thinking that Marlowe and Vivian had called from his ranch house, Mars goes to Geiger's place to set up an ambush but finds Marlowe waiting. After extracting a confession from Mars, Marlowe fires some shots and forces Mars to go out the front door, where he is gunned down by his own men. Safe inside the house, Marlowe and Vivian await the arrival of the police.

Los Angeles adds a horizontal dimension to film noir. In

place of the looming monoliths and endless urban alley-ways of the Eastern cityscape, there is a physical and moral sprawl, a chain of suburbs full of legal and illegal activities linked by wide boulevards and expressways. Chandler saw this and made *The Big Sleep*, like all his other stories set in Los Angeles, a series of journeys across a mythical landscape of darkened bungalows, decaying office buildings, and sinister nightspots. As Chandler wrote in "The Simple Art of Murder," his critical essay on the genre of detective fiction, "Down these mean streets a man must go who is not himself mean, who is neither tarnished nor afraid."

What Chandler's detective rediscovered each time he drove down those streets is something akin to the film noir vision of the world. Unlike many protagonists original to film noir, Chandler's Philip Marlowe enters that world with a number of prescriptive literary qualities that insure his survival. Although Marlowe may seem just a fallen idealist, capable of being physically worn out or romantically duped, he is neither mean, tarnished, nor afraid because, as Chandler asserted, "The detective in this kind of story must be such a man…the best man in his world." For Chandler the intricate web of motivations in *The Big Sleep* are the stylistic analogue of the dark streets and lonely houses the movie Marlowe explores. *The Big Sleep,* as film, evokes the chaotic underworld of the novel through setting and visualization rather than plot. The complexities of narrative are still there, but they no longer constitute the main ground against which the noir figure of Marlowe is defined. *The Big Sleep* stresses characterization and visual style rather than events and, it ultimately reduces a story line that is irretrievably tangled to minor significance.

Both the novel Marlowe and the film Marlowe are outsiders. They enter the world of men like Gen. Sternwood and court women like his daughters Vivian by invitation only. They seem to search in that world for fleeting glimpses of compassion, of simple human feeling; but they are unwilling to be the first to betray such feelings in themselves. In fact, both Marlowes guard their private ground so tenaciously that they are viscerally outraged when Carmen Sternwood invites herself in and violates it with attempted seduction. Both versions of Marlowe possess a fairly explicit sense of, if not morality per se, at least right conduct. The presence of such amoral men and women as Carmen, Canino, Eddie Mars, and Agnes casts a heavy pall of pessimism over the film's background characterizations, which is broken only in Marlowe's scenes with Vivian Sternwood. In effect, Vivian's tough broad facade ill conceals a desperate concern about her psychotic sister and sickly father; and Marlowe's hard guy pose is a thin veneer easily pierced by his admiration for the loyal heroism of a "little man" like Harry Jones.

After the initial inscription of the noir underworld—in the dark compositions of the opening sequences and in several cynical exchanges of dialogue, such as that between Marlowe and Mars puzzling over the blood stain in Geiger's house: "Got any ideas, soldier?" asks Mars; and Marlowe replies, "A couple. Somebody gunned Geiger, or somebody got gunned by Geiger who ran away, or Geiger

had meat for dinner and likes to do his butchering on the parlor floor."—*The Big Sleep* becomes a series of character encounters in which the drama of trust tendered, trust betrayed, and trust restored is played out. For Marlowe, whose world is always associated with such concepts as "gunning," "running away," and "butchering," trust is a different concept entirely: one that is both difficult and necessary for him. Marlowe needs at least one person which to anchor his own shaken code of beliefs. He has one for a brief interlude in Harry Jones and his fidelity to the worthless Agnes; and when Canino viciously compels Jones's suicide, Marlowe comes close to losing his equilibrium. Beaten and unable to overcome Canino alone, Marlowe is forced to the realization that his life is *en prise* and its continuance depends on the sufferance of those he does not fully trust.

Vivian frees him; and that act is a consummation of their uncertain relationship established in earlier scenes. The sexual tension between Marlowe and Vivian is suggested by their mannerisms in their first encounter and supported by subsequent dialogue (Marlowe: "You've got a touch of class, but I don't know how you'd do over a stretch of ground." Vivian: "A lot depends on who's in the saddle."). Against her own better judgment, Vivian cannot rid herself of Marlowe. She goes to his office with that idea in mind but ends by sitting on his desk and helping him throw the police off track. Moreover the interpretation of Marlowe and Vivian by Bogart and Bacall is full of nonverbal expressions of sympathy that quickly undermine the initial antagonism of the characters. By the time Vivian frees Marlowe at the ranch house, they have realized that mutual trust is essential to their survival. With that understanding established, Marlowe succeeds in killing both Canino and Mars; and Vivian concedes to Marlowe that there's nothing wrong with her that he can't fix.

To a considerable extent the film version romanticizes Chandler's concept of *The Big Sleep,* particularly in the final image of Marlowe and Vivian huddled in the darkened parlor of Geiger's house while the sounds of approaching sirens and Max Steiner's orchestration are combined on the sound track. Ultimately *The Big Sleep* is faithful to the noir vision because that final image has an underlying irony. Visually the couple is surrounded by dark corners; aurally ominous sirens encroach on the romantic score; and they stand all the while near the bloodstain, the emblem of Geiger's death and the beginning of a series of murders and betrayals. Although both Marlowe and Vivian have survived that violent chain reaction, they cannot have been untouched by it.

—J.P., J.K., A.S.

BLACK ANGEL (1946)

Director: Roy William Neill
Producers: Tom McKnight, Roy William Neill (Universal)

Screenplay: Roy Chanslor; from the novel by Cornell Woolrich
Director of Photography: Paul Ivano
Special Photography: David S. Horsley
Sound: Bernard B. Brown, Joe Lapis
Music Score: Frank Skinner
Songs: "Heartbreak," "I Wanted to Talk About," "Time Will Tell," and "Continental Gentleman" by Edgar Fairchild and Jack Brooks; sung by June Vincent
Art Directors: Jack Otterson, Martin Obzina
Set Decoration: Russell A. Gausman, E.R. Robinson
Costumes: Vera West
Makeup: Jack P. Pierce
Hairstyles: Carmen Dirigo
Dialogue Director: Raymond Kessler
Assistant Director: Charles S. Gould
Film Editor: Saul A. Goodkind

CAST: Dan Duryea (Martin Blair), June Vincent (Catherine), Peter Lorre (Marko), Broderick Crawford (Capt. Flood), Constance Dowling (Marvis Marlowe), Wallace Ford (Joe), Hobart Cavanaugh (Jake), Freddie Steele (Lucky), Ben Bard (Bartender), John Phillips (Kirk Bennett), Junius Matthews (Dr. Courtney), Maurice St. Clair, Vilova (Dance Team), Pat Starling (Tap Dancer).
BITS: Marion Martin (Flo), Wally Webb (Banjo Player), Mary Fields (Maid), Steve Olsen (Bartender), Florence Auer (Madame), Eddy Chandler (Sgt. Baker), Dorothy Granger (Woman), Mauritz Hugo (Gambler), Robert Williams (2nd Detective), Eula Guy (Neighbor Lady), Dick Wessel (Doorman), Michael Branden (Mitchell), Clark Kuney (Announcer), Ralph Brooks (Intern), Chuck Hamilton (Man), Ann Lawrence (Girl Clerk), Shephard Houghton, Bob Crosby, Bud Lawler, Gary Delmar (Specialty Dancers).
Location: Hollywood, California
Filming Completed: May 17, 1946
Released: Universal, August 2, 1946
Running Time: 83 minutes

After his treacherous wife, Marvis, leaves him, composer Marty Blair becomes an alcoholic. Marvis lives in a luxurious apartment and Marty goes there one night to see her but is refused admittance on Marvis's instructions. Later, Marvis is found murdered. Marty is the logical suspect, but he was sleeping in his room at the time of the murder. Kirk Bennett, who went to Marvis's apartment to retrieve incriminating letters before they were sent to his wife Catherine, is convicted of the crime. In spite of her husband's involvement with Marvis, Catherine believes him innocent and enlists the aid of Marty, who remembers a stranger leaving Marvis's apartment the night of the murder. This was Marko, a shady nightclub operator, who hires Marty and Catherine to play and sing in his club. They work for Marko, hoping to find a jeweled, heart-shaped brooch that Marty had given to Marvis. The brooch, which disappeared the night of the murder, can incriminate Marko. But Marko is innocent of the murder and was in fact

being watched by the police at the time of her death. Marty is convinced that Bennett did the killing; he asks Catherine to start a new life with him, but she rejects Marty, declaring that she still loves her husband. Despondent and in an alcoholic haze, Marty sees Marvis's jeweled heart on a woman in a bar and realizes that it was he who murdered his wife, subsequently blocking it from his mind. Marty calls the police just in time to save Bennett's life.

The Black Angel is a modest but imaginative film, with an ingenious script. Dan Duryea, a very interesting actor unfortunately too often typed for his successful portraits of pathological villains and insidious pimps, not only has the leading role but is allowed to play an affectingly romantic character. This unusual casting of Duryea (also a distinguishing feature of *World For Ransom* and *The Burglar* in the 1950s) makes the dramatic thrust of the story even more interesting. While Duryea is the murderer, he remains the most sympathetic character in the film and far worthier of the heroine than her weak and disloyal husband, the "innocent" Bennett.

Certainly, the opening sequence with its complex boom shot from the street to the interior of Marvis's penthouse apartment and the expressionistic re-creation of the murder through Marty's drunken consciousness effectively realize the potential of the material. Likewise, the Duryea character is so carefully drawn that the climax of the story has a feeling of genuine tragedy. The encouragement given to art directors and photographers in B films is very much in evidence in *The Black Angel*. The design of Marko's nightclub, in particular, belie the limitations of a modest budget.
—B.L.

BLAST OF SILENCE (1961)

Director: Allen Baron
Producer: Merrill Brody (Malda Productions)
Screenplay: Allen Baron
Director of Photography: Merrill Brody
Sound: Lee Bost
Music: Meyer Kupferman
Art Director: Charles Rosen
Assistant Director: Carole Brody
Film Editor: Merrill Brody

CAST: Allen Baron (Frank Bono), Molly McCarthy (Lorrie), Larry Tucker (Big Ralph), Peter Clume Troiano), Canny Meehan (Petey), Milda Memonas (Troiano's Girl), Dean Sheldon (Nightclub Singer), Charles Creasap (Contact Man), Joe Bubbico (Gangster), Bill DePrato (Sailor), Erich Kollmar (Bellhop), Ruth Kaner (Building Supervisor), Gil Rogers, Jerry Douglas (Gangsters), Don Saroyan (Lorrie's Boyfriend), Jeri Sopanen (Waiter), Mel Sponder (Drummer), Betty Kovac

THE BLUE DAHLIA

(Troiano's Wife), Bob Taylor, Ernest Jackson (Gangsters).
Location: Manhattan, Brooklyn, Staten Island, New York
Filming Completed: 1961
Released: Universal-International, August 1961
Running Time: 77 minutes

A train hurtles out of a tunnel toward Manhattan, bringing with it Frank Bono, a hired killer. A cautious professional brought to town by the syndicate to eliminate one of their own number, Bono insists on taking the time to chart the movements of his intended victim. In the course of his work, he reencounters a former girl friend. He is disturbed to discover that he is still attracted to her, as that might interfere with his assignment. A misunderstanding over the "clean" gun to be used in the job leads Bono to kill Big Ralph, a grossly overweight, minor hood. Despite lingering doubts about the problems he has had, Bono fulfills his contract. When he goes to a prearranged spot at a nearby bench to collect the remainder of his fee, he is shot down.

Coming as it does after the close of the 1950s, certain elements of *Blast Of Silence* may seem to be unconscious caricatures of classic noir motifs. The bulky Big Ralph, Troiano's moll, and an odd assortment of other street people provide the stereotypical local color to punctuate Bono's unrelentingly grim odyssey. The fact that almost the entire cast of this low-budget, New York-based production were nonprofessionals before its release, does not mitigate the occasional sense of "Hollywood" types playing against each other. At the same time, the anonymous, gray background fused from a succession of location exteriors effectively counteracts the probing asides of the unseen, third-person narrator and restrains the viewer from penetrating Bono's physical and emotional isolation. As neither the theme nor the visual treatment is particularly complex, it is Allen Baron's portrayal of the stolid, compulsive Bono, rather than his direction, that supports the noir mood of *Blast Of Silence*. After the explosive opening of the film—a sustained shot of a train taking several minutes to traverse a tunnel and finally roaring out—Baron is content to situate his dark figure simply and effectively in the various urban settings; in a way this contrasts graphically with, but is figuratively analogous to, the aspect of the cautious assassin, White Suit, in *The Dark Corner*: a man playing out a role and quietly awaiting his inexorable betrayal.

—A.S.

THE BLUE DAHLIA (1946)

Director: George Marshall
Producer: John Houseman (Paramount)
Screenplay: Raymond Chandler
Director of Photography: Lionel Lindon

Process Photography: Farciot Edouart
Sound: Gene Merritt, Joel Moss
Music: Victor Young
Art Directors: Hans Dreier, Walter Tyler
Set Decoration: Sam Comer, Jimmy Walters
Costumes: Edith Head
Property Master: Pat Delaney
Assistant Director: C.C. Coleman, Jr.
Film Editor: Arthur Schmidt

CAST: Alan Ladd (Johnny Morrison), Veronica Lake (Joyce Harwood), William Bendix (Buzz Wanchek), Howard da Silva (Eddie Harwood), Doris Dowling (Helen Morrison), Tom Powers (Capt. Hendrickson), Hugh Beaumont (George Copeland), Howard Freeman (Corelli), Don Costello (Leo), Will Wright (Dad Newell), Frank Faylen (the Man), Walter Sande (Heath, Gangster). **BITS:** Vera Marshe (Blond), Mae Busch (Jenny, the Maid), Gloria Williams (Assistant Maid), George Barton, Jack Gargan (Cab Drivers), Harry Hayden (Mr. Hughes, Assistant Hotel Manager), Harry Barris (Bellhop), Paul Gustine (Doorman), Roberta Jonay (Girl Hotel Clerk), Milton Kibbee (Night Hotel Clerk), Dick Winslow (Piano Player at Party), Anthony Caruso (Marine Corporal), Matt McHugh (Bartender), Arthur Loft (the "Wolf"), Stan Johnson (Naval Officer), Ernie Adams (Joe, Man in Coveralls), Henry Vroom (Master Sergeant), Harry Tyler (Clerk in Bus Station), Jack Clifford (Plainclothes Dick), George Sorel (Paul, Captain of Waiters), James Millican, Albert Ruiz (Photographers), Charles A. Hughes (Lt. Lloyd), Leon Lombardo (Mexican Bellhop), Nina Borget (Mexican Waitress), Douglas Carter (Bus Driver), Ed Randolph (Cop), Bea Allen (News Clerk), Perc Launders (Hotel Clerk), Jimmy Dundee (Driver of Gangster Car), Tom Dillon (Cop in Prowl Car), Dick Elliott (Motor Court Owner), Clark Eggleston (Elevator Operator), George Carleton (Clerk, DeAnza Hotel), Lawrence Young (Clerk), Franklin Parker (Police Stenographer), Noel Neill, Mavis Murray (Hatcheck Girls), Brooke Evans, Carmen Clifford, Audrey Westphal, Lucy Knoch, Audrey Korn, Beverly Thompson, Jerry James, Charles Mayon, William Meader (Guests at Cocktail Party).
Location: Miramar Hotel, Santa Monica, Encino, Malibu, Hollywood, California
Filming Completed: May 22, 1945
Released: Paramount, April 19, 1946
Running Time: 98 minutes

A war veteran, Johnny Morrison, returns home to find that his wife, Helen, has not been faithful. Disgusted, he leaves her. Soon afterward she is found murdered and Johnny is suspected of the crime. In his big flight from the police, a mysterious woman attempts to befriend Johnny but he is mistrustful of her. Later, he discovers that she is Joyce, the wife of Eddie Harwood, a nightclub owner who played a prominent role in his wife's infidelity. In the meantime, Johnny's buddies Buzz and George try to clear their friend of the murder charges. The clues, however, suggest that

Johnny Morrison (Alan Ladd) and Joyce Harwood (Veronica Lake) in The Blue Dahlia.

Buzz actually murdered Johnny's wife while suffering a blackout caused by a lingering war wound. A series of brutal beatings and private sleuthing carried out by Johnny and Mrs. Harwood ultimately lead to a final confrontation, and Harwood is accidentally shot by his own henchmen. Dad Newell, a hotel detective, is tricked by the police investigator and is shot after confessing the murder of Johnny's wife when his blackmail plot involving Harwood failed to gain him the required results.

As an original screenplay by Raymond Chandler, *The Blue Dahlia* is an important postwar film noir. The inclusion of amnesia, helplessness, and dissillusionment contribute to the film's noir mood. Originally, Chandler wanted Buzz to be the actual killer, blinded and desensitized by the brutalizing effects of the war. The studio met with objections from the Navy and forced Chandler to rewrite the film implicating Dad as the murderer. The ambience of Chandler's hard-boiled novels was given a strong visual impact from Ladd's emotionless characterization and Bendix's frenzied amnesia. The overriding sense of corruption hidden below the surfaces of many of the film's characters—combined with atmosphere provided by director George Marshall—make *The Blue Dahlia* a fascinating example of postwar noir sensibility. The elements of the film are more exciting than the ultimate production, so that in lieu of Chandler's initial plot, *The Blue Dahlia* surfaces less as a quintessential film noir than as merely an interesting and stylish thriller.

—C.M.

THE BLUE GARDENIA (1953)

Director: Fritz Lang
Producer: Alex Gottlieb (Alex Gottlieb Productions)
Screenplay: Charles Hoffman; from the short story "Gardenia" by Vera Caspary
Director of Photography: Nicholas Musuraca
Special Effects: Willis Cook
Sound: Ben Winkler
Music: Raoul Kraushaar
Song: "The Blue Gardenia" by Bob Russell and Lester Lee, arranged by Nelson Riddle; sung by Nat "King" Cole
Art Director: Daniel Hall
Assistant Director: Emmett Emerson
Film Editor: Edward Mann

CAST: Anne Baxter (Norah Larkin), Richard Conte (Casey Mayo), Ann Sothern (Crystal Carpenter), Raymond Burr (Harry Prebble), Jeff Donnell (Sally Ellis), Richard Erdman (Al), George Reeves (Police Capt. Haynes), Ruth Storey (Rose Miller), Ray Walker (Homer), Nat "King"

BODY AND SOUL

Cole (Himself), Celia Lovsky (Blind Woman), Frank Ferguson (Drunkard), Alex Gottlieb (Man).
Filming Completed: December 24, 1952
Released: Warner Brothers, March 28, 1953
Running Time: 90 minutes

Norah Larkin, depressed at having received a "Dear Jane" letter from her fiancé in Korea, impulsively accepts a blind date with a man calling for her roommate, Crystal. They meet at the Blue Gardenia, a Hollywood restaurant, where the beautiful but naive Norah is easy prey for playboy Harry Prebble. He plies her with liquor during dinner and then takes her to his apartment where he attempts to seduce her. When he becomes too intimate, she panics and strikes out at Prebble then loses consciousness. The following day, she is unable to account for her movements the previous evening—until, reading that Prebble has been beaten to death. She remembers and is certain she has committed murder. A clever, aggressive reporter, Casey Mayo, writes a story captioned "Letter to An Unknown Murderess" to coax the killer into giving herself up to him. Norah calls him at the paper, posing as a "friend" of the murderess, and arranges a series of meetings. She begins to fall in love with Casey, who promises her the newspaper's protection and finally persuades her to confess. Feeling responsible, Casey assists police Capt. Haines's investigation of another suspect. This suspect attempts suicide with a piece of broken glass, but the police arrest her and discover that she is Prebble's pregnant girl friend, Rose. The night of the murder, she arrived at Prebble's house shortly after Norah had fled, and when he refused to marry her she killed him with the poker.

Fritz Lang is one of the few major directors whose name is repeatedly associated with the noir cycle in the 1950s through such films as *Clash By Night, The Blue Gardenia, The Big Heat,* and *Human Desire.* Tied to a narrative that was rather unimaginative, *The Blue Gardenia* was the weakest of the four; yet Lang, together with a capable cast and photographer, was able to imbue it with his sense of the *maudit.* A newspaper-oriented melodrama, which makes connection with a host of neurotic personalities, is an appropriate vehicle in the 1950s for a study of middle-class alienation. An indication of the changing aspect of the noir cycle is that *The Blue Gardenia* as directed by Lang and as photographed by Nicholas Musuraca was largely composed of flat, neutral gray images most representative of 1950s television with its overhead lighting. The diminished influence of a particular studio or visual style is evidenced by Musuraca, whose presence helped define the noir style at RKO but who contributes only a few expressionistic moments in *The Blue Gardenia:* an occasional rain-streaked window or Prebble's murder reflected in the glass of a broken mirror. Despite this high-key visual style, Lang does exploit to advantage certain technical developments in motion pictures. The location work complements the images in giving the film a surface value in a realistic rather than expressionistic tradition. Lang also uses the mobility of the crab dolly to

follow his characters with a nervous insistence that anticipates the hand-held camera. The circling motions around the unfortunate Norah become vectors in a relentless determinism that is most typical of Lang's noir vision.

—B.P. & A.S.

BODY AND SOUL (1947)
[Working title: AN AFFAIR OF THE HEART]

Director: Robert Rossen
Producer: Bob Roberts (Enterprise Productions)
Screenplay: Abraham Polonsky
Director of Photography: James Wong Howe
Sound: Frank Webster
Music Score: Hugo Friedhofer
Song: "Body and Soul," music by Johnny Green, lyric by Edward Hewman, Robert Sour, Frank Eyton
Music Director: Rudolph Polk
Art Director: Nathan Juran
Set Decoration: Edward J. Boyle
Costumes: Marion Herwood Keyes
Makeup: Gustaf M. Norin
Production Manager: Joseph Gilpin
Assistant Director: Robert Aldrich
Special Montages: Guenther Fritsch
Film Editor: Robert Parrish
Supervising Film Editor: Francis Lyons

CAST: John Garfield (Charlie Davis), Lilli Palmer (Peg Born), Hazel Brooks (Alice), Anne Revere (Anna Davis), William Conrad (Quinn), Joseph Pevney (Shorty Polaski), Canada Lee (Ben Chaplin), Lloyd Goff (Roberts), Art Smith (David Davis), James Burke (Arnold), Virginia Gregg (Irma), Peter Virgo (Drummer), Joe Devlin (Prince), Shimin Rushkin (Grocer), Mary Currier (Miss Tedder), Milton Kibbie (Dan), Tim Ryan (Shelton), Artie Dorrell (Jack Marlowe), Cy Ring (Victor), Glen Lee (Marine), John Indrisano (Referee), Dan Tobey (Fight Announcer).
Filming Completed: April 1947
Released: United Artists, August 22, 1947
Running Time: 105 minutes

Charlie Davis, a young man of the slums, is determined to be a success and escape from his life of poverty. He enters into a partnership with Roberts, a gambler and fight promoter, and tries to use his skill as a boxer to acquire the material wealth he has always wanted. His search for money and glory alienates Charlie from those closest to him He rejects Peg, the woman who loves him, for Alice, a girl friend of Roberts and his gambler cohorts. He also grows increasingly distant from his mother. Heeding neither his best friend, Shorty Polaski, nor his faithful trainer and sparring partner, Ben Chaplin, Charlie even stands by when Roberts eventually causes Shorty's death. His final act of corruption, deliberately planning to throw a fight at Roberts's request, is a turning point in Charlie's life. When Ben dies, Charlie begins to question his values and decides to try and win the fight, going against Roberts and the mob.

Body and Soul contains many elements of the early social dramas made in the 1930s; in some ways it can be seen as one of the last cries of liberalism before the House Un-American Activities Committee investigations were to crush many of its principals. Basically about corruption, the ever present temptation of the dollar is constantly dangled before the eyes of Charlie Davis, the fighter hero of the film. All along the way, Charlie rejects the virtuous choices of his mother, his girl friend and his longtime friend Shorty. Finally, it is the death of the last remaining "good" person in his life, the aging Ben, that leads him to perform the positive act that sets him free from the gangsters. This shift to affirmation and growth at the end of the film is partly a reflection of director Robert Rossen's own idealism and partly that of writer Abraham Polonsky's social conscience.

The visualization is restrained in terms of expressionistic devices but does include techniques that reinforce Davis's sense of being trapped in a certain milieu. For instance, the long craning shot in the training camp moves slowly over the ring and other unused paraphernalia then in through a window, where it reveals Davis lying awake on his bed. This third-person camera relentlessly tracking the protagonist acquires a subjective quality in the actual fight sequences, when the hand-held camera alternately lunges at Davis and his opponent, accentuating the alienating violence of his profession with a graphic naturalism.

—J.C. & A.S.

BORDER INCIDENT (1949)
[Working Title: BORDER PATROL]

Director: Anthony Mann
Producer: Nicholas Nayfack (MGM)
Screenplay: John C. Higgins; from an unpublished story by John C. Higgins and George Zuckerman
Director of Photography: John Alton
Sound: Douglas Shearer, Charles E. Wallace
Music Director: André Previn
Art Directors: Cedric Gibbons, Hans Peters
Set Decoration: Edwin B. Willis, Ralph S. Hurst
Makeup: Jack Dawn
Production Manager: William Kaplan
Assistant Director: Howard Koch
Script Supervisor: Don MacDougall
Film Editor: Conrad A. Nervig

CAST: Ricardo Montalban (Pablo Rodriguez), George Murphy (Jack Bearnes), Howard da Silva (Owen Parkson), James Mitchell (Juan Garcia), Arnold Moss (Zopilote), Alfonso Bedoya (Cuchillo), Teresa Celli (Maria), Charles McGraw (Jeff Amboy), Jose Torvay (Pocoloco), John Ridgely (Mr. Neley), Arthur Hunnicutt (Clayton Nordell), Sig Ruman (Hugo Wolfgang Ulrich), Otto Waldis (Fritz), Harry Antrim (John Boyd), Tony Barr (Luis), Rozene Jones (Senora), John McGuire (Norson), Jack Lambert (Chuck), Nedrich Young (Happy), Fred Graham (Leathercoat), Lynn Whitney (Bella Amboy). **BITS:** Jose Dominguez, Rogue Ybarra, George L. Derrick, Charles Rivero, Albert Haskell, Samuel Herrera, Jerry Riggio, David Cota, Danilo Valente, Mitchell Lewis, Robert Cabal, Elias Gamboa, Miguel Contreras (*Braceros*), Martin Garralaga (Col. Alvarado), Paul Marion (One-Armed Man), Gerald Echaverria (Padre Ignacio), Manual Lopez (Mexican Lieutenant), Enrique Escalante (Mexican Sergeant), William Phillips (Jim), Lita Barron (Rosita), Frank Conlan (Clerk), Ed Max (Doc Kelso), Gordon Harris, Riley Sunrise (Bandits).
Location: Mexicali, Mexico
Filming Completed: May 24, 1949
Released: MGM, November 19, 1949
Running Time: 96 minutes

A crooked rancher, Owen Parkson, smuggles Mexicans with phony work permits into the California valleys, where the Mexicans are exploited. The criminal operation leads to murder; and immigration officials on both sides of the border join forces to investigate. A U.S. agent, Jack Bearnes, and a Mexican agent, Pablo Rodriguez, infiltrate. The former poses as a petty crook in Parkson's gang while the latter is disguised as a *bracero* delivered to Parkson's ranch. Pablo and Jack witness the inhuman treatment of the Mexicans by the psychopathic Parkson and his sadistic henchman. Jack's true identity is discovered, and he dies horribly as the helpless Pablo watches. Finally, Pablo and the immigration authorities destroy Parkson and smash his gang.

The reputation made by Anthony Mann and John Alton with *T-Men* and their other Eagle-Lion pictures, rapidly earned them work at MGM; and it is no surprise that Mann directed a film modeled closely on *T-Men*. *Border Incident* features two undercover men, this time immigration officials rather than Treasury agents, and in a egalitarian spirit, one is an American while the other is Mexican and they are equally sympathetic. The scene in *T-Men* in which O'Brien must watch Genaro be killed, is matched in *Border Incident* by the scene of Bearnes run down by a tractor as Pablo looks on. The latter scene is more visually impressive as a close wide-angle shot vividly captures Bearnes's terror as he desperately claws at dirt to save himself. Certainly this death scene is one of the most grisly in this period of film history and was later copied by the makers of *Prime Cut*. However, the comparable scene in *T-Men* includes a more complex emotional exchange between O'Brien and the heroic Genaro.

Border Incident's photography by John Alton consists primarily of deep focus compositions with high contrast. In the Mexican sequences, chiaroscuro lighting enhances the visual impression. Additionally, the landscape of the California Southwest is used for the first time by Mann to enhance dramatically the moral and emotional thrust of the action, prefiguring the Westerns he would begin making the following year.

—B.L.

BORN TO KILL (1947)
[Working Title: DEADLIER THAN THE MALE]

Director: Robert Wise
Executive Producer: Sid Rogell (RKO)
Producer: Herman Schlom
Screenplay: Eve Greene and Richard Macaulay; from the novel *Deadlier than the Male* by James Gunn
Director of Photography: Robert de Grasse
Special Effects: Russell A. Cully
Sound: Robert H. Guhl, Roy Granville
Music Score: Paul Sawtell
Music Director: Constantin Bakaleinikoff
Art Directors: Albert S. D'Agostino, Walter E. Keller
Set Decoration: Darrell Silvera, John Sturtevant
Costumes: Edward Stevenson
Assistant Director: Sam Ruman [Robert Weiss?]
Film Editor: Les Millbrook

CAST: Claire Trevor (Helen Trent), Lawrence Tierney (Sam Wild), Walter Slezak (Arnold Arnett), Philip Terry (Fred Grover), Audrey Long (Georgia Staples), Elisha Cook, Jr. (Marty Waterman), Isabel Jewell (Laury Palmer), Esther Howard (Mrs. Kraft), Kathryn Card (Grace), Tony Barrett (Danny), Grandon Rhodes (Inspector Wilson). **BITS:** Sam Lufkin, Sayre Dearing, Sammy Shack, Joe Dixon (Crap Dealers), Ruth Brennan (Sally), Tom Noonan (Bellboy), Al Murphy (Cab Driver), Phil Warren (Chauffeur), Ben Frommer (Delivery Boy), Netta Packer (Mrs. Perth), Lee Frederick (Desk Clerk), Demetrius Alexis (Maitre d'Hotel), Martha Hyer (Maid), Beatrice Maude (Cook), Ellen Corby (2nd Maid), Jean Fenwick (Margaret Macy), Reverend Neal Dodd (Clergyman), Napolean Whiting (Porter), Perc Launders (Detective Bryson), Stanley Stone (Train Conductor), Jason Robards, Sr. (Conductor).
Filming Completed: June 21, 1946
Released: RKO, May 3, 1947
Running Time: 92 minutes

Sam Wild, a former boxer and rancher, is in Reno gambling with his friend, Marty Waterman. Sam is alternately morose and cruel, and his violent nature has got him into trouble many times. Marty is calm and cool and attempts to hold Sam's passions in check, but when Sam sees a girl friend of his, Laury Palmer, out with another man, he kills them both in a jealous rage. The bodies are discovered that evening in Mrs. Kraft's boarding house by a tenant, Helen Trent, who does not report the murders because she is leaving town that night and returning to San Francisco. Sam flees to San Francisco and Marty delays his own departure so that he can keep track of the murder investigation in Reno. Meeting on the train, Helen is attracted to Sam's good looks and cocky manner but refuses to arrange a date. She is the adopted sister of a newspaper heiress, Georgia Staples, and is engaged to a young steel heir, Fred Grover. Sam visits Helen at the Staples mansion but when he learns of her engagement, he courts Georgia. Not realizing that he is only interested in her wealth, Georgia and Sam are soon married. Marty attends the wedding but is followed by Arnold Arnett, a dishonest private detective hired by Mrs. Kraft to find Laury's murderer. Arnett sells his information to Marty, who plans to kill Mrs. Kraft to protect Sam. Meanwhile, Sam jealously suspects Marty of having an affair with Helen. When Marty lures Mrs. Kraft to a lonely stretch of beach and prepares to kill her, Sam intervenes and murders Marty. Despite everything, Helen cannot overcome her perverse attraction for Sam and forces Mrs. Kraft to drop her investigation. Helen calls for the police in an attempt to extricate herself from criminal involvement, and Georgia realizes Helen has always hated her and is in love with Sam. Spiteful, Helen makes Georgia witness Sam's adulterous passion and then convinces Sam to shoot Georgia, but the arrival of the police stops him. When Sam learns who sent for the police, he shoots Helen and is then killed by the police.

Born To Kill is a grim and complicated melodrama, which is nonetheless intriguing, for it is the first of a number of noir films directed by Robert Wise, who had previously been associated with Orson Welles and then with the Val Lewton group at RKO. This leads to the interesting speculation that RKO developed the quintessential noir style of the 1940s due to a unique synthesizing of the expressionistic style of Welles and the moody, Gothic atmosphere of Lewton. *Born To Kill* is an excellent example of an RKO style, not only for its visuals but also for its offhanded depiction of perturbed sexuality and extreme brutality.

—B.P.

BRAINSTORM (1965)

Director and Producer: William Conrad (Warner Brothers)
Screenplay: Mann Rubin; from an unpublished story by Larry Marcus
Director of Photography: Sam Leavitt
Sound: M.A. Merrick
Music: George Duning
Art Director: Robert Smith
Set Decoration: Hoyle Barrett
Makeup: Gordon Bau
Hairstyles: Jean Burt Reilly
Unit Manager: James Vaughn

Assistant Director: Howard L. Grace, Jr.
Film Editor: William Ziegler

CAST: Jeff Hunter (James Grayam), Anne Francis (Lorrie Benson), Dana Andrews (Cort Benson), Viveca Lindfors (Dr. Elizabeth Larstedt), Stacy Harris (Josh Reynolds), Kathie Browne (Angie DeWitt), Phillip Pine (Dr. Ames), Michael Pate (Dr. Mills), Joan Swift (Clara), George Pelling (Butler), Victoria Meyerink (Julie), Strother Martin (Clyde), Steven Roberts (Judge), Pat Cardi (Bobby), Robert McQueeney (Sgt. Dawes). **BITS:** Pamelyn Ferdin (Little Girl in Lobby), Julie VanZandt (Mother), Byron Keith, Ray Montgomery (Guards), George Neise, Barbara Dodd, Wendy Russell, James O'Hara, Elaina Martone (Party Guests), James Seay (Judge at Scavenger Hunt), Lloyd Kino (Mr. Komato), Suzanne Benoit, Isabelle Cooley (Nurses), Biff Elliott, Al Shelly, Harry Bartell (Detectives), Steve Ihnat (Intern), John Mitchum, Roberto Contreras, Victor Rodman, Richard Kiel, Joe Mell (Inmates), Charles Maxwell (Patient), William Quinn (Psychiatrist), Maurice Wells (Judge), Wil Duffy, Don Chaffin (Orderlies).
Filming Completed: February 19, 1965
Released: Warner Brothers, May 5, 1965
Running Time: 114 minutes

A brilliant scientist, James Grayam, saves Lorrie Benson from suicide and subsequently has an affair with her. She is the wife of Grayam's employer, a powerful, sadistic industrialist named Cort Benson, who tries to break up his wife's affair and destroy Grayam's career by arranging incidents to make it appear that the scientist, who once had a nervous breakdown, is going insane. At the urging of a helpful friend, Grayam undergoes therapy and meets Dr. Elizabeth Larstedt, a dedicated, but mysterious, psychiatrist. At her office he throws an angry, somewhat irrational tantrum that triggers a destructive fit in a young patient. As the industrialist's persecution continues, Grayam enlists Lorrie's unenthusiastic help and turns the tables by masquerading as insane. He then publicly murders Benson, hoping to be sent temporarily to a mental institution. At the trial, Dr. Larstedt seems to realize Grayam is faking, yet helps him anyway by testifying he is insane. Once he is committed to an institution, Lorrie deserts him and, trapped in this bleak environment, Grayam gradually deteriorates. Having become truly psychotic, he escapes in order to tell the psychiatrist the truth and persuade her to release him. After listening to his nearly incoherent story she returns him to the asylum.

Brainstorm, a minor masterpiece of the 1960s, was directed by actor William Conrad who directed or produced a number of other interesting genre pieces during this period including *An American Dream* and *My Blood Runs Cold.* Along with films like *Psycho, Brainstorm* is one of the best examples of the 1960s counterpart of 1940s film noir. At the core of the film's quality is a complex, compelling plot. Like *Nightmare Alley* and *Double Indemnity,* which in a narrative

sense it closely resembles, *Brainstorm* follows a typical noir pattern from romance, to melodrama, to crime, and finally to horror. But unlike these films, which deal only tangentially with insanity, *Brainstorm* is primarily an exploration of that theme. The plot carries its scientist-protagonist, a man of considerable knowledge who is initially a seemingly innocent bystander, deeper and deeper into insanity. First, he is seduced into an unhealthy and doomed affair; next, as he is persecuted by the industrialist, into self-destructive paranoia, then into maniacal murder and finally into a complete psychotic breakdown. Additionally, *Brainstorm* equates the world of the absolutely powerful industrialist with the world of the indifferent asylum. Both are equally frightening and overwhelming, filled with forces that are impossible for the individual to resist.

Brainstorm also contains a number of complex images and striking visual effects. For example, while the scientist has his stormy and irrational argument with the psychiatrist, a boy is shown in the background through a two-way mirror wildly smashing all the objects in the room. The film is a good example of associational editing for narrative impact, but even more its energetic, somewhat jarring style contributes greatly to the film's disturbing and frenzied mood.
—D.L.W.

THE BRASHER DOUBLOON (1947)
[Working Title: THE HIGH WINDOW]

Director: John Brahm
Producer: Robert Bassler (20th Century-Fox)
Screenplay: Dorothy Hannah; adapted by Dorothy Bennett and Leonard Praskins; from the novel *The High Window* by Raymond Chandler
Director of Photography: Lloyd Ahern
Special Photographic Effects: Fred Sersen
Sound: Eugene Grossman, Harry M. Leonard
Music Score: David Buttolph
Music Director: Alfred Newman
Orchestration: Maurice de Packh
Art Directors: James Basevi, Richard Irvine
Set Decoration: Thomas Little, Frank E. Hughes
Costumes: Eleanor Behm
Makeup: Ben Nye
Assistant Director: Hal Herman
Film Editor: Harry Reynolds

CAST: George Montgomery (Philip Marlowe), Nancy Guild (Merle Davis), Conrad Janis (Leslie Murdock), Roy Roberts (Lt. Breeze), Fritz Kortner (Vannier), Florence Bates (Mrs. Murdock), Marvin Miller (Blaire), Houseley Stevenson (Morningstar), Bob Adler (Sgt. Spangler), Jack Conrad (George Anson), Alfred Linder (Eddie Prue), Jack Overman (Manager), Jack Stoney (Mike), Ray Spiker (Figaro), Paul Maxey (Coroner), Reed Hadley

THE BREAKING POINT

(Dr. Moss). **BITS:** Edward Gargan (Truck Driver), Ben Erway (Shaw).
Location: Hollywood and Los Angeles, California
Filming Completed: September 13, 1946
Released: 20th Century-Fox, February 6, 1947
Running Time: 72 minutes

A stolen gold coin brings Philip Marlowe into the employ of a rich and eccentric widow, Mrs. Murdock. Her motives for discovering the whereabouts of her rare doubloon become moot as soon as Marlowe realizes that there is more to this case than a simple robbery. The trail leads from robbery and blackmail to murder, with Marlowe in the middle. When Marlowe feels he finally has a clear picture of the events surrounding the brasher doubloon, he suffers a savage beating at the hands of the grotesque Vannier. Then, while attempting to straighten out a blackmail scheme involving Mrs. Murdock's mentally disturbed secretary, Merle Davis, Marlowe finally puts the pieces of this bizarre puzzle together. His investigation comes full circle as his original client, Mrs. Murdock, is revealed as a murderess and the perpetrator of the entire affair.

In transferring the ambience and hard-boiled character of Raymond Chandler's novel *The High Window* to the screen, *The Brasher Doubloon* may not succeed in carrying over the complexity of the novel but it definitely succeeds as a film noir. Visually, the film is filled with moody, low-key images supported by a dense and occasionally threatening background. The script is bland, yet it is filled with the type of dialogue and grotesque characterizations that distinguish the noir film from an ordinary thriller. Still, director John Brahm gives *The Brasher Doubloon* a comparatively understated style. There is little out of the ordinary or flamboyant in Brahm's hard-boiled world. The environment is a far cry from his classic period noir films like *The Lodger* and *Hangover Square*. Even the music, usually so important in film noir, is strangely absent in most of the film. Still, *The Brasher Doubloon* functions as a film noir because of the power of Chandler's world and the creatures populating it. Most of the acting in the film is undistinguished with the exception of Fritz Kortner, a veteran actor molded in the expressionist cinema of Germany in the 1920s. His depiction of Vannier brings a sense of aberrant vitality to Chandler's truncated story.

—C.M.

THE BREAKING POINT (1950)

Director: Michael Curtiz
Producer: Jerry Wald (Warner Brothers)
Screenplay: Ranald MacDougall; from the novel *To Have and Have Not* by Ernest Hemingway
Director of Photography: Ted McCord
Sound: Leslie G. Hewitt
Music: Ray Heindorf
Art Director: Edward Carrere
Set Decoration: George James Hopkins
Costumes: Leah Rhodes
Makeup: Bill Phillips
Hairstyles: Myra Stoltz
Dialogue Director: Norman Stuart
Second Unit Director: David C. Gardner
Assistant Director: Sherry Shourds
Script Supervisor: Irva Ross
Film Editor: Alan Crosland, Jr.

CAST: John Garfield (Harry Morgan), Patricial Neal (Leona Charles), Phyllis Thaxter (Lucy Morgan), Juano Hernandez (Wesley Park), Wallace Ford (Duncan), Edmond Ryan (Rogers), Ralph Dumke (Hannagan), Guy Thomajan (Danny), William Campbell (Concho), Sherry Jackson (Amelia), Donna Jo Boyce (Connie) Victor Sen Yung (Sing), Peter Brocco (Macho), John Doucette (Gotch), James Griffith (Charlie). **BITS:** Norman Fields (Dock Attendant), Juan Hernandez (Joseph), Juan Duval (Bartender), Spencer Chan (1st Chinese Cook), Helene Hatch (Mrs. Cooley), Donna Gibson, George Hoagland, Bob McLean (Leona's Party), Beverly Mook (Kid), John Close (Deputy), Alex Gerry (Mr. Phillips), Benny Long (Bartender), Mary Carroll (Girl), Glen Turnbull (Taxi Driver), John Morgan, John Alvin (Reporters), Dave McMahon (Coast Guardsman), Paul McGuire (Leona's Escort), Gregg Rhinelander (Intern), Bob Williams (Doctor), Len Hendry (Boatswain).
Location: Newport Bay, California
Filming Completed: May 10, 1950
Released: Warner Brothers, September 30, 1950
Running Time: 97 minutes

Harry Morgan is the owner of a Newport, California, charter boat, the *Sea Queen.* He is trying to support his wife Lucy and two daughters but business is bad. A flashy sports fisherman, Hannagan, and his mistress Leona Charles charter Harry's boat to Mexico. Hannagan leaves without paying his bill and Harry is stranded in Mexico without money to pay his docking fee. A disreputable lawyer, Duncan, offers a proposition to smuggle Chinese into the United States for $200 each and Harry feels obliged to agree. The leader of the Chinese, Sing, double-crosses Harry and is killed. Harry makes the other Chinese jump ship in shallow Mexican waters. But the Coast Guard has heard of the smuggling attempt and impounds Harry's ship. Harry returns home despondent and has a brief affair with Leona. Duncan secures a court order to release Harry's boat and blackmails him to accept another illegal charter party. Harry and his alcoholic first mate, Wesley Park, take a group of hoodlums to Catalina Island to deliver stolen race track receipts. En route, Wesley is killed by the criminals, and Harry realizes they intend to kill him also. One by one, Harry kills each of the thieves and is severely wounded by them. A Coast Guard cutter finds Harry and brings him to home port. Lucy persuades Harry that she still loves him and that he must let the doctors amputate his wounded arm or die. Harry agrees and lives to start a new life with Lucy.

As its story indicates, *The Breaking Point* has many of the fatalistic tendencies associated with film noir although, strictly speaking, it is equally a romantic melodrama, ranging from California to Mexico and exploiting its coastal locations. *The Breaking Point* is a remake of *To Have And Have Not*, but is altogether more faithful to the Hemingway novel than Howard Hawks's film. A pervasive feeling of hopelessness and futility surrounds the protagonist and, although he displays the characteristic toughness of the action hero, his vulnerability and capacity for suffering make him an archetypally defeated noir figure. John Garfield gives one of his best performances in the role, which is matched by that of Juano Hernandez as the first mate. Photographically, the work is in deep focus, which allows for a rewardingly detailed *mise-en-scène*.

—B.L.

THE BRIBE (1949)

Director: Robert Z. Leonard
Producer: Pandro S. Berman (MGM)
Screenplay: Marguerite Roberts; from the short story by Frederick Nebel
Director of Photography: Joseph Ruttenberg
Special Effects: Warren Newcombe, A. Arnold Gillespie
Sound: Douglas Shearer, Fred MacAlpin
Music Score: Miklos Rozsa
Song: "Situation Wanted" by Nacio Herb Brown and William Katz
Art Directors: Cedric Gibbons, Malcolm Brown
Set Decoration: Edwin B. Willis, Hugh Hunt
Costumes: Irene
Hairstyles: Sydney Guilaroff
Makeup: Jack Dawn
Production Manager: Edward Woehler
Assistant Director: Bert Glazer
Script Supervisor: Tess Primrock
Film Editor: Gene Ruggiero

CAST: Robert Taylor (Rigby), Ava Gardner (Elizabeth Hintten), Charles Laughton (A.J. Bealer), Vincent Price (Carwood), John Hodiak (Tug Hintten), Samuel S. Hinds (Dr. Warren), John Hoyt (Gibbs), Tito Renaldo (Emilio Gomez), Martin Garralaga (Pablo Gomez). **BITS:** Pepe Hernandez, Robert Cabal, Richard Lopez, David Cota (Bellboys), Nacho Galindo, Felipe Turich (Clerks), Walter A. Merrill, Frank Mayo (Ad Lib Americans), Marcel de la Brosse, Albert Pollet (Ad Lib Frenchmen), Juan Duval, Albert Morin, Joe Dominguez (Waiters), Ernesto Morelli (Bartender), Julian Rivero (Boatman), William Haade (Walker), Alfonso Pedrosa (Hotel Proprietor), Charles Gonzales (Bouncer), Fernando Alvarado (Flute Player),

Peter Cusanelli (Rhumba Dancer), Jerry Pina (Stunt Juggler), Harry Vejar (Indian).
Filming Completed: Agust 2, 1948
Released: MGM, February 3, 1949
Running Time: 98 minutes

Federal Agent Rigby is sent to a small South American island to break up a ring dealing in contraband war surplus materials. The organization is headed by Carwood, an apparently naive American playboy-sportsman. Carwood is assisted by the cynical and slovenly A.J. Bealer and by Tug Hintten, who smuggles the goods out on his ship. When Tug becomes ill with a heart ailment and is totally dependent upon his wife, Elizabeth, Carwood makes new arrangements. Carwood realizes the agent's identity and plots Rigby's "accidental" death on a fishing trip, but Emilio Gomez, a young native guide, is killed. Rigby enlists the aid of Emilio's father to break up the ring and, meanwhile, Carwood kills Tug. Rigby and Elizabeth are romantically involved and Bealer blackmails her to drug the agent so that the contraband can be transported while he is unconscious. Rigby recovers in time to foil their plans and Bealer turns against Carwood. The playboy-smuggler fights with Rigby during a spectacular fireworks display, and the agent defeats Carwood.

The Bribe contains elements of fairly stock postwar intrigue, which are rather tangential to the film noir tradition. However, it does show the effects of the noir tradition in its depiction of pervasive corruption abetted by a romanticized setting and the physical and iconographic presence of heavies like Charles Laughton and Vincent Price. The film incorporates a spattering of stylized sequences, particularly in the ending, the shots of mirror images, and others of Elizabeth through rain-streaked windows. Also, a hint of traditional romantic *angst* is conveyed by Rigby's narration as he tells most of the story in flashback while recovering from the drugs. Indeed, Rigby at one point decided to forego career and honor for the love of Elizabeth Hintten and although he emerges victorious at the end, he is narrating from the noir position of defeat and betrayal.

—B.P.

THE BROTHERS RICO (1957)

Director: Phil Karlson
Producer: Lewis J. Rachmil (A William Goetz Production)
Screenplay: Lewis Meltzer and Ben Perry; from the novelette *Les Freres Rico* by Georges Simenon
Director of Photography: Burnett Guffey
Sound: Lambert Day
Music Score: George Duning
Conductor: Morris Stoloff
Orchestrations: Arthur Morton
Art Director: Robert Boyle

BRUTE FORCE

Set Decoration: William Kiernan, Darrell Silvera
Costumes: Jean Louis
Makeup: Clay Campbell
Hairstyles: Helen Hunt
Assistant Director: Jack Berne
Film Editor: Charles Nelson

CAST: Richard Conte (Eddie Rico), Dianne Foster (Alice Rico), Kathryn Grant (Norah), Larry Gates (Sid Kubik), James Darren (Johnny Rico), Argentina Brunetti (Mrs. Rico), Lamont Johnson (Peter Malaks), Harry Bellaver (Mike Lamotta), Paul Picerni (Gino Rico), Paul Dubov (Phil), Rudy Bond (Gonzales), Richard Bakalyn (Vic Tucci), William Phipps (Joe Wesson), Mimi Aguglia (Julia Rico), Maggie O'Byrne (Mrs. Felici), George Cisar (Dude Cowboy), Peggy Maley (Jean), Jane Easton (Nellie). **BITS:** James Waters (Laundry Truck Driver), Pat Donahue (Miss Van Ness), Estelle Lawrence (Counter Girl), Darren Dublin (Bellboy), George Lewis (Desk Clerk), Don Orlando (Cabbie #1), Mimi Gibson (Felici, Little Girl), Marvin Bryan (Ticket Clerk), Samuel Finn (Cabbie #2), Ernesto Morelli (Pizza Maker), Jerry Summers (Bellboy), Bonnie Bolding (Stewardess), Dean Cromer (Narco Felici), Nesdon Booth (Burly Man), Pepe Hern (Bank Clerk), Robert Malcolm (Bank Guard), Rankin Mansfield (Bank Official), Betsy Jones Moreland (Looping Voice).
Filming Completed: December 27, 1956
Released: Columbia, September 1957
Running Time: 92 minutes

An ex-mobster turned successful businessman, Eddie Rico, is contacted by the syndicate to locate his younger brothers who have apparently double-crossed their gangland associates. He feels obliged to search for his brothers, not only to protect their lives but the lives of his family as well. As he tracks his brothers down, the elder Rico begins to suspect ulterior motives for his frenzied manhunt. Finding his brother Johnny secluded in a rundown resort house, the entire puzzle unravels itself. The power play of the mob was merely a way of seeking revenge for a crime committed against the mob by the Rico brothers. Unable to save his brothers, the elder Rico extricates himself from the treachery he has been connected with, and returns to his wife and family scarred by the deadly affair.

Utilizing material adapted from the writing of French mystery writer Georges Simenon, director Phil Karlson creates in *The Brothers Rico* a thriller deeply rooted in the postnoir style of police thrillers like *The Line-Up* and *Phoenix City Story*. In these films the subtly ritualized violence and dark ambience of the film noir was replaced by an overt emphasis on crude violence and a dull, almost flat visual style. This type of thriller became the heir apparent to the rapidly declining noir output of the 1950s. Throughout *The Brothers Rico*, Richard Conte provides the only physical link to the noir pattern set during the 1940s. In this film he seems to characterize a personality out of step with the rest of society. His meaningless quest and inability to control events was not common during the late 1950s. These feelings of hopelessness and impotence lead *The Brothers Rico* onto a noir plane. However, the conventions of true noir film making—which emphasizes a world devoid of order and possessed of a sentiment rejecting compassion and sensitivity—had long since wasted away for lack of usage. *The Brothers Rico* is a simple thriller that displays very little in the way of noir ambience, a film constructed from archaic conventions and petty obstacles that strongly point to the decline of the noir series during the 1950s.

—C.M.

BRUTE FORCE (1947)

Director: Jules Dassin
Producer: Mark Hellinger (Mark Hellinger Productions)
Associate Producer: Jules Buck
Screenplay: Richard Brooks; from an unpublished story by Robert Patterson
Director of Photography: William Daniels
Special Photography: David S. Horsley
Sound: Charles Felstead, Robert Pritchard
Music Score: Miklos Rozsa
Art Directors: Bernard Herzbrun, John F. DeCuir
Set Decoration: Russell A. Gausman, Charles Wyrick
Costumes: Rosemary Odell
Makeup: Bud Westmore
Hairstyles: Carmen Dirigo
Technical Adviser: Jacques Gordon
Assistant Director: Fred Frank
Film Editor: Edward Curtiss

CAST: Burt Lancaster (Joe Collins), Hume Cronyn (Capt. Munsey), Charles Bickford (Gallagher), Yvonne DeCarlo (Gina), Ann Blyth (Ruth), Ella Raines (Cora), Anita Colby (Flossie), Sam Levene (Louie), Howard Duff (Soldier), Art Smith (Dr. Walters), Roman Bohnen (Warden Barnes), John Hoyt (Spencer), Richard Gaines (McCollum), Frank Puglia (Ferrara), Jeff Corey (Freshman), Vince Barnett (Muggsy), James Bell (Crenshaw), Jack Overman (Kid Coy), Whit Bissell (Tom Lister), Sir Lancelot (Calypso), Ray Teal (Jackson), Jay C. Flippen (Hodges), James O'Rear (Wilson), Howland Chamberlain (Gaines), Kenneth Patterson (Bronski), Crane Whitley (Armed Guard in Drain Pipe), Charles McGraw (Andy), John Harmon (Roberts), Gene Stutenroth (Hoffman), Wally Rose (Peary), Carl Rhodes (Strella), Guy Beach (Convict Foreman), Edmund Cobb (Bradley), Tom Steele (Machine Gunner #1). **BITS:** Alex Frazer (Chaplain), Will Lee (Kincaid), Ruth Sanderson (Miss Lawrence), Francis McDonald (Regan), Jack S. Lee (Sergeant), Virginia Farmer (Sadie), Paul Bryar (Harry), Glenn Strange (Tompkins), Al Hill (Plonski), Peter Virgo, Eddy Chandler, Kenneth R. MacDonald, Howard

Left to right: Wilson (James O'Rear) is driven to his death by Spencer (John Hoyt) in Brute Force.

Mitchell, Al Ferguson, Jerry Salvail (Guards), Herbert Heywood (Chef), Rex Lease (Hearse Driver), Lee Kendall (Shorty), Blanche Obronska (Young Girl), Hal Malone (Young Inmate), Don McGill (Max), Harry Wilson (Tyrone, Homely Prisoner), Rex Dale, Billy Wayne, Frank Marlo, William Cozzo (Prisoners), Sam Rizhallah (Convict Son), Kippee Valez (Visitor).

Filming Completed: April 19, 1947
Released: Universal-International, June 6, 1947
Running Time: 95minutes

Behind the walls of an isolated prison, convicts are dehumanized to the point of absurdity by the sadistic Capt. Munsey. Not being able to stand idly by as inmates are tortured and exploited by the captain of the guards, Joe Collins and his comrades from cell R17 begin plans for their liberation. The escape plot includes the help of the big man, Gallagher, whose influence with the rest of the convicts is essential for the success of their plan. After his informer is forced to fall into a huge punch press, Munsey resorts to acts of uncontrollable brutality in order to get information regarding the planned breakout. At the designated moment, however, Gallagher stages a protest in the prison yard as a diversion for Collins and his men, who are working the mine detail. The subsequent breakout turns into a savage

and incredible eruption of fatal violence that destroys the escaping convicts and Munsey.

The essence of Jules Dassin's *Brute Force* is violence. Functioning as a blatant allegory for an existential vision of the world (Sartre's *No Exit* can be seen as a theatrical counterpart), the prison of *Brute Force* becomes a living hell from which escape is impossible. This hopeless situation is echoed by the remarks of the prison doctor who constantly reminds anyone willing to listen, "Nobody escapes, nobody ever escapes." It remains for the violent action found throughout the film to serve as a liberating force for the inmates, as well as indicating a way of life adopted by the sadistic, Nazi-like Munsey. Dassin has constructed a microcosm of the world in this film as a perverse sense of order surrounds the activities of Munsey and his henchmen. Their treatment of the prisoners is far from noble; and Munsey's villainy is taken to the point of absurdity. Yet it is his outrageously brutal attitudes that serve as a catalyst, turning the variety of inmates in cell R17—personalities ranging from the totally passive to the unpredictably volatile—into the liberators of their comrades from the crude, hellish nightmare. Written by Richard Brooks, whose films include *Crossfire, Key Largo* and *The Blackboard Jungle, Brute Force* is concerned with meaninglessness

THE BURGLAR

transcended only by an act of violence, because "outside" life becomes valueless in the confines of the prison. The overtly romantic flashbacks detailing the various reasons for some of the inmates' imprisonments under the scrutiny of Capt. Munsey lack the vitality needed to make their previous lives attractive. The only goal that seems to matter is the destruction of Munsey. With this single purpose in mind, the inmates play out a strange ritualized existence. Dassin's direction, fleshed with a taut urgency, makes the stylized tortures conceived by Munsey a striking counterpoint to the magnificent brutality of the abortive prison breakout. There are aspects of despair, corruption, and displacement at the core of every element of *Brute Force*. These aspects, essential to films of a noir character, transform the film into an indictment of a contemporary society tolerating a brutal, desensitized, and insular world beyond its control.

—C.M.

THE BURGLAR (1957)

Director: Paul Wendkos
Producer: Louis W. Kellman (Samson Productions)
Screenplay: David Goodis; from his novel
Director of Photography: Don Malkames
Sound: Ed Johnstone, Albert Gramalla
Supervising Sound Editor: Norman Kasow
Sound Effects: John Peckham
Music: Sol Kaplan
Song: "You Are Mine," by Bob Marcucchi and Pete Deangelo; sung by Vince Carson
Bassoon solo: S. Schoenbach of the Philadelphia Orchestra
Art Director: Jim Leonard
Makeup: Josephine Clannella
Hairstyles: Gary Elliot
Production Manager: Ben Berk
Continuity: Deedee Schwartz
Technical Adviser: Maurice R. Pilner, Philadelphia Police Department
Film Editor: Herta Horn

CAST: Dan Duryea (Nat Harbin), Jayne Mansfield (Gladden), Martha Vickers (Della), Peter Capell (Baylock), Mickey Shaughnessy (Dohmer), Wendell Phillips (Police Captain), Phoebe Mackay (Sister Sara), Stewart Bradley (Charlie), John Facenda (News Commentator), Frank Hall (News Reporter), Bob Wilson (Newsreel Narrator), Steve Allison (State Trooper), Richard Emery (Harbin as a Child), Andrea McLaughlin (Gladden as a Child), Frank Orrison, Sam Elber, Ned Carey, John Boyd, Michael Rich, George Kane, Sam Cresson, Ruth Burnat (People).
Location: Philadelphia, Pennsylvania
Filming Completed: 1956
Released: Columbia, June 1957
Running Time: 90 minutes

Gladden helps Nat Harbin and his two henchmen, Baylock and Dohmer, successfully steal a diamond necklace from a spiritualist's mansion. But the gang was spotted by the police and must carefully plan their next move. Nat is an ophan who was raised by Gladden's father and now is guardian of Gladden. When Dohmer makes a pass at her, Nat sends her to Atlantic City. One night Nat meets Della and later overhears her plotting with a dishonest policeman, Charlie, to steal the necklace from Nat's gang by kidnapping Gladden. Taking Dohmer and Baylock, Nat drives to Atlantic City to rescue Gladden but Dohmer is killed en route. When Nat arrives at Gladden's hotel she is talking to Charlie, innocent of his real intentions. Nat hides the necklace under her pillow and cannot convince her to leave town. Charlie discovers Baylock's hiding place and kills him, also confronting Nat and forcing him to reveal where the necklace is hidden. Della stays with Nat while Charlie hurries to Gladden's hotel. Nat escapes from Della and meets Gladden on the boardwalk where she has slipped past Charlie and carries the necklace. Chased, Gladden and Nat are cornered on the Steel Pier. Nat gives the necklace to Charlie in return for Gladden's freedom and Charlie kills Nat. When the police arrive, Charlie swears that the necklace was thrown into the ocean and that he killed Nat in self-defense. But Della arrives, reveals their plot, and Charlie is arrested for murder and theft.

Like other works by David Goodis, *The Burglar* is more concerned with the feelings of its characters than with its melodramatic pulp story. Some of this feeling is expressed by the direction of Paul Wendkos; but in the main he is concerned in this film, his first directorial effort, with ostentatious imagery in the manner of Orson Welles. Affinities between the Steel Pier sequence and the fun house sequence of *The Lady From Shanghai*, as well as the burglary that begins the story with a visual tour de force of tense close-ups and startling cuts, demonstrates Wendkos's pretensions. Like many late noir films, *The Burglar* suffers from a self-consiousness which makes its artistry less impressive than that of earlier works with a more subtle ambience.

—B.L.

CAGED (1950)
[Working Title: LOCKED IN]

Director: John Cromwell
Producer: Jerry Wald (Warner Brothers)
Screenplay: Virginia Kellogg and Bernard C. Schoenfeld
Director of Photography: Carl Guthrie
Sound: Stanley Jones
Music Score: Max Steiner
Orchestration: Murray Cutter
Art Director: Charles H. Clarke
Set Decoration: G.W. Berntsen
Makeup: Perc Westmore, Ed Voight
Hairstyles: Myrl Stoltz
Technical Adviser: Doris Whitney
Assistant Director: Frank Mattison
Script Supervisor: Jean Baker
Film Editor: Owen Marks

CAST: Eleanor Parker (Marie Allen), Agnes Moorehead (Ruth Benton), Ellen Corby (Emma), Hope Emerson (Evelyn Harper), Betty Garde (Kitty Stark), Jan Sterling (Smoochie), Lee Patrick (Elvira Powell), Olive Deering (June), Jane Darwell (Isolation Matron), Gertrude Michael (Georgia), Sheila Stevens (Helen), Joan Miller (Claire), Marjorie Crossland (Cassie), Gertrude Hoffman (Millie), Lynn Sherman (Ann), Queenie Smith (Mrs. Warren), Naomi Robison (Hattie), Esther Howard (Grace), Marlo Dwyer (Julie), Wanda Tynan (Meta), Peggy Wynne (Lottie), Frances Morris (Mrs. Foley), Edith Evanson (Miss Barker), Yvonne Rob (Elaine), Ann Tyrell (Edna), Eileen Stevens (Infirmary Nurse), June Whipple (Ada), Sandra Gould (Skip), Grace Hayes (Mugging Matron), Taylor Holmes (Sen. Donnolly), Don Beddoe (Commissioner Walker), Charles Meredith (Chairman), George Baxter (Jeffries), Guy Beach (Mr. Cooper), Harlan Warde (Dr. Ashton). **BITS:** Bill Hunter (Guard), Barbara Esback, Marjorie Wood, Evelyn Dockson, Hazel Keener, Jane Crowley (Matrons), Gail Bonney, Doris Kemper, Lovyss Bradley, Ezelle Poule, Margaret Lambert, Eva Nelson, Rosemary O'Neil, Jean Calhoun, Nita Talbot, Marie Melish, Pauline Creasman, Joyce Newhard, Helen Eby-Rock, Sheila Stuart, Claudia Cauldwell, Tina Menard, Carole Shannon, Gladys Roach, Virginia Engels (Inmates), Bill Haade (Laundryman), Ruth Warren (Miss Lyons), Davison Clark (Doctor), Pauline Drake (Doctor's Wife), Gracille LaVinder (Visit-ing Room Matron), Bill Wayne (Ada's Father), Doris Whitney (Woman Visitor), Grace Hampton, Helen Mowery, Helen Spring, Frances Henderson (Women).

Filming Completed: September 10, 1949
Released: Warner Brothers, May 19, 1950
Running Time: 97 minutes
[FACTUAL BASIS: Virginia Kellogg spent two weeks in one woman's prison and surveyed others intensively.]

Sentenced to a term in prison for having helped her husband in a small robbery, Marie Allen changes from a naive and fundamentally innocent young woman to a hardened and knowing adult. The warden of the prison, Ruth Benton, is a sympathetic and well-meaning woman who means to rehabilitate the prisoners; but the prison is actually run by a sadistic matron, Evelyn Harper, who holds her job because of crooked political influence. Marie is already a woman of tragic circumstances as her husband was shot in the robbery and she suffered a miscarriage. As she witnesses the corrupting influence of Evelyn Harper on her fellow inmates and suffers the cruelties of prison life, Marie is disillusioned but determined to go straight. Kitty, the leader of a shoplifting ring, recruits her for work on the outside when she is paroled. Marie resists her advances and also those of Elvira Powell, who is the influential head of a lucrative prostitution organization. Later, Kitty kills Evelyn Harper and another inmate goes "stir crazy" when denied parole. For the chance of an early parole, Marie capitulates and is released from prison to become a prostitute. The Warden observes that Marie will be back.

The best woman's prison film ever made (not necessarily high praise in itself), *Caged* represents a union between the semirealistic and socially conscious dramas made by Warner Brothers in the 1930s and the more stylized world of film noir. With this film, Warner Brothers extends the potential of its powerful but often simplistic social dramas while retaining the virtues of the earlier films. *Caged* is totally unsentimental, damning the society that could corrupt the soul of a Marie Allen but refusing to absolve the character herself and depict her as a complete victim. It is equally clear that her fellow inmates, many of them cynical and apparently insentitive, have followed the same route as Marie. The film's conclusion is pessimistic; the implication is that all humans, if punished long enough and cruelly enough, will look for an easy way out and willingly turn their back on the positive values they once cherished. Marie exits from the prison to her criminal life with a hardened smile on her face. John Cromwell reaches his peak in the direction of this gritty Warners film, controlling every element of the work. Eleanor Parker gives the best performance of her career under Cromwell and creates a convincing metamorphosis from a shy and innocent young girl to a woman of the world. She gives a multiplicity of nuances to her playing of all her scenes, which are both low-keyed and emotionally charged. As the sadistic and presumably lesbian matron, the physically imposing Hope Emerson adds to the list of her portrayals of female villains of film noir. Equally impressive is Cromwell's visual realization of the claustrophobia of prison life, aided by the low key and high contrast photography of Carl Guthrie. Each shot is complexly composed and lit, and many images become nightmarish tableaux.

—B.L.

CALCUTTA (1947)

Director: John Farrow
Producer: Seton I. Miller (Paramount)
Screenplay: Seton I. Miller
Director of Photography: John F. Seitz
Process Photography: Farciot Edouart
Special Effects: Gordon Jennings
Sound: Stanley Cooley, Walter Oberst
Music Score: Victor Young
Song: "This is Madness" by Bernie Wayne and Ben Raleigh
Art Directors: Hans Dreier, Franz Bachelin
Set Decoration: Sam Comer, Jack de Golconda
Costumes: Dorothy O'Hara
Makeup: Wally Westmore
Technical Advisers: Maj. M.H. Whyte, Capt. Joe Rosbert, Dr. Paul Singh
Choreography: Roberta Jonay
Assistant Director: William H. Coleman
Film Editor: Archie Marshek

CAST: Alan Ladd (Neale Gordon), Gail Russell (Virginia Moore), William Bendix (Pedro Blake), June Duprez (Marina Tanev), Lowell Gilmore (Eric Lasser), Edith King (Mrs. Smith), Paul Singh (Mul Raj Malik), Gavin Muir (Inspector Kendricks), John Whitney (Bill Cunningham), Benson Fong (Young Chinese Clerk). **BITS:** Don Beddoe (Jack Collins), Milton Parsons (Desk Clerk), Leslie Fong (Chinese Radio Man at Dinjhan), Jimmy Aubrey (Mac, Mechanic), Lee Tung Foo (Kim), Joey S. Ray (Bodyguard to Lasser), Beal Wong (Native Foreman at Dinjhan), Bruce Wong (Chinese Radio Man at Ed's Place), Eddie Das (Native Boss), Morton Lowry (Scarred Man), Mahmed Tahir (Native Waiter), Robert R. Stephenson, Fred Giermann, Harry Cording (Tea Planters), Marilynn Chow (Chinese Stewardess), Len Hendry (Starter), Eddie Hall (Copilot), Bobby Barber (Taxi Driver), Fred

Nurney (Man in Cafe), Peter Cusanelli (Headwaiter), Carmen Beretta (Woman), John Benson (Pilot), Albert Pollet, Julio Bonini (Men), Erno Verebes (Frenchman), George Sorel (Croupier), Charles Stevens (Strangler), Adrienne D'Ambricourt (Croupier's Assistant), Moy Ming (Elderly Chinese Clerk), Shirley Lew (Mrs. Smith's Assistant Hairdresser), Barbara Jean Wong (Mrs. Smith's Manicurist), Leyland Hodgson, Frank Baker, Bruce Carruthers, Colin Kenny (Police Officers), Wong Artarne (Copilot), Madge E. Schofield (Hindu Servant Woman), Anandi Dhalwani (Hindu Woman), Eddie Leo (Jim Wong, Bank Clerk), Hassan Khayyam (Hindu Man), Suran Singh (Doorman), Lal Chand Mehra (Bar Captain), George Kirby (Day Desk Clerk), Bhogwan Singh (Bar Boy), George Broughton (Hotel Guest), Aminta Dyne (Sleepy Woman), Bill Nind (Police Sergeant), Diane Ervin, Joy Harington (Hotel Guests).

Location: Hollywood, California
Filming Completed: August 9, 1945
Released: Paramount, May 30, 1947
Running Time: 83 minutes

Neale, Pedro, and Bill are commercial pilots based in India and close friends. Bill becomes engaged to be married but is mysteriously killed. Neale, suspicious by nature and especially distrustful of women, brutally questions Bill's fiancée, Virginia Moore. But once Virginia's innocence is ascertained, Neale is friendly. Neale "borrows" a scarab diamond given to Virginia by Bill, and traces it to a sinister Indian smuggler, Mr. Malik. When a star sapphire and a cache of diamonds are discovered hidden aboard, Neale realizes that they are being used to transport illegal jewelry. Neale is threatened by Malik with a knife but subdues him. Malik is shot before he can reveal any information. Again suspicious of Virginia, Neale questions the hotel clerk who refutes her alibi. When she denies her guilt, Neale slaps a confession out of her. He is stopped by Mr. Lasser, a sophisticated owner of a local club and part of the smuggling ring. In the ensuing melee, Lasser is shot by Neale, who is impervious to Virginia's pleas not to turn her over to the authorities.

At first glance, *Calcutta* appears to be a typical action-adventurer geared to appeal to Alan Ladd's fans. Closer inspection reveals the strong influence of the tough guy fictional tradition, not only in the glacial performance of Ladd but especially in his attitude toward women. Later, Ladd and Paramount would become more aware of his large popularity with young boys, so *Calcutta* is unusual because of his sexual involvement with women. Paramount alternated Veronica Lake and Gail Russell as romantic "damsels in distress" in Ladd's films, but in a shrewd bit of reverse casting, Russell is allowed to play the *femme fatale* in Calcutta, and a nasty one at that. Russell's exotic features, warm manner, and soft voice invariably gave her a connotation of innocence and vulnerability, which were capitalized on in most of her films. By contrast, when Ladd rips a pendant from her neck or slaps her around, it makes him appear all the more impervious to women. Their interaction holds this film together and demonstrates the misogynistic strain of hard-boiled fiction; it is a strain implicit in much of post-war American society as well. It is Ladd's resistance to feminine wiles that allows him to survive, as indicated in a number of classic exchanges between him and Russell. He quotes for her an old Gurkha saying, "Man who trust woman walk on duckweed over pond." When she tells him he had nothing in common with his dead pal, that he's "cold, sadistic, egotistical," he replies, "Maybe, but I'm still alive." Finally, paraphrasing Sam Spade's ultimate rejection of Brigid in *The Maltese Falcon*, Neale tells Virginia, "You counted on your beauty with guys, even ones you were going to kill."

—B.P.

CALL NORTHSIDE 777 (1948)

Director: Henry Hathaway
Producer: Otto Lang (20th Century-Fox)
Screenplay: Jerome Cady and Jay Dratler, adapted by Leonard Hoffman and Quentin Reynolds; from *Chicago Times* articles by James P. McGuire
Director of Photography: Joe MacDonald
Special Photographic Effects: Fred Sersen
Wirephoto: Associated Press
Sound: W.D. Flick, Roger Heman
Music Director: Alfred Newman
Orchestration: Edward Powell
Art Directors: Lyle Wheeler, Mark-Lee Kirk
Set Decoration: Thomas Little, Walter M. Scott
Costumes: Kay Nelson
Wardrobe Director: Charles LeMaire
Makeup: Ben Nye, Dick Smith, Thomas Tuttle
Hairstyles: Myrtle Ford
Production Manager: Sam Wurtzel
Assistant Directors: Abe Steinberg, Joe Richards
Script Supervisor: Stanley Scheuer
Film Editor: J. Watson Webb, Jr.

CAST: James Stewart (McNeal), Richard Conte (Frank Wiecek), Lee J. Cobb (Brian Kelly), Helen Walker (Laura McNeal), Betty Garde (Wanda Skutnik), Kasia Orzazewski (Tillie Wiecek), Joanne de Bergh (Helen Wiecek-Rayska), Howard Smith (Palmer), Moroni Olsen (Parole Board Chairman), John McIntire (Sam Faxon), Paul Harvey (Martin Burns), George Tyne (Tomek Zaleska), Richard Bishop (Warden), Otto Waldis (Boris), Michael Chapin (Frank, Jr.), E.G. Marshall (Rayska), Truman Bradley (Narrator). **BITS:** John Bleifer (Jan Gruska), Addison Richards (John Albertson), Richard Rober (Larson), Eddie Dunn (Patrolman), Percy Helton (Mailman), Charles Lane (Prosecuting Attorney), Norman McKay, Walter Greaza (Detectives), William Post, Jr. (Police Sergeant), George Melford, Charles Miller, Joe Forte, Dick Ryan (Parole Board Members), Lionel Stander (Corrigan), Jonathan Hale (Robert Winston), Lew Eckles (Policeman), Freddie Steele, George Turner (Holdup Men), Jane Crowley (Anna Felczak), Robert Karnes (Spitzer), Larry Blake, Robert Williams, Perry Ivins, Lester Sharpe (Technicians), Helen Foster (Secretary), Abe Dinovitch, Jack Mannick (Polish Men), Henry Kulky (Bartender in Drazynski's Place), Cy Kendall (Bartender in Bill's Place), Dollie Caillet (Secretary), Joe Ploski, Peter Seal (Men), George Spaulding (Man on Parole Board), Wanda Perry, Ann Staunton (Telephone Operators), Rex Downing (Copy Boy), Edward Peil, Jr., Buck Harrington (Bartenders), George Cisar, Philip Lord (Policemen), Stanley Gordon (Prison Clerk), Carl Kroenke (Guard), Arthur Peterson (Keeler's Assistant), Duke Watson, George Pembroke (Policemen).

Location: Chicago and the Illinois State Prison, Illinois
Filming Completed: November 15, 1947
Released: 20th Century-Fox, February 18, 1948
Running Time: 111 minutes

A woman inserts a classified advertisement in a Chicago newspaper, offering a reward of $5,000 for information that may lead to her son's release from prison. A newspaper editor sees the ad and sends McNeal, a skeptical reporter, out to investigate. He discovers that the woman, Tillie Wiecek, has been scrubbing floors for eleven years, saving nickels and dimes until able to offer the $5,000. The advertisement thus becomes a human interest story, and the newspaper involves itself in a crusade for her son's liberation. McNeal goes to the state prison to talk to Frank Wiecek, sentenced to life imprisonment for killing a policeman during a grocery store robbery. Wiecek insists that he was framed and was at home with his wife during the robbery. His conviction was based on his being named in a lineup by Wanda Skutnik, who claimed to have seen him at the scene of the crime. McNeal has Wiecek submit to a lie detector test, which comes out in the prisoner's favor. Next, Wiecek's ex-wife and child are interviewed by the paper and their picture featured on the front page. This upsets Wiecek terribly; he insists that the paper drop the investigation fearing his son's future will be jeopardized. But McNeal is convinced of the man's innocence and seeks out Wanda Skutnik. She refuses to change her story, and the police withhold information from McNeal. The paper decides to drop the proposed hearing for Wiecek due to lack of evidence. But McNeal finds a newspaper photograph of Wanda Skutnik and Wiecek walking in the police station together. He reschedules the hearing, has the picture enlarged, and convinces the hearing board that the date on the photo proves that Wanda first saw Wiecek at the time he was booked, not at the time of the crime. Wiecek is set free and McNeal watches his touching reunion with his son.

Shot in a realistic, almost documentary style, *Call Northside 777* is a fine example of what might be called "newspaper noir." The hard-boiled world of a big city daily newpaper is examined, with James Stewart portraying the reporter to whom the story is everything. His cynical veneer gradually cracks as he becomes convinced of Wiecek's innocence. But it does not matter what he thinks. The outside world of the police, the hearing board, and the politicians makes the rules. The police department's role is particularly interesting. Not exactly corrupt, the police do not like to be proved wrong, especially since Wiecek was accused of shooting a patrolman. Instead of helping McNeal on his search for evidence, the police continually throw obstacles in his path, such as withholding police records that are technically open to anyone. As McNeal gets deeper and deeper into the case, he sees that justice and the law are not always the same. When the woman who convicted Wiecek will not change her story, the newspaper is unwilling to continue what appears to be a losing battle and wants to drop the case. But it is McNeal's personal quest. He continues to look for the one piece of evidence that will free Wiecek, who has become not only his story, but his conscience. Thus, the reporter's victory in freeing the prisoner becomes a triumph not only for the forces of justice, but for a man who pitted himself against the apparatus of the state. In typical noir fashion, all is not sewn up neatly. Wanda Skutnik, who obviously committed perjury, never changes her story and remains at large. Wiecek's wife remarried long ago, leaving him alone in his newly found freedom with only occasional weekends with his son. His eleven years in prison cannot be given back to him; but, at least, his mother did not waste her $5,000.

—J.C.

CANON CITY (1948)

Director: Crane Wilbur
Executive Producer: Bryan Foy (Bryan Foy Productions)
Producer: Robert T. Kane
Screenplay: Crane Wilbur
Director of Photography: John Alton
Second Unit Cameraman: Walter Strenge
Photographic Effects: George J. Teague
Sound: Leon S. Becker, Hugh McDowell
Music Director: Irving Friedman
Art Director: Frank Durlauf
Set Decoration: Armor Marlow, Clarence Steenson
Costumes: Frances Ehren
Hairstyles: Joan St. Oegger, Beth Langston
Makeup: Ern Westmore, Frank Westmore
Production Supervisor: James T. Vaughn
Dialogue Director: Burk Symon
Second Unit Director: James Leicester
Assistant Directors: Allen K. Wood, Ridgeway Callow
Script Supervisor: Arnold Laven
Film Editor: Louis H. Sackin

CAST: Scott Brady (Jim Sherbondy), Jeff Corey (Schwartzmiller), Whit Bissell (Heilman), Stanley Clements (New), Charles Russell (Tolley), De Forest Kelley (Smalley), Ralph Byrd (Officer Gray), Warden Roy Best (Warden), Henry Brandon (Freeman), Alfred Linder (Lavergne), Ray Bennett (Klinger), Bob Bice (Turley), Bob Kellard (Officer Williams), Richard Irving (Trujillo), Bud Wolfe (Officer Clark), Mabel Paige (Mrs. Oliver), Reed Hadley (Narrator). **BITS:** Bob Reeves (Guard), Donald Kerr (Convict Waiter), Victor Cutler (Convict Photographer), Lynn Millan (May), James Ames (Convict Mug), Ruth Warren (Mug's Wife), Brick Sullivan (Guard), Henry Hall (Guard Captain), Cay Forester (Sherbondy's Sister), Bill Walker (Prisoner), Officer McLean (Himself), Paul Scardon (Joe Bondy), Ralph Dunn (Convict Blacksmith), Alvin Hammer (Convict Tailor), Capt. Kenny (Himself), John Shay, Paul Kruger (Officers), Raymond Bond (Mr. Oliver), Esther Summers (Mrs. Higgins), Mack Williams (Mr. Higgins), Capt. Gentry (Himself), Howard Negley (Richard Smith), Virginia Mullens (Mrs. Smith), Bill Clauson (Joel), Shirley Martin (Judith), Elysabeth Goetten (Barbara), Margaret Kerry (Maxine), Eve March (Mrs. Bauer), John Doucette (Mr. Bauer), Phyllis Gallow (Myrna), Anthony Sydes (Jerry), Jack Ellis (Man at Roadblock), John Wald (Radio Commentator).
Location: Canon City, Colorado
Filming Completed: May 1948
Released: Eagle-Lion, June 30, 1948
Running Time: 82 minutes
[FACTUAL BASIS: Based on the December 30, 1947, prison break at the Colorado State Penitentiary at Canon City, Colorado.]

A group of convicts successfully escape from the Colorado State Penitentiary in Canon City. Forcing another inmate, Jim Sherbondy to go along against his will, they flee over the desolate snow-covered countryside terrorizing local citizens. Ultimately, all but Sherbondy are killed, and he takes refuge in Mr. Bauer's farmhouse. When the Bauer boy has an attack of appendicitis, Sherbondy allows Mrs. Bauer to leave to get help then takes off to try and escape on foot. A grateful Mr. Bauer, realizing Sherbondy is not a hardened criminal, picks him up in his car and tries to help him, but the convict is recaptured at a police roadblock.

Canon City is a semidocumentary of the penitentiary, which was shot on location in Colorado and even opens with interviews of the warden and some of the actual convicts. The director, Crane Wilbur, began as a screenwriter in the silent era and became something of a specialist in gangster and prison films throughout the 1930s and 1940s. Subsequent to this he scripted the classic *He Walked By Night* as well as *Outside The Wall*, which he also directed. Neither the semidocumentary approach, enhanced by Reed Hadley's stentorian narration, nor John Alton's photography give this film the noir ambience of productions like *T-Men* and *He Walked By Night*, which indicates that Anthony Mann's contribution, (uncredited in the case of the second film) was rather substantial.

—B.P.

CAPE FEAR (1962)

Director: J. Lee Thompson
Producer: Sy Bartlett (Melville-Talbot)
Screenplay: James R. Webb; from the novel *The Executioners* by John D. MacDonald
Director of Photography: Samuel Leavitt
Sound: Waldon O. Watson, Corson Jowett
Music: Bernard Herrmann
Art Directors: Alexander Golitzen, Robert Boyle
Set Decoration: Oliver Emert
Costumes: Mary Wills
Makeup: Frank Prehods, Thomas Tuttle
Hair Styles: Virginia D'Arcy
Production Manager: Ernest B. Wehmeyer
Assistant Director: Ray Gosnell, Jr.
Film Editor: George Tomasini

CAST: Gregory Peck (Sam Bowden), Robert Mitchum (Max Cady), Polly Bergen (Peggy), Lori Martin (Nancy), Martin Balsam (Chief Dutton), Jack Kruschen (Grafton), Telly Savalas (Sievers), Barrie Chase (Diane), Paul Comi (Garner), Page Slattery (Deputy Kersek), Ward Ramsey (Officer Brown), Thomas Newman (Lt. Gervasi), Edward Platt (Judge), Will Wright (Dr. Pearsall). **BITS:** Alan Reynolds (Vernon), Mack Williams (Dr. Lowney), Joan Staley (Waitress), Herb Armstrong (Waiter), Bunny Rhea (Pianist), John McKee (Officer Marconi), Paul Levitt (Police Operator), Norma Yost (Ticket Clerk), Alan Wells, Allan Ray (Young Men), Jack Richardson (Deputy), Carol Sydes (Betty), Al Silvani (Man), Josephine Smith (Librarian), Joseph Jenkins (Janitor), Marion Landers (Cross), Bob Noble, Jack Elkins (Pedestrians).
Location: Rural area near Savannah, Georgia
Released: Universal-International, April 12, 1962
Running time: 105 minutes

A violent psychopath, Max Cady, seeks revenge against the lawyer, Sam Bowden, whom he holds responsible for sending him to prison. The psychopath terrorizes Bowden's wife, Peggy, and teen-age daughter, Nancy, until the entire family is in torment; but Cady does so without breaking any laws. Realizing he must trap the psychopath, Bowden hides Peggy and Nancy in a houseboat on the Cape Fear River, where he expects Cady will find them. As Max attacks the two women, Bowden overpowers him in the river and has the evidence needed to send Cady back to a life term in prison.

Many films have taken the subject of a secure family threatened by dark and violent outside forces. Usually, however, there is a dramatic meaning to the portrayal of this kind of situation. At its most bourgeois and uninteresting, it is the affirmation of the family unit, as in *The Desperate Hours,* where tensions extant in the family are resolved by the crisis. At its most complex and moving, it is the qualification of the family's values by the persuasiveness of the intruder's values, especially if the dark intruder is himself a member of the complacent family. Hitchcock's *Shadow Of A Doubt* is the supreme example of the latter, made even more compelling because of the character of young Charlie, poised between the family and the intruder whom Charlie alone comprehends. *Cape Fear* does not exploit the possibilities of such a situation; and the family is fundamentally unchanged at the end. The sole point of the motion picture seems to be that the evil character is able to circumvent the law and drive the good character to a perfectly reasonable desire for violence.

However simplistic the thrust of this film, it does possess distinction in the very effective score of Bernard Herrmann (although it is a further reminder of the film's sub-Hitchcock quality) and the performance of Robert Mitchum as the psychopath. Although Mitchum's twisted preacher in *The Night Of The Hunter* is a more complex and subtly created character, his swaggering presence in *Cape Fear* has a menacing authority. His ability to appear reptilian as he crawls up the riverbank seems totally antithetical to the sensitive emotional responses that distinguish his more archetypal characterizations.

—B.L.

THE CAPTIVE CITY (1952)
[Working Title: TIGHTROPE]

Director: Robert Wise
Producer: Theron Warth (Aspen Productions)
Screenplay: Karl Kamb and Alvin M. Josephy, Jr.; from an unpublished story by Alvin M. Josephy, Jr.
Prologue/Epilogue: Senator Estes Kefauver
Director of Photography: Lee Garmes
Sound: James G. Stewart
Music Score: Jerome Moross
Music Director: Emil Newman
Production Design: Maurice Zuberano
Assistant Director: Ivan Volkman
Film Editor: Ralph Swink

CAST: John Forsythe (Jim Austin), Joan Camden (Marge Austin), Harold J. Kennedy (Don Carey), Ray Teal (Chief Gillette), Marjorie Crossland (Mrs. Sirak), Victor Sutherland (Murray Sirak), Hal K. Dawson (Clyde Nelson), Geraldine Hall (Mrs. Nelson), Martin Milner (Phil Harding), Gladys Hurlbut (Linda Percy), Ian Wolfe (the Reverend Nash), Jess Kirkpatrick (Anderson). **BITS:** Paul Newlan (Krug), Frances Morris (Mrs. Harding), Charles Waggenheim (Phone Man), Paul Rinegar (Police Sergeant), Vic Romito (Fabretti), Charles Regan (Gangster).
Filming Completed: February 1952
Released: United Artists, March 26, 1952
Running Time: 90 minutes

Jim Austin and his wife Marge flee from their home in

CAUGHT

Kennington, a "nice town" of 300,000, to reach Washington, D.C., and appear before Senator Kefauver's Committee to Investigate Organized Crime. Fearful, they stop at a small-town police station and await the return of the Chief of Police, hoping he will escort them to Washington. Meanwhile Austin tape records his story as a precaution against an "accident." Austin, the editor of the *Kennington Journal*, first learned of organized crime in his town when a private detective, Nelson, explained to him about investigating a local bookie, Murray Sirak, as part of a divorce action. Nelson was harassed by the local police and eventually his license was revoked by the state. Austin is dubious of Nelson and is reassured by Kennington Police Chief Gillette that there are no town rackets. But when Nelson is killed, and the police seem uninterested in finding the murderer, Austin becomes suspicious. Investigating on his own, Austin discovers the Kennington police are controlled by the mob. After Murray Sirak threatens Austin, he leaves town quietly with his wife, in hopes that an appearance before Senator Kefauver's committee will help. A crime syndicate representative offers him money at the hearing if Austin will forget the whole thing. Of course, Austin turns him down.

Captive City is an important transitional film, for it represents an uneasy synthesis of the noir style with the exposé format. The exposé film represents one of a handful of film genres, such as the police documentary, the caper film, and the "social problem" film, that grew out of the film noir tradition as it fragmented along new lines before disappearing altogether in the 1950s. Through skillful use of *mise-en-scène* and photography, Wise and Garmes almost completely recapture the romanticized style of the earlier noir films with lonely cars prowling the night, muffled footsteps in an alley, and frightened faces emerging from the shadows. But the majority of the film conflicts with its documentary conventions of underplayed acting styles; overrhetorical music; and, in particular, the opening and closing segments in which Senator Kefauver speaks directly to the audience. It is also apparent that the film was designed to capitalize on the public's renewed interest in organized crime, due in part to the fame of the Kefauver Committee's investigations, which began in 1950. However, the public's preoccupation with a nationwide criminal organization such as the Mafia was not strong enough in the 1950s to displace the Communist paranoia, and thus the films that illustrated efforts to contain the Communist menace were much more successful than those describing organized crime.

—B.P.

CAUGHT (1949)

Director: Max Ophuls [Uncredited: John Berry]
Producer: Wolfgang Reinhardt (Enterprise Productions)

Screenplay: Arthur Laurents; from the novel *Wild Calendar* by Libbie Block
Director of Photography: Lee Garmes
Process Photography: Mario Castegnaro
Montage: Michael Luciano
Sound: Max Hutchinson
Music Score: Frederick Hollander
Music Director: Rudolph Polk
Art Director: P. Frank Sylos
Set Decoration: Edward G. Boyle
Costumes: Louise Wilson
Makeup: Gus Norin
Hairstyles: Larry Germaine
Production Manager: Joe C. Gilpin
Assistant Director: Albert Van Schmus
Technical Director: Dr. Leo Morton Schulman
Film Editor: Robert Parrish

CAST: James Mason (Larry Quinada), Barbara Bel Geddes (Leonora Eames), Robert Ryan (Smith Ohlrig), Ruth Brady (Maxine), Curt Bois (Franzi), Frank Ferguson (Dr. Hoffman), Natalie Schaefer (Dorothy Dale), Art Smith (Psychiatrist), Sonia Darrin (Miss Chambers), Bernadene Hayes (Mrs. Rudecki), Ann Morrison (Miss Murray), Wilton Graff (Gentry), Jim Hawkins (Kevin), Vicki Raw Stiener (Lorraine).
Filming Completed: 1948
Released: MGM-Enterprise, February 17, 1949
Running Time: 88 minutes

Brainwashed by fashion magazines, a charm school course, and the empty chatter of her girl friends, department store model Leonora Eames believes that the way for a woman to be happy is to marry a rich man. She gets her chance when she meets Smith Ohlrig, a neurotic, reclusive millionaire, who takes her as his wife to spite his psychiatrist. Although the marriage is headlined as a "Cinderella story," Leonora is miserable, alternately neglected and vilified by the paranoid Ohlrig. Night after night, she waits for him while he conducts business, her only companion Ohlrig's slimy parasite Franzi. After Ohlrig humiliates her once too often, Leonora leaves him, hiding her true identity to get a job as a receptionist for the dedicated young Dr. Quinada. Ohlrig entices her back for one night by promising that things will be different, but when he immediately schedules a business trip, she returns to Quinada's office. Soon she is happy in her work and with Quinada, who proposes to her. But discovering that she is pregnant by Ohlrig, she leaves Quinada and returns to the prison of the millionaire's mansion in order to secure financial security for her child. Quinada comes to the mansion and implores her to come away with him. Ohlrig refuses to give her a divorce unless she gives him custody of the child. Leonora sends Quinada away. Ohlrig tortures her through the remaining months of her pregnancy, waking her at odd hours of the night and giving her no peace. Ultimately, she rebels and Ohlrig has one of his psychosomatic attacks. Filled with remorse, because she believes Ohlrig will die, Leonora has a

Smith Ohlrig (Robert Ryan) and his wife, Leonora (Barbara Bel Geddes), in Caught.

Smith Ohlrig (Robert Ryan) in Caught.

miscarriage. Finally, although she loses her baby, she is free to leve her torturer and begin again with Quinada.

From its opening scene, Max Ophuls's *Caught* concentrates on the sharp—and often tragic—difference between dream and reality. Opening on a shot of a woman's hands languidly turning the pages of a slick fashion magazine while a disdainful voice declares that "mink is so everyday," Ophuls's mobile camera swiftly pulls back to reveal a shabby flat peopled by two ordinary shopgirls with dreams of marrying "a handsome young millionaire." With graphic strength, Ophuls and scenarist Arthur Laurents demonstrate what might happen if that dream came true.

Ophuls develops Ohlrig's character in a terrifying session with his helpless psychiatrist. When Robert Ryan's Ohlrig, his face a closed, tight mask, says through clenched teeth, "I have these attacks because I have a bad heart," the cut to Leonora underscores its ominous implications. Soon she is ensconced in jeweled splendor in Ohlrig's gloomy mansion and is a prisoner of her own fantasies.

In a dazzling set piece, Leonora, her face a smear of misery, waits for her errant husband while his lackey, the egregious Franzi torments her. Pounding out Viennese schmaltz on the piano and taunting "Tough, tough, darling" as Leonora begs him to stop, Franzi takes it as part of the ritual when she finally slaps him across the face. "That's all right," he says. "It saves him [Ohlrig] from getting it—that's what I'm paid for." In fact, Franzi, Leonora, and his business associates are all Ohlrig's paid objects, trapped as much by their own desire for some ill-defined "security" as by the millionaire's coercive methods. Even when she discovers love and fulfillment with the blessedly sane and charming Dr. Quinada, Leonora is relentlessly drawn back to Ohlrig, unable to shake her ingrained need for all the things that she thinks money can buy. She is willing to stay with a man who tells her, "All I care about is breaking you," because she has been taught since birth that money and power are the supreme objects of desire and worship.

The ending of *Caught*, while curiously impassive, is nevertheless appropriate to the powerful theme of the film. Leonora does not break away from Ohlrig out of any personal strength of her own. Rather, in the process of losing her child, she is bodily borne away by Quinada. Only the epilogue, in which Quinada's associate tells a nurse bearing Leonora's mink that the young woman will not want it anymore, seems forced. We are left with the suspicion that Leonora, and many like her, will always be willing to barter freedom and self-respect for the unsubtle enticements of men like Smith Ohlrig.

—J.K.

CAUSE FOR ALARM (1951)

Director: Tay Garnett
Producer Tom Lewis (MGM)

Screenplay: Mel Dinelli and Tom Lewis; from an unpublished story by Larry Marcus
Director of Photography: Joseph Ruttenberg
Sound: Douglas Shearer
Music Score: André Previn
Art Directors: Cedric Gibbons, Arthur Lonergan
Set Decoration: Edwin B. Willis, Alfred E. Spencer
Makeup: William J. Tuttle
Hairstyles: Sydney Guilaroff
Assistant Director: Jack Greenwood
Film Editor: James E. Newcom

CAST: Loretta Young (Ellen Jones), Barry Sullivan (George Z. Jones), Bruce Cowling (Dr. Ranney Grahame), Margalo Gillmore (Mrs. Edwards), Bradley Mora (Hoppy Billy), Irving Bacon (Mr. Carston, Postman), Georgia Backus (Mrs. Warren), Don Haggerty (Mr. Russell), Art Baker (Superintendant), Richard Anderson (Lonesome Sailor). **BITS:** Greta Granstedt (Mom), George McDonald (Butch), Margie Liszt, Kathleen Freeman (Women), Ivor James, Teddy Infuhr, Robert Easton, Carl "Alfalfa" Switzer, Gerald Courtermarche (Boys), Helen Winston (Nurse), Earl Hodgins (Postman), Jack Daley (Elderly Man), Bonnie Kay Eddy (Girl), Edward Kilroy (Crossing Guard), Lou Merrill (Dr. Philipps's Voice).
Filming Completed: May 11, 1950
Released: MGM, January 29, 1951
Running Time: 74 minutes

An insanely jealous husband, George Z. Jones, who is recuperating from some lingering heart disease begins to fantasize that his wife, Ellen, is having an affair with the family doctor. He informs her that he is about to kill himself after he watches her mail a letter for him that denounces both Ellen and the doctor as his murderers. Frantic, Ellen tries to recover the incriminating letter before it is too late. Stopped at every turn, Ellen's life becomes a nightmare as her normal suburban routine takes on a menacing attitude, and she is at wit's end by the cruel torture perpetrated on her. When all hope has left her, the letter is serendipitously returned, freeing her from the jealous plotting of her psychotic husband.

A melodrama with a noir flair, *Cause For Alarm* is an exercise in paranoia and claustrophobia. Directed by Tay Garnett, the film presents the Jones house as a threatening maze filled with hidden evil. The film takes every opportunity to subvert normal, everyday situations into perverse visions of madness. The true noir flavor comes in the total dehumanization experienced by Ellen Jones. She might survive the ordeal brought about by her warped husband, but her life will never be the same. Stylistically, the film owes more to television staging than it does to film noir. *Cause For Alarm* falls into a group of melodramas like *The Trial* and *Autumn Leaves*, where the world percieved by the camera may be normal, and yet, seen through the eyes of the characters, it becomes distinctly bleak and hopeless.

—C.M.

THE CHASE (1946)

Director: Arthur Ripley
Producer: Seymour Nebenzal (Nero Producers)
Associate Producer: Eugene Frenke
Screenplay: Philip Yordan; from the novel *The Black Path of Fear* by Cornell Woolrich
Director of Photography: Franz F. Planer
Special Photographic Effects: Ray O. Binger
Sound: Corson Jowett
Music Score: Michel Michelet
Music Director: Heinz Roemheld
Music Supervision: David Chudnow
Art Director: Robert Usher
Set Decoration: Victor A. Gangelin
Costumes: Bill Edwards; Peter Tuesday for Michele Morgan
Makeup: Don Cash
Hairstyles: Marjorie Lund
Production Manager: Joe Popkin
Assistant Director: Jack Voglin
Film Editor: Edward Mann

CAST: Michele Morgan (Lorna), Robert Cummings (Chuck Scott), Steve Cochran (Eddie Roman), Lloyd Corrigan (Emmerick Johnson), Jack Holt (Commander Davidson), Don Wilson (Fats), Alexis Minotis (Acosta), Nina Koschetz (Madame Chin), Peter Lorre (Gino), Yolanda Lacca (Midnight), James Westerfield (Job), Jimmy Ames (the Killer), Shirley O'Hara (Manicurist).
Filming Completed: October 12, 1946
Released: United Artists, November 22, 1946
Running Time: 86 minutes

Chuck Scott, a veteran down on his luck, becomes chauffeur for wealthy Miami businessman Eddie Roman as a reward for returning his lost wallet intact. Roman lives extravagantly with his wife, Lorna, and his aide, Gino, who is his only confidant. Chuck learns that Roman is cruel and not altogether a legitimate businessman when he has Gino eliminate a business rival, Emmerick Johnson. Lorna is unhappy and asks Chuck to help her escape to Havana. He agrees, and they plan to leave the next evening. That afternoon Chuck suffers a recurrence of malarial fever and lies down on his bed to rest. He dreams that after arriving in Havana with Lorna, she is stabbed to death and he is quickly arrested for murder. Escaping from the police, Chuck ultimately discovers Gino is the killer and is murdered by him. Chuck awakens from the nightmare but does not remember his plans to leave with Lorna until he speaks with his doctor, Commander Davidson. Meanwhile, Roman has discovered Lorna's plans and rushes with Gino to make the midnight boat to Havana. With Gino at the wheel of the limousine while Roman controls the speed through a special device, the two are killed attempting to overtake a train. Chuck and Lorna arrive safely in Havana where the coachman from Chuck's dream drops them off at the same nightclub as in his dream.

The Phantom Lady excepted, *The Chase* is the best cinematic equivalent of the dark, oppressive atmosphere that characterizes most of Cornell Woolrich's best fiction. He is certainly the most expressionistic if not the most skilled writer of the *Black Mask* school. Director Ripley has something of a cult following, but he has not made another picture quite like *The Chase*. Its fine pictorial quality may be largely the result of a fortuitous creative synthesis of producer, director, and the rich visual texture of Woolrich's fiction, which was expertly photographed by Franz Planer, a refugee from the classic period of German cinema.

The film is also notable for containing almost equal quantities of those qualities that Borde and Chaumeton (in *Panorama du Film Noir American*) see as quintessentially noir: its oneirism, in which a dreamlike atmosphere prevails, especially at the conclusion, which collapses the distinction between dream and reality; its eroticism, particularly in the scene where Roman sexually badgers and then abuses his female barber and manicurist; its unprecedented elements, such as the dreamed death of the hero; and its aspects of cruelty and ambivalence, as best illustrated in what begins as a comic scene, when Johnson is looking over Roman's wine cellar accompanied by Gino and ends up being trapped there with a killer dog.

—B.P.

CHICAGO DEADLINE (1949)
[Working Title: ONE WOMAN]

Director: Lewis Allen
Producer: Robert Fellows (Paramount)
Screenplay: Warren Duff; from the novel *One Woman* by Tiffany Thayer
Director of Photography: John F. Seitz
Process Photography: Farciot Edouart
Sound: Harold Lewis, Gene Garvin
Music Score: Victor Young
Art Directors: Hans Dreier, Franz Bachelin
Set Decoration: Sam Comer, Ross Dowd
Costumes: Mary Kay Dodson
Makeup: Wally Westmore, Hal Lierley
Hairstyles: Elaine Ramsey
Production Managers: C. Mick, J. Cottrell
Assistant Director: Alvin Ganzer
Script Supervisors: Charles Morton, Gene Buck, Jr.
Film Editor: LeRoy Stone

CAST: Alan Ladd (Ed Adams), Donna Reed (Rosita Jean d'Ur/Ellen Rainer), June Havoc (Leona), Irene Hervey (Belle Dorset), Arthur Kennedy (Tommy Ditman), Berry Kroeger (Solly Wellman), Harold Vermilyea (Anstruder), Shepperd Strudwick (Blacky Franchot), John Beal (Paul Jean d'Ur), Tom Powers (Howard), Gavin Muir (G.G. Temple), Dave Willock (Pig), Paul Lees (Bat).
BITS: Howard Freeman (Hotspur Shaner), Margaret

Field (Minerva), Harry Antrim (Gribbe), Roy Roberts (Jerry Cavanaugh), Marietta Canty (Hazel), Celia Lovsky (Mrs. Schleffler), Ottola Nesmith (Sister John), Jack Overman (Lou Horan), Clarence Straight (Nelson), Dick Keene (Spingler), Leona Roberts (Maggie), Carole Mathews (Secretary), Gordon Carveth (Marty), Laura Elliott (Marcia), Paul Bryar, Jack Gargan (Bartenders), Douglas Carter (Waiter), Phyllis Kennedy (Maid), Donald Wilmot (Copy Boy), Jerry James, Eric Alden, Bill Meader, Charley Cooley, Hal Rand, Ralph Montgomery, Lyle Moraine, Douglas Spencer (Reporters), Frances Sanford (Telephone Operator), Marie Blake (Operator), Joane and Robert Rexer (Specialty Act), Joe Whitehead (Actor), Dulce Daye (Woman), Helen Chapman (Girl), Julia Faye (Nurse), Pat Lane (Assistant Undertaker), Harry Cheshire (Minister), Arthur Space (Peterson), Jack Roberts, George Magrill (Handlers), Jim Davies (Second), Ralph Peters (Taxi Driver), Michael Brandon (Reporter).

Location: Hollywood, California
Filming Completed: September 18, 1948
Released: Paramount, November 2, 1949
Running Time: 87 minutes

A journalist, Ed Adams, discovers the body of a young girl, Ellen Rainer, dead of tuberculosis in a cheap hotel room. Falling in love with this emaciated but exquisite corpse, he steals her address book before the police arrive and commits himself to the rehabilitation of her memory. Using her book as a guide in his investigation, he meets a diverse group of individuals, some of whom are at first reluctant to acknowledge her, which makes Ed press on all the more steadfastly. As each person, tells his story in flashback, a variety of differing images of the girl, whose real name was Rosita Jean d'Ur, is presented. Ultimately, Ed uncovers two murders and several blackmail attempts connected with Rosita's friends. His life is threatened, but Ed tricks the killer, Solly, who dies instead. At the girl's funeral Ed burns her address book, and her brother, Tommy, tells him that he probably knew Rosita better than anybody.

As Borde and Chaumeton point out (in *Panorama du Film Noir American*), *Chicago Deadline* would have been a classic film noir· in the manner of *Laura* had a more mordant sensibility prevailed. They feel this might have been the case had "the makers insisted upon the peculiarity of the investigation and the morbid character of Adams's devotion to the dead girl…if the hero, tired but victorious, had died of his wounds in the final scene, after having listened to the final mass given for the purified martyr; if Alan Ladd had not played a superman whose look dominated all situations…" These faults are attributed to the director, Lewis Allen, but it is more likely that the character and noir tone that they demand would not have been allowed by the producers of a Ladd starring vehicle, since his one film about romantic defeat, *The Great Gatsby*, had done poorly at the box office earlier in the year.

—V.P.

CHINATOWN (1974)

Director: Roman Polanski
Producer: Robert Evans (Paramount-Penthouse-The Long Road Productions)
Associate Producer and Unit Production Manager: C.O. Erickson
Screenplay: Robert Towne
Director of Photography: John A. Alonzo [Technicolor; Panavision]
Camera Operator: Hugh Gagnier
Special Effects: Logan Frazee
Sound: Larry Jost, Bud Grenzbach
Sound Editor: Robert Cornett
Music: Jerry Goldsmith
Songs: "I Can't Get Started" by Ira Gershwin and Vernon Duke; "Easy Living" by Leo Robin and Ralph Rainger; "The Way You Look Tonight" by Jerome Kern and Dorothy Fields; "Some Day" and "The Vagabond King Waltz" by Brian Hooker and Rudolf Friml
Production Designer: Richard Sylbert
Art Director: W. Stewart Campbell
Set Design: Gabe Resh, Robert Resh
Set Decoration: Ruby Levitt
Costumes: Anthea Sylbert
Wardrobe: Richard Bruno, Jean Merrick
Makeup: Hank Edds, Lee Harmon
Hairstyles: Susan Germaine, Vivienne Walker
Casting: Mike Fenton, Jane Feinberg
Production Assistant: Gary Chazan
Script Supervisor: Mary Wale Brown
Assistant Director: Howard W. Koch, Jr.
Titles: Wayne Fitzgerald
Film Editor: Sam O'Steen

CAST: Jack Nicholson (J.J. Gittes), Faye Dunaway (Evelyn Mulwray), John Huston (Noah Cross), Perry Lopez (Escobar), John Hillerman (Yelburton), Darrell Zwerling (Hollis Mulwray), Diane Ladd (Ida Sessions), Roy Jenson (Mulvihill), Roman Polanski (Man with Knife), Dick Bakalyan (Loach), Joe Mantell (Walsh), Bruce Glover (Duffy), Nandu Hinds (Sophie), James O'Reare (Lawyer), James Hong (Evelyn's Butler), Beaulah Quo (Maid), Jerry Fujikawa (Gardener), Belinda Palmer (Katherine), Roy Roberts (Mayor Bagby), Noble Willingham, Elliott Montgomery (Councilmen), Rance Howard (Irate Farmer), George Justin (Barber), Doc Erickson (Customer), Fritzie Burr (Mulwray's Secretary), Charles Knapp (Mortician), Claudio Martinez (Boy on Horseback), Federico Roberto (Cross's Butler), Allan Warnick (Clerk), John Holland, Jesse Vint, Jim Burke, Denny Arnold (Farmers in the Valley), Burt Young (Curly), Elizabeth Harding (Curly's Wife), John Rogers (Mr. Palmer), Cecil Elliott (Emma Dill), Paul Jenkins, Lee DeBroux, Bob Golden (Policemen).

Location: Los Angeles, California
Released: Paramount, June 21, 1974
Running Time: 130 minutes   **MPAA Rating:** R

Evelyn Mulwray (Faye Dunaway) in Chinatown.

Left to right: Noah Cross (John Huston) and J. J. Gittes (Jack Nicholson) in Chinatown.

CHRISTMAS HOLIDAY

Los Angeles in 1937 is suffering through a drought. J.J. Gittes, an ex-cop and private detective specializing in "matrimonial" work, is hired by a woman claiming to be Evelyn Mulwray to discover whether her husband, the water commissioner, is faithful. Gittes spies on Hollis Mulwray and sees him with a young girl. The story makes front-page headlines and Gittes learns he has been duped in a plot to discredit the commissioner, who opposes construction of a water reservoir in the San Fernando Valley farmlands near Los Angeles. The authentic Mrs. Mulwray, who is the daughter of powerful magnate Noah Cross, threatens to sue Gittes. But when her husband is found murdered, she asks Gittes to find the criminal. The detective uncovers a crooked land deal, whereby acreage in the San Fernando Valley is being purchased cheaply by Noah Cross and his associates under false names for speculation pending the reservoir's construction. Gittes is aided and hinderd by the anguished Evelyn Mulwray. He learns that the young girl spotted with Hollis Mulwray is Evelyn's daughter *and* sister, Kathryn, the offspring of Noah's rape of Evelyn when she was fifteen years old. Gittes falls in love with Evelyn and agrees to help her smuggle Kathryn out of the country. However, the police follow his trail to Chinatown, where Evelyn and Kathryn await Gittes. Noah Cross arrives also, and Evelyn wounds her father while attempting to flee with Kathryn. Handcuffed, Gittes is powerless to help and must watch while Evelyn is fatally shot by the police and Cross comforts his granddaughter, who is also his daughter.

Screenwriter Robert Towne has devised a metaphor in *Chinatown* that is easily applicable to film noir in general. Many noir characters have shadowy pasts and are plagued by subconscious fears. Gittes's worries stem from "Chinatown"; a state of mind and a spiritual landscape where monstrous deeds are performed in the name of progress and eyes are quickly averted. If 1937 Los Angeles, as viewed in this film, has a definable personality, then *Chinatown* is its id. It does not appear as a location until the end of the story, but its ambience permeates the film. The mere mention of it causes people to respond in the manner that children react to the "bogeyman." J.J. Gittes referred to it obliquely: "You may think you know what you're dealing with, but believe me, you don't," and "Talking about the past bothers everyone who works in Chinatown because you can't always tell what's going on..."

Based on an incident in Los Angeles history, Towne's script clothes its symbols with the trappings of a hard-boiled pulp detective yarn. It is structured in the conventional private-eye style in which a straightforward investigation proves to be just the tip of the iceberg. Importantly, however, *Chinatown*'s protagonist is no Philip Marlowe who prides himself on the fact that he doesn't do divorce work. It is J.J. Gittes's specialty, and he is a tasteless little gumshoe with pretensions to class. Traditionally, the private eye is a man with a code, who functions like a wandering knight. He is outside the law, which is usually either corrupt or ineffectual. Gittes is an unlikely Sir Galahad, as his main concern is getting paid. It is hinted, however, that while patrolling Chinatown he tried to prevent something terrible from happening to a woman he cared for, but his interference only hastened the calamity, and he quit the force. He continually clashes with his former colleagues, even though they are bound together in unspoken ways. When Gittes attempts to save Evelyn Mulwray, he literally gets into deep water and finds history foredoomed to repeat itself.

Water is one of the many ingenious symbols used in the film. Los Angeles has been utilized effectively many times for its symbolic resonances. It is the city of eternal sunshine where prayers are answered, but it is also the dead end of the continent. When there are no more mountains to cross, the lemmings run into the sea. In *The Day of the Locust*, Nathanael West saw it as the place people come to die. Horace McCoy staged his marathon dance of death in *They Shoot Horses, Don't They?* in a squalid ballroom on a pier jutting into the Pacific Ocean. In *Chinatown*, Los Angeles is in the midst of a drought, a parched community desperately in need of both water and spiritual relief; and the film chronicles the chicanery behind the building of a reservoir in the San Fernando Valley. The chief villain, ironically named Noah, is a craggy old robber baron whose incestuous rape of his daughter is paralleled by his violation of the land. The daughter, Evelyn Mulwray, is a traditional noir heroine. A genuine black widow, she ensnares the detective in a web of opposing allegiances and motives. As a professional snoop, "sticking his nose in other people's business," Gittes has his nostril slashed with a knife, brandished by Roman Polanski as one of the villain's minions. It becomes his scarlet letter, and he sports it like a badge of courage.

Roman Polanski and Robert Towne clashed over the ending, as Towne had written that Mrs. Mulwray murders her father and Gittes spirits her daughter/sister across the Mexican border. Polanski prevailed and the finale is despairing; but more consistent with all that has preceded it. The mordant tone is in accord with Polanski's chilly temperament. Shots are composed in a constricting fashion, giving the impression that things of importance are happening just beyond the frame, on the fringes of our perception. This gives the film an airless, suffocating feeling that befits the dusty, hot climate. In collaboration with his gifted cinematographer, John Alonzo, Polanski chose elemental colors to enhance this desertlike aura, using earthy browns and sun-drenched yellows;

Chinatown is ample proof that the noir film is not dead. It is a melancholy and savage film. Robert Towne may have set the plan in motion, but it is Polanski who wields the knife.

—J.B.

CHRISTMAS HOLIDAY (1944)

Director: Robert Siodmak
Producer: Frank Shaw

Executive Producer: Felix Jackson (Universal Pictures)
Screenplay: Herman J. Mankiewicz; from the novel by W. Somerset Maugham
Director of Photography: Woody Bredell
Special Photography: John P. Fulton
Sound: Joe Lapis
Music: Hans J. Salter
Songs: "Spring Will Be a Little Late This Year" by Frank Loesser; "Always" by Irving Berlin
Art Directors: John B. Goodman, Robert Clatworthy
Set Decoration: Russell A. Gausman, E.R. Robinson
Costumes: Vera West; Deanna Durbin's gowns by Muriel King and Howard Greer
Assistant Director: William Holland
Film Editor: Ted Kent

CAST: Deanna Durbin (Jackie Lamont, Abigail Mannette), Gene Kelly (Robert Manette), Richard Whorf (Simon Fenimore), Dean Harens (Charles Mason), Gladys George (Valerie de Merode), Gale Sondergaard (Mrs. Manette), David Bruce (Gerald Tyler). **BITS:** Minor Watson (Townsend), the Reverend Neal Dodd (Minister), Robert Homans, James Flavin, Charles McMurphy (Policemen), Cy Kendall (Jordan), Eddie Dunn, Charles Cane (Detectives), Cy Ring, Larry Steers, Heinie Conklin, Arthur Stuart Hull, Frank Austin, James Farley, Jack C. Smith (Jurymen), Charles Jordan (Bailiff), John Hamilton (Foreman), Oliver Prickett (Lawyer), George Irving (Judge), John Berkes (Waiter), Frank Marlowe (Bellboy), Joseph Crehan (Steve, Bartender), Katherine York (Woman Clerk), Edwin Stanley (Room Clerk), Louise Currie (Stewardess), Clyde Fillmore (Colonel), Joe Kirk (Airline Attendant).
Location: Hollywood, California
Filming Completed: February 12, 1944
Released: Universal, June 30, 1944
Running Time: 93 minutes

Lt. Charles Mason, en route to San Francisco for Christmas furlough, is forced to stay over in New Orleans by a rainstorm. He meets a local chanteuse, Jackie Lamont, and accompanies her to midnight mass. The girl cries during the mass and later tells Mason her story. Her real name is Abigail Mannette and her husband, Robert, is serving a life sentence for murdering a bookie. Abby first met Robert at a concert and, impressed by his cultured charm, learned that he and his mother were the surviving members of an important New Orleans family. Robert's mother approves of Abby but cryptically tells her that she would like Robert to fall in love with a woman who would bring him strength. After they are married, Abby refuses to recognize Robert's faults. He is a wastrel whose surface charm belies a violent temper. Abby ignores indications that he and his mother conspire to conceal a murder. When Robert is convicted, his mother berates Abby for her lack of courage in refusing to see him as he really was. Her sad story finished, Abby says goodbye to Lt. Mason and returns to her cabaret job. Meanwhile, Robert has escaped from jail and is holding a

reporter hostage in Abby's dressing room. She is trapped by her husband, who hates her for what she has become. Abby explains that she took the job so that she might also be in prison, albeit an emotional one. Before Robert kills Abby, he is fatally shot by a policeman and exclaims, "You can let go now, Abby."

Christmas Holiday is perhaps the most unusual, although scarcely the most successful, of Siodmak's noir films. Mankiewicz's transposition of Maugham's novel had problems that were intensified by Deanna Durbin's rejection of Siodmak's efforts to deglamorize her. For anyone who has seen the synthetic sexuality of Ella Raines's impersonation of a floozy in *The Phantom Lady*, it is obvious that Siodmak was attempting the same transformation in *Christmas Holiday*, especially when Durbin sings. Moreover, the reverse casting of Gene Kelly as Robert is almost perfect. It is unfortunate that Kelly's sinister side—first expressed in Broadway's hit musical, *Pal Joey*, through artificial smiles and a measured gait—was never again fully exploited on the screen after *Christmas Holiday*. Siodmak's Germanic sensibility allowed him deeply to undercut that almost Rockwellian portrait of a smiling mother, son, and daughter-in-law gathered around a piano. This scene of American harmony is disrupted by suggestions of incest and homosexuality. Present are relationships of love and sex that are so perverse they evoke the noir underworld as if it were a foundation of corruption, like Eliot's skull beneath the skin, underlying an ostensibly attractive reality. Finally, Hans Salter's use of Wagner's "Tristan" theme to open and close Robert and Abby's relationship, and the slow, highly syncopated rendition of "Always" that he forces on Deanna Durbin as a reaffirmation of the love that destroys as it consumes, reinforce the noir conceptions of the film.

—B.P.

CITY STREETS (1931)

Director: Rouben Mamoulian
Producer: E. Lloyd Sheldon (Paramount)
Screenplay: Max Marcin and Oliver H. P. Garrett, adapted by Max Marcin; from a story by Dashiell Hammett Marcin; from a story by Dashiell Hammett
Director of Photography: Lee Garmes, William Shea
Sound: J.A. Goodrich, M.M. Paggi
Music: Sidney Cutner

CAST: Gary Cooper (the Kid), Sylvia Sydney (Nan Cooley), Paul Lukas (Big Fella Maskal), William Boyd (McCoy), Guy Kibbee (Pop Cooley), Stanley Fields (Blackie), Wynne Gibson (Agnes), Betty Sinclair (Pansy), Terry Carroll (Esther March), Bob Kortman (Servant), Barbara Leonard (Girl), Edward LeSaint, Hal Price (Shooting Gallery Patrons), Robert E. Homans (Inspector), Willard Robertson (Detective), Ethan Laid-

CITY THAT NEVER SLEEPS

law (Prison Killer), George Regas (Machine Gunner), Leo Willis, Nick Thompson (Henchmen), Allan Cavan (Policeman), Matty Kemp (Stabbed Man), Norman Foster, (Man on Midway), Bill Elliott (Dancer), Bill O'Brien (Waiter).

Released: Paramount, April 18, 1931
Running Time: 83 minutes

A carnival employee known as the Kid falls in love with Nan Cooley, the daughter of underworld assassin, Pop Cooley. She tries to persuade the Kid to join the mob, where the rewards are easy money and fast living; but he refuses. Later, after Nan is railroaded into prison for not squealing on her father, who murdered a rival racketeer, she begins to perceive the shortcomings of a criminal life. The Kid, an excellent marksman, is eventually recruited into the service of Maskal, a big-time bootlegger. Quickly pulling himself up through the ranks of Maskal's organization, the Kid discovers how easy it is to take out on his own. On Nan's release, she pleads with Maskal not to destroy the Kid. Maskal's moll, feeling double-crossed, murders her lover and locks Nan in the room with the corpse. The Kid returns and rescues Nan from the clutches of the enraged mobsters; they leave the city and its corruption behind them.

Adapted from an original screenplay by Dashiel Hammett, *City Streets* is an unusually decadent and stylish gangster film. Directed by Rouben Mamoulian, it displays none of the staccato violence associated with gangster films of that period. Rather, Mamoulian prefers to fill the production with iconography and strong visual symbols. The resulting film evokes a mood of corruption redeemed only by the love of Nan and the Kid. There are hints of Hammett's unique gangland environment in both Maskal's complex mob and the subtle touches of criminal savvy, (such as the use of the long ash on Pop Cooley's cigar for an alibi). Mamoulian's films almost always displayed a stunning visual style, and *City Streets* is no exception. Heavy chiaroscuro lighting and the dark milieu of the underworld reinforce the noir attitude of Hammett's expert characterizations.

—C.M.

CITY THAT NEVER SLEEPS (1953)

Director and Associate Producer: John H. Auer
Executive Producer: Herbert J. Yates (Republic)
Screenplay: Steve Fisher
Director of Photography: John L. Russell, Jr.
Special Effects: Howard and Theodore Lydecker
Sound: Dick Tyler, Howard Wilson
Music: R. Dale Butts
Art Director: James Sullivan
Set Decoration: John McCarthy, Jr., Charles Thompson

Costumes: Adele Palmer
Makeup: Bob Mark
Hairstyles: Peggy Gray
Technical Adviser: Sgt. Wilbur F. Parker, Chicago Police Department
Assistant Director: Herb Mendelson
Film Editor: Fred Allen

CAST: Gig Young (Johnny Kelly), Mala Powers (Sally Connors, "Angel Face"), William Talman (Hayes Stewart), Edward Arnold (Penrod Biddel), Chill Wills (Sgt. Joe, the "Voice of Chicago"), Marie Windsor (Lydia Biddel), Paula Raymond (Kathy Kelly), Otto Hulett (Sgt. John Kelly, Sr.), Wally Cassell (Gregg Warren), Ron Hagerthy (Stubby), James Andelin (Lt. Parker), Thomas Poston (Detective), Bunny Kacher (Agnes), Philip L. Boddy (Maitre d'Hotel), Thomas Jones (Fancy Dan), Leonard Diebold (Cab Driver).
BITS: Emmett Vogan (Doctor), Tom Irish (Bellboy), Walter Woolf King (Hotel Manager), Helen Gibson (Woman), Gil Herman, Clark Howatt (Patrolmen).

Location: Chicago, Illinois
Filming Completed: January 5, 1953
Released: Republic, August 8, 1953
Running Time: 90 minutes

Johnny Kelly, a young police officer, is on mobile patrol duty one night but stops by a nightclub and visits his lover, Sally, a stripper. She warns him that she is soon leaving town; she tells him that if he will not come with her she is going with Gregg Warren, her ex-boyfriend who pretends to be a "mechanical man" in the nightclub's display window. Smothered in his marriage anyway, Johnny agrees to leave with Sally and plans on quitting the police force the next day, because it is a job he took to appease his father, who is also a cop. He continues with the night's duties and meets Penrod Biddel, an older, affluent lawyer. Biddel wants to trap his wife, Lydia, with her lover, Stewart, and promises Johnny enough money to "give your life dignity" if he will arrest Stewart, who is Johnny's friend. However, Biddel confronts the lovers first and is killed by Stewart, who, with Lydia, attempts to find Johnny, believing he will help them escape. But Johnny's father, Sgt. John Kelly, Sr., stops them at the nightclub and is killed by Stewart who also shoots Lydia, unaware that the "mechanical man" has witnessed the act and is a real person. Gregg Warren agrees to continue his window routine and act as a decoy to encourage Stewart's return. Sally tries to convince Gregg to leave his dangerous position, and Gregg begins to cry at her promise of a new life together. Seeing the tears, spectators draw the attention of the hidden Stewart to the fact that the "mechanical man" is real. Stewart shoots at Gregg but misses, and flees with Johnny in close pusuit. They fight on the elevated streetcar tracks, and Stewart falls to his death. At dawn, Johnny meets his wife, Kathy, in the street and they kiss, as "Sgt. Joe," the "Voice of Chicago," tells us that Johnny has been born again.

Hayes Stewart (William Talman) in
City That Never Sleeps.

City That Never Sleeps attempts to do for Chicago what *The Naked City* did for New York, although it lacks the impact of the earlier film. It successfully combines the two conventions of the 1950s thrillers; the semidocumentary study of a city and the socially vignetted night with a police unit; but the film exchanges a sardonic tone for sentimentality by embodying the "Voice of Chicago" in the person of Sgt. Joe. However the location photography is quite good, William Talman achieves his usual degree of menace, and Wally Cassell brings something more than pathos to this performance of the "mechanical man," Gregg Warren. The motifs of self-debasement, alienation, and dehumanization, so typical of the noir cycle, are perhaps nowhere better exemplified than in this character who fantasized new life with the stripper, the sight of the teardrops streaming down his "gilded" face are memorable images.

—B.P.

CLASH BY NIGHT (1952)

Director: Fritz Lang
Executive Producer: Jerry Wald (Wald-Krasna Productions.)
Producer: Harriet Parsons
Screenplay: Alfred Hayes, with contribution by David Dortort; from the play by Clifford Odets
Director of Photography: Nicholas Musuraca
Special Photographic Effects: Harold Wellman
Sound: Jean L. Speak, Clem Portman
Music: Roy Webb
Song: "I Hear A Rhapsody" by Joe Gasparre, Jack Baker, and George Fragos; sung by Tony Martin
Music Director: Constantin Bakaleinikoff
Art Directors: Albert S. D'Agostino, Carroll Clark
Set Decoration: Darrell Silvera, Jack Mills
Film Editor: George J. Amy

CONFLICT

CAST: Barbara Stanwyck (Mae Doyle D'Amato), Paul Douglas (Jerry D'Amato), Robert Ryan (Earl Pfeiffer), Marilyn Monroe (Peggy), J. Carroll Naish (Uncle Vince), Keith Andes (Joe Doyle), Silvio Minciotti (Papa D'Amato). **BITS:** Diane and Deborah Stewart (Twin Babies), Roy D'Armour, Gilbert Frye (Men), Nancy Duke, Sally Yarnell, Irene Crosby, Helen Hansen, Dan Bernaducci, Dick Coe, Al Cavens (Guests), Julius Tannen, William Bailey (Waiters), Bert Stevans, Mario Siletti (Bartenders), Bill Slack, Art Dupuis (Customers), Frank Kreig (Art), Tony Dante (Fisherman).
Location: Monterey, California
Filming Completed: February 20, 1952
Released: RKO, June 18, 1952
Running Time: 104 minutes
[NOTE: William H. Mooring, film critic of *Tidings,* a Roman Catholic weekly, persuaded Jerry Wald and Harriet Parsons that two scenes of *Clash By Night* belittled the church and ridiculed religion. The scenes were subsequently cut.]

Disillusioned by big city high life, Mae Doyle returns to her home town of Monterey after a long absence. Her sophisticated air attracts the attention of Jerry D'Amato, a good-natured fisherman she knew in her youth, and his movie-projectionist friend, the cynical Earl Pfeiffer. Mae's brother Joe is engaged to a young woman, Peggy, who longs to live with the freedom she believes Mae represents. Although Mae and Earl are immediately drawn to each other, their mutual cynicism prevents a relationship from developing. Mae decides to marry the kindly but unexciting Jerry, who genuinely loves her. They have a child and live uneventfully but happily together for a short time. Soon, however, Mae wearies of her life with Jerry and embarks on an affair with Earl. When Jerry learns of her infidelity, Mae decides to go off with Earl. But she discovers that his cynicism disgusts her and she returns to Jerry, asking him to take her back and they are reunited.

Clash By Night is a film with a modest scenario, but the plot's eternal triangle is transformed by characters that are subtly graded, complex creations, never wholly one thing or another. Stanwyck's portrayal of Mae, a free-living woman of dubious past who cuckolds her husband, is also a character of liberated imagination, and one who can ultimately see the flaws in a situation of her own creation. Robert Ryan's caustic cynic, Earl Pfeiffer, is capable of coldly informing Mae that in every decisive circumstance "somebody's throat has to be cut," but he is the same person who cries, "Help me, Mae, I'm dying of loneliness!"

As in many noir films, Ryan delivers *Clash by Night*'s most anguished performance. As the model of the alienated man, pain constantly flickers beneath the sardonic mask of his face, although he holds his mouth tightly in check and his powerful body in a useless rigidity. Ryan etches a complex portrayal of an unhappy personality whose miseries are expressed in acts of cruelty but who is accepted with some degree of audience understanding. Earl Pfeiffer's imprisonment in his milieu is reinforced by the extraordinary

opening of *Clash By Night,* which details the day-to-day work of fishermen and cannery laborers. Fritz Lang referred to this documentary sequence as "three hundred feet of introduction," and it situates the film firmly in a naturalistic reality that supports the middle-class alienation of its characters.

—J.K.

CONFLICT (1945)
[Working Title: THE PENTACLE]

Director: Curtis Bernhardt
Producer: William Jacobs (Warner Brothers)
Screenplay: Arthur T. Horman and Dwight Taylor; from an original story by Robert Siodmak and Alfred Neumann
Director of Photography: Merritt Gerstad
Sound: Oliver S. Garretson
Music Score: Frederick Hollander
Song: "Tango of Love"
Music Director: Leo F. Forbstein
Orchestration: Jerome Moross
Art Director: Ted Smith
Set Decoration: Clarence I. Steensen
Costumes: Milo Anderson
Makeup: Perc Westmore
Unit Manager: Al Alleborn
Dialogue Director: James Vincent
Assistant Director: Elmer Decker
Film Editor: David Weisbart

CAST: Humphrey Bogart (Richard Mason), Alexis Smith (Evelyn Turner), Sydney Greenstreet (Dr. Mark Hamilton), Rose Hobart (Katherine Mason), Charles Drake (Professor Norman Holdsworth), Grant Mitchell (Dr. Grant), Patrick O'Moore (Detective Lt. Egan), Ann Shoemaker (Nora Grant), Frank Wilcox (Robert Freston), James Flavin (Detective Lt. Workman), Edwin Stanley (Phillips), Mary Servoss (Mrs. Allman). **BITS:** Doria Caron (Nurse), Ray Hanson, Billy Wayne (Cab Drivers), Ralph Dunn (Highway Patrolman), John Harmon (Hobo), Bruce Bilson (Bellboy), Marjorie Hoshelle (Telephone Operator), Frances Morris (Receptionist), George Carleton (Harris), Oliver Prickett, Harlan Briggs (Pawnbrokers), Wallis Clark (Professor Berens), Jack Mower (Desk Clerk), Emmett Vogan (Luggage Salesman).
Filming Completed: August 25, 1943
Released: Warner Brothers, June 15, 1945
Running Time: 86 minutes

Richard and Katherine Mason are not so happily married as they appear; but when Richard admits that he loves Katherine's sister, Evelyn, Katherine refuses to give him up. One night, driving home from a dinner party given by their friend, psychiatrist Mark Hamilton, Richard injures his leg in an auto accident. He later conceals that it has healed and declines Katherine's invitation to join her for a stay at a mountain resort. Instead, he intercepts her car on a lonely mountain road, strangles her, and then pushes her car off a cliff into a log-filled ravine. Shortly after reporting her missing, a series of strange incidents occur causing Richard to doubt Katherine's death: the odor of her perfume in a room; the reappearance of a piece of her jewelry and her handkerchief; and finally a letter in her handwriting. These occurrences, when reinforced by anonymous phone calls and the glimpse of a woman dressed in her clothes, lead Richard to doubt his sanity. Making matters worse, Evelyn denies they ever had a romance and believes Katherine will always stand between them. Richard seeks help from Hamilton, and the psychiatrist gives him a rational explanation for the events but tells him that he must cure himself since Richard is obviously not completely candid. Richard returns to the scene of the crime to prove to himself that Katherine is really dead. Once there, however, Hamilton and the police arrive. Richard discovers that the entire series of incidents were part of an ingenious plan contrived by Hamilton, who had spotted a flaw in Richard's initial description of Katherine's last appearance. Mason had described her as wearing a rose; a detail he couldn't possibly have known about because Hamilton had given it to her that day, after she left Richard.

What might have been little more than a trite mystery is given a noir ambience by the effective performances of the Warner Brothers stock players. More importantly, the romantic fatalism so prevalent in mid-1940s film noir is present in *Conflict*, contrived by the heavy Germanic influence of author Robert Siodmak and director Curtis Bernhardt, another expatriot of German expressionism. The film is particularly memorable for the use of the song "Tango of Love" as leitmotif to indicate the putative reappearance of Katherine, with the background strings translating the scent of perfume; the opening trucking shot through the rain-soaked night up to the window of the Mason house, which allows the audience to eavesdrop on the dinner party; and the sinister appearance of Bogart as he steps out of the shadows to murder his wife.

—B.P.

CONVICTED (1950)

[Working Title: ONE WAY OUT]

Director: Henry Levin
Producer: Jerry Bresler (Columbia)
Screenplay: William Bowers, Fred Niblo, Jr., and Seton I. Miller; from the play *Criminal Code* by Martin Flavin
Director of Photography: Burnett Guffey
Sound: Lodge Cunningham
Music Score: George Duning
Music Director: Morris Stoloff
Art Director: Carl Anderson

Set Decoration: James Crowe
Makeup: Newt Jones
Hairstyles: Helen Hunt
Production Manager: Jack Fier
Assistant Director: Frederick Briskin
Script Supervisor: Charlsie Bryant
Film Editor: Al Clark

CAST: Glenn Ford (Joe Hufford), Broderick Crawford (George Knowland), Millard Mitchell (Malloby), Dorothy Malone (Kay Knowland), Carl Benton Reid (Capt. Douglas), Frank Faylen (Ponti), Will Geer (Mapes), Martha Stewart (Bertie Williams), Henry O'Neill (Detective Dorn), Douglas Kennedy (Detective Baley), Ronald Winters (Vernon Bradley), Ed Begley (Mackay), Frank Cady (Eddie), John Doucette (Tex), Ilka Gruning (Martha Lorry), John A. Butler (Curly), Peter Virgo (Luigi), Whit Bissell (Owens). **BITS:** Fred Sears (Fingerprint Man), Fred Graham, Eddie Parker, James Millican, Ray Teal, Robert Malcolm, James Bush, Bill Tannen, Clancy Cooper (Guards), William E. Green (Dr. Masterson), Charles Cane (Sergeant), Wilton Graff (Dr. Agar), Vincent Renno (Freddie), Harry Cording (Brick, 3rd Convict), Griff Barnett (Mr. Hufford), Richard Hale (Judge), William Vedder (Whitey, 2nd Convict), Alphonse Martell (Melreau), Harry Harvey, Marshall Bradford, Bradford Hatten (Patrolmen), Jimmie Dodd (Grant), Benny Burt (Blackie), Thomas Kingston (Conductor), Jay Barney (Nick), Chuck Hamilton, Charles Sherlock (Policemen).
Filming Completed: January 19, 1950
Released: Columbia, August 1950
Running Time: 91 minutes
[NOTE: *Convicted* is a remake of the 1932 film *The Criminal Code.*

An innocent man, Joe Hufford, is put in prison, accused of murdering a member of an important family, a man he had met in a bar. The district attorney, George Knowland, feels that Joe is innocent, but he is helpless after the lawyer assigned to defend the suspect totally mishandles the case. Given a lighter sentence at the district attorney's prompting, Joe becomes a model prisoner. A concentrated effort on both sides of the prison walls finally reveals the real killer and frees the soured inmate. His charges are dropped and he gains his freedom after losing the respect of both his family and friends.

Prison pictures rarely become noir films. The inherent claustrophobic atmosphere allows fewer opportunities to express the hopelessness and feelings of alienation, which give a film a dark, cynical noir attitude; and there can be little anticipation of redemption. *Convicted* is a film that lacks originality. Its overworked themes and obvious amelioration are opposed to the noir framework; but there is a noir quality in the film due primarily to the presence of Glenn Ford. Ford's presence in many of the noir films of Columbia Pictures during that period (*Framed, Undercovered Man,* and the superb *Gilda*), established a screen personality that, of

CORNERED

itself, articulated a close affinity to the noir world. The ironies of the plot, playing off Ford's assumed persona, inbue *Convicted* with a noir sensibility that would have been unattainable without Ford.

—C.M.

CORNERED (1945)

Director: Edward Dmytryk
Producer: Adrian Scott (RKO)
Screenplay: John Paxton; from an unpublished story by John Wexley
Director of Photography: Harry J. Wild
Sound: Richard Van Hessen, James G. Stewart
Music: Roy Webb
Music Director: Constantin Bakaleinikoff
Orchestration: Gil Grau
Art Directors: Albert S. D'Agostino, Carroll Clark
Set Decoration: Darrell Silvera
Costumes: Renie

Dialogue Director: Leslie Urbach
Assistant Director: Ruby Rosenberg
Film Editor: Joseph Noriega

CAST: Dick Powell (Gerard), Walter Slezak (Incza), Micheline Cheirel (Mme. Jarnac), Nina Vale (Señora Camargo), Morris Carnovsky (Santana), Edgar Barrier (DuBois), Steven Geray (Señor Camargo), Jack La Rue (Diego), Luther Adler (Marcel Jarnac), Gregory Gay (Perchon). **BITS:** Jean Del Val (First Prefect), Igor Dolgoruki (Swiss Hotel Clerk), Ellen Corby (French Maid), Louis Mercier (Rougon), Jacques Lory (French Clerk), Martin Cichy (Jopo), George Renevant (Second Prefect), Nelson Leigh (Dominion Official), Leslie Dennison (Finance Officer), Tanis Chandler (Airline Hostess), Egon Brecher (Insurance Man), Gloria De Guarda, Beverly Bushe (Girls), Hans Moebus, Joaquin Elizondo, Warren Jackson (Men), Byron Foulger (Night Clerk), Michael Mark (Elevator Operator), Ken McDonald (Businessman), Al Murphy (Bartender), Al Walton, Milton Wallace (Waiters), Cy Kendall (Detective), Belle Mitchell (Hotel Maid), Simone La Brousse (Maria), Carlos Barbe (Regules), Hugh Prosser (Police Assistant), Jerry De

Gerard (Dick Powell) in Cornered.

Castro (Taxi Driver), Stanley Price (Hotel Clerk), Nestor Paiva (Police Official), Frank Mills (Stumblebum), Carl De Lora (Mean-faced Man), Richard Clark (Cab Driver), Paul Bradley (Policeman), Rod De Medici (Bellboy).
Filming Completed: August 17, 1945
Released: December 25, 1945
Running Time: 102 minutes

Laurence Gerard, a Canadian pilot recently released from a prisoner of war camp, begins a quest to avenge the death of his young French war bride, who was betrayed by Marcel Jarnac, a Vichy official. Jarnac is a man of mystery. Few people can recall his appearance, and Gerard, skeptical of the official report of Jarnac's death, follows his trail. It leads to Swizerland and ultimately to Buenos Aires. There, Mme. Jarnac is part of a set of wealthy expatriates and local gentry, including Mr. DuBois, Señor Santana, and Mr. and Mrs. Thomas Camargo. Gerard is suspicious of the whole group, unaware that DuBois, Santana, and the servant Diego belong to an organization dedicated to ferreting out former Nazis and collaborators. Gerard's brusque manner and headstrong actions inadvertently bring about the death of Diego and force Santana to reveal the existence of the anti-Fascist group to Gerard, who refuses an offer to join them. Gerard learns that Mme. Jarnac has never seen Jarnac but married him by proxy to escape France, since she and her war-injured sister were the daughters of collaborators. Keeping close tabs on collaborator Thomas Camargo and his wife, Gerard discovers that a mysterious figure he assumes is Jarnac has meetings at the Bar Fortunato. Going there alone, Gerard finds Incza, a petty informant, and Camarago in a back room. Jarnac steps out of the shadows with a gun, kills the unreliable Incza, and instructs the weak-willed Camarago to kill Gerard. A scuffle ensues, disabling Camarago, and Jarnac attacks Gerard with a knife. During the fight Gerard goes into a momentary "trance", an affliction plaguing him since his release from the POW camp. Regaining his senses he finds that he has beaten Jarnac to death, but Santana and DuBois, having followed Gerard, promise to help him with the authorities.

Director Dmytryk, star Powell, photographer Wild, and the writer-producer team of Paxton and Scott had earlier made *Murder, My Sweet,* which established more effective archetypes and motifs for the noir private eye series than the excellent, but too early, *Maltese Falcon.* Although Dmytryk does not embellish *Cornered* with all the expressionistic devices of *Murder, My Sweet,* the film has more graphic ingenuity than the average postwar thriller. In it, Dick Powell achieves his finest delineation of the tough guy, adept enough at quick action and cynical dialogue but romantic enough to cry at the memory of his lost wife. *Cornered* also contains a now-dated attack on Fascism which is not surprising given the ideological proclivities of many of the people associated with it, some of whom (Dmytryk, Scott, Carnovsky, and Adler) were ironically to suffer later at the hands of American ultraconservatives.

—B.P.

CRACK-UP (1946)

Director: Irving Reis
Executive Producer: Jack J. Gross (RKO)
Screenplay: John Paxton, Ben Bengal, and Ray Spencer; from the short story "Madman's Holiday" by Fredric Brown
Director of Photography: Robert de Grasse
Special Effects: Russell A. Cully
Sound: John Cass and Terry Kellum
Music: Leigh Harline
Music Director: Constantin Bakaleinikoff
Art Directors: Albert S. D'Agostino, Jack Okey
Set Decoration: Darrell Silvera, Michael Orenbach
Costumes: Renie
Dialogue Director: Leslie Urbach
Assistant Director: James Anderson
Film Editor: Frederick Knudtson

CAST: Pat O'Brien (George Steele), Claire Trevor (Terry Cordeau), Herbert Marshall (Traybin), Ray Collins (Dr. Lowell), Wallace Ford (Cochrane), Dean Harens (Reynolds), Damian O'Flynn (Stevenson), Erskine Sanford (Mr. Barton), Mary Ware (Mary). **BITS:** Harry Harvey (Moran), Robert Bray (Man with Drunk), Tom Noonan (Vendor), Bob White, Eddie Parks (Drunks), Chef Milani (Joe), Al Hill, Carl Hansen, Roger Creed, Gloria Jetter (Gamblers), Horace Murphy (Conductor), Alvin Hammer (Milquetoast), Tiny Jones, Dorthea Wolbert (Old Ladies), Sam Lufkin, Carl Faulkner (Detectives), Ed Gargan, Harry Shannon, Tex Swan, Cap Somers, George Bruggerman, Philip Morris (Cops), Joe Kamaryt (Waiter), Harry Monty (Midget), Bob Pepper (Intern), Frank Moran (Bartender), Kernan Cripps (Ticket Clerk), Rose Plummer (Impatient Woman), Frank Shannon (Gateman), Sam McDaniels (Porter), Lee Elson (Man), Shemen Ruskin (Wide-eyed Man), Bonnie Blair (Dorothy), Dick Rush (Ship's Captain), Delmar Costello (Deck Hand), Jimmy O'Gatty (Mate), Guy Beach (Station), Johnny Indrisano (Detective), Richard Ryen (Butler), Ellen Corby (Maid), Jack Cheatham (Attendant), Belle Green (Woman in Audience), Alf Haugan (Man in Audience), John Ince, Fred Hueston, Alex Akimoff, J.C. Fowler, John Ardell (Men).
Filming Completed: February 16, 1946
Released: RKO, October 6, 1946
Running Time: 93 minutes

George Steele, who had been an expert on art forgeries for the army during the war, is suspended from his position as lecturer and tour guide at the New York Metropolitan Museum due to his erratic behavior there one night. He appears to have been drunk; but Steele claims his condition was the result of involvement in a train wreck. However, he has no recollection of what happened between the time of the wreck and his appearance at the museum—and the police find there is no record of the train accident. Under suspicion, Steele retraces his movements during the eve-

Left to right: George Steele (Pat O'Brien) and Dr. Lowell (Ray Collins) in Crack-Up.

ning of the "wreck." He uncovers a devious plot for substituting forgeries for several of the masterpieces on loan at the museum. Many substantial dealers and collectors in the area, and even the museum's supervisor, Mr. Barton, are forced to go along with the scheme. Apparently, Steele's suspension from the museum was engineered to keep him from X-raying a masterpiece as part of a lecture and thus inadvertently uncovering a forgery. Steele is assisted by his girl friend, newspaper columnist Terry Cordeau, who, unknown to Steele is also assisting an undercover Scotland Yard agent, Traybin, to discover the source of the forgeries. Steele, avoiding arrest by the police for murder, finds proof of the forgeries but is kidnapped and delivered to Dr. Lowell, the mastermind of the scheme. To get information, Lowell puts Steele under the influence of sodium pentothal, the same drug the doctor used on him to simulate the train wreck. Lowell plans to kill both Steele and Terry, but they are rescued in the nick of time by Traybin, who had been waiting outside to gain the necessary evidence against Lowell.

Crack Up, a much negelected thriller, is certainly a key film in the noir cycle because of its consideration of the role of art. Much has been written regarding the use and abuse of art in such films as *The Big Sleep, Laura,* and *The Dark Corner.* Here, however, the place of art in the noir world—a world embodied in typical RKO stylized chiaroscuro—is given prominence. First, the hero is a spokesman of "art for the masses": his aesthetic bias is strongly in favor of personal taste. Opposed to him are the officials, critics, collectors, and snobs who lack his democratic sensibility and who often use art merely as a means of social climbing. The fact that Steele turned up Nazi forgeries during the war not only parallels the Nazi desire to hoard art with that of the villain, but helps to explain the association of high art with villainy, a common gambit in many postwar films. Lowell is, of course, the spokesman for the elitist bias: "Did you ever want to possess something that was unattainable? These masters became everything in life to me...unfortunately museums have a habit of wasting good art on dolts who can't distinguish between it and trash." Like art, technology can be used or misused: in the hands of a Steele it can be used to expose falsehood (forgeries); in the hands of a Dr. Lowell it is used as a means of mastering others. Ironically both the X-ray and narcosynthesis are means of discovering "truth"; and when Lowell reminds us that narcosynthesis was a byproduct of the war, American concern with the abuse of technology is linked again to the war that culminated with the atomic bomb. Finally, the film's bias against surrealism (an art style dismissed rather jokingly by Steele) is reminiscent of an era when modernism was looked upon in many quarters as somehow subversive and tainted with radicalism.

—B.P.

CRIME OF PASSION (1957)
[Working Title: LOVE STORY]

Director: Gerd Oswald
Executive Producer: Bob Goldstein (Bob Goldstein Productions)
Producer: Herman Cohen
Screenplay: Jo Eisinger
Director of Photography: Joseph LaShelle
Sound: Francis J. Scheid
Music: Paul Dunlap
Art Director: Leslie Thomas
Set Direction: Morrie Hoffman
Film Editor: Marjorie Fowler

CAST: Barbara Stanwyck (Kathy Ferguson), Sterling Hayden (Bill Doyle), Raymond Burr (Inspector Tony Pope), Fay Wray (Alice Pope), Royal Dano (Capt. Alidos), Virginia Grey (Sara), Dennis Cross (Detective Jules), Robert Griffin (Detective James), Jay Adler (Nalence), Malcolm Atterbury (Officer Spitz), John S. Launer (Chief of Police), Brad Trumbull (Detective Johns), Skipper McNally (Detective Jones), Jean Howell (Mrs. Jules), Peg La Centra (Mrs. James), Nancy Reynolds (Mrs. Johns), Marjorie Owens (Mrs. Jones), Robert Quarry (Reporter), Joe Conley (Delivery Boy), Stuart Whitman (Lab Technician).
Filming Completed: July 1956
Released: United Artists, January 9, 1957
Running Time: 85 minutes

Kathy Ferguson is a lovelorn columnist in San Francisco who gets her big break when she convinces a murderess to give herself up. On her way to a better job in New York City, Kathy stops off in Los Angeles to have dinner with her new friend, Detective Lt. Bill Doyle of the Los Angeles Police Department. The dinner leads to deeper involvement, and she forsakes her career to marry Doyle and settle down in a typical Los Angeles suburban house. Becoming bored with her husband's circle of friends, she decides her marriage has become a prison and that Bill must enhance his status on the force. With this in mind, she "arranges" for them to become sociable with Doyle's boss, Inspector Tony Pope, and his wife, Alice. Kathy influences Pope to favor her husband over Bill's chief rival and good friend, Capt. Alidos. She eventually destroys their friendship and, through a series of poison-pen letters, succeeds in having Alidos transferred. Kathy uses her affair with Pope to extract his promise to appoint Doyle his successor on retirement, which is hastened by his wife's ill health. In a moment of decency, however, Pope appoints Alidos to replace him. Distraught, Kathy calls on Pope at home alone one evening and announces she can only justify their affair if her husband is promoted. Pope argues that her efforts to further Doyle's career have been adequately realized. When he remains oblivious to her entreaties, she fatally shoots him with a gun stolen from the police station. Lt. Doyle, investigating the death, eventually discovers the murder weapon and how it disappeared from the precinct. Ultimately he is forced to arrest his wife.

Crime of Passion is quite typical of most 1950s film noir in that it relies more on scripting and strong performances than on the expressionistic visual style that characterized the 1940s productions. The 1950s witnessed a shift in interest from the romantic fatalism of tales of innocent victims, bourgeois murderers, and the private eyes to "routine" police detection (usually of startling cases), robbery capers, and more serious social concerns. The suburban disquietude that began with *Mildred Pierce*, although *Pitfall* is more central to this theme, reaches its fruition in the 1950s, and *Crime of Passion* with its suggestions of malaise infecting suburbia was a prime example. Ironically, at the film's beginning, Kathy Ferguson's job as a columnist makes her quite cynical of the melodramatic problems about which her middle-class correspondents complain; and yet before *Crime of Passion* has concluded, she finds herself involved in a genuine melodramatic problem of her own creation, one far more outlandish than any she has ever written about.

—B.P. & A.S.

CRIME WAVE (1954)
[Working Titles: DON'T CRY BABY; THE CITY IS DARK]

Director: Andre DeToth
Producer: Bryan Foy (Warner Brothers)
Screenplay: Crane Wilbur, adapted by Bernard Gordon and Richard Wormser; from the *Saturday Evening Post* story "Criminals Mark" by John and Ward Hawkins
Director of Photography: Bert Glennon
Sound: Stanley Jones
Music: David Buttolph
Art Director: Stanley Fleischer
Assistant Director: James McMahon
Film Editor: Thomas Reilly

CAST: Gene Nelson (Steve Lacey), Phyllis Kirk (Ellen), Sterling Hayden (Detective Sgt. Sims), James Bell (Daniel O'Keefe), Ted De Corsia (Doc Penny), Charles [Bronson] Buchinsky (Ben Hastings), Ned Young (Gat Morgan), Jay Novello (Otto Hessler), Walter Dub Taylor (Gus Snider), Richard Benjamin (Mark), Mack Chandler (Sully), Gayle Kellogg (Detective), James Hayward (Zenner), Timothy Carey (Johnny Haslett). **BITS:** Sandy Sanders, Harry Lauter, Dennis Dengate, Joe Bassett, Fred Boby (Officers), Diane Fortier, Mary Alan Hokanson, Ruth Lee, Eileen Elliott (Police Announcers), Fritz Feld, Bill Schroff (Men), Shirley O'Hara, Shirley Whitney (Girls), Charles Cane, Don Gibson, Bert Moorhouse, Jack Kenney (Detectives), Harry Wilson (Parolee), Jack Woody (Stoolie), Hank Worden (Sweeney), Ted Ryan (Janitor), Tommy Jackson (Guard), Iris Adrian (Hastings's Girl Friend), Mary Newton (Mrs. O'Keefe), Faith Kruger, Tom Clarke (Salvation Army Singers), Guy Wilkerson, Lyle Latell (Hoodlums).

Location: Los Angeles, Glendale, California
Filming Completed: December 3, 1952
Released: Warner Brothers, January 12, 1954
Running Time: 73 minutes

Steve Lacey, an ex-convict, is implicated in a holdup by two former inmates of the same prison. Steve who has now gone straight, is forced to cooperate with the two thugs in order to protect his wife, Ellen, and their family. But the hardened detective, Sims, is after Steve, apparently convinced of the young man's guilt. Steve finally foils the two crooks but is not off the hook until Sims reverses his position and helps Steve to clear himself.

Crime Wave is an engaging low-budget film that maintains visual excitement through its 73-minute running time by imaginative compositions in the noir tradition and vivid photography in the city exteriors, as well as offbeat touches of character. Although the premise is familiar, considerable sympathy is established for the hero, Steve, who does not have the tiresome moral righteousness of many wronged protagonists. Curiously, Andre DeToth directed few film noir—*Crime Wave* and *Pitfall* are the only two examples of his work in the cycle—although the influence of film noir is felt strongly in his Westerns, *Ramrod, Man in The Saddle,* and *Day Of The Outlaw.* DeToth's treatment of betrayals and reversals of character of the ambiguously motivated Sims in *Crime Wave* is direct and free of moral posturing. The final image, in which Sims, who chews toothpicks throughout because he is attempting to quit smoking cigarettes, finally lights up, takes one drag, throws the cigarette away and walks off, chewing a match, is memorable for its offhand and semicomic paraphrasing of the noir archetype of alienation.

—B.L.

THE CRIMSON KIMONO (1959)

Director, Producer, and Screenplay: Samuel Fuller (Globe Enterprises
Director of Photography: Sam Leavitt
Sound: John Livadary, Josh Westmoreland
Music: Harry Sukman
Orchestration: Leo Shuken, Jack Hayes
Art Directors: William E. Flannery, Robert Boyle
Set Decoration: James A. Crowe
Costumes: Bernice Pontrelli
Makeup: Clay Campbell
Hairstyles: Helen Hunt
Film Editor: Jerome Thoms

CAST: Victoria Shaw (Christine Downs), Glenn Corbett (Detective Sgt. Charlie Bancroft), James Shigeta (Detective Joe Kojaku), Anna Lee (Mac), Paul Dubov (Casale), Jaclynne Greene (Roma), Neyle Morrow (Hansel), Gloria Pall (Sugar Torch), Barbara Hayden (Mother), George Yoshinaga (Willy Hidaka), Kaye Elhardt (Nun), Aya Oyama (Sister Gertrude), George Okamura (Karate), the Reverend Ryosho S. Sogabe (Priest), Robert Okazaki (Yoshinaga), Fuji (Shuto). **BITS:** Robert Kino (Announcer), Rollin Moriyama, Jack Carol, (Men), Brian O'Hara (Police Captain), Carol Nugent (Girl), David McMahon (Police Officer), Harrison Lewis (Waiter), Walter Burke (Ziggy), Torau Mori (Kendo Referee), Edo Mita (Gardener), Chiyo Toto (Woman), Katie Sweet (Child), Stafford Repp (City Librarian), Nina Roman (College Girl), Allen Pinson, Stacey Morgan (Stunt Doubles).

Location: Little Tokyo, Los Angeles, California
Filming Completed: March 10, 1959
Released: Columbia, October 1959
Running Time: 82 minutes

Detectives Charlie Bancroft and Joe Kojaku are best friends who live and work together in Los Angeles. When a stripper, Sugar Torch, is murdered, they are assigned to the case and meet a beautiful artist, Christine. Both men fall in love with her and she, a Caucasian, reciprocates the feelings of Joe, a Nisei, who has been more reticent to express his feelings for her than Charlie. Charlie is jealous but Joe mistakes his friend's reaction for racism against Joe and Christine as an integrated couple. In a traditional Kendo match, Joe loses control and beats Charlie senseless. The murder investigation continues and, in a final chase, Joe shoots Roma, the killer, who confesses that she killed Sugar Torch because Roma mistakenly believed her lover Hansel preferred the stripper. The killer's situation forces Joe to see his problems clearly and he and Christine are united.

Many of Fuller's films shockingly juxtapose moments of sensitivity and gentleness with others of vulgarity and violence. *The Crimson Kimono* is the one most consistent in revealing character emotion and runs counter to the view that Fuller is abrasive and unsubtle. There is nothing primitive or naive about the unusual love triangle in which the heroine prefers a Nisei to a Caucasian, especially as both men are likable and attractive. The love story is well integrated into the central narrative, which is the pursuit of the killer; Joe's neurosis over his racial identity is challenged by the self-understanding he gains in discovering the cause of the murder. Similarly, the use of actual locations in Little Tokyo and metropolitan Los Angeles reinforce the personal, cultural, and racial considerations of the narrative.

As usual in a Fuller film, there are numerous imaginative elements of characterization, action, and style. The alcoholic artist, Mac, played by Anna Lee, is another offbeat mother figure in the tradition of Thelma Ritter in *Pickup On South Street* and anticipates Beatrice Kay in *Underworld U.S.A.* The violence in the film—notably Charlie and Joe's fight

Left to right: Detectives Joe Kojaku (James Shigeta) and Charlie Bancroft (Glenn Corbett) interrogate Hansel (Neyle Morrow) in Crimson Kimono.

Christine Downs (Victoria Shaw) falls in love with Detective Joe Kojaku in The Crimson Kimono.

Roma (Jaclynne Green) in The Crimson Kimono.

with a huge Korean and the chase down Little Tokyo's streets amidst the masked figures of the Japanese New Year festival—reflects on the film's themes of racial unity and on Joe's ambivalence toward his own culture—a culture celebrated by Fuller. Some sequences, such as Joe playing the piano for Christine, are directed in an unobtrusive manner while at other times, as during the Kendo match, Fuller appropriately accelerates the pace of his cutting. His close-ups maintain their expressiveness, particularly in the striking moment of Joe's changing look as he holds Roma and listens to her dying words. The final shot of Joe and Christine in a feverish kiss is erotically charged.

In spite of its police melodrama origins, *The Crimson Kimono* presents an unusually positive view of a racially and culturally integrated society. Fuller's *House of Bamboo*, on the other hand, because it occurs in Tokyo rather than the harsher milieu of Los Angeles, does not have the same dramatic thrust and sense of cultural alienation. In retrospect, the film seems to represent a temporary optimism on the part of Fuller, as it was followed by his pessimistic trilogy of modern America: *Underworld U.S.A.*, *Shock Corridor*, and *The Naked Kiss*.

—B.L.

CRISS CROSS (1949)

Directo: Robert Siodmak
Producer: Michel Kraike (Universal International)
Screenplay: Daniel Fuchs; from the novel by Don Tracy
Director of Photography: Franz Planer
Special Effects: David S. Horsley
Sound: Leslie I. Carey, Richard DeWeese
Art Directors: Bernard Herzbrun, Boris Leven
Music Score: Miklos Rozsa
Set Decoration: Russell A. Gausman, Oliver Emert
Costumes: Yvonne Wood
Makeup: Bud Westmore, Ernest Young
Hairstyles: Carmen Dirigo, Gaye McGarray
Production Manager: Keith Weeks
Assistant Director: Fred Frank
Script Supervisor: Constance Earle
Film Editor: Ted J. Kent

CAST: Burt Lancaster (Steve Thompson), Yvonne De Carlo (Anna), Dan Duryea (Slim Dundee), Stephen McNally (Pete Ramirez), Richard Long (Slade Thompson), Esy Morales (Orchestra Leader), Tom Pedi (Vincent), Percy Helton (Frank), Alan Napier (Finchley), Griff Barnett (Pop), Meg Randall (Helen), Joan Miller (Lush), Edna M. Holland (Mrs. Thompson), John Doucette (Walt), Marc Krath (Mort), James O'Rear (Waxie), John Skins Miller (Midget), Robert Osterloh (Mr. Nelson), Vincent Renno (Headwaiter), Charles Wagenheim (Waiter). **BITS:** Tony Curtis (Gigolo), Beatrice Roberts, Isabel Randolph (Nurses), Stephen Roberts (Doctor), Garry Owen (Johnny), Kenneth Paterson, Gene Evans

Left to right: Slim Dundee (Dan Duryea) threatens Steve Thompson (Burt Lancaster) and Anna (Yvonne De Carlo) in Criss Cross.

(Guards), George Lynn (Andy), Michael Cisney (Chester), Robert Winkler (Clark), Lee Tung Foo (Chinese Cook), Ann Staunton, Dolores Castle, Diane Stewart, Geraldine Jordan, Kippee Valez, Jean Bane (Girls), Vito Scotti (Track Usher), Timmy Hawkins (Boy), John Roy (Bartender).

Location: Los Angeles, California
Filming Completed: July 28, 1948
Released: Universal-International, January 12, 1949
Running Time: 88 minutes

Steve Thompson, an armored car guard, is drinking heavily and unable to reorganize his life a year after his divorce. Still haunted by the image of his ex-wife, Anna, Thompson frequents a nightclub where they previously spent time together and is surprised to see Anna on the dance floor. Anna tells him that she is planning to marry Slim Dundee, a gambler with syndicate connections; but although Dundee has given her the wealth that Thompson never could, Anna suggests that the physical intensity of her first marriage has not been equalled. Encouraged by Anna's hints of dissatisfaction and despite warnings that she is no good from his family and from his detective friend, Pete Ramirez, Thompson begins to see Anna again while Dundee is out of town or otherwise occupied. Dundee catches them together in his house, and Thompson hastily improvises an explanation: he has plans to rob the armored car company for which he works and wants Dundee's help. Anna convinces Thompson to actually go through with the robbery and promises to leave Dundee once Thompson has money. Dundee, on his part, still believes Anna and Thompson are having an affair and plans to double-cross him. During the robbery, Dundee's men murder Thompson's partner and wound Thompson, who kills two of them. Although Thompson is hospitalized and praised for his heroics, Ramirez suspects his complicity. Because Anna has disappeared with the money, Dundee has Thompson kidnapped; but Thompson bribes his abductor into taking him to Anna's hideout instead. Terrified by Thompson's arrival and the knowledge that Dundee will soon be tipped off,

Anna prepares to abandon the wounded man. Before she can leave, Dundee arrives with the police in pursuit. He kills Thompson and Anna then runs out toward the sound of approaching sirens.

From the opening aerial shot across the darkened city and into the parking lot of a small nightclub, *Criss Cross* invokes the indicators of fatality in film noir: a distanced view of an anonymous urban landscape, the frenetic chords of Miklos Rozsa's score gradually ceding to the dance music from within the club, the preordained movement inward, drawn by an unknown object or person. As the image dissolves from an omniscient perspective to a particularized one, as the headlights of a car sweep across the parking lot and illuminate two figures embracing, the deterministic quality of the narrative is effectively anticipated. This introduction of the protagonists, Steve and Anna Thompson, exploits the noir conventions to plunge the viewer abruptly into their point-of-view and to isolate a moment that mixes fear of discovery with sexual excitement. Only through subsequent flashbacks is the true nature of Thompson's relationship to Anna detailed. "From the start, it all went one way. It was in the cards or it was fate or a jinx or whatever you want to call it." The fear and excitement so obvious in that first scene are components of Thompson's fatal obsession, components present when he recalls his reencounter with Anna. Alone at the bar, not dissolute but seeking escape, the viewer intrudes into his reverie. As Thompson tries to dispel his ill-defined disquiet, a point-of-view shot abruptly compels the audience to coexperience what he sees. Through the hazy room a long lens isolates one couple dancing languorously. As Thompson strains for a better look, the woman turns; for a moment, her face is visible then lost again in the crowd. The woman is Anna, Thompson's former wife, with whom he is still emotionally and physically obsessed. Not only do the formal elements of the shot idealize Anna's appearance, but the use of point-of-view makes an economic, nonverbal connection between that appearance and Thompson's opinion of her. Anna is suddenly there, oneirically before him, as if sprung from the depths of that initial reverie. In fact, Thompson might at first suspect that he is hallucinating, since there is no reason, other than his overwhelming desire, for her to be in the nightclub. Because this articulation of the relationship between Thompson and Anna is purely visual, it defies misconstrual. The audience is given a perspective that cannot be literally what Thompson sees—the long lens and slow motion belie that—but is rather a composite of what he sees as distorted by what he feels.

This sequence is the key to *Criss Cross* and to the ultimate destruction of its protagonist. The daylit exteriors of Angel's Flight, where Thompson lives, and those of his visits to Anna at Dundee's spacious home or the full-lit shots of him at work are all naturalistic in their lighting and composition. But, as informed by the first scenes, they become functionally if not stylistically noir, for they reflect Thompson's rekindled dissatisfaction with his drab environment. The expressionistic staging of the robbery with its violence, its

dark, masked figures moving apprehensively through smoke-filled frames, and its deadly excitement becomes a nightmarish variant—again from Thompson's point-of-view—of the sexual promise of the initial sequence. This carries over into the claustrophobic paranoia of Thompson in the hospital, where, in a new series of anxious close shots echoing the introductory ones of him, he hopes simultaneously for and against Anna's arrival. Finally, the slow pan down to Thompson's and Anna's bodies fallen together in a mortal repose undisturbed by the rising blare of sirens, reverses the inward sweep of the film's first shot under Rozsa's same ominous score.

By beginning with the dynamics of the relationship between Thompson and Anna and by establishing that quickly, precisely, and solely through the *mise-en-scène*, Siodmak irrevocably ties all these events that follow to that first fatal moment in the nightclub, a moment that will govern Thompson's destiny with an irresistible force. In so doing, he makes *Criss Cross* one of the most tragic and compelling of film noir.

—A.S.

THE CROOKED WAY (1949)

Director: Robert Florey
Producer: Bendict Bogeaus (La Brea Productions)
Associate Producer: Arthur M. Landau
Screenplay: Richard H. Landau; from the radio play "No Blade Too Sharp" by Robert Monroe
Director of Photography: John Alton
Sound: Max Hutchinson
Music Score: Louis Forbes
Production Design: Van Nest Polglase
Set Decoration: Joseph Kish
Makeup: Lee Greenway
Hairstyles: Lillian Shore
Production Manager: Herman Webber
Production Assistant: James Stacy
Assistant Director: Horace Hough
Script Supervisor: Mary Gibsone
Film Editor: Frank Sullivan

CAST: John Payne (Eddie Rice), Sonny Tufts (Vince Alexander), Ellen Drew (Nina), Rhys Williams (Lt. Williams), Percy Helton (Petey), John Doucette (Sgt. Barrett), Charles Evans (Capt. Anderson), Greta Granstedt (Hazel), Harry Bronson (Danny), Hal Fieberling (Coke), Crane Whitley (Dr. Kemble), John Harmon (Kelly), Snub Pollard (News Vendor).
Filming Completed: December 1948
Released: United Artists, April 22, 1949
Running Time: 87 minutes

Eddie Rice, awarded the Silver Star, is finally released from the veterans' rehabilitation ward, victim of a war wound that has left him a permanent amnesiac. The only information he has concerning himself is that he comes from Los Angeles, so he returns there to try and recover his past. Arriving at Union Station, he runs into Lt. Williams with policemen who know him as Eddie Ricardi. Williams is skeptical of Eddie's memory loss, and informs him that prior to the war Ricardi had been the partner of a local racketeer named Vince Alexander. Eddie meets Nina Martin, who is his ex-wife, and she takes him to the hotel where he used to live. Later, Vince Alexander has his ex-partner escorted to his office and beaten up because Vince believes that Eddie enlisted in the armed forces under a phony name leaving Vince to take the blame for a crime. Vince warns Eddie to leave town soon and instructs Nina to seduce Eddie so that Vince is informed of Eddie's plans. Confronted by Lt. Williams about a recent murder, Vince shoots the policeman and has Eddie set up to take the blame. But Eddie escapes and Nina is convinced he has become a new man. Although wounded by Vince's henchmen, she instructs Eddie to find an old friend, Petey, who is hiding in a Santa Monica warehouse. Petey informs Vince of Eddie's visit and a gun battle ensues between the two men. When the police arrive, Vince uses Eddie as a shield but is shot by Petey. Losing his cover, Vince turns on the cops and is shot to death. Nina and Eddie are finally reunited, and Eddie hopes that his old personality will never return.

The Crooked Way is a minor film noir, possibly because its narrative was originally conceived for radio. It is nonetheless tied directly to the cycle through the use of an ambiguous hero, and, more overtly, the theme of an amnesiac functioning as detective, as in the superb *Somewhere In The Night* (1946). *The Crooked Way*'s photographer, John Alton, imbued location photography with a noir style better than anyone else, and does so here with Los Angeles locales. The concluding warehouse sequence is particularly baroque; a combination of Alton's talents with those of the director, Robert Florey. Beginning his career as an assistant to Louis de Feuillade, Florey moved from an apprenticeship in impressionism and surrealism to a director of American B films. Most memorable of all in *The Crooked Way* is the rodentlike performance of Percy Helton as the pathetic Petey, coughing and wheezing in his warehouse lair, surrounded by his beloved cats.

—B.P.

CROSSFIRE (1947)

Director: Edward Dmytryk
Executive Producer: Dore Schary (RKO)
Producer: Adrian Scott
Screenplay: John Paxton; from the novel *The Brick Foxhole* by Richard Brooks
Director of Photography: J. Roy Hunt
Special Effects: Russell A. Cully
Sound: John E. Tribby, Clem Portman

Music: Roy Webb
Music Director: Constantin Bakaleinikoff
Art Directors: Albert S. D'Agostino, Alfred Herman
Set Decoration: Darrell Silvera, John Sturtevant
Makeup: Gordon Bau
Dialogue Director: William E. Watts
Assistant Director: Nate Levinson
Film Editor: Harry Gerstad

CAST: Robert Young (Finlay), Robert Mitchum (Keeley), Robert Ryan (Montgomery), Gloria Grahame (Ginny), Paul Kelly (the Man), Sam Levene (Joseph Samuels), Jacqueline White (Mary Mitchell), Steve Brodie (Floyd), George Cooper (Mitchell), Richard Benedict (Bill), Richard Powers (Detective), William Phipps (Leroy), Lex Barker (Harry), Marlo Dwyer (Miss Lewis), **BITS:** Harry Harvey (Man), Carl Faulkner (Deputy), Jay Norris, Robert Bray, George Turner, Don Cadell (Military Police), Philip Morris (Police Sergeant), Kenneth McDonald (Major), Allen Ray (Soldier), Bill Nind (Waiter), George Meader (Police Surgeon).
Filming Completed: March 28, 1947
Released: RKO, July 22, 1947
Running Time: 85 minutes

Four army buddies, Leroy, Montgomery, Floyd, and Mitchell go on leave. They meet Joseph Samuels and his girl friend, Miss Lewis, in a nightclub and Mitchell is invited to Samuel's apartment. Floyd follows and later, while Montgomery and Mitchell are arguing with Samuels, a Jew, Montgomery beats him to death. The police suspect Mitchell, who hides in an all-night movie house, but Sgt. Keeley helps Detective Finlay discover the real killer. Montgomery then kills Floyd to avoid capture as Samuel's murderer. The police suspect Montgomery and use Leroy to set a trap for the killer, who tells that Floyd wants to see him. Confused, Montgomery returns to where he killed Floyd to see why the man is still alive and the waiting police arrest him.

Authentic film noir or message picture? *Crossfire* is probably both but leans strongly toward the latter, vitiating the force inherent in the Richard Brooks novel on which the film is based. A further problem is the direction of Edward Dmytryk, who does little to alleviate the visually static nature of many scenes, such as that in which Robert Young delivers his sermon to the hapless Southern boy, Leroy, but pretentiously stages the subsequent sequence between Montgomery and Leroy with a tricky use of mirrors. In other words, *Crossfire* is a film of stylistic flourishes but lacks a meaningful style. On the whole, the characters have little individual depth. Such actors as Mitchum, Ryan, and Grahame bring a semblance of noir iconography to any film by their collective presence. Ryan's performance, in particular, has a certain reputation; but he has played psychopaths in many films, and even a comparable role as a bigot in *Odds Against Tomorrow* possesses more fascinating twists and turns of character. The one truly unusual characteri-

Left to right: Montgomery (Robert Ryan) is interrogated by Keeley (Robert Mitchum) and Finlay (Robert Young) in Crossfire.

zation is by Paul Kelly as Gloria Grahame's boyfriend; but the role is undeveloped by a predictable structure that dominates the story's development except in Ryan's lying flashback. Racial prejudice is an apt theme for a film with noir overtones; but this subject is much more compelling in such a film as Fuller's *The Crimson Kimono*, where the bigotry is bound to the intimate personal relationships between the central characters.

—B.L.

CRY DANGER (1951)

Director: Robert Parrish
Producers: Sam Wiesenthal and W.R. Frank (Olympic Productions)
Screenplay: William Bowers; from an unpublished story by Jerome Cady

Director of Photography: Joseph F. Biroc
Sound: William Lynch
Music Score: Emil Newman, Paul Dunlap
Song: "Cry Danger," music by Hugo Friedhofer, lyric by Leon Pober
Art Director: Richard Day
Set Decoration: Joseph Kish
Costumes: Elois Jenssen
Men's Wardrobe: Jack E. Miller
Makeup: Kiva Hoffman
Dialogue Director: Rodney Amateau
Production Supervisor: Herman E. Webber
Production Assistant: Maurice Binder
Assistant Director: Lowell J. Farrell
Film Editor: Bernard W. Burton

CAST: Dick Powell (Rocky), Rhonda Fleming (Nancy), Richard Erdman (Delong), William Conrad (Castro), Regis Toomey (Cobb), Jean Porter (Darlene), Jay Adler (Williams), Joan Banks (Alice Fletcher), Gloria Saunders

(Cigarette Girl), Hy Averbach (Bookie), Renny McEvoy (Taxi Driver), Lou Lubin (Hank), Benny Burt (Bartender).
Location: Los Angeles, California
Released: RKO, February 21, 1951
Running Time: 79 minutes

Rocky, framed for a murder and robbery of $100,000, has his case reviewed and is released after five years. However, his best friend, Danny, also framed, remains in prison. Rocky sets out to clear Danny and seeks revenge on the man responsible, a racketeer named Castro. Complicating matters is the renewed affection between Rocky and Danny's wife, Nancy, who had been Rocky's girl before her marriage. Rocky finally pins the crime on Castro but not before finding out that Danny really was the accomplice and that Nancy has known it all along, keeping half of the stolen money as payment for remaining silent.

Familiar as the plot is, with its characteristically devious woman, betrayals, and infringement of the past upon the present, the emotional tone of *Cry Danger* is dissimilar to other noir films of its type. Rather than a pessimistic and harsh view of human nature like *Out Of The Past* and *Criss Cross,* it emphasizes the essential health of the hero, who is humanly disappointed in his friend and the girl he loves but is ready to continue by himself in what will be a better life. In this respect, this modest picture thematically anticipates work in other genres by its director Robert Parrish, films such as *The Purple Plain* and *The Wonderful Country.* All three films show the hero in the last, therapeutic stages of abandoning the vestiges of a neurotic and crippling past.

The positive self-direction of the hero in *Cry Danger* finds literal expression in the encouragement he gives an alcoholic ex-marine. In contrast to this sympathetic relationship, Rocky otherwise finds himself in the company of a bookie and *femmes fatales* who are virtually unreal characters—although characteristic types of the milieu—but who misrepresent themselves and foreshadow the eventual revelation regarding Danny and Nancy. The characters and milieu identify themselves as belonging to the noir world; but the compositions, lighting, and editing are unusually stable and without the asymmetry expected of an archetypal film noir. Parrish's pacing in *Cry Danger* is fast compared to the languorous tempos of his other films and much less distinctive for that very reason, although consistent with the overall realization of the film.

—B.L.

CRY OF THE CITY (1948)
[Working Titles: THE CHAIR FOR MARTIN ROME; THE LAW AND MARTIN ROME]

Director: Robert Siodmak
Producer: Sol Siegel (20th Century-Fox)

Screenplay: Richard Murphy; from the novel *The Chair for Martin Rome* by Henry Edward Helseth
Director of Photography: Lloyd Ahern
Special Photographic Effects: Fred Sersen
Sound: Eugene Grossman, Roger Heman
Music Score: Alfred Newman
Music Director: Lionel Newman
Orchestral Arrangements: Herbert Spencer, Earle Hagen
Art Directors: Lyle Wheeler, Albert Hogsett
Set Decoration: Thomas Little, Ernest Lansing
Wardrobe Director: Charles LeMaire
Costumes: Bonnie Cashin
Hairstyles: Linda Cross
Makeup: Ben Nye, Harry Maret, Pat McNally
Production Manager: Sid Bowen
Assistant Director: Jasper Blystone
Script Supervisor: Rose Steinberg
Film Editor: Harmon Jones

CAST: Victor Mature (Lt. Candella), Richard Conte (Martin Rome), Fred Clark (Lt. Collins), Shelley Winters (Brenda), Betty Garde (Mrs. Pruett), Barry Kroeger (Niles), Tommy Cook (Tony), Debra Paget (Teena Riconti), Hope Emerson (Rose Given), Roland Winters (Ledbetter), Walter Baldwin (Orvy), June Storey (Miss Boone), Tito Vuolo (Papa Roma), Mimi Aguglia (Mama Roma), Konstantin Shayne (Dr. Veroff), Howard Freeman (Sullivan). **BITS:** Dolores Castle (Rosa), Claudette Ross (Rosa's Daughter), Tiny Francone (Perdita), Elena Savonarola (Francesca), Thomas Ingersoll (Priest), Vito Scott (Julio), Robert Karnes, Charles Tannen (Interns), Oliver Blake (Caputo), Antonio Filauri (Vaselli), Joan Miller (Vera), Ken Cristy (Loomis), Emil Raneau (Dr. Niklas), Eddie Parks (Mike), Charles Wagenheim (Counterman), Kathleen Howard (Mrs. Pruett's Mother), John Cortay (Policeman), George Melford (Barber), Harry Carter (Elevator Operator), Robert Adler, Harry Seymour (Men), Jane Nigh, Ruth Clifford (Nurses), Tom Moore (Doctor), George Beranger (Barber), Michael Stark (Cop), Martin Begley (Bartender), Davison Clark (Mounted Policeman), Helen Troya (Girl), Michael Sheridan (Detective), Tommy Nello (Julio).
Location: New York, New York
Filming Completed: February 24, 1948
Released: 20th Century-Fox, September 29, 1948
Running Time: 96 minutes
[NOTE: An undated press release from 20th Century-Fox states that Lon McCallister will play the title role in *The Chair for Martin Rome* to be scripted by Ben Hecht and Charles Lederer and filmed in San Francisco. Another Fox press release, dated January 14, 1948, explains Victor Mature was switched from the title role to the part of Candella, the Italian cop, while Richard Conte becomes Martin Rome in *The Chair for Martin Rome.*]

Wounded in a battle in which he killed a cop, tough, young, Martin Rome refuses to reveal to homicide officer Lt.

CRY OF THE CITY

Candella the identity of a girl who secretly visited him the previous night in the hospital. Candella grew up with Martin in New York's Little Italy and is a friend of his family, but Candella believes the mystery girl is implicated in a jewel robbery, known as the de Grazia case. Martin uses his charm and persuades Nurse Pruett to find and hide the young, innocent girl, Teena. Transferred to a prison ward, Martin escapes and murders Niles, a crooked lawyer who balks at giving him money to escape, and then discovers the de Grazia jewels in Niles's safe. Candella almost traps Martin in Teena's apartment, but the gangster is tipped off by his brother, Tony. Later Candella stumbles onto Martin at the home of his parents, but the ganster escapes. Suffering from his wounds, Martin asks his former girl friend, Brenda, to find a doctor who will treat him in a car. Martin offers Rose Given, a masseuse, the key to a subway locker containing the de Grazia jewels in exchange for $5,000 and steamship tickets to South America. When the deal is made, Martin informs Candella where to pick Rose up. Suspicious, Rose forces Martin to accompany her to the subway locker, and when she sees the police she aims to shoot Martin, but hits Candella instead. Martin escapes once more. Wounded, Candella visits Nurse Pruett, who reveals that Teena is meeting Martin in a neighborhood church. Meanwhile, Martin persuades Tony to help him "borrow" money for a getaway from their parents. In the church, Martin convinces Teena that he has only killed in self-defense and just as she is about to elope with him, Candella arrives. Candella persuades Teena to leave and, without a gun, challenges Martin to shoot it out, bluffing Martin into turning his gun over to him and walking outside. Once there, Candella sinks to the sidewalk weak from loss of blood, and Martin makes a break for it. Candella warns him to stop, and when Martin refuses he kills him. As Martin lies dead on the darkened sidewalk, Tony arrives, crying, unable to steal from his parents. Candella takes the young boy under his wing, and they go off together.

Cry Of The City is certainly complex enough visually to sustain a thorough structural or iconographic analysis; yet it is perhaps more important for what its narrative implies. It represents an effort on the part of a director, Robert Siodmak, most closely associated with the highly artificial, expressionistic style of the studio film noir, to exploit a semidocumentary, location style that was purportedly incompatible with the former production method. Siodmak himself stated that he was not completely satisfied working on location. However, he was able to extract from the discordant elements of this pseudorealism—with its extraneous sights and sounds; its brief, incisive, character studies; and a stunning jailbreak scene—without sacrificing the sociological implications of a naturalistic Italian ghetto. The location touches in *Cry Of The City* may have implied that Siodmak was Americanizing his style, but surely the noir psychology of the film—its cruel eroticism in the person of Rose Given, its insistence on urban corruption, and finally its use of interiors with enclosed spaces and expressionistic lighting—give it as much of an oppressive atmosphere as Siodmak's earlier studio films. It also confirms that the studio films were not stylistically at odds with the later semidocumentary ones. Looking at the latter from the perspective of today's naturalistic techniques, it is evident that the audience's conventional sense of reality was conditioned by these films. The *mise-en-scène* of *T-Men, Kiss of Death, Street With No Name,* and even the early television "Dragnet," is highly controlled, its realism an artificial one that, location work and all, could be manipulated by adept photographers and directors to produce a world as hermetic and stylized as the best studio films. In fact, an element such as Alfred Newman's musical street scene theme, a trademark of the Fox noirs, only becomes a veritable cry of the city when it is imposed with its manifest stylization over the naturalistic images of New York.

—B.P.

D.O.A. (1950)

Director: Rudolph Maté
Executive Producer: Harry M. Popkin (Harry M. Popkin Production)
Producer: Leo C. Popkin
Associate Producer: Joseph H. Nadel
Screenplay: Russell Rouse and Clarence Green
Director of Photography: Ernest Laszlo
Sound: Ben Winkler, Mac Dalgleish
Music Score: Dimitri Tiomkin
Art Director: Duncan Cramer
Set Decoration: Al Orenbach
Costumes: Maria Donovan
Makeup: Irving Berns
Assistant Director: Marty Moss
Script Supervisor: Arnold Laven
Film Editor: Arthur H. Nadel

CAST: Edmond O'Brien (Frank Bigelow), Pamela Britton (Paula Gibson), Luther Adler (Majak), Beverly Campbell (Miss Foster), Lynn Baggett (Mrs. Philips), William Ching (Halliday), Henry Hart (Stanley Philips), Neville Brand (Chester), Laurette Luez (Marla Rakubian), Jess Kirkpatrick (Sam), Cay Forrester (Sue), Virginia Lee (Jeanie), Michael Ross (Dave).
Location: Los Angeles, San Francisco, California
Filming Completed: November 1949
Released: United Artists, April 30, 1950
Running Time: 83 minutes

Frank Bigelow, a certified public accountant, leaves his home town of Banning, California, for a vacation in San Francisco. After enjoying a night on the town, he feels ill the next day and undergoes a medical examination. The doctor informs him that he has suffered radiation poisoning and has only a few days to live. While preparations are made to admit him to a hospital, Bigelow escapes and is determined to find his killers. Calling his fiancée and secretary, Paula, Bigelow traces a shipment of iridium, which he notorized, and learns it later fell into criminal hands. At the Los Angeles firm that handled the shipment's transportation, he discovers that the company's boss at the time of the iridium shipment has also mysteriously died of poison. Suspecting the same people are responsible for his poisoning Bigelow is confronted by the actual killer. After a frenetic chase through Los Angeles, Bigelow kills his assassin and explains his story to the police just before his death.

D.O.A. is an unusually cynical noir film. The concept of a murder victim who functions as his own detective combined with the coincidental nature of the murder motive and entire incident, gives *D.O.A.* a unique point of view. Directed by Rudolph Maté, the film is fast-paced and designed as a thriller. *D.O.A.* becomes noir through certain key sequences. After a conventional beginning, the basic atmosphere of the film is significantly reversed during a scene in a sleazy, waterfront nightclub. The intense use of jazz music, interpreted through the tight close-ups of sweating musicians caught up in the fury of their music combines with images of patrons lost in the pounding jazz rhythms and approaches a chaotic climax. This chaos is compromised by an unseen assassin who exploits the exotic locale as a screen behind which he can poison an unsuspecting witness to a prior crime. As the doomed Frank Bigelow, Edmond O'Brien is transformed from an ordinary man into an obsessed avenger bent on discovering the reason behind his imminent death. His quest leads him into an ever-darkening nightmare world filled with grotesque and crazed people. Chester, played by Neville Brand, is the archetypal noir killer, who is a caricature of psychotic reality. His wild excesses do not seem out of place amid the chaos of the jazz club, and he cannot be overcome by the sad and ambivalent people of a drugstore to whom Bigelow appeals for help. As Bigelow tries to escape from Chester in a car, the psychopath follows and gleefully increases the speed of the chase to a suicidal rate.

The inspiration for *D.O.A.* comes from a 1931 German film entitled *Der Mann, Der Seinen Morder Sucht,* directed by Robert Siodmak, which deals with a dying man's attempt to discover the cause of his approaching unnatural demise. Utilizing this basic story, *D.O.A.* is a prime example of a thriller accentuated by factors of cynicism, alienation, chaos, and the corrupt nature of society to convey a dark vision of contemporary America. This noir vision remains solid throughout the film except for the strangely humorous quality provided by Dimitri Tiomkin's music. His intent in offering silly musical reinforcements to Bigelow's wolfish womanizing combined with a pretentious score works to vitiate the chaotic atmosphere created in the jazz sequence. The portrait of Bigelow and the nightmarish world into which he stumbles transcend Tiomkin's score to evoke the

Frank Bigelow (Edmund O'Brien) is informed he has iridium poisoning in D.O.A.

sordid underworld of film noir. *D.O.A.* may not be a perfect film noir, yet it typifies the hopeless plight of people manipulated by forces they are unable to control or comprehend; and it is through this existential outlook that *D.O.A.* contributes to the noir canon.

—C.M.

THE DAMNED DON'T CRY (1950)

Director: Vincent Sherman
Producer: Jerry Wald (Jerry Wald Productions)
Screenplay: Harold Medford and Jerome Weidman; from a story by Gertrude Walker
Director of Photography: Ted McCord
Sound: C.A. Riggs
Music Score: Daniele Amfitheatrof
Music Director: Ray Heindorf
Orchestration: Maurice de Packh
Art Director: Robert Haas
Set Decoration: William L. Kuehl
Costumes: Sheila O'Brien

Makeup: Perc Westmore, Otis Malcolm
Hairstyles: Gertrude Wheeler, Ray Forman
Production Manager: Eric Stacey
Assistant Director: Al Alleborn
Script Supervisor: Wanda Ramsey
Film Editor: Rudi Fehr

CAST: Joan Crawford (Ethel Whitehead/Lorna Hansen Forbes), David Brian (George Castleman), Steve Cochran (Nick Prenta), Kent Smith (Martin Blackford), Hugh Sanders (Grady), Selena Royle (Patricia Longworth), Jacqueline de Wit (Sandra), Morris Ankrum (Mr. Whitehead), Sara Perry (Mrs. Whitehead), Richard Egan (Roy), Jimmy Moss (Tommy), Edith Evanson (Mrs. Castleman), Eddie Marr (Walter Talbot).
Released: Warner Brothers, May 13, 1950
Running Time: 103 minutes

After the death of her son Tommy, Ethel Whitehead leaves her husband Roy and makes a life of her own in New York City. She capitalizes on her beauty and soon moves from the job of a cigar store clerk to that of a model for a cheap fashion wholesaler. Another model, Sandra, advises Ethel to accept high-priced dates with businessmen. Introducing the valuable accounting talents of her friend, the naive

Martin Blackford, to a crime-syndicate chief, Ethel enters the inner circle of George Castleman, who is a refined but ruthless gangster. He finances Ethel's transformation into a socially prominent Texas heiress dubbed "Lorna Hansen Forbes," and she becomes Castleman's mistress. She and her mentor, Patricia, are sent to a Western desert city to trap Nick Prenta, a rebellious member of Castleman's gang. Lorna falls in love with Nick and tries to sabotage Castleman's plans. A bitter and corrupted Blackford visits Lorna and reminds her of her duties; but Castleman arrives and kills Nick despite Lorna's attempt to save him. Blackford, still in love with Lorna, persuades Castleman that she is still a useful tool in the gang's activities. Lorna escapes and returns to her parents' home. Castleman follows and wounds her as she calmly confronts him. Blackford kills Castleman, and Lorna's future is undecided but she is free of criminal influence.

The problems of the protagonist, Ethel, in *The Damned Don't Cry* originate in a clearly delineated situation of class oppression and economic misery. The first scene's images of giant oil rigs appearing like carnivorous dragons or prehistoric birds hovering over the depressed home of Ethel's parents expresses her original status clearly; and the contrast later between her wealth and education, financed by dirty money, further equates the upper class with the forces of oppression and exploitation. The film, however, like many of the noir cycle, takes a view of circumstance that is at once romantic and deterministic. From the universe presented in the film, it would appear that there are only two choices in life: honest grinding poverty or ill-gotten opulence. Although Ethel's decision to follow the high life and damn the consequences is represented throughout the film as somewhat justified because of her squalid beginnings (and is reinforced by the similar behavior of Sandra and Patricia), her lack of moral foresight is her tragic mistake. Her learning experience is brutal and pragmatic but morally incomplete, since she is unable to grasp the implications of her corrupt life. Joan Crawford's portrayal of the unsophisticated but ambitious woman who undergoes a metamorphosis into an elegant society woman is striking. At first modest and unpretentious, Ethel eventually feels superior to Sandra's avaricious schemes; and once Ethel realizes how little she has to deliver to receive luxury, she outreaches her "teacher's" ability. She learns to hide her disgust so well that she eventually believes herself above any passion except selfishness. Sunning herself luxuriously at poolside, her serenity is disrupted when Blackford appears: and the shadow that he casts over her gracious form externalizes the pall over her soul. In a dynamic close-up as Ethel looks up, the sun is brilliantly reflected in her sunglasses; but she has to take them off and confront the ugliness of Blackford's vicious squabbling. Suddenly, she realizes her emotions are not dead, and she is obligated to save Nick's life. When she fails, Lorna seems calm and drained of emotion. Returning to her parents' home and confronting Castleman, she appears not to care what occurs. Most noir protagonists are disillusioned with life,

and many are misanthropic; but few noir characters trace Ethel's development from a disillusionment with the romantic notions of love and family to an ultimate and complete disillusionment with oneself. *The Damned Don't Cry* is in a sense a romantic tragedy, as Ethel realizes she has destroyed herself; and it is equally a film noir because of the manner in which the protagonist is debased by the criminal underworld, sex, and deception.

—E.M. & E.W.

DANGER SIGNAL (1945)

Director: Robert Florey
Producer: William Jacobs (Warner Brothers)
Screenplay: Adele Commandini and Graham Baker; from the novel by Phyllis Bottome
Director of Photography: James Wong Howe
Special Effects: Harry Barndollar, Edwin DuPar
Sound: Everett Brown
Music Score: Adolph Deutsch
Music Director: Leo F. Forbstein
Orchestration: Murray Cutter
Art Director: Stanley Fleischer
Set Decoration: Jack McConaghty
Costumes: Milo Anderson
Dialogue Director: Jack Daniels
Assistant Director: Elmer Decker
Film Editor: Frank Magee

CAST: Faye Emerson (Hilda Fenchurch), Zachary Scott (Ronnie Mason/Marsh), Dick Erdman (Bunkie Taylor), Rosemary DeCamp (Dr. Silla), Bruce Bennett (Dr. Andrew Lang), Mona Freeman (Anne Fenchurch), John Ridgely (Thomas Turner), Mary Servoss (Mrs. Fenchurch), Joyce Compton (Katie), Virginia Sale (Mrs. Crockett). **BITS:** Howard Mitchell, Jack Smart (Roomers), Addison Richards (Inspector), Clancy Cooper (Captain), Robert Arthur (Young Boy), Monte Blue, James Notaro (Policemen).
Location: Hollywood, California
Filming Completed: May 22, 1945
Released: Warner Brothers, November 14, 1945
Running Time: 78 minutes
[NOTE: After a serious back injury, Ann Blyth was replaced by Mona Freeman.]

Ronnie Mason is a smooth scoundrel who makes his living by preying on unhappy women. He steals the wedding ring and money from a young woman who is lying dead in an Eastern hotel room and escapes with his loot through the window. The newspapers report the death as a suicide; but an investigator, as well as the woman's husband, Thomas Turner, are suspicious of the role played by the woman's boyfriend, a mysterious artist known only as Marsh. Mason takes a bus to Los Angeles, steals a service pin, and disguises himself as an injured veteran named Ron Marsh. He rents a room in the Fenchurch house, occupied by Hilda, a former stenographer, and Anne, her spirited teen-age sister. Although Hilda has an established courtship with Dr. Andrew Lang, a typical absent-minded professor, she succumbs easily to Ronnie's persuasive charms. But when Ronnie learns that Anne will soon receive a large inheritance, he romances her, which leaves Hilda broken-hearted and suspicious. She confides her troubles to her friend, Dr. Silla, a psychoanalyst who quickly discerns Ronnie's personality. Anne refuses to heed Hilda's warnings, so Hilda and Dr. Silla scheme to get Ronnie alone at Silla's beach house where they can break him down. Hilda decides at the last moment to poison Ronnie while they are both alone at the beach house. Her plan is discovered by Dr. Silla and, with Dr. Lang, she rushes to stop Hilda. But the woman cannot commit the murder. Ronnie leaves, only to encounter Mr. Turner, the husband of the dead woman. Attempting to flee, Ronnie falls to his death from a cliff.

Danger Signal is an attempt to transpose the essential ingredients of Hitchcock's *Shadow Of A Doubt* to an urban setting. Regrettably, *Danger Signal* contains little of its predecessor's suspense and develops so slowly that even the abrupt increase in its tempo by using the wheel-screeching race against time is ineffective. Zachary Scott, of course, has an established noir persona; and Howe's photography provides an appropriately dark style, particularly in the opening sequence when Ronnie flees through an open window in the shadowy, mysterious night.

—B.P.

DARK CITY (1950)
[Working Title: NO ESCAPE]

Director: William Dieterle
Producer: Hal Wallis (Hal Wallis Productions)
Screenplay: John Meredyth Lucas and Larry Marcus, with contributions from Leonardo Bercovici, and adapted by Ketti Frings; from an unpublished story by Larry Marcus
Director of Photography: Victor Milner
Process Photography: Farciot Edouart
Sound: Don McKay, Walter Oberst
Music Director: Franz Waxman
Songs: "If I Didn't Have You" by Jack Elliott and Harold Spina; "That Old Black Magic" by Harold Arlen and Johnny Mercer; "I Wish I Didn't Love You So" by Frank Loesser; "I'm In The Mood For Love" by Jimmy McHugh and Dorothy Fields; "Letter From a Lady in Love"
Art Directors: Hans Dreier, Franz Bachelin
Set Decoration: Sam Comer, Emile Kuri
Costumes: Edith Head
Makeup: Wally Westmore, Bill Wood
Hairstyles: Hedy Mjorud
Production Manager: Richard Blaydon

Assistant Director: Richard McWhorter
Script Supervisor: Lupe Hall
Film Editor: Warren Low

CAST: Charlton Heston (Danny Haley), Lizabeth Scott (Fran), Viveca Lindfors (Victoria Winant), Dean Jagger (Capt. Garvey), Don DeFore (Arthur Winant), Jack Webb (Augie), Ed Begley (Barney), Henry Morgan (Soldier), Walter Sande (Swede), Mark Keuning (Billy Winant), Mike Mazurki (Sidney Winant), Stanley Prager (Sammy), Walter Burke (Bartender). **BITS:** Byron Foulger (Motel Manager), Ralph Peters (Proprietor), Greta Granstedt (Margie), Stan Johnson (Room Clerk), Otto Waldis (Benowski), John Bishop (Fielding), Sally Corner (Woman), Mike Mahoney (Cashier), James Dundee (Detective), Dewey Robinson, Jeffrey Sayre, Bill Sheehan (Gamblers), Robin Camp (Boy), Jack Carroll (Pianist), William J. Cartledge (Bellhop), Edward Rose (Shoeshine Boy), Fred Aldrich (Civilian Detective), Owen Tyree (Desk Clerk), Franz F. Roehn (Photographer), Jay Morley (MacDonald), Mike P. Donovan (Sergeant).
Location: Los Angeles, California; Las Vegas, Nevada
Filming Completed: May 10, 1950
Released: Paramount, October 18, 1950
Running Time: 98 minutes
[NOTE: Hal Wallis originally purchased *Dark City* by Richard Bodkin as well as *No Escape* by Larry Marcus, planning that Burt Lancaster would star in the production.]

After losing a considerable sum of money to Danny Haley in a somewhat questionable poker game, Arthur Winant commits suicide. This situation forces the gambling racketeers to hesitate before cashing a check signed over to them by the now dead Winant. Tension begins to mount when another gambler is found murdered, his limp body dangling grotesquely from a thin cord. Eventually Haley goes to visit Winant's widow. Once there, he confirms suspicions that Winant's brother, Sidney, is a homicidal maniac. Haley's tough exterior is penetrated by Victoria Winant's dedication to her family and struggle to make a home for her fatherless son. Haley travels to Las Vegas in an attempt to win some money to ease her problems. Ultimately Sidney is apprehended and the nightmare of terror is finally put to an end.

The basic premise of *Dark City* is certainly noir. The characteristic grotesques are present: Ed Begley's snarling, garish gambler, Barney; Jack Webb's gutless small-time hood, Augie; and Mazurki's diabolical killer, Sidney. There is a tension and atmosphere that recalls the crisp, dark streets and unsavory elements of films like *Street With No Name, Where The Sidewalk Ends* and even *T-Men*. Charlton Heston rejects the potent nature of his physical presence to become the classy, but ultimately punk gambler, Danny. The basic noir elements are there, but the overriding sense of hope and compassion leads *Dark City* away from its invocation of the noir world. While Lizabeth Scott, as Haley's girl friend, spends most of her time singing dull and

Fran (Lizabeth Scott) and Danny Haley (Charlton Heston) in Dark City.

Left to right: Arthur Winant (Don DeFore), Danny Haley (Charlton Heston), and his strong-arm man (Henry Morgan) in Dark City.

raspy torch songs, there is no surrendering to the noir *angst* and aura of helplessness. Haley's transformation into a hero as the film moves toward its climax displaces much of the noir feeling that is built up by Director William Dieterle and cameraman Victor Milner. *Dark City* is a vision of the noir world without the emphasis of the noir ethos.

—C.M.

THE DARK CORNER (1946)

Director: Henry Hathaway
Producer: Fred Kohlmar (20th Century-Fox)
Screenplay: Jay Dratler and Bernard Schoenfeld; from the short story by Leo Rosten
Director of Photography: Joe MacDonald
Special Photographic Effects: Fred Sersen
Sound: W.D. Flick, Harry M. Leonard
Music: Cyril Mockridge
Music Director: Emil Newman
Orchestration: Maurice de Packh
Art Directors: James Basevi, Leland Fuller
Set Decoration: Thomas Little, Paul S. Fox
Costumes: Kay Nelson
Makeup: Ben Nye
Assistant Director: Bill Eckhardt
Film Editor: J. Watson Webb

CAST: Mark Stevens (Bradford Galt), Lucille Ball (Kathleen), Clifton Webb (Hardy Cathcart), William Bendix (White Suit), Kurt Kreuger (Tony Jardine), Cathy Downs (Mari Cathcart), Reed Hadley (Lt. Frank Reeves), Constance Collier (Mrs. Kingsley), Eddie Heywood and His Orchestra (Themselves), Molly Lamont (Lucy Wilding). **BITS:** Forbes Murray (Mr. Bryson), Regina Wallace (Mrs. Bryson), John Goldsworthy (Butler), Charles Wagenheim (Foss), Minerva Urecal (Mother), Raisa (Daughter), Matt McHugh (Milkman), Hope Landin (Scrubwoman), Gisela Werbisek (Mrs. Schwartz), Vincent Graeff (Newsboy), Thomas Louden (Elderly Man), Frieda Stoll (Frau Keller), Thomas Martin (Majordomo), Mary Field (Cashier), Ellen Corby (Maid), Eloise Hardt (Saleswoman), Steve Olsen (Barker), Eugene Goncz (Practical Sign Painter), Lee Phelps, Donald MacBride, Tommy Monroe, Charles Cane, John Kelley, John Russell, Ralph Dunn (Policemen), Charles Tannes (Cabbie), Colleen Alpaugh (Little Girl), Alice Fleming, Isabel Randolph (Women), John Elliott, Pietro Sosso, Peter Cusanelli (Men), Lynn Whitney (Stenographer).
Filming Completed: March 15, 1946
Released: 20th Century-Fox, April 9, 1946
Running Time: 99' minutes

Bradford Galt, a private detective released from jail after being framed for a crime by his ex-partner, Tony Jardine, finds himself followed by a man in a white suit for unknown reasons, but he suspects Jardine is responsible. Actually, a vicious and cultured art dealer, Hardy Cathcart, has hired White Suit to tail Galt in the hopes that he will suspect Jardine and be provoked into murdering him, thereby eliminating Jardine, who is having an affair with Cathcart's beautiful wife, Mari. When Galt does not act against Jardine, White Suit kills him and hides the body under Galt's bed, where it is found by the apartment maid. Cathcart double-crosses White Suit and pushes him out of a skyscraper window, before Galt can speak with him. With the help of his secretary, Kathleen, Galt ties Cathcart into the crime. Pursued by the police for Jardine's murder, Galt confronts Cathcart at his art gallery. Mari walks in and, listening to Galt's accusations, is convinced that Cathcart is responsible for Jardine's death. As Cathcart prepares to kill Galt and report him as a robber, Mari shoots her husband.

In many ways, *The Dark Corner,* released in 1946, is the prototypical reflection of postwar malaise in film noir and, albeit metaphorically, a more effective statement about the price of social readjustment than such a self-conscious film as *The Best Years of Our Lives.* Like the protagonists of *Nobody Lives Forever* and *Somewhere In The Night,* Bradford Galt is discharged at the film's beginning; unlike them, his release is not from the army but from prison. Initially, Galt, portrayed with terse sullenness by Mark Stevens, attempts to reassume his role as a tough private detective. Harassed by the police and bitterly unable to reconcile himself to his incarceration after betrayal by a partner, Galt suddenly finds himself framed again, this time by unknown enemies. The immediate result is a cry of existential anguish, captured in the remark to his secretary: "I feel all dead inside. I'm backed up in a dark corner and I don't know who's hitting me."

The extreme nature of Galt's alienation must be partially attributed by the viewer to events that occurred before the film began. By invoking the dark past as the fundamental cause of Galt's affliction, the narrative acquires deterministic overtones that reinforce the hopelessness of Galt's position in his "dark corner." Visually, darkness becomes a pervasive motif of Galt's environment. Although the streets he walks are frequently daylit, and Galt's nemesis dresses in an unusual white suit, his office and apartment are filled with ominous shadows. They leave isolated wedges of light on the back walls and bisect figures and faces.

This visual instability conveyed by cinematographer MacDonald's broken shafts of cross-light is incorporated by director Hathaway into a pattern of narrative irony that balances Galt's uncertainty with Cathcart's intellectual arrogance and amoral self-assurance. Although he cannot know of its intensity, Cathcart assumes the existence of Galt's anguish. In fact, he regards and even relishes it with the self-satisfaction of an author who has created a convincing portrait of a tormented character. Cathcart himself is more fully ensnared by the narrative of *The Dark Corner* than he realizes. Despite his ruthless murder of White Suit, his obsession with *his* melodrama causes him to take too much time talking to Galt before killing him. Mari's subsequent intrusion and Cathcart's destruction are not part of a victory of proletarianism over decadent intellectualism, as much as actuality and emotion represented by Galt's desperation and Mari's hatred of the theatricality and effete mannerism of Cathcart. As Mari pitilessly empties her gun into Cathcart's body, Galt is stripped of any sense of triumph over those dark forces afflicting him; he is allowed only relief that they have of their own abated.

—A.S.

THE DARK MIRROR (1946)

Director: Robert Siodmak
Producer: Nunnally Johnson (Inter-John, Inc.)
Screenplay: Nunnally Johnson; from an unpublished story by Vladimir Pozner
Director of Photography: Milton Krasner
Special Photographic Effects: J. Devereaux Jennings, Paul Lerpae
Sound: Fred Lau, Arthur Johns
Music Score: Dimitri Tiomkin
Production Designer: Duncan Cramer
Set Decoration: Hugh Hunt
Costumes: Irene Sharaff
Makeup: Norbert Miles
Hairstyles: Mary Freeman
Dialogue Director: Phyllis Loughton
Assistant Director: Jack Voglin
Film Editor: Ernest Nims

CAST: Olivia De Havilland (Terry Collins/Ruth Collins), Lew Ayres (Dr. Scott Elliott), Thomas Mitchell (Detective Stevenson), Dick Long (Rusty), Charles Evans (District Attorney Girard), Garry Owen (Franklin), Lester Allen (George Benson), Lela Bliss (Mrs. Didriksen), Marta Mitrovich (Miss Beade), Amelita Ward (Photo Double). **BITS:** William Halligan (Sgt. Temple), Ida Moore (Mrs. O'Brien), Charles McAvoy (O'Brien, Janitor), Jack Cheatham (Policeman), Barbara Powers (Girl), Ralph Peters (Dumb Policeman), Rodney Bell (Fingerprint Man), Lane Watson (Mike, Assistant), Ben Erway (Police Lieutenant), Jean Andren (District Attorney's Secretary), Jack Gargan (Waiter), Lane Chandler (Intern).
Filming Completed: March 29, 1946
Released: Universal-International, October 18, 1946
Running Time: 85 minutes

A set of identical twins, Terry and Ruth Collins, are scrutinized by the police when a gentleman caller of one of the young ladies is found dead. Although the twins are physically identical, mentally they are complete opposites. Ruth is a kind, passive, and loving person; but Terry is a ruthless, aggressive, and spiteful human being. A psychologist, Dr. Elliott, begins talking to the women in the hopes of discovering if either twin was responsible for the murder.

Finding the pressures of this scrutiny too great the evil sister plans to do away with her counterpart and take her place. The plan almost succeeds. Fortunately the psychologist is able to detect slight differences in their characters, the police close in, and Terry is revealed as the murderess.

The Dark Mirror reflects noir attitudes and style mainly through Robert Siodmak's capable direction. His particular interest in the aberrant behavior of disturbed minds—as explored in his earlier *Spiral Staircase*—is underscored to a much greater extent in *The Dark Mirror*'s contemporary, urban setting. There is none of the visual objectifications that made the *Spiral Staircase* a fine example of American Gothic filmmaking. Rather, Siodmak deals with the subject of the doppelgänger. The implications of two people who are seemingly identical but have completely different psychological attitudes is the defining noir motif in this film. This use of the double had been a classic film motif since the 1913 film *Der Student Von Prag* directed by Stellan Rye. However, this expressionistic device of revealing the dark side of people's personalities found little exposure in the films of that period. For the most part American noir films substitute mirror images and reflections for the actual doppelgänger. It becomes much more apparent in *The Dark Mirror*, with the title hinting at the perverse imagery, that Siodmak returned to the initial, simplistic double image. The Collins twins are characterized through a facile interpretation of Freudianism, which is prevalent in many noir films. Lost and confused in a world that seems to reward alienation and depression, the twins spin through a macabre dance of rejection and isolation.

—C.M.

DARK PASSAGE (1947)

Director: Delmar Daves
Producer: Jerry Wald (Warner Brothers)
Screenplay: Delmer Daves; from the novel by David Goodis
Director of Photography: Sid Hickox
Special Effects Photography: H.F. Koenekamp
Sound: Dolph Thomas
Music Score: Franz Waxman
Music Director: Leo F. Forbstein
Orchestration: Leonid Raab
Art Director: Charles H. Clarke
Set Decoration: William Kuehl
Costumes: Bernard Newman
Assistant Director: Richard Mayberry
Film Editor: David Weisbart

CAST: Humphrey Bogart (Vincent Parry), Lauren Bacall (Irene Jansen), Bruce Bennett (Bob), Agnes Moorehead (Madge Rapf), Tom D'Andrea (Sam, Taxi Driver), Clifton Young (Baker), Douglas Kennedy (Detective), Rory

Mallinson (George Fellsinger), Houseley Stevenson (Dr. Walter Coley). **BITS:** Bob Farber, Richard Walsh, Ian MacDonald (Policemen), Anita Sharp Bolster, Mary Fields (Women), Clancy Cooper, Dude Maschemeyer, Lennie Bremen, John Arledge (Men), Pat McVey (Taxi Driver), Tom Fadden (Waiter), Shimin Ruskin (Driver), Tom Reynolds (Hotel Clerk), Michael Daves, Deborah Daves (Children), John Alvin (Blackie), Ross Ford (Driver), Ramon Ros (Waiter), Craig Lawrence (Bartender).
Location: San Francisco, California
Filming Completed: January 30, 1947
Released: Warner Brothers, September 27, 1947
Running Time: 106 minutes

Vincent Parry, wrongly convicted of his wife's murder, escapes from San Quentin prison. He rolls down a hill and hitches a ride on the highway. The first to pick him up is Baker, with whom Vincent fights and knocks unconscious. Irene, a beautiful and wealthy San Francisco artist, seeks Vincent out and takes him home with her. While she is out buying him new clothes with which he can escape safely out of the country, her friend Madge knocks on the door and calls out for Irene. Vincent recognizes her voice because she was coincidentally a friend of his wife's, and it was her false testimony which helped to convict Vincent. Vincent tells Madge to go away, and she, puzzled, obeys. Vincent finds a newspaper clipping in Irene's room stating that her father was executed for murdering his wife, who was Irene's stepmother. Irene subsequently explains her father was innocent. Later, Vincent visits his friend George before undergoing plastic surgery. Returning to George's for rest after the operation, Vincent finds the man dead. Weak, Vincent returns to Irene's apartment and hides, but he has been followed by Baker. Madge arrives and tries to convince Irene to hide her from Vincent; but Irene is not concerned. When Vincent's bandages come off, he leaves for a hotel insisting that Irene cannot be further involved in his life. Baker trails him and attempts blackmail; But Vincent fools the punk and Baker is accidentally killed. Vincent confronts Madge with his knowledge that she is responsible for murdering his wife and George. But Madge commits suicide rather than confess to the police. Vincent prepares to leave the country; but at the last moment he reconsiders and calls Irene. They agree to meet in Peru. Later, they dance together in a South American nightclub overlooking the ocean and plan a new life.

Dark Passage is an interesting film that carries its basic visual premise too far. The exclusive use of the first person point-of-view camera for the first half of the film is unusual but also somewhat unsuccessful at invoking the physical existence of a protagonist. The film is thirty minutes old before even a shadowed glimpse of Bogart's figure, as Vincent Parry, is seen; and it is a full sixty-two minutes before his "new" face appears on the screen. However, the subjective camera is an interesting device and more integral to this film's plot than that of *Lady In The Lake*, which used the

similar camera technique a year earlier. Thirty-two pages of production notes were originally appended to *Dark Passage*'s script to tackle special problems such as achieving "natural" effects of the first person point-of-view shots of walking, sitting, and lying down. Suggestions were made to accommodate set construction and enhance camera effects, including a lens mask (not used in the final film) to simulate eyelids and lashes. The initial effect of this point-of-view device actually does involve the viewer emotionally and forces an identification with Vincent while he rolls down a hill and escapes. But the device diminishes in impact as it continues beyond its novelty value. Audience identification is also weakened by the fact that Vincent's voice and narration is so easily recognizable as Bogart's; therefore the viewer knows what Vincent looks like all along. A less-well-known actor or less identifiable voice might have been better suited to this visual premise. Some low-key lighting and San Francisco fog and rain add to the noir atmosphere created by the point-of-view camera; but this film is not fully immersed in the noir style. Vincent is an innocent man framed by a villainous "spiderwoman" type, stalked by a vulturous punk, and the police, whose net is close around him. However, unlike the central figure in many noir films, Vincent is not entangled in this net through his own weakness or stubborness; all of the causality is external. The more characteristic noir figures generate much of their own misery through misconceptions or dogged persistence; and efforts of extrication only tangle them more hopelessly into dangerous circumstances. These external pressures are further mitigated in *Dark Passage* by Irene, who generously provides Vincent with the means to escape and with whom he is reunited at the end of the film. Vincent's union with the woman in the South American resort might seem both unearned and undeserved, because he was at least the catalyst, if not the cause, of the two semiaccidental deaths of Madge and Baker, and George's murder. It is more typical for the noir protagonist to suffer some less delightful consequences of fear, guilt, and legal retribution. In spite of the attempt to exploit noir stylistic devices, this film ultimately lacks much of the internal structure of human weakness and fatalism central to the complete film noir.

—E.M.

THE DARK PAST (1948)
[Working Titles: THE BLIND ALLEY, HEARSAY]

Director: Rudolph Maté
Producer: Buddy Adler (Columbia)
Screenplay: Philip MacDonald, Michael Blankfort, and Albert Duffy, adapted by Malvin Wald and Oscar Saul; from the play, *Blind Alley* by James Warwick
Director of Photography: Joseph Walker
Sound: George Cooper

Music Score: George Duning
Music Director: Maurice W. Stoloff
Art Director: Cary Odell
Set Decoration: Frank Tuttle
Costumes: Jean Louis
Makeup: Clay Campbell
Hairstyles: Helen Hunt, Flora Jaynes
Assistant Director: Milton Feldman
Script Supervisor: Dorothy Cummings
Film Editor: Viola Lawrence

CAST: William Holden (Al Walker), Nina Foch (Betty), Lee J. Cobb (Dr. Andrew Collins), Adele Jergens (Laura Stevens), Stephen Dunne (Owen Talbot), Lois Maxwell (Ruth Collins), Barry Kroeger (Mike), Steven Geray (Professor Fred Linder), Wilton Graff (Frank Stevens), Robert Osterloh (Pete), Kathryn Card (Nora), Bobby Hyatt (Bobby), Ellen Corby (Agnes), Charles Cane (Sheriff), Robert B. Williams (Williams). BITS: Phil Tully (Policeman), Jimmy Lloyd (Fuller), Gay Nelson (Woman), Hermine Sterler (Mrs. Linder), Harry Harvey, Jr. (John Larrapoe), Edward Earle (McCoy), Selmer Jackson (Warden), G. Pat Collins (Father), Jack Gordon, Edwin Mills (Prisoner), Pat McGeehan (Commentator).
Filming Completed: June 21, 1948
Released: Columbia, December 22, 1948
Running Time: 74 minutes
[NOTE: The Dark Past is a remake of the 1939 film Blind Alley also based on James Warwick's play.]

Andrew Collins explains to the police why criminals should be rehabilitated through careful psychiatric treatment by relating a personal experience. Dr. Collins and his wife, Ruth, are spending a weekend at their lakeside cabin with their son Bobby, and their friends, Frank and Laura Stevens. They are awaiting the arrival of Fred Linder when a radio news bulletin announces that a notorious killer, Al Walker, has escaped from jail. Suddenly the criminal and his girl friend, Betty, and two henchmen, Mike and Pete, intrude on the vacationers and hold them hostage while awaiting transportation to freedom. Through the course of their terror, Dr. Collins gradually unravels the motivation behind Al's behavior. The realization that he was responsible for his father's death when he betrayed the man to the police, changes Al and he cannot fire the trigger of his gun when confronted by the police. He and his gang are captured and the vacationers are safe.

A remake of the 1939 film Blind Alley, The Dark Past is a prime example of Hollywood's simplification of Freudian psychology. Using the analysis of dreams to serve as the basis for criminal and aberrant psychological problems, The Dark Past flows in the tradition of Alfred Hitchcock's morose Spellbound. The unique quality is found in the dream sequences and the typically crude, tough guy persona exhibited by William Holden as the criminal Al.
—C.M.

DEAD RECKONING (1947)

Director: John Cromwell
Producer: Sidney Biddell (Columbia)
Screenplay: Oliver H.P. Garrett and Steve Fisher, adapted by Allen Rivkin; from an unpublished story by Gerald Adams and Sidney Biddell
Director of Photography: Leo Tover
Sound: Jack Goodrich
Music Score: Marlin Skiles
Music Director: M.W. Stoloff
Song: "Either It's Love Or It Isn't"by Allan Roberts and Doris Fisher
Art Directors: Stephen Goosson, Rudolph Sternad
Set Decoration: Louis Diage
Costumes: Jean Louis
Makeup: Clay Campbell
Hairstyles: Helen Hunt
Assistant Director: Seymour Friedman
Film Editor: Gene Havlick

CAST: Humphrey Bogart (Rip Murdock), Lizabeth Scott (Coral Chandler), Morris Carnovsky (Martinelli), Charles Cane (Lt. Kincaid), William Prince (Johnny Drake), Marvin Miller (Krause), Wallace Ford (McGee), James Bell (Father Logan), George Chandler (Louis Ord), William Forrest (Lt. Col. Simpson), Ruby Dandridge (Hyacinth). BITS: Lillian Wells (Pretty Girl), Charles Jordan (Mike, Bartender), Robert Scott (Band Leader), Lillian Bronson (Mrs. Putnam), Maynard Holmes (Desk Clerk), William Lawrence (Stewart), Dudley Dickerson (Waiter), Syd Saylor (Morgue Attendant), George Eldredge (Policeman), Chester Clute (Martin), Joseph Crehan (Gen. Steele), Gary Owen (Reporter), Alvin Hammer (Photographer), Pat Lane (General's Aide), Frank Wilcox (Desk Clerk), Stymie Beard (Bellboy), Matty Fain (Ed), John Bohn, Sayre Dearing (Croupiers), Harry Denny, Kay Garrett (Dealers), Jack Santoro (Raker), Joe Gilbert (Croupier), Sam Finn (Raker), Dick Gordon (Dealer), Ray Teal (Motorcycle Policeman), Hugh Hooker (Bellboy), Chuck Hamilton, Robert Ryan (Detectives), Grady Sutton (Maitre d'Hotel), Jesse Graves (Waiter), Byron Foulger (Night Attendant), Tom Dillon (Priest), Isabel Withers (Nurse), Wilton Graff (Surgeon), Paul Bradley (Man), Alyce Goering (Woman).
Filming Completed: September 4, 1946
Released: Columbia, January 22, 1947
Running Time: 100 minutes

The disappearance of an army buddy pricks Rip Murdock's curiosity. His subsequent investigation leads him to Coral Chandler, his friend's old girl friend. From Coral, Rip receives a confusing series of clues. His conclusions are brought into focus when Rip discovers that Coral actually "belongs to Martinelli," a local gangster who operates a gambling joint and is keeping her marriage to the crime boss a secret. Coral and Martinelli are involved in the circumstances surrounding the death of Rip's friend. Dredging up these facts causes Rip to become a target for Martinelli's sadistic henchmen. He succeeds in smashing their operation and killing Martinelli but only after being beaten and hunted like an animal. Rip then confronts Coral. Almost falling into her seductive trap, he is jolted back to reality by an automobile crash that proves fatal for the corrupted Coral Chandler.

In a departure from his tough guy roles, Bogart as Rip Murdock becomes a man caught in a web of circumstances, a genuine noir hero. He resorts to tough-guy tactics yet never really surrenders to them. He becomes a noir icon of a man who is at once the hunted and the hunter. The film is structured as a confession of guilt; and Rip feels compelled to retell the story as a doomed romance. Director John Cromwell, whose early work in the late 1920s and early 1930s included some underworld films, uses the postwar milieu to develop a particularly noir vision of love. Filled with oblique angles and low-key lighting, the visualization of Coral's entrapped world constantly reinforces the fated nature of her emotional ties Even her death—seen as a parachute drifting into a black void—signifies not just a visual gimmick but also a strangely satisfying image for the implications of Rip and Coral's doomed love. A sometimes brutal yet oddly sensitive film *Dead Reckoning* is an example of the *femme fatale's* inability to transcend the limitations of her persona.

—C.M.

DEADLINE AT DAWN (1946)

Director: Harold Clurman
Executive Producer: Sid Rogell (RKO)
Producer: Adrian Scott
Screenplay: Clifford Odets. from the novel by William Irish [Cornell Woolrich]
Director of Photography: Nicholas Musuraca
Special Effects: Vernon L. Walker
Sound: Earl A. Wolcott, James G. Stewart
Music: Hanns Eisler
Music Director: Constantin Bakaleinikoff
Art Directors: Albert D'Agostino, Jack Okey
Set Decoration: Darrell Silvera
Costumes: Renie
Assistant Director: William Dorfman
Film Editor: Roland Gross

CAST: Susan Hayward (June Goth), Paul Lukas (Gus), Bill Williams (Alex Winkley), Joseph Calleia (Bartelli), Osa Masson (Helen Robinson), Lola Lane (Edna Bartelli), Jerome Cowan (Lester Brady), Marvin Miller (Sleepy Parsons), Roman Bohnen (Collarless Man), Steven Geray (Holie), Joe Sawyer (Babe Dooley), Constance Worth (Mrs. Raymond), Joseph Crehan (Lt. Kane). **BITS:**

Jason Robards, Sr. (Policeman), Sammy Blum (Sam, Taxi Driver), Emory Parnell (Capt. Bender), Lee Phelps (Philosophical Policeman), Ernie Adams (Waiter), Larry McGrath (Whispering Man), Connie Conrad (Mrs. Bender), Carl Faulkner (Policeman Drawing Diagram), Dorothy Curtis (Giddy Woman), Mike Pat Donovan (Sweating Trickster), Fred Aldrich (Beefy Guest), Pearl Varvalle (Woman), John Ince (Elderly Sleeper), Billy Wayne (Billy White), Jack Kenny (Headwaiter), Edmund Glover, Al Eben (Taxi Drivers), Betty Gillette (Woman with Dog), Annelle Hayes (Society Woman), Larry Wheat (Derelict), Shimen Ruskin (Sam), Myrna Dell (Hatcheck Girl), George Tyne (Ray), Larry Thompson (Drunk), Ed Gargan (Bouncer), Edgar Caldwell (Dancer), Florence Pepper (Dancing Girl), Dorothy Grainger (Ticket Girl), Eddy Chandler, Philip Morris (Policemen), Phil Warren (Jerry Robinson), John Elliott (Sleepy Man), Louis Quince (Markey), Alan Ward (Yerkes), Dick Rush (Policeman), Armand Curly Wright (Fruit Peddler), John Barton (One-legged Man), Dick Elliot (Chap), Earle Hodgins (Barker), Walter Soderling (Husband), Virginia Farmer (Janitress), Al Bridge (Detective Smiley), Ralph Dunn (Capt. Dill), Jack Cheatham, Dick Rush, Frank Meredith, Roger Creed (Policemen), Jerome Franks, Billy Bletcher (Waiters), Tommy Quinn, Peter Breck (Countermen), Jack Daley (Snoring Man), Eddie Hart (Policeman), William Challee (Ray).
Filming Completed: July 3, 1945
Released: RKO, April 3, 1946
Running Time: 83 minutes

Alex Winkley, a young sailor on 24-hours leave, discovers that he inadvertently took some money from a girl, Edna Bartelli, that he was with while drunk. Enlisting the aid of a dancer, June Goth, he goes to return the money and finds Edna dead in her apartment. Winkley can't remember what happened when he was with Edna, but June believes he is innocent of her murder and agrees to help him discover the truth. They have but a few short hours, for Winkley is due to be back aboard ship in the morning. A kindly, philosophical taxi driver agrees to take them wherever they wish to go free of charge and they meet a number of possible suspects: Sleepy Parsons, a blind pianist, who had argued with the dead girl over money; the girl's brother; a man with whom she had been involved; and a timid little businessman, Holie, who follows June. By dawn, they discover the real murderer is actually the taxi driver, who killed Edna, a vicious tramp, to prevent her from hurting any more people.

By virtue of *mise-en-scene* alone, *Deadline At Dawn* captures a major ingredient of Woolrich's ethos: the quiet despair of the nighttime people in New York City. The film is filled with those odd personalities for whom Woolrich seemed to have such an affection, such as Steven Geray's Holie; and the strange, repressed businessman with a fetish for dancing with his gloves on, who refuses to stop following June once having danced with her. Woolrich's narrative and

Musuraca's RKO-style of shadowy lighting make this a rather typical film noir. Ironically, the dialogue of Clifford Odets, a writer of much greater reputation than Woolrich, is the one incongruous element in the film. Odets's patronizing concern for the common people and, even worse, his pseudopoetic, elliptical dialogue are out of place in the lower-class locales of the film.

—B.P.

DECOY (1946)

Director: Jack Bernhard
Producers: Jack Bernhard, Bernard Brandt (Bernhard-Brandt)
Screenplay: Ned Young, from an unpublished story by Stanley Rubin
Director of Photography: L.W. O'Connell
Special Effects: Augie Lohman
Sound: Tom Lambert
Music Director: Edward J. Kay
Art Director: Dave Milton
Set Decoration: Ray Boltz
Costumes: Lorraine MacLean
Assistant Directors: William Calihan, Kenny Kessler
Film Editor: Jason Bernie

CAST: Jean Gillie (Margot Shelby), Edward Norris (Jim Vincent), Herbert Rudley (Dr. Lloyd Craig), Robert Armstrong (Frank Olins), Sheldon Leonard (Sgt. Joseph Portugal), Marjorie Woodworth (Nurse), Philip Van Zandt (Tommy), John Shay (Al). **BITS:** Bill Self (Station Attendant), Madge Crane (First Visitor), Betty Lou Head (Second Visitor), Jody Gilbert (Fat Woman), Louis Mason (Thin Attendant), Ferris Taylor (Fat Attendant), Donald Kerr (Elevator Operator), Bill Ruhl (Guard), Franco Corsaro (Kelsey), Harry Tyler (Counterman), Carol Donne (Waitress), Rosemary Bertrand (Ruth), Austin McCoy (Piano Player), Walden Boyle (Chaplain), Dick Elliott (Driver), Pat Flaherty (Policeman), Virginia Farmer (Maid), Bert Roach (Bartender), Kenneth Patterson (Joe), Ray Teal (Policeman), Don MacCracken (Prison Guard).
Filming Completed: May 11, 1946
Released: Monogram, September 14, 1946
Running Time: 76 minutes

Dazed and weakened, Dr. Lloyd Craig enters the apartment of Margot Shelby, the pretty but vicious brains of a gang of thieves, and shots ring out. Sgt. Joseph Portugal arrives to find the doctor dead and Margot dying on the couch. Asking "Sgt. Jojo" to come closer, she whispers that she will tell him the whole story because he is an honest cop. Margot admits that she became an associate of Frankie Olins, who hid a stolen $400,000 before being sentenced to die in the gas chamber for killing a cop. Frankie wouldn't reveal where the money was hidden; but Margot devised an intricate plan to rescue Frankie's body immediately after the execution so that he could be given an antidote to cyanide gas. Margot acquires the cooperation of Dr. Lloyd Craig, who certifies the prison deaths. The plan succeeds without a hitch; Frankie's body is brought to their hideout and revived. He draws a map of the money's hiding place and gives half of the map to Margot. When he tries to kiss her, Vincent, the third member of Margot's gang, shoots Frankie and takes the other half of the map. Vincent and Margot force the doctor to help them search for the money. Driving, Margot simulates a flat tire which Vincent gets out to repair. She ruthlessly runs the man over and continues driving on to the money's hiding place. When the doctor digs up the money box, she opens it. In paroxysms of laughter, Margot shoots the doctor. But he recovers and returns to her apartment for revenge. Her story finished, Margot laughs at Sgt. Jojo and then dies. The policeman opens the money box to find a single dollar bill and a note stating that Frankie left the dollar to double-crossers and the rest of the money to the worms.

Decoy's opening shot of hands being washed in a filthy service station sink and then a tiltup to a fragmented mirror that reveals the disheveled face of Dr. Lloyd Craig, sets the tone for the entire film. Although the plot contains inconsistencies, the film features the exciting performance of British actress Jean Gillie as Margot, the most vicious *femme fatale* of the noir cycle prior to Annie Laurie Starr in *Gun Crazy.* Margot uses men without qualm and admits receiving particular pleasure from seducing Dr. Craig because she thereby smashed the fortress of his ideals. Her sadism is revealed when she runs her car back and forth over the hapless Jim Vincent, then calmly gets out of the car, takes his portion of the treasure map away from his body and replaces the jack in the car's trunk before resuming her journey. Unregenerate to the very end, Margot even attempts to degrade the police sergeant by the use of the pet name "Jojo" and laughing in his face.

—B.P.

DESPERATE (1947)

Director: Anthony Mann
Producer: Michel Kraike (RKO)
Screenplay: Harry Essex, with additional dialogue by Martin Rackin; from an unpublished story by Dorothy Atlas and Anthony Mann
Director of Photography: George E. Diskant
Special Effects: Russell A. Cully
Sound: Earl A. Wolcott, Roy Granville
Music: Paul Sawtell
Music Director: Constantin Bakaleinikoff
Art Directors: Albert S. D'Agostino, Walter E. Keller
Set Decoration: Darrell Silvera

DESTINATION MURDER

Assistant Director: Nate Levinson
Film Editor: Marston Fay

CAST: Steve Brodie (Steve Randall), Audrey Long (Anne Randall), Raymond Burr (Walt Radak), Douglas Fowley (Pete), William Challee (Reynolds), Jason Robards, Sr. (Ferrari), Freddie Steele (Shorty), Lee Frederick (Joe), Paul E. Burns (Uncle Jan), Ilka Gruning (Aunt Klara).
BITS: Larry Nunn (Al Radak), Robert Bray (Policeman), Carl Kent (Detective), Carol Forman (Mrs. Roberts), Erville Alderson (Simon Pringle), Teddy Infuhr (Richard), Perc Launders (Manny), Ralfe Harolde (Doctor with Walt), Kay Christopher (Nurse), Bill Wallace, Carl Saxe (Policemen), Grahame Covert (Man), Jay Norris (Villager), Milt Kibbee (Mac), Dick Elliot (Hat Lewis), Charles Flynn (State Trooper), Art Miles, Glen Knight (Truck Drivers), Hans Herbert (the Reverend Alex), Michael Visaroff, Ernie Adams (Villagers), Elena Warren (Mrs. Oliver), Robert Clarke (Bus Driver), Netta Packer (Woman on Train), George Andrson (Man on Train), Don Kerr (Vendor on Train), Frank O'Connor (Conductor), William Bailey, Marshall Ruth (Traveling Salesmen), Jack Baxley (Dr. Wilson), Joe Recht (Bellhop), Eddie Parks (Mr. Franks), Leza Holland (Nurse).
Filming Completed: December 26, 1946
Released: RKO, May 20, 1947
Running Time: 73 minutes

A young newlywed, Steve Randall, is the innocent dupe in a warehouse racketeering scheme. The plans of several small-time gangsters fail, resulting in the death of a policeman and the capture of one of the gang members. The captured criminal, who is the brother of the gang's head man, Walt Radak, is found guilty of murder and is sentenced to die in the electric chair. In a move designed to clear their condemned associate, the remaining fugitives attempt to blackmail Randall into confessing to be the sole party responsible for the murder and apparent robbery. If he fails to confess, Randall's wife, Anne, would become a target for the desperate criminals. Seeing no way out of this frustrating dilemma, the young man takes his bride, and they run for their lives Their frantic escape leaves the two young lovers in the questionable safety of an isolated farm owned by relatives. The peaceful solitude of this pastoral setting is eventually invaded by the gangsters. The innocent couple are saved seconds before the criminals can carry out their plans of retribution.

As the first in a series of noir films directed by Anthony Mann, *Desperate* is a perversion of middle-class values and structure. The paranoia of the young married couple is derived not out of fear of the law, but rather from fear of the criminals' vengeance. There is a sense of hopelessness in this situation, which brings the film fully within the noir sphere; and there is a tone of cynicism and brutality that impugns American social life. Violence exists as a "real" entity in Mann's films, as there is no distortion of brutality through innuendo or subtlety, and *Desperate* has a raw

impact unmatched in most noir films of the period. Even in an early Mann film like *Desperate*, the visual quality of the violence is well defined. The brutal beating of Randall in a dank basement hideout—illuminated by a single electric light bulb flashing on a variety of images as it is battered about from the vigorous movement of the blows—is a startling example of American expressionist film making.

—C.M.

DESTINATION MURDER (1950)

Director: Edward L. Cahn
Producers: Edward L. Cahn, Maurie M. Suess (Prominent Pictures)
Screenplay: Don Martin
Director of Photography: Jackson J. Rose
Sound: Garry A. Harris
Music Score: Irving Gertz
Art Director: Boris Leven
Set Decoration: Jacque Mapes
Costumes: Maria P. Donovan (Women), Jerry Bos (Men)
Makeup: Henry Vilardo
Hairstyles: Lillian Shore
Film Editor: Philip Cahn

CAST: Joyce MacKenzie (Laura Mansfield), Stanley Clements (Jackie Wales), Hurd Hatfield (Stretch Norton), Albert Dekker (Armitage), Myrna Dell (Alice Wentworth), James Flavin (Lt. Brewster), John Dehner (Frank Niles), Richard Emory (Sgt. Mulcahy), Norma Vance (Inebriated Lady), Suzette Harbin (Harriett, Nightclub Maid), Buddy Swan, Bert Wenland (Messenger Boys), Franklyn Farnum (Mr. Mansfield).
Filming Completed: 1949
Released: RKO, June 8, 1950
Running Time: 72 minutes

Laura Mansfield witnesses the murder of her father, a local big shot, by a youth dressed in a messenger suit. Later she recognizes Jackie Wales as the messenger boy and agrees to date him to discover more about her father's murder. Jackie brings her to the Vogue Nightclub, owned by a figure known as Armitage and run by his first lieutenant, Stretch Norton, who is actually in command. Romantic intrigues complicated by blackmail end with Jackie's death; and Stretch pretends to help Laura get proof that Armitage is her father's murderer. But Stretch kills Armitage in such a way as to make Laura believe she committed the crime. Stretch now "discovers" Armitage's confession, a letter he had kept secret, and gives it to the police; but the whole case appears too convenient to satisfy Lt. Brewster. Attempting to learn more about Stretch, Brewster releases Frank Niles, the man Stretch framed for Mansfield's murder. Niles announces he is taking over the city's rackets. Stretch overpowers Niles in a fight; and when Brewster arrives they scuffle, but another policeman shoots and kills Stretch.

Destination Murder is another in a long line of B thrillers in the RKO style, with a plot more complicated than *The Big Sleep*. Albert Dekker here plays what would become a traditional noir role for him, that of the criminal aesthete, made more arresting by idiosyncrasies that outdo *Kiss Me Deadly*'s Dr. Soberin. Not only does Armitage like good music, own an exquisitely decorated mansion filled with works of art, but he is capable of brutal acts only when accompanied by Tchaikovsky on the player piano. That Armitage refers to himself in the third person indicates that "Armitage" is merely a persona, a creation perhaps of Stretch Norton's; and the theme of the doggelgänger takes on new and unusual ambiguities. For Hurd Hatfield's rather oblique portrayal of Stretch Norton (a descent from the epicurean delights of his Dorian Gray) and his early admission that he dislikes women, casts doubt upon the nature of his relationship with Armitage. There are hints of both the exotic and the homosexual. Unfortunately, these implications are left undeveloped by a convoluted and often meaningless plot.

—B.P.

DETECTIVE STORY (1951)

Producer and Director: William Wyler (Paramount)
Associate Producers: Robert Wyler and Lester Koenig
Screenplay: Philip Yordan and Robert Wyler; from the play by Sidney Kingsley
Director of Photography: Lee Garmes
Process Photography: Farciot Edouart
Sound Supervisor: Leon Becker
Sound Recording: Hugo Grenzbach, John Cope
Art Directors: Hal Pereira, Earl Hedrick
Set Decoration: Emile Kuri
Costumes: Edith Head
Makeup: Wally Westmore
Hairstyles: LaVaughn Speer
Assistant Director: C.C. Coleman, Jr.
Film Editor: Robert Swink

CAST: Kirk Douglas (Jim McLeod); Eleanor Parker (Mary McLeod); William Bendix (Lou Brody); Cathy O'Donnell (Susan); George Macready (Karl Schneider); Horace McMahon (Lt. Monahan); Gladys George (Miss Hatch); Joseph Wiseman (First Burglar); Lee Grant (Shoplifter); Gerald Mohr (Tami Giacoppetti); Frank Faylen (Gallagher); Craig Hill (Arthur); Michael Strong (Lewis Abbott); Luis Van Rooten (Joe Feinson); Bert Freed (Dakis); Warner Anderson (Sims); Grandon Rhodes (O'Brien); William "Bill" Phillips (Callahan); Russell Evans (Barnes). **BITS:** Edmund F. Cobb (Ed,

Detective); Burt Mustin (Janitor); James Maloney (Mr. Pritchett); Howard Joslin (Gus Keogh); Lee Miller (Policeman); Mike Mahoney (Coleman); Catherine Doucet (Mrs. Farragut); Ann Codee (Frenchwoman); Ralph Montgomery (Finney); Pat Flaherty (Desk Sergeant); Jack Shea (2nd Desk Sergeant); Bob Scott (Mulvey); Harper Goff (Gallantz); Charles D. Campbell (Newspaper Photographer); Donald Kerr (Taxi Driver); Kay Wiley (Hysterical Woman).
Filming Completed: March 24, 1951
Released: Paramount, November 6, 1951

[NOTE: Paramount announced on December 19, 1949, that Dashiell Hammett had signed a contract to write the screenplay for *Detective Story*.]

Jim McLeod, a New York detective, believes that people's tendencies toward lawbreaking should be stamped out before they begin a career of crime. His prosecution verges on persecution, as he metes out justice to a variety of characters that come into the police station on one particular day. His superior officer becomes suspicious when McLeod is particularly ruthless to an abortionist. The suspect's lawyer accuses McLeod of having personal reasons for his unprofessional behavior toward the doctor, and it is revealed that McLeod's wife had had an abortion early in her life, performed by the same doctor whom her husband now holds in the station. McLeod cannot bring himself to forgive his wife, even though she is the one person he loves; his confusion becomes so great that he deliberately steps into the line of fire from a desperate hoodlum who pulls a gun attempting to escape from the station. As he dies in his wife's arms, McLeod recites the Act of Contrition.

Dashiell Hammett was supposed to write the screenplay of Sidney Kingsley's Broadway play, and one wonders what qualities the sadistic McLeod would have acquired in Hammett's hands. As it is, *Detective Story* is a modern morality play set in a New York police station. Kirk Douglas, as Detective McLeod, represents virtue driven mad by evil around him. For unclarified reasons, McLeod sees himself as an almighty avenger and shows no mercy toward anyone—an uncomfortable and dangerous position for a man representing the law. His actions narrow the gap between the so-called justice of the law and the justice of the streets. Outside the precinct station, crimes against society are perpetrated, while inside the station, McLeod commits crimes against individuals. Using the events in one day of his harried life, *Detective Story* exposes McLeod's breaking point: he collapses when his harsh judgmental stance toward sin and mankind clashes with, and destroys, his faith in the one person he loves. In the escaping criminal's gun, McLeod finds his own escape from a world in which he is obsolete.

Director William Wyler begins the film in a naturalistic style, but the claustrophobia of the one-room police station presses in relentlessly, increasing the pace and ultimately

DETOUR

illustrating the panic created by McLeod's hysteria. The uselessness of McLeod's death is not redeemed by his final prayers. As a noir figure, his righteousness is simply overwhelmed by the modern world.

—J.C. & E.W.

DETOUR (1945)

Director: Edgar G. Ulmer
Producer: Leon Fromkess (Producers Releasing Corporation
Associate Producer: Martin Mooney
Screenplay: Martin Goldsmith
Director of Photography: Benjamin H. Kline
Sound: Max Hutchinson
Music Score: Leo Erdody
Art Director: Edward C. Jewell
Set Decoration: Glenn P. Thompson
Makeup: Bud Westmore
Costumes: Mona Barry
Dialogue Director: Ben Coleman
Production Manager: Raoul Pagel
Film Editor: George McGuire
Assistant Director: William A. Calihan, Jr.

CAST: Tom Neal (Al Roberts), Ann Savage (Vera), Claudia Drake (Sue), Edmund MacDonald (Charles Haskell, Jr.), Tim Ryan (Diner Proprietor), Roger Clark, Pat Gleason (Men).
Filming Completed: June 30, 1945
Released: PRC, November 30, 1945
Running Time: 68 minutes

Al Roberts is a pianist in a New York nightclub where his girl friend, Sue, is a singer. The two plan to marry, but Sue is ambitious and leaves for "stardom" in Hollywood. Left alone, Roberts calls her one night and Sue tells him that she works as a waitress. He decides to hitchhike West and join her. Eventually, he is picked up by Haskell, who is carrying a lot of cash and driving all the way to Los Angeles. Haskell talks about a female hitchhiker who scratched him viciously when he made a sexual advance. Later, he goes to sleep while Roberts drives. When it begins to rain, Roberts attempts rousing Haskell to put up the convertible top, but Haskell is mysteriously dead, although his head hits a rock when Roberts accidentally causes the body to fall out of the car. Roberts, believing the police will never accept his innocence, hides the body and drives on alone. The next day Roberts picks up Vera, initially unaware that she is the same woman who scratched Haskell. Questioning him about the man's death, she does not believe Robert's story but agrees to remain silent if he will follow her plans. Arriving in Los Angeles, they rent a room; and Vera plans that Roberts will sell the car using Haskell's identity. But when she discovers that Haskell was the heir of a dying millionaire and that his family has not seen him for years,

she plans to pass Roberts off as Haskell. That night they quarrel about this scheme, and Vera runs into the other room threatening to call the police but collapses drunkenly on the bed with the telephone cord entwined about her neck. Roberts pulls on the cord from the other side of the locked door, inadvertently strangling her. Without ever seeing his fiancée, Robert flees to Reno, where he sits in a diner and reflects on the strange circumstances that have put him in such a hopeless situation.

As a "poverty row quicky," *Detour* is a film that does not need to affirm conventional values and can embrace the subversive implications of film noir more completely than many more obviously distinguished productions. Edgar G. Ulmer is paradoxically a director who thrives at this level of production, which is usually scorned by the accomplished artist. The story of *Detour*, fraught with outrageous coincidence, would be ridiculous in most hands; but Ulmer possesses the temperament to make it convincing and to persuade the audience to reflect on its premise that, in the protagonist's final words, "Fate or some mysterious force can put the finger on you or me for no good reason at all."

Bitter at his fiancée, Roberts would certainly like to punish her for abandoning him, as demonstrated in his punishment of the piano during his crazed interpretation of a Brahms waltz; but Roberts deludes himself that he desires to join her. In fact, he has a need for Haskell and Vera, as they provide him with the opportunity to redirect his suppressed emotions. His struggle against fate is self-defeating, for in spite of his protestations to the contrary, the "detour" is really the road he wants to travel. How appropriate that Haskell and Vera are both predatory and dying of fatal diseases. Roberts must always encounter the same projection of his own sense of pessimism and doom in rebellion against his soft and accommodating nature. Vera is his true female complement, however intolerable and hateful she seems to him. It is not Vera's bizarre schemes but their behavior as a couple that keeps them together in the Los Angeles motel room; and the claustrophobic visuals seem to affirm that they belong together. The tawdry complexity of Vera—complete with strange classical allusions: Vera is compared to both Camille and Caesar in dialogue that is well up to the riotous standards set by other portions of the script—owes much to the performance of Ann Savage.

In his mind, Roberts restructures his journey with Vera; it is both externalized in his memory images and internalized by the incessant confessional tone of his narration. Ulmer's camera, shackled by his modest production budget, obviously never really moves from New York to Los Angeles. If the journey is made, it is because Roberts voyages metaphorically to an understanding of his immediate present through images and the sound of his own voice, through the process of reviewing his arrival and imagining the closed door of his future. Such an understanding precludes the self-awareness that could reveal to him that his own character has determined the twists of the road.

—B.L.

90

DIRTY HARRY (1971)
[Working Title: DEAD RIGHT]

Director and Producer: Don Siegel
Executive Producer: Robert Daley (Malpaso Company)
Associate Producer: Carl Pingitore
Screenplay: Harry Julian Fink, R.M. Fink, and Dean Riesner; from an unpublished story by Harry Julian Fink and R.M. Fink
Director of Photography: Bruce Surtees [Technicolor]
Sound: William Randall
Music: Lalo Schifrin
Art Director: Dale Hennesy
Set Decoration: Robert DeVestel
Costumes: Glenn Wright
Hairstyles: Jean B. Reilly
Dialogue Supervisor: Scott Hale
Unit Production Manager: Jim Henderling
Production Assistant: George Fargo
Assistant Director: Robert Rubin
Film Editor: Carl Pingitore

CAST: Clint Eastwood (Harry Callahan), Reni Santoni (Chico), Harry Guardino (Bressler), Andy Robinson (Killer), John Mitchum (DeGeorgio), John Larch (Chief), John Vernon (Mayor), Mae Mercer (Mrs. Russell), Lyn Edgington (Norma), Craig G. Kelly (Sgt. Reineke), James Nolan (Liquor Proprietor), Joe DeWinter (Miss Willis), William Paterson (Bannerman), Josef Sommer (Rothko), Maurice S. Argent (Sid Kleinman). **BITS:** Melody Thomas (Ann Mary Deacon, Photographer), Ruth Kobart (Bus Driver), Albert Popwell, Ernest Robinson (Robbers), Diana Davidson (Swimmer), David Gilliam, Richard Lawson (Homosexuals), George Fargo (Homicide Detective), Angela Paton (Homicide Detective), John W. Peebles (Walkie-Talkie Policeman), George R. Burrafato (Taxi Driver), Raymond Johnson, Leslie Fong, John Tracy, Kristoffer Tabori, Frederic D. Ross, Charles A. Murphy, Al Dunlap, Vincent P. Deadrick (Men), Kathleen Harper, Diann Henrichsen, Ann Bowen, Janet Wisely, Laury Monk, Jana D'Amico, Lolita Rios, Ann Noland, Kathleen O'Malley (Women), Charles Dorsett (Television Watcher), Dean Webber, Scott Hale (Newsmen), Joy Carlin (Communications Secretary), Allen Seaman (Orderly), Stuart P. Klitsner, Eddie Garrett (Policemen), Diane Darnell (Mayor's Secretary), Marc Hertsens (Doctor), Lois Foraker (Hot Mary), John F. Vick (Fired Chief), Tony Dario (Police Sergeant), John Garber, Maxwell Gail, Jr., Christopher Pray (Tunnel Hoodlums), Charles C. Washburn (Intern), Woodrow Parfrey (Mr. Jaffee), Mary Ann Neis (Miss Van Sachs), Debbi Scott (Ann Mary Deacon), Denise Dyer, Diane Dyer, Jack Hanson, Derek Jue, Sean Maley, Richard Samuelson, Pamela Tanimura (Bus Kids), Victor Paul (Car Driver), Bob Harris, Joe Finnegan (Men in Truck), Stephen Zacks (Lake Kid), Charles Hicks (Flower Vendor), Wayne Van Horn, Robert J. Miles, Jr., Jerry Maren, Bennie E. Dobbins, Raylene Holliday, Paula Martin, Emory Souza, Carl Rizzo, Billy Curtis, Regina Parton, John Hudkins, Everett Louis Creach, Fred Lerner, Julie Ann Johnson, George C. Sawaya, Larry Duran, Richard Crockett, Boyd "Red" Morgan, Walter Scott, Mark Thomas, Alex A. Brown, Richard A. Washington, Bill Lane, Fred Stromsoe, Alex Sharp, Willie Harris, Eddie Smith, Jane Aull, William T. Couch, Vincent Deadrick (Stunts and Stunt Doubles), Leon Russom, Phil Clark, John Finnegan, James Joyce, Joanne Morre Jordan, Darlene Connelly, Fred Draper, Arnold F. Turner, Michele Tobin, Darren Moloney, Michael Freeman, Wendy Tochi, Jill Riha, Don Haggerty (Voices).

Location: San Francisco, California
Completed: June 18, 1971
Released: Warner Brothers, December 23, 1971
Running Time: 103 minutes
MPAA Rating: R
[NOTE: Frank Sinatra's Bristol Productions originally acquired the screenplay of *Dirty Harry* for production of a film entitled *Dead Right*, to be directed by Irvin Kershner. Subsequently, Sinatra withdrew from the production due to a hand injury and Malpaso Productions acquired the screenplay and restored its original title.]

"Dirty Harry" Callahan, an inspector with the San Francisco police force, has earned his nickname and his reputation not only because he is most frequently assigned to the dirty work of the department but also because of his rough and frequently unethical treatment of criminals. A loner on the force, his superiors often castigate him as his methods are frequently the source of bad police publicity. Nevertheless, his record for effectiveness is unrivaled, even though unorthodox. When the city is terrorized by a kidnapping sniper, Harry takes the case. The maniac is holding a girl underground and threatening to suffocate her. Harry decides to deliver the ransom himself, and although he is instructed to complete the exchange without taking aggressive action, he disobeys, scuffles with this so-called Scorpio Killer and wounds him. However, the psychotic escapes and the girl is not released. Harry finally tracks the criminal to a small shack, which he illegally enters without a warrant. But the kidnapper is not there and Harry finally corners him in a huge stadium where the policeman kicks him repeatedly in his injured leg, till the psychotic confesses the girl's hiding place. The body of the girl is recovered, but the young man is not convicted of rape and murder, because Harry's illegal search of the apartment provides a loophole for the criminal's release. Harry becomes obsessed with trapping the killer and harasses him, even after his superiors warn him to stop. The Scorpio Killer pays a thug to beat him up and then charges Harry with assault; a restraining order against Harry is issued that curtails the policeman's vengeance. However, the psychopath kidnaps a schoolbus full of children. After a protracted and unaided chase, Harry catches the bus, saves the children, and pursues the criminal to the edge of a lake. When the Scorpio Killer reaches for a weapon several feet away, Harry taunts him and then shoots him dead. Realizing that his action will be reprimanded by the police force, Harry removes his badge in disgust and tosses it into the swamp, thereby leaving in doubt the question of his future police career.

An early scene in *Dirty Harry* both celebrates and critiques the central theme of the film. While eating lunch at a diner, Harry spots a robbery in progress, and, with hot dog still in hand, he foils the crime. After cornering one of the criminals, Harry taunts him to escape, threatening to shoot him, *if* he has any bullets left in his gun. The gun is empty; and Harry leaves the robber in other hands and strolls back to the diner to finish his lunch after single-handedly destroying a city block. The criminals were caught and several of them shot down, but in the process a vendor's business was ruined, a car wrecked, and a fire hydrant exploded, spewing a huge ejaculation over this macho combat. The audience is made both to contemplate the destruction and to wonder what person could wreak such havoc in the name of preserving law and order.

It is this tension between the satisfaction in and the repulsion by the violence committed on both sides of the law that places *Dirty Harry* in the noir category. But this is not just the story of Harry versus the Scorpio Killer, roughly modeled on the actual San Francisco Zodiac Killer. Rather *Dirty Harry* is an enormous unresolved morality play in which both cop and criminal meet in a city that, like the sports arena where the gladiatorial encounter occurs, has become a theater of violence. The alienation and frustration of Harry, a simple man with simplistic values (who is portrayed with interesting ironic texture by Eastwood), are a result of being caught in a complex world with an impossible job enforcing the unenforceable in an indifferent city already rife with anomie. Harry is complemented by the murderer; both are driven to insane and brutal violence, and each side of the duel has certain advantages provided by the law and society. The film presents the law's protection of police tactics as being diminished by recent events and makes the conflict between policeman and criminal into a war between outcasts, with society suffering the greatest casualties. The film implies at some levels that, whereas society used to sympathize with the police in this war, society is now in favor of maintaining a criminal's civil rights. The young psychotic killer is portrayed as so exceedingly debased, horrible, and subhuman that he deserves to be slaughtered without consideration. The use of progressively uglier makeup, a full-face ski mask, a large bandage on the nose, and progressively wider lenses transform the appearance of the criminal into a physical monster. Although his crimes of child rape, kidnapping, and murder are horrible and horribly recounted, it is principally the killer's maniacal glee and his physical repugnance that justify, in terms of the film, Harry's vengeance and the audience's identification with that vengeance. At the same time, images are employed to link and equate the inspector and the psychotic: Harry's badge dissolves to the sniper's muzzle, and, as Harry subdues the killer in the giant stadium, the camera pulls back until they are lost in the darkness together. But sympathetic develop-

ment of Harry's character is implicit in the film's opening sequence, which lists the San Francisco police officers who have been killed in action. The vigilante spirit of *Dirty Harry* is ultimately disturbing. Crime is not seen as a social phenomenon; rather all crimes and all criminals are equated with the psychotic Scorpio Killer. Although the question of how to control and maintain society without licensing indiscriminate violence by either police or criminals may be seen as a central issue by the liberal viewer, it is finally a personal empathy and support for Dirty Harry Callahan that the structure of the film offers as a primary gratification to its audience.

—E.M.

DOUBLE INDEMNITY (1944)

Director: Billy Wilder
Executive Producer: B.G. DeSylva (Paramount)
Producer: Joseph Sistrom
Screenplay: Raymond Chandler and Billy Wilder; from the novel by James M. Cain
Director of Photography: John F. Seitz
Process Photography: Farciot Edouart
Sound: Stanley Cooley
Music Score: Miklos Rozsa [original music and arrangements], and the D Minor Symphony by César Franck
Art Director: Hal Pereira
Supervising Art Director: Hans Dreier
Set Decoration: Bertram Granger
Dialogue Director: Jack Gage
Assistant Director: C.C. Coleman, Jr.
Film Editor: Doane Harrison

CAST: Fred MacMurray (Walter Neff), Barbara Stanwyck (Phyllis Dietrichson), Edward G. Robinson (Barton Keyes), Porter Hall (Mr. Jackson), Jean Heather (Lola Dietrichson), Tom Powers (Mr. Dietrichson), Byron Barr (Nino Zachette), Richard Gaines (Mr. Norton), Fortunio Bonanova (Sam Gorlopis), John Philliber (Joe Pete).
BITS: George Magrill (Man), Bess Flowers (Secretary), Kernan Cripps (Conductor), Harold Garrison (Redcap), Oscar Smith (Pullman Porter), Betty Farrington (Maid), Constance Purdy (Woman), Dick Rush (Pullman Conductor), Frank Billy Mitchell (Pullman Porter), Edmund Cobb (Train Conductor), Floyd Shackelford (Pullman Porter), Sam R. McDaniel (Garage Attendant), Clarence Muse (Black Man), Judith Gibson (Pacific All-risk Telephone Operator), Miriam Franklin (Keyes's Secretary).
Location: Los Angeles, California
Filming: September 27, 1943 - November 24, 1943
Released: Paramount, September 7, 1944
Running Time: 106 minutes
[NOTE: Walter Neff's execution scene was cut before release. The scene featured Alan Bridge (Execution Chamber Guard), Edward Hearn (Warden's Secretary), George

Phyllis Dietrichson (Barbara Stanwyck) hides as Walter Neff (Fred MacMurray) watches Inspector Keyes leave in Double Indemnity.

Anderson (Warden), Boyd Irwin, George Melford (Doctors), William O'Leary (Chaplain), Lee Shumway (Door Guard).
FACTUAL BASIS: in 1927, Albert Snyder of Queens Village, New York City, was murdered by his wife, Ruth, and Judd Grey to collect Synder's insurance benefits.]

Phyllis Dietrichson seduces an insurance agent, Walter Neff, into devising a brilliant scheme to murder her husband and collect on his accident insurance policy. But after the crime is committed, Neff's passion for Phyllis sours. Further, the deceitful Phyllis has used Neff for her own purposes. There is even some doubt as to whether the policy will be paid. The cunning Barton Keyes, chief claims investigator and Neff's best friend, is suspicious of the circumstances of the apparent accident. Neff plans to kill Phyllis, hoping to pin her death as well as the original crime on her other lover, Zachette, the supposed boyfriend of her stepdaughter Lola, after Lola informs Neff of Phyllis's past.

But Phyllis is one jump ahead of Neff and they shoot each other, with Phyllis proclaiming at the last moment that she loves Neff. The mortally wounded Neff dictates a confession at his insurance office, where he is found by Keyes. Claiming he will escape to Mexico, Neff collapses before reaching the elevator.

Double Indemnity is based on a novel by the allegedly hard-boiled author, James M. Cain, and its script is coauthored by another famous novelist, Raymond Chandler; but the nature of the film seems to have been determined more by coscenarist and director Billy Wilder than by either Cain or Chandler, in spite of their strong personalities. This was Wilder's first and truest film noir, for *Sunset Boulevard* is flawed by sentimentality in the hero's relationship with the nice girl and the harsh cynicism of *The Big Carnival (Ace In The Hole)* smacks of overprotestation. A perverse sense of humor informs *Double Indemnity*'s grim story, in the exchanges between Neff and Phyllis, and tellingly, between

A DOUBLE LIFE

Neff and Keyes in the final scene. The apparent "throwaway" of having Neff continually light the cigars of the "matchless" Keyes has an extraordinary payoff in the final moments of the film, when Keyes tenderly lights the cigarette of the bleeding Neff. Night-for-night exteriors and moodily lit interiors (notably the meeting at Neff's apartment between Neff and Phyllis) coupled with the rhythmic flow of MacMurray's narration and the transposition of the story to flashback, anticipate other important film noir such as *Out Of The Past, The Killers,* and *Criss Cross.* The black widow played by Stanwyck is an archetypal construction. Evidentally Wilder deeply appreciated the ambience of Cain's novel and followed the narrative closely. While respecting Chandler's contributions, Wilder used the noir structure to color and restrict the romanticism of Neff's character and emphasize instead the doomed and obsessive qualities of his entanglement in Phyllis's web. Supported by Seitz's photography and Miklos Rozsa's score, the ultimate noir statement of *Double Indemnity* is the characteristically unrelenting fatality of Neff's" ride to the end of the line."

—B.L.

A DOUBLE LIFE (1948)
[Working Title: THE ART OF MURDER]

Director: George Cukor
Producer: Michael Kanin (Kanin Productions)
Screenplay: Ruth Gordon and Garson Kanin
Director of Photography: Milton Krasner
Special Photography: David S. Horsley
Sound: Leslie I. Carey, Joe Lapis
Music Score: Miklos Rozsa
Production Design: Harry Horner
Art Directors: Bernard Herzbrun, Harvey Gillett
Set Decoration: Russell A. Gausman, John Austin
Costumes: Yvonne Wood, Travis Banton for Signe Hasso
Hair Styles: Carmen Dirigo
Makeup: Bud Westmore
Production Assistants: George Yohalem, Jack Murton
Adviser on *Othello* **Sequences:** Walter Hampden
Assistant Director: Frank Shaw
Film Editor: Robert Parrish

CAST: Ronald Colman (Anthony John), Signe Hasso (Brita), Edmond O'Brien (Bill Friend), Shelley Winters (Pat Kroll), Ray Collins (Victor Donlan), Philip Loeb (Max Lasker), Millard Mitchell (Al Cooley), Joe Sawyer (Pete Bonner), Charles La Torre (Stellini), Whit Bissell (Dr. Stauffer), John Drew Colt (Stage Manager), Peter Thompson (Assistant Stage Manager), Elizabeth Dunne (Gladys), Alan Edmiston (Rex), Art Smith, Sid Tomack (Wigmakers), Wilton Graff (Dr. Mervin), Harlan Briggs (Oscar Bernard), Claire Carleton (Waitress), Betsy Blair, Janet Warren, Marjory Woodworth (Girls in Wig Shop). CAST in *Othello*: Fay Kanin (Guy Bates Post), Frederic

Worlock (Leslie Denison), Arthur Gould-Porter (David Bond), Boyd Irwin (Virginia Patton), Percival Vivian (Thayer Roberts). CAST in *A Gentleman's Gentleman:* Mary Young (Elliott Reid), Percival Vivian (Georgia Caine). **BITS:** Curt Conway (Reporter), Robert E. Keane (2nd Photographer), Kay Lavelle (Large Woman), Sarah Selby (Anna), Alexander Clark (Barry), Harry Bannister (2nd Actor), Joann Dolan (Ellen), Joyce Matthews (Janet), Harry Oldridge, Nick Dennis, Barry Macollum, Frank Richards (Stagehands), Janet Manson, Augusta Roeland (Girls in Lobby), Angela Clarke (Lucy), Paddy Chayefsky (1st Photographer), Russ Conway, Reginald Billado (Reporters), Fernanda Eliscu (Landlady), Joe Bernard (Husband), Charles Jordan (Bartender), Walter McGrail (Steve), Joey Ray (Boyer), Nina Gilbert, Hazel Keener, Ethyl May Halls, Maue Fealy (Women), Jameson Shade, Harry Hays Morgan, George Sherwood, Cedric Stevens (Guests), Bruce Riley, Wayne Treadway, Don McGill (Men at Party), Carl Milletaire (Customer), Hal Melone (Head Usher), George Manning (Usher), William N. Bailey, Elmo Lincoln (Detectives), Ed Wragge (Actor), John Derek (Police Stenographer), Phil MacKenzie (Police Photographer), Buddy Roosevelt (Fingerprint Man), Howard Mitchell (Tailor), Watson Downs (Bootmaker), Albert Pollett (Costume Designer), Laura Kasley Brooks (Dowager), Fred Hoose (Laughing Man), Countess Elektra Rozanska, Mary Worth, Beatrice Gray, Katharine Marlowe, Yvette Reynard, Clare Alden, Doretta Johnson, Diane Lee Stewart, John Morgan, Mike Stokey, Leader De Cordova, George Douglas, James F. Cade, Jerry Salvail (Audience).

Location: The Empire Theatre, New York, New York
Filming Completed: August 18, 1947
Released: Universal-International, December 25, 1947
Running Time: 103 minutes

Anthony John, an actor who is so obsessed with his stage roles that he cannot leave them in the theater, tackles the part of Othello. His misgivings are shared by his former but still friendly wife, Brita, the actress who will play Desdemona. Anthony first begins to act strangely toward Pat Kroll, a pathetically lonely waitress, who invites him to her apartment and ultimately to her bed. By opening night, Anthony is feeling the jealous madness of Othello in real life. He suspects the play's press agent, Bill Friend, of having an affair with Brita. When she quarrels with Anthony about this, he drifts inexorably to Pat's place. As he recites lines from the play, he chokes the helpless woman to death and smothers her with a kiss. Bill, hearing of Pat's death, devises a publicity scheme linking it with the play. Anthony goes into a rage, arousing Bill's suspicion. Aided by a homicide detective, Bill sets Anthony up by arranging for a girl disguised as Pat to confront him. Anthony's horrified surprise confirms the detective's suspicions, and he plans to arrest the actor after that night's performance of *Othello*. But Anthony, sensing that he has been exposed, plunges a dagger into his heart while performing and dies in the wings.

Anthony John (Ronald Colman) in A Double Life.

George Cukor's only excursion into the noir genre, *A Double Life* is an appropriate vehicle for the director's special talents. Unlike most noir films, it boasts the "high-toned" background of theater, and, excepting Shelley Winters's pathetic proletarian waif, equally high-toned characters. The film's re-creation of the theatrical world is meticulous, with the theater-bred director and writers Ruth Gordon and Garson Kanin drawing on their firsthand knowledge of that special world to lend verisimilitude to an unusual story.

Milton Krasner's chiaroscuro cinematography aids in creating a landscape of glittering, shifting surfaces beneath which lurk the black depths of psychological disturbance. With Ronald Colman on stage, the viewer must squint out past the glare of the footlights into a void haunted by bodyless voices. With him we walk rainwashed streets gleaming under the streetlights and stretching away into empty night. Virtually every shot in this film is a visual metaphor for Colman's state of mind, glinting with lucidity and wit one moment, plunging into bizarre and haunted depths the next.

Although it has been suggested that Colman was not sufficiently demonic for the part of Anthony John/Othello, he gives a powerful, highly original performance, a portrait of disintegration, if not of evil. The least vain of actors despite his matinée-idol looks, Colman allows his character's mental anguish to emerge from within and distort his perfect features in appropriate Jekyll-and-Hyde fashion.

As its title suggests, *A Double Life* is truly a picture of opposing forces, mirror images and deadly doubles. Anthony John is at war with Othello, the elegant world of the theater is opposed to the squalid existence of Shelley Winters's Pat Kroll, and illusion versus reality are all conveyed in the opposing lights and darks of Krasner's luminous photography.

—J.K.

DRIVE A CROOKED ROAD (1954)
[Working Titles: LITTLE GIANT, SPEEDY SHANNON]

Director: Richard Quine
Producer: Jonie Taps (Columbia Pictures)
Screenplay: Blake Edwards, adapted by Richard Quine; from an unpublished story by James Benson
Director of Photography: Charles Lawton, Jr.
Sound: George Cooper
Music Director: Ross Dimaggio
Art Director: Walter Holscher
Set Decoration: James Crowe
Assistant Director: Jack Corrick
Film Editor: Jerome Thoms

CAST: Mickey Rooney (Eddie Shannon), Dianne Foster (Barbara Mathews), Kevin McCarthy (Steve Norris), Jack Kelly (Harold Baker), Harry Landers (Ralph), Jerry Paris (Phil), Paul Picerni (Carl), Dick Crockett (Don), Mort

EDGE OF DOOM

Mills (Garage Foreman), Peggy Maley (Marge). **BITS:** Mike Mahoney, George Paul, John Damler, John Close (Police Officers), Patrick Miller (Teller), Diana Dawson, Irene Bolton, Linda Danson (Women), Mel Roberts (Customer), John Fontaine (Wells), Howard Wright, Jean Engstrom, Richard Cutting (People).

Location: Los Angeles, California
Filming Completed: November 3, 1953
Released: Columbia Pictures, April 2, 1954
Running Time: 83 minutes

Eddie Shannon is a mechanic and amateur racing driver who leads a lonely existence until he meets Barbara Mathews. He is persuaded that she is romantically interested in him; but she is actually the mistress of Steve Norris, who wants to use Eddie in a Palm Springs bank robbery. Norris needs a driver of Eddie's caliber to get over a difficult road in a matter of minutes, thereby eluding the police roadbocks on the main highway. Eddie hesitates to participate but Barbara convinces him. The robbery is a success; but Eddie discovers he has been duped. Over the protestations of the guilty Barbara, Steve and his partner, Harold, decide to kill Eddie. At gunpoint, Harold forces Eddie to drive to a secluded spot, but Eddie purposefully crashes the car and kills Harold. Seriously injured, Eddie returns to Steve's house and finds him beating Barbara. After killing Steve, Eddie consoles Barbara as the police arrive.

In the 1950s, the expressionistic lighting and camera angles associated with film noir of the 1940s gave way to a more modest style, typified in this film. The story moves forward clearly and directly, taking advantage of readily available locations, such as the beach and the streets of Los Angeles neighborhoods, with interiors that have sparse and functional decor. Eddie's apartment is expressive of his hopes and dreams in the racing trophies he displays; but it emphasizes his anonymity in virtually every other way. The same moderation of style extends to the characterizations, as Dianne Foster's and Kevin McCarthy's portrayals seem more down-to-earth and reasonable in their smooth treachery than their 1940s counterparts. In fact, Foster makes Barbara's remorse over destroying Eddie seem genuine, although there is probably nothing that would have made her do otherwise.

The lack of pretentiousness in a film like *Drive A Crooked Road* could be mistaken for a lack or artistic zeal; but such films take the motifs of the cycle out of the dark corners of a noir underworld and bring them into the sunlight, where human nature remains as corrupt as it is in the dark. The doomed noir hero played by Rooney is all the more poignant for being a very ordinary human being who suffers from the simplest of alienated emotional states: heterosexual loneliness. The most striking shot in the film shows Eddie tossing and turning on his bed when Barbara refuses to see him, a brief but evocative moment. —B.L.

EDGE OF DOOM (1950)

Director: Mark Robson, with additional scenes by Charles Vidor
Producer: Samuel Goldwyn (Samuel Goldwyn Productions)
Screenplay: Philip Yordan, with additional scenes by Ben Hecht; from the novel by Leo Brady
Director of Photography: Harry Stradling
Sound: Fred Lau
Music Score: Hugo Friedhofer
Music Director: Emil Newman
Art Director: Richard Day
Set Decoration: Julia Heron
Costumes: Mary Wills
Makeup: Blague Stephanoff

Hairstyles: Marie Clark
Production Manager: Raoul Pagel
Assistant Directors: Ivan Volkman, Ed Garvin
Script Supervisor: Jim Yarbrough
Film Editor: Daniel Mandell

CAST: Dana Andrews (Father Roth), Farley Granger (Martin Lynn), Joan Evans (Rita Conroy), Robert Keith (Mandel), Paul Stewart (Craig), Mala Powers (Julie), Adele Jergens (Irene), Harold Vermilyea (Father Kirkman), John Ridgeley, Douglas Fowley (Detectives), Mabel Paige (Mrs. Pearson), Howland Chamberlain (Mr. Murray), Houseley Stevenson, Sr. (Mr. Stevenson), Jean Innes (Mrs. Lally), Ellen Corby (Mrs. Moore), Ray Teal (Ned Moore), Mary Field (Mary Jane Glennon), Virginia Brissac (Mrs. Dennis), Frances Morris (Mrs. Lynn).

Location: Los Angeles, California
Filming Completed: January 10, 1950; additional sequences shot August 24, 1950
Released: RKO, August 3, 1950 in New York City; general release September 27, 1950
Running Time: 99 minutes
[NOTE: In response to criticism and poor business at the New York premier engagement, Goldwyn hired Ben Hecht to enlarge Dana Andrews's part (Father Roth) and give the film a prologue and epilogue.]

Martin Lynn, a floral delivery clerk, is a frustrated young member of New York's poverty row because he cannot save enough money to marry his girl, Julie, or to send his mother, dying of consumption, to an area where she might regain her health. Although he is a hard worker, Martin's boss procrastinates over giving him a raise. His mother dies; and encourged by Mr. Craig, a neighbor and small-time grifter, Martin goes to the local Catholic Church to demand money for a proper funeral. Although his mother died a pious Catholic, Martin had been antagonistic toward the church and especially his pastor, Father Kirkman, because he refused to give Martin's father, a suicide, a Catholic burial. This evening Father Kirkland is alone in the rectory. Remembering Martin, he agrees to help with the funeral expenses. But Martin demands a fancy funeral and Kirkman explains that his a very poor parish. Martin loses control completely and kills Kirkman, bludgeoning him with a crucifix. The boy attempts to rush home, but a nearby box office theft leads police to arrest him as a suspect. The next day Father Roth, who becomes pastor at Kirkman's death, hears of Martin's arrest and persuades Inspector Mandel to release him to his custody. After demanding an expensive floral arrangement from his boss, Martin is fired. The mortician, Mr. Murray, agrees to extend credit for a lavish funeral until he hears Martin is unemployed. Martin subsequently but accidentally confronts the corpse of Father Kirkman, which upsets him further. Meanwhile, Father Roth discovers that Martin is guilty. Grief-stricken, Martin prays before his mother's body and finally confesses to Father Roth, explaining that he will turn himself in if he is allowed to attend his mother's funeral.

Father Roth has told Martin's story as a lesson to a younger priest who wishes to leave St. Steven's because he could not cope with the hopelessness of its parishioners. Roth explains he saw God in Martin "when conscience triumphed over fear and despair." Roth goes on to state that Martin writes him from prison and looks forward to one day kneeling again in front of St. Steven's altar.

A film noir produced by Samuel Goldwyn, *Edge Of Doom* is in many respects an anomaly. The pessimistic bias of the film noir runs counter to a Catholic setting and moral. The film's *mise-en-scéne* subverts that outlook; for although Father Roth may have seen God in Martin, it is unlikely that the audience will. *Edge Of Doom* captures as well as any film the hopelessness and despair of those who dwell at the bottom of society and, together with films like *The Window*

and *He Ran All The Way*, uses the vertically oriented background of New York City to create a graphic sense of claustrophobia and entrapment.

—B.P.

THE ENFORCER (1951)
[Great Britain: MURDER, INC.]

Director: Bretaigne Windust and (uncredited) Raoul Walsh
Producer: Milton Sperling (United States Pictures)
Screenplay: Martin Rackin
Director of Photography: Robert Burks
Sound: Dolph Thomas
Music Score: David Buttolph
Orchestration: Maurice de Packh
Art Director: Charles H. Clarke
Set Decoration: William Kuehl
Assistant Director: Chuck Hansen
Film Editor: Fred Allen

CAST: Humphrey Bogart (Martin Ferguson), Zero Mostel (Big Babe Lazich), Ted de Corsia (Joseph Rico), Everett Sloane (Albert Mendoza), Roy Roberts (Capt. Frank Nelson), Lawrence Tolan (Duke Malloy), King Donovan (Sgt. Whitlow), Robert Steele (Herman), Patricia Joiner (Teresa Davis/Angela Vetto), Don Beddoe (Thomas O'Hara), Tito Vuolo (Tony Vetto), John Kellogg (Vince), Jack Lambert (Zaca), Adelaide Klein (Olga Kirshen), Susan Cabot (Nina Lombardo), Mario Siletti (Louis).
BITS: Alan Foster (Shorty), Harry Wilson (B.J.), Robert Strong (Secretary), Mike Lally (Detective), George Meader (Medical Examiner), Barry Reagan, Pete Kellett (Interns), Dan Riss (Mayor), Ralph Dunn (Sergeant), Perc Launders (Police Sergeant), Art Dupuis (Keeper), Tom Dillon (Policeman), John Maxwell (Doctor), Howard Mitchell (Chief), Bud Wolfe (Fireman), Brick Sullivan (Police Chauffeur), Greta Granstedt (Mrs. Lazick), Louis Lettieri (Boy), Monte Pittman (Intern), Chuck Hamilton, Jay Morley (Policemen), Richard Bartell (Clerk), Karen Kester (Nina, as a child), Eula Guy (Landlady), Creighton Hale (Clerk), Patricia Hayes (Teenager).
Filming Completed: August 31, 1950
Released: Warner Brothers, February 24, 1951
Running Time: 88 minutes

Assistant District Attorney Martin Ferguson is ready to prosecute Albert Mendoza for a number of seemingly unrelated and unsolved homicides when his only witness, Joseph Rico, is killed on the eve of the trial. Ferguson and Police Capt. Frank Nelson spend the night going through the collected prosecution files and tape recordings, putting together a grisly picture of Mendoza's scheme to sell murder by hiring gunmen to kill for a fee, thereby eliminating all chance of detection through motive. At the last moment, Ferguson finds a clue that leads to the discovery of another witness and secures his case against Mendoza.

The Enforcer is one of the first films to deal realistically with the criminal business of killing as represented by Murder, Inc. (also known as the Syndicate or the Mob). *The Enforcer* borrows the semidocumentary flavor of earlier film noir such as *The House On 92nd Street* and *Naked City*, but is also a topical film, produced about the same time that Senator Estes Kefauver's committee was investigating organized crime.

Bogart plays Martin Ferguson, the assistant district attorney. He is determined to put Albert Mendoza in prison for his part in creating the murder organization that embodies the perfect murder method for the paranoid noir psychology, dealing as it does in motiveless, unexplainable, nightmare crime. Everett Sloane as Mendoza is only one of a cast of familiar noir faces, including Jeff Corey, King Donovan, Ted de Corsia, and, in a brief but unusual role, Zero Mostel. *The Enforcer* is briskly paced, for the story, told primarily in flashback, is of an urgent job that must be completed in twelve hours. The harsh photography by Robert Burks complements the relentless tone of the film; but it is principally Raoul Walsh's (uncredited) direction that plays Ferguson's barely repressed outrage against Mendoza's lethal self-assurance that he can deal with any threat.

The finale of *The Enforcer* is positive but curiously ambiguous. The witness that Ferguson needed to ensure his case's success has been found; but there are no scenes of the trial, and the film has already suggested that justice is often blind when dealing with the cold-blooded killers of Murder, Inc. In this world of shifting values and uncertain motivation where anything may happen, the viewer is left to speculate on whether justice will triumph and, if so, for how long.

—M.B. & A.S.

EXPERIMENT IN TERROR (1962)

Director and Producer: Blake Edwards (Geoffrey-Kate Productions)
Associate Producer: Don Peters
Screenplay: Gordon Gordon and Mildred Gordon; from their novel *Operation Terror*
Director of Photography: Philip Lathrop
Sound: Charles J. Rice, Lambert Day
Music: Henry Mancini
Orchestration: Leo Shuken, Jack Hayes
Art Director: Robert Peterson
Set Decoration: James M. Crowe
Makeup: Ben Lane
Script Supervisor: Betty Abbott

Assistant Director: Sam Nelson
Film Editor: Patrick McCormack

CAST: Glenn Ford (John "Rip" Ripley), Lee Remick (Kelly Sherwood), Stefanie Powers (Toby), Roy Poole (Brad), Ned Glass (Popcorn), Anita Loo (Lisa), Patricia Huston (Nancy), Gilbert Green (Special Agent), Clifton James (Capt. Moreno), Al Avalon (Man Who Picked Up Kelly), William Bryant (Chuck), Dick Crockett (1st F.B.I. Agent), James Lanphier (Landlord), Warren Hsieh (Joey Soong), Sidney Miller (Drunk), Clarence Lung (Attorney Yung), Frederic Downs (Welk), Sherry O'Neil (Edna), Mari Lynn (Penny), Harvey Evans (Dave), William Sharon (Raymond Burkhardt), Ross Martin (Red Lynch). **BITS:** Fred Coby, Kelly McCormick, Bill Neff, Richard Norris, Kenny Jackson, James Callahan, David Tomack, Ken Wales (F.B.I. Agents), Edward Mallory (Dick), Judee Morton (Louella), Ray Kellogg (Man at Ballpark), Claire Griswold (Peggy), Fay McKenzie (Hospital Superintendent), Audrey Swanson (Nurse), Mario Cimino (Cook), Helen Jay (Waitress), Beal Wong (Pastor), Tommy H. Lee (Chinese Waiter), Barbara Collentine (Janie), George Moorman (Radio Man), William Remick (Coroner), Bob Carraher (Police Lieutenant), Gil Perkins (Taxi Driver), Mike Foran (Danny), Bob Dempsey (Helicopter Pilot), Mary Ellen Popel (Secretary), Robert Coffey (Announcer), Russ Whiteman (T.V. Director), Karen Norris (Saleswoman), Peggy Patten (Housekeeper).
Location: Oakland Bay Bridge, Candlestick Park, San Francisco, California
Filming Completed: November 11, 1961
Released: Columbia, April 13, 1962
Running Time: 123 minutes

Kelly Sherwood, a young, single bank teller, is apprehended in her garage late one night by a man who seems to know a great deal about her life. Invisible in the darkness and with an asthmatic voice, he threatens her and her younger sister with harm if she will not comply with his wishes and give him $100,000 from the bank where she works. Against her assailant's instructions, Kelly calls the F.B.I. Agent John Ripley handles the case, posting guards around Kelly and her sister, and informing the president of the bank. The F.B.I. discovers the identity of the extortionist. Red Lynch, through the clue of his having asthma and with the help of informants, who are later found murdered. When Kelly's sister is kidnapped to ensure that she carry out the plan, the F.B.I. advises her to steal the money as stipulated. Kelly does so, and Lynch tells her to meet him at Candlestick Park during a ball game. F.B.I. agents infiltrate the crowd and Lynch is killed in a shoot-out as he attempts to escape.

Film noir is associated with urban settings, and for his locale, Edwards effectively utilizes the graceful bridges and leisurely cable cars of San Francisco. By placing his menace in a sophisticated milieu, Edwards heightens the threat, expressing the noir concern that the city is outwardly respectable but inwardly seething with nameless terrors that spring to life when least expected. His use of the Bay Area as a location is rivaled only by Don Siegel in *The Line-Up* and *Dirty Harry*. In all of these films leaving your heart in San Francisco is not only a lyric fancy but a grim possibility.

The heroine is surrounded by people but is still very alone, defenseless, and vulnerable to attack from the criminal who has singled her out as his prey. She is most susceptible in the place that people normally feel most secure: her home. Additionally, although her dangerous position is known by the F.B.I., their plans leave her unprotected. In film noir's urban landscapes, one is safe nowhere.

The killer is a rarely seen, shadowy presence, with an asthmatic wheeze that hints of whispery evil. Heavies in film noir often have distinct physical deformities, such as Everett Sloane's limp in *The Lady From Shanghai*, or vivid mannerisms, such as Richard Widmark's high-pitched giggle in *Kiss Of Death*, to correspond to their tainted souls. In *Experiment In Terror*, Ross Martin's throaty susurrations give the heroine and the audience a sense of quiet but deadly menace. Henry Mancini scored the film with a slow autoharp that echoes the slithery sounds of the villain's voice. Throughout, there is effective manipulation of sound

and image. The end of one scene is punctuated by the piercing scream of a young woman; the cut shows us the yelp of fear emanating from a girl about to be tossed off the diving board of a public swimming pool. Tension slackens momentarily as the scream is revealed as a cry of pleasure, only to be tightened seconds later when she is kidnapped. The murder of one informant takes place in the auditorium of a silent movie theater during a frenetic slapstick comedy accompanied by a raucous piano.

The climax of the film is at Candlestick Park during a crowded Giants baseball game. The killer, like an unreal figure from the subconscious, bursts out of the mob against the background of this great American pastime. Wearing a hooded parka and sunglasses he is cornered and makes his last move on the pitchers mound under the glaring lights and before thousands of spectators. Like the Dodger pitcher in the bottom of the ninth, he faces sudden death. Like an insect, he is ground down by something larger, the whirring helicopter overhead. In a large sense, the whole of America is an arena for the nightmare conflicts epitomized by film noir. Therefore, whether it is the deserted Kezar Stadium where the protagonist of *Dirty Harry* apprehends the sniper or a teeming Candlestick Park in *Experiment In Terror*, it is appropriate that such epic, symbolic confrontations in American life take place in stadiums. —J.B.

FALL GUY (1947)

Director: Reginald LeBorg
Producer: Walter Mirisch (Monogram)
Screenplay: Jerry Warner, with additional dialogue by John O'Dea; from the short story "Cocaine" by Cornell Woolrich
Director of Photography: Mack Stenger
Special Effects: Augie Lehman
Sound: Tom Lambert
Music Director: Edward J. Kay
Art Director: Dave Milton
Set Decoration: Vin Taylor
Production Manager: William Calihan
Assistant Director: Frank Fox
Film Editor: William Austin, [Edward Mann?]

CAST: Clifford Penn (Tom Cochrane), Teala Loring (Lois Walter), Robert Armstrong (Mac McLaine), Virginia Dale (Marie), Elisha Cook, Jr. (Joe), Douglas Fowley (Shannon), Charles Arnt (Uncle Jim Grossett), Harry Strang (Taylor). **BITS:** Iris Adrian (Mrs. Sindell), John Harmon (Mr. Sindell), John Bleifer (Clerk), Lou Lubin (Benny), Christian Rub (Swede), George Backus (Police Physician), Jack Overman (Mike), Theodore Gottlieb (Inmate), Franklin Dix, Monty Ford, Wally Walker (Men), Katherine Marlowe, Edna Harris, Marlyn Gladstone (Women), Bob Carleton (Pianist).
Filming Completed: November 22, 1946
Released: Monogram, March 15, 1947
Running Time: 64 minutes

Tom, a pleasant young man, is arrested for the murder of an

attractive young woman. Tom has no memory of the night she was murdered; but all the evidence, including the possession of the blood-stained murder knife, implicates him. Luckily, he has a friend on the police department Mac McLaine, who frees him so that they can trace the clues together. Tom remembers only bits and pieces of the evening, such as drinking liquor at a party and finding a woman in a closet. Ultimately, the truth is revealed. Uncle Jim, who is the guardian of Tom's girl friend, Lois Walters, was having an affair with the victim who was also blackmailing the distinguished gentleman. Uncle Jim was jealous of Tom's relationship with Lois and concocted a plan to induce amnesia in Tom by means of a powerful narcotic, then frame Tom for his mistress's murder. Uncle Jim is arrested after a police battle, and Lois and Tom are reunited.

Fall Guy, a cheaply made Monogram release, has an uneven and eclectic visual style. It qualifies as a film noir because of its development of a typical Woolrich plot. His stories utilized strange ideas regarding the influence of narcotics to indicate man's loss of self-determination. Woolrich's characters similarly commit crimes and suffer from amnesia, recurrent nightmares, and entrapment while in drug-induced states in such films as *Fear In The Night, Nightmare, Deadline At Dawn,* and *The Chase.*

—B.P.

FALLEN ANGEL (1946)

Director and Producer: Otto Preminger (20th Century-Fox)
Screenplay: Harry Kleiner; from the novel by Marty Holland
Director of Photography: Joseph LaShelle
Special Photographic Effects: Fred Sersen
Sound: Bernard Freericks, Roger Heman, Harry M. Leonard
Music: David Raksin
Music Director: Emil Newman
Song: "Slowly" by David Raksin and Kermit Goell
Art Directors: Lyle Wheeler, Leland Fuller
Set Decoration: Thomas Little, Helen Hansard
Costumes: Bonnie Cashin
Makeup: Ben Nye
Assistant Director: Tom Dudley
Film Editor: Harry Reynolds

CAST: Alice Faye (June Mills), Dana Andrews (Eric Stanton), Linda Darnell (Stella), Charles Bickford (Mark Judd), Anne Revere (Clara Mills), Bruce Cabot (Dave Atkins), John Carradine (Madley), Percy Kilbride (Pop), Olin Howlin (Joe Ellis). BITS: Hal Taliaferro (Johnson), Mira McKinney (Mrs. Judd), Jimmy Conlin (Hotel Clerk), Leila McIntyre (Bank Clerk), Garry Owen (Waiter), Horace Murphy (Sheriff), Martha Wentworth (Hotel Maid), Paul Palmer, Paul Burns (Detectives), Dave Morris, Herb Ashley (Reporters), Stymie Beard (Shoeshine Boy), Dorothy Adams (Woman), William Haade, Chick Collins (Bus Drivers), J. Farrell MacDonald (Bank Guard), Max Wagner (Bartender), Betty Boyd (Bank Clerk).
Location: Orange, California
Released: 20th Century-Fox, February 6, 1946
Running Time: 98 minutes

Down to his last dollar, Eric Stanton arrives by bus in a little northern California town where he immediately becomes interested in Stella, a waitress, and pretends to be a medium. He succeeds in impressing one of the town's most respectable women, June Mills, although her sister Clara is skeptical of his intentions. Eric plans to romance June to acquire her money and then marry Stella, who remains aloof. Several other men are also interested in Stella, including Pop, proprietor of the café where she works, and the slick Dave Atkins. A former New York detective, Mark Judd, comes into the café regularly and drinks coffee. Eric tries but is unable to get hold of June's money without marrying her. When Stella is murdered, Eric is the main suspect. The relentless Judd investigates, and Eric flees to San Francisco with June, discovering that he loves her. He returns to the town and proves that Judd is actually the murderer.

Made as a follow-up to the highly successful *Laura,* this less celebrated film boasts many of the same qualities, including Joseph LaShelle's imaginative lighting, a romantic David Raksin melody that complements the action, and the ideal Preminger actor, Dana Andrews, whose presence encourages a moral uncertainty. Preminger's *mise-en-scène* and subtle development of characters who are ambiguous and fascinating belie his resolutions, which are often disappointing simplifications of complex moral and visual structures. *Fallen Angel* avoids this because of the two women with whom the protagonist is involved: one light and the other dark. June is guileless in her attractiveness, while Stella exploits her sexuality for everything she can. Preminger forces contemplation of the meaning behind the visual and behavioral qualities of the two women by cutting from a close-up of one to the other at key moments, and in the dance sequence, connecting them with an ostentatious, sustained shot. There is a possible interpretation that the protagonist stands between an angel and a devil, heaven and hell; or the title can support the implication that he is a Lucifer figure, particularly since his past is mysterious and his attachments suspect. The real emotional pull in the film is away from Stella and toward June. Eric's apparent desire to possess Stella seems more willed than felt; and he quickly forgets her after she is dead. Thus it makes metaphorical sense that the complementary Lucifer figure, Judd, is Stella's killer because his descent into hell was not stopped by an "angel" such as June.

Another notable aspect of *Fallen Angel* is Preminger's direction of the scenes in the café. The counter is slightly curved, facilitating arresting and graceful moves of the camera. Eric and Judd are always situated on opposite sides of the cash register, when they drink their coffee—like mirror images of each other—as Pop and Stella work. Although Stella, Pop, and Eric apparently dominate these scenes, the dramatic core is characteristically provided by the actions of Judd, the nonparticipant. Ritualistically, he comes in, sips his coffee, and plays the same song on the jukebox, "Slowly I open my eyes," then he leaves. This is the extent of his involvement in the story before Stella's murder; but it is remarkably sufficient. The ritual actions become retrospectively dramatic when Judd repeats them as a central character accused of murder.

—B.L.

FAREWELL, MY LOVELY (1975)

Director: Dick Richards
Executive Producers: Elliott Kastner and Jerry Bick (E.K. ITC Production)
Producers: George Pappas, Jerry Bruckheimer
Screenplay: David Zelag Goodman; from the novel by Raymond Chandler
Director of Photography: John A. Alonzo [Fujicolor; Panavision]
Camera Operator: Chris Schwiebert
Special Effects: Chuck Gaspar
Sound Mixers: Tom Verton, Dick Portman
Sound Effects: Bill Phillips
Music Editor: Ralph James Hall
Music: David Shire
Songs: "Sunday" by Jule Styne, Ned Miller, Chester Cohn, and Bennie Krueger; "I've Heard That Song Before" by Jule Styne and Sammy Cahn
Production Designer: Dean Tavoularis
Art Director: Angelo Graham
Set Decoration: Bob Nelson
Costumes: Tony Scarano
Wardrobe: Silvio Scarano (Men's), Sandy Berke (Women's)
Makeup: Frank Westmore
Hairstyles: Judy Alexander
Title Design: Wayne Fitzgerald
Casting Director: Louis Di Giaimo
Unit Production Manager/First Assistant Director: Tim Zinnemann
Assistant Directors: Henry Lange, Jr., David O. Sosna
Film Editors: Walter Thompson, Joel Cox

CAST: Robert Mitchum (Philip Marlowe), Charlotte Rampling (Mrs. Grayle), John Ireland (Nulty), Sylvia Miles (Mrs. Florian), Anthony Zerbe (Brunette), Harry Dean Stanton (Billy Rolfe), Jack O'Halloran (Moose Malloy), Joe Spinell (Nick), Sylvester Stallone (Jonnie), Kate Murtagh (Frances Amthor), John O'Leary (Marriott), Walter McGinn (Tommy Ray), Burton Gilliam (Cowboy), Jim Thompson (Mr. Grayle), Jimmie Archer (Georgie), Ted Gehring (Roy), Logan Ramsey (Commissioner), Margie Hall (Woman), Jack Bernardi (Louis Levine). **BITS:** Ben Ohta (Patron in Pool Hall), Jerry Fujikawa (Fence), Richard Kennedy (1st Detective), John O'Neill, Mark Allen (Detectives), Andrew Harris (Mulatto Child), Napoleon Whiting (Hotel Clerk), John Eames (Butler), Rainbeaux Smith (Doris), Stu Gilliam, Roosevelt Pratt (Men), Dino Washington (Bouncer), Harry Caesar (Bartender), Bill Gentry (Hood), Cory B. Shiozaki (Waiter), Noelle North (Girl), Wally Berns (Father), Lola Mason (Mother), Joan Shawlee (Woman in Ballroom), Edra Gale (Singer), Karen Gaston (Prostitute).

Location: Los Angeles and H.M.S. Queen Mary, Long Beach, California
Filming Completed: April 21, 1975
Released: Avco Embassy, August 20, 1975
Running Time: 97 minutes
MPPA Rating: R

Private detective Philip Marlowe is hired by a hulking ex-con, Moose Malloy, to find his missing girl friend, Velma. At the same time, a somewhat peculiar gentleman hires Marlowe to help him buy back a stolen necklace for a mysterious Mrs. Grayle. Working simultaneously on both cases, Marlowe becomes involved with murder: he is drugged and almost murdered himself at a brothel run by a sadistic madam, Frances Amthor, and finds himself attracted to the seductive Mrs. Grayle. When he finds Mrs. Grayle has connections with a sharpster named Brunette who runs an exclusive high-stakes gambling ship, Marlowe surreptitiously boards the vessel and confronts Brunette. Unknown to Marlowe, he is followed by Moose. Mrs. Grayle is also present; and it becomes apparent that she is Moose's faithless Velma. Moose is shot, but he manages to kill Velma before Marlowe can stop him; and the ineffectual detective is left with only his baseball hero, Joe DiMaggio, to believe in.

Robert Mitchum is an icon of the cinema noir films of the 1950s; and it is his presence, nothing short of mythic, that lends force to *Farewell, My Lovely*. The result is a film more atmospherically faithful to the ethos of Chandler's novel than *Murder My Sweet*, the 1944 version, which starred a hard-boiled Dick Powell. Mitchum's shell may be as tough as Powell's but within he is a turmoil of unspoken passions and lost dreams. The hooded eyes in the life-creased face may seem remote at first glance; but they are fastened on idealistic dreams and veil a hidden vulnerability.

A slow, neon-lit pan first reveals Mitchum's physiognomy, while in voice-over, he speaks in his familiar, unemotional tones about the winter creeping into his bones and heart. Like Mitchum, this is a tough-shelled film with a soft core of sentimentality; but it never, amazingly, descends into the maudlin. The period production design by Dean Tavolouris utilizes the Los Angeles locations with clearheadedness and respect. Moody color cinematography by John Alonzo and a jazz-oriented score by David Shire, balance the performances and compensate for an occasionally confusing script. But the main element is Mitchum as Marlowe, moving with disillusioned but steady tread, taken with Joe DiMaggio, love-struck thugs, and wise-eyed women, all of whom will disappoint him, but all of whom he will go on loving anyway, in his weary fashion.

—J.K.

FEAR (1946)
[Working Title: SUSPENSE]

Director: Alfred Zeisler
Producer: Lindsley Parsons (Monogram)
Screenplay: Alfred Zeisler and Dennis Cooper
Director of Photography: Jackson Rose
Special Effects: Bob Clark
Sound: Tom Lambert
Art Director: Dave Milton
Set Decoration: Charles Thompson, Vin Taylor
Production Manager: Glenn Cook
Dialogue Director: Leonard Zurit
Assistant Director: Clarence Bricker
Film Editor: Ace Herman

CAST: Warren William (Capt. Burke), Anne Gwynne (Eileen), Peter Cookson (Larry Crain), James Cardwell (Ben), Nestor Paiva (Schaefer), Francis Pierlot (Professor Morton Stanley), Johnny Strong (John), William Moss (Al), Darren McGavin (Chuck), Henry Clay (Steve), Almira Sessions (Mrs. Williams). **BITS:** Ernie Adams (Painter), Charles Calvert (Doc), Fairfax Burger (Magician), Cedric Stevens (Man), Bubbles Hecht (Woman), Lee Lasses White (Janitor), Ken Broeker (Uniformed Officer), Carl Leviness (Tailor), Dewey Robinson (Bartender), Brick Sullivan (Policeman), Jack Richardson, Winnie Nard, Phyllis Ayres, Hy Jason (Pedestrians), Chester Conklin (Switchman).
Filming Completed: July 26, 1945
Released: Monogram, March 2, 1946
Running Time: 68 minutes

His scholarship discontinued, medical student Larry Crane is forced to pawn his few possessions with Professor Stanley. Still lacking sufficient funds, Larry convinces himself that Stanley has exploited him and kills the professor. Unfortunately, he forgets to steal the money and leaves clues behind. However, his situation improves when a romance blossoms with a recent aquaintance, Eileen; and his article is published in the *Periodical Review,* which pays him $1,000 and motivates the faculty to renew his scholarship. The premise of the article, that exceptional people are above the law, arouses the suspicions of police Capt. Burke who is investigating the murder of Professor Stanley. Larry

accuses the police of persecuting him, while simultaneously he drops "hints" that implicate him. Distraught, Larry attempts suicide but is saved by a stranger. He finally confesses his crime to Eileen, but shortly thereafter Burke apologizes to him and explains that another suspect has confessed. Larry gets tickets to leave town but is hit by a car. At this point, Larry wakes up and realizes that he has been dreaming. Professor Stanley visits him, gives him a "discounted" loan, and announces he has been awarded a new scholarship. The next day Larry meets the girl in his dream.

This low budget film is hardly pure Dostoevsky, but it has a visual style superior to and more cohesive than the typical Monogram product. The framing device of the dream, trite from a literary viewpoint, actually reinforces the noir quality of *Fear* by virtue of its oneirism. This is further supported by a visual style full of oblique angles, depth-staging, and expressionistic lighting.

—B.P.

FEAR IN THE NIGHT (1947)

Director: Maxwell Shane
Producers: William H. Pine, William C. Thomas (Pine-Thomas)
Associate Producer: L.B. Merman
Screenplay: Maxwell Shane; from the short story "Nightmare" by William Irish [Cornell Woolrich]
Director of Photography: Jack Greenhalgh
Sound: Frank Webster
Art Director: F. Paul Sylos
Set Decoration: Elias H. Reif
Assistant Director: Howard Pine
Film Editor: Howard Smith

CAST: Paul Kelly (Cliff Herlihy), De Forest Kelley (Vince Grayson), Ann Doran (Lil Herlihy), Kay Scott (Betty Winters), Robert Emmett Keane (Lewis Belnap), Jeff York (Torrence), Charles Victor (Capt. Warner), Janet Warren (Mrs. Belnap), Michael Harvey (Bob Clune), John Harmon (Mr. Bilyou), Gladys Blake (Bank Clerk), Stanley Farrar (Patron), Julia Faye (Mrs. Tracey-Lytton), Dick Keane (Mr. Kern), Joey Ray (Contractor), Chris Drake (Elevator Operator), Loyette Thomson (Waitress), Jack Collins, Leander de Cordoba (Men).
Location: Los Angeles, California
Filming Completed: 1946
Released: Paramount, April 18, 1947
Running Time: 71 minutes

In a small room composed entirely of mirrored doors, a woman stands over a man who cuts into a safe with a torch. Somnambulistically, Vince Grayson enters through one of the doors; and the men struggle. Vince grabs a drill from the woman's hand and thrusts it into the man's heart. The woman disappears through one of the doors and Vince, stuffing the body into a closet, runs through another door, clutching a button from the victim's jacket and the key to the closet door. Waking the next morning, Vince finds the key and the button, indicating that he was not simply dreaming. Upset, Vince seeks the aid of his brother-in-law, police detective Cliff Herlihy, who insists it was just a nightmare. Later, Cliff and his wife Lil are joined by Vince and his girl friend, Betty, on a picnic. When Vince is thoroughly familiar with every room in a large mansion where the group seeks shelter from a storm, Cliff is convinced that Vince committed murder. Cliff delays arresting Vince for the sake of his wife, and his sympathies are aroused when he saves Vince from suicide. Cliff learns that the middle-aged roomer next door visited Vince the night of the murder carrying a candle. He is wealthy Mr. Belnap, owner of the mystery mansion and husband of the woman in Vince's "dream" who was killed in an auto accident after leaving the mansion that night. Cliff suspects Belnap hypnotized Vince. After Mrs. Belnap's funeral, Vince confronts Belnap in the mirrored room, which has been wired to a recorder in the basement The man admits he hypnotized Vince and murdered his wife. To get further proof, Vince allows Belnap to hypnotize him again and, in the trance, writes a confession of the killings, preparatory to drowning himself in a lake. But Cliff and the police arrive to save Vince, and chase the fleeing Belnap, who is killed in an auto accident.

The low budget Pine-Thomas organization at Paramount adapted this typical Woolrich story. Greenhalgh's photography is effectively stylized, particularly in the opening sequence. One shot is especially impressive: at his sister's house, Vince's mind flashes back to the murder, superimposes his irises in a huge close-up of his eyes over the remembered event. The major weakness of the film is the development of Vince's character, which lacks verisimilitude in its somnabulism carried over from Woolrich's story. Shane remade this story in the 1950s with a bigger budget, as *Nightmare*, but despite the title, it lacks the emphasis on oneirism contained in *Fear In The Night*.

—B.P.

THE FILE ON THELMA JORDON (1950)

Director: Robert Siodmak
Producer: Hal B. Wallis (Hal B. Wallis Productions)
Screenplay: Ketti Frings; from an unpublished story by Marty Holland
Director of Photography: George Barnes
Special Effects: Gordon Jennings
Process Photography: Farciot Edouart
Sound: Harry Lindgren, Walter Oberst
Music: Victor Young

Art Director: Hans Dreier, Earl Hedrick
Set Decoration: Sam Comer, Bertram Granger
Costumes: Edith Head
Makeup: Wally Westmore, R. Ewing, J. Stinton
Hairstyles: Dorothy Cole
Production Manager: Curtis Mick
Assistant Director: Francisco Day
Script Supervisor: Irving Cooper
Film Editor: Warren Low

CAST: Barbara Stanwyck (Thelma Jordon), Wendell Corey (Cleve Marshall), Paul Kelly (Miles Scott), Joan Tetzel (Pamela Marshall), Stanley Ridges (Kingsley Willis), Richard Rober (Tony Laredo), Minor Watson (Judge Calvin Blackwell), Barry Kelley (District Attorney Pierce), Laura Elliott (Dolly), Basil Ruysdael (Judge Hancock), Jane Novak (Mrs. Blackwell), Gertrude W. Hoffman (Aunt Vera Edwards), Harry Antrim (Sidney), Kate Lawson (Clara), Theresa Harris (Esther), Byron Barr (McCary), Geraldine Wall (Matron), Jonathan Corey (Timmy Marshall), Robin Corey (Joan Marshall). **BITS:** Garry Owen (Bailiff), Clancy Cooper (Chase), Stephen Robert (Jury Foreman), Ottola Nesmith (Mrs. Asher), Stan Johnson (Young Melvin Pierce), Virginia Hunter (Secretary to the District Attorney), Nolan Leary (Court Clerk), Rodney Bell (Withers), Dorothy Klewer, Michele Ann Barrett, Fairy Cunningham, Geraldine Jordon, Lynn Whitney, Dot Farley (Women Prisoners), Lee Phelps (Chauffeur), Kenneth Tobey (Police Photographer), Tony Merrill, Eric Alden, Jack Roberts, Howard Gardiner, Jerry James, Bill Meader, Nick Cravat (Reporters), Lew Harvey (Court Reporter), Bill Hawes (Spectator) Jim Davies (Bailiff), Gertrude Astor (Juror), Caroline Fitzharris (Cook's Daughter), John Cortay (Deputy Sheriff), Ethel Bryant (Woman Deputy), William Hamel, Harry Templeton (Newsmen), Sam McDaniel (Porter), Lynn Whitney, Dot Farley (Women Prisoners), Ezelle Poule, Lorna Jordon (Women), Mary Gordon (Charwoman), Eddie Parks (Proprietor).
Filming Completed: April 2, 1949
Released: Paramount, January 18, 1950
Running Time: 100 minutes

Late one evening, Thelma Jordon walks into the district attorney's office of a small town to discuss attempted burglaries at her elderly aunt's mansion, where Thelma also resides. But only the assistant district attorney, Cleve Marshall, is there. A love affair begins between them despite Cleve's marriage. Thelma's affections appear confused when she is met one evening by Tony Laredo, a sinister man who apparently knows her quite well. Later, Thelma tells Cleve she is married to Tony but never wants to see him again. Thelma's aunt is killed, and her safe burgled of an emerald necklace. An intricate series of events compels Cleve to the scene of the crime before it has been discovered by the police but after Thelma has cleaned up evidence that she fears implicates Tony. Advising Thelma to feign sleep, Cleve is seen escaping but not recognized by the butler, who discovers Aunt Vera's body. Thelma, protesting innocence, is arrested for murder the following day; and Tony Laredo is established as being in Chicago at the time of the crime. Slowly, Cleve learns of Thelma's corrupted past, but nevertheless he anonymously pays for her lawyer, Kingsley Willis, and plans her case, although he is the prosecuting attorney. Meanwhile, the police cannot find "Mr. X," the unidentified man the butler saw escape, and Thelma's guilt cannot be proven. Acquitted, Thelma and Tony arrange to leave town, but Cleve confronts her. Bitterly, she confesses that their affair was all a plot. Tony beats Cleve unconscious and departs with Thelma. On a mountain road, Thelma's remorse overwhelms her and she causes their car to plunge over a cliff. Tony is killed, but Thelma survives long enough to confess her crimes to the police with Cleve in attendance. She still refuses to reveal "Mr. X," however, explaining that she truly loves him. Cleve admits to his partner, Miles, that he is "Mr. X," but Miles has deduced that fact. Knowing his life and career are ruined, Cleve walks off into the shadows.

As Thelma Jordan, Barbara Stanwyck portrays a different type of *femme fatale* than Phyllis Dietrichson in *Double Indemnity,* whom Thelma nonetheless resembles in method and motivation. Although she ensnares the innocent Cleve Marshall to ensure the success of a criminal plan to benefit herself and another man, Thelma falls in love with her victim. Phyllis was emotionally frozen and only admitted to loving Walter Neff as she shot him in a futile attempt to save herself. Additionally, Cleve is much more innocent than Walter, who admittedly considered many illicit methods of collecting insurance money before he met Phyllis. Whereas Cleve's actions are impulsive and he improvises his plans to save Thelma, Walter times every moment of his crime. Phyllis and Walter are chillingly logical while Cleve and Thelma are guilt-ridden and romantic. The crucial moment that determines Thelma's fate is not when she murders her aunt, but when Cleve confronts her at the mansion after her acquittal. Cleve faces her squarely, but his presence in the room is shadowed by Tony Laredo. Literally a man of darkness with an animalistic sexuality, Tony is irresistible to Thelma; and she cannot break with him despite Cleve's cleancut normality and self-sacrificing love. As she looks from one man to the other Thelma knows they are equally bound to her because they know the truth; but she realizes that her lies have left her with no choice, that she belongs in the shadows with Tony. Romantically, she attempts redemption through the flaming car crash and confession, in a desperate belief that her death will salvage Cleve's shattered life. But Cleve, the noir hero unwittingly pulled into a nightmare, cannot be redeemed. He is not completely ostracized from society, but he is scarred immeasurably. An emotional Sisyphus, Cleve must from then on bear the weight of his tragic mistake "because of his children and because of the years."

—E.W.

FOLLOW ME QUIETLY (1949)

Director: Richard Fleischer
Producer: Herman Schlom (RKO)
Screenplay: Lillie Hayward; from an unpublished story by Francis Rosenwald and Anthony Mann
Director of Photography: Robert de Grasse
Sound: Phil Brigandi, Clem Portman
Music Score: Leonid Raab
Music Director: Constantin Bakaleinikoff
Art Directors: Albert S. D'Agostino, Walter E. Keller
Set Decoration: Darrell Silvera, James Altwies
Makeup: Gordon Bau, H.W. Phillips
Hairstyles: Hazel Rogers, Annabell Levy
Assistant Director: James Casey
Script Supervisor: Anita Speer
Film Editor: Elmo Williams

CAST: William Lundigan (Grant), Dorothy Patrick (Ann), Jeff Corey (Collins), Nestor Paiva (Benny), Charles D. Brown (Mulvaney), Paul Guilfoyle (Overbeck), Edwin Max (the Judge), Frank Ferguson (McGill), Marlo Dwyer (Waitress), Michael Brandon (Dixon), Douglas Spencer (Phony Judge). **BITS:** Maurice Cass (Bookstore Owner), Wanda Cantlon (Waitress), Howard Mitchell (Don, Bartender), Cy Stevens (Kelly), Robert Emmett Keane (Coroner), Paul Bryar (Sgt. Bryce), Lee Phelps, Art Dupuis (Detectives), Walden Boyle (Intern), Joe Whitehead (Ed), Martin Cichy (Cop), Virginia Farmer (Woman), Nolan Leary (Larson).
Filming Completed: September 4, 1948
Released: RKO, July 7, 1949
Running Time: 59 minutes

A mysterious assassin, known only as the Judge, commits a series of brutal murders to rid the world of scum. The police cannot get a complete description of the killer. Utilizing what little eye-witness evidence they obtain, the police construct a mannequin that approximates the criminal's stature. As time goes by, the case seems unsolvable, and several police officers begin talking to the mannequin. But the killer takes the place of the mannequin and sits in the shadows of the dingy office and listens to the frustrated detective explain his inadequacies. A break in the case give the police an important clue. They stake out the area where they believe the Judge lives. He walks into the trap and a wild chase begins. Finally, cornering the murderer on the catwalks of a refinery, the Judge is revealed as a middle-aged eccentric whose unattractive appearance and cruel disposition led him to become a murderer. In the fight with police that ensues, the killer falls to his death.

Based on an original story by Francis Rosenwald and Anthony Mann, *Follow Me Quietly* is a strangely obsessive film noir. Conceived as an extremely low-budget second feature directed by Richard Fleischer, the film is only 59 minutes long. Yet in that brief period, the special ambience of Mann's earlier noir films was captured and exploited, including the usual grotesques that inhabit Mann's noir universe. The Judge is a prime example of the expressionistic use of actors to convey specific emotional and psychological meanings, and one of the most effective scenes in the film comes as the mannequin, perched on a chair in the empty office, reveals itself to the audience as the Judge. Fleischer's direction is direct, the dialogue tough, and the characters of the film infused with proper noir sensibilities. *Follow Me Quietly* is patterned in the mold of *He Walked By Night*. The police serve as a means of exploring the bizarre and decadent underworld that surfaced after World War II.

—C.M.

FORCE OF EVIL (1948)
[Working Titles: TUCKER'S PEOPLE: THE NUMBERS RACKET; THE STORY OF TUCKER'S PEOPLE.]

Director: Abraham Polonsky
Producer: Bob Roberts (Roberts Productions)
Screenplay: Abraham Polonsky and Ira Wolfert; from the novel *Tucker's People* by Ira Wolfert
Director of Photography: George Barnes
Sound: Frank Webster
Music Score: David Raksin
Music Director: Rudolph Polk
Art Director: Richard Day
Set Decoration: Edward Boyle
Costumes: Louise Wilson
Makeup: Gus Norin
Hairstyles: Lillian Lashin
Production Manager: Joseph C. Gilpin
Casting Director: Jack Baur
Dialogue Director: Don Weis
Unit Manager: George Yohalem
Assistant Director: Robert Aldrich
Script Supervisor: Don Weis
Editing Supervisor: Walter Thompson
Film Editor: Art Seid

CAST: John Garfield (Joe Morse), Beatrice Pearson (Doris Lowry), Thomas Gomez (Leo Morse), Howland Chamberlain (Freddy Bauer), Roy Roberts (Ben Tucker), Marie Windsor (Edna Tucker), Paul McVey (Hobe Wheelock), Tim Ryan (Johnson), Sid Tomack (Two & Two Taylor), Georgia Backus (Sylvia Morse), Sheldon Leonard (Ficco), Jan Dennis (Mrs. Bauer), Stanley Prager (Wally). **BITS:** Jack Overman (Juice), Raymond Largay (Bunte), Paul Frees (Elevator Operator), Bert Hanlon (Cigar Man), Bob Williams (Elevator Starter), Barbara Woodell (Receptionist), Bill Neff (Law Clerk), Frank Pharr (Bootblack), Joe Warfield (Collector), Beau Bridges (Frankie Tucker), Perry Ivans (Mr. Middleton), Cliff Clark (Police Lieutenant), Larry Blake (Detective), Phil Tully, Paul Newlan, Max Wagner, Chuck Hamilton, Carl Saxe, Capt. Fred Sommers, George Magrill, Ralph Dunn, Jim Davies, Bob Reeves, Bud Wiser, Brick Sullivan, Ray Hyke (Policemen), Jimmy Dundee (Dineen), Mickey McGuire (Boy), Bud Fine (Butcher), Douglas Carter, Sam Ash (Men), Milton Kibbee (Richards), Esther Somers (Mrs. Lowry), Barry Kelley (Egan), Allen Mathews (Badgley), Mervin Williams (Goodspeed), Frank O'Connor (Bailiff), Charles Evans (Judge), Will Lee (Waiter), David McKim (Cashier), William Challee, Joey Ray, David Fresco (Gunmen) John Indrisano (Henchman), Stanley Waxman (Manager), Eileen Coghlin, Barbara Stone, Estelle Etterre, Helen Eby-Rock (Secretaries), Margaret Bert, Jesse Arnold, Betty Corner, Jim Toney, Sherry Hall, Shimen Ruskin (Sorters), Jim Drum, Carl Sklover, John Butler (Bankers), Dick Gordon, Roger Cole, Jay Eaton, Carl Hanson, Ralph Brooks, Dick Elmore, Bert Davidson (Attorneys), Arthur O'Connell (Link Hall), Murray Alper (Comptroller), Robert Strong (Court Reporter), Joel Fluellen (Father), Mildrey Boyd (Mother), Louise Saraydar (Hatcheck Girl), Ray Hirsch (Newsboy), Barbara Combs, John Collum, William H. O'Brien (Dancers), Bob Stebbins (Norval), Ann Duncan (Norval's Girl Friend), Diane Stewart (Girl), Ed Peil, Sr. (Counterman).

Location: Manhattan, New York, New York
Filming Completed: August 10, 1948
Released: Enterprise Studio presentation and MGM Release, December 26, 1948
Running Time: 88 minutes
[NOTE: Roberts Productions acceded to the demands of the Motion Picture Code Administration not to use any title incorporating the phrase "numbers racket."]

A gambling syndicate lawyer, Joe Morse, is inextricably bound to a set of ethics that he doesn't fully understand. His bitter fear of failure and the ability to make easy money allow him to justify his role in "legalizing" a large-scale numbers racket. The only obstacle is his brother, Leo, who runs a small, independent bookie joint and who will not relinquish his independence to join the syndicate. Eventually the situation is taken out of Joe's hands and the larger syndicate moves in and destroys Leo's small-time operation. The corrupted lawyer begins to realize the true character of his business. Joe battles to break loose of the syndicate with the help of a young woman who worked for his brother; but, involved beyond the point of salvation Leo perishes and Joe exposes the syndicate.

Written and directed by Abraham Polonsky, *Force Of Evil* is a noir film with strong social leanings. After his association with Robert Rossen and John Garfield in *Body And Soul*, Polonsky retained Garfield to act in this socially conscious indictment of organized crime. Using the iconography and personalities of the noir series, Polonsky was able to mask

105

his methods of social criticism under a melodramatic veneer of gangsterism and corruption. It is an extraordinarily existential vision that transcends the mythic aspects of the underworld to delineate the gambling rackets as a surrogate reality reinforced by Polonsky's use of location and semidocumentary threatment of the government reformers. In effect, *Force Of Evil* brings racketeering into focus as a form of capitalism, with John Garfield as the individual who is unable to differentiate morality from achievement. Marie Windsor co-stars in a pivotal role as a *femme fatale* who is used to manipulate Garfield into accepting the brutal destruction of his brother's organization and maintaining the artificial legality of the syndicate's racket.

When Joe Morse is finally radicalized by his brother's death and the sudden self-image of his own corruption, his revolt is as much existential as it is political. Joe makes a revelation of his betrayal to the mobsters at a rendezvous by the East River, fully realizing and even anticipating that it may precipitate his own murder. In contrast to the claustrophobic reality of his parting with Doris in the back seat of a taxi (photographed by Polonsky in a long take of a two-shot), a bridge with its span of steel girders looms over the final sequence on the riverbank like a piece of expressionistic stage dressing. Not only does Joe play out his personal drama dwarfed by this manifestation of the power and immensity of mankind as a whole, but the scene acquires a theatrical aura, which is entirely appropriate to the way in which Joe has "staged" his death. Although there is clearly more than just one death at stake in the climax of *Force Of Evil*, it is this clear sense of Joe's "staging" it—as compared with the similar but more impromptu suicide of Harry Fabian for the sake of his girl friend in *Night And The City*—which valorizes Joe's sacrifice and which puts the stress on individual rather than societal action. Polonsky's *mise-en-scène* both highlights this attitude of Joe's and reveals the other more social forces at work behind it without compromising the noir ambience of the film as a whole.

—C.M. & A.S.

FRAMED (1947)
[Working Title: THEY WALK ALONE]

Director: Richard Wallace
Producer: Jules Schermer (Columbia)
Screenplay: Ben Maddow; from an unpublished story by Jack Patrick.
Director of Photography: Burnett Guffey
Sound: George Cooper
Music: Marlin Skiles
Music Director: M.W. Stoloff
Art Director: Stephen Gooson
Set Decoration: Wilbur Menefee, Sidney Clifford, Fay Babcock

Costumes: Jean Louis
Assistant Director: Herman Webber
Film Editor: Richard Fantl

CAST: Glenn Ford (Mike Lambert), Janis Carter (Paula Craig), Barry Sullivan (Stephen Price), Edgar Buchanan (Jeff Cunningham), Karen Morley (Mrs. Price), Jim Bannon (Jack Woodworth), Sid Tomack (Bartender), Barbara Wooddell (Jane Woodworth), Paul Burns (Assay Clerk). **BITS:** Charles Cane (Manager, Truck Company), Art Smith (Hotel Clerk), Robert Stevens (Young Man), Lillian Wells (Young Woman), Fred Graff (Bank Clerk), Michael Towne (Boy in Jail), Walter Baldwin (Assistant Manager), Eugene Borden (Julio), Martin Garralaga (Sweeper), Kenneth MacDonald, Crane Whitley (Policemen), Alan Bridge (Judge), Snub Pollard (Dishwasher), Jack Baxley (Bank Guard), Stanley Andrews, Gene Stutenroth (Detectives), David Fresco (Newsboy), Mabel Smaney (Fat Woman), Cecil Weston (Woman in Jail), Harry Strang (Jail Guard), Cy Malis (Crap Shooter), Nacho Galindo (Mexican Shooter), William Stubbs (Houseman), Mel Wixson (Man).
Filming Completed: October 30, 1946
Released: Columbia, May 25, 1947
Running Time: 82 minutes

Mike Lambert, an unemployed mining engineer, takes work as a truck driver. He is seduced by Paula Craig, a waitress, who wants to use him as part of a plan she has concocted with her lover, Stephen Price. Price married into a prominent family and is vice-president of the local bank. He and Paula plan to embezzle $250,000 and run off together, if they can find someone who looks sufficiently like Stephen to frame for the crime. Mike is chosen, but Paula falls in love with him. After the robbery, she double-crosses and kills her former lover, Stephen. She tells Mike she killed Stephen while drunk, but when Mike's friend Jeff is arrested for the murder, Mike refuses to let him take the blame. Mike finally realizes that Paula is guilty and traps her into incriminating herself, so that she is arrested.

Framed is photographed by Burnett Guffey in his usual "flat" style. The plot line owes much to the middle-class milieu first created in literature by James M. Cain. *Framed* benefits from a portrayal by Janis Carter, who had she not remained in low budget films, might have rivaled Barbara Stanwyck as the leading noir actress of the 1940s. Carter was adept at adding sexual overtones to sadistic acts. As Paula she exhibits a decidedly sexual excitement as Stephen's car goes off the cliff, which rivals a sequence in the earlier film *Night Editor*, in which she becomes frenzied while watching a girl being beaten to death. In a singular example of the perfidious nature of the fatal woman, she poisons Mike's coffee when he seems adverse to her plans, only to withdraw the coffee at the last moment when his conversation takes on a more reassuring tone.

—B.P.

THE FRENCH CONNECTION (1971)

Director: William Friedkin
Executive Producer: G. David Schine (D'Antoni Productions)
Producer: Philip D'Antoni
Associate Producer: Kenneth Utt
Screenplay: Ernest Tidyman; from the book by Robin Moore
Director of Photography: Owen Roizman [DeLuxe Color]
Camera Operator: Enrique Bravo
Special Effects: Sass Bedig
Sound: Chris Newman, Theodore Soderberg
Music: Don Ellis
Song: "Everyone Gets To Go To The Moon" by Jim Webb; sung by The Three Degrees
Art Director: Ben Kazaskow
Set Decoration: Ed Garzero
Costumes: Joseph Fretwell, III
Wardrobe: Joseph W. Dehn, Florence Foy
Makeup: Irving Buchman
Unit Production Manager: Paul Ganapoler
Technical Consultants: Eddie Egan, Sonny Grosso
Stunt Coordinator: Bill Hickman
Casting: Robert Weiner
Location Consultant: Fat Thomas
Assistant Directors: William C. Gerrity, Terry Donnelly
Script Supervisor: Nick Sgarro
Film Editor: Jerry Greenberg

CAST: Gene Hackman (James "Popeye" Doyle), Fernando Rey (Alain Charnier), Roy Scheider (Buddy Russo), Tony LoBianco (Sal Boca), Marcel Bozzuffi (Pierre Nicoli), Frederic De Pasquale (Devereaux), Bill Hickman (Mulderig), Ann Rebbot (Marie Charnier), Harold Gary (Weinstock), Arlene Farber (Angie Boca), Eddie Egan (Simonson), Andre Ernotte (La Valle), Sonny Grosso (Klein), Pat McDermott (Chemist), Alan Weeks (Drug Pusher), Al Fann (Informant), Irving Abrahams (Police Mechanic), Randy Jurgensen (Police Sergeant), William Coke (Motorman), the Three Degrees (the Band), Ben Marino (Lou Boca), Maureen Mooney (Bicycle Girl), Robert Weil (Auctioneer).
Location: New York, New York; Washington, D.C.; Marseilles, France
Released: 20th Century-Fox, October 7, 1971
Running Time: 104 minutes
MPAA Rating: R
[FACTUAL BASIS: In 1961, New York narcotics squad officers Egan and Grosso confiscated 120 pounds of heroin valued at $32,000,000. However, no one was killed in their two and a half year investigation.]

Popeye Doyle and Buddy Russo are New York narcotics detectives whose job consists mainly of arresting Harlem dealers and addicts. A huge heroin shipment is coming from Marseilles, and Doyle and Russo investigate. Behind the shipment is a cultured, brilliant archcriminal, Charnier, who personally arrives in New York to help close the deal. The obstinate Doyle is outsmarted in following Charnier, who decides to have Doyle killed. Instead, after a grueling car chase through the streets of New York, Doyle kills the assassin. The police finally determine the locale of the illegal transaction and close in. Most of the dope ring is killed in the raid, but Charnier escapes, while Doyle mistakenly shoots a fellow policeman, believing him to be the Frenchman. Censured by his colleagues, Popeye Doyle immediately resumes his pursuit of Charnier.

At one time, thrillers, detective films, and film noir received little critical attention. *The French Connection*, unimpressive visually but filled with "crowd-pleasing" action sequences, has generated a large amount of critical acclaim but is a counterfeit of the noir movement. In spite of an impressively hot and edited car chase (which is less fully integrated into the narrative than an analogous sequence in, for example, *The Lineup*), the prevailing impression is of a cynical, exploitative work. The behavior of Doyle, the central character, is at times offbeat and interesting but lacks a critical *raison d'etre*. The chase, for instance, is a flurry of precisely choreographed action for vehicles and pedestrians, in which Doyle and the unidentified criminal he chases are less characters than performers. By stressing the mechanics of the violence of Doyle and others—and, by extension, exposing the "automaton" mentalities of Doyle and his partner—the brutality demanded of Doyle by the narrative always seems more gratuitous than obsessive. Doyle is never characterized as psychopathic (compare Jim Wilson at the beginning of *On Dangerous Ground*) but simply as someone conditioned to separate emotions or conscience from official actions. Accordingly his outrage against Charnier becomes less a personal grudge against one who has outwitted him than a mechanistic repugnance for a criminal who refuses to be duly processed.

—B.L. & A.S.

FRENCH CONNECTION II (1975)

Director: John Frankenheimer
Producer: Robert L. Rosen (20th Century-Fox)
Screenplay: Alexander Jacobs, Robert Dillon, and Lauri Dillon; from an unpublished story by Robert Dillon and Lauri Dillon
Director of Photography: Claude Renoir [DeLuxe Color]
Camera Operator: Charles-Henri Montel
Special Effects: Logan Frazee
Sound: Bernard Bats, Ted Soderberg
Music: Don Ellis
Production Designer: Jacques Saulnier
Art Directors: Gerard Viard, Georges Glon
Costumes: Jacques Fonterary
Wardrobe: Pierre Nourry
Makeup and Hairstyles: Monique and Alex Archambault

THE FRIENDS OF EDDIE COYLE

Production Supervisor: Pierre Saint-Blancat
Stunt Coordinator: Hal Needham
Casting: Margot Capelier
Publicity Director: Gordon Arnell
Stills Photographer: Serge Moritz
Assistant Directors: Bernard Stora, Thierry Chabert
Script Supervisor: Lucie Lichtig
Film Editor: Tom Rolf

CAST: Gene Hackman (James "Popeye" Doyle), Fernando Rey (Alain Charnier), Bernard Fresson (Barthelemy), Jean-Pierre Castaldi (Raoul Diron), Charles Millot (Miletto), Cathleen Nesbitt (Old Lady), Pierre Collet (Old Pro), Alexandre Fabre (Young Tail), Philippe Leotard (Jacques), Jacques Dynam (Inspector Benevoix), Raoul Delfosse (Dutch Captain), Patrick Floersheim (Manfredi).
Location: Marseilles, France
Filming Completed: October 25, 1974
Released: 20th Century-Fox, May 21, 1975
Running Time: 118 minutes
MPAA Rating: R
[NOTE: James Poe was originally contracted to write the script for D'Antoni's production of *French Connection II*.]

Popeye Doyle goes to Marseilles, France, to continue searching for the elusive Alain Charnier. The New York City detective is an official observer at the Marseilles police department and treated with contempt by the French detective, Barthelemy. Doyle is completely out of his element with his crude language, loud dress, total lack of manners, and fractured French conversation. Seemingly ignored by the city's police, he is unknowingly being used to lure Charnier into the open. But the plan fails when Doyle eludes his police protection. Charnier kidnaps Doyle and turns him into a drug addict but decides against murder and releases him when it is determined that the American cop knows very little about the organization. Doyle is aided by Barthelemy in defeating his addiction and, when he recovers, is even more determined to capture Charnier. The French police succeed in breaking into the drug ring's headquarters but once again Charnier escapes and Doyle chases him on foot. The criminal boards a small boat and is sailing out of the harbor when Doyle spots him. After an arduous, superhuman run, Doyle reaches the edge of a dock from which he calls Charnier's name. The man instinctively turns and Doyle shoots him.

While its predecessor is a film without depth of characterization, *French Connection II* is one of the most noir films of recent years. Doyle emerges as a man with a meaning, returning from near death and oblivion to become an impassioned revenge figure. At the same time, Charnier evolves as more than a gentleman who insidiously deals in dope; he rises to the level of an evil figure whom the audience wants to see destroyed. Without becoming more sympathetic in any superficial way, Doyle wins viewer respect, most notably in the concise montage that shows his

change of dress from raincoat to sports shirt, as he walks the streets following his recovery.

After years of undistinguished films following the early and brilliantly conceived *The Manchurian Candidate, French Connection II* demonstrates that director John Franhenheimer still has the ability to draw a fine-line portrait of the alienated loner. In its riveting final sequence, and above all in its cathartic last frames, this film is one of the few recent works in American cinema which can be readily described as noir.

—B.L.

THE FRIENDS OF EDDIE COYLE (1973)

Director: Peter Yates
Producer: Paul Monash (Paramount)
Associate Producer: Charles Maguire
Screenplay: Paul Monash; from the novel by George V. Higgins
Director of Photography: Victor J. Kemper [Technicolor; Panavision]
Sound: Dick Raguse, Dick Voriscek, Ron Kalish
Music: Dave Grusin
Production Designer: Gene Callahan
Set Decoration: Don Galvin
Costumes: Eric Seelig
Makeup: Irving Budhman
Casting: Marion Dougherty Associates, Vic Ramos
Assistant Director: Peter Scoppa
Second Assistant Director: Sal Scoppa
Film Editor: Pat Jaffe

CAST: Robert Mitchum (Eddie Coyle), Peter Boyle (Dillon), Richard Jordan (Dave Foley), Steven Keats (Jackie), Alex Rocco (Scalise), Joe Santos (Artie Van), Mitchell Ryan (Waters), Peter MacLean (Partridge), Kevin O'Morrison (Second Bank Manager), Marvin Lichterman (Vernon), Carolyn Pickman (Nancy), James Tolkan (Contact Man), Margaret Ladd (Andrea), Matthew Cowles (Pete), Helena Carroll (Sheila Coyle), Jane House (Wanda), Michael McCleery (the Kid), Alan Koss (Phil), Dennis McMullen (Webber), Judith Ogden Cabot (Mrs. Partridge), Jan Egleson (Kid), Robert Anthony (Moran), Gus Johnson (Ames), Ted Maynard (Sauter), Sheldon Feldner (Ferris).
Location: Boston, Massachusetts
Filming Completed: December 1972
Released: Paramount, June 27, 1973
Running Time: 102 minutes
MPPA Rating: R

Realizing that an upcoming trial might force him to live the rest of his life behind bars, a middle-aged, three-time-loser named Eddie Coyle is out on bail. He decides to become a police informant and engage in plea bargaining with treasury agent Dave Foley. But Coyle also continues to transport illegal goods across state lines for the mob. While the police pressure Eddie for information without any intention of shortening his probable jail sentence, the mob also manipulates him. Coyle's underworld contact and friend, Dillon, is hired by the mob to kill the apparent informer. Finding out that the contract is for Eddie, Dillon is still determined to go through with the assassination. Like a pig fattened up before the slaughter, Coyle is treated to a last fling by his eventual murderer. After a hockey game and several drinks, Eddie Coyle is driven to a lonely spot, killed, and left in an abandoned car.

Adapted from a novel by George V. Higgins, *The Friends Of Eddie Coyle* comes closer to capturing the feeling and mood of the noir films of the late 1940s than most contemporary thrillers. Many of the elements that define the noir bias are present in the film. Not only is there an overwhelming mood of corruption complicated by an ethos of hopelessness and fatalism, but there is equally a sharp sense of alienation and fear. *The Friends Of Eddie Coyle* deals with a contemporary world still confined by the goals and situations of the noir environment. There even remains a ritualization of violence, as indicated by the elongated execution of Eddie Coyle, that recalls the best work of Anthony Mann and Dassin. Robert Mitchum provides a physical link to the 1940s noir film because, by the time of *Eddie Coyle*, his well-established persona developed in such noir films as *Out Of The Past, Crossfire,* and *The Racket* had decomposed into the aged protrait of a man faced with the reality of no real escape. The cynical nature of the police and the young punks with whom Coyle comes in contact merely reinforce the noir ambience present in the film. The downbeat ending and ultimate grotesqueness of the portrayals by Peter Boyle and the assorted young hoods— along with the other more debasing characteristics of the film—place *The Friends Of Eddie Coyle* closer to the true noir cycle than the homage offered by such films as *Chinatown* and *Farewell, My Lovely.*

—C.M.

FURY (1936)
[Working Titles: THE MOB, MOB RULE]

Director: Fritz Lang
Producer: Joseph L. Mankiewicz (MGM)
Screenplay: Bartlett Cormack and Fritz Lang; from the story "Mob Rule" by Norman Krasna
Director of Photography: Joseph Ruttenberg
Music: Franz Waxman
Art Directors: Cedric Gibbons, William A. Horning, and Edwin B. Willis
Costumes: Dolly Tree
Assistant Director: Horace Hough
Film Editor: Frank Sullivan

CAST: Spencer Tracy (Joe Wheeler), Sylvia Sydney (Catherine Grant), Walter Abel (District Attorney), Edward Ellis (Sheriff), Walter Brennan (Buggs Meyers), Bruce Cabot (Bubbles Dawson), George Walcott (Tom), Frank Albertson (Charlie), Arthur Stone (Durkin), Morgan Wallace (Fred Garrett), George Chandler (Milt), Roger Gray (Stranger), Edwin Maxwell (Vickery), Howard C. Hickman (Governor), Jonathan Hale (Defense Attorney), Leila Bennett (Edna Hooper), Esther Dale (Mrs. Whipple), Helen Flint (Franchette). **BITS:** Edward Le Saint (Doctor), Everett Sullivan (New Deputy), Murdock MacQuarrie (Dawson's Friend), Ben Hall (Goofy), Janet Young, Jane Corcoran, Mira McKinney, Mary Foy, Edna Mae Harris (Women), Edwin J. Brady, James Quinn, Al Herman, Frank Mills (Dawson's Friends), George Offerman, Jr. (Defendant), Frank Sully, Dutch Hendrian (Miners), Albert Taylor (Old Man), Ray Brown (Farmer), Guy Usher (Assistant Defense Attorney), Nora Cecil (Albert's Mother), Frederick Burton (Judge Hopkins), Tom Mahoney (Bailiff), Tommy Tomlinson (Reporter), Sherry Hall (Court Clerk), Carlos Martin (Donelli), Jack Daley (Factory Foreman), Duke York (Taxi Driver), Charles Coleman (Innkeeper), Will Stanton (Drunk), Esther Muir (Girl), Bert Roach (Waiter), Raymond Hatton (Hector), Victor Potel (Jorgeson), Clara Blandick (Judge's Wife), Erville Alderson (Plumber), Herbert Ashley (Oscar), Harry Hayden (Look-up Keeper), Si Jenks (Hillbilly), Christian Rub (Ahem), Carl Stockdale (Hardware Man), Elsa Newell (Hot Dog Stand Owner), Alexander Cross, Robert E. Homans (Guards), Arthur Hoydt, Ward Bond, Franklin Parker, Wally Maher, Huey White, Clarence Kolb (Men), Gertrude Sutton (Mrs. Tuttle), Minerva Urecal (Fanny), Daniel Haynes (Taxi Driver), Sam Hayes (Announcer), Harvey Clark (Pippen).

Filming Completed: April 25, 1936
Released: MGM, June 5, 1936
Running Time: 90 minutes

Joe Wheeler is on his way to rejoin his fiancée, Catherine, when he is arrested as a suspected kidnapper. He is held in the local jail on the basis of circumstantial evidence— specifically the possession of a bill that was part of a ransom payment. As word spreads through the town that someone has been arrested, people congregate around the jail seeking information. They are dispersed by the sheriff, but angry words are exchanged. While the sheriff convinces the governor to alert the national guard in the event of a lynch mob, a deputy inadvertently tells the mob leaders of the evidence against Wheeler. This ignites the patrons of the local tavern into action, and they gather supporters as they march on the jail. While the sheriff fights to hold them off, the governor is persuaded that dispatching the guard would be political folly. Even after the deputies have been overpowered, the lynchers cannot break through to the cells, so they set fire to the building. By the time the governor does release the guardsmen, the jail has been gutted by flames and dynamite.

FURY

Unseen by anyone, Wheeler escapes from the blaze; but, infuriated by the attempt to kill him, he remains in hiding even after the actual kidnapper is caught and confesses. Believing that Wheeler perished in the fire, the district attorney indicts two dozen townspeople for murder. Despite the refusal of any witness, including the sheriff, to testify against his neighbors, the district attorney supports his charges with a newsreel film showing the defendants taking part in the riot. The defense contention that Wheeler may not even have been in his cell is dispelled when Catherine takes the stand and explains that she arrived on the scene just in time to see Joe at a window of the burning building. Finally, the district attorney produces Wheeler's charred engagement ring, which prompts a woman defendant to confess and implicate the others. Only after twenty persons are found guilty and sentenced does Wheeler reveal that he survived.

What classifies Fritz Lang's *Fury* as one of the earliest of film noir is less its socially conscious, antilynching theme than its portrayal of a newly-embittered protagonist unrelentingly set on revenge. In fact, the "fury" of the title could apply just as strongly to the emotional state of Joe Wheeler in the second half of the film as it does to that of the mob in the first portion. By dividing his picture into two parts and focusing in turn on social and individual anger, Lang suggests the potential for transference between the two, that alienation or *angst* are both personal and mass ills. Moreover, Lang adapts the fateful visual style of his earlier German expressionism, full of Freudian and cryptoreligious symbolism, to the more prosaic reality of the American depression

The film opens with an alternation of static and moving shots following Joe and Catherine just before her departure for a better-paying job in another state. The couple gaze at a window display of bedroom furniture, consider going to a movie, and finally, not knowing what to do with their last few hours, simply walk in the rain. When they reach out to each other in the station, the train jerks them apart, until Catherine is lost in a haze of lights. From the beginning the acting and editing convey an underlying, ominous sense of disquiet. Lang multiplies the details of milieu and the couple's relationship rapidly, establishing a context for his personal notions of destiny. At the same time, the economic necessity of the couple's separation maintains the film's contemporary relevance.

Having introduced this background of both personal and social instability, Lang injects a deterministic plot twist in the form of Wheeler's arrest and his possession of an incriminating bill (ironically, his problems continue to be linked to money). After indulging in some sardonic metaphors (for instance, the gossiping townswomen spreading word of Joe's arrest are intercut with hens in a barnyard), Lang returns to a direct, if visually diffracted, statement for the lynching: Wheeler "meets his fate" in a flurry of flashing torches, shattered glass, and bodies hurled up against barred windows.

The trial of the lynch party that follows is a sequence that could be described as semidocumentary and yet verges on expressionism. While the prosecutor reads aloud figures about lynching and recapitulates the defendants' various alibis in voice-over, the newsreel footage shows them throwing rocks and breaking up furniture for the fire. Lang intercuts between freeze-frames of a mechanic spreading kerosene, a houswife hurling a firebrand, and another man severing a fire hose and close-ups of the same people on the stand. The final bit of manipulation is reserved for the melodramatic climax of the trial sequence: the verdict. As a sober-voiced clerk reads the jury's decisions, he begins with two "not guiltys," at which point all the defendants turn to congratulate each other; he then follows with a chain of "guiltys," as each one named, in ironic parallel to the newsreel, "freezes" in disbelief.

Although Wheeler reappears to spare the mob members further punishment, it cannot be assumed that he does so out of forgiveness. It may be that he has become conscious of his own unjust behavior toward Catherine—that, too, is not made clear. In either case, Lang does not imply that the people of the town have learned their lesson. He does imply that Wheeler's existence has been permanently altered by his ordeal; and that, like many noir heroes to follow, he may never entirely escape the disturbing specter of his past.

—A.S.

THE GANGSTER (1947)

Director: Gordon Wiles
Producers: Maurice and Frank King (King Brothers)
Screenplay: Daniel Fuchs; from his novel *Low Company*
Director of Photography: Paul Ivano
Special Effects: Roy W. Seawright
Sound: William Randall
Music Score: Louis Gruenberg
Conductor: Irvin Talbot
Song: "Paradise" by Gordon Clifford and Nacio Herb Brown
Art Director: F. Paul Sylos
Set Decoration: Sidney Moore
Costumes: Norma
Makeup: Ern Westmore
Dialogue Director: Sidney Moore
Technical Adviser: Herman King
Production Assistant: Arthur Gardner
Assistant Director: Frank S. Heath
Film Editor: Walter Thompson

CAST: Barry Sullivan (Shubunka), Belita (Nancy Starr), Joan Lorring (Dorothy), Akim Tamiroff (Nick Jammey), Henry Morgan (Shorty), John Ireland (Karty), Fifi D'Orsay (Mrs. Ostroleng), Virginia Christine (Mrs. Karty), Sheldon Leonard (Cornell), Leif Erickson (Beaumont), Charles McGraw (Dugas), John Kellogg (Sterling), Elisha Cook, Jr. (Oval), Ted Hecht (Swain). **BITS:** Clancy Cooper, Jeff Corey, Peter Whitney (Brothers-in-law), Edwin Maxwell (Politician), Murray Alper (Eddie), Bill Kennedy, Mike Conrad (Thugs), Rex Downing (Boy with Note), Shelley Winters (Hazel), Ruth Allen (Girl Singer), Billy Gray (Little Boy), Norma Jean Nilsson (Little Girl), Dewey Robinson (Pool Player), Jack Reynolds, Larry Thompson (Thugs), Greta Grandstedt, Marguerita Padula (Women), Larry Steers (Headwaiter), Mike Lally, Sammy Shack (Men), Jean Calhoun, Helen Alexander (Women), Pat Emery (Miss Callister), Lennie Bremen, Alec Pope, Mike Gaddis (Men), Maxine Semon (Hotel Maid), Marie Blake (House Mistress), Anita Turner (Essie), Phyllis Ayres (Wife on Street), Dolores Castle (Cigarette Girl), Sidney Melton (Stage Manager), Delese Daudet, Jean Harrison (Dancers), Tommy Reilly (Piano Player), Don Haggerty (Stranger), Griff Barnett (Dorothy's Father), Jay Eaton (Man), Zona Eaton, Irene Brooks (Women), Ralph Freto, Gene Collins (Boys),

Andy Andrews, Phil Arnold (Men), Michael Vallon (Man on Boardwalk), Jane Weeks (Girl in Corridor), Parker Gee (Man in Corridor).
Filming Completed: March 12, 1947
Released: Allied Artists, October 6, 1947
Running Time: 84 minutes

A neurotic gangster, Shubunka, reaches the crossroads of his life. A rival, Cornell, is trying to take over his nefarious activities and Shubunka will not listen to the desperate warning of his associate, Jammey. Shubunka is giving all his attention to his mistress, Nancy, over whom he is insanely jealous. In moments of relative calm, the ill-fated gangster hangs out in an ice cream parlor where he is severely judged by a young girl, Dorothy, whose good opinion means something to him, and where he is entreated for money by a desperate gambler, Karty. Finally Karty's losses drive him to sell out Shubunka to Cornell. Shubunka, after alienating Nancy, is shot down by Cornell's men on the rainy streets.

The Gangster has little in common with the traditional gangster film that characteristically illustrates the history of a criminal protagonist's rise and fall. Even a film made as late as 1960, *The Rise And Fall Of Legs Diamond*, can be traditional and actually describes and categorizes itself as such by its title. The rise and fall of Shubunka is implicit in *The Gangster*, but it is compressed into a single turn of events occurring when the central figure is already doomed. Consequently, this film is a mood piece.

Owing too little to traditional structure and too much to a style that it does not really grasp, *The Gangster* is arty and affected, as director Gordon Wiles has gravitated toward the creation of a theatrical rather than a visual impression. A film—and the most visually exciting of film noir bear this out—can show discernment and restraint when there are pretentious aspects implicit in the material. An occasional composition that is subtle rather than flamboyant and understated editing rather than ostentatious asymmetry would benefit a film like *The Gangster* in which the characters seem to have stepped out of the pages of elitist poetry. The theatrical qualities of this picture are easily discerned by noting how a cast of seasoned motion picture actors—such as Sullivan, Tamiroff, Ireland, Morgan, and Lorring—emote throughout as if the third-act curtain were only minutes away. A possible explanation for the ambitions of such a modest picture might be the script, confirmed as the uncredited work of Dalton Trumbo, a writer whose tendency to portentuous significance is only contained by such directors as Otto Preminger.

—B.L.

THE GARMENT JUNGLE (1957)
[Working Title: THE GARMENT CENTER]

Directors: Vincent Sherman [Uncredited: Robert Aldrich]
Producer: Harry Kleiner (Columbia)
Screenplay: Harry Kleiner; from a series of articles "Gangsters In the Dress Business" by Lester Velie
Photography: Joseph Biroc
Sound: John Livadary
Music: Leith Stevens
Orchestration: Arthur Morton
Art Director: Robert A. Peterson
Set Decoration: William Kiernan, Frank A. Tuttle
Costumes: Jean Louis
Makeup: Clay Campbell
Hairstyles: Helen Hunt
Assistant Director: Irving Moore
Film Editor: William Lyon

CAST: Lee J. Cobb (Walter Mitchell), Kerwin Matthews (Alan Mitchell), Gia Scala (Theresa Renata), Richard Boone (Artie Ravidge), Valerie French (Lee Hackett), Robert Loggia (Tulio Renata), Joseph Wiseman (Kovan), Adam Williams (the Ox), Harold J. Stone (Tony), Wesley Addy (Mr. Paul), Willis Bouchey (Dave Bronson), Robert Ellenstein (Fred Kenner), Celia Lovsky (Tulio's Mother).
BITS: Jon Shepodd (Alredi), Judson Taylor (Latzo), Dick Crockett (Miller), Suzanne Alexander (Joanne), Ellie Kent (Stephanie), Gloria Pall (Fitting Model), Millicent Deming, Shirley Buchanan (Announcers), Ann Carroll, Laurie Mitchell, Kathy Marlowe, Peggy O'Connor, Bonnie Bolding, Marilyn Hanold, June Tolley (Models), Madeline Darrow, Jan Darlyn, June Kirby (Models on Line), Jean Lewis (Receptionist), Joan Granville (Girl Operator), Irene Seidner (Old Lady Operator), Betsy Jones Moreland (Secretary), Dale Van Sickel (Helper), Irene King (Model), Hal Taggart, Paul Knight, Paul Weber, Donald Kirke, Paul Power (Salesmen), Archie Savage (Elevator Operator), Dorothe Kellogg, Lillian Culver, Kenneth Gibson, (Buyers), Sidney Melton (Male Operator), Bob Hopkins (Bartender), Betty Koch (High Fashion Model), Frank Marlowe (Onlooker), Diane DeLaire (Head Seamstress), George Robotham (Truck Driver).
Location: New York, New York
Filming Completed: December 20, 1956
Released: Columbia, May 22, 1957
Running Time: 88 minutes
[NOTE: Vincent Sherman replaced Aldrich as director on December 4, 1956, five days before the scheduled comple-

tion of shooting and sixteen days before the actual completion. Aldrich claims that he has never seen the finished picture and is uncertain of how much of his footage was reshot.]

Korean War veteran Alan Mitchell returns to New York to join his widowed father Walter Mitchell's dress manufacturing business. The garment industry itself is under pressure from local unions to sign shop contracts; and Alan is suspicious that this turmoil may be connected with the death of his father's partner in a fall down an elevator shaft.

Alan is somewhat alienated by his father's adamance at keeping out the union and his long-term liaison with a young buyer, Lee Hackett. Eventually Alan learns that Walter has been paying protection money to a small union-busting syndicate run by Artie Ravidge. Alan decides to go to the union to get their side of the issue and, if possible, more information about Artie Ravidge's mob. There he meets Tulio Renata and his wife, Theresa. Tulio's arguments for unionization are fully as emotional as Walter Mitchell's are against it; Tulio appeals to Alan's liberalism to break with his father and help them organize the Mitchell employees. Alan decides to try and convince his father to unionize or, at least, break with Ravidge. Walter, believing he can control his hired thugs, still refuses and passes on information from his discussion with Alan to Ravidge. The result is Tulio's brutal murder in a dark alley near his home. This radicalizes Alan to the point where he promises to get evidence to connect Ravidge (and possibly his father) with the crime. Walter, shocked by Ravidge's violence, attempts to disconnect himself from the mobster. This leads only to his own murder at the hands of Ravidge's men. Alan, who has already assumed some responsibility for Theresa and her child, now finds himself head of the Mitchell firm but still unable to implicate Ravidge. Freed from the promise of secrecy by Walter's death, Lee admits to Alan that she has his father's record of payoffs to Ravidge. While that material is taken to the district attorney, Alan goes to vent his anger and frustration in a physical confrontation with Ravidge. His fight is broken up by the arrival of Theresa with the police who arrest the beaten Ravidge.

Made near the end of the noir cycle, *The Garment Jungle* combines the traditional character of the weary veteran with Robert Aldrich's precise visualization of the noir viewpoint. At the beginning of the film, Alan Mitchell is an uncertain and ineffective figure, bullied in turn by his father, his father's hired thug, and Renata, the union organizer. Renata draws Mitchell out of the semi-insular world of Roxton Fashions, where sustained camera and full light create an aura of stability, into a darker universe. As Mitchell is both fascinated and repelled by Renata's revelations, Aldrich alters his composition to include more low angles punctuated by top-light and side-light that cast irresolute shadows on the protagonist's faces. Renata also exposes Michell to the ire of Artie Ravidge, who with his even white teeth flashing from a pock-marked face personifies the menace of the noir underworld. This cliched, quasi-satirical characterization satisfies the expectations of Mitchell's liberal sensibilities; it also suggests that Ravidge, who keeps people at a distance with the tip of a burning cigarette, may be more effete and assailable than he appears.

The conflicting forces at work in the narrative are underscored by a variety of stylistic devices, including Aldrich's favorite metaphor for subsurface chaos: the ceiling fan. As Ravidge's hoods close in on a union official, a low angle medium shot reveals a web of twisting shadows from such a fan thrown on all the surrounding walls. As the distracting shadows and odd angles visually inject instability, the actuality of Ravidge's violence sustains it on a narrative level. The murders of Renata and Walter Mitchell, like the image of the black elevator shaft down which the elder Mitchell's partner plummets at the film's beginning, evoke the ever-present threat of annihilation with a shuddering simplicity. The final sequence in which Alan Mitchell physically defeats Ravidge offers some reduction of that threat. But Mitchell himself is quickly subsumed by the demands of the business and, perhaps in existential terms, is annihilated by it almost as thoroughly as he might have been by Ravidge. The film ends, sardonically, on a shot of a Roxton Fashions operator as she mechanically switches lines and informs callers that "Mr. Mitchell is busy."

—A.S.

GILDA (1946)

Director: Charles Vidor
Producer: Virginia Van Upp (Columbia)
Screenplay: Marion Parsonnet, adapted by Jo Eisinger; from an original story by E.A. Ellington
Director of Photography: Rudolph Maté
Sound: Lambert Day
Music Director: Morris Stoloff
Songs: "Put the Blame on Mame" and "Amado Mio" by Doris Fisher and Allan Roberts
Orchestration: Marlin Skiles
Art Directors: Stephen Goosson, Van Nest Polglase
Set Decoration: Robert Priestly
Costumes: Jean Louis
Makeup: Clay Campbell
Hairstyles: Helen Hunt
Producer's Assistant: Norman Deming
Assistant Director: Art Black
Film Editor: Charles Nelson

CAST: Rita Hayworth (Gilda), Glenn Ford (Johnny Farrell), George Macready (Ballin Mundson), Joseph Calleia (Obregon), Steven Geray (Uncle Pio), Joe Sawyer (Casey), Gerald Mohr (Capt. Delgado), Robert Scott (Gabe Evans), Lionel Royce (German Agent), S.Z. Martel (Little Man).

Released: Columbia, May 15, 1946
Running Time: 110 minutes

Johnny Farrell is a down-on-his-luck gambler; but his loaded dice change his whole situation as he cleans out all the customers of a Buenos Aires waterfront dive. Johnny is rescued from a thug who tries to rob him of his winnings by the owner, Ballin Mundson, who wields a cane and dagger in Johnny's defense. He then hires Johnny as manager of his casino. All is well until Mundson returns from a trip with his beautiful new wife, Gilda. Johnny is surprised that Mundson would marry without telling him, and there is tension between Gilda and Johnny because they were once lovers. Mundson discovers their past romance and jealously plots to use one against the other, as a method of insuring his control over each. Mundson gives Johnny the unpleasant responsibility of spying on the recklessly amorous Gilda, who resents both Mundson and Johnny for their treatment of her. She later creates a sensation in Mundson's nightclub by performing a strip tease to the song "Put the Blame on Mame." She frequently taunts Johnny and attempts to get him in trouble with Mundson, since Johnny refuses to betray his friend by having an affair with Gilda. Mundson, now fronting for an international Nazi-controlled cartel, gets into a fight and kills a man. He rushes home and, finding Johnny struggling with a drunken Gilda, assumes they have renewed their affair. Mundson boards an escape plane, which crashes in the ocean immediately after takeoff. Believing Mundson dead, Johnny is very upset; but Gilda tells Johnny she is glad because she loves him. He marries her planning to punish her for cheating on her husband, his best friend. Gilda flees this horrible relationship and finds a job singing, but Johnny uses his money and resources to have her brought back. Gilda and Johnny finally realize they are in love; but Ballin reappears and tries to resume the old arrangement. He is shot by an aging janitor, who was Gilda's only friend at the nightclub; and Johnny and Gilda remain together.

The friendship between Ballin Mundson and Johnny Farrell is remarkable for its lack of self-consciousness in the face of its overt pathological aspects. No mere boss-henchman duo, they promise to be loyal and not to let others strain this sacred bond. The question of sexuality is completely suppressed, whether toward one another or toward women. It is Johnny's blind devotion to Mundson and his unhealthy, exclusive affection for the older man that cause Johnny not only to be jealous of Gilda but eventually to try to destroy her, a woman he had once loved. Johnny's aggressive behavior toward Gilda can be seen as symptomatic of his pain over compounded rejections. Originally Gilda rejected Johnny, then Mundson displaced Johnny with Gilda. Finally, Gilda commits the ultimate sin by rejecting Johnny's beloved friend Mundson and shaming him in public. When Johnny eventually has the opportunity to marry Gilda, his feelings toward her are so complex that he cannot return to the simple love he had for her before he ever knew Ballin. Indeed, Johnny seems to be punishing

THE GLASS KEY

Gilda both for loving and for leaving Mundson. *Gilda* presents a highly unusual picture of a woman who clearly realizes that she is used and abused by the men in her life. Her insight into the relationship between Mundson and Johnny may falter at times, but her knowledge of her own terrible position is all too clear. Having married Mundson as an easy out from a hard life, she believes that loving Johnny is a chance to mend her sterile emotional condition and salvage some good from a generally unhappy past. When both men clearly demonstrate her status is that of an object, Gilda turns to the only defense she has: revenge and sexual humiliation. The lyrics of the song "Put the Blame on Mame" are more to the point than any of the dialogue in the film, as Gilda sings about a woman who knows exactly what a threat she is to men and how unfair that image is. Hayworth is constumed and photographed in this film to give her portrayal of Gilda an unusual combination of sensuality and sophistication and, at the same time, the air of a vulnerable adolescent. Tightly fitted dresses emphasize her figure and full loose hairstyles frequently hide her face and occasionally give her a shy demeanor. Even makeup and soft lighting, especially in close-ups toward the end of the film, combine to lend an air of perhaps unwarranted youth and innocence to her character.

—E.M.

THE GLASS KEY (1942)

Director: Stuart Heisler
Executive Producer: B. G. DeSylva (Paramount)
Associate Producer: Fred Kohlmar
Screenplay: Jonathan Latimer; from the novel by Dashiell Hammett
Director of Photography: Theodor Sparkuhl
Music: Victor Young
Art Directors: Hans Dreier, Haldane Douglas
Assistant Director: Arthur Black
Film Editor: Archie Marshek

CAST: Brian Donlevy (Paul Madvig), Veronica Lake (Janet Henry), Alan Ladd (Ed Beaumont), Bonita Granville (Opal Madvig), Joseph Calleia (Nick Varna), Richard Denning (Taylor Henry), Moroni Olsen (Senator Henry), William Bendix (Jeff), Margaret Hayes (Eloise Matthews), Arthur Loft (Clyde Matthews), George Meader (Tuttle), Eddie Marr (Rusty), Frances Gifford (Nurse), Joe McGuinn (Lynch), Frank Hagney (Groggins), Joseph King (Fisher).
Filming Completed: March 30, 1942
Released: Paramount, October 15, 1942
Running Time: 85 minutes

Ed Beaumont, whom political boss Paul Madvig took from the gutter to become his chief aide, is quite loyal to his boss but is opposed to Madvig's decision to support Senator

Henry's "reform" ticket in the upcoming election. Ed believes that the senator and his beautiful daughter, Janet, to whom Paul is engaged, are simply using Madvig. Moreover, the reform platform calls for the elimination of vice and gambling, which will arouse the enmity of local racketeer Nick Varna. Senator Henry's wastrel son Taylor, who has been having an affair with Opal Madvig, Paul's sister, is killed. Paul is implicated; but he refuses to do anything to clear his name despite a series of accusatory letters sent to District Attorney Farr. Parting company from Paul, Ed pretends to work for Varna, to foil the gangster's plans to set Paul up for murder. When discovered, Ed is held captive and beaten unmercifully by Varna's sadistic henchman, Jeff. Though badly injured, Ed escapes and gets word to Paul of Varna's plans. Janet is romantically drawn to Ed, but he rejects her because of his loyalty to Paul. Leaving his sick bed, Ed uncovers another plan of Varna's to have newspaper publisher Matthews print Opal's accusations that her brother is Taylor's murderer. Matthews commits suicide and Ed destroys his holographic will, which appoints Varna executor. Ed does this so that Paul can appoint another executor and prevent the paper from falling into the racketeer's hands. Ed then discovers that it is Janet who is writing the letters and who believes that Paul is guilty. Guessing the identity of the real killer, Ed has the police arrest Janet for murder. The arrest leads Senator Henry to confess that he accidentally killed his son when they fought outside the Henry mansion and that Paul, a witness, covered up for the senator. Later, when Paul discovers that Janet and Ed "got it bad for each other," he removes his engagement ring from Janet's finger and gives them his blessing.

The Maltese Falcon excepted, the 1942 version of *the Glass Key* remains the best adaptation of a Hammett story, although the film lacks the powerful ending of the original novel. Alan Ladd's stoic portrayal makes Beaumont even more of a cipher than in the novel; and aside from the film's insistence on his inherent loyalty to Madvig, Beaumont's character in the film is considerably more amoral than in the novel. He encourages Mrs. Matthews to respond to him sexually, which leads directly to her husband's suicide; and then he callously steals Matthews's will. He stands idly by while Jeff strangles Varna, whereas in the book he tells Jeff he wants no part of a killing. Finally, he is even willing to sacrifice Janet to get a confession, proclaiming to the police, "I was getting worried—afraid we'd have to hang the girl to make the old man crack." Most memorable, however, are the scenes between Bendix and Ladd. Bendix, playing Jeff, emphasizes his vulgarity by spitting on the floor and stuffing his mouth with food; and his relationship with Beaumont has more than just a tinge of the homoerotic: he fondles Beaumont, calls him "sweetheart" and "baby", and enjoys beating him almost literally to death. Although Beaumont's masochism is deemphasized from the novel by eliminating his suicide attempt and alcoholism, there exists a brutal, almost symbiotic link between the two men. Sparkuhl's low-key photography is an evocative change from the full-lit 1935 version of *The Glass Key*, as is former pulp writer Latimer's catalogue of "tough" lines such as "He trow'd another Joe," "We got to give him the works," or the oft-repeated "Gimme the roscoe."

—B.P.

rich's original atmosphere of suspense remain. This is particularly true of the surprise finale in which the apparently innocent protagonist, Mike, turns out to be the guilty party. This ironic reversal is both a Woolrich trademark and typical of the noir cycle.

—B.P.

THE GUILTY (1947)

Director: John Reinhardt
Producer: Jack Wrather (Monogram)
Associate Producer: James C. Jordan
Screenplay: Robert R. Presnell, Sr.; from the short story "Two Men in a Furnished Room" by Cornell Woolrich
Director of Photography: Henry Sharp
Sound: J.T. Corrigan
Music: Rudy Schrager
Music Director: David Chudnow
Art Director: Oscar Yerge
Production Manager: Ben Berk
Assistant Director: William Forsyth
Film Editor: Jodie Caplan

CAST: Bonita Granville (Estelle Mitchell/Linda Mitchell), Don Castle (Mike Carr), Wally Carsell (Johnny Dixon), Regis Toomey (Detective Heller), John Litel (Alex Tremholt), Ruth Robinson (Mrs. Mitchell), Thomas Jackson (Tim McGinnis), Oliver Blake (Jake), Caroline Andrews (The Whistler).
Filming Completed: November 27, 1946
Released: Monogram, March 22, 1947
Running Time: 71 minutes

Mike Carr returns to his old neighborhood, attracted by Estelle Mitchell whom he has been trying to forget. While waiting for her he tells a bartender the story of why he left the area a year ago: Linda, Estelle's twin sister, disappeared after leaving Johnny Dixon's apartment. The girls' mother called the police, and Detective Heller found Linda's body stuffed into an incinerator. Evidence pointed to Dixon, who escaped. Later, based on facts uncovered by Mike, the police arrested Alex Tremholt, who murdered Linda, because he believed she was the perfidious Estelle, whom he loved. Finishing the story, Mike greets Estelle and kissing her, he discovers she no longer exerts the same charm. Leaving the bar, Mike goes to the scene of the crime, where he is arrested on newly discovered evidence, which indicates that he killed Linda because he also thought she was the faithless Estelle. He had done so because she had threatened to break up Mike's romance with Linda, which occurred before Mike's involvement with Estelle.

The Guilty is based upon a short story by Cornell Woolrich, whose convoluted plot requires more than the low-budget treatment it is given here to be convincing. Despite poor acting and unimaginative photography, vestiges of Wool-

GUILTY BYSTANDER (1950)

Director: Joseph Lerner
Executive Producer: Edmund L. Dorfman (Laurel Films and Edmund L. Dorfman)
Producer: Rex Carlton
Associate Producer: Peter Mayer
Screenplay: Don Ettlinger; from the novel by Wade Miller
Director of Photography: Gerald Hirschfeld
Sound: James Shields
Music Score: Dimitri Tiomkin
Production Designer: Leo Kerz
Makeup: Ira Senz
Production Manager: Jack Aichele
Assistant Director: James DiGangi
Film Editor: Geraldine Lerner

CAST: Zachary Scott (Max Thursday), Faye Emerson (Georgia), Mary Boland (Smitty), Sam Levene (Capt. Tonetti), J. Edward Bromberg (Varkas), Kay Medford (Angel), Jed Prouty (Dr. Elder), Harry Landers (Bert), Dennis Harrison (Mace), Elliot Sullivan (Stitch), Garney Wilson (Harvey), Ray Julian (Johnny).
Location: New York, New York
Filming Completed: 1949
Released: Film Classics, April 21, 1950
Running Time: 92 minutes

Max Thursday is a former police detective who was discharged for alcoholism, after repeated newspaper criticisms of him during a tough case. He is now the house detective for the tawdry Bridgeport Hotel. His lovely ex-wife Georgia enters his bare, unkempt room and wakes him from a drunken stupor to ask his help in finding their son, who has been kidnapped. The boy was taken by her brother, Fred Mace, while on an errand for Dr. Elder to whom Mace was financially indebted. Thursday, shaky but sober, decides to visit Elder's office. Elder is waiting to meet him with a mysterious person known as St. Paul and, after plying Thursday with liquor, knocks him out. Thursday wakens in the police station to learn from his old friend Capt. Tonetti that Elder has been murdered and that Max could easily be charged with the crime, but Georgia has provided Max's alibi. He returns to his hotel and asks its proprietress, Smitty, a woman who is intimate with underworld circles, if she knows a man named Varkas, who is associated with Elder. Varkas is a smuggler with offices in a Brooklyn warehouse. Thursday is surprised when he meets

Max Thursday (Zachary Scott) and Smitty (Mary Boland) in Guilty Bystander.

Varkas to learn that he is also seeking St. Paul. Stopping at a bar frequented by Mace's sadistic girl friend, Angel, Thursday is told by her that Mace was supposed to pick up smuggled jewelry for Elder; but that he kept the contraband for himself and she is hiding him. On the way to Angel's apartment, Thursday is waylaid by Varkas's henchmen and Mace disappears. Thursday is wounded and ready to admit defeat; but, when he discovers that Varkas and his hoodlums are dead, he discovers a clue. Returning to the Bridgeport Hotel, Thursday knows that the mysterious St. Paul is actually Smitty, and he forces her to lead him to Mace, who reveals where Thursday's son is hidden. Ignoring Smitty's offers to share her ill-gotten gains with him, Thursday turns her over to the police. He finds his son and, together with Georgia, walks away from his corrupt surroundings to start his life over.

Guilty Bystander is marred by budget limitations that lead to an overreliance on verbal exposition, a device that fails to mask an extremely contrived plot and a great deal of uninteresting photography despite the use of New York locations. Its redeeming aspect is that, heightened by the use of locale, *Guilty Bystander* is able to portray a world populated by losers. Scott's Max Thursday is the bottom-of-the-line private detective, an alcoholic who is forced into action but keeps returning to the bottle. The hypochondriac Varkas is portrayed by heavy-lidded Bromberg in properly oblique fashion. Finally, Mary Boland, grown fat and gross,

brings pathos to her portrayal of the principal villain, Smitty, who double-crossed the smugglers so that she might live out her old age in comfort.

—B.P.

GUN CRAZY (1950)
[Original Release Title: DEADLY IS THE FEMALE]

Director: Joseph H. Lewis
Producer: Frank and Maurice King (King Brothers)
Screenplay: MacKinlay Kantor and Millard Kaufman: from the *Saturday Evening Post* story "Gun Crazy" by Mackinlay Kantor [Uncredited: Dalton Trumbo]
Director of Photography: Russell Harlan
Sound: Tom Lambert
Music: Victor Young
Orchestration: Leo Shuken, Sidney Cutner
Music Editor: Stuart S. Frye
Production Designer: Gordon Wiles
Set Decoration: Raymond Boltz, Jr.
Costumes: Norma for Peggy Cummins
Production Assistant: Arthur Gardner
Assistant Director: Frank Heath
Film Editor: Harry Gerstad

CAST: Peggy Cummins (Annie Laurie Starr), John Dall (Bart Tare), Berry Kroeger (Packett), Morris Carnovsky (Judge Willoughby), Anabel Shaw (Ruby Tare), Harry Lewis (Clyde Boston), Nedrick Young (Dave Allister), Trevor Bardette (Sheriff Boston), Mickey Little (Bart Tare, Age 7), Rusty Tamblyn (Bart Tare, Age 14), Paul Frison (Clyde Boston, Age 14), Dave Bair (Dave Allister, Age 14), Stanley Prager (Bluey-Bluey), Virginia Farmer (Miss Wynn), Anne O'Neal (Miss Sifert), Frances Irwin (Danceland Singer), Don Beddoe (Man from Chicago), Robert Osterloh (Hampton Policeman), Shimen Ruskin (Taxi Driver), Harry Hayden (Mr. Mallenberg).

Filming Completed: July 1949

Released: United Artists, as *Deadly Is The Female* on January 26, 1950; rereleased as *Gun Crazy* on August 24, 1950

Running Time: 87 minutes

A young man's fascination with weapons leads him to feel important only when he is using a gun. After spending his youth in a corrective institution and taking a tour of duty in the army, Bart Tare returns to his home town. He accompanies two old friends to a carnival, where he is fascinated by the sideshow "Annie Oakley," Annie Laurie Starr. When she challenges someone from the audience to shoot against her onstage, Bart accepts and wins. His ability impresses Packett, the sideshow owner, and Bart is hired to join the act. After a few weeks on tour, Bart and Annie Laurie's affair leads to intimacy. At this point, they are fired by Packett, whose interest in Annie Laurie has been thwarted by Bart. As their money runs out, their life style degenerates, until Annie Laurie convinces Bart to stage a holdup, and the couple become outlaws. They quickly graduate from filling stations and liquor stores to banks, and their notoriety increases proportionally. Although Bart is an expert marksman, he abhors the thought of murder; but Annie Laurie thrives on violence, and Bart's sexual fascination with her carries him through a variety of violent crimes.

After several months of robberies and flight through the U.S. Southwest, the couple arrive in California where they plan one big job to be followed by a flight across the border to Mexico. They take jobs in a meat-packing plant and plan meticulously; but their attempt to steal a large payroll is

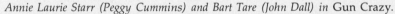

Annie Laurie Starr (Peggy Cummins) and Bart Tare (John Dall) in Gun Crazy.

marred when Annie Laurie kills two employees. Cut off by the police from crossing the border but unwilling to go underground separately, the couple return to Bart's home town. Bart is unable to find sanctuary with his family, and his boyhood friends, now sheriff's deputies come to arrest him and Annie Laurie. Bart takes her and flees on foot across nearby mountains. As night falls and their pursuers close in, Bart is torn between his loyalty to his wife and his desire to keep his boyhood memories pure and unaffected by his criminal activities. In a futile gesture, Bart shoots Annie Laurie before they are cut down by police bullets. Their bodies fall together in a final, lifeless embrace.

Although it may still be often referred to as a forerunner of *Bonnie And Clyde,* the prototypical noir style, grim narrative, and pervasive aura of eroticism in *Gun Crazy* have given it a growing reputation as a key film of the noir cycle. The narrative core—the fugitive couple—is a concept found in the earliest of noir films; but whereas the doomed love of Jo and Eddie in the early *You Only Live Once* or of Bowie and Keechie in the more contemporary *They Live By Night* have an asexual serenity that almost permits their salvation, the atavistic, precipitous *amour fou* of Annie Laurie Starr and Bart Tare in *Gun Crazy* is the root cause of their destruction. Moreover, while Lang and Ray underplay both the sexuality and violence of their lovers, *Gun Crazy* contains no scenes of domesticity to belie the couple's basic lawlessness. For Joseph H. Lewis in *Gun Crazy*, sex and violence are the major motifs of the noir universe. This attitude, evident later in his *The Big Combo*, not only contrasts with the perspectives of Lang and Ray but also anticipates and, to some degree, goes beyond the similar aspect of Penn's more modern *Bonnie and Clyde*. When Clyde first shows Bonnie his gun in Penn's film, she expresses her arousal by fondling the barrel. Such an action seems understated next to Bart's initial encounter with Annie Laurie in the sideshow. Lewis's introductory shot is taken from an emphatic low angle as she strides into frame wearing a cowgirl costume and firing two pistols above her head. Bart accepts the challenge to his shooting skill and, figuratively, to his masculinity, and the two square off onstage. The winner of the exhibition will be the one who can light the most matches worn in a crown on the opponent's head by grazing them with .45 caliber bullets. Lewis ends the sequence with an exchange of glances between the two: Annie Laurie smiling encouragingly; Bart, the victor with his potency amply established, grinning from ear to ear.

At this point, the relationship of Annie Laurie and Bart is one of the most purely sexual in film noir. He abandons his friends and family to join her in the sideshow. She denies further sexual favors to Packett, the owner, which ultimately leads to their being fired. Despite Bart's fascination with guns, it is Annie Laurie who must initiate their criminal activity. When they have run out of money, she sexually blackmails him to prevent him from pawning his collection of sidearms. She also argues that they could earn more by staging their shooting exhibitions in banks rather than carnival tents. When he hesitates, she sits down on the edge of a broken-down motel bed, demurely slips on her stockings, and threatens to leave him unless he agrees.

Lewis's choice of rural rather than an urban locale for most of the action supports the narrative concept of obsessive and destructive sexuality Isolated in small towns or hiding out in country motels, Annie and Bart have nothing to distract them from themselves and their lack of prospects. Alternately, Lewis recruits familiar icons such as automobiles, guns, clothes (Annie favors berets and tight sweaters when not in her cowgirl regalia), and in the early sequences the sights and sounds of the carnival to create an underlying sense of ostracism and decay. When they drive into Hampton to rob the local bank during a Western festival, they dress in Western shirts and Stetsons to make themselves seem a part of it; but the inescapable visual metaphor is that their primitive *amour fou* is as anachronistic as their garb, part of an earlier, lawless era.

In that same sequence, Lewis uses a single long take to underscore the equation of sex and violence at a stylistic level. The camera mounted in the backseat of their car begins by recording their nervousness and anxiety, like teenagers on their first date, on the outskirts of town. Their excitement mounts as they approach the savings and loan building: with Annie Laurie behind the wheel, they worry over whether things will go as planned, whether there will even be a place to park in front of the building. During the actual robbery, the camera remains in the car with Annie and only pans over to the sidewalk when she must slip out to distract a passing policeman by admiring his revolver. When Bart emerges, she clubs the policeman with her gun. Even after this climactic moment, the single shot and its visual tension are maintained as their vehicle races out of town. Annie Laurie glances back, short of breath, at the camera, while leaning toward Bart as if to embrace him, and sees that they are not being followed. Lewis ends the sequence and the shot by fading out on her look, secure, gratified, and now smiling lasciviously as she did when Bart won the shooting contest.

Lewis's staging of a violent crime as if it were a sexual act is not unique in film noir; but his consistent stylization of *Gun Crazy* in those terms inbues the sexuality of Annie Laurie and Bart with a desperation and fatality that defines the noir vision. Moreover, Lewis gives his characters a greater self-consciousness of their *amour fou* than the fugitive couples of *You Only Live Once, They Drive By Night,* and even *Bonnie and Clyde*. It is lingering beneath the surface when, as Packett observes to Annie Laurie, they first look at each other "like wild animals." Bart, in particular, once he has been initiated into the sexual thrill of violence by Annie Laurie, seems existentially aware of his position and the consequences of his choice. He replies fatalistically to her suggestion, at one point, that they split up because she is destroying him by observing with a most appropriate simile that they cannot separate because "we go together…like guns and ammunition." That statement characterizes both the explosive and fateful qualities of their relationship: they are made for each other but only in the context of violence and death. That awareness also leads Lewis's couple—

unlike Ray's Bowie and Keechie, innocents who move slowly from platonic interdependence to sexual experience—from an initial, chance encounter and simple sexual attraction to a final position of self-destructive romanticism. Perhaps the most telling sequence is the wordless one after Annie Laurie has convinced Bart to take a separate route for a while and rejoin her later. After he drives her to where a second car is waiting, they start off in opposite directions. Abruptly and at the same instant, the cars veer around as if irresistibly drawn back together and almost collide. In that sequence, the machines express what their drivers have understood but never fully verbalized.

The expressionistic conclusion of *Gun Crazy* with the couple pursued across country by Bart's former friends recapitulates the irrational, noir quality of *amour fou*. Bart's return to the locus of his childhood and the nascency of his "gun-craziness" may be either a search for the causes of his impending annihilation or a flagrant display to his childhood friends of his sociopathic freedom (for both). In any case, the stylized setting and the ritual of the fugitive couple's death, fallen together in the foggy marshland, add an unusual, quasi-operatic final note to their *amour fou*. Both the "gun-craziness" and the "mad love" of the protagonists are typical of the noir world; yet no other film integrates these concepts as fully on a variety of levels as *Gun Crazy*. The viewer would have understood from convention the inevitable result of Annie Laurie and Bart's passion even if Lewis had left them standing in each other's arms between their idling cars in the middle of the highway. The actual ending, with its drastic shift in *mise-en-scène*, reminiscent of *You Only Live Once*, becomes almost an afterstatement, a detached affirmation of *amour fou*'s necessary death.

—A.S. & C.M.

THE HARDER THEY FALL (1956)

Director: Mark Robson
Producer: Philip Yordan (Columbia)
Screenplay: Philip Yordan; from the novel by Budd Schulberg
Director of Photography: Burnett Guffey
Sound: Lambert Day, John Livadary
Music: Hugo Friedhofer
Music Director: Lionel Newman
Orchestration: Arthur Morton
Art Director: William Flannery
Set Decoration: William Kiernan, Alfred E. Spencer
Makeup: Clay Campbell
Hairstyles: Helen Hunt
Technical Director: John Indrisano
Assistant Director: Milton Feldman
Film Editor: Jerome Thoms

CAST: Humphrey Bogart (Eddie Willis), Rod Steiger (Nick Benko), Jan Sterling (Beth Willis), Mike Lane (Toro Moreno), Max Baer, Sr. (Buddy Brannen), Jersey Joe Walcott (George), Edward Andrews (Jim Weyerhause), Harold J. Stone (Art Leavitt), Carlos Montalban (Luis Agrandi), Nehemiah Persoff (Leo), Felice Orlandi (Vince Fawcett), Herbie Faye (Max), Rusty Lane (Danny McKeogh), Jack Albertson (Pop), Val Avery (Frank), Tommy Herman (Tommy), Vinnie De Carlo (Joey), Pat Comiskey (Gus Dundee), Matt Murphy (Sailor Rigazzo), Abel Fernandez (Chief Firebird), Marian Carr (Alice), Joe Greb (Ex-Fighter). **BITS:** J. Lewis Smith (Brannen's Manager), Everett Glass (Minister), William Roerick (Lawyer), Lillian Culver (Mrs. Harding), Jack Daly, Richard Norris, Don Kohler, Ralph Gamble, Charles Tannen, Mark Scott, Russ Whiteman Mort Mills, Stafford Repp, Sandy Sanders, Emily Belser (Reporters), Paul Frees (Priest), Joe Herrera, Frank Hagney (Referees), Diane Mumby, Elaine Edwards (Vince's Girl Friends), Tina Carver (Mrs. Benko), Anthony Blankley, Penny Carpenter (Nick's Children), Pat Dane (Shirley).
Filming Completed: December 29, 1955
Released: Columbia, May 9, 1956
Running Time: 108 minutes

[NOTE: The novel's screen rights were purchased by RKO for a proposed film directed by Edward Dmytryk, starring Robert Mitchum and with a screenplay by Budd Schulberg.

FACTUAL BASIS: Based on the career of Primo Carnera, an Italian who became heavyweight boxing champion. Max Baer, Sr., recreated his 1934 prizefight defeat of Carnera for the film. The interview of Joe Greb, an ex-fighter, was not scripted or rehearsed.]

HE RAN ALL THE WAY

Eddie Willis, once a well-known sports columnist, is now down on his luck. He is hired for his abilities and contacts in the sports world, by Nick Benko, the head of a fight promotion syndicate. His job is to promote the syndicate's latest acquisition, a blundering Argentinian boxer, Toro Moreno. Formidable looking and gigantic, Moreno is an inept fighter with a glass jaw. Nevertheless, Moreno wins a series of fixed bouts, arranged to give him a shot at the championship fight. Moreno is matched against the ex-champ, Gus Dundee. Dundee loses and subsequently dies of a brain hemorrhage. Thinking himself to blame, Moreno suffers great guilt. Willis informs him that all of his fights have been fixed and that the cause of Dundee's death was a beating he had taken from champ Buddy Brannen in a previous fight. Determined to fight Brannen anyway and take the prize money back home to his family in South America, Moreno is severely beaten in the ring. When Willis goes to collect Moreno's winnings from Benko, he is told that the total profit is a mere $49.07. Giving in to the disgust he has felt all along, Willis gives his $26,000 share of the profits to Moreno and puts him on a plane to Argentina. Willis then sits down to write a series of articles exposing Benko and his syndicate. Although threatened with harm, Willis is determined to outlaw boxing in the United States "if it takes an act of Congress to do it."

The Harder They Fall is an exposé or organized crime's influence in the world of professional boxing. The film's treatment of the topic and the general tone of outrage are reminiscent of the Warner Brothers' style of socially realistic motion pictures of the 1930s with their sense of immediacy.

Humphrey Bogart's presence particularly links *The Harder They Fall* with the Warner Brothers pictures of the 1930s.

Bogart is a key iconographic figure in all of film noir, since the roles he played throughout his lengthy career touched on all of the cycle's major thematic concerns. Whether as a gangster, detective, or an initially aloof figure straddling the fence, Bogart's characters were often beyond the law. One of his early Warner Brothers appearances, in *Kid Galahad*, was as a fight-fixing mobster. In *The Harder They Fall* he is an ex-sports columnist turned boxing promoter; and Bogart plays the cynical loner for the last time. It is his most popular on-screen persona and a key noir character trait. A cynic is a reformed idealist who has experienced too much pain and disillusionment to risk sticking his neck out for anyone because the fear of reactivating the old hurt is ever present. But, if action defines character then the character must act, finally, when something crucial is at stake. The name may be Rick as in *Casablanca,* or Harry Morgan in *To Have And Have Not,* but Bogart's roles eventually shed their hard shells and respond to a moral code that had been hibernating. The strong cynical edge of this film, rooted in the script by Philip Yordan, is supported by the harsh black-and-white photography and unsentimental direction and editing.

—J.B.

HE RAN ALL THE WAY (1951)

Director: John Berry
Producer: Bob Roberts (Bob Roberts Productions)
Associate Producer: Paul Trivers
Screenplay: Guy Endore and Hugo Butler; from the novel by Sam Ross [Uncredited: Dalton Trumbo]
Director of Photography: James Wong Howe
Music: Franz Waxman
Art Director: Harry Horner
Assistant Director: Emmett Emerson
Film Editor: Francis D. Lyon

CAST: John Garfield (Nick Robey), Shelley Winters (Peg Dobbs), Wallace Ford (Mr. Dobbs), Selena Royle (Mrs. Dobbs), Bobby Hyatt (Tommy Dobbs), Gladys George (Mrs. Robey), Norman Lloyd (Al Molin). **BITS:** Clancy Cooper (Stan), Keith Hetherington (Captain of Detectives), Renny McEvoy (Attendant), Dale Van Sickle (Policeman), Cameron Grant (Fat Man), James Magill (Workman), Robert Davis (Delivery Boy), Vici Raaf (Marge), John Morgan (Police Doctor), Ralph Brooks (Detective Lieutenant), Jimmy Ames (Clerk), Robert Karnes (Detective), Mark Lowell (Boy), Lucille Sewall (Mrs. Marsden).
Filming Completed: March 13, 1951
Released: United Artists, July 13, 1951
Running Time: 77 minutes

Nick Robey, a small-time thief, joins his friend Al in a payroll robbery. The thieves panic and Al and a guard are wounded. Nick runs with the money to a nearby public swimming pool where he meets Peg Dobbs. When the pool closes, he escorts Peg to her home and is introduced to her parents and younger brother. The family goes to a movie, leaving Nick and Peg at home. When the parents return, Nick thinks they have found out about him and holds them at gunpoint. The morning paper reveals that the guard that he shot died; and Nick is now wanted for murder. He holds the family hostage, alternately befriending and terrorizing them. Nick trusts only Peg, whom he gives money to buy a car so that they can both escape. When the car fails to arrive, Nick panics and turns on Peg, forcing her out of the apartment where her father stands ready to kill him. Choosing between her father and Nick, she shoots Nick just as the car he wanted pulls up.

He Ran All the Way was the first film to use the theme of a family trapped in their own home by hostile outside forces. It is similar in mood to William Wyler's *The Desperate Hours* but instead of a middle-class family being held by a trio of inarticulate and violent escaped convicts, in *He Ran All The Way* the killer and the family share the same background, which adds an interesting ambivalence to their relationship. John Garfield as Nick conveys the feeling of a wounded animal rather than a cold-blooded killer. As a man rejected by his own family, he tries to become part of the family. The film continually points out how much alike the killer and his hostages are, and how similarly they view society. In other circumstances, they might well be on the same side. Written and directed by two victims of McCarthyism, John Berry and Hugo Butler, Nick's paranoia is matched throughout the film by references to a paranoid society. The father hesitates to call the police, because, like firemen at a fire, "they chop, chop, chop."

The ambivalence between the killer and his prey makes the relationship of Nick and Peg believable. However, in the final explosive sequence when Peg must choose between her father and her lover, her moral sense leaves her no choice. She shoots the intruder to the accompaniment of Franz Waxman's cacophony, and the camera pans away to an image of desolation, the rain-splashed streets.

—J.C.

HE WALKED BY NIGHT (1949)
[Working Titles: TWENTY-NINE CLUES; THE L.A. INVESTIGATOR]

Director: Alfred Werker [Uncredited: Anthony Mann]
Producer: Robert Kane (Bryan Foy Productions)
Screenplay: John C. Higgins and Crane Wilbur, with additional dialogue by Harry Essex [and uncredited contributions from Beck Murray]; from an unpublished story by Crane Wilbur
Director of Photography: John Alton
Photographic Effects: George J. Teague
Sound: Leon S. Becker, Hugh McDowell
Music: Leonid Raab
Music Director: Irving Friedman
Art Director: Edward Ilou
Special Art Effects: Jack R. Rabin
Set Decoration: Armor Marlowe, Clarence Steenson
Makeup: Ern Westmore, Joe Stinton
Production Supervisor: James T. Vaughn
Dialogue Director: Stewart Stern
Assistant Director: Howard W. Koch
Film Editor: Alfred DeGaetano
CAST: Richard Basehart (Morgan), Scott Brady (Sgt. Marty Brennan), Roy Roberts (Capt. Breen), Whit Bissell (Reeves), Jimmy Cardwell (Chuck Jones), Jack Webb (Lee), Bob Bice (Detective Steno), Reed Hadley (Narrator). **BITS:** Chief Bradley (Chief Bradley), John McGuire (Rawlins), Lyle Latell (Sergeant), Jack Bailey (Pajama Top), Mike Dugan, Garrett Craig (Patrolmen), Bert Moorhouse, Gaylord Pendleton, Robert Williams, Doyle Manor (Detectives), Bernie Suss (Business Suspect), George Chan (Chinese Suspect), George Goodman (Fighter Suspect), Carlotta Monti (Woman), Louise Kane (Mrs. Rawlins), Kay Garrett (Doctor), Florence Stephens (Receptionist), Tom Browne Henry (Dunning), Harry Harvey (Detective Prouty), Virginia Hunter (Miss Smith), Ruth Robinson (Mrs. Rapport), John Parrish (Vitale), Earl Spainard (Kelly), Alma Beltran (Miss Montalvo), Anthony Jochim (Thompson), Paul Fierro (Mexican Detective), Jane Adams (Nurse Scanlon), John Dehner (Assistant Chief), Byron Foulger (Avery), Felice Ingersoll (Record Clerk), Wally Vernon (Postman), Dorothy Adams (Housewife), Dick Mason, Donald Kerr (Mailmen), Charles Lang (Policeman), Mary Ware (Dolores), Ann Doran (Woman Dispatcher), Harlan Warde (C.B. Officer), Kenneth Tobey (Detective), Frank Cady (Suspect), Paul Scardon (Father), Charles Meredith (Desk Sergeant), Tim Graham (Uniformed Sergeant), Jim Nolan, Rory Mallinson (Detectives), Bill Mauch, John Perri, Tom Kelly, Rex Downing (Young Men), Stan Johnson (Artist).
Location: Los Angeles, California
Filming Completed: October 8, 1948
Released: Eagle-Lion, February 6, 1949
Running Time: 79 minutes
[FACTUAL BASIS: Based on the Pasadena, California, murder of two policemen by a young staff member of the police fingerprinting department.]

Ray Morgan, alias Roy Martin, is a brilliant, technically adept young man and a thief. He kills a police officer who observed him attempting to burglarize an electronics store. Although Martin's skills at intercepting police calls, altering his appearance and changing his *modus operandi* to escape detection are considerable, the police department is determined to capture this unique killer. A composite drawing of Martin is made from various descriptions and he is traced to an electronics firm owned by Paul Reeves, to whom Martin rents out equipment he has stolen and modified. With Reeves's cooperation, the police set a trap to capture Martin there at night; but he proves too wary and, after a gun battle with the police, he flees through the flood-control district channels beneath Los Angeles. Sgt. Brennan, disguised as a milk man, locates Martin's hideout in a small Hollywood bungalow and the police surround him; but once again Roy slips out and escapes via the sewers. Police trap the criminal when an automobile that is parked over a manhole cover blocks his escape route. Even his hidden arsenal cannot save him, and Martin is hunted down and shot.

He Walked by Night may not rank among the most imaginative of the semidocumentary thrillers, but it is from it that Jack Webb drew the inspiration for the popular radio series, "Dragnet." As a result, the combination of noir and documentary styles became a major influence on the police shows of early television. All of the familiar conventions are present, including a stentorian narrator (Reed Hadley) who is accompanied by the appropriate visual montage while telling about the city of Los Angeles and its police department and announcing the case to be a true story in which "only the names" have been changed. The film catalogues small details of police work and the interior operations of the police department. This had been done before, and to greater effect, in such films as *T-Men*. Since John Alton photographed *He Walked by Night* and Anthony Mann

Marty Brennan (Scott Brady), left center, and Capt. Breen (Roy Roberts), right center, in He Walked By Night.

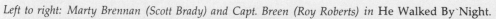

Left to right: Marty Brennan (Scott Brady) and Capt. Breen (Roy Roberts) in He Walked By Night.

directed a good deal of it uncredited, it is quite likely that they are responsible for its strongest qualities. Plot deficiencies and a lack of character development are the film's most obvious shortcomings, although the police are not made to appear as heroic as they might in contrast to the police shows currently on television. The character with the most appeal is Roy Martin, subtly enacted by a young Richard Basehart, who takes Martin's shallowness and makes it compelling. Basehart's Roy Martin becomes the epitome of the "underground man." Misanthropic, lonely, and friendly only to a small dog (which compares to the fondness for cats expressed by the killer in *This Gun for Hire*), Martin is a scientific wizard who almost matches the resources of the entire police department. The scenes of him alone at night with his dog, operating on himself to extract a bullet, or nocturnally roaming the sewers, characterize the completely alienated noir protagonist.

—B.P.

HELL'S ISLAND (1955)
[Working Titles: THE RUBY VIRGIN; LOVE IS A WEAPON]

Director: Phil Karlson
Producers: William H. Pine, William C. Thomas (Pine-Thomas Productions)
Screenplay: Maxwell Shane; from an unpublished story by Jack Leonard and Martin M. Goldsmith
Director of Photography: Lionel Lindon [Technicolor, Vista-Vision;]
Technicolor Consultant: Richard Mueller
Sound: Harry Lindgren, Gene Garvin
Music Supervisor: Irvin Talbot
Art Directors: Hal Pereira, Al Y. Roelofs
Film Editor: Archie Marshek

CAST: John Payne (Mike Cormack), Mary Murphy (Janet Martin), Francis L. Sullivan (Barzland), Arnold Moss (Paul Armand), Paul Picerni (Eduardo Martin), Eduardo Noriega (Inspector Pena), Walter Reed (Lawrence), Sandor Szabo (Torbig), Robert Cabal (Miguel).
Released: Paramount, May 6, 1955
Running Time: 83 minutes

Mike Cormack is a former district attorney who, after losing his job because of drinking, is employed as a bouncer in a Las Vegas casino. There he is approached by Barzland, a wheel-chair bound "financier" of questionable reputation, and offered $5,000 to recover a missing ruby, which was possibly lost in a plane that crashed while en route from the Caribbean. After he accepts, Cormack learns that he was solicited because his former fiancèe, Janet Martin, is now married to the man suspected of sabotaging the plane carrying the ruby. Although she had left him desolate, Janet greets Cormack warmly and asks for his help in clearing her husband of murder charges. Cormack agrees; but, after being beaten by Barzland's henchmen and detained by the local police, he learns that Janet has been abducted and taken to Hell's Island. Despite the warnings of a police inspector, Cormack attempts to rescue her. Succeeding, he discovers that Janet was responsible for the plane crash in hopes of killing her husband for his insurance, after she stole the ruby. When Barzland and his men realize this, Cormack kills them in self-defense and then turns Janet over to the authorities.

Hell's Island comes near the end of the noir cycle, after numerous other noir and related films featuring its star John Payne, including *99 River Street* and *Kansas City Confidential*, which were also directed by Phil Karlson. By the time of *Hell's Island*, Payne's world-weariness has become symptomatic of the movement and his particular unsmiling and fatigued expression has become something of a noir icon. Payne's portrayal of Cormack, like that of Ernie Driscoll, the fallen prizefighter in *99 River Street*, develops from that of a defeated and hopeless figure to someone tenaciously clinging to a second chance. As he moves, shoulders slumped, first out of place in a tuxedo among the casino patrons and then framed alone against the visually idyllic tropical backgrounds, Cormack carried with him the resilience of one who knows he cannot be beaten down any further. Because Janet Martin represents not merely a lost woman but, in the sexual transference of the film noir, lost self-esteem, Cormack willingly endures both bodily injury and emotional humiliation to win her back. By developing the narrative as a flashback from Cormack on an operating table, Karlson permits the first-person narration to become heavily ironic. As Cormack dispassionately recalls the events leading to Janet's arrest, he is also chronicling his own blindness to her true nature, which caused him to be deceived a second time. As such, the entire narrative becomes a compelling confession of human weakness. His record of mental suffering and the graphic depiction of physical punishment become purgative rituals by which Cormack ultimately restores his own being.

—A.S.

HICKEY & BOGGS (1972)

Director: Robert Culp
Executive Producer: Richard L. O'Connor (Film Guarantors)
Producer: Fouad Said
Associate Producer: Joel Reisner
Screenplay: Walter Hill
Director of Photography: Wilmer Butler
Assistant Cameramen: Earl Clark, Eddie Rio, Jr.
Special Effects: Joe Lombardi
Second Unit Photography: Rex Hosea
Sound: Gene Cantamessa
Music: Ted Ashford
Costumes: Bill Thiese, Pauline Campbell

HICKEY & BOGGS

Production Manager: Elliot Schick
Assistant Director: Edward Teets
Script Supervisor: Hope Williams
Film Editor: David Berlatsky

CAST: Bill Cosby (Al Hickey), Robert Culp (Frank Boggs), Rosaland Cash (Nyona), Sheila Sullivan (Edith Boggs), Isabel Sanford (Nyona's Mother), Ta-Ronce Allen (Nyona's Daughter), Lou Frizzell (Lawyer), Nancy Howard (Apartment Manager's Wife), Bernard Nedell (Used Car Salesman), Carmen (Mary Jane), Louis Moreno (Quemando, Prisoner), Ron Henriquez (Quemando, Florist), Cary Sanchez (Mary Jane's Daughter), Jason Culp (Mary Jane's Son), Robert Mandan (Mr. Brill), Michael Moriarty (Ballard), Bernie Schwartz (Bernie), Denise Renfro (Brill's Daughter), Bill Hickman (Monte), Matt Bennett (Fatboy), Tommy Signorelli (Nick), Gerald Peters (Jack), Keri Shuttleton, Wanda Spell, Winston Spell (Playground Kids), Vincent Gardenia (Papadakis), Jack Colvin (Shaw), James Woods (Lt. Wyatt), Ed Lauter (Ted), Joe Tata (Coroner's Assistant), Lester Fletcher (Rice), Gil Stuart (Farrow), Sil Words (Mr. Leroy), Jerry Summers (Bledsoe), Dean Smith (Bagman).
Location: Los Angeles, California
Filming Completed: October 1, 1971
Released: United Artists, October 4, 1972
Running Time: 111 minutes
MPAA Rating: PG

Impoverished private detectives Al Hickey and Frank Boggs are hired for $200 a day by an effeminate lawyer named Rice to locate his girl friend, Mary Jane. Rice gives them a list of people to contact about her whereabouts, but each one is soon killed. The police become suspicious of Hickey and Boggs, and Rice disappears after paying off the two. Hickey and Boggs discover that Mary Jane is married to one of the Quemando brothers, who are Chicano radicals currently in prison. The woman is holding onto $400,000 stolen from a Pittsburgh bank in a heist designed by Mr. Brill, a syndicate chieftain, and is sending sample $1,000 bills to those interested in purchasing the stolen money from her. Hickey and Boggs decide to retrieve the stolen money and collect the $25,000 reward. They interrupt a meeting between Mary Jane and her buyers at the Los Angeles Coliseum and save the woman's life; but she escapes with the money. The detectives are warned off the case by all involved, including Rice, who actually works for Leroy, the head of a black power organization. But when Hickey's estranged wife is brutally murdered by Brill's henchmen, the detectives pursue the killers and the stolen money with a vengeance. Ultimately, they force the recently released Quemando to lead them to the beach where he and Mary Jane have set up Leroy for the syndicate. Brill and his mobsters arrive in a helicopter and battle fiercely with Leroy's guerrilla organization. Hickey and Boggs are the sole survivors as the sun sets over the ocean.

Film noir has often used the character of a private detective to illustrate the alienated and obsessive nature of postwar America. These detectives become involved in dangerous situations that they feel compelled to control and change, reestablishing morality in a world that appears to ignore it. While the detectives of *Hickey and Boggs* share the independent spirit of their earlier counterparts, they differ in the extent to which they can control their situation. Through ten years, the film noir protagonist has steadily lost ability to effect change in a modern world, and this increasing powerlessness is a correlative of diminishing social morality. This powerlessness is expressed by Frank Boggs several times in the film when he says, "I gotta get a bigger gun. I can't hit anything." His revolvers, small and large—trademarks of his profession and, therefore, symbols of his personal power—are nothing compared to the modern arsenal possessed by the gangsters and the political guerrillas, who annihilate each other with carbines and Browning automatic rifles at the film's climax. Hickey and Boggs are too small, too unimportant, to control anything; and even the film's plot only marginally involves them. Nonetheless, they are the film's protagonists because *Hickey and Boggs* is more a character study than a narrative thriller. Initially used by Rice as a decoy, Hickey and Boggs are then ignored by the guerrillas. Even though the syndicate "soldiers" murder Hickey's wife in an attempt to frighten the detectives from continuing their investigation and to avenge Boggs's killing of their associate in an earlier shoot-out, it does not seem to matter to them that Hickey and Boggs continue their pursuit. The nature of the syndicate killers is mechanical and psychopathic, but in certain ways their peculiar code is a counterpart to Hickey and Boggs's fallen romanticism. Hickey and Boggs seem to alternate in their desire for money and revenge. Hickey is stunned and may realize that vengeance is futile. He had previously explained that "There's nothing left of this profession, it's all over. It's not about anything." But Boggs, the dissolute believer of a bygone heroism, seems to understand their existential dependence on this profession and insists it is important to "try and even it up, make it right." As the smoke clears, Hickey says, "Nobody came, nobody cares. It's still not about anything," and Boggs replies, "Yeah, you told me."

To illustrate the disorder of the modern world in *Hickey and Boggs*, all of the mystery sequences take place during broad daylight and the private lives of the detectives are shown at night. Breaking archetypes, these men are not handsome, romanticized loners but are weary, displaced persons. Hickey's arrival home at night scares and angers his wife, who complains that she is not running a boarding house. Boggs is an alcoholic who spends most of his spare time in bars watching television commercials and brooding about his ex-wife. His singular enjoyment is watching her striptease act in a seedy nightclub, where she psychologically castrates him.

Instead of the anonymity provided in many film noir by busy and crowded urban streets, the action of *Hickey and Boggs* occurs in large areas of unoccupied public space. The violence that takes place in a deserted coliseum, ball park, neighborhood park, and open beach with the backdrop of the cityscape, illustrates society's ineffectiveness in controlling its domain and the antagonistic forces within it. The absurdity of the gangsters' and guerrillas' overkill in the film's climax also underlines the absurdity of modern violence as effectively as the "eternal whatsis" in *Kiss Me Deadly*. In a sardonic variant of the old-fashioned happy ending, the detectives walk off into the sunset. Hickey and Boggs are the only survivors; but they have survived only because they are unimportant.

—E.W.

HIGH SIERRA (1941)

Director: Raoul Walsh
Producer: Hal B. Wallis (Warner Brothers-First National)
Associate Producer: Mark Hellinger

Screenplay: John Huston and W.R. Burnett; from the novel by   W.R. Burnett
Director of Photography: Tony Gaudio
Special Effects: Byron Haskin, H.F. Koenekamp
Sound: Dolph Thomas
Music: Adolph Deutsch
Music Director: Leo F. Forbstein
Art Director: Ted Smith
Costumes: Milo Anderson
Dialogue Director: Irving Rapper
Assistant Director: Russ Saunders
Film Editor: Jack Killifer

CAST: Humphrey Bogart (Roy Earle), Ida Lupino (Marie), Alan Curtis (Babe), Arthur Kennedy (Red), Joan Leslie (Velma), Henry Hull (Doc Banton), Barton MacLane (Jake Kranmer), Henry Travers (Pa), Elisabeth Risdon (Ma), Cornel Wilde (Louis Mendoza), Minna Gombell (Mrs. Baugham), Paul Harvey (Mr. Baugham), Donald MacBride (Big Mac), Jerome Cowan (Healy), John El-

Left to right: Red (Arthur Kennedy), Babe (Alan Curtis), Roy Earle (Humphrey Bogart), and Marie (Ida Lupino) in High Sierra.

dredge (Lou Preiser), Isabel Jewell (Blond), Willie Best (Algernon), Arthur Aylsworth (Auto Court Owner), Robert Strange (Art), Wade Boteler (Sheriff), Sam Hayes (Radio Commentator), **BITS:** George Lloyd (Gangster), Erville Alderson (Farmer), Gerald Mackey (Boy), Spencer Charters (Ed), Carl Harbaugh (Fisherman), Cliff Saum (Shaw), Frank Mayo, De Wolfe Hopper, Peter Ashley, Robert Emmett Keane, Tony Hughes, Louis Jean Heydt (Men), George Meeker (Pfiffer), Eddy Chandler, Lee Phelps, James Blaine, Clancy Cooper, Jack Mower, Frank Moran, Davison Clark, Jack Rutherford, James Flavin (Police), Richard Clayton (Bellboy), Charlotte Wynters, Maris Wrixon, Lucia Carroll (Women), Dorothy Appleby (Margie), Garry Owen (Joe), Eddie Acuff (Bus Driver), Harry Hayden (Druggist), Ralph Sanford (Fat Man), Frank Cordell (Marksman).

Location: Sierra Mountains, California
Filming Completed: September 16, 1940
Released: Warner Brothers, January 4, 1941
Running Time: 100 minutes

Notorious criminal "Mad Dog" Roy Earle is helped to escape from prison by Big Mac, an old gangland associate who wants him to go to California to engineer the holdup of a resort hotel. On the way, Roy meets the Goodhues and their granddaughter, Velma, a clubfooted girl for whom he feels a sympathetic attraction. Arriving at a mountain hideout, Roy finds that Red and Babe, the henchmen assigned to him, have brought along a dance-hall girl, Marie. At first opposed to her presence, Roy soon comes to trust her, while she quickly falls in love with him. But his mind is on Velma; after planning the holdup with the inside help of Mendoza, a corrupt clerk at the hotel, he goes to visit the girl, giving her money for an operation to correct her clubfoot. The holdup takes place, and Roy makes his getaway with Marie; but Babe and Red are killed in a car crash. Mendoza talks, setting the police after Roy, who has gone to Big Mac for help, only to find him dead. Roy then goes to a now-cured Velma, but she has thrown him over for another man. He gives the ring intended for Velma to Marie, and the two misfits go on the run together. But the police are closing in; Roy puts Marie on a bus before heading for a mountain pass in the High Sierras; but he is trapped. Hearing about her lover's last stand, Marie halts her flight and comes after him, arriving just in time to see him killed.

The reputation of Raoul Walsh is based largely on his talents as an action-adventure director. But such films as *They Died With Their Boots On, White Heat, The Roaring Twenties, They Drive By Night,* and *High Sierra*—while indeed boasting action sequences also offer affecting character studies of strongly defined individuals operating both in and out of society. Walsh's protagonists are people struggling, in the words of *High Sierra's* Roy Earle, "to crash out" to an unfettered, free life of which they are both maker and master.

High Sierra may well be Walsh's most powerful expression of the individual's quest for freedom, a fact that in some ways seems to divorce it from the noir cycle. The sun shines generously; the characters are freed from the stricture of bleak little rooms and are led out into grassy parks and lush mountain pathways where the night skies are filled with stars rather than fogged with neon. But Walsh's lavish display of the glories of the natural world reinforce, by contrast, his grim view of human existence. Surrounded by magnificence, man is miserable. The superbly soaring peaks of the Sierras mock his insignificance and are monuments to his unreachable desires.

Walsh's sense of a cruel, inexorable fate viewed in *High Sierra* with a mordant humor, is also a noir conception. Velma's defection after Roy has literally turned her life around, Big Mac's badly timed death, and the wind's disposal of Roy's note absolving Marie of collaboration in his crimes—all seem like hideous practical jokes perpetrated against the film's helpless protagonists.

Still, Walsh's characters are far more than pathetic victims. Doomed from the start, as Roy's face seems stamped with death and Marie has the bruised look of a fallen angel, they nevertheless struggle toward freedom. Roy looks up at a starry sky and observes to an untouched Velma that the earth seems to him like "a little ball turning through the night, with us hanging on to it." In fact, Roy does hang on, with what can only be called a noble tenacity. His last flight is straight up, to a mountain's peak, to the last clear patch of sky and finally, to death. The conclusion of *High Sierra* is unusually exultant, even mystical. With Roy shot down from his mountaintop, a stricken Marie turns to a policeman and asks him the meaning of Roy's reiterated desire "to crash out." The man tells her that it means to be free. And murmuring "free" over and over to herself like an incantation, Marie raises her tear-stained face to the sky. In tight closeup, her tears are gone, and she wears an expression of joyful exaltation. Roy is free; and soon, perhaps, Marie will join him.

—J.K.

THE HIGH WALL (1947)

Director: Curtis Bernhardt
Producer: Robert Lord (MGM)
Screenplay: Sydney Boehm and Lester Cole; from the novel and play by Alan R. Clark and Bradbury Foote
Director of Photography: Paul Vogel
Special Effects: Warren Newcombe, A. Arnold Gillespie
Montage Effects: Peter Ballbusch
Sound: Douglas Shearer, Charles E. Wallace
Music: Bronislau Kaper
Art Directors: Cedric Gibbons, Leonid Vasian
Set Decoration: Edwin B. Willis, Joseph W. Holland
Makeup: Jack Dawn
Hairstyles: Sydney Guilaroff

Assistant Director: Al Raboch
Film Editor: Conrad A. Nervig

CAST: Robert Taylor (Steven Kenet), Audrey Totter (Dr. Ann Lorrison), Herbert Marshall (Willard I. Whitcombe), Dorothy Patrick (Helen Kenet), H.B. Warner (Mr. Slocum), Warner Anderson (Dr. George Poward), Moroni Olsen (Dr. Philip Dunlap), John Ridgeley (David Wallace), Morris Ankrum (Dr. Stanley Griffin), Elisabeth Risdon (Mrs. Kenet), Vince Barnett (Henry Cronner), Jonathan Hale (Emory Garrison), Charles Arnt (Sidney X. Hackle), Ray Mayer (Tom Delaney), Dick Wessell (Jim Hale), Robert Emmet O'Connor (Joe), Celia Travers (Maggie), Mary Servoss (Aunt Martha), Bobby Hyatt (Richard, Age 5), Eula Guy (Vera Mercer), Jack Davis (Detective Halloran), Tom Quinn (Detective Schaeffer).
BITS: Frank Jenks (Drunk), Irving Bacon (Gas Station Proprietor), Bernard Gorcey (Hirsch), Bert Hanlon (Bored Clerk), Selmer Jackson (Inspector Harding), John R. Hamilton (Police Surgeon), Lee Phelps (Telephone Man), Matt Willis (Admittance Clerk), Bob Williams, Eddy Dunn (Deputies), Jim Drumm, Paul Kruger, Jack Worth (Orderlies), Lisa Golm (Dr. Golm), Gordon Rhodes (Dr. Edermann), John Beck (Patient), Henry Sylvester, Phil Dunham, Skeets Noyes (Patients), Perry Ivens (Cackling Patient), Dorothy Vaughn (Harriett), Jean Andren (Nurse), Marta Mitrovich, Kate McKenna, Russell Arms, Al Hill, Erville Alderson, William Fawcett, Stanley Price, Joel Friedkin (Patients), Helen Eby-Rock (Josephine), Milton Kibbee (Counterman), George Bunny, Bob Wendal, Sammy Shack, Hank Worden (Customers), Georgia Caine (Miss Twitchell), Boyd Davis (Mrs. Grant), Henry Hall (the Reverend Holmsby), Howard Michell (Attendant), Frank Darien (Old Man in the Tub), Dorathea Neumann (Mrs. Miller), Guy Beach, Frank Marlowe (Patients), Ray Teal (Lieutenant of Police), Dan Quigg, Tay Dunn (Police Clerks), Rhea Mitchell (Woman), Abe Dinovich (Cab Driver), Jack Chefe, Jack Baxley (Bartenders).
Filming Completed: August 26, 1947
Released: MGM, December 25, 1947
Running Time: 100 minutes

Steven Kenet, an ex-army pilot, is found unconscious behind the wheel of a wrecked car next to his wife, Helen, who has been strangled, and he is arrested for murder. Steven has headaches and blackouts, which are the result of a wartime brain injury, and a hematoma has developed that should be operated on. Steven refuses, realizing that he will not be executed for murder if he cannot be judged legally sane; and he is committed to a veterans mental institution which is surrounded by a high wall. He arouses the interest and sympathy of Dr. Ann Lorrison, who persuades him to undergo the necessary operation. After the operation he still cannot recall the events leading to Helen's death and agrees to undergo narcosynthesis. Under its influence he relates to Dr. Lorrison that his wife was bored at home and

became a secretary to Willard Whitcombe, an executive with a religious book publishing company. Steven found her one night at Whitcombe's apartment with her overnight bag. In a burst of temper, Steven began to strangle her and then blacked out. Revisiting the Whitcombe apartment with Dr. Lorrison, Steven realizes that his wife's overnight bag was missing following her death. A few days later he is visited at the sanatorium by Mr. Whitcombe, who wishes to arouse him so that he will be thought unbalanced. Whitcombe confesses to killing Helen, and Steven loses control of himself. Later, however, he escapes from the institution and, joined by Dr. Lorrison, makes his way back into Whitcombe's apartment. When Whitcombe arrives they scuffle, but Steven knocks Whitcombe out and Dr. Lorrison administers sodium pentothal to Whitcombe, who confesses to the murder under the drug's influence.

German refugee Curtis Bernhardt, apparently drawn to thrillers with psychological overtones such as *Conflict* and *The Possessed* embellishes the straightforward plot of this otherwise ordinary melodrama with a noir *Mise-en-scène*, supported by Vogel's fine camerawork and MGM production values. Elements such as Robert Taylor's narration and images of lonely cars on dark rain-soaked steets respectively reinforce the basic romanticism of Kenet's relationship with his therapist, Ann Lorrison, and provide objective correlatives to his personal despair. Even more imaginative is the use of subjective camera in the murder flashback. Herbert Marshall, equally adept as villain or victim, lends ambiguity to his portrayal of the stodgy Whitcombe, whose sexual passion betrays his desire to succeed in that most conservative of businesses, religious book publishing. The manner in which he kills Cronner, a witness to his crime, is one of those chilling noir scenes in which killing is reduced to an offhand gesture. Cronner is on a stool repairing an elevator, as Whitcombe casually slips the handle of his umbrella around the stool's leg, pulling it and sending Cronner plummeting down the elevator shaft to his death.

—B.P.

HIS KIND OF WOMAN (1951)
[Working Title: SMILER WITH A GUN]

Director: John Farrow
Producer: Robert Sparks (RKO—A Howard Hughes Presentation)
Screenplay: Frank Fenton and Jack Leonard; from the unpublished story "Star Sapphire" by Gerald Drayson Adams
Director of Photography: Harry J. Wild
Sound: John Tribby, Clem Portman
Music Score: Leigh Harline
Music Director: Constantin Bakaleinikoff

HIS KIND OF WOMAN

Songs: "Five Little Miles from San Berdoo" by Ben S. Coslow; "You'll Know" by Jimmy McHugh and Harold Adamson
Production Designer: J. McMillan Johnson
Art Director: Albert S. D'Agostino
Set Decoration: Darrell Silvera, Ross Dowd
Costumes: Howard Greer
Makeup: Mel Berns
Hairstyles: Larry Germaine
Assistant Director: Sam Ruman
Film Editors: Eda Warren, Frederic Knudtson

CAST: Robert Mitchum (Dan Milner), Jane Russell (Lenore Brent), Vincent Price (Mark Cardigan), Tim Holt (Bill Lusk), Charles McGraw (Thompson), Marjorie Reynolds (Helen Cardigan), Raymond Burr (Nick Ferraro), Leslye Banning (Jennie Stone), Jim Backus (Myron Winton), Philip Van Zandt (José Morro), John Mylong (Martin Krafft), Carleton G. Young (Hobson), Erno Verebes (Estaban), Dan White (Tex Kearns), Richard Bergren (Milton Stone), Stacy Harris (Harry), Robert Cornthwaite (Hernandez). **BITS:** Jim Burke (Barkeep), Paul Frees, (Corle), Joe Granby (Arnold), Daniel De Laurentis (Mexican Boy), John Sheehan (Husband), Sally Yarnell (Wife), Anthony Caruso (Tony), Robert Rose (Corle's Servant), Tol Avery (the Fat One), Paul Fierro, Mickey Simpson, (Hoodlums), Ed Rand, Jerry James (Policemen), Joel Fluellen (Sam), Len Hendry (Customer), Gwen Caldwell, Don House, Stuart Holmes, Jim Davies, Barbara Freking, Oliver Cross, Joan Olander, Joy Windsor, Jerri Jordan, Mary Brewer (Guests), Maria Sen Young (Waitress), Marietta Elliott (Redhead), Saul Gorss (Viscount), Dan Borzage (Bartender), Dorothy Abbot (Card Player), Mike Lally (Henchman), Peter Brocco (Short and Thin), Bud Wolfe (Seaman), Henry Guttman (Man), Ralph Gomez (Mexican Foreman), Howard Batt (Plane Pilot), Albert Morin (Rodriguez), William Justine (Gyppo), Bill Nelson (Capt. Salazar).
Filming Completed: May 23, 1950
Released: RKO, August 1951
Running Time: 120 minutes
[NOTE: Warren Duff originally contracted to produce *His Kind Of Woman*. Jerry Wald and Norman Krasna made unspecified changes to *His Kind Of Woman* prior to its release.]

Nick Ferraro, a deported syndicate boss in exile in Naples, wants desperately to return to the United States to oversee his troubled criminal holdings. He radios three of his men at a Mexican resort to put into effect a plan calling for him to assume the identity of a U.S. citizen. One of the men goes to Los Angeles, where he sets up Dan Milner for a beating from three of a bookmaker's strong-arm men. Milner, a gambler just released from a short term in a county jail, is then made an offer: $50,000 to leave the United States for a year. Having no other prospects, Milner agrees to go to Mexico and await further instructions. In a Mexican cantina near his initial rendezvous point, Milner meets Lenore

Brent, a singer posing as an heiress and traveling south to pursue an affair with film star Mark Cardigan. Milner is told to fly to Morro's Lodge, an exclusive resort in Baja California, which is also Lenore's destination. Lenore is attracted to Milner but has already spent almost all her savings trying to get Cardigan to marry her. Once they arrive at Morro's she finds that Cardigan is more interested in going hunting with Milner than spending time with her.

Milner questions Morro but learns nothing. He then pays a nocturnal visit to the room of a man named Krafft, whom he suspects of working for Ferraro. He is interrupted by Thompson, another Ferraro henchman, who tells Milner that his job is to keep Milner and Krafft there but that he knows no more than that. Milner has no choice but to wait. He passes the time with Lenore and assists a young couple who have run up a large gambling debt to a vacationing financier. It is not until the arrival of Bill Lusk, an undercover agent from the U.S. immigration department, that Milner learns why he is there. Lusk warns Milner that Ferraro plans to undergo plastic surgery from Krafft, a doctor and former Nazi, then dispose of Milner, and assume his identity. Lusk is caught in Thompson's room while searching for his radio transmitter. After he overhears a message from Ferraro in Morse code, Thompson struggles with the agent and kills him. After the arrival of Cardigan's wife, Lenore and Milner have left the lodge to walk along the beach where they discover Lusk's body. Milner takes her back to her room and warns her to remain there. In his own room, he finds Thompson waiting with two accomplices, one of whom comes up behind Milner and disarms him. As they prepare to take him to Ferraro's yacht which has anchored offshore, Lenore arrives with a gun she has stolen from Cardigan for Milner. Milner tells her pointedly to take it back to him; instead she waits and sees him being taken away then goes to Cardigan for help.

As Cardigan goes toward the beach, Milner jumps from a boarding ladder capsizing Thompson's dinghy. He swims back to shore, with Thompson and his men close behind, and finds Cardigan waiting. While Cardigan holds them off, Milner takes a gun and slips back aboard ship to confront Ferraro, but he is cornered below deck and recaptured. Using his familiarity with the terrain, Cardigan shoots Thompson's men and captures Thompson. When he returns to Morro's he finds a squad of police called to investigate Lusk's death and recruits them into a posse completed by hotel guests armed with Cardigan's stock of hunting rifles. While their initial assault on the boat fails because their rowboat sinks, Milner is savagely beaten by Ferraro's men and thrown into an engine room filled with steam from a pipe he had blown out. When Cardigan and his men approach in a second boat, Krafft convinces Ferraro to let him give Milner a mind-destroying injection that will cause death within a year. As Cardigan storms aboard the yacht, Milner breaks free. Cardigan stops Ferraro's men as they try to lower an escape boat, and Milner shoots Ferraro when he tries to come up behind Cardigan. Back at Morro's, Cardigan holds a triumphant press conference and Milner is reunited with Lenore.

On a literal level—because it is set almost entirely at night—*His Kind Of Woman* is among the most oppressively dark of film noir. Narratively, it culminates by balancing and intercutting comedy that verges on slapstick, as Cardigan leads his unlikely band of rescuers against Ferraro's ship, with scenes of Milner's prolonged beating and torture: first he is whipped with the buckle end of a belt and thrown into the steam-filled engine room; then Ferraro revives him to point a gun between his eyes while he murmurs, "Wake up, little boy, I want you to see it coming"; and finally Krafft has him held down for a fatal injection. The effect of such abrupt shifts in narrative tone and content—from Milner doubling over under vicious body blows to the hapless Cardigan standing in the sunken bow quoting from *The Tempest* ("Now would I give a thousand furlongs of sea for an acre of barren ground") after his boat has floundered from an excess burden of men and guns and back to the bare-chested Milner struggling against a half dozen hands as the deadly, glistening needle draws nearer to his skin—is both grisly and chaotic. On the one hand, Farrow's staging isolates and to some degree exaggerates familiar icons of film noir: from the complex group shots when Ferraro's men bring Milner in—composed initially with Ferraro reclining on a sofa so that the crime boss's rim-lit face seems to float at the bottom edge of the frame, then restructured with a wide-angle lens so that when he sits up Ferraro's face becomes an oversized silhouette in the right foreground—to the simple close-ups of Krafft's needle as he prepares an overdose of anesthetic. On the other hand, the elaborate comic scenes with Cardigan—from his melodramatic declaration as he locks Lenore in a closet ("If I'm not here by Wednesday, chop that door down") to his absurd posturing before his "volunteers" ("Survivors will get parts in my next picture")—satirizes and debunks the very conventions of the "serious" events aboard the yacht. Rather than undercut the stereotypical reality of the leering Ferraro obsessed with liquidating the "welsher" Milner, his pragmatic ex-Nazi surgeon, or his simple-minded, brutal thugs, Cardigan's comic antics concentrate narrative tension and viewer apprehension on those sequences with Milner. Ferraro and his minions become less personalities than the embodiment of the vague impersonal peril that has threatened Milner throughout the film, and each cutaway to Cardigan reemphasizes the illogical chaos of Milner's situation and prolongs his ordeal in a manner suggestive of the hazards and incongruities of the noir universe.

In a sense, *His Kind Of Woman* deals only in archetypes of the noir world, in a series of ambiguous characters and events—from the songstress Liz Brady playing the role of the heiress Lenore Brent and the insecure Mark Cardigan unable to escape his film star persona to Krafft wearing dark glasses while he plays chess with himself or the dispassionate Thompson who is "ignorant and happy to be that way"—all clustered around the central confrontation between Milner, the aimless, laconic "hero," and Ferraro, the determined, rapacious crime boss. Actually, Milner is uncertain for much of the film whether his suspicions are justified. He knows that something is being done to him; but, surrounded by an unrelenting, literal, and metaphorical darkness, he cannot perceive what it is or by whom. Although Ferraro is physically absent through most of the narrative, he is represented in every threatening or apprehensive moment coexperienced by Milner and the viewer. Appropriately, Ferraro is introduced first: a bulky figure in a white suit slowly striding forward into the foreground of a medium shot. The close-up that ends the shot is back-lit to reveal eyes flashing in a somber visage and stylized to underscore his archetypal menace. Milner, as portrayed by Mitchum, is an equally exaggerated characterization: weary, sardonic, unexcited but critically unaware that the components of a fateful plot, which will ensnare him and compel him into action, are already in motion. In a *mise-en-scène* that combines long takes with compositions in which wedges of light and bizarre shadows clutter the frame and distract the viewer, Milner is the only predictable element, he is the only emblem of stability, however uncertain. Milner's introduction in the late night diner is fully as stylized as Ferraro's as he explains to an acquaintance behind the counter that he is out of money and has just spent thirty days on a county road gang for an implicit vagrancy. The counterman gives Milner a free meal but his stance with his back to the gambler with occasional glances over his shoulder betray a distance and inability to understand Milner's life-style—a style that types the gambler, despite his constant weary smile, as a friendless loner. The suggestion that Milner inhabits the noir underworld is reinforced in the next sequence. First a long shot isolates Milner on a dark street, where he climbs a set of wooden steps to a cheap second-floor apartment. Inside Milner finds three men waiting. In the course of a long take Milner shrugs off their accusations of reneging on a bet and finally, after telling them it would "be nice if you guys cleaned up this mess before you got out of here," snubs out a cigarette in the palm of one of the men. The sustained shot is broken as Milner falls out of frame under the fists of the other two.

Milner's self-destructive defiance is symptomatic of his world-weariness. When, after this first of many beatings he will endure during the course of the film, Ferraro's man calls with his proposition, Milner offhandedly tells him, "I was just getting ready to take my tie off ... wondering whether I should hang myself with it." But for all his postures of fatigue and weariness, Milner is most at home in the noir underworld. Clearly the white-walled, expensively furnished home he visits to hear Ferraro's offer makes him uncomfortable: as he discusses the proposition in a sustained three shot, Milner paces back and forth, finally slumping against a Greek-styled column and remarking on the offer, "I'm not knocking it, man, I'm just trying to understand it." For Milner, who understands the complexities of odds, something for nothing is a puzzle. He moves through Mexico almost like a somnambulist in search of a waking reality. In typically noir values, there is some degree of that reality to be found, but only in money and in sexuality as represented by Lenore. At that, Milner's relationship with sex and money is somewhat eccentric. He jokingly remarks to the vacationing financier that he buries his money in the ground. When Lenore drops by his room late at night, she finds him ironing currency: "When I have nothing to do and can't think, I always iron my money." Clearly, Milner is not avaricious; he could easily fleece the financier but restricts himself to helping the young husband win back what he has lost. Nor is he as likely to inflict violence as to endure it. Cardigan thinks more in those terms, however fantastically, and makes the equation with sexuality by telling Milner, after both men catch sight of Lenore, that "I've got a little Winchester I'd like you to try. If it feels right to you, I'll let you use it." Milner refuses to equate Lenore either with violence or with money. Although he is clearly drawn to her, her claim to being wealthy is not enticing to him. The fact that her off-screen voice draws him around the bar at the cantina and the choker close-ups of both of them suddenly inserted as he watches her sing suggest an immediate fascination with her. Yet there is also an indication of an underlying sexual tension between them in their initial conversation after Milner buys her champagne; and their awkward movements when they find themselves together in the plane to Morro's reinforce the sense of a mutual reluctance toward a precipitous intimacy. Nonetheless, Lenore is more real for Milner than any of the film's other characters. The only day scene, which occurs midway through the narrative, features Milner with her at the resort's private beach. Ultimately Lenore's presence, whether she is being openly solicitous (Lenore: "You're in trouble." Milner: "Everybody's in trouble.") or merely engaging in odd sexual banter (Lenore:"What do you press when you're broke?" Milner: "When I'm broke, I press my pants."), permits sequences of relative verisimilitude that contrast with Milner's other encounters. In terms of film noir conventions, because Lenore is his kind of woman, Milner's relationship with her despite its sexual tension is crucial to his survival. He survives; and the tension is finally dissipated in the film's last shot, the comic sexual metaphor of an iron burning Milner's pants while he and Lenore embrace.

—A.S.

THE HITCH-HIKER (1953)
[Working Title: THE PERSUADER]

Director: Ida Lupino
Producer: Collier Young (The Filmakers)
Associate Producer: Christian Nyby
Screenplay: Collier Young and Ida Lupino, adapted by Robert Joseph; from an unpublished story by Daniel Mainwaring
Director of Photography: Nicholas Musuraca
Photographic Effects: Harold E. Wellman
Sound: Roy Meadows, Clem Portman
Music: Leith Stevens
Music Director: Constantin Bakaleinikoff

Art Directors: Albert S. D'Agostino, Walter E. Keller
Assistant Director: William Dorfman
Film Editor: Douglas Stewart
CAST: Edmond O'Brien (Ray Collins), Frank Lovejoy (Gilbert Bowen), William Talman (Emmett Myers), José Torvay (Capt. Alvarado), Sam Hayes (Sam), Wendell Niles (Wendell), Jean Del Val (Inspector General), Clark Howat (Government Agent), Natividad Vacio (José), Rodney Bell (William Johnson), Nacho Galindo (Proprietor), Martin Garralaga (Bartender), Tony Roux (Gas Station Owner), Jerry Lawrence (News Broadcaster), Felipe Turich, Joe Dominguez (Men), Rose Turich (Woman), Orlando Veltran, George Navarro (Salesmen), June Dinneen (Waitress), Al Ferrara (Gas Station Attendant), Henry Escalante (Mexican Guard), Taylor Flaniken (Mexican Cop), Wade Crosby (Joe, Bartender), Kathy Riggins (Child), Gordon Barnes (Hendrickson), Ed Hinton (Chief of Police), Larry Hudson (F.B.I. Agent)
Filming Completed: December 1952
Released: RKO, April 29, 1953
Running Time: 71 minutes
[FACTUAL BASIS: Based on a crime committed in the early 1950s.]

Emmett Myers is a psychotic killer who hitchhikes, rides, then robs and murders his benefactors. He is hunted by the police, so when he is picked up by Ray Collins and Gil Bowen, two men on a fishing trip to Mexico, he makes them his prisoners, at least until he finds safety in Mexico. Myers's curious personality may be the result of parental hatred compounded by the physical deformity of a right eye that cannot close, even when he is asleep. The two vacationers are perpetually in his gun sights, and Myers toys with them, deprecating their softness and proclaiming the superiority of those strong enough to take what they want. They arrive at a small Mexican village where they wait to ferry across a river. Bowen leaves his wedding ring on a service station gas pump. The ring tips off the police and they eventually capture the killer.

The Hitch-Hiker is the only film noir directed by a woman; but it probably owes much of its noir sensibility to Daniel Mainwaring's original story (which went uncredited because Mainwaring's then "radical" reputation made him persona non grata at RKO, then controlled by Howard Hughes). Although the film is purportedly based on a true story, it is less a warning to beware of hitchhikers than a reflection of a more generalized American paranoia that in the 1950s ran the gamut from "authentic" aliens (as illustrated by the "pods" of Mainwaring's script for Invasion of the Body Snatchers) to nuclear reactions and Communists. The Hitch-Hiker's desert locales, although not so graphically dark as a cityscape at night, isolate the protagonists in a milieu as uninviting and potentially deadly as any in film noir. As with Vanning in Nightfall, the upheaval of the lives of Collins and Bowen is sudden, ill-chanced, and impersonal—a typical noir reflection of the lack of security or stability in everyday living, no matter how commonplace.
—B.P. & A.S.

Left to right: Gilbert Bowen (Frank Lovejoy) and Ray Collins (Edmund O'Brien) in The Hitch-Hiker.

HOLLOW TRIUMPH (1948)
[Working Title: THE SCAR]

Director: Steve Sekely
Executive Producer: Bryan Foy *(Hollow Triumph, Inc.)*
Producer: Paul Henreid
Screenplay: Daniel Fuchs; from the novel by Murray Forbes
Director of Photography: John Alton
Photographic Effects: George J. Teague
Sound: Leon S. Becker, Hugh McDowell
Music Score: Sol Kaplan
Music Director: Irving Friedman
Music Conductor: Charles Previn
Art Directors: Edward Ilou, Frank Durlauf
Set Decoration: Amor Marlowe, Clarence Steenson
Costumes: Kay Nelson for Joan Bennett
Makeup: Ern Westmore, Frank Westmore
Hairstyles: Joan St. Oegger, Merle Reeves
Production Supervisor: James T. Vaughn
Dialogue Director: Stewart Stern
Assistant Director: Emmett Emerson
Script Supervisor: Arnold Laven
Film Editor: Fred Allen

CAST: Paul Henreid (John Muller/Dr. Bartok) Joan Bennett (Evelyn Nash), Eduard Franz (Frederick Muller), Leslie Brooks (Virginia Taylor), John Qualen (Swangron), Mabel Paige (Charwoman), Herbert Rudley (Marcy). **BITS:** Paul Burns (Clerk), Charles Trowbridge (Deputy), Ann Staunton (Blond), Mack Williams (Cashier), Franklyn Farnum (Big Winner), Morgan Farley (Howard Anderson), Joel Friedkin (William), Phillip Morris (Doorman), Rennie McEvoy (Clerk), Tom Stevenson (Lester), Benny Rubin (Cabbie), Charles Arnt (Coblenz), Sid Tomack (Artell, Manager), George Chandler (Aubrey, Assistant), Alvin Hammer (Jerry), Jerry Marlowe (Hiker), Cliff Clark, Eddie Dunn (Men), Constance Purdy (Mrs. Neyhmer), Cay Forester (Nurse), Carmencita Johnson (Elevator Operator), Lucien Littlefield (Davis), Norma Varden (Mrs. Gerry), Catherine Doucet (Mrs. Nielson), Victor Jones (Bellboy), Babe London (Lady with Orchid), Flo Wix, Lulu Mae Bohrman (Guests), Cy Ring (Croupier), Sam Finn (Patron), Dulcy Day (Woman), Joaquin Elizando (Housekeeper), Felice Ingersoll (Woman), Steve Carruthers (Man), Lyle Latell (Official), Ray Bennett (Man), Bob Bice, Dave Shilling (Thugs), Nolan Leary (Newcomer), Joan Myles, Vera Marshe, Jeanne Blackford (Women), Tony Horton (Patron), Sayre Dearing (Man), Rovert Ben Ali (Rosie), Henry Brandon (Big Boy), Bud Wolfe (Al), Tom Henry (Stansyck), Jack Webb (Bullseye), Dick Wessell (Sidekick)

131

HOUSE OF BAMBOO

Location: Los Angeles, California
Filming Completed: March 1948
Released: Eagle Lion, October 28, 1948
Running Time: 82 minutes

When Johnny Muller, a former medical student, confidence artist, and phony psychologist, is convicted of a payroll theft and later released from jail, his brother Fred suggests a low-paying but safe job with a medical supply firm. However, Johnny soon takes up with his old mob and persuades them to rob a gambling club owned by racketeer Rocky Stansyck. The robbery does not go off as planned, and only Johnny and his friend Marcy get out alive. After they split the stolen $60,000, Marcy heads for Mexico while Johnny returns to his job. Discovering that a nearby psychiatrist, Dr. Victor Bartok, is his exact look-alike except for a scar that Bartok carries on his cheek, Johnny romances Bartok's secretary, Evelyn Nash. Through her he learns about the doctor's practice and obtains a copy of his signature. Johnny quits his job and becomes a parking attendant in the garage where Bartok keeps his car. A photographer makes an enlargement of Bartok's picture for Johnny and, using a scalpel, he makes a duplicate incision on his face. What Johnny does not know is that the photographer "flopped" the negative and printed the scar on the wrong cheek. Only after he kills the unsuspecting Bartok does Johnny realize that the scar is wrong. But no one notices the change in the location of the scar; and his patients prefer his new bedside manner. "Bartok" even fools Fred who comes to tell Johnny that he is now safe. Evelyn discovers the impersonation and, bitter at being used, decides to leave town. Johnny refuses to let her go and arranges for them to travel by ship to Honolulu the next evening. As he is rushing to join Evelyn on the ship, he is stopped by two hoods who inform him that Bartok owed a gambler $90,000. Johnny explains that he is not Bartok, but the hoods pay no attention. Realizing he may miss the boat, he attempts to escape and they shoot him. Johnny dies while crawling to the ship and people pass unheedingly by him.

The Hollow Triumph's fine use of Los Angeles exteriors demonstrates again that John Alton was a master at photographing the location thriller. As in many of these *B* thrillers, the plot is contrived although the film's conclusion is as downbeat as any noir film since *Scarlet Street*. The acting in *The Hollow Triumph* — particularly by Joan Bennett who, as the cynical Evelyn, has the film's best line: "You can't go back and start again. The older you get, the worse things get." — matches the low-key visual style in its understated menace. Although the viewer realizes that Paul Henreid interprets both the distracted Bartok and the unmitigatedly villainous Johnny Muller, Henreid's suggestion of Muller's unfailing confidence in his own criminal guise greatly adds to the film's central irony: Muller dies because he has finally outsmarted himself.

— B.P. & A.S.

HOUSE OF BAMBOO (1955)

Director: Samuel Fuller
Producer: Buddy Adler (20th Century-Fox)
Screenplay: Harry Kleiner, with additional dialogue by Samuel Fuller
Director of Photography: Joe MacDonald [De Luxe Color; CinemaScope]
Color Consultant: Leonard Doss
Special Photographic Effects: Ray Kellogg
Sound: John D. Stack, Harry M. Leonard
Musical Score: Leigh Harline
Orchestration: Edward B. Powell
Musical Director: Lionel Newman
Art Directors: Lyle R. Wheeler, Addison Hehr
Set Decoration: Walter M. Scott, Stuart A. Reiss
Costumes: Charles LeMaire
Makeup: Ben Nye
Hair Styles: Helen Turpin
Assistant Director: David Silver
Film Editor: James B. Clark

CAST: Robert Ryan (Sandy Dawson), Robert Stack (Eddie Kenner/Spanier), Shirley Yamaguchi (Mariko), Cameron Mitchell (Griff), Brad Dexter (Capt. Hanson), Sessue Hayakawa (Inspector Kito), Biff Elliot (Webber), Sandro Giglio (Ceram), Elko Hanabusa (Japanese Screaming Woman), Harry Carey (John), Peter Gray (Willy), Robert Quarry (Phil), De Forest Kelley (Charlie), John Doucette (Skipper). **BITS:** Teru Shimada (Nagaya), Robert Hosai (Doctor), Jack Maeshiro (Bartender), May Takasugi (Bath Attendant), Robert Okazaki (Mr. Hommaru), Neyle Morrow (Army Corporal), Kazue Ikeda, Clifford Arashiro, Robert Kino (Policemen), Frank Kwanaga (File Clerk), Rollin Moriyama (Pearl Man), Reiko Sato (Charlie's Girl), Sandy [Chikaye] Azeka (Charlie's Girl at Party), Fuji, Frank Jumagai (Pachinko Managers), Harris Matsushige (Office Clerk), Kinuko Ann Ito (Servant), Barbara Uchiyamada (Japanese Girl), Fred Dale (Man).
Location: Tokyo, Japan
Filming Completed: March 28, 1955
Released: 20th Century-Fox, July 1, 1955
Running time: 105 minutes

Sandy Dawson has organized a criminal ring of former G.I.'s in Tokyo after the war. The army sends a man, Kenner, under the false identity of Spanier, to infiltrate the gang. In order to cover himself after joining Sandy's gang, Kenner must live with Mariko, the widow of one of Sandy's men, who has assumed the false identity of a "kimono girl." Sandy breaks his own rule during a robbery and spares Kenner's life. Thereafter, Kenner is first in Sandy's affection, replacing Griff, whom Sandy kills when it becomes evident someone is betraying the gang. When Sandy discovers that Kenner/Spanier is the real betrayer, he tries to set him up to be shot by the army, but fails. Kenner pursues him to an amusement park on the roof of an office building, where the two engage in a gunfight on a whirling globe. Sandy is finally killed; and Kenner is reunited with Mariko.

House of Bamboo, in color and CinemaScope, is a remake of *Street With No Name*, a typical undercover-man film noir. The Sam Fuller film is a totally rethought work, transposing certain generic elements into a setting that renders them unconventional by virtue of cultural contrasts. The pachinko parlors, Kabuki troupe, Great Buddha, whirling globe, and cherry blossoms have an almost surreal relationship to the criminal activities of Sandy's gang. Rather than appearing to be an incidental background, these aspects of the *mise-en-scène* express the subject of the film: that one culture may absorb and contain another, even if the alien culture expresses itself in a violent and disruptive way. The American occupation of Japan has never been presented, even metaphorically, as criminal except by Fuller, who indirectly posits this idea and modifies it through the sympathetic interracial romance between Kenner and Mariko. Their love story is handled literally and symbolically: the screen that separates the couple at night visually reinforces their sense of psychological estrangement. Fuller's feeling for the visual subject is expressed in the colors and dynamic compositions of Joe MacDonald's photography. The violent scenes have particular power. The tracking shot of the factory robbery with black-coated hunched and running figures has a compelling visual sweep; and the climactic battle between Sandy and Kenner on the whirling globe is choreographed with the precision of a Noh drama.

The homosexuality of Sandy, which is implied in his treatment of Mariko and his blind trust of Kenner, makes him a particularly vulnerable figure despite his villainy and lack of compunction over murder. Kenner is forced to assume a strange role as *ichi-ban* ("number one man") after Sandy has saved his life; but although he does so reluctantly and his army duty compels him to take advantage of Sandy's sexual attraction and good will, Kenner's deception is not altogether sympathetic. Under the perverse circumstances, Kenner is like Thelma Jordon or any other sexual exploiter in film noir; and he feels uncomfortable in his role as betrayer.

—B.L. & A.S.

HOUSE OF STRANGERS (1949)
[*Working Title: EAST SIDE STORY*]

Director: Joseph L. Mankiewicz
Producer: Sol C. Siegel (20th Century-Fox)
Screenplay: Philip Yordan; from the novel *I'll Never Go There Again* by Jerome Weidman
Director of Photography: Milton Krasner

Special Photographic Effects: Fred Sersen
Sound: W.D. Flick, Roger Heman
Music Score: Daniele Amfitheatrof. Recording of "Largo Al Factotum," sung by Lawrence Tibbett
Orchestration: Maurice de Packh
Art Directors: Lyle Wheeler, George W. Davis
Set Decoration: Thomas Little, Walter M. Scott
Wardrobe: Charles LeMaire
Makeup: Ben Nye, Dick Smith
Production Manager: Sid Bowen
Assistant Director: William Eckhardt
Script Supervisor: Weslie Jones
Film Editor: Harmon Jones

CAST: Edward G. Robinson (Gino Monetti), Susan Hayward (Irene Bennett), Richard Conte (Max Monetti), Luther Adler (Joe Monetti), Paul Valentine (Pietro Monetti), Efrem Zimbalist, Jr. (Tony), Debra Paget (Maria Domenico), Hope Emerson (Helena Domenico), Esther Minciotti (Theresa Monetti), Diana Douglas (Elaine Monetti), Tito Vuolo (Lucca), Albert Morin (Victoro), Sid Tomack (Waiter), Thomas Henry Brown (Judge), David Wolfe (Prosecutor), John Kellogg (Danny), Ann Morrison (Woman Juror), Dolores Parker (Nightclub Singer). **BITS:** Mario Siletti, Tommy Garland, Maurice Samuels, Frank Jacquet (Men), Charles J. Blynn, Howard Mitchell, Phil Tully (Guards), Joseph Mazzuca (Bat Boy), John Pedrini, Charles McClelland, James Little (Cops), Scott Landers, Fred Hillebrand (Detectives), Argentina Brunetti, Rhoda Williams (Women), Donna La Tour, Maxine Ardell, Sally Yarnell, Jeri Jordan, Marjorie Holliday (Chorus Dancers), Bob Castro, Eddie Saenz (Preliminary Fighters), Herbert Vigran (Neighbor), Mushy Callahan (Referee), George Spaulding (Doorman), John "Red" Kullers (Taxi Driver).
Location: Little Italy, New York, New York
Filming Completed: February 23, 1949
Released: 20th Century-Fox, July 1, 1949
Running Time: 101 minutes

Gino Monetti, patriarch of an Italian-American family, runs his sons with an iron hand, except for his favorite, Max, who is a lawyer. All of the sons work at their father's bank and suffer in silence as he berates them and plays opera records during dinner. Max, although engaged to a girl approved by his family, falls in love with Irene Bennett, a chic woman from the other side of town; but Gino maintains his affection for Max. When it is discovered that Gino has broken banking laws by giving high-interest loans for little or no collateral, the bank is ruined. He turns over the assets to his wife, who gives them to his vindictive sons. Max cannot get assistance from his brothers in defense of their father, and the eldest son, Joe, has Max arrested for attempting to bribe a juror. Gino is freed but Max goes to prison for seven years and returns home to find that his father has died and his brothers have reopened the bank. Afraid of Max's bitterness, Joe tries to kill him; but one of the other brothers kills Joe instead. Max is happily reunited with Irene and begins a new life.

House of Strangers exploits the traditional concept of the immigrant family in order to develop a corrosive story of a patriarchal domination that is destroyed from within. Usually, films about large families emphasize the loyalty of the family members in unifying against outside forces. *House of Strangers* is exceptional in illustrating the hatred generated when a man insists on being the master of his family in the tradition of older generations and foreign cultures. Paradoxically, while the other sons have bitter dreams of freedom from their father's rule, Max is both the most independent and the most loyal. As a result, the relationship between Max and Irene, a conventional romance, acquires a distinctive tension by virtue of her existence as an outsider relative to his family's cultural preference.

Director Mankiewicz, generates theatrical expansiveness in sequences involving large gatherings. Because the film is in flashback form, with Max recalling the story's events on the day of his release from prison, the introduction of his father (at the opening of the flashback) descending a staircase to the strains of Rossini toward his waiting family gathered below, is appropriately stylized like a personal memoir. The side-light and detailing in the Monetti home both evokes the milieu and suggests something of the suffocating monomania of Gino's patriarchal despotism.

Conte's performance as Max, in particular, exploits the fact that he is not conventionally associated with heroic parts (*Thieves' Highway, Call Northside 777*) to the exclusion of villainous ones (*Cry Of The City, The Big Combo*) to imbue his portrayal with an ambiguous morality that is only resolved during his father's crisis. That Max is ultimately punished by his brothers and society for his father's crimes is doubly ironic. Not only does it perpetuate the traditions of older cultures, which held the sons responsible for the sins of their fathers, but it also makes Max the victim of a cataclysmic turn of events from which, in a noir universe, no amount of glibness or worldly cynicism can protect him.

—B.L. & A.S.

HOUSE ON 92nd STREET (1945)
[Working Title: NOW IT CAN BE TOLD]

Director: Henry Hathaway
Producer: Louis de Rochemont (20th Century-Fox)
Screenplay: Barre Lyndon, Charles G. Booth, and John Monks, Jr.; from an unpublished story by Charles G. Booth
Director of Photography: Norbert Brodine
Special Photographic Effects: Fred Sersen
Sound: W.D. Flick
Music: David Buttolph
Music Direction: Emil Newman
Art Directors: Lyle Wheeler, Lewis Creber

Set Decoration: Thomas Little, William Sittel
Costumes: Bonnie Cashin
Makeup: Ben Nye
Casting Director: William Newberry
Assistant Director: Henry Weinberger
Film Editor: Harmon Jones

CAST: William Eythe (Bill Dietrich), Lloyd Nolan (Inspector Briggs), Signe Hasso (Elsa Gebhardt), Gene Lockhart (Charles Ogden Roper), Leo G. Carroll (Hammershon), Lydia St. Clair (Johanna Schwartz), William Post, Jr. (Walker), Harry Bellaver (Max Coburg), Bruno Wick (Adolphe Lange), Harro Meller (Conrad Arnulf), Charles Wagenheim (Gus Huzmann), Alfred Linder (Emil Kline), Renee Carson (Luise Vadja), John McKee (Dr. Appleton), Edwin Jerome (Major General), Elisabeth Newmann (Freda Kassel), George Shelton (Jackson), Alfred Zeisler (Col. Strassen), Reed Hadley (Narrator). **BITS:** Rusty Lane (Admiral), Salo Douday (Von Wirt), Paul Ford (Sergeant), William Adams (Customs Officer), Lew Eckles, Fred Hillebrand (Policemen), Tom Brown (Intern), Bruce Fernald, Jay Wesley, (F.B.I. Agents), Benjamin Burroughs (Aide), Douglas Rutherford (Colonel), Frieda Altman, William Beach, Hamilton Benz, Henry Cordy, Mita Cordy, James J. Coyle, Hans Hansen, Kenneth Konopka, Scott Moore, Delmar Nuetzman, John Zak, Gertrude Wottitz, Bernard Lenrow (Saboteurs), George Brandt (German Man), Yoshita Tagawa (Japanese Man), Sheila Bromley (Customer), Elmer Brown, Jack Cherry (Scientists), Victor Sutherland (Toll Guard), Stanley Tackney (Instructor), Robert Culler, Vincent Gardenia, Carl Benson, Frank Richards, Ellsworth Glath, Edward Michaels, Harrison Scott, Anna Marie Hornemann, Sara Strengell, Eugene Stuckmann, Marriott Wilson (Trainees), Frank Kreig (Travel Agent), Antonio J. Pires (Watchmaker), Danny Leone (Delivery Boy), Edward Marshall (Attendant at Morgue).
Location: The Federal Bureau of Investigation, Washington, D.C.; New York, New York
Filming Completed: August 29, 1945
Released: 20th Century-Fox, September 26, 1945
Running Time: 89 minutes
[FACTUAL BASIS: Based on Federal Bureau of Investigation files.]

A brilliant student, Bill Dietrich, is approached by the Nazis and asked to join the German cause; but he informs the F.B.I. of this attempted recruitment. They ask him to become an undercover agent and report the activities of German espionage and subversion. As the United States enters World War II, Dietrich proves to be a valuable contact for the F.B.I. Discovering that the Germans have been getting information concerning the top secret American A-bomb project, Dietrich is determined to discover the identity of the high-level traitor. The Germans discover that Dietrich is a spy but not before he learns the name of the agent providing the Nazis with their data. The

F.B.I., headed by Inspector Briggs, arrive in time to rescue their agent and rout the Germans. As the Nazis flee, one of them shoots Elsa Gebhart, the leader of the espionage ring, in the mistaken belief that she is Dietrich.

Produced by Louis de Rochemont, whose *March of Time* newsreel series became standard theatrical fare in the late 1930s and early 1940s, *House on 92nd Street* took the style and conventions of the earlier newsreels and applied them to fiction film making. Utilizing location photography and a stentorian narrator, the film possesses a surface realism not common to movies of that period. The film boasted that it was based on actual F.B.I. cases, with only the names being changed; and director Hathaway chose to shoot the film in the actual locales of the original incidents. Many of the actors in the film were nonprofessional and some were even actual F.B.I. personnel. Although these concepts were outside the sensibilities of film noir, the flat characterizations and the naturalistic atmosphere juxtaposed with the menacing, stereotyped Nazis created a semidocumentary, yet threatening, aura that influenced a number of subsequent noir films to exploit the newsreel style of *House on 92nd Street*, most notably *T-Men*, *Walk a Crooked Mile*, and *The Naked City*.

—C.M. & A.S.

THE HOUSE ON TELEGRAPH HILL (1951)

Director: Robert Wise
Producer: Robert Bassler (20th Century-Fox)
Screenplay: Elick Moll and Frank Partos; from the novel *The Frightened Child* by Dana Lyon
Director of Photography: Lucien Ballard
Photographic Effects: Fred Sersen
Sound: George Leverett, Harry M. Leonard
Music Score: Sol Kaplan
Music Director: Afred Newman
Orchestration: Edward Powell, Maurice de Packh
Art Directors: Lyle Wheeler, John DeCuir
Set Decoration: Thomas Little, Paul S. Fox
Costumes: Rennie
Wardrobe Supervisor: Charles LeMaire
Makeup: Ben Nye
Assistant Director: Horace Hough
Film Editor: Nick DeMaggio

CAST: Richard Basehart (Alan Spender), Valentina Cortesa (Victoria Kowelska), William Lundigan (Maj. Marc Anders), Fay Baker (Margaret), Gordon Gebert (Chris). **BITS:** Kei Thing Chung (Houseboy), Steve Geray (Dr. Burkhardt), Herbert Butterfield (Callahan), John Burton (Mr. Whitmore), Katherine Meskill (Mrs. Whitmore), Mario Siletti (Tony), Charles Wagenheim (Man at Accident), David Clarke (Mechanic), Tamara Schee (Maria), Natasha Lytess (Karin), Ashmead Scott (Inspector Hardy), Mari Young (Chinese Girl Singer), Tom McDonough (Farrell), Henry Rowland (Sergeant-Interpreter), Les O'Pace (UNRRA Sergeant), Don Kohler (Chemist), Harry Carter (Detective Ellis).
Location: San Francisco, California
Filming Completed: October 12, 1950
Released: 20th Century-Fox, May 13, 1951
Running Time: 92 minutes

Victoria Kowelska assumes the identity of Karin de Nakova, a woman who died in a German concentration camp, in order to gain permission to enter the United States after World War II. DeNakova's young son, Chris, has lived since birth with his wealthy great-aunt in San Francisco, and Victoria travels to join them. Before she arrives however, the aunt dies and Victoria maintains Karin's identity and inherits the aunt's estate, which includes a mansion atop Telegraph Hill. Victoria falls in love with the estate's trustee, Alan Spender, and they marry. Soon, however, unexplainable accidents cause Victoria to fear that Alan and the child's governess, Margaret, are not only plotting her death but murdered the aunt to assume control of the estate. Alan attempts to poison Victoria, but she tricks him and he dies instead because Margaret refuses to call a doctor to help him. The police arrest Margaret for murder, and she tells Victoria "to let her conscience be her guide."

A film that borders on the Gothic, *The House on Telegraph Hill* is film noir because of the atmospheric photography of Lucien Ballard; the fatalistically romantic narration of Valentina Cortesa, who tells Victoria's story in flashback; the devious characterization of Alan Spender by Richard Basehart; and the glacial performance of Fay Baker as the governess, Margaret. Additionally, the hints of sexual aberration, the intrusions of an enigmatic past, and the isolation and ultimate entrapment of the heroine in the old mansion combine the paranoia of a modern setting while exploiting certain conventions of noir-related period films such as *Gaslight* and *The Spiral Staircase*. Like them, *The House on Telegraph Hill* has a climactic scene that reveals that the victim's peril is not imaginary—specifically when Alan and Victoria confront each other in the child's playhouse, and it appears momentarily that Alan plans to push his wife through the hole in the wall making her fall to her death at the base of the steep hill.

—B.P.

HUMAN DESIRE (1954)

Director: Fritz Lang
Producer: Lewis J. Rachmil (Columbia)
Screenplay: Alfred Hayes; from the novel, *La Bête Humaine*, by Émile Zola
Director of Photography: Burnett Guffey
Sound: John Livadary

HUSTLE

Music Score: Daniele Amfitheatrof
Conductor: Morris Stoloff
Art Director: Robert Peterson
Set Decoration: William Kiernan
Hairstyles: Helen Hunt
Assistant Director: Milton Feldman
Film Editor: William A. Lyon

CAST: Glenn Ford (Jeff Warren), Gloria Grahame (Vicki Buckley), Broderick Crawford (Carl Buckley), Edgar Buchanan (Alec Simmons), Kathleen Case (Ellen Simmons), Diane DeLaire (Vera Simmons), Grandon Rhodes (John Owens), Dan Seymour (Bartender), John Pickard (Matt Henley), Paul Brinegar (Brakeman), Dan Riss (Prosecutor Gruber), Victor Hugo Greene (Davidson), John Zaremba (Russell), Carl Lee (John Thurston), Olan Soule (Lewis).

Location: Rock Island Railroad lines, Oklahoma
Filming Completed: January 25, 1954
Released: Columbia, August 6, 1954
Running Time: 90 minutes

Carl Buckley asks his wife Vicki to use her influence with Mr. Owens, a wealthy shipper, to save his railroad job which he is in danger of losing due to his hot temper. At first hesitant, she agrees to meet with Owens and Carl's position is saved. But her husband suspects adultery. Haunted by jealousy, he forces his wife to rendezvous with Owens onboard a train and, confronting them alone in a compartment, Carl kills Owens. Vicki was observed near Owen's compartment by Jeff Warren, an off-duty railroad engineer. At the postmortem Jeff lies to protect Vicki and they eventually engage in an adulterous liaison. Meanwhile Carl is obsessed that Vicki was "somebody's leftover," and when she refuses to maintain a sexual relationship with him, he degenerates into alcoholism. However, Carl still loves Vicki and keeps her through holding an incriminating letter of hers. When he is ultimately fired, Carl wants to leave town with Vicki but she persuades Jeff to waylay her drunken husband one night and make his murder appear an accident. Jeff cannot kill Carl and only retrieves the letter, returning it to Vicki. Disgusted, Vicki leaves town with Carl. On the train she taunts the hapless husband by telling him of her plan to kill him and of her sexual exploits. Carl loses control of himself and kills her. The film closes, as it opened, with Jeff and his friend Alec in the locomotive's cabin.

Much of the sexual perversities of Jean Renoir's film *La Bête Humaine* (1938) had to be eliminated in the contemporized 1954 American film version. However, Gloria Grahame's portrayal of Vicki is as sexually motivated as Simone Simon's in the French film; and her final confrontation with Carl, when she details her sexual adventures, is more perverse than any aspect of Simon's rather kittenish portrayal of the same character. Visually *Human Desire* is constructed with a graphic determinism that is more relentless than any usage in Renoir's original film. The metaphorically ominous shots of a dark sea seen under the titles of Lang's production of *Clash By Night* are superseded in his direction of *Human Desire* by opening and closing shots of a myriad of railroad tracks randomly interweaving and separating in a switching yard. The obvious metaphor for human paths crossing and affecting each other by chance is linked directly to Jeff Warren because the image is taken as a point-of-view from the cab of an engine. As the narrative develops, every line and bar shadow added as a background detail recalls those fateful vectors of the film's beginning, vectors that mock the ineffectual attempts by the film's characters to redeem their desolate lives with desperate pleasures.

—B.P. & A.S.

HUSTLE (1975)
[Working Titles: HOME FREE; CITY OF THE ANGELS]

Director: Robert Aldrich
Executive Producer: Burt Reynolds (RoBurt Productions-Paramount in association with Churchill Service Company)
Producer: Robert Aldrich
Associate Producer: William Aldrich
Screenplay: Steve Shagan
Director of Photography: Joseph Biroc [Eastmancolor]
Camera Operators: Kenneth Peach, Jr.; Roger Sherman, Jr.
Special Effects: Henry Miller
Sound: Jack Solomon
Music: Frank DeVol
Songs: "Yesterday When I Was Young" by Charles Aznavour with English lyric by Herbert Kretzmer, sung by Charles Aznavour; "So Rare" lyric by Jack Sharpe, music by Jerry Herst; "A Man and a Woman" by Francis Lai; "Mission Impossible" music by Lalo Schifrin; "Begin the Beguine" by Cole Porter.
Art Director: Hilyard Brown
Set Decoration: Raphael Bretton
Costumes: Oscar Rodriguez (Men), Betsy Cox (Women)
Makeup: Tom Ellingwood
Hairstyles: Marlene Williams
Dialogue Supervisor: Alvin Greenman
Script Supervisor: Adell Aldrich
Still Photographer: Jack Gereghty
Production Supervisor: Eddie Saeta
Production Assistant: Walter Blake
Casting: Jack Baur
First Assistant Director: Malcom Harding
Film Editor: Michael Luciano

CAST: Burt Reynolds (Lt. Phil Gaines), Catherine Deneuve (Nicole Britton), Ben Johnson (Marty Hollinger), Paul Winfield (Sgt. Louis Belgrave), Eileen Brennan (Paula Hollinger), Eddie Albert (Leo Sellars), Ernest Borgnine (Santoro), Jack Carter (Herbie Dalitz), Sharon Kelly (Gloria Hollinger), James Hampton (Bus Driver), David

Spielberg (Bellamy), Catherine Bach (Peggy Summers), Chuck Hayward (Morgue Attendant), David Estridge (Albino), Peter Brandon (Minister), Naomi Stevens (Woman Hostage), Med Flory (Cop beating Albino), Steve Shaw, Dino Washington (Cops in Elevator), Anthony Eldridge (Laugher), John Duke Russo (Man in Phone Booth), Don Billett (Cop in Tee Shirt), Hal Baylor (Police Captain), Nancy Bonniwell (Girl in Airport Bar), Don "Red" Barry (Airport Bartender), Karl Lukas (Charley), Gene Chronopoulos (Bartender), Patrice Rohmer (Linda, a Dancer), Alvin Hammer (Liquor Store Clerk), Dave Willock (Liquor Store Clerk), Queenie Smith, Marilyn Moe (Customers), Robert Englund (Holdup Man), George Memoli (Foot Fetish Man), Fred Willard (Interrogator), Thad Geer (Second Holdup Man), Kelly Wilder (Nancy Gaines), Ben Young (First Detective), Tasso Bravos, Jimmy R. Hampton, Nathan Harding (Boys on Beach), John Furlong (Waiter), Jason Wingreen (Jim Lang), Ron Nyman (Pan Am Clerk), Victoria Carroll (Guest).

Location: Los Angeles, Pasadena, Marina del Rey, California
Filming Completed: February 11, 1975
Released: Paramount, December 25, 1975
Running Time: 120 minutes
MPAA Rating: R

Police Lt. Phil Gaines's morning off is interrupted when a young woman's body is found by children on a beach outing. Leaving the home he shares with Nicole, a French-born prostitute, Gaines joins his partner, Sgt. Louis Belgrave, and suspects that the dead woman is Gloria Hollinger. Asking her parents to identify the body, Gaines is knocked down by Hollinger when he sees his daughter's nude body. Told that Gloria's death was probably due to a self-induced drug overdose, Hollinger accuses the police of covering up a murder because his family are "nobodies." Although convinced the death is a suicide, Gaines agrees to investigate the identity of a man whose photograph was found in Gloria's possession. First, Gaines must kill a psychopath, whom he had previously arrested but who is now free and holding hostages in a factory. Discovering that the man in Gloria's photograph is Leo Sellars, a prominent but corrupt attorney who is responsible for bringing Nicole to the United States, Gaines confronts him about Gloria. The attorney is candid about knowing the woman but assures Gaines that there would be no reason for anyone to murder her. On his return home, Gaines and Nicole have another quarrel about her profession; but she will not abandon it unless Phil can accept her and offer financial as well as emotional security. Meanwhile, Hollinger investigates on his own and is brutally beaten by thugs at the nightclub where Gloria worked. When Mrs. Hollinger informs Gaines about her husband's beating, she also relates that he is suffering from shellshock and that Gloria's estrangement from home was partly due to her daughter's awareness of Mrs. Hollinger's infidelity. Gaines hopes to reason with Hollinger by revealing his daughter's perform-

ances in pornographic films; but his plan backfires. Hollinger is more outraged and tracks down Leo Sellars. Alerted, Gaines and Belgrave rush to protect the attorney but arrive just after Hollinger has killed him. While lecturing against vigilantism, Gaines tampers with the evidence to make it appear Hollinger acted out of self-defense. Before returning to the office, Gaines telephones Nicole to meet him at the airport for a weekend in San Francisco. On his way there, Gaines intercedes in a liquor store burglary and is killed by the robbers.

In counterpart to the tired private detectives in *Hickey and Boggs*, Phil Gaines represents the contemporary noir policeman. Although he is, in the manner of Callahan in *Dirty Harry*, fundamentally disillusioned with the course of his life's work and the system that supports it—as illustrated by his remark, "Don't you know what country you live in? Can't you smell the bananas? You live in Guatemala with color television."—Gaines's response is much more introspective and less inclined to violence than Harry Callahan's. With his painful awareness of the impermanence of both social institutions and personal relationships, Gaines's characterization is typically noir, as are his attempts to detach himself emotionally from both Nicole and his job. But his jealousy over Nicole's profession and his outrage over the fact that "everybody hustles" are never really in control.

More than in any of his earlier film noir, Aldrich keys the *mise-en-scène* to Gaines's own alienated point-of-view. The initial sequence in his and Nicole's home is remarkably diffracted, beginning with an aerial shot that moves in, followed by two cuts pulling back, then another in to Nicole's face. The color and details of setting are attenuated by the high contrast and the hard edge in the lighting. The dialogue between them is photographed mostly in close-ups, which isolate Gaines and Nicole; the two shots are framed tightly, cutting into their foreheads. Gaines's expensive home is made to seem unattractive and claustrophobic, even as he is visually distanced from the woman with whom he lives. The first shots in Gaines's office, after he has been knocked down by Hollinger in the morgue, reveal an even less appealing locus: dark, grimy pens separated by dingy frosted glass and illuminated by a few traces of yellow sunlight, which cannot dispel the pervasive shadows.

Whereas Harry Callahan takes to the streets in search of catharsis, Gaines retreats from the oppressive realities into self. His nostalgia, "I like the thirties, Cole Porter, Dizzy Dean," is symptomatic of the same fallen romanticism that plagued Mike Callahan in *World For Ransom*. Because he may feel compelled to kill—as when he gives a *coup de grace* to a homicidal mental patient, so that he may never be allowed to go free again—Gaines adopts metaphors for his violence, his favorite being the movie version of *Moby Dick*. If Gaines sees himself as Ahab, driven mad by his own moral outrage, he must also see himself reflected in the felons and psychos, who are waging their own war against the system, so that each action against them ultimately

becomes an act against self. As the myths begin to lose their therapeutic potency—Nicole returns home to find Gaines watching *Moby Dick* on television and crouched in the shadows like Charlie Castle in *The Big Knife*—Gaines initiates a noir transference with the pitiful Marty Hollinger.

Hollinger, the Korean War veteran who is still affected by shellshock, is identified with Gaines on both visual and narrative levels. The balanced framing between the two men, as they stand beside the body of Hollinger's daugher in the morgue, is carried over into matching low angles and side-light on Gaines and Hollinger in their respective homes. Both men are haunted by memories of an ostensibly happier past, which are incorporated into the narrative as brief flashbacks; and although only Gaines is aware of it, both were sexually betrayed by their wives. Finally, both hate syndicate attorney Leo Sellars, Gaines for his corruption of Nicole, Hollinger for that of his daughter. Gaines further despises Sellars as a symbol of the decadence in the system that employs him; but, when Sellars asks him, "Why single me out?"; Gaines must reply, "I can't get everyone." Through his surrogate, Gaines does get Sellars; but, to make the transference complete, he unwittingly makes himself liable for the moral retribution and is gunned down in the liquor store. Whether or not Gaines has a moment of realization, before dying, about the causes of his destruction is tangential to *Hustle's* noir statement. Unlike Harry Callahan, Gaines lacks the intensity or simply the inclination to act alone whenever possible; as a consequence, when he tries, he perishes.

—A.S.

I AM A FUGITIVE FROM A CHAIN GANG (1932)

Director: Mervyn LeRoy
Producer: Hal Wallis (Warner Brothers)
Screenplay: Howard J. Greene and Brown Holmes; from Robert E. Burns's autobiography, *I Am A Fugitive From A Georgia Chain Gang*
Director of Photography: Sol Polito
Art Director: Jack Okey
Costumes: Orry-Kelly
Technical Advisers: S.H. Sullivan, Jack Miller[Uncredited: Robert E. Burns]
Film Editor: William Holmes

CAST: Paul Muni (James Allen), Glenda Farrell (Marie Woods), Helen Vinson (Helen), Preston Foster (Pete), Allen Jenkins (Barney Sykes), Edward Ellis (Bomber Wells), John Wray (Nordine), Hale Hamilton (the Reverend Robert Clinton Allen), Harry Woods (Guard), David Landau (Warden), Edward J. McNamara (Second Warden), Robert McWade (Ramsey), Willard Robertson (Prison Commissioner), Noel Francis (Linda), Louise Carter (Mrs. Allen), Berton Churchill (Judge), Sheila Terry (Allen's Secretary), Sally Blane (Alice), James Bell (Red), Edward LeSaint (Chairman, Chamber of Commerce), Douglas Dumbrille (District Attorney), Robert Warwick (Fuller). **BITS:** Charles Middleton, Reginald Barlow, Jack LaRue, Charles Sellon, Erville Alderson, George Pat Collins, William Pawley, Lew Kelly, Evertt Brown, William LeMaire, George Cooper, Wallis Clark, Walter Long, Frederick Burton, Irving Bacon, Lee Shumway, J. Frank Glendon, Dennis O'Keefe (Men).
Released: Warner Brothers, November 10, 1932
Running Time: 93 minutes

James Allen is a hometown boy returning from the World War with a few medals and a sense of dissatisfaction. He finds his old factory job stultifying and cannot adjust to smalltown life. His family finds this difficult to understand, and they are baffled and relieved when he leaves home to find a more rewarding life. Unable to locate a job, Allen stays in a flophouse filled with other unemployed men, many of them also veterans. One of the men suggests that they panhandle a meal at a local diner. Allen's new acquaintance, however, tries to rob the diner and kills the owner. The police arrive and the gunman is shot, but the innocent Allen is convicted and sent to a brutal Southern prison farm. The prison is a hell of beatings, torture, and murder. Allen escapes to the North, changes his name, and locates work. As a construction worker, his diligent application and his desire "to build, to create" bring success; and he eventually becomes a respected engineer. Along the way, he marries Marie, a bar girl who had befriended him after his escape. Her vulgarity later becomes a burden and embarrassment to Allen. Allen meets an elegant woman

named Helen at a dinner with business associates and falls in love with her. She urges him to return to prison because she believes that his great success in life will mitigate his sentence and break Marie's hold on him, as his wife has been holding Allen with threats of exposing his prison escape. The authorities assure Allen that his cooperation will earn a pardon within a short time. The pardon is refused, however, and appeals are rejected again and again. Betrayed, he escapes a second time and blows up a bridge, a telling reversal on his former success at building them. Allen sees Helen one last time at night and then fades into the darkness. His face is no longer visible when he answers her question about how he lives by saying, "I steal."

Although *I Am A Fugitive From A Chain Gang* was made too early in the 1930s to be considered a bona fide film noir, it is certainly one of the most important forerunners of the type. The relatively undeveloped technology precluded the use of high contrast, low-key lighting characteristic of noir films, yet much of the film takes place in darkness. There is a conscious use of shadows and silhouettes, and the daylight scenes are stark and unrelieved in shading and texture. More than just its visual style, however, marks *Chain Gang* as a prototype of film noir. The film's desperate and unrelieved vision of the world as a perilous place for the common man suggests that honor, honesty, and work are paper values in a brutal jungle where savagery and dishonor are institutionalized.

I Am A Fugitive From A Chain Gang is one of the most famous of the Warner's "social problem" films, and its appearance during the middle of the Great Depression accounts for much of its pessimism. It is especially interesting as a reflection of the extreme bitterness over the veterans issue. The veterans' Bonus March on Washington took place in 1932, the same year this film was released, and the agitation for veterans benefits had been a public issue since the early 1920s. The entire film is actually placed within the context of the disillusioned, ignored, and mal-treated veteran; and it is this ill fortune of James Allen that starts his life on the downward spiral. One of the most memorable moments in the film is the scene where Allen tries to pawn his war medals, only to be shown a cardboard box filled with similarly worthless medals and ribbons. In its antiromantic attitude toward the national myth of individual responsibility, *Chain Gang* differs significantly from the glamorous existentialism of the average film noir. James Allen is nothing but a victim and his involvement in crime is totally unwitting. Furthermore, his efforts to untangle himself and go straight are successful; his return to prison, and the second, more violent escape are motivated by other people. On one point, however, Allen seems a less-than-noble character, and that is his callous attitude towards his lower-class wife, Marie. His self-betterment program acquires an unpleasant opportunism when he decides to abandon his uneducated wife for an attractive, rich, and cultured "equal." The shrewish and vengeful characterization of the wife sustains audience identification with Allen's rejection of her. The sympathetic portrayal of

Allen by Paul Muni adds verisimilitude and supports audience empathy for the character's increasing paranoia and ultimate psychosis, even while they may fear such a person's subsequent actions. The last image of a haunted and paranoid animal is an effective indictment of a society which could force James Allen to blow up a bridge like those he worked and dreamed for years to construct.

—E.M.

I DIED A THOUSAND TIMES (1955)
[Working Title: THE JAGGED EDGE]

Director: Stuart Heisler
Producer: Willis Goldbeck (Warner Brothers)
Screenplay: W.R. Burnett; from his novel *High Sierra*
Director of Photography: Ted McCord [Warner Color; CinemaScope]
Second Unit Photography: Edwin DuPar
Sound: Charles Lang
Music: David Buttolph
Orchestration: Maurice de Packh, Gus Levene
Art Director: Edward Carrere
Set Decoration: William L. Kuehl
Costumes: Moss Mabry
Makeup: Gordon Bau
Dialogue Supervisor: Eugene Busch
Assistant Director: Chuck Hansen
Second Unit Director: Russ Saunders
Second Unit Assistant: Al Alleborn
Film Editor: Clarence Kolster

CAST: Jack Palance (Roy Earle), Shelley Winters (Marie Gibson), Lori Nelson (Velma), Lee Marvin (Babe), Earl Holliman (Red), Perry Lopez (Louis Mendoza), Gon-zalez Gonzalez (Chico), Lon Chaney, Jr. (Big Mac), Howard St. John (Doc Banton), Ralph Moody (Pa), Olive Carey (Ma), Joseph Millikin (Kranmer), Richard Davalos (Lon Preisser), Bill Kennedy (Sheriff), Peggy Maley (Kranmer's Girl). **BITS:** Dub Taylor (Ed), Dick Reeves, Chris Alcaide, Larry Hudson, John Pickard (Deputies), Karolee Kelly (Cigar Counter Vendor), John Stephenson (Pfeiffer), Mae Clarke (Mabel Baughman), Hugh Sanders (Mr. Baughman), Howard Hoffman (Fisherman), Nick Adams, Darren Dublin (Bellboys), Myrna Fahey (Margie), Herb Vigrain (Art), Dennis Hopper (Joe), David McMahon (Owner of Auto Court), Paul Brinazar (Bus Driver), Wendell Niles (Radio Announcer), John Daheim, Dennis Moore, Mickey Simpson (Officers), Steve Darrell (Detective), Gil Perkins (Slim), Larry Blake (Healy), Nesdon Booth, Ed Fury, Larve Farlow, Hubie Kerns, Tony Hughes, Mary Benoit, Paul Power, Charles Watts, Don Dillaway, Fay Baker, James Seay (People).
Location: Mount Whitney, California
Filming Completed: April 4, 1955
Released: Warner Brothers, November 9, 1955

I, THE JURY

Running Time: 109 minutes
[NOTE: Frank Sinatra was originally considered for the part of Roy Earle]

Roy Earle, a pardoned ex-convict, is to lead the robbery of a resort hotel. While setting up the raid, Roy begins an affair with a member of the robbing gang, Marie, and also befriends a mongrel dog. Meanwhile, Roy meets Velma, a "good" girl. Velma is crippled; but after Roy buys her an operation that cures her, she rejects him. The robbery is badly bungled and Roy and Marie go on the run. Rich in jewels but with no cash, Roy drives alone into Los Angeles to fence the gems. He is wounded in a double cross and chased into the California Sierras by the police. Roy is cornered and a crowd gathers to witness his killing. Marie watches helplessly as Roy is shot down.

Although *High Sierra* may be esthetically more satisfying and historically more significant, *I Died A Thousand Times* is in some respects a more cohesive film, probably because of its screenwriter, W.R. Burnett. There are large sections of this film that duplicate *High Sierra* but there are also significant narrative differences and a general sharpening of dramatic focus in the screenplay of the later film. While it is slightly longer than *High Sierra*, Burnett has, in fact, cut material from the original and brought *I Died A Thousand Times* closer to the novel as well as closer to creating a first person point-of-view.

The openings of the respective versions illustrate this difference. While *High Sierra* begins with a series of clumsy vignettes about Roy's rural childhood, his membership in the Dillinger gang, and his arranged pardon, *I Died A Thousand Times* opens with Jack Palance as Roy Earle already driving through the desert, with the Sierras and his ambiguous destiny looming ahead of him. Throughout his chance meeting with Velma and her family and his fatalistic conversation with a gas station attendant,he is noticeably affected by the landscape around him. It is not until the film's second scene, the arrival at Shaw's camp, that Earle's name and his past are revealed. What was exposition and sentimentality in *High Sierra* becomes an ironic sequence in the later film. Not only does it set the film's mood, it establishes a unity of place and time by beginning Earle's story in geographical proximity to where it will end. By making Earle a more mysterious figure it produces a stronger sense of his existential isolation; and because considerable action occurs before Roy is identified as a criminal on a job, the film is structured as a character study and not as a genre piece.

While *High Sierra* contains a realistic emphasis on sex and violence, it is also the skills of Humphrey Bogart as Roy and Ida Lupino as Marie that prevent the film from becoming hopelessly melodramatic. If *I Died A Thousand Times* is more blatant in this respect it is also more naturalistic. For instance, the episode in which Roy returns to find his two hooligans, Red and Babe, fighting over Marie is much more sexual, violent, and disturbing than the equivalent scene in *High Sierra*; Roy's dog has been kicked, Marie's face is badly bruised, and Red is lurking in the woods waiting to kill Babe. That Roy wants Marie to pistol whip and "to mark" her attacker suggests a volatile combination of ruthlessness, sadism, and avenging justice not seen in Bogart's characterization of Earle. Throughout the film, Roy experiences his sexual desires and emotional needs in defiance of his oppressive surroundings; and passionate scenes with Marie consistently dissolve into long shots of the jagged mountains.

The massive and omnipresent mountains and vast desert spaces foreshadow Earle's final death journey; but *I Died A Thousand Times* does not match *High Sierra's* climactic chase. Director Heisler (or second unit director Saunders) staged and shot the chase precisely as in *High Sierra* with the locations, camera setups, and even the screen direction identical. Yet the potential of this footage is mitigated by editing these shots into short pieces that fail to develop the pace and organization of the *High Sierra* sequence with its tension and sense of inexorable fate. Even the originally long pan from Earle's car to those of the police as they make a hairpin curve has inserts cut into its counterpart scene in the later film. Contrasted with *High Sierra*, Palance as Earle has an interesting proletarian quality that may have thematic implications of the small man made great by his fate. But he does not have nearly the same aura of tragedy that Bogart gives the role. However, Lee Marvin as Babe and Earl Holiman as Red add a realistic coarseness to their roles that is lacking in the earlier film.

—D.L.W.

I, THE JURY (1953)

Director: Harry Essex
Producer: Victor Saville (Parklane Productions)
Screenplay: Harry Essex; from the novel by Mickey Spillane
Director of Photography: John Alton [Black-and-White; Dunning 3-Dimensional]
Sound: Joe Edmundson
Music: Franz Waxman
Art Director: Ward Ihnen
Production Manager: Norman Cook
Assistant Director: Jack Greenwood
Film Editor: Fredrick Y. Smith

CAST: Biff Elliot (Mike Hammer), Preston Foster (Capt. Pat Chambers), Peggie Castle (Charlotte Manning), Margaret Sheridan (Velda), Alan Reed (George Kalecki), Frances Osborne (Myrna), Robert Cunningham (Hal Kines), Elisha Cook, Jr. (Bobo), Paul Dubov (Marty), Mary Anderson (Eileen Vickers), Tani Seitz (Mary Bellamy), Dran Seitz (Esther Bellamy), Robert Swanger (Jack Williams), John Qualen (Dr. Vickers).
Location: Los Angeles, California
Filming Completed: April 30, 1953

Released: United Artists, August 14, 1953
Running Time: 88 minutes

Jack Williams, an amputee, is shot several times by a mysterious intruder as he attempts to crawl to his gun. His best friend, private detective Mike Hammer, swears vengeance on the killer even though he has been warned against using illegal tactics by his friend, Pat Chambers of the New York Police Department. Checking out everyone present at a party that Jack gave before he was killed, Hammer discovers an array of types including Myrna, a former heroin addict and Jack's fiancèe; psychiatrist Charlotte Manning; the apparently love-starved but beautiful Bellamy twins; and George Kalecki, a fight promoter turned art collector. As Hammer investigates, his path is strewn with corpses. Finally, the detective discovers that Kalecki is the head of a narcotics racket and kills him. But it is not the end of Kalecki's organization. The clues lead Hammer to confront his own fiancèe, Charlotte, with his knowledge that she wanted to take over Kalecki's racket and is responsible for several murders. As Hammer continues with his accusations, the woman stops denying the charges and partially disrobes. Embracing Hammer, she reaches for a hidden gun; but before she can use it, the detective shoots her.

I, The Jury was the first of the Saville-produced Spillane series and is probably the only film noir to be shot in the 3-Dimensional technique. John Alton's photography is, as always, brilliant although budget limitations force the use of such devices as Christmas card scenes instead of establishing shots. Also detrimental is Biff Elliott as Mike Hammer. Elliott has little presence and no conventional persona on which to draw for dramatic impact. Most of the sadism of the Spillane novels is missing here, except for the startling opening and closing sequences. In the first, a faceless assassin toys with the vicim by letting the amputee crawl slowly to his gun before killing him, while "Hark, The Herald Angels Sing" plays in the background. This contrapuntal use of Christmas music throughout the film is reminiscent of Robert Montgomery's Lady In The Lake. In the closing scene, a more explicit version of Double Indemnity's climax, Hammer shoots the almost nude Charlotte in the stomach as they embrace. When she asks, "How could you?" he replies simply, "It was easy." Despite the fact that other elements of the novel's violence are eliminated, the tone of its machismo sexuality remains, including Spillane's basic misogyny and distaste for homosexuals.

—B.P.

I WAKE UP SCREAMING (1942)
[Working Title: HOT SPOT]

Director: H. Bruce Humberstone
Executive Producer: Darryl F. Zanuck (20th Century-Fox)

Producer: Milton Sperling
Screenplay: Dwight Taylor; from the novel by Steve Fisher, serialized in Photoplay-Movie Mirror.
Director of Photography: Edward Cronjager
Sound: Bernard Freericks, Roger Heman
Music Director: Cyril J. Mockridge
Art Directors: Richard Day, Nathan Juran
Set Decoration: Thomas Little
Costumes: Gwen Wakeling
Makeup: Guy Pearce
Assistant Director: Ad Schaumer
Film Editor: Robert Simpson

CAST: Betty Grable (Jill Lynn), Victor Mature (Frankie Christopher), Carole Landis (Vicky Lynn), Laird Cregar (Ed Cornell), William Gargan (McDonald), Alan Mowbray (Robin Ray), Allyn Joslyn (Larry Evans), Elisha Cook, Jr. (Harry Williams), Chick Chandler (Reporter), Morris Ankrum (Assistant District Attorney), May Beatty (Mrs. Handel). **BITS:** Cyril Ring, Basil Walker, Bob Cornell (Reporters), Charles Lane (Florist), Frank Orth (Caretaker), Gregory Gaye (Headwaiter), Stanley Clements, George Hickman (Newsboys), Dick Rich, James Flavin, Stanley Blystone, Tim Ryan, Ralph Dunn, Wade Boteler, Eddie Dunn, Phillip Morris (Detectives), Cecil Weston (Police Matron), Harry Strang, Russ Clark (Policemen), Edward McWade, Paul Weigel (Old Men), Harry Seymour (Bartender), Pat McKee (Newsman), Albert Pollet (Waiter), Dorothy Dearing (Girl), Forbes Murray (Mr. Handel).
Filming Completed: August 26, 1941
Released: 20th Century-Fox, January 16, 1942
Running Time: 82 minutes
[NOTE: I Wake Up Screaming was previewed for the press on October 16, 1941 under the title Hot Spot.]

Promoter Frankie Christopher is accused of the murder of Vicky Lynn, a young actress he "discovered" as a waitress with the aid of ex-actor Robin Ray and gossip columnist Larry Evans. Frankie hides out with Vicky's sister Jill, with whom he has fallen in love but is captured. The relentless and obsessive investigating officer, Ed Cornell, admits that he knows Frankie is innocent but because evidence is completely incriminating says, "That won't prevent you from going to the hot chair." Frankie realizes he must find Vicky's murderer himself, so he escapes and tries to find clues. Ultimately, he traps Vicky's neighbor, Harry Wiliams, in his room, which is decorated with photographs of the dead woman, and the pimply-faced elevator operator confesses that he murdered Vicky. Harry also relates that he confessed to Cornell but was told to keep silent because both men were jealous of Frankie and agreed to see him executed for the murder. Frankie turns in his evidence to Cornell's superiors and is now free to enjoy his romance with Jill.

I Wake Up Screaming is an example of the developing film noir style in the early stages of the cycle. The locations, casting, and camerawork, particularly the shadowy, low-key lighting, develop a quasi-naturalistic and threatening ambience. Part of the original novel's interest, by hard-boiled pulp writer Steve Fisher, is its insider's view of Hollywood; but Zanuck had tabooed "Hollywood" pictures and forced the film makers to switch the story's location to New York City with its atmospheric haunts of nightclubs, ritzy apartments, police stations, and movie theaters.

H. Bruce "Lucky" Humberstone, the director, was not known for his work in melodrama but his *mise-en-scene* exploits the dark Fox-style lighting of cinematographer Edward Cronjager. It is high contrast and full of interesting and disturbing shadows, particularly the slanting shadows of venetian blinds. This visual contrast is complemented by the film's casting, which pits the darkly gleaming Victor Mature against the blonde freshness of Carole Landis and Betty Grable (in her first nonmusical role); and the literally "heavy" Laird Cregar, against nervous, birdlike, Elisha Cook, Jr. In minor roles, character actors like Alan Mowbray as a conceited ham actor and Allyn Joslyn as the ruthless gossip columnist contribute respectively to the sardonic and brutal undercurrents of the film. As do many noir films, *I Wake Up Screaming* contains suggestions of sexual perversity. Jill finds herself irresistably attracted to the man who presumably murdered her sister. The scene in which Frankie wakes to find Cornell seated beside his bed and obsessed with proving Frankie's guilt, also hints at Cornell's repressed homosexual passion.

I Wake Up Screaming is exemplary of what the developing noir style could do for a movie. The plastic beauty inherent in such a style creates a mood and resonance that are often beyond the implication of the script. Using the icons of the style, many unremarkable directors did their best work in film noir.

—M.B. & A.S.

I WALK ALONE (1948)

Directo: Byron Haskin
Producer: Hal B. Wallis (Hal B. Wallis Productions)
Screenplay: Charles Schnee, adapted by Robert Smith and John Bright; from the play, *Beggars are Coming to Town* by Theodore Reeves
Director of Photography: Leo Tover
Process Photography: Farciot Edouart
Sound: Harry Lindgren, Walter Oberst
Music: Victor Young
Songs: "Don't Call It Love" by Ned Washington and Allie Wrubel; "Isn't It Romantic" by Richard Rodgers and Lorenz Hart; "My Ideal" by Leon Robin, Richard A. Whiting, and J. Newell Chase; "It's Easy To Remember" by Richard Rodgers and Lorenz Hart; "Two Sleepy People" by Frank Loesser and Hoagy Carmichael; "Heart and Soul" by Frank Loesser and Hoagy Carmichael; "I'm Yours" by E.Y. Harburg and Johnny Green; and "You

Leave Me Breathless" by Fred Hollander and Ralph Freed. Performed by The Regency Three.
Art Directors: Hans Dreier, Franz Bachelin
Set Decoration: Sam Comer, Patrick Delaney
Costumes: Edith Head
Makeup: Wally Westmore
Dialogue Director: Joan Hathaway
Assistant Director: Richard McWhorter
Film Editor: Arthur Schmidt

CAST: Burt Lancaster (Frankie Madison), Lizabeth Scott (Kay Lawrence), Kirk Douglas (Noll Turner), Wendell Corey (Dave), Kristine Miller (Mrs. Richardson), George Rigaud (Maurice), Marc Lawrence (Nick Palestro), Mike Mazurki (Dan), Mickey Knox (Skinner), Roger Neury (Felix). **BITS:** John Bishop (Ben), Bruce Lester (Charles), Jean Del Val (Henri), Gino Corrado (George), Freddie Steele (Tiger), Dewey Robinson (Heinz), Fred G. Somers (Butcher), Charles D. Brown (Lt. Hollaran), Walter Anthony Merrill (Schreiber), Bobby Barber (Newsboy), Jack Perrin (Policeman), Bert Moorehouse (Toll Gate Policeman), Olin Howlin (Watchman), James Davies (Masseur).
Filming Completed: March 1947
Released: Paramount, January 22, 1948
Running Time: 98 minutes

In the days of bootlegging, Frankie Madison and Noll Turner were partners. Chased by the cops on a night run, they struck a deal whereby Turner would attempt to escape on foot while Madison would stick with the truck, so that if one was caught, the other could keep their nightclub operating and save half the profits for the unlucky partner to collect when free. Madison is released from prison some years later and returns to claim his share. His brother Dave is now working as an accountant for Turner, who owns a new club. Attempting to placate Madison with favors and attention from lovely singer Kay Lawrence, who works at the club and is Turner's girl, Turner makes it clear that he will not split profits evenly with Madison because the old club was sold and Madison will only receive half of that club's modest profits. Betrayed, Madison is particularly enraged that his own brother has helped Turner. Only Kay is sympathetic.

Dave overcomes his cowardice and stands up to Turner, who has him killed. Madison gets even, enters a legitimate business, and wins Kay's love.

I Walk Alone incorporates a subjective quality into a story about bitterness and vengeance that is unusual in film noir of this period. The gangsters speak of corporate structures and bewilder the straightforward Madison, whose racketeering dates from a less complicated era. But also, director Byron Haskin supports this with an ambience of romanticism in such scenes as the arranged dinner between Madison and Kay (a similar generosity of humor and romantic nuance informs a film as different as the director's film about a rancher and his mail-order bride, *The Naked*

Kay Lawrence (Lizabeth Scott) and Frankie Madison (Burt Lancaster) in I Walk Alone.

Jungle). *I Walk Alone* is Haskin's first film and introduces these sympathetic virtues, particularly in the character of Kay whose singing is warmly evocative of postwar idealism. Curiously, the anguish one expects from Frankie Madison's character as the film noir protagonist is more apparent in the character of the remorseful brother, Dave, played by Wendell Corey. Frankie is absent in the film's most dramatic moment, when Dave is killed and in which Corey makes a lasting impression.

—B.L.

I WAS A COMMUNIST FOR THE F.B.I. (1951)

Director: Gordon Douglas
Producer: Bryan Foy (Warner Brothers)
Screenplay: Crane Wilbur; from the *Saturday Evening Post* article "I Posed as A Communist for the F.B.I." by Matt Cvetic as told to Pete Martin
Director of Photography: Edwin DuPar
Sound: Leslie G. Hewitt
Art Director: Leo K. Kuter
Set Decoration: Lyle B. Reifsnider
Makeup: Gordon Bau
Assistant Director: Al Alleborn
Film Editor: Folmar Blangsted

CAST: Frank Lovejoy (Matt Cvetic), Dorothy Hart (Eve Merrick), Philip Carey (Mason), Dick Webb (Crowley), James Millican (Jim Blandon), Ron Hagerthy (Dick Cvetic), Paul Picerni (Joe Cvetic), Frank Gerstle (Tom Cvetic), Russ Conway (Frank Cvetic), Hope Kramer (Ruth Cvetic), Kasia Orzazekski (Mrs. Cvetic), Eddie Norris (Harmon), Ann Morrison (Miss Nova), Konstantin Shayne (Gerhardt Eisler), Roy Roberts (Father Novac). **BITS:** Paul McGuire (McIntyre), Douglas Evans (Chief Agent), Janet Barrett, Karen Hale (Secretaries), Joseph Smith, Jim O'Gatty (Goons), Frank Marlowe, Barry Sullivan (Workers), Mike Ross (Foreman), Lenita Lane (Principal), Alma Mansfield (Teacher), Ann Kimball, Paula Sowl (Students), Charles Sherlock, George MacGrill (Men), Grace Lenard (Wife), Eric Neilsen (Jackie), Roy Engle (Jackie's Father), Bill Lester (Brown), John Crawford (McGowan), Ernest Anderson, Sugarfoot Anderson (Black Men), Johnny Bradford (Dobbs), Jimmy Gonzales (Brennan), David MacMahon (Masonvitch), Charles Horvath (Good Leader), Phil Tully (Irish Mick), Howard Negley (Union Chairman), Bobby Gilbert, James Adamson (Pickets), Mary Hokanson, Mildred Boyd (Women), Barry Reagan (Officer), Hugh Sanders (Garson), Lyle Latell (Cahill), Chuck Colean (Brakeman), Dick Gordon, William Bailey, Paul Bradley, Buddy Shaw (Lawyers), William Forrest (Senator Wood), Bert Moorhouse (Senator Gray).

I WOULDN'T BE IN YOUR SHOES

Location: Los Angeles and Burbank, California
Filming Completed: February 22, 1951
Released: Warner Brothers, May 2, 1951
Running Time: 84 minutes

Matt Cvetic, a Pittsburgh steel company worker, has joined the Communist Party; but, unknown to anyone including his family, he is an undercover agent for the F.B.I. His family is embarrassed and hostile to him because he is a "slimy red." Matt's immediate superiors in the party are Blandon and Harmon, who are part of a large-scale plan to disrupt the nation by making sure that there are Communists in key positions in industry and unions. When Matt is made the chief party organizer, he is spied on by other Communists as part of their strategy for ferreting out traitors. Matt's son gets in a fight at school over Matt and the boy, upset and disheartened, turns on his father. Matt foolishly writes a letter to his son explaining that he is working for the F.B.I.; but it is accidentally lost and picked up by Eve Merrick, his son's teacher and a Communist Party member. Eve does not turn the letter in because she is upset with Communist Party tactics. Matt is forced to report her unhappiness to his superiors and they plan to get rid of her. Rescuing Eve, Matt is followed by a Communist agent and, in a fight in a train tunnel, shoots him. A federal probe of Communist activities takes place and Matt testifies. His true role becomes known and he is redeemed in the eyes of family and friends.

I Was A Communist For The F.B.I., a quite obvious product of the red hysteria of the 1950s, demonstrates how easily the conventions of noir thrillers could be used for these propaganda pieces, which were produced by the motion picture studios for more political reasons than for commercial value. Of all of them, including *The Red Menace, Iron Curtain, I Married A Communist,* and *The Whip Hand, I Was A Communist For The F.B.I.* is the most visually noir. Its popular success is indicated by the famous spin-off TV series "I Led Three Lives," based on the memoirs of undercover agent Herb Philbrick. *I Was A Communist* also recruits the conventions of the police documentary, beginning when the stentorian narrator testifies to the story's veracity. Throughout the film, the undercover cop or federal agent has been replaced by an "average" citizen, Matt Cvetic, and "Commies" take the place of gangsters.

—B.P.

I WOULDN'T BE IN YOUR SHOES (1948)

Director: William Nigh
Producer: Walter Mirisch (Monogram)
Screenplay: Steve Fisher; from the novel by Cornell Woolrich
Director of Photography: Mack Stengler
Sound: Max Hutchinson
Music Score: Edward J. Kay

Art Director: Dave Milton
Set Decoration: Raymond Boltz, Jr.
Hairstyles: Lela Chambers
Production Supervisor: Glenn Cook
Assistant Directors: William Calihan, Ed Morey, Jr.
Script Supervisor: Ilona Vas
Film Editor: Roy Livingston
Supervising Editor: Otho Lovering

CAST: Don Castle (Tom), Elyse Knox (Ann), Regis Toomey (Judd), Charles D. Brown (Inspector Stevens), Rory Mallinson (1st Detective), Robert Lowell (Kosloff), Bill Kennedy (2nd Detective). **BITS:** Ray Dolciame (Shoeshine Boy), William Ruhl (Police Lieutenant), Esther Michelson (Mrs. Finkelstein), Steve Darrell (District Attorney), John Sheehan (Judge), Herman Cantor (Jury Foreman), John H. Elliott (Lawyer), Tito Vuolo (Grocer), Jimmy Aubrey (Tramp), John Shay (Salesman), Donald Kerr (Vaudeville Man), Joe Bernard (Janitor), Stanley Blystone (McGee), Dorothy Vaughan (Mrs. Alvin), Matty Fain, John Doucette, Dan White, Bill Walker (Prisoners), Ray Teal, Paul Bryar (Guards), Walden Boyle (Priest), Hugh Charles (Counterman), Laura Treadwell (Mrs. Stevens), Wally Walker (Clerk), Edwin Parker (Policeman).
Filming Completed: February 6, 1948
Released: Monogram, May 23, 1948
Running Time: 70 minutes

Tom and Ann are a husband and wife dance team down on their luck. They come into some unearned money; but Tom's pair of dance shoes, which had been accidentally discarded, are found to be clues in a murder. Since they are custom-made, they are quite easily traced back to him; and Tom is arrested and eventually sentenced for murder. Ann, with the aid of detective Judd, attempts to continue the investigation on her own and eventually uncovers sufficient evidence to clear her husband. In a surprise ending, Judd turns out to be the killer.

This film is rather standard Monogram fare, photographed competently by Stengler and acted in the same manner by the cast. Plot inconsistencies are commonplace in a narrative adapted from Woolrich's work. But this film's faults are redeemed by a straightforward performance by Toomey who, as a murderous detective who uncovers his own crime, anticipates to some extent the compulsive newspaper editor of the 1952 *Scandal Sheet*.

—B.P.

IN A LONELY PLACE (1950)
[Working Title: BEHIND THIS MASK]

Director: Nicholas Ray
Producer: Robert Lord (Santana Productions)

Associate Producer: Henry S. Kesler
Screenplay: Andrew Solt, adapted by Edmund H. North; from the novel by Dorothy B. Hughes
Director of Photography: Burnett Guffey
Sound: Howard Fogetti
Musical Score: George Antheil
Music Director: Morris Stoloff
Art Director: Robert Peterson
Set Decoration: William Kiernan
Costumes: Jean Louis
Makeup: Clay Campbell
Hairstyles: Helen Hunt
Technical Adviser: Rodney Amateau
Assistant Director: Earl Bellamy
Script Supervisor: Charlsie Bryant
Film Editor: Viola Lawrence

CAST: Humphrey Bogart (Dixon Steele), Gloria Grahame (Laurel Gray), Frank Lovejoy (Brub Nicolai), Carl Benton Reid (Capt. Lochner), Art Smith (Mel Lippman), Jeff Donnell (Sylvia Nicolai), Martha Stewart (Mildred Atkinson), Robert Warwick (Charlie Waterman), Morris Ankrum (Lloyd Barnes), William Ching (Ted Barton), Steven Geray (Paul), Hadda Brooks (Singer), Alice Talton (Frances Randolph), Jack Reynolds (Henry Kesler), Ruth Warren (Effie), Ruth Gillette (Martha), Guy Beach (Swan), Lewis Howard (Junior). **BITS:** Mike Romanoff (Himself), Arno Frey (Joe), Pat Barton (2nd Hatcheck Girl), Cosmo Sardo (Bartender), Don Hamin (Young Driver), George Davis (Waiter), Billy Gray (Young Boy), Melinda Erickson (Tough Girl), Jack Jahries (Officer), David Bond (Dr. Richards), Myron Healey (Post Office Clerk), Robert Lowell (Airline Clerk), Tony Layng, Robert Davis, Laura K. Brooks, Jack Santoro, Frank Marlowe, Evelyn Underwood, Hazel Boyne, Mike Lally, John Mitchum, Joy Hallward, Allen Pinson, Oliver Cross, June Vincent, Charles Cane (People).
Location: Los Angeles, California
Filming Completed: December 1, 1949
Released: Columbia, May 17, 1950
Running Time: 94 minutes

A Hollywood writer, Dixon Steele, blacklisted because of alcoholism and belligerancy, invites the hatcheck girl at a local bar to his apartment, so she can tell him the story of a book he may turn into a movie. She flirts with him; but he gives her a kindly brush-off and sends her home in a taxi. The next morning, her brutally battered body is discovered, and Steele is questioned by the police on suspicion of murder. But his new neighbor, Laurel Gray, tells the police that she saw the hatcheck girl enter Steele's apartment and leave alone later. Although he is still a suspect, Steele is released. After becoming acquainted, Steele and Laurel fall in love. Under Laurel's influence, Steele returns to writing and the work goes well. But his violent temper and jealousy, along with the continuing suspicion of the police, unnerve Laurel; and she begins to suspect that he may have been involved in the murder. Sensing her distrust, Steele's violence increases in a series of alarming incidents. Although she promises to marry him, Laurel is afraid of him and tries to leave town on the very day of the proposed wedding. Steele stops her and, in a murderous rage, tries to strangle Laurel. Just then, the phone rings. It is the police; the real murderer is the hatcheck girl's jealous boyfriend, who has just confessed. But the confession comes too late for Steele and Laurel; her distrust and his rage have torn them apart forever.

Like its title, *In A Lonely Place* is strange, sad, and hauntingly romantic. A peculiar kind of film noir, it combines a harsh murder mystery in a somewhat sleazy milieu with a colorful, semi-hard-boiled cast of characters. Like almost all of Nicholas Ray's films, *In A Lonely Place* concerns alienation, effort, failure, and loss. It seems hardly to matter that the characters of Dixon Steele and Laurel Grey love each other genuinely and passionately; nor does it make any difference that, in many ways, they are good for one another, each lifting the other briefly from a common morass of cynicism and depression. Their inherent goodness and their efforts to relate are all in vain.

Ray sees the world as dark with distrust; it is a disease that eats its way even into the bones of those who resist it most by doing that hardest thing of all: opening themselves to others. This candor renders Steele, in particular, vulnerable to suspicion. When he reveals his dark side to Laurel her distrust of him becomes inevitable.

That Laurel's distrust does become a brutal betrayal that is a grievous, albeit understandable, failing is largely due to the structuring of the film. Until the end, the viewer cannot be absolutely certain of Steele's innocence and comes to share Laurel's suspicions and bewilderment at how this man who is kind and loving in some instances can be abruptly brutal in others. Steele's life guilt and *angst* become sinister qualities that make the film's love scenes, by contrast, reverberate with a tenuous sexuality.

In spite of the violence and hardness of much of the film, *In A Lonely Place* is understated and naturalistic in its portrayal of a love affair between two people who left their innocence behind long ago. It is no moonlit and misty-eyed Hollywood version of romance; in fact, Steele is almost proletarian when he tells Laurel that his idea of two people in love is two people like them: a guy cutting grapefruit and a girl with sleep in her eyes. But Steele is basically a fallen romantic, as his coda-like remarks quoted by Laurel at the film's end reveal: "I was born when you kissed me. I died when you left me. I lived a few weeks while you loved me." Steele's inability to reconcile the worthlessness of his past successes adds to the obsessive burden of his current failure at the film's beginning. If Laurel redeems him momentarily, it is only because she distracts him from the concentrated, existential anguish of his position. The violence that expresses his malaise is ultimately suicidal; but that, too, fails. In Ray's vision of the noir universe, destructive impulses such as Steele's must eventually short-circuit the sexual and creative potency that Laurel temporarily inspires. Like the forced melodrama of his screenplays and of his final remarks, Steele is a noir hero trapped in a compulsive role; caught, almost frozen, between the dark past and a bleak future, he is unable to see a continuum that valorizes the present except through Laurel. Hence Steele is literally and figuratively in a lonely place. The final image, which frames Steele and Laurel together but not facing each other, renders them alien and alone once again.

—J.K. & A.S.

JOHNNY ANGEL (1945)

Director: Edwin L. Marin
Producer: Jack Gross (RKO)
Associate Producer: William Pereira
Screenplay: Steve Fisher, adapted by Frank Gruber; from the novel *Mr. Angel Comes Aboard* by Charles Gordon Booth, serialized in *Liberty* magazine
Director of Photography: Harry J. Wild
Special Effects: Vernon L. Walker
Montage: Harold Palmer
Music: Leigh Harline
Song: "Memphis in June," by Hoagy Carmichael and Paul Webster
Music Director: Constantin Bakaleinikoff
Art Directors: Albert S. D'Agostino, Jack Okey
Set Decoration: Darrell Silvera, William Stevens
Costumes: Rennie
Assistant Director: Sam Ruman
Film Editor: Les Millbrook

CAST: George Raft (Johnny Angel), Claire Trevor (Lilah), Signe Hasso (Paulette), Lowell Gilmore (Sam Jewell), Hoagy Carmichael (Celestial O'Brien), Marvin Miller (Gustafson), Margaret Wycherly (Miss Drumm), J. Farrell McDonald (Capt. Angel), Mack Gray (Bartender).
BITS: Jason Robards, Sr., Marc Cramer (Officers), Bill Williams (Big Sailor), Robert Anderson, Bryant Washburn, Russell Hopton, Carl Kent (Reporters), Chili Williams (Redhead), Rusty Farrell (Blond), Virginia Belmont (Cigarette Girl), Rosemary LaPlanche (Hatcheck Girl), Ann Codee (Charwoman), Wade Crosby (Watchman), O.M. Steiger (Frenchman), Eddy Hart (Seedy Sailor), Johnny Indrisano (Al), Jack Overman (Biggsy), Bert Holm (Isherwood), Eddie Lewis (Black Boy), Aina Constant (Secretary), Ed Dearing, Philip Morris (Cops), Louis Mercier (Cigar Maker), Theodore Rand (Head-waiter), James Flavin (Mate), Don Brodie (Clerk on Putnam), Kernan Cripps, Perc Launders (Officials), John Hamilton (Ship Captain), Marcel De La Bross (French Civilian), Al Rhein (Checker), Joe Ray (3rd Mate), Leland Hodgson (Paul Jewell), Alf Haugan, Charles Sullivan, Jimmy O'Gatty (Sailors), Ernie Adams (Leslie), Al Murphy (Lookout), George Magril (Man).
Filming Completed: January 16, 1945
Released: RKO, December 27, 1945
Running Time: 76 minutes

Johnny Angel, a ship captain, discovers his father's ship abandoned and his father killed. He returns to his home port of New Orleans to find the killer. The owner of Angel's ship, Gusty Gustafson, who has been pampered since childhood by his nurse, Miss Drumm, does not take any interest in the murder mystery. Angel is aided by his friend, a taxi driver named Celestial O'Brien; and they find Paulette, a witness to the crime. Celestial hides the woman who then reveals the true story: Gusty killed Capt. Angel, double-crossed the other smugglers, and escaped with the gold. Johnny confronts Gusty, who confesses to the killings and claims that his wife, Lilah, forced him to steal. He then prepares to shoot Johnny, but Miss Drumm kills him, and Johnny turns Lilah over to the police.

Johnny Angel was photographed by Harry Wild, who followed in the tradition of Nick Musuraca as an exponent of RKO expressionism. That style is most notable here in the especially threatening ambience of Raft's nighttime foray down the back streets of New Orleans. Claire Trevor's portrayal of Lilah epitomizes the lethal black widow, while Marvin Miller as Gustafson, ruthless in a petulant way in *Brasher Doubloon* and *Dead Reckoning,* is reduced here to the role of a man-child spoiled by a sensual, avaricious wife and an overbearing mother figure who fittingly kills the monster she helped to create.

—B.P.

JOHNNY EAGER (1942)

Director: Mervyn LeRoy
Producer: John W. Considine, Jr. (MGM)
Screenplay: John Lee Mahin and James Edward Grant; from an unpublished story by James Edward Grant
Director of Photography: Harold Rosson
Musical Score: Bronislau Kaper
Art Directors: Cedric Gibbons, Stan Rogers
Assistant Director: Al Shenberg
Film Editor: Albert Akst

CAST: Robert Taylor (Johnny Eager), Lana Turner (Lisbeth Bard), Edward Arnold (John Benson Farrell), Van Heflin (Jeff Hartnett), Robert Sterling (Jimmy Lanthrop), Patricia Dane (Garnet), Glenda Farrell (Mae Blythe), Barry Nelson (Lew Rankin), Henry O'Neil (A.J. Verne), Charles Dingle (A. Frazier Marco), Cy Kendall (Bill Halligan), Don Costello (Billiken), Paul Stewart (Julio).
BITS: Diana Lewis (Judy Sanford), Lou Lubin (Benjy), Connie Gilchrist (Peg Fowler), Robin Raymond (Matilda Fowler), Cliff Danielson (Floyd Markham), Leona Maricle (Miss Mines), Joseph Downing (Ryan), Bryon Shores (Joe Agridowski), Nestor Paiva (Tony), Douglas Newland (Cop), Gladys Blake, Janet Shaw (Girls in Verne's Office), Alonzo Price, Edward Earle, Hooper Atchley, Stanley Price (Men), Beryl Wallace (Mabel), Georgia Cooper (Wife), Richard Kipling (Husband), Sheldon Bennett (Headwaiter), Joyce Bryant (Woman), Anthony Warde (Guard), Elliott Sullivan (Ed), Pat West (Hanger-on), Jack Carr (Cupid), Art Miles (Lt. Allen), Mike Pat Donovan (Switchman), Gohr Van Vleck (Frenchman), Joe Whitehead (Ruffing), Alice Keating (Maid), John Dilson (Pawnbroker), Charles Thomas (Bus Conductor), Art Belasco, Larry Clifford, Harrison Greene, James C. Morton (Card Players), Alex Pollard (Butler).
Filming Completed: October 28, 1941
Released: February 19, 1942
Running Time: 102 minutes

In a taxi driver's uniform, Johnny Eager reports on his success in the legitimate world to parole officer A.J. Verne, who introduces to him two sociology students, Lisbeth Bard and Judy Sanford. Johnny returns to his cab and drives to his office at the new dog-racing track, which he plans to open soon with the help of bribed politicians. After taking care of the day's business with nightclub owner Lew Rankin and his associate Marco, he is visited by his alcoholic lawyer, Jeff Hartnett, who baffles everyone with his constant literary allusions. That night, Johnny threatens nightclub owner Rankin and finds Lisbeth at Rankin's club. He escorts her home and learns that she is the daughter of John Benson Farrell, the district attorney whose case against Eager sent him to the penitentiary. Farrell threatens to reimprison Johnny if he sees Lisbeth again. Insulted and hoping to blackmail Farrell, the gangster invites Lisbeth to his apartment and stages a brutal fight between himself and

Julio, calling out for her to shoot his assailant. Lisbeth complies but is shocked to find herself capable of murder. Meanwhile, Rankin struggles for control of the city's rackets. Johnny kills the renegade but now has to hide from Rankin's associates and the police. Lisbeth suffers a mental breakdown over her alleged crime and Farrell begs Johnny to tell her the truth. But it is Jeff Hartnett who convinces Johnny to meet with Lisbeth and convince her that she is innocent of any crime. As Rankin's men close in on him, Lisbeth refuses to leave Johnny. Knocking her unconscious so that she will be safe, Johnny exposes himself to the police and is killed by a policeman he had befriended.

In this early film noir, the supporting characters of Jeff Hartnett and Lisbeth Bard display more overt noir characteristics of disillusion and weakness than the protagonist, Johnny Eager. Hartnett is a wounded soul, the gangster's lawyer who realizes that he has betrayed himself by perverting his profession to serve the purposes of crime. He hides his self-hate behind an alcoholic haze and cryptic quotations, which the gangster, Johnny Eager, finds amusing but unintelligible. Lisbeth Bard is literally an innocent schoolgirl who is attracted to the underworld's excitement. Rich and secure, she complacently believes herself to be in control of her destiny. When she discovers her vulnerability and is ensnared in a "murder," she breaks with reality rather than cope with her situation. Even Lisbeth's powerful father, the district attorney, realizes that he does not control fate when the gangster forces him to sacrifice his ideals to save his daughter. The charming and brash Johnny Eager is transformed when Jeff makes the racketeer realize that his power has corrupted him beyond what is necessary to survive and achieve his criminal goals. Significantly, however, Johnny's attempts to reverse the damage he caused Lisbeth is futile. She does not even hear his confession that Julio's "murder" was staged, and he must inflict more damage on her to save her life. As a surviving noir heroine, Lisbeth is permanently scarred. In a moment of existential self-emulation Johnny demands a more tangible punishment and proof that he is mortal. Yelling, "Come and get me," he dies in the dark, wet street, killed by a policeman who was his friend but who failed to recognize him.

—E.W.

JOHNNY O'CLOCK (1947)

Director: Robert Rossen
Producer: Edward G. Nealis (J.E.M. Productions)
Associate Producer: Milton Holmes
Screenplay: Robert Rossen; from an unpublished story by Milton Holmes
Director of Photography: Burnett Guffey
Sound: Jack Haynes
Music Score: George Duning

JOURNEY INTO FEAR

Music Director: Morris Stoloff
Art Directors: Stephen Goosson, Cary Odell
Set Decoration: James Crowe
Costumes: Jean Louis
Technical Adviser: John P. Barrett
Production Assistant: Lehman Katz
Assistant Director: Carl Hiecke
Film Editors: Warren Low, Al Clark

CAST: Dick Powell (Johnny O'Clock), Evelyn Keyes (Nancy Hobbs), Lee J. Cobb (Inspector Koch), Ellen Drew (Nelle Marchettis), Nina Foch (Harriet Hobbs), Thomas Gomez (Pete Marchettis), John Kellogg (Charlie), Jim Bannon (Chuck Blayden), Mabel Paige (Slatternly Woman), Phil Brown (Hotel Clerk), Jeff Chandler (Turk), Kit Guard (Punchy). **BITS:** Charles Mueller, Allen Mathews (Bodyguards), Virginia Farmer (Mrs. Wilson), Pat Lane (Onlooker), Robert Ryan (Policeman), Jerry Franks (Man), Jesse Graves (Redcap), Matty Fain (Fleming), Cy Malis, Bob Perry, Cy Schindell, Charles Perry, Sam Shack, Charles St. George, Gene Delmont, Ralph Volkie (Dealers), Brooks Benedict, Bill Wallace, Jeffrey Sayre, Paul Bradley, Richard H. Gordon (Card Players), Jack Smith, Fred Beecher, Ralph Freedman, Thomas H. O'Neil, Joe Helper, Bill Stubbs, John Terrano, Edward Margolis, George Zouzaniles, George Alesko (Practical Dealers), Raoul Freeman, Carl Saxe (Detectives), Shimen Ruskin (Storekeeper), Robin Raymond (Hatcheck Girl), John P. Barrett (Floorman), Charles Wexler (Bartender), Victoria Faust (Marion), John Berkes (Waiter), Al Hill, George Lloyd (Workmen), Ken MacDonald (Customer), Charles Marsh (Businessman).
Filming Completed: September 6, 1946
Released: Columbia, March 27, 1947
Running Time: 95 minutes

Johnny O'Clock is a junior partner in a New York gambling casino owned by Pete Marchettis. A bribed policeman, Chuck Blayden, decides to replace Johnny in the organization and also breaks off with his girl friend, Harriet, who works in the gambling club. Blayden disappears after Harriet's body is found in her apartment, an apparent suicide. The woman's sister, Nancy, arrives in town to investigate and is attracted to Johnny O'Clock. Marchettis's wife, Nelle, also loves Johnny and presents him with a diamond watch that is identical to her husband's. Inspector Koch suspects both Johnny and Marchettis of murder when Blayden's body is found in the river and the coroner discovers that Harriet was poisoned. Marchettis learns of Johnny's diamond watch and orders his thugs to eliminate his partner. But Johnny escapes and confronts Marchettis to dissolve their business arrangement. Marchettis shoots Johnny, who retaliates and kills the senior partner. When Johnny rejects Nelle, she informs the police that Johnny murdered her husband in cold blood. Surrounded outside the office by the police, Johnny takes Inspector Koch as hostage and plans to escape. But when he sees that Nancy is also outside, he realizes that their love is too important to

waste by spending the rest of their lives as fugitives and gives himself up.

After writing a series of gangster thrillers in the 1930s and one particularly noir film in the mid-1940s, *The Strange Love Of Martha Ivers*, Robert Rossen turned his attention to the possibility of serving as director as well and *Johnny O'Clock* was his first directorial effort. He utilized many of the standard conventions of the noir period including the characteristic photographic style, the use of the tough guy, and the contemporary underworld setting. Even the choice of Dick Powell to portray the slick gambler who had fallen on bad times betrayed a certain adherence to noir convention. However, the film is emotionally detached and the character portrayed by Powell was not obviously vulnerable. It is through a sense of the protagonist's weakness that most films of this nature approach the noir classification. But *Johnny O'Clock* is not privy to this important attitude, although the motivations are correct and the settings are particularly corrupt and ambiguous. The elements lacking are a sense of fear and powerlessness. Rossen managed to capture that noir objective in his later films, most notably *The Undercover Man*, which he produced, *Desert Fury*, which he wrote, and the direction of his masterpiece of sustained tension and corruption, *Body and Soul*.

—C.M.

JOURNEY INTO FEAR (1943)

Director: Norman Foster [and Orson Welles, uncredited]
Executive Producer: George J. Schaefer (Mercury Productions)
Producer: Orson Welles
Screenplay: Joseph Cotten and Orson Welles; from the novel by Eric Ambler
Director of Photography: Karl Struss
Special Effects: Vernon L. Walker
Sound: Richard Van Hessen, James G. Stewart
Music: Roy Webb
Music Director: Constantin Bakaleinikoff
Songs: "C'est Mon Coeur" [also known as "Chagrin d'Amour"]; "Three Little Words" by Harry Ruby and Bert Kalmar
Art Directors: Albert S. D'Agostino, Mark-Lee Kirk
Set Decoration: Darrell Silvera, Ross Dowd
Costumes: Edward Stevenson
Assistant Director: Dewey Starkey
Film Editor: Mark Robson

CAST: Joseph Cotten (Howard Graham), Dolores Del Rio (Josette Martel), Orson Welles (Col. Haki), Ruth Warrick (Stephanie Graham), Agnes Moorehead (Mrs. Mathews), Everett Sloane (Kopeikin), Jack Moss (Banat), Jack Durant (Gogo), Eustace Wyatt (Dr. Haller), Frank Readick (Mathews), Edgar Barrier (Kuvetli), Stefan

Schnabel (Purser), Hans Conreid (Oo Lang Sang, the Magician), Robert Meltzer (Steward), Richard Bennett (Ship's Captain), Shifra Haran (Mrs. Haklet), Herbert Drake, Bill Roberts (Men).

Released: RKO, March 18, 1943
Running Time: 71 minutes
[NOTE: *Journey Into Fear* was previewed June 7, 1942, with a running time of 69 minutes. Welles reshot the final sequence and the film was released in March 1943.]

The attempted assassination of Howard Graham, a naval engineer, is the first hint of a dangerous Nazi conspiracy. Warned by Col. Haki, a Turkish military official, that he has information vital to the Nazi war effort, Graham is hastily ushered out of Turkey and befriended by the evasive Kopeikin and an exotic dancer named Josette. Graham's escape route takes him aboard a sinister steamship populated by a host of suspicious characters. Banat, a grotesque Nazi assassin, silently watches Graham throughout the trip; and a variety of agents and double agents are promptly disposed of until Graham is unsure of everyone he meets. Finally captured by Nazi agents, Graham makes a desperate escape and rejoins his wife, who is unaware of the intrigue surrounding her husband. Banat follows Graham and chases him onto the rain-drenched ledge of a hotel three stories above the street. Graham is saved thanks to the efforts of Col. Haki; and the rain, which obscures Banat's vision during a barrage of gunfire, causes him to fall to his death.

Deeply rooted in a tradition of international intrigue, *Journey Into Fear* is a marginal film noir. The whimsical flavor of Graham's narration is a deflating counterpoint to the threatening noir atmosphere and sardonic characterization exhibited by Banat. Orson Welles's Mercury company produced the film, with Welles contributing to the direction and ultimate visual quality of the film. It is an early noir film, but *Journey Into Fear* presents interesting flashes of a sensibility that Welles would develop more fully in *The Stranger* and *The Lady From Shanghai*. The overriding sense of dread that permeates *Journey Into Fear* combines with a visual style that uses contrasts between light and shade as a metaphor for the instability and futility typical of the noir universe. However, few films dealing with this type of intrigue are fully realized film noir because they require a broad base of action and a more socialized hero, which forces the film to reject the alienated attitudes found in noir films of the 1940s for a more conventional bias.　—C.M.

KANSAS CITY CONFIDENTIAL (1952)

Director: Phil Karlson
Producer: Edward Small (Associated Players and Producers, Edward Small Productions)
Screenplay: George Bruce and Harry Essex; from an unpublished story by Harold R. Greene and Rowland Brown
Director of Photography: George E. Diskant
Sound: Fred Lau
Music: Paul Sawtell
Art Director: Edward L. Ilou
Production Supervisor: Ben Hersh
Assistant Director: Ralph Black
Film Editor: Buddy Small

CAST: John Payne (Joe Rolfe), Coleen Gray (Helen), Preston Foster (Timothy Foster), Dona Drake (Teresa), Jack Elam (Harris), Neville Brand (Kane), Lee Van Cleef (Tony), Mario Seletti (Timaso), Howard Negley (Andrews), Ted Ryan (Morelli), George Wallace (Olson), Vivi Janiss (Mrs. Rogers), Helen Keeb (Mrs. Crane). **BITS:** Archie Twitchell, House Peters, Jr., George Dockstader, Don House, Brick Sullivan, Jack Shea, Tom Dillon, Tom Greenway, Paul Fierro (Police), Kay Wiley (Woman), Harry Hines (News Vendor), Don Orlando (Diaz), Al Hill, Mike Lally (Shooters), Charles Sherlock, Frank Scannell (Stickmen), Charles Sullivan, Carlos Rivero, Sam Scar, Barry Brooks, Eddie Foster (Players), Joe Ray (Houseman), Paul Hogan (Bouncer), Paul Dubov (Eddie), Ric Roman (Brother), Sam Pierce (Workman), Eduardo Coch (Airline Clerk), William Haade (Detective Barney), Charles Cane (Detective Mullins), Ray Bennett (Prisoner), Orlando Beltran (Por-

149

ter), Carleton Young (Assistant District Attorney Martin), Phil Tead (Collins), Lee Phelps (Jailer).
Filming Completed: August 1952
Released: United Artists, November 28, 1952
Running Time: 98 minutes

Timothy Foster is a retired Kansas City police captain embittered by his meager pension. He blackmails three felons on whom he possesses incriminating evidence into implementing his plans for an armored car robbery. Foster remains anonymous and brings the men together wearing masks, so that none will know the others' identities. Part of the plan involves escape in a facsimile of a florist's van that makes a daily delivery next door to the bank. The police arrest the driver of the real van, an ex-convict named Joe Rolfe, question him brutally about the robbery, but eventually release him for lack of evidence. Angered by this frame-up, Rolfe gets a lead from former underworld contacts and tracks one of the robbers to Tijuana. After Rolfe beats more information out of him, he is killed by local police; and Rolfe assumes his identity. Summoned to a rendezvous in a resort town further south, Rolfe makes the acquaintance of Foster's daughter, Helen. When he goes to the meeting, Rolfe discovers that Foster is planning to turn in the men and collect the insurance company's reward, as well as embarrass the Kansas City police force. A gun battle breaks out in which the two accomplices are killed and Foster is mortally wounded. When Helen arrives with the police, Rolfe lies and credits Foster with helping find the robbers and clear his name.

Kansas City Confidential combines elements of the semi-documentary style of the productions of De Rochemont and Hellinger at Fox and Universal respectively with two central noir figures: the embittered ex-cop, Foster, and the equally embittered ex-con, Rolfe. The narrative scheme, which brings them by chance into direct conflict, not only reverses their previous roles as criminal and policeman but ironically keeps them unaware of the other's true identity and purpose until the film's conclusion. As in his other noir films, *99 River Street* and *Hell's Island*, Phil Karlson uses physical violence and the acting of John Payne to characterize the conflicting forces of menace and endurance at work in the noir underworld. Like Galt in *The Dark Corner*, Rolfe is assailed and nearly destroyed by unknown forces, forces that he will discover bore him no personal malice. His unrelenting and brutal search is both a moral vindication and a simple assertion of existential outrage. Because Rolfe's disruption of Foster's plans is to some extent unwitting, the ultimate irony of *Kansas City Confidential* is that Rolfe brings down the same type of mischance—albeit more deadly—that Foster had visited on him from the same unknowledgeable position. Thus each man, in turn, becomes the deterministic key to the other's destiny with Foster, the noir antagonist, the appropriately last victim of the fatal mechanism that he set in motion.

—A.S.

KEY LARGO (1948)

Director: John Huston
Producer: Jerry Wald (Warner Brothers)
Screenplay: Richard Brooks and John Huston; from the play by Maxwell Anderson
Director of Photography: Karl Freund
Special Effects: William McGann, Robert Burks
Sound: Dolph Thomas
Music Score: Max Steiner
Song: "Moanin' Low" by Howard Dietz and Ralph Rainger
Orchestration: Murray Cutter
Art Director: Leo K. Kuter
Set Decoration: Fred M. MacLean
Costumes: Leah Rhodes, Ted Schultz (Men), Marie Blanchard (Women)
Makeup: Frank McCoy
Hairstyles: Betty Delmont
Unit Manager: Chuck Hansen
Continuity: Jean Baker
Assistant Director: Arthur Lueker
Second Assistant Director: John Prettyman
Script Supervisor: Jean Baker
Film Editor: Rudi Fehr

CAST: Humphrey Bogart (Frank McCloud), Edward G. Robinson (Johnny Rocco), Lauren Bacall (Nora Temple), Lionel Barrymore (James Temple), Claire Trevor (Gaye Dawn), Thomas Gomez (Curley), Harry Lewis (Toots), John Rodney (Deputy Sawyer), Marc Lawrence (Ziggy), Dan Seymour (Angel), Monte Blue (Ben Wade), Jay Silver Heels, Rodric Redwing (Osceola Brothers). **BITS:** Joe P. Smith (Bus Driver), Albert Marin (Skipper), Pat Flaherty (Man), Jerry Jerome, John Phillips, Lute Crockett (Ziggy's Henchmen), Felipa Gomez (Old Indian Woman).
Filming Completed: March 13, 1948
Released: Warner Brothers, July 16, 1948
Running Time: 100 minutes

Frank McCloud, an ex-army officer, comes to Key Largo and stays at a run-down hotel owned by wheel-chair invalid James Temple. Living with Temple is his widowed daughter-in-law, Nora, whose husband was a war buddy of McCloud's. Frank is present when the hotel is taken over by gangster Johnny Rocco and his henchmen and even has the chance to kill Rocco but is too disillusioned by life to involve himself. A fierce storm grips the island, which panics Rocco but imbues Frank with courage; he is outraged by Rocco's treatment of Gaye Dawn, the gangster's alcoholic mistress, but gets a beating for his efforts to help her. When Sheriff Ben Wade comes searching for his deputy and finds him dead, Rocco blames two local Indians who are killed by the sheriff when they try to escape. Frank finally realizes how dangerous Rocco is and plans to eliminate him by making Rocco think he will pilot a boat to Cuba for Rocco and the gang. After a cat-and-mouse battle on the small cruiser, Frank kills Rocco although he is himself wounded. Frank then heads back to Key Largo and Nora, with whom he has fallen in love.

Key Largo was Edward G. Robinson's last major gangster portrayal. He plays Johnny Rocco with the mannerisms and verve of his famous role in *Little Caesar*; but Rocco and his hoods are not young anymore. They are clearly out of their time, relics of an old order that has passed. Based on a play by Maxwell Anderson, *Key Largo* is a gangster-gothic. Director John Huston retains some of Anderson's poetic intentions; but the film is really an ode to Robinson as the aging gangster-madman. Johnny Rocco is evil incarnate, surrounded by his boozy tart and over-the-hill henchmen. It is an unusual setting, as the gangsters are not in a dark city but in an isolated, shabby hotel on one of the Florida keys. The exotic scenery, the storm at sea, and the closed-in feeling of the hotel lounge combine and create a heavy, humid atmosphere that is laden with claustrophobic tension. Humphrey Bogart and Lauren Bacall are cast in the equally alienated roles of a disillusioned veteran and an embittered widow. Their acting is low-keyed compared to Robinson's cigar-chomping, swaggering Rocco. The gangster is the complete antiromantic; a sadist and a misogynist.

Hating women was always a part of the Robinson's gangster image, but at no other time is he as cruel to females as in *Key Largo* when he forces his alcoholic mistress to sing her pathetic rendition of "Moanin' Low" and then refuses to give her a drink. Robinson's performance during the storm scene, when he suffers uncontrollable shakes, is an example of broad physical acting to reveal the emotional state of a character. His performance reflects the desperate nostalgia of one who has been "A Somebody." It personifies a typically noir, ill-fated threat against Frank and Nora, most effectively evokes the noir universe of *Key Largo*.

—J.C.

THE KILLER IS LOOSE (1956)

Director: Budd Boetticher
Producer: Robert L. Jacks (Crown Productions)
Screenplay: Harold Medford; from the story by John and Ward Hawkins published in *The Saturday Evening Post*
Director of Photography: Lucien Ballard

Grace (Dee J. Thompson) and Otto Flanders (John Larch) are terrorized by Leon "Foggy" Poole (Wendell Corey) in The Killer Is Loose.

THE KILLER THAT STALKED NEW YORK

Sound: Frank Webster
Music: Lionel Newman
Art Director: Leslie Thomas
Film Editor: George Gittens

CAST: Joseph Cotten (Sam Wagner), Rhonda Fleming (Lila Wagner), Wendell Corey (Leon "Foggy" Poole), Alan Hale, Jr. (Denny), Michael Pate (Chris Gillespie), Virginia Christine (Mary Gillespie), John Larch (Otto Flanders), John Beradino (Mac), Paul Bryar (Greg), Dee J. Thompson (Grace Flanders).
Filming Completed: August 27, 1955
Released: United Artists, March 2, 1956
Running Time: 73 minutes
[NOTE: Daniel Fuchs was originally contracted to write the screenplay of A Killer Is Loose for Crown Productions.]

Foggy Poole, so named because of his extreme myopia, is a bank clerk who acts as the inside man in a holdup. When the other robbers are caught, Poole is identified and the police arrest him. Poole's wife is accidentally shot and killed, and a devastated Poole blames the arresting officer, Sam Wagner. At his trial, Poole's vengeful plan to kill Lila, the officer's wife, is revealed. Poole is a model prisoner and is soon sent to a prison farm, from which he escapes. As he heads back to the city, it is obvious that his psyche has become dangerously deranged and he menaces several hostages. Meanwhile, Sam Wagner is worried and tries to marshal the forces of the police to protect Lila and capture Poole at the same time. Wagner reluctantly agrees to let Lila be used as bait, and Poole almost succeeds in killing her before he is shot down.

The Killer Is Loose is a characteristic thriller of the 1950s, possessing relatively naturalistic decor and lighting as compared to the preceding decade of film noir. Its tautness is the result of a concise screenplay, unmannered composition, and effective crosscutting. The action is situated largely in unpoeticized suburban settings; and the only character given any distinctive treatment is Poole.

Director Budd Boetticher is best known for his Randolph Scott Westerns, specifically those written by Burt Kennedy. They are consistently distinctive, but many of his other films are impersonal and routine. The Killer Is Loose immediately precedes the cycle of Westerns, which are followed by the director's only other significant contribution to the urban crime genre, The Rise and Fall Of Legs Diamond. Both of the modern subjects confirm Boetticher's way with villains and relate to the Westerns in interesting ways. The charming, pathological Legs Diamond is a logical and imaginative extension of the gregarious, colorful antagonists of the Westerns. Poole, on the other hand, is a thematic forerunner of the Randolph Scott hero, who typically seeks revenge for his wife's death. This coincidence, is noteworthy because the characterization of Poole is the most outstanding quality of The Killer Is Loose. The thick glasses required by his myopia, immediately striking when associated with a villain, are a visual manifestation of helpless-

ness; and Wendell Corey seizes on this trait as an opportunity to project a subtle pathos.

—B.L.

THE KILLER THAT STALKED NEW YORK (1951)
[Working Title: FRIGHTENED CITY]

Director: Earl McEvoy
Producer: Robert Cohn (Columbia)
Screenplay: Harry Essex; from a *Cosmopolitan* magazine article "Smallpox: The Killer That Stalked New York" by Milton Lehman
Director of Photography: Joseph Biroc
Sound: Russell Malmgren
Music Score: Hans Salter
Music Director: Morris Stoloff
Art Director: Walter Holscher
Set Decoration: Louis Diage
Makeup: Bob Schiffer
Hairstyles: Helen Hunt
Production Manager: Jack Fier
Assistant Director: James Nicholson
Script Supervisor: Arlene Cooper
Film Editor: Jerome Thoms

CAST: Evelyn Keyes (Sheila Bennet), Charles Korvin (Matt Krane), William Bishop (Dr. Ben Wood), Dorothy Malone (Alice Lorie), Lola Albright (Francie Bennet), Barry Kelley (Johnson), Carl Benton Reid (Commissioner Ellis), Ludwig Donath (Dr. Cooper), Art Smith (Moss), Whit Bissell (Sid Bennet), Roy Roberts (Mayor), Connie Gilchrist (Belle), Dan Riss (Skrip), Harry Shannon (Officer Houlihan), Beverly Washburn (Welda Kowalski), Celia Lovsky (Mrs. Kowalski), Richard Egan (Owney), Walter Burke (Danny), Peter Virgo (Joe Dominic), Arthur Space (Dr. Penner), Don Kohler (Ted James), Jim Backus (Willie Dennis), Peter Brocco (Tom), Tommy Ivo (Jerry), Angela Clarke (Mrs. Dominic).
Released: Columbia, January 4, 1951
Running Time: 79 minutes
[FACTUAL BASIS: New York City was threatened by a smallpox epidemic in 1946, but the crisis was met without panic.]

Sheila Bennet returns to New York City from Cuba, where she had carefully followed her husband Matt's plan to obtain stolen diamonds and mail them back to him in the United States. Not suspecting that she has contracted smallpox and is a carrier of the disease, she is followed by a Treasury agent. Matt, who is having an affair with his wife's sister, Francie, instructs Sheila to stay at a hotel. Feeling ill, she sneaks out and, after losing the Treasury agent, visits the office of Dr. Wood, where she infects a young girl. The doctor treats Sheila's symptoms as a cold but later, when the young girl dies of smallpox, medical authorities realize that

Sheila is a carrier and try to locate her. Sheila stays with Matt who does not inform her that the diamonds have arrived because he intends to run off with Francie. Dr. Woods and the T-Men realize they are searching for the same woman and trace her to her brother's flophouse. Meanwhile, Sheila has discerned her husband's infidelity and plans to kill him but falters. However, Matt dies when he falls from a building. Sheila gives the doctor a full list of all the people she contacted before she succumbs to the disease.

The Killer That Stalked New York is one of a number of films dealing with the dangers of foreign contamination, which is another aspect of the 1950s cold war paranoia. The talented Joseph Biroc, later to photograph a good deal of television as well as Robert Aldrich's films, evokes the proper New York City atmosphere, particularly in the night scenes. By centering its attention on the criminal who becomes progressively sicker and more alienated rather than on the efforts of the young doctor to combat the plague, *The Killer That Stalked New York* is considerably more noir than the 1950 film, *Panic In The Streets*.

—B.P.

THE KILLERS (1946)

Director: Robert Siodmak
Producer: Mark Hellinger (Mark Hellinger Productions)
Screenplay: Anthony Veiller; from the short story by Ernest Hemingway
Director of Photography: Woody Bredell
Special Photography: David S. Horsley
Sound: Bernard B. Brown, William Hedgecock
Music: Miklos Rozsa
Art Directors: Jack Otterson, Martin Obzina
Set Decoration: Russell A. Gausman, E.R. Robinson
Costumes: Vera West
Makeup: Jack P. Pierce
Production Assistant: Jules Buck
Assistant Director: Melville Shyer
Film Editor: Arthur Hilton

CAST: Edmond O'Brien (Riordan), Ava Gardner (Kitty Collins), Albert Dekker (Colfax), Sam Levene (Lubinsky), John Miljan (Jake), Virginia Christine (Lilly), Vince Barnett (Charleston), Burt Lancaster (Swede), Charles D. Brown (Packy), Donald MacBride (Kenyon), Phil Brown (Nick), Charles McGraw (Al), William Conrad (Max), Queenie Smith (Queenie), Garry Owen (Joe), Harry Hayden (George), Bill Walker (Sam), Jack Lambert (Dum Dum), Jeff Corey (Blinky), Wally Scott (Charlie), Gabrielle Windsor (Ginny), Rex Dale (Man). **BITS:** Harry Brown (Paymaster), Beatrice Roberts (Nurse), Howard Freeman (Police Chief), John Berkes (Plunther), John Sheehan, George Anderson (Doctors), Charles Middle-

ton (Farmer Brown), Al Hill (Customer), Noel Cravat (Lou Tingle), The Reverend Neal Dodd (Minister), Vera Lewis (Mrs. Hirsch), Howard Negley, Perc Launders, Geoffrey Ingham (Policemen), Milton Wallace, Nolan Leary, John Trebach (Waiters), Ann Staunton (Stella), William Ruhl (Motorman), Therese Lyon (Housekeeper), Ernie Adams (Little Man), Jack Cheatham (Police Driver), Ethan Laidlaw (Conductor), Michael Hale (Pete), Wally Rose (Bartender), Audley Anderson (Assistant Paymaster), Mike Donovan (Timekeeper).
Filming Completed: June 28, 1946
Released: Universal, August 28, 1946
Running Time: 105 minutes

A pair of hired killers, Max and Al, enter a small town and systematically track down their intended target, Swede. They find him silently waiting in a darkened room; and he offers no resistance. The killers leave, satisfied that they performed their job well. Riordan, an insurance investigator who learns of the murder's circumstances while following up a routine claim for a very minor amount of money, becomes obsessed with finding out why Swede would sit back and allow two men to murder him. His investigation leads him to a variety of people, and it becomes apparent that the victim was involved with a gang of thieves. Riordan also learns that Swede's double cross by a woman caused him to become a shell of a man, and it was only a matter of time until his past caught up with him. The insurance investigator, desiring to see justice done, receives the reward for recovering money stolen by this same group of thieves and sets himself up as a decoy to catch the criminals.

Seen as a quintessential noir film, *The Killers* derives its inspiration from a great many sources. As an adaptation of a Hemingway short story, the film fulfills the premise established by the author's tough, hard-boiled style. The actors who portray the killers, William Conrad and Charles McGraw, completely typify the personae of the noir world. However Hemingway's story ends with the departure of the killers. The film, directed by Robert Siodmak and scripted by Anthony Veiller, merely uses this sequence to serve as a prologue in order to deal with the real story of why someone would lose the desire to live. The entire production was supervised by Mark Hellinger, a famous reporter who became a film producer.

The sensibilities of Siodmak and Veiller and the hard-boiled realism of Hellinger combine to exemplify the most interesting aspects of noir film making. Initially the structure of the film isolates *The Killers* from more conventional noir films. Utilizing a convoluted time structure, the story of Swede, portrayed by Burt Lancaster, is unfolded in a series of disconnected flashbacks much in the same way as *Citizen Kane*. This use of time, disjointed and at times overlapping, creates an unusual texture for the film. The alienating disjunction felt by Swede and his subsequent surrender to the nightmarish trap of a classic *femme fatale*, Kitty Collins, is reaffirmed by the basic structure of the film.

KILLER'S KISS

The overwhelmingly corrupt universe in which the young boxer-turned-criminal involves himself is simply the noir world. An undercurrent of violence exists throughout the film and there is also an existential anger present that serves to create a chaotic environment, dark motives, and hopeless situations. No vindication or amelioration exists in *The Killers*. Rather, the entire structure of good and evil has been pared down to melodramatic essentials. Investigator Riordan uses the situation of Swede to move beyond the boring routine of his job and enter a world of corruption and chaos. His efforts produce the required results, yet nobody really triumphs. Riordan's outrage over Kitty's corruption and Swede's hopelessness is a personal not a social response; in Siodmak's vision, the noir universe endures.

On a final note, *The Killers* was remade in 1964 by Don Siegel. The basic elements of the plot are the same, but in the new version it is the killers who track down information to discover why their victim would face his death with relative indifference. Even the use of Angie Dickinson as the *femme fatale* took on a different meaning. The implications in the 1940s of a woman who could take a man on a sexual joyride that was far removed from the ordinary was lost by the time of the mid-1960s. The *femme fatale* existed as a form without substance. Seen too often in film after film, this particular noir character was canonized and became another fixture in a world already cluttered by clichés.
—C.M.

leave the city and begin a new life but the coziness of their newfound relationship is short-lived. Vince, the owner of the nightclub where Gloria works, has "plans" for his lovely blond dancer and does not like interference from outsiders, especially from a down-on-his luck boxer. At every opportunity Vince attempts to seduce his unwilling employee, even while they watch Davy box on television. Frustrated by Gloria's teasing but ultimate rejection of him, Vince becomes violent. He kidnaps Gloria in a warehouse used to store dismantled mannequins and waits for Davy. When the boxer appears, Gloria betrays him to save herself. The boxer and the grim nightclub owner engage in a brutal and deadly fight. Ultimately, Davey walks away alone and decides to leave the city and return home. At the last moment on the train platform, he is joined by Gloria and they leave together.

Killer's Kiss is Stanley Kubrick's second feature film, and it displays a visual unity unusual in a low-budget, independently produced film. The atmosphere Kubrick creates in the film is dark and unwholesome; an overwhelming sense of violence lurks below the surface of the people populating the New York of *Killer's Kiss*. Much of the film, however, is an experiment. Kubrick's use of obtuse flashbacks and surreal nightmare sequences, presented on negative film stock, give the film an alienating visual quality. Yet the most striking element of *Killer's Kiss* is its tendency to associate sex and violence, as illustrated by the attempted seduction of Gloria, which is accelerated by the brutal prizefight on television and in the finale in which disjointed parts of female mannequins and a fire axe are used as weapons in a fistfight.
—C.M.

KILLER'S KISS (1955)
[Working Title: KISS ME, KILL ME]

Director: Stanley Kubrick
Producers: Stanley Kubrick and Morris Bousel (Minotaur)
Screenplay: Stanley Kubrick
Director of Photography: Stanley Kubrick
Music: Gerald Fried
Choreography: David Vaughan
Film Editor: Stanley Kubrick

CAST: Frank Silvera (Vincent Rapallo), Jamie Smith (Davy Gordon), Irene Kane (Gloria Price), Jerry Jarret (Albert, the Fight Manager), Mike Dana, Felice Orlandi, Ralph Roberts, Phil Stevenson (Hoodlums), Julius Adelman (Owner of Mannequin Factory), David Vaughn, Alec Rubin (Conventioneers).
Location: New York, New York
Released: United Artists, November 1955
Running Time: 67 minutes

Living in a less than luxurious apartment building, two lonely people, Gloria Price and Davy Gordon, are drawn together. Gloria, a dancer in a sinister nightclub, is ultimately befriended by Davy, a young boxer, when he rescues her from an apparent assault. They make plans to

THE KILLING (1956)

Director: Stanley Kubrick
Producer: James B. Harris (Harris-Kubrick)
Screenplay: Stanley Kubrick, with additional dialogue by Jim Thompson; from the novel *The Clean Break* by Lionel White
Director of Photography: Lucien Ballard
Art Director: Ruth Sobotka Kubrick
Production Supervisor: Clarence Eurist
Film Editor: Betty Steinberg

CAST: Sterling Hayden (Johnny Clay), Coleen Gray (Fay), Vince Edwards (Val Cannon), Jay C. Flippen (Marvin Unger), Marie Windsor (Sherry Peatty), Ted deCorsia (Randy Kennan), Elisha Cook, Jr. (George Peatty), Joe Sawyer (Mike O'Reilly), Timothy Carey (Nikki Arane), Jay Adler (Leo), Kola Kwarian (Maurice Oboukhoff), Joseph Turkell (Tiny), James Edwards (Parking Attendant).
Filming Completed: November 1955

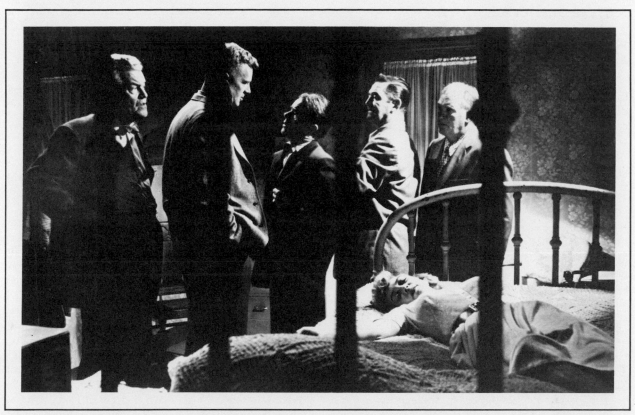

Left to right: **The Killing** *Marvin Unger (Jay C. Flippen), Johnny Clay (Sterling Hayden), George Peatty (Elisha Cook, Jr.), Randy Kennan (Ted de Corsia), and Sherry Peatty (Marie Windsor).*

Johnny Clay (Sterling Hayden) in **The Killing.**

KISS ME DEADLY

Released: United Artists, May 20, 1956
Running Time: 84 minutes

Ex-convict Johnny Clay, a small-time criminal, plots a daring race-track robbery with the assistance of a corrupt cop, Randy Kennan; the track bartender, Mike O'Reilly; the betting window teller, George Peatty; a chess-playing wrestler; and a sharpshooter, Nikki Arane. The heist goes off as planned, while the shooting of a race horse serves as a diversion. During the getaway the sharpshooter is killed. The avaricious wife, Sherry Peatty, of the timid teller has learned of the plan and tips off her boyfriend. He and a crony attempt to rob the robbers as they assemble to divide the loot. A shoot-out occurs, laying waste to the mob. Mortally wounded, the teller staggers home and murders his unfaithful wife. Clay arrives late at the scene of the slaughter and takes the money. He is apprehended at the airport, attempting to escape, when the money-laden suitcase falls off a baggage cart and scatters the bills in the wind.

The Killing presents what has become a familiar Stanley Kubrick theme: the fallibility of man and his plans. Just as the supposedly fail-safe devices in *Dr. Strangelove* go awry and hasten the end of the world, and the ultimate computer, Hal, rebels in *2001: A Space Odyssey*, the perfect crime charted in *The Killing* falls to pieces due to greed and human error, leaving the majority of the protagonists bullet-ridden corpses.

Detailing a robbery through the eyes of the participants is a device that became popular during the 1950s and 1960s. Where *The Killing* differs most strikingly from its generic predecessors is in its use of time. The flashback is a standard narrative ploy in many noir films, such as *The Killers, Dead Reckoning,* and *Out Of The Past. The Killing,* however, plays with time in a different manner. The plot is developed in bits and pieces as we are introduced to the various members of the gang and the roles they will play in the holdup. Once a character is established, the film leaps backwards, and picks up another character until all the component parts come together like the pieces of a jigsaw puzzle. This motif is again used for the robbery itself. Using a shot of dray horses pulling the starting gate into position for the race as a time reference, we see how each gang member fulfills his function until the robbery is completed. It is a unique structure for a film of this kind but successfully solves the problem of showing several actions occurring simultaneously.

The film is shot in a raw, nervy style and while it may often seem forcedly hard-boiled, there are many memorable touches, such as the grotesquely grinning, rubber clown mask Hayden uses to hide his face; the offbeat puppy-loving sharpshooter played by Timothy Carey, whose permanent death rictus of a smile foreshadows his own death; and the shrieking parrot that accompanies a marital squabble.

—J.B.

KISS ME DEADLY (1955)

Director and Producer: Robert Aldrich
Executive Producer: Victor Saville (Parklane Productions)
Screenplay: A.I. Bezzerides; from the novel by Mickey Spillane
Director of Photography: Ernest Laszlo
Art Director: William Glasgow
Music: Frank DeVol
Song: "Rather Have the Blues," lyric and music by Frank DeVol; sung by Nat "King" Cole
Assistant Director: Robert Justman
Film Editor: Michael Luciano

CAST: Ralph Meeker (Mike Hammer), Albert Dekker (Dr. Soberin), Paul Stewart (Carl Evello), Maxine Cooper (Velda), Gaby Rodgers (Gabrielle/Lily Carver), Wesley Addy (Pat), Juano Hernandez (Eddie Yeager), Nick Dennis (Nick), Cloris Leachman (Christina), Marian Carr (Friday), Jack Lambert (Sugar), Jack Elam (Charlie Max), Jerry Zinneman (Sammy), Percy Helton (Morgue Doctor), Fortunio Bonanova (Carmen Trivago), Silvio Minciotti (Mover), Leigh Snowden (Girl at Pool), Madi Comfort (Singer), James Seay (F.B.I. Man), Mara McAfee (Nurse), Robert Cornthwaite (F.B.I. Man), James McCallian (Super), Jesslyn Fax (Mrs. Super), Mort Marshall (Piker), Strother Martin (Truck Driver), Marjorie Bennett (Manager), Art Loggins (Bartender), Bob Sherman (Gas Station Man), Keith McConnell (Athletic Club Clerk), Paul Richards (Attacker), Eddie Beal (Sideman).

Location: Los Angeles, California
Filming Completed: December 23, 1954
Released: United Artists, May 18, 1955
Running Time: 105 minutes

While he is returning to Los Angeles at night, private investigator Mike Hammer's car is flagged down by a woman named Christina. She tries to evade Hammer's questions about where she is escaping from—barefoot and wearing only a trenchcoat—but he learns that she is from a nearby asylum. Nonetheless, he takes her through a roadblock. A few miles beyond, after a stop for gas at which she tells him that should anything happen to "Remember me," Hammer's car is run off the road. Hammer is semiconscious while Christina is tortured and killed, and he is thrown clear when his car is pushed off a cliff.

Hammer comes to in a hospital, where his secretary Velda and a detective of his acquaintance, Pat, inform him that a federal investigating board wants to question him. Their interest and Christina's cryptic message prompt him to ignore all warnings and begin his own investigation. He follows up a number of disconnected leads, all of which point to a conspiracy against a murdered scientist named Raymondo, which has been organized by a local gangster, Carl Evello. The conspirators first try to buy Hammer off with a conciliatory phone call and a new sports car, from which he has his mechanic, Nick, remove two bombs. When he visits Evello's house, his sister Friday tries to seduce

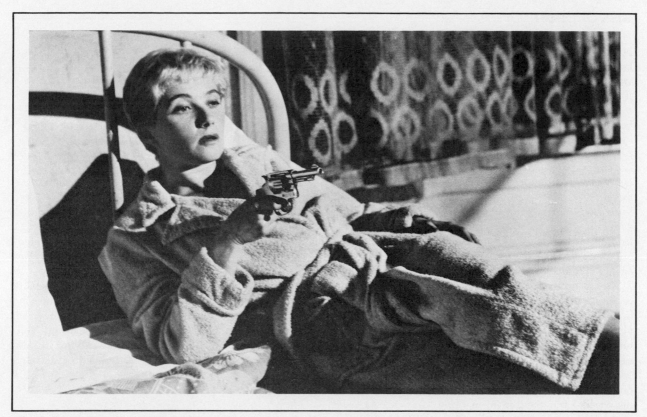

Lily Carver (Gaby Rogers) in Kiss Me Deadly.

Hammer; after subduing Evello's thugs, he is offered money by Evello. Hammer refuses; he traces Christina's roommate, Lily Carver, and hides her in his apartment. Before he can go further, Nick the mechanic is killed and Hammer is abducted by Evello's men. At the gangster's beach house he encounters Dr. Soberin, whose voice Hammer recognizes as that of Christina's killer. Overcoming the influence of sodium pentothal administered by Soberin, Hammer overpowers Evello and kills one of his men, then returns home to find Velda missing; but with Lily Carver he decodes Christina's message through a poem by Christina Rossetti. From a morgue attendant Hammer obtains a key that leads to a locker containing what Velda had dubbed "the great whatsit." He leaves it in the locker but goes out to find Carver gone. At his apartment, the police are waiting. He is told that the box contains radioactive material being sought by foreign agents. When the locker is found empty, Hammer again follows his own lead to a patient of Soberin's and gets the doctor's address through a prescription bottle. Arriving at Soberin's beach house, Hammer discovers that Lily Carver has killed him to gain sole possession of the box. Carver shoots Hammer and opens the container. The radioactive material sets her on fire and begins a chain reaction. Hammer struggles through the house, finds Velda, and frees her. Together they stumble into the surf as the house explodes.

At the core of *Kiss Me Deadly* are speed and violence. The adaptation of Mickey Spillane's novel takes Mike Hammer from New York to Los Angeles, where it situates him in a landscape of somber streets and decaying houses. Much like Hammer's fast cars, the movie swerves frenziedly through a series of disconnected and cataclysmic scenes. As such, it typifies the frenetic, post-atomic-bomb Los Angeles of the 1950s with its malignant undercurrents; it records the degenerative half-life of an unstable universe as it moves towards critical mass. When it reaches the fission point, the graphic threat of machine-gun bullets traced in the door of a house on Laurel Canyon (as in *The Big Sleep*) is superseded, as a beach cottage in Malibu becomes ground zero.

Kiss Me Deadly's central character is less heroic, than he is egocentric, callous, and brutal. In the film, Hammer is incorporated into a system of moral determinism, where crime breeds countercrime, and thieves and murderers fashion the implements of their own destruction. Christina, arguably the most conventionally "sensitive" of the picture's characters (she reads poetry and, although mockingly, lyricizes her own predicament) is ironically the "loony," the one institutionalized by society, yet quickest to penetrate Hammer's tough guy pose. In the first scene, she helps to reveal that the hero of *Kiss Me Deadly* is more typically related to other characters in Robert Aldrich's work than in Mickey Spillane's. Point-of-view, for instance—the haziness when Hammer is "sapped"; the shots of feet as he lies semiconscious on the floor; the tilted angle when his head is lying to one side—becomes a quasi-objective expression of Hammer's environment, of angularity, construction, and instability, and, by extension, of the violent and disruptive forces lingering beneath the surface. If the Aldrich and Bezzerides conception of Hammer is more objective than Spillane's, it is because his conception begins with but ultimately emerges from more than a modification of the plot, characters, or dialogue.

Hammer *is* a quester. He is not so much an outsider as he is a part of a generic underworld (or otherworld), from the everyday or commonplace. Deception is the key to this milieu. Deception, not detection, is Hammer's trade—his livelihood depends on the divorce frame-up and the generally shady deal. Deception is Lily Carver's game also, from the false name she assumes to the vulnerable pitch of her voice and the pathetic way she brings her hand up against her face like a wing of Christina's dead canary.

This deception, as in most film noir, lays the groundwork for *Kiss Me Deadly*'s melodramatic tension. Because the plot line has all the stability of one of Nick's "Va-vavooms", the viewer comes to anticipate the sinister and malign. The first torpedo, set to go off when the ignition key is turned, necessarily posits the second rigged to explode at a higher speed. From the viewer's objective vantage, the shift from one level of appearances to another may occasionally be discerned—as in the transformation of the sensual Carver, framed behind a bedpost and swinging a hip up to expose more of her leg through the fold of the terry cloth robe, then becoming shrill and waiflike for Hammer's benefit. Usually, though, the viewer is also deceived and disjunction is the rule.

The sensational elements in *Kiss Me Deadly* follow this rule. The craning down and the hiss of the hydraulic jack as the screaming Nick is crushed under the weight of a car; the pillar of fire that consumes Lily Carver; the eerie growl of the black box; even a simple "Pretty pow!" as Nick jams a fist into his open palm—these have no organizing principles but transcend context to deliver shock that is purely sensory.

As in Aldrich's *World For Ransom,* the trap is a part of *Kiss Me Deadly*'s figurative scheme; and, again, its constructs are primarily visual. But the elaborate "capture" of Callahan in the earlier picture is distilled down to single shots in *Kiss Me Deadly.* For example, in the high-angle long shot of Hammer outside Lily Carver's room, the dark foreground of stairway and balustrades are arrayed concentrically about his figure and seem to enclose him.

What most distinguishes *Kiss Me Deadly*'s figurative usage from that of other Aldrich films is an explicit, aural fabric of allusions and metaphor: the recurring Christina Rossetti poem, "Remember Me"; the Caruso recording with which Carmen Trivago sings is a Flotow opera, *Martha*; Tchaikovsky plays on the radio in Christina's room ("She was always listening to that station"); a prize fight is being broadcast in the background when Evello and Sugar Smallhouse are killed. While these latter examples may not be as fully incorporated into the narrative structure as the poem, they all provide immediate textural contrast if not subsidiary meaning. The fight broadcast, in particular, and

even some one-line gags—for instance, Velda approaches Mike asking, "But under any other name, would you be as sweet?"; and he, not paying attention to her, says, "Kowalski"—are easily appreciated as non sequiturs or confusions of ritual (the prize fight) and reality (death), where responses and intentions work at cross purposes or get misplaced. These concepts run parallel to Hammer's own search for meaning in the cryptic pentameter of the poem ("But when the darkness and corruption leave/A vestige of the thoughts that once we had"). Myth becomes even more of a surface value in the case of the "great whatsit." Pat Murphy's "few harmless words" ("…just a bunch of letters scrambled together, but their meaning is very important…Manhattan project…Los Alamos…Trinity.") are just as much words to conjure with as Soberin's pedantic analogies. For Soberin's "Cerberus barking with all his heads" is too archaic and unfrightening to keep Lily Carver from opening her Pandora's box. In the final analysis, the "great whatsit" contains pure phlogiston. The quest for it becomes the quest for the cleansing, combustible element, for the spark of the purifying fire that reduces the nether world of *Kiss Me Deadly* to radioactive ash.

—A.S.

KISS OF DEATH (1947)

Director: Henry Hathaway
Producer: Fred Kohlmar (20th Century-Fox)
Screenplay: Ben Hecht and Charles Lederer; from an unpublished story by Eleazar Lipsky
Director of Photography: Norbert Brodine
Special Photographic Effects: Fred Sersen
Sound: W.D. Flick, Roger Heman
Music Score: David Buttolph
Music Director: Lionel Newman
Orchestration: Earle Hagen
Art Directors: Lyle Wheeler, Leland Fuller
Set Decoration: Thomas Little
Costumes: Charles LeMaire
Makeup: Ben Nye
Assistant Director: Abe Steinberg
Film Editor: J. Watson Webb, Jr.

CAST: Victor Mature (Nick Bianco), Brian Donlevy (D'Angelo), Coleen Gray (Nettie), Richard Widmark (Tom Udo), Karl Malden (Sgt. William Cullen), Taylor Holmes (Earl Howser), Howard Smith (Warden), Anthony Ross (Williams), Mildred Dunnock (Ma Rizzo), Millard Mitchell (Max Schulte), Temple Texas (Blondie), J. Scott Smart (Skeets). **BITS:** Wendell Phillips (Pep Magone), Lew Herbert, Harry Kadison, Lawrence Tiernan, Bernard C. Sell, Jack Rutherford, Arthur Holland, George Smith, Pat Malone, Bill O'Leary (Policemen), John Kullers (Prisoner), Victor Thorley, Rollin Bauer,

Arthur Foran, Jr., James Doody, William Zuckert (Sing Sing Guards), Paul Lilly, Herbert Holcombe (City Jail Guards), Steve Roberts, Dennis Bohan, Greg Martell, Richard Midgley (Guards), Iris Mann (Congetta), Marilee Grassini (Rosaria), Norman McKay (Capt. Dolan), Harry Cooke, Richard Taber, Jesse White (Taxi Drivers), Robert Karnes (Hoodlum), Harry Carter, Robert Adler, Charles McClelland (Detectives), Yvonne Rob, Carl Milletaire (Customers), Gloria O'Connor, Consuela O'-Connor (Girls), Harold Crane (Mr. Moremann), Mel Ruick (Moremann's Assistant), John Marley (Al), Lee Sanford (Chips Cooney), John Stearns (Harris), Eda Heinemann (Mrs. Keller), Eva Condon, Irene Shirley (Nuns), Mary Morrison (Mother Superior), Alexander Campbell (Train Conductor), George Shelton, David Fresco (Waiters), Harold Gary (Doorman), Dort Clark (Man in Car), Arthur Kramer (Mr. Sulla), Perc Launders (Lieutenant), Olga Borget (Cashier), Don Giovanni (Gangster), Tito Vuolo (Luigi).

Location: Chrysler Building, Tombs Prison, Criminal Courts Building, Hotel Marguery, New York, New York; Sing Sing Penitentiary, Ossining, New York; The Academy of the Holy Angels, Fort Lee, New Jersey
Filming Completed: May 17, 1947
Released: 20th Century-Fox, August 27, 1947
Running Time: 98 minutes

Everyone in New York City is enjoying Christmas but Nick Bianco, a man with a criminal record and no job. He goes Christmas shopping for his children by robbing a jewelry store. The jeweler trips the alarm, however, and Nick is wounded in a battle with the police. History is repeating itself because the same thing happened to Nick's father twenty years ago, and Nick watched his father die from a police bullet. After Nick recovers, he is taken to Assistant District Attorney D'Angelo, who offers Nick a reduced sentence if he informs on other criminals. Nick refuses and is sent to prison. He worries about his family when his letters are returned unopened; and he soon learns that his wife has committed suicide and his children are in an orphanage. Nettie, who used to baby-sit Nick's kids visits him in prison and relates good news of his children, but sad tales of his wife's affair with a gangster named Rizzo. Nick contacts D'Angelo and offers information even though it will not free him. D'Angelo conceals Nick's cooperation from other criminals by implicating Rizzo as a police informant. The mob sends out a contract on Rizzo. Nick, out on parole, visits Nettie and falls in love. They marry, but D'Angelo constantly demands information from Nick about criminal activities, thereby endangering his family's safety. The district attorney forces Nick to testify against a sadistic killer, Tommy Udo. When Udo is acquitted, Nick lives in fear of the killer's revenge. Sending his family away, Nick seeks out Udo but is ambushed and shot repeatedly. Udo is killed by the police. Although he is seriously wounded, Nick is taken from the scene in an ambulance. The viewer is led to believe that he will survive and begin a new life reunited with his family.

Although praised in 1947 for its realism, *Kiss Of Death* displays an uncomfortable alliance of documentarylike locations and stylized script and characterizations. Norbert Brodine's photography contributes to the aspect of stylization by making a row house in Queens look like a soundstage set. The cast and crew were transported both to Sing Sing prison and the Tombs in New York City and, in "method" acting spirit, were processed through these institutions as though they were convicts. None of this dissipates the melodramatic atmosphere of the script. Nick's wife, Nettie, narrates the story in voice-over; and the use of a female narrator is somewhat unusual in film noir. However, the exploration of actual social inequities, of the jobless turning to crime because of lack of alternatives, which is introduced by her narration, is never substantially developed. Rather the contradictions in this narrative's content suggest either an attempt to approximate Nettie's biased viewpoint or a weak social commentary to bolster the ambience of realism initiated by the location work. Simplistically, the narrator introduces Nick Bianco to the viewer as an unlucky individual who steals only to purchase Christmas presents for his children; yet it is soon revealed that his criminal record dates back to his adolescence. Aside from the mention in passing of the fact that Nick's father was also a felon, there is no probing of the economic or environmental causes of Nick Bianco's misspent life. The result is the naive suggestion that criminal inclinations are inherited like a family business.

Victor Mature's interpretation of Nick—although like Widmark's celebrated, leering portrayal of Udo overly dramatized in context—suggests a character trapped by his compulsive behavior and elicits viewer sympathy despite his criminal past. But the script again fails to define this figure further except through clichéd encounters with the police, other criminals, and his family. The overt theme of a "reformed" man inevitably sucked back into the criminal world is less innovative than the brief scenes of illegal deals made by corrupt district attorneys or the intrigues of the script's truest villain, the shyster lawyer who protects the criminal and betrays both the law and the reformed convict. That character and Widmark's psychotic rendering of the sadistic Udo, who pushes old women in wheelchairs down stairs for kicks or gleefully empties his automatic into Nick's body, are also undeveloped. Ultimately, a figure like Udo becomes an incongruous gargoyle of a truly noir world trapped in a narrative of facile social consciousness.

—E.M.

KISS THE BLOOD OFF MY HANDS (1948)
[Working Title: THE UNAFRAID]

Director: Norman Foster
Executive Producer: Harold Hecht (Harold Hecht-Norma)
Producer: Richard Vernon
Associate Producer: Norman Deming

KISS TOMORROW GOODBYE

Screenplay: Leonardo Bercovici, with additional dialogue by Hugh Gray, adapted by Ben Maddow and Walter Bernstein; from the novel by Gerald Butler
Director of Photography: Russell Metty
Special Photography: David S. Horsley
Sound: Leslie I. Carey, Corson Jowett
Music Score: Miklos Rozsa
Art Directors: Bernard Herzbrun, Nathan Juran
Set Decoration: Russell A. Gausman, Ruby R. Levitt
Makeup: Bud Westmore
Hairstyles: Carmen Dirigo
Production Manager: John Hambleton, Keith Weeks
Technical Adviser: Hugh Gray
Assistant Director: Jack Voglin
Script Supervisor: Connie Earle
Film Editor: Milton Carruth

CAST: Joan Fontaine (Jane Wharton), Burt Lancaster (Bill Saunders), Robert Newton (Harry Carter), Lewis L. Russell (Tom Widgery), Aminta Dyne (Landlady), Grizelda Hervey (Mrs. Paton), Jay Novello (Sea Captain), Colin Keith-Johnston (Judge), Reginald Sheffield (Superintendent), Campbell Copelin (Publican), Leland Hodgson (Tipster), Peter Hobbes (Young Father). **BITS:** Thomas P. Dillon (Welshman), Joseph Granby (Theater Manager), Robin Hughes, Harry Cording, Art Foster, Don MacCracken (Policemen), Harry Allen (Drunk), Valerie Cardew (Change Girl), Ben H. Wright (Cockney Tout), Wally Scott (Hanger-on), Harold Goodwin (Whipper), Keith Hitchcock (Official), Alec Harford (Doctor), Lora Lee Michel (Little Girl), Jimmy Aubrey (Taxi Driver), Leslie Denison (Constable), Arthur Gould-Porter, Kenneth Harvey, Tommy Hughes, Tom Pilkington (Bookies), Charles McNaughton (Telescope Man), Filippa Rock (Woman), Timothy Bruce, Anne Whitfield, Suzanne Kerr, Patty King (Children), Colin Kenny (Proprietor), Ola Lorraine (Donald's Mother), Frank Hagney, James Logan, David McMahon (Seamen), Al Ferguson (Marker), David Dunbar (Large Man), Richard Glynn (Donald), Marilyn Williams (Barmaid), Jack Stoney (Man), Mildred Hale (Woman), James Fowler, Robert Hale, Fred Fox, Jack Carol (Tipsters), George Bunny (Bookie), Harry Wilson (Man in Pub), Duke Green, Wesley Hopper (Men).
Filming Completed: May 8, 1948
Released: Universal-International, October 29, 1948
Running Time: 79 minutes
[NOTE: After a dispute with the Motion Picture Production Code Administration to retain the title of the novel as the film's title, Universal-International announced its decision to "change title of *Kiss The Blood Off My Hands* back to *The Unafraid* tag under which it was produced...as the *Kiss* tag was 'too gruesome,'"although the film had already been released. However, there is no record that the film was ever released as *The Unafraid*.]

Bill Saunders, an embittered war veteran, goes into a rage in an English pub and kills the proprietor. Running from the police, he takes refuge in the room of a shy nurse, Jane, and a sympathetic relationship develops. But he is recognized by the insidious Harry, who witnessed the killing and wants to draw Bill into criminal activities. Bill shuns Harry but, because of his violent temper, he is sentenced to six months in prison and a whipping after assaulting a policeman. More bitter and lonely than before, Bill finds Jane after his release from prison; and she gets him a job as truck driver at the clinic where she works. But Harry blackmails Bill into stealing medicine for him to sell on the black market. When Jane becomes an unexpected passenger in his truck on the designated assignment, Bill does not go through with the plan. Harry comes to Jane's flat later and attempts to gain her cooperation by playing on her feelings of love and protectiveness toward Bill. In self-defense, Jane kills the menacing Harry; and Bill plans to flee the country with her. At the last minute Bill changes his mind, knowing that if he tells the whole truth, he will be punished for the killing of the innkeeper but Jane will go free for the justifiable killing of Harry.

Conjuring up images of murder, anguish, and love, *Kiss The Blood Off My Hands* is one of the most evocative titles of any film noir. However, the film itself is simply another entry in the Burt Lancaster cycle of masochistic melodramas, in which a tormented Lancaster journeys through a treacherous world accompanied by the dissonant strains of Miklos Rozsa's music. Joan Fontaine's sincere heroine is in contrast to the destructive women played by Ava Gardner and Yvonne De Carlo in *The Killers* and *Criss Cross* and even to the ambiguous, but ultimately sympathetic, Lizabeth Scott character of *I Walk Alone*. The material itself is inconsistent and the lack of pacing in Robert Newton's performance causes the well-written character of Harry to lapse from an initially strong impression into monotony. The whipping of Lancaster, however, is staged for maximum effectiveness; and Bill and Jane's visit to a zoo, where he is disturbed by his kinship to the animals, is well presented. Taking full advantage of the cinematography of Russell Metty, the director makes the most of Bill's nocturnal flights from the police. Admittedly, it is not entirely clear why the story is set in London, in contrast to *Night And The City*, which offers a pointed relationship between the hustling American, Harry Fabian, and the city of his curious self-exile.

—B.L.

KISS TOMORROW GOODBYE (1950)

Director: Gordon Douglas
Producer: William Cagney (A William Cagney Production)
Screenplay: Harry Brown; from the novel by Horace McCoy
Director of Photography: J. Peverell Marley
Special Effects: Paul Eagler

Sound: William Lynch
Music Score: Carmen Dragon
Production Design: Wiard Ihnen
Set Decoration: Joe Kish
Costumes: Adele Parmenter
Makeup: Otis Malcolm
Assistant Director: William Kissell
Film Editors: Truman K. Wood, Walter Hannemann

CAST: James Cagney (Ralph Cotter), Barbara Payton (Holiday Caldwell), Helena Carter (Margaret Dobson), Ward Bond (Inspector Weber), Luther Adler (Cherokee Mandon), Barton MacLane (Reece), Steve Brodie (Jinx Raynor), Rhys Williams (Vic Mason), Herbert Heyes (Ezra Dobson), John Litel (Chief of Police Tolgate), William Frawley (Byers), Robert Karnes (Gray), Kenneth Tobey (Fowler), Dan Riss (District Attorney), Frank Reicher (Doc Green), John Halloran (Cobbett), Neville Brand (Carleton). **BITS:** George Spaulding (Judge), Mark Strong (Bailiff), Jack Gargan (Clerk of Court), Frank Marlowe (Joe, Milkman), Mack Williams (Hartford), Ann Tyrrell (Miss Staines), Clark Howatt (Intern), John Day, William Murphy (Motorcycle Policemen), Dan Ferniel (Highness), Matt McHugh (Satterfield), Georgia Caine (Julia), Charles Meredith (Mr. Golightly), King Donovan (Driver), Dick Rich, Ric Roman (Collectors), Gordon Richards (Butler), Fred Revelala (Rafael), Frank Wilcox (Doctor), Thomas Dillon (Apperson).
Filming Completed: May 16, 1950
Released: Warner Brothers, August 4, 1950
Running Time: 102 minutes

After escaping from a prison farm, Ralph Cotter, and a fellow inmate, Jinx Raynor, find refuge in a corrupt, out-of-the-way small town. It takes a shrewd criminal like Cotter little time to discover which police can be bribed; and he plans to blackmail a couple of dishonest cops, Weber and Reece, while stealing money from the mob. Cotter's flamboyant road to the top is paved with the bodies of those inessential to his plans. Even his mistress, Holiday, is sidestepped to allow Cotter the freedom to soil the reputation of a local politician's daughter. He leaves after receiving a large payoff and information that gives him considerable political leverage. The vile schemes of Ralph Cotter come to a cruel and violent end when Holiday kills him rather than give him up to someone else. Justice is served, and the town's corrupt elements are sentenced to jail.

A tough and unrelenting film from the novel by Horace McCoy, *Kiss Tomorrow Goodbye* is one of the most brutal and cynical noir films. The presence of Cagney as a totally corrupt individual begins where *White Heat* ends. As Cody Jarrett, there was some sympathy developed for Cagney. The role of Ralph Cotter is not burdened by this soft shell. His evil nature completely overshadows the rest of the cast, painting a vivid portrait of the complete noir villain. Directed by Gordon Douglas, *Kiss Tomorrow Goodbye* em-

phasizes violence and sadistic brutality. There is never a hint of compassion in the nature of Cotter. However, his man, Jinx, is weak and filled with the anxieties common to most noir characters. His uncertainty forms a sharp contrast to Cotter and his push for the top. There is no glamour in Cotter's death, killed unexpectedly just as he was about to celebrate his latest triumph; yet Cotter, who trusts only his automatic, summons the grim strength to mock Holiday when the revolver she is using to kill him misfires once. *Kiss Tomorrow Goodbye* is one of the noir films that leaves a bitter aftertaste; order is restored at the expense of suffering.

—C.M.

KNOCK ON ANY DOOR (1949)

Director: Nicholas Ray
Producer: Robert Lord (Santana Productions)
Associate Producer: Henry S. Kesler
Screenplay: Daniel Taradash and John Monks, Jr.; from the novel by Willard Motley
Director of Photography: Burnett Guffey
Sound: Frank Goodwin
Music Score: George Antheil
Music Director: Morris W. Stoloff
Art Director: Robert Peterson
Set Decoration: William Kiernan
Costumes: Jean Louis
Makeup: Clay Campbell
Hairstyles: Helen Hunt
Technical Advisers: National Probation and Parole Association
Assistant Director: Arthur S. Black
Script Supervisor: Frances McDowell
Film Editor: Viola Lawrence

CAST: Humphrey Bogart (Andrew Morton), John Derek (Nick Romano), George Macready (District Attorney Kerman), Allene Roberts (Emma), Susan Perry (Adele), Mickey Knox (Vito), Barry Kelley (Judge Drake), Dooley Wilson (Piano Player), Cara Williams (Nelly), Jimmy Conlin (Kid Fingers), Sumner Williams (Jimmy), Sid Melton (Squint), Pepe Hern (Juan), Dewey Martin (Butch), Robert A. Davis (Sunshine), Houseley Stevenson (Junior), Vince Barnett (Bartender), Thomas Sully (Officer Hawkins), Florence Auer (Aunt Lena), Pierre Watkin (Purcell), Gordon Nelson (Corey), Argentina Brunetti (Ma Romano), Dick Sinatra (Julian Romano), Carol Coombs (Ang Romano), Joan Baxter (Maria Romano). **BITS:** Evelyn Underwood, Mary Emery, Franz Roehn, Betty Hall, Jack Jahries, Rose Plumer, Mabel Smaney, Joy Hallward, John Mitchum, Sidney Dubin, Homer Dickinson, Netta Packer (Jury Members), Ann Duncan, Lorraine Comerford (Teenagers), Chuck Hamilton, Ralph Volkie, Frank Marlo (Bailiffs), Joe Palma, Dick Bartell, Eddie Randolph, Eda Reiss Merin,

Joan Danton (Reporters), Donald Kerr (Court Clerk), Myron Healey (Assistant District Attorney), Jane Lee, Dorothy Vernon (Women), John Indrisano, Blackie Whiteford, Charles Sullivan, Ray Johnson, Jack Perry, Joe Brockman, Franklin Farnum, Dudley Dickerson, Tex Swan, Harry Wilson, Joe Dougherty, George Hickman, Eddie Borden, Cliff Heard, Jeff York, Paul Kreibich, Charles Camp, Charles Colean (Men), Connie Conrad, Ann Cornwall, Beulah Parkington, Betty Taylor, Hazel Boyne, Roberta Haynes (Women), Jack Clisby, Glen Thompson, Paul Baxley, Lee Phelps (Policemen), Gary Owen (Larry), Chester Conklin (Barber), George Chandler (Cashier), Theda Barr (Girl), Wesley Hopper (Boss), Sid Tomack (Duke), Frank Hagney, Peter Virgo (Suspects), George Hickman, Saul Gorss, Al Hill, Phillip Morris (Detectives), Helen Mowery (Miss Holiday), Jody Gilbert (Gussie), Curt Conway (Elkins), Edwin Parker, Al Ferguson (Guards).

Filming Completed: September 17, 1948
Released: Columbia, February 22, 1949
Running Time: 100 minutes
[NOTE: Mark Hellinger purchased *Knock On Any Door*, and Humphrey Bogart, and Marlon Brando were to star in his production. Robert Lord, Humphrey Bogart, and Morgan Maree formed a corporation to produce the film after Hellinger died on December 31, 1947.

A pictorialization of the novel was published by *Look* magazine in the September 30, 1947, issue. Subsequently, *Look* published still photographs from the film and compared them with their 1947 photographs in the March 15, 1949, issue.]

When a policeman is killed during a robbery, Nick Romano, a rebellious youth with a record as a hoodlum, is put on trial for the crime. Andrew Morton, an attorney who knows Romano well because of their mutual slum background, defends him and believes in his innocence. As the trial proceeds, Romano's history is revealed. Bitter toward an oppressive society, poverty stricken, and without a father, Nick became a juvenile delinquent, committing many petty crimes. Morton tried to help Nick; but after seeming to reform, Nick robbed Morton and the older man turned his back on the youth, although for personal reasons he continued to feel responsible for Nick. The influence of a girl, Emma, finally reformed Nick; and the two married. But Nick could not keep a job and he gambled in attempts to improve things for Emma. When she became pregnant, Nick became more dissolute; and his desperate young wife finally killed herself. Insane with grief and anger, Nick committed the robbery that resulted in the policeman's death. Morton is winning Nick's case when the district attorney pressures Nick about Emma's death, and he confesses to killing the policeman. Stunned by Nick's guilt, Morton speaks passionately about environment and circumstamces combining to make Nick what he is. Nevertheless, Nick is sentenced to die in the electric chair; and Morton visits him only moments before the young man goes to his death.

Knock On Any Door is a film that suffers from the explicitness of its social consciousness. All of Nicholas Ray's films have a strong sense of social and moral issues. Usually, however, this social and moral sense is implicit in Ray's treatment and the viewer accepts Ray's attitudes because the director has generated a deep emotional response. Further, there is a complexity in most of his work that is denied in *Knock On Any Door* by the simplification of Nick Romano's character. He is the only Ray protagonist who is solely the victim of his environment. No such assumption is made about the similar characters of Bowie in *They Live By Night* and of Jim in *Rebel Without A Cause*. Despite this, however, the character of Nick Romano, as realized in individual scenes, is compelling. John Derek (making his film debut here), played a very similar role as Davey Bishop in Ray's Western, *Run For Cover*. One of the reasons that film is so much more successful than *Knock On Any Door* is that the relationship between the misguided youth and the older man, Mat Dow, who tries to help him is a neurotic one. Mat Dow betrays psychological flaws by his continuing faith in the Davey Bishop character, while the comparable Bogart character, Andrew Morton, in *Knock On Any Door* never seems essential to the plot.

Visually, this is one of Ray's plainer films, especially in the courtroom scenes. The casting of George Macready as the prosecutor helps somewhat; and Bogart's long speech is delivered with conviction in spite of the contrived nature of the speech itself. The one memorable moment in these scenes occurs when Nick is sentenced and the camera cranes up to look down pityingly on the doomed Nick and the unhappy Morton. However, some of the feeling of film noir is present in the flashbacks with their evocation of city streets, pool halls, and impoverished flats; and in the close-ups and dissolves of Nick following Emma's death. Additionally, Nick undercuts and contradicts the solemnity of the film's message when he says, "Live fast, die young and have a good-looking corpse."

—B.L.

THE KREMLIN LETTER (1970)

Director: John Huston
Producers: Carter De Haven, III; Sam Wiesenthal (20th Century-Fox)
Screenplay: John Huston and Gladys Hill; from the novel by Noel Behn
Director of Photography: Ted Scaife [DeLuxe Color; Panavision]
Camera Operator: Dudley Lovell
Special Effects: Augie Lohman
Sound: Basil Fenton-Smith, Renato Cadueri
Music: Robert Drasnin
Production Designer: Ted Haworth
Art Director: Elven Webb
Scenic Artist: Fred Tuch

Set Decoration: Dario Simoni
Costumes: John Furniss
Makeup: Amato Garbini
Continuity: Lucy Litchig
Assistant Directors: Gus Agosti, Carlo Cotti
Film Editor: Russell Lloyd

CAST: Bibi Andersson (Erika), Richard Boone (Ward), Nigel Green (Janis, alias "the Whore"), Dean Jagger (Highwayman), Lila Kedrova (Sophie), Micheal MacLiammoir (Sweet Alice), Patrick O'Neal (Rone), Barbara Parkins (B.A.), Ronald Radd (Potkin), George Sanders (Warlock), Raf Vallone (Puppet Maker), Max Von Sydow (Kosnov), Orson Welles (Bresnavitch), Sandor Eles (Grodin), Niall MacGinnis (Erector Set), Anthony Chinn (Kitai), Guy Deghy (Professor), John Huston (Admiral), Fulvia Ketoff (Sonia). **BITS:** Vonetta McGee (Black Woman), Marc Lawrence (Priest), Cyril Shaps (Police Doctor), Christopher Sandford (Rudolph), Hana-Maria Pravda (Mrs. Kazar), George Pravda (Mr. Kazar), Ludmilla Dudarova (Mrs. Potkin), Dimitri Tamarov (Ilya), Pehr-Olof Siren (Receptionist), Daniel Smid (Waiter), Victor Beaumont (Dentist), Steve Zacharias (Dittomachine), Laura Forin (Elena), Saara Rannin (Mikhail's Mother), Sacha Carafa (Mrs. Grodin), Rune Sandlunds (Mikhail).
Location: Helsinki, Finland; The Museum of the Hispanic Society of America, Central Park Zoo, Greenwich Village, New York, New York; Mexico
Filming Completed: June 5, 1969
Released: 20th Century-Fox, February 2, 1970
Running Time: 121 minutes
MPPA Rating: M
[NOTE: John Huston and Steve McQueen formed a partnership for Huston to direct and McQueen to star in *The Kremlin Letter*.]

Charles Rone, a naval intelligence officer with a cold and computerlike brain, is drafted into a bizarre gang of spies who have been hired to recover from the Soviet Union a compromising U.S. State Department letter discussing a US-USSR plan to attack Red China. The group includes an expert in vice, Janis; a homosexual, Warlock; a sinisterly hearty professional spy, Ward; a young and innocent master safecracker, B.A.; and their dying leader, Highwayman, who is a protègé of Sturdevant, one of the last great independent spies, now rumored to be dead.

Once inside Russia the group uses moral and sexual corruption to accomplish their goals. But in a sudden raid, all the agents are captured except Rone. He blackmails Breznavitch, a prominent member of the Soviet politburo, into freeing Ward, who is presumably the only surviving captive. Rone and Ward prepare for a routine flight home; but Ward abruptly murders a woman, Erika, who was protecting Rone. Her husband, Kosnov, head of the Soviet secret service, seeks revenge but is confronted by Ward, who is actually the famous Sturdevant and who tortures and murders Kosnov to avenge Kosnov's betrayal of him

during World War II. Additionally, Sturdevant now works with Bresnavitch as the new head of the Soviet secret service. Sturdevant attempts to blackmail Rone into working for him to save B.A.; but Rone cannot make a decision between the deaths of a Soviet politician's family or of B.A.

Beginning in the early 1960s the spy film divided into two contrasting subgenres; one emphasized action, fantasy, superheroes, and supervillains (e.g., *Goldfinger, Our Man Flint,* and *The Silencers*) and the second cynical, nonheroic, and often political realism (e.g., *The Spy Who Came In From The Cold, The Ipcress File,* and *The Quiller Memorandum*). While there are no 1940 films other than an occasional serial or Bulldog Drummond programmer that resembles a James Bond movie, there are a number of important noir films allied with a realistic and political tradition, among them *This Gun For Hire, Confidential Agent, Ministry of Fear, Background to Danger, Mask of Dimitrios,* and *Journey Into Fear.* However, it is surprising that with the possible exception of *Confidential Agent,* these films fail to be as black as they might be, given the nature of the Graham Greene and Eric Ambler novels upon which they are based. That these films tend to be highly conventionalized versions of the novels is doubly perplexing because of the pessimism and bleakness so common in the treatment of other genres such as the gangster and detective film during the 1940s. But twenty years later the essentially noir elements of the 1940s espionage novel did begin to turn up with some consistency in films such as *The Kremlin Letter* and those cynical and politically realistic films mentioned above, which have to be seen as part of an older, more noir tradition to be fully understood.

The Kremlin Letter is not simply a study of espionage or political corruption. These elements are there; but it is the way in which they are combined that makes *The Kremlin Letter* both emotionally disturbing and structurally allied to the noir cycle. The film's qualities are grounded in the peculiar progression and cumulative impact of its narrative. Also, in the noir tradition, none of its characters is ever in control of his life; no one is ever sure if his associates or adversaries are what they seem; and unknown forces pilot everyone's fate, eventually forcing all of them to give up those they love. Like pawns, people move from one insecure position to another and are isolated and defenseless.

When not seen as a composition of these episodes in time, *The Kremlin Letter* seems a conglomeration of sex, sadism, and torture. But in context, such elements are neither blatant nor obtrusive; What emerges are the very human motivations that lead not only to violence but, the experience of being trapped in a world of perversion, degradation, violence, and death makes the characters desperate. It also leads them to the discovery of their need for trust and compassion. The traditional icons and clichés of the spy film move into the background and reveal *The Kremlin Letter* as, in the noir tradition, an existential set-piece of which Rone's inability to choose is the ironic climax.

—D.L.W.

THE LADY FROM SHANGHAI (1948)

Director and Producer: Orson Welles (Columbia)
Associate Producers: Richard Wilson, William Castle
Screenplay: Orson Welles; from the novel *Before I Die* by Sherwood King
Director of Photography: Charles Lawton, Jr.
Special Mirror Effects: Lawrence Butler
Sound: Lodge Cunningham
Music Score: Heinz Roemheld
Music Director: Morris Stoloff
Song: "Please Don't Kiss Me," by Allan Roberts and Doris Fisher
Art Directors: Stephen Goosson, Sturges Carne
Set Decoration: Wilbur Menefee, Herman Schoenbrun
Costumes: Jean Louis
Hairstyles: Helen Hunt
Assistant Director: Sam Nelson
Script Supervisor: Dorothy Cormack
Film Editor: Viola Lawrence

CAST: Rita Hayworth (Elsa Bannister), Orson Welles (Michael O'Hara), Everett Sloane (Arthur Bannister), Glenn Anders (George Grisby), Ted de Corsia (Sidney Broome), Erskine Sanford (Judge), Gus Schilling (Goldie), Carl Frank (District Attorney), Louis Merrill (Jake), Evelyn Ellis (Bessie), Harry Shannon (Cab Driver), Wong Show Chong (Li), Sam Nelson (Yacht Captain). **BITS:** Tiny Jones (Woman), Edythe Elliott (Old Lady), Peter Cusanelli (Bartender), Joseph Granby (Police Lieutenant), Al Eben, Norman Thomson, Edward Coke, Harry Strang (Policemen), Gerald Pierce (Waiter), Maynard Holmes (Truck Driver), Jack Baxley, Ed Peil, Heenan Elliott (Guards), Dorothy Vaughn (Old Woman), Philip Morris (Port Steward/Policeman/Peters), Steve Benton, Milt Kibbee, Phil Van Zandt (Policemen), William Alland, Alvin Hammer, Mary Newton, Robert Gray, Byron Kane (Reporters), John Elliott (Clerk), Charles Meakin (Jury Foreman), Jessie Arnold (School Teacher), Mabel Smaney, George "Shorty" Charello, Vernon Cansino (People), Doris Chan, Billy Louie (Chinese Girls), Joe Recht (Garage Attendant), Jean Wong (Ticket Seller), Artarne Wong (Ticket Taker), Grace Lem (Chinese Woman), Preston Lee (Chinese Man), Joseph Palma (Cab Driver).
Location: Central Park, the Maritime Union Headquarters, New York, New York; the Aquarium, Chinese Mandarin Theatre, San Francisco; Walhalla Bar and Cafe, Sausalito, California; Acapulco, Mexico; and aboard the yacht, *Zaca*, owned by Errol Flynn.

Filming Completed: February 27, 1947
Released: Columbia, June 10, 1948
Running Time: 86 minutes

Michael O'Hara comes to the aid of a mysterious and beautiful woman who is being mugged. After a brief and flirtatious conversation, the woman vanishes into the night. Soon afterward Michael is hired as a crew member for a pleasure cruise south of the border on a yacht owned by Arthur Bannister, who is the husband of his mystery lady, Elsa Bannister. Arthur is a brilliant trial lawyer but is severely crippled. Husband and wife seem to have an odious reason for wanting Michael aboard ship. O'Hara is introduced to Bannister's associate, Grisby, and is slowly implicated in a bizarre and constantly changing program of murder and fraud. The resulting death of Grisby is blamed on the ill-fated Michael. He is defended in court by Bannister who, although he has never lost a case, is determined to see Michael convicted. O'Hara escapes before the verdict is decided and hides out in a Chinatown theater, where he is followed by Elsa. Several of her oriental associates drug O'Hara and bring him to an abandoned amusement park, where he confronts the cruel and demanding Elsa for the last time. However, Bannister forces his wife into a final showdown in a hall of mirrors. Amid shattering images of Elsa and the crippled lawyer, the truth about Grisby's death is revealed. Michael walks away from the dying Elsa, alone and ultimately ambivalent to the entire affair.

Remembered most for its final sequence with the celebrated hall of mirrors confrontation, Orson Welles's *The Lady From Shanghai* is an unusual noir film. It can be seen as the complete opposite of the hard-boiled tradition explored by writers like Chandler and Hammett; and yet it contains elements of chaos and obtuseness common to both writers. At the same time, Elsa Bannister is an original *femme fatale*, her only rival being Brigid O'Shaughnessy from Hammett's *The Maltese Falcon*. The incomprehensible motives for a great deal of the action is outweighed by Welles's exotic visual style. The film is full of shifting imagery. The city is quickly replaced by the lush tropical locale of the Caribbean, which in turn gives way to the trial and Chinatown. The return to civilization is part of a baffling and confusing plot in which nothing seems to make sense to Michael or anyone else. What takes place is a wild nightmare, which Welles illustrates with baroque juxtaposition and illusive imagery. The quality of illogic that forms the basis of development for *The Lady From Shanghai* stems from an unconscious association with the noir style. Welles most often was able to transcend his various genres to create wholly original works; but his particular conception of the world complemented the noir vision. His films from *Journey Into Fear* through *Touch Of Evil,* with the exception of his Shakespearean works, are all noir oriented. His style at times undercuts basic noir tendencies, and accounts for the inconsistencies of films like *The Stranger* and to a lesser degree *The Lady From Shanghai*. Because the film remains closely rooted to its hard-boiled heritage of an elliptical and inscrutable logic, it constantly confounds and unsettles through its quasi-romantic narration and the elusive quality of demanding yet unmotivated and unresolved relationships. *The Lady From Shanghai* radically deconstructs itself in a way that alienates the viewer but offers no alternate reading.

—C.M.

LADY IN THE LAKE (1947)

Director: Robert Montgomery
Producer: George Haight (MGM)
Screenplay: Steve Fisher; from the novel by Raymond Chandler
Director of Photography: Paul C. Vogel
Special Effects: A. Arnold Gillespie
Sound: Douglas Shearer
Music Score: David Snell
Choral Director: Maurice Goldman
Art Directors: Cedric Gibbons, Preston Ames
Set Decoration: Edwin B. Willis, Thomas Theuerkauf
Costumes: Irene
Makeup: Jack Dawn
Hairstyles: Sydney Guilaroff
Assistant Director: Dolph Zimmer
Film Editor: Gene Ruggiero

CAST: Robert Montgomery (Philip Marlowe), Lloyd Nolan (Lt. DeGarmo), Audrey Totter (Adrienne Fromsett), Tom Tully (Capt. Kane), Leon Ames (Derace Kingsby),

Philip Marlowe (Robert Montgomery) in Lady In The Lake.

LADY IN THE LAKE

Jayne Meadows (Mildred Haveland), Morris Ankrum (Eugene Grayson), Lila Leeds (Receptionist), Richard Simmons (Chris Lavery), Ellen Ross (Elevator Girl), William Roberts (Artist), Kathleen Lockhart (Mrs. Grayson). **BITS:** Cy Kendall (Jaibi), Ralph Dunn (Sergeant), Wheaton Chambers (Property Clerk), Frank Orth (Greer), William McKeever Riley (Bunny), Robert Williams (Detective), Fred E. Sherman (Reporter), Jack Davis, John Gallaudet, Tom Murray George Magrill, Budd Fine, John Webb Dillon (Policemen), Billy Newell (Drunk), Robert Spencer (Montgomery Double), Eddie Acuff (Coroner), Nina Ross, Charles Bradstreet, George Travell, William O'Leary, Bert Moorehouse, Florence Stephans, Sandra Morgan, Fred Santley, Laura Treadwell,, Kay Wiley, Frank Dae, David Cavendish, James Nolan, Sherry Hall, Ann Lawrence, Roger Cole (Christmas Party Guests).

Filming Completed: July 5, 1946
Released: MGM, January 23, 1947
Running Time: 105 minutes

Philip Marlowe, a private investigator, meets with Adrienne Fromsett, editor-in-chief of a series of crime magazines published by Derace Kingsby, to discuss Marlowe's submission of a mystery story. But Adrienne actually wants to hire Marlowe to find Kingsby's missing wife, Crystal, so that Kingsby's divorce proceedings can begin. Marlowe visits Crystal's gigolo/boyfriend, Chris Lavery; but Lavery knocks him unconscious. Marlowe wakes up to find himself at the police station where he is warned by Capt. Kane and the belligerent Lt. Degarmo that they do not like private investigators harassing their citizens. A corpse is found in the lake near Kingsby's vacation cabin. Marlowe suspects it is Crystal but discovers it is Muriel Chess, the wife of Kingsby's caretaker, whose real name is Mildred Haveland. Derace Kingsby learns of Adrienne's plotting and fires her, insisting that he does not plan to divorce Crystal and marry her. However, he does want Marlowe to find Crystal. Marlowe returns to Lavery's house and meets his scatterbrained landlady. She leaves, and Marlowe discovers Lavery's body. The police arrive and suspect Marlowe is the killer, especially after the detective fights with Lt. Degarmo. It is Christmas Eve, however, and Capt. Kane lets Marlowe go when his alibi proves him innocent of Lavery's killing. Subsequently, Marlowe is driving home along a deserted road when another car forces him off the road and into a ditch. Barely conscious, liquor is poured over him by Lt. Degarmo and Marlowe realizes he is being framed for drunk driving. Later, a celebrating passerby peeks into Marlowe's car. The detective knocks the man out and changes identification cards with him. Marlowe is severely hurt and then crawls to a phone booth and calls Adrienne for help. They realize they love each other and spend a quiet Christmas making future plans. On Christmas evening, Derace Kingsby rushes in with the news that Crystal wants $5,000 delivered to her. Leaving a trail of rice so that Adrienne can follow him, Marlowe meets Crystal and affirms what he suspected: she is the woman who

posed as Lavery's landlady and also as Muriel Chess but is actually Mildred Haveland. The real Crystal was the woman whom Mildred drowned in the resort lake. Mildred prepares to kill Marlowe, but Degarmo arrives. The cop followed the rice trail and kicked it aside so that no one else will find them. Degarmo, in love with Mildred, prepares to kill her and Marlowe in order to stop the murderess from killing anyone else, and he plans to make it apparent that they killed each other. Degarmo shoots Mildred; but Capt. Kane arrives and shoots Degarmo before he can kill Marlowe. Adrienne and Marlowe are happily reunited.

One of the most unusual of Hollywood film experiments, *Lady In The Lake* was almost entirely photographed from a subjective point-of-view, with the camera serving as the eyes of detective Marlowe. The only break from the subjective set-up is when Marlowe sits behind his desk and introduces various confusing elements of the plot while encouraging the audience to unravel the mystery themselves and "expect the unexpected." By restricting the field of vision to a subjective viewpoint, the tension and effectiveness of any surprise violence foisted upon Marlowe is heightened, as in the scenes when Lavery hits him, he is doused with liquor, he crawls across the street and struggles to reach a phone, and is threatened by Mildred Haveland's gun. Particularly interesting is the use of mirrors to complement the action. When Marlowe visits Lavery, he turns to look at a clock situated near a mirror. Although Marlowe seems not to notice, the audience can see Lavery's fleeting reflection as he prepares to hit the detective, just before the actual blow lands and the screen fills with blackness. Additionally, the subjective camera records Marlowe's impressions while he listens to a character speak. For example, as he is interviewed by Adrienne Fromsett, her alluring receptionist enters the room and Marlowe follows her every move while she answers his "stare" with seductive expressions. Not only does this technique increase visual interest, it also contrasts Adrienne's pretentiousness with Marlowe's more honest, albeit coarse, personality. A year later, Delmer Daves directed *Dark Passage* with a subjective camera for half that film's length, and, although the gimmick is integrated into the film to make the camera's subjectivity more meaningful to the plot, it lacks the consistent personalization of the camera as employed in *Lady In The Lake*. *Dark Passage*'s camera never wanders tellingly about a room or examines a person inch-by-inch.

Lady In The Lake's screenwriter, Steve Fisher, integrated his firsthand experience with pulp fiction to give Raymond Chandler's novel a new cinematic beginning. Fisher amusingly substituted *Lurid Detective* and *True Horror* magazine (to which Marlowe has submitted a story entitled, "If I Should Die Before I Wake"), for the novel's "Gillerlain Regal, the Champagne of Perfumes," and effectively transposed Chandler's corrupt tycoon environment to a commercial literary business run by hypocrites. The dialogue is tough and gritty; and Fisher retained much of Chandler's cynical "Marlowe" speeches, as when Adrienne says, "I don't like your manner," and Marlowe replies, "I'm not selling it." Fisher makes Adrienne Fromsett a complete character and initially, Marlowe's chief antagonist, while Chandler kept her half hidden as her boss's devoted mistress. When the film's Marlowe breaks up Adrienne's mercenary wedding plans, she bitterly asks him, "On what corner do you want me to beat my tambourine?" Marlowe has little idea that it should be on his corner; and Fisher keeps their verbal rivalry active until the mystery is almost at a close. When Marlowe and Adrienne admit their attraction to each other, it is a sentimental surprise dependent on the film maker's presumption that the audience demanded a romantic, happy ending no matter how contrived.

Ultimately, what happens in *Lady In The Lake* is immaterial because the visual discipline and suspension of conventional perception required of the viewer eliminate the necessity for complete dramatic development, much in the same way that the narrative confusion of *The Big Sleep* is functionally irrelevant. Robert Montgomery, as the director and star of *Lady In The Lake*, sustains the film's one-dimensional style with noir touches, such as the body of the murdered gigolo found behind a bullet-shattered glass shower door, the oppressive antagonism of the police, and the dilapidation of Mildred's hideout. However, it wasn't until Montgomery's next directorial effort, *Ride The Pink Horse*, that he found a character *and* a style fully evocative of the social constriction and existential anguish of film noir.

—C.M. & E.W.

LADY ON A TRAIN (1945)

Director: Charles David
Producer: Felix Jackson (Universal)
Associate Producer: Howard Christie
Screenplay: Edmund Beloin and Robert O'Brien, from an unpublished story by Leslie Charteris
Director of Photography: Woody Bredell
Special Photography: John P. Fulton
Sound: Joe Lapis
Music Score: Miklos Rozsa
Music Director for Deanna Durbin: Edgar Fairchild
Songs: "Gimme a Little Kiss, Will Ya, Huh?" by Turk-Smith-Pinkhard; "Silent Night" by Collier; "Night and Day" by Cole Porter
Art Director: John B. Goodman
Set Decoration: Russell A. Gausman
Assistant Director: William Holland
Film Editor: Ted Kent

CAST: Deanna Durbin (Nikki Collins), Ralph Bellamy (Jonathan), Edward Everett Horton (Mr. Haskell), George Coulouris (Mr. Saunders), Allen Jenkins (Danny), David Bruce (Wayne Morgan), Patricia Morison (Joyce), Dan Duryea (Arnold), Maria Palmer (Margo),

Elizabeth Patterson (Aunt Charlotte), Samuel S. Hinds (Mr. Wiggam), William Frawley (Sergeant Christie), Jacqueline de Wit (Miss Fletcher), Thurston Hall (Josiah Waring), Clyde Fillmore (Cousin), Ben Carter (Maxwell), Mary Forbes (Cousin), Sarah Edwards (Cousin), Nora Cecil (Woman with Umbrella), Hobart Cavanaugh (Drunk). **BITS:** Alfred La Rue (Waiter), Poni Adams, Kathleen O'Malley (Photographers), Jean Trent, Barbara Bates (Hatcheck Girls), Karen Randle (Cigarette Girl), Tom Dugan (Turnkey), Addison Richards (Captain), Joseph Crehan (Mr. Smith), Chester Clute (Conductor), Ralph Peters (Taxi Driver), Charles Cane (New York Policeman), Andre Charlot (Man with Carnation), Eddie Bruce, George Lewis, Charles Sherlock, Bert Moorehouse (Reporters), Eddie Acuff (New York Cab Driver), Alice Fleming (Mrs. Brown), Ed Waller (Mr. Brown), Eddie Dunn (Clerk), Jack Norton (Santa Claus), Matt McHugh (Drunk), George Chandler (Customer), Charles Deschamps (Hairdresser), Bert Roach (Fat Man), Robert Dudley (Honeywell), George Lloyd, Al Ferguson (Workmen), Eddie Bartel (Sound Track), Mabel Forrest (Wife), Sam McDaniel, Ernest Anderson (Porters), Lockard Martin (Doorman), Dick Hirbe (Newsboy), Perc Launders (New York Policeman), Ethel Mae Halls (Haughty Woman).

Filming Completed: May 28, 1945
Released: Universal, August 24, 1945
Running Time: 94 minutes
[NOTE: This film is a remake of the English motion picture, *Lady In Distress*.]

Nikki Collins is meeting her family lawyer, Mr. Haskell, in New York City. As her train pulls into Grand Central station, she witnesses through the car window, a murder in a nearby office building but is only able to see the murderer's back. Brushing the ineffectual Haskell aside, Nikki enlists the unwilling aid of mystery writer Wayne Morgan. Nikki learns that the murder victim was a wealthy shipping magnate, Waring. She visits his eccentric family, which includes two nephews, the dotty Jonathan and the handsome but sinister Arnold. It is disclosed that Waring left the bulk of his estate to his mistress, a nightclub singer. Nikki goes to the club where she discovers that the woman is dead and narrowly escapes Danny and Saunders, two menacing individuals in the employ of the murderer, whom she suspects is Arnold. When he tries to get her alone in the Waring Building, Nikki avoids him and is befriended by Jonathan. He takes her into the room that she recognizes as the scene of the crime and suddenly realizes that he is the killer. Arnold comes in with a gun followed by Wayne, who mistakes Arnold as the guilty party, takes the gun from him and gives it to Jonathan. Fortunately, the police arrive in time to prevent any further killing.

Lady On A Train is one of the rare noir comedies that is not a parody of private detective stories. Instead, it parodies Cornell Woolrich's aura of fateful circumstance and quaint or pathological characters. The opening scene is especially

A LADY WITHOUT PASSPORT

derivative of Woolrich as the young, beautiful woman on a train watches helplessly from her rain-streaked Pullman window as a man is murdered. The photography of Woody Bredell evokes the same atmospheric New York that he captured a year earlier in *Phantom Lady*. It combines with Charteris's original story, the eccentric characterizations of Coulouris, Bellamy, and Duryea, and the haunting music of Miklos Rozsa to provide a noir setting for a film that even gives Deanna Durbin a chance to sing.

—B.P.

A LADY WITHOUT PASSPORT (1950)

Director: Joseph H. Lewis
Producer: Samuel Marx (Samuel Marx Production)
Screenplay: Howard Dimsdale, adapted by Cyril Hume; from a story by Lawrence Taylor
Director of Photography: Paul C. Vogel
Music: David Raksin
Art Directors: Cedric Gibbons, Edward Carfagno
Film Editor: Frederick Y. Smith

CAST: Hedy Lamarr (Marianne Lorress), John Hodiak (Pete Karczag), James Craig (Frank Westlake), George Macready (Palinov), Steven Geray (Frenchman), Bruce Cowling (Archer Delby James), Nedrick Young (Harry Nordell), Steven Hill (Jack), Robert Osterloh (Lt. Lannahan), Trevor Bardette (Lt. Carfagno), Charles Wagenheim (Ramon Santez), Renzo Cesana (A., Sestina), Esther Zeitlin (Beryl Sandring), Carlo Tricoli (Mr. Sandring), Marta Mitrovitch (Elizabeth Alonescu), Don Garner (Dimitri Matthias), Richard Crane (Navy Flyer), Nita Bieber (Dancer).
Location: Stock footage exteriors of Cuba
Released: MGM, August 3, 1950
Running Time: 72 minutes

A government plot to break up an illegal alien smuggling racket involves undercover work by special agent Pete Karczag. Impersonating a Hungarian immigrant stranded in Cuba who wishes to enter the United States without a passport, Karczag gets involved with a beautiful refugee, Marianne Lorress, also seeking asylum in America. She is smoothly manipulated by Karczag into working for the government. It is Marianne who ultimately infiltrates the organization headed by Palinov. However, Karczag blows his cover and is almost killed by the smugglers. Panicked by the discovery of an infiltrator, Palinov takes the still unsuspected Marianne and attempts to escape to America in a small plane. Unable to control the craft, the smuggler crashes the plane in the Florida everglades. A final shootout in the misty swampland results in Palinov's death and the rescue of Marianne.

There is a quaint, almost juvenile, noir quality to Joseph H.

Lewis's *A Lady Without Passport*. Utilizing a number of noir conventions, ranging from the exotic *femme fatale* to decadent villainy and hard-boiled heroes, without any real noir insight, this production falls into that category of films made during the noir period that reproduce the look but not the very complex ethos of true film noir. Most of what is noir in *A Lady Without Passport* stems from Lewis's particular brand of exoticism, which is somtimes expressionistic and decidedly surreal. Unlike Henry Hathaway and Anthony Mann who treated similar "authentic police dramatizations" with a sense of documentary realism, Lewis instilled his films with an atmosphere of unreality. His more interesting noir films, such as *My Name Is Julia Ross* and *Gun Crazy* possess an ambience that rejects normal sensibilities while substituting surrealism. *A Lady Without Passport*, although not one of Lewis's most interesting films, still draws on this stylistic preoccupation to give a strange and occasionally fascinating treatment to a stereotypical narrative.

—C.M.

LAURA (1944)

Director and Producer: Otto Preminger (20th Century-Fox)
Screenplay: Jay Dratler, Samuel Hoffenstein, and Betty Reinhardt; from the novel by Vera Caspary
Director of Photography: Joseph La Shelle
Sound: E. Clayton Ward
Special Effects: Fred Sersen
Music Score: David Raksin
Music Director: Emil Newman
Song: "Laura," lyric by Johnny Mercer, music by David Raksin
Art Directors: Lyle Wheeler, Leland Fuller
Set Decoration: Thomas Little
Costumes: Bonnie Cashin
Assistant Director: Tom Dudley
Film Editor: Louis Loeffler

CAST: Gene Tierney (Laura Hunt), Dana Andrews (Mark McPherson), Clifton Webb (Waldo Lydecker), Vincent Price (Shelby Carpenter), Judith Anderson (Ann Treadwell), Dorothy Adams (Bessie Clary), James Flavin (McAvity), Clyde Fillmore (Bullitt), Ralph Dunn (Fred Callahan), Grant Mitchell (Corey), Kathleen Howard (Louise). **BITS:** Harold Schlickenmayer, Harry Strang, Lane Chandler (Detectives), Frank La Rue (Hairdresser), Alexander Sacha, Dorothy Christy, Aileen Pringle, Terry Adams, Jean Fenwick, Yolanda Lacca. Forbes Murray, Cyril Ring, Nester Eristoff, Kay Linaker, Cara Williams, Gloria Marlin, Beatrice Gray, Kay Connors, Frances Gladwin, William Forrest (People), Buster Miles (Office Boy), Jane Nigh (Secretary), John Dexter (Jacoby).
Filming Completed: June 29, 1944

Released: 20th Century-Fox, October 11, 1944
Running Time: 88 minutes

Investigating the murder of career girl Laura Hunt, Detective Mark McPherson questions her mentor, noted radio personality Waldo Lydecker. It becomes clear that the caustic Lydecker regarded Laura not only as his finest creation but also as his personal property, using his biting wit to stave off her many suitors—all except one. The single exception is Shelby Carpenter, to whom Laura was engaged at the time of her death, much to the chagrin of Lydecker and Ann Treadwell, an older woman in love with Shelby. As Mark continues his investigation, he, too, falls under Laura's spell. As he is going over her apartment for evidence, he falls into a daze, staring at a stunning portrait of the dead woman. Suddenly, the door opens and in walks Laura. She explains that she's been in the country to decide whether or not to marry Shelby. The detective gets a call informing him that the disfigured body believed to be Laura's is actually that of a model, Diane Redfern. Mark has four suspects in the girl's murder: the jealous Lydecker and Anne Treadwell, each of whom could have killed Diane believing her to be Laura; Shelby, who admits he invited Diane to Laura's place to brush her off; and Laura, who could have jealously murdered the model. Resisting the love he feels for her, Mark is initially most suspicious of Laura. Ultimately, however, he discovers the murder weapon hidden in a clock given to Laura by Lydecker, whom he goes to arrest while leaving Laura alone. As Laura listens to Lydecker's pre-recorded radio broadcast, Lydecker sneaks into her apartment to finish the job he bungled. Vowing that if he can't have her, no one can, Lydecker attacks Laura; but Mark bursts in just in time to save her—for himself.

Laura posits a world in which everyone is implicated, in which everyone not only has a motive for, but is seemingly capable of, committing a heinous crime. Given such a premise, the ostensibly happy ending of the film, with Laura and Mark embarking on a new life together, seems strangely overshadowed. The ambiguity that distinguishes the film is further emphasized by the puzzling spectacle of Mark and Lydecker, entirely different in temperament and personality, yet both enthralled by a woman who reveals little of herself to either of them. Mark is the "hero" and Lydecker the "villain," but both are driven by the same obsession: the Laura that each creates in his own mind.

Preminger's gliding, probing camera is the perfect visual analogue to Lydecker's and particularly Mark's obsession. Following Mark as he moves around Laura's apartment, peering into her closets, examining her possessions, poring over her letters and diary, it makes the audience a party to Mark's insatiable curiosity, conveyed in subtle yet intense terms by Dana Andrews. Overshadowed by Clifton Webb's marvelously idiosyncratic performance as Lydecker, Andrews's quieter portrayal deserves more attention. With his haunted eyes, taut yet sensitive mouth, and softly insinuating voice, Andrews is a highly evocative screen presence, conveying more with a look than many actors do with a soliloquy. As the pragmatic, unromantic cop who, when asked by Lydecker if he's ever been in love, replies, "A doll in Washington Heights got a fox fur out of me once," he is only able to love the perfumed ghost of a woman he believes is dead, and who becomes a dream expressed in a work of art.

—J.K.

LEAVE HER TO HEAVEN (1945)

Director: John M. Stahl
Producer: William A. Bacher (20th Century-Fox)
Screenplay: Jo Swerling; from the novel by Ben Ames Williams
Director of Photography: Leon Shamroy [Technicolor]
Technicolor Directors: Natalie Kalmus, Richard Mueller
Special Photographic Effects: Fred Sersen
Sound: E. Clayton Ward, Roger Heman
Music Score: Alfred Newman
Orchestration: Edward B. Powell
Art Directors: Lyle Wheeler, Maurice Ransford
Set Decoration: Thomas Little, Ernest Lansing
Costumes: Kay Nelson
Makeup: Ben Nye
Assistant Director: Joseph Behm
Film Editor: James B. Clark

CAST: Gene Tierney (Ellen Berent), Cornel Wilde (Richard Harland), Jeanne Crain (Ruth Berent), Vincent Price (Russell Quinton), Mary Phillips (Mrs. Berent), Ray Collins (Glen Robie), Gene Lockhart (Dr. Saunders), Reed Hadley (Dr. Mason), Darryl Hickman (Danny Harland), Chill Wills (Leick Thorne), Paul Everton (Judge), Olive Blakeney (Mrs. Robie), Addison Richards (Bedford), Harry Depp (Catterson), Grant Mitchell (Carlson), Milton Parsons (Medcraft). **BITS:** Earl Schenck (Norton), Hugh Maguire (Lin Robie), Betty Hannon (Tess Robie), Kay Riley (Nurse), Guy Beach (Sheriff), Audrey Betz (Cook at Robie's Ranch), Jim Farley (Conductor), Charles Tannen (Man).
Location: Bass Lake, Monterey, Busch Gardens in Pasadena, California; Sedona Basin near Flagstaff, Granite Dells near Prescott, Arizona
Released: 20th Century-Fox, December 25, 1945
Running Time: 110 minutes

Ellen Berent is insanely jealous and possessive of her husband, writer Richard Harland, who resembles her dead father to whom she was also completely devoted. In order to be Richard's sole companion at his "Back of the Moon" lodge in Maine, Ellen sends his handyman Thorne away, lets his crippled brother Danny drown, and then murders their unborn child by throwing herself down a staircase. Ellen continues to fear Richard's alienation and feels threatened by the presence of her adopted sister, Ruth. Ellen hysterically admits to Richard that the recent accidents were planned by her to maintain their love; and he prepares to leave her. Ellen kills herself with poison in such a way as to suggest that she was murdered by Richard and Ruth. They are acquitted of Ellen's murder, although Richard is convicted as an accessory to Ellen's crimes because he did not reveal her criminal negligence. When Richard is released from prison, Ruth is waiting for him at the lodge.

Leave Her To Heaven is arguably the most vividly colored film noir. There are those for whom the very idea of a film noir in color is impossible, a contradiction in terms in a type of film that demands black-and-white photography for its treatment of rain-washed streets and harsh oblique shadows. The country settings of *Leave Her To Heaven* do not suit the urban locale usually associated with film noir. Yet, to quote a popular 1940s novelist, John Franklin Bardin, "The words 'I love you,' spoken on a sun-streaked terrace during a joyous day, can cement a betrayal."* This is the precise source of the extraordinary power and tension of *Leave Her To Heaven;* that the noir theme of a woman obsessed, whose love is so all-consuming that she must murder to retain exclusive possession of her beloved, is enacted under the sunniest of skies in the most beautiful of country settings. The glowing, healthy colors of nature are echoed in the costumes and makeup used to enhance Gene Tierney's masklike beauty and serve to make her unnatural actions as Ellen Berent all the more disturbing.

The predominant color of Leon Shamroy's photography is an orange—which seems to have been his favorite color throughout his career—that suggests the same sickness and corruption as the high-contrast photography of black-and-white film noir and also dominates other noir films shot in color, such as John Alton's *Slightly Scarlet*. In contrast with cold blue shadows and night exteriors, the warm amber glow of *Leave Her To Heaven* occurs in the films of many of the most prominent photographers of this pre-1954 Technicolor period, giving a distinctive tone that can be, in context, as ominous as the grays and blacks of standard film noir.

A strong mythic element runs through *Leave Her To Heaven*, from Ellen Berent's Electra-like adoration of her father, her Hippolytean stance as she scatters her father's ashes on horseback, and the Medea-like murder of her husband's young brother and unborn child. This mythic aspect of the story is emphasized by the smooth, marble planes of Gene Tierney's face and the straight-line, classical clothes she wears. Her face during the film's most frightening scene, as she watches her husband's crippled brother drown only a few feet from her, is as impassive as any statue's. She commits murder by inaction rather than violence. Ellen goes into a trance, becoming for one

moment a pure object; and without her support, acceptance, and love, the male must drown.

Ellen's expression is made more blank and statuelike by her heart-shaped sunglasses. They hold an almost cosmic significance as she uses them to conceal her spirit as well as her eyes. Contemporary audiences found it necessary to condemn her as an evil person and ignore the admonition of the title, but psychoanalysis would support the title's reference to a higher plane of reality and point out that she interacts with her society as an alien and should not be accountable to its temporal laws. In fact, mental illness was first referred to as alienism, and psychologists as alienists. This corresponds to director John Stahl's unusual conception of his heroines as super-real, emotionally alive individuals frustrated by their dull surroundings and unimaginative men. Society might see these women as unnatural and mentally ill, but to Stahl they are profoundly provocative beings. When one of them happens to be a murderess, he is completely unrestrained and makes the extreme contrast between her and her surroundings even more wild, hinting at inner tension and complexity that the other characters in the film could never suspect. Cornel Wilde is given only token sympathy as a "normal" man and Vincent Price gets none as the predatory male.

—M.B. & L.S.

THE LETTER (1940)

Director: William Wyler
Producer: Hal B. Wallis (Warner Brothers-First National)
Associate Producer: Robert Lord
Screenplay: Howard Koch; from the story by W. Somerset Maugham
Director of Photography: Tony Gaudio
Sound: Dolph Thomas
Musical Score: Max Steiner
Music Director: Leo F. Forbstein
Orchestration: Hugo Friedhofer
Art Director: Carl Jules Weyl
Costumes: Orry-Kelly
Makeup: Perc Westmore
Technical Advisers: Louis Vincenot, John Villasin
Unit Manager: Robert Ross
Assistant Director: Sherry Shourds
Film Editor: George Amy

CAST: Bette Davis (Leslie Crosbie), Herbert Marshall (Robert Crosbie), James Stephenson (Howard Joyce), Frieda Inescort (Dorothy Joyce), Gale Sondergaard (Mrs. Hammond), Bruce Lester (John Withers), Elizabeth Earl (Adele Ainsworth), Cecil Kellaway (Prescott), Sen Yung (Ong Chi Seng), Willie Fung (Chung Hi), Doris Lloyd (Mrs. Cooper), Tetsu Komai (Head Boy).
Filming Completed: July 18, 1940

*p. 209, Introduction to *The Last Of Philip Banter* in *The John Franklin Bardin Omnibus*, Baltimore: Penguin, 1976

170

Released: Warner Bros.-First National, November 22, 1940
Running Time: 95 minutes

On a plantation in the tropics, Leslie Crosbie shoots her lover in a jealous rage and fabricates a skillfully-told lie indicating self-defense to justify the killing. When her case goes to trial, her husband's closest friend, Howard Joyce, is employed as Leslie's attorney. A letter exists which proves Leslie's relationship to the dead man, and the lawyer prevails on Leslie's husband for authority to buy it, without disclosing its nature. The lawyer clears Leslie in court but the truth comes out afterward. Her husband forgives her, but Leslie declares, "I still love the man I killed." Walking outside, she is killed by an assassin employed by her lover's native mistress.

The Letter employs compelling long takes in key scenes between Leslie and the lawyer, with elaborate visual techniques reserved almost exclusively for the opening and closing sequences that have a precociously noir atmosphere for a 1940 film. Critical complaints have been directed at the closing sequence for being arbitrarily melodramatic. Actually, it was imposed to satisfy code requirements that a murderer must die. But it is precisely this kind of sudden, poetically rendered violence that epitomizes the deterministic fatality of film noir; and, in that respect *The Letter*'s finale is even more interesting than the tracking shot with which Wyler opens the film.

The Letter is also noteworthy for the moral shading of its most interesting character, the lawyer, who is simultaneously drawn to and repelled by the murderess. Ambiguous, intensely sympathetic, and thoughtfully realized, the character seems to express the film's true meaning as his reluctant complicity in Leslie's lie leads him to an implied psychological self-destruction. He is a precursor of the countless protagonists destroyed by women in the later classics of the noir cycle.

—B.L.

THE LINEUP (1958)

Director: Don Siegel
Producer: Jaime Del Valle (A Frank Cooper-Pajemar Production)
Screenplay: Stirling Silliphant; from characters created by Lawrence L. Klee in the CBS Television series "The Lineup"
Director of Photography: Hal Mohr
Sound: Stanford Haughton, John Livadary
Music: Mischa Bakaleinikoff
Art Director: Ross Bellah
Set Decoration: Louis Diage
Technical Adviser: Inspector John Kane, San Francisco Police Department
Second Unit Director: Lawrence Butler

Producer's Assistant: William Beaudine, Jr.
Assistant Director: Irving Moore
Film Editor: Al Clark

CAST: Eli Wallach (Dancer), Robert Keith (Julian), Warner Anderson (Inspector Guthrie), Richard Jaeckel (Sandy McLain), Mary La Roche (Dorothy Bradshaw), William Leslie (Larry Warner), Emile Meyer (Inspector Al Quine), Marshall Reed (Inspector Fred Asher), Raymond Bailey (Philip Dressler), Vaughn Taylor (The Man), Cheryl Callaway (Cindy), Bert Holland (Porter), George Eldredge (Dr. Turkel), Robert Bailey (Staples). **BITS:** Charles Stewart, Jack Carol (Lab Men), Dee Pollock, Chuck Courtney (Boys), Junius Matthews (Jeffers), Frank Tang (Housekeeper), Clayton Post (Communications Sergeant), Francis de Sales (Chester McPhee), Kay English (Supervisor), Al Merin (Porter Foreman), Billy Snyder (Salisbury), Bill Marsh (Manager), John Maxwell (Norm Thompson), Kathleen O'Malley (Stewardess), Jack Moyles (Attendant).
Location: San Francisco, California
Filming Completed: October 29, 1957
Released: Columbia, June 11, 1958
Running Time: 85 minutes

A ship's porter throws a bag into a taxicab. The taxicab hits a cop and a chase ensues, which ends when the cabbie is shot by the police. The bag contains heroin, and detectives Guthrie and Quine must find the source of the heroin shipments. Later, the professional killer, Dancer, and his older associate, Julian, who likes to make notes of people's last words before they die, arrive by plane. Their assignment is to retrieve three separate parcels of heroin that were unwittingly smuggled into San Francisco by three groups of travelers. The first packet is held by a merchant seaman who knows what is in it, and Dancer kills him. The second packet was brought in by a married couple, who are not at home. Their servant hesitates to accept Dancer's story about switched suitcases and is also killed. The final packet is concealed in a Japanese doll belonging to a little girl. Dancer befriends her mother, and he and Julian are invited to her apartment; but the little girl has discovered the packet and used it to powder her doll's face. He and Julian take the mother and daughter with them to explain to The Man, who is waiting for their heroin delivery in an arcade. The Man, a pitiless individual in a wheelchair, will not accept Dancer's explanations and coldly declares they will be killed. Dancer pushes The Man over a railing onto the skating rink; and they all run to escape. The police pursue the criminals in a dizzying chase until their driver, McLain, makes a wrong turn onto a half-built freeway and has nowhere to go. Killing McLain and Julian, Dancer dies while shooting it out with the cops.

The characters of Julian, McLain, The Man, and, especially, Dancer are the core of *The Lineup*. Don Siegel has a flair for developing ostracized characters and Dancer is a good example of what Andrew Sarris refers to as Siegel's "anti-

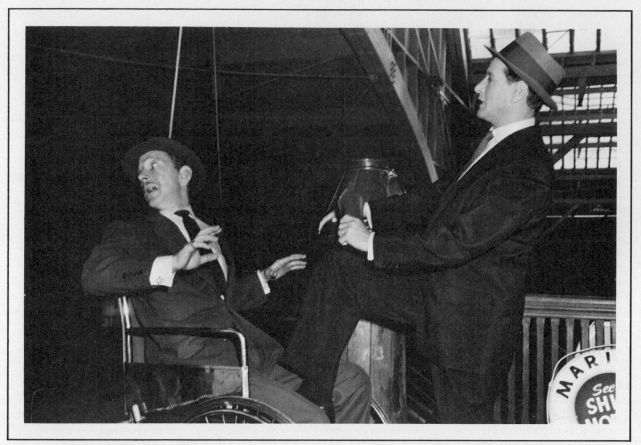

Dancer (Eli Wallach) pushes "The Man" (Vaughn Taylor) to his death in The Lineup.

Larry Warner (William Leslie) is shot by Dancer (Eli Wallach) in The Lineup.

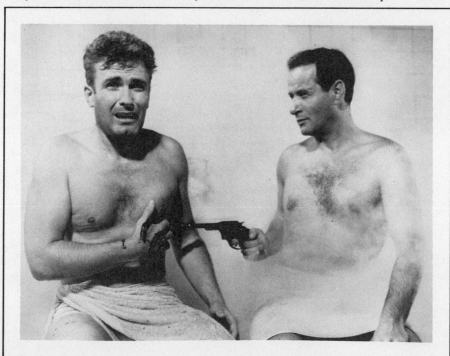

social outcasts." Julian's efforts to give Dancer social polish are both humorous relief and chilling indications of Dancer's imbalance. Whatever Dancer appears to be learning, any crisis causes him to revert to his true role of the psychopathic killer.

Thrillers like *The Lineup* do not possess the poetic iconography of their predecessors. While 1940s noir films follow their characters again and again down dark, rain-soaked streets in an endless night, late 1950s thrillers are often enacted in glaring sunshine. *The Lineup* is very much of this latter type but uses imaginative locales of the skating arcade, props such as the Japanese doll, and absurdist twists in the action occurring on a half-built freeway to make the film distinctively fatalistic. The final chase, although half of it takes place before a back-projection screen, is more visually precise than many spectacular chases in recent films. McLain's turn onto the unfinished exit is a subtly ill-fated moment in which the very cityscape thwarts Dancer. It also precipitates the outraged Dancer's query to the disdainful Julian before the younger man shoots his partner, "How about some last words for the book?"

—B.L.

LOAN SHARK (1952)

Director: Seymour Friedman
Producer: Bernard Luber (Bernard Luber Productions)
Screenplay: Martin Rackin and Eugene Ling; from an unpublished story by Martin Rackin
Director of Photography: Joseph Biroc
Sound: Frank Webster
Art Director: Feild Gray
Assistant Director: Carl Hiecke
Film Editor: Al Joseph

CAST: George Raft (Joe Gargen), Dorothy Hart (Ann Nelson), Paul Stewart (Donelli), Helen Westcott (Martha), John Hoyt (Phillips), Henry Slate (Paul Nelson), William Phipps (Ed Haines), Russell Johnson (Thompson), Benny Baker (Tubby), Larry Dobkin (Walter Karr), Charles Meredith (Rennick), Harlan Warde (Lt. White), Spring Mitchell (Nancy), Margie Dean (Ivy), Ross Elliott (Norm), Robert Bice (Steve Casmer), Robert Williams (Scully), Michael Ragan (Maxie), Virginia Caroll (Netta).
Filming Completed: January 1952
Released: Lippert, May 23, 1952
Running Time: 79 minutes

Released from prison, Joe Gargen goes to live with his sister's family. When his hard-working brother-in-law becomes the murdered victim of a loan-shark racket, Joe promises to avenge the killing and infiltrates the gang. The racket ensnares local factory employees who need cash by encouraging them to borrow from the racket at tremendous

interest rates. The racketeers extract their repayment in blood if the money is withheld. Joe uncovers the racket's mysterious leader, Mr. Phillips, and destroys him in a final showdown.

This film is a low-budget attempt to capitalize on the success of such films as *The Enforcer*. It is distinguished primarily by the characterizations of Paul Stewart as Donelli and John Hoyt as Phillips, as well as by some vivid photography. The brutal showdown between Phillips and Joe, which takes place in a cleaning plant, is full of evocative, menacing shadows. Joe, overpowering the gangster, throws him into one of the cleaning vats where he is boiled to death.

—B.P.

THE LOCKET (1947)

Director: John Brahm
Executive Producer: Jack J. Gross (RKO)
Producer: Bert Granet
Screenplay: Sheridan Gibney
Director of Photography: Nicholas Musuraca
Special Effects: Russell A. Cully
Sound: John L. Cass, Clem Portman
Music Score: Roy Webb
Conductor: Constantin Bakaleinikoff
Art Directors: Albert D'Agostino, Alfred Herman
Set Decoration: Darrell Silvera, Harley Miller
Costumes: Michael Woulfe
Dialogue Director: William E. Watts
Assistant Director: Harry D'Arcy
Film Editor: J.R. Whittredge

CAST: Laraine Day (Nancy Blair), Brian Aherne (Dr. Blair), Robert Mitchum (Norman Clyde), Gene Raymond (John Willis), Sharyn Moffett (Nancy, age 10), Ricardo Cortez (Mr. Bonner), Henry Stephenson (Lord Wyndham), Katherine Emery (Mrs. Willis), Reginald Denny (Mr. Wendall), Fay Helm (Mrs. Bonner), Helene Thimig (Mrs. Monks), Nella Walker (Mrs. Wendall), Queenie Leonard (Woman Singer), Lilian Fontaine (Lady Wyndham), Myrna Dell (Thelma), Johnny Clark (Donald). **BITS:** Vivian Oakland (Mrs. Donovan), Nancy Saunders (Miss Wyatt), George Humbert (Luigi), Trina Varella (Luigi's Wife), Nick Thompson (Waiter), Connie Leon (Bonner Maid), Dave Thursby (Dexter), Tom Chatterton (Art Critic), Sam Flint (District Attorney), Tom Coleman (Stenoypist), J.W. Johnston, Allen Schute, Eddie Borden (Men), Virginia Keiley (Ambulance Driver), Wyndham Standing (Butler), Fred Worlock, Henry Mowbray (Doctors), Cecil Weston (Nurse), Colin Kenny (Chauffeur), Leonard Mudie (Air Raid Warden), Pat Malone (London Bobby), Jacqueline Frost (Girl), Polly Bailey (Cook), Ellen Corby, Jean Ransom (Kitchen Girls), Keith Hitchcock (Orville), Gloria Donovan (Karen), Carol Donell, Martha Hyer, Kay Christopher (Bridesmaids), Ben Erway (2nd Willis Butler), Mari Aldon (Mary), Charles Flynn, Joe Ray, Bob Templeton (Photographers), Broderick O'Farrell (Minister), Dorothy Curtis (Maid).

Filming Completed: May 11, 1946
Released: RKO, March 19, 1947
Running Time: 85 minutes

John Willis and Nancy Blair are to be married; but on their wedding day, Dr. Blair, Nancy's former husband, comes to Willis and reveals Nancy's history of kleptomania. Blair was ignorant of her illness until Nancy's previous lover, a painter named Norman Clyde, informed him of the unhappiness her kleptomania had caused him. As a child, Nancy coveted a locket that she was denied. Later, she was accused of stealing it. Although Clyde killed himself in anguish, Dr. Blair persistently doubted Clyde's story until an incident in London during the war confirmed Nancy's criminal tendencies. Now Willis refuses to believe Blair; and the marriage goes on as planned. Just prior to the ceremony, however, the locket is given to Nancy and her entire past flashes across her mind. Collapsing, she suffers a mental breakdown and is institutionalized.

The Locket is an unusual psychological melodrama in the visual style of RKO. It is distinctive in its flashbacks within flashbacks, with the story often being told by a third or fourth person removed. This device is handled effectively in preparation for the climactic flashback, which reveals the truth. Also, given the psychological nature of the subject, the complex time structure is much more appropriate and evocative than in the similarly structured *Passage To Marseilles* made at Warner Brothers a few years earlier. The character of Nancy is well realized by the performance of Laraine Day, with less visible affectation than a similar character in Hitchcock's *Marnie*. Although there is a suggestion that Nancy's illness infects her various relationships with men, the sexual content of *The Locket* is much less pronounced than that of *Marnie*; a film that gains a great deal of its emotional tension from the leading character's frigidity.

—B.L.

THE LONG GOODBYE (1973)

Director: Robert Altman
Executive Producer: Elliott Kastner (Lion's Gate Films)
Producer: Jerry Bick
Associate Producer: Robert Eggenweiler
Screenplay: Leigh Brackett; from the novel by Raymond Chandler
Director of Photography: Vilmos Zsigmond
Sound: John V. Speak
Music Score and Conductor: John Williams

Song: "The Long Goodbye," lyric by Johnny Mercer, music by John Williams
Costumes: Kent James (Men), Marjorie Wahl (Women)
Makeup: Bill Miller
Hair Styles: Lynda Gurasich
Gaffer: Randy Glass
Key Grip: Ken Adams
Script Supervisor: Adel Bravos
Assistant Director: Tommy Thompson
Film Editor: Lou Lombardo

CAST: Elliott Gould (Philip Marlowe), Nina van Pallandt (Eileen Wade), Sterling Hayden (Roger Wade), Mark Rydell (Marty Augustine), Henry Gibson (Dr. Verringer), David Arkin (Harry), Jim Bouton (Terry Lennox), Warren Berlinger (Morgan), Jo Ann Brody (Jo Ann Eggenweiler), Jack Knight (Hood), Pepe Callahan (Pepe), Vince Palmieri, Arnold Strong (Hoods), Rutanya Alda, Tammy Shaw (Marlowe's Neighbors), Jack Riley (Piano Player), Ken Sansom (Colony Guard), Danny Goldman (Bartender), Sybil Scotford (Real Estate Woman), Steve Coit (Detective Farmer), Tracy Harris (Detective), Jerry Jones (Detective Green), Rodney Moss (Clerk).

Location: Hollywood, Westwood, and Malibu, California; Tepoztlan and Chiconcuac, near Cuernavaca, Mexico
Released: United Artists, March 7, 1973, in Los Angeles, Philadelphia, and Chicago. Released with new advertising campaign in New York on October 28, 1973. Subsequently rereleased in Los Angeles and major cities in December 1973.
Running Time: 113 minutes
[NOTE: The screen rights to *The Long Goodbye* were first acquired by Jerry Gershwin and Elliott Kastner for production at Warner Brothers in October 1965. But Gabriel Katzka purchased the screen rights for the film on June 9, 1967, to be produced by MGM. Stirling Silliphant began work on the screenplay after completion of his screenplay for *The Little Sister*, which was released as *Marlowe* (1969). In 1971, Elliott Kastner signed an agreement with United Artists to produce *The Long Goodbye* with a screenplay by Leigh Brackett. Kastner announced in May 1972, that Robert Altman would direct the film, starring Elliott Gould and Dan Blocker, who died on May 13, 1972. Sterling Hayden was later cast to replace Blocker in the part of Roger Wade, and the film was dedicated to Blocker's memory.]

Late one night, Los Angeles private detective Philip Marlowe is urgently requested by his friend, Terry Lennox, to drive him to the Mexican Border at Tijuana. Marlowe returns to Los Angeles and is interrogated and incarcerated by the police, who are investigating the brutal murder of Terry's wife, Sylvia. Three days later, Marlowe is released when the police receive from Mexico Terry's suicide note, which also confesses to killing Sylvia. Incredulous, Marlowe is determined to find out who is the actual killer. Meanwhile, he accepts a new case from Eileen Wade who requests that the detective find her alcoholic husband,

Philip Marlowe (Elliott Gould) in The Long Goodbye.

writer Roger Wade. A virtual prisoner at the mysterious sanitorium operated by the unscrupulous Dr. Verringer, Roger is rescued by Marlowe. A short thank you and goodbye note from Terry Lennox with a $5,000 bill enclosed arrives in Marlowe's mail. Subsequently, he is visited by gangster Marty Augustine who insists the detective knows where Lennox hid the gangster's money and threatens him with violence if he doesn't retrieve it. Marlowe follows Augustine and watches from outside while the gangster intimidates Eileen Wade, who had previously told Marlowe that she was not well acquainted with her neighbors, the Lennoxes. The next day, Marlowe asks Roger and Eileen about Augustine and receives conflicting stories. Marlowe travels to Mexico and confirms Lennox's death through photographs taken by the village officials. He returns to Los Angeles and attends a party at the Wades' beach home where he witnesses Roger's humiliation by Dr. Verringer who demands his fee. The party disperses, Roger passes out in an alcoholic stupor, and Eileen asks Marlowe to stay for dinner. While the detective confronts Eileen about Lennox, Roger Wade commits suicide by drowning. Eileen confesses to Marlowe that she thinks her husband killed Sylvia Lennox, as he was having an affair with the woman. The police ignore

Marlowe's entreaties to reopen the Lennox case. Augustine confronts Marlowe and again threatens death, until suddenly the missing money is returned. Marlowe sees Eileen Wade leave Augustine's office building and chases her but is hit by a car. He refuses to give up, leaves the hospital, and returns to the Mexican village where he bribes the city officials and discovers that Lennox bribed them to engineer proof of his death. Marlowe finds Lennox luxuriating about a pool and kills his manipulative friend. As the detective leaves Lennox's hideout, he passes the arriving Eileen Wade.

The Long Goodbye is about friendship and betrayal, not about murder. Marlowe's primary purpose is to clear his friend's name and to help a woman find her disturbed husband, whom he believes she loves very much. The mystery that ensnares the characters is something that Philip Marlowe stumbles upon and does not wish to unravel but cannot help doing so.

Marlowe is a man lost in a world he does not understand. He constantly attempts to convince himself that each antagonizing incident is "O.K. with me;" but obviously it is not. As a man who lives by a mythical code of chivalry, nothing is as it seems and nothing is right. Marlowe can ignore the whacked-out girls next door or the rude market clerk; but he cannot ignore what he supposes is a convenient frame-up of his friend and, finally, he cannot be indifferent to his friends exploitation of Marlowe's trust. When Terry Lennox tells him, "But that's you, Marlowe... you'll never learn, you're a born loser," Marlowe righteously kills him because Terry is wrong. Marlowe is not a loser; he is motivated by a code far different from Lennox's manipulations. A code that, for one, doesn't permit women to be beaten—murderously like Sylvia, cruelly like Eileen Wade, or willfully like Augustine's girl friend. The first thing Marlowe notices about Eileen Wade is the bruise she tries to hide with her long blond hair. When Marlowe touches it gently, she politely ignores his concern and he admires her stoicism. Correspondingly, she admires the friendship he has shown Lennox.

Marlowe and Eileen Wade greatly resemble each other, which is a vast departure from Raymond Chandler's novel, wherein Eileen is a *femme fatale* and murderess. In the film she, like Marlowe, tries to hide her alienation. But her method is through a veneer of cheerfulness and beauty. She attempts to hide her bruised face, a symbol of her internal suffering, and her belief that her husband murdered Sylvia Lennox. She knows Roger Wade is capable of extreme violence when drunk, and she wears the mark of it; but she cannot betray him. Conversely, she has been deceived with Marlowe into believing that Lennox is incapable of murder. Ironically, Marlowe and Eileen work at cross purposes to achieve the same goal, neither realizing that the goal is worthless. This is the additional conflict that Altman and Brackett have imposed on Raymond Chandler's popularized detective character and the Los Angeles milieu of his novels.

The Long Goodbye qualifies as a film noir because of the powerlessness, in this instance through ignorance and stubborness, of its independent protagonists Philip Marlowe and Eileen Wade to untangle a moral dilemma in a modern, corrupt world. As a private detective, Marlowe is conventionally expected to understand and discern a solution to this puzzle; but even the police know more than he does.

Unlike the attitudes of the police conveyed in film noir of the 1940s and 1950s, the modern corruption of the police in *The Long Goodbye* is not caused by individual ambition and greed, but by overload. All the police want is their paperwork completed, a murder confessed, and a suicide certified by the proper official. They desire simple solutions regardless of conflicting facts because they lack energy and time. While Chandler's novels use the police as identifiable personalities and antagonists, Altman keeps the police anonymously surly, interchangeable, and unimportant. A policeman's face is never lingered upon in the film without a distracting element occurring simultaneously. When Marlowe is interrogated at the station, he is in the center of the frame while the police circle about him like gnats firing questions; and all the while Marlowe plays with the inky smears left on his fingers by the police's arrest procedure. Later, when he confronts them at the scene of Wade's suicide, Marlowe drunkenly waves a wine glass in their faces while they exhibit little expression.

The use of glass in the film expresses the illusory nature of clarity and appearances over and over again, to reinforce the plot's revelation that Lennox has deceived everyone and that Roger, for all his rowdiness, directs his murderous violence inward. The Wades' beach house is made almost entirely of glass. While Roger and Eileen stand inside and watch Marlowe out on the beach, Roger intimates the detective is an ignorant slob. A few minutes later, Marlowe watches the couple argue fiercely; and his image is placed between the two of them in the window's reflection, indicating that he brought them back together but that he may have to protect each one from the other. But with a quizzical look on his face, Marlowe isn't sure what he wants to do. Later, Marlowe and Eileen argue behind the window while Roger commits suicide, and the plain view of his actions does not increase their ability to help him. Marlowe watches through the window while the gangster Augustine intimidates Eileen; but is unable to make a clear connection between the two until he sees her leave Augustine's building after the money arrives. The undraped picture windows in the gangster's office do not hinder Augustine's attempt to get at the truth through disrobing and would not impair his killing Marlowe, even though, symbolically, the whole city could view the crime. But the city is silent and indifferent. As Augustine's girl friend is taken past screaming and bleeding profusely, the neighboring girls are too self-engrossed to notice the girl's plight. Malibu neighbors crowd around the scene of Roger's suicide with tinkling wine glasses and music they have carried from their parties. In *The Long Goodbye*, Altman adds society's indifference to the long list of alienating elements that comprise film noir.

—E.W.

THE LONG WAIT (1954)

Director: Victor Saville
Producer: Lesser Samuels (Parklane Productions)
Screenplay: Alan Green and Lesser Samuels; from the novel by Mickey Spillane
Director of Photography: Franz Planer
Sound: Joseph Edmondson
Music: Mario Castlenuova-Tedesco
Song: "Once" by Harold Spina and Bob Russell
Conductor: Irving Gertz
Art Director: Boris Leven
Assistant Director: William McGarry
Film Editor: Ronald Sinclair

CAST: Anthony Quinn (Johnny McBride), Charles Coburn (Gardiner), Gene Evans (Servo), Peggie Castle (Venus), Mary Ellen Kay (Wendy), Shawn Smith (Carol), Dolores Donlon (Troy), Barry Kelley (Tucker), James Millican

(Lindsey), Bruno Ve Sota (Packman), Jay Adler (Bell-boy), John Damler (Logan), Frank Marlowe (Pop Henderson.
Filming Completed: November 30, 1953
Released: United Artists, July 2, 1954
Running Time: 94 minutes

Johnny McBride, an amnesia victim who lost his memory in a car accident, is arrested as a murder suspect. He is released after tests on his burnt fingers fail to produce usable fingerprints as evidence for a conviction. He returns to his old hometown in order to clear his name of the presumed murder charges. He literally tears the town apart in his zeal to get to the bottom of a contradictory set of circumstances. Henchmen working for the local mob leader, Servo, try to end McBride's meddling. This results in their death. McBride is double-crossed when he visits a woman named Venus. After a savage beating, he regains consciousness but finds himself tied up and bathed in the glare of a solitary spotlight. Venus crawls to Johnny's side. She pulls a gun and, in the ensuing bloodbath, kills Servo, and frees Johnny McBride. He makes his way to the house of Mr. Gardiner, his ex-employer, who is the financier behind the activities of Servo's mob, including the murder blamed on McBride. Johnny exposes the corrupt set-up and in the process regains his self-respect.

Turning Mickey Spillane's novel into a depressing excursion through small-town corruption, *The Long Wait* displays a cynicism and milieu strongly influenced by the noir films of the late 1940s and early 1950s. The inclusion of amnesia, giving the hero a sense of hopelessness compounded by the frustration of his loss of identity, instills a distinct existential bias into McBride's search. This attitude combines with a pervading sense of corruption and dehumanization to give *The Long Wait* a fatalistic noir ethos. There is a quality of violence and brutality, as exhibited by Johnny McBride and Venus, which lies below the surface of many characters populating the fictional town of Lyncastle. *The Long Wait* presents the most low-key vision of Mickey Spillane's hard-boiled universe without the discipline provided by his detective Mike Hammer. This allows the film to exhibit an *angst* found in very few of Spillane's filmed works.

—C.M.

LOOPHOLE (1954)
[Working Title: OFF THE RECORD]
Director: Harold Schuster
Producer: Lindsley Parsons (Lindsley Parsons Productions)
Associate Producer: Warren Douglas
Screenplay: Warren Douglas; from an unpublished story by George Bricker and Dwight V. Babcock
Director of Photography: William Sickner
Sound: Tomas Lambert

Music: Paul Dunlap
Art Director: David Milton
Set Decoration: Ben Bone
Makeup: Ted Larsen
Production Manager: Rex Bailey
Continuity: Bobbie Sierks
Assistant Director: Joe Wonder
Film Editor: Ace Herman

CAST: Barry Sullivan (Mike Donovan), Charles McGraw (Gus Slavin), Dorothy Malone (Ruthie Donovan), Don Haggerty (Neil Sanford), Mary Beth Hughes (Vera), Don Beddoe (Herman Tate), Dayton Lummis (Mr. Starling), Joanne Jordan (Georgia), John Eldredge (Mr. Temple), Richard Reeves (Pete Mazurki).
Location: Los Angeles, California
Filming Completed: October 28, 1953
Released: Allied Artists, March 12, 1954
Running Time: 79 minutes

Teller Herman Tate enters a Hollywood bank on inspection day and, pretending to be one of a group of examiners, absconds with $50,000 from the drawer of teller Mike Donovan. Donovan is under suspicion, and the fact that he waits until Monday morning to report the loss further implicates him. However, the bank manager, police detective Neil Sanford, and even the F.B.I. are eventually willing to accept Mike's plea of innocence. But Gus Slavin, special investigator for the bonding company that insured the loss, is convinced of Mike's guilt, and hounds him to turn over the money. The bonding company refuses to underwrite Mike, so he must give up his bank position and look for new work. Every time Mike gets another job Gus informs his new employer that Mike is a criminal. One day Mike, now a taxi driver, joins his wife who is depositing money in their meager account and recognizes Tate, who is one of the tellers. Mike forces Tate to take him back to his apartment on the pretense of demanding a share of the loot. Tate hands him part of the money, but they are interrupted by the criminals's girl friend, Vera, who threatens to kill Mike. Before she can shoot however, she and Tate are frightened by Gus, who refuses to believe Mike's claims that he was on the track of the true criminals. Escaping from Gus, Mike follows the criminals to a remote beach house and is unaware that it is a trap. Before entering the house, Mike calls Neil, who dispatches the police. Vera confronts Mike and demands he hand over the money previously given him; she also insists that Tate shoot Mike. When Tate refuses, Vera shoots both men. But Mike is only wounded and subdues Vera until the police arrive.

Loophole is too much of a 1950s film to be more than a marginal film noir, and even its use of Los Angeles exteriors lacks stylization. It is most interesting for its plot and characterization, particularly that of Mike Donovan, who is the familiar vulnerable innocent whose life is all but ruined by a random occurrence. But it is not the workings of a nameless fate that continue to keep Mike from succeeding.

Rather, it is the perverse persecution of a private investigator that is the cause of Mike's continuing deprivation after the initial happenstance. The film's conclusion is extremely ambiguous and indicates that this persecution may continue. The narrator says that Mike is back at his job "and everything is Rosy, or is it?" while Mike looks up from his desk in the bank to see Slavin ominously stationed outside for no logical reason.

—B.P.

M (1951)

Director: Joseph Losey
Producer: Seymour Nebenzal (Superior Films)
Associate Producer: Harold Nebenzal
Screenplay: Norman Reilly Raine and Leo Katcher, with additional dialogue by Waldo Salt; based on the 1931 screenplay by Thea von Harbou, with Paul Falkenberg, Adolf Jansen, and Kark Vash; from an article by Egon Jacobson
Director of Photography: Ernest Laszlo
Sound: Leon Becker
Music Score: Michel Michelet
Conductor: Bert Shefter
Art Director: Martin Obzina
Set Decoration: Ray Robinson
Makeup: Ted Larsen
Production Supervisor: Ben Hersh
Production Layout: John Hubley
Assistant Director: Robert Aldrich
Film Editor: Edward Mann

CAST: David Wayne (M), Howard da Silva (Carney), Martin Gabel (Marshall), Luther Adler (Langley), Steve Brodie (Lt. Becker), Glenn Anders (Riggert), Norman Lloyd (Sutro), Walter Burke (McMahan), Raymond Burr (Pottsy).
Location: Los Angeles, California
Released: Columbia, June 10, 1951
Running Time: 87 minutes

A child murderer is terrorizing Los Angeles. He has killed four children and the police have only the clue that he always takes the shoes of his victims. The killer claims his fifth victim, Elsie Coster, after entertaining her by playing his tin flute and buying her a balloon from a blind vendor. The head of the investigation, Inspector Carney, gives a list of newly released mental asylum inmates to his assistant, Lt. Becker, to check out. On the list is Martin Harrow. In the solitude of his urban apartment, Martin plays his flute, fondles the shoelaces from his victims' shoes, and molds a clay figure of a child, only to crush it into a lumpen mass when he is finished. The operations of the Los Angeles underworld have been disturbed by the police search for the killer. The local syndicate chieftain, Charles Marshall, plans that the underworld will capture the killer themselves and "take the heat off." Eventually Harrow is drawn toward a sixth victim. He buys her a balloon from the same blind vendor, who recognizes the tune Harrow is playing on the flute and informs a pool hustler who plants the chalk letter "M" as an identification mark on the killer's back. Later, the little girl points out the letter, and Harrow, frightened, runs away. Marshall's men converge and pursue him to the Bradbury building; there they capture Harrow and take him to Marshall's cab company garage. A kangaroo court is convened, and Marshall appoints Langley, a drunken ex-lawyer, as Harrow's defense. Harrow pleads his own case and begs to be punished. Langley tells the crowd to take him, but the enraged Marshall shoots Langley, as the mob starts madly for the killer. The vigilantes are stopped by the arrival of the police.

Losey's *M* is almost an exact remake of the Fritz Lang film, but by placing it in an American setting and by a skillful manipulation of the location shots, the film takes on the atmosphere of an American film noir. Although more problematic than Lang's film, because the type of underworld camaraderie conventionally acceptable in Germany did not translate convincingly, Losey's film can stand on its own. It is particularly notable for the scenes when David Wayne, as the killer, is alone in his apartment. His illness and perversion are disturbingly explicit in this version, as it seems apparent that he gets a sexual thrill from the manipulation of the children's shoelaces and the clay doll.

—B.P.

The psychopath (David Wayne)
in M.

MACAO (1952)

Director: Josef von Sternberg [Uncredited: Nicholas Ray]
Executive Producer: Samuel Bischoff (RKO)
Producer: Alex Gottlieb
Screenplay: Bernard C. Schoenfeld and Stanley Rubin; from an unpublished story by Bob Williams
Director of Photography: Harry J. Wild
Sound: Earl Wolcott, Clem Portman
Music: Anthony Collins
Music Director: Constantin Bakaleinikoff
Songs: "One For My Baby" by Johnny Mercer and Harold Arlen; "You Kill Me" by Jule Styne and Leo Robin; "Ocean Breeze" by Lerios-Jenkins. Sung by Jane Russell
Art Directors: Albert S. D'Agostino, Ralph Berger
Assistant Director: Lowell Farrell
Film Editors: Samuel E. Beetley, Robert Golden

CAST: Robert Mitchum (Nick Cochran), Jane Russell (Julie Benson), William Bendix (Lawrence Trumble), Thomas Gomez (Lt. Sebastian), Gloria Grahame (Margie), Brad Dexter (Halloran), Edward Ashley (Martin Stewart), Philip Ahn (Itzumi), Vladimir Sokoloff (Kwan Sum Tang), Don Zelaya (Gimpy). **BITS:** Emory Parnell (Ship Captain), Nacho Galindo (Bus Driver), Philip Van Zandt (Custom Official), George Chan (Chinese Photographer), Sheldon Jett (Dutch Tourist), Genevieve Bell (Woman Passenger), Tommy Lee (Chinese knifed in Water), Alex Montoya, Manuel Paris (Bartenders), Spencer Chan, James B. Leong, Alfredo Santos (Hoodlums), Marc Krah (Desk Clerk), May Taksugi (Barber), Lee Tung Foo (Merchant), Maria Sen Young, Iris Wong

(Croupiers), Abdullah Abbas (Arabian), Everett Glass (Garcia), Walter Ng (Fisherman), Rico Alaniz (Bus Driver), Trevor Bardette (Alvaris), Weaver Levy (Chang), W.T. Chang (Old Fisherman), Michael Visaroff (Russian Doorman), Phil Harron (Sikh), William Yip (Rickshaw Driver), Art Dupuis (Portuguese Pilot).
Location: Stock footage of Macao exteriors
Filming Completed: October 19, 1950
Released: RKO, April 30, 1952
Running Time: 81 minutes

Three Americans enter Macao, the Portuguese colony south of Hong Kong. They are Nick Cochran, an ex-G.I. escaping from a minor criminal charge in the United States, chanteuse Julie Benson, and a detective posing as a salesman named Lawrence Trumble. Trumble intends to capture Vincent Halloran, Macao's leading gambling club owner, because he is wanted for committing murder in New York. Cochran's and Trumble's identities are switched when Julie lifts Cochran's wallet while kissing him. The local policeman, Lt. Sebastian, reports to Halloran—who has killed three previous detectives sent from the United States on similar missions —that the ex-G.I. represents the latest attempt by U.S. law enforcement to capture the gambler. Meanwhile, Julie is hired to sing in Halloran's club and causes his girl friend, Margie, to be jealous. Trumble exploits Cochran's mistaken identity by offering him a chance to dispose of a large diamond, which is bait to lure Halloran beyond Macao's borders. When Halloran recognizes the gem as one of his own from a bungled smuggling scheme, he plans to murder the ex-G.I.; but the assassin mistakes the authentic Trumble for Cochran, thereby mortally wounding the true detective. Before dying, Trumble promises that Cochran's criminal offense will be forgotten in the United States if he can deliver Halloran to the waiting authorities outside Macao's three-mile limit. After a vicious battle, Cochran succeeds in subduing Halloran and leaves for the United States with Julie.

Initially planned as a project to be directed by Josef von Sternberg at RKO, *Macao*, was almost totally reshot after its completion by director Nicholas Ray. Von Sternberg managed to instill his own brand of exotic, sometimes vulgar pictorialism into *Macao* even though very few of his sequences remain intact in the film. Neither Ray nor von Sternberg professed much interest in the making of this film, considering it just another assignment for Howard Hughes at RKO. What *is* interesting about *Macao* is the way in which Robert Mitchum and William Bendix, two of the noir films' most hulking icons, are set against one another. Bendix, who portrayed typical heavy roles in earlier noir films like *The Glass Key, Dark Corner,* and *Gambling House,* is slightly mellower in the role of Trumble in *Macao*. As Cochran, Mitchum maintains a persona that rejects the typical trenchcoated, tough-guy sentimentality, replacing it with a sleepy ambivalence that seems to blend with the dreamlike imagery created by von Sternberg and maintained by Nicholas Ray. Furthermore, the noir dilemma of mistaken identity and shifting allegiances is enhanced by Cochran's ignorance. Mistaken for Trumble, Cochran does not bother to protest the indignities irrationally visited upon his head; the world is irrational, so he just puts up his fists and slugs his way out.

Macao's female characters, Julie and Margie, are each typical noir examples of the good-bad girl. But von Sternberg deifies these two women as he had Marlene Dietrich. Encasing Jane Russell and Gloria Grahame in metallic gowns, von Sternberg thematically contrasts the women who are kept separated by beaded curtains and surrounded by much of the same exotic paraphernalia that von Sternberg used earlier in *The Shanghai Gesture*.

Considering the problems of completing a film directed separately by two different artists, *Macao* may not reflect the full potential of its contributors; but it nevertheless functions as a brutal and competent noir thriller.

—M.B. & C.M.

MADIGAN (1968)

Director: Don Siegel
Producer: Frank P. Rosenberg (Universal)
Screenplay: Henri Simoun and Abraham Polonsky; from the novel *The Commissioner* by Richard Dougherty
Director of Photography: Russell Metty [Technicolor; Techniscope]
Title Backgrounds: Graeme Ferguson
Matte Supervisor: Albert Whitlock

Sound: Waldon O. Watson, Lyle Cain, Ronald Pierce
Music: Don Costa
Music Supervisor: Joseph Gershenson
Art Directors: Alexander Golitzen, George C. Webb
Set Decoration: John McCarthy, John Austin
Makeup: Bud Westmore
Hairstyles: Larry Germain
Dialogue Coach: Scott Hale
Second Unit Production Manager: Wes Thompson
Assistant Director: Joe Cavalier
Film Editor: Milton Shifman

CAST: Richard Widmark (Daniel Madigan), Henry Fonda (Commissioner Russell), Inger Stevens (Julia Madigan), Harry Guardino (Rocco Bonaro), James Whitmore (Chief Inspector Charles Kane), Susan Clark (Tricia), Michael Dunn (Castiglioni), Steve Ihnat (Barney Benesch), Sheree North (Jonesy), Don Stroud (Hughie), Warren Stevens (Capt. Ben Williams), Raymond St. Jacques (Dr. Johnston), Bert Freed (Chief-of-Detectives Lynch), Harry Bellaver (Mickey Dunn), Frank Marth (Lt. James Price), Woodrow Parfrey (Marvin), Dallas Mitchell (Tom Gavin), Richard O'Brien (Detective O'Brien), Lloyd Gough (Earl Griffin), Robert Granere (Buster), Rita Lynn (Rita Bonaro), Gloria Calomee (Policewoman Doris Hawkins), Ray Montgomery (Detective O'Mara), Albert Henderson (Lt. Strong). **BITS:** Henry Beckman (Philip Downes), Toian Matchinga (Rosita), Abel Fernandez (Detective Rodriguez), Robert Ball (Prisoner), Virginia Gregg (Esther Newman), Lloyd Haines (Sam Woodley), Paul Sorensen, Bob Biheller, Ollie O'Toole, Al Dunlap, Pepe Hern, Scott Hale, Sean Kennedy, Bob O'Connell, Conrad Bain, Ed Crowley, Tom Rosqui (Men), Diane Sayer, Mina Martinez, Kay Turner, Kathleen O'Malley, Elizabeth Fleming, Madeline Clive, Phillippa Bevans, Nina Varela, Kate Harrington (Women), Al Ruban (Kowalski), Lincoln Kilpatrick (Patrolman Grimes), Seth Allen (Nick), Ralph Smiley (Captain).
Location: New York, New York
Filming Completed: June 23, 1967
Released: Universal, March 29, 1968
Running Time: 101 minutes

New York detectives Dan Madigan and Rocco Bonaro break into a tenement room to bring in a small-time hood, Barney Benesch, for questioning. Distracted by the naked woman whom Benesch pushes out of his bed, the policemen find themselves suddenly under Benesch's gun, in which position they must surrender their own weapons and permit Benesch to escape. Only later do they learn that Benesch is wanted for a recent murder. The police commissioner, already plagued by charges of racist brutality during a recent arrest and by evidence that his chief inspector has been the victim of syndicate extortion, threatens Madigan and Bonaro with suspension unless the suspect is captured within 72 hours. Madigan and Bonaro begin an intense on- and off-duty search for information. They terrorize a woman to find out the whereabouts of a dwarf bookie with a grudge against Benesch, deal with him for the name of a man who provides Benesch with women, and through this man set a trap. It fails; but Benesch is pursued through Spanish Harlem and cornered in an apartment house. As the police surround the building, Madigan and Bonaro impatiently charge in. Benesch is killed; but Madigan is mortally wounded and dies in a nearby hospital.

From its opening shots of the deserted New York City streets at daybreak, *Madigan* evokes the ambience of a decade earlier. Siegel's narrative is a complicated one, intercutting freely between the politically significant efforts of Commissioner Russell to maintain departmental integrity and the personally significant efforts of Madigan and Bonaro to correct their blunder. These frequent cutaways could be interpreted as gratuitous moralizing and filler for the time gaps in the two detectives' search; but, while the conflicts that Siegel defines may be simplistic, they are not isolated or unrevealing. If Russell regards Madigan as a poor example of a policeman, the commissioner's sexual estrangement, like that of Madigan's wife, betrays an unrealistic view of human nature by which Madigan is not troubled. Madigan's own alienation is, in the noir tradition, more narrowly focused and more purely existential. Although he is not a rogue cop nor an embezzler as in Siegel's *Private Hell #36*, Madigan does accept the meager privileges of his job. Being stripped of his gun by a felon should not be read in Freudian terms as a castration but in noir films as a threat to his life style and, by extension, his being. In this context, the casualness of Madigan's violence—overturning the secretary's desk; meancing the dwarf on the beach— or the unscrupulous blackmail of Benesch's parttime pimp become the only possible responses to an oppressive quirk of fate. Madigan perishes then not in expiation for corruption (if anything the scenes with Russell establish, relatively, Madigan's honesty) or immorality (he is too tired to indulge in the sexual transgressions that plague Russell and tempt Madigan's wife) but in a final assertion of identity as fleeting and explosive as the bursts from his gun.

—A.S.

THE MALTESE FALCON (1941)
[Working Title: THE GENT FROM FRISCO]

Director: John Huston
Producer: Hal B. Wallis (Warner Brothers)
Associate Producer: Henry Blanke
Screenplay: John Huston; from the novel by Dashiell Hammett
Director of Photography: Arthur Edeson
Sound: Oliver S. Garretson
Music: Adolph Deutsch
Music Director: Leo F. Frobstein
Orchestration: Arthur Lange

Art Director: Robert Haas
Costumes: Orry-Kelly
Makeup: Perc Westmore
Dialogue Director: Robert Foulk
Assistant Directors: Jack Sullivan, Claude Archer
Film Editor: Thomas Richards

CAST: Humphrey Bogart (Samuel Spade), Mary Astor (Brigid O'Shaughnessy), Gladys George (Iva Archer), Peter Lorre (Joel Cairo), Barton MacLane (Lt. Detective Dundy), Sydney Greenstreet (Kasper Gutman), Ward Bond (Detective Tom Polhaus), Jerome Cowan (Miles Archer), Elisha Cook, Jr. (Wilmer Cook), James Burke (Luke), Murray Alper(Frank Richman), John Hamilton (Bryan), Emory Parnell (Mate of *La Paloma*). **BITS:** Robert Homas (Policeman), Creighton Hale (Stenographer), Charles Drake, Bill Hopper, Hank Mann (Reporters), Jack Mower (Announcer), Walter Huston (Man Delivering the Falcon).
Filming Completed: July 22, 1941
Released: Warner Brothers, October 3, 1941
Running Time: 100 minutes
[NOTE: The title, *The Maltese Falcon*, was changed to *The Gent From Frisco* on September 5, 1941. The original title was restored five days later.]

After his partner, Miles Archer, is killed while shadowing a man named Thursby for a mysterious Miss Wonderly, detective Sam Spade is determined to find Miles's killer. He first confronts Miss Wonderly, who confesses that her real name is Brigid O'Shaughnessy and that the same person who killed Miles—and, it turns out, Thursby—is also threatening her. Attracted to her, Spade agrees to help her. His investigation leads him to the strange trio of the foppish Joel Cairo, Kasper "Fat Man" Gutman, and Wilmer, Gutman's inept gunsel. All are on the trail of the Maltese Falcon, a bird figurine whose encrustation of priceless gems has been coated with black enamel. Eventually, Spade discovers that Brigid, a psychopathic liar, is as deeply involved in pursuit of the falcon as the others; and, when the bird falls into his hands via a murdered ship's captain, Spade cleverly draws the cutthroat group together to find out the true story. Learning that Wilmer, working for Gutman, was responsible for the deaths of Thursby and the captain, Spade produces the bird, which turns out to be a fake. The bitterly disappointed Gutman, Wilmer, and Cairo flee. Spade sends the cops after them, and then forces a confession out of Brigid. She killed Miles, hoping to rid herself of her partner, Thursby, by pinning the murder on him. Although she pleads with Spade, wildly professing her love, he turns her over to the police.

As an artifact of popular culture, *The Maltese Falcon* seems peculiarly invulnerable to criticism. It is amusing to watch and tends to make one forget that it is as much a caricature than a motion picture, because its characters are so one-dimensional that they are scarcely characters at all. Bogart is the tough guy with the soft heart; Mary Astor, the lying

Brigid O'Shaughnessy (Mary Astor), Sam Spade (Humphrey Bogart) and Joel Cairo (Peter Lorre) in The Maltese Falcon.

bitch of innocent demeanor; Sidney Greenstreet the threatening, chortling Fat Man, Peter Lorre, the mincing menace; Elisha Cook, Jr., the twitchy, stupid little punk. It is difficult to summon up more than such brief phrases to describe the shadowy, undeveloped figures that populate *The Maltese Falcon*.

The film's chief assets are its crisp dialogue and the bravura performances of the principals. That these performances are overloaded with mannerisms is inconsequential in a film that depends on emphasis of the superficial for its effect. More distressing here is the textbook camerawork (e.g., shooting Greenstreet from low angles to emphasize his bulk) and the general attitude of contemptuous misanthropy, which is common to most of director John Huston's films.

While it is certainly true that most films in the noir genre are despairing in nature, the best are realized in such a way that even the most neurotic characters are endowed with a human dimension and allowed a fascinating ambiguity. But there are no shades of gray in Huston's *The Maltese Falcon*. Sam Spade himself, while spouting the obligatory "When your partner gets killed, you gotta do something about it" speech, is brushing off that same partner's frantic wife, with whom he has been conducting a casual affair. Only lip service is given here to the private codes of honor that motivate other noir characters.

In the end *The Maltese Falcon* itself suffers from its own contempt. As Spade deliberately lays out the pros and cons

of letting Brigid "take the fall," he balances her murderous, lying nature against the notion that "Maybe you love me and maybe I love you." Ostensibly, we should feel sympathy for Spade at such a crossroads, forced to make a painful decision between justice and love. But it all rings false as there have been no intimations of anything like love between Spade and Brigid, who are two manipulators par excellence. The thrill felt at the end of *The Maltese Falcon* is not a poignant one; it is something a little uglier. With Huston's Spade, the viewer is getting a thrill out of sending Brigid over.

—J.K.

THE MAN WHO CHEATED HIMSELF (1951)
[Working Title: THE GUN]

Director: Felix E. Feist
Producer: Jack M. Warner (Jack M. Warner Productions)
Screenplay: Seton I. Miller and Phillip MacDonald; from an unpublished story by Seton I. Miller
Director of Photography: Russell Harlan
Special Effects: Rex Wimpy
Sound: William Lynch
Music: Louis Forbes
Production Design: Van Nest Polglase

Costumes: Elois Janssen
Makeup: Abe Haberman
Production Manager: Herman Webber
Assistant Directors: Joe Depew, Marty Moss
Film Editor: David Weisbart

CAST: Lee J. Cobb (Ed Cullen), John Dall (Andy Cullen), Jane Wyatt(Lois), Lisa Howard (Janet), Alan Wells (Nito Capa), Harlan Warde (Howard Frazer), Tito Vuolo (Pietro Capa), Mimi Aguglia (Mrs. Capa), Charles Arnt (Mr. Quimby), Marjorie Bennett (Mrs. Quimby), Bud Wolfe (Blair), Morgan Farley (Rushton), Howard Negley (Olson). **BITS:** William Gould (Medical Examiner), Art Milan (Airport Clerk), Gordon Richards(Butler), Terry Frost (Detective), Mario Siletti (Machetti), Charles Victor (Attorney).
Location: San Francisco, California
Filming Completed: July 25, 1950
Released: 20th Century-Fox, February 8, 1951
Running Time: 81 minutes

The Cullen brothers work together as policemen. Lt. Ed Cullen, a tough old pro, is a bachelor and something of a playboy. His younger brother Andy is happily married to a pretty young wife. Ed is having an affair with Lois Frazer, a wealthy socialite who is divorcing her husband, Howard. Howard fakes leaving his home for good. Instead of flying out of town, he returns home to rob the house, having set up an alibi of being at the airport during the time of the robbery. But Lois shoots him with his own gun. She then calls Ed,who comes over immediately and helps her cover up the killing. Ed puts the body in his car and drives back to the airport, so that it will look as if Howard was killed there. Unfortunately Ed leaves clues: the toll bridge officer recognizes him, and two airport witnesses can identify the car he was driving. Ironically, Ed leads the murder investigation and is assisted by Andy, who eventually suspects his brother. After confronting Ed with the evidence, Andy is knocked unconscious. Ed and Lois hide in an abandoned building near the base of the Golden Gate Bridge where Ed and Andy played as children. Andy goes there, not realizing that he is followed by other police who arrest Ed and Lois. Waiting outside the courtroom for the trial to begin, Ed notices that a successful lawyer has replaced him in Lois's affections.

The Man Who Cheated Himself adeptly interweaves two familiar noir elements, a bad cop, and a double-crossing wife, to maintain interest and suspense. The film is enhanced by Russell Harlan's skillful use of San Francisco locales and credible performances. In a unique bit of reverse casting, John Dall plays a "normal" nice guy while Jane Wyatt, usually the typical American housewife,plays a convincing *femme fatale*. The film's message, that a staid married life is better than a fast single one, is appropriate for an American about to embark on a steady diet of Eisenhower and a baby boom. The central irony—like that of *The Scandal Sheet*—in which a man is compelled to investigate a

crime that he committed, reinforces the social judgment against bachelorhood since the root causes of Ed Cullen's predicament are his lack of permanent sexual ties and Lois's offhanded dissolution of her marriage.

—B.P. & A.S.

THE MANCHURIAN CANDIDATE (1962)

Director: John Frankenheimer
Executive Producer: Howard W. Koch (M.C. Productions/Essex Productions)
Producers: George Axelrod and John Frankenheimer
Screenplay: George Axelrod and John Frankenheimer; from the novel by Richard Condon
Director of Photography: Lionel Lindon
Special Effects: Paul Pollard
Photographic Effects: Howard Anderson Company
Camera Operator: John Mehl
Sound: Joe Edmondson, Buddy Myers
Sound Effects Editor: Del Harris
Music: David Amram
Music Editor: Richard Carruth
Music Recording: Vinton Vernon
Production Designer: Richard Sylbert
Assistant Art Director: Philip M. Jefferies
Set Decoration: George R. Nelson
Costumes: Moss Mabry
Wardrobe: Wesley V. Jefferies
Hairstyles: Gene Shacove for Janet Leigh: Mary Westmoreland
Makeup: Bernard Ponedel, Jack Freeman, Ron Berkeley
Dialogue Coach: Thom Conroy
Script Supervisor: Amelia Wade
Assistant Director: Joseph Behm
Film Editor: Ferris Webster

CAST: Frank Sinatra (Bennett Marco), Laurence Harvey (Raymond Shaw), Janet Leigh (Rosie), Angela Lansbury (Raymond's Mother), Henry Silva (Chunjin), James Gregory (Senator John Iselin), Leslie Parrish (Jocie), John McGiver (Senator Thomas Jordan), Khigh Dhiegh (Yen Lo), James Edwards (Cpl. Melvin), Douglas Henderson (Colonel), Albert Paulsen (Zilkov), Madame Spivy (Berezovo), Barry Kelly (Secretary of Defense), Joe Adams (Psychiatrist), Lloyd Corrigan (Mr. Gaines), Whit Bissell (Medical Officer), Mimi Dillard (Melvin's Wife), Anton van Stralen (Officer), John Laurence (Gossfeld), Tom Lowell (Lembeck), Richard LaPore (Mavole), Nick Bolin (Berezovo), NickyBlair (Silvers), William Thourlby (Little), Irving Steinberg (Freeman), John Francis (Haiken), Robert Riordan (Nominee), Reggie Nalder (Gomel), Miyoshi Jingu (Miss Gertrude), Anna Shin (Korean Girl), Helen Kleeb, Maye Henderson (Chairladies), Mickey Finn, Richard Norris, Johnny Indrisano

MANHANDLED

(Reporters), Lou Krugg (Manager), Mike Masters, Tom Harris (F.B.I. Men), Mariquita Moll (Soprano), Robert Burton (Convention Chairman), Karen Norris (Secretary), Bess Flowers (Gomel), Jean Vaughn (Nurse), Ray Spiker (Policeman), Merritt Bohn (Jilly), Frank Basso (Photographer), Harry Holcomb (General), Julie Payne, Lana Crawford, Evelyn Byrd (Guests at Party), Ray Dailey (Page Boy), Estelle Etterre, Mary Benoit, Rita Kenaston, Maggie Hathaway, Joan Douglas, Frances Nealy, Evelyn Byrd, Ralph Gambina, Sam "Kid" Hogan (People in Hotel Lobby), James Yagi, Lee Tung Foo, Raynum Tsukamoto (Chinese Men in Hotel Lobby).
Location: Santa Monica, California; New York, New York
Released: United Artists, October 24, 1962
Running Time: 126 minutes

Bennett Marco, a major in Army Intelligence, is troubled by recurring nightmares of the Korean War in which he sees Raymond Shaw, a former comrade, murder two other soldiers. Marco mentions his worries to supervisors, who conclude that he is exhausted and give him sick leave. He suffers an anxiety attack on the New York-bound train and is comforted by a young woman named Rosie. She helps him again after he visits Shaw's apartment and is attacked by Chunjin, Shaw's servant, who was formerly the patrol's Korean guide. Marco meets Shaw and learns of Shaw's hatred for his mother and Red-baiting stepfather, Senator John Iselin, and that another member of their patrol has written to Shaw complaining of nightmares similar to Marco's. Military superiors are dubious about the origin of these dreams, since Shaw holds the Congressional Medal of Honor at Marco's recommendation; but they authorize Marco to investigate. He discovers that the entire patrol was brainwashed in Korea. Shaw is a living time bomb and is a programmed murderer. He is under the supervision of Communist agent Zilkov who uses playing cards, specifically the queen of diamonds, to trigger Shaw's hypnotic obedience. The hypnotic bond is tested when Shaw murders his employer, his new wife, and his father-in-law. Shaw's American contact is his own mother, who intends to profit by her son's condition and make her reactionary husband President of the United States. Shaw becomes suspicious of himself and tries to fight hypnosis when he is instructed to assassinate the presidential nominee of Iselin's party. Marco attempts to stop him; but Shaw turns the gun on Senator Iselin, his mother, and finally on himself.

A cold war thriller that typifies the updating and transformation of film noir, *The Manchurian Candidate* is a contemporary nightmare perpetrated by extreme political thinking. The film uses a great many noir conventions. The photography by Lionel Lindon is heavily influenced by its many noir predecessors. The atmosphere is corrupt and oppressive, and many of the characters in the film function as grotesques. The most notable among these correlatives of evil are Henry Silva as the predatory Chunjin and Angela Lansbury as the aging, ambitious mother. John Franken-

heimer directed the film with an interest in maintaining an intellectual as well as physical suspense. The major difference that occurs between the noir thriller of the late 1940s and *The Manchurian Candidate* is in the sophistication of the film makers who realize that they are working in a tradition while avoiding convention. Eliptical direction and an undercurrent of violence is compounded by the characters' overwhelming confusion. This attempt to move toward the brink of sanity and stretch the suspension of disbelief gives *The Manchurian Candidate* an interesting noir ambience. However, the universe of the tough guy, a world populated by losers and con men is replaced by the slick and pretentious world of politics. The same types of grim and hopeless characters exploit this upper-crust world, only this time the rats wear tuxedos. Frankenheimer returned to this world that verges on noir sensibilities several times during the early 1960s in films like *Seconds* and *Seven Days In May*. After a hiatus of several years, Frankenheimer's *99 and 44/100% Dead* became a parody of the type of film he created in his earlier thrillers.

—C.M. & E.M.

MANHANDLED (1949)
[Working Titles: BETRAYAL; A MAN WHO STOLE A DREAM]

Director: Lewis R. Foster
Producers: William H. Pine, William C. Thomas (Pine-Thomas)
Screenplay: Lewis R. Foster and Whitman Chambers; from the short story "The Man Who Stole A Dream" by L.S. Goldsmith
Director of Photography: Ernest Laszlo
Sound: William Fox
Music Score: Darryl Calker
Music Director: David Chudnow
Art Director: Lewis H. Creber
Set Decoration: Alfred Keggeris
Costumes: Edith Head, Odette Myrtil
Makeup: Paul Stanhope, Emil Lavigne
Hairstyles: Doris Harris
Production Manager: Doc Merman
Assistant Director: Howard Pine
Script Supervisor: Sam Freedle
Film Editor: Howard Smith

CAST: Dorothy Lamour (Merl Kramer), Dan Duryea (Karl Benson), Sterling Hayden (Joe Cooper), Irene Hervey (Ruth Bennett), Philip Reed (Guy Bayard), Harold Vermilyea (Dr. Redman), Alan Napier (Alton Bennett), Art Smith (Lt. Dawson), Irving Bacon (Sgt. Fayle).
Filming Completed: December 1948
Released: Paramount, May 25, 1949
Running Time: 97 minutes

Alton Bennett recounts to psychiatrist Dr. Redman a dream

he had in which he kills his wife Ruth on learning she has been seeing another man. When Mrs. Bennett is found dead with some of her jewels missing, Bennett is suspected by police Lt. Dawson and insurance investigator Joe Cooper. Actually, Dr. Redman's innocent secretary, Merl Kramer, was duped by her boyfriend, Karl Benson, an unscrupulous private detective. Benson learned about the Bennett dream and jewelry from Merl, had a duplicate key made to the Bennett apartment, and was following Mrs. Bennett the night of the murder. The real killer, however, is Dr. Redman, who also wanted the jewels and killed Mrs. Bennett for them. However, he was in turn robbed by Benson who ended up with the jewelry. Redman knows that it was Karl who subdued him, so Karl attempts to persuade him to help frame Merl for the murder because the jewels are too hot to fence. Dr. Redman disagrees and, locking Karl in a closet, escapes with the jewels. Karl breaks out quickly and traps Redman in a blind alley where he runs over the doctor with his car. Returning to Merl's apartment to proceed with his plans, Karl learns that she will implicate him. He attempts to throw Merl off the building's roof; but is stopped in time by the police.

With Dan Duryea in the main role of Karl Benson, a crooked private eye, *Manhandled* might have been a classic in that series of thrillers dealing with the degraded cop or investigator. As it is, due to the extremely convoluted plot and slack direction, the film lacks suspense and it never develops the potential of its characters and locales. However, the opening dream sequence and the scene in which Benson crushes Redman with his car are quite evocative of the noir style.

—B.P.

MARLOWE (1969)
[Working Title: THE LITTLE SISTER]

Director: Paul Bogart
Producers: Gabriel Katzka, Sidney Beckerman (Katzka-Berne Productions—Cherokee-Beckerman Productions)
Screenplay: Stirling Silliphant; from the novel *The Little Sister* by Raymond Chandler
Director of Photography: William H. Daniels [Metrocolor]
Camera Operator: Bill Johnson
Special Effects: Virgil Beck
Sound: Franklin Milton
Music: Peter Matz
Art Directors: George W. Davis, Addison Hehr
Set Decoration: Henry Grace, Hugh Hunt
Costumes: Jimmy Taylor, Florence Hackett
Makeup: Phil Rhodes
Hairstyles: Sherry Wilson, Charles James
Unit Manager: Sergei Petschnikoff
Script Supervisor: Jeanne Lippman

Assistant Director: Bud Grace
Film Editor: Gene Ruggiero

CAST: James Garner (Philip Marlowe), Gayle Hunnicutt (Mavis Wald), Carroll O'Connor (Lt. Christy French), Rita Moreno (Dolores Gonzales), Sharon Farrell (Orfamay Quest), William Daniels (Mr. Crowell), Sonny Steelgrave (H.M. Wynant), Jackie Coogan (Grant W. Hicks), Kenneth Tobey (Sgt. Fred Beifus), Nate Esformes (Paleface), Bruce Lee (Winslow Wong), Christopher Cary (Chuck), George Tyne (Oliver Hady), Corinne Comacho (Julie), Paul Stevens (Dr. Vincent Lagardie), Roger Newman (Orrin Quest), Read Morgan (Gumpshaw). **BITS:** Warren Finnerty (Manager), Bartlett Robinson (Munsey), Ted Derby (Tiger Man), Carolan Daniels, Marlain Kallevig (Women), Chet Stratton (Harold Munsey), Hoke Howell (Intern), Mark Allen (Attendant), Jason Wingreen (Clerk), Ann Carroll (Mona), Emil Alegata (Waiter), Isabel Colley (Receptionist), Bert L. Bantle, Tony Conkle (Pilots), Dee Carroll (Nurse), Jack English (Director), Lou Whitehill (Assistant Director), Mary Wilcox (YWCA Clerk), Tom Monroe (Policeman), Nicole Jaffe (Lilly), Camille Grant (Belly Dancer), Fay Wilkie (Psychologist), Buddy Garion (Maitre D'), Paul Micale (Waiter), Angus Duncan (TV Actor).
Location: Largo Club, Mt. Wilson, Bradbury Building, Hotel Alvarado, Los Angeles, California
Filming Completed: February 1969
Released: MGM, October 22, 1969
Running Time: 95 minutes
MPPA Rating: M

Philip Marlowe is hired by Orfamay Quest to find her missing brother Orrin and traces him to a hippie hotel entitled the Infinite Pad, run by Dr. Lagardie. Told by Grant W. Hicks that Orrin has checked out, Marlowe eventually finds Orrin with an ice pick embedded in his torso, a trademark of gangster H.M. Wynant. Marlowe suspects that the entire affair is connected with a plot to blackmail Mavis Wald, a prominent television actress involved with Wynant, and is hired by her publicity agency to protect her. Marlowe is threatened and intimidated by the police and particularly by Wynant's henchman, Winslow Wong, a karate expert. When Mavis hysterically claims she killed Wynant, Marlowe arranges the evidence to appear as though the gangster committed suicide. Although he does not fool police Lt. Christy French, no arrests are made. The following morning, Mavis and Orfamay confront Marlowe and explain that Orfamay and Orrin were blackmailing Mavis about Wynant. Orrin refused to share the loot with Orfamay and disappeared. Meanwhile, Mavis admitted to murdering Wynant as she wrongly believed Orfamay to be the killer. While the two sisters battle viciously, Marlowe leaves his office. Later, he accuses Wynant's previous lover, a stripper named Dolores Gonzales, of jealously murdering the gangster. But before Marlowe can tell the police,

THE MASK OF DIMITRIOS

Dolores is killed by her ex-husband Lagardie, who then kills himself.

The modern *Marlowe* loses much of the existential bias so aptly characterized by the hard-boiled detective of the 1940s. James Garner, as Marlowe, is an anachronism unable to adapt his knightly considerations to a world jaded beyond his capacity to affect it. The chaos inherent in the postwar years of the 1940s is somewhat approximated by the Vietnam *angst*. But no matter how strained these associations become, *Marlowe* cannot evoke the aura of a society filled with hidden corruptions and decadent grotesques. These particular elements are presented as a normal part of the environment, and therefore no longer hold the apprehension found in the noir films of the 1940s.

—C.M.

THE MASK OF DIMITRIOS (1944)

Director: Jean Negulesco
Producer: Henry Blanke (Warner Brothers)
Screenplay: Frank Gruber; from the novel *A Coffin For Dimitrios* by Eric Ambler
Director of Photography: Arthur Edeson
Sound: Oliver S. Garretson
Music: Adolph Deutsch
Music Director: Leo F. Forbstein
Orchestral Arrangements: Jerome Morross
Art Director: Ted Smith
Set Decoration: Walter Tilford
Makeup: Perc Westmore
Technical Adviser: Michael D. Kadri
Dialogue Director: Herschel Daugherty
Unit Manager: Lou Baum
Assistant Directors: Jack Sullivan, Don Page
Film Editor: Frederick Richards

CAST: Sydney Greenstreet (Mr. Peters), Zachary Scott (Dimitrios), Faye Emerson (Irana Preveza), Peter Lorre (Cornelius Latimer Leyden), George Tobias (Fedor Muishkin), Victor Francen (Wladislaw Grodek), Steve Geray (Bulic), Florence Bates (Madame Chavez), Eduardo Ciannelli (Marukakis), Kurt Katch (Col. Haki), Marjorie Hoshelle (Anna Bulic), Georges Metaxa (Hans Werner), John Abbott (Mr. Pappas), Monte Blue (Dhris Abdul), David Hoffman (Konrad). **BITS:** Philip Rock, Rita Holland, Rola Stewart (People on Beach), Georges Ranavent (Fisherman), Peter Helmers (Reporter), Lal Chand Mehra, Jules Molnar, Walter Palm (Servants), Pedro Regas (Morgue Attendant), Nino Pipitone (Hotel Clerk), Eddie Hyans, Antonio Filauri, Alfred Paix, Saul Gorss (Men), Frank Lackteen (Soldier), Nick Thompson (Porter), Hella Crossley (Hostess), Carmen D'Antonio (Nightclub Dancer), Fred Essler (Bostoff), John Bleifer (Coach Driver), Alvert Van Antwerp (Landlord), Edgar Licho (Cafe Proprietor), Michael Visaroff, Louis Mercier (Policemen), Felix Basch (Vaxoff), Leonid Snegoff (Stambulisky), Gregory Golubeff (Doorkeeper), Carl Neubert (Secretary), Lotte Palfi (Receptionist), John Mylong (Druhar), May Landa (Flower Girl), Alphonse Martell (Croupier), Ray de Ravenne (Taxi Driver), Marek Windheim (Hotel Clerk), Charles Andre (Conductor).
Filming Completed: January 27, 1944
Released: Warner Brothers, June 23, 1944
Running Time: 95 minutes

Cornelius Latimer Leyden, a mystery writer, is intrigued when the Istanbul police chief shows him the murdered body of Dimitrios, an internationally known criminal. Out of professional and personal curiosity Leyden decides to reconstruct Dimitrios's life and death. He meets people from Dimitrios's past who recount the man's career of murder, pimping, political assassination, double-crossing, and espionage. In his mission, Leyden is helped by Mr. Peters, one of Dimitrios's previous victims, who eventually reveals that Dimitrios is not dead but has faked his own murder in order to live a safe and prosperous life. Peters uses Leyden to blackmail Dimitrios, who retaliates by attempting to murder the extortionists. After a struggle, Peters and Dimitrios kill each other.

Although noir film makers have done relatively well when adapting American crime fiction, they have consistently overlooked the potential of the British thriller. Hollywood's three attempts in the 1940s to film Eric Ambler's novels are a case in point. *Background To Danger* is reduced to a secret agent programmer and *Journey Into Fear*, although the most literal and appropriately cast Ambler, dissipates its suspense by concentrating more on the mechanics of the central character's mission than on the psychological implications of his plight. *The Mask Of Dimitrios* is the most ambitious of the three.

The novel's great strengths are its approach to character and structure. Leyden, for instance, is an ordinary man; we can identify with him and, as a result, share his curiousity and then his fear. The book is constructed in a series of flashbacks as Leyden resurrects Dimitrios's career. Each flashback functions on its own; each also carries forward the plot and its sense of sinister inevitability by positing, but only partially answering, the questions "Who is Dimitrios?"; "Why did he die?"; and "Is he dead?"

Both of these virtues are undercut in the film. Zachary Scott makes a remarkable Dimitrios, but Greenstreet is a predictable Peters and Lorre is completely at odds with Leyden's common-man role. Even more problematic are the film's low-key lighting effects, stylized sets, and sententious dialogue. They do not support the characters, plot, and structure as effectively as a simple, straightforward style might have; instead, they seem superficial atmospherics. The best indication of this is the unpretentious and direct "Belgrade 1926" flashback; it is the film's most impressive and evocative episode.

The Mask Of Dimitrios has both the visual style and narrative content associated with noir; yet it lacks the emotional effect of a noir film. It is possible that Ambler's characters are not cynical enough for American noir or that his point of view is more radical than existential.

—D.L.W.

MILDRED PIERCE (1945)

Director: Michael Curtiz
Producer: Jerry Wald (Warner Brothers)
Screenplay: Ranald MacDougall; from the novel by James M. Cain
Director of Photography: Ernest Haller
Special Effects: Willard Van Enger
Montage: James Leicester
Sound: Oliver S. Garretson
Music: Max Steiner
Music Director: Leo F. Forbstein
Orchestration: Hugo Friedhofer
Art Director: Anton Grot
Set Decoration: George James Hopkins
Costumes: Milo Anderson
Makeup: Perc Westmore
Dialogue Director: Herschel Daugherty
Assistant Director: Frank Heath
Film Editor: David Weisbart

CAST: Joan Crawford (Mildred Pierce), Jack Carson (Wally Fay), Zachary Scott (Monte Beragon), Eve Arden (Ida), Ann Blyth (Veda Pierce), Bruce Bennett (Bert Pierce), George Tobias (Mr. Chris), Lee Patrick (Maggie Binderhof), Moroni Olson (Inspector Peterson), Jo Ann Marlowe (Kay Pierce), Barbara Brown (Mrs. Forrester). **BITS:** Charles Trowbridge (Mr. Williams), John Compton (Ted Forrester), Butterfly McQueen (Lottie), Garry Owen, Clancy Cooper, Tom Dillon, Charles Jordan (Policemen), James Flavin, Jack O'Connor (Detectives), Larry Rio (Reporter), George Anderson (Peterson's Assistant), Johnny Walsh (Delivery Man), Robert Arthur (High School Boy), Joyce Compton, Lynne Baggett, Marion Lessing, Doria Caron, Marjorie Kane, Elyse Brown (Waitresses), Jimmy Lono (Houseboy), Mary Servoss (Nurse), Manart Kippin (Dr. Gale), David Cota (Pancho), George Meader, Harold Miller, Robert Lorraine (Men), Joan Wardley (Wife), Don Grant (Bartender), Chester Clute (Mr. Jones), Robert Evans (Sailor), Wallis Clark (Wally's Lawyer), Perk Lazello (Attorney's Clerk), Angela Green, Betty Alexander, Ramsay Ames, Helen Pender (Party Guests), Joan Winfield (Piano Teacher), John Christian (Singing Teacher), Leah Baird (Police Matron), Paul Panzer (Waiter), William Alcorn (Soldier), John Sheridan (Clerk), Dick Kipling, Wheaton Chambers, William Ruhl (Personnel Men), Mary Ellen Meyran, Jean Lorraine (Women).

Filming Completed: February 28, 1945
Released: Warner Brothers, September 28, 1945
Running Time: 113 minutes

The murder of wealthy Monte Beragon unveils the past of Mildred Pierce. A bored, middle-class housewife, married to real estate broker Bert Pierce, Mildred is obsessed with providing luxuries for her daughter Veda, which Bert cannot provide, so she separates herself from him. Mildred takes a job as a waitress to support her two daughters; but Veda discovers her mother's position and is humiliated. Mildred's plan to open a restaurant placates Veda's snobbery. With the help of Wally Fay, Bert's old partner, Mildred obtains land for a restaurant sponsored by Monte Beragon, an indolent Southern California heir who is looking for a little excitement. Veda is attracted to Monte and breaks her engagement to a wealthy man in order to seduce him. Wanting to be even closer to Veda since the death of Kay, her younger daughter, Mildred divorces Bert and offers her wealth to Monte. He marries her and quickly bankrupts the chain of restaurants, which have originated from Mildred's initial success. Mildred suffers a final humiliation when she sees Monte embrace Veda. In defense, Monte describes Veda as a "rotten little tramp;" and the girl kills him. Shocked, Mildred vows to protect Veda and tries to convince the police that she is the murderess. But Veda is arrested; and Mildred is left to piece together her life, reunited in sorrow with her first husband, Bert.

Like Dashiell Hammett and Raymond Chandler, James M. Cain feels the need for a tough guy hero. Unlike those two, Cain cannot imagine one. The toughest character he develops in his novels is Keyes in *Double Indemnity*. But by the time *Mildred Pierce* reached the screen in 1945, filmic conventions of violence and ill-fated love affairs existed, and they altered the form of Cain's original novel so that Mildred Pierce became a tough guy, albeit an unwilling one.

The film *Mildred Pierce* uses the act of murder to develop a dramatic focus and force that elude the book. Thus Monte's killing, which does not even take place in the original novel, is the film's focal point. The entire film flashes back from the moment of Beragon's death and each flashback is arranged so that violence informs and dominates it.

Although Mildred is not a detective, she is perhaps the hard-boiled detective's counterpart in the only way suited to a 1940s heroine. Mildred has opted out of her socially well-defined milieu to become a free agent and successful businesswoman; she makes or breaks herself, acting without the benefit of the community's moral support. Like a Marlowe or a Spade, she is subjected to beatings in the course of her work, which are appropriately financial rather than physical. Significantly, Mildred misplaces her love and trust not in an evil man but in her daughter Veda, who is the same type of *femme fatale* that wreaks havoc throughout film noir. Veda demands obsessive passion and Mildred sacrifices herself. When she is finally freed from Veda's clutches, Mildred, like the tough guy, does not triumph but merely survives.

187

MINISTRY OF FEAR

Mildred Pierce makes use of all the visual motifs that predominate in film noir: low key lighting, diagonals, dark interiors, and night exteriors. The introductory shot of Veda, the murderess, is also typical of many noir films because it reveals that reality is not what it seems. Veda is first seen wearing a white dress and flowers, photographed from a low angle. The angle gives her a dominating, threatening aspect at odds with the innocent clothing; and the contradictory image adds mystery, ambiguity, and a sense of danger to her character. Additionally, Curtiz juxtaposes Veda's personality and Mildred's consuming motherly devotion with the musical correlative of "You Must Have Been A Beautiful Baby."

Mildred's climb up the ladder of success alienates her from society because it does not achieve what she desires. Continually rejected by Veda, Mildred essentially rejects her younger daughter, Kay, who later dies. However, Mildred encourages everyone to exploit her and erode her foundation of confidence and industry until there is nothing left. Mildred's escape from a routine marriage leads to a nightmarish realm of inconsistent realities and selfish desires.

—E.K. & C.M.

MINISTRY OF FEAR (1945)

Director: Fritz Lang
Executive Producer: B. G. DeSylva (Paramount)
Associate Producer: Seton I. Miller
Screenplay: Seton I. Miller; from the novel by Graham Greene
Director of Photography: Henry Sharp
Sound: W. C. Smith
Musical Score: Victor Young
Art Directors: Hal Pereira, Hans Dreier
Set Decoration: Bert Granger
Assistant Director: George Templeton
Film Editor: Archie Marshek

CAST: Ray Milland (Stephen Neale), Marjorie Reynolds (Carla Hilfe), Carl Esmond (Willi Hilfe), Hillary Brooke (the Second Mrs. Bellaire), Percy Waram (Prentice), Dan Duryea (Cost/Travers), Alan Napier (Dr. Forrester), Erskine Sanford (Mr. Rennit), Thomas Louden (Mr. Newland), Aminta Dyne (the First Mrs. Bellaire), Eustace Wyatt (Blind Man), Mary Field (Miss Penteel), Byron Foulger (Mr. Newby), Lester Matthews (Dr. Norton). BITS: Helena Grant (Mrs. Merrick), Grayce Hampton, Ottola Nesmith, Connie Leon, Jessica Newcombe, Evelyn Beresford, Anne Curson, Hilda Plowright (Women), Frank Dawson (Vicar), Harry Allen, Cyril Delevanti, Frank Leigh, Francis Sayles, Arthur Blake, Edward Fielding, Matthew Boulton, Edmond Russell, Leonard Carey (Men), Eric Wilton, Boyd Irwin, Frank Baker, Colin Kenny (Scotland Yard Men), Bruce Carruthers (Police Clerk), David Clyde (English Bobby), Wilson Benge (Air Raid Warden), Clive Morgan, George Broughton, Olaf Hytten (Men in Tailor's Shop).
Filming Completed: August 30, 1943
Released: Paramount, February 7, 1945
Running Time: 86 minutes

During World War II in London, Stephen Neale is released from prison after serving a term for a mercy killing that he did not commit. He attends a parish bazaar, unknowingly speaks a secret word, and is handed a cake that is intended for a Nazi spy. The cake contains microfilm of the British plans for the invasion of Europe and Stephen is immediately chased by the Nazi espionage ring. He hires a detective to help him; but the man is murdered and the spies implicate Neale as the killer. Realizing the police believe him guilty because of his past criminal record, Neale must break the espionage ring himself. His girl friend, Carla, who is an Austrian refugee, helps Neale but ultimately discovers that her own brother Willi is a Nazi and kills him. After eluding attempts on his life, Neale exposes the spies and is free of criminal charges.

Based on Graham Greene's novel, *Ministry of Fear* is an early attempt to incorporate the mood and tone of the developing noir sensibility into the framework of intrigue surrounding World War II. Much in the same way as Welles's earlier *Journey into Fear*, this thriller directed by Fritz Lang has its share of grotesques. Foremost among them is Dan Duryea, one of Lang's favorite villains, whose scissors-stabbing sequence is a tour de force of contrived menace. *Ministry of Fear* is highly atmospheric and reminiscent of Paramount's earlier *Among the Living; Street of Chance;* and another Graham Greene adaptation, *This Gun for Hire.* Lang, who had wanted to make a film of *Ministry of Fear* for some time, was brought into the production without any authority to change the script; and seldom is Lang's particularly deterministic bias evoked. Carla's betrayal however, is a distinctly noir element of the narrative.

—C.M.

MR. ARKADIN (1955)
[Great Britain Release Title: CONFIDENTIAL REPORT]

Director: Orson Welles
Producer: Louis Dolivet (Filmorsa; Cervantes Film Organization, Sevilla Studios [Spain]/Film Organization [France]; a Mercury Production)
Screenplay: Orson Welles; from his novel
Director of Photography: Jean Bourgoin
Sound: Jacques Lebreton, Jacques Carrère

Music: Paul Misraki
Art Director, Costumes: Orson Welles
Production Manager: Michel J. Boisrond
Assistant Directors: José María Ochoa, José Luis De la Serna, Isidoro Martínez Ferri
Film Editor: Renzo Lucidi

CAST: Orson Welles (Gregory Arkadin), Paola Mori (Raina Arkadin), Robert Arden (Guy Van Stratten), Akim Tamiroff (Jacob Zouk), Michael Redgrave (Burgomil Trebitsch), Patricia Medina (Mily), Mischa Auer (the Professor), Katina Paxinou (Sophie), Jack Watling (Marquis of Rutleigh), Grégoire Aslan (Bracco), Peter Van Eyck (Thaddeus), Suzanne Flon (Baroness Nagel), Tamara Shane (Woman in Apartment), Frederic O'Brady (Oskar).
Location: France, Spain, Germany, Italy
Filming Completed: August 1954
Released: Warner Brothers, in Great Britain on August 11, 1955; M & A Alexander Productions, in the United States on October 11, 1962
Running Time: 100 minutes

A bizarre shoot-out near the Milan waterfront involves Guy Van Stratten in a complex web of mystery and double cross. Coming to the aid of a dying man, Guy's mistress Mily is told two names: Gregory Arkadin and Sophie. Knowing that Arkadin is one of the richest men in the world, Van Stratten believes the dying man's words could mean money. He trails Arkadin to a resort area in Spain and approaches Arkadin through his daughter, Raina. At an exotic costume party, Arkadin exposes Van Stratten as a petty adventurer and a small-time con man. Shortly afterward, however, he is hired by Arkadin to investigate the tycoon's past because it is a total blank to the man. The first memories that Arkadin recollects are of wandering through Eastern Europe with a small fortune stuffed in the pockets of his coat. Guy accepts the job as well as Arkadin's demand never to see his daughter again. As Van Stratten traces the past of this rich and powerful man, he uncovers the history of a white slaver who used the flesh of innocent women to build a fortune. Mysteriously, everyone Van Stratten comes in contact with is soon killed. Van Stratten finally realizes that he is merely a tool helping to destroy all traces of Arkadin's sordid past. To save himself, Guy persuades Raina to tell her father that she knows everything about him. Arkadin, flying home, calls on the radio and is informed of Raina's knowledge. Destroyed emotionally, he jumps to his death from the plane.

Probably one of the most elliptical films directed by Orson Welles, *Mr. Arkadin* remains an unusually haunting portrait of a man obsessed with the past. Drawing from the "pulp" traditions of the 1930s and 1940s in the formation of his mystery novel and screenplay, Welles complements his plot with a totally baroque visual style filled with obtuse camera angles and wildly cluttered environments causing total disorientation.

Although reminiscent of *Citizen Kane*'s investigation into the past of a powerful and wealthy man, *Mr. Arkadin* becomes a more personalized and highly romanticized vision of power and corruption. (Not only did Welles make a film of this story, he also wrote and starred in a radio version of it on his "Third Man" show a few years prior to the film's production. This particular episode was entitled "Man of Mystery" and Welles, portraying Harry Lime, traced the past of Mr. Arkadin. Additionally, Welles wrote the novel, *Mr. Arkadin,* on which the screenplay is based. The film is hampered by a limited budget, which forced Welles to abandon his original screenplay, entitled *Masquerade,* for the less poetic version finally released. Robert Arden's portrayal of Guy Van Stratten also mars the film because of his inability to sustain audience identification; but the cameo appearances by Michael Redgrave, Akim Tamiroff, and Katina Paxinou offer diverse performances that compensate for Arden's weak screen presence. It seems that initially Welles may have desired Michel Simon to play Arkadin, as the cosmetic makeup for the role suggests. The film's association with the noir sensibility comes less from characterization than from its exotic visual style and from its attempt to deglamorize the wealthy by placing them at the root of corruption. Ultimately, that corruption—like the nature of the scorpion who, Arkadin explains, cannot keep himself from stinging the frog that carries it across the river—is the deterministic force which destroys Arkadin and his cohorts.

—C.M.

THE MOB (1951)
[Working Titles: WATERFRONT; REMEMBER THAT FACE]

Director: Robert Parrish
Producer: Jerry Bresler (Columbia Pictures)
Screenplay: William Bowers; from the novel *Waterfront* by Ferguson Findley
Director of Photography: Joseph Walker
Sound: Lodge Cunningham
Music Score: George Duning
Music Director: Morris Stoloff
Art Director: Cary Odell
Set Decoration: Frank Tuttle
Makeup: Clay Campbell
Hairstyles: Helen Hunt
Assistant Director: James Nicholson
Film Editor: Charles Nelson

CAST: Broderick Crawford (Johnny Damico), Betty Buehler (Mary Kiernan), Richard Kiley (Thomas Clancy), Otto Hulett (Lt. Banks), Matt Crowley (Smoothie), Neville Brand (Gunner), Ernest Borgnine (Joe Castro), Walter Klavun (Sgt. Bennion), Lynne Baggett (Peggy), Jean Alexander (Doris), Ralph Dumke (Police Commissioner), John Marley (Tony), Frank de Kova (Culio), Jay Adler (Russell), Duke Watson (Radford), Emile Meyer (Gas Station Attendant), Carleton Young (District Attorney). **BITS:** Fred Coby (Plainclothesman), Ric Roman (Police Officer), Art Millan, Paul Bryar (Officers), Michael McHale (Talbert), Kenneth Harvey (Paul), Don Megowan (Bruiser), Richard Irving (Prowl Cop Driver), Robert Fould, Tom Greenway, Dick Pinner, Jack Finley (Men), Al Mellon (Joe), Don De Leo (Cigar Store Proprietor), Peter Prouse (Fred), Sidney Mason, David McMahon (Cops), Ernie Venneri (Crew Member), Robert Anderson (Mate), Jess Kirkpatrick (Mason), Charles Marsh (Waiter), Charles [Bronson] Buchinski (Jack), Mary Alan Hokanson, Virginia Chapman (Nurses), William Pullen (Plotter), Peter Virgo (Bakery Truck Driver), Larry Dobkin (Doctor), Harry Lauter (Daniels), Paul Dubov (Johnson).

Filming Completed: February 8, 1951
Released: Columbia, October 17, 1951
Running Time: 87 minutes

Going underground to smoke out the mobsters who are controlling the docks, policeman Johnny Damico soon finds that the waterfront is rife with corruption. His initially brazen, hard-boiled attitude causes the mob to send over a couple of boys, Gunner and Joe Castro, to educate the newcomer in the finer points of waterfront life. Convincing them that he is on the level, Johnny is soon working for the mob in a superficial capacity. Damico is befriended by Tom Clancy, also an undercover cop assigned to ferret out Smoothie, the leader of the mob. In their attempts to discover the ringleader's identity, the two undercover agents use luminous liquid, which drips from the rear of the mobster's car, to trail him as he threatens informants with physical violence. They finally discover Smoothie, which leads to his death at the hands of the police.

A violent film populated with sordid characters and events epitomizing corruption and brutality, *The Mob* is a rehash of several gangster thrillers inspired by the crackdown on organized crime following World War II. What distinguishes *The Mob* from these other films is its depiction of the ruthless hard-boiled character of both the police and the criminals. At times it becomes hard to differentiate between the undercover cops and the mobsters. Broderick Crawford takes the simple role of Johnny Damico and converts it into a noir characterization of toughness and vulgarity. *The Mob* also exploits the staccato pacing of the 1930s gangster films while playing off the postwar preoccupations of a society returning to normality. The result is an eclectic film noir held together by the conventions and social interests of the period.

—C.M.

MOONRISE (1949)

Director: Frank Borzage
Producer: Charles Haas (Charles K. Feldman Group Productions)
Screenplay: Charles Haas; from the novel by Theodore Strauss
Director of Photography: John L. Russell
Special Effects: Howard and Theodore Lydecker
Sound: Earl Crain, Sr., Howard Wilson
Music: William Lava
Songs: "It Just Dawned On Me" by William Lava and Harry Tobias; "Lonesome" by Theodore Strauss and William Lava. Sung by David Street.
Production Designer: Lionel Banks
Set Decoration: John McCarthy, Jr., George Sawley
Costumes: Adele Palmer
Makeup: Bob Mark
Hairstyles: Peggy Gray
Assistant Director: Lee Lukather
Film Editor: Harry Keller

CAST: Dane Clark (Danny Hawkins), Gail Russell (Gilly Johnson), Ethel Barrymore (Grandma), Allyn Joslyn (Clem Otis), Rex Ingram (Mose), Henry Morgan (Billy Scripture), David Street (Ken Williams), Selena Royle (Aunt Jessie), Harry Carey, Jr. (Jimmy Biff), Irving Bacon (Judd Jenkins), Lloyd Bridges (Jerry Sykes), Houseley Stevenson (Uncle Joe Jingle), Phil Brown (Elmer), Harry V. Cheshire (J. B. Sykes), Lila Leeds (Julie). **BITS:** Virginia Mullen (Miss Simpkins), Oliver Blake (Ed Conlon), Tom Fadden (Homer Blackstone), Charles Lane (Man In Black), Clem Bevans (Jake), Helen Wallace (Martha Otis), Michael Branden, Bill Borzage, Tiny Jimmie Kelly, Ed Rees, Casey MacGregor (Barkers), John Harmon (Baseball Attendant), Monte Lowell (Man), Jimmie Hawkins, Gary Armstrong, Buzzy Henry, Jimmy Crane, Harry Lauter, Bob Hoffman, Joel McGinnis (Boys), Timmie Hawkins (Alfie), Doreen McCann, Candy Toxton (Girls), Steven Peck (Danny, Age 7), Johnny Calkins (Danny, Age 13), Tommy Ivo (Jerry, Age 7), Michael Dill (Jerry, Age 13), Linda Lombard, Stelita Ravel (Dancers), Renee Donatt (Ticket Seller), George Backus, Monte Montague (Hunters).

Completed: February 5, 1948
Released: Republic, March 6, 1949
Running Time: 90 minutes

[NOTE: *Moonrise* was planned as a Marshall Grant Production, to be directed by William Wellman and starring either James Stewart or John Garfield, from a screenplay written by Vladimir Posner. Charles K. Feldman purchased the motion picture rights to the book from Marshall Grant.]

Danny, a young man whose father was hanged as a murderer, is constantly reminded of his "unsavory" heritage as he grows up. His struggle to become a part of his small Southern community meets with constant rejection and harassment. Eventually, his preoccupation with the past leads him to kill Jimmy, one of his archtormentors, in self-defense. He is plagued with the fears that he might be discovered and becomes obsessed with the notion that he might have "bad blood." His fears of becoming a criminal ultimately force him to leave his sympathetic girl friend and schoolteacher, Gilly, and live in the swamps. It is here that Danny ultimately confronts his past through talking to Grandma and is able to see that he is what he makes of himself. Wending his way back from the swamps, Danny rejoins society and surrenders to the authorities with relief.

It is interesting to see how an overtly romantic director like Frank Borzage develops a story with the noir overtones found in *Moonrise*. Rather than take an expressionistic approach, which might have left the film cold and ruthless, Borzage maintained his relatively impressionistic style and gave *Moonrise* a close association with the works of the French poetic realists. The opening sequence of Danny's father being led to the gallows is a stunning vision, which becomes a central image of the film. It is an image that Borzage returns to in the process of establishing the patterns of existence for Danny and the others. Danny is constantly trapped, threatened, and walled in by the *mise-en-scène*. His escape through the swamp up the hill to his grandmother's cabin and his parents' graves becomes increasingly lighter and liberated; like a mythical journey from his own private hell to the heaven of freedom from guilt and pain.

The element of redemption is a factor that has little potency in many noir films. However, it is necessary in Borzage's treatment of the world and, in this instance, with particularly noir circumstances. Danny's return to civilization—much in the same way as Robert Ryan's reestablishment of personal relationships in Nicholas Ray's *On Dangerous Ground*—fulfills the film. Without this sense of redemption, which is uncharacteristic of the noir sensibility yet totally acceptable in the context of these films, neither work would be complete.

—M.B. & C.M.

MURDER IS MY BEAT (1955)
[Working Title: THE LONG CHANCE]

Director: Edgar G. Ulmer
Producer: Aubrey Wisberg (Masthead)
Associate Producer: Ilse Lahn
Screenplay: Aubrey Wisberg; from an unpublished story by Aubrey Wisberg and Martin Field
Director of Photography: Harold E. Wellman
Special Photography: Elmer Dyer
Sound: Robert William Roderick

Music: Al Glasser
Art Director: James Sullivan
Set Decoration: Harry H. Reif
Makeup: Jack Byron
Assistant Director: Raoul Pagel
Film Editor: Fred R. Feitshans, Jr.

CAST: Paul Langton (Ray Patrick), Barbara Payton (Eden Lane), Robert Shayne (Bert Rawley), Selena Royle (Mrs. Abbott), Roy Gordon (Abbott), Tracey Roberts (Patsy Flint), Kate McKenna (Landlady), Henry A. Harvey, Sr. (Gas Station Attendant), Jay Adler (Bartender).

Filming Completed: November 1954
Released: Allied Artists, February 27, 1955
Running Time: 77 minutes

The body of a Mr. Deane is found with his head in a fireplace, his features burned beyond recognition. Police detectives Ray Patrick and Bert Rawley arrest a nightclub singer, Eden Lane, for the crime, and she is convicted. While Ray and a police matron travel with her to prison, Eden sees a man through the train window that she identifies as the Deane she was convicted of murdering. Ray believes her, and he and Eden leap from the train when it slows for a grade. They walk back to town and days pass while they search in vain. Ray finds Patsy Flint, Eden's old roommate, registered at a hotel under an assumed name. Returning to the motel, he discovers Eden gone and his partner Rawley waiting to arrest him. Ray pleads for 24 more hours, and Rawley agrees to help. They locate Deane in a ceramics factory he owns under the name of Abbot. Abbot had fallen in love with Eden and hired a private eye to keep track of her; but he murdered the detective when the man threatened blackmail. Patsy Flint's body is found in her hotel room, where she was slain by Mrs. Abbot in response to another blackmail attempt. Eden, who gave herself up to the warden at the state prison, is freed and Ray is waiting to marry her.

Murder Is My Beat uses flashbacks, elliptical editing, and a general lack of establishing shots to illustrate a destructive and disordered universe. It may lack the classic dimensions of the same director's *Detour*, but benefits from the presence of Barbara Payton as an ambiguous *femme fatale*. Ulmer extracts the maximum narrative tension from the viewer's uncertainty over Eden Lane's guilt, an uncertainty reinforced by Payton's portrayal of Eden in a "neutral" manner. Although Eden ultimately proves to be the factor that binds the diverse elements of the narrative together, Payton's performance permits the suggestion of instability beneath the surface calm of Eden's visage. In a film that lacks any strong visual or narrative center, this added element of ambiguity compounds the alienating effect of a discontinuous *mise-en-scène*.

—B.P. & A.S.

MURDER MY SWEET

MURDER, MY SWEET (1944)
[Original Release Title: FAREWELL, MY LOVELY]

Director: Edward Dmytryk
Executive Producer: Sid Rogell (RKO)
Producer: Adrian Scott
Screenplay: John Paxton; from the novel *Farewell, My Lovely* by Raymond Chandler
Director of Photography: Harry J. Wild
Special Effects: Vernon L. Walker
Montage: Douglas Travers
Sound: Bailey Fesler, James E. Stewart
Music: Roy Webb
Music Director: Constantin Bakaleinikoff
Art Directors: Albert S. D'Agostino, Carroll Clark
Set Decoration: Darrell Silvera, Michael Ohrenbach
Costumes: Edward Stevenson
Dialogue Director: Leslie Urbach
Assistant Director: William Dorfman
Film Editor: Joseph Noreiga

CAST: Dick Powell (Philip Marlowe), Claire Trevor (Velma/Mrs. Grayle), Anne Shirley (Ann), Otto Kruger (Amthor), Mike Mazurki (Moose Malloy), Miles Mander (Mr. Grayle), Douglas Walton (Marriott), Don Douglas (Lt. Randall), Ralf Harolde (Dr. Sonderborg), Esther Howard (Mrs. Florian). **BITS:** John Indrisano (Chauffeur), Jack Carr (Short Guy), Shimen Ruskin (Elevator Operator), Ernie Adams (Bartender), Dewey Robinson (the Boss), Larry Wheat (Butler), Sammy Finn (Headwaiter), Bernice Ahi (Dancer), Don Kerr (Taxi Driver), Paul Phillips (Detective Nulty), Ralph Dunn, George Anderson (Detectives), Paul Hilton (Boy).

Filming Completed: July 1, 1944
Released: RKO, as *Farewell, My Lovely* in Minneapolis, Minnesota, on December 18, 1944; as *Murder, My Sweet* in New York, New York, on March 8, 1945
Running Time: 95 minutes

After his release from prison, Moose Malloy hires private investigator Philip Marlowe to find his missing girl friend Velma. While Marlowe comes up against a blank wall in his search for Velma, he is hired to accompany an effeminate patsy as he ransoms a cache of stolen jewels. The patsy is killed and Marlowe is knocked unconscious. Informing the owner of the stolen jewels, Mrs. Grayle, that her friend has been murdered, Marlowe is assigned to recover the jewels and find out who the murderer is. The search for Velma is sidetracked as he moves from the seedy environment of cheap flophouses into the slick upper-class world of corruption. Meddling into Mrs. Grayle's past, Marlowe is beaten and drugged until the facts surrounding his investigation become confused. Finally putting the events of the two cases together, Marlowe realizes that Velma and Mrs. Grayle are the same person. He contrives a meeting between all interested parties at a beach house. Moose, Mrs. Grayle, and her husband shoot each other as their past is revealed, and emotions of hate and deception surface.

One of the quintessential noir films, *Murder, My Sweet* opens with a disorienting shot of a glaring ceiling light as voices level accusations of murder at someone. The camera tilts down and comes to rest on Dick Powell as Philip Marlowe, sitting jacketless and with bandaged eyes at a small table. Marlowe begins to tell his story, prompted by a policeman, and the camera cuts to city lights at night. Pulling in through a window, the camera reveals Marlowe watching the evening and the flashing lights outside. Suddenly, each flash of light reflects a brooding face in the windowpane and a huge presence hulks in the darkness behind Marlowe.

The disorienting angles, low-key and high-contrast lighting, the reflection towering over Marlowe, and the private eye's blindness in the first scenes point to a disordered and ominous world beyond control. *Murder, My Sweet* is a fascinating blend of the hard-boiled tradition and a hybrid form of muted expressionism. Taking Raymond Chandler's *Farewell, My Lovely* and transforming it into a film with a dark ambience unknown in most films of this period, director Edward Dmytryk succeeded in transcending the conventions of tough dialogue and mystery films by creating a singularly cynical vision of society. Dmytryk and screenwriter John Paxton were especially careful in evoking this vision through Marlowe's character. They molded the previously uninspired, juvenile crooner persona of Dick Powell into a model of hard-boiled toughness that became a classic icon of the noir period. A vulnerable hero, Powell's soft, almost baby face and perpetual hang-dog expression make him a doubtful sort of protagonist. When he lashes out at characters in the film, he's like a spoiled child who hasn't got his way and doesn't know how to get it except by throwing a tantrum.

Murder, My Sweet develops within a closed system as Marlowe narrates the flashback and knows the unhappy end. Thus the entire text of the film becomes one of reflection and pause; both because it occurs in flashback and because Marlowe continually interrupts his tale with wry comments on the action: "I gave her a drink. She was a gal who would take a drink if she had to knock you over to get it." But the dialogue sequences are less important than the narrative. It is not his repartee but his search through the nightmarish landscape devoid of order and ripe with chaotic images that governs the mood of the film. Filled with shadows and half-lit realities, *Murder, My Sweet* has a visual quality that became characteristic of the period. Contrast is all important. The inclusion of dream images when Marlowe is drugged, complete with threatening symbols and a surreal sense of perversion, create an atmosphere of fear and dislocation. *Murder, My Sweet* is also filled with a succession of grotesque characters that have little relation to the real world. They exist as icons or images of the twilight world of film noir. Ultimately *Murder, My Sweet* is the archetype for a number of films made later. The use of the *femme fatale,* an atmosphere of paranoia, the vulnerability of the hero, the motivation of violence, the predominance of grotesque characters, and the threatening environment all contribute to this noir ambience. There is nothing sweet in *Murder, My Sweet,* a film that remains not

only a highly stylized and complex detective thriller but also an uncompromising vision of corruption and decay.
—E.K. & C.M.

MY NAME IS JULIA ROSS (1945)
[Working Title: THE WOMAN IN RED]

Director: Joseph H. Lewis
Producer: Wallace MacDonald (Columbia)
Screenplay: Muriel Roy Bolton; from the novel *The Woman In Red* by Anthony Gilbert
Director of Photography: Burnett Guffey
Sound: Lambert Day
Music: Mischa Bakaleinikoff
Art Director: Jerome Pycha, Jr.
Set Decoration: Milton Stumph
Assistant Director: Milton Feldman
Film Editor: James Sweeney

CAST: Nina Foch (Julia Ross), Dame May Whitty (Mrs. Hughes), George Macready (Ralph Hughes), Roland Varno (Dennis Bruce), Anita Bolster (Sparkes), Doris Lloyd (Mrs. Mackie), Leonard Mudie (Peters), Joy Harrington (Bertha), Queenie Leonard (Alice), Harry Hays Morgan (Robinson), Ottola Nesmith (Mrs. Robinson), Olaf Hytten (the Reverend Lewis), Evan Thomas (Dr. Keller). **BITS:** Marilyn Johnson (Nurse), Milton Owens, Leland Hodgeson (Policemen), Reginald Sheffield (McQuarrie), Charles McNaughton (Gatekeeper).
Filming Completed: August 4, 1945
Released: Columbia, November 8, 1945
Running Time: 64 minutes

Julia Ross, badly in need of a job, is offered the position of resident secretary to Mrs. Williamson Hughes, a wealthy matron, and her son, Ralph. Greeted by Ralph, who explains that the servants are off, she is taken to her room and given a meal. Julia awakens from a drugged sleep to find herself in different clothes and in a room that overlooks the Cornwall seacoast far below. She is informed that she is Ralph's wife, Marian, and that she has just come home from a mental institution. Escaping from the house, she finds the grounds are surrounded by a ten-foot wall with a locked and guarded gate. One day, however, Ralph takes her into the village and she secretly mails a note to her boyfriend, Dennis, for help. Later, she overhears Ralph and his mother plot to fake Julia's suicide to cover up Ralph's murder of the authentic Marian Hughes. Julia pretends to take poison to have a doctor called; but Mrs. Hughes has the butler, Peters, pose as the doctor and Julia tells him of the note she mailed. Peters goes to London to intercept the letter, and, when he is caught trying to steal it, he confesses the entire plan to the police. Dennis and the police rush to Cornwall and arrive just as Ralph prepares to kill Julia. Mrs. Hughes is arrested,

Ralph is killed trying to escape, and Dennis and Julia return to London to plan their future life together.

My Name Is Julia Ross is the first of a series of film noir directed by Joseph H. Lewis and is the film that Lewis likes to consider as the "real" beginning of his career. It marks a long association with Columbia and photographer Guffey and is notable for the opening scene of Julia in the rain with her shadow on the wall of the employment agency and the 360° pan around the room when she first awakens in Cornwall. Additionally, the use of windows as a subjective perspective to the world; as Lewis's central characters always seem to see "through a glass, darkly," foreshadow a consistent motif in his future films.
—B.P.

MYSTERY STREET (1950)
[Working Title: MURDER AT HARVARD]

Director: John Sturges
Producer: Frank E. Taylor (MGM)
Screenplay: Sydney Boehm and Richard Brooks; from an unpublished story by Leonard Spigelgass
Director of Photography: John Alton
Sound: Douglas Shearer, J. Edmondson
Music: Rudolph G. Kopp
Art Directors: Cedric Gibbons, Gabriel Scognamillo
Set Decoration: Edwin B. Willis, Ralph S. Hurst
Makeup: Jack Dawn, Sam Palo
Hairstyles: Sydney Guilaroff, Ethel Neejus
Production Manager: Charles Hunt
Assistant Director: Sid Sidman
Script Supervisor: Don MacDougall
Film Editor: Ferris Webster

CAST: Ricardo Montalban (Lt. Peter Morales), Sally Forrest (Grace Shanway), Bruce Bennett (Dr. McAdoo), Elsa Lanchester (Mrs. Smerrling), Marshall Thompson (Henry Shanway), Jan Sterling (Vivian Heldon), Edmon Ryan (James Joshua Harkley), Betsy Blair (Jackie Elcott), Wally Maher (Tim Sharkey), Ralph Dumke (Tattooist), Willard Waterman (Mortician), Walter Burke (Ornithologist), Don Shelton (District Attorney), Brad Hatton (Bartender). **BITS:** Douglas Carter (Counterman), William F. Leicester (Doctor), Arthur Loew, Jr. (Sailor), Sherry Hall (Clerk), James Hayward (Constable Fischer), Eula Guy (Mrs. Fischer), Virginia Mullen (Neighbor), King Donovan, George Cooper, Ralph Brooks, George Sherwood, John Crawford (Reporters), Fred E. Sherman, Allen O'Locklin (Photographers), Melvin H. Moore (Oyster Shucker), Ned Glass (Dr. Levy), Matt Moore (Dr. Rockton), Maurice Samuels (Tailor), John Maxwell (Kilrain), Robert Foulk (O'Hara), Louise Lorimer (Mrs.

Mrs. Smerrling (Elsa Lancaster) seated in Mystery Street.

Shanway), Napoleon Whiting (Red Cap), Jack Shea (Policeman), Mary Jane Smith, Juanita Quigley (Daughters), Lucille Curtis (Mrs. Harkley), Charles Wagenheim (Clerk), David McMahon (Garrity), Michael Patrick Donovan (Porter), Frank Overton (Guard), Bert Davidson (Dr. Thorpe), May McAvoy (Nurse), Mack Chandler (Doorman), Elsie Baker (Elderly Lady), Ralph Montgomery (Waiter), Jim Frasher (High School Boy), Ernesto Morelli (Portuguese Fisherman), Robert Strong (Cop), George Brand (Man in Bedroom), Fred Santley (Pawnbroker), Perry Ivins (Alienist), Peter Thompson (Law Student).

Location: Cape Cod, Boston, Cambridge, and Harvard University, Massachusetts

Filming Completed: December 9, 1949

Released: MGM, July 27, 1950

Running Time: 94 minutes

Vivian Heldon is a cheap blond who has been having an affair with a married man, Harkley, a descendant of one of Boston's oldest families. Realizing that she is pregnant, Vivian arranges a meeting with him on a remote stretch of beach but first meets a stranger, Henry Shanway, in a bar where she is drowning her sorrow. Henry, later drives her part way to her rendezvous; and she dupes him and takes his car. When she meets Harkley and announces her pregnancy, he shoots her, strips her body and throws it into the ocean, then pushes the car so that it sinks into a nearby bog. Meanwhile, Henry reports his car as stolen. Eventually Vivian's skeleton is found on the beach and a police team, headed by Lt. Peter Morales, investigates. Morales is aided by a brilliant Harvard scientist, Dr. McAdoo, and discovers the girl's identity from her skeleton and that she has been shot. They drag the bog and find the car, which leads them to arrest Shanway. Lt. Morales is not satisfied with Shanway's guilt and uncovers a link between Hartley and Vivian. Hartley meanwhile is blackmailed by Mrs. Smerrling, the dead girl's avaricious landlady, who found his phone number and stole the murder weapon from Hartley's desk. He calls on her intending to kill her but is interrupted by Grace Shanway and Morales. Hartley escapes but Morales discovers the key to a locker in Trinity Station, where Mrs. Smerrling has hidden the gun. He corners Hartley there the next morning.

Mystery Street is one of a mini series of thrillers produced by MGM during the reign (1948–56) of Dore Schary as production head. Certainly it was Schary who provided a favorable atmosphere for the talents of Anthony Mann, John Alton, Sidney Boehm, and others who were previously long associated with low budget thrillers. It was an atmosphere that went against the grain of Louis B. Mayer and the older executives who still saw MGM as the studio "with more stars than there are in heaven." In any case, Alton was thoroughly familiar with a photographic style that could enhance the detailed scientific investigation and become the bizarre background for a crime as illustrated by the reconstruction of an adult skeleton, dredging a swamp for a car, and sifting beach sand to discover and reconstruct the skeleton of a fetus. In this, the film has much of the lurid detail of *The Enforcer*. There is a bit of social consciousness, too, that is characteristic of the 1950s, as one of America's aristocrats is not only a murderer but an elitist who resents the authority of an "ethnic" type like Morales. Morales, also born and raised in the Boston area, handles the snobbery of the rich well and weds the ethnic virtues of the common man to the technological acumen of a representative of the Harvard intellectual community.

—B.P.

THE NAKED CITY (1948)
[Working Title: HOMICIDE]

Director: Jules Dassin
Producer: Mark Hellinger (Mark Hellinger Productions)
Associate Producer: Jules Buck
Screenplay: Albert Maltz and Malvin Wald; from an unpublished story by Malvin Wald
Director of Photography: William Daniels
Sound: Leslie I. Carey, Vernon W. Kramer
Music: Miklos Rozsa, Frank Skinner
Music Supervisor: Milton Schwarzwald
Art Director: John F. DeCuir
Set Decoration: Russell A. Gausman, Oliver Emert
Costumes: Grace Houston
Makeup: Bud Westmore
Hairstyles: Carmen Dirigo
Assistant Director: Fred Frank
Film Editor: Paul Weatherwax

CAST: Barry Fitzgerald (Lt. Dan Muldoon), Howard Duff (Frank Niles), Dorothy Hart (Ruth Morrison), Don Taylor (Jimmy Halloran), Ted de Corsia (Garzah), House Jameson (Dr. Stoneman), Anne Sargent (Mrs. Halloran), Adelaide Klein (Mrs. Batory), Grover Burgess (Mr. Batory), Tom Pedi (Detective Perelli), Enid Markey (Mrs. Hylton), Frank Conroy (Capt. Donahue), Mark Hellinger (Narrator). **BITS:** Walter Burke (Backalis), David Opatoshu (Ben Miller), John McQuade (Constantino), Hester Sondergaard (Nurse), Paul Ford (Henry Fowler), Ralph Bunker (Dr. Hoffman), Curt Conway (Nick), Kermit Kegley (Qualen), George Lynn (Fredericks), Arthur O'Connell (Shaeffer), Jean Adair (Little Old Lady), Nicholas Joy (McCormick), Virginia Mullen (Martha), Beverly Bayne (Mrs. Stoneman), Celia Adler (Proprietor), Grace Coppin (Miss Livingston), Robert Harris (Druggist), James Gregory (Hicks), Edwin Jerome (Publisher), Amelia Romano (Shop Girl), Anthony Rivers (Ed Garzah), Bernard Hoffman (Wrestler), Elliott Sullivan

Garzah (Ted de Corsia) in The Naked City.

THE NAKED KISS

(Trainer), Charles P. Thompson (Ticket Taker), G. Pat Collins (Freed), John Marley (Managing Editor), Russ Conway (Ambulance Doctor), Joe Kerr (Ned Harvey), William Cottrell (Bisbee), Mervin Williams (Clerk), John Randolf (Policeman), Cavada Humphrey (Mother), Stevie Harris (Halloran's Son), Al Kelley (Newsboy), Johnny Dale (Mr. Stillman), Judson Laire (Publisher), Ray Greenleaf (City Editor), Joyce Allen (Shop Girl), Sarah Cunningham (Nurse), Ralph Simone (Old Gentleman), Pearl Gaines (Maid), Alexander Campbell (Policeman), Harris Brown (Janitor), Carl Milletaire (Young Man), Kathleen Freeman (Stout Girl), Lee Shumway (Patrolman), Perc Launders (Police Photographer), Earle Gilbert (Banker), Victor Zimmerman, David Kermen, George Sherwood (Patrolmen), Andre D. Foster (Jeweler), Blanche Obronska (Mother), William Green (Man), Marion Leeds (Nurse), Joseph Karney (Wrestler), Janie Leslie Alexander (Little Girl), Richard W. Shankland (Blind Man), Retta Coleman (Crippled Girl), Mildred Stronger, Carole Selvester, Clifford Sales, Maureen Latorella, Charles Latorella, Denise Doyle, Margaret McAndrew, Marsha McClelland, Bobbie Gusehoff, John Joseph Mulligan, Reggie Jouvain, Judith Suzanne Locker, Norma Jane Marlowe, Diana Pat Marlowe (Children), Harold Crane (Man).

Location: Stillman's Gym, Roxy Theater, Whitehall Building, the City Morgue, Roosevelt Hospital, Universal Building , and Williamsburg Bridge, in New York, New York
Released: Universal-International, March 4, 1948
Running Time: 96 minutes

The seemingly unexplained murder of a beautiful young woman sets off a police investigation headed by veteran detective Dan Muldoon. Working with a younger and uninspired assistant, Jimmy Halloran, the two detectives begin by tracing down a number of unsubstantial leads. The investigators eventually narrow the search down to two suspects: one, Frank Niles, is the pampered son of a wealthy family who is filled with a passion for high living; the other, Garzah, serves as the strong arm of the pair and is an aberrant muscle boy. Satisfied that Niles and Garzah are responsible for killing the young woman, the police begin to close in. Niles is taken without much difficulty, but Garzah panics and takes off on a frantic race for freedom through the slums and tenement section of New York City. Finally cornered on the girders of the Brooklyn Bridge, the murderer is gunned down by the police below.

Existing as a sort of amalgamation of producer Mark Hellinger's familiar urban landscape, *The Naked City* remains a prime example of Hollywood's assimilation of documentary style film making. There is not much to associate *The Naked City* and film noir. Rather, functioning as a *film policier*, *The Naked City* moves on the periphery of the noir sensibilities. Using on-location photography, which won William Daniels an Academy Award, *The Naked City* tells the story of a typical police investigation embellished

by the antielitism of Albert Maltz's screenplay and the crisp assurance of Jules Dassin's direction. The real star of the film becomes the city, which can take on a variety of personalities. It is truly a mysterious entity imbued with all sorts of stories and affectations. *The Naked City* is unlike most of Dassin's other films, as it is a vision of the world that forsakes subtlety and deals almost exclusively with black and white absolute truths. There is a thematic elegance to Dassin's other noir films such as *Brute Force, Night and the City,* and *Thieves Highway,* that is absent in *The Naked City.*
—C.M.

THE NAKED KISS (1964)
[Working Title: THE IRON KISS]

Director and Producer: Samuel Fuller (Leom Fromkess-Sam Firks Productions)
Screenplay: Samuel Fuller
Director of Photography: Stanley Cortez
Camera Operator: Frank Dugas
Sound: Alfred J. Overton, Bert Hallberg
Music: Paul Dunlap
Art Director: Eugene Lourie
Set Decoration: Victor Gangelin
Costumes: Einar H. Bourman (Men), Hazel Allensworth (Women)
Makeup: Harry Thomas
Hairstyles: Marie Timme
Production Manager: Herbert G. Luft
Script Supervisor: John Dutton
Assistant Director: Nate Levinson
Film Editor: Jerome Thoms

CAST: Constance Towers (Kelly), Anthony Eisley (Griff), Michael Dante (Grant), Virginia Grey (Candy), Patsy Kelly (Mac), Betty Bronson (Miss Josephine), Marie Devereux (Buff), Karen Conrad (Dusty), Linda Francis (Rembrandt), Barbara Perry (Edna), Walter Mathews (Mike), Betty Robinson (Bunny), Gerald Michenaud (Kip), Christopher Barry (Peanuts), George Spell (Tim), Patty Robinson (Angel Face). **BITS:** Neyle Morrow (Officer Sam), Monte Mansfield (Farlunde), Fletcher Fist (Barney), Gerald Milton (Zookie), Breena Howard (Redhead), Sally Mills (Marshmallow), Edy Williams (Hatrack), Michael Barrere (Teenager), Patricia Gayle (Nurse), Sheila Mintz (Receptionist).
Filming Completed: 1964
Released: Allied Artists, October 28, 1964
Running Time: 92 minutes

A warm-hearted prostitute with a violent temper, Kelly takes a long look in her mirror one morning and decides to become respectable. She gets a job nursing handicapped children in a small town, establishes a wary relationship with Griff, a local cop who knows about her past, and meets

Grant, a wealthy intellectual who regales her with tales of Venice. Gaining self-respect from her highly successful work with the children and from the affection of the townspeople, Kelly tells Grant about her compromised past. To her relief, he "forgives" her and asks her to marry him. Overjoyed, she agrees, although there is something about his kiss that disturbs her. Just before they are to be married, she witnesses him in the act of molesting a little girl. When he tells her that they belong together because of their mutual "perversions," she kills him. The whole town turns against her, not believing that a respected citizen like Grant could actually be a pervert. But she convinces Griff to help her find the little girl who ran out of Grant's house as Kelly confronted him. The child is found, tells the truth, and Kelly is acclaimed as a heroine by the town; but she is so disgusted by this experience that she leaves the community.

Samuel Fuller could be described as a primitive talent never introduced to the restraint of polite society. *The Naked Kiss* is, above all, an impolite film, lingering over the uncomfortable subjects of prostitution, perversion, and physical handicaps. From its opening sequence of Kelly's brutal battle with her pimp, during which her wig is snatched off and her shaved head is revealed, *The Naked Kiss* presents a series of increasingly bizarre images: Kelly, dressed garishly and with a suitcase at her side, sits primly on a bench in a small town square; children with withered limbs and sunken eyes are incongruously clad in pirate hats; Kelly stuffs money down the throat of a madam who attempts to lure a young nurse into her shady business; a child skips blithely from the room where she has narrowly escaped the "attentions" of a pervert; and Kelly bludgeons her lover to death with a telephone receiver. This is a nightmarish vision; but it is Fuller's reality, unflinchingly captured by Stanley Cortez's hard, sharply delineated black-and-white photography.

That such a bizarre vision of the world proves convincing is due largely to Constance Towers's performance as Kelly. Tough, cynical, and violent, she fulfills the role of the traditionally male film noir protagonist better than many men could; and, like them, she follows a certain code of honor. Her violence, while excessive, is never without motive. It stems from a sense of moral outrage against the pimp who cheats her, the whore who would corrupt innocence, and the lover whose cultured veneer deceives her and hides his unnatural lusts.

If Kelly's presence is anarchic, it is because Fuller considers anarchy a healthy antidote to the strictures of modern society. The handicapped children, sunk in hopelessness prior to Kelly's arrival, are briefly liberated by the workings of her unbridled imagination. Herself a misfit, Kelly appeals to the little band of outsiders by releasing the wilder aspects of their natures, which have been stifled by the reality of their handicaps and by a constrained society that prefers to ignore them. Kelly arrays the children in pirate hats and encourages the outlaw in them, telling them that if they pretend hard enough, they will be free. Through cinematic fantasy, one of the most pathetic of the children actually runs, leaps, and gambols in joyful abandon.

Like the other moment of pure fantasy in the film, in which Kelly and Grant float together in a Venetian gondola while enveloped in a fog of dreams, this happy vision cannot be sustained. Reality prevails in *The Naked Kiss*. The children can run and play only in their newly freed imaginations; Kelly can only dream of romantic love; and the "bluebird of happiness," which the children sing about in the haunting little melody taught them by Kelly, is forever out of reach.

—J.K.

THE NARROW MARGIN (1952)
[Working Title: THE TARGET]

Director: Richard Fleischer
Producer: Stanley Rubin (RKO)
Screenplay: Earl Fenton; from the unpublished story by Martin Goldsmith and Jack Leonard
Director of Photography: George E. Diskant
Sound: Clem Portman, Francis Sarver
Art Directors: Albert S. D'Agostino, Jack Okey
Set Decoration: Darrell Silvera, William Stevens
Film Editor: Robert Swink

CAST: Charles McGraw (Walter Brown), Marie Windsor (Mrs. Neil), Jacqueline White (Ann Sinclair), Gordon Gebert (Tommy Sinclair), Queenie Leonard (Mrs. Troll), David Clarke (Kemp), Peter Virgo (Densel), Don Beddoe (Gus Forbes), Paul Maxey (Jennings), Harry Harvey (Train Conductor) **BITS:** Mike Lally (Taxi Driver), Don Dillaway, George Sawaya (Reporters), Tony Merrill (Officer Allen), Howart Mitchell (Train Conductor), Milton Kibbee (Tenant), Don Haggerty (Detective Wilson), Johnny Lee, Ivan H. Browning, Clarence Hargrave, Edgar Murray (Waiters), Napoleon Whiting, Bobbie Johnson (Redcaps), Will Lee (Newsstand Owner), Franklin Parker (Telegraph Attendant), Jasper Weldon (Porter).
Filming Completed: December 20, 1951
Released: RKO, May 4, 1952
Running Time: 71 minutes

[NOTE: In 1949, Lou Breslow completed a screenplay entitled *Narrow Margin,* to be produced by Milton Sperling at United States Productions and be released by Warner Brothers.]

Detective Walter Brown and his partner, Gus Forbes, are assigned to escort Mrs. Neil, a racketeer's widow, by train to appear as a witness against organized crime. Forbes is immediately killed by gangsters; and, although Brown must protect a woman of dubious character so that she will live to give testimony, he feels nothing but contempt for her, believing that his partner's life was of greater value. During the train journey, Brown befriends the refined Ann Sinclair, who is traveling with her son. The gangsters attempt to bribe and intimidate Brown without success, so they kill Mrs. Neil, who was a policewoman posing as the witness in order to protect the real gangster's widow, Ann Sinclair. Brown is shamed by the death of an associate whom he had too readily judged on the basis of her appearance and manner. He learns that the reason he was not informed of Mrs. Neil's true identity was that his superiors were not confident that he would not succumb to bribery. The authentic Mrs. Neil arrives safely at her destination, protected by the chastened, honest cop.

A film of considerable reputation, *The Narrow Margin* is actually modest, unaffected, and direct but not particularly powerful in its noir statement. The film benefits from the surprises in its story and the good roles afforded to Windsor and McGraw. It is probable that its excellent use of the confined space in the train is the distinguishing quality for which it is critically valued; but other films have made better use of trains, although not always for so much of their length: notably certain works of Hitchcock as well as *The Tall Target, La Bête Humaine, Human Desire,* and *The Manchurian Candidate.* Cinematographer George Diskant, remembered for his films with Nicholas Ray, achieves fine effects in the glistening corridors. Richard Fleischer's direction is sometimes imaginative and supple, more so than in certain of his later, more expansive films. Although the final impression of *The Narrow Margin* might not qualify it as a minor classic, it is possible to respect an honest work in which the moral stature of the characters is relative and that reflects the noir view of an unstable and deceiving surface reality.

—B.L.

NEW YORK CONFIDENTIAL (1955)

Director: Russell Rouse
Producer: Clarence Greene (Greene-Rouse, an Edward Small Presentation)
Screenplay: Clarence Greene and Russell Rouse; suggested by the book by Jack Lait and Lee Mortimer
Director of Photography: Edward Fitzgerald
Special Effects: Willis Cook
Sound: John Kean, Roger Heman
Sound Effects Editor: Henry Adams
Music: Joseph Mullendore
Music Editor: Robert Tracey
Orchestration: Walter Sheets
Production Designer: Fernando Carrere
Set Decoration: Joseph W. Holland
Costumes: Ernest Newman, Norman Martien
Makeup: Harry Thomas
Hairstyles: Carla Hadley
Production Supervisor: Maurie M. Suess
Producer's Assistant: Winston Jones

Assistant Director: James W. Lane
Film Editor: Grant Whytock

CAST: Broderick Crawford (Charlie Lupo), Richard Conte (Nick Magellan), Marilyn Maxwell (Iris Palmer), Anne Bancroft (Kathy Lupo), J. Carrol Naish (Ben Dagajanian), Onslow Stevens (Johnny Achilles), Barry Kelley (Frawley), Mike Mazurki (Arnie Wendler), Celia Lovsky (Mama Lupo), Herbert Heyes (James Marshall), Steven Geray (Morris Franklin). **BITS:** Bill Phillips (Whitey), Henry Kulky (Gino), Nestor Paiva (Martinelli), Joe Vitale (Batista), Carl Milletaire (Sumak), William Forrest (Paul Williamson), Ian Keith (Waluska), Charles Evans (Judge Kincaid), Mickey Simpson (Hartmann), Tom Powers (District Attorney Rossi), Lee Trent (Ferrari), Lennie Bremen (Larry), John Doucette (Shorty), Frank Ferguson (Dr. Ludlow), Hope Landon (Mrs. Wesley), Fortunio Bonanova (Señor).
Filming Completed: 1954
Released: Warner Brothers, February 18, 1955
Running Time: 87 minutes

The New York syndicate is headed by Charlie Lupo, one of a handful of men who control a nationwide crime cartel, which is run like a large corporation. At one of the board meetings it is decided to liquidate one of the minions who made an unauthorized "hit," so Lupo arranges for Chicago chief Johnny Achilles to send out Nick Magellan. He completes his assignment masterfully, and Lupo borrows Nick from Achilles to act as his bodyguard. Lupo is a widower and has a daughter, Kathy, who hates his gangland involvement and would like to leave home. She is attracted to Nick, but he is wary of any relationship with her. The syndicate's plans for a petroleum-shipping contract with foreign nations under federal subsidy go awry when the lobbyist who is to arrange for this sells out the syndicate. At another meeting of the board, the gangsters decide to kill the lobbyist despite Lupo's protest. New York is the target area and Lupo must make the arrangements. Three men kill the lobbyist but they leave clues, and Lupo dispatches Nick to get rid of them. He eliminates two, but the third, Arnie, escapes and turns to the police. Lupo decides to hide but the syndicate chieftains vote that he must take the rap to protect the organization. Meanwhile Kathy Lupo gets drunk and kills herself in an auto accident. Lupo decides to disclose syndicate secrets to the police, but first the syndicate instructs Nick, now Lupo's closest friend, to kill him. Although he would prefer not to, Nick obeys orders and, welcomed by a smiling Lupo, eliminates both Lupo and his mistress, Iris. Nick is eliminated by another of the syndicate murderers, thus ensuring the continuance of the system.

New York Confidential is as good as most of the exposé thrillers of the 1950s, although the best remains *The Enforcer.* Based on the supposedly "confidential" series of exposés by Jack Lait and Lee Mortimer, which popularized the term "crime syndicate," *New York Confidential* exploited the American fear of a deadly underground, typified by the

Mafia, which was spawned by the Kefauver Committee's investigation into organized crime. The narrative entanglement of the characters and the series of double crosses coordinated by the criminal corporate structure anticipates the nihilism of many gangster melodramas of the 1960s. Conte as Nick Magellan gives the character both a moral ambivalence based on his earlier roles and a fatalism that anticipates his own destruction with almost existential stoicism.

—B.P. & A.S.

NIAGARA (1953)

Director: Henry Hathaway
Producer: Charles Brackett (20th Century-Fox)
Screenplay: Charles Brackett, Walter Reisch, and Richard Breen
Director of Photography: Joe MacDonald [Technicolor]
Special Photographic Effects: Ray Kellogg
Color Consultant: Leonard Doss
Sound: W. D. Flick, Roger Heman
Music: Sol Kaplan
Song: "Kiss" by Lionel Newman and Haven Gillespie; sung by Marilyn Monroe
Music Director: Lionel Newman
Orchestration: Edward Powell
Art Directors: Lyle Wheeler, Maurice Ransford
Set Decoration: Stuart Reiss
Costumes: Dorothy Jeakins
Wardrobe Director: Charles LeMaire
Makeup: Ben Nye
Assistant Director: Gerd Oswald
Film Editor: Barbara McLean

CAST: Marilyn Monroe (Rose Loomis), Joseph Cotten (George Loomis), Jean Peters (Polly Cutler), Casey Adams (Ray Cutler), Dennis O'Dea (Inspector Sharkey), Richard Allan (Patrick), Don Wilson (Mr. Kettering), Lurene Tuttle (Mrs. Kettering), Russell Collins (Mr. Qua), Will Wright (Boatman). BITS: Lester Matthews (Doctor), Carleton Young (Policeman), Sean McClory (Sam), Minerva Urecal (Landlady), Nina Varela (Wife), Tom Reynolds (Husband), Winifield Hoeny (Straw Boss), Neil Fitzgerald (Customs Officer), Norman McKay (Morris), Gene Wesson (Guide), George Ives (Carillon Tower Guide), Patrick O'Moore (Detective), Arch Johnson, Harry Carey, Jr. (Taxi Drivers), Henry Beckman, Willard Sage (Motorcycle Cops), Bill Foster, Robert Ellis (Young Men), Gloria Gordon (Dancer).
Location: Niagara Falls, Canada and the United States
Filming Completed: July 24, 1952
Released: 20th Century-Fox, January 21, 1953
Running Time: 92 minutes

Arriving in Niagara Falls on a belated honeymoon, Polly and Ray Cutler encounter Rose and George Loomis, a newly married couple in the motel room next door. They seem oddly matched; Rose openly flaunts her sexuality while explaining that George, her much older husband, has recently been released from a veterans mental hospital. Sightseeing, Polly witnesses Rose kissing a younger man, Patrick, by the falls. The illicit couple are planning to murder George and make it appear that he committed suicide. When George is reported missing, Rose is called to the morgue and discovers that Patrick is dead. Not revealing the man's true identity, she faints and is taken to the hospital. Later, Polly sees George, but Ray convinces her that she is mistaken. Fearing George's vengeance, Rose leaves the hospital but is pursued by her husband and strangled. When George tries to escape from the Ontario police by stealing a motorboat, Polly is inadvertently aboard. The boat runs out of gas and is caught by the water flowing toward the falls. George pushes Polly off on a ledge as the boat is slowed temporarily by a rock, but he is unable to save himself and is hurled over the falls to his death on the rocks below. Polly is rescued by a helicopter and reunited with Ray.

On the surface *Niagara* may seem less a film noir than a melodramatic showcase designed by 20th Century-Fox to exploit its contract star, Marilyn Monroe, after establishing her through small roles in *The Asphalt Jungle* and *Clash by Night.* Despite her beginnings in such films, Marilyn Monroe was not to become a conventional film noir actress such as Gloria Grahame, Jane Greer, or even Joan Bennett. Although the sexual domination of Rose over George Loomis may be roughly analogous in character terms to the part played by Joan Bennett in *Scarlet Street,* there is no invocation in Monroe's performance of the stereotypical *femme fatale,* at once scornful and seductive. Clearly, Rose Loomis is treated initially in *Niagara* as little more than a sexual object; her tight dresses and adolescent mannerisms are meant to titillate the viewer as much as George Loomis. But *Niagara* does not treat Rose's sexuality and its potential destructiveness in the usual manner of film noir. To begin with, the abnormality of Rose's relationship to her much older husband is contrasted and underscored by the presence of the Cutlers. That their marriage has other aspects than the purely sexual is made clear in their introduction at a customs station: while they explain that they are visiting Canada on a honeymoon delayed for practical reasons, the agent checking the luggage is amused by his discovery of books in the husband's suitcase. Although Ray Cutler is not so taken up with reading that he fails to notice Rose's appearance, Polly seems to typify conventional mores. That both are basically conventional in their attitudes is clear from their reaction to an encounter with Rose and George after the latter couple have obviously just enjoyed a sexual interlude. Ray is somewhat taken aback to find the normally jittery and suspicious George suddenly calm, witty, and terribly pleased with himself; and Polly's sense of sexual intimidation is directly expressed when she replies to Ray's suggestion that she might try wearing a dress like Rose's: "You have to start laying your plans at thirteen for a dress like that."

Nonetheless, Polly is fascinated by the very existence of Rose and George as a couple; and her perceptions become a meaningful filter both for the viewer and for the film's underlying noir vision. The core of that latter conception is George Loomis. Although he is temporally removed from the disturbed veterans of earlier film noir, George is as insecure and unable to readjust to society after nearly a decade as they were when newly returned from the war. Like the viewer, George's interest in Rose must initially be as an object; but she becomes in his disturbed psyche an emblem of the youth he lost to the aftereffects of war. Therefore, his paranoia over the possibility of her sexual betrayal is as much a fear for the loss of his delicate mental balance as it is over her faithlessness. Ultimately, all the literal and metaphoric sexuality of *Niagara*—even such oversized examples as the bell tower where George strangles Rose to the orgasmic accompaniment of the bells on the sound track—does prove destructive. In that sense, *Niagara* recruits the icon of the falls themselves—the sexual symbolism of which has been appreciated by thousands of actual honeymooners who preceded George and Rose— for its final statement on sex and destruction. It is at the foot of the falls that a high-angle long shot reveals Rose's body floating in a now incongruous bright red dress; and it is over the falls that George follows her to his own death.

—A.S. & M.B.

THE NICKEL RIDE (1975)

Director and Producer: Robert Mulligan
Executive Producer: David Foster, Lawrence Turman (Boardwalk Productions)
Screenplay: Eric Roth
Director of Photography: Jordan Cronenweth [DeLuxe Color]
Sound: Don Bassman, Gene Catamessa
Music: Dave Grusin
Art Director: Larry Paull
Set Decoration: Jack Stevens
Assistant Director: Daniel J. McCauley
Film Editor: O. Nicholas Brown

CAST: Jason Miller (Cooper), Linda Haynes (Sarah), Victor French (Paddie), John Hillerman (Carl), Bo Hopkins (Turner), Richard Evans (Bobby), Brendan Burns (Larry), Lou Frizzell (Paulie), Jeanne Lange (Jeannie), Bart Burns (Elias), Harvey Gold (Chester), Mark Gordon (Tonozzi).
Location: Los Angeles, California
Filming Completed: Spring 1974
Released: 20th Century-Fox, November 15, 1975

Running Time: 114 minutes
MPAA Rating: PG

Cooper is a low-level syndicate crime boss who is on his way out. The new lawyers and money men who run the organization no longer approve of his neighborhood "Godfather" style of operation. Cooper is trying hard to close a deal for an abandoned warehouse where the mob can cache stolen goods. His superiors are irritated at his inability to conclude this business, so they assign a new and obnoxious henchman, Turner, to keep an eye on Cooper. Meanwhile, Cooper's assistant, Bobby, roughs up an uncooperative prize fighter and kills the fighter's manager without Cooper's permission or knowledge. When Cooper learns of the murder he disciplines Bobby—and is immediately reprimanded by his superiors. Cooper takes the criticism badly and suspects that the seemingly simple, cowboy-type Turner is slated to be his assassin. Taking his girl friend, Sarah, to the country for the weekend, where he is supposed to make the final contacts for closing the warehouse deal, Cooper is snubbed and the whole arrangement falls through. Paranoid, Cooper has terrifying fantasies of being followed by Turner who shoots Sarah. Fearing a real showdown, Cooper sends Sarah to Las Vegas and promises to follow her next day. He confronts his superior in the organization with his belief that a murder contract has been taken out on him, but the man denies this and makes a date to meet with Cooper later. While Cooper is dressing that evening, Turner walks in and shoots him. The men struggle and Cooper eventually strangles the assassin; but his gunshot wound is serious. The next morning, Cooper's body is found sitting on a bench and his huge ring of keys falls from his hand to the pavement.

The Nickel Ride is a gritty portrait of a man who is no longer a winner, who has grown too old, and whose style and self-image are no longer in tune with the "corporation." The exact reason for his downfall is unimportant and unclear. But his neighborhood still respects and supports him; and there is a vague implication that Cooper's current lack of success in closing deals is really due to bad publicity started by his own superiors, as one contact even mentions to him that he has heard "Coop" is on his way out. This murky origin of Cooper's troubles, his bewilderment and growing paranoia because he knows how "these things" can be arranged, identify Cooper as a noir protagonist. Jason Miller's portrayal of the neighborhood boss is interesting for the brooding power he brings to the role. Cooper is a character who has always been able to hold things together by the main force of his personality; Miller plays him as a strong man who is perceptive enough to sense changes but impotent to stop his fate.

The color photography in the city sequences is grainy and nearly colorless. It convey's Cooper's neighborhood as a small and inconsequential part of a large city. It is obvious that the territory was never a prime location and, like him, it has grown old without prospering.

The fantasy sequences of paranoia and violence are adroitly handled and well-integrated into the film. They appear to be actual plot developments until they are over; so that the viewer coexperiences the same shaken relief and yet continuing terror of a man who is losing his grip on his destiny.

—E.M.

NIGHT AND THE CITY (1950)

Director: Jules Dassin
Producer: Samuel G. Engel (20th Century-Fox)
Screenplay: Jo Eisinger; from the novel by Gerald Kersh
Director of Photography: Max Greene
Sound: Peter Handford, Roger Heman
Music: Franz Waxman
Orchestration: Edward Powell
Art Director: C. P. Norman
Costumes: Oleg Cassini for Gene Tierney, Margaret Furse for Googie Withers
Assistant Directors: George Mills, Percy Hermes
Film Editors: Nick De Maggio, Sidney Stone

CAST: Richard Widmark (Harry Fabian), Gene Tierney (Mary Bristol), Googie Withers (Helen Nosseross), Hugh Marlowe (Adam Dunn), Francis L. Sullivan (Phil Nosseross), Herbert Lom (Kristo), Stanislaus Zbyszko (Gregorius), Mike Mazurki (Strangler), Charles Farrell (Beer), Ada Reeve (Molly), Ken Richmond (Nikolas).
BITS: Elliot Makeham (Pinkney), Betty Shale (Mrs. Pinkney), Russell Westwood (Yosh), James Hayter (Figler), Tomy Simpson (Cozen), Maureen Delaney (Anna Siberia), Thomas Gallagher (Bagrag).
Location: Silver Fox Café, St. Martin's Lane, London, England.
Filming Completed: October 11, 1949
Released: 20th Century-Fox, June 9, 1950
Running Time: 95 minutes

Harry Fabian is a tout for Phil Nosseross's London clip joint, luring gullible tourists in with the suggestion of illicit entertainments. He has aspirations of making a mark as a promoter, despite the urgings of his girl friend, Mary Bristol, a singer at Nosseross's club, that he get an ordinary job. While looking for marks in one of the wrestling auditoriums controlled by a sports promoter named Kristo, Fabian overhears a conversation between Kristo's father, Gregorius, and his protegé, Nicolas, and witnesses Gregorius's disgusted departure from what he considers a degrading display. Before Kristo's men come to evict him, Fabian learns that Gregorius is a legendary figure in Greco-Roman wrestling. Outside, by feigning aesthetic outrage, Fabian quickly cons Gregorius into believing that he can promote Greco-Roman bouts to compete with Kristo's exhibitions. Kristo, knowing that his father has been taken

in, tells Fabian he will be allowed to stage Greco-Roman contests but only those. Despite his confidence that he has found a safe entry into the lucrative field that Kristo monopolizes by force, Fabian cannot convince Nosseross to loan him money to begin operation. Nosseross's wife, however, offers to make Fabian a partner, if he will bribe officials to get her a nightclub license. Fabian buys her a forged license and then uses her money to get matching funds from Nosseross. The latter suspects Fabian of having an affair with his wife and is infuriated when she leaves him; he goes to Kristo and offers to help entrap Fabian.

Nosseross tells Fabian that he will withdraw his backing unless an attraction such as the Strangler, a thug particularly despised by Gregorius, is secured. Desperately, Fabian goads the Strangler into coming to the gym and challenging Nicolas. Gregorius agrees to permit Nicolas to fight the Strangler, but while Fabian prepares a contract, the drunken wrestler and Gregorius exchange taunts that lead to a combat in earnest. The older Gregorius wins, but the exertion causes a stroke. Kristo arrives just before he dies; and Fabian flees in terror. Kristo mobilizes the London underworld to find Fabian by offering a large reward. After dodging Kristo's men all night Fabian is found on a barge at daybreak by Mary. Convinced that he will never escape and wanting to repay money he had taken from her, Fabian runs out crying to Kristo that Mary has betrayed him. He is killed by the Strangler, and his body thrown in the Thames.

In its opening scenes *Night and the City* recruits the formal conventions of film noir to convey an unmistakable presentiment of fatality. Harry Fabian, the "hero," returns home pursued, anxious, physically out of breath. The *mise-en-scène* reveals him moving diagonally past dark buildings and stumbling down alleyways, and reduces him to a black outline, constricted and redirected by an impersonal cityscape. The wedges of light glistening off the walls and gutters, the angularity and tension of the framing, supported by the insistent, frenetic chords of Franz Waxman's score, stalk him until he reaches an apartment house. There a long shadow spreads out and stops at the foot of the stairs, as does Fabian, exhausted and leaning against an interior wall. At that moment and, metaphorically, for the remainder of the film, Fabian is caught halfway, transfixed between top and bottom trying to catch his breath.

Stylistically, the beginning of *Night and the City* is depersonalized. The urban setting—reinforced by the third-person narration that dispassionately announces: "This is London"—is not photographed in a naturalistic manner; but the viewpoint that affects and distorts the images is not Fabian's. Rather, the connotations are of the exterior, deterministic forces of the noir universe. Other elements of visual usage are keyed to characters and relationships. The extensive use of top-light and side-light, even at the moment of Fabian's triumph, cast shadows under his eyes to suggest fatigue—accentuated by Widmark's gaunt features—or obscure half his face to underscore his indecisiveness. Nosseross, Fabian's corpulent employer is photographed with a wide-angle lens that artificially enhances his bulk. Another wide-angle lens, as Fabian challenges the Strangler, not only links the characters within the depth of a single frame—anticipating the transference in which Harry, not the Strangler, will be blamed by Kristo for his father's death—but also distorts Fabian's features grotesquely to match his behavior. Ultimately, both exterior and interior connotations may be present in a single sequence. For instance, when Nosseross reveals his treachery to Fabian, as he jeeringly tells him, "You're a dead man, Harry Fabian, a dead man," his large figure constricts Fabian's in the two-shot that encloses them both. At the same time, textured, bar-shaped shadows all about the room externalize the tangled web in which Fabian has enmeshed himself; and mirrored reflections from the rotating ballroom globe flash by at increasing speed, as if foreshadowing the blur of street lights that will streak past in the background of Fabian's flight.

For all its visual diversity, *Night and the City* is an extremely concentrated work. If Harry Fabian's frantic greed is endemic of a certain type of figure, then his prolonged and ultimately futile run across the typically noir landscape of foggy streets, derelict buildings, construction sites, and wharves is an easily read metaphor for the world's antipathy to his plight and his ordinariness. In his overriding need to be someone, Fabian overlooks the needs of others, of whom Gregorius is the fatal example. The long take of Harry and the old blackmarketeer, Anna, on her barge is a summation of Harry's meaningless life. Within the tension and enclosure of the shot, Harry sits with his back to her speaking of "How close I came" and "The things I did." There is no real exchange between them—he does not even look at her; she is just an audience for his lament. Footsteps, which he does not know to be Mary's, bring Fabian to his feet. This ruptures the shot and leads to a final side-lit close-up. Mary's presence breaks his indecision and inspires his one selfless gesture. It is, of course, not nearly enough to alter the course of his destruction predestined from the opening frame.

—A.S.

NIGHT EDITOR (1946)

Director: Henry Levin
Producer: Ted Richmond (Columbia)
Screenplay: Hal Smith; from the radio program "Night Editor" by Hal Burdick and the short story "Inside Story" by Scott Littleton
Directors of Photography: Burnett Guffey, Philip Tannura
Sound: Lambert Day
Music: Mischa Bakaleinikoff
Art Director: Robert Peterson
Set Decoration: James Crowe
Assistant Director: Ivan Volkman
Film Editor: Richard Fantl

CAST: William Gargan (Tony Cochrane), Janis Carter (Jill Merrill), Jeff Donnell (Martha Cochrane), Coulter Irwin (Johnny), Charles D. Brown (Crane Stewart), Paul E. Burns (Ole Strom), Harry Shannon (Capt. Lawrence), Frank Wilcox (Douglas Loring), Robert Stevens (Doc Cochrane), Roy Gordon (Benjamin Merrill), Michael Chapin (Doc, as a Boy), Robert Emmett Keane (Max), Anthony Caruso (Tusco), Edward Keane (Chief of Police Barnes), Jack Davis (District Attorney Halloran), Lou Lubin (Necktie), Charles Marsh (Swanson). **BITS:** John Tyrell (Street Sweeper Driver), Jimmy Lloyd (Clerk), Murray Leonard (Proprietor), Douglas Wood (Bank Manager), Ronnie Ralph (Small Boy), William Kahn, Joseph Palma (Newsboys), Emmett Vogan (Coroner), Johnny Calkins (Boy), Donald Kerr (Reporter), Betty Hill (Elaine), Frank Dae (Butler), Herman Marks, Frank McLure, Cy Malis (Men), Harry Tyler (Bartender), Charles Wagenheim (Phillips), Jack Frack (Reporter), Wally Rose (Photographer), Ed Chandler (Dickstein), Vernon Dent (Fat Man).
Filming Completed: January 12, 1946
Released: Columbia, March 29, 1946
Running Time: 66 minutes

A police detective, Tony Cochrane, is having an affair with Jill Merrill. Their rendezvous is the site of a brutal murder, which they witness in complete silence. Unable to report the killing due to fear of the scandal that might arise, Cochrane resigns himself to silence. Jill is not so inactive. She discovers the killer and attempts to blackmail him while an innocent man is held for the crime. Rejecting Cochrane, Jill enjoys the social power afforded by her blackmail scheme. In a final attempt to allow Jill to come forth with the truth, Cochrane meets her at a lavish party. His pleas fall on deaf ears as Jill grabs an ice pick and stabs the detective in the stomach. She is taken to jail and Tony Cochrane leaves the police force, only to surface as the narrator of this bizarre story.

Night Editor is a definite B product linked to the noir cycle in its depiction of sadistic brutality and violence. As Tony and Jill are kissing in a secluded spot, the murder they witness seems to function as a sexual stimulus for her. She insists on seeing the body that has been battered by repeated blows from a tire iron. There is little pity in the film, which uses every opportunity to describe people as "rotten through and through," or as "something they serve at the Ritz that has been laying out in the sun too long." The cruelty and lack of compassion found in Jill gives her the quality of a traditionally noir *femme fatale,* as she uses sex to get what she wants. *Night Editor* even uses the convention of the doomed or romantic narrator to tell its story. Conceived as a pilot film for a series of movies introduced by a "night editor," the film failed in that respect but succeeds as a perverse example of the affinity between sex and violence in the noir universe.

—C.M.

Jean Courtland (Gail Russell) and John Triton (Edward G. Robinson) in Night Has A Thousand Eyes.

NIGHT HAS A THOUSAND EYES (1948)

Director: John Farrow
Producer: Endre Bohem (Paramount)
Screenplay: Barre Lyndon and Jonathan Latimer; from the novel by Cornell Woolrich
Director of Photography: John F. Seitz
Process Photography: Farciot Edouart
Sound: Hugo Grenzbach, Gene Garvin
Music: Victor Young
Art Directors: Hans Dreier, Franz Bachelin
Set Decoration: Sam Comer, Ray Moyer
Costumes: Edith Head
Makeup: Wally Westmore
Production Manager: Roy Burns
Assistant Director: William H. Coleman
Script Supervisor: Irving Cooper
Editor: Eda Warren

CAST: Edward G. Robinson (John Triton), Gail Russell (Jean Courtland), John Lund (Elliott Carson), Virginia Bruce (Jenny), William Demarest (Lt. Shawn), Richard Webb (Peter Vinson), Jerome Cowan (Whitney Court-land), Onslow Stevenson (Dr. Walters), John Alexander (Mr. Gilman), Roman Bohnen (Melville Weston, Special Prosecutor), Luis Van Rooten (Mr. Myers). **BITS:** Henry Guttman (Butler), Mary Adams (Miss Hendricks), Philip Van Zandt (Chauffeur), Douglas Spencer (Dr. Ramsdell), Jean King (Edna), Dorothy Abbott (Maid), Bob Stephenson (Gowan), William Haade (Bertelli), Stuart Holmes (Scientist), Jean Wong, Minerva Urecal, Anna Tom (Women), Artarne Wong (Waiter), Jane Crowley (Newsstand Woman), Joey Ray (Radio Announcer), Eleanore Vogel (Scrubwoman), Betty Hannon, Renee Randall, Marilyn Gray, Helen Chapman (Secretaries), Jerry James, Len Hendry, Billy Burt, Joey Ray (Policemen), Antonio Filauri, Edward Earle, Weaver Levy (Men), Frank Hagney (Truckman), James Davies (Jailer), Lyle Latell, Jim Drum, Jimmie Dundee, Pat Flaherty (Policemen), Harry Allen (MacDougall), Lester Dorr, Gladys Blake (Mr. and Mrs. Byers), Frances Morris (Mother), Harland Tucker (Husband), Regina Wallace (Mother-in-law), Violet Goulet (Deb's Mother), Marie Thomas (Girl), George Nokes (Newsboy), Philip Van Zandt (Cigar Attendant), Audrey, Raymond, and Russell Saunders, Walter Cook (Tumbling Act), John Sheehan (Doorman),

THE NIGHT HOLDS TERROR

Albert Pollet (Frenchman Toto), Margaret Field (Agnes), Julia Faye, Rae Patterson (Companions), Major Sam Harris (Deb's Father).
Location: Los Angeles, California
Released: Paramount, October 13, 1948
Running Time: 81 minutes

Elliott Carson stops his fiancée Jean Courtland from suicide one starry night. They go to a café and meet with John Triton, who tells them his life story. Triton had a mind-reading act twenty years ago in which he was assisted by Jenny, his fiancée, and Whitney Courtland. During one of his acts, Triton received a true premonition and sent a woman in the audience home to save her small son from burning in a fire. During the next few weeks, Triton received many premonitions, including one of Jenny's death in childbirth. Leaving the act, he lived in a deserted gold mine and communicated with no one for five years. Hearing that Jenny married Whitney Courtland and died giving birth to a baby girl, Triton moves to Los Angeles to be near Courtland, now a wealthy industrialist, and his daughter, Jean. He does not reveal himself to them until he receives a premonition of Courtland's death, and then contacts Jean. Elliott Carson thinks that Triton is a fake; but Jean is convinced of his powers when her father is killed in a plane crash. Jean attempted suicide because Triton had a vision of her lying under the stars, which she took as a portent of her death. Elliott contacts the police, and Triton is taken into custody to investigate possible sabotage of Courtland's plane. When Triton makes a correct prediction concerning a prisoner's suicide, the police let him go to Jean, whom he believes is still in a great deal of danger. Reaching her side just in time to stop her from being killed by one of her father's crooked business associates, Triton rushes to her defense and the police accidentally shoot him. In his pocket they find a note predicting his own death that night.

Supported by an appropriately eerie score composed by Victor Young, *The Night Has a Thousand Eyes* is a psychological thriller with its seer hero poised on the brink of doom. It is precisely the feeling of doom throughout the film that separates it from most mysteries. John Triton is a man with a gift he never asked for; his power to see flashes of future events could be beneficent, but everything he sees is tragic. Death is usually the subject of his vision. Even his seemingly harmless race track predictions or stock market tips add up to death for Whitney Courtland, who became wealthy because of these tips. For Triton, there is no way out. Despite living as a recluse for twenty years, events pointed him toward his inevitable end. Farrow's direction of Lyndon and Latimer's script is entirely realistic. The audience must believe that such things happen in an otherwise normal world. Although reasonable explanations are given by the skeptical police inspector of Triton's predictions, there is never any doubt that Triton is authentic. In a noir sense, man cannot control or rationalize the future. Life is pathetic for the seer, who is helpless and useless despite his efforts to avoid tragedy. Triton's dilemma is epitomized when he tells his best friend's daughter, "I had become a reverse zombie, the world was dead and I was living." *The Night Has a Thousand Eyes* depicts the noir universe at its darkest. The night itself is the enemy, and the stars fatally oversee every misadventure.

—J.C.

THE NIGHT HOLDS TERROR (1955)
[Working Title: TERROR IN THE NIGHT]

Director, Producer, and Screenplay: Andrew Stone (Andrew Stone Productions)
Director of Photography: Fred Jackman, Jr.
Sound: Theron Triplett
Music Score: Lucien Cailliet
Song: "Every Now and Then" by Virginia Stone
Assistant Director: Melville Shyer
Film Editor: Virginia Stone

CAST: Jack Kelly (Gene Courtier), Hildy Parks (Doris Courtier), Vince Edwards (Victor Gosset), John Cassavetes (Robert Batsford), David Cross (Luther Logan), Edward Marr (Capt. Cole), Jack Kruschen (Detective Pope), Joyce McCluskey (Phyllis Harrison), Jonathan Hale (Bob Henderson), Barney Phillips (Stranske), Charles Herbert (Steven), Nancy Dee Zane (Deborah), Joel Marston (Reporter).
Location: Lancaster, California
Filming Completed: December 20, 1954
Released: Columbia, September 14, 1955
Running Time: 85 minutes
[FACTUAL BASIS: The film combines incidents concerning the 1953 Gene Courtier kidnapping case and the 1954 Leonard Moskowitz kidnapping cases.]

Returning to his desert home in Lancaster, Gene Courtier picks up a young hitchhiker, Victor Gosset, who pulls a gun on him and is soon joined by two other criminals: the psychopathic leader of the bunch, Robert Batsford, and the gentler Luther Logan. The three men hold Courtier, his wife Doris, and their two small children hostage. The family spends a terrified night but believes that the nightmare will end in the morning when Courtier sells his car for the cash the men seek. But in the morning, Batsford announces a new plan and holds Courtier for ransom as he has learned that Courtier's father is rich. The F.B.I., in cooperation with the telephone company, attempts to trace the source of the criminals' telephone calls and Courtier attempts to escape several times, almost succeeding when the weak Logan becomes frightened at the immensity of the crime. Finally, the efforts of the phone company and the law, as well as Courtier's own resourcefulness, results in the death of the three kidnappers and Courtier is safely returned to his family.

Based on a true story, *The Night Holds Terror* is one of a series of suspense motion pictures written and directed by Andrew Stone in the 1950s, in which the contribution of his wife, editor Virginia Stone, is of paramount importance. Complex cross-cutting between the activities of the law and the phone company, and the drama of the captives and the criminals, effectively creates tension and gives an impression of unusual density for a film of 85-minute duration. Of even more interest than this display of technique, however, is the more genuine noir vision of this film compared to *The Desperate Hours,* a higher-budgeted and considerably more prestigious production on the same subject. *The Desperate Hours* betrays not only its theatrical source but also the complacency of William Wyler when presented with a middle-class family of the 1950s; and it appears that Wyler's reason for making the film is to indulge his ostentatious but empty predilection for staging scenes in deep focus, especially on staircases as noted in the climactic confrontation. *The Night Holds Terror* also uses deep focus compositions but with more fluidity and less self-consciousness. Stone does not use his terrorized family to confirm the virtues of the middle-class life-style as does Wyler, but as a reflection of the unforeseen perils of the noir underworld. Stone's family is simply terrorized and needs to summon a little more courage and cunning than is their custom to survive the ordeal. Similarly, Wyler's melodramatic heavies are considerably less frightening than the more realistically presented trio of the Stone film. All in all, Stone's cast of newcomers is superior to the seasoned actors of the Wyler cast. John Cassavetes, always effective in pathological roles, is especially subtle and compelling in the Stone film.
—B.L.

NIGHT MOVES (1975)
[Working Title: THE DARK TOWER]

Director: Arthur Penn
Producer: Robert M. Sherman (Warner Brothers)
Associate Producer: Gene Lasko
Screenplay: Alan Sharp
Director of Photography: Bruce Surtees [Technicolor]
Special Effects: Marcel Vercoutere, Joe Day
Sound: Jack Solomon
Rerecording: Richard Voriscek
Music: Michael Small
Production Designer: George Jenkins
Set Decoration: Ned Parsons
Costume Supervisor: Rita Riggs
Makeup: Bob Stein
Hairstyles: Irene Aparicio, Bruce Jossen
Unit Production Manager: Thomas J. Schmidt
Casting: Nessa Hyams
Producer's Assistant: Bonnie Bruckheimer
Script Supervisor: Marshall Schlom

Assistant Director: Jack Roe
Film Editor: Dede Allen

CAST: Gene Hackman (Harry Moseby), Susan Clark (Ellen), Edward Binns (Ziegler), Harris Yulin (Marty Heller), Kenneth Mars (Nick), Janet Ward (Arlene Iverson), James Woods (Quentin), Anthony Costello (Marv Ellman), John Crawford (Tom Iverson), Melanie Griffith (Delly Grastner), Jennifer Warren (Paula). **BITS:** Ben Archibek (Charles), Maxwell Gail, Jr. (Tony), Victor Paul, Louis Elias, Carey Loftin, John Moio (Cops), Susan Barrister, Larry Mitchell (Airline Ticket Clerks), Tim Haldeman (Delivery Boy), Jacque Wallace (Man), Dennis Dugan (Young Man), C. J. Hincks (Girl), Phil Altman, Bob Templeton (Crewmen), Terry Leonard, Fred Waugh, Ron Rondell, Chuck Parkison, Jr., Glen Wilder, Betty Raymond, Dean Englehardt, Chuck Hicks, Ted Grossman, Richard Hackman, Rick Lockwood, Walter Scott, Ernie Orsatti (Stunt and Stunt Doubles), Avril Gentles, Sandra Diane Seacat, Rene Enriquez, Simon Deckard, Michael Ebert (Voices).
Location: Southern California; the Florida Keys
Released: Warner Brothers, July 2, 1975
Running Time: 99 minutes

Harry Moseby is a small-time private detective with an obsession for "finding out" things. He searched for his father for years, only to refuse at the last moment to see or speak to a man he neither knew nor loved. Harry is shattered when he discovers his wife is having an affair. Against this backdrop of his unhappy life, Harry is hired by an aging film star, Arlene, to find her runaway daughter, Delly. The actress only wants the girl back so she can continue to control her daughter's trust fund; and she suggests that a stepfather, Tom Iverson, has lured Delly to Florida. Harry first traces the wild and promiscuous Delly to a film location in the Southwest where she supposedly is living with a stunt pilot; but the girl is gone. Harry finds her at Tom Iverson's fishing cabin in the Florida Keys and Delly refuses to leave. Harry is attracted to Paula, Tom's mistress, and they begin an affair. Delly discovers the sunken, crashed plane of her stuntman lover while swimming and, horrified, agrees to return to her mother. Harry returns to his wife and takes Delly back to her Los Angeles home. The next day Delly is killed while filming a movie stunt. Harry watches the footage repeatedly and is convinced that she was murdered. Returning to Florida, he discovers that Iverson and Paula have committed several murders to cover up their smuggling of pre-Columbian art into the United States. After a fight, a chase, and a plane crash that kills the smugglers, a wounded Harry is left stranded and helpless in a motor boat, which runs in ever-widening circles.

The chief motivation behind the narrative structure of *Night Moves* is Harry Moseby's compulsive "need to know." But whereas this curiosity, combined with emotional detachment, was Philip Marlowe's strength, it is Harry's fatal flaw.

NIGHTFALL

The traditional detective derived his power not just from the ability to track one clue to the next but from the insight that enabled him to see the larger picture, to justify the sordidness of his search by creating meaning out of mystery. In this sense, Harry is impotent. Times have changed since Marlowe and the Continental Op. Harry stands under the light of modern psychologizing; and what was once investigation is now recognized as cheap spying and a vicarious emotional life. Far from giving him power over the people he deals with, his aloofness leaves him weak, abandoned, and lonely. Harry resembles Delly; both suffer the same adolescent dilemma of being smart but not smart enough. The illusion that each can control his or her life, make choices, and impose meaning on other people's choices, obscures the one truth of their universe: that there is no truth and no amassing of evidence will make any difference. Knowledge is no longer power; the final image of the man trapped in a boat that travels in concentric circles around the site of a disaster caps the futility of Harry's life.

—E.M.

NIGHTFALL (1957)

Director: Jacques Tourneur
Producer: Ted Richmond (Copa Productions)
Screenplay: Stirling Silliphant; from the novel by David Goodis
Director of Photography: Burnett Guffey
Sound: Ferol Redd, John Livadary
Music Score: George Duning
Music Conductor: Morris Stoloff
Orchestration: Arthur Morton
Song: "Nightfall," lyric by Sam M. Lewis, and music by Peter DeRose and Charles Harold; sung by Al Hibbler
Art Director: Ross Bellah
Set Decoration: William Kiernan, Louis Diage
Costumes: Jean Louis
Makeup: Clay Campbell
Hairstyles: Helen Hunt
Assistant Director: Irving Moore
Film Editor: William A. Lyon

CAST: Aldo Ray (James Vanning), Brian Keith (John), Anne Bancroft (Marie Gardner), Jocelyn Brando (Laura Fraser), James Gregory (Ben Fraser), Frank Albertson (Dr. Edward Gurston), Rudy Bond (Red), George Cisar (Bus Driver), Eddie McLean (Taxi Driver), Lillian Culver, Maya Van Horn (Women), Orlando Beltran, Maria Belmar (Spanish Couple), Walter Smith (Shoeshine Boy). **BITS:** Monty Ash (Clerk), Art Bucaro (Cashier), Arline Anderson (Hostess), Gene Roth (Bartender), Robert Cherry (Man), Jane Lynn, Betty Koch, Lillian Kassan, Joan Fotre, Pat Jones, Annabelle George (Models), Winifred Waring (Fashion Narrator).
Filming Completed: April 9, 1956

Released: Columbia, January 23, 1957
Running Time: 80 minutes

Fearing he is being followed, Jim Vanning takes refuge in a restaurant where he meets Marie Gardner, who has been stood up by a friend and has no money to pay for her drink. Vanning offers to buy her dinner; but when they leave, he is abducted at gunpoint by two thugs named John and Red. They take him to a deserted oil derrick by the ocean and prepare to torture him for information; but while they are momentarily inattentive, Vanning escapes. Believing she may have betrayed him, Vanning goes to Gardner's apartment. He learns that she is innocent but discovers that a piece of paper with her name and address is missing, probably taken by John and Red. As they flee together, Vanning explains the cause of his dilemma. During a hunting trip in the mountains with a doctor friend, Vanning had considered broaching the subject of sexual advances made to him by the doctor's wife. Before anything was said, the two men witnessed a car accident. Going to aid the occupants, they were taken prisoner by John and Red, who were escaping after a robbery. After killing the doctor and thinking Vanning mortally wounded, the pair continued their flight but mistook the doctor's bag for one containing their loot. Fearing he would be a prime suspect in the doctor's death, the wounded Vanning concealed the bag of money in a snowbank and went into hiding until he recovered. However, pursued by both John and Red and an insurance investigator named Fraser, he has been unable to return for it. Marie agrees to help him retrieve the money, and they leave for Wyoming. When they arrive, they are confronted by Fraser but convince him to join them in their search. Vanning finds the spot; but the bag is gone. Going to a nearby ghost town off the highway, they find John and Red arguing over the money. Red kills his partner, but Vanning grabs his rifle. Red takes cover in the cab of a snowplow and drives towards Fraser and Marie in a small shack, but Vanning pulls him from the cab, and Red falls under the mechanism.

Despite being made near the end of the cycle, the dilemma of *Nightfall*'s protagonist is typically noir. Although he is a victim of several mischances, Vanning's paranoia compounds these problems significantly. Tourneur relegates those causal incidents to a flashback halfway through the film; but he does not allow them to be distorted by Vanning's point-of-view. Rather, they reflect Vanning's struggle to comprehend how such violent but basically simple past occurrences have put him in such a dangerous and complicated present predicament. This usage recalls the narrative structure of *Out of the Past*; it also reveals the unlikely chain of events to the viewer after their visible effects, thereby adding considerable credibility to them as they conspire to afflict Vanning. In fact, when Vanning is first seen skulking in the shadows of a back street, the visual inscription could easily be that of a culpable figure trying to avoid detection. This contrasts markedly with the introduction of Jeff Bailey in *Out of the Past*, who is at work at his service station. Yet it permits the ironies of that earlier film to be extended. Because Vanning is basically innocent of any wrongdoing, whereas Bailey clearly was not, the trap into which he has fallen can only be interpreted as impersonal or deterministic, not retributive. Because Vanning has a socially motivated paranoia—stronger than any of Bailey's apprehensions—of being misjudged and incriminated in the doctor's death, he is unable to restore equilibrium to his life, as Bailey did for a considerable amount of time. His initial belief that Marie—whose ultimate influence on Vanning is as beneficent as Kathie's effect on Bailey was malign—has betrayed him to John and Red is symptomatic of how Vanning's trauma has distorted his outlook.

Vanning is not haunted by a particularly dark or distant past but driven by an unsettled and immediate one; and the most subtle ironies that Tourneur attaches to this situation are visual rather than narrative. Contrary to archetype, for Vanning the black streets promise some measure of safety while the bright snow-covered landscape recalls pain and near death. Low angles and side-light around the oil derrick turn the mechanism into a huge, nightmarish mantis waiting to devour Vanning. In the climactic sequence, the snowplow lumbering after him like a gigantic beast becomes the final metaphor for the larger-than-life terrors that have plagued him.

—A.S.

THE NIGHT RUNNER (1957)

Director: Abner Biberman
Producer: Albert J. Cohen (Universal-International)
Screenplay: Gene Levitt; from the *Cosmopolitan* magazine story by Owen Cameron
Director of Photography: George Robinson
Sound: Leslie I. Carey, Corson Jowett
Music: Joseph Gershenson
Art Directors: Alexander Golitzen, Robert Boyle
Set Decoration: Russell A. Gausman, Ray Jeffers
Assistant Director: George Lollier
Film Editor: Al Joseph

CAST: Ray Danton (Roy Turner), Colleen Miller (Susan Mayes), Willis Bouchey (Loren Mayes), Merry Anders (Amy Hansen), Harry Jackson (Hank Hansen), Eddy C. Waller (Vernon), Robert Anderson (Ed Wallace), Jean Inness (Miss Dodd), Jane Howard (Typist), John Stephenson (Dr. Crawford), Richard Cutting (Man Interviewer), Alexander Campbell (Dr. Royce), Steve Pendleton (Capt. Reynolds), John Pickard (Dr. Fisher), Paul Weber (Dr. Rayburn), Jack Lomas (Real Estate Man), Natalie Masters (Miss Lowell), William Erwin (McDermott), George Barrows (Bus Driver), Ethyl May Halls (Elderly Woman), Sam Flint (Elderly Man), Marshall Bradford (Mailman), Diana Darrin (Waitress), Lola Ken-

drick (Secretary), Dale Van Sickel (Bus Driver), Alex Sharp (Deputy), Jay Berniker (Boy).
Filming Completed: September 5, 1956
Released: Universal, February 1957
Running Time: 79 minutes

Roy Turner is an inmate at a state mental hospital under treatment for schizophrenia. Because of overcrowding at the hospital, Turner is made an outpatient; as he is given his freedom by his psychiatric overseer, he is warned to avoid emotionally charged situations. After taking a bus south, Turner finds a motel and decides to remain there indefinitely because he is attracted to the nearby beach. He is also attracted to Susan Mayes, the daughter of the motel owner. When she reciprocates his interest, her father looks into Turner's past and discovers his history of mental illness. After ridiculing him, Mayes threatens to have Turner recommitted unless he leaves his daughter alone. The sudden stress imbalances Turner, and he kills Mayes. He begins to flee with Susan down the beach and considers killing her and himself. After he pushes her into the sea, the shock restores his equilibrium. He rescues her and then turns himself in to the authorities.

Many of *The Night Runner*'s story elements are curiously reminiscent of Hitchcock's *Psycho,* a film it antedates by three years. In fact, the narrative particulars of a schizophrenic young man coming to a secluded motel and capturing the sympathy of the owner's daughter seem almost a planned inversion of the roles in the later film. What makes *The Night Runner* truly noir, rather than a neo-Gothic or psychological melodrama, is the characterization of the "hero," Roy Turner. While Hitchcock regards his psychopath somewhat sardonically, *The Night Runner*'s portrayal is sympathetic. The very title suggests what the introductory sequences at the mental hospital confirm expositionally: that the main character is acting under the dark compulsion of an aberration for which he is not morally responsible and of which he is only partially aware. Ray Danton's interpretation is lacking in nervous tics, darting eyes, or other clichéd mannerisms and does not alienate the viewer from the character's quasi-normality.

The Night Runner's imagery is equally restrained. Roy Turner's fascination with birds is, unlike Norman Bates's in *Psycho,* based not on their rapacious traits but their freedom to fly wherever they choose. Mainly, the film draws on the contrasting aspects of the rundown motel and the expansive beach nearby to externalize the conflicting side of Roy Turner's psyche, as he attempts to readjust to society. It does contain moments—such as the tracking shot and abrupt subjective tilting when Turner goes mentally "over the brink"—that are visually striking.

This shot, like those of Turner rapturously watching the seabirds or gloomily side-lit in his room, is a sensorily direct and fairly effective moment of stylistic irony. The central irony of *The Night Runner,* however, is thematic and most typically noir: Turner is undone not by his illness but because his semblance of normality leads to the beginnings of a relationship with Susan Mayes and, in turn, to his unwitting murder of her possessive father.

—A.S.

NIGHTMARE (1956)

Director: Maxwell Shane
Producers: William C. Pine, William C. Thomas (Pine-Thomas-Shane)
Screenplay: Maxwell Shane; from the short story by William Irish [Cornell Woolrich]
Director of Photography: Joe Biroc
Sound: Jack Solomon
Music: Herschel Burke Gilbert
Songs: "What's Your Sad Story?" by Dick Sherman; "The Last I Ever Saw of My Heart," lyric by Doris Houck, music by Herschel Burke Gilbert
Vocal and Instrumental Arrangements: Billy May
Art Director: Frank Sylos
Set Decoration: Edward Boyle
Film Editor: George Gittens

CAST: Edward G. Robinson (René Bressard), Kevin McCarthy (Stan Grayson), Connie Russell (Gina), Virginia Christine (Sue), Rhys Williams (Torrence), Gage Clark (Belnap), Barry Atwater (Warner), Marian Carr (Madge), Billy May (Louie Simes).
Location: New Orleans, Louisiana
Filming Completed: December 1955
Released: United Artists, May 11, 1956
Running Time: 89 minutes

New Orleans jazz musician Stan Grayson dreams that he stabs a man to death in a mirrored room and wakes to find scratches, bruises, and other indications that it was not a dream. He relates the incident to his brother-in-law, police detective René Bressard, who assures him it was a dream. The thought that he may be a killer haunts him, as does a strange, exotic tune that runs through his mind. He prowls the jazz bars on Bourbon Street, hoping to find someone who is familiar with the song but with no success. Hoping to cure Stan's melancholia, René invites him to picnic with his sister and girl friend, Gina. A sudden rainstorm forces them into the car, but its windshield wipers are broken and, in an effort to find shelter, Stan directs them to a large, empty mansion, which is the house in his dream. He discovers the strange song was nothing more than a popular tune, played on the record player at a slower speed. Then he and René find the mirrored room. Later, when René is informed by

Stan Grayson (Kevin McCarthy), left, in Nightmare.

the local police that a murder did take place there, he believes Stan tried to dupe him. He takes Stan back to his hotel room, informing him that he should leave town for he will turn him in the next day. When Stan attempts to jump from the building's ledge, René saves him and begins to believe his story. Stan then tells about Mr. Britton, his next door neighbor, who had once insisted that he take one of his cough drops and who, on the night of the murder, came into Stan's room with a lighted candle. René suspects Stan was hypnotized and discovers that the mansion is owned by Mr. Belnap, whose wife was killed in a car accident the evening of the murder. By doctoring a photograph of Belnap, René has Stan identify it as Mr. Britton and decides to set a trap for Belnap. After Mrs. Belnap's funeral, Stan is outfitted with a microphone to record the conversation and he confronts Belnap in the mirrored room with the information that he was never under hypnosis but had only pretended, so that he could blackmail Belnap later. Belnap hypnotizes Stan again, escapes with him through one of the mirrored doors and instructs Stan to walk into the bayou. However, the police arrive quickly and, as they shoot Belnap, René rescues Stan from a watery death.

Nightmare is a remake of Shane's 1947 adaptation of Woolrich's story, entitled *Fear in the Night*. The remake benefits from superior acting, particularly by McCarthy, a bigger budget, an inventive jazz score, and the use of New Orleans locations. The photography in this film, from the opening credits done in wax over McCarthy's eyes illuminated by candle, is markedly more expressionistic and is aptly reinforced by the score. The use of McCarthy's narration, the exotic bayous and strange nocturnal odyssey down Bourbon Street, combine with the mutated version of the jazz piece and contribute to the film's oneiristic tone.

—B.P.

NIGHTMARE ALLEY (1947)

Director: Edmund Goulding
Producer: George Jessel (20th Century-Fox)
Screenplay: Jules Furthman; from the novel by William Lindsay Gresham
Director of Photography: Lee Garmes
Special Photographic Effects: Fred Sersen
Sound: E. Clayton Ward, Roger Heman
Music Score: Cyril Mockridge
Music Director: Lionel Newman
Orchestral Arrangements: Maurice de Packh, Earle Hagen
Art Directors: Lyle Wheeler, J. Russell Spencer
Set Decoration: Thomas Little, Stuart Reiss
Costumes: Bonnie Cashin
Wardrobe Director: Charles LeMaire
Makeup: Ben Nye
Technical Advisers: Jimmy Woods, Mink DeRonda, Ed Mundy

Assistant Director: Gaston Glass
Film Editor: Barbara McLean

CAST: Tyrone Power (Stanton Carlisle), Joan Blondell (Zeena), Colleen Gray (Molly), Helen Walker (Dr. Lilith Ritter), Taylor Holmes (Grindle), Mike Mazurki (Bruno), Ian Keith (Pete), Julia Dean (Mrs. Peabody), James Flavin (Hoatley), Roy Roberts (McGraw), James Burke (Town Marshal). **BITS:** Maurice Navarro (Fire Eater), Leo Gray (Detective), Harry Hays Morgan (Headwaiter), Albin Robeling (Captain), George Beranger (Geek), Marjorie Wood (Mrs. Prescott), Harry Cheshire (Mr. Prescott), Edward Clark (Farmer), Eddy Waller (Old Farmer), Mike Lally (Charlie), George Davis (Waiter), Hollis Jewell (Delivery Boy), Laura Treadwell (Woman), Nina Gilbert (Worried Mother), Bill Free (Man in Spode Room), Henry Hall (Man), Jerry Miley (Friend in Spode Room), Gilbert Wilson (Husband in Spode Room), June Bolyn (Maid in Grindle Room), Gene Stutenroth (Masseur), Charles Flickinger (Bellboy), Florence Auer (Housekeeper), Al Herman (Cab Driver), George Chandler, Oliver Blake, Emmett Lynn, George Lloyd, Jack Raymond (Hoboes), John Wald (Radio Announcer).
Filming Completed: July 31, 1947
Released: 20th Century-Fox, October 9, 1947
Running Time: 110 minutes
[NOTE: The Patterson-Yankee Carnival was rented and rebuilt on 10 acres of the 20th Century-Fox backlot.]

Stanton Carlisle, a small-time carnival operator with the Hoatley and Henny Carnival, obtains the secrets of a fake mind reader and becomes successful in Chicago by setting himself up as a spiritualist. He acquires two partners, Zeena, a sideshow fortune teller, and Dr. Lilith Ritter, a psychologist. His young wife, Molly, reluctantly becomes a part of his act. Just as "The Great Stanton" seems on the verge of riches because of his exploitation of wealthy clients, Molly exposes him during a particularly heinous exhibition where she is supposed to act as a man's dead mistress. Stan's fall is as swift as his success. He is ruined and drifts from one tavern to another, until he must return to the shoddy carnival as a "geek," a freak-show attraction who eats live chickens to earn his living.

Nightmare Alley was adapted by Jules Furthman from the novel by William Lindsay Gresham. Gresham was fascinated by the darker side of the entertainment world; he wrote about carnivals and circuses and ultimately committed suicide. The film is a study of the traveling carnival, which is of the "lower depths" of show business. The film's subject and the exposition of its milieu through Lee Garmes's low-key photography is strongly expressionistic. From the dark, shadowy world of the second-rate carnival to the moneyed, jewelled rooms of bright nightclubs, Stan is a man trapped by his own cunning fate. His fall is hinted early in the film when he reveals his horror and repugnance of the geek, who is the lowest form of carnival life. Tyrone Power, whose more usual screen persona was as a romantic lead and who had encompassed near-sainthood in *The Razor's Edge,* was cast against type as "The Great Stanton," an unmitigated cad who goes too far and hits bottom.

The characterizations in *Nightmare Alley* are studies in film noir. People are shown as venal, gullible, and obsessed with success at any price. Besides Stan's obvious brand of fakery, there is Lilith, his clever psychologist accomplice, who acts with an icy intelligence and suggests a woman of soulless ambition. Additionally, Cyril Mockridge's score eerily underlines the film's evocation of bizarre terror.

—J.C.

99 RIVER STREET (1953)
[Working Title: CROSSTOWN]

Director: Phil Karlson
Producer: Edward Small (World Films, Inc.)
Screenplay: Robert Smith; from an unpublished story by George Zuckerman
Director of Photography: Franz Planer
Sound: Lambert Day
Music: Emil Newman, Arthur Lange
Art Director: Frank Sylos
Assistant Director: Ralph Black
Film Editor: Buddy Small

CAST: John Payne (Ernie Driscoll), Evelyn Keyes (Linda James), Brad Dexter (Victor Rawlins), Frank Faylen (Stan Hogan), Peggie Castle (Pauline Driscoll), Jay Adler (Christopher), Jack Lambert (Mickey), Eddy Waller (Pop Dudkee), Glen Langan (Lloyd Morgan), John Day (Bud), Ian Wolfe (Walde Daggett), Peter Leeds (Nat Finley), William Tannen (Director), Gene Reynolds (Chuck).
Filming Completed: July 12, 1953
Released: United Artists, October 3, 1953
Running Time: 83 minutes

Bitter over an eye injury that halted his career as a professional prizefighter, Ernie Driscoll drives a taxi for a living and becomes increasingly estranged from his wife Pauline, who constantly berates him for his failure to earn as much money as he had previously made by fighting. Ernie is consoled only by his friend Stan, a taxi dispatcher, and by Linda James, an aspiring actress with whom he drinks coffee at a drug store. When Pauline threatens to leave Ernie, Stan suggests that having a child might help his rocky marriage. Ernie takes a box of candy to the shop where Pauline works and when he sees her kissing another man he angrily confronts them before driving off in his car. Pauline is not greatly concerned, and she plans to run off with the man, Victor Rawlins, who has just executed a jewel robbery. Rawlins is unable to fence the jewels with a man named Christopher, who objects to Pauline's involvement. Meanwhile, Linda James asks Ernie for help. She claims to have murdered a man and takes Driscoll to the theater where it happened. Driscoll offers to help her conceal

evidence of the crime but, it is revealed that Linda's problem is a hoax; the producer's idea of an acting test. Ernie is humiliated and strikes the producer. The same night, Rawlins kills Pauline to appease Christopher. Ernie is then sought by the police as the leading murder suspect. The actual murderer forces Christopher to give him the money for the jewels and then prepares to depart the country but is followed by Christopher. Also following the murderer are Ernie and a remorseful Linda. She detains Rawlins in a tavern while Ernie waits for the police to find them. At the last minute, Rawlins escapes. A chase ensues in which Christopher crashes his car and Ernie fights with Rawlins—during which time the fighter relives in his mind the fight that finished his boxing career. Rawlins is finally captured by the police, enabling Ernie and Linda to look forward to a happier life.

A compelling and unusual film, *99 River Street* contains ideas not often found in a film noir. Although the squalid marriage of Ernie and Pauline and the criminal activities of Rawlins and Christopher are standard elements, the script's structure gives weight to contrasts between life and theater, as well as between violence as a spectacle and as private destiny.

In the opening scene, Ernie is severely beaten in the fight ring, and the camera draws back to reveal that he is watching a television film of his last fight and that he has joined the film's audience as a spectator. Later, audience expectations are cheated again in the theater scene when Linda gives her very effective performance in one long claustrophobic take, with the camera holding on Linda as she moves about the stage. The boxing ring is also a kind of theater but the fight contrasts to Linda's performance because it is an honest spectacle rather than a lie. Additionally, violence actually occurred in the fight film while Linda's violence, although backed up by a "corpse," is not real. These ideas are still further developed when Ernie inflicts actual violence—to the producer—on the stage following the revelation of the charade. Additionally, Linda's "act" as a seductress in the tavern with her captive audience is more convincing than her overplayed confession of murder (which was successful only because the naïve Ernie believed it). Finally, Ernie's beating of Rawlins at the finale, a private act of revenge for his wife's murder, is transformed and becomes in Ernie's mind the spectacle in the ring that was witnessed at the opening of the film, a fight he had lost but that he now "wins."

The reality of artifice and the sometimes unreal flow of actual events in a person's life are provocative concepts. One expects to see these concepts explored in films about imaginative characters—dreamers and artists—not in a film dealing with desperate men and women looking for a fast buck, a sordid embrace, and a hard punch to the jaw from a mindless thug. But these ideas work very effectively in a film noir context. For film noir, with its unreal atmosphere and extremes of passion and violence, is itself a style conscious of both mocking life and stylizing it.

—B.L.

Left to right: Pop Gruber (Walter Brennan), Nick Blake (John Garfield), and Al Doyle (George Tobias) in Nobody Lives Forever.

NOBODY LIVES FOREVER (1946)

Director: Jean Negulesco
Producer: Robert Buckner (Warner Brothers)
Screenplay: W. R. Burnett
Director of Photography: Arthur Edeson
Special Effects: William McGann
Sound: Dolph Thomas
Music Score: Adolph Deutsch
Orchestration: Jerome Moross
Art Director: Hugh Reticker
Set Decoration: Casey Roberts
Costumes: Milo Anderson
Dialogue Director: Herschel Daugherty
Assistant Director: Reggie Callow
Film Editor: Rudi Fehr

CAST: John Garfield (Nick Blake), Geraldine Fitzgerald (Gladys Halvorsen), Walter Brennan (Pop Gruber), Faye Emerson (Toni), George Coulouris (Doc Ganson), George Tobias (Al Doyle), Robert Shayne (Chet King), Richard Gaines (Charles Manning), Dick Erdman (Bellboy), James Flavin (Shake Thomas), Ralph Peters (Windy Mather). **BITS:** Allen Ray (Art), Roger Neury (Headwaiter), Jack Chefe (Waiter), Harry Seymour (Master of Ceremonies), Rudy Friml, Jr. (Orchestra Leader), Fred Kelsey (Railroad Conductor), Wallace Scott (Drunk), Albert Von Antwerp (Tough Waiter), Charles Sullivan (Bartender-Waiter), Alex Havier (Telesfero), Paul Power (Hotel Clerk), George Meader (Evans), Virginia Patton (Switchboard Operator), Robert Arthur (Bellhop), Marion Martin (Blond), Cyril Ring (Blond's Escort), William Edmunds (Priest), William Forrest (Mr. Johnson), Grady Sutton (Counterman), Adrian Droeshout (Man at Slot Machine), Joel Friedkin (Storekeeper), Ralph Dunn (Ben), Lee Phelps (Police Officer).

Filming Completed: November 10, 1944
Released: Warner Brothers, November 1, 1946
Running Time: 100 minutes
[NOTE: A Warner Brothers press release originally announced that Humphrey Bogart would star in *Nobody Lives Forever* after completion of *To Have and Have Not.*]

Ex-G.I. and New York gambler, Nick Blake, returns from the service to find that both his girl friend, Toni, and his gambling operation have been taken over. After extorting a substantial payoff for his investment, he and a henchman, Al Doyle, leave for California, where Blake wants only to take a vacation from both war and larceny. A former mentor and con man, Pop Gruber, is enlisted by some broken-down sharpsters led by Doc Ganson to convince Blake to assist them in a scheme that involves Gladys Halvorsen, a lonesome widow with a considerable fortune. Ganson's gang merely want Blake to finance the venture; but, after seeing the "mark," Blake decides to handle the job himself and split the profits with Ganson later. As he puts the plan

211

into operation, Blake finds himself falling for the attractive widow and decides to pull out. When he offers to pay off Ganson with his own money, a recently arrived Toni convinces Ganson that Blake is trying to double-cross him. Ganson and his men kidnap Gladys and hold her for ransom on a deserted pier. Alerted by Pop, Blake rescues her; but in the process Pop and Ganson are killed, each by the other's gun.

Like several other productions released the year after World War II, *Nobody Lives Forever* confronts the question of postwar disorientation through the noir conventions. The protagonist, Nick Blake, is not merely an ex-serviceman but also an ex-gambler, stripped of his status in a manner that must have been familiar to many veterans. Unlike the ordinary G.I., Blake can afford the luxury of a retreat from society to nurse his psychological wounds. Money, however, does not mitigate his dissatisfaction; nor does his hermitage fulfill the need for activity. His encounter with Pop Gruber, a former big-time operator reduced to selling views through a telescope, only sharpens Blake's sense of estrangement.

The visuals associated with Blake's uneasy condition in *Nobody Lives Forever* are not so unrelentingly dark as they are for Bradford Galt in *The Dark Corner* or the amnesiac George Taylor in *Somewhere in the Night*. In contrast, Blake's beach house and the sunlit nearby stretch of sand where he takes solitary walks become the locus for his moments of most acute malaise. It is equally ironic that the unused pier, with its uninviting expanse of creaking, sea-sprayed timbers surrounded by a black ocean, is the unlikely setting in which Blake recommits himself to social interaction. There, in a typical noir transference, the used-up Pop Gruber dies under Ganson's gun in Blake's stead. His dying comment—at once existential and grimly reminiscent of the larger holocaust from which Blake has recently returned—gives voice sardonically to the words of the title: "Nobody lives forever."

—A.S.

NOCTURNE (1946)

Director: Edwin L. Marin
Executive Producer: Jack J. Gross (RKO)
Producer: Joan Harrison
Screenplay: Jonathan Latimer; from an unpublished story by Frank Fenton and Rowland Brown
Director of Photography: Harry J. Wild
Special Effects: Russell A. Cully
Montage: Harold Palmer
Sound: Jean L. Speak, Terry Kellum
Music Score: Leigh Harline
Music Director: Constantin Bakaleinikoff
Songs: "Nocturne," music by Leigh Harline, lyric by Mort Greene; "Why Pretend" and "A Little Bit Is Better Than None" by Eleanor Rudolph

Production Designer: Robert Boyle
Art Director: Albert S. D'Agostino, Robert Boyle
Set Decoration: Darrell Silvera, James Altwies
Costumes: Renie
Technical Advisor: Barney Ruditsky
Assistant Director: James Anderson
Film Editor: Elmo Williams

CAST: George Raft (Joe Warne), Lynn Bari (Frances Ransom), Virginia Huston (Carol Page), Joseph Pevney (Fingers), Myrna Dell (Susan), Edward Ashley (Vincent), Walter Sande (Halberson), Mabel Paige (Mrs. Warne), Bernard Hoffman (Torp), Queenie Smith (Queenie), Mack Gray (Gratz). **BITS:** Pat Flaherty (Cop with Susan), Lorin Raker (Police Chemist), William Challee (Police Photographer), Greta Grandstedt (Clara), Lillian Bond (Mrs. Billings), Carol Forman, Betty Farrington, Connie Evans, Doris Stone, Monya Andre, Dorothy Adams, Lillian Bronson, Gladys Blake, Betty Hill, Carol Donell, Eleanor Counts, Norma Brown (Women), Robert Malcolm (Earn), Jim Pierce, Willie Bloom, Roger Creed, Ed Dearing, Al Hill, Dick Rush (Policemen), John Banner (Shawn), Rudy Robles (Eujemio), Janet Shaw (Grace), Ted O'Shea (Dancer), Harry Harvey (Police Doctor), Robert Anderson (Pat), Broderick O'Farrell (Butler), Virginia Edwards (Mrs. O'Rourke), Virginia Keiley (Lotus Evans), Antonio Filauri (Nick Pappas), Al Rhein (Waiter), Benny Burt (Bartender), Bert Moorehouse (Director), George Goodman (Manager of the Keyboard Club), Bob Terry, Edward Clark, Sam Flint, Matt McHugh, Lloyd Dawson, Phil Baribault, Tex Swan, Lee Frederick, James Carlisle, Paul Stader, Jack Norton, Mex Wixon, John Rice (Men), William Wright (Mr. Billings), Donald Kerr (Gaffer), Lucille Casey (Bessie).
Filming Completed: June 14, 1946
Released: RKO, November 9, 1946
Running Time: 87 minutes

A composer is shot while working at his piano and detective Joe Warne is among the police assigned to the case. Despite Warne's suspicions that one of the cast-off women from the composer's many and notorious affairs may have murdered him, the official conclusion of the investigation is that he committed suicide. Warne remains unconvinced; and he continues to make inquiries and search for a woman referred to in one of the victim's songs as "Dolores." His persistence causes him to annoy numerous suspects, and their complaints lead to Warne's suspension from the police force. Unabashed, Warne interprets this as a sign that he is getting close to the truth. He concentrates his efforts on Frances Ransom to whom he is reluctantly attracted. Ultimately, Warne discovers that Ransom has lied to him to protect not herself but her sister, Carol Page, a singer who is also "Dolores." Warne confronts Page and Ransom after hours in the nightclub where the former works. As Page is about to confess her involvement, her accompanist, Fingers, appears and discloses that he is the murderer.

Nocturne opens with a long traveling shot across a landscaped model of the Hollywood Hills and into the window of an isolated house. An optically matched dissolve continues the movement through the window, into the room, and toward a man sitting at a piano. As the camera comes up close behind him, a gun fires point-blank at his head. This opening shot, in which the third-person camera seems to be drawn over the dark terrain by the sound of the piano, builds visual tension through a long take and surprises the viewer with the explosion from the gun just before the cutaway. It also initiates a complex irony that will be maintained throughout the film. Just as the audience cannot anticipate from the visual treatment the presence of another person in the composer's house or the sudden intrusion into the frame of the flash and smoke from the gun's discharge, Joe Warne will possess information they do not have throughout the entire narrative. Conversely, while Warne is confident that the death is not suicide, only the viewer can be certain of that from having witnessed the murder. By endistancing the audience from the protagonist in this way, Joe Warne's investigation becomes from their viewpoint less a quest for the fact of the murder than for its motives. But what inspires his obsessive behavior, undeterred by the physical punishment he suffers in the course of his search, is never clarified.

Nocturne's noir statement resides in the possibility that Warne is most fascinated by the life-style of the victim, whose photographs of numerous amorous conquests hang on the walls of an expensive home that is in marked contrast to the modest interior of the small house Warne shares with his mother. Warne's fascination may be roughly analogous to that of Mark McPherson in *Laura*, but his attraction to Frances Ransom is certainly not as compulsive. To some extent, Warne—particularly as underplayed by George Raft —is a cipher, a figure exploring nightclubs, backrooms, and even movie lots to find an answer for the audience without ever revealing his own motives. Actually, it is the act of investigation rather than any result that interests Warne. For if the composer is the real focus of his obsession, it is the investigation that compels his songs to be heard and his former women to be followed. The visual tension of the opening sequence may be diminished after Warne's appearance; but its irony never is, becoming instead the foundation for an existential melodrama in which Warne is defined only in terms of his quest. When that quest is resolved and the killer found, Warne's vicarious existence is terminated.

—A.S.

NORA PRENTISS (1947)
[Working Title: THE SENTENCE]

Director: Vincent Sherman
Producer: William Jacobs (Warner Brothers)
Screenplay: Richard Nash [with uncredited contributions by Philip McDonald]; from an unpublished story by Paul Webster and Jack Sobell
Director of Photography: James Wong Howe
Special Effects: Harry Barndollar, Edwin DuPar
Montage: James Leicester
Sound: Charles Lang
Music Score: Franz Waxman
Music Director: Leo F. Farbstein
Orchestration: Leonid Raab
Songs: "Would You Like A Souvenir?" and "Who Cares What People Say?" music by Moe K. Jerome, lyrics by Jack Scholl
Art Director: Anton Grot
Set Decoration: Walter Tilford
Costumes: Travilla
Makeup: Perc Westmore
Assistant Director: Jim McMahon
Film Editor: Owen Marks

CAST: Ann Sheridan (Nora Prentiss), Kent Smith (Dr. Richard Talbot), Bruce Bennett (Dr. Joel Merriam), Robert Alda (Nick Dinardos), Rosemary DeCamp (Lucy Talbot), John Ridgely (Walter Bailey), Robert Arthur (Gregory Talbot), Wanda Hendrix (Bonita Talbot), Helen Brown (Miss Judson), Rory Mallinson (Fleming), Harry Shannon (Police Lieutenant), James Flavin (District Attorney), Douglas Kennedy (Doctor), Don McGuire (Truck Driver), Clifton Young (Policeman). **BITS:** John Newland, John Compton, Ramon Ros (Reporters), Jack Mower (Sheriff), Philo McCullough (Warden), Fred Kelsey (Turnkey), Louis Quince (Judge), Lottie Williams (Agnes), Gertrude Carr (Mrs. Dobie), Richard Walsh (Bystander), Tiny Jones (Flower Woman), Georgia Caine (Mrs. Sterritt), Dean Cameron (Rod, Piano Player), Roy Gordon (Oberlin), David Fresco (Newsboy), Jack Ellis, Lee Phelps (Doormen), Creighton Hale (Captain of Waiters), Ed Hart, Clancey Cooper, Alan Bridge (Policemen), Ross Ford (Chauffeur, Billie), Adele St. Maur (Nurse), Ralph Dunn, Ed Chandler (Detectives), Charles Marsh (Bailiff), Matt McHugh, Wallace Scott (Drunks), George Campeau (Man), Charles Jordan (Clerk at Court), John Elliott (Chaplain), Herb Caen, Bill McWilliams, Mike Musura, Jerry Baulch, Fred Johnson, Jack Dailey, Bill Best, Seymore Snaer, James Nickle (Newspapermen at Ferry Building).
Location: San Francisco, California
Filming Completed: April 20, 1946
Released: Warner Brothers, February 22, 1947
Running Time: Previewed at 153 minutes; general release at 111 minutes

A successful San Francisco doctor, Richard Talbot, leads an unsatisfying and ordinary life with his wife and two children. He and a nightclub singer, Nora Prentiss, begin an affair that seems hopeless because Talbot cannot summon the courage to ask for a divorce. Nora moves to New York to work in a new nightclub. Desolate, Talbot takes advantage of his patient's sudden death to fake his own death and leaves home to join Nora in New York. Later, he reads that police are investigating his death as a possible murder. Talbot is frightened to leave Nora's apartment and becomes alcoholic while her career proceeds well. He imagines Nora is romancing her boss, Phil, and Talbot starts a drunken brawl with the man. Believing he has murdered Phil, Talbot flees from the nightclub and has a serious automobile accident. Undergoing plastic surgery to repair his badly burned face, Talbot no longer looks like himself. He considers the new appearance a blessing and is surprised when he is arrested for the death he faked in California. None of his family or friends recognizes him at the trial and Talbot forces Nora to remain silent so that his family will be spared any further shame. Talbot is convicted of his own murder and Nora says goodbye to him in death row.

If there were a category of "women's noir," *Nora Prentiss* should certainly rank at the top. Unlike such other Ann Sheridan or Joan Crawford motion pictures as *The Unfaithful*, *Flamingo Road*, and *The Damned Don't Cry*, *Nora Prentiss* does not lapse into a romantic melodrama that might detract from their *maudit* sensibility, the quintessential element of film noir. *Nora Prentiss* is photographed by James Wong Howe in typically expressionistic style, the closed form of which enhances the entrapment of both principal players: Nora and Dr. Talbot. This is especially true in two key scenes. In one, the scarred Talbot is alone in his prison cell thinking as the story unfolds in flashback. The other is when their relationship has become badly strained by the long hours spent together in their small New York apartment because the pathetic Talbot is frightened to go out and risk being recognized.

—B.P.

NOTORIOUS (1946)

Director and Producer: Alfred Hitchcock (RKO)
Assistant Producer: Barbara Keon
Screenplay: Ben Hecht
Director of Photography: Ted Tetzlaff
Special Effects: Vernon L. Walker, Paul Eagler
Sound: John E. Tribby, Terry Kellum
Music Score: Roy Webb
Music Director: Constantin Bakaleinikoff
Art Directors: Albert S. D'Agostino, Carroll Clark
Set Decoration: Darrell Silvera, Claude Carpenter
Costumes: Edith Head
Assistant Director: William Dorfman
Film Editor: Theron Warth

CAST: Cary Grant (Devlin), Ingrid Bergman (Alicia Huberman), Claude Rains (Alexander Sebastian), Louis Calhern (Paul Prescott), Madame Konstantin (Mme. Sebastian), Reinhold Schunzel (Dr. Anderson), Moroni Olsen (Walter Beardsley), Ivan Triesault (Eric Mathis), Alex Minotis (Joseph), Wally Brown (Mr. Hopkins), Gavin Gordon (Ernest Weylin), Sir Charles Mendl (Commodore), Ricardo Costa (Dr. Barbosa), Eberhard Krumschmidt (Hupka), Fay Baker (Ethel). **BITS:** Antonio Moreno (Señor Ortiza), Frederick Ledebur (Knerr), Luis Serrano (Dr. Silva), William Gordon (Adams), Charles D. Brown (Judge), Ramon Nomar (Dr. Silva), Peter Von Zerneck (Rossner), Fred Nurney (Huberman), Herbert Wyndham (Mr. Cook), Aileen Carlyle, Lillian West, Beulah Christian, Alameda Fowler, Leota Lorraine (Women), Harry Hyden (Defense Council), Dink Trout (Court Clerk), John Vasper, Eddie Bruce, Don Kerr, Ben Erway, Emmett Vogan, Paul Bryan, Alan Ward, James Logan (Reporters), Howard Negley, George Lynn, Frank Marlowe (Photographers), Warren Jackson (District Attorney), Howard Mitchell (Bailiff), Tom Coleman (Court Stenographer), Garry Owen, Lester Dorr (Motorcycle Police), Patricia Smart (Mrs. Jackson), Candido Bonsato, Ted Kelly (Waiters), Tina Menard (Maid), Richard Clark, Frank McDonald (Men), Frank Wilcox (F.B.I. Agent), Bee Benadaret, Virginia Gregg, Bernice Barrett (Clerks).
Filming Completed: January 17, 1946
Released: RKO, August 22, 1946
Running Time: 101 minutes

As World War II comes to an end, Alicia Huberman is a sophisticated playgirl living in Florida while her father—a Nazi spy—is imprisoned elsewhere in the United States. She had never approved of her father's politics and is persuaded by Devlin, a federal agent, to assist him in a Rio de Janeiro undercover operation to ensnare a Nazi friend of her father's, Alexander Sebastian, who protects a group of Nazi conspirators now living there. Alicia and Devlin are attracted to each other, but Devlin cannot accept her past. Sebastian welcomes Alicia into his home and soon proposes marriage to her. Alicia accepts his offer when it is obvious that Devlin is only interested in the success of their espionage and not in her happiness. Meanwhile, Sebastian's mother is highly suspicious of Alicia. During a large party at her new home, Alicia and Devlin take advantage of the situation and discover a cache of uranium hidden in the wine cellar. The next day, Sebastian realizes that Alicia is a spy and is convinced that it is essential to keep the truth concealed from his Nazi friends. He and his mother begin slowly to poison Alicia in order to make her death appear as if caused by a natural illness. Devlin is eventually concerned by Alicia's failure to contact him further. He brazens his way into the Sebastian mansion and finds her at the edge of death. Assuring her of his love, Devlin carries her boldly out of the house and into his waiting car while Sebastian—surrounded by Nazi friends—must look on helplessly.

Although it is ostensibly a romantic thriller, Hitchcock incorporates familiar film noir themes into *Notorious*. The customary seeds of suspicion and betrayal are sown in several ways but the most interesting, perhaps, is Hitchcock's treatment of the "bad woman," a noir staple. Ingrid Bergman's portrayal of Alicia is initially presented as a woman who is cynical, promiscuous, and alcoholic. Cary Grant's character of Devlin is apparently correct in distrusting her and views her with an equally cynical eye. Gradually, Hitchcock reveals that misery and self-pity are the demons that have driven this sensitive woman to various excesses. Moreover, she responds out of a sense of patriotism, which, although she denies its existence, is revealed when Devlin plays a recording of her violent argument with her father concerning his Nazi activities. Her deeply romantic nature is revealed by the tremulous, pathetically eager-to-please way in which she blossoms under Devlin's reluctant but sincere attentions and is a clear indication of Alicia's fundamental innocence.

In a noir manner, Devlin is neurotically obsessed with Alicia's past and represses his profound attraction to her, contemptuously comparing her to a leopard that "can't change its spots." Perversely, he pushes her back into the very kind of life for which he condemned her. As a final irony, Hitchcock generates audience sympathy for the duped Sebastian by plainly indicating that he loves Alicia unreservedly, something that the strait-laced, unimaginative Devlin cannot do.

Hitchcock exploits a noir style while inverting several of the noir conventions. Alicia, his "bad woman"—like such later examples of his antiheroines as Eve Kendall in *North by Northwest* and Madeleine/Judy in *Vertigo*—is bad not by nature or design but as a result of circumstances. At a passing glance, Alicia is not unlike the predatory Kathie of *Out of the Past*, the deceptive Kitty of *The Killers*, or the traitorous Anna of *Criss Cross*; but Alicia is later revealed as a woman inured to misery while still ready to risk herself for emotional fulfillment. Devlin, although similar to other noir heroes in his inability to see beyond a woman's facade, is flawed not by trusting too much but rather by not trusting enough.

—J.K.

ODDS AGAINST TOMORROW (1959)

Director and Producer: Robert Wise (Harbel Productions)
Associate Producer: Phil Stein
Screenplay: John O. Killens and Nelson Gidding; from the novel by William P. McGivern
Director of Photography: Joseph Brun
Camera Operator: Sol Midwall
Sound: Edward Johnstone, Richard Voriscek
Music: John Lewis
Art Director: Leo Kerz
Set Decoration: Fred Ballmeyer
Costumes: Anna Hill Johnstone
Makeup: Robert Jiras
Production Manager: Forrest E. Johnston
Script Supervisor: Marguerite James
Assistant Director: Charles Maguire
Film Editor: Dede Allen

CAST: Harry Belafonte (Johnny Ingram), Robert Ryan (Earl Slater), Gloria Grahame (Helen), Shelley Winters (Lorry), Ed Begley (Dave Burke), Will Kuluva (Bacco), Mae Barnes (Annie), Carmen DeLavallade (Kitty), Richard Bright (Coco), Lou Gallo (Moriarity), Fred J. Scollay (Cannoy), Lois Thorne (Eadie). **BITS:** Wayne Rogers (Soldier), Zohra Lampert (Girl in Bar), William Zuckert (Bartender), Burt Harris (George), Ed Preble (Hotel Clerk), Mel Stewart (Elevator Operator), Marc May (Ambulance Attendant), Paul Hoffman (Garry), Cicely Tyson (Fra), Robert Jones (Guard), William Adams (Bank Guard), John Garden (Bus Station Clerk), Allen Nourse (Police Chief).

Location: Upstate New York
Filming Completed: May 1959
Released: United Artists, October 15, 1959
Running Time: 96 minutes

Earl Slater, a racially prejudiced ex-con, is asked by Dave Burke, an ex-cop who was disgracefully dismissed from the force, to join in his plan to rob a small-town bank in upstate New York. Johnny Ingram, a black singer, reluctantly joins Burke and Slater because a hoodlum named Bacco has threatened Johnny's ex-wife and small daughter with harm if he does not repay a debt soon. Everything goes wrong during the robbery. A service station attendant recognizes Earl, and Johnny is stopped as a witness to an accident; but he manages to put himself in the place of the black sales clerk who brings food and drinks into the bank at night.

When the real clerk arrives, a cop wounds Burke, who cannot pass the getaway car's keys to his partners, and he kills himself rather than be arrested. Racial antagonisms come to the fore as Earl and Johnny fight, and Johnny chases Earl while both are pursued by the police to the top of some oil storage tanks. The two criminals take aim and fire at each other, igniting the tanks. The next day, someone sorting through the wreckage asks of the two corpses, "Which is which?" and another person replies, "Take your pick."

Odds Against Tomorrow, if measured in terms of its visual style, may well qualify as the last film of the noir cycle. It is a worthy descendant of the caper film series inaugurated by *The Asphalt Jungle* and is updated by the use of a jazz background, the inclusion of a homosexual hoodlum, and racial themes. The ending of this film recalls the climax of *White Heat* and is a fitting epitaph for film noir because *Odds Against Tomorrow* contains hints of many of the subgenres into which film noir evolved (i.e., the productions that deal with infamous gangsters, psychotic killers, racial conflicts, and other socially conscious issues). The noir look of the late 1940s and early 1950s is maintained in *Odds Against Tomorrow* through night-for-night location exteriors and a number of effective interior scenes featuring dark rooms modulated by the diagonal lines of venetian blinds. Gloria Grahame's performance is of the ultimate black widow *femme fatale,* particularly when she begs Robert Ryan to excite her before they make love by relating how it feels to kill someone.

— B.L.

ON DANGEROUS GROUND (1952)

[Working Titles: DARK HIGHWAY, MAD WITH MUCH HEART]

Director: Nicholas Ray
Producer: John Houseman (RKO)
Screenplay: A. I. Bezzerides, adapted by A. I. Bezzerides and Nicholas Ray; from the novel *Mad With Much Heart* by Gerald Butler
Director of Photography: George E. Diskant
Special Effects: Harold Stine
Sound: Phil Brigandi, Clem Portman
Music Score: Bernard Herrmann
Music Director: Constantin Bakaleinikoff; viola d'amore played by Virginia Majewski
Art Directors: Albert S. D'Agostino, Ralph Berger
Set Decoration: Darrell Silvera, Harley Miller
Makeup: Mel Berns
Hairstyles: Larry Germain
Assistant Director: William Dorfman
Film Editor: Roland Gross

CAST: Ida Lupino (Mary Malden), Robert Ryan (Jim Wilson), Ward Bond (Walter Brent), Charles Kemper (Bill Daly), Anthony Ross (Pete Santos), Ed Begley (Capt. Brawley), Ian Wolfe (Carrey), Sumner Williams (Danny Malden), Gus Schilling (Lucky), Frank Ferguson (Willows), Cleo Moore (Myrna), Olive Carey (Mrs. Brent), Richard Irving (Bernie), Pat Prest (Julie). **BITS:** Bill Hammond (Fred), Gene Persson, Tommy Gosser, Ronnie Garner, Dee Garner, Harry Joel Weiss, (Boys), Ruth Lee (Helen), Kate Lawson, Esther Zeitlin (Women), William Challee (Thug), Eddie Borden, Steve Roberts, Budd Fine, Mike Lally, Don Dillaway, Al Murphy, Art Dupuis, Frank Arnold, Homer Dickinson (Men), Ken Terrell (Crook), W. J. O'Brien (Hotel Clerk), Nita Talbot (Woman in Bar), Joe Devlin (Bartender), Jim Drum (Stretcher Bearer), Al. I. Bezzerides (Gatos), Tracy Roberts (Peggy Santos), Vera Stokes (Mother), Nestor Paiva (Bagganierri), Leslie Bennett (Sgt. Wendell), Jimmy Conlin (Doc Hyman), John Taylor (Hazel).

Filming Completed: May 10, 1950
Released: February 12, 1952
Running Time: 82 minutes

Jim Wilson, a New York City policeman, is on the verge of a nervous breakdown. He lives alone in a cheerless apartment and knows no one except his partners, Daly and Santos, and the assortment of criminals he encounters as part of his job. This life has made Wilson bitter and violent. Daly and Santos try to help him, but he rejects their reasoning. Finally, as punishment for his most recent display of brutality, Wilson is sent out of town on a case. A disturbed teenager, Danny Malden, has molested and killed a girl. Wilson must initially calm the girl's irate father, Walter Brent, who wants to kill the youth. Danny's blind sister, Mary, pleads with Wilson to bring her brother in unharmed; but Brent's interference prompts the murderer to flee in panic across the snow-covered countryside. Losing his grip as he tries to scale some rocks, Danny falls to his death. Wilson consoles Mary, and their emotional rapport promises a new beginning for each of them; but a rupture occurs and he heads back to the city. Realizing that desolation is all that awaits him in New York, he returns to Mary.

Nicholas Ray's visual treatment of despair and salvation is one of the most moving in film noir. Although the elements of the plot are somewhat arbitrary and contrived, the central character of Wilson is conceived and delineated with great impact. The structural division of the film is in two parts, city and country. It creates a narrative framework of a journey that is literally from city to country and, subtextually, an inner journey of self-realization. Beginning as an archetypal film noir in its violent amd brooding city "overture" (defining the probable "dangerous ground" of the title), the film becomes more profound as the setting changes and Mary is introduced to alter the entire tone of the work. High contrast lighting pervades the city sequences, and the action is harsh and quick with each scene concisely staged. The country sequences are relatively slower and photographed more naturally as the visual style emphasizes the snowy landscape's beauty or light from Mary's fireplace as it casts strange shadows about her living room. However, the intensity and imbalance of the protagonist's emotional state is expressed also through subjective shots of the road as Wilson drives. That emotion carries over to and from other moments (rendered subjectively with a hand-held camera), such as the chase of a suspect in the city sequence or his subduing of the brutal Brent.

The special qualities of *On Dangerous Ground* are primarily attributable to Nicholas Ray. Strangely, he regards it as a failure, perhaps because of the "miracle" ending in which a series of dissolves of the anguished face of Wilson driving, the country in daylight, and the city street at night, abruptly brings Wilson back into Mary's house and the warmth of her embrace. "I don't believe in miracles," Ray has said. And yet he has suggested in the film that Wilson's violence results from a spiritual crisis precipitated by the dehumanizing nature of his occupation clashing with his innate sensitivity—an internal conflict that cannot withstand the pressure placed on him by a violent environment and that only begins to dissipate in his very first moments with Mary. The film is both psychologically realistic and spiritually mysterious; and, if Ray would not concede this, he could not deny specific virtues found in the creative responses of certain of the film's participants. George E. Diskant (also photographer of Ray's first film, *They Live By Night*) captures exactly the contrasting moods of the city and country locales. Bernard Herrmann contributes one of his most beautiful scores, unusual in its use of horns during the chase and in its viola d'amore theme for Mary. Above all, there is the mesmerizing presence of Ida Lupino and Robert Ryan. Ryan's face expresses the motif of alienation that pervades Ray's work better than any dialogue could. As played by Ryan, Wilson's violent interrogation of a suspect, asking "Why do you punks make me do it?" is one of the most neurotic and self-destructive actions in film noir, so that the character's return to his apartment later that night becomes a gripping vision of loneliness. Wilson looks for a moment at his sports trophies, which are the only positive symbols left in his life and bitterly asks, "Who cares?" Few actors could give this simple line as evocative a reading.

—B.P.

THE OTHER WOMAN (1954)

Director and Producer: Hugo Haas (Hugo Haas Productions)
Associate Producer: Robert Erlick
Screenplay: Hugo Haas
Director of Photography: Eddie Fitzgerald
Sound: Earl Snyder
Music: Ernest Gold
Art Director: Rudi Feld
Film Editor: Robert S. Eisen

CAST: Hugo Haas (Darmen), Cleo Moore (Sherry), Lance Fuller (Ronnie), Lucille Barkley (Mrs. Darmen), Jack Macy (Lester), John Qualen (Papasha), Jan Arvan (Collins), Carolee Kelly (First Assistant Director), Mark Lowell (Second Assistant Director), Melinda Markey (Actress).
Released: 20th Century-Fox, December 21, 1954
Running Time: 81 minutes

Darmen is an émigré director whose Hollywood career is helped because his wife is the daughter of the production chief for a large motion picture company. One day he refuses to use an aspiring actress. She resents his decision and schemes to blackmail him, persuading him to take her home to her apartment one evening after work. Once there, she serves him a drugged drink that makes him sleep. When he awakens, she pretends they have had sexual relations. Sherry later announces her pregnancy to Darmen and demands he get her $50,000 from his father-in-law to avoid a scandal. The director, realizing his future is finished if he goes to his father-in-law, plans to murder the woman. For an alibi, he engineers a sound loop on his editing room's moviola so that it appears to his secretary that he is busy working while he is actually committing the crime. When a police detective sees through Darmen's alibi, the film director confesses.

It is interesting to speculate whether Hugo Haas, an émigré director, was working out one of his own worst fantasies in *The Other Woman*. The film is one of countless low-budget "cheapies" such as *Pickup, Bait,* and *Strange Fascination* that Haas made as director, writer, and star opposite 1950s B-movie, "sexpot" actresses like Beverly Michaels or Cleo Moore, who was also his wife. However, *The Other Woman* comes closer in style and substance to true film noir than any other of Haas's efforts, due to the Fox production values of dark, glistening sets and an expressionistic visual style, which is characterized by the enclosed space of small rooms. Additionally, the film collapses the distinction between victim and artist because Haas, as director, speaks directly of his entrapment: first, in the film's opening, when Haas as Darmen tells an actor how to perform a scene in a jail set; and secondly, at the film's close, when Darmen is confined in prison and relates to the audience that in real life there are no happy endings.

OUT OF THE PAST (1947)
[Working Title: BUILD MY GALLOWS HIGH]

Director: Jacques Tourneur
Executive Producer: Robert Sparks (RKO)
Producer: Warren Duff

OUT OF THE PAST

Screenplay: Geoffrey Homes (Daniel Mainwaring); from his novel *Build My Gallows High*. [Uncredited: Frank Fenton]
Director of Photography: Nicholas Musuraca
Special Effects: Russell A. Cully
Sound: Francis M. Sarver, Clem Portman
Music Score: Roy Webb
Conductor: Constantin Bakaleinikoff
Art Directors: Albert S. D'Agostino, Jack Okey
Set Decoration: Darrell Silvera
Costumes: Edward Stevenson
Makeup: Gordon Bau
Assistant Director: Harry Mancke
Film Editor: Samuel E. Beetley

CAST: Robert Mitchum (Jeff Bailey), Jane Greer (Kathie Moffett), Kirk Douglas (Whit Sterling), Rhonda Fleming (Meta Carson), Richard Webb (Jim), Steve Brodie (Fisher), Virginia Huston (Ann), Paul Valentine (Joe), Dickie Moore (the Kid), Ken Niles (Eels). **BITS:** Lee Elson (Policeman), Frank Wilcox (Sheriff Douglas), Mary Field (Marney), José Portugal (Waiter), Jess Escobar, James Bush (Doormen), Hubert Brill (Car Manipulator), Brooks Benedict, Mike Lally, Homer Dickenson, Bill Wallace (Kibitzers), Primo Lopez (Bellhop), Mildred Boyd (Woman), Ted Collins (Man), Caleb Peterson (Man with Eunice), Theresa Harris (Eunice), Wesley Bly (Headwaiter), Tony Roux (José Rodriguez), Sam Warren, Euminio Blanco, Vic Romito (Waiters), Michael Branden (Rafferty), Wallace Scott (Petey), John Kellogg (Baylord), Oliver Blake (Tillotson), William Van Vleck (Cigar Store Clerk), Phillip Morris (Porter), Charles Regan (Mystery Man), Harry Hayden (Canby Miller), Adda Gleason (Mrs. Miller), Manuel Paris (Croupier).
Location: Reno, Nevada; Lake Tahoe, San Francisco, Los Angeles, California; Mexico City, Acapulco, Mexico
Filming Completed: January 9, 1947
Released: RKO, November 25, 1947
Running Time: 96 minutes
[NOTE: Dick Powell was announced to star in *Build My Gallows High* after completing *Johnny O'Clock*.

In 1976, Jerry Bick and John Ptak announced plans to remake *Out Of The Past* as *Build My Gallows High*, to be directed by Jerry Schatzberg from a screenplay by Marilyn Goldin.]

In the little town of Bridgeport, California, Jeff Bailey runs a gas station with the assistance of a mute boy, Jimmy, and courts Ann. Joe Stefanos drives into town and informs Jeff that Whit Sterling, a racketeer, wants to see him. Jeff relates his life's story to Ann as they drive to Sterling's Lake Tahoe mansion. As a private detective named Jeff Markham, he was hired to find Sterling's mistress, Kathie Moffett, who had shot Sterling and escaped with $40,000. Jeff found Kathie in Mexico but fell in love with her and believed her claim that she did not steal any money. They moved to San Francisco and lived anonymously until Fisher, Jeff's former partner, found them. Kathie killed Fisher and Jeff discovered evidence that proved she lied

about the money. Disillusioned, Jeff moved to his new life at Bridgeport. Arriving at Sterling's, Jeff assures Ann before she departs that he no longer loves Kathie. Meeting with Sterling, Jeff is surprised to see Kathie. She secretly tells him that Sterling is blackmailing her about Fisher's murder to stay with him. The racketeer blackmails Jeff to obtain tax records from Eels, a renegade accountant of Sterling's gang, but Jeff is being used as a patsy: Eels is to be killed by Stefanos, who will frame Jeff for the murder. When Jeff discovers the plot, he unsuccessfully tries to prevent the crime and realizes that Sterling has false evidence that also implicates him as Fisher's murderer. Hunted by the police, Jeff flees to Bridgeport and finds that Ann still believes in him. After eluding Stefanos, Jeff confronts Sterling, who agrees to reveal Kathie as Fisher's murderer, but Sterling is killed by her. Kathie tells Jeff that they belong together and should escape the country. He appears to agree but alerts the police and the two are both killed as she attempts to drive through a roadblock. Jeff's assistant, Jimmy, conveys the impression to Ann that Jeff actually loved Kathie so that Ann can reject Jeff's memory and free herself from the past to build a new life.

Out Of The Past is a title evocative of the noir cycle as well as descriptive of this particular film. The existential figure of the ill-fated noir protagonist Jeff, incarnated by Robert Mitchum, is restrained, joyless, and with a look of doom in his sad eyes. The erotic and lethal female Kathie, is vividly portrayed by Jane Greer. Daniel Mainwaring's complex screenplay uses narration like the voice of fate over a flashback into Jeff's past, which inescapably determines the present and future. The shadowy lighting of a cinematographer attuned to noir, Nicholas Musuraca, combines with the tragic sensibility of the director, Jacques Tourneur, and is well-suited to the downbeat nature of the genre.

However, to say that this is one of the key works of film noir is not necessarily to accept it as unflawed. It can be faulted both for its excessively complex plotting, notably in the San Francisco section, and for a solemnity that almost becomes tedious. Its best section is the flashback sequence that follows an ominous opening sequence reminiscent in mood of Hemingway's "The Killers" and the faithful recreation of that story in Siodmak's film. In the flashback sequence, the combination of Mitchum's mesmerizing narration as Jeff waits for Kathie and eventually sees her walking out of the sunlight into the Mexican café, the romantic interlude on the beach, and their desperate flight conspires to give the film the perfect noir mood. Elsewhere, in the film's second half, the Mainwaring screenplay seems protracted and overly emphatic of Jeff's capitulation to his fate and Kathie's duplicity. The melodramatic climax of the film, and one of the strongest visual moments, occurs when Kathie shoots Fisher and Jeff turns, registering the shock of seeing Kathie's true nature revealed.

Its many other merits aside and its faults taken into account, *Out of the Past* is, with *Criss Cross*, one of the two films that best evoke a subject central to the genre: the

Kathie Moffett (Jane Greer) in Out Of The Past.

destruction of a basically good man by a corrupt woman he loves. In both films the heroine vacillates between the hero and another man, which results in the destruction of all three, and a flashback traces the hero's "fall." But the two films are quite different, even in the nature of their flashbacks. In the *Criss Cross* flashback, Steve Thompson is already haunted by Anna, his former wife, and his first view of her in the nightclub recreates his former desire. In the *Out of the Past* flashback, Bailey encounters Kathie for the first time when she walks into the Mexican café so the turning point of his life seems more immediate and placed within the film. The most interesting difference, however, is that Bailey knows before the flashback is over that Kathie is destroying him. The film traces the course in which he gradually accepts this fate and even embraces it, spiritually if not physically. Thompson, on the other hand, in spite of bad experiences with Anna in the past, convinces himself that he trusts her and only fully understands her and her betrayal of him in the very last scene.

But in these two fundamentally different visions of male-female relationships, there is one constant: the woman herself. Film noir is filled with such women as these and the instances in which the woman who is loved represents the best part of the hero rather than the worst, such as Keechie in *They Live by Night*, are the exceptions. This vision of women is resonant in many noir films, such as *Criss Cross, Angel Face, Hell's Island,* and *Double Indemnity* and the noir milieu powerfully underscores it. Alternately, such films as *Pitfall, Nightfall, The Big Sleep, Notorious,* and *Chinatown*

suggest the other side of this theme. In each, the hero presumes at some point the heroine's betrayal but is found to be wrong. Still, this presumption never threatens their lives as forcefully as the true betrayal of *Out of the Past.* Although it would seem that some alternative version of *Out of the Past*'s narrative—in which the hero's lack of faith, his failure to trust, destroys them—should be possible, the noir vision will not admit a male protagonist's simple, possibly tragic error in judgment so readily as it will a misguided and fatal obsession.

—B.L.

THE OUTFIT (1973)

Director and Screenplay: John Flynn; from the novel by Richard Stark [Donald E. Westlake]
Producer: Carter De Haven (MGM)
Director of Photography: Bruce Surtees (Metrocolor)
Music: Jerry Fielding
Song: "Your Guess Is As Good As Mine" by Steve Gilette and Jeremy Kronsberg
Art Director: Tambi Larsen
Set Decoration: James I. Berkey
Sound: Richard Raguse, Hal Watkins
Stunt Coordinator: Ron Rondell
Film Editor: Ralph E. Winters

THE OUTFIT

Production Manager: Jim Henderling
Assistant Director: William McGarry

CAST: Robert Duvall (Earl Macklin), Karen Black (Bett Jarrow), Joe Don Baker (Cody), Robert Ryan (Mailer), Timothy Carey (Jake Menner), Richard Jaeckel (Chemy), Sheree North (Buck's wife), Marie Windsor (Madge Coyle), Jane Greer (Alma), Henry Jones (Doctor), Joanna Cassidy (Rita), Tom Reese (1st Man), Elisha Cook, Jr. (Carl), Bill McKinney (Buck), Anita O'Day (Herself), Archie Moore (Parkard), Tony Young (Accountant), Roland LaStarza (Hit Man), Edward Ness (Ed Macklin), Roy Roberts (Caswell), Toby Anderson (Parking Attendant), Emile Meyer (Amos), Roy Jensen (Al), Philip Kenneally (Bartender), Bern Hoffman (Sinclair), John Steadman (Station Attendant), Paul Genge (Payoff Man), Francis De Dales (Jim), James Bacon (Bookie), Army Archerd (Butler), Tony Trabert (Himself).
Released: MGM, September 1973
Running Time: 103 minutes

A professional thief named Earl Macklin is released from prison and learns that his brother had been murdered under circumstances indicating that it was done by syndicate gunmen. Before he is also hit, Macklin's girl friend, Bett, confesses that she has been forced to set him up by Jake Menner, a syndicate underling. Menner has been commissioned to eliminate Macklin, his brother, and their partner Cody for inadvertently robbing a syndicate bank. Macklin intercepts Menner's hit man, beats him, then goes off himself to confront Menner with a defiant declaration of war. Macklin travels North to bury his brother, has a rendezvous with Cody, and enlists his aid in a scheme to get even with the mob. Together they stage a succession of raids on syndicate gambling rooms and bookie joints. Mailer, the local syndicate chief, summons Menner and issues an ultimatum: kill Macklin or forfeit his own life. Menner's ambush on a country road misfires. He and his cohorts are killed by Macklin and Cody; but Bett also dies in the exchange of gunfire. Macklin now decides to strike at Mailer himself in retribution. First he and Cody penetrate Mailer's security manor home and set a bomb to cover their retreat. Macklin then tracks Mailer down through the manor's inner rooms and mercilessly shoots him. Cody is wounded; but both men escape in the confusion of fire trucks and police responding to the explosion.
[NOTE: The television version of *The Outfit* ends with Macklin and Cody ostensibly trapped in a back room as the police and fire trucks arrive.]

The Outfit is loosely adapted from one of the sequels to Richard Stark's first "Parker" novel, *The Hunter*, which became the film *Point Blank*. As in the previous book, the central figure is a free-lance robber who finds himself suddenly under attack from organized crime and decides that his best chance of survival lies in active retaliation. The adaptors of *The Outfit* confront a central narrative that suggests an existential set piece in which a loner salves his alienation through murderous violence. It is also a mock

epic in which the "little man" defeats the dehumanized, organizational machine. The closing shot of *The Outfit* (a freeze-frame of Macklin and Cody smiling in exhilaration at their victory) would seem to fall into the latter category, particularly in contrast to the ambiguous conclusion of Boorman's *Point Blank*. But this ending with its single, frozen moment does not controvert the fundamentally noir vision of the film, which situates itself wholly in an underworld where the uncertainty of surface appearances undermines the very concepts of victory or defeat. That uncertainty is present in the film's prologue in which men who appear to be a priest and a cab driver murder Macklin's brother. It is elaborated on in a later sequence when Macklin is shown a souped-up car that looks like a Volkswagen but, as the mechanic laments, "I just can't make her sound like a Volkswagen." In the face of these masquerades, Macklin realizes that he cannot take the advice of his brother's common-law wife, who asks, "What do you want it [money] for? You got a woman; you got time." In Macklin's perception of how things stand or fall, money and time are both symbolic values, both keys to survival.

Macklin's position in these early scenes—recently released from prison, hiding out in a dingy motel room, betrayed by Bett—is drawn from a number of familiar noir motifs. Macklin's response to his situation, accentuated by Robert Duvall's laconic performance reminiscent of Robert Montgomery's in *Ride the Pink Horse*, recalls similar noir figures, all mindful of their own possible destruction but obsessed with evening the score. More than most of those precursors, Macklin had the tools to accomplish this. He has the ruthlessness of Hammer in *Kiss Me Deadly* without his egocentricity, the inside knowledge of Kelvaney in *Rogue Cop* without his indecision, and the sheer killing ability of Callahan in *Dirty Harry* without any pretense of abiding by the law. Macklin can forgive Bett's potentially deadly betrayal; or he can with equal dispassion release the man sent to kill him with the offhand remark, "Die someplace else."

If Macklin appears to move through the array of noir icons arrayed against him—from Robert Ryan and the maniacal Timothy Carey as the syndicate man to such familiar bit players as Elisha Cook, Jr., Marie Windsor, and Emile Meyer—it may be because they evoke, like the old car parked outside Macklin's first heist, an antique vision of the noir underworld. Unlike Dancer in *The Line-Up*, infuriated by his exasperating inability to reconcile the syndicate boss to his honest mistake, Macklin understands from the start that procedure is the only element of stability in that noir underworld. By systematically disrupting it, he almost becomes a cipher for that underworld turning destructively in against itself. The protest of Mailer's wife against hiding in the safety of his manor—"How long are we going to stay cooped up in this mausoleum?"—betrays the true nature of the cardboard killers who Bett remarks "act like they own the world" but whom Macklin easily defeats. Having metaphorically lost faith as their own institutions become noir artifacts, they are beaten as much by time as they are by the free lancers.

—A.S.

PANIC IN THE STREETS (1950)
[Working Title: OUTBREAK]

Director: Elia Kazan
Producer: Sol C. Siegel (20th Century-Fox)
Screenplay: Richard Murphy, adapted by Daniel Fuchs; from an unpublished story by Edna and Edward Anhalt
Director of Photography: Joe MacDonald
Special Photographic Effects: Fred Sersen
Sound: W. D. Flick, Roger Heman
Music: Alfred Newman
Orchestration: Edward Powell, Herbert Spencer
Art Directors: Lyle Wheeler, Maurice Ransford
Set Decoration: Thomas Little, Fred J. Rode
Costumes: Travilla
Wardrobe Director: Charles LeMaire
Makeup: Ben Nye
Production Manager: Joseph Behm
Assistant Director: F. E. Johnston
Script Supervisor: Stanley Scheuer
Film Editor: Harmon Jones

CAST: Richard Widmark (Dr. Clinton Reed), Paul Douglas (Police Capt. Warren), Barbara Bel Geddes (Nancy Reed), Walter [Jack] Palance (Blackie), Zero Mostel (Fitch), Dan Riss (Neff), Alexis Minotis (John Mefaris), Guy Thomajan (Poldi), Tommy Cook (Vince). **BITS:** Edward Kennedy (Jordan), H. T. Tsiang (Cook), Lewis Charles (Kochak), Ray Miller (Dubin), Lenka Peterson (Jeanette), Pat Walshe (Pat), Paul Hostetler (Dr. Gafney), George Ehmig (Kleber), John Schilleci (Lee), Waldo Pitkin (Ben), Leo Zinser (Sgt. Phelps), Beverly C. Brown (Dr. Mackey), William A. Dean (Cortelyou), H. Waller Fowler, Jr. (Mayor Murray), Red Moad (Wynant), Irvine Vidacovich (Johnston), Val Winter (Commissioner Quinn), Wilson Bourg, Jr. (Charlie), Mary Liswood (Mrs. Fitch), Aline Stevens (Rita), Stanley J. Reyes (Redfield), Darwin Greenfield (Violet), Emile Meyer (Beauglyde), Herman Cottman (Scott), Al Theriot (Al), Juan Villasana (Hotel Proprietor), Robert Dorsen (Coast Guard Lieutenant), Henry Mamet (Anson), Tiger Joe Marsh (Bosun), Arthur Tong (Lascar Boy).
Location: New Orleans, Louisiana
Released: 20th Century-Fox, August 4, 1950
Running Time: 96 minutes

The unidentified body of a murder victim is discovered to be carrying a deadly communicable disease. Dr. Clinton Reed of the Public Health Service realizes he has 48 hours to track down the murderers who have been exposed to the disease. If he is too late, the disease will become virulent and a large-scale epidemic will result. Meeting resistance from police Capt. Warren, who is assigned to the murder case, Reed decides to take matters into his own hands and investigate for himself. He searches the dilapidated dockside section of New Orleans and faces suspicion and distrust from the people he meets. But he finds the killers, and they are captured after a chase through the New Orleans dock area.

For years, gangsters and criminals have been referred to in films as rats and scum, as a menace to society. *Panic in the Streets* takes this thought to its logical conclusion, making it literally as well as figuratively true. The murderous thugs have been exposed to a deadly plague, brought into the country by the illegal alien whom they killed over a card game. Their arrest becomes a race to avert an epidemic of huge proportions. The film gains its suspense from the fact that the viewer knows the narrative essentials from the beginning. The film continually cuts back and forth between the efforts of the Public Health official to find the murderers; and the culprits themselves, who become increasingly baffled at what seems an undue interest on the part of the police to track them down. It is emphasized that, although a man has been murdered, the police would normally not go out of their way to find the killers of an illegal alien. This gives the film an ironic edge, as the killers are initially smug because they assume nothing will be done about the murder. It is not the criminals alone, however, who are suspicious and xenophobic. The lower-class community is wary of the outside world. When Reed begins prowling the cafés, houseboats, and union halls of the district, he is regarded with distrust. A café owner with an important lead is dissuaded from telling what he knows by his wife, who does not wish to get involved. Her reluctance is doubly distressing because she already has symptoms of the disease.

The ordinary attitudes of the criminal and lower-class segment of society are thrown into relief by an extraordinary situation. The protagonist in many noir films is the man who walks alone, who is forced to travel a path beyond the limits of the law. Reed, as portrayed by Widmark, is forced to take the law into his own hands for the sake of the society at large. Faced with stubborn official resistance, personified by Paul Douglas as the police captain—who, like the criminals, does not realize the enormity of the

221

danger—Reed is required to hunt the guilty by immersing himself in the noir underworld. *Panic in the Streets* evokes that particular underworld through an apt choice of locations. The actual use of the New Orleans wharf district adds graphic reality to the danger and disease. Adding to this unhealthy aura are the characterizations of the criminals. Zero Mostel as Fitch is sweaty, wormy, and obsequious in his devotion to Blackie, played by Jack Palance. Their archetypical performances underscore their symbolic value to the film as human malignancies. The most memorable visual simile comes at the film's climax, when the symbolic and literal action merge in one telling image. Cornered in the dockside area, Blackie attempts to escape by crawling up the mooring of a ship. The obstacle he encounters is a hawser designed to prevent rats from climbing aboard. It works: like a rat, Blackie falls into the ocean and is caught.

—J.B.

PARTY GIRL (1958)

Director: Nicholas Ray
Producer: Joe Pasternak (Euterpe Productions)
Screenplay: George Wells; from an unpublished story by Leo Katcher
Director of Photography: Robert Bronner (Metrocolor; CinemaScope)
Color Consultant: Charles K. Hagedon
Sound: Dr. Wesley C. Miller
Music: Jeff Alexander
Song: "Party Girl" by Nicholas Brodszky and Sammy Cahn; sung by Tony Martin
Choreography: Robert Sidney
Art Directors: William A. Horning, Randall Duell
Set Decoration: Henry Grace, Richard Pefferle
Assistant Director: Erich von Stroheim, Jr.
Film Editor: John McSweeney, Jr.

CAST: Robert Taylor (Thomas Farrell), Cyd Charisse (Vicki Gaye), Lee J. Cobb (Rico Angelo), John Ireland (Louis Canetto), Kent Smith (Jeffrey Stewart), Claire Kelly (Genevieve), Corey Allen (Cookie), Lewis Charles (Danny Rimett), David Opatoshu (Lou Forbes), Kem Dibbs (Joey Vulner), Patrick McVey (O'Malley), Barbara Lang (Tall Blond Party Girl), Myrna Hansen (Joy Hampton), Betty Utey (Showgirl). **BITS:** Jack Lambert (Nick), Sam McDaniel (Jesse), Floyd Simmons (Assistant Prosecutor), Sydney Smith (Judge Bookwell), Rusty Lane (Judge John A. Dasen), Michael Dugan (Jenks), Irving Greenberg, Richard Devine, Georges Saurel (Rico's Hoods), Carl Thayler, Mike Pierce, John Franco, Ken Perry (Cookie's Henchmen), Barrie Chase, Sanita Pelkey, Sandy Warner (Showgirls), Burt Douglas (P.A. Voice), Harry Tom McKenna (Politician), Erich von Stroheim, Jr. (Police Lieutenant), Herbert Armstrong (Intern), Carmen Phillips (Rico's Secretary), Pat Cawley (Farrell's Secretary), Marshall Bradford (District Attorney), Tom Hernandez (Sketch Artist), David McMahon (Guard), Andrew Buck (Chauffeur), Aaron Saxon (Frankie Gasto), Vaughn Taylor (Dr. Caderman), Peter Bourne (Cab Driver), Vito Scotti (Hotel Clerk), Ralph Smiley (Hotel Proprietor), Herbert Lytton (Judge Alfino), Benny Rubin (Mr. Field), Paul Keast (Judge Davers), Jerry Schumacher (Newsboy), John Damler (Detective), Geraldine Wall (Day Matron), Robert B. Williams (Guard), Dolores Reed (Woman), David Garcia (Newsman), Harry Hines (Newsboy), Jack Gargan (Officer), Margaret Bert (Wardrobe Woman), Hy Anzel (Man), Maggie O'Byrne (Woman).

Filming Completed: July 22, 1958
Released: MGM, October 28, 1958
Running Time: 99 minutes

Thomas Farrell, a crippled lawyer who represents members of Rico Angelo's gang in 1930s Chicago, meets nightclub dancer Vicki Gaye at Rico's party celebrating Farrell's latest courtroom victory. Vicki asks Farrell to take her home and they discover that her roommate, Joy Hampton, has committed suicide. Farrell consoles Vicki; and a romance begins, which brings hope into both of their lonely lives. Rico assigns Farrell to defend the hoodlum Cookie from an indictment. Cookie jumps bail and the prosecutor arrests Farrell for bribing a juror. When Farrell won't reveal anything about Rico's activities, the prosecutor sends the word out that Farrell has talked and then releases him. Realizing that Rico will kill him or, worse, harm Vicki Farrell cooperates with the prosecutor and reveals all he knows. Farrell confronts Rico just before the police arrive to capture him; Rico has kidnapped Vicki and threatens to disfigure her in revenge for Farrell's betrayal. The police arrive, and Rico is killed. Farrell and Vicki leave sordid Chicago behind and start a new life together.

Party Girl stands out as Nicholas Ray's most antisocial, self-indulgent film. While most of his other works try, no matter how feebly to set a "realistic" social context—such as Miami of the early 1900s in *Wind Across the Everglades,* North Africa of World War II in *Bitter Victory,* and the urban jungle in *Knock on Any Door*—or to deal with social problems—such as drugs in *Bigger Than Life,* war in *Bitter Victory,* police brutality in *On Dangerous Ground,* ecology in *Wind Across the Everglades,* and the generation gap in *Rebel Without a Cause*—*Party Girl* makes no such pretense. Even *They Live by Night,* which shares with *Party Girl* the primary theme of two lovers in conflict with society, fails to approach the surreal, fantastical quality of the latter film. At no point in *They Live by Night* is the oppressive social atmosphere that drove these two young people to loneliness and despair forgotten, whereas *Party Girl* makes ample use of exotic dance sequences, costumes, and sets to create its surreal atmosphere. With the ambiguous opening title—"Chicago in the early '30s"—superimposed over a chiaroscuro backdrop of that city, the "unreal" tone of the entire film is set. Although the film is filled with easily recognizable Hollywood archetypes of a brutal yet childlike gangster czar, drooling henchmen, ambitious young punks, loose women with pure hearts, and self-righteous government investigators, *Party Girl* is far from the typical gangster product. Rather it restates one of the most insistent dualities in Ray's work. There is a personal division between his self-acknowledged duty to be involved as a social critic with civilization and his yearning to regress to a more primitive and emotionally pure existence and experience. The final scene of *Party Girl*, for example, illustrates Ray's stylization of violence as a hallucinatory and antisocial force. After turning in evidence on the mob in fear for Vicki's life (as only this danger can spur him to societal action), Farrell goes to Rico's hideout to confront the gangster. The room is filled with colored lights, decorations, and broken glass, which are the remnants of an all-night celebration. Rico sits on his wooden throne with his coat draped over him like a royal cape and calmly pours acid over a red, papier-mâché bell, thereby draining it of all color and "life." After this demonstration of Rico's power, the kidnaped Vicki is brought in with her face wrapped in bandages. Farrell stares at her in dread that she has already been disfigured. With excruciating slowness, the bandages are removed until her unscathed face is revealed. Farrell breathes easier but now Rico calls for their death. Farrell stalls for time by using a cynical trick he often used to draw sympathy from jurors. Rico has almost believed the complimentary ruse, when police sirens are heard and searchlights fill the festive room, followed by sprays of bullets and bursting glass. The acid intended for Vicki is splashed in Rico's face and he frantically, but with horrifying grace, falls through a window to his death. With Rico's death Farrell's and Vicki's connection with society is severed completely, and they walk away from the police and crowd of spectators into the deserted streets. Their action visually sums up the central theme of the movie and of noir sexuality: it can either destroy them or allow them to transcend the boundaries of society.

Compounding the theme of mad love are the dual natures of the hero and heroine and of society's underworld and legitimate "upperworld." Vicki and Farrell have both suffered spiritually: and Farrell is also physically handicapped. In consequence, as required in film noir, they have adopted cynicism to bandage their wounds. Vicki relates her philosophy very early in the film, when she tells another call girl, to "Never get crowded into a corner. Never let them get too close." Farrell expresses his bitterness when he explains, "That's my business—mouthpiece for the mob, guardian angel for punks and gunmen . . . I'm a great believer in the easiest way." Within this duality, Ray constructs a complex relationship among Rico, Farrell, and Vicki. Rico Angelo is the incarnation of evil, tempting Farrell with money and, later, threatening violence. Vicki is Farrell's redemption: curiously, this is revealed by Rico who has nicknamed her Angel. Ray's society, typically of film noir, divides into two distinct yet overlapping worlds. The underworld is violent, chaotic, and decadent; but it is always oriented to success, as is the "upperworld," repre-

sented by Jeffrey Stewart, which imposes order and stability. "Harmful" passions are suppressed, although controlled coercion against the two lovers is accepted. As in the underworld—consider Fabian in *Night and the City*—success is the overriding concern: it legitimizes questionable activity. Farrell, while in jail, asks Stewart, "Incidentally, when do they start pushing you for Senator?" and Stewart replies, "The day you start talking." The difference between Stewart's world and Rico's is in the former's repression of base instincts; and yet his success hinges on the destruction and revelation of the latter's activities.

—J.U.

THE PEOPLE AGAINST O'HARA (1951)

Director: John Sturges
Producer: William H. Wright (MGM)
Screenplay: John Monks, Jr.; from the novel by Eleazar Lipsky
Director of Photography: John Alton
Special Effects: A. Arnold Gillespie
Sound: Douglas Shearer
Music Score: Carmen Dragon
Art Directors: Cedric Gibbons, James Basevi
Set Decoration: Edwin B. Willis, Jacques Mapes
Costumes: Helen Rose
Makeup: William Tuttle
Hair Styles: Sydney Guilaroff
Assistant Director: Herbert Glazer
Film Editor: Gene Ruggiero

CAST: Spencer Tracy (James Curtayne), Pat O'Brien (Vincent Ricks), Diana Lynn (Ginny Curtayne), John Hodiak (Louis Barra), Eduardo Cianeli (Knuckles Lanzetta), James Arness (Johnny O'Hara), Yvette Duguay (Mrs. Lanzetta), Jay C. Flippen (Sven Norson), William Campbell (Frank Korvac), Richard Anderson (Jeff Chapman), Henry O'Neill (Judge Keating), Arthur Shields (Mr. O'Hara), Louise Lorimer (Mrs. O'Hara), Ann Doran (Betty Clark), Emile Meyer (Capt. Tom Mulvaney), Regis Toomey (Fred Colton), Katherine Warren (Mrs. Sheffield), Paul Bryar (Detective Howie Pendleton), Peter Mamakos (James Korvac), Perdita Chandler (Gloria Adler), Frank Fergusson (Al), Don Dillaway (Monty), C. Anthony Hughes (George), Lee Phelps (Emmett Kimbaugh), Lawrence Tolan (Vincent Korvac), Jack Lee (Court Clerk), Tony Barr (Little Wolfie). BITS: Jan Kayne, Virginia Hewitt (Girls), Richard Landry (Sailor), "Billy" Vincent (William Sheffield), Frankie Hyers (Bartender), Michael Dugan (Charlie, Detective), Lennie Bremen (Harry), Jim Toney (Officer Abrams), Benny Burt (Sammy), John Maxwell (Thayer Connolly), Mae Clarke (Receptionist), Paul McGuire (Male Stenographer), Kay Scott (Secretary), Angi O. Poulis (Watch-

Left to right: Ricks (Pat O'Brien), radio technician, and Bara (John Hodiak) in The People Against O'Hara.

Left to right facing: Ricks (Pat O'Brien), Curtayne (Spencer Tracy) and Bara (John Hodiak) in The People Against O'Hara.

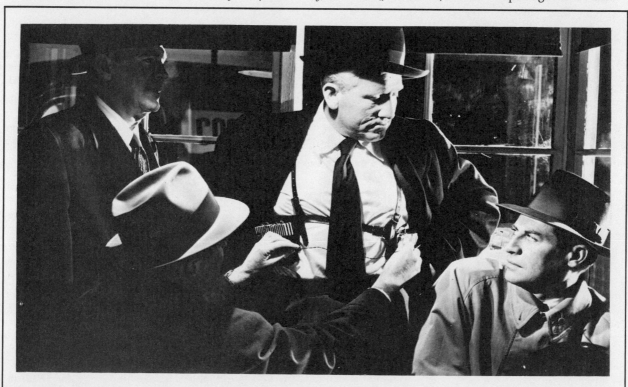

man), Julius Tannen (Toby Baum), Dan Foster (Assistant District Attorney), Harry Cody (Photographer), Ned Glass (Magistrate), John Butler, (Court Clerk), Lou Lubin (Eddie), Michael Mark (Workman), Phyllis Graffeo (Mary), Maurice Samuels (Papa Lanzetta), Celia Lovsky (Mrs. Korvac), Charles [Bronson] Buchinsky (Angelo Korvac), Bill Fletcher (Pete Korvac), Richard Bartlett (Tony Korvac), Joyce Otis (Thelma), "Tiny" Jimmie Kelly (Leigh Keighly), Fred Essler (Augie), John Albright (Waiter), John Sheehan (Postal Clerk), Jack Kruschen (Detective), William Self (Technician), Jonathan Cott (Policeman), William Schallert (Intern), Sammy Finn, Brooks Benedict (Gamblers), Frank Sully, Ernesto Morelli (Fishmongers), Jeff Richards (Ambulance Driver), George Magrill (Court Attendant), Bud Wolfe (Fingerprint Technician).
Filming Completed: April 20, 1951
Released: MGM, September 5, 1951
Running Time: 102 minutes

James Curtayne is an ex-district attorney whose alcoholism forced his early retirement. Now on the wagon, Curtayne would like to make a comeback as a lawyer, although his daughter, Ginny, who has been postponing marriage to take care of him, is worried lest the pressures of another case drive him back to drink. However, Curtayne takes the case of an acquaintance, Johnny O'Hara, as a favor to his parents who do not have the money for a good lawyer. Johnny is accused of gunning a man down in the streets; but he swears to Curtayne that he is innocent, although he will not say where he was at the time of the murder. On the basis of evidence offered by Frankie Korvac, reputedly a friend of Johnny's, the district attorney, Barra, feels he has a strong case. Curtayne's old friend, detective Vince Ricks, helps him discover that Johnny was out with his former girl friend that fatal night but refused to make this known for fear of getting her in trouble with her husband, gangster Knuckles Lanzetta. Also, Frankie Korvac and his brothers are no real friends of Johnny's, and it is possible that Frankie is the guilty party. Curtayne finds a seaman who witnessed the shooting from across the street, but the man refuses to testify in Johnny's favor unless he is paid. Curtayne reluctantly gives the man money, fearing he cannot win the case without his testimony. During the summation Curtayne's physical condition weakens his presentation. However, Barra discovers the bribe and Curtayne decides to redeem himself by hiding a microphone on himself, which will broadcast to a hidden police van. Since he is meeting with the Korvacs to sell them information, Barra realizes that Curtayne is setting himself up as a clay pigeon. When the Korvacs emerge from a parked car, the police descend on them but not in time to prevent Curtayne's death.

John Alton's photography evokes a cluttered and chaotic environment in his use of the New York locations; and his night shots, particularly the long odyssey of Curtayne at the film's climax, are as dark and uninviting as any in *T-Men*. *People Against O'Hara* is another one of the MGM noirs directed by John Sturges and it is rather strange to see some of the MGM stars in this sort of film, particularly an actor like Spencer Tracy, who, perhaps for the first and only time in his career, portrays an indecisive alcoholic.

—B.P.

PHANTOM LADY (1944)

Director: Robert Siodmak
Executive Producer: Milton Feld (Universal)
Associate Producer: Joan Harrison
Screenplay: Bernard C. Schoenfeld; from the novel by William Irish (Cornell Woolrich)
Director of Photography: Woody Bredell
Sound: Bernard B. Brown, Joe Lapis
Music Director: Hans J. Salter
Music Staging: Lester Horton
Song: "Chick-ee-Chick," music by Jacques Press, lyric by Eddie Cherkose; sung by Aurora
Art Directors: John B. Goodman, Robert Clatworthy
Set Decoration: Russell Gausman, L.R. Smith
Costumes: Vera West, the "phantom hat" created by Kenneth Hopkins
Assistant Directors: Seward Webb, Willard Sheldon
Film Editor: Arthur Hilton

CAST: Franchot Tone (Jack Marlow), Ella Raines (Carol "Kansas" Richman), Alan Curtis (Scott Henderson), Aurora (Estela Monteiro), Thomas Gomez (Inspector Burgess), Fay Helm (Ann Terry), Elisha Cook, Jr. (Cliff March), Andrew Tombes, Jr. (Bartender), Regis Toomey (Detective), Joseph Crehan (Detective), Doris Lloyd (Kettisha), Virginia Brissac (Dr. Chase), Milburn Stone (District Attorney).
Filming Completed: October 28, 1943
Released: Universal, February 17, 1944
Running Time: 87 minutes

Scott Henderson, a successful young businessman, is arrested for the murder of his wife, who was strangled in their apartment with his tie. On the night of the murder, he explains, he met a young lady in a bar and persuaded her to join him in attending a musical show. Part of their arrangement was that they would withhold each other's names, so all he knows about her is that she was wearing a flamboyant hat which was identical to the one that the lead Latin American singer in the show was wearing. Since neither the cabdriver, the bartender, nor the singer can (or will) confirm his story, Scott is tried, convicted, and sentenced to die in eighteen days. Scott's faithful secretary, Kansas, believes his story and decides to find the real murderer with assistance from police Inspector Burgess, who is also convinced of Scott's innocence. She haunts the

Kansas accompanies Jack back to his studio-apartment to wait for Burgess, where she discovers her stolen purse and realizes Jack is the murderer. As Jack unties his scarf to strangle her, Burgess arrives and Jack jumps out the apartment window. Scott is freed from prison and is welcomed home by Kansas.

The Phantom Lady not only boosted the American career of director Robert Siodmak, but also gave him a *métier* in which his special Germanic temperament would find its happiest medium—the film noir. For all of its silly dialogue and reliance on one of the pulpier Woolrich novels, it, as much as any other film, defines the studio noir. Siodmak and his brilliant cinematographer, Woody Bredell, have provided *The Phantom Lady* with the essential ingredients of Woolrich's world, from the desperate innocent at loose at night in New York City, a city of hot sweltering streets, to the details of threatening shadows, jazz emanating from low-class bars, and the click of high heels on the pavement. The whole noir world is developed here almost entirely through *mise-en-scène*. The second half of the film, in which Franchot Tone predominates as a domestic version of the crazed artist—whose preoccupation with his hands is a throwback to the German classic, *The Hands of Orlac* [*Orlacs Händes*]—is certainly the weaker part of the film and the denouement does stress verisimilitude. But these defects can be easily overlooked because of the film's tour de force jazz as sex sequence. Intercutting shots of Elisha Cook, Jr., reaching orgiastic fervor as he climaxes his drum solo with shots of the wordless sexual innuendos of Ella Raines, Siodmak brilliantly interweaves expressionistic decor with American idiom. If watched without sound, the scene could be from one of the classic German films of the 1920s.

—B.P.

Left to right: Carol "Kansas" Richman (Ella Raines), and prisoner Scott Henderson (Alan Curtis) in Phantom Lady.

bar where Scott first met the "phantom lady," and pressures the bartender to inform; but he is killed in a car accident. Disguising herself as a prostitute, Kansas seduces Cliff March, a trap drummer in the musical show who had given the "phantom lady" the eye. Cliff admits that he has been paid off to "forget" the woman. When Kansas unfortunately drops her purse and Cliff sees the police sheet on him, which she is carrying, he is upset and pursues her. She escapes to call Burgess; but Cliff is strangled with a scarf by Jack Marlow, who takes Kansas's purse. Marlow, Scott's best friend, is a schizophrenic artist who was having an affair with Scott's wife, and killed her when she refused to run away with him. Jack meets Kansas at the prison when both are visiting Scott, and he agrees to help her find the murderer. Through a cooperative milliner, they trace the hat to Ann Terry, who gives them the hat. Overjoyed,

PICKUP ON SOUTH STREET (1953)

Director: Samuel Fuller
Producer: Jules Schermer (Jules Schermer Productions)
Screenplay: Samuel Fuller; from an unpublished story by Dwight Taylor
Director of Photography: Joe Macdonald
Special Photographic Effects: Ray Kellogg
Sound: Winston H. Leverett
Music: Leigh Harline
Music Director: Lionel Newman
Orchestration: Edward Powell
Art Directors: Lyle Wheeler, George Patrick
Set Decoration: Al Orenbach
Costumes: Travilla
Wardrobe Director: Charles LeMaire
Makeup: Ben Nye
Assistant Director: Ad Schaumer
Film Editor: Nick De Maggio

CAST: Richard Widmark (Skip McCoy), Jean Peters (Candy), Thelma Ritter (Moe), Murvyn Vye (Capt. Dan Tiger), Richard Kiley (Joey), Willis B. Bouchey (Zara), Milburn Stone (Winoki), Henry Slate (MacGregor), Jerry O'Sullivan (Enyart), **BITS:** Harry Carter (Dietrich), George E. Stone (Police Clerk), George Eldredge (Fenton), Stuart Randall (Police Commissioner), Frank Kumagi (Lum), Victor Perry (Lightning Louie), Maurice Samuels (Peddler), Parley Baer (Stranger), Jay Loftin (Librarian), Virginia Carroll (Nurse), Roger Moore (Mr. Victor), Clancy Cooper (Lean Man), John Gallaudet (Campion), Wilson Wood (Driver), Ray Montgomery, Ray Stevens (F.B.I. Agents), Ralph Moody (Captain).
Location: Los Angeles, California; New York, New York
Filming Completed: October 16, 1952
Released: 20th Century-Fox, June 17, 1953
Running Time: 83 minutes

A New York City pickpocket and "three-time loser" named Skip McCoy inadvertently lifts some microfilm from the purse of Candy, the former mistress of a Communist spy, Joey. McCoy's nemesis on the police force, Capt. Tiger, cooperates with the federal agent who maintained surveillance over Candy. Tiger learns that McCoy has the microfilm from Moe, an old woman who supplements her income from selling ties by peddling information. But Skip denies that the film exists and does not yield to the federal agent's patriotic appeal or Tiger's promise to overlook the crime. Moe sells Skip's waterfront address to Candy because she must retrieve the microfilm by any means possible. She and Skip are sexually attracted to one another; but this does not affect his price for the microfilm. Candy refuses to cooperate with Joey when she learns he is a Communist, and she confides in Moe. Joey tries to buy Skip's address from Moe; but he kills her when she refuses to reveal it to a Communist at any price. He then savagely beats and shoots Candy, who had acquired the film but was cooperating with the federal agents. A piece is missing from the film; and Joey, who has obtained Skip's address, goes to meet the pickpocket. Skip avoids the spy and follows him on the subway, where he lifts both the microfilm and Joey's gun. After breaking up Joey's rendezvous, Skip pursues Joey and beats him mercilessly to avenge Candy's shooting and Moe's death. Candy and Skip are reunited, and he is free of any criminal charges.

Much has been written about the contradictions of Fuller's politics. *Pickup on South Street* is anti-Communist, but the sympathetic Americans of the film are not members of respectable society. A pickpocket, a prostitute, and a stool pigeon fight for their country even though they will remain in its gutter. Fuller laughs in the face of righteous patriotic sentiment. When the pious federal man asks solemnly, "Do you know what Communism is?" Skip breezily replies, "Who cares?"

In spite of the provocative nature of these themes, the real distinction of Fuller's film is his visual realization.

Pickup benefits from Joe MacDonald's high-contrast black-and-white photography and from the vividly created settings of subways, the waterfront, and Moe's shabby room. Fuller is never stylistically redundant. Long takes, such as the moving shot that stalks Candy as Joey assaults her, alternate with rhythmically cut sequences. Intense close-ups often dominate, but at other times the camera glides over the action, coming to rest and resuming movement at unexpected intervals.

Contrast is characteristically a part of the action and Fuller's violent love scenes are the best example. The eroticism of Skip and Candy's encounter is heightened by Skip's readiness to punch Candy in the mouth and then caress the bruise he has created. Equally, she will unhesitatingly knock him unconscious after making love in order to get what she wants. *Pickup* features what is perhaps the most compelling example in all of Fuller's films of his mingling of violence and tenderness. Most of the action is hard, tough, and brutal; but the scene of Moe's death is unexpectedly sensitive and touching. Thelma Ritter's Moe is one of the most embellished supporting characters in film noir. Exhausted by life, her romantic phonograph record accompanies her last moments, when she heroically repulses Joey's threats. The camera holds tellingly on Moe's face as the shabby woman becomes proudly beautiful.
—B.L.

THE PITFALL (1948)

Director: André de Toth
Producer: Samuel Bischoff (Regal Films)
Screenplay: Karl Kamb, from the novel by Jay Dratler
Director of Photography: Harry Wild
Sound: Frank Webster
Music: Louis Forbes
Art Director: Arthur Lonergan
Set Decoration: Robert Priestley
Makeup: Robert Cowan
Hairstyles: Hedvig Mjorud
Production Manager: Ben Hersh
Assistant Director: Joe Depew
Script Supervisor: Cora Palmatier
Film Editor: Walter Thompson

CAST: Dick Powell (John Forbes), Lizabeth Scott (Mona Stevens), Jane Wyatt (Sue Forbes), Raymond Burr (MacDonald), John Litel (District Attorney), Byron Barr (Bill Smiley), Jimmy Hunt (Tommy Forbes), Ann Doran (Maggie), Selmer Jackson (Ed Brawley), Margaret Wells (Terry), Dick Wassel (Desk Sergeant).
Location: Los Angeles, California
Filming Completed: March 18, 1948
Released: United Artists, August 24, 1948
Running Time: 86 minutes

John Forbes (Dick Powell) is nursed by his wife Sue (Jane Wyatt), and son, Tommy (Jimmy Hunt) in The Pitfall.

John Forbes, a successful insurance agent married to his high school sweetheart, Sue, lives with her and their young son, Tommy, in a suburb of Los Angeles. John feels that their youthful plans have failed to materialize and he is bored with the routine of his existence. His firm has paid off on a robbery committed by Bill Smiley, who is now in jail. John is aided by private detective Mack MacDonald in recovering some of the goods that Smiley had bought with the stolen money. The items are traced to Mona Stevens, Smiley's beautiful blond girl friend, who is a model living near a marina, where she enjoys taking her motorboat out for pleasure rides. Mona is disappointed, of course, that she must give up Smiley's gifts. John is attracted to her, and what starts out as an innocent adventure becomes a love affair. Mack warns John to stay away from Mona, since he also wishes to court her despite her obvious dislike of him. John ends his affair with the woman; but Mack arranges for Smiley's bail and plies him with liquor to arouse the criminal's jealousy and hostility towards John. Mona warns the insurance agent, who puts his family to bed and waits downstairs with a gun. Smiley breaks into the house and is fatally shot. John reveals the entire affair to his wife, who is unsure of her emotions. Meanwhile, Mack forces Mona to run off with him but she kills him. John is exonerated while Mona is arrested. As John and Sue drive home from the courthouse, Sue explains that she will remain his wife although their relationship may never be the same.

The Pitfall is the key film noir detailing the fall of the errant husband from the grace of bourgeois respectability. The casting underscores this aspect of the film: a pre-Perry Mason Raymond Burr is both reprehensible and pathetic as Mack, attempting to gain the affection of Mona, portrayed by Lizabeth Scott, the classic good-bad girl aptly described once by Humphrey Bogart in *Dead Reckoning* as "Cinderella with a husky voice." Dick Powell's cherubic good looks, which made him the most vulnerable of the tough guys, and his usually sour disposition enhance the boredom exhibited by the husband whose life has fallen into a rut. Finally, Jane Wyatt is the stereotypical wife and mother, and she provides a visual contrast to Lizabeth Scott in a reversal of the classic "dark" and "light" women of romantic fiction. In exposing the chinks in the facade of the American middle-class dream of suburban life, *Pitfall* looks forward to such films as *Bigger than life; Rebel Without a Cause;* and *No Down Payment.* From today's perspective, Tommy Forbes's nightmares—which may be caused by more than his reading comic books, despite his father's glib assurance to the contrary—are telling indicators of the pervasive malaise of the American middle class as expressed in film noir.

—B.P.

PLUNDER ROAD (1957)

Director: Hubert Cornfield
Executive Producer: E. J. Baumgarten (Regal Films)
Producers: Leon Chooluck, Laurence Stewart
Screenplay: Steven Ritch and Jack Charney; from an unpublished story by Steven Ritch
Director of Photography: Ernest Haller (Regalscope)
Sound: Harold Hanks, Harry M. Leonard
Music: Irving Gertz
Art Director: Robert Gill
Assistant Directors: Louis Brandt, Nat Merman

Producer's Assistant: Michael Fox
Film Editors: Warren Adams, Jerry S. Young

CAST: Gene Raymond (Eddie), Jeanne Cooper (Fran), Wayne Morris (Commando), Elisha Cook, Jr. (Skeets), Stafford Repp (Roly Adams), Steven Ritch (Frankie), Nora Hayden (Hazel), **BITS:** Helen Heigh (Society Woman), Paul Harber, Michael Fox, Charles Conrad (Troopers), Douglas Bank, Richard Newton (Guards), Don Garrett, George Keymas (Policemen), Jim Canino (Tibbs), Robin Riley (Don), Harry Tyler (Ernie Beach), Stacy Graham, Michael Fox, Douglas Bank (Narrators).
Location: Los Angeles, California
Filming Completed: July 26, 1957
Released: 20th Century-Fox, December 5, 1957
Running Time: 82 minutes

A gang robs a train of the gold bound for the San Francisco mint. The gang members are: Eddie, a college man who planned the theft; Commando, a widowed ex-con who plans to retire to Rio with his son; Frankie, an ex-race car driver; Skeets, a good-natured former stunt man; and Roly, a gum-chewing truck driver. After the robbery the gold ingots are divided into three lots and hidden on three different vehicles: a moving van, a freight truck supposedly hauling coffee, and a tanker supposedly filled with chemicals. Roly leaves first in the moving van. When he forgets to turn off the police radio on his truck and arouses suspicion at a roadblock, he panics and is killed. Next to depart are Commando and Skeets in the freight truck. At a weighing station, their load gives them away and they are captured. Eddie and Frankie, in the tanker, manage to make it to Los Angeles. They unload the gold at an iron foundry where arrangements have been made by Eddie's girl friend, Fran. They melt down and cast the gold into bumpers, which they chrome and place on a Cadillac. The next day as they drive to board a ship, an accident backs up traffic, and a gawking woman locks bumpers with their car. When a pair of policemen attempt to help uncouple the cars, the chrome is scraped off. Frankie draws his gun and is shot; Eddie tells Fran to run and heads off for the freeway overpass. With the police in pursuit, he jumps off the bridge, trying to land on the top of a truck on the freeway below. He is unable to secure himself, rolls off the truck's top, and is crushed in the oncoming traffic.

Plunder Road makes the most of a very limited budget by dividing its narrative into three major segments and following its characters through a variety of locations atmospherically photographed by Ernest Haller. Both the visual style and the presence of actors such as Elisha Cook, Jr., and Stafford Repp, archetypal losers from numerous noir films of the 1940s, anticipate the most noir aspect of *Plunder Road*, the overriding determinism of its narrative. Unlike Kubrick's *The Killing* of a year earlier, *Plunder Road* eschews overlapping scenes or any pointedly analytical devices in favor of a basic, dramatic irony in which the

criminals are defeated by their own elaborate safeguards. Perhaps Eddie has an instant of anguished realization, as he plummets off the overpass, that if only he had simply put the ingots in the trunk of the car rather than doing as he did, he might have succeeded. However, that is less significant than the totality of the actions leading up to that moment. The final shot, pulling back from the freeway clogged with vehicles, underscores the fatally noir statement of the film even as it abandons its characters to existential oblivion.

—B.P. & A.S.

POINT BLANK (1967)

Director: John Boorman
Producer: Judd Bernard, Robert Chartoff (BCW)
Screenplay: Alexander Jacobs, David Newhouse, and Rafe Newhouse; from the novel *The Hunter* by Richard Stark (Donald Westlake)
Director of Photography: Philip H. Lathrop (Metrocolor; Panavision)
Special Effects: Virgil Beck
Color Consultant: Bill Stair
Sound: Franklin Milton, Larry Jost, Frank Artunez
Music: Johnny Mandel
Art Directors: George W. Davis, Albert Brenner
Set Decoration: Henry Grace, Keogh Gleason
Costumes: Margo Weintz
Makeup: John Truwe
Dialogue Coach: Norman Stewart
Script Supervisor: Doris Grau
Assistant Director: Al Jennings
Film Editor: Henry Berman

CAST: Lee Marvin (Walker), Angie Dickinson (Chris), Keenan Wynn (Yost), Carroll O'Connor (Brewster), Lloyd Bochner (Frederick Carter), Michael Strong (Stegman), John Vernon (Mal Reese), Sharon Acker (Lynne), James Sikking (Hired Gun), Sandra Warner (Waitress), Roberta Haynes (Mrs. Carter), Kathleen Freeman (Citizen), Victor Creatore (Carter's Man), Lawrence Hauben (Car Salesman), Susan Holloway (Customer), Sid Haig, Michael Bell (Guards), Priscilla Boyd (Receptionist), John McMurtry (Messenger), Ron Walter, George Strattan (Men), Nicole Rogell (Carter's Secretary), Rico Cattani, Roland LaStarza (Reese's Gura Guards). **BITS:** Jerry Catron, Joe Mell (Men), Ted White (Football Player), Casey Brandon, Roseann Williams, Bonnie Dewberry, Carey Foster (Dancers), Karen Lee (Waitress), Bill Hickman, Chuck Hicks (Guards), Louis Whitehill (Policeman), Felix Silla (Bellhop), Andrew Orapeza (Desk Clerk).
Location: Alcatraz Island, San Francisco, Los Angeles, California
Filming Completed: April 27, 1967
Released: MGM, September 18, 1967

POSSESSED

Running Time: 92 minutes
MPAA Rating: R

A man, Walker, is shot point-blank in a cell on deserted Alcatraz prison island by his friend Reese, with whom he has been hijacking a crime syndicate's money. Walker's wife, Lynne, is also present and, as he becomes unconscious, it is clear that Lynne has been unfaithful and helped Reese betray him. But somehow, Walker survives. Later, he meets a mysterious man, Yost, who offers Walker support in a plan for revenge and recovery of the $93,000 taken by Reese and Lynne. Walker goes to Los Angeles, shooting Lynne's bed full of holes but unable to kill her. She later dies of an overdose of sleeping pills. Walker finds he must not only revenge himself on Reese but also collect his money from the top members of the syndicate, who are Carter, Brewster, and Fairfax. He uses Lynne's friend, Chris, to set up Reese by seducing him. Walker enters the security penthouse but Reese is so frightened by Walker that he accidentally falls from the roof. Walker attempts to get his money from Carter, who plans to have him shot. At the designated place, the sniper shoots at long range and kills Carter instead. Taking Chris with him, Walker goes to Brewster's house to wait. When Brewster arrives, he tells Walker that they have to go to Alcatraz for the money, but this is to lure Walker into a trap. Yost, who is in fact Fairfax, is also at Alcatraz and has Brewster killed by the same sniper who killed Carter. As Fairfax shouts at Walker to come and get his money, Walker withdraws into the shadows.

Point Blank is not a literal narrative. The shooting of Walker at point-blank range realistically suggests that he is dead from the first few moments of the film. His inexplicable survival and subsequent reserve dominates even violent moments, and his face is a mask permanently registering the emotions of the exact moment when he comprehended his betrayal. The technical complexity of the film, which at times is powerfully expressive, supports the view that the film actually tells a story that is in Walker's mind. He considers the possibilities of revenge open to him *if* he had lived and, at last, determines that they lead nowhere.

This fascinating premise is influenced by the films of Alain Resnais, manifesting a profound concern with the ambiguities of time and space. In addition, *Point Blank* brings film noir into a contemporary world of cold glass and steel, of gray suits and modish decor. Telephoto lenses and unbalanced compositions, emphasizing Walker's total alienation, enhance the presentation of Walker as a noir hero situated in a world where women take tranquilizers and gangsters have no personality. John Boorman's attention to every aspect of the work is remarkable, and his direction of Lee Marvin as Walker and Angie Dickinson as Chris results in unusual and notable performances. Although the extroverted role of Carroll O'Connor as the gangster, Brewster, is disruptive to the film, the first few reels are hypnotic, especially the sequence of Walker's walk through the Los Angeles airport intercut with shots of Lynne in her apartment, which combine the loud reverberation of his footsteps over each image.

—B.L.

POSSESSED (1947)
[Working Titles: THE SECRET, ONE MAN'S SECRET]

Director: Curtis Bernhardt
Producer: Jerry Wald (Warner Brothers)
Screenplay: Sylvia Richards and Ranald MacDougall; from the *Cosmopolitan* magazine novelette *One Man's Secret* by Rita Weiman
Director of Photography: Joseph Valentine
Special Effects: William McGann, Robert Burks
Sound: Robert B. Lee
Music Score: Franz Waxman
Music Director: Leo Forbstein
Orchestration: Leonid Raab
Art Director: Anton Grot
Set Decoration: Fred M. MacLean
Costumes: Bernard Newman, Adrian
Makeup: Perc Westmore
Unit Manager: Lou Baum
Dialogue Director: Herschel Daugherty
Assistant Director: Sherry Shourds
Film Editor: Rudi Fehr

CAST: Joan Crawford (Louise Howell Graham), Van Heflin (David Sutton), Raymond Massey (Dean Graham) Geraldine Brooks (Carol Graham), Stanley Ridges (Dr. Harvey Williard), John Ridgely (Harker), Moroni Olsen (Dr. Ames), Erskine Sanford (Dr. Max Sherman), Gerald Perreau (Wynn Graham), Isabel Withers (Nurse Rosen), Lisa Golm (Elsie), Douglas Kennedy (Assistant District Attorney), Monte Blue (Norris), Don McGuire (Dr. Craig), Rory Mallinson (Coroner's Assistant), Clifton Young (Intern), Griff Barnett (Coroner). **BITS:** Ralph Dunn (Motorman), Max Wagner, Dick Bartell (Men in Cafe), Frank Marlowe (Proprietor), Rose Plummer (Woman in Cafe), Jane Harker (Woman's Voice), Robert Lowell, Richard Walsh (Faces), Jack Mower (Man), James Conaty (Foreman), Creighton Hale (Secretary), Jane Harker (First College Girl), Martha Montgomery (Second College Girl), Tristram Coffin (Man at Concert), Jacob Gimpel (Walter Sveldon), Nell Craig, Bunty Cutler (Nurses), Henry Sylvester (Dean's Secretary), Sara Padden (Caretaker's Wife), Wheaton Chambers (Waiter), Eddie Hart (Bartender), Philo McCullough (Butler), Paul Bradley, Peggy Leon (Wedding Guests).
Filming Completed: November 12, 1946
Released: Warner Brothers, May 29, 1947
Running Time: 108 minutes

Wealthy Mrs. Louise Graham is found at dawn, wandering in downtown Los Angeles and asking for "David" as if in a trance. Taken to the hospital, doctors learn her story through narcosynthesis. As Louise Howell, she was employed by industrialist Dean Graham as a nurse to his wife, Pauline, an invalid with symptoms of mental illness. Louise is in love with a young engineer, David Sutton, who rejects her and takes a job in Canada. Meanwhile, Pauline Graham imagines a liaison between her husband and Louise and drowns herself. Some time later Mr. Graham proposes marriage to Louise and she accepts. Unexpectedly, David attends the wedding reception and begins to court Carol, Graham's daughter. Louise's mind begins to falter and she imagines killing Carol. After seeing a psychiatrist under an assumed name, Louise refuses to heed his warnings about her potential mental breakdown. She confronts David, and attempts to arouse his pity and cause him to break with Carol; but he refuses, and Louise kills him. This act precipitates her catatonic state.

Possessed reflects Curtis Bernhardt's penchant for psychological themes, as did *Conflict* and *The High Wall*. A past master at the creation of *stimmung*, or atmosphere, Bernhardt evokes the ethos of film noir in a variety of scenes, such as the opening location shot, which is an evocative mixture of downtown exteriors in the early morning half-light with the odyssey of the entranced woman; the disorienting shot of Louise being wheeled into the hospital and her point-of-view looking up from the bed; the associational dissolve from the hospital water pitcher to the mountain lake where Mrs. Graham commits suicide; and the use of rain-streaked windows, which frame the mournful face of Louise. By developing the plot from the point-of-view of a neurotic and skillfully using flashback and fantasy scenes in a straightforward manner, the distinction betwen reality and Louise's imagination is blurred. That makes *The Possessed* a prime example of oneirism, the dreamlike tone that is a seminal characteristic of film noir.

—B.P.

THE POSTMAN ALWAYS RINGS TWICE (1946)

Director: Tay Garnett
Producer: Carey Wilson (MGM)
Screenplay: Harry Ruskin and Niven Busch; from the novel by James M. Cain
Director of Photogrpahy: Sidney Wagner
Sound: Douglas Shearer
Music Score: George Bassman
Orchestration: Ted Duncan
Art Directors: Cedric Gibbons, Randall Duell
Set Decoration: Edwin B. Willis
Costumes: Irene
Wardrobe: Marion Herwood Keyes
Makeup: Jack Dawn
Assistant Director: William Lewis
Film Editor: George White

CAST: Lana Turner (Cora Smith), John Garfield (Frank Chambers), Cecil Kellaway (Nick Smith), Hume Cronyn (Arthur Keats), Leon Ames (Kyle Sackett), Audrey Totter (Madge Gorland), Alan Reed (Ezra Liam Kennedy), Jeff York (Blair), Charles Williams (Jimmie White), Cameron Grant (Willie), Wally Cassell (Ben), William Halligan, Morris Ankrum (Judges). **BITS:** Garry Owen (Truck Driver), Dorothy Phillips (Nurse), Edward Earle (Doctor), Byron Foulger (Picnic Manager), Sondra Morgan (Matron), Jeffrey Sayre, Walter Ridge, Dick Crockett, James Darrell (Reporters), Brick Sullivan, Paul Krueger (Officers), Phillip Ahlm, John Alban, Harold Miller, Reginald Simpson (Photographers), Betty Blythe, Helen McLeod, Hilda Rhodes (Customers), Joel Friedkin (John X. MacHugh), Jack Chefe (Headwaiter), George Noisom (Telegraph Messenger), Frank Mayo, Bud Harrison (Bailiffs), Virginia Randolph (Snooty Woman), Tom Dillon (Father McConnell), Howard Mitchell, John M. Sullivan (Doctors), James Farley (Warden), Edward Sherrod, Dan Quigg, Oliver Cross, Paul Bradley (Men), Paula Ray (Woman).
Filming Completed: October 26, 1945
Released: MGM, May 2, 1946
Running Time: 113 minutes

[NOTE: MGM officials joined with producers of a French version of James M. Cain's novel to block worldwide distribution of the 1942 Italian production *Ossessione*, directed by Luchino Visconti, which was an unauthorized film version of *The Postman Always Rings Twice*.]

A drifter, Frank Chambers, arrives at a small California roadside café and is immediately attracted to Cora Smith, a beautiful young woman married to the elderly proprietor of the restaurant. Staying on as an employee, Frank falls hopelessly in love with Cora. They plan to leave together, but after quickly discovering the harsh realities of life on the road they return to the café before her husband discovers them missing. Cora convinces Frank that the only way to stay together is to kill her husband and make it appear an accident. Their initial attempts fail. Finally, on a trip to Santa Barbara, the murder is committed. But Frank cannot get out of the car fast enough, and he plunges over the cliff with the doomed husband. While recuperating in the hospital, Frank is placed in a compromising situation. The district attorney is bent on pinning the murder on Cora, and Frank is hustled into signing a complaint against her. The trial never goes to court for lack of evidence, and in a fatal gesture, Cora marries Frank. Their relationship is complicated by an unnecessary affair and various attempts at blackmail by an unscrupulous lawyer who had initially forced a confession out of the frightened Cora at the time of the accident. Finally, believing all their problems to be behind them, Cora and Frank resolve to begin a new life. But they have another automobile accident and Cora is killed. Frank is falsely convicted of her murder and is condemned to die in the electric chair.

THE PRETENDER

Evil and corruption lie just below the surface of the mundane in *The Postman Always Rings Twice*. Virtually the entire film takes place in a bright, rather shabby roadside café, one that is, as the narrator informs us at the opening of the film, just like thousands of other roadside restaurants. James M. Cain's novel of treachery and murder becomes a classic vision of the noir films' ability to depict *amour fou*, a love which goes beyond the bounds of normal relationships. As a *femme fatale*, Cora Smith is a far cry from Cain's cold-blooded Phyllis Dietrichson, portrayed by Barbara Stanwyck in *Double Indemnity*. Cora is helpless, trapped in a world of abundant ironies. Her marriage to Nick in order to "get away" leaves her bored and restless. The love affair with Frank ends with both parties dead. She offered Frank a world removed from the ordinary, but in doing so, Cora condemned each of them to a nightmarish existence. Phyllis, on the other hand, constructs her plots with calculating precision, and she manipulates her cast of characters to her whims. Her death at the hands of Walter Neff completes the bizarre ritual of love and death she embraced; and she dies without love or pity. Cora, however, remains a sympathetic character throughout *The Postman Always Rings Twice*, as she is caught in a situation from which there is no real escape and moves inevitably toward her doom. Tay Garnett's direction highlights this paradox, lending it a surreal quality, as in the sequence in which Frank and Cora swim far out into the deep ocean at night to cleanse themselves of suspicion and reaffirm their love to one another. The dark ocean suggests the surrounding doom and danger that has become a part of their lives and threatens to drown them. Many of Garnett's scenes also consist of two or three simple shots with little tracking or moving of the camera. The claustrophobia of these static shots, which the lovers share with Cora's unwanted husband, seem to compel the lovers toward murderous action as the only way to force her husband to give them breathing room. This link between sex and violence is explicit throughout the film, as Frank tells Cora, "Give me a kiss or I'll sock ya," early in the story. And when she tells him, after the murder, that she wants "kisses that come from life, not death," their fate has already been sealed by their own actions. She is killed in a car wreck caused by giving Frank that kiss from life. As the car door opens after the crash, her arm falls, and her hand releases a tube of lipstick, which drops to the ground. This symbolically reverses the events of their first meeting, when Frank stoops to pick up a lipstick tube rolling toward him; he then looks up to see Cora standing over him with a waiting hand outstretched to receive her possession.

Important also is that Frank narrates the story, as Walter Neff did in *Double Indemnity*, prior to his execution. In flashback, Frank attempts to examine and understand what went wrong and enables *The Postman Always Rings Twice* to capture the ambience of the film noir world without compromising the fatalistic nature of Cain's novel.

—E.K. & C.M.

THE PRETENDER (1947)

Director and Producer: W. Lee Wilder (W. W. Productions)
Screenplay: Don Martin, with additional dialogue by Doris Miller
Director of Photography: John Alton
Sound: Herbert Norsch
Music Director: Paul Dessau
Art Director: F. Paul Sylos
Costumes: I. R. Berne
Makeup: Don Cash
Production Manager: George Moskov
Assistant Director: Mack Wright
Film Editor: Asa Boyd Clark
Supervising Film Editor: John F. Link

CAST: Albert Dekker (Kenneth Holden), Catherine Craig (Claire Worthington), Charles Drake (Dr. Leonard Koster), Alan Carney (Victor Korrin), Linda Stirling (Flo Ronson), Tom Kennedy (Fingers Murdock), Selmer Jackson (Charles Lennox), Charles Middleton (William, Butler), Ernie Adams (Thomas, Butler), Ben Welden (Mickie), John Bagni (Hank Gordon), Stanley Ross (Stranger), Forrest Taylor (Dr. Stevens), Greta Clement (Margie), Peggy Wynne (Miss Chalmers), Eula Guy (Nurse), Cay Forrester (Evelyn Cossett), Peter Michael (Stephen), Michael Mark (Janitor), Dorothy Scott (Miss Michael).

Filming Completed: April 2, 1947
Released: Republic, August 13, 1947
Running Time: 69 minutes

Kenneth Holden, a handsome, middle-aged investment broker, embezzles from an estate and then plans to marry the estate's heiress, Claire Worthington, thereby covering up his crime. But Claire rejects Ken's proposal because she is already engaged. He then arranges with Vic Korrin, a nightclub owner, to have Claire's fiancé killed, saying that the victim's photograph will appear in the newspaper's society section. When Claire suddenly breaks her engagement with young Dr. Koster and marries Ken, a photo of the newlyweds is published in the paper. Realizing his life is threatened, Ken, under the alias of Mr. Foster, tries to call off his deal with Korrin but discovers the man is dead. Ken cannot contact Korrin's successor, Fingers Murdock, and becomes increasingly paranoid. He spends long hours locked in his room, subsisting on canned goods and crackers. Claire tries to help, but Ken does not respond. One evening, Ken sees a man's figure lurking in the street beneath his window and shoots at him. Escaping from the house in his car, Ken drives away followed by his wife's vehicle and two other cars. Ken is killed in an accident and never realizes that the pursuing cars were driven by people attempting to help him. One car was driven by the bodyguard Claire had hired to protect her husband and the other by Fingers Murdock, who was returning Ken's money and knew that the murder contract had been called off.

Despite stilted dialogue, static direction, and other script deficiencies, *The Pretender* is a penetrating example of the noir vision and it is mostly the result of John Alton's brashly expressionistic photography and Dekker's stylized performance as Ken. Sets were built with forced perspective to permit depth-staging, as in the scene when Dekker is on the phone, lost in pools of darkness, while a brightly-lit party is going on in the background. Rooms are filled with grotesque personalities, such as Charles Middleton as the butler, and equally bizarre bric-a-brac. The film has a quintessential noir sequence in the objective shot of Ken, peeking out at night through the venetian blind of his darkened room, followed by a cut to his point-of-view of a trench-coated figure standing below beneath a streetlight. The scene of Ken seated on the floor of his darkened, locked room eating crackers and cold canned food is the ultimate noir illustration of entrapment and paranoia. The use of the theremin underscores this mood on the soundtrack with an aural suggestion of neurotic tension. (This musical instrument was first used by Miklos Rozsa for *Spellbound* and was added to many subsequent film noir scores until it became a cliché in the science fiction films of the 1950s.)

—B.P.

PRIVATE HELL 36 (1954)

Director: Don Siegel
Producer: Collier Young (Filmakers)
Associate Producer: Robert Eggenweiler
Screenplay: Collier Young and Ida Lupino
Director of Photography: Burnett Guffey
Sound: Thomas Carmen, Howard Wilson
Music: Leith Stevens
Song: "Didn't You Know" by John Franco; sung by Ida Lupino
Art Director: Walter Keller
Production Manager: James Anderson
Film Editor: Stanford Tischler

CAST: Ida Lupino (Lilli Marlowe), Steve Cochran (Cal Bruner), Howard Duff (Jack Farnham), Dean Jagger (Capt. Michaels), Dorothy Malone (Francey Farnham), Bridget Duff (Baby Farnham). **BITS:** Jerry Hausner (Nightclub Boss), Dabbs Greer (Bartender), Chris O'Brien (Coroner), Ken Paterson (Officer), George Dockstader (Fugitive), Jimmy Hawkins (Delivery Boy).
Location: Hollywood Park, Los Angeles, California
Released: Filmakers, September 3, 1954
Running Time: 81 minutes

In New York, a daring elevator robbery results in murder and the theft of a huge sum of money, later to play an important part in the lives of Los Angeles detectives Cal Bruner and Jack Farnham. The two are friends, although Farnham is a family man and Bruner is an emotionally remote loner. Both show signs of bitterness over the chances they take for relatively low pay; and when another cop is killed on the job, Bruner shrugs it off cynically while Farnham shares his feelings with his wife Francey. The search for the money from the elevator robbery leads to Lili Marlowe, a nightclub singer; and Farnham and Bruner accompany her each day to the race track hoping that she can spot the man who gave the money to her as a tip. Bruner and Lili begin seeing each other in the evenings as well; but, although their mutual attraction is intense, Lili sees no future in the relationship as he lacks the wealth she desires. Finally, the crook is spotted leaving the track. Bruner and Farnham chase his car, but the crook drives off the road and dies. Bruner pockets a considerable amount of the remaining money, and a reluctant Farnham goes along with him when Bruner reminds him about Francey and his child. Their superior, Capt. Michaels, is apparently not suspicious; but Farnham begins to betray emotional guilt. Meanwhile, Bruner makes his pitch to Lili; but she guesses where the money came from and relents in her demands, now believing that perhaps they could be happy without it. A partner of the dead criminal blackmails Farnham and Bruner by telephone. They arrange to meet him at the trailer park where the money is stashed; but Farnham has already made up his mind that he wants to return the money and take the consequences. In a final battle, Farnham is wounded by Bruner, who in turn is killed by the police. Michaels reveals that there was no partner and that he had suspected the two men from the start.

This film is fairly routine in narrative content and is somewhat given over to moralizing on the ethics of law enforcement. In terms of visual action, too, it is a second-rate Siegel production, having no sequences comparable to the car chase in *The Lineup* or the unforgettable shoot-out that climaxes *Madigan*, although an opening gun battle between Bruner and some thieves in a store at night is visually effective. *Private Hell 36* does have merit as a character study. Bruner is the first of a line of noir detective heroes in Siegel's films (Madigan and Harry Callahan are notable successors); and he is effectively contrasted to Farnham, whose basic decency is stressed repeatedly in domestic scenes with his wife, which also provide contrast to the scenes between Bruner and Lili. Bruner is ambiguous throughout most of the film; he is unemotional, competent, and amoral but he reveals unexpected feeling with his sudden outburst of desire and desperation in opposition to Lili's ambivalence. That moment gives great irony to Farnham's judgment of Bruner in a later scene: "You're sick, Cal. You don't care about anyone or anything." But although Cal is less warped and more comprehensible than his partner realizes, he is never sentimentalized. He is depicted as a complex human being rather than a stereotyped rogue cop. Steve Cochran's interpretation of this role, and the presence of Ida Lupino (who was also coscenarist of the film) as Lili, prevent the figures from being romanticized by the film's social context. They retain the appropriate, conventional aspects of the doomed film noir couple.

—B.L.

THE PROWLER (1951)
[Working Titles: THE COST OF LOVING; THE COST OF LIVING]
Director: Joseph Losey
Producer: S. P. Eagle [Sam Spiegel] (Horizon Pictures)
Associate Producer: Samuel Rheiner
Screenplay: Hugo Butler; from an unpublished story by Robert Thoeren and Hans Wilhelm [Uncredited: Dalton Trumbo]
Director of Photography: Arthur Miller
Sound: Benny Winkler
Music Score and Conductor: Lyn Murray
Music Director: Irving Friedman
Song: "Baby" by Lyn Murray
Art Director: Boris Leven
Set Decoration: Jacques Mapes
Costumes: Maria Donovan
Hairstyles: Marie Clark
Production Manager: Joseph H. Nadel
Dialogue Director: Gladys Hills
Assistant Director: Robert Aldrich
Script Supervisor: Don Weis
Film Editor: Paul Weatherwax

CAST: Van Heflin (Webb Garwood), Evelyn Keyes (Susan Gilvray), John Maxwell (Bud Crocker), Katharine Warren (Mrs. Crocker), Emerson Tracy (William Gilvray), Madge Blake (Martha Gilvray), Wheaton Chambers (Doctor James), Louise Lorimer (Motel Manager), Robert Osterloh (Coroner), Sherry Hall (John Gilvray). **BITS:** Louise Bates (Doctor's Wife), Steve Carruthers (Mr. Talbot), Betty Jane Howarth (Mrs. Talbot), Fred Hoose (Foreman), Alan Harris (Clerk).
Filming Completed: May 1, 1950
Released: United Artists, July 2, 1951
Running Time: 92 minutes

Patrolmen Webb Garwood and Bud Crocker respond to a report of a prowler at the Los Angeles home of Susan Gilvray, wife of a late night radio disc jockey; but they fail to find anyone. Webb returns later "to check up on things," admires Susan's home, and tells her he hopes to own a Las Vegas motel one day, "which will make money for you even while you sleep." Learning that her husband's will provides Susan with a small fortune and knowing she feels trapped in her marriage, Webb seduces her. One night, Webb pretends to be a prowler outside the Gilvray house and then responds to their police call for help. Mr. Gilvray is outside with a gun, looking for the prowler, and Webb orders him to "Halt!" Mr. Gilvray begs the policeman not to shoot; but Webb kills him and then shoots himself with Gilvray's gun to that it appears Gilvray shot him first. Although suspicious of Webb, Susan does not reveal their affair and a coroner's jury rules her husband's death was accidental. Ultimately convinced of Webb's innocence, Susan marries him; and they use her money to buy a motel in Las Vegas. But they soon move to a deserted ghost town because Susan is pregnant, and Webb fears the baby may be

incriminating evidence that he killed Gilvray, who was sterile. Preparing to deliver the baby himself, Webb is forced to call a doctor when Susan's labor proves difficult. The doctor safely delivers the child, but Webb frantically confesses he murdered Gilvray; and Susan realizes he plans to kill the doctor. She helps the doctor escape and he calls the police. When they arrive, Webb attempts to flee. When he doesn't halt after their warning, the police shoot him.

Like most of Losey's American films, *The Prowler* is concerned with complex social issues, which make it marginal to the film noir series. *The Prowler* is nonetheless a film that reveals the dark underside of the American dream of status and success. In many respects Webb Garwood is the all-American guy: the high school star who never quite makes it in college, drinks nothing but milk, who reads *Muscle Power* magazine, and who hopes to improve himself so greatly that one day he "can make money while he sleeps." Like Webb, Susan desires status and security, for which reason she married Gilvray; but she is willing to give that up for Webb. The policeman, who in his own way loves Susan, never sees the shallowness of his desires and, in the first scene following their wedding, he lecherously eyes a young woman who is checking into their motel. Losey's most telling indictment of social values is the fact that both Webb and those around him base their judgments on appearances. Webb is successful in his crime because his good looks and assured manner support his image as a model policeman. Ironically, Webb is too enmeshed in those values to survive. His paranoia over Susan's pregnancy is based on his own suspicions and hypocrisy rather than any real threat. The final irony is that his lapse into sentimentality in summoning the doctor precipitates his destruction.

—B.P. & A.S.

PUSHOVER (1954)
[Working Titles: THE KILLER WORE A BADGE, 322 FRENCH STREET]

Director: Richard Quine
Producer: Jules Schermer (Columbia)
Associate Producer: Philip A. Waxman
Screenplay: Roy Huggins; from the serialized story "The Killer Wore a Badge" by Thomas Walsh; from the novel *The Night Watch* by Thomas Walsh; and from the novel *Rafferty* by William S. Ballinger
Director of Photography: Lester H. White
Sound: John Livadary
Music Score: Arthur Morton
Conductor: Morris Stoloff
Art Director: Walter Holscher
Set Decorator: James Crowe
Costumes: Jean Louis

Makeup: Clay Campbell
Hairstyles: Helen Hunt
Assistant Director: Jack Corrick
Film Editor: Jerome Thoms

CAST: Fred MacMurray (Paul Sheridan), Kim Novak (Leona McLane), Phil Carey (Rick McAllister), Dorothy Malone (Ann), E. G. Marshall (Lt. Carl Eckstrom), Allen Mourse (Paddy Dolan), Phil Chambers (Briggs), Alan Dexter (Fine), Robert Forrest (Billings), Don Harvey (Peters), Paul Richards (Harry Wheeler), Ann Morris (Ellen Burnett). **BITS:** Dick Crockett (Young Man), Marion Ross (Young Woman), Kenneth L. Smith (Bank Guard), Joe Bailey (Hobbs), Hal Taggart (Bank Executive), John De Simone (Assistant Bank Manager), Ann Loos (Teller), Walter Beaver (Schaeffer), Mel Welles (Detective), Richard Bryan (Harris), Jack Wilson (Detective), Paul Picerni, Tony Barrett (Men), Mort Mills, Robert Carson (Bartenders), John Tarangelo (Boy), James Anderson (Beery).
Location: Los Angeles, California
Filming Completed: February 13, 1954
Released: Columbia, July 30, 1954
Running Time: 88 minutes

Harry Wheeler's gang robs a bank of $210,000 and kills one of the guards. Wheeler's girl friend, Leona, meets Paul Sheridan after attending a movie, and a romance begins. Sheridan reports to his superior, Detective Lt. Carl Eckstrom, of his success with Leona; and Paul, Rick McAllister, and Paddy Dolan are assigned to watch Leona's apartment for Wheeler's return. That evening, Leona leaves her apartment. Following her, Paul is surprised when she drives to his apartment, where she exposes him as a policeman but admits loving him. She suggests that he kill Wheeler in the line of duty and escape with her and the stolen money. Paul is disgusted at the scheme and rejects her. Meanwhile, Rick has become fascinated watching Leona's neighbor, Ann, who appears to lead a happy and normal existence. Paul returns and explains Leona made no attempt to contact Wheeler. After several days separation, Paul becomes sexually obsessed with Leona. Meeting her secretly, Paul agrees to her plan and arranges the details. When Leona finally receives a message from Wheeler that he is arriving shortly, she leaves and draws Rick away from the apartment. Paul kills Wheeler; but the killing is witnessed by Paddy. Then Ann spots Paul leaving Leona's apartment after delivering their all-clear signal. Rick returns from following Leona and Lt. Eckstrom arrives with the news that Wheeler has been seen in the vicinity. Paul kills Paddy to conceal his crime and then kidnaps Ann to use as a shield for his and Leona's escape. But Eckstrom and Rick have realized Paul's deception. He is wounded severely in the ensuing chase, while Ann is unharmed.

Initially, *Pushover* resembles *Double Indemnity* with its plot of murder for money, in which a cool, beautiful blond seduces a man into betraying his profession and his colleagues. The

male protagonists in both films are similarly vulnerable, superficially clever but unwise men. They conceal their romantic disillusionment behind cynicism and must develop dual personalities simultaneously to engineer their crime and then begin a sham investigation of it. As the actor who portrayed Walter Neff and now plays Paul Sheridan, Fred MacMurray adds a significant physical resemblance between the two characters but also a significant difference, because the actor is ten years older and the years have not been kind. Walter Neff was an attractive, expensive dresser; he was a fast talker and a successful, ambitious man. Paul is slower and his face has a puffiness that betrays an inactive and unrewarding life as effectively as his rumpled rain coat. Walter is tempted by Phyllis but also by the thrill of cheating an insurance company that knows all the angles. But Paul is tempted only by Leona; and the huge sum of money becomes a way to protect himself from the difference in their ages. While in the police observation room early in the film, Paul's younger partner Rick sits by the window in the glow thrown off by the outside world and remarks, "Money's nice, but it doesn't make the world go round." But Paul retorts, "Don't it? . . . I promised myself as a kid that I'd have plenty of dough." Paul makes a slight guffaw and admits his failure, but the dream is no less of a desire.   Like Phyllis Dietrichson and Walter Neff in *Double Indemnity*, Paul and Leona are sexually fascinated with each other; and the *mise-en-scène* of their moments together in Paul's apartment is remarkably similar, almost shot as a mirror reverse of the former film but significantly less glamorous, despite or perhaps because Leona's naïve sexuality has replaced Phyllis's sophisticated lust. Unlike their counterparts, Paul and Leona do not redirect their sexual frustrations into a double cross. Instead, Paul confuses the money with a guarantee of Leona's fidelity. Confronted by the police, Leona urges Paul to forget the money. But he has transferred his obsession to it and realizes too late, as he lies face down in the street, that "We really didn't need the money, did we?" Although Leona is a true *femme fatale* in the noir sense, her ambitions are misguided; and she suffers due to inexperience, whereas Phyllis Dietrichson was a calculating murderess. Additionally, Leona does not manipulate Paul. Although he initially accuses her of this, it is obvious how little power she has over him because he controls all elements of their plot and only gives her simple directions, which she follows unhesitatingly. One of Leona's few independent moments occurs when Paul criticizes her for accepting Wheeler's favors. Vehemently denouncing squalor, she turns abruptly away and, in a medium close-up, states, "Money isn't dirty, just people." Paul's face is visible behind her as it registers understanding of her implicit disgust of Wheeler. His expression also foreshadows his subsequent self-betrayal of his existence as he destroys his connection with the law and society.

Besides the obvious contrast between the neighboring women's personalities, *Pushover* contrasts the renegade attitudes of its protagonists with the subplot of Rick and Ann's gradual and rational attraction. The conventional behavior of the career woman and the stalwart policeman seems to provide positive emphasis of society's values, while illustrating the increasing alienation of Paul and Leona. However, the moralizing tone is undercut by the aspects of voyeurism that Rick exhibits as he literally window shops for the right woman. Also, Ann's character displays unconventional sensitivity when she, immediately after being rescued from the threat of Paul's gun, runs to the wounded man instead of to Rick, who has fired two bullets into his friend.

—E.W.

THE RACKET (1928)

Director: Lewis Milestone
Producer: The Caddo Company (Presented by Howard Hughes)
Screenplay: Harry Behn and Del Andrews, adapted by Bartlett Cormack; from his play
Titles: Eddie Adams
Director of Photography: Tony Gaudio
Film Editor: Tom Miranda

CAST: Thomas Meighan (Capt. McQuigg), Marie Prevost (Helen Hayes, an Entertainer), Louis Wolheim (Nick Scarsi), Richard Skeets Gallagher (Miller), Lee Moran (Pratt), Lucien Prival (Chick), Tony Marlow (Chick's Chauffeur), Henry Sedley (Corcan), Sam De Grasse (District Attorney), Burr McIntosh (Old Man), G. Pat Collins (Policeman Johnson).
Released: Paramount Famous Players Lasky, June 30, 1928
Running Time: 85 minutes

Police Capt. McQuigg is an honest cop in a corrupt Chicago police department and Nick Scarsi is a mobster whom McQuigg is determined to destroy. McQuigg is eventually allowed to attack the criminal because Scarsi's fall has become convenient for the police, the city administration, and the underworld who plan to replace Scarsi. Despite McQuigg's efforts, the Chicago underworld continues unchecked.

Although *The Racket* is not a true gangster film because it is only partly from a gangster's point of view and has a policeman for its nominal hero, it is also not an old style crime film in which the police triumph over evil. Nick Scarsi is the first modern gangster protagonist. Not only is he completely unlike Bull Weed in *Underworld*, who is closer to a Raffles than a Capone, Scarsi is the prototype of Rico Bandello in *Little Caesar* or Tony Camonte in *Scarface*. He is of immigrant stock, dresses flamboyantly, and is leery of women, while being clearly based on actual gangster celebrities of his day with political as well as criminal power. Most importantly, he is treated as a hero with weaknesses but also with definite strengths and virtues.

The Racket is as much a political exposé as it is a genre piece because it was set in contemporary Chicago, while *Little Caesar* and *Scarface* draw on an earlier, less complex era of crime. *The Racket* makes accusations of specific officials and accuses the mayor of Chicago of not just selling protection in return for votes but of murder; and for the first and perhaps only time on film, federal prohibition agents are said to be on the gangster payroll.

Because this film is lost today, it is impossible to judge if its acting, adaption, and visuals convey the drama of its theatrical source. But whether the 1928 *The Racket* has artistic merit that would hold up today is moot; there seems little doubt that it was a watershed film and that both by shaping subsequent gangster films and by legitimizing the use of topical material, it also influenced film noir.

—D.L.W.

THE RACKET (1951)

Director: John Cromwell
Producer: Edmund Grainger (RKO)
Screenplay: William Wister Haines and W. R. Burnett; based on the play by Bartlett Cormack
Director of Photography: George E. Diskant
Sound: Frank McWhorter, Clem Portman

Music: Constantin Bakaleinikoff
Song: "A Lovely Way To Spend An Evening," music by Jimmy McHugh, lyric by Harold Adamson
Art Directors: Albert S. D'Agostino, Jack Okey
Set Decoration: Darrell Silvera, William Stevens
Costumes: Michael Woulfe
Makeup: Mel Berns
Hairstyles: Larry Germain
Production Manager: Cliff Broughton
Assistant Director: James Casey
Film Editor: Sherman Todd

CAST: Robert Mitchum (Capt. McQuigg), Lizabeth Scott (Irene), Robert Ryan (Scanlon), William Talman (Johnson), Ray Collins (Welch), Joyce MacKenzie (Mary McQuigg), Robert Hutton (Ames), Virginia Huston (Lucy Johnson), William Conrad (Turck), Walter Sande (Delaney), Les Tremayne (Chief Craig), Don Porter (Connolly), Walter Baldwin (Sullivan), Brett King (Joe Scanlon), Richard Karlan (Enright), Tito Vuolo (Tony). **BITS:** Howland Chamberlain (Higgins), Ralph Peters (Davis), Iris Adrian (Sadie), Jane Hazzard, Claudia Constant (Girls), Jack Shea, Eric Alden, Mike Lally (Sergeants), Howard Joslyn (Sgt. Werker), Bret Hamilton, Joey Ray (Reporters), Duke Taylor, Miles Shepard (Policemen), Dulcie Day, Hazel Keener (Secretaries), Steve Roberts (Schmidt), Pat Flaherty (Clerk), Milburn Stone (Foster), Max Wagner (Durko), Richard Reeves (Leo), Johnny Day (Menig), Don Beddoe (Mitchell), Matthew Boulton (Simpson), Don Dillaway (Harris), Barry Brooks (Cameron), George Sherwood (Douglas), Jack Gargan (Lewis), Herb Vigran (Headwaiter), Bud Wolfe (Detective), Ronald Lee (Elevator Boy), Dick Gordon, Allen Mathews, Ralph Montgomery (Men), Al Murphy (Newsboy), Bob Bice, Sally Yarnell, Jane Easton, Kate Belmont (Operators), Harriet Matthews (Librarian), Curtis Jarrett, Art Dupuis, Harry Lauter (Policemen), Ed Parker (Thug).
Filming Completed: May 14, 1951
Released: RKO, December 12, 1951
Running Time: 88 minutes

Police Capt. McQuigg and mobster Nick Scanlon struggle against the backdrop of a corrupt Midwestern city during the final days of a municipal election. McQuigg, an honest cop, is infuriated by the crime and graft he sees about him and directs his anger at Scanlon, who is just a middle-level member of the underworld but who symbolizes everything McQuigg hates. The policeman's superiors, Inspector Turck and City Prosecutor Welch, are controlled by the organization and warn him to take it easy. Meanwhile, Scanlon struggles with his superiors—who want him to become a more modern, less violent, and more businesslike gangster—and with a rival hoodlum whom he finally must arrange to have murdered. This assassination leads directly to his own death, as it becomes convenient for the city's political and criminal "Big Boys" to let McQuigg destroy Scanlon. The city's reformers are defeated in the election, the rackets continue as usual. Scanlon is replaced by a more sinister lieutenant. McQuigg remains powerless, and it is hinted that the city's real crime lord is the state governor.

Corruption in *The Racket* is not some kind of abstract force or entity. It is the aggregate of all the desires, ambitions, and compromises of a city; and the film makes no moralistic, good-bad distinctions. Even the worst characters are not evil, sadistic, or very dangerous. Turck, for instance is shown to be far more intelligent and sensitive than McQuigg. Welch has a streak of honesty counterbalanced by one of pragmatism. When he is asked why he sold out, he answers because he was promised a judgeship. Scanlon, in fact, is the film's most fully drawn and sympathetic character. He is alone, alienated, and doomed by the evolution of one form of gangsterism into another, and by his existential refusal to lose his identity by changing with it.

McQuigg's role is at least as ambiguous. If Scanlon is an old-style mobster, McQuigg is an equally conservative cop who sees his job not as providing justice but maintaining law and order. Welch says that for McQuigg honesty is a kind of disease; and the film offers a great deal of evidence that this is the case. His extreme honesty is as destructive and violent as Scanlon's brute force approach to graft. McQuigg is not a mobster, but he is similar because his methods are outside the law; he tears up writs of habeas corpus, frames suspects, and, finally, allows Scanlon to be killed. His goal is not reform; he does these things to bring down Scanlon, not the corruption. Howard Hughes was always sensitive to the commercial and aesthetic potentials of underworld material. Bartlett Cormack's play *The Racket* was the second property Hughes filmed in 1927 (it was released in 1928) when he turned his attention to motion pictures. A remake of *The Racket* was one of the first projects announced by the newly Hughes controlled RKO in 1948. Samuel Fuller was the first writer to work on the project, and he envisioned a film grounded in post-World War II society, not the Prohibition era. When he delivered an essentially original script, writer William Haines and director John Cromwell replaced him. They developed a more faithful adaption of the play, nominally set in the late 1940s but drawing its conflicts and plot from Chicago in the 1920s. Halfway through production, Howard Hughes personally hired writer W.R. Burnett to rewrite the film. Even with Burnett's expertise (he had written the novels and/or scripts on which *Little Caesar, Scarface, High Sierra,* and *The Asphalt Jungle* are based), $500,000 worth of retakes and the work of a half dozen fine actors, the film is little more than a competent commercial picture; and its situations and characters are somehow out of date and unreal. However, it is politically more sophisticated than *The Asphalt Jungle,* which is closely resembles. *The Racket's* problem may be that because it is not really rooted in a specific time or place, its legitimate claim to being the most complex treatment of political, police, and criminal forces in equilibrium is obscured.

—D.L.W.

RAILROADED

RAILROADED (1947)

Director: Anthony Mann
Producer: Charles F. Riesner (Producers Releasing Corporation)
Screenplay: John C. Higgins; from a story by Gertrude Walker
Director of Photography: Guy Roe
Special Effects: George J. Teague
Sound: Leon Becker, John Carter
Music Score: Alvin Levin
Music Director: Irving Friedman
Art Director: Perry Smith
Set Decorations: Armor Marlowe, Robert P. Fox
Costumes: Frances Ehren
Makeup: Ern Westmore, Tom Tuttle
Hairstyles: Eunice, Evelyn Bennett
Dialogue Director: Stewart Stern
Production Manager: Ben Stoloff
Assistant Director: Ridgeway Callow
Supervising Editor: Alfred DeGaetano
Film Editor: Louis H. Sackin

CAST: John Ireland (Duke Martin), Sheila Ryan (Rosa Ryan), Hugh Beaumont (Mickey Ferguson), Jane Randolph (Clara Calhoun), Ed Kelly (Steve Ryan), Charles D. Brown (Capt. MacTaggart), Clancy Cooper (Chubb), Peggy Converse (Marie), Hermine Sterler (Mrs. Ryan), Keefe Brasselle (Cowie), Roy Gordon (Ainsworth).
Filming Completed: August 9, 1947
Released: P.R.C., October 30, 1947
Running Time: 71 minutes

The robbery of a beauty shop that served as a front for a gambling racket results in the death of a policeman and the apprehension of one of the robbers, Cowie, whose face was badly disfigured. Interrogated by the police at his bedside, the fatally wounded criminal implicates an innocent friend, Steve Ryan, as his accomplice. Not believing that her brother is capable of such heinous crimes, his sister, Rosa, convinces police investigator Ferguson to reopen the case. Their suspicions center on Duke Martin, a gunman who double-crossed the gambling racket that hired him by stealing the booty. As Ferguson and Rosa hunt down witnesses who might link Duke to the robbery, the trigger-happy gunman stays ahead of them and leaves a number of corpses in his wake. He ritualizes each murder by perfuming his bullets and polishing his gun before he commits his crime, and this affectation finally gives him away. In a final shoot-out in a deserted bar, Ferguson kills the sadistic Duke.

Railroaded is another low-budget noir extravaganza directed by Anthony Mann and, like the earlier *Desperate,* it is a crisp, well-made thriller. The real tone of the noir sensibility is revealed by John Ireland's grotesque portrayal of Duke Martin. There is an erotic quality to his ritualizing anointment of the bullets and the self-satisfying response to the massaging of his gun barrel. The almost ludicrous Freudian association between sex and violence is carried off so convincingly that Duke's obsession is never questioned or laughed at. In *Railroaded,* Mann was more concerned with the dealings of the noir antagonist, Duke, than in the vindication of the wrongly accused fall guy. The retribution for the crimes committed by Duke are inconsequential. What matters in *Railroaded* is that the aberrant nature of Duke's character was not compromised. The lack of redemption attests to the noir code, and the screenplay by John C. Higgins (who also wrote *T-Men, Raw Deal, He Walked by Night,* and *Border Incident* for Anthony Mann) is strongly rooted in the hard-boiled tradition of pulp magazines of the period.

—C.M.

RAW DEAL (1948)

Director: Anthony Mann
Producer: Edward Small (Edward Small Production)
Screenplay: Leopold Atlas and John C. Higgins, from a story by Arnold B. Armstrong and Audrey Ashley
Director of Photography: John Alton
Special Effects: George J. Teague
Sound: Leon S. Becker, Earl Sitar
Music Score: Paul Sawtell
Music Director: Irving Friedman
Art Director: Edward L. Ilou
Set Decoration: Armor Marlowe, Clarence Steensen
Makeup: Ern Westmore, Ted Larsen
Hairstyles: Joan St. Oegger, Anna Malin
Production Manager: James T. Vaughn
Dialogue Director: Leslie Urbach
Assistant Director: Ridgeway Callow
Script Supervisor: Dick Welton
Film Editor: Alfred De Gaetano

CAST: Dennis O'Keefe (Joe Sullivan), Claire Trevor (Pat), Marsha Hunt (Ann Martin), John Ireland (Fantail), Raymond Burr (Rick Coyle), Curt Conway (Spider), Chili Williams (Marcy), Richard Fraser, Whitner Bissell, Cliff Clark (Men).
Released: Eagle-Lion, July 8, 1948
Running Time: 79 minutes

A gangster, Joe Sullivan, is framed by his associates and vows revenge when he is released from prison. Unable to wait, he breaks jail with the help of his girl, Pat. But his old gang kidnaps Ann Martin, a stranger who sympathetically corresponded with Joe while he was in jail. As his plans to exact revenge are complicated by Ann's presence, Joe finds a way to work her into his plans. He decides to seduce her into his world of violence and murder. A fight with the vicious Fantail ends when the losing Joe convinces Ann to shoot his attacker in the back. After this act of murder, Ann decides she is in love with Joe. Relenting, he sends her away from his nightmarish world and goes to kill Rick, the man who was a key factor in Joe's initial frame-up. Rick's fascination with fire becomes a method of execution. Surprised by Joe's sudden intrusion, Rick shoots him and inadvertently starts a fire. Trapped, Rick crashes through the upper-story window to his death. Ann nestles the dying Joe in her arms as Pat resigns herself to a lonely future.

Anthony Mann transcended the typically brutal environment in the gangster film and created an interesting paradox of sex and violence in *Raw Deal.* Joe Sullivan exists as a *homme fatal,* seducing Ann Martin into a world filled with violent action and murder, enticing her with a promise of sexual fulfillment that goes beyond the realm of normal relationships. She surrenders completely to Joe, committing murder as the ultimate expression of her love. Along with this apparent twist of classic noir archetypes, *Raw Deal* creates an atmosphere in grotesquerie and fetishism that reveals the sordid nature of the noir world. Complementing the mood and tone inherent in the film, John Alton's photography suggests a half-lit world magnified by the strong use of shadows and cluttered composition. The ironic narration provided by Pat, develops the romantic undercurrent evident in many noir films. It remains for the true noir film to debase any sense of pity or love that may be present, replacing it with a tough, cynical nature.

—C.M.

THE RECKLESS MOMENT (1949)

Director: Max Ophuls
Producer: Walter Wanger (Walter Wanger Productions)
Screenplay: Henry Garson and Robert W. Soderberg, adapted by Mel Dinelli and Robert E. Kent; from the short story "The Blank Wall" by Elisabeth Saxnay Holding
Director of Photography: Burnett Guffey
Sound: Russell Malmgren
Music Score: Hans Salter
Music Director: Morris Stoloff
Art Director: Cary Odell
Set Decoration: Frank Tuttle
Costumes: Jean Louis
Makeup: Newt Jones
Hairstyles: Carmen Dirigo, Ella Perkins
Assistant Director: Earl Bellamy
Script Supervisor: Francis McDowell
Film Editor: Gene Havlick

CAST: James Mason (Martin Donnelly), Joan Bennett (Lucia Harper), Geraldine Brooks (Bea Harper), Henry O'Neil (Mr. Harper), Shepperd Strudwick (Ted Darby), David Bair (David Harper), Roy Roberts (Nagle), Frances Williams (Sybil). **BITS:** Paul E. Burns (Desk Clerk), Danny Jackson (Drummer), Claire Carleton (Blond), Billy Snyder (Gambler), Peter Brocco (Bartender), Karl "Killer" Davis (Wrestler), Virginia Hunter (Girl), Cosmo Sardo, Holger Bendixen, Evelyn Moriarity, Al Bayne, Robert Gordon, Ed Pine, Jack Baker, Kenneth Kendall, Richard Mickelson, John Roy, David Levitt, Barbara Hatton, Gail Bonney, Dorothy Phillips, George Dockstader, Barry Regan, Byron Poindexter (People), Joseph Palma (Card Player), Bobby Hyatt (Mud), Penny O'Connor (Liza), Bruce Gilbert Norman (Dennie), Sharon Monaghan (Bridget), Charles Marsh (Newsman), Harry Harvey (Post Office Clerk), Boyd Davis (Tall Man), Norman Leavitt (2nd Postal Clerk), Ann Shoemaker (Mrs. Feller), Everett Glass (Drug Clerk), Buddy Gorman (Magazine Clerk), Louis Mason (Mike), Pat Barton (Receptionist), John Butler (Pawnbroker), Kathryn Card (Mrs. Loring), Pat O'Malley (Bank Guard), Charles Evans (Bank Official), Jessie Arnold (Old Lady), Sue Moore (1st Woman), Charles Jordan (Man #1), Celeste Savoi (Waitress), Joe Recht (Newsboy), Mike Mahoney, Glenn Thompson, John Monaghan (Policemen), William Schallert (Lieutenant).

Location: Balboa and Los Angeles
Filming Completed: April 15, 1949
Released: Columbia, December 29, 1949
Running Time: 81 minutes

Lucia Harper leads an upper middle-class existence in a quaint house in Balboa, California, with her children, Bea and David, husband, father-in-law, and servant, Sybil. While her husband is traveling on business, she discovers that Bea has fallen in love with an unscrupulous older man, Ted Darby, who attempts to blackmail the Harpers. Lucia tells Bea of Darby's scheme, and Bea meets with him in the Harper boathouse. They have a fight; and, after hitting him over the head with a flashlight, she runs off. Darby staggers after her but falls over the guardrail into the water and dies. Lucia finds the body and hides it to protect her daughter. Unfortunately, Darby had given Bea's love letters to him to a loan shark, Nagle, who learns the police are investigating Darby's murder. Nagle sends his partner, Martin Donnelly, to blackmail Lucia for $5,000 but she can only raise $800. Donnelly, romantically drawn to her, tells her not to worry because the police have arrested one of Darby's shady associates for the murder, although Lucia claims she does not want an innocent man to suffer. Nagle feels Donnelly is too soft and goes to Balboa to wait for Lucia. He and Donnelly fight and Lucia's new friend chokes the blackmailer to death after being severely hurt himself. Lucia discover's Donnelly's wounds, but he drives off with Nagle's corpse before she can bandage his cuts. Lucia follows with Sybil, to whom she relates the whole story. Catching up with Donnelly shortly after he has smashed his car, he tells Lucia to leave and promises he will take care of the problem. Donnelly confesses to both murders to save Lucia before he dies as a result of the car accident. Not realizing what Lucia has undergone for their sake, the Harper family eagerly awaits the return of their father.

The Reckless Moment is narratively distinct among film noir. Although its story-line is roughly analogous to such diverse predecessors in the cycle as *Woman in the Window* and *Detour* in that it involves an attempt to conceal a crime and

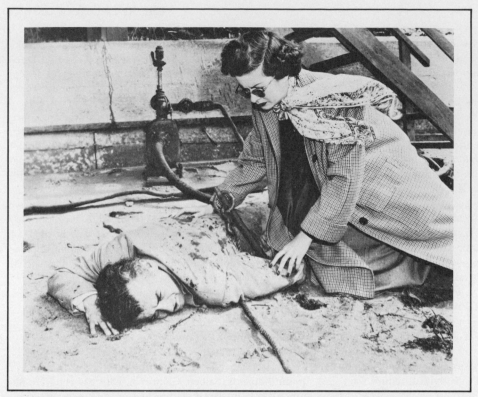

Lucia Harper (Joan Bennett) and Darby (Shepperd Strudwick) in Reckless Moment.

subsequent blackmail, there is a crucial character difference in *The Reckless Moment*. While its protagonist is as morally innocent as the men in those earlier films, the person who is enmeshed by circumstances in *The Reckless Moment* is a woman, a part played as it happens by Joan Bennett, the actress who was the *femme fatale* of Dr. Wanley's fantasy in *Woman in the Window*. Finally, unlike the women in *Mildred Pierce* and *The Accused*, the central irony of Lucia Harper's situation is not in her actual guilt or innocence but in her stereotypical middle-class background. Lucia does break the law when she conceals Darby's body; but, again unlike Mildred Pierce who is paying a psychological price for her own overriding ambition in the form of her malign daughter Veda's criminality, Lucia protects Bea because her middle-class values cannot accept such an unforeseen and precipitous disruption of her nuclear family. In this sense, Lucia's reaction is instinctive and socially "normal." The fact that the viewer is encouraged to believe that Lucia had been emotionally ordinary before the events surrounding Darby's death makes the character even further removed from the psychologically troubled Wilma Tuttle in *The Accused* than she is from Mildred Pierce. If all three of these female characters are taken as essentially realistic in the detailing of their actions and motivations, the comparison with the ruthlessly ambitious Mildred Pierce and her business enterprises or the sexually paranoiac Wilma Tuttle and her academic environment further underscores the commonplace qualities of Lucia Harper and her milieu.

Although the narrative does identify Lucia as a housewife who enjoys such upper-class privileges as an expensive home and a servant. Ophuls's visualization stresses the ordinary aspects of her person and surroundings. Unlike *Caught*, in which Ophuls fills Ohlrig's mansion with dark corners waiting to swallow the hapless Leonora Eames, the full light in the Harper house seems to reduce its size and reveal worn surfaces on its furnishings. Lucia's light-colored suits and dresses are not dowdy by any means, but they do suggest a different kind of woman than the one in a dark evening gown and with an exotic shawl over her head who suddenly appears reflected in the window before Dr. Wanley. The change in Bennett's appearance from that earlier film is completed by the hair-styling, makeup, and lighting on her face, free of shadows that might suggest the unusual or ominous. Even as he is visually emphasizing the plainness of Lucia and her customary surroundings, Ophuls also delineates a prototypical noir underworld into which she is thrust by Darby's death. The fact that it is prototypical adds a level of irony to the narrative; literally, it is all presented as a flashback from Lucia's point-of-view; figuratively, Ophuls's images have a graphic reality inscribed through long takes and fluid camera movement. These stylistic filters add a somnambulistic quality that implies a noir universe that is but partially real and partially what a woman such as Lucia would imagine it to be.

Donnelly is, in character terms, the principal noir fixture of *The Reckless Moment*; yet his hopeless fascination with Lucia and his self-sacrifice to protect her are not the "realistic" actions of a small-time crook. Ophuls accentuates this unreality by casting James Mason against type as Donnelly. Thus Donnelly becomes an introspective loner as much out of place with his criminal associates as he is with Lucia but ideally suited to her needs; and when

Ophuls's camera follows Donnelly through a smoke-filled barroom, it is as much that need—Lucia's point-of-view—as it is the staging that seems to separate him from that blurred background evoking the noir underworld.

All of Ophuls's ironies and the depth of his noir vision center on this identification of Lucia's middle-class viewpoint. Donnelly may see Lucia as his hope for spiritual salvation. He does not realize, nor does Lucia, that the only salvation lies in the anonymity of her social values. The final irony then must be that, after Donnelly's death, the momentarily disrupted elements of Lucia's world fall so easily back into place.

—A.S. & B.P.

RED LIGHT (1950)

Director and Producer: Roy Del Ruth (Roy Del Ruth Productions)
Associate Producer: Joe Kaufman
Screenplay: George Callahan
Director of Photography: Bert Glennon
Sound: Frank Webster
Music: Dimitri Tiomkin
Art Director: F. Paul Sylos
Production Manager: Joe C. Gilpin
2nd Unit Director: D. Ross Lederman
Assistant Director: Mel Dellar
Film Editor: Richard Heermance

CAST: George Raft (John Torno), Virginia Mayo (Carla North), Gene Lockhart (Warni Hazard), Barton MacLane (Sarecker), Henry Morgan (Rocky), Raymond Burr (Nick Cherney), Arthur Franz (Jess Torno), Arthur Shields (Father Redmond), Frank Orth (Stoner), Philip Pine (Pablo), Movita Castenada (Trina), Paul Frees (Bellhop), Claire Carleton (Waitress), Soledad Jiminez (Pablo's Mother).
Location: San Francisco, California
Filming Completed: March 30, 1949
Released: United Artists, January 15, 1950
Running Time: 84 minutes

Johnny Torno, the aggressive owner of the Los Angeles based Torno Freight Company, welcomes his brother Jess, a Roman Catholic chaplain, back from the war. Unknown to Johnny, his ex-employee who was convicted of embezzlement, Nick Cherney, is plotting to get even with Johnny by killing Jess. One evening, Johnny visits his brother's hotel room and finds him dying of a bullet wound. Johnny asks him who did it, but Jess can only answer, "In the Bible," before dying. Later Johnny reasons that his brother was referring to the hotel room's Gideon Bible, which is now missing. Johnny hunts for the missing Bible with the help of Carla North and leaves Warni Hazard in charge of the freight company. The Bible is found with the passage "Vengeance is mine . . . saith the Lord," clearly marked.

Ultimately, Johnny learns Nick is responsible and chases him to the top of the Torno Freight Company sign. Ready to shoot, Johnny remembers his brother's message and drops his gun. But Nick accidentally breaks the neon sign and is electrocuted. Another sign, stating "24 Hour Service," blazes in the background.

Red Light is a rather strange film as the conventions of film noir do not readily accommodate its religious message. It does, however, contain one classic noir scene: Warni, in a state of abject fear, goes down to the darkened truck garage and discovers the distributor wires of his car have been cut. Becoming more fearful, he runs in fright, stumbles, and then climbs under the truck trailer. We see only the pair of legs of his pursuer, who walks up to the trailer and casually kicks one of the jacks out while Warni screams. Then the camera pans up to a shot of the sinister Raymond Burr as Cherney, smoking and smiling.

—B.P.

RIDE THE PINK HORSE (1947)

Director: Robert Montgomery
Producer: Joan Harrison (Universal-International)
Screenplay: Ben Hecht and Charles Lederer; from the novel by Dorothy B. Hughes
Director of Photography: Russell Metty
Sound: Leslie I. Carey, Jack A. Bolger, Jr.
Music: Frank Skinner
Orchestration: David Tamkin
Art Directors: Bernard Herzbrun, Robert Boyle
Set Decoration: Russell A. Gausman, Oliver Emert
Costumes: Yvonne Wood
Makeup: Bud Westmore
Hairstyles: Carmen Dirigo
Assistant Director: John F. Sherwood
Film Editor: Ralph Dawson

CAST: Robert Montgomery (Gagin), Thomas Gomez (Pancho), Rita Conde (Carla), Iris Flores (Maria), Wanda Hendrix (Pila), Grandon Rhodes (Mr. Edison), Tito Renaldo (Bellboy), Richard Gaines (Jonathan), Andrea King (Marjorie), Art Smith (Bill Retz), Martin Garralaga (Barkeeper), Edward Earle (Locke), Harold Goodwin (Red), Maria Cortez (Elevator Girl), Fred Clark (Frank Hugo). BITS: Paul Maxey (Portly Man), Howard Negley, Jimmy Ames, John Doucette, Jack Worth (Thugs), Leon Lenoir (Workman), Beatrice Roberts (Manager), Julian Rivero, Ernest Hilliard, Jerry De Castro, Kenneth Ross, Mac Kenzie (Men), Virginia Wave, Ralph Montgomery (Waiters), Amadita Garcia, Connie Asins, Rose Marie Lopez, Martha Brenes, Olga Perez, Carmen Pallais, Margarita Savilla (Girls), Miguel Tapia, Roque Ybarra, Jr., Enrique Valades, Robert Cabal, Robert Espinsoa, Harry Garcia (Boys), Donald Kerr (Headwaiter).
Filming Completed: July 3, 1947

Blackie Gagin (Robert Montgomery) meets "G-Man" Retz (Art Smith) in Ride the Pink Horse.

Released: Universal-International, October 8, 1947
Running Time: 101 minutes
[NOTE: The antique Tio Vivo Carousel, built in 1882 in Taos, New Mexico, was the model for the carousel in the novel *Ride The Pink Horse.* This carousel was purchased by Universal-International and shipped from Taos to Universal City where it was reconstructed for use in the film.]

An ex-G.I. known only as Gagin comes to a small New Mexico town during its annual fiesta. Gagin's intention is to confront and blackmail a mobster named Frank Hugo. While he waits for Hugo's arrival at the local hotel, Gagin is approached by Bill Retz, an F.B.I. agent, who suspects that Gagin possesses incriminating material on Hugo and asks him to turn it over. Gagin claims to be in town merely as a tourist and denies having any information. Followed by Retz, Gagin does tour the town, spending a good portion of the day near an old carousel operated by Pancho and frequented by Pila, an Indian girl who attaches herself to Gagin. Despite Gagin's efforts to discourage her, she follows him around town and, after his initial meeting with Hugo, witnesses an attempt to kill him. She and Pancho nurse the badly beaten Gagin but cannot dissuade him from approaching Hugo again. This time Gagin defeats the mobster but is tricked by his associates. Retz, alerted by Pila, intervenes and Hugo is killed.

Among the various portraits of weary veterans contained in film noir, Gagin is perhaps most literally devoid of identity.

He has no first name—only Gagin, clipped, guttural, almost an epithet for Robert Montgomery's taciturn portrayal. The epithet the villagers give him as he wanders through San Pablo is "the man with no place," an appropriate choice of words for someone who comes from nowhere in particular and lacks any ultimate destination. As to Gagin's personal connections, he describes them succinctly to the inquisitive Pila: "I'm nobody's friend."

Initially, the *mise-en-scène* supports this self-image of Gagin. He descends from the bus, and the camera tracks him through the terminal as he deposits an envelope in a locker, conceals the key, then exits and enters the town proper. The actions are simple enough; but the single moving shot in which they are inscribed rivets the audience's attention and compels them to extrapolate some sense of Gagin's character from the mere fact of his silent, methodical activity. At the same time, the sustained camera graphically imprisons Gagin within the unattractive realities of the bus depot and the dusty road to town.

Gagin is not a cipher. The typical qualities of the embittered loner, which the figure invokes through the visual inscription, and the subsequent narrative exposition of his hatred for Frank Hugo are the film's seminal definitions of a complex protagonist. As a result, the original assertion of Gagin's identity is grounded in conflict—both an understated but immediate conflict with his environment and an imminent clash with the criminal archetype, Hugo. Ostensibly, San Pablo offers nothing, other than the presence of Hugo, to mollify the alienation that Gagin carries so visibly, no alternate reality to that revealed in the naturalistic images of the bus terminal, central San Pablo, or the hotel lobby peopled by Hugo's henchmen and agent Retz. Only after Gagin's quest to extort Hugo and vindicate his dead friend is momentarily suspended does he discover Pancho, Pila, and the Tio Vivo Carousel.

It is not merely because it gives the film its title that Tio Vivo is the central image of *Ride the Pink Horse.* Somewhat like Rica's apartment in *Thieves' Highway,* it offers a haven, and not merely for Gagin. Well before Pancho and Pila take him there literally to regain his strength, Gagin is made uneasy by the unusual relationship between the carousel and its patrons. On his first visit there, Pila asks Gagin, the stranger, which horse to ride. Approaching the merry-go-round Gagin uncovers the horse nearest to him and remarks laconically, "Why don't you ride the pink one?" To Gagin, it makes no difference which horse she chooses; all are substantially the same, all travel in the same circle. To Pila, who understands instinctively the significance of choice, it makes all the difference. The carousel is at once one of the most stylized objects in the film—by nature, as a theatrical amusement, and because it is photographed on a sound stage under a neutral gray light that differs markedly from the high contrast shots made on actual location—and one of the most free of artificial restraints. Aside from its theatricality and the aspects of ritual that its patrons attach to it, Tio Vivo is a quintessential, noir set piece. Gagin, who comes to it burdened by the complicated codes of the noir underworld, specifically the belief that he must extract vengeance for his friend, cannot see it as representative of existential choice, which Pila without benefit of sophisticated terminology clearly does. Again like Nick Garcos in *Thieves' Highway,* only after Gagin accepts the carousel, albeit reluctantly, as sanctuary, does he begin to comprehend its meaning. Conditioned as he is to living with alienation, as part of the role that he feels compelled to take on, he still rejects Tio Vivo in favor of another chance at Hugo. That rejection, in itself, represents a truer choice than Gagin had previously made; and choice, in the noir world, ultimately guarantees either annihilation or salvation.

—A.S.

ROADBLOCK (1951)

Director: Harold Daniels
Producer: Jewis J. Rachmil (RKO)
Screenplay: Steve Fisher and George Bricker; from a story by Richard Landau and Geoffrey Homes
Director of Photography: Nicholas Musuraca
Sound: Frank Sarver, Clem Portman
Music Score: Paul Sawtell
Music Director: Constantin Bakaleinikoff
Song: "So Swell of You" by Leona Davidson
Art Directors: Albert S. D'Agostino, Walter E. Keller
Set Decoration: Darrell Silvera, Jack Mills
Costumes: Michael Woulfe
Assistant Director: James Casey
Film Editor: Robert Golden

CAST: Charles McGraw (Joe Peters), Joan Dixon (Diane), Lowell Gilmore (Kendall Webb), Louis Jean Heydt (Harry Miller), Milburn Stone (Egan), Joseph Crehan (Thompson). **BITS:** Joe Forte (Brissard), Barry Brooks, Frank Marlowe (Policemen), Ben Cameron, Joey Ray (Hoods), Harold Landon (Bartender at Larry's Club), Martha Mears (Singer at Larry's Club), John Butler (Hotel Clerk), Peter Brocco (Bank Heist Man), Dewey Robinson (Mike, Bartender), Harry Lauter (Saunders), Howard Negley (Police Captain), Dave McMahon (Radio Operator), Phyllis Planchard (Bobbie Webb), Steve Roberts (De Vita), Richard Irving (Partos), Taylor Reid (Green), Clarence Straight (Talbot), Jean Dean (Airline Hostess), Janet Scott (Mrs. MacDonald), Dave Willock (Airport Clerk).
Filming Completed: October 19, 1950
Released: RKO, September 17, 1951
Running Time: 73 minutes

Joe Peters and Harry Miller are insurance investigators who have completed an important case. On the plane back to Los Angeles, Joe meets Diane Marley and allows her to pose as his wife to fly half-fare. Due to bad weather, they spend an innocent night together in a hotel. Diane calls him "Honest Joe" and explains that they could never be happy together because she cares too much about money while he doesn't care about it at all. Some time later, Harry and Joe investigate a fur robbery and talk to one of the suspects, nightclub owner Kendall Webb. Joe often visits Diane, who works for Webb; and although she is falling in love with Joe, she tells him she cannot live on his small salary. Joe offers Webb information regarding a shipment of used money on its way to be destroyed in exchange for part of the booty. Diane marries Joe regardless of money, but it is too late for Joe to extricate himself from the robbery attempt. According to plan, the newlyweds go to a mountain cabin for their honeymoon, where Joe will receive his share of the money. But the robbery went badly and a postal clerk was killed. Joe tries to frame Webb by murdering him and leaving the body with part of the stolen money. Harry, Joe's friend, confronts him with knowledge of Joe's complicity. Joe tries to escape from Los Angeles with Diane, but the roads are all blocked. In desperation, Joe drives into the dry Los Angeles riverbed and is followed by the police. Realizing he is caught, Joe pushes Diane out of the vehicle and continues on but soon abandons it. Refusing to give himself up, Joe is shot by the police.

Like the corrupted policemen in *The Prowler* and *Pushover,* Joe Peters's destruction is irrevocably tied to sex and

ROAD HOUSE

money. Coscreenwriter Steve Fisher and coauthor Geoffrey Homes take a pulp mystery plot and combine it with an aura of middle-class malaise and pervasive corruption in *Roadblock* to provide a motivation for Peters's alienation and fall. Charles McGraw plays, atypically, a weak hero. His usual, stolid image—based on his full figure and square-set facial features—contrasts ironically with his portrayal of a sexually obsessed and ineffectual criminal. Like Paul Sheridan in *Pushover*, Peters learns too late that the impossible object, Diane, could in fact be possessed without recourse to criminal activity. Unlike Sheridan, Peters is misled by his own notions of economic determinism than by Diane's cynical apprehension of falling back into the poverty from which she escaped. The staging of Peters's death in the dry channels of the Los Angeles riverbed graphically reinforces his fatal position of entrapment.

—B.P. & A.S.

ROAD HOUSE (1948)

Director: Jean Negulesco
Producer: Edward Chodorov (20th Century-Fox)
Screenplay: Edward Chodorov; from an unpublished story
by Margaret Gruen and Oscar Saul
Director of Photography: Joseph La Shelle
Special Effects: Fred Sersen
Sound: Alfred Bruzlin, Harry M. Leonard
Music Score: Cyril Mockridge
Music Director: Lionel Newman
Orchestrations: Herbert Spencer, Earle Hagen
Art Directors: Lyle Wheeler, Maurice Ransford
Set Decoration: Thomas Little
Costumes: Kay Nelson
Wardrobe Director: Charles LeMaire
Makeup: Ben Nye, Tom Tuttle, Bill Riddle
Hairstyles: Myra Stolz, Catherine Reed
Production Manager: Sid Bowen
Assistant Director: Tom Dudley
Script Supervisor: Rose Steinberg
Film Editor: James B. Clark

CAST: Ida Lupino (Lily), Cornel Wilde (Pete), Celeste Holm (Susie), Richard Widmark (Jefty), O. Z. Whitehead (Arthur), Robert Karnes (Mike), George Beranger (Lefty), Ian MacDonald (Sheriff), Grandon Rhodes (Judge), Jack G. Lee (Sam). **BITS:** Marion Marshall (Millie), Lee MacGregor, Don Kohler, Jack Edwards, Jr., Edgar Caldwell (Men), Tom Moore (Foreman), Geraldine Jordan, Kathleen O'Malley, Blanche Taylor, Cecil Weston (Women), Ray Teal, Charles Flynn, Clancy Cooper, Robert Foulk (Policemen), Douglas Gerrard (Waiter), Robert Cherry (Pinboy).
Filming Completed: May 11, 1948

Released: 20th Century-Fox, November 7, 1948
Running Time: 95 minutes

Jefty owns a roadhouse in a town near the Canadian border, and his best friend Pete is the manager. He hires a singer and pianist, Lily, and she becomes an immensely popular entertainer. Jefty falls in love with her while Pete remains aloof. Meanwhile, Susie, the cashier, keeps her tender feelings for Pete to herself. But when Jefty goes on a hunting trip, Pete and Lily fall in love. Jefty returns with plans to marry Lily and when Pete tells him what has happened, the psychotic side of Jefty is revealed. He frames Pete for criminal charges by stealing money from the roadhouse profits and making his employee appear guilty. When Pete is charged, Jefty pretends a change of heart and persuades the judge to release Pete in his custody. Pete and Lily must live in the roadhouse, subject to constant psychological torment by Jefty. Finally, Jefty takes Pete, Lily, and Susie to his cabin near the border where he plans to torment Pete to the point where the man will attempt to escape across the border at which time Jefty will shoot him. Pete and Lily do make a run for it when they feel they have a chance. Susie obtains evidence of Jefty's machinations and follows them. But Jefty wounds Susie as she tries to warn the fugitives. Pete and Jefty fight, and Lily shoots and kills Jefty. Pete carries the injured Susie, and Lily walks beside him on the way back home.

Road House impresses first of all with its sharp dialogue exchanges between the characters and the bizarre look of the interiors. The roadhouse itself is designed in such a way as to conjure up a synthetic vision of the postwar period, seeming at once modern and rustic. The ambience of the scenes in these interiors is strongly supported by the characteristically moody noir lighting of La Shelle. This unusual setting is the background for scenes in which Ida Lupino as Lily sits at the piano, burning grooves into the top of the instrument with her forgotten cigarettes as she sings torch songs in her inimitable voice, prompting the line, "She does more without a voice than anyone I ever heard." When the story moves to a new setting in the final reels and Jefty becomes totally berserk, the artificial milieu becomes a sound-stage forest in which the characters file towards an unreal lake that rests beneath a painted sky. The artificiality of the noir style was seldom so severe; yet the look of these scenes arguably complements the flamboyant behavior of the characters.

Road House does contain a reasonably subtle and effective contrast between the two characters suffering from unrequited love. Jefty's crazed actions are mostly attributable to the demands of the noir style. On the other hand, Susie, suffering in good-natured silence over Pete's attraction to Lily, demonstrates in a very credible way the reaction most normal individuals would have. Ironically, such a reaction is made to seem almost perverse in the context of the film, especially as it ends in self-destructive heroism.

—B.L.

ROGUE COP (1954)
[Working Title: KELVANEY]

Director: Roy Rowland
Producer: Nicholas Nayfack (MGM)
Screenplay: Sydney Boehm; from the novel by William P. McGivern
Director of Photography: John Seitz
Special Effects: A. Arnold Gillespie
Sound: Wesley C. Miller
Music: Jeff Alexander
Art Directors: Cedric Gibbons, Hans Peters
Set Decoration: Edwin B. Willis, Keogh Gleason
Costumes: Helen Rose (Women)
Makeup: William Tuttle
Hairstyles: Sydney Guilaroff
Assistant Director: Ridgeway Callow
Film Editor: James E. Newcom

CAST: Robert Taylor (Christopher Kelvaney), Janet Leigh (Karen Stephanson), George Raft (Dan Beaumonte), Steve Forrest (Eddie Kelvaney), Anne Francis (Nancy Corlane), Robert Ellenstein (Sidney Y. Myers), Robert F. Simon (Ackerman), Anthony Ross (Father Ahearn), Alan Hale, Jr. (Johnny Stark), Peter Brocco (Wrinkles Fallon), Vince Edwards (Langley), Olive Carey (Selma), Roy Bancroft (Lt. Vince D. Bardeman), Dale Van Sickel (Manny), Ray Teal (Patrolman Mullins). **BITS:** Guy Prescott (Detective Ferrari), Dick Simmons (Detective Ralston), Phil Chambers (Detective Dirksen), Herbert Ellis (Bartender), Lillian Buyeff (Gertrude), Jimmy Ames (News Dealer), Joe Waring (Rivers), Paul Brinegar (Clerk), Nesdon Booth (Detective Garrett), Connie Marshall (Frances), Nicky Blair (Marsh), Richard Deacon (Stacey), Gilda Oliva (Italian Girl), Paul Hoffman (Clerk), Dick Ryan (Elevator Man), Dallas Boyd (Patrolman Higgins), George Taylor (Dr. Leonard), Paul Bryar (Patrolman Marx), Russell Johnson (Patrolman Carland), Michael Fox (Rudy), Milton Parsons (Tucker), Robert Burton (Inspector Cassidy), Carleton Young (District Attorney Powell), George Selk (Parker), Benny Burt (Proprietor), Gene Coogan (Truck Driver), Mitchell Kowall (Guard), Jack Victor (Orderly).
Filming Completed: May 14, 1954
Released: MGM, September 17, 1954
Running Time: 87 minutes

Christopher Kelvaney is notorious among his fellow policemen as a rogue cop who finances his imported suits and other expensive items through payoffs from various criminals. His brother Eddie, a rookie patrolman, is determined to restore family honor by his integrity. After Eddie witnesses a knife murder by Wrinkles Fallon, the latter asks for help from a syndicate boss, Dan Beaumonte, over whom he holds incriminating evidence of a killing Beaumonte had committed. Beaumonte in turn tells his hired cop, Chris Kelvaney, to offer his brother money to drop the charges. Kelvaney enlists the aid of Karen Stephanson, Eddie's girl friend, impressing her of the seriousness of Beaumonte's intentions. When both their appeals and threats from Beaumonte fail, Kelvaney advises the mobster to back off. Infuriated, Beaumonte rails against Kelvaney until Kelvaney beats both the mobster and his bodyguard and vows to kill Beaumonte if his brother is harmed. Beaumonte brings in an out-of-town killer named Langley to dispose of the Kelvaney brothers; and he succeeds in ambushing and killing Eddie on the street. Learning of his brother's death, Kelvaney finds himself ostracized by all his fellow policemen except Sid Myers, a victim of department anti-Semitism. Alone, Kelvaney questions Beaumonte's moll, Nancy Corlane, and gets information. Langley finds Nancy hidden in Karen's apartment and kills her; but Kelvaney captures the assassin. Desperate, Beaumonte sets a trap for the policeman. With Myers, Kelvaney walks into the setup. In the ensuing gun battle all the criminals are killed and both policemen wounded, Kelvaney seriously. Riding the ambulance to the hospital, Myers assures Kelvaney that he has restored his honor.

Rogue Cop and Rowland's *Scene of the Crime* are among the few film noir produced at MGM. The intricacies of the criminal activities of that earlier production are abandoned in *Rogue Cop* with the focus instead on the corrupt Chris Kelvaney and his inability to cope with the dissolution of his carefully constructed life-style. Kelvaney's self-justification for being on the syndicate payroll is a personal distaste for the brutality of everyday police work. Accordingly, he uses his money to insulate himself from what he sees as sordid and demeaning. His sense of superiority causes him to pity all those around him: his brother and fellow officers for ill-paying integrity, Karen Stephanson for her physical impediment (a limp), Nancy Corlane for her inanity, and even Beaumonte for being unable to remove the stench of cheap criminality with any amount of expensive cologne. Kelvaney's "business" relationship with Beaumonte has become so routine that he is unprepared to respond when Beaumonte resorts to force. Although he beats the mobster physically, he lacks the ability to prevent his brother's assassination. The final portion of the film concerns a vendetta, but Kelvaney carries it out as much to restore his own sense of identity as to avenge his brother. When Beaumonte takes out the contract on Kelvaney, the corrupt cop is suddenly reimmersed in a chaotic underworld. He stalks the streets for information and captures Langley with a rediscovered authority. Then, like Joe Morse in *Force of Evil*, Kelvaney purposely falls for the mobster's trap in expectation of his own destruction as well as Beaumonte's.

Rowland visually reinforces the dichotomy between Kelvaney's world and that of the streets, and, to some extent, subjectifies the film according to Kelvaney's viewpoint. Initially, Kelvaney is seen only in well-lit rooms, relaxed and well groomed as he goes through a charade of police work. Eddie is photographed on his nightly beat, cautiously patrolling neighborhoods of cheap bars and flophouses separated by dark alleyways. Kelvaney's fight with Beaumonte is his first brush with physical violence.

SCANDAL SHEET

Ironically, it takes place in the mobster's luxurious apartment, so that as Kelvaney breaks up his expensive furnishings he is also destroying the basis of his own insular mentality. The graphic brutality of that scene, so seemingly out of place, also initiates a predictable transference between the two brothers. When Beaumonte's fury cannot reach Chris, it kills Eddie; and suddenly Chris Kelvaney reverts to depending on a shadowy world of informants and back rooms for survival. Whether he survives or not is never made clear, as the film ends with the ambulance ride through the very streets Kelvaney despised. But that follows a final confrontation that is both an existential catharsis and a moral expiation in which Kelvaney and Beaumonte mindlessly blast away at each other until their revolver hammers fall on empty chambers and their bodies crumple to the ground. —A.S.

SCANDAL SHEET (1952)

[Working Title: THE DARK PAGE]
Director: Phil Karlson
Producer: Edward Small (Motion Picture Investors Production)
Screenplay: Ted Sherdeman, Eugene Ling, and James Poe; from the novel *The Dark Page* by Samuel Fuller
Director of Photography: Burnett Guffey
Sound: Jack Goodrich
Music: George Duning
Musical Director: Morris Stoloff
Art Director: Robert Peterson
Set Decoration: William Kiernan
Costumes: Jean Louis
Makeup: Clay Campbell
Hairstyles: Helen Hunt
Assistant Director: Frederick Briskin
Film Editor: Jerome Thoms

CAST: John Derek (Steve McCleary), Donna Reed (Julie Allison), Broderick Crawford (Mark Chapman), Rosemary DeCamp (Charlotte Grant), Henry O'Neill (Charlie Barnes), Henry Morgan (Biddle), James Millican (Lt. Davis), Griff Barnett (Judge Hacker), Jonathan Hale (Frank Madison), Pierre Watkin (Baxter), Ida Moore (Needle Nellie), Ralph Reed (Joey), Luther Crockett (Jordan), Charles Cane (Heeney), Jay Adler (Bailey), Don Beddoe (Pete). **BITS:** Shirlee Allard, Pat Williams (Telephone Operators), Raymond Largay (Conklin), Edna Holland (Mrs. Penwick), Kathryn Card (Mrs. Rawley), Cliff Clark (O'Hanlon), Victoria Horne (Mary), Matt Willis (Joe), Eugene Baxter (Edwards), Helen Brown (Woman), Katherine Warren (Mrs. Allison), Mike Mahoney, Peter Virgo, Ric Roman, Tom Kingston, Charles Colean (Reporters), Harry Hines, Harry Wilson, Ralph Volkie, John "Skins" Miller, Gary Owen (Bums), Guy Wilkerson (Janitor), Duke Watson (Policeman).
Filming Completed: May 18, 1951
Released: Columbia, January 16, 1952
Running Time: 82 minutes

Mark Chapman becomes editor of an almost defunct newspaper, the *New York Express,* and successfully increases its circulation by a series of brash stunts. Steve McCleary is Chapman's protegé, and in love with feature writer Julie Allison, who objects to Chapman's unethical tactics. Chapman organizes a Lonely Hearts Club and sponsors a huge ball to publicize the paper. But Charlotte Grant, his poverty-stricken wife whom Chapman deserted years ago, appears at the ball and later, at her apartment, threatens to expose her ruthless husband. Chapman is furious and strikes her down, killing her. He places her in her bathtub and tries to make it appear that she drowned. Escaping unseen, Chapman removes all traces of her identity. Concussion is determined as the cause of Charlotte's death and McCleary investigates the murder for the newspaper. He finds a pawn ticket belonging to the dead woman, which is accidentally given to his friend, ex-reporter Charley Barnes. Redeeming the ticket, Barnes discovers a photograph of Charlotte with Mark Chapman, who kills him before he can inform McCleary. But Julie and McCleary track down the judge who married Charlotte and Chapman; and he identifies the victim's husband. Mark threatens the group with a gun; but the police arrive and kill him. Disillusioned and sorrowful, Steve writes Chapman's front-page obituary.

Left to right: Mark Chapman (Broderick Crawford), Steve McCleary (John Derek), Julie Allison (Donna Reed) and newspaper staff in Scandal Sheet.

The real presence behind *Scandal Sheet* is Samuel Fuller. Based on his award-winning novel *The Dark Page*, the screenplay explores the dark world of yellow journalism. It is drawn from Fuller's experience in the newspaper world and begins with the transformation of a respectable, conservative newspaper into a sensationalist tabloid—all accomplished by the heavy hand of Mark Chapman. As played by Broderick Crawford, Chapman is a bullish, overbearing, yet ultimately sympathetic editor who employs every technique from browbeating "stuffed shirt" stockholders to sensationalizing the news in order to make his periodical "number one." The carefully established surrogate father-son relationship between Chapman and McCleary is the central irony of this film. Chapman has so effectively imparted his brand of journalistic skill to McCleary that the protegé becomes the instrument of Chapman's punishment. Because the "father" murdered in a moment of rashness, the "son" becomes the avenger-reporter and the story takes a classical turn. The elder newspaperman can only watch with fear and trepidation as the machinery he has created is manipulated by McCleary and turned against him. As his tragic flaws are finally revealed to his protegé and to the world, it is obvious that Chapman has masterminded his own downfall.

—J.U.

SCARLET STREET (1945)

Director and Producer: Fritz Lang
Executive Producer: Walter Wanger (Diana Productions)
Screenplay: Dudley Nichols; from the novel and play, *La Chienne,* by Georges de la Fouchardiere in collaboration with Mouezy-Eon
Director of Photography: Milton Krasner
Special Photography: John P. Fulton
Sound: Bernard B. Brown, Glenn E. Anderson
Music Score: Hans J. Salter
Art Director: Alexander Golitzen
Paintings: John Decker
Set Decoration: Russell A. Gausman, Carl Lawrence
Costumes: Travis Banton
Makeup: Jack P. Pierce
Hair Stylist: Carmen Dirigo
Assistant Director: Melville Shyer
Editor: Arthur Hilton
CAST: Edward G. Robinson (Christopher Cross), Joan Bennett (Kitty March), Dan Duryea (Johnny Prince), Jess Barker (Janeway), Margaret Lindsay (Millie), Rosalind Ivan (Adele), Samuel S. Hinds (Charles Pringle), Arthur Loft (Dellarowe), Vladimir Sokoloff (Pop Lejon), Charles Kemper (Patcheye), Russell Hicks (Hogarth), Anita

Bolster (Mrs. Michaels), Cyrus W. Kendall (Nick); Fred Essler (Marchetti), Edgar Dearing, Tom Dillon (Policemen), Chuck Hamilton (Chauffeur), Gus Glassmire, Ralph Littlefield, Sherry Hall, Howard Mitchell, Jack Statham (Employees), Rodney Bell (Barney). **BITS:** Henri de Soto (Waiter), Milton Kibbee (Saunders), Tom Daly (Penny), George Meader (Holliday), Lou Lubin (Tiny), Clarence Muse (Ben), John Barton (Hurdy Gurdy Man), Emmett Vogan (Prosecution Attorney), Horace Murphy (Milkman), Will Wright (Loan Office Manager), Joe Devlin (Williams), George Lloyd (Conway), Syd Saylor (Crocker), Dewey Robinson (Derelict), Herbert Heywood (Bellboy), Charles C. Wilson (Watchman), Constance Purdy (Matron), Fritz Leiber (Evangelist), Wally Scott (Drunk), Arthur Gould-Porter, Boyd Irwin, Richard Abbott (Critics), Byron Foulger (Jones), Thomas Jackson (Chief of Detectives), Edward Deane, Dick Wessel, Dick Curtis (Detectives), Robert Malcolm, Lee Phelps, Matt Willis, William Hall, Ralph Dunn (Policemen), Richard Cramer (Principal Keeper), the Reverend Neal Dodd (Priest), Kerry Vaughn (Blond Girl), Beatrice Roberts (Secretary).

Filming Completed: October 8, 1945
Released: Universal, December 28, 1945
Running Time: 102 minutes

Christopher Cross is a lonely man, tied to a shrewish wife and a dreary cashier's job. All that sustains him is his hobby, painting. When he meets Kitty March, he becomes infatuated and she encourages his attentions, believing that he is a famous and wealthy painter. Egged on by her con man lover, Johnny Prince, Kitty persuades Chris to establish her in a lavish apartment where he can paint her portrait. Although he must embezzle company funds to pay for Kitty's luxuries, Chris is happy for the first time in his life. Johnny then passes Kitty off as the painter of Chris's canvases, which enjoy sudden critical acclaim. Chris discovers the deception; but Kitty charms him and he forgives her. His wife's first husband is discovered still alive, and Chris runs to tell Kitty that they can marry. But he discovers her in the arms of Johnny and realizes he has been manipulated. When Johnny leaves, Chris stabs Kitty to death and then escapes. Johnny is convicted of her murder and executed. Meanwhile, Chris loses his job when his embezzlement is discovered. Unable to go to the police and unable to paint because his name has been usurped, he suffers a mental breakdown and is haunted by the taunting voices of Kitty and Johnny.

In typical Fritz Lang fashion, *Scarlet Street* is a bleak film in which a common man, under the influence of the corrupting forces of evil, succumbs first to vice and then to murder. Kitty March and Johnny Prince are certainly two of film noir's most casual villains, amoral and reeking of a heady kind of sin. Kitty is the ultimate sex object wrapped in her see-through plastic raincoat like a bonbon in cellophane, ready and waiting for consumption. Johnny is strutting and

sexy with his butterscotch-slick hair and straw boater, drawling an insinuating, "Hello, Lazy Legs" to a spraddle-limbed Kitty. Horrific as these two are, Lang cynically invests them with an irresistible allure and an energy that makes Christopher Cross's fall seem not only believable but inevitable. Additionally, Cross has an incredibly dreary job and an unremittingly shrewish wife who verges on caricature. Nothing could be more pathetic than his testimonial dinner, a brilliant set piece that opens the film. But Fritz Lang seems to imply that this is all that Chris could hope for—and when he desperately reaches for the scented warmth and understanding that he thinks Kitty represents, he is doomed.

Christopher Cross's disintegration relies heavily on Milton Krasner's dramatic cinematography to convey precise psychological states. The stark white light of passion illuminates the luxurious boudoir in which Chris murders Kitty by stabbing at her ice-cold heart with the most appropriate of weapons, an ice pick; this white-hot light reveals a look of furious lust on his face as he finally penetrates her long-withheld body. As the shadows encroach on Chris's mind, they also creep into the film's frame; their shapes and origins are strange and unexplained. At the film's end, with his sensibility clouded and his life in ashes, Chris moves through a vague, befogged landscape devoid of significant detail or meaning.

Christopher Cross is an artist who is undeniably talented but pathetically weak and vulnerable, a patsy in the hands of those who would use him for their own mercenary ends. There is some pity in Lang's noir vision of this character, but a touch of contempt as well. *Scarlet Street* conveys the attitude that those who live by the imagination can become helpless victims in a cruelly realistic world.

—J.K.

SCENE OF THE CRIME (1949)

Director: Roy Rowland
Producer: Harry Rapf (MGM)
Screenplay: Charles Schnee; from the short story "Smashing The Bookie Gang Marauders" by John Bartlow Martin
Director of Photography: Paul C. Vogel
Special Effects: A. Arnold Gillespie
Sound: Douglas Shearer, John A. Williams
Music Score: André Previn
Art Directors: Cedric Gibbons, Leonid Vasian
Set Decoration: Edwin B. Willis, Alfred E. Spencer
Costumes: Irene
Makeup: Jack Dawn
Hairstyles: Sydney Guilaroff
Production Manager: Dave Friedman
Assistant Director: Jack Greenwood

Script Supervisor: John Banse
Film Editor: Robert J. Kern

CAST: Van Johnson (Mike Conovan), Gloria De Haven (Lili), Tom Drake (C. C. Gordon), Arlene Dahl (Gloria Conovan), Leon Ames (Capt. Forster), John McIntire (Fred Piper), Norman Lloyd (Sleeper), Donald Woods (Herkimer), Richard Benedict (Turk Kingby), Anthony Caruso (Tony Rutzo), Tom Powers (Umpire Menafoe), Jerome Cowan (Arthur Webson), Mickey Kuhn (Ed Monigan), William Haade (Lafe Douque), Caleb Peterson (Loomis), Robert Gist (Pontiac), Romo Vincent (Hippo), Tom Helmore (Norrie Lorfield). **BITS:** Thomas E. Breen (Boy), Mary Jane Smith, Bette Arlen (Girls), G. Pat Collins (Monigan), Ray Teal (Patrolman), Don Haggerty, Allen Mathews, Gregg Barton, Mickey McCardle, James Scott, William J. Tannen, Paul Fierro, Anthony Merrill, George Magrill, Ralph Montgomery (Detectives), Forrest Taylor (Captain of Detectives), Minerva Urecal, Margaret Bert (Women), Charles Wagenheim (Nervous Man), William McCormick (Older Man), Victor Paul (Young Punk), Guy Kingsford (Ballistics Man), Ray Bennett (Sheriff Kiesling), Jack Shea (Fighter), Cameron Grant (Fighter), Jean Carter (Marlene), Jimmy Dundee (Captain of Waiters), Douglas Carther (Sanitation Man), Lucille Barkley (Corrine), Gladys Balke, Sarah Berner (Girl Voices), Mack Chandler, Fred Murray (Men On Table), William Phipps (Young Man), Richard Irving, Harris Brown, John Phillips (Doctors), Wilson Wood (Gateman), Billy Snyder, Eddie Foster, Zon Murray, Micael Jordan, Michael Barrett, Billy Dix (Gangsters), Jeffrey Sayre (Manager of the Fol De Rol), Erin Selwyn (Hatcheck Girl), Sam Finn, Charles Regan, Jimmy Dunn (Patrons), John McKee (Recorder), Robert Strong (Police Stenographer), Allan Ray (Wounded Officer).
Filming Completed: March 12, 1949
Released: MGM, July 28, 1949
Running Time: 94 minutes

When officer Monigan is killed and $1,000 is discovered on his person, it appears he was protecting bookie joints from a pair of thieves. Monigan's son blames officer Mike Conovan for his father's death because Mike had recently dropped Monigan and taken on a new partner, young C. C. Gordon. Mike wants to clear Monigan's name, but the only clues are that the murderer was reported to have a mottled face and a twisted hand. Mike decides to locate the two men suspected of robbing the bookie joints, Turk and Lafe. He persuades Lili, a stripper and Turk's ex-mistress, to cooperate with him. They find Lafe in a run-down hotel asleep, with the radio playing. While Mike searches the room, Lafe awakens, and after a vicious fight Mike subdues him. As Lafe is taken to headquarters, shots ring out. Lafe is killed and Mike lies wounded. The murder weapon is found and traced to a man with a twisted hand. Mike's young wife, Gloria, is frightened because of his injury and urges him to take a better job. Frustrated over the Monigan case and worried about

his marriage, Mike quits the force. Meanwhile, Lili leaves a tip for Mike to meet with an informant; but an older officer, Fred Piper, takes Mike's place and is killed. Realizing Lili has been helping Turk, Mike returns to the force despite his wife's threat to leave him. The police are tipped to a robbery and discover the crooks are led by Turk in an armored car. Mike commandeers a truck and rams the robbers' car, which bursts into flames. A dying Turk confesses to the murders and to the deformed disguise. Gloria reconsiders and remains with Mike.

It seems a bit incongruous to have an actor like Van Johnson in a film noir, although this sort of anomaly was typical of the short-lived noir series produced at MGM during the Dore Schary years. And yet MGM provided a smooth transition from the 1930s gangland films to the film noir with its "Crime Does Not Pay" series of shorts and such mysteries as *Kid Glove Killer, Grand Central Murder,* and *Rage in Heaven.*

Scene of the Crime contains several elements that are brutally naturalistic, from McIntire's portrayal of the martyred policeman Fred Piper, to the savage fight sequence between Lafe and Mike, and finally Turk's dying epithet to this faithful moll, Lili: "I hate a tramp . . . ya always gotta tell 'em, 'I love you, baby,' . . . a waste of time." Like his later *Rogue Cop,* Rowland's *Scene of the Crime* exploits the traditional noir locales through Paul Vogel's stylish photography of the dark streets and the back rooms of old warehouses that are so uncharacteristic of the MGM look. Moreover, Rowland exploits the conventional personae of such actors as Johnson and McIntire to partially play against type and extend his naturalistic treatment to the police force. Gordon, the brash rookie, and Piper, the resigned veteran, contrast with Conovan's laconic competence; and yet Conovan is duped by Lili, even as he feels guilty for exploiting her. Conovan's awareness of the monolithic nature of crime—underscored by the early sequence in which he is allowed to witness the syndicate policing itself—compounds his disillusionment with his "career goals" and causes him to acquiesce to his wife's pressure and to accept a job from her former suitor. The violent climax, like that of *Rogue Cop,* is a spiritual catharsis but only a partial reestablishment of Conovan's sense of his own ability, which must be permanently overshadowed by his failure with Lili and his temporary withdrawal from the police force.

—B.P. & A.S.

THE SCOUNDREL (1935)
[Working Title: MIRACLE IN 49TH STREET]

Directors and Producers: Ben Hecht and Charles MacArthur
Screenplay: Ben Hecht and Charles MacArthur

THE SECOND WOMAN

Director of Photography: Lee Garmes
Sound: Joseph Kane
Music Director: Frank Tours
Art Director: Walter E. Keller
Set Decoration: Albert Johnson
Production Manager: Arthur Rosson
Assistant Director: Harold Godsoe
Film Editor: Arthur Ellis

CAST: Noël Coward (Anthony Mallare), Julie Haydon (Cora Moore), Stanley Ridges (Paul Decker), Rosita Moreno (Carlotta), Martha Sleeper (Julia Vivian), Hope Williams (Margie), Ernest Cossart (Jimmy Clay), Everly Gregg (Mildred Langwiter), Eduardo Cianneli (Maurice Stern), Helen Strickland (Mrs. Rolinson), Lionel Stander (Rothenstein), Harry Davenport (Slezack), William Ricciardi (Luigi), Isabelle Foster (Scrub Woman), Madame Shushkina (Fortune Teller).
Released: Paramount, May 2, 1935
Running Time: 75 minutes

A New York publisher, Anthony Mallare, creates a ruthless environment in which exploitation and self-flattery become a way of life. Mallare finds it an amusing pastime to manipulate the lives of people he feels are beneath him. His flirtatious games sometimes lead to tragedy. After exploiting a young writer, Cora Moore, and her lover, Paul Decker, to a point of ignoble satisfaction, Mallare's life is cursed. His vicious whims are cut short when a plane in which he is traveling crashes. All the passengers, including Mallare are killed. But he is returned to life by a mystical force that orders him to find someone who will mourn his death. His eternal salvation hinges on finding a sympathetic person in his disturbing smug world. A final declaration to God allows Mallare the satisfaction that his decadent life had denied him.

Written and directed by Ben Hecht and Charles MacArthur, *The Scoundrel* is a modern morality play set in the nightmarish world of contemporary cynicism and decadence. It is a film that, inspired by Hecht's earlier novel, *Fantazius Mallare*, reveals a world held together by a self-serving demigod. *The Scoundrel* is unique in its early development in film of attitudes that are decidedly existential, creating an atmosphere of meaninglessness and intense hopelessness relieved only by the film's metaphysical ending. As photographed by Lee Garmes, *The Scoundrel* creates a stunning visual correlative for an earthly hell. Although not involved with the underworld and crime, the film succeeds in exposing the noir underworld of a society governed by high-class socialites. The images of corruption are simply presented. The ultimate redemption, however unconvincing, anticipates the inability of future noir characters to transcend their fated existence.

—C.M.

THE SECOND WOMAN (1951)
[Former Titles: HERE LIES LOVE; ELLEN; TWELVE MILES OUT]

Director: James V. Kern
Executive Producer: Harry M. Popkin (Harry M. Popkin Productions)
Producers: Mort Briskin, Robert Smith
Associate Producer: Joseph H. Nadel
Screenplay: Robert Smith and Mort Briskin
Director of Photography: Hal Mohr
Sound: Ben Winkler, Mac Dalgleish
Music: Nat W. Finston, themes from Peter Ilyich Tchaikovsky
Music Director: Joseph Nussbaum
Set Decoration: Jacques Mapes
Production Designer: Boris Leven
Costumes: Maria Donovan
Makeup: Henry Vilardo
Hairstyles: Kay Shea
Assistant Director: Maurie M. Suess
Film Editor: Walter Thompson
CAST: Robert Young (Jeff Cohalan), Betsy Drake (Ellen Foster), John Sutton (Keith Ferris), Florence Bates (Amelia Foster), Morris Carnovsky (Dr. Hartley), Henry O'Neill (Ben Sheppard), Jean Rogers (Dodo Ferris), Raymond Largay (Maj. Badger), Shirley Ballard (Vivian Sheppard), Vici Raaf (Secretary), John Galludet (Mac), Jason Robards, Sr. (Stacy Rogers), Steven Geray (Balthazar Jones), Jimmy Dodd (Mr. Nelson), Smokey Whitfield (Porter), Cliff Clark (Police Sergeant).
Location: Monterey and Carmel, California
Released: United Artists, February 1, 1951
Running Time: 91 minutes

Jeff Cohalan, a guest at his Aunt Amelia's house, attempts suicide by carbon monoxide poisoning. His problems are explained by his girl friend, Ellen, beginning with their first meeting on a train some months ago. As a young architect working for Ben Sheppard, a wealthy California landowner, Jeff was engaged to Ben's daughter, Vivian, prior to her death in an auto accident that also injured him. He suffers from blackouts and memory lapses and doubts his sanity because of a series of incidents that have occurred since the accident. Jeff lives alone at a beautiful ocean view "house with wings" he designed for his future bride, until it mysteriously burns down. A friend, a psychiatrist named Dr. Hartley, believes Jeff caused the fire and other accidents because he feels responsible for his fiancée's death. Ellen discovers that Keith Ferris, another of Shepperd's employees, resents Jeff because Keith and Vivian were lovers and were running off together when the fatal car accident occurred. Jeff was following them and claimed he was with Vivian in the car to cover up her scandal. Her father then avenged Vivian's death by creating Jeff's "accidents" and the fire. Confronted with the true story, Ben threatens Jeff and Ellen with a gun, explaining that Vivian's mother had been a tramp. Confused, Ben believes that Ellen is Vivian but fails in an attempt to kill her, wounding Jeff instead. Dr. Hartley takes Ben to a hospital, explaining that he may eventually recover from the shock of Vivian's death and his subsequent psychosis. Jeff is now free of the past and unafraid of his future. His suicidal depression ends and his romance with Ellen is renewed.

The overriding creative sensibility in *The Second Woman* is producer Harry M. Popkin, who was responsible for a number of low-budget film noir. In *Impact* and *The Thief,* Popkin unsuccessfully strove for respectability but his production of *D.O.A.* is a classic. Hal Mohr's photography in *The Second Woman* keeps this film visually exciting despite Robert Young's subdued performance as the impotent architect. This film does not make the broad statements about creative genius and tyranny that abound in *The Fountainhead,* but because *The Second Woman*'s villain is a prominent real estate developer the film makes an oblique social criticism of the tract housing that was dramatically altering the postwar California landscape.

—B.P.

THE SET-UP (1949)

Director: Robert Wise
Producer: Richard Goldstone (RKO)
Screenplay: Art Cohn; from the poem by Joseph Moncure March
Director of Photography: Milton Krasner
Sound: Phil Brigandi, Clem Portman
Music Director: Constantin Bakaleinikoff
Art Directors: Albert S. D'Agostino, Jack Okey
Set Decoration: Darrell Silvera, James Altwies
Makeup: Gordon Bau, Joe Norrin, Bill Phillips
Hairstyles: Hazel Rogers, Gale Roe McGarry
Technical Adviser: John Indrisano
Assistant Director: Edward Killy
Script Supervisor: Dan Ullman
Film Editor: Roland Gross

CAST: Robert Ryan (Stoker), Audrey Totter (Julie), George Tobias (Tiny), Alan Baxter (Little Boy), Wallace Ford (Gus), Percy Helton (Red), Hal Fieberling (Tiger Nelson), Darryl Hickman (Shanley), Kenny O'Morrison (Moore), James Edwards (Luther Hawkins), David Clarke (Gunboat Johnson), Phillip Pine (Souza), Edwin Max (Danny). **BITS:** Dave Fresco (Mickey), William E. Green (Doctor), Abe Dinovitch (Ring Caller), Jack Chase (Hawkins's Second), Mike Lally, Arthur Sullivan, William McCarther, Gene Delmont (Handlers), Herbert Anderson, Jack Raymond (Husbands), Helen Brown, Constance Worth (Wives), Walter Ridge (Manager), Jess Kirkpatrick, Paul Dubov (Gamblers), Frank Richards (Bat), Jack Stoney (Nelson's Second), Archie Leonard (Blind Man), John Butler, Ralph Volke, Tony Merrill, Carl Sklover, Sam Shack, Herman Bodel, Andy Carillo, Charles Sullivan, Al Rehin, Tom Noonan, Dan Foster, Everett Smith, Brian O'Hara, Donald Kerr (Men), Lillian Castle, Frances Mack, Ruth Brennan (Women), Lynn Millan (Bunny), Bernard Gorcey (Tobacco Man), Charles Wagenheim (Hamburger Man), Billy Snyder (Barker), W. J. O'Brien (Pitchman), Frank Mills (Photographer), Bobby Henshaw (Announcer), Dwight Martin (Glutton), Noble "Kid" Chissel (Handler), Ben Moselle (Referee), Arthur Weegee Fellig (Timekeeper).
Filming Completed: November 11, 1948
Released: RKO, March 29, 1949
Running Time: 72 minutes

While his wife Julie waits in a shabby hotel room, Stoker, a 35-year-old fighter past his prime, goes to fight the last bout on a night's card, which follows the main event. Although Stoker knows he is no longer at his best and has been losing most of his recent fights, he believes that he might defeat his younger opponent. But his manager, Tiny, has arranged with the opposition for him to lose and is so confident that Stoker will be beaten that he does not tell the fighter to "take a dive." Stoker waits in the dressing room with the other fighters, all of whom have their private fears and obsessions, until it is time for his fight. In the early rounds, Stoker receives a lot of punishment and Tiny is sure it will be over at any moment. However, Stoker endures and gets the

Stoker (Robert Ryan) in The Set-Up.

251

advantage of his less experienced opponent. Tiny finally tells him of the deal; but Stoker refuses to cooperate and, dismayed at being sold out by his manager, he goes on to win the fight. Afterward, the crooks who made the deal with Tiny give Stoker a vicious beating. With broken hands but unbroken spirit, Stoker returns to Julie.

The Set-Up has a gritty atmosphere and decor and occurs entirely in a night world, a darkness that sets it apart as film noir in visual and emotional terms. Its story includes an ensemble of parasitic characters that are enlivened by offbeat casting. The part of Tiny is an unusual one for George Tobias, who is normally a figure of comic relief; and the strange, high-voiced Percy Helton (familiar from a role in *Kiss Me Deadly*) plays Red, Stoker's second. By contrast to the petty greed of these characters, Stoker himself possesses an unarticulated nobility that is subtly projected by Robert Ryan. One of the most important noir actors, Ryan possesses not only the physical appearance of a fighter—which he in fact was at one time—but gives a benighted dignity to Stoker that is necessary to make him an existential hero.

—B.L.

711 OCEAN DRIVE (1950)

Director: Joseph M. Newman
Producer: Frank N. Seltzer (Essaness Pictures)
Screenplay: Richard English and Francis Swan
Director of Photography: Franz F. Planer
Sound: James Gaither
Music Score: Sol Kaplan
Music Director: Emil Newman
Production Designer: Perry Ferguson
Set Decoration: Howard Bristol
Costumes: Odette Myrtil, Athena
Wardrobe: Greta Isgrigg
Makeup: Jack Byron
Hairstyles: Ann Locker
Technical Advisers: Lt. William Burns (Los Angeles Police Department), Edwin Block
Dialogue Director: Jack Herzberg
Production Manager: Orville Fouse
Assistant Director: Charles L. Smith
Film Editor: Bert Jordan

CAST: Edmond O'Brien (Mal Granger), Joanne Dru (Gail

Mal Granger (Edmund O'Brien), center, in 711 Ocean Drive.

Mason), Donald Porter (Larry Mason), Sammy White (Chippie Evans), Dorothy Patrick (Trudy Maxwell), Barry Kelley (Vince Walters), Otto Kruger (Carl Stephans), Howard St. John (Lt. Pete Wright), Robert Osterloh (Gizzi), Bert Freed (Marshak), Carl Milletaire (Joe Gish), Charles La Torre (Rocco), Fred Aldrich (Peterson), Charles Jordan (Tim), Sidney Dubin (Mendel Weiss).

Location: Los Angeles, Palm Springs, California; Lake Mead and Boulder Dam (Hoover Dam), Nevada
Filming Completed: 1950
Released: Columbia, July 19, 1950
Running Time: 102 minutes

Mal Granger is a hard-working and ingenious telephone repairman. One day he makes a repair call to a bookie joint, run by two distinguished businessmen, Larry Mason and Vince Walters. Impressed with Mal's technical acumen, they persuade him to engineer a telephone wire service connecting the racing results of all the West Coast tracks. Mal is successful and, desirous of money and power, eventually takes over Mason's operation and his beautiful wife by having the man murdered. The coastal wire service does so well that the big boys back East, headed by Carl Stephans, decide to incorporate it into the national crime syndicate and freeze Granger out. Mal is forced to flee to Las Vegas. Trapped near Hoover Dam, he attempts to escape by crossing the dam on foot but is shot and falls to his death below.

In *711 Ocean Drive* Edmond O'Brien assumes a role quite similar to that of the skilled master of technology he played in *White Heat*. In this case, however, he is on the other side of the law. His death at the base of Hoover Dam is an ironic memorial to the perishability of criminal genius. Moreover, unlike the case of Joe Morse in *Force of Evil*, the syndicate is not wiped out with his death. Rather, at the end of the film, a smiling Otto Kruger (again playing the master criminal) remains firmly in control.

—B.P.

SHADOW OF A DOUBT (1943)

Director: Alfred Hitchcock
Producer: Jack H. Skirball (Universal)
Screenplay: Thornton Wilder, Sally Benson, and Alma Reville; from a story by Gordon McDonell
Director of Photography: Joseph Valentine
Sound: Robert Pritchard
Music Score: Dimitri Tiomkin
Music Director: Charles Previn
Art Director: John B. Goodman, Robert Boyle

Set Decoration: R. A. Gausman, E. R. Robinson
Assistant Director: William Tummel
Film Editor: Milton Carruth

CAST: Teresa Wright (Young Charlie), Joseph Cotten (Uncle Charlie Oakley), Macdonald Carey (Jack Graham), Henry Travers (Joseph Newton), Patricia Collinge (Emma Newton), Hume Cronyn (Herbie Hawkins), Edna Mae Wonacott (Ann Newton), Wallace Ford (Fred Saunders), Irving Bacon (Station Master), Charles Bates (Roger Newton), Clarence Muse (Railroad Porter), Janet Shaw (Louise), Estelle Jewell (Girl Friend), Minerva Urecal (Mrs. Henderson), Isabel Randolph (Mrs. Green), Earle S. Dewey (Mr. Norton). **BITS:** Eily Malyon (Librarian), Edward Fielding, Sarah Edwards (Doctor and Wife on Train), Vaughn Glaser, Virginia Brissac (Dr. and Mrs. Phillips), Grandon Rhodes, Ruth Lee (the Reverend and Mrs. MacCurdy), Edwin Stanley (Mr. Green), Frances Carson (Mrs. Poetter), Byron Shores, John McGuire (Detectives), Constance Purdy (Mrs. Martin), Shirley Mills (Young Girl).
Filming Completed: October 28, 1942
Released: Universal, January 12, 1943
Running Time: 108 minutes

The mysterious but charming Charlie Oakley arrives in Santa Rosa ostensibly to visit his family, but he actually is eluding two investigators. He is welcomed by his adoring niece and namesake, Charlie. However, she gradually suspects that her beloved uncle may be wanted by the police for the murder of several wealthy widows. Her suspicions are shared by detective Jack Graham, who meets the family by pretending to be a pollster. At the same time, another suspect in the case is accidentally killed and the inquiry is officially closed. But Uncle Charlie becomes aware of his niece's suspicions and decides to kill her. After two unsuccessful attempts, he tries to push her off a train into the path of an oncoming engine. In the ensuing scuffle, he falls off and is killed. At his funeral, Uncle Charlie is honored by the townspeople, while the secret knowledge of his guilt draws his niece and the detective together.

Like many of Hitchcock's films, *Shadow of a Doubt* focuses on the character of a psychopath. Charlie's evil is defined initially through contrasts with the normal behavior of his relatives in the small California town. His violent verbal outbursts against mankind in general—"Do you know the world is a foul sty? Do you know if you ripped the fronts off houses you'd find swine?"—and the women he has murdered in particular—"Useless women, drinking the money, eating the money, smelling of money."—shatter his niece's security and illusions about life.

Hitchcock makes his points about Charlie's character with a variety of effects; the most celebrated and cinematic is the ominous cloud of black smoke that hangs over the train station as Charlie arrives in Santa Rosa, giving the impression, as François Truffaut has pointed out in his book

SHAKEDOWN

Hitchcock, that "the devil was coming to town." Charlie is very like a devil, self-endowed with all the power of a fallen god, passing judgment on the world. He is a killer with a mission, bent on the destruction of what he sees as ugly, his crazed eye fixed on a vision of a lost time when, as he tells his beloved niece, "Everybody was sweet and pretty, the whole world—not like today."

Charlie makes most of the declarations of his strange philosophy to his niece, who is, quite literally, his better half. The bond between them is telepathic: they share the same name and the same thoughts. She tells him, "We're sort of like twins"; and he tells her, "The same blood runs in our veins." The crucial difference between them is that of right and wrong. But Hitchcock is not content with such a neat, black-and-white schematization. The title, *Shadow of a Doubt,* refers not only to young Charlie's suspicions about her uncle, but also to the shadows that impinge upon her goodness. The will to destroy is the motivating force of Uncle Charlie's life; shockingly it turns out that this is yet another thing that young Charlie shares with him, if only momentarily, by accident and by necessity. For in the end, Uncle Charlie is brought down by his better half—and young Charlie is driven to destroy the thing she loves.

—J.K.

SHAKEDOWN (1950)

Director: Joe Pevney
Producer: Ted Richmond (Universal-International)
Screenplay: Alfred Lewis Levitt and Martin Goldsmith; from a story by Nat Dallinger and Don Martin
Director of Photography: Irving Glassberg
Sound: Leslie I. Carey, Robert Pritchard
Music Director: Joseph Gershenson
Art Directors: Bernard Herzbrun, Robert Clatworthy
Set Decoration: Russell A. Gausman, Ruby R. Levitt
Costumes: Yvonne Wood
Makeup: Bud Westmore, Del Armstrong
Hairstyles: Joan St. Oegger, Helen Turpin
Production Manager: Lew Leary
Assistant Directors: Joe Kenney, George Lollier
Script Supervisor: Pat Betts
Film Editor: Milton Carruth

CAST: Howard Duff (Jack Early), Brian Donleavy (Nick Palmer), Peggy Dow (Ellen Bennett), Lawrence Tierney (Coulton), Bruce Bennett (David Glover), Anne Vernon (Nita Palmer), Stapleton Kent (City Editor), Peter Virgo (Roy), Charles Sherlock (Sam). **BITS:** Will Lee, Carl Sklover (Taxi Drivers), Josephine Whittell (Mrs. Worthington), Steve Roberts (Magazine Representative), John Miller (Brownie), Ken Patterson (Thurman), Leota Lorraine (Guest), Charles Flynn (Fireman), Jack Reitzen (Fat Man), Roy Engel (Captain), Jack Rice (Floorwalker), Bert

Davidson, Ralph Brooks, Doug Carter (Photographers), Kay Riehl (Mrs. Spencer), Wendy Waldron (Information Clerk), Elsie Baker (Maid), Donald Kerr (Newsboy), Doretta Johnson (Nurse), Jack Chefe (Proprietor), Forbes Murray (Mr. Spencer), William Marks (Detective), Steve Wayne (Reporter), Joe Dougherty, Bill O'Brien, James Garwood, Chester Conklin (Men).
Filming Completed: April 27, 1950
Released: Universal-International, September 23, 1950
Running Time: 80 minutes

Jack Early is an opportunistic photographer who parlays a probationary job with a major San Francisco newspaper into an important assignment by romancing his boss, Ellen Bennett, and delivering two sensational photos. His next assignment is to photograph Nick Palmer, a camera-shy hoodlum. Jack persuades Palmer that complimentary pictures are in his best interest and Palmer offers him a job photographing one of his unruly henchmen, Harry Coulton, robbing a store. Jack takes the incriminating picture and then blackmails Coulton to prevent the photo from being published. Informing Coulton that Palmer attempted to frame him, Jack follows Coulton and takes photographs while the hoodlum places a bomb in Palmer's car. Jack gets a perfect picture of Palmer's death as the bomb goes off. This photograph makes Jack famous. He becomes photographer for a national magazine and hides the incriminating pictures of Coulton in Ellen's apartment for future use. She breaks off their relationship when she realizes Jack is unscrupulous and is also seducing Palmer's widow. Some time later, Jack is assigned to photograph a high society party and arranges to have Coulton's gang rob the guests of their jewelry and split the profits with him. But Coulton convinces Nita Palmer that her new lover killed her husband and she threatens to kill Jack. He begs Ellen to bring the incriminating photographs of Coulton to Nita, but Ellen does not believe the pictures exist. Nita is accidentally shot, and Jack attempts to escape but is shot by Coulton. As he dies, Jack squeezes the shutter on his camera and takes a picture of his murderer. This photograph is published by Jack's old newspaper alongside his complimentary obituary.

Shakedown is not a pejorative depiction of the newspaper business as was the 1930 classic, *Five Star Final,* or any of the versions of *The Front Page.* It is an indictment of the American drive for success and the extent to which ambition leads Jack Early to misuse the tremendous power given to him by the press. The complex narrative of ironic counterpurposes would be simplified in later film noir such as *Scandal Sheet.* In *Shakedown,* Howard Duff, radio's "Sam Spade," again displays his ability to personify a sympathetic heel, a role he had played earlier in *The Naked City.* Lawrence Tierney was physically dissipated by the time of *Shakedown's* production, but he brings to the role an iconic identity as among the most menacing of film noir villains.

—B.P.

THE SHANGHAI GESTURE (1941)

Director: Josef von Sternberg
Producer: Arnold Pressburger (Arnold Pressburger Productions)
Associate Producer: Albert de Courvill
Screenplay: Josef von Sternberg, Karl Vollmoeller, Geza Herczeg, Jules Furthman; from the play by John Colton
Director of Photography: Paul Ivano
Music Score: Richard Hageman
Art Director: Boris Leven
Set Decoration: Howard Bristol
Murals: Keye Luke
Cotumes: Oleg Cassini for Gene Tierney; Royer for Ona Munson
Wigs: Hazel Rogers
Technical Advisers: Tom Bubbins, Aline Sholes
Assistant Directors: Charles Kerr, Fred Pressburger
Film Editor: Sam Winston

CAST: Gene Tierney (Poppy), Walter Huston (Sir Guy Charteris), Victor Mature (Dr. Omar), Ona Munson (Mother Gin Sling), Phyllis Brooks (Dixie Pomeroy), Albert Basserman (Commissioner), Maria Ouspenskaya (Amah), Eric Blore (Bookkeeper), Ivan Lebedeff (Gambler), Mike Mazurki (Coolie), Clyde Fillmore (Comprador), Rex Evans (Counselor Brooks), Grayce Hampton (Social Leader), Michael Delmatoff (Bartender), Marcel Dalio (Croupier), Mikhail Rasumni (Cashier), John Abbott (Escort).

Filming Completed: December 1941
Released: United Artists, December 26, 1941
Running Time: 106 minutes

Mother Gin Sling is the owner of a Shanghai casino which, despite her bribes, the local authorities have decided to close under pressure from British financier Sir Guy Charteris. Charteris has his own plans for the property and refuses to accept any of Gin Sling's calls to discuss it. She has him investigated and learns that as a young man he was engaged in questionable activities in China, married a native woman, then fled with money from her estate and their infant daughter. At the same time, she discovers that this daughter, Poppy, now grown, has become a habitué of her establishment. Through one of her associates, Dr. Omar, Mother Gin Sling encourages Poppy's gambling until she has run up a considerable debt. Poppy, although enraged at Gin Sling's contemptuous treatment of her and suspicious of Omar's fidelity, nonetheless thwarts her father's attempt to send her out of the city and continues to patronize the casino. In order to get his daughter out of this environment, Charteris feels compelled to accept an invitation to Gin Sling's New Year's dinner and to hear her implicit blackmail demands. Ultimately, Gin Sling reveals to the incredulous Charteris that she is the wife whom he presumed killed and whose money he appropriated. Shaken, Charteris explains that he thought she had died after betraying him; but Poppy is unable to accept under any circumstances that Gin Sling could be her mother and hysterically denounces the woman. Infuriated by her own daughter's vilification, Gin Sling loses control and shoots her.

The nightmarish, almost Baroque environment that von Sternberg creates in *The Shanghai Gesture* contains much of what was to become a standard expression of the noir vision. Numerous changes in the 1925 Broadway play were mandated by the Hays Office—which had rejected nearly three dozen earlier film treatments. In Jules Furthman's screen version, for example, Mother Goddamn becomes Mother Gin Sling and her brothel becomes a gambling house. Despite all these changes, Sternberg evokes an underworld more tangible and more threatening than anything in such noir precursors as *Underworld* and *Thunderbolt*. The true nature of Gin Sling's establishment is, in effect, revealed in such early scenes as her "purchase" of Dixie, a blond playgirl, from the police and culminates in the New Year's auction of women suspended in cages outside the casino. Despite such exotic embellishments or the title disclaimer that "Our story has nothing to do with the present," *Shanghai Gesture* obviously anticipates and has everything to do with the postwar noir vision fatality and inexplicable malaise.

Poppy is the key characterization of that fatality. She is both the physical and psychological child of the youthful liaison between Gin Sling and Charteris; and, in the latter capacity, she embodies the emotional estrangement that both her parents suffered in assuming betrayal by the other. Sternberg uses Poppy's fascination with vice and her subsequent degeneration as an emblem of the more gradual process by which her parents have alienated themselves from normal relationships. In contrast to the artificial Gin Sling, whose masklike makeup and exotic headdress outwardly suggest a lifeless doll, and Charteris, who takes satisfaction in frustrating his sycophants by lighting his own cigarette, Poppy initially reacts to Gin Sling's gambling house with an open and natural disdain, "What a witches' sabbath . . . so incredibly evil. I didn't think such a place existed except in my own imagination—like a half-remembered dream. Anything could happen here, at any moment." Poppy's words are, of course, in the narrative convention of film noir, prophetic ones. The effects of her surrender to the dark side of her "own imagination" are apparent. Her gambling, drinking, and infatuation with Omar are examples, as are her altered appearance, haggard and slow-moving, and her frequently slurred words. Her drug addiction is not explicit but abundantly suggested by her own name, her mercurial behavior, and her increasing dependence on Omar.

Sternberg visually underscores the concept of Poppy's "evil, half-remembered dream" with numerous diffused close-ups, many of them on the half-familiar faces of well-known character actors that portray Gin Sling's minions: Maria Ouspenskaya as the Amah, Gin Sling's attendant; Eric Blore as the bookkeeper; Marcel Dalio as the croupier who controls the gamblers' fates; and Mike Mazurki as the hulking coolie who banters with Charteris in Pidgin English. From cuts of intent faces watching the spinning of the roulette wheel, Sternberg pulls back to overhead long shots of the smoke-filled hall with its cramped figures arranged into tiers around the wheel like a rendering of Dante's Inferno in evening dress. In a world where normal relationships are impossible, Sternberg isolates moments of either detachment or fury. In contrast to the increasingly frenzied Poppy, who senses herself being slowly crushed as surely as the wax figurine that Gin Sling rends with her polished nails, there is the imperturbable Omar, as laconic and icily unreachable as the Dietrich figures in Sternberg's earlier films. Omar's dark skin, hair slick with oil, and hooded eyes complement the moment when he spreads his cape around Poppy like a vampire before kissing her, almost suggesting an incubus who personifies the destruction of the noir underworld.

Charteris's final appearance in this underworld precipitates the violent denouement, which is a return to the darker vision of Sternberg's earlier films, a much bleaker vision than that found in the fates of the quixotic figures of the later *Macao*. Poppy's death not only verifies her observation that "anything could happen here, at any moment" but also denies any possibility of regeneration. The irony of Gin Sling's earlier remark that occasionally "Shanghai decides to clean itself like a swan in a muddy lake," is that the characters have no such option but are trapped in a miasma of their own dissolution. For the murdered Poppy, the question of "paying" for her sins is moot. For Gin Sling and for Charteris, who stumbles out of the casino to suffer a final taunt from the coolie ("You likee Chinee New Year?"), the question is left open-ended.

—A.S. & M.B.

SHIELD FOR MURDER (1954)

Directors: Edmond O'Brien and Howard W. Koch
Producer: Aubrey Schenck (Camden Productions)
Screenplay: Richard Alan Simmons and John C. Higgins, adapted by Richard Alan Simmons; from the novel by William P. McGivern
Director of Photography: Gordon Avil
Sound: Ben Winkler
Music: Paul Dunlap
Production Designer: Charles D. Hall
Assistant Director: Eugene Anderson, Jr.
Film Editor: John F. Schreyer

CAST: Edmond O'Brien (Barney Nolan), Marla English (Patty Winters), John Agar (Mark Brewster), Emile Meyer (Capt. Gunnarson), Carolyn Jones (Girl At Bar), Claude Akins (Fat Michaels), Larry Ryle (Laddie O'Neil), Herbert Butterfield (Cabot), Hugh Sanders (Packy Reed), William Schallert (Assistant District Attorney),

David Hughes (Ernest Sternmueller), Richard Cutting (Manning).
Filming Completed: May 25, 1954
Released: United Artists, August 27, 1954
Running Time: 80 minutes

Barney Nolan, a corrupt policeman, murders a small-time hood who tried to hold back a payoff and steals $25,000 from the corpse. His justification—that the murder was in the line of duty—convinces his superiors. Unfortunately, the entire affair was witnessed by an elderly gentleman who reports it to the police. As no connection is made with the earlier killing, Nolan is assigned to investigate the case. He eventually eliminates the old man and plans to establish himself in suburbia with his fiancée, Patty, in a newly built model home. But Nolan is pursued by a gangster, Packy Reed, and becomes a target for revenge. Mark Brewster, another detective, has meanwhile learned of Nolan's killings and the rogue cop becomes a fugitive hunted by both the police and the gangster. Nolan finds temporary sanctuary at the site of his new home but the police surround the area and gun him down on the lawn.

Starring and co-directed by Edmond O'Brien, a familiar noir actor, *Shield for Murder* was produced late in the cycle and explodes the myth of suburbia. The corruption found in the police officer is carried over into his cozy environment of builtin dishwashers and two-car garages. O'Brien transcends his characterization of the policeman on the take and becomes a symbol of decaying middle-class values. The film is explicit in its violence and brutal in its depiction of greed and lust warped by the false sense of power present behind the police badge. The destruction of the bad cop, Nolan, is inevitable. He follows a course that leads to death, because the redemption he seeks in the shelter of his new home is as insubstantial as the house's stucco facade. Nolan dies, crumpled up on his unplanted front lawn, nothing more than a piece of debris cluttering up the outline of sameness found in the tract of houses.

—C.M.

SIDE STREET (1950)

Director: Anthony Mann
Producer: Sam Zimbalist (MGM)
Screenplay: Sydney Boehm
Director of Photography: Joseph Ruttenberg
Sound: Douglas Shearer, Charles E. Wallace
Special Effects: A. Arnold Gillespie
Music Score: Lennie Hayton
Art Directors: Cedric Gibbons, Daniel B. Cathcart
Set Decoration: Edwin B. Willis, Charles de Crof
Makeup: Jack Dawn
Hairstyles: Sydney Guilaroff
Production Manager: Charles Hunt

Assistant Director: Howard Koch
Script Supervisor: Don MacDougall
Film Editor: Conrad A. Nervig

CAST: Farley Granger (Joe Norson), Cathy O'Donnell (Ellen Norson), James Craig (Georgie Garsell), Paul Kelly (Capt. Walter Anderson), Edmon Ryan (Victor Backett), Paul Harvey (Emil Lorrison), Jean Hagen (Harriet Sinton), Charles McGraw (Stanley Simon), Ed Max (Nick Drummon), Adele Jergens (Lucille "Lucky" Colner), Harry Bellaver (Larry Giff), Whit Bissell (Harold Simpsen), John Gallaudet (Gus Heldon), Esther Somers (Mrs. Malby), Harry Antrim (Mr. Malby), George Tyne (Detective Roffman), Kathryn Givney (Miss Carter), King Donovan (Gottschalk), Norman Leavitt (Pete Stanton), Sid Tomack (Louie). **BITS:** Joe Verdi (Vendor), Don Terranove (Patrolman), James Westerfield (Patrolman), Gail Bonney, Marjorie Liszt (Women's Voices), Brett King (Pigeon Man), Peter Thompson (Mickey), John A. Butler (Elevator Man), Herbert Vigran (Photographer), Robert Malcolm (Charlie), Paul Marion (Dave), William Ruhl (Manny), Ransom Sherman (Superintendent), Ruth Warren (Housekeeper), Eula Guy (Florence), Ed Glover (Fingerprint Expert), William Hansen (Dr. Harry Sternberg), Tom McElhany (Newsboy), Jack Diamond (Bum), George David (Syrian Proprietor), Don Haggerty (Rivers), Mildred Wall (Mrs. Glickburn), Angi O. Poulos (Ahmed), Albert Morin (Ismot Kimal), W. P. McWatters, James O'Neil (Men), Peter DeBear (Tommy Drummon, Jr.), Bee Humphries (Mrs. Farnol), Sarah Selby (Nurse Williams), Margaret Brayton (Woman Clerk), Charles McAvoy (Bank Guard), George Lynn (Frank, Technician), John Maxwell (Monitor's Voice), Nolan Leary (Doorman), Ralph Riggs (Proprietor), Ben Cooper (Young Man), Marie Crisis (Headwaitress), Lynn Millan (Hatcheck Girl), David Wolfe (Smitty), Ralph Montgomery (Milkman), Minerva Urecal (Landlady), Ollie O'Toole (Voice), Walter Craig (Radio Clerk), Helen Eby-Rock (Mother), Frank Conlon (Night Elevator Operator), John Phillips (Detective), Ellen Lowe (Mrs. Rivers), James O'Neil (Priest).
Location: New York, New York
Filming Completed: June 8, 1949
Released: MGM, March 23, 1950
Running Time: 83 minutes

Needing a little money to provide his pregnant wife with the "finer" things in life, a private mail carrier, Joe Norson, steals an envelope filled with cash from an office on his route. Unknown to Norson, the money is a payoff in a blackmail scheme that involves several murders. Taking some of the stolen money, Norson begins to construct his dream world. However, he starts having second thoughts about his crime. Attempting to return the remaining cash, he is met with feigned ignorance of its existence. Fearful of the consequences that may arise, Norson tells his wife, Ellen, that an out-of-town job opportunity compels him to leave home for a short time. Norson then hides in a cheap

hotel and leaves the money with a friend who absconds with it. Several hoodlums involved with the original blackmail plot find Norson and force him to reveal where he has hidden the money. His escape and subsequent efforts to undo his crime, lead Norson into a desolate world of sleazy nightclubs and underworld hangouts. Accused of a series of murders that he did not commit and hounded by an overwhelming sense of guilt, Norson is hunted by both the police and the hoodlums. He is captured by the criminals who plan to eliminate him. In a high-speed chase through the streets of New York City, the police finally catch up with Joe Norson and his unlikely companions. Although wounded, Norson is reunited with his wife and family.

Trying to capitalize on the relative success of Nicholas Ray's *They Live By Night,* MGM brought Cathy O'Donnell and Farley Granger together again under the directorial guidance of Anthony Mann. The result is a taut thriller shot on location and filled with a sense of despair but lacking the more romantic outlook of Ray's earlier film. Farley Granger is usually associated with such portrayals of ill-fated hopelessness as *Edge of Doom* and *I Want You,* yet in *Side Street* he transcends the melodramatic core of his role and gives the character of Joe Norson a naturalism most characteristic of film noir. *Side Street* deflates the American dream by confounding it with the inherent corruption and violence that rests below the surface of American culture. The impotence of Norson's situation, an ordinary man caught up in a situation he cannot control, goes far beyond the implications of doomed love. *Side Street* brings into focus the strained ambitions of a normal person, Norson, who is driven to desperate and illegal acts by mischance and a momentary moral lapse. Mann eschews his usual expressionistic lighting in favor of a more neutral style that complements the location exteriors. Such a style permits figurative usages like the high-angle shots of Norson pursued through narrow streets lined by tall buildings, suggesting an animal struggling through a maze, while the gray tones of the images underscore the naturalistic aspects of Norson's dilemma.

—C.M. & A.S.

SLEEP, MY LOVE (1948)

Director: Douglas Sirk
Producers: Charles Buddy Rogers, Ralph Cohn (Triangle Productions)
Associate Producer: Harold Greene
Screenplay: St. Clair McKelway and Leo Rosten, with contributions from Cyril Endfield and Decla Dunning; from the novel by Leo Rosten
Director of Photography: Joseph Valentine
Sound: William Randell
Music: Rudy Schrager

THE SLEEPING CITY

Music Supervisor: David Chudnow
Art Director: William Ferrari
Set Decoration: Howard Bristol
Costumes: Sophie, Margaret Jennings
Makeup: Burris Grimwood
Hairstyles: Marjorie Lund
Production Manager: Robert M. Beche
Assistant Director: Clarence Eurist
Script Supervisor: Mary Gibsone Whitlock
Film Editor: Lynn Harrison

CAST: Claudette Colbert (Alison Courtland), Robert Cummings (Bruce Elcott), Don Ameche (Richard Courtland), Rita Johnson (Barby), George Coulouris (Charles Vernay), Hazel Brooks (Daphne), Queenie Smith (Mrs. Tomlinson), Keye Luke (Jimmie), Fred Nurney (Haskins), Maria San Marco (Jeannie), Raymond Burr (Lt. Strake), Lillian Bronson (Helen), Ralph Morgan (Dr. Rhinehart).
Filming Completed: August 1, 1947
Released: United Artists, February 18, 1948
Running Time: 96 minutes

Alison Courtland is startled when she wakes up aboard a night train to Boston, as she has no recollection of leaving her home in New York City. Assisted by matronly Mrs. Tomlinson, she contacts her husband Richard, who purposefully allows the police to overhear their conversation, as Alison does not remember that she threatened Richard with a gun. On the plane home, Alison meets a charming friend of a friend, Bruce Elcott, who falls in love with her. Richard convinces his wife to undergo psychiatric treatment at her home with Dr. Rhinehart, who intimidates her and then mysteriously disappears. Richard excuses himself for a business meeting, but he keeps a rendezvous with Daphne; and it is revealed that the illicit couple have conspired with a photographer, Charles Vernay, to pose as Dr. Rhinehart and drive Alison to suicide so that Dick can inherit his wife's fortune. When Bruce finds Alison sleepwalking and about to jump off a balcony, he becomes suspicious of Richard's activities and investigates. Discovering Vernay's photography studio and claiming to need a passport picture, Bruce finds evidence that links Vernay as the man who posed as Dr. Rhinehart. Meanwhile, Richard believes he has drugged Alison and hypnotically suggests that she must kill Dr. Rhinehart to protect herself. But Vernay has realized he is being double-crossed and shocks Alison out of her stupor. Richard kills Vernay and prepares to shoot his wife, but Alison is saved by Bruce's arrival.

Sleep, My Love adds the noir elements of drugs, hypnosis, nightmares, and seemingly innocent but dangerous circumstance to its melodramatic plot of adultery and wife murder. Additionally, the climactic confrontation between Richard, Vernay, Alison, and Bruce derives noir impact because the scene develops in a way none of the characters intended and ensnares them all in revolving positions of helplessness. Alison, only half-drugged as she only half believes her husband capable of deceiving her, is urged by Richard to shoot Vernay's indistinct shadow, which appears through a frosted glass door. But the shadow looms forward and opens the door, and Vernay quickly relates to Alison the vicious truth about her recent neurosis. Richard drops all of his civilized pretensions and savagely shoots Vernay who falls back through the glass, literally shattering all of Alison's illusions about her husband. As Richard turns on her and affirms Vernay's revelations, Alison cowers in a corner, moaning "No, no no . . ." and the shadow of the stairway's railing figuratively imprisons her. Surprisingly, a figure emerges from behind Richard and kills him. Bruce Elcott's belated arrival undercuts his character's confident control over all situations and initially deludes the audience who believes that Vernay has struggled to his feet to avenge his betrayal.

This final scene overrides the lighthearted and bland characterizations provided by Claudette Colbert as the wife who is afraid but not horrified or alienated by her fear; and Robert Cummings as the sincere, brash hero, Bruce, who never doubts that his instincts are correct. The antagonists are more fully developed as noir characters: Don Ameche's cloying portrayal of the husband with schizophrenic desires; Daphne's icy sensuality; and especially George Coulouris's multifaceted Vernay highlight the motion picture. The scene with these latter three in the photography studio plotting their psychological crime is heightened by the illusory nature of Vernay's profession, photography, and the superficiality of Daphne's skill as a model, someone who bitterly understands that she can only sit in the studio wearing expensive clothes and will never be allowed to actually live a normal life clothed in them.

—E.W.

THE SLEEPING CITY (1950)
[Working Title: WEB OF THE CITY; CONFIDENTIAL SQUAD]

Director: George Sherman
Producer: Leonard Goldstein (Universal-International)
Screenplay: Jo Eisinger
Director of Photography: William Miller
Sound: Leslie I. Carey, Corson Jowett
Music Score: Frank Skinner
Art Directors: Bernard Herzbrun, Emrich Nicholson
Set Decoration: Fred Ballmeyer
Costumes: Rosemary Odell
Makeup: Ira Senz
Hairstyles: Donoene Lambert
Production Manager: Lew Leary
Script Supervisor: Josephine Cohn
Assistant Director: John Sherwood
Film Editor: Frank Gross

CAST: Richard Conte (Fred Rowan), Coleen Gray (Ann Sebastian), Peggy Dow (Kathy Hall), John Alexander

(Inspector Gordon), Alex Nicol (Dr. Bob Anderson), Richard Taber (Pop Ware), James J. Van Dyk (Dr. Sharpley), Hugh Reilly (Dr. Foster), Michael Strong (Dr. Connell), Frank M. Thomas (Lt. Lally), Richard Kendrick (Dr. Druta), Henry Hart (Dr. Nester), Robert Strauss (Lt. Marty Miller), Herbert Ratner (Detective Reese), Mickey Cochran (Detective Diamond), Ernest Saracino (Detective Abate). **BITS:** Russell Collins (Medical Examiner), Mrs. Priestly Morrison (Miss Wardly), James O'Neill (Engle), Frank Tweddell (Kingdon), Victor Sutherland (Holland), Jack Lescoulie (Paulsen), Carroll Ashburn (Surgeon), Tom Hoirer (Gaye), William Martell (Male Nurse), James Little (Travers), Terry Denim, Harold Bayne, Frank Baxter, James Daly, Dort Clark (Interns), Mimi Strongin (Little Girl), Rod McLennan (Detective), Ralph Hertz (Patient with Broken Leg).
Location: Bellevue Hospital, New York, New York
Filming Completed: December 10, 1949
Released: Universal-International, September 20, 1950
Running Time: 85 minutes

[NOTE: Universal-International agreed to appease New York City Mayor O'Dwyer's opposition to *The Sleeping City* by inserting a prologue, spoken by Richard Conte, that the film's story does not describe any particular U.S. city.]

An intern at a metropolitan hospital is murdered and police inspector Gordon assigns an undercover agent, Fred Rowan, to pose as a new intern to discover what is behind the death. His investigation exposes the victim's tormented roommate; a mysteriously criminal nurse, Ann; and an elderly elevator operator, Pop Ware, who extorts the hospital staff to obtain drugs for the black market.

The Sleeping City is an especially disturbing film noir because its plot concerns corruption within a hospital and involves depriving patients of needed drugs. The interns and nurses upon which the story focuses are shown as depressed and neurotic individuals, bitter and desperate people with little chance for a good future, rather than the noble crusaders usually associated with medical stories. The noir heroine of Ann Sebastian, played by Coleen Gray, is a nurse who abuses her patients for the sake of aiding a sick child who is not her own. The ending of the film is very similar to that of *The Maltese Falcon* but divides audience sympathy between the nurse and the undercover agent who now loves her. The agent watches her being arrested with a regret that suggests that he has not condemned her; and her bleak view of life has been reinforced by the film's images to the point that it has left a stronger emotional impression upon him than his devotion to duty regardless of his final compliance with that duty. George Sherman directed *The Sleeping City* with an imaginative visual interpretation, as in the tracking shot preceding the murder at the film's opening; and he guided interesting performances, notably the representatives of the law who—excepting the hero—are unusually hard and cynical.

—B.L.

SLIGHTLY SCARLET (1956)

Director: Allan Dwan
Producer: Benedict Bogeaus (Filmcrest Productions)
Screenplay: Robert Blees; from the novel *Love's Lovely Counterfeit* by James M. Cain
Director of Photography: John Alton [Technicolor; Superscope]
Sound: Jean Speak, Terry Kellum
Music Score: Louis Forbes
Art Director: Van Nest Polglase
Assistant Director: Nate Watt
Film Editor: James Leicester

CAST: John Payne (Ben Grace), Arlene Dahl (Dorothy Lyons), Rhonda Fleming (June Lyons), Kent Taylor (Jansen), Ted de Corsia (Sol Caspar), Lance Fuller (Gauss), Buddy Baer (Lenhardt), Frank Gerstle (Dietz), Ellen Corby (Martha).
Filming Completed: August 6, 1955
Released: RKO, February 29, 1956
Running Time: 99 minutes

[NOTE: Kurt Neumann was originally contracted to direct *Slightly Scarlet.*]

Ben Grace is a petty criminal working for Sol Caspar, criminal boss of a metropolis. When an honest man runs for mayor, Ben receives information concerning the politician's lovely secretary, June Lyons, and the prison record of her sister Dorothy. Romancing June, Ben gives her incriminating material on Caspar, causing the violent boss to kill an important newspaperman. Caspar must flee the city and Ben takes over, leading an ambiguous existence as a dishonest gang boss with some good instincts while also being genuinely in love with June. Meanwhile, June is apprehensive as Dorothy is attracted to Ben. When Caspar returns to avenge himself, Ben suffers being shot with bullet after bullet so that Caspar may be caught by the police with a gun in his hand. A severely wounded Ben is taken away as Dorothy and June follow.

This rendering of James M. Cain's *Love's Lovely Counterfeit* considerably alters the story, in which Dorothy enters late in the narrative and becomes Ben's lover, ennobling both of them. In the film, Ben is faithful to June; but Dorothy, although her presence is less motivated from a narrative standpoint, becomes the most interesting character: neurotic, unpredictable, and captivatingly immoral. It may be that Allan Dwan, with his passion for symmetry, introduced Dorothy at the beginning of the story to utilize Rhonda Fleming and Arlene Dahl as complementary redheaded visual objects throughout the film. In any event, the film does succeed visually as a stylistic representation of a triangle, in spite of the fact that the relationship of Ben, Dorothy, and June does not really support it. In the last shot, equal distances separate the three as they exit, with June presented as a figure caught in space between the man

THE SNIPER

whom she loves and the sister whom she obsessively protects.

Slightly Scarlet is one of a series of films made by RKO which Allan Dwan directed, John Alton photographed, and on which Van Nest Polglase was art director. Although made with extremely modest budgets, these films are among the most richly colored and decorated of the period and confirm that Alton's imagination in lighting is as distinctive in color as it is in black and white. As *Slightly Scarlet* is the only modern subject of this Dwan-Alton series, it is perhaps also the most interesting photographically, being a Technicolor film noir akin to the Leon Shamroy photography of *Leave Her to Heaven*. Alton continues to utilize extensive shadows and large black areas, while also accentuating a garish array of pinks, greens, and oranges, producing a startling effect in many scenes.

—B.L.

THE SNIPER (1952)

Director: Edward Dmytryk
Executive Producer: Stanley Kramer (Stanley Kramer Company)
Associate Producers: Edna and Edward Anhalt
Screenplay: Harry Brown; from an unpublished story by Edna and Edward Anhalt
Director of Photography: Burnett Guffey
Sound: Frank Goodwin
Music Score: George Antheil
Music Director: Morris Stoloff
Production Designer: Rudolph Sternad
Art Director: Walter Holscher
Set Decoration: James Crowe
Technical Adviser: William T. Whalen
Production Manager: Clem Beauchamp
Assistant Director: Milton Feldman
Film Editor: Aaron Stell
Supervising Editor: Harry Gerstad

CAST: Adolphe Menjou (Lt. Kafka), Arthur Franz (Eddie Miller), Gerald Mohr (Sgt. Ferris), Marie Windsor (Jean Darr), Frank Faylen (Inspector Anderson), Richard Kiley (Dr. James G. Kent), Mabel Paige (Landlady), Marlo Dwyer (May Nelson), Geraldine Carr (Checker), Jay Novello (Pete), Ralph Peters (Police Interlocutor), Max Palmer (Chadwick), Sidney Miller (Intern), Hurb Latimer (Sam), Dani Sue Nolan (Sandy), Harry Cheshire (Mayor), Cliff Clark (Chief of Police). **BITS:** Robert Foulk, Vern Martell, Fred Hartman, Don Michaelian, Renaldo Viri, Kernan Cripps, Rory Mallinson, J. Anthony Hughes (Policemen), John Bradley (Rookie Policeman), Danny Mummert (Boy), George Dockstader (Mapes), Les Sketchley (Flaherty), Carl Benton Reid (Liddell),

Byron Foulger (Pete Eureka), Roy Maypole (TV Announcer), Paul Marion (Al), Grandon Rhodes (Mr. Fitzpatrick), Kay Sharpe (Millie), Harlan Warde (Harper), John Brown (Wise), John Eldredge (Stonecroft), Patricia Toun, Helen Linstrom, Wanda Wirth, Luanna Scott, Kathleen O'Rielly, Elsa Weber, Helen Eliot, Aline Watson, Mary Holly, Alice Bartlett, Betty Shute, Gail Bonney, Sarah Selby, Robin Raymond, Marlene Lyden, Jean Willes, Kathleen O'Mally, Adrienne Marden, Jessie Arnold (Women), Elizabeth Whitney (Nurse), John H. Algate, Thomas Heidt, Richard Freye, Harry Bechtel, Willis West, Norman Nazarr, Robert Day, Nolan Leary, Billy Wayne, Paul Du Bov, Charles Lane, Harry Harvey, John A. Butler, Frank Sully, Donald Kerr (Men), Ralph Smiley (Tony Debiaci, Suspect), John Pickard (Allen Martin, Suspect), Ralph Volkie (Suspect), Joe Miksak, Richard Glyer, Howard Negley, David McMahon, Robert Malcolm, Charles Watts, Steve Darrell (Detectives), Frank Shaw (Anna Potch), Frank Kreig (Jailer), Victor Sen Young (Waiter), Gaylord Pendleton (Ambulance Man), Clark Howat (Police Photographer), Dudler Dickerson (Cleaner), Edgar Novack, Mike Lally, George Chesbro (Concessionaires), Charles Marsh (Manager), Lillian Bon (Mrs. Fitzpatrick), Donald Kerr, Joe Palma, Frank Sully (Men), Barry Brooks (Attendant), Bruce Cameron (Motorcycle Policeman), Tommy Hawkins (Outfielder), Lucas Farara (Child), Al Hill (Bartender), Ralph O. Clark (Man Who Falls from Smokestack).
Location: San Francisco, California
Filming Completed: October 20, 1951
Released: Columbia, May 9, 1952
Running Time: 87 minutes
[FACTUAL BASIS: The screenwriters claim they based the Eddie Miller character on the composite personalities of men who were convicted of violent crimes against women. Coincidentally, between the time they sold their screenplay and the film's release, a sniper named Evan Charles Thomas was arrested (on April 16, 1952) and admitted he killed one woman and wounded three women and a ten-year-old girl during the preceding year.]

A mentally disturbed young man, Eddie Miller, feels compelled to kill women. His attempts to find help are met with lack of interest and apathy. Breaking down, he shoots women from rooftops throughout the city. A scruffy and initially unsympathetic policeman, Lt. Kafka, is assigned to capture the sniper. As his investigation zeros in on the unbalanced killer, Kafka realizes that this killing spree is inspired not out of criminal lust but rather from deep psychological problems. Finally trapping the sniper in a cheap hotel room, the police close in. They force their way into his lightly barricaded room and find their suspect surrounded by a small arsenal of weapons. He offers no resistance, and a solitary tear of relief appears on his stoic countenance.

Directed by Edward Dmytryk, *The Sniper* possesses a visual

force reminiscent of his earlier noir efforts, including *Murder My Sweet, Crossfire,* and *Cornered.* However, the noir tone and ambience merely serves as a vehicle for the film's indictment of contemporary society for failure to deal with mental problems and urban alienation. But significantly, the film's verdict is lost amid the impact of ritualized violence and the thrill of the police manhunt, and society's status quo is maintained. The characters found in *The Sniper* exist in a netherworld that permits humanitarian speculation to surface through scenes of humiliation and *angst.* Although Dmytryk, along with such directors as Nicholas Ray and Elia Kazan, blended social awareness with a noir sensibility, *The Sniper* remains closer to the central noir vision than their films *Knock on Any Door* or *On the Waterfront,* respectively.

—C.M.

SO DARK THE NIGHT (1946)

Director: Joseph H. Lewis
Producer: Ted Richmond (Columbia)
Screenplay: Martin Berkeley and Dwight Babcock; from an unpublished story by Aubrey Wisberg
Director of Photography: Burnett Guffey
Sound: Frank Goodwin
Music: Morris W. Stoloff, Hugo Friedhofer
Art Director: Carl Anderson
Set Decoration: William Kiernan
Assistant Director: Chris Beaute
Film Editor: Jerome Thorms

CAST: Steven Geray (Henri Cassin), Micheline Cheirel (Nanette Michaud), Eugene Borden (Pierre Michaud), Ann Codee (Mama Michaud), Egon Brecher (Dr. Boncourt), Helen Freeman (Widow Bridelle), Theodore Gottlieb (Georges), Gregory Gay (Commissioner Grande), Jean Del Val (Dr. Manet), Paul Marion (Leon Achard), Emil Ramu (Pere Cortot), Louis Mercier (Jean Duval). **BITS:** Billy Snyder (Chauffeur), Frank Arnold (Antoine), Adrienne d'Ambricourt (Newspaper Woman), Marcelle Corday (Proprietor), Alphonse Martel (Bank President), André Marsaudon (Postmaster), Francine Bordeaux (Flower Girl), Esther Zeitlin (Peasant Woman), Cynthia Gaylord (Bootblack).
Filming Completed: December 12, 1945
Released: Columbia, October 10, 1946
Running Time: 70 minutes

Henri Cassin, the top detective of the Paris Sûreté, takes his first vacation in eleven years at the Michaud family inn in the quiet country village of St. Margot and is immediately attracted to pretty, young Nanette Michaud. Mama Michaud does her best to promote her daughter's new romance despite Nanette's engagement to a young local farmer, Leon Archard, since marriage to Henri is an opportunity to enhance her status and live in Paris. While Leon is out of town, Nanette encourages the proper and middle-aged Henri and soon they announce their engagement. M. Michaud warns Henri against the marriage. Leon accuses Mme. Michaud of "arranging things," and tells Henri that if he marries Nanette, Leon will pursue her and she will never be truly Henri's. Leon leaves and is followed by Nanette, who does not return. Henri is disconsolate. When her body is found in the river, Henri discovers that she has been strangled. Leon's body is found at his farm and has also been strangled. The only clue is the killer's footprint in the wet dirt beneath the body. Agreeing to help the local police, Henri swears to find the killer of his beloved Nanette. He receives a note stating "There will be another murder," and soon the body of Mme. Michaud is discovered. Henri returns to Paris to consult with his superior, Commissioner Grande and gives the Sûreté artist the killer's physical description as deduced from the footprint. The artist remarks that it resembles Henri. Suspecting himself, Henri writes one of the murder notes with his left hand. It conforms to the others and Henri insists he be put under custody. The police doctor explains it is possible for Henri to have a split personality. Henri relapses and escapes back to the Michaud Inn. Poised to kill M. Michaud, the police arrive and shoot Henri through the window.

So Dark the Night, Joseph Lewis's second venture in the noir cycle indicates his ability to infuse a pastoral setting with *maudit* elements. More importantly, Lewis forced cinematographer Burnett Guffey into an uncharacteristic visual style utilizing an unusual range of deep blacks, depth staging, and shooting through windows, to lend the necessary expressionistic touch. Though a relatively obscure film, *So Dark the Night* should stand at the summit of those films that deal with the degraded detective. For Henri Cassin, a veritable Sherlock Holmes of the Sûreté, is reduced to murder because of those very talents that have made him so great; particularly his ability to cut himself off from the rest of the world. The pressures of his job and the unhappy affair of the heart, with all of its implications of *l'amour fou,* are what precipitate his split personality, which kills when divorced from his rational mind. The consistent visual motif of this film—shooting through windows—identifies the audience with the detective as voyeur. In the startling final scene all is made clear as Henri, forced to admit he is a murderer and dying of a bullet wound, returns his gaze to the inn's window and sees himself as he appeared when he first arrived: a smiling, famous police detective. This image merges with that of him as a killer, whereupon Henri smashes the window and eliminates both of his "reflections." Recognizing the two sides of his nature, perhaps for the first time, he exclaims: "Henri Cassin is no more. I have caught him and killed him."

—B.P.

SOMEWHERE IN THE NIGHT

SOMEWHERE IN THE NIGHT (1946)

Director: Joseph L. Mankiewicz
Producer: Anderson Lawler (20th Century-Fox)
Screenplay: Howard Dimsdale and Joseph L. Mankiewicz, adapted by Lee Strasberg; from a story by Marvin Borowsky
Director of Photography: Norbert Brodine
Special Effects: Fred Sersen
Sound: Eugene Grossman, Harry M. Leonard
Music: David Buttolph
Music Direction: Emil Newman
Orchestral Arrangements: Arthur Morton
Art Directors: James Basevi, Maurice Ransford
Set Decoration: Thomas Little, Ernest Lansing
Costumes: Kay Nelson
Makeup: Ben Nye
Assistant Director: Johnny Johnston
Film Editor: James B. Clark

CAST: John Hodiak (George Taylor), Nancy Guild (Christy Smith), Lloyd Nolan (Lt. Donald Kendall), Richard Conte (Mel Phillips), Josephine Hutchinson (Elizabeth Conroy), Fritz Kortner (Anzelmo), Margo Woode (Phyllis), Sheldon Leonard (Sam), Lou Nova (Hubert), John Russell (Marine Captain), Houseley Stevenson (Conroy), Charles Arnt (Little Man), Al Sparlis (Anzelmo's Henchman). **BITS:** Richard Benedict (Technical Sergeant), John Kellogg (Medical Attendant), Phil Van Zandt (Navy Doctor), Whit Bissell (Bartender), Forbes Murray (Executive), Jeff Corey (Bank Teller), Polly Rose (Nurse), Mary Currier (Miss Jones, Nurse), Sam Flint (Bank Guard), Henry Morgan (Swede), Charles Marsh (Hotel Clerk), Clancy Cooper (Attendant), Jack Davis (Dr. Grant), Louis Mason (Brother William), Henri DeSoto (Headwaiter), Milt Kibbee (Proprietor), Elaine Langan (Hatcheck Girl), Edward Kelly, Jr., Cy Schindel (Men at Bar), Maynard Holmes (Police Stenographer).
Filming Completed: April 5, 1946
Released: 20th Century-Fox, June 12, 1946
Running Time: 110 minutes

George Taylor, an ex-marine, is a victim of amnesia with only two clues to his past: a bitter letter from a girl who hated him and another equally mysterious letter signed "Larry Cravat." Taylor goes to Los Angeles to find Cravat. His presence at a nightclub attracts the malevolent attention of two thugs and he escapes via the dressing room of entertainer Christy Smith. Outside, he is beaten by two mobsters named Anzelmo and Hubert, who believe that Taylor knows where Cravat is. Taylor finds sanctuary in Christy's apartment; and she promises the help of her boss, Mel Phillips, and police Lt. Donald Kendall, who explains that Cravat disappeared about the same time Taylor joined the marines. Cravat is wanted for murder and a robbery of $2 million. The lone witness to the murder, Conroy, has been mortally wounded as Taylor arrives to question him;

but before dying the man tells Taylor that the stolen money is hidden under a San Pedro dock and that two men are involved in the murder. Taylor and Christy find the suitcase full of money and a man's suit that reads, "W. George, Tailor"; and Taylor realizes he is actually Larry Cravat. Shots ring out, and he and Christy take refuge. Phillips helps them escape; but Taylor remembers that the club owner is his old partner and the actual killer. Phillips demands the money; but Taylor leads him into a trap and Lt. Kendall kills Phillips as he attempts to escape. Taylor and Christy are free to begin a new life.

Somewhere in the Night is the quintessential film whose protagonist is an amnesiac veteran. This film, very much a part of the Fox noir cycle, is directed by Joseph Mankiewicz and filled with grotesques like Sheldon Leonard, Henry Morgan, Charles Arnt, and especially Fritz Kortner, a veteran of Max Reinhardt's Berlin theater. The film is tied closely to a war psychology; in fact, the $2 million was supposed to have entered America from Germany. Also, Larry Cravat had been a none too scrupulous private eye as he had cruelly rejected a girl who was later killed and was also involved in a shady scheme to get the contraband money. Even in his new personality, George Taylor, he exploits a lonely and frightened girl to find her father, the lone witness to a murder.

—B.P.

SORRY, WRONG NUMBER (1948)

Director: Anatole Litvak
Producers: Hal B. Wallis, Anatole Litvak (Hal Wallis Productions)
Screenplay: Lucille Fletcher; from her radio play
Director of Photography: Sol Polito
Photographic Effects: Farciot Edouart, Gordon Jennings
Music Score: Gene Merritt, Walter Oberst
Art Directors: Hans Dreier, Earl Hedrick
Set Decoration: Sam Comer, Bertram Granger
Costumes: Edith Head
Makeup: Wally Westmore
Jewels: Ruser
Production Manager: Richard Blaydon
Assistant Director: Richard McWhorter
Script Supervisor: Marvin Weldon
Film Editor: Warren Low

CAST: Barbara Stanwyck (Leona Stevenson), Burt Lancaster (Henry Stevenson), Ann Richards (Sally Lord Dodge), Wendell Corey (Dr. Alexander), Harold Vermilyea (Waldo Evans), Ed Begley (James Cotterell), Leif Erickson (Fred Lord), William Conrad (Morano), John Bromfield (Joe, Detective), Jimmy Hunt (Peter Lord), Dorothy Neumann (Miss Jennings), Paul Fierro (Harpootlian). **BITS:** Kristine Miller (Dolly, Dr. Alexander's

Girl Friend), Suzanne Dalbert (Cigarette Girl), George Stern (Drug Store Proprietor), Joyce Compton (Blond) Tito Vuolo (Albert), Garry Owen (Bingo Caller), Holmes Herbert (Wilkins, Butler), Neal Dodd (Minister), Louise Lorimer (Nurse), Yola D'Avril (French Maid), Pepito Perez (Boat Operator), Ashley Cowan (Clam Digger), Igor Dega, Grace Poggi (Dance Team), Cliff Clark (Sergeant Duffy).

Filming Completed: March 1948
Released: Paramount, September 1, 1948
Running Time: 89 minutes

Leona Stevenson, an invalid heiress, is alone in her New York apartment one evening when, because of crossed telephone wires, she overhears two men planning to kill a woman. When the police can't investigate on her sketchy information, she makes phone calls to learn more about the murder and discovers that the intended victim is herself. Previously stubborn and self-indulgent, Leona has developed a psychosomatic cardiac condition. Her henpecked husband, Henry, has been blackmailed by a sinister man named Morano into plotting to hasten Leona's "imminent" death so that Henry would inherit her estate. But when he learns Leona's condition is psychosomatic, Henry attempts to call off the plan. Morano refuses to wait and forces Henry to leave town so that his wife's death will appear as the result of a robbery attempt. Changing heart, Henry telephones a warning to Leona. She answers the phone but is unable to escape and screams, then drops the phone as the murderer approaches. It is picked up eventually and a man replies, "Wrong number." As Henry leaves the phone booth he is arrested by the police who have discovered his plot.

Sorry, Wrong Number was originally a 22-minute radio script written by Lucille Fletcher. Performed by Agnes Moorehead, the radio program is a virtual monologue and was rebroadcast seven times between 1943 and 1948 and translated into fifteen languages. The film is not as tightly constructed as the radio play, but it is a fine example of how the hermetic world of film noir creates a sense of entrapment. Director Anatole Litvak, who arrived in the United States via Russia, Germany, and France, uses a variety of surrealistic and expressionistic devices. Leona's self-imprisonment is described by a circling camera that moves from the array of useless medicines on her bedside table to Leona herself clothed in lace and ensconced in her elegant bed. Believing herself to be helpless, she watches the murderer's shadow creep up the stairs. Her only link with the outside world, the telephone, is voided by her screams and the depersonalized leather glove of the killer. Although cast against type, Lancaster as the ineffectual and bespectacled Henry, the ordinary man menaced by the hulking Morano, contrasts with Leona's poorly suppressed hysteria and adds a level of verisimilitude lacking in the original version.

—B.P. & L.S.

SOUTHSIDE 1-1000 (1950)

Director: Boris Ingster
Producers: Maurice and Frank King (King Brothers Productions)
Screenplay: Leo Townsend and Boris Ingster; from an unpublished story by Milton M. Raison and Bert C. Brown
Director of Photography: Russell Harlan
Sound: John Kean
Music Score: Paul Sawtell
Song: "Je T'aime" by Fritz Rotter and Harold Stern; sung by Kippee Valez
Music Editor: Stuart Frye
Production Designer: Edward S. Haworth
Art Director: David Milton
Set Decoration: Raymond Blotz, Jr.
Costumes: Norma
Production Manager: Allen K. Wood
Continuity: Richard Evans
Technical Adviser: Herman King
Dialogue Coach: Leon Charles
Assistant Director: Frank S. Heath
Film Editor: Christian Nyby

CAST: Don DeFore (John Riggs/Nick Starns), Andrea King (Nora Craig), George Tobias (Reggie), Barry Kelley (Evans), Morris Ankrum (Eugene Deane), Robert Osterloh (Albert), Charles Cane (Harris), Kippee Valez (Singer).
Location: San Quentin Prison, Los Angeles, California
Filming Completed: June 30, 1950
Released: Allied Artists, November 2, 1950
Running Time: 73 minutes

Master counterfeit engraver Deane has grown old and sick serving a life sentence in prison. His major solace appears to be religion; and he is always reading his Bible, which conceals the counterfeit plates that he works on in his cell. The plates are sneaked out of the prison in a minister's valise and are later picked up by Reggie, a member of a gang headed by Nora Craig, who is ostensibly the respected manager of a Los Angeles hotel but is actually Deane's daughter. Alerted, Treasury Department agent John Riggs finds evidence of the counterfeit plates in Deane's cell. Tracing the bogus money to Nora's hotel, Riggs assumes the identity of Nick Starns, a gambler wanted by the F.B.I. He strikes up a romance with Nora who arranges for him to buy some of the counterfeit bills. But she finds a sketch drawn by her father titled "Agent Riggs" and realizes Nick is a T-Man. She locks him in the gang's house, which is then set afire. The police and federal men show up, to capture all of the gang except Nora. They free Riggs, who pursues Nora through the darkened downtown area and into the freight yards, where he finally catches her. She tries to throw him off a narrow ledge; but falls to her death on the tracks below.

Although not so fully realized as *T-Men, Southside 1-1000* is significant if only because it was written and directed by Boris Ingster, who also directed what is probably the first true film noir, *Stranger on the Third Floor*. Unlike that earlier studio effort, this film is in the style of the pseudodocumentary, but with much chiaroscuro and location work. The last sequence, in which the righteous agent pursues his former lover across a trestle bridge, is particularly ironic. After a moment in which they are locked in a passionate embrace of love and hate, the chase culminates with her Freudian leap into the darkness below. The bitch-heroine, Nora Craig, is excellently portrayed by Andrea King in a role similar to her part of Marjorie in *Ride the Pink Horse*, where she is described by Gagin as "a dead fish with perfume on the outside."

—B.P.

THE SPLIT (1968)
[Working Title: RUN THE MAN DOWN]

Director: Gordon Flemyng
Producers: Irwin Winkler and Robert Chartoff (Spectrum Productions)
Screenplay: Robert Sabaroff; from the novel *The Seventh* by Richard Stark [Donald Westlake]
Director of Photography: Burnett Guffey [Metrocolor, Panavision]
Special Effects: Virgil Beck
Sound: Franklin Milton
Music: Quincy Jones
Songs: "It's Just a Game, Love," lyric by Ernie Shelby, music by Quincy Jones, sung by Arthur Prysock; "A Good Woman's Love," lyric by Sheb Wooley, music by Quincy Jones, sung by Sheb Wooley
Art Directors: Urie McCleary, George W. Davis
Set Decoration: Keogh Gleason, Henry Grace
Unit Manager: Jim Henderling
Script Supervisor: Les Hoyle
Assistant Director: Al Jennings
Film Editor: Rita Roland

CAST: Jim Brown (McClain), Diahann Carroll (Ellie), Julie Harris (Gladys), Ernest Borgnine (Bert Clinger), Gene Hackman (Lt. Walter Brill), Jack Klugman (Harry Kifka), Warren Oates (Marty Gough), James Whitmore (Herb Sutro), Donald Sutherland (Dave Negli), Jackie Joseph (Jackie), Harry Hickox (Detective), Joyce Jameson (Jenifer), Warren Vanders (Mason). **BITS:** George Cisar (Doorman), Karen Norris (Proprietress), Duane Grey, Reg Parton, Cal Brown, Jon Kowal, John Orchard (Guards), Barry Russo (Maccione, Top Guard), Ron Stokes (Detective), Anne Randall (Negli's Girl), Beverly Hills (Receptionist), Robert Foulk (Sergeant), Howard Curtis, Chuck Kicks, Bill Couch, Carl Saxe, Gene LeBell, George Robotham (Physical Instructors), Fabian Dean, Thordis Brandt (Clerks), Dee Carroll, Edith Evanson

(Women), Lou Whitehill, Ron McCavour (Policemen), Orriel Smith, Cherie Lamour (Teenagers), Chance Gentry (Policeman), José Gallegos (Father), Tina Menard (Mother), Priscilla Ann (Daughter), Anthony Carbone (Man), Vanessa Lee (Little Girl), Jonathan Hole (Ticket Seller), Geneva Pacheco (Concessionaire).
Location: Los Angeles, California
Filming Completed: April 17, 1968
Released: MGM, October 14, 1968
Running Time: 91 minutes

McClain and Gladys recruit a gang of professional criminals to carry out their plan to steal the receipts of a sold-out football game in the Los Angeles Coliseum. Each prospective member of the group is tested by McClain: he picks a fight with strong-arm man Bert Clinger; he engages in an armed duel with shootist Dave Negli; he has a drag race with racing driver Harry Kifka; and he uses a prostitute to trap escape artist Marty Gough. Meticulous planning results in the robbery of $500,000; and the money is hidden with McClain's estranged wife, Ellie, who will not reconcile with McClain unless he gives up crime. McClain promises to go legitimate with his share of this robbery's proceeds. But Ellie is raped and killed by her landlord, Herb Sutro, who discovers the money and steals it. Lt. Brill investigates the murder and ties it in with the Coliseum robbery. Meanwhile, the gang members suspect that McClain has stolen the cash and pursue him. McClain makes a deal with Brill to track down the murderer of Ellie in return for information about the stolen money. Brill apprehends the killer and hijacks the $500,000. McClain demands a cut of the money and Brill cooperates, but the gang has followed McClain. He and Brill engage in a successful shoot-out against the gang. As a result, Brill becomes a police hero and lets McClain escape with a share of the stolen money; but the criminal is haunted by the memory of his wife.

A downbeat thriller, *The Split* is an adaptation of one of the "Parker" novels of Richard Stark [Donald Westlake]. These contemporary novels, which focus on an underworld character who proves that the distinctions between hero and antihero are relatively minor, present an interesting correlative to the noir world of the late 1940s and early 1950s. The ritualization of violence, the aura of corruption, the quality of hopelessness, and an intense feeling of alienation combine to give *The Split* a definite noir tone. The ambience is remarkably similar to a great many noir films. Even the environment is surprisingly decayed and dingy. Several of Stark's novels have been filmed in the past few years, most notably Jean-Luc Godard's *Made in U.S.A.*, adapted from the novel *The Jugger*; John Boorman's *Point Blank*, adapted from *The Hunter*; and, most recently, *The Outfit*, from the novel of the same name. Each of these films update certain noir attitudes and objectives into contemporary film making. Stylistically, *The Split*, directed by Gordon Flemyng, is filled with low-key images and tight claustrophobic settings. Rather than physically recreating the 1940s milieu either for atmosphere or as homage as do films like *Chinatown* and *Farewell, My Lovely*, *The Split* attempts, perhaps unconsciously, to recapture the spirit of the classic noir films.

—C.M.

STORM FEAR (1956)

Director and Producer: Cornel Wilde (Theodora Productions)
Screenplay: Horton Foote; from the novel by Clinton Seeley
Director of Photography: Joseph La Shelle
Sound: Glen Glenn Sound Company
Music: Elmer Bernstein
Production Design: Rudi Feld
Film Editor: Otto Ludwig

CAST: Cornel Wilde (Charlie), Jean Wallace (Elizabeth), Dan Duryea (Fred), Lee Grant (Edna), David Stollery (David), Dennis Weaver (Hank), Steven Hill (Benjie), Keith Britton (Doctor).
Filming Completed: May 1955
Released: United Artists, February 1, 1956
Running Time: 88 minutes

Charlie and two surviving members of his gang, Benjie and Edna, take refuge after a bank robbery in his older brother Fred's New England farmhouse. While Benjie and Edna wait anxiously to continue their flight, Charlie tends to a gunshot wound in his leg and plans to elude police roadblocks by going on foot over nearby mountains. Charlie also attempts a reconciliation with his brother's young wife, Elizabeth, with whom he previously had an affair and whose son, David, is actually Charlie's own child. When Hank, Fred's hired hand, escapes from the farm to alert the police, the criminals must hastily prepare to leave. Charlie convinces David to guide them across the snow-covered mountain; and when Fred resists this, he is shot by Benjie. As they cross the open country, Edna breaks her ankle and is abandoned by Charlie, which shocks David who had thought his "uncle" was a basically good man. Nonetheless, when Benjie attempts to overpower Charlie near the summit and escape alone with the loot, David grabs the gun dropped during the criminals' struggle and shoots Benjie. David helps Charlie, whose wound has been reopened, to the summit. But before he can get over, Charlie is shot by the rifle of the pursuing Fred and dies in the local hospital.

Released one year after such cynical and apocalyptic films as *Kiss Me Deadly* and *The Big Combo*, the latter also starring Cornel Wilde and Jean Wallace, *Storm Fear*'s noir

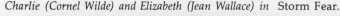

Charlie (Cornel Wilde) and Elizabeth (Jean Wallace) in Storm Fear.

characteristics stem less from its violence or any gritty city-scapes (there are none), than from the claustrophobic quality of the fugitive's sojourn in the farmhouse. Here the illicit past relationships between the criminal and his brother's seemingly normal family are revealed; and the remembered passion of Charlie and Elizabeth's past affair is translated into their unspoken contest for the present affections of their son. These underlying tensions carried over from the guilty past are separated from the main narrative line dealing with the gang's plan to elude capture yet coupled to such diverse morbid details as Benjie's socio-pathic hatred of all present, Charlie's self-conscious stammer caused by the disapproval of his older brother, and even the cheap dog collar that the family has used to decorate the Christmas tree after their pet's death, so that the melodrama develops with Ibsen-like pretensions. In the hospital epilogue, Charlie's guilt finally precipitates a rather gratuitous plea for forgiveness. In contrast with Lewis's direction of *The Big Combo*, Wilde removes the self-assurance and glamour from his and Jean Wallace's respective roles in *Storm Fear*. The use of locations for the flight over the mountain finally reduces the diverse interior conflicts to a graphically defined struggle between small, dark figures and a vast, snow-covered landscape.

—A.S.

STRANGE ILLUSION (1945)
[Also Released As: OUT OF THE NIGHT]

Director: Edgar G. Ulmer
Producer: Leon Fromkess (Producers Releasing Corporation)
Screenplay: Adele Commandini; from an original story by Fritz Rotter
Director of Photography: Philip Tannura
Sound: Frank McWhorter
Music Director: Leo Erdody
Art Director: Paul Palmentola
Set Decoration: Elias H. Reif
Costumes: Harold Bradow
Properties: Charles Stevens
Production Manager: Albert Herman
Assistant Director: Ben Kadish
Film Editor: Carl Pierson

CAST: James Lydon (Paul Cartwright), Warren William (Brett Curtis), Sally Eilers (Virginia Cartwright), Regis Toomey (Dr. Vincent), Charles Arnt (Professor Muhlbach), George H. Reed (Benjamin), Jayne Hazard (Dorothy Cartwright), Jimmy Clark, Mary McLeod, Pierre Watkin, John Hamilton, Sonia Sorrel, Vic Portel (People).
Filming Completed: October 16, 1944
Released: PRC, March 31, 1945
Running Time: 84 minutes

Adolescent Paul Cartwright believes that his father's death and his mother's plans for remarriage are not merely coincidental. This suspicion becomes solidified after he receives a letter written by his father before the man was found dead. Spurred on by this message from beyond the grave, Paul decides to feign insanity in the hopes of catching his mother's suitor off guard and exposing him as his father's murderer. Committed to an asylum by his mother at the prompting of her fiancé, Brett Curtis, the youth is subjected to intense scrutiny by the hospital staff. The plan nearly backfires in the sinister surroundings of the asylum, which drives Paul to the edge of sanity. Finally, the youth gathers enough evidence to convict his mother's lover as his father's murderer.

Strange Illusion is another stylish, low-budget feature directed by Edgar G. Ulmer; but unlike his other noir efforts, notably *Detour* and *Ruthless, Strange Illusion* is a relatively actionless production. The most interesting aspect of the film rests in its updating of *Hamlet,* complete with the message from beyond the grave and the faked insanity, into a contemporary thriller. The noir tone of *Strange Illusion* is accentuated by both Warren William's portrayal of the lecherous cad and the claustrophobic atmosphere of the mental hospital. William, who for the previous decade had been one of the Warner's studios matinee idols, adds a naturalistic dimension to the character of the suave, middle-aged gigolo Brett who leers at teenage girls lounging around a private pool. The asylum sequences, on the other hand, are controlled visions of chaos and corruption, a mental hell sardonically defined by Ulmer.

—C.M.

THE STRANGE LOVE OF MARTHA IVERS (1946)

Director: Lewis Milestone
Producer: Hal B. Wallis (Hal B. Wallis Productions)
Screenplay: Robert Rossen; from an unpublished story "Love Lies Bleeding" by Jack Patrick
Director of Photography: Victor Milner
Process Photography: Farciot Edouart
Sound: Harold Lewis, Walter Oberst
Music: Miklos Rozsa
Song: "Strange Love" by Haynes and Lyons
Art Directors: Hans Dreier, John Meehan
Set Decoration: Sam Comer, Jerry Welch
Costumes: Edith Head
Assistant Directors: Richard McWhorter, Robert Aldrich
Film Editor: Archie Marshek

CAST: Barbara Stanwyck (Martha Ivers), Van Heflin (Sam Masterson), Lizabeth Scott (Toni Marachek), Kirk Douglas (Walter O'Neil), Judith Anderson (Mrs. Ivers), Roman Bohnen (Mr. O'Neil), Darryl Hickman (Sam Masterson, as a boy), Janis Wilson (Martha Ivers, as a girl), Ann

Sam Masterson (Van Heflin) and Toni Marachek (Lizabeth Scott) in The Strange Love Of Martha Ivers.

Doran (Secretary), Frank Orth (Hotel Clerk), James Flavin (Detective #1), Mickey Kuhn (Walter O'Neil, as a boy), Charles D. Brown (Special Investigator). **BITS:** Matt McHugh (Bus Driver), Walter Baldwin (Dempsey, Garage Owner), Catherine Craig (French Maid), Sayre Dearing, Jarry Leonard (Crap Shooters), William Duray (Waiter), Payne B. Johnson (Bellboy), Max Wagner (Detective #2), Tom Fadden (Taxi Driver), Gladden James (John O. Butler), Bert Roach, Ricky Ricardi, Billy Burt, Gene Ashley (Men), Robert Homans (Policeman), John Kellogg (Detective), Al Murphy (Waiter), Kay Deslys (Jail Matron), Bob Perry (Bartender), Olin Howlin (Newspaper Clerk), Blake Edwards (Sailor), Betty Hill (Waitress), Tom Dillon (Detective), Tom Schamp, Kerman Cripps (Policemen), Thomas Louden (Lynch, Butler).

Filming Completed: December 7, 1945
Released: Paramount, July 24, 1946
Running Time: 115 minutes

An unusual childhood situation results in murder; and young Martha Ivers inherits a large family fortune. In the next twenty years, she maintains control of a large industrial plant in a small Midwestern town. An accidental reunion with a childhood friend, Sam Masterson, rekindles old passions and long-forgotten feelings of guilt in Martha. Her weak and alcoholic husband, District Attorney O'Neil, is not pleased when he discovers Masterson's presence and attempts to force him out of town by using a young woman, Toni Marachek as bait. Masterson quickly realizes that he is being compromised and decides to confront O'Neil but first flatters Martha in order to discover her true motives. When he realizes that she did indeed murder her aunt, it is O'Neil who foresees complications. He taunts Masterson about his affair with Martha and then falls down the stairs in a drunken rage. Martha urges her supposed lover to murder her husband; but he refuses and leaves Martha alone with the crumpled O'Neil. The couple realize that circumstances will force them to reveal the crime they committed long ago. O'Neil gives his wife a pistol, which she turns on herself. He then uses the same pistol to shoot himself. Masterson leaves town with Toni, remarking casually, "I wanted to see if I could be lucky twice."

In the postwar period, Hal Wallis's predilection for producing extremely romantic novels and stories often placed his films in a category of their own. His major characters suffered from psychological obsessions and neuroses but were infrequently criminals from the lower classes, whose presence can give film noir a lurid appeal. Wallis selected material that enabled veteran directors, notably Dieterle, Litvak, and Milestone, to have a certain freedom of expres-

THE STRANGER

sion; but patterns of Wallis's authorship occur most frequently in these films, such as the concerned but uninvolved characters played by Ann Richards in *Love Letters* and *Sorry, Wrong Number*; the method in which the *mise-en-scène* is grotesquely overstated at crucial moments to evoke the audience's private romantic fantasies; or the many characters who return to places that hold traumatic associations for them and rekindle suppressed passions.

Miklos Rozsa wrote the music for *Strange Love of Martha Ivers,* and it illustrates the conventional Holywood leitmotif technique of film scoring. This technique associates a musical theme with each character, setting, or situation, thus heightening the dramatic flux and the audience's unconscious understanding and expectation of the film's story. It should be pointed out that the popular song "Strange Love" represents the sweetness of Toni and the happy ending, not the hardness of Martha. Rozsa overscores to the point that nonmusical moments in his films amount to negative emphasis.

The Strange Love of Martha Ivers is filled with noir implications as the characterizations of Martha and the two principal male characters make an absurd love triangle. Dealing in a relationship based on fear, guilt, and cruelty, the noir characters exhibit an emotional imbalance caused by romantic zeal. Heflin functions as a catalyst. He enters the town and his mere presence is responsible not only for the disruption of normal activities but also the death of the leading citizens. Milestone has created a film that is a testimony to both the affinity between sex and violence and the cruel manipulations of a fatal woman. Kirk Douglas's portrayal of O'Neil reflects the tendency of noir films from this period to cast conventionally strong personalities in a fictional position of impotence. By the same token, Masterson also has little potency and merely reacts to the manifestations of Martha Ivers's aura of control. The unusual double suicide once again associates film noir with the surrealist concept of *amour fou* in presenting a love that finds justification only in death.

—C.M. & L.S.

THE STRANGER (1946)

Director: Orson Welles
Executive Producer: William Goetz (International Pictures)
Producer: S. P. Eagle [Sam Spiegel]
Screenplay: Anthony Veiller [with uncredited contribution from John Huston and Orson Welles]; from a story by Victor Trivas
Director of Photography: Russell Metty
Sound: Corson F. Jowett
Musical Score: Bronislav Kaper
Production Designer: Perry Ferguson
Costumes: Michael Woulfe
Production Manager: Bernard F. McEveety

Assistant Director: Jack Voglin
Film Editor: Ernest Nims

CAST: Edward G. Robinson (Wilson), Loretta Young (Mary Longstreet), Orson Welles (Franz Kindler/Professor Charles Rankin), Philip Merivale (Judge Longstreet), Billy House (Mr. Potter), Richard Long (Noah Longstreet), Konstantin Shayne (Konrad Meinike), Martha Wentworth (Sara), Byron Keith (Dr. Lawrence), Pietro Sosso (Mr. Peabody).
Filming Completed: November 21, 1945
Released: RKO, July 21, 1946
Running Time: 95 minutes

The seemingly peaceful surroundings of a small New England college community is invaded by a fugitive war criminal. His escape was engineered by government agents in the hopes of trailing the zealous Nazi to his superiors. Wilson, the agent sent to follow their human bait, is knocked out before he is able to identify the object of his intense search. Franz Kindler alias Charles Rankin, a supposed college professor, wastes no time in disposing of the unwanted visitor from his Nazi past. He murders his ex-comrade and conceals the body scant hours before he is to wed Mary Longstreet, a prominent young society woman. The small-town atmosphere begins to take on a distinctly morose personality manipulated by Kindler and assaulted by the constant probings of Wilson, the government agent. Ultimately Kindler makes mistakes and his actions betray his deep-rooted Nazi philosophies. Only after exposing Kindler/Rankin's wife to the atrocities committed by him during the war does the agent begin to tighten the net around the war criminal. Unable to completely believe that the man she loves could be capable of such heinous crimes, Mrs. Rankin confronts her husband for the last time. However Kindler/Rankin has gone over the edge of sanity and attempts to murder her. Cornered by the police and agent Wilson, Kindler falls to his death impaled by a mechanism connected to a huge clock tower.

Probably the most conventional of Orson Welles's films, *The Stranger* nevertheless is an unusual film noir. Working through a tradition of international intrigue in the mode of writers like Eric Ambler or Graham Greene, Welles and his screenwriters Anthony Veiller and John Huston introduce sensations of irrationality into a small-town environment. Atypically of Welles's work, the images found in *The Stranger* are neither complex or baroque. Rather the characters tend to be ciphers, mired in cryptic illusions of purpose and rationale. Each of the main characters is a stranger: Franz Kindler, due not only to the fact that he is an alien but also because he masquerades as a completely different person; Wilson, an outsider whose presence upsets the balance of typical routine in the college community; and Mary Longstreet, who never reveals her character until the film's conclusion. The movie is filled with perverse relationships and equally perverse characterizations. Besides the obvious nature of Kindler's Nazi allegiances, even someone as seemingly harmless as Mr. Potter, the proprietor of the local grocery store becomes a dark-sided elf, cheating at checkers, overtly suspicious of strangers, and easily convinced of conspiracies. The relationship between Charles Rankin and his wife is surreal in its implications. A viewer may find it implausible that no one, particularly his wife, would be able to see the hidden current of Nazi madness in Rankin/Kindler's personality. The growing relationship in their young marriage is a mild example of mad love as it extends beyond the bounds of normal relationships. Ultimately the mockery of a marriage and the underlying thread of violence found in Kindler's pulpish characterization underscore the noir quality to *The Stranger*. *The Stranger* exists as an answer to the critics who complained that Welles could not make a "program" picture. He did, and it has found a niche in the canon of the film noir.

—C.M.

STRANGER ON THE THIRD FLOOR (1940)

Director: Boris Ingster
Producer: Lee Marcus (RKO)
Screenplay: Frank Partos
Director of Photography: Nicholas Musuraca
Montage: Vernon L. Walker
Art Director: Van Nest Polglase
Assistant Director: James Casey
Film Editor: Harry Marker

CAST: Peter Lorre (Stranger), John McGuire (Mike Ward), Margaret Tallichet (Jane), Charles Waldron (District Attorney), Elisha Cook, Jr. (Joe Briggs), Charles Halton (Meng), Ethel Griffies (Mrs. Kane), Cliff Clark (Martin), Oscar O'Shea (Judge), Alec Craig (Defense Attorney), Otto Hoffman (Police Surgeon). BITS: Charles Judels (Nick), Frank Yaconelli (Jack), Paul McVey (Lt. Jones), Robert Dudley (Postman), Frank O'Connor, Don Kelly, James Farley (Policemen), Emory Parnell, Jack Cheatham, Dell Henderson (Detectives), Herbert Vigran, Robert Weldon, Terry Belmont, Gladden James (Reporters), Harry C. Bradley (Court Clerk), Greta Grandstedt, Bess Wade, William Edmunds (Housekeepers), Jane Keckley (Landlady), Bud Osborne (Bartender), Lyton Brent, Lee Phelps, Max Hoffman (Taxi Drivers), Broderick O'Farrell (Minister), Henry Roquemore (Boss McLean), Ralph Sanford (Truck Driver), Betty Farrington, Katherine Wallace (Women), Ray Cooke (Attendant), Bobby Barber (Italian).
Filming Completed: July 3, 1940
Released: RKO, September 1, 1940
Running Time: 64 minutes

Newspaper reporter Mike Ward is the star witness at the trial of a taxi driver, Briggs, accused of a brutal throat-slashing murder. Although Mike's evidence is circumstan-

tial, it secures a guilty verdict and capital punishment from a rather detached judge and jury. Mike's fiancée, Jane, believes Briggs is innocent and encourages Mike to help prove it. One night on his way into his apartment, he sees a stranger with a white scarf first outdoors and then lurking in the shadows on the stairwell. Subsequently noticing that he cannot hear the usual snoring of his elderly next-door neighbor, Albert Meng, Mike begins to worry that Meng might be dead but falls asleep in his chair. Mike dreams that he is arrested, tried, and convicted for Meng's murder. Finally strapped into the electric chair, Meng himself, cruelly laughing, enters to witness Mike's execution. Waking from this nightmare, Mike rushes next door, and finds Meng's throat slashed. Suspecting the white-scarfed stranger, Mike reports the murder to the police, who suspect him. Jane scours the neighborhood looking for the stranger and, seeing a bizarre little man, she asks to walk with him for protection. She presses him for information, but the stranger becomes afraid. He threatens Jane but she runs across the street. The stranger gives chase, but he is hit by a truck and killed. Mike and Jane are married, and a smiling Briggs, now free, ushers them into his taxicab.

Stranger on the Third Floor is the first true film noir; and it represents a distinct break in style and substance with the preceding mystery, crime, detection, and horror films of the 1930s. To begin with, there is the oneiristic blurring of the distinction between dream and reality. But more significantly, this unheralded B film noir, made a full year before *Citizen Kane*, demonstrates the most overt influence yet of German expressionism on American crime films to that time. Partos's story and script, which stresses paranoia and claustrophobia, is given form through the highly artificial *mise-en-scène* of studio setting. Ingster's Germanic direction is given additional force through the heavily gestured performances of Peter Lorre as the stranger and John McGuire as Mike Ward and also through Van Nest Polglase's art direction. Polglase's career at RKO was later capped by *Citizen Kane*, but in *Stranger on the Third Floor* he collaborated on many seminal noir techniques with Albert S. D'Agostino, who was to be head of RKO's art department throughout the noir cycle. Finally, *Stranger on the Third Floor* exploits the Baroque photography of Nick Musuraca, whose mannered style would later be further refined in films made by Orson Welles and Val Lewton.

—B.P.

STRANGERS ON A TRAIN (1951)

Director and Producer: Alfred Hitchcock (Warner Brothers)
Assistant Producer: Barbara Keon
Screenplay: Raymond Chandler and Czenzi Ormonde, adapted by Whitfield Cook; from the novel by Patricia Highsmith

STREET OF CHANCE

Director of Photography: Robert Burks
Special Effects: H. F. Koenekamp
Sound: Dolph Thomas
Music Score: Dimitri Tiomkin
Music Director: Ray Heindorf
Art Director: Ted Haworth
Set Decoration: George James Hopkins
Costumes: Leah Rhodes
Makeup: Gordon Bau
Assistant Director: Mel Dellar
Film Editor: William H. Ziegler

CAST: Farley Granger (Guy Haines), Ruth Roman (Anne Morton), Robert Walker (Bruno Antony), Leo G. Carroll (Senator Morton), Patricia Hitchcock (Barbara Morton), Laura Elliott (Miriam), Marion Lorne (Mrs. Antony), Jonathan Hale (Mr. Antony), Howard St. John (Capt. Turley), John Brown (Professor Collins), Norma Varden (Mrs. Cunningham), Robert Gist (Hennessey), John Doucette (Hammond). **BITS:** Howard Washington (Waiter), Dick Wessell (Baggage Man), Edward Clark (Mr. Hargreaves), Leonard Carey (Butler), Edna Holland (Mrs. Joyce), Tommy Farrell, Rolland Morris (Miriam's Boyfriends), Louis Lettieri (Boy), Murray Alper (Boatman), John Butler (Blind Man), Roy Engle, Joel Allen (Policemen), Eddie Hearn (Sgt. Campbell), Mary Alan Hokanson (Secretary), Janet Stewart, Shirley Tegge (Girls), George Renevant, Odette Myrtil (M. and Mme. Darville), Charles Meredith (Judge Dolan), Minna Phillips, Monya Andre (Dowagers), Laura Treadwell (Mrs. Anderson), J. Louis Johnson (Butler), Sam Flint, Ralph Moody (Men), Harry Hines (Man Under Merry-Go-Round).
Location: New York, New York; Washington, D.C.; Darien, Connecticut; amusement park constructed on Rowland V. Lee's ranch, Los Angeles, California
Released: Warner Brothers, June 30, 1951
Running Time: 101 minutes

Guy Haines, a champion tennis pro, is approached by Bruno Antony, a professed fan, while on a train. Armed with an astonishing knowledge of Guy's personal life, Bruno proposes an unusual arrangement: criss-cross murders, with Bruno killing Guy's wife, who refuses to give him a divorce so he can remarry, and Guy murdering Bruno's strict father. Appalled, Guy jokingly rejects the proposal; but the psychotic Bruno carries out his part of the plan by strangling Guy's wife in an amusement park. Guy is unable to provide a solid alibi to the police; and they keep him under observation. Bruno demands Guy carry out his part of the so-called bargain. Guy is evasive; but his feelings of guilt cause him to appear increasingly suspicious to the police. Bruno threatens to implicate Guy by planting the tennis pro's lighter at the scene of the crime. Guy must race through a scheduled tennis match in order to catch up with Bruno before he plants the evidence. In the end, Bruno is crushed to death by a runaway merry-go-round, and Guy is cleared of the crime.

Guilt, if only by association, is a theme that Hitchcock returns to obsessively, most often focusing on a basically innocent man who, by some accident of character or circumstance, is implicated in a crime he did not commit. Henry Fonda as Manny Balestrero in *The Wrong Man* is hounded by the police and sent to jail because he coincidentally resembles a real criminal. In *Spellbound*, the strange behavior of Gregory Peck as J.B. derives from the buried torment he feels at having witnessed his brother's childhood death and causes him to fall under suspicion. The voyeurism of James Stewart as Jeff in *Rear Window* implicates him in a murder he inadvertently uncovers. But in *Strangers on a Train*, Guy's innocence is a technicality. The character of Guy, incarnated by Farley Granger in appropriately oily fashion, is self-serving, clearly opportunistic, and is at least partially responsible—in his refusal to take Bruno seriously—for his wife's murder. Certainly it serves his purpose only too well: he becomes free to make a politically advantageous marriage. Guy's rebuff of Bruno's proposal is weak enough to imply a certain assent and his subsequent actions seem motivated more by a desire to avoid trouble than to bring Bruno to justice.

Bruno, the actual murderer, is a carefree individual. Slyly played by Robert Walker, Bruno is witty, straightforward, and sadly sympathetic. He seems far more a victim than the obnoxious Guy; after having honored his part of what he believes is a bargain, he is betrayed.

The world of *Strangers on a Train*, wherein the guilty are innocent and the innocent are guilty, is characteristically noir but more characteristically Hitchcock's world, a world in which no one, it seems, can escape blame—not even the audience. In *Psycho*, there is a scene in which the murderer disposes of his victim's body by placing it in a car that he then pushes into a pond. There is a moment when the car stops sinking; and the audience sympathetically hopes that it will go all the way down, burying all the evidence of a heinous crime. In short, the audience sides with the killer. *Strangers on a Train* has a similar sequence: on his way to plant Guy's lighter at the scene of his wife's murder, Bruno drops the incriminating object down a grate. His struggles to retrieve it, intercut with scenes of Guy feverishly trying to finish a tennis match so that he can go after Bruno, are agonizing—and the end result, again, is that the audience sympathizes with a killer.

—J.K.

STREET OF CHANCE (1942)
[Working Title: THE BLACK CURTAIN]

Director: Jack Hively
Associate Producer: Burt Kelly (Paramount)
Screenplay: Garrett Fort; from the novel *The Black Curtain* by Cornell Woolrich
Director of Photography: Theodor Sparkuhl

Music: David Buttolph
Art Directors: Hans Dreier, Haldane Douglas
Assistant Director: Alvin Ganzer
Film Editor: Arthur Schmidt

CAST: Burgess Meredith (Frank Thompson), Claire Trevor (Ruth Dillon), Louise Platt (Virginia Thompson), Sheldon Leonard (Joe Marucci), Frieda Inescort (Alma Diedrich), Jerome Cowan (Bill Diedrich), Adeline de Walt Reynolds (Grandma Diedrich), Arthur Loft (Sheriff Lew Stebbins), Clancy Cooper (Burke), Paul Phillips (Schoeder), Keith Richards (Intern), Ann Doran (Miss Peabody), Cliff Clark (Policeman Ryan), Edwin Maxwell (Stillwell, District Attorney). **BITS:** Gladden James (Mr. Clark), Reed Porter (Counterman), Kenneth Chryst, Kernan Cripps (Taxi Drivers), Sonny Boy Williams (Small Boy), Helen MacKellar (Mrs. Webb, Landlady), Ruth Gillette (Blond), Harry Tyler (Proprietor of Clothing Store), Besse Wade (Landlady), Ralph Dunn (Fireman), James C. Morton (Bartender), Milton Kibbee (Barber), George Watts (Proprietor of Pawnshop), Gloria Williams (Woman).
Filming Completed: February 19, 1942
Released: Paramount, November 18, 1942
Running Time: 74 minutes

After blacking out when hit by a falling beam, Frank Thompson awakens in an unfamiliar section of New York, carrying a cigarette case and hat marked with the initials "D.N." Returning home, he discovers his wife has moved and traces her to where she lives under her maiden name of Virginia Morrison. Recovering from the initial shock of seeing Frank, Virginia explains that he disappeared completely over a year ago, but Frank has no memory of what has happened during that time. Fortunately, he is allowed back at his position of accountant; but, upon returning to the office the next day, he notices a sinister individual watching him from outside the building. Leaving work that evening, Frank is aware that the same man follows him home and waits outside. Leaving via the fire escape, Frank tells Virginia to go to her mother's where he will contact her after he attempts to discover what happened during the missing year of his life. He haunts the area where the accident occurred, and one evening a girl calls to him. Pretending to know her, Frank discovers she knows him as Dan Nearing and that her name is Ruth Dillon. He is shocked to discover from Ruth, who claims to be his fiancée, that as Nearing he is wanted for the murder of Ruth's employer, Harry Diedrich. Persuading Ruth to take him with her to the Diedrich mansion, Frank hopes to prove his innocence. He also learns that his sinister pursuer is Detective Joe Marucci. At the mansion, Frank meets Grandma Diedrich, an invalid. Working out an eye code with Grandma, Frank discovers it was Ruth who killed Harry Diedrich. Ruth admits her guilt and Frank confesses his amnesia. She pulls a gun on Frank, but is shot by Detective Marucci. Realizing Ruth has only moments to live, Frank claims the amnesia was a lie and that he loves her. Marucci hears Ruth's dying confession and Frank is free to return to his normal existence.

Although somewhat obscure, *Street of Chance* is an important early entry in the noir cycle; it establishes a number of conventions that later helped to define film noir and set it off from its predecessors. It is the first adaption of a Cornell Woolrich work and it authentically captures the atmosphere of Woolrich's universe: the hapless and desperate individual at loose in New York City; a sense of doom and foreboding; and the use of amnesia. Woolrich's greatest weakness is in his plotting of contrivances, coincidences, and contradictions, which lack any sense of coherency. Yet, it is this very weakness that helps develop the whole black and chaotic world that is unique to Woolrich and makes his narratives compatible to film noir. It is tempting to dismiss the contribution of director Jack Hively in favor of Woolrich's originality and the special visual sensibility of Theodore Sparkuhl. Veteran of German expressionism and French poetic realism, Sparkuhl had previously helped give an appropriate low-key look to *Among the Living*. The *mise-en-scène* contrasts markedly with that of similar melodramas produced in the 1930s, particularly because of a distinctive use of space: rooms with lowered ceilings to enhance a sense of enclosure; the use of forced perspective to allow greater depth staging; and much less reliance on areas of white, which are now broken up by patterns of diagonal and vertical lines. Additionally, *Street of Chance* has an early emphasis on the use of jazz background music as opposed to orchestrally staged numbers.

—B.P.

THE STREET WITH NO NAME (1948)

Director: William Keighley
Producer: Samuel G. Engel (20th Century-Fox)
Screenplay: Harry Kleiner
Director of Photography: Joe MacDonald
Special Photographic Effects: Fred Sersen
Sound: Roger Heman, W. D. Flick
Music: Lionel Newman
Art Directors: Lyle Wheeler, Chester Gore
Set Decoration: Thomas Little
Wardrobe Director: Charles LeMaire
Costumes: Kay Nelson
Makeup: Ben Nye, Tommy Tuttle
Production Manager: Gene Bryant
Assistant Director: Henry Weinberger
Script Supervisor: Kathleen Fagan
Film Editor: William Reynolds

CAST: Mark Stevens (Gene Cordell), Richard Widmark (Alec Stiles), Lloyd Nolan (Inspector Briggs), Barbara Lawrence (Judy), Ed Begley (Chief Harmatz), Donald Buka (Shivvy), Joseph Pevney (Matty), John McIntire

(Cy Gordon), Howard Smith (Commissioner Demory), Walter Greaza (Lt. Staller), Joan Chandler (Joan Mitchell), Bill Mauch (Mutt), Sam Edwards (Whitey), Don Kohler (F.B.I. Agent Atkins), Roger McGee (Joe), Vincent Donahue (Cholly), Phillip Pine (Monk), Buddy Wright (Giveno), Larry Anzalone (Sparring Partner), Robert Karnes (Dave), Robert Patten (Danker). **BITS:** Joan Blair (Valentine Leval), Kitty McHugh (Waitress), Jack Herrick (Pug), Joe Haworth (Sgt. Bryant), Randy Stuart (Helen), Marion Marshall (Singer), Mike Killian (Police Sergeant), Edmund Cobb (Desk Sergeant), Johnny Kern (Fighter), Philip Van Zandt (Manager of Bonding Company), Al Thompson (Hotel Clerk), George Leonard (Ticket Taker), Don Jessee (Scar-Faced Tough), Joe McGurk (Fight Manager), Billy Wayne (Fight Trainer), Wally Scott (Ring Manager), Kid Wagner (Old Pug), Charles Tannen (Cab Driver), Fred Graham (Bank Clerk), Michael Sheridan, Lyle Latell (Officers), Sammy Shack (Bartender), Robert B. Williams (Sergeant).

Location: Los Angeles, California; Washington, D.C.
Filming Completed: March 7, 1948
Released: 20th Century-Fox, July 14, 1948
Running Time: 91 minutes

When an innocent woman is killed in a nightclub holdup in the Midwestern town of Center City, the F.B.I. investigates. Inspector Briggs discovers that the primary suspect, Ed Danker, was framed, arrested, then released on bail and mysteriously killed. Realizing that the crime wave is the work of a well-organized gang, Briggs and his assistant, Cy Gordon, bring in Gene Cordell as undercover agent. Given the identity of Joe Manley, a drifter with a police record, Cordell arrives in Center City by bus. As Manley, he meets fight promoter Alec Stiles and several of his men and impresses Stiles with his boxing ability. When Manley's wallet is missing, he knows the cover is working. His wallet is found as evidence in a robbery, and Manley is arrested and his bail is arranged. Manley continues to ingratiate himself with Stiles and informs Gordon of the details of the gang's next robbery attempts. Stiles learns the police are aware of his plans from his informant, Commissioner Demory, and calls the crime off. When Manley steals a bullet from Stiles's luger to compare it with the murder weapon used in a past robbery, Stiles discovers fingerprints, which Demory links to Manley. Realizing he is an undercover agent, Stiles devises a plan to kill Manley during a robbery. But when the police arrive, they shoot Stiles instead. Police Chief Harmatz had discovered that Demory was the gangster's informant in time to thwart Stiles's plot.

Street with No Name is an example of the semidocumentary thrillers produced by Fox. It was directed by William Keighley, who directed several classic gangster films in the 1930s at Warner Brothers. Extensive location filming and minor parts played by actual F.B.I. personnel are used with a stentorian narrator extolling the virtues of that organization. But the photography of Joe MacDonald, who is closely associated with the semidocumentary of this period, such as *Call Northside 777* and *Panic in the Streets*, evokes a sense of the corrupt city through stylized and shadowy images not too different from such studio films as *I Wake Up Screaming* and *Dark Corner*. Lloyd Nolan and John McIntire play stereotypical roles with which they are conventionally associated, while Mark Stevens's low-keyed performance as Cordell recalls his character of Bradford Galt in *The Dark Corner* and has an understated intensity reminiscent of Alan Ladd. There is an attempt on the part of both writer and actor to tone down the psychotic characteristics of Widmark's earlier and startling performance as Tom Udo in *Kiss of Death*; but Widmark's presence underscores his portrayal of Alec Stiles with numerous neurotic idiosyncrasies: the misogynism evident in Stiles's brutal treatment of his wife; the muted homosexual relationship with Manley; his manic laugh; his use of a nasal inhaler and his obsession with the dangers of fresh air and germs. Even more unusual in Stiles's character is its accommodation to the postwar society, in his desire to run the gang like an army, to "build an organization along scientific lines."

—B.P.

THE STRIP (1951)

Director: Leslie Kardos
Producer: Joe Pasternak (MGM)
Screenplay: Allen Rivkin
Director of Photography: Robert Surtees
Special Effects: A. Arnold Gillespie, Warren Newcombe
Montage: Peter Ballbusch
Sound: Douglas Shearer
Music: Georgie Stoll
Orchestration: Leo Arnaud, Pete Rugolo
Songs: "A Kiss To Build A Dream On" by Bert Kalmer, Harry Ruby, and Oscar Hammerstein II; "Shadrack" by Robert MacGimsey; "La Bota" by Charles Wolcott and Haven Gillespie II; "Basin Street Blues" by Spencer Williams; "Don't Blame Me" by Jimmy McHugh and Dorothy Fields
Art Directors: Cedric Gibbons, Leonid Vasian
Set Decoration: Edwin B. Willis, Alfred E. Spencer
Costumes: Helen Rose
Makeup: William Tuttle
Hairstyles: Sydney Guilaroff
Dance Director: Nick Castle
Assistant Director: Sid Sidman
Film Editor: Albert Akst, A.C.E.

CAST: Mickey Rooney (Stanley Maxton), Sally Forrest (Jane Tafford), William Demarest (Fluff), James Craig (Delwyn "Sonny" Johnson), Kay Brown (Edna), Louis Armstrong & Band (Band), Tommy Rettig (Artie), Tom

Powers (Bonnabel), Jonathan Cott (Behr), Tommy Farrell (Boynton), Myrna Dell (Paulette Ardrey), Jacqueline Fontaine (Frieda), Vic Damone, Monica Lewis (Singers). **BITS:** Robert Foulk, John McGuire, Russell Trent, Fred Graham, Don Haggerty, William Tannen (Deputies), Frank Hyers (Sergeant), John Maxwell, Sherry Hall, Tom Quinn (Doctors), Fred Datig, Jr., Dan Foster, Jeff Richards (G.I.'s), Dolores Castle, Joyce Jameson (Girls), Art Lewis (Sam), Samuel London (Fred), Larry Hudson, Roger Moore, Sam Finn, Tay Dunne, Bert Davidson, Don Kerr, Sig Frohlich (Clerks in Bookie Joint), Helen Spring (Elderly Secretary), Alex Frazer (Horticulturist), Lester Dorr (Police Surgeon), Robert Malcolm (Deputy), Earle Hodgins (Technician), Bette Arlen, Betty Jane Howarth (Charleston Dancers), Carl Saxe, Joel Allen (Two Boyfriends), Wilson Wood (Patron), Dee Turnell, Carmen Clifford, Ward Ellis, Jack Regas, Leo Scott, Bert May (Specialty Dancers).
Location: Sunset Boulevard, Hollywood, California
Filming Completed: February 9, 1951
Released: MGM, August 1951
Running Time: 84 minutes

An aspiring actress, Jane Tafford, is dying of a gunshot wound and her lover, Sonny Johnson, is dead. The police arrest jazz drummer Stan Maxton, Jane's ex-boyfriend, on suspicion of murder. He tells the police that he is a Korean War veteran who came to Los Angeles to resume his music career but initially was involved in Sonny Johnson's racketeering. Later, Stan met Jane who introduced him to a jazz nightclub owner, and Stan performed with some of the greatest musicians, such as Louis Armstrong. Hoping Sonny could help Jane with her acting career through his many contacts, Stan introduces them to each other. Jane and Sonny become romantically involved and Stan jealously warns Jane about Sonny's criminal connections. Sonny's thugs beat Stan up to encourage him to leave town. Jane protests Sonny's tactics and is shot in the ensuing argument. To protect Jane, Stan claims he murdered Sonny but the police do not believe him. He admits that Jane killed Sonny after she dies. Free from suspicion, Stan unhappily returns to his musical career.

The Strip is one of a series of minor noir films that Mickey Rooney starred in and often produced during the 1950s, and in which he usually portrays a sincere little guy who is victimized by life. However this film has the backing of an MGM production and, in particular, makes use of some fine jazz interludes. James Craig plays Sonny Johnson with just the right flair. His flower fixation is reminiscent of the noir gangster's strange estheticism. The existential overtones of *The Strip* are quite pronounced. Rooney's performance as the musician whose pain makes him withdraw into his music, looks backward to Tom Neal as Al Roberts in *Detour* and forward to Charles Aznavour as Charlie Koeller in *Shoot the Piano Player.*

—B.P.

SUDDEN FEAR (1952)

Director: David Miller
Producer: Joseph Kaufman (Joseph Kaufman Productions)
Screenplay: Lenore Coffee and Robert Smith; from the novel by Edna Sherry
Director of Photography: Charles Lang, Jr.
Sound: T. A. Carman, Howard Wilson
Music: Elmer Bernstein
Songs: "Afraid" by Elmer Bernstein and Jack Brooks; "Sudden Fear" by Irving Taylor and Arthur Altman
Art Director: Boris Leven
Set Decoration: Edward G. Boyle
Makeup: Edwin Allen for Joan Crawford; Josef Norin for Jack Palance
Costumes: For Joan Crawford: gowns by Sheila O'Brien, furs by Al Teitelbaum, lingerie by Tula, hats by Rex, Inc., jewels by Ruser
Hairstyles: Jane Gorton
Production Supervisor: Henry Spitz
Production Assistant: B. C. Wylie
Assistant Director: Ivan Volkman
Second Unit Director: Ralph Hoge
Film Editor: Leon Barsha

CAST: Joan Crawford (Myra Hudson), Jack Palance (Lester Blaine), Gloria Grahame (Irene Neves), Bruce Bennett (Steve Kearney), Virginia Huston (Ann), Touch [Mike] Conners (Junior Kearney).
Location: San Francisco, California
Released: RKO, August 7, 1952
Running Time: 110 minutes

Myra Hudson, a successful playwright and San Francisco heiress, is in New York to help cast her new play. During the auditions she vetoes actor Lester Blaine because he doesn't look like a romantic lead. Meeting her again on the train to San Francisco, Lester romances Myra, and they soon marry. Lester meets with Irene Neves, his flashy ex-girl friend, and makes it clear that he married for reasons other than love; but he warns Irene against attempting to break up his marriage. Lester uses Irene's connections to find out about his wife's finances and discovers that Myra plans to donate her father's estate to a heart foundation and live solely on her income as a playwright. Secretly meeting in Myra's study, Lester and Irene find a new will leaving Lester $10,000 per year until he remarries. This will was devised by Myra's lawyer, Steve Kearney, without Myra's consent; and Lester is unaware that his wife has already dictated a new, more generous will. Irene informs Lester the will cannot become valid until after the weekend and urges Lester to arrange for Myra to have a fatal accident soon. By chance, Myra had left her dictating machine running, inadvertently recording the lovers' conversation. Listening to the machine, Myra realizes Lester's intentions. She goes to bed that evening terrified and stays awake the whole night devising a plan to kill Lester. The next day she enters Irene's apartment, where she finds the poison meant for her and a

Myra Hudson (Joan Crawford) and Lester Blaine (Jack Palance) in Sudden Fear.

gun. Arranging for Lester to meet with Irene that evening in the apartment, Myra waits for him with Irene's gun. She also forges a note from Lester instructing Irene to meet him in a nearby garage, thus insuring that Irene will be held for Lester's murder. When he arrives, Myra is incapable of firing the gun. Dropping the weapon, she runs from the apartment; and Lester pursues her in his car. Not finding Lester in the garage, Irene returns to her apartment. Dressed similarly, Lester mistakes Irene for Myra and starts to run her down. As she screams, he recognizes Irene and attempts to swerve the car but kills both Irene and himself.

Sudden Fear, a late entry in the RKO noir cycle, has an overly contrived plot partially camouflaged by some stylish and typically RKO photography by Charles Lang and by naturalistic performances by the three lead actors. Gloria Grahame, as Irene, displays further nuances of sexual masochism than in past roles, at one point asking Lester, who has just threatened to beat her, to "crush" her as they kiss. But the height of perturbed sexuality is in the marriage relationship of Myra and Lester. As the husband, Palance strikes a balance between a romantic and a sinister person-

ality while his wife, portrayed by Crawford, keeps her affections under strict control and effectively conveys a suppressed but growing hysteria and resentment. One scene especially embodies the noir love-hate relationship: Lester is calmly reading Myra to sleep, all the while planning to kill her; Myra realizes this and uses all her strength to appear calm, betrayed only by a telltale hand squeezing a handkerchief.

—B.P.

SUDDENLY (1954)

Director: Lewis Allen
Producer: Robert Bassler (Libra Productions)
Screenplay: Richard Sale
Director of Photography: Charles Clarke
Camera Operator: Bob Gough
Sound: Joe Edmonson, Win Hancock
Music: David Raksin

Art Director: Frank Sylos
Set Decoration: Howard Bristol
Costumes: Jack Masters
Makeup: Bill Buell
Production Manager: Charles Hall
Script Supervisor: Doris Drought
Assistant Director: Hal Klein
Film Editor: John F. Schreyer

CAST: Frank Sinatra (John Baron), Sterling Hayden (Tod Shaw), James Gleason (Pop Benson), Nancy Gates (Ellen Benson), Kim Charney (Pidge), Paul Frees (Benny Conklin), Christopher Dark (Bart Wheeler), Willis Bouchey (Dan Carney), Paul Wexler (Slim Adams), Jim Lilburn (Jud Hobson), Charles Smith (Bebop), Ken Dibbs (Wilson), Clark Howatt (Haggerty), Dan White (Burge), Richard Collier (Hawkins). BITS: Roy Engel, Ted Stanhope (Drivers), Charles Waggenheim (Kaplan), John Bernardino (Trooper).
Filming Completed: May 1, 1954
Released: United Artists, October 7, 1954
Running Time: 77 minutes

The peaceful surroundings of a small California town are quietly invaded by a trio of hired assassins who intend to kill the President of the United States. Forcing their way into a house that overlooks a train depot where the President is secretly scheduled to transfer to a private motorcar, the gunmen hold the Benson family and the local policeman, Tod Shaw, hostage as they await the train's arrival. John Baron is in charge of this operation and seizes every opportunity to frighten, humiliate, and bully his hostages. After what seems like an endless period of psychopathic threats, the assassination plan is put into effect. Shaw finds a way to escape and subdues the would-be killers only moments before the train pulls into the station.

Just as its title implies, *Suddenly* is a taut, fast-paced thriller that emphasizes the vicious sadism of the key conspirator, John Baron. His boastful, Machiavellian attitude links *Suddenly* with the more brutal noir films of the 1950s such as *The Big Night* and *Kiss Me Deadly*. Beyond this preoccupation with violence, the sense of claustrophobia and despair unleashed by the assassins in *Suddenly* is completely amoral, and totally opposite of the style of harrassment found in such non-noir, socially redemptive films as *The Desperate Hours*. The criminals in *Suddenly* have a purpose that director Lewis Allen and writer Richard Sale exploit only as action; they exclude any significant level of social protest or criticism. There are no reasons given, or asked for, regarding the assassination—the entire incident functions as a nightmare, a very real nightmare that invades the serenity of a small town. At the end of the film it is apparent that the Benson family will never be the same, suddenly scarred by people out of nowhere who irrevocably disrupt their middle-class tranquility.

—C.M.

SUNSET BOULEVARD (1950)

Director: Billy Wilder
Producer: Charles Brackett (Paramount)
Associate Producer: Maurice Schorr [uncredited]
Screenplay: Charles Brackett, Billy Wilder, and D. M. Marshman, Jr.
Director of Photography: John F. Seitz
Special Photographic Effects: Gordon Jennings
Process Photography: Farciot Edouart
Sound: Harry Lindgren, John Cope
Music Score: Franz Waxman
Song: "The Paramount Don't Want Me Blues" by Jay Livingston and Ray Evans
Art Director: Hans Dreier, John Meehan
Set Decoration: Sam Comer, Ray Moyer
Costumes: Edith Head
Makeup: Wally Westmore, Karl Silvera
Hairstyles: Nellie Manley, Vera Tomei
Production Manager: Hugh Brown
Assistant Director: C. C. Coleman, Jr.
Script Supervisor: Lupe Hall
Film Editor: Arthur Schmidt
Supervising Editor: Doane Harrison

CAST: William Holden (Joe Gillis), Gloria Swanson (Norma Desmond), Erich von Stroheim (Max Von Mayerling), Nancy Olson (Betty Schaefer), Fred Clark (Sheldrake), Lloyd Gough (Morino), Jack Webb (Artie Green), Cecil B. DeMille, Hedda Hopper, Buster Keaton, Anna Q. Nilsson, H. B. Warner (Themselves), Franklyn Farnum (Undertaker), Sidney Skolsky, Ray Evans, Jay Livingston (Themselves). BITS: Larry Blake, Charles Dayton (Finance Men), Eddie Dew (Assistant Coroner), Roy Thompson (Shoeshine Boy), Michael Brandon, Kenneth Gibson (Salesmen), Peter Drynan (Tailor), Ruth Clifford (Sheldrake's Secretary), Bert Moorhouse (Gordon Cole), E. Mason Hopper (Doctor), Yvette Vedder (Girl on Telephone), Virginia Randolph (Courtier), Al Ferguson (Phone Standby), Stan Johnson (1st Assistant Director), William Sheehan (2nd Assistant Director), Julia Faye (Hisham), Gertrude Astor, E. Mason Hopper, Frank O'Connor (Courtiers), Ralph Montgomery (1st Prop Man), Eva Novak (Courtier), Bernice Mosk (Herself), Gertie Messinger (Hair Dresser), John Skins Miller (Hog Eye, Electrician), John Cortay (Young Policeman), Robert E. O'Connor (Old Policeman), Gerry Ganzer (Connie), Joel Allen (2nd Prop Man), Tommy Ivo (Boy), Emmett Smith (Man), Ottola Nesmith (Woman), Jay Morley (Fat Man), Howard Negley (Captain of Police), Ken Christy (Captain of Homicide), Len Hendry (Police Sergeant), Arthur A. Lane, Archie R. Dalzell (Camera Operators), James Hawley, Edward Wahrman (Camera Assistants). Sanford E. Greenwald (Newsreel Cameraman), Howard Joslin (Police Lieutenant).
Location: Los Angeles, California
Filming Completed: June 18, 1949

SUSPENSE

Released: Paramount, August 10, 1950
Running Time: 115 minutes

Pursued by creditors who want to confiscate his car, down-and-out screenwriter Joe Gillis turns into a Sunset Boulevard driveway and finds shelter in a crumbling garage flanked by a massive, faded mansion. The half-ruined estate is occupied only by Norma Desmond, a long-forgotten silent film star, and her faithful butler, Max, who was once her husband and a famous director. Attracted to Joe, Norma offers him a job helping her prepare the script of her comeback film, *Salome.* Because he is broke, Joe accepts and moves into a room over the garage at Norma's insistence. The spineless writer soon becomes Norma's kept man, accepting fancy clothes and expensive jewelry in exchange for suffering Norma's smothering affection and her strident insistence that new days of stardom are around the corner. Bored and fed up with Norma's world of past glories, Joe escapes one evening to a local hangout, where he meets Betty Schaefer, a young studio reader. Together they try to write a screenplay, and Joe sneaks out at night observed only by the everwatchful Max. Soon falling in love with Betty, Joe tries to make a clean break with Norma but is pulled back into her orbit when she attempts suicide. Norma goes too far, however, when she finds out about Joe's clandestine meetings with Betty and tells the young girl that the man she loves is really no more than a weak gigolo. Joe finally summons up enough courage to walk out, but as he does so, the hysterical Norma kills him. Faced by a barrage of police and reporters, Norma goes mad. Descending her staircase as the newsreel cameras roll, she believes that she is making her comeback in *Salome.*

It is the rare film that declares itself as immediately as does *Sunset Boulevard.* Opening with the sardonic narration of a dead man commenting mordantly on the circumstances of his own murder, this highly unusual work announces itself as a bleak but irresistably sardonic motion picture, a trenchant observation of Hollywood's most bizarre human artifacts. (One can only imagine the effect of the film's original opening, which was shot but discarded; it featured the dead Joe Gillis sitting up on his slab in the morgue and telling his story to a captive audience of corpses.)

The fusion of writer-director Billy Wilder's biting humor and the classic elements of film noir make for a strange kind of comedy, as well as a strange kind of film noir. There are no belly laughs here, but there are certainly strangled giggles: at the pet chimp's midnight funeral, at Joe's discomfited acquiescence to the role of gigolo; at Norma's Mack Sennett-style "entertainments" for her uneasy lover; and at the ritualized solemnity of Norma's "waxworks" card parties, which feature such former luminaries as Buster Keaton as Norma's has-been cronies.

It should be noted that, although much of *Sunset Boulevard*'s peculiar brand of humor derives from the strange circumstances of Norma's life, very little—if any—of that humor is actually at Norma's expense. The real buffoon of

the piece is the weak, wavering Joe, played with highly appropriate, slack-jawed prettiness by William Holden. Norma herself, as portrayed by Gloria Swanson, is a tragic figure, imbued by Wilder with powerful romantic presence. A woman obsessed, she clings to her vision with a tenacity that must ultimately be granted a grudging admiration, and she is the only character in the film, with the possible exception of Erich Von Stroheim's fanatically loyal Max, who inspires genuine sympathy. Watching herself on screen in an old movie, she leaps into the projector's murderous blast of light and cries, "They don't make faces like that anymore!" It is difficult for the viewer to favor Joe's cynicism over her fervor, however misguided or self-centered it may be.

—J.K.

SUSPENSE (1946)

Director: Frank Tuttle
Producer: Maurice and Frank King (King Brothers)
Screenplay: Philip Yordan
Director of Photography: Karl Struss
Special Effects: Jack Shaw, Ray Mercer
Sound: Tom Lambert
Music: Daniele Amfitheatrof
Music Editor: Al Teeter
Art Director: F. Paul Sylos
Set Decoration: George J. Hopkins
Costumes: Robert Kalloch
Skating Sequences: Nick Castle
Technical Adviser: Herman King
Production Manager: Clarence Bricker
Dialogue Coach: Leon Charles
Assistant Director: Frank S. Heath
Film Editor: Dick Heermance
Supervising Editor: Otho Lovering

CAST: Belita (Roberta Elba), Barry Sullivan (Joe Morgan), Albert Dekker (Frank Leonard), Eugene Pallette (Harry), Bonita Granville (Ronnie), Edith Angold (Nora), George Stone (Max). **BITS:** Billy Nelson, Robert Middlemass, Lee "Lasses" White (Woodsmen), Byron Foulger (Cab Driver), Leon Belasco (Pierre), Nestor Paiva, Dewey Robinson (Men with Blond), Marian Martin (Blond), George Chandler (Louie), Frank Scannell (Monk), Sidney Melton (Smiles), Bobby Ramos (Vocalist), Jack Chefe (Waiter), Billy Grey (Small Boy), Norma Jean Nilsson (Little Girl), Paul Kruger (Stranger), Bernard Sell (Peanut Vendor), Charlie Wilson (Police Officer), Chris Pin Martin (Mexican Waiter), Hugh Prosser (Photographer), Ernie Adams (Watchman), Kid Chrissell (Workman), Capt. Summers (Truck Driver), Don Clarke, Jack Richardson, Charles Sherlock, Joey Cappo, Jack Kenney

(Poker Players), Edward Brian (Reporter), Parker Gee, Martha Clemmons, Jo Ann Deen, Harisse Brin (Spectators), Kristine Miller, Beverly Haney, Beverly Hawthorne, Virginia Owen, Zaz Vorka, Alice Kirsten, Phyllis Henry, Barbara Swanson, Mario Icido, Mercedes, Susanne Rosser, Evelyn Moriarity, (Models), Tiny Lipson (Man in Audience), Bobby Barber (Delicatessen Man), Dave Shore (Clerk).

Location: Los Angeles, California
Filming Completed: December 7, 1945
Released: Monogram, June 15, 1946
Running Time: 101 minutes

Joe Morgan, a former promoter, gets a job selling peanuts with Frank Leonard's Los Angeles ice show. After devising a dangerous "hoop" of swords through which his boss's wife, skating star Roberta Elba, will jump, Joe is promoted to the show's ringmaster. A romance begins between Roberta and Joe, and the suspicious Frank persuades his wife to vacation with him at their mountain lodge. Joe is accosted by Ronnie, an ex-girl friend from Chicago, who wishes to rekindle their romance but Joe refuses. He goes up to Frank's lodge on a pretext of business and is invited to stay. After pretending to retire early, Frank observes his wife embrace Joe. The next day Joe and Roberta are ice skating when someone shoots at Joe with a rifle but misses and causes an avalanche. Discovering both Frank and a rifle missing from the lodge, the couple believe Frank fired the shot and was buried in the avalanche. Joe takes over administration of the ice show and their romance continues although the memory of Frank haunts them. Roberta ultimately realizes that Joe killed Frank and stuffed his body in the rolltop desk that he later burned. When Roberta refuses to agree with his plans, Joe decides to kill her by loosening one of the swords in her act. But seconds before she is to jump, she fixes the sword. Explaining that the ringmaster's hat never fit him anyway, Joe walks out of the show and into the night. However, Ronnie has not got over being jilted and kills him as he approaches the street.

Suspense, the first of Monogram's A budget films, is not so cohesive in its noir framework as Monogram's next large projection, *The Gangster,* but it is worthy of consideration. Philip Yordan's script compares favorably to the many of his other thrillers and Frank Tuttle reuses some of the angular compositions of *This Gun for Hire.* With photographer Karl Struss, Tuttle demonstrates what can be done visually even on a limited budget. Struss, Tuttle and the art director Paul Sylos compensate for the lapses in the drama and the lengthy musical numbers by a *mise-en-scène* that suggests a surrealist nightmare, exemplified by the huge head through which Roberta first appears. As in *The Gangster,* Barry Sullivan expresses a good deal of pathos with his portrayal of Joe, and Dekker's personality expertly embodies the cool, cryptic character of Frank.

—B.P.

SWEET SMELL OF SUCCESS (1957)

Director: Alexander MacKendrick
Producer: James Hill (Norma-Curtleigh Production)
Screenplay: Clifford Odets, adapted by Ernest Lehman; from the short story "Tell Me About it Tomorrow" by Ernest Lehman
Director of Photography: James Wong Howe
Sound: Jack Soloman
Music: Elmer Bernstein
Art Director: Edward Carrere
Film Editor: Alan Crosland, Jr.

CAST: Burt Lancaster (J. J. Hunsecker), Tony Curtis (Sidney Falco), Susan Harrison (Susan Hunsecker), Martin Milner (Steve Dallas), Sam Levene (Frank D'Angelo), Barbara Nichols (Rita), Jeff Donnell (Sally), Joseph Leon (Robard), Edith Atwater (Mary), Emile Meyer (Harry Kello), Joe Frisco (Herbie Temple), David White (Otis Elwell), Lawrence Dobkin (Leo Bartha), Lurene Tuttle (Mrs. Bartha), Queenie Smith (Mildred Tam), Autumn Russell (Linda), Jay Adler (Manny Davis), Lewis Charles (Al Evans).

Location: New York, New York
Filming Completed: May 1957
Released: United Artists, June 27, 1957
Running Time: 96 minutes [The press screening was 103 minutes.]

Sidney Falco is a success-starved publicity agent on Broadway who is being ignored by the monomaniacal top Broadway columnist, J. J. Hunsecker, because Falco has not completed a favor for him. Falco was requested to break up a romance between Hunsecker's sister, Susan, and a young guitarist, Steve Dallas. Desperate to regain the columnist's good graces, Falco attempts blackmail and then pimps for other columnists until he can get an item published that identifies the musician as crazed by marijuana use and a "card-carrying" Communist. When the item appears, Hunsecker pretends to be a sympathetic ally and pulls strings to get Steve his job back. Confronting the guitarist and his sister, Hunsecker demands a show of gratitude. Steve refuses, revealing that he realizes that the columnist somehow contrived the entire incident. Steve asks Susan to choose between them; but Hunsecker insists she does not have to make that choice. Susan leaves during the argument and later tells Hunsecker she will not see Steve again. But she does, and he convinces her that her brother manipulates her. Hunsecker is outraged at Steve's ingratitude, and he implies that he will give Falco a three-month guest editorship of his column if the press agent will plant marijuana on Steve and then call Kello, a policeman who is indebted to Hunsecker. Steve is arrested and Falco celebrates his good fortune; but he is called to Hunsecker's apartment where he finds Susan undressed and about to commit suicide. Hunsecker enters and assumes that Falco has sexually assaulted his sister. Falco leaves as Hunsecker calls the police to arrest Falco for planting the marijuana on Steve. Susan packs a small suitcase and announces that she is leaving her brother's home for good. As Susan crosses the street in front of the apartment building, Falco is beaten by the police and taken into custody.

Noir films about the entertainment business often center on the parasites of that industry who are not creative themselves but prey off the artistic talents of others. The sycophantic press agent epitomized by Sidney Falco and described as "the man with the ice cream face . . . who has the scruples of a guinea hen and the morals of a gangster," is also the character of Smiley Coy in *The Big Knife*, who willingly commits manslaughter to ingratiate himself with an actor, and of hustler Harry Fabian of *Night and the City*. What makes these characters noir protagonists is their desperate, misguided ambition, and their delusion that they are important people about to achieve greatness, when actually they are cruelly manipulated by almost everyone they meet. Because of their lack of self-awareness, these men commit crimes or actions that hopelessly ensnare them into traps created by men more powerful than they. Falco, Coy, and Fabian are expendable pawns to their respective kingpins, Hunsecker, Hoff, and Kristo. They become sympathetic characters because they are pitiable in their ignorance and because their selfish actions are not as disgusting as those kingpins' cold-blooded manipulations.

While Falco realizes the extent of his callousness but not his insignificance, J. J. Hunsecker believes himself to be Broadway's avenging angel and is righteous because millions of Americans put their faith in his opinions each morning over breakfast. Subliminally realizing that this faith is dependent upon illusion, Hunsecker wants the mocking guitarist destroyed to prove his omnipotence. Hunsecker's arrogance is equal to the attitudes of Waldo Lydecker in *Laura*, or Hardy Cathcart in *Dark Corner*. The major difference, of course, is that Hunsecker's status (and life) is not literally destroyed at film's end by those he manipulated, whereas Lydecker and Cathcart are proved to be dangerous criminals. But *Sweet Smell of Success* is less a classic film noir than either *Dark Corner* or *Laura*, both of which use murder, detection, and retribution as plot elements to express entrapment and alienation. Rather, *Sweet Smell of Success* is an expressionistic character study that uses deception and manipulation to achieve the same premise as 1940s film noir.

The character of Hunsecker's sister, Susan, is contrastingly used to define Hunsecker's noir milieu. She is the film's only character freed from the alienating force of her brother's possessiveness as she literally crosses over onto the sunny side of the street to start a new life. The only other times she is seen in daylight is when she leaves the shadowy arena of a theater to talk with Steve by the river's edge. Susan initially protests that their love will never work; but he is able to convince her that she can make the choice her brother denies exists and can be free of him and her useless, nocturnal existence. Her ultimate rejection of Hunsecker is the only retribution that is leveled against him; but it is portrayed as a serious emotional punishment. Additionally, Susan manipulates her brother and uses Falco to avenge Steve's difficulties. Although very little of this vengeance seems planned, when Falco turns to her and says, "You've grown up, cute!," she seizes the opportunity she has created. Importantly, Steve does not arrive to rescue her and she does not mention him as she leaves. Susan is not running from one man's dominion to another's but has become truly independent. Susan's independence is atypical of a noir heroine, but not unusual for a noir protagonist, who when the smoke clears, the drugs wear off, or the day breaks, rises up to survive but not forget. —E.W.

T-MEN (1948)

Director: Anthony Mann
Executive Producer: Edward Small (Reliance Pictures)
Producer: Aubrey Schenck
Associate Producer: Turner Shelton
Screenplay: John C. Higgins; from an unpublished story by Virginia Kellogg based upon the files of the U.S. Treasury Department
Director of Photography: John Alton
Photographic Effects: George J. Teague
Sound: Leon Becker, Frank McWhorter
Music Score: Paul Sawtell
Musical Director: Irving Friedman
Orchestration: Emil Cadkin
Art Director: Edward C. Jewell
Special Art Effects: Jack R. Rabin
Set Decoration: Armor Marlowe
Costumes: Frances Ehren
Makeup: Ern Westmore, Joe Stinton
Hairstyles: Joan St. Oegger, Alma Armstrong
Dialogue Director: Stewart Stern
Assistant Director: Howard W. Koch
Editorial Supervision: Alfred DeGaetano
Film Editor: Fred Allen

CAST: Dennis O'Keefe (Dennis O'Brien), Alfred Ryder (Tony Genaro), Mary Meade (Evangeline), Wallace Ford (Schemer), June Lockhart (Tony's Wife), Charles McGraw (Moxie), Jane Randolph (Diana), Art Smith (Gregg), Herbert Heyes (Chief Carson), Jack Overman (Brownie), John Wengraf (Shiv), Jim Bannon (Lindsay), William Malten (Paul Miller). **BITS:** Reed Hadley (Narrator), Vivian Austin (Genevieve), James Seay (Hardy), Lyle Latell (Isgreg), John Newland (Jackson Lee), Victor Cutler (Snapbrim), Tito Vuolo (Pasquale), John Parrish (Harry), Curt Conway (Shorty), Ricki Van Dusen (Girl on Plane), Irmgard Dawson (Hostess on Plane), Robert Williams (Detective Captain), Anton Kosta (Vantucci), Paul Fierro (Chops), Louis Bacigalupi (Boxcar), Trevor Bardette (Rudy), William Yip (Chinese Merchant), Al Bridge (Agent in Phone Booth), Keefe Brasselle (Cigar Attendant), Les Sketchley (Big Guy), George M. Manning, Paul Hogan (Men), Jerry Jerome, Bernie Sell, Ralph Brooks, John Ardell (Dice Players), Sandra Gould (Girl at Phone), Cuca Martinez (Dancer in Club), Salvadore Barroga (Housekeeper), Tom McGuire, Mira McKinney (Couple at Car), Frank Ferguson (Secret Service Man), Cecil Weston (Woman Proprietor), Frank Hyer (Ollie), George Carleton (Morgue Attendant).
Location: Los Angeles, California
Filming Completed: September 1947
Released: Eagle-Lion Films, January 22, 1948
Running Time: 92 minutes

A Treasury agent is close to breaking a counterfeiting ring when he is killed. Two new agents, O'Brien and Genaro, are brought into the case. Assuming the identities of small-time hoods, they begin their undercover work by joining the Vantucci mob in Detroit. A man named Schemer in Los Angeles is involved, and O'Brien goes there to pursue it. Vantucci harshly interrogates Genaro, who takes it for awhile but then gives him a phony story. Introduced into the counterfeiting ring, O'Brien produces a phony bill for which he claims to have the plates and sends for his partner. O'Brien and Genaro bargain with the ring for a deal on the plates while they investigate. They room with Schemer who is frightened that he is going to be killed by the ring. One day, in the market, Schemer and Genaro run into the agent's wife; they pretend not to know each other, but Schemer is suspicious and bargains with his potential killer, Moxie, by giving him this information. Genaro finds the key that will lead to Schemer's coded information just as the ring, with O'Brien among them, comes to kill him. O'Brien watches helplessly as Moxie shoots Genaro, but not before Genaro tips his partner about the key. With the information in the government's hands, O'Brien is still in danger. One member of the ring, Paul Miller, knows O'Brien's plates are the work of a counterfeiter currently in prison. Miller tries to bargain with O'Brien in private but is shot; and a wounded O'Brien avenges Genaro by killing Moxie, as the other TMen arrive and break the counterfeiting ring.

T-Men established the reputations of its director, Anthony Mann, and its photographer, John Alton. Within a year, both were hired by MGM on the strength of this Eagle-Lion sleeper. The realization of this film creates its true subject, which is not the heroic accomplishments of Treasury agents but rather the perversity and unreality of life as an undercover agent. At the outset of the film, it is explained that the story is a composite case from Treasury files; but the very first shot, opening a night scene, in which mysterious figures shoot it out, staged in strange perspectives, contradicts the matter-of-fact introduction. As a stolid narrative voice continues to trace the activities of the two agents, the *mise-en-scène* and the manner in which the agents behave as criminals directs our attention to a level of meaning denied by the narration. O'Brien and Genaro are consumed by their roles. Their placement in the compositions emphasizes their ease in the criminal milieu. The pull of the story itself is such as to make them schizophrenic: narratively they are stalwart heroes, visually they are brutal hoods. Mann emphasizes the poignancy of this dichotomy in close-ups of the two men. Genaro is ostentatiously displaced from the background in a close-up when he looks at his wife. Similarly, O'Brien reacts to Genaro's death with an involuntary twitching of his face and slight lowering of the head, while shots are heard over his close-up.

Many of Mann's films feature interesting villains; but although Wallace Ford's Schemer is an arresting characterization, it is the two T-Men who dominate this film. Dennis O'Keefe and Alfred Ryder, as O'Brien and Genaro, blend like chameleons into the noir atmosphere as if to deny their existence as human beings independent of their jobs. In fact, the film does not explore their "real" personalities. They come alive in the moment when they step into the expensive clothes they will wear in their criminal identities and introduce themselves to each other. All that is divulged of their personal life is that Genaro has been married only a few months. The bravery and resourcefulness of both men is secondary in the film's realization to the mystery surrounding their true natures.

Alton's photography is a primary dramatic force in the film. The placement of characters at opposite ends of the frame in deep focus on a diagonal plane illustrates how the photography complements the direction. Examples are the nightclub scene in which O'Brien watches Schemer; the strange shot in the market in which Genaro and Schemer are reflected in one window while reflected from another window at a double remove; and the eerie lighting of the steam room sequence in which Schemer is killed and the black screen is filled with flourishes of light. Each shot with its distortions of space and unpredictable, dissonant lighting, forces an awareness of the visual narrative so that the jingoism of the Treasury Department may be ignored and a vision of the noir underworld may emerge.

—B.L.

TALK ABOUT A STRANGER (1952)

Director: David Bradley
Producer: Richard Goldstone (MGM)
Associate Producer: Sol Baer Fielding
Screenplay: Margaret Fiits; from the short story "The Enemy" by Charlotte Armstrong
Director of Photography: John Alton
Sound: Douglas Shearer

Music: David Buttolph
Art Directors: Cedric Gibbons, Eddie Imazu
Film Editor: Newell P. Kimlin

CAST: George Murphy (Robert Fontaine, Sr.), Nancy Davis (Marge Fontaine), Billy Gray (Robert Fontaine, Jr.), Lewis Stone (Mr. Wardlaw), Kurt Kasznar (Matlock), Anna Glomb (Camille), Katharine Warren (Dr. Dorothy Langley), Teddy Infuhr (Gregory). **BITS:** Stanley Andrews (Mr. Wetzell), Maude Wallace (Mrs. Wetzell), Cosmo Sardo (Barber), Jon Gardner, Donald Gordon, Warren Farlow, Wayne Farlow, Gary Stewart (Boys), Margaret Bert (Woman's Voice), Tudor Owen (Policeman), Harry Lauter (Canavan), Dan Riss (Mr. Taylor), Charles La Torre (Batastini), Kathleen Freeman (Rose), Burt Mustin (Mr. McEley), Ralph Moody (Short), Jack Williams (Truck Driver), Jack Moore (Sailor), William Tannen (Driggs), Leslie K. O'Pace (MacLarnin), Harry Hines (Talmadge), Edward Cassidy (Soloway), Virginia Farmer (Mrs. Campbell).
Released: MGM, April 18, 1952
Running Time: 65 minutes

Bobby, the young son of Robert Fontaine, a citrus rancher, encounters an unfriendly stranger in the supposedly empty house next door. Bobby thinks that the stranger, Matlock, is an enemy; and when the boy finds his dog dead, he believes that Matlock poisoned it. Mr. Wardlaw, the editor of the local newspaper, listens sympathetically to Bobby's story but gently cautions him to get evidence before making accusations. The boy gathers proof that he believes will establish that Matlock has murdered a human being as well as the dog. Taking vengeance into his own hands, Bobby unplugs Matlock's oil tank, which depletes the local ranchers' supply of vital fuel for smudge pots needed during a freezing spell. The mystery is solved when the newspaper editor discovers that Matlock is a doctor who retreated from the world after his son's death. Bobby's dog was accidentally poisoned by someone else. As a friendly gesture, the doctor gives Bobby a new pet and the citrus crop is saved when oil trucks arrive with more fuel.

The most disturbing aspect of *Talk About a Stranger* is its central character: a paranoid and destructive juvenile with whom the viewer is led to identify throughout most of the film. The effective use of John Alton's location photography in the opening scenes around the orange groves, the family ranch house, and the dusty streets of a Southern California farm town economically establish a realistic milieu of which Bobby Fontaine seems a normal part. The death of Bobby's dog and the genuinely dour aspect of the new neighbor, Matlock, further support the credibility of Bobby's assumption that the man has malignant intentions. At this point, the audience might be directed to shift its identification to Bobby's father or to the newspaper editor who offers him counsel; but neither of these characters is developed in a manner that would encourage this. Instead, as Bobby searches for hard evidence on the editor's advice, the film shifts from daylit scenes to a series of night sequences. As darkness falls and the orange groves become menacing tangles of light and shadow—an appropriate, nightmare landscape in which Bobby can situate his fantasies—the boy's mania leads him to tamper with Matlock's oil tank. The wide-angle, low-key shot as Matlock looms over the boy by a pool of escaping oil is the Wellesian climax to a succession of strikingly Gothic compositions.

It is only when the viewer learns that Bobby's accusations have been unfounded and his actions criminally unjust, that these images acquire a psychological as well as decorative value. By causing the viewer to participate in the visual and narrative point-of-view of the disturbed child, David Bradley ultimately reveals that his expressionistic *mise-en-scène* was not merely directorial flourish but a subjective visualization aptly keyed to Bobby's confusion and fear.

—A.S.

THE TATTERED DRESS (1957)

Director: Jack Arnold
Producer: Albert Zugsmith (Universal-International)
Screenplay: George Zuckerman
Director of Photography: Carl E. Guthrie [Technicolor; CinemaScope]
Sound: Leslie I. Carey, Robert Pritchard
Music: Frank Skinner
Music Director: Joseph Gershenson
Art Directors: Alexander Golitzen, Bill Newberry
Set Decoration: Russell A. Gausman, John P. Austin
Assistant Director: Dale Silver
Film Editor: Edward Curtiss

CAST: Jeff Chandler (James Gordon Blane), Jeanne Crain (Diane Blane), Jack Carson (Nick Hoak), Gail Russell (Carol Morrow), Elaine Stewart (Charleen Reston), George Tobias (Billy Giles), Edward Andrews (Lester Rawlings), Philip Reed (Michael Reston), Edward C. Platt (Ralph Adams), Paul Birch (Frank Mitchell), Alexander Lockwood (Paul Vernon), Edwin Jerome (Judge), William Schallert (Court Clerk), Joseph Granby (Second Jury Foreman), Frank Scannell (Cal Morrison). BITS: Floyd Simmons (Larry Bell), Ziva Shapir (Woman on Train), Marina Orschel, Ingrid Goude (Girls by Pool), Billy Snyder (Rod Staley), Helene Marshall (Newspaper Woman), Charles J. Conrad, John Phillips (Reporters), Forrest Stanley (Hank Bell), Vincent G. Perry, Gordon Morehouse (Poker Players), Jack Shutta (Gas Station Proprietor), Dick Wilson (Foreman of First Jury), Clar-

ence Straight (Bailiff), June McCall (Girl at Slot Machine), Robert Malcolm (Elderly Citizen), Todd Ferrell (Timmy), Charles Herbert (Johnny), Napoleon Whiting (Willie, Porter), Freda Jones (Sarah Bell), King Lockwood (Steward), Joseph Gilbert, Arthur Tovey, Danny Dowling, Murray Pollack, Maurice Marks, Mary Bayless, Jack Del Rio, Jeffrey Sayre, Jerry Elliott, Charles E. Perry, Donald Chaffin, Beau Anderson, Richard Dale Clark, Lillian Ten Eyck (People).
Location: Hollywood, California
Filming Completed: September 14, 1956
Released: Universal-International, March 14, 1957
Running Time: 93 minutes

A brilliant and amoral lawyer James Gordon Blane, comes to a resortlike desert town in California to defend a rich misfit, Michael Reston, in a murder case. Reston is accused of the murder of a man who, he claims, assaulted his provocative wife Charleen. The dead man was popular in the region, and Blane makes no friends by defending his killer, especially as Charleen Reston is considered a tramp. But Blane wins the case, partly by undermining the testimony of the local sheriff, Nick Hoak. Afterward, however, the vengeful sheriff produces charges of bribing a juror, and Blane must defend himself. His estranged wife Diane comes to his side; and the two are reconciled as Blane realizes that his reputation is based on clever courtroom tactics that mock justice. Although most of his clients have been guilty, Blane is innocent and fights passionately for his acquittal. He wins and is further vindicated when Carol Morrow, the woman juror who made the bribery charge, is revealed as Hoak's mistress. As Blane goes free, Carol shoots and kills Hoak on the courthouse steps.

Although *The Tattered Dress* is a modest thriller, it has several noir elements. The hero only becomes sympathetic because of the trouble his own arrogance brings him; and the critical tone toward his morality is reserved until the final reels. As a tarnished lawyer, he is a forerunner of the hero of Nicholas Ray's *Party Girl*, although Blane's crisis does not have the emotional complexity found in Ray's film. The character of Nick Hoak is perhaps more singularly interesting, and provokes ambivalent feelings of sympathy and distaste reminiscent of the antagonists of many film noir. Hoak is portrayed by Jack Carson, who excelled in a number of offbeat characterizations in this period of his career, such as those he played in *A Star Is Born* and *The Tarnished Angels*.

The main interest of the film, however, is the visual style of Jack Arnold. The desert setting recalls certain of his horror films, such as *It Came from Outer Space* and *Tarantula*; and it reveals that in this wasteland he finds a certain beauty that is very modern and strangely affecting. It is cleverly contrasted to the contemporary decors in which the characters exist and expresses a moral, as well as physical, desert.

—B.L.

THE TATTOOED STRANGER

THE TATTOOED STRANGER (1950)

Director: Edward J. Montagne
Producer: Jay Bonafield (RKO)
Associate Producer: Douglas Travers
Screenplay: Phil Reisman, Jr.
Director of Photography: William Steiner
Sound: Francis Woolley
Music Score: Alan Schulman
Music Director: Herman Fuchs
Art Directors: Sam Corso, William Saulter
Production Manager: Frank Mayer
Assistant Director: Peter Scoppa
Film Editor: David Cooper

CAST: John Miles (Detective Tobin), Patricia White (Mary Mahan), Walter Kinsella (Lt. Corrigan), Frank Tweddell (Capt. Lundquist), Rod McLennan (Capt. Gavin), Henry Lasko (Joe Canko), Arthur Jarrett (Johnny Marseille), Jim Boles (Fisher), William Gibberson (Aberfoyle).
Location: New York, New York
Filming Completed: September 1949
Released: RKO, February 9, 1950
Running Time: 64 minutes

A rookie detective searches for a mysterious stranger who is responsible for a series of extremely brutal murders. His investigation leads him to the underside of New York City. After tracking down a number of leads hinting that the murders were crimes of passion, the rookie begins to attract the attention of the killer. The rookie closes in on the tattooed stranger in a granite works area. Framed by an ocean of gravestones, the detective and crazed murderer shoot it out. The rookie's flurry of bravado is postscripted by his return to work as a noninvestigating police officer.

One of the seediest films ever made, *The Tattooed Stranger* remains a unique testament to independent film makers. Taking to the streets, the film is populated with nonprofessional actors who suggest, rather than act out, the intrinsic fear and loathing found in many urban slums. Beyond this implication, the film is rather mundane, relieved briefly at the end by the Baroque sequence of the gravestones.

—C.M.

TAXI DRIVER (1976)

Director: Martin Scorsese
Producers: Michael and Julia Phillips (Bill/Phillips Production, an Italo-Judeo Production)
Associate Producer: Phillip M. Goldfarb
Screenplay: Paul Schrader
Director of Photography: Michael Chapman
Camera Operator: Fred Schuler

Visual Consultant: David Nichols
Second Unit Camera: Michael Zingale
Special Effects: Tony Parmelee
Sound: Roger Pietschman, Tex Rudloff
Sound Effects: Frank E. Warner
Music Score: Bernard Herrmann
Songs: "Too Late for the Sky" by Jackson Browne; "Hold Me Close," lyric by Keith Addis, music by Bernard Herrmann
Art Director: Charles Rosen
Set Decoration: Herbert Mulligan
Scenic Artist: Cosmo Sorice
Costume Design: Ruth Morley
Wardrobe: Al Craine
Special Makeup: Dick Smith
Makeup: Irving Buchman
Hairstyles: Mona Orr
Script Supervisor: Kay Chapin
Casting: Juliet Taylor, Sylvia Faye
Still Photographer: Josh Weiner, Steve Shapiro
Title Design: Dan Perri
Creative Consultant: Sandra Weintraub
Assistant Director: Peter R. Scoppa
Film Editors: Tom Rolf, Melvin Shapiro
Supervising Editor: Marcia Lucas

CAST: Robert DeNiro (Travis Bickle), Jodie Foster (Iris), Albert Brooks (Tom), Peter Boyle (Wizard), Cybill Shepherd (Betsy), Leonard Harris (Senator Palantine), Harvey Keitel (Sport), Murray Mosten (Timekeeper), Richard Higgs (Secret Service Agent), Vic Argo (Melio, Delicatessen Owner), Steven Prince (Gun Salesman), Martin Scorsese (Weird Passenger). **BITS:** Dianne Abbot (Concession Girl), Frank Adu (Angry Black Man), Gino Aroito (Policeman at Rally), Garth Avery (Iris's Friend), Harry Cohn (Cabbie in Bellmore), Copper Cunningham (Prostitute), Harry Fischler (Dispatcher), Nat Grant (Stickup Man), Vic Magnotta (Secret Service Photographer), Robert Maroff (Mafioso), Norman Matlock (Charlie T), Bill Minkin (Tom's Assistant), Harry Horthup (Doughboy), Gene Palma (Street Drummer), Carey Poe (Campaign Worker), Peter Savage (Man), Brenda Dickson, Beau Kayser (Soap Opera Couple).
Location: New York, New York
Released: Columbia, February 1976
Running Time: 113 minutes
MPAA Rating: R

Travis Bickle, an ex-Marine and lonely drifter in New York City, takes a job as a cab driver on the night shift. He can find neither rest nor peace and considers the city filthy. Meeting Betsy, a pretty blond campaign worker for presidential candidate Senator Charles Palantine, Travis arranges a date; but Betsy is disgusted when he takes her to a pornographic film and leaves him. Travis's depression increases and he buys guns and puts himself through a series of rigid physical exercises. He meets Iris, a twelve-year-old prostitute, and buys time with her from her pimp, Sport, to

Travis Bickle (Robert DeNiro) in Taxi Driver.

persuade her to return to school. Now sure of his "mission," Travis goes fully armed to a Palantine rally at Columbus Circle. Chased away by Secret Service men, he goes to Iris's place instead and shoots Sport, his crony, and Iris's customer. After being treated as a hero by the press, Travis acts cool toward Betsy when she rides in his cab.

By the 1950s the two types of noir hero had merged into a basically good man who had been psychologically scarred and became obsessed with attaining a goal. His obsession usually leads to a violent act, which he later regrets, as exemplified by Barney Nolan in *Shield for Murder* and Howard Tyler in *Try and Get Me.* Travis Bickle of *Taxi Driver* resembles Cain's and Chandler's protagonists, the first type of noir hero, because he is a man who moves through the city at night and whose frustrated and repressed emotions focus on "angelic" blonds. But like the later noir hero of the 1950s Travis is obsessed with attaining the admiration of these women and saving them from what he considers to be

a malevolent society. Importantly however, Travis does not regret his violence; instead he receives praise and gains self-confidence, rejecting the woman he once desired. Travis's alienation and loneliness has not dispersed, and he may again reach a boiling point where he explodes into violence.

Taxi Driver's visual style also derives from the classic period of film noir. From the opening shot of a hazy, neon New York as seen by Travis's blurring vision, the city is presented as a hard, elusive, cold, and corrupt enemy. Bernard Herrmann's score movingly states the alternating themes of alienation and self-terror that Travis feels. Paul Schrader, who has written at length on film noir, provides a spare, Bressonian script style that director Martin Scorsese's firsthand knowledge of the New York streets makes into a film that owes much to Hollywood's past, yet reflects the self-destructive urges and the craze for vengeance that preoccupied the American screen in the 1970s.

—J.C.

TENSION

TENSION (1950)

Director: John Berry
Producer: Robert Sisk (MGM)
Screenplay: Allen Rivkin; from an unpublished story by John Klorer
Director of Photography: Harry Stradling
Sound: Douglas Shearer, A. Norwood Fenton
Music Score: André Previn
Art Directors: Cedric Gibbons, Leonid Vasian
Set Decoration: Edwin B. Willis, Jack D. Moore
Production Manager: Ruby Rosenberg
Assistant Director: George Rhein
Script Supervisor: William Hole
Film Editor: Albert Akst

CAST: Richard Basehart (Warren Quimby), Audrey Totter (Claire Quimby), Cyd Charisse (Mary Chanler), Barry Sullivan (Lt. Collier Bonnabel), Lloyd Gough (Barney Deager), Tom D'Andrea (Freddie), William Conrad (Lt. Edgar Gonsales), Tito Renaldo (Naroo), Philip Van Zandt (Lt. Schiavone). BITS: Tommy Walker (Man at Counter), Dewey Robinson, Tim Ryan, Jack Davis, Jack Daley (Men), Hayward Soo Hoo (Kid), Stephen Roberts (Attendant), Virginia Brissac (Mrs. Andrews), John Indrisano (Handler), Ray Bennett (House Manager), Kitty McHugh (Waitress), John Gallaudet (Newspaperman), Peter Brocco (Technician), Carl Sklover, Bert Davidson, Mike Morelli (Reporters).
Filming Completed: June 22, 1949
Released: MGM, January 11, 1950
Running Time: 95 minutes

An unassuming, mild-mannered druggist, Warren Quimby is crushed when his wife, Claire, decides to leave him for another man. He begins to create a second identity, an alter ego, that will provide him with an alibi for his plan to dispose of the unfaithful pair. In his new identity, however, he meets and is attracted to a young woman, Mary Chanler, which gives him a reason not to go through with his premeditated plans for murder. Yet drawn to the beach house of his wife's new lover, he discovers that someone has already killed his rival, Barney Deager. Warren is sought in connection with the killing. As the net slowly tightens around the frightened Quimby, Lt. Collier Bonnabel suspects that Claire murdered her new boyfriend. He traps this sullen woman into revealing herself as the killer and takes her to jail.

Tension is a taut thriller developed with noir motifs and style. The film is populated by a host of characters who embody the cynical essence of the noir world. Claire is a classic *femme fatale,* a woman who drives men to the brink of disaster merely on a whim; Warren is a weak man trapped in a pointless world and forced to extremes completely alien to his normal way of life; Bonnabel serves as the hard-boiled voice whose philosophy makes him explore the breaking point of human rationality. The film utilizes the image of a taut rubber band as a visualization of the tension that the characters of the film must face. Director John Berry has filled the film with low-key images and presented a visual contrast between Mary Chanler and Claire. Warren's degeneration leaves no room for salvation. His obsession with his wife's infidelity propels him over the edge of reason.

—C.M.

THEY LIVE BY NIGHT (1948)
Working Title: YOUR RED WAGON; Original Release Title: THE TWISTED ROAD]

Director: Nicholas Ray
Executive Producer: Dore Schary (RKO)
Producer: John Houseman
Screenplay: Charles Schnee, adapted by Nicholas Ray; from the novel *Thieves Like Us* by Edward Anderson
Director of Photography: George E. Diskant
Special Effects: Russell A. Cully
Sound: John Cass, Clem Portman
Musical Score: Leigh Harline
Music Director: Constantin Bakaleinikoff
Song: "Your Red Wagon" by Richard M. Jones, Don Raye, and Gene DePaul
Art Director: Albert S. D'Agostino, Al Herman
Set Decoration: Darrell Silvera, Maurice Yates
Makeup: Gordon Bau
Assistant Director: James Lane
Film Editor: Sherman Todd

CAST: Cathy O'Donnell (Keechie), Farley Granger (Bowie), Howard Da Silva (Chickamaw), Jay C. Flippen (T-Dub), Helen Craig (Mattie), Will Wright (Mobley), Marie Bryant (Singer), Ian Wolfe (Hawkins), William Phipps (Young Farmer), Harry Harvey (Hagenheimer). BITS: Regan Callais (Young Wife), Frank Marlowe (Mattie's Husband), Jim Nolan (Schreiber), Charles Meredith (Commissioner Hubbell), J. Louis Johnson (Porter), Myra Marsh (Mrs. Schaeffer), Tom Kennedy (Cop-Bumper Gag), Stanley Prager (Short Order Man), Suzi Crandall (Lulu), Fred Graham (Motorcycle Cop), Lewis Charles (Parking Lot Attendant), Dan Foster (Groom), Marilyn Mercer (Bride), Jimmy Dobson (Boy at Parking Lot), Lynn Whitney (Waitress), N. L. Hitch (Bus Driver), Carmen Morales (Mother), Ralph Dunn (Policeman), Paul Bakanas, Mickey Simpson (Shadows), Boyd Davis (Herman), Kate Lawson (Tillie), Guy Beach (Plumber), Byron Foulger (Lambert), Teddy Infuhr (Alvin), Gail Davis (Girl at Parking Lot), Curt Conway (Man in Tuxedo), Chester Jones (Waiter in Nightclub),

Douglas Williams (Drunk), Helen Crozier (Nurse), Jimmy Moss (Boy), Erskine Sanford (Doctor), Frank Ferguson (Bum), Eula Guy (Mrs. Haviland), Will Lee (Jeweler), Russ Whitman, Jane Allen (People).
Filming Completed: August 16, 1947
Released: RKO, June 28, 1948, as *The Twisted Road*; re-released November 4, 1949, as *They Live By Night*
Running Time: 95 minutes

Two hardened criminals, Chickamaw and T-Dub, are joined in a prison break by a naïve youth, Bowie. Together the three rob a bank. Subsequently, Bowie is hurt in an auto accident caused by Chickamaw and nursed back to health by Keechie, the daughter of a man who helped in the prison escape. Bowie and Keechie fall in love and marry, trying to forget the past as they live on his share of the holdup money; but Chickamaw and T-Dub force Bowie into another robbery. T-Dub is killed; and Chickamaw and Bowie quarrel in the getaway car and part company. Later, Chickamaw is killed by the police. T-Dub's sister, Mattie, negotiates to have her own husband released from prison. She turns Bowie in to the police as he is about to go on the run again, leaving the pregnant Keechie alone until he finds a new home. Bowie is shot down and Keechie is desolate; but his love is confirmed when she finds a letter he wrote to her moments before being killed.

The pre-credit shot shows the lovers deep in the warmth of their affection, even as this warmth is frozen by the writing on the screen, which seals their doom: "This boy and this girl were never properly introduced to the world we live in." The following credit sequence cuts to an overhead of a swiftly moving car full of men destined for violence. Nicholas Ray, as director, establishes visual and emotional contrasts that pervades the entire treatment. His romanticism is punctuated by unexpected moments of unusual violence, as in the moment in which Chickamaw clumsily breaks a Christmas tree ornament; symbolically destroying the possibilities of a normal life for the fugitive lovers. Violence is a trap that consumes some, such as Chickamaw, and renders it impossible for others, such as Bowie and Keechie, to tighten their tenuous hold on their dream. The self-destruction of Chickamaw and the destruction of Bowie by Mattie harshly indicate that the lovers can neither escape nor forget the dark world into which fortune has cast them.

For his first film, Nicholas Ray followed Lang's and Walsh's examples and dealt with the theme of lovers on the run. However, the youth and vulnerability of Bowie and Keechie set them apart from their prototypes in *You Only Live Once* and *High Sierra*; and the gentleness and warmth of Keechie particularly contrasts with her contemporary counterpart, Annie Laurie Starr in Lewis's *Gun Crazy*. Keechie is anything but the customary black widow, being more akin to a madonna and adding a quasi-religious tone to the film. Additionally, the concept of fate is modified in *They Live By Night* by pauses in the thrust of the action in

which the lovers' doomed course is forgotten as Ray lingers on their momentary intimacy. This subtle modification makes the predictable denouement uncommonly tragic.

Counterpointing their relationship to a hostile world is the relation of the lovers to each other. Initially mistrustful, they regard each other uneasily in the long scene in which Keechie tends to Bowie's wounds and their love is inarticulately expressed. After their marriage, he gains an adult sense of responsibility. When he is betrayed and killed, Keechie, with the sound of tenderness on her unseen lips, walks away with her back to the camera as she reads Bowie's letter, and then turns toward the camera to echo the final words of "I love you," at the film's end. In this fade-out, Ray underlines the inevitability of the desolation that accompanies fugitive love and suggests that their happiness, illustrated in the opening image, could provide only a fleeting, existential moment in the face of eternity.

—B.L.

THEY WON'T BELIEVE ME (1947)

Director: Irving Pichel
Executive Producer: Jack J. Gross (RKO)
Producer: Joan Harrison
Screenplay: Jonathan Latimer; from an unpublished story by Gordon McDonell
Director of Photography: Harry J. Wild
Special Effects: Russell A. Cully
Sound: John Tribby, Clem Portman
Music: Roy Webb
Conductor: Constantin Bakaleinikoff
Art Directors: Albert S. D'Agostino, Robert Boyle
Set Decoration: Darrell Silvera, William Magginetti
Makeup: Gordon Bau
Costumes: Edward Stevenson
Assistant Director: Harry D'Arcy
Film Editor: Elmo Williams

CAST: Robert Young (Larry Ballentine), Susan Hayward (Verna Carlson), Jane Greer (Janice Bell), Rita Johnson (Gretta), Tom Powers (Trenton), George Tyne (Lt. Carr), Don Beddoe (Thomason), Frank Ferguson (Cahill), Harry Harvey (Judge Fletcher). **BITS:** Wilton Graff (Patrick Gold), Janet Shaw (Susan Haines), Glen Knight (Parking Lot Attendant), Anthony Caruso (Tough Patient), George Sherwood (Highway Cop), Perc Launders (Police Stenographer), Byron Foulger (Mortician), Hector Sarno (Nick), Carl Kent (Chauffeur), Lee Frederick (Detective), Elena Warren (Mrs. Bowman), Herbert Heywood (Sheriff), Lillian Bronson (Mrs. Hines), Paul Maxey (Mr. Bowman), Jean Andren (Maid), Martin Wilkins (Sailor), Dot Farley (Emma), Milton Parsons (Court Clerk), Lee Phelps (Bailiff), Frank Pharr (Patrick Collins), Bert LeBaron (Joe Pots), Ellen Corby (Screaming

THE THIEF

Woman), Bertha Ledbetter (Mrs. Oaks), Polly Bailey (Untidy Woman), Matthew McHugh (Tiny Old Man), Bob Pepper (Officer guarding Larry), Ira Buck Woods (Waiter), Charles Flynn (Masseur), Freddie Graham (Deputy Sheriff), Irene Tedrow (1st Woman), Bob Thom (Hotel Clerk), Lida Durova (Girl at Newsstand), Jack Gargan (Bartender), Madam Borget (Mrs. Roberts), Alben Roberling (Headwaiter), George Morrell (Rancher), Harry Strang (Ryan), Bud Wolfe (Driver), Sol Gorss (Gus), Helen Dickson (Woman), Lovyss Bradley (Miss Jorday), Harry D'Arcy (Fisherman), Ivan Browning (Bartender), Jack Rice (Tour Conductor), William Gillespie (Waiter), Netta Packer (Spinster), Ann Cornwall (Screaming Woman).

Filming Completed: October 12, 1946
Released: RKO, July 16, 1947
Running Time: 95 minutes

Larry Ballentine, on trial for the murder of his girl friend, Verna Carlson, is described by his lawyer Cahill as a man of "many derelictions but not murder." Then Ballentine takes the stand and tells his story. Ballentine married his wife Gretta only for money and social position. While they lived in New York, Ballentine had an affair with Janice Bell and planned to leave his wife. Gretta persuaded Ballentine to move with her to Los Angeles, where she purchased him a stock brokerage firm. He agreed, but soon began a liaison with a young secretary, Verna Carlson. Gretta found out about the second affair and moved with Ballentine to a remote ranch. He could not endure life there and ran off with Verna to Reno, where he planned a quick divorce and remarriage. On the way, they had an auto accident and Verna burned to death. Ballentine allowed the police to believe that it was his wife who died and returned home to find that Gretta had committed suicide. To cover up his lies, he dragged her body into a nearby lake. A former admirer of Verna's became suspicious of her disappearance and had the police investigate, leading to the discovery of Gretta's body. When Ballentine finishes his story, the jury leaves to deliberate. They return; but before the verdict is given, Ballentine kills himself by jumping out of the courtroom window. Ironically, the jury's verdict is not guilty.

A contemporary review suggested that the popularity of Billy Wilder's adaptation of James M. Cain's *Double Indemnity* had had a deleterious influence upon American films, as illustrated by *They Won't Believe Me*. It is certainly true that the spirit of Cain seems present in the story's adultery and middle-class malaise; but it adds to the value of the film. *They Won't Believe Me* is an atypical film for director Irving Pichel, but not for producer Joan Harrison, who has been primarily associated with such sardonic directors as Hitchcock and Siodmak. Additionally, the post-*Murder, My Sweet* expressionistic photography of Harry Wild and the cunning reverse casting of Robert Young in the role of the cad make this a very unusual and underrated film noir.
—B.P.

THE THIEF (1952)

Director: Russell Rouse
Executive Producer: Harry M. Popkin (Fran Productions)
Producer: Clarence Greene
Screenplay: Clarence Greene and Russell Rouse
Director of Photography: Sam Leavitt
Music: Herschel Burke Gilbert
Production Designer: Joseph St. Amand
Production Supervisor: Maurie Suess
Production Assistant: Winston Jones
Assistant Director: Leon Chooluck
Film Editor: Chester Schaeffer

CAST: Ray Milland (Allan Fields), Martin Gabel (Mr. Bleek), Rita Gam (the Girl), Harry Bronson (Harris), John McKutcheon (Dr. Linstrum), Rita Vale (Miss Philips), Rex O'Malley (Beal), Joe Conlin (Walters).
Location: Washington, D.C.; New York, New York
Filming Completed: June 13, 1952
Released: United Artists, October 15, 1952
Running Time: 87 minutes

Without the benefit of dialogue, the story of Dr. Allan Fields, a scientist at the Atomic Energy Commission in Washington who sells classified secrets to the Communists, is narrated. Working by a "phone code" with his contacts, Fields passes information on microfilm. While filming important documents, Dr. Fields is almost caught but exits the room without arousing suspicion. The microfilmed documents make their way to New York City, where they will then travel by plane to the Middle East. But one of the contacts is killed in New York with the microfilm still clutched in his hand, and the F.B.I. is called in to investigate. While tracing the information, all A.E.C. employees are investigated. Fields receives a telegram warning him that he must leave the country; the F.B.I. has a record of the telegram but discover that the name and address of the sender are fictitious. After driving to New York City, Fields abandons his car and takes the subway to a locker in Grand Central Terminal, where he receives a note, a suitcase, and a key to a tenement room in a cheap section of the city. In the tenement, Fields reads his instructions to meet a woman atop the Empire State Building who has his cruise tickets. On a given phone signal, Fields departs for his rendezvous; but the woman is followed by an F.B.I. agent. After receiving his tickets, Fields is trapped atop the building. He steps on an agent's hand as the man is climbing to reach him, and the agent falls to his death. Escaping, Fields is visibly shaken by the sight of the corpse on the sidewalk. Returning to his room, he breaks down and cries; but that night with tickets in hand, he goes to embark upon the ship that will take him out of the country. However, he throws his phony passport papers away and, at dawn, waits outside the F.B.I. building to give himself up.

With a major star and budget and a new gimmick, *The Thief* was the most publicized of the anti-Red films produced as a political ploy in the early 1950s. In many respects the script, which relies solely on visuals and sound effects, is ingenious, but after awhile the silence, as much a part of the spy's world as it may be, becomes tedious and obviously contrived. *The Thief* remains superior to most other propaganda films—the loss of dialogue in itself is an asset in toning down didacticism—and director Russell Rouse, experienced in the noir cycle, imbues the film with the necessary elements of fear, persecution, alienation, and loneliness. It is characterized by the necessarily dark visual style that works against the documentary nature of the location photography. As the amateur spy, Ray Milland's performance is full of understated tension as he nervously awaits the ring of the rooming house telephone, eyed by an exotic woman who is waiting for the same phone's bell; as he desperately searches for a hidden microphone (in a scene similar to his alcoholic frenzy in *The Lost Weekend*); as he smokes alone in a seedy New York tenement in the dark with only the blinking neon signs for illumination; and finally, as he cries piteously when the guilt of the F.B.I. agent's death is too much to bear.

—B.P.

THIEVES' HIGHWAY (1949)
[Working Titles: HARD BARGAIN; THIEVES' MARKET]

Director: Jules Dassin
Producer: Robert Bassler (20th Century-Fox)
Screenplay: A. I. Bezzerides; from his novel *Thieves' Market*
Director of Photography: Norbert Brodine
Special Photographic Effects: Fred Sersen
Sound: Alfred Bruzlin, Harry M. Leonard
Music Score: Alfred Newman
Music Director: Lionel Newman
Orchestration: Earle Hagen
Art Directors: Lyle Wheeler, Chester Gore
Set Decoration: Thomas Little, Fred Roe
Costumes: Kay Nelson
Wardrobe Director: Charles LeMaire
Makeup: Ben Nye
Production Manager: Gene Bryant
Assistant Director: Henry Weinberg
Script Supervisor: Stanley Scheur
Film Editor: Nick De Maggio

CAST: Richard Conte (Nick Garcos), Valentina Cortesa (Rica), Lee J. Cobb (Figlia), Barbara Lawrence (Polly), Jack Oakie (Slob), Millard Mitchell (Ed), Joseph Pevney (Pete), Morris Carnovsky (Yanko), Tamara Shayne (Parthena Garcos), Kasia Orzazewski (Mrs. Polansky), Norbert Schiller (Polansky), Hope Emerson (Midgren), George Tyne (Charles), Edwin Max (Dave), David Clarke (Mitch), Walter Baldwin (Riley), David Opatoshu (Frenchy). **BITS:** Ann Morrison (Mable), Percy Helton (Proprietor), Maurice Samuels (Mario), Saul Martell

(Stukas), Howard Chamberlin (Mr. Faber), Irene Tedrow (Mrs. Faber), Frank Richards (Pig), Mario Siletti (Pietro), Jim Nolan, Robert Foulk (Policemen).
Location: San Francisco, Oakland, Highway 99, Sebastopol, Calistoga, Santa Rosa, Hueneme, and Oxnard, California
Filming Completed: January 6, 1949
Released: 20th Century-Fox, September 23, 1949
Running Time: 94 minutes

Ex-G.I. Nick Garcos returns home to find that his father has been crippled under suspicious circumstances in a truck accident. Although he had planned to marry his girl friend, Polly, Nick is upset by his parents' poverty and convinced to invest his savings in a surplus troop truck by Ed, a driver of his father's acquaintance. Followed by Pete Bailey and Slob, Ed's former partners, the men leave with two truckloads of apples for the produce market in San Francisco. En route, Nick is injured while fixing a flat, when his truck slips off the jack. Ed rescues Nick but is unable to keep pace in his older vehicle. Arriving exhausted, Nick parks in front of the establishment of a wholesaler named Figlia but decides to wait for Ed before selling his load. Figlia pays a refugee named Rica to entice Nick to her apartment and then sells Nick's produce. Nick falls asleep briefly at Rica's, but she wakes him to warn that Figlia has disposed of his apples on consignment. Learning the amount Figlia received, Nick compels him to turn it all over. After calling Polly, Nick starts back to the apartment with Rica but is intercepted and robbed by two of Figlia's henchmen. Rica attempts to escape with Nick's money but is cornered. When she returns to her apartment, she must convince an angry Nick that she had no part in the ambush. He decides to rest and wait for Ed before taking any action. Ed, however, loses control of his truck on a steep grade outside the city and is killed when it crashes and burns. When Pete and Slob arrive with this news, Figlia offers them money to collect the apples scattered from Ed's truck. While Pete accepts the offer and goes out with Figlia, Polly arrives at Rica's apartment. Seeing Rica and learning that Nick has lost all his money, she breaks off their engagement. Enraged, Nick goes to Figlia's warehouse where Slob tells him of Ed's death. Together they go to the site of the crash and confront Figlia at a roadside café. Pete, discovering Figlia has cheated him, confirms Figlia's reputation for arranging "accidents" for drivers that oppose him. Nick breaks Figlia's hand and, as the wholesaler literally throws back his money, beats him savagely, until the police, alerted by Rica, arrive. Nick returns to San Francisco and proposes marriage to Rica.

The narrative organization of *Thieves' Highway* is suggestive of conflicts that are at once mythic (Nick's return home to find his father disfigured, thereby inspiring his desire for revenge) and proletarian (the exploitation of drivers played against each other by Figlia). Also unusual is the fact that the anger and alienation of the noir hero, who is a veteran, is not initially motivated by the disruptive experience of war. Many of the characters in *Thieves' Highway* appear to be displaced persons; and some, such as Rica, are much more victimized by the war than Nick. The war actually provides Nick with a grubstake he never had before; and its remnants in the form of the cheaply purchased surplus truck continue to serve him when discovery of his father's injury alters his original plans.

In the opening sequences set in the farmlands of central California, Nick functions with more freedom of choice than the typical noir hero. Only after the trip to the produce mart of the nearest urban center is undertaken does Nick start to experience personal difficulties. The near-fatal accident with his truck is a seemingly minor episode but indicative of the threatening instability of the environment toward which Nick is traveling.

Throughout *Thieves' Highway,* the visualization supports this concept of a journey into a hostile or chaotic universe. The images in the Garcos home—with the exception of the odd-angled shot when Nick first realizes his father has lost his legs—are composed at eye level and full-lit, as are those of Ed and Nick loading their trucks at the orchard. As Nick moves along the highway, the framing becomes more constricted; traffic moving past and, at night, headlights flashing through the cab undercut the static compositions. By the time of Nick's mishap with the tire, night has fallen, so that strongly side-lit low angle and overhead shots are justified and continue to appear after Nick reaches his destination and begins his confrontation with Figlia. Appropriately, of all the locations in the city, only Rica's apartment is photographed with some measure of normality: more fill light, medium two-shots, and balanced close-ups of Nick and Rica predominate. This visual treatment reinforces the narrative suggestion against type that Rica, despite her foreignness, explicit sexuality, and questionable morality, is worthier of Nick's attention than the blond, Waspish Polly.

—A.S.

THE THIRTEENTH LETTER (1951)
[Working Title: THE SCARLET PEN]

Director and Producer: Otto Preminger (20th Century-Fox)
Screenplay: Howard Koch; from a story and screenplay *Le Corbeau* by Louis Chavance
Director of Photography: Joseph LaShelle
Special Photographic Effects: Fred Sersen
Sound: Arthur L. Kirbach, Roger Heman
Music Score: Alex North
Music Direction: Lionel Newman
Orchestration: Maurice de Packh
Art Director: Lyle Wheeler, Maurice Ransford
Set Decoration: Thomas Little, Walter M. Scott
Costumes: Edward Stevenson
Wardrobe Director: Charles LeMaire

Makeup: Ben Nye
Assistant Director: Dick Mayberry
Film Editor: Louis Loeffler

CAST: Linda Darnell (Denise), Charles Boyer (Dr. Laurent), Michael Rennie (Dr. Pearson), Constance Smith (Cora Laurent), Françoise Rosay (Mrs. Sims), Judith Evelyn (Sister Marie), Guy Sorel (Robert Helier), June Hedin (Rochelle). **BITS:** Camille Ducharme (Fredette), Paul Guevremont (Postman), George Alexander (Dr. Fletcher), J. Leo Cagnon (Dr. Helier), Ovila Legare (Mayor), Wilford Davidson, Arthur Groulx, Sheila Coonan, L. P. Herbert, Odie Lemire, Gilles Pelletier, C. Bosvier, J. L. Roux, Blanche Gauthier, Jerry Rowan, Louis Roux, Eleanor Stuart, Lucie Boitres (Townspeople), Jacques Auger (Priest), Patrick O'Moore, Robin Hughes (Interns), Stanley Mann, Vernon Steele (Officers).
Location: St. Hyacinthe, St. Denis, St. Charles, St. Hilaire, and St. Marc, Quebec, Canada
Filming Completed: October 20, 1950
Released: 20th Century-Fox, February 21, 1951
Running Time: 88 minutes

Dr. Pearson is a young, highly talented doctor working in a small French-Canadian village hospital. Upset because his wife had left him, he abandoned a great career in the city to forget his pain and lives a solitary life with only his clock collection as a diversion. His solitude is shattered when Cora Laurent, the pretty young wife of the older, revered Dr. Paul Laurent, receives a poison pen letter accusing her of having an affair with Dr. Pearson. The letters continue and are signed only by the mysterious name of "Raven." A number of townspeople are suspected as the letters' author: Dr. Pearson himself; Denise, Dr. Pearson's clubfooted patient who tried unsuccessfuly to seduce him; Cora's older sister, a nurse, who previously accused Cora of enticing other men; and a woman whose son, a paranoid veteran, is being treated by Dr. Pearson. The veteran receives a letter from "Raven," which falsely informs him that he has incurable cancer, and he commits suicide. When another poison pen letter drops out of the choir loft onto the church congregation, Dr. Laurent assumes control of the investigation. Despite comparing the handwriting of all 18 choir members, Laurent fails to establish the author's identity. Dr. Pearson finally discovers the truth. Cora Laurent, attracted to the aloof Pearson, wrote the first letter in a moment of weakness. When her husband discovered this, he forced her to continue writing the letters to demonstrate his theory of "an insanity of two"; that is, that one person's mad act can inspire cooperation in another. The veteran's mother avenges her son's death by slitting Dr. Laurent's throat as he writes a final letter.

Because it changes the locale to Quebec and drops the vicious portraits of a variety of local types, Preminger's *The Thirteenth Letter* is much less corrosive than Clouzot's

Dr. Laurent (Charles Boyer) and Dr. Pearson (Michael Rennie) in The Thirteenth Letter.

original *Le Corbeau*. Preminger's film is another example of how easily French suspense films could be adapted as American thrillers, as *La Bête Humaine* became *Human Desire*, *La Chienne* became *Scarlet Street*, and as *Le Jour Se Leve* became *The Long Night*. While *The Thirteenth Letter* is not necessarily superior to the original French film, it does fall under the influence of the noir cycle. Rennie's portrayal of Dr. Pearson is that of a man with guarded sensibilities who has been severely hurt by life; and his alienation is well revealed in the 360° pan around his room, which is filled with clocks. Boyer's apparently kind old Dr. Laurent, who is actually vicious and insane, is equally well described by the scene borrowed from the original when Laurent, while his face moves in and out of the light cast by a swinging overhead lamp tells Pearson, "Good and evil can change places like light and shadow." Linda Darnell's conventional voluptuousness and seductiveness become ironic when she reveals her clubfoot. Denise is yet another character with a false front and traumatized soul. *The Thirteenth Letter* has a good deal of the original's suspense, and, although it never aroused as much controversy as Clouzot's film, it could have because of the latent sexual perversity carried over into the American version.

—B.P.

THIS GUN FOR HIRE (1942)

Director: Frank Tuttle
Producer: Richard M. Blumenthal (Richard M. Blumenthal Productions)
Screenplay: Albert Maltz and W. R. Burnett; from the novel by Graham Greene
Director of Photography: John Seitz
Music: Frank Loesser and Jacques Press
Film Editor: Archie Marshek

CAST: Alan Ladd (Phillip Raven), Veronica Lake (Ellen Graham), Robert Preston (Michael Crane), Laird Cregar (Willard Gates), Tully Marshall (Alvin Brewster). **BITS:** Mikhail Rasumny (Slukey), Marc Lawrence (Tommy), Pamela Blake (Annie), Harry Shannon (Finnerty), Frank Ferguson (Albert Baker), Bernadene Hayes (Baker's Secretary), James Farley (Night Watchman), Virita Campbell (Crippled Girl), Roger Imnof (Senator Burnett), Victor Kilian (Brewster's Secretary), Olin Howland (Fletcher), Emmett Vogan (Charlie), Chester Clute (Mr. Stewart), Charles Arnt (Will Gates), Virginia Farmer (Woman in Shop), Clem Bevans (Old Timer), Harry Hayden (Restaurant Manager), Tim Ryan (Guard),

Phillip Raven (Alan Ladd) in This Gun For Hire.

Ellen Graham (Veronica Lake) and Phillip Raven (Alan Ladd) in This Gun For Hire.

Yvonne De Carlo (Show Girl), Ed Stanley (Police Captain), Eddy Chandler (Foreman), Louise La Planche (Dancer), Richard Webb (Young Man), Lora Lee (Girl in Car), Cyril Ring (Waiter), William Cabanne (Laundry Truck Driver).

Location: Los Angeles, California
Released: Paramount, May 13, 1942
Running Time: 80 minutes

Phillip Raven, a psychologically disturbed young assassin, is hired in San Francisco by Willard Gates to commit murder. Gates, an overweight, unctuous epicure, is in turn an agent of Alvin Brewster, the elderly and crippled head of a large, Los Angeles-based chemical firm. Brewster is making millions selling chemical formulas to the Nazis, and the victim is a possible police informant. Raven completes his job successfully and is paid off by Gates. Gates however has given him "hot" money, and a San Francisco police detail headed by Detective Michael Crane are soon pursuing Raven. He escapes and heads for Los Angeles in an effort to get even with Gates for setting him up. On the train there, he accidentally becomes involved with Ellen Graham, Crane's fiancée, who is secretly working as an agent for federal authorities in an attempt to discover the Nazi spy. Ellen is initially used by Raven as a tool to escape police and get to Gates, as she is a singer at Gates's nightclub. Ellen begins to sympathize with Raven because she realizes that he has been sorely treated by life. The cynical Raven gradually begins to see her as more than "just a skirt." She asks him to use Gates to find out who his boss is; he leaves her behind and eludes the police. Raven ultimately discovers the identity of the traitor, as well as the fact that Ellen is engaged and has been using him in an effort to aid the government. Nevertheless, when Brewster is alerted that Ellen is a government spy he holds her prisoner in his building. Raven infiltrates his office and becomes locked in with Brewster, Ellen, and Brewster's servant. The hired gun forces Brewster to sign a confession whereupon the servant shoots him. Crane follows Ellen to Brewster's office and knows Raven is with her. He lowers himself down to the window from a higher floor and shoots Raven. The assassin dies without bitterness, realizing that he has helped the only person who has ever been kind to him. The French consider *This Gun for Hire* one of the most important early film noir due to its connection to the British thriller via the original and also due to Alan Ladd's performance as a stoical killer. The film fails in some respects to live up to its reputation. The propaganda value of the film has dated badly, the musical interludes slow the action, and the role of Veronica Lake as a combination faithful fiancée, undercover agent, entertainer, and confidante to Ladd is overly complicated. Stripped of her patriotic guise, Ellen is revealed as a noir *femme fatale* who leads Raven to his destruction; he would have been better off following his own dictum: to only love cats. For all its weaknesses, *This Gun for Hire* helps to establish a number of conventions of the genre. John Seitz evokes an exotic atmosphere by a skillful blending of studio and location shots—

particularly the chase scene in the freight yards—figures darting in and out of shadows in the foggy night; fugitives hiding in a huge dynamo room; finally a sensational climax with people grotesquely garbed in uniforms and gas masks. Notable too are the characterizations: the wizened Tully Marshall, an ineffectual Mabuse confined to a wheelchair and speaking only in a hoarse whisper; the silken-voiced Laird Cregar, already defined as a somewhat perverse personality with his taste for fine women and chocolate mints and his abhorrence of violence; finally, Ladd as Raven, breaking with the 1930s criminal characteristics by being given a Freudian rationale: he killed his vicious stepmother who struck him with an iron, deforming his wrist. Discounting the ending, Raven is a tough guy reminiscent of Bogart's Spade: the angelic face that hides the inner demon; the tough dialogue (well handled by an actor with experience in radio); the alienated posture. His whole being is defined in a well-devised opening sequence: he loads his gun and casts one last glance at his cat, then sternly tells the young maid to watch out for it. Out of spite, she quickly drives the animal away; but he returns to catch her. Without saying a word he slaps her twice, knocking her down and ripping her dress. As she lies whimpering, he pours a little more milk for the cat, pets him a bit, then, still silent and indecipherable, leaves to complete his job.

—B.P.

THUNDERBOLT (1929)

Director: Josef von Sternberg
Producer: Paramount Famous Players Lasky
Screenplay: Jules Furthman, dialogue by Herman J. Mankiewicz; from a story by Charles and Jules Furthman
Titles: Joseph Mankiewicz
Director of Photography: Henry Gerrard
Sound: M. M. Paggi
Song: "Thinkin' About My Baby" by Sam Coslow
Art Director: Hans Dreier
Film Editor: Helen Lewis

CAST: George Bancroft (Thunderbolt Jim Lang), Fay Wray (Ritzy), Richard Arlen (Bob Morgan), Tully Marshall (Warden), Eugenie Besserer (Mrs. Morgan), James Spottswood (Snapper O'Shea), Fred Kohler (Bad Al Frieberg), Robert Elliott (Prison Chaplain), E. H. Calvert (District Attorney McKay), George Irving (Mr. Corwin), Mike Donlin (Kentucky Sampson), S. S. Stewart (Convict), William L. Thorne (Police Inspector).
Released: Paramount Famous Players Lasky, June 20, 1929
Running Time: Sound version, 95 minutes, silent version, 81 minutes

An underworld boss, Thunderbolt Jim Lang, tries hard to keep his beautiful mistress, Ritzy, interested. He is jealously

TOO LATE FOR TEARS

on the prowl for anyone who might divert her attention from him. Thunderbolt blunders, however, and is sent to prison. Once behind bars, Thunderbolt's fears about his relationship with Ritzy become a reality. A local small-time hustler, Bob Morgan, falls in love with Ritzy, and she is attracted to him. Thunderbolt learns of this apparent infidelity and eventually sets up a frame that sends Morgan to prison. Placed in the same environment as the jealous gangland boss, Morgan's chances for survival seem slim as Thunderbolt is a leader of the convicts. He is called upon by the warden to quash an occasional riot or prison escape. When Morgan's situation seems hopeless, Ritzy marries him in a preposterous wedding ceremony, which takes place on death row, and Thunderbolt realizes the true meaning of love. Before he is marched off to the electric chair, he confesses to having Morgan framed for a crime he did not commit. Thunderbolt goes to his death with a cleaner conscience, as Ritzy and Bob begin a new life outside the prison walls.

Von Sternberg's last underworld thriller, *Thunderbolt* is filled with an ambience and tone far removed from his earlier films, including *Dragnet, The Case of Lena Smith,* and even *Underworld.* In *Thunderbolt* the moral nature of the gangster is scrutinized in the constricting environment of a prison. There is no freedom to explore the underworld and no real hint as to the scope and character of the gangsters that existed there. Chaos is absent from this particular vision of the world. Rather, von Sternberg substitutes an inappropriate sense of romanticism into the film that works against his usual brand of visual exoticism. *Thunderbolt* is filled with strong personalities who transcend their illegal professions and function substantively as heroes. Because this quality in *Thunderbolt* is not particularly noir, the dark sensibility of the film derives from von Sternberg's shadowy visuals and the occasional flashes of cynicism lurking in Jules Furthman's screenplay. It is interesting to realize that less than twenty years later Jules Furthman would write one of the bitterest and most uncompromising noir films ever made, *Nightmare Alley*; it is a far cry from the meanderings of *Thunderbolt,* a dark thriller forced to exist without many thrills.

—C.M.

TOO LATE FOR TEARS (1949)

Director: Byron Haskin
Producer: Hunt Stromberg (Hunt Stromberg Productions)
Screenplay: Roy Huggins; from the *Saturday Evening Post* serialization of his novel.
Director of Photography: William Mellor
Special Effects: Howard and Theodore Lydecker
Optical Effects: Consolidated Film Industries

Sound: Earl Crain, Sr., Howard Wilson
Music Score: Dale Butts
Music Director: Morton Scott
Art Director: James Sullivan
Set Decoration: John McCarthy, Jr., Charles Thompson
Costumes: Adele Palmer
Makeup: Bob Mark
Hairstyles: Peggy Gray
Production Manager: Lou Rosso
Production Assistant: Bob Sterling
Assistant Director: Dick Moder
Script Supervisor: Marvin Weldon
Film Editor: Harry Keller

CAST: Lizabeth Scott (Jane Palmer), Don DeFore (Don Blake), Dan Duryea (Danny Fuller), Arthur Kennedy (Alan Palmer), Kristine Miller (Kathy Palmer), Barry Kelley (Lt. Breach). **BITS:** Denver Pyle (Youth), Virginia Mullen (Woman), Richard Irving (1st Bindlestiff), George K. Mann (Texan), Harry Vejar (Teniente), June Storey (Girl), Jimmy Ames (Fat Man), Jim Nolan (Parker), John Butler (Little Man), Smokie Whitfield (Pete), William Halop (Boat Attendant), Jimmie Dodd (2nd Bindlestiff), David Clarke (Sharber), Denny O'Morrison, Jack Shea, Charles Flynn, Robert Kellard, Robert Bice, George Backus (Policemen), John Mansfield (Carlos), Garry Owen (Officer at Switchboard), Gregg Barton (Clerk, Missing Bureau), William O. Wayne (Gas Station Attendant), Patricia Wallace (Woman), Perry Ivins (Attendant at Stand), Alex Montoya (Customs Officer), Robert Neff (Man in Black Car), Renee Donatt (Young Girl), Carl Thompson (Young Boy).
Filming Completed: October 15, 1948
Released: United Artists, August 14, 1949
Running Time: 98 minutes

Alan Palmer and his wife, Jane, are driving to a party one night and have an argument, which causes their car to swerve off the road and blink its lights. Another car mistakes this for a signal, and a bag containing $60,000 is thrown into the Palmers' convertible as the two cars pass. Alan would like to turn the money over to the police, but Jane persuades him to keep it and check it into a luggage stand in Union Station the next day. A man calls on Jane at home and claims the money, identifying himself as a private detective named Danny Fuller. They haggle and he finally agrees to split the sum with her. Realizing her husband will never consent to keeping any of the money, she kills him and hides the baggage claim check. Stalling Fuller, she reports her husband has disappeared to the police and to Alan's sister, Kathy. Some days later a stranger named Don Blake arrives at Jane's house and explains that he is Alan's old army buddy. Blake is actually the brother of Jane's first husband, whom he suspects she murdered. Meeting Kathy, Blake confides his true identity and she reveals her suspicions about Alan's disappearance. She discovered a

292

baggage claim ticket in his bureau drawer where he usually kept his gun. Jane is aware of Kathy's surveillance and plans to poison her, but she discovers the truth about Blake and must retrieve the claim ticket from him and Kathy at gunpoint. After hiding briefly at Fuller's motel, she poisons him and departs for Mexico city. Blake finds her and calls the police. As she hurries to elude them, Jane falls from the balcony to her death and the money flutters down after her.

Dan Duryea's portrayal of the corrupt and slimy detective pales in contrast to Lizabeth Scott's avaricious Jane Palmer. Although the detective pretends to be tough, he must get drunk before he has the courage to purchase poison for Jane's plans and, by falling in love with her, permits her to murder him with the same poison. *Too Late for Tears* is a minor piece, but it is a good example of the way low budget films made good use of Los Angeles locales. Importantly, the film indicates a growing middle-class dissatisfaction illustrated in the extreme by Jane who murdered two husbands because she wanted "to move out of the ranks of the middle-class poor."

—B.P.

TOUCH OF EVIL (1958)

Director: Orson Welles [Additional scenes by Harry Keller]
Producer: Albert Zugsmith (Universal-International)
Screenplay: Orson Welles; from the novel *Badge of Evil* by Whit Masterson
Director of Photography: Russell Metty
Sound: Leslie I. Carey, Frank Wilkinson
Music: Henry Mancini
Music Director: Joseph Gershenson
Art Directors: Alexander Golitzen, Robert Clatworthy
Set Decoration: Russell A. Gausman, John P. Austin
Costumes: Bill Thomas
Production Manager: F. D. Thompson
Assistant Directors: Phil Bowles, Terry Nelson
Film Editors: Virgil M. Vogel, Aaron Stell

CAST: Charlton Heston (Ramon Miguel "Mike" Vargas), Janet Leigh (Susan Vargas), Orson Welles (Hank Quinlan), Joseph Calleia (Pete Menzies), Akim Tamiroff (Uncle Joe Grandi), Joanna Moore (Marcia Linnekar), Marlene Dietrich (Tanya), Ray Collins (Adair), Dennis Weaver (Motel Manager), Victor Millan (Manolo Sanchez), Lalo Rios (Risto), Valentin de Vargas (Pancho), Mort Mills (Schwartz), Mercedes McCambridge (Hoodlum), Wayne Taylor, Ken Miller, Raymond Rodriguez (Gang Members), Michael Sargent (Pretty Boy), Zsa Zsa Gabor (Owner of Nightclub), Keenan Wynn (Man), Joseph Cotten (Detective), Phil Harvey (Blaine), Joi Lansing (Blond), Harry Shannon (Gould), Rusty Wes-

coatt (Casey), Arlene McQuade (Ginnie), Domenick Delgarde (Lackey), Joe Basulto (Hoodlum), Jennie Dias (Jackie), Yolanda Bojorquez (Bobbie), Eleanor Corado (Lia).

Location: Venice, California
Filming Completed: April 1, 1957
Released: Universal-International, May 21, 1958
Running Time: 95 minutes
[NOTE: The University of California at Los Angeles Film Archive has discovered a 105-minute version of *Touch of Evil*, which is now included in the American Film Institute Archive at the Library of Congress.]

One night on the Mexican border, a millionaire named Linnekar is blown up along with his blond companion by a time bomb planted in his car. At odds in the investigation are Mike Vargas, a Mexican narcotics investigator on his honeymoon with his American wife, Susan, and Hank Quinlan, a shrewd stateside detective. Quinlan believes that a young Mexican, Sanchez, is guilty of the murder and plants evidence to frame him. Discovering this, Vargas seeks to expose Quinlan. The outraged Quinlan, who has routinely framed suspects ever since he failed to bring his wife's murderer to justice, retaliates by enlisting the help of racketeer Uncle Joe Grandi, who is seeking to discredit Vargas so that the mobster's brother will not go to prison. Grandi sends a gang of punks to the American motel where Susan Vargas is staying to set her up as an apparent drug addict. To cover his tracks, Quinlan kills Grandi in the hotel room to which Susan has been brought, but Quinlan's devoted partner, Menzies, discovers Quinlan's cane in the room and is pressured by Vargas to expose Quinlan. Menzies gets Quinlan's confession, which is surreptitiously recorded by Vargas. Quinlan discovers the betrayal and shoots Menzies, who in turn shoots him. The two men die as news arrives that Sanchez has confessed to the initial bomb murder. Clear of the drug charge, Susan asks her husband to take her away while Tanya, Quinlan's old friend, has a last philosophical word to say about the once powerful cop.

Initially underrated by all but a few, *Touch of Evil* is now perhaps a bit overrated, at least in relation to some less widely known but equally impressive noir films. Of course, Orson Welles is a substantial presence off and on the screen; and it must be admitted that there is more subtle artistry in *On Dangerous Ground, White Heat, Criss Cross, Angel Face* and *The Big Heat,* to name only a few; nevertheless, they cannot tarnish Welles's vivid creation of a Mexican nightmare out of the strange decor of Venice, California, or his realization of a host of characters who are colorful and resonant. Welles utilizes his bravura style so effectively that it cannot always be discerned which moments create the dramatic thrust of the film and which are simply full of sound and fury.

The opening shot, lasting over three minutes, displays Welles's propensity for the moving camera and the long-take, and immediately establishes the premise around which the narrative is structured. The camera begins on a close-up of a time bomb and then cranes up to reveal the bomb being planted in a car. Linnekar and his girl friend emerge out of the background darkness and, as they enter the car and begin to drive away, the high craned camera travels up and back, moving with them along the streets toward the border. Slowly, the camera descends as Vargas and Susan cross the street at a traffic light where Linnekar is stopped. Tracking alongside and in front of the couple, the camera then cranes up again as the car moves past them and onward to the customs station. The camera continues moving with Vargas and Susan when suddenly there is a blinding explosion as the bomb goes off in the car. The shot is completed with a close-up of the car engulfed in flames, followed by a reverse zoom away from the wreck. The uninterrupted fluidity of this opening shot works in direct opposition to the violence of the imagery, and the suspense which the visual style engenders is heightened by the fact that only the spectator is aware of the bomb's presence. This cinematic fluidity is continued throughout *Touch of Evil* and is not only tensing as a visual device, but it is appropriate to the shadowy characters and their complex, rapid, comings and goings across the border.

Russell Metty's camerawork exhibits film noir lighting at its peak in the matching of studio shots with Venice locations and is especially effective in the scene of Grandi's murder. The sometimes clichéd device of an exterior neon light flashing into a room is powerfully expressive as Quinlan and Grandi move in and out of the darkness within a restricted space. Welles varies the tempo in the similarly lit sequence of Sanchez's interrogation, which is dominated by a long take that is remarkable for its constantly varying composition.

In the character of Hank Quinlan, Welles gives one of his most persuasive performances. Visually, his vast paunch, his limp, his half-closed eyes, and his fondness for cigars and candy bars, all contribute to the seediness of the character he portrays. And yet, Welles creates a sympathetic antagonist who exhibits a human, almost wistful quality when speaking of the wife he lost years before. Through such characters as the fortune telling Tanya and police assistant Menzies, Quinlan demonstrates that he is capable of inspiring devotion. Equally essential in creating an atmosphere of lurking evil are the secondary characters of the obscene and vulgar Grandi, with his hair slicked down and popping eyes; his sadistic gang, which includes a lesbian hoodlum; and the ineffectual night man at the motel, whose nervousness and incoherent, mumbling speech becomes more exaggerated as he is confronted by Vargas. Ultimately Welles makes Hank Quinlan into an imposing and driven figure whose face reflects the ancient but still intense anguish of his wife's ambiguous murder and the fatal corruption that will destroy him. The sight of Quinlan staggering down an embankment to die in a river of garbage is a moment at once grotesque and tragic, underscored by Tanya's epitaph that "He was some kind of man."

—B.L. & T.T.

TRY AND GET ME (1950)
[Original Release Title: THE SOUND OF FURY]

Director: Cyril Endfield
Executive Producer: Robert Stillman (Robert Stillman Productions)
Associate Producer: Seton I. Miller
Screenplay: Jo Pagano; from his novel *The Condemned*
Director of Photography: Guy Roe
Sound: Jean Speaks, Hal McNiff
Music Score: Hugo Friedhofer
Music Director: Emil Newman
Art Director: Perry Ferguson
Set Decoration: Howard Bristol
Assistant Director: Ivan Volkman
Film Editor: George Amy

CAST: Frank Lovejoy (Howard Tyler), Kathleen Ryan (Judy Tyler), Richard Carlson (Gil Stanton), Lloyd Bridges (Jerry Slocum), Katherine Locke (Hazel), Adele Jergens (Velma), Art Smith (Hal Clendenning), Renzo Cesana (Dr. Simone), Irene Vernon (Helen Stanton), Lynn Gray (Vi Clendenning), Cliff Clark (Sheriff Demig), Dabbs Greer (Mike), Mack Williams (Professor Martin), Jane Easton (Barbara Colson), John Pelletti (Herb Colson), Mary Lawrence (Kathy), Donald Smelick (Tommy Tyler).

Location: Phoenix, Arizona
Filming Completed: August 28, 1950
Released: United Artists, as *The Sound of Fury* on December 12, 1950; the title changed to *Try and Get Me* on March 26, 1951, while the film was still in general release
Running Time: 90 minutes

[FACTUAL BASIS: In 1933, two men were arrested in San Jose, California, for kidnapping and murdering Brooke Hart. The suspects confessed and were lynched by a mob of townspeople.]

A down-on-his-luck veteran, Howard Tyler, finds that after returning from the war he is unable to provide his family with such material goods as television sets, clothes, and entertainment, which he feels they want. Out of desperation he teams up with a casual acquaintance in order to pull off a robbery and come away with the needed cash. The robberies evolve into a kidnapping plot that quickly results in the unnecessary death of the victim. With no money and tremendous anxieties, Howard and Jerry Slocum try to wait out the storm of civic passion that follows the killing in hopes that the crime will not be traced to them. Howard's marriage slowly crumbles as he becomes a moody irrational neurotic. When Howard and Jerry are captured, Gil Stanton's series of irresponsible newspaper articles so enrages the local citizens over this brutal crime that, after they gather in front of the jail, a riot develops. Bursting into the jail, the mob reaches the two accused murderers and savagely beats them to death while the police stand by helpless.

Howard Tyler (Frank Lovejoy), left, kidnap victim and Jerry Slocum (Lloyd Bridges) in Try and Get Me *(Sound of Fury was working title).*

Howard Tyler (Frank Lovejoy) and his wife, Judy (Kathleen Ryan) in Try And Get Me.

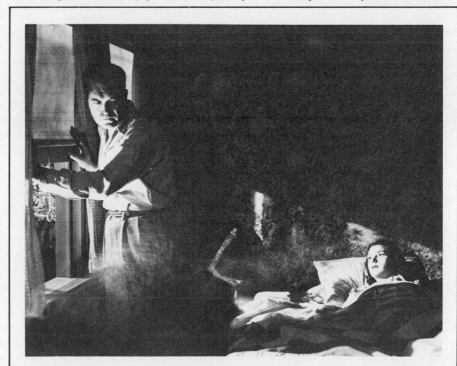

THE TURNING POINT

Utilizing a strained structural device that incorporates a European humanitarian as the voice of social relevance throughout the film, *Try and Get Me* functions better as a film noir than it does as a quasi-documentary exposing environment as the true producer of crime, because the film chronicles the inevitable destruction of a man hopelessly lost in his own society. There is no redemption in Howard Tyler's world, and yet there is no sin either. His situation is completely out of his control. Directed by Cy Enfield, who was later blacklisted due to his strong social and political philosophies, *Try and Get Me*'s brutal, modern irony plays against the transparent background of novelist Jo Pagano's script. After the mob violence subsides and the message of social consciousness is delivered, the striking chiaroscuro images of alienation and confusion remain deeply rooted as the core of the film. Reminiscent of both Fritz Lang's *Fury* and Mervin Leroy's *They Won't Forget*, *Try and Get Me* concentrates less on the result of the lynching than on the collapse of decency in both the criminals and the townspeople.

—C.M.

THE TURNING POINT (1952)
[Working Title: THIS IS DYNAMITE]

Director: William Dieterle
Producer: Irving Asher (Paramount)
Screenplay: Warren Duff; from an unpublished story by Horace McCoy
Director of Photography: Lionel Lindon
Special Photographic Effects: Gordon Jennings
Process Photography: Farciot Edouart
Sound: Gene Merritt, John Cope
Music Direction: Irving Talbot
Art Directors: Hal Pereira, Joseph McMillan Johnson
Set Decoration: Sam Comer, Grace Gregory
Costumes: Edith Head
Makeup: Wally Westmore
Assistant Director: Michael Moore
Film Editor: George Tomasini

CAST: William Holden (Jerry McKibbon), Edmond O'Brien (John Conroy), Alexis Smith (Amanda Waycross), Tom Tully (Matt Conroy), Ed Begley (Eichelberger), Dan Dayton (Ackerman), Adele Longmire (Carmelina), Ray Teal (Clint), Ted De Corsia (Harrigan), Don Porter (Joe Silbray), Howard Freeman (Fogel), Neville Brand (Red). **BITS:** Peter Baldwin (Boy), Judith Ames (Girl), Mary Murphy (Secretary), Leonard George (Lefty), Ben Cameron (Gates), Russell Johnson (Herman), Leonard Bremen (Doc), Eugene White (Pinky), Buddy Sullivan, Robert Rockwell, Joel Marston, Russell Conway (Reporters), George Ford, Charles Sherlock,

Lee Phelps, Chalky Williams, George Dempsey (Policemen), Charles Campbell (Cameraman), Albin Robeling (Waiter), Jean Ransome (Maid), Gretchen Hale (Mrs. Conroy), Grace Hayle (Mrs. Martin), Ruth Packard, Hazel Boyne, Carolyn Jones (Women), Whit Bissell (Buck), Harry Hines (Maintenance Man), Franz F. Roehn (Cashier), Tony Barr (Garcia), Tom Moore (Drugstore Proprietor), Jamesson Shade (Staff Member), Jerry James (Man), John Maxwell (Ed), Soledad Jiminez (Mrs. Manzinates), Diane Garrett (Woman at Detroit Joint), Ralph Sanford (Harry), Ralph Montgomery (Driver).
Location: Los Angeles, California
Filming Completed: November 6, 1951
Released: Paramount, November 14, 1952
Running Time: 85 minutes

John Conroy, an honest, aggressive lawyer and politician, is head of a special committee investigating organized crime in a large Midwestern city. His friend, investigative reporter Jerry McKibbon, is shocked to discover that Conroy's father, Matt, was once a policeman on the syndicate payroll; but McKibbon decides not to tell Conroy about his father. As the committee puts pressure on the syndicate chieftain, Eichelberger, the gangsters decide that Matt Conroy must be killed. John Conroy redoubles his efforts to indict the syndicate, while McKibbon writes newspaper exposés with information gleaned from underworld contacts. The committee subpoenas incriminating records from Eichelberger, which could mean the end of his empire. The files are stored in a downtown tenement, and Eichelberger burns the building down and kills many of the people who live there. Ultimately, a witness to a murder committed by Eichelberger's aide reveals herself to the committee. Meanwhile, McKibbon walks into a trap set by Eichelberger by attending a prizefight where a hired assassin awaits him. Conroy learns of the plot, but McKibbon is shot and killed before the police can arrive.

The Turning Point, with its emphasis on the work of an investigative committee, was obviously inspired by the publicity given the Kefauver Committee hearings. Horace McCoy's story, however, emphasizes an atmosphere of pervasive corruption. Corruption is only mildly included in the film, chiefly with Matt Conroy's illicit mob connection. To reinforce the realistic milieu in which the syndicate operates, there is a good use of location shots photographed in semidocumentary fashion. They are very obviously of Los Angeles, although the fictional locale is a "Midwestern" city. Two individual scenes are memorable: Ed Begley's portrayal of Eichelberger contains a mute distillation of corruption. As he calmly drinks a glass of water and decides to burn down the apartment building, his utter inhumanity is revealed in his sweaty face and gleaming animalistic eyes. Finally, the nighttime sequence of the fire, with men, women, and children screaming in the midst of the conflagration, and scores of charred bodies in the debris surely qualifies as among the most brutal scenes in film noir.

—B.P.

UNCLE HARRY (1945)

[Also released as THE STRANGE AFFAIR OF UNCLE HARRY]

Director: Robert Siodmak
Executive Producer: Milton H. Feld (Charles K. Feldman Productions)
Producer: Joan Harrison
Screenplay: Stephen Longstreet, adapted by Keith Winter; from the play by Thomas Job
Director of Photography: Paul Ivano
Special Photography: John P. Fulton
Second Unit Photography: Bill Miller
Music Director: H. J. Salter
Art Directors: John Goodman, Eugene Lourie
Set Decoration: Russell A. Gausman
Costumes: Travis Banton
Assistant Director: Melville Shyer
Film Editor: Arthur Hilton

CAST: George Sanders (John Quincy), Geraldine Fitzgerald (Lettie Quincy), Ella Raines (Deborah Brown), Sara Allgood (Nona), Moyna MacGill (Hester), Samuel S. Hinds (Dr. Adams), Harry Von Zell (Ben), Ethel Griffies (Mrs. Nelson), Judy Clark (Helen), Craig Reynolds (John Warren), Will Wright (Mr. Nelson), Arthur Loft (Mr. Follinsbee), Irene Tedrow (Mrs. Follinsbee), Coulter Irwin (Biff Wagner), Dawn Bender (Joan Warren), Ruth Cherrington (Matron), Rodney Bell (Joe, The Greek). **BITS:** Harry Hayden (Slavin), Holmes Herbert (Warden), William Hall, Matt McHugh (Moving Men), Harlan Briggs (Hangman), Barbara Pepper (Annie), Robert Malcolm (Connors), Robert Dudley (Stationmaster), Sara Selby (Alice), Walter Soderling (Jed Jessup), the Reverend Neal Dodd (Minister), Fred Santley (Waiter), Bob McKenzie (Manager), Wally Scott (Barman), Frank Jaquet (Salesman), Robert Anderson, Gregory Muradian, Billy Gray, Mike Clifton (Children), Bill Henderson (Johnny), Norman Nielson, Clarence Badger, Alan Watson, Jan Williams (Quartette).
Location: Second unit photography in New Hampshire
Filming Completed: June 16, 1945
Released: Universal, as *The Strange Affair of Uncle Harry,* August 17, 1945.
Running Time: 80 minutes
[NOTE: *Uncle Harry* was previewed in Los Angeles with five different endings aimed at appeasing the Hays Office and receiving the seal of approval under the Production Code. The producer, Joan Harrison, quit Universal when the "dream ending" was selected.]

John Quincy lives a dull life with his domineering sisters, Lettie and Hester, in their family mansion in Corinth, New Hampshire. He meets Deborah Brown, a visiting fashion expert from New York City, at the Quincy mill. Soon their friendship becomes love, and he asks her to marry him. Deborah meets John's family and, although Hester is happy for her brother, Lettie is jealous of Deborah and feigns a heart attack on learning of their engagement. Frustrated and angry at Lettie's attempt to spoil his happiness, John plans to murder her; but Hester drinks the poison intended for Lettie and dies. Lettie is convicted of her sister's murder but does not incriminate John, because she knows that her death will prevent him from marrying Deborah. John wakes up and discovers that the entire situation has been a dream.

The central narrative of *Uncle Harry,* with its portrayal of unnatural, even obsessive, love between sister and brother —and with its consequent suggestions of incest—is developed in the same straightforward manner as such other films directed by Siodmak as *Phantom Lady* and *The Dark Mirror.* Geraldine Fitzgerald's interpretation of Lettie, the possessive sister, is punctuated by the same moments of pathological hysteria as Franchot Tone's deranged killer in *Phantom Lady* and Olivia de Havilland's disturbed twin in *The Dark Mirror.* Lettie's self-destructive failure to exonerate herself as part of a plan to prevent John's marriage by the fact of her execution, further delineate a monomania that ranks with the most severe depicted in film noir. The ending, which discloses that John's plan to murder Lettie and free himself has all been a dream, may seem to take *Uncle Harry* out of the realm of noir melodrama and closer to such black comedies as Siodmak's own *Fly by Night,* a parody of formula thrillers like Hitchcock's *Saboteur.* But *Uncle Harry* is not a parody, for what the ending—ironically, selected to mollify the MPAA code administrators—reveals, in the manner of the framing device in Lang's *Woman in the Window,* is that the most disturbed psyche in the film may actually have been that of the protagonist. John Quincy's infatuation with Deborah Brown does appear to be threatened, in what becomes a dream narrative told from his point-of-view, by Lettie's dominance of his emotions. At the same time, the physical resemblance between Deborah

THE UNDERCOVER MAN

and Lettie and the exaggerated dream portrait that John renders of his sister betray the possibility that John's nightmare is more accurately a reflection of his own suppressed, socially unacceptable desires than they are of Lettie's. Similarly, his recourse to an elaborate murder scheme rather than a direct, adult confrontation reinforce the likelihood that his reverie is a manifestation not just of deep-rooted psychological dependency on his sister but also of profound guilt over his sexual attraction to her. Like Richard Wanley in *Woman in the Window,* John awakens from an intolerable dream situation with relief but finds himself no less oppressed by reality than he was before.

—A.S.

THE UNDERCOVER MAN (1949)
[Working Title: CHICAGO STORY]

Director: Joseph H. Lewis
Producer: Robert Rossen (Robert Rossen Productions)
Screenplay: Sydney Boehm, with additional dialogue by Malvin Wald, based on a screen story by Jack Rubin; from an article "Undercover Man: He Trapped Capone" by Frank J. Wilson

Director of Photography: Burnett Guffey
Sound: Jack Goodrich
Music Score: George Duning
Music Director: M. W. Stoloff
Art Director: Walter Holscher
Set Decoration: William Kiernan
Costumes: Jean Louis
Assistant Director: Wilbur McGaugh
Script Supervisor: Frances McDowell
Film Editor: Al Clark

CAST: Glenn Ford (Frank Warren), Nina Foch (Judith Warren), James Whitmore (George Pappas), Barry Kelley (Edward O'Rourke), David Wolfe (Stanley Weinburg), Frank Tweddell (Inspector Herzog), Howard St. John (Joseph S. Horan), John F. Hamilton (Sergeant Shannon), Leo Penn (Sidney Gordon), Joan Lazer (Rosa Rocco), Esther Minciotti (Maria Rocco), Angela Clarke (Theresa Rocco), Anthony Caruso (Salvatore Rocco), Robert Osterloh (Manny Zanger), Kay Medford (Gladys LaVerne), Patricia White (Muriel Gordon), Peter Brocco (Johnny), Everett Glass (Judge Parker), Joe Mantell (Newsboy), Michael Cisney (Fred Ferguson), Marcella Cisney (Alice Ferguson), Sidney Dubin (Harris), William Vedder (Druggist). **BITS:** James Drum, Pat Lane, Allen Mathews, Robert Malcolm, Brian O'Hara, Joe Palma

Frank Warren (Glenn Ford), left, in Undercover Man.

(Policemen), Esther Zeitlin, Irene Martin, Virginia Farmer, Rose Plumer, Stella LeSaint (Women), Harlan Warde, Cy Malis, Jack Gordon, Paul Marion, Ted Jordan, Glen Thompson, Roy Darmour, Wally Rose, Saul Gorss (Hoodlums), Tom Coffey, William Rhinehart (Gunmen), Ralph Volkie (Big Fellow/Man In White), Ken Harvey (Big Fellow), Al Murphy, Daniel Meyers, Franklin Parker, Robert Haines, Sam LaMarr, Bernard Sell, Edwin Randolph (Men), Silvio Minciotti (Vendor), John Butler (Grocer), Richard Bartell (Court Attendant), Ben Erway (Court Clerk), Franklin Farnum (Federal Judge), Frank Mayo (Jury Foreman), Wheaton Chambers (Secretary), George Douglas (District Attorney), Helen Wallace (Mrs. O'Rourke), Peter Virgo (Cigar Store Owner), Edwin Max (Manager), Billy Nelson (Bouncer), Billy Stubbs (Crap Dealer), Tom Hanlon (Newsreel Announcer).

Location: Union Station, Los Angeles; Chicago, Illinois
Filming Completed: April 20, 1948
Released: Columbia, April 20, 1949
Running Time: 85 minutes

A group of undercover agents working for the Internal Revenue Service attempt to discover information that would prove a top mobster guilty of tax evasion. Frank Warren, an extremely dedicated family man, and his partner, George Pappas, begin questioning people who had access to the bookkeeping records. Their first contact is shot down by unknown assassins. The tedious, painstaking job of locating another individual willing to jeopardize his life in order to see the mob leader behind bars takes Warren and Pappas into a strange twilight world of intense paranoia. After a second witness is savagely murdered in broad daylight, the entire scheme seems doomed to failure. The agents finally get the information from the murdered bookkeeper's wife. Indictments are handed down. The pressures of the investigation cause one officer to commit suicide. The final double-crossing of the "big fellow" by his lawyer, who is willing to sell out for a pardon, leaves the shyster dead and Warren in a position to expose a handful of jurors bought off by the mob.

Another in an unrelated cycle of noir films made during the late 1940s that approach the subject of organized crime through the conventions of supposed documentary technique, *The Undercover Man* emphasizes the ability of the noir film to suspend disbelief. The nature of the unresolved murders in the film coupled with Joseph H. Lewis's eclectic direction gives the film a very episodic quality. Lewis draws heavily from a base of pure romanticism, embellished with stylistic touches of American expressionism and his own natural flare for the surreal. The convention of this type of film, much in the same manner as *T-Men, Naked City,* or even *House on 92nd Street,* plays on the ability to relate a great deal of the action with newsreel style film footage. The grotesqueness of the characters and the unorthodox nature of much of the action allows these films to become noir while maintaining their alleged documentary flavor.

—C.M.

UNDERCURRENT (1946)

Director: Vincente Minnelli
Producer: Pandro S. Berman (MGM)
Screenplay: Edward Chodorov, with contributions from Marguerite Roberts and [uncredited] George Oppenheimer; from the novel *You Were There* by Thelma Strabel
Director of Photography: Karl Freund
Sound: Douglas Shearer
Music Score: Herbert Stothart (Brahms Fourth Symphony)
Art Directors: Cedric Gibbons, Randall Duell
Set Decoration: Edwin B. Willis, Jack D. Moore
Costumes: Irene
Makeup: Jack Dawn
Hairstyles: Sydney Guilaroff
Assistant Director: Norman Elzer
Film Editor: Ferris Webster

CAST: Katharine Hepburn (Ann Hamilton), Robert Taylor (Alan Garroway), Robert Mitchum (Michael Garroway), Edmund Gwenn (Professor Dink Hamilton), Marjorie Main (Lucy), Jayne Cotter (Sylvia Burton), Clinton Sundberg (Mr. Warmsley), Dan Tobin (Professor Herbert Bangs), Kathryn Card (Mrs. Foster), Leigh Whipper (George), Charles Trowbridge (Justice Putnam), James Westerfield (Henry Gilson), Billy McLain (Uncle Ben).
BITS: Milton Kibbee (Minister), Jean Andren (Mrs. Davenport), Forbes Murray (Senator Edwards), Bert Moorehouse (1st Man), David Cavendish, Ernest Hilliard, Clive Morgan, Reginald Simpson, Oliver Cross, Harold Miller, Frank Leigh, Dick Earle, James Carlisle, Ann Lawrence, Florence Fair, Laura Treadwell, Ella Ethridge, Hazel Keener, Maxine Hudson, Bess Flowers, Hilda Rhoades, Joan Thorsen, Barbara Billingsley (Guests), Sarah Edwards (Manager), Ellen Ross (Gwen), Betty Blythe, Moyna Andre (Saleswomen), Helyn Eby-Rock (Fitter), Sylvia Andrew (Nora), Eula Guy (Housekeeper), Wheaton Chambers (Proprietor), James Westerfield (Henry Gilson), Gordon Richards (Headwaiter), Frank Dae (2nd Man), Nina Ross, Dorothy Christy, Jane Green (Women), Dan Kerry (Elevator Man), Sydney Logan (Model), Hank Worden (Attendant), Robert Emmet O'Connor (Stationmaster), Rudy Rama (Headwaiter), William Eddritt (Butler), Phil Dunham (Elevator Man), Jack Murphy, William Cartledge (Messengers).
Filming Completed: April 27, 1946
Released: MGM, November 28, 1946
Running Time: 114 minutes

Ann Hamilton leads a sheltered life with her father, a gentle professor, until she meets handsome and charming Alan Garroway, an airplane manufacturer. They fall in love and are married but Alan is emotionally disturbed and obsessed with hatred for his long-missing brother, Michael. Alan claims that Michael cheated him in business and then disappeared. Ann gradually discovers the truth from other sources, and a new portrait of Michael emerges, that of a gentle and sensitive man who may be missing because Alan has killed him. Curious, Ann visits Michael's ranch where she meets a man she assumes is the caretaker but who is actually Michael. Later, Michael confronts Alan because he is concerned that his brother will ruin Ann's life. Michael left the family business because he knew that Alan killed an inventor who worked for him and assumed credit for the ideas responsible for the company's success. Alan persuades Michael not to interfere by claiming that he loves Ann. However, realizing that Ann no longer loves him, Alan attempts to kill her but is killed himself by Michael's horse. Ann and Michael meet later and she confesses that she somehow knew it was he at the ranch and, despite the terror of her marriage, she has now found a man worthy of her love.

Film noir encompasses much of the most imaginative work of great directors, as illustrated by the works of Lang, Ray, Preminger, and Mann. Unfortunately, the lone contribution to the cycle by Minnelli is a confusing and convoluted work, not without interesting qualities but ultimately lacking in power. This is regrettable because the premise is characteristic of Minnelli's best work. The heroine discovers the reality of a world outside her sheltered niche to be a nightmare—personified by her husband, Alan—from which she finds refuge by falling in love with a dream—personified by Michael. Katharine Hepburn gives one of her most controlled performances in this role but that tone is not supported by Minnelli's indulgence of the obvious symbolism of Michael's horse or the motif of the flickering fireplaces in each key setting.

Although Minnelli is customarily more precise in his characteristic visual usages, certain sequences manifest an awareness of the noir style: the confrontation between Michael and Alan, for instance, is dramatically heightened by the swinging lamp in the stable where they talk. The most memorable moment occurs when Ann is alone on a train at night; and, as she is unable to sleep, her face reflects waking nightmares both real and imagined. Curiously, Minnelli, who has painted profound portraits of madness in such films as *Madame Bovary, Cobweb,* and *Lust for Life,* seems ill at ease with the character of Alan, perhaps because his illness is a melodramatic contrivance of the story rather than a subjective state the director understands and with which he feels some kinship. Yet the inferiority and persecuted hysteria suffered by Alan is very characteristic of film noir.

Curiously, Minnelli asserted himself in an unexpected musical context with the "Girl Hunt Ballet" of *The Bandwagon,* which says more about film noir in ten minutes than *Undercurrent* does in two hours. The "Girl Hunt Ballet" is a satire of detective fiction and incorporates the elements of the literary genre into a visually exotic style. Minnelli combines the imaginative choreography by Michael Kidd with a romantic jazz score by Arthur Schwartz and places it within expressionistic sets of stairs that lead nowhere, mazes of decor, and multilevel stages of action. Brilliant colors, a trademark of Minnelli's style, identify the archetypal characters as good or bad, dangerous or innocent.

Fred Astaire dances while his understated narration, written by Minnelli and filled with amusing yet evocative literary clichés, details the latest chapter in the life of detective Rod Riley. Two mysterious women, neither of whom are what they seem, are portrayed through dance by Cyd Charisse. The detective is alone at night in the "sleeping city," with "all the rats in their holes . . . and the lonesome sound of a horn..." when he is interrupted by an apparently innocent blond woman's dilemma and a murder. Rod is suspicious of a seemingly dangerous female cabaret dancer (a brunet dressed in a red-sequined costume) but later discovers the dishonesty of the blond who is a murderess and the faithfulness of the woman in red. Having already avowed that "I hate killers and when I hate, I hate hard," Rod proclaims that "Killers have to die," and shoots the blond. As he and the red-dressed siren walk away into the still sleeping city, he reaffirms that "She was bad . . . she was dangerous. I wouldn't trust her any further than I could throw her. But she was my kind of woman."

—B.L. & E.W.

UNDERWORLD (1927)

Director: Josef von Sternberg
Producer: Hector Turnbull; presented by Adolph Zukor, Jesse L. Lasky (Paramount Famous Players Lasky)
Screenplay: Robert N. Lee, adapted by Charles Furthman; from a story by Ben Hecht
Titles: George Marion, Jr.
Director of Photography: Bert Glennon
Art Director: Hans Dreier

CAST: George Bancroft (Bull Weed), Clive Brook (Rolls Royce), Evelyn Brent (Feathers McCoy), Larry Semon (Slippy Lewis), Fred Kohler (Buck Mulligan), Helen Lynch (Mulligan's Girl Friend), Jerry Mandy (Paloma), Karl Morse (High Collar Sam).
Released: Paramount Famous Players Lasky, August 21, 1927
Running Time: 85 minutes

A top gangster, Bull Weed, maintains a strong grip over the activities of the Chicago underworld. His world is invaded by Rolls Royce, an alcoholic intellectual who, while bringing himself up out of the gutter, falls for Bull's moll, Feathers McCoy. Complications arise for the trio when Bull murders his arch rival in the underworld, Buck Mulligan, and is sent to prison. Feeling betrayed by Feathers and Rolls Royce, Bull's plans for escape include disposal of his two unfaithful comrades. But as the police close in on the jealous fugitive, Rolls and Feathers convince Bull of their complete loyalty. They attempt to fight off the police alongside Bull in his specially equipped apartment. Bull, however, ushers his two young friends out a convenient hidden exit and faces his fate alone.

An unconventional film for its time, *Underworld* may be regarded as the first modern gangster film in which the heroes are actually criminals. There were serious films that dealt with the world of crime and gangsterism prior to *Underworld,* films that were limited by a strong moral code and hampered by a social rationale such as D. W. Griffith's *Musketeers of Pig Alley* and *Dream Street* as well as Allan Dwan's *The Perfect Crime* and *Manhandled. Underworld* eliminated most of the causes for crime and focused on the criminals themselves. The atmosphere of this underworld is enhanced immeasurably by the exotic visual preoccupations of director Josef von Sternberg, which encompass a range of original symbols and imagery. Beyond the stylized nature of von Sternberg's direction, the script, as written by ex-newspaperman Ben Hecht, realistically details the personalities populating the sordid speakeasies and dingy dwellings of the gangsters. As a result, they take on a subtle, almost naturalistic, identity. Hecht's characters contain a strange blend of humor and brutality. Although *Underworld* is not truly a film noir, the overriding implications of claustrophobia, alienation, and corruption combine with the dark ambience of this highly romanticized criminal environment and mark the film as an important noir predecessor.

—C.M.

UNDERWORLD U.S.A. (1961)

Director and Producer: Samuel Fuller (Globe Enterprises)
Screenplay: Samuel Fuller; from the *Saturday Evening Post* articles by Joseph F. Dinneen
Director of Photography: Hal Mohr
Sound: Charles J. Rice, Josh Westmoreland
Music: Harry Sukman
Art Director: Robert Peterson
Set Decoration: Bill Calbert
Costumes: Bernice Pontrelli
Assistant Director: Floyd Joyer
Film Editor: Jerome Thoms

CAST: Cliff Robertson (Tolly Devlin), Dolores Dorn (Cuddles), Beatrice Kay (Sandy), Paul Dubov (Gela), Robert Emhardt (Conners), Larry Gates (Driscoll), Richard Rust (Gus), Gerald Milton (Gunther), Allan Gruener (Smith), David Kent (Tolly at 12), Tina Rome (Woman), Sally Mills (Connie), Robert P. Lieb (Officer), Neyle Morrow (Barney), Henry Norell (Prison Doctor). **BITS:** David Fresco (Convict), Peter Brocco (Vic Farrar), Joni Beth Morris (Jenny), Alan Aaronson, Donald Gamble (Boys), Rickie Sorenson (Harry), Audrey Swanson (Mother), Tom London, Bob Hopkins (Drunks), Charles Sterrett, Bernie Hamilton (Investigators), Jerry Mann (Cashier), Don Douglas (Man), James R. Bacon (Newspaperman).
Filming Completed: August 8, 1960

Released: Columbia, May 13, 1961
Running Time: 99 minutes
[NOTE: a short promotional film, directed by Roy Brickner, was made in which Samuel Fuller explained how and why he wrote *Underworld U.S.A.,* followed by scenes from the production.]

Twelve-year-old Tolly Devlin, the motherless son of a hoodlum, is befriended by Sandy, a speakeasy owner who once loved Tolly's father. They witness the murder of his father by four men, and Tolly swears vengeance. As an adult, Tolly is in prison and recognizes an inmate, Vic Farrar, as one of his father's killers. Dying, Vic tells Tolly the names of the other three murderers who are crime syndicate leaders: Gela, Smith, and Gunther, all working for a gangster named Conners. Tolly is released from prison and returns to see Sandy, whose bar has been taken over by Gela. Tolly fortuitously saves one of Gela's workers, Cuddles, from harm; and she leads Tolly to a cache of heroin. Cuddles is hidden with Sandy while Tolly convinces Gela to hire him, although the mobster knows Tolly is Devlin's son. Tolly persuades Cuddles to identify Smith as a murderer to Driscoll, a government man investigating the crime syndicate; and Smith is arrested. Assigned by Conners to raid Driscoll's files, Tolly arranges with the government man to provide the mobster with phony files incriminating Gela and Gunther as government witnesses; and Conners orders them killed. His father avenged, Tolly refuses to help Driscoll trap Conners, and goes to visit the mobster chieftain. Meeting Gus, one of Conner's hired assassins, Tolly learns he is expected to murder Cuddles. Confronting Conners, Tolly is mortally wounded and dies before Cuddles and Sandy can save him. Cuddles is determined to avenge Tolly's death by testifying against the mob.

Samuel Fuller is a director with a noir bias comparable to that of Nicholas Ray, Robert Siodmak, and Don Siegel. These four men each have different viewpoints, but all of them are singularly suited to film noir and have created films utilizing noir style in all genres. Additionally, Fuller's filmography contains numerous war films and *Underworld U.S.A.* reflects that: it is a war fought between the F.B.I. and the crime syndicate, both of which are described in militaristic terms. The protagonist of *Underworld U.S.A.,* Tolly Devlin, is not only a soldier in the war but also one of its refugees, as an orphan who desires revenge, and ultimately one of its casualties. Like one inured to war's horrors, Tolly is incapable of human response apart from what is needed for the success of his quest. His sexuality, for instance, is dominated by his need for information about his enemies, and making love is essential for eliciting information from Cuddles. Fuller also exploits brutal violence for visual impact. Both Tolly's and Cuddles's faces are marred by vivid bruises and large bandages throughout much of the film; and their visages passively reflect the fundamental and pervasive influence that violence exerts on their lives. Under that influence Tolly is unrelentingly and mechanistically devoted to his personal battle plan, a plan that puts

Tolly Devlin (Cliff Robertson) and Cuddles (Dolores Dorn) in Underworld U.S.A.

Young Tolly (David Kent) and Sandy (Beatrice Kay) find Tolly's father brutally murdered in **Underworld U.S.A.**

him in opposition, supported by Fuller's staging and composition, to both criminal and legal forces. In that self-centered position, Tolly resembles Skip McCoy in Fuller's *Pickup on South Street*. Unlike McCoy, Tolly Devlin is not saved by the influence of Cuddles and Sandy as McCoy was by the similar characters of Candy and Moe in the earlier film. Perhaps because Devlin's overriding motivation is revenge rather than simple avarice, perhaps because the efforts of Cuddles and Sandy in his behalf are not so self-destructive as those of Candy and Moe for McCoy, Devlin does not survive. Like an exhausted warrior, Tolly is literally and figuratively finished when his revenge is complete; and he dies, alone, in the same alley where his father perished to the ironic strains of "Auld Lang Syne."

—M.B. & A.S.

UNION STATION (1950)

Director: Rudolph Maté
Producer: Jules Schermer (Paramount)
Screenplay: Sydney Boehm; from an unpublished story by Thomas Walsh
Director of Photography: Daniel L. Fapp
Process Photography: Farciot Edouart
Sound: Hugo Grenzbach, Gene Garvin
Music Director: Irvin Talbot
Art Directors: Hans Dreier, Earl Hedrick
Set Decoration: Sam Comer, Ray Moyer
Costumes: Mary Kay Dodson
Makeup: Wally Westmore
Production Managers: C. Kenneth DeLand, John Coonan
Assistant Director: Eddie Salven
Script Supervisor: Harry Hogan
Film Editor: Ellsworth Hoagland

CAST: William Holden (Lt. William Calhoun), Nancy Olson (Joyce Willecombe), Barry Fitzgerald (Inspector Donnelly), Lyle Bettger (Joe Beacom), Jan Sterling (Marge Wrighter), Allene Roberts (Lorna Murcall), Herbert Heyes (Henry Murcall), Don Dunning (Gus Hadder), Fred Graff (Vince Marley), James Seay (Detective Shattuck). **BITS:** Parley E. Baer (Gottschalk), Ralph Sanford (Fay), Richard Karlan (George Stein), Bigelow Sayre (Ross), Charles Dayton (Howard Kettner), Jean Ruth (Pretty Girl), Paul Lees (Young Man Masher), Harry Hayden (Conductor Skelly), Ralph Byrd (Priest), Edith Evanson (Mrs. Willecombe), Queenie Smith (Landlady), George M. Lynn (Moreno), Richard Barron (Halloran), Joe Warfield (Manny), Trevor Bardette, Robert Wood, Mike Mahoney (Patrolmen), Robert R. Cornthwaite (Orderly), Clifton Young, Freddie Zendar (Ambulance Drivers), Howard J. Negley (Conductor), Dick Elliott (Employee), Douglas Spencer (Stationmaster), Byron Foulger (Horace), Edgar Dearing, Thomas E. Jackson, Al Ferguson, Howard Mitchell (Detectives),

Sumner Getchell (Police Car Driver), Bob Easton (Cowboy), Bob Hoffman (Messenger), Ralph Montgomery, Jerry James (City Slickers), Bernard Szold (Counterman), Joe Recht (Messenger), John Crawford (Hackett, Clerk), Gil Warren, Eric Alden, Charles Sherlock (Doctors), Jack Gargan (Police Stenographer), Bill Meader (Projectionist), Hans Moebus (Charles, Chauffeur), Jack Roberts (Freddie), Mike P. Donovan (Watchman), Laura Elliot, Barbara Knudson, Gerry Ganzer, Charmienne Harker, Freddie Zendar, Isabel Cushin (Clerks), June Earle (Nurse), Betty Corner (Woman).
Location: Los Angeles, California
Filming Completed: March 7, 1950
Released: Paramount, October 4, 1950
Running Time: 80 minutes

A tense situation develops at Chicago's Union Station when a grotesque loser, Joe Beacom, kidnaps a blind girl. The head of depot security, Lt. Calhoun, must contend with the crisis without causing a panic in the busy train terminal. The police, headed by Inspector Donnelly, are called in when the kidnapper escapes with the child and a concentrated search turns up two of Beacom's accomplices. One is chased into a stockyard where the ensuing gunfire stampedes a herd of cattle ready for slaughter, which leaves the petty hood trampled to death. The second accomplice is easier to catch. When they are unable to get the necessary information out of their suspect, the police threaten to throw him "accidentally" into the path of an oncoming train; and this ruthless tactic secures the needed information. The police arrive at Beacom's hideout only to find the kidnapper and his victim gone. Beacom's mistress tells the police of his plans to murder the girl after he receives the ransom money, and she is shot by Beacom for her treachery. A frantic chase takes place, ending up in an underground tunnel laced with high-tension wires. In a desperate shootout in the electrified tunnel, Calhoun kills Beacom as the ransom money flutters out of the opened suitcase and drifts down the deserted tunnel.

The dehumanization of Joe Beacom, an average man turned into a vile kidnapper, is a characteristic symptom of the sense of helplessness inherent in noir films. There is a cynical outlook that moves beyond the simple apprehension of the criminals. Even the actions of the police, in forcing the suspected kidnapper to talk under the threat of death, suggest an acceptance of their unnecessarily brutal tactics as normal police procedure. The cheapness of life and the level of destructive irony needed to restore order betray a definite noir outlook, despite the routine plot development in *Union Station*. The characters explored in this film exist in a twilight world in which freedom of choice is unknown and temptations fostered by an ill-defined fate lead men through a moral maze as figuratively constricting as the tunnels through which Beacom is pursued and in which he perishes.

—C.M.

THE UNKNOWN MAN

THE UNKNOWN MAN (1951)

[Working Titles: BEHIND THE LAW; THE THIN KNIFE; THE BRADLEY MASON STORY; THE KNIFE]

Director: Richard Thorpe
Producer: Robert Thomsen (MGM)
Screenplay: Ronald Millar and George Froeschel
Director of Photography: William Mellor
Special Effects: A. Arnold Gillespie
Sound: Douglas Shearer
Music Score: Conrad Salinger
Art Directors: Cedric Gibbons, Randall Duell
Set Decoration: Edwin B. Willis, Jacques Mapes
Costumes: Helen Rose
Assistant Director: Al Jennings
Film Editor: Ben Lewis

CAST: Walter Pidgeon (Dwight Bradley Mason), Ann Harding (Stella Mason), Barry Sullivan (Joe Buckner), Keefe Brasselle (Rudy Wolchek), Lewis Stone (Judge Hulbrook), Eduard Franz (Andrew Jason Layford), Richard Anderson (Bob Mason), Dawn Addams (Ellie Fansworth), Phil Ober (Wayne Kellwin), Mari Blanchard (Sally Tever), Konstantin Shayne (Peter Hulderman), Don Beddoe (Fingerprint Man). **BITS:** Holmes Herbert (the Reverend Michael), Jean Andren (Secretary), Richard Hale (Eddie Caraway), Jeff York (Guard), John Maxwell (Doctor Palmer), Margaret Brayton (Mother), Rush Williams (Delivery Man), John Butler, Harry Hines, Ronald Brogan, Robert Scott, Robert Griffin, Frank Gerstle, Jimmy Dodd, Larry Carr, Eric Sinclair (Reporters), King Donovan, Frank Scannell (Photographers), Katherine Meskill (Telephone Operator), Phil Tead (Attendant), Dabbs Greer (Driver), Mira McKinney (Maid), Wheaton Chambers (Bailiff), Richard Karlan (Lieutenant), Bradford Hatton (Plainclothesman), Robert Fould (Sergeant), Emmett Vogan (Court Clerk), Paul Kruger (Prison Guard), Jack Gargan (Male Secretary), Fred Rapport (Butler), Monya Andre, Anna Q. Nilsson, Bess Flowers (Guests), Mae Clarke Langdon (Stella's Friend), Estelle Etterre (Saleswoman), Fred Aldrich (Bailiff), Harte Wayne (Court Clerk), Tay Dunne (Court Reporter), Harry Cody (Detective), Frank Pershing (Foreman of Jury), John Alvin (Photographer), Jack Shea (Sash), Rhea Mitchell (Maid).
Filming Completed: February 2, 1951
Released: MGM, November 16, 1951
Running Time: 88 minutes

District Attorney Joe Buckner, substituting for deceased attorney Dwight Bradley Mason as keynote speaker before a graduating class of law students, which includes Mason's son, tells them the story he believes Mason would want them to hear. Dwight Mason defended Rudy Wolcheck, who was accused of murder, and won the young man's acquittal. Afterwards, Mason suspected Rudy was guilty and found the murder weapon, a long knife hidden in Rudy's walking cane. Mason sought the advice of Andrew

Jason Layford, head of an influential citizen's crime commission, only to discover Layford was leader of the racket that encouraged Rudy to commit murder. Layford boasted that the city was in the palm of his hand, and Mason killed him for "laughing at the law." Rudy was arrested for Layford's murder and, defended by Mason, was convicted and sentenced to death. Mason then admitted his guilt to District Attorney Buckner, who chose to ignore Mason's confession. Requiring punishment, Mason confessed to Rudy in the man's prison cell and dropped a dagger within his reach in hopes of provoking Rudy's vengeance. The plan worked and Rudy stabbed Mason to death, thereby relieving Mason of his guilt before ultimately paying for the murder of his original victim.

As in most of the MGM noir films, production value and acting stylize a conventional, socially conscious plot. It is rather strange to see a romantic actor such as Walter Pidgeon playing the entrapped protagonist and supported by such featured players as Lewis Stone and Ann Harding, who were probably more familiar in comedy or period contexts. Barry Sullivan seems less out of place, and his presence reinforces the thematic insistence on the way an innocent person can be drawn into a crime—and in this instance not a helpless middle-class individual but a powerful and respected attorney. It is also one more fictionalization of the pervasiveness of crime and corruption that seemed to preoccupy America in the 1950s, well summed up by Pidgeon: "This is a city teeming with pride and corruption, where crime operates out of skyscrapers and plush hotels."

—B.P.

THE UNSUSPECTED (1947)

Director: Michael Curtiz
Producer: Charles Hoffman (Michael Curtiz Productions)
Associate Producer: George Amy
Screenplay: Ranald MacDougall, adaptation by Bess Meredyth; from the novel by Charlotte Armstrong
Director of Photography: Woody Bredell
Special Effects: David C. Kertesz, Harry Barndollar, Robert Burks
Sound: Everett A. Brown, Leslie Hewitt
Music Score: Franz Waxman
Music Director: Leo F. Forbstein
Orchestration: Leonid Raab
Art Director: Anton Grot
Set Decoration: Howard Winterbottom
Costumes: Milo Anderson
Makeup: Perc Westmore
Dialogue Director: Jack Meredyth Lucas
Unit Manager: Al Alleborn
Assistant Director: Robert Vreeland
Film Editor: Frederick Richards

CAST: Joan Caulfield (Matilda Frazier), Claude Rains (Alexander Grandison), Audrey Totter (Althea Keane), Constance Bennett (Jane Moynihan), Hurd Hatfield (Oliver Keane), Michael North (Steven Francis Howard), Fred Clark (Richard Donovan), Harry Lewis (Max), Jack Lambert (Mr. Press), Ray Walker (Donovan's Assistant), Nana Bryant (Mrs. White), Walter Baldwin (Justice of the Peace). **BITS:** Barbara Woodell (Roslyn), Douglas Kennedy (Bill), Ross Ford (Irving), Art Gilmore (Announcer), Lucile Vance (Frizzy Haired Woman), David Leonard (Dr. Edelman), Cecil Stewart (Al, Piano Player), Faith Kruger, Bunty Cutler (Women), George Meader (Fritz), Bob Alden (Messenger), Dick Walsh, Ross Ford, Ray Montgomery (Reporters), Ed Parks (Waiter), Walter Baldwin (Dr. White), Eleanor Counts (Bride), Alan Ray (Groom), Jean Andren (Mother of the Bride), Hal Craig, Jack Cheatam (Policemen), Joleen King (Maid), Harriet Matthews (Mannish Woman), Martha Crawford, Wendy Lee (Guests).

Filming Completed: March 15, 1947
Released: Warner Brothers, October 3, 1947
Running Time: 103 minutes

A young woman is murdered by her employer, Alexander Grandison, a noted radio personality, who makes the slaying appear as a suicide. His appetite for death and deception is fed by his radio mystery programs, which detail murder and brutality with shocking accuracy. His well-constructed web of intellectual evil is disturbed when the mysterious Steven Howard returns from the war and attempts to avenge his dead fiancée, Grandison's murdered secretary. Howard uses a number of unsavory methods, including impersonation, to force Grandison to confess to the murder. He tries to convince Grandison's niece, Matilda, that he is her lost husband who wants to help her recover from a nervous breakdown. Finding that the only way to maintain control of the family fortune and keep young Howard from exposing him as a murderer is to strike first, Grandison contacts a fugitive that he is blackmailing and forces him to dispose of the troublesome Howard. Meanwhile, Grandison fails in an attempt to poison Matilda and make it look like a suicide. Howard is saved from death; and Grandison is made to pay for his crimes.

The Unsuspected is one of the few noir films that consciously emphasizes the element of style. Charlotte Armstrong's story serves merely as a framework for Michael Curtiz to construct a visual portrait of a decadent murderer trapped in a world of his own machinations. The use of expressionist lighting, filled with threatening shadows epitomizes the noir pattern. The imaginative direction, highlighted by Woody Bredell's chiaroscuro cinematography links the upper class world of Grandison with that of the unsavory underworld. There is a sequence in *The Unsuspected* that epitomizes the quality of paranoia and claustrophobia so often found in noir films. Jack Lambert as the blackmailed killer lies in bed smoking. The radio is on and Alexander Grandison is detailing the story of his particular crime. The only source of illumination in this dingy hotel room comes from a partially obscured flashing neon sign. The letters that are visible through the window seem to echo the thoughts of the uncomfortable murderer as it keeps blinking "KILL . . . KILL . . . KILL."

—C.M.

VICKI (1953)

Director: Harry Horner
Producer: Leonard Goldstein (20th Century-Fox)
Screenplay: Dwight Taylor, with additional dialogue by Harold Greene and Leo Townsend; from the novel *I Wake Up Screaming* by Steve Fisher
Director of Photography: Milton Krasner
Special Photographic Effects: Ray Kellogg
Sound: E. Clayton Ward, Roger Heman
Music: Leigh Harline
Music Director: Lionel Newman
Song: "Vicki" by Ken Darby and Max Showalter
Orchestration: Edward B. Powell
Art Directors: Lyle Wheeler, Richard Irvine
Set Decoration: Claude Carpenter
Costumes: Renie
Wardrobe Direction: Charles LeMaire
Makeup: Ben Nye
Assistant Director: William Eckhardt
Film Editor: Dorothy Spencer

VICKI

CAST: Jeanne Crain (Jill), Jean Peters (Vicki Lynn), Elliott Reid (Steve Christopher), Richard Boone (Lt. Ed Cornell), Casey Adams (Larry Evans), Alex D'Arcy (Robin Ray), Carl Betz (McDonald), Aaron Spelling (Harry Williams). **BITS:** Roy Engel, Parley Baer, Stuart Randall, Russ Conway, Jack Gargan, Frank Gerstle, Norman Stevens, Jack Mather, Jerome Sheldon, Mike Stark (Detectives), Billy Nelson (Wino), John Dehner (Chief), Richard Garland (Reporter), Ramsay Ames (Café Photographer), Frank Fenton (Eric), Izetta Jewel (Mrs. Mc-Vale), Helene Hayden (Connie), Harry Seymour (Bartender), Irene Seidner (Cleaning Woman), Robert Adler, Harry Carter, Paul Kruger (Policemen), Charles Wagenheim, Al Hill, Kenneth Gibson, Hershel Graham, R. C. McCracken, Brandon Beach, Heinie Conklin (Men), June Glory, Ethel Bryant (Women), Richard West (Delivery Man), Chet Brandenburg (Milkman), Bonnie Paul (Girl), Ron Hargrave (Boy), Kathryn Sheldon (Hotel Clerk), Burt Mustin (Bellboy).
Filming Completed: April 4, 1953
Released: 20th Century-Fox, September 7, 1953
Running Time: 85 minutes

[NOTE: *Vicki* was originally planned to be produced in a stereoscopic process.]

Vicki Lynn, a popular New York model, is murdered, and Detective Lt. Ed Cornell cuts short his vacation to return to the city and take over the investigation. Cornell's suspicions focus on Steve Christopher, Vicki's publicity man, whom the policeman interrogates at length. A flashback discloses the events leading to his discovery of Vicki when she was a waitress in a café and his agreement to promote her into a celebrity. Vicki solidified her newfound status by encouraging the attentions of several prominent men, including Christopher. Cornell's partner questions Vicki's sister, Jill, who provides more information about Vicki's success and her subsequent negotiation without Christopher's assistance of a Hollywood contract; but Jill defends Christopher's reaction to that betrayal of confidence as well as his general motives for handling Vicki. Jill is suggesting that the police search for a man who used to watch Vicki at the café when Cornell enters, and she recognizes him as that very man. Cornell reacts by claiming that surveillance is part of his job and accusing Jill of covering up for Christopher out of infatuation with him. Jill admits that she found Christopher alone with her sister's body; but under renewed interrogation the publicity man will not admit guilt to Cornell. Cornell's superior releases him, on his own assumption that Harry Williams, the night clerk at Vicki's hotel, is guilty; but Cornell clears Williams and renews his harassment of Christopher. When he follows Christopher to a meeting with Jill and overhears her admit to concealing an incriminatory note, Cornell tries to arrest the publicity man but is knocked out by Jill. Now handcuffed, Christopher aranges to meet Jill later but arrives to witness her arrest by Cornell. Christopher goes to the detective's apartment to bargain for Jill's release but is turned away by a panic-stricken Cornell. Instead Christopher makes a deal with Cornell's partner and tricks Williams into confessing. Williams also claims that Cornell knew of his guilt but told him to keep quiet. When the group breaks into Cornell's apartment, they find it filled with photos and other memorabilia of Vicki Lynn. Cornell admits his own love for Vicki and hatred of Christopher for taking her out of his reach.

Vicki, a second adaptation of Steve Fisher's *I Wake Up Screaming,* uses a complicated flashback structure to unmask the self-serving motivations of virtually all its characters. The vacationing Cornell's reaction to the newspaper story detailing the death of Vicki Lynn immediately suggests the obsessive nature of his involvement with the crime. His persecution of the prime suspect, Steve Christopher, is reminicent of Mark McPherson's insistent probing in Preminger's *Laura.* But while the class-conscious McPherson found himself suddenly immersed in a milieu of snobbish sophistication only to discover that Laura was ultimately obtainable, Cornell's relationship to Vicki, as the subsequent narrative illustrates, is abrogated before the film begins. Moreover, the pre-credit night sequence of Vicki's body being carried out of her tenementlike hotel initially associates the dead woman with a background far different from that of Laura's richly furnished apartment. In contrast to Laura, Vicki is of a fundamentally proletarian background; and that background, particularized by the café where Cornell spied on her and fantasized her into a love object is the ironic cause of her death. Cornell's refurnishing of his apartment into a shrine to Vicki, where Christopher and the others discover him amid his pictures and votive candles, celebrates Vicki as he knew her, as a proletarian idol.

This revelation of Cornell's incipient madness is only one aspect of *Vicki*'s sardonic structure. The character of Vicki is presented as exploitive and ruthlessly ambitious with little regard for those who have helped her. The relentless investigation of her murder by Cornell becomes, in this context, a legalistic formality without benefit of audience empathy. The amount of empathy focused on Christopher is also questionable, since, although he is physically guiltless of Vicki's murder, his motives for promoting her are suspect and his tricking of Williams is technically illegal. A triangular relationship develops between Cornell, Christopher, and Williams both because of their fascination with Vicki and because Cornell knew of Williams's guilt. In fact, Cornell's reaction is not unlike Kristo's pursuit of Fabian rather than the strangler after his father's death in *Night and the City*—both bypass the man who actually killed to focus on one whom they consider morally responsible. Cornell's belief that Christopher has casually corrupted Vicki—and ultimately caused her death—by promoting her almost on a whim is at minimum partly true. As all of its characters lose audience sympathy, *Vicki* becomes even more a study in total alienation, underscored by the final shot that moves ironically from Christopher and Jill to a billboard overhead where Vicki's likeness is being replaced by that of another.
— WRE & A.S.

WHEN STRANGERS MARRY (1944)

Director: William Castle
Executive Producer: Maurice King (King Brothers)
Producer: Franklin King
Screenplay: Philip Yordan and Dennis J. Cooper; from an unpublished story by George V. Moscov
Director of Photography: Ira Morgan
Sound: Tom Lambert
Music Score: Dimitri Tiomkin
Music Editor: Leon Birnbaum
Art Director: Paul Sylos
Assistant Director: Clarence Bricker
Film Editor: Martin G. Cohn

CAST: Dean Jagger (Paul), Kim Hunter (Millie), Robert Mitchum (Fred Graham), Neil Hamilton (Blake), Lou Lubin (Houser), Milt Kibbee (Charlie), Dewey Robinson (Newsstand Man), Claire Whitney (Middle-aged Woman), Edward Keane (Middle-aged Man), Virginia Sale (Chambermaid), Dick Elliot (Sam Prescott), Lee "Lasses" White (Old Man).
Filming Completed: August 7, 1944
Released: Monogram, August 21, 1944
Running Time: 67 minutes

Sam Prescott, attending a Lions Club convention in New York City, is drunk in a bar and foolishly reveals he is carrying a large sum of money. He meets a man in the bar who has no hotel room and after he offers to share his room, Prescott leaves with the stranger. The next morning Prescott is found strangled and his money gone. Shortly afterward, Millie Baxter checks into Prescott's hotel where she is to be reunited with her new husband, Paul. In the lobby she coincidentally meets her old boyfriend, Fred Graham, who tells her of the murder and offers best wishes for her recent marriage. Paul fails to arrive and Millie spends a lonely night in the hotel room. The next day, Fred urges her to report Paul's disappearance to the police. Later, Paul telephones her and asks her to meet him secretly. His subsequent behavior causes Millie to fear he is involved with Prescott's murder. As they elude the police together, Paul confesses to Millie that he was the stranger in the bar. Although tempted, Paul claims that he did not take the money, and that when he left Prescott's room the man was alive. As Paul finishes his story, the police capture the newlyweds. But new evidence indicates Fred Graham com-

mitted the murder, and the police arrest him at the hotel as he attempts to slip the stolen money into a mail slot.

Despite a convoluted, Woolrich-like plot, *When Strangers Marry* is a good example of the B thriller structure and represents the initial contributions of writer Philip Yordan and the King Brothers to the noir cycle. In this early success, director William Castle (who quickly moved on to suspense-exploitation films), is influenced by the styles of Alfred Hitchcock and Val Lewton as he creates an oppressive New York atmosphere in studio sets. This artificial setting is laced with those undertones of fear and hysteria that constitute some of the definitive motifs of the noir studio film. Millie Baxter is alone and frightened in a hotel room with jazz blaring next door, while the neon "dancing" sign alternately fills the room with light then leaves it in darkness. A fear-ridden bartender agonizes over the dim memory of a murderer's appearance and the once-jovial dead man, whose face was grotesquely covered by a lion's head. A young woman rushes home through a dark urban tunnel haunted by the huge faces superimposed over her lonely figure. Finally, Robert Mitchum, as Fred Graham, loses his cool exterior, and for the first time reveals a portrayal of perverse lunacy that would dominate such later motion pictures as *Night of the Hunter* and *Cape Fear*.

—B.P.

WHERE DANGER LIVES (1950)
[Working Title: WHITE ROSE FOR JULIE]

Director: John Farrow
Producer: Irving Cummings Jr. (Cummings-Allen-RKO)
Associate Producer: Irwin Allen
Screenplay: Charles Bennett; from an unpublished story by Leo Rosten
Director of Photography: Nicholas Musuraca
Sound: John Tribby, Clem Portman
Music Score: Roy Webb
Music Director: Constantin Bakaleinikoff
Art Directors: Albert S. D'Agostino, Ralph Berger
Set Decoration: Darrell Silvera, John Sturtevant
Costumes: Michael Woulfe
Makeup: Mel Berns
Hairstyles: Larry Germain

WHERE THE SIDEWALK ENDS

Production Manager: Eddie Donahoe
Assistant Director: Samuel Ruman
Script Supervisor: Irving Cooper
Film Editor: Eda Warren

CAST: Robert Mitchum (Jeff Cameron), Faith Domergue (Margo Lannington), Claude Rains (Frederick Lannington), Maureen O'Sullivan (Julie), Charles Kemper (Police Chief), Ralph Dumke (Klauber), Billy House (Mr. Bogardus), Harry Shannon (Dr. Maynard), Philip Van Zandt (Milo DeLong), Jack Kelly (Dr. Mullenbach), Lillian West (Mrs. Bogardus). **BITS:** Ruth Lewis (Nurse Collins), Julia Faye (Nurse Seymour), Dorothy Abbott (Nurse Clark), Gayelord Pendleton, Joey Ray, Lestor Dorr, Jerry James (Policemen), Art Dupuis (Intern), Stanley Andrews (Dr. Mathews), Jack Kruschen (Casey), Elaine Riley (Nurse Bates), Gordon Clark (Attendant), Geraldine Wall (Annie), David Stollery (Boy), Sherry Jackson (Girl in Iron Lung), Clifford Brooke (Butler), Jim Dundee (Taxi Driver), Tol Avery (Honest Hal), Ann Zika (Woman), Robert Stevenson (Clerk), Ethan Laidlaw, Earle Hodgins, William Bailey (Men), Gene Barnes (Tipsy Youth), Ray Teal (Joe Borden), Duke York (Cowboy), Earle Hodgins, Marie Allison, Grace MacNaughton (Girls), Julian Rivero (Pablo), George Sherwood (Quartz Miner), Len Henry, Don House (Policemen), John Sheehan (Quartz Miner), James Brick Sullivan, Carlos Albert, Mike Lally, Philip Ahlm (Customs Officers), Tina Menard (Cashier), Stuart Holmes, Frank Leyuda, Carl Sklover (Men), Jeraldine Jordan, Hazel Boyne (Women), Erno Verebes (Waiter), Betty Hannon (Girl), Florence Hamblin, Amilda Cuddy (Hawaiians), Allen Mathews (Waiter), Maxine Gates (Girl in Act), Phil Boutelje (Pianist), Herschel Daugherty (Desk Clerk), Linda Johnson (Airport Announcer), Marie Thomas, Gerry Ganzer (Stewardesses), Bob Coleman (Airport Official), Carl Saxe, Marvin Jones (Policemen), Helen Brown (Nurse), William E. Green (Doctor).
Filming Completed: February 22, 1950
Released: RKO, July 14, 1950
Running Time: 82 minutes

Margo, the young wife of wealthy Frederick Lannington, is mentally ill and has had many love affairs. After attempting suicide, she is treated by a young doctor, Jeff Cameron, who is unaware of her mental condition and is attracted to her. He breaks off with his girl friend, Julie, when Margo insinuates that Lannington is her father. Later, Jeff learns the truth but is heedless of Lannington's warnings regarding Margo's mental state. One night the two men fight and Lannington is knocked out. When Jeff leaves the room for a moment, Margo smothers Lannington with a pillow and Jeff believes he has killed him. Convincing Jeff that they must leave the country, they begin driving to Mexico at once despite Jeff's symptoms of a concussion. They suspect the police are chasing them and make secret and expensive arrangements to cross the border. Before they cross, however, Jeff realizes Margo is psychotic. She attempts to kill him and enter into Mexico alone; but Jeff struggles to follow and stop her. At the border, Margo shoots Jeff and is subsequently shot by the police and confesses to her husband's murder before dying. Jeff recovers and is reunited with Julie.

Where Danger Lives is in many respects quite similar to Preminger's film, *Angel Face,* particularly the role played by Robert Mitchum as Jeff. A domestic scene enlivened by sex and murder is rather a cliché of the noir series by this time; but veteran director John Farrow (at the peak of his form when working with John Seitz in *The Big Clock),* and RKO cameraman Nick Musuraca imbued this film with a typically dark visual style that isolates details of an imaginative *mise-en-scène* from Claude Rains's mischievous smile to Faith Domergue's pouting sexuality unrelenting even as she is gunned down in a spotlight at the border fence. Once again the sloe-eyed Mitchum does well in exhibiting his passive vulnerability, as Domergue seduces him into being a murder accomplice after the fact and takes him on a nightmare journey from the manors of Northern California and the prestige of a medical practice to being a fugitive in a dingy border town. Jeff's infatuation with the exotic Margo makes him a considerably weaker character than the one he portrays in Farrow's *His Kind of Woman;* but unlike the ambulance driver in *Angel Face,* he does possess the underlying strength to realize his error and to survive.
—B.P. & A.S.

WHERE THE SIDEWALK ENDS (1950)
[Working Title: NIGHT CRY]

Director and Producer: Otto Preminger (20th Century-Fox)
Associate Producer: Frank P. Rosenberg
Screenplay: Ben Hecht, adapted by Victor Trivas, Frank P. Rosenberg, and Robert E. Kent; from the novel *Night Cry* by William L. Stuart
Director of Photography: Joseph LaShelle
Special Effects: Fred Sersen
Sound: Alfred Bruzlin, Harry M. Leonard
Music: Cyril Mockridge
Music Director: Lionel Newman
Orchestration: Edward Powell
Art Directors: Lyle Wheeler, J. Russell Spencer
Set Decoration: Thomas Little, Walter M. Scott
Costumes: Oleg Cassini
Wardrobe Director: Charles LeMaire
Makeup: Ben Nye
Production Manager: Sam Wurtzel
Assistant Director: Henry Weinberger
Script Supervisor: Kathleen Fagan
Film Editor: Louis Loeffler

CAST: Dana Andrews (Mark Dixon), Gene Tierney (Morgan Taylor), Gary Merrill (Scalise), Bert Freed (Klein),

Mark Dixon (Dana Andrews) drags Ken Paine's (Craig Stevens) body in Where The Sidewalk Ends.

Tom Tully (Jiggs Taylor), Karl Malden (Lt. Thomas), Ruth Donnelly (Martha), Craig Stevens (Ken Paine), Robert Simon (Inspector Foley), Harry von Zell (Ted Morrison), Don Appell (Willie), Neville Brand (Steve), Grace Mills (Mrs. Tribaum), Lou Krugman (Mike Williams), David McMahon (Harrington), David Wolfe (Sid Kramer), Steve Roberts (Gilruth), Phil Tully (Tod Benson), Ian MacDonald (Casey), John Close (Hanson), John McGuire (Gertessen), Lou Nova (Ernie). **BITS:** Oleg Cassini (Mayer), Louise Lorimer (Mrs. Jackson), Lester Sharpe (Friedman), Chili Williams (Teddy), Robert Foulk (Feeney), Eda Reiss Merin (Mrs. Kelin), Mack Williams (Morris), Duke Watson (Cab Driver), Clancy Cooper (Lt. Arnaldo), Bob Evans (Sweatshirt), Joseph Granby (Fat Man), Barry Brooks, Ott George (Thugs), Wanda Smith, Shirley Tegge (Models), Louise Lane (Secretary), Gus Lax (Cab Driver), John P. Barrett (Dealer), Milton Gowman, Lee MacGregor (Men), John Daheim, Tony Barr (Hoodlums), John Marshall, Clarence Straight (Detectives), John Trebach (Bartender), Herbert Lytton (Joe), Kathleen Hughes (Secretary), Peggy O'Connor (Model).
Location: New York, New York

Released: 20th Century-Fox, July 7, 1950
Running Time: 95 minutes

A police officer with a history of unnecessary brutality, Mark Dixon, inadvertently kills a robbery suspect while trying to get some information out of him. He camouflages the accidental slaying by making the whole incident appear a gangland murder. However, the circumstantial evidence leads to Jiggs Taylor, a cab driver whose daughter, Morgan, was involved with the murdered man. Through the course of the investigation, Morgan falls in love with Dixon. This unexpected relationship causes the entire situation to become extremely complicated. In a final attempt to swing the evidence away from Morgan's father and into the lap of Scalise, an important underworld figure, Dixon comes face to face with the mobster and his henchmen. A shoot-out at Scalise's meeting place leaves the mobster dead and Jiggs and Dixon apparently clear of the murder charges. But in a final moment of moral reassessment, Dixon confesses to the original killing and goes to jail satisfied in the knowledge that Morgan will be waiting for him when he gets out.

Written by Ben Hecht and directed by Otto Preminger,

WHILE THE CITY SLEEPS

Where the Sidewalk Ends concerns itself with a hero of questionable virtue and limited potency trying to react to a society of confused moral values. The character of Mark Dixon is plagued by the shadow of his father, a onetime mobster. His brutal treatment of criminal suspects gives a strangely distorted and easily corruptible quality to the image of authority he portrays; and this brand of corruption, linked with the potential for violence lurking below the veneer of urban society, is an important noir motif. Hecht takes this situation one step further by presenting the police, in the guise of Dixon, as violent and unstable. It is this lack of control, and the eventual nightmare it produces, which forms the central noir statement of the film. In attempting to come to grips with the obvious incongruities of his position, Dixon becomes an archetypical noir hero, a man both existentially adrift and trapped by circumstance, whose redemption—but not salvation—is made possible by his own ironic sense of justice. Hecht's film scripts in the late 1940s replaced such grotesque figures as Tony Camonte in *Scarface* and Anthony Mallare in *The Scoundrel* with such noir everymen as Mark Dixon in *Where the Sidewalk Ends* and Gagan in *Ride the Pink Horse*. There is a common feeling of alienation and loneliness that molds these characters of Hecht's imagination. Not only do the heroes of Hecht's screenplays change drastically, but the underworld he created has been transformed into a realistic backdrop, ideal for the criminal acts and capers of dark personalities. It is a vision of the urban jungle far removed from the gallant settings of *Underworld* and *Scarface*. *Where the Sidewalk Ends* reunites many of the elements of Preminger's earlier noir film *Laura*. However, under Hecht's influence, the decadent world of the corrupted upper class explored in *Laura* has been replaced by a gritty, naturalistic milieu. Both *Laura* and *Where the Sidewalk Ends* do demonstrate Preminger's precise visual style. But the quasi-romantic preoccupation that embellishes Vera Caspary's mystery works against Hecht's major concerns. One film remains noir due mainly to its exposure of corruption on a high social level; the other becomes noir through detailing the exploits of a less-than-powerful hero involved in a deeply corrupted society.

—C.M.

WHILE THE CITY SLEEPS (1956)
[Working Title: NEWS IS MADE AT NIGHT]

Director: Fritz Lang
Producer: Bert Friedlob (Bert E. Friedlob Productions)
Screenplay: Casey Robinson; from the novel *The Bloody Spur* by Charles Einstein
Director of Photography: Ernest Laszlo
Sound: Jack Solomon, Buddy Myers
Music: Herschel Burke Gilbert
Art Director: Carroll Clark
Costumes: Bob Martien, Jackie Spitzer

Assistant Director: Ronnie Rondell
Supervising Editor: Gene Fowler, Jr.

CAST: Dana Andrews (Edward Mobley), Rhonda Fleming (Dorothy Kyne), George Sanders (Mark Loving), Howard Duff (Lt. Burt Kaufman), Thomas Mitchell (John Day Griffith), Vincent Price (Walter Kyne, Jr.), Sally Forrest (Nancy Liggett), John Barrymore, Jr. (Robert Manners), James Craig (Harry Kritzer), Ida Lupino (Mildred Donner), Robert Warwick (Amos Kyne), Ralph Peters (Meade), Vladimir Sokoloff (George Pilski), Mae Marsh (Mrs. Manners), Sandy White (Judith Fenton).

Filming Completed: 1955
Released: RKO, May 16, 1956
Running Time: 99 minutes

A series of brutal sex murders is terrifying the city, and the yet unidentified murderer is dubbed the "lipstick killer." Dilettante Walter Kyne, Jr., has just inherited one of the city's major newspapers and announces a competition among his staff editors to find the killer. The winner will be the paper's new editor in chief. Griffith, the city editor, enlists the aid of his friend, reporter Edward Mobley, who in turn is a friend of a policeman investigating the case. Debonair Mark Loving, the wire service editor, uses Mildred Donner, his attractive mistress who is also a reporter, to get information from Mobley. The photo editor, Harry Kritzer, uses his romantic influence with Kyne's wife, Dorothy, to secure the new position for himself. Mobley is persuaded to use his girl friend Nancy Liggett as "bait" for the killer, which almost costs her life. Finally the pursuit of the crazed killer—a delivery boy—ends in the subway, where Mobley captures him. Griffith wins the new job, while Mobley and Nancy patch up their relationship.

This film is a multifaceted drama, in which two equally interesting threads—the lipstick killings and the competition for the newspaper's editorship—are woven together by a well-constructed screenplay. The pitiable murderer, given to outbursts of bitterness and rage in the company of his mother, emerges as a vivid and fully realized character in his own right despite the narrative emphasis on the newspaper people. They are admittedly an interesting and realistic ensemble, especially as played by Dana Andrews, Ida Lupino, and George Sanders. Since the killer cannot help himself and is even compulsively given to writing "Catch me before I kill again," there is an unusual reversal in which he is more sympathetic than the newspaper people who will do anything to get ahead (even Mobley's participation is initially due to financial considerations). Indeed, the fact that three men in this story willingly use their girl friends as "bait" of one kind or another does not speak well for their fundametnal humanity.

Fritz Lang's style had become very refined by the time of this film, one of his last; and it is revealing of how an effective film noir can be created without recourse to a great deal of the stylistic mannerisms of moody lighting and bizarre camera angles. Lang remained subtly expressionistic in his use of decor as illustrated by Kyne's apartment, which is reminiscent of the silent "Dr. Mabuse" films; but the simple formal beauty of *While the City Sleeps* is disdainful of affectation that would undermine the lucidity of its presentation. Lang effectively undercuts viewer certainty about anything, including the intrusions of the killer and the motives of the characters. Affinities of composition and judicious editing integrate the killer into the world in which the "normal" people move; and in the climax both killer and reporter run through the darkness of the subway tunnels that lie beneath the city streets. The true suspense of the film is manifest in the narrative probing of the critical relationship between society's illnesses and its normality; and the formal precision of each scene reasserts the existence of this relationship. One of the central values implicit in film noir is that there is no separation between the disturbed depths of a society (its noir underworld) and the acceptable modes of living within that society.

—B.L.

WHITE HEAT (1949)

Director: Raoul Walsh
Producer: Lou Edelman (Warner Brothers)

Screenplay: Ivan Goff and Ben Roberts; suggested by a story by Virginia Kellogg
Director of Photography: Sid Hickox
Special Effects: Roy Davidson, H. F. Koenekamp
Sound: Leslie G. Hewitt
Music Score: Max Steiner
Orchestration: Murray Cutter
Art Director: Edward Carrere
Set Decoration: Fred M. MacLean
Costumes: Leah Rhodes
Assistant Director: Russell Saunders
Script Supervisor: Irva Mae Ross
Film Editor: Owen Marks

CAST: James Cagney (Cody Jarrett), Virginia Mayo (Verna Jarrett), Edmond O'Brien (Hank Fallon/Vic Pardo), Margaret Wycherly (Ma Jarrett), Steve Cochran (Big Ed Somers), John Archer (Phillip Evans), Wally Cassell (Cotton Valetti), Fred Clark (the Trader), Ford Rainey (Zuckie Hommell), Fred Coby (Happy Taylor), G. Pat Collins (the Reader), Mickey Knox (Het Kohler), Paul Guilfoyle (Roy Parker), Robert Osterloh (Tommy Ryley), Ian MacDonald (Bo Creel), Ray Montgomery (Trent).
BITS: Jim Toney (Brakeman), Leo Cleary (Fireman), Murray Leonard (Engineer), Terry O'Sullivan (Radio Announcer), Marshall Bradford (Chief of Police),

Left to right: Cody Jarrett (James Cagney), Verna Jarrett (Virginia Mayo) and Hank Fallon (Edmund O'Brien) in White Heat.

George Taylor (Police Surgeon), Milton Parsons (Willie Rolf), John Pickard, Eddie Phillips (Government Agents), Joel Allen (Operative), Claudia Barrett (Cashier), Buddy Gorman (Vendor), DeForest Lawrence (Jim Donovan), Garrett Craig (Ted Clark), George Spaulding (Judge), Sherry Hall (Clerk), Ray Bennett, Harry Strang, Lee Phelps (Guards), Sid Melton (Russell Hughes), Carl Harbough (Foreman), Jack Worth, Bob Fowke, Art Foster, Arthur Miles, Jim Thorpe (Guards), Ralph Volkie (Lawyer), Fern Eggen (Margaret Baxter), Eddie Foster (Lefeld), Perry Ivins (Prison Doctor), Larry McGrath (Clocker), Grandon Rhodes, John McGuire (Psychiatrists), Herschel Dougherty (Policeman), Norman Leary (Attendant), Joey Ray, Bob Carson (Agents), John Butler (Man).

Released: Warner Brothers, September 2, 1949
Running Time: 114 minutes

After robbing a train, Cody Jarrett and his gang, including his mother, take refuge in a mountain cabin. Cody suffers from blinding headaches relieved only by the attentions of Ma Jarrett, while one gang member, Big Ed, covets both the gang's leadership and Cody's wife, Verna. Cody confesses to a lesser crime in order to avoid implication in the murder of a railroad man. In prison, he is befriended by Vic Pardo, who is actually Hank Fallon, an undercover police detective. Cody learns that Big Ed and Verna have murdered Ma and he breaks down hysterically in the prison dining hall. With Fallon's help Cody escapes and kills Big Ed, but Verna persuades him that she is innocent of Ma's murder. Cody then plans a payroll robbery, which is frustrated by Fallon and results in the deaths of all of the gang members. Mortally wounded, Cody shoots it out from the top of a huge tank of explosive gas, which finally blows up as he shouts to his dead mother that he is "on top of the world."

White Heat's Cody Jarrett is one of film noir's most crippled and maladjusted protagonists. Nevertheless, on the strength of James Cagney's interpretation of the role and Walsh's direction, Cody is a believable figure whose violent nature and desire for a perverse kind of glory prevent the character from becoming a caricature. In contrast, the ostensible hero of the film, Fallon, has a monotonous and impersonal normality and seems more a betrayer than an agent of justice, especially in view of the psychological methods he uses to gain Cody's trust. *White Heat* is not notable for expressionistic lighting or oppressive doom-laden camera angles. But it is a film noir, with a visual character appropriate to the cycle. In place of the more common characteristics, Walsh employs arresting moves of the camera, which build tension by virtue of their economy. The introduction of Verna in close-up and the following of her movements as she gets out of bed in this shot, as well as the sudden move back from Cody as he has his first headache and slumps to the floor in agony, are effective moments of *mise-en-scène*. Other shots establish the fatal links between characters, such as the one in which Big Ed and Verna kiss while chewing gum and the camera pans

rapidly to Ma observing them from a window. The energy of Walsh's camera style in the prison dining room sequence, which combines high angles and dynamic tracking shots, complements the celebrated playing of this scene by Cagney. The presence of conventional sequences and characters in the law enforcement episodes sets off the darker scenes, which focus on Cody, Verna, Big Ed, and Ma and which are the core of the narrative. The tone of individual scenes is alternately stark, humorous, violent, brooding, and, finally, powerful. Further, while the myth of the heroic outlaw is time honored, the strategy of inducing the audience to accept a psychotic protagonist as representative of this myth is intuitively modern. In keeping with this approach, Walsh subtly modifies his traditional style without sacrificing it. A tragic grandeur, often elusive in the postwar cinema, is achieved through this style and culminates in Cody's delirious and explosive self-immolation atop a metallic pyre.

—B.L.

THE WINDOW (1949)

Director: Ted Tetzlaff
Producer: Frederic Ullman, Jr. (RKO)
Screenplay: Mel Dinelli; from the novelette *The Boy Cried Murder* by Cornell Woolrich
Director of Photography: William Steiner
Special Effects: Russell A. Cully
Sound: Earl A. Wolcott, Terry Kellum
Music Score: Roy Webb
Music Director: Constantin Bakaleinikoff
Art Directors: Walter E. Keller, Sam Corso
Set Decoration: Darrell Silvera, Harley Miller
Production Manager: Walter Daniels
Assistant Director: Sal Scoppa, Jr., Earl Harper
Script Supervisor: Bill Shanks
Film Editor: Frederic Knudtson

CAST: Barbara Hale (Mrs. Woodry), Bobby Driscoll (Tommy), Arthur Kennedy (Mr. Woodry), Paul Stewart (Joe Kellerton), Ruth Roman (Mrs. Kellerton). **BITS:** Anthony Ross (Ross), Richard Benedict (Drunken Seaman), Jim Nolan (Stranger on Street), Ken Terrell (Man), Lee Phelps, Eric Mack, Charles Flynn, Budd Fine, Carl Faulkner, Lloyd Dawson, Carl Saxe (Police Officers), Lee Kass (Reporter), Tex Swan (Milkman).
Location: New York, New York
Filming Completed: January 6, 1948
Released: RKO, August 1949
Running Time: 73 minutes

The Woodrys are a working-class family living in a tenement in New York's Lower East Side. Their young son, Tommy, often tells innocent lies that embarrass the family. One hot summer night, Tommy goes out onto the fire

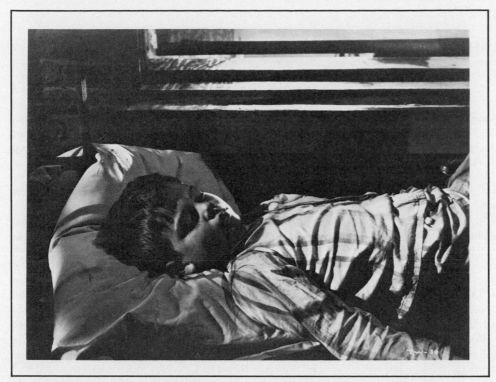

Tommy (Bobby Driscoll) in The Window.

escape to sleep and climbs up one floor to cool off. There he observes the Kellertons through the window robbing and killing a drunken seaman. Frightened, Tommy runs back to his apartment and tells what he saw, but his parents do not believe him. So he sneaks out and reports the incident to the police, who send an investigator posing as a building inspector. When he finds nothing, he informs Mrs. Woodry that Tommy visited the police; and she forces Tommy to apologize to Mrs. Kellerton. Tommy now feels threatened because the Kellertons realize he witnessed their crime. The following evening Mrs. Woodry must leave Tommy alone in the apartment; and he writes a note saying that he is running away and adding a postscript that he really did witness the murder. His father returns to the apartment before departing for work, catches Tommy, locks him in his room and nails the windows shut. Then Mr. Woodry leaves for work unaware of Tommy's note. Later, Joe Kellerton enters the Woodry apartment; he finds the note and carefully rips off the postscript. He "helps" Tommy escape and says they are going to tell the police the truth. Tommy evades Kellerton's grasp, but he is recaptured on the subway and knocked unconscious. Returning to the apartment, Kellerton places the child on the fire escape ledge expecting him to fall. Mrs. Kellerton tries to prevent the fall; and Tommy escapes to a condemned building next door, followed by the Kellertons. Meanwhile Mr. Woodry comes

home early and, suspicious, asks the police to find Tommy. The boy stumbles across the drunk's corpse in the condemned building and runs up the staircase as the building begins to collapse. He climbs out on a bare rafter and Kellerton follows, but Tommy causes him to fall. The police arrest Mrs. Kellerton and persuade Tommy to jump into a net. Safe, Tommy promises never to lie again.

The Window, one of the most financially successful thrillers of 1949, exploits the ironies of childhood paranoia of adults. Director Tetzlaff uses experience gained as the cinematographer of several Hitchcock films and benefits from a well-constructed script by Mel Dinelli, who also wrote *Spiral Staircase,* to transpose Woolrich's darkly oppressive vision of New York City into the studio settings of *The Window.* This film uses location shots to create an American urban landscape that seems almost infernal with its decaying tenement buildings baking in the hot sun while laundry, hanging on clotheslines outside, provides the only glimpse of cleanliness. The neighborhood's disreputable streets are enclosed by the elevated train and parallel the quality of the inhabitants' lives. Such a world represents the inverse of the American dream of freedom; and it is not surprising that when his mother tells him not to go out of the apartment, Tommy replies ingenuously that "There's no place for me to go."
　　　　　　　　　　　　　　　　　　　　　　　—B.P.

313

WITNESS TO MURDER

WITNESS TO MURDER (1954)

Director: Roy Rowland
Producer and Screenplay: Chester Erskine (Chester Erskine Productions)
Director of Photography: John Alton
Sound: Jack A. Goodrich, Joel Moss
Music: Herschel Burke Gilbert
Song: [Title unknown] by Herschel Burke Gilbert and Sylvia Fine
Art Director: William Ferrari
Film Editor: Robert Swink

CAST: Barbara Stanwyck (Cheryl Draper), George Sanders (Albert Richter), Gary Merrill (Lawrence Mathews), Jesse White (Eddie Vincent), Harry Shannon (Capt. Donnelly), Claire Carleton (the Blond), Lewis Martin (Psychiatrist), Dick Elliott (Apartment Manager), Harry Tyler (Charlie), Juanita Moore (Woman), Joy Hallward (Woman's Coworker), Adeline DeWalt Reynolds (Old Lady), Gertrude Graner (Policewoman).
Filming Completed: December 1953
Released: United Artists, April 15, 1954
Running Time: 81 minutes

One evening Cheryl Draper is awakened by the wind and, closing her window, she witnesses a man murder a young woman in the apartment directly across the way. The man is Albert Richter, a historical writer; and he is killing his mistress before she upsets his approaching marriage to a wealthy woman. Cheryl calls the police; but Richter hides the body in an unoccupied apartment, and the police inform Cheryl that she was mistaken. Learning that Cheryl reported the incident, Richter visits her socially and tampers with her lock, so that he can get into the apartment when she is gone. He writes and mails a series of threatening letters to himself on her typewriter and later shows them to the police as evidence that she is harassing him and is mentally disturbed. She is temporarily committed to a mental hospital when she breaks down under the strain of Richter's accusations. When she is released, she observes Richter reading newspaper stories telling that his victim's body has been discovered. Cheryl deduces how Richter framed her and she confronts him. Unafraid of her "neurotic" accusations, Richter reveals his neo-Nazi beliefs and claims that the woman's life was insignificant compared to the importance of his future. He threatens to forge a suicide note and murder Cheryl, but she escapes. Pursued by Richter, she runs into a building under construction and climbs up onto the wooden scaffolding. The police arrive and Richter falls to his death in a fight, while Cheryl is saved before the scaffolding collapses.

When *Witness to Murder* was released in 1954 it was promoted as "topping the thrills of *Double Indemnity* and *Sorry, Wrong Number.*" A well-constructed film that generates some suspense, *Witness to Murder* is compromised by its position late in the noir cycle, by which time most of its formal devices—an innocent witness to murder, a hysterical victim to whom the city is indifferent, and a woman trapped in a psycho ward—had become conventions. The sequence of Stanwyck in the mental ward, repulsed by the other patients and interviewed by a psychiatrist, is shot from an exceedingly high angle with a number of oblique shadows to heighten the feeling of entrapment in a manner reminiscent of *The Snake Pit* and *The Lost Weekend.* Of course, Stanwyck effectively constructs what is for her a composite of many past roles, and the same is true of George Sanders's performance; but the narrative concept of a crypto-fascist rising to power was quite dated by 1954. Alton's photography is, as always, evocative—especially in the opening shot of the hot, nocturnal wind blowing the awning of one of those all-too-typical West Los Angeles apartments that frames the figure of Stanwyck rising and walking to the window, only to become a witness to murder. Unlike *Scene of the Crime* and *Rogue Cop,* director Rowland does not organize the elements of *Witness to Murder* in such a way as to suggest a surrounding noir milieu of explosive instability. Richter's threat to Cheryl is much more personal and physical than the vague, criminal underworld that thwarts and menaces the police characters in those other films. In fact, the central irony of *Witness to Murder* is that Richter is able to recruit the agencies of social stability to persecute the hapless Cheryl. Cheryl's fortuitous survival undercuts to some degree the noir statement of the film and reduces the symbolic value of Richter's character to that of a simple stereotype.

—B.P. & A.S.

THE WOMAN IN THE WINDOW (1945)

Director: Fritz Lang
Producer: Nunnally Johnson (International Pictures)
Screenplay: Nunnally Johnson; from the novel *Once Off Guard* by J. H. Wallis
Director of Photography Milton Krasner
Special Effects: Vernon Walker
Sound: Frank McWhorter
Music Score: Arthur Lange
Art Director: Duncan Cramer
Set Decoration: Julia Heron
Costumes: Muriel King for Joan Bennett
Still Photographer: Ed Henderson
Assistant Director: Richard Harlan
Film Editors: Marjorie Johnson, Gene Fowler, Jr.
Supervising Editor: Paul Weatherwax

CAST: Edward G. Robinson (Ricahrd Wanley), Joan Bennett (Alice Reed), Raymond Massey (Frank Lalor), Edmond Breon (Dr. Barkstane), Dan Duryea (Heidt), Thomas E. Jackson (Inspector Jackson), Arthur Loft (Mazard), Dorothy Peterson (Mrs. Wanley), Frank Dawson (Steward), Carol Cameron (Elsie), Bobby Blake (Dickie). **BITS:** Frank Melton, Don Brodie (Men in front of Art Gallery), Alec Craig (Garageman), Frank Mills (Garage Attendant), Ralph Dunn, Fred Graham, Eddie Chandler (Policemen), Lane Watson, James Beasley (Men), Joe Devlin (Toll Collector), Tom Hanlon (Radio Announcer), Calvin Emery (Newsreel Cameraman), Spanky McFarland (Boy Scout), Harry Hayden (Druggist), Jack Gardner (Lalor's Chauffeur), Arthur Space (Capt. Kennedy), Harold McNulty, Joel McGinnis, Donald Kerr, Frank McClure (Elevator Operators), Ann O'Neal, Fred Chapman (Mother and Child), Anne Loos, Frances Morris (Stenographers), Thomas P. Dillon (Flynn), Iris Adam (Prostitute), Ruth Valmy (Magazine Model), Hal Craig (News Vendor), Fred Rapport (Club Manager), Alex Pollard (Headwaiter), James Harrison, Jack Gargan (Stewards), Lawrence Lathrop, William Dyer (Pageboys), Brandon Beach, Austin Bedell, Al Benault, Paul Bradley, James Carlisle, William Holmes, Fred Hueston, Sheldon Jett, J. W. Johnston, Charles Meakin, Harold Minjer, Ralph Norwood, Wedgewood Nowell, Louis Payne, David Pepper, Roy Saegar, Scott Seaton, Wyndham Standing, Larry Steers (Men At Club).

Filming Completed: June 3, 1944
Released: RKO, January 25, 1945
Running Time: 99 minutes

Professor Richard Wanley, a sedentary, middle-aged intellectual, sees his family off on vacation and goes to his club for a drink. On his way, he passes an art gallery and later remarks to his friends at the club about a painting of a beautiful woman in the show window. The friends tease one another with jokes about "wild nights on the town." Wanley stops to look at the painting again on his way home and is startled when the model suddenly appears next to him reflected in the glass. He buys the young woman, whose name is Alice Reed, a drink and sees her home. While he is having an innocent nightcap in her apartment, her hulking boyfriend arrives in a jealous rage and fights Wanley. As he struggles desperately, Alice hands Wanley a pair of scissors, and he kills the boyfriend. Alice and the professor are frightened and plan to dispose of the body. Wanley gets his car and, after various alarms, dumps the body behind a deserted fence in the woods but cuts his hand, tears his coat, and contracts poison ivy in the process. Wanley thinks the episode is finished; but the body is discovered. The police inspector is Wanley's close friend, so he is forced to listen politely and discuss the sensational murder. Meanwhile, Alice is contacted by Heidt, the dead man's bodyguard, who says he knows of the killing and wants money. Alice informs Wanley of the blackmail demands, and Wanley decides they must turn themselves in. Unable to face scandal and disgrace, Wanley prepares to

swallow poison. However, Heidt is killed in a gun battle with police, who suspect that he murdered his boss. Heidt dies outside Alice's apartment, and she calls to tell Wanley they are saved; but Wanley has apparently swallowed the poison and cannot hear the phone ringing. The camera travels back to reveal the professor is slumped in his armchair, but it is only because he has fallen asleep at his club and had a nightmare. Waking, Wanley is greatly relieved, and on his way home, a flashy woman approaches him as he passes the same gallery window. The startled and chastened professor shuns her and hurries home, his desire for adventure completely dissipated.

The central motif of *Woman in the Window* is the *doppelgänger* and the good and evil universe it implies. Wanley himself is the key to this double system: on the one hand a middle-class family man, sober, responsible, and just a little bored; on the other, Wanley is the impulsive adventurer, whose one flirtation leads inevitably to murder and suicide. The clear dividing line is the family, and it is not until Wanley's family departs that his desires and interests as an individual can express themselves. Wanley bids goodbye at the station to the epitome of the bourgeois family. The children are engrossed in their comic books and the husband and wife say farewell without so much as a public embrace. Wanley is not really in flight from this de-eroticized relationship; but he does allow his mind to wander over the possibilities, couching it all in wistful joking and male camaraderie with his friends at the club. He is permitted to imagine and fantasize a sexual identity as long as the object of his dreams remains safely abstracted in a painting. The sudden appearance of the real woman, both in reflection and in the flesh, opens the door to the other world, where desires are gratified instead of repressed. The inevitability of sordidness, crime, and disaster may seem less justified in *Woman in the Window* than it does in Lang's parallel *Scarlet Street*; but any transgression of bourgeois morality must be punished, whether the sinner is escaping from a horrible shrewish wife or whether he is an innocent merely daydreaming about adultery. Indeed, Wanley desires to be discovered and punished, while at the same time he struggles desperately to conceal the evidence of his crime. He constantly suggests to the district attorney that all the evidence could point to him, an inconsequential little professor, as the archvillain of this scenario. From his initial lecture on Freud and the criminal mind to his final self-punishment, Wanley struggles with and is finally overcome by the gigantic superego of middle-class rectitude. Hundreds of mirrors and window reflections throughout the film reinforce both the Freudian and *doppelgänger* aspects of the characters and situations. Wanley is permitted this glance over the edge of the abyss as a learning experience; and the object of the lesson is demonstrated to be effective when Wanley refuses to give even a match to a passing streetwalker and runs chastened back to his safely circumscribed life.

—E.M.

WOMAN ON THE RUN

WOMAN ON THE RUN (1950)

Director: Norman Foster
Producer: Howard Welsch (Fidelity Pictures)
Screenplay: Alan Campbell and Norman Foster; from an *American* magazine story by Sylvia Tate
Director of Photography: Hal Mohr
Process Photography: Loyal Griggs, Robert Hansard
Sound: Fred Lau, Mac Dalgleish
Music Score: Emil Newman, Arthur Lange
Art Director: Boris Leven
Set Decoration: Jacques Mapes
Costumes: Martha Bunch, William Travilla for Ann Sheridan
Hairstyles: Vera Peterson
Production Supervisor: Ben Hersh
Dialogue Director: Ross Hunter
Assistant Director: Maurie M. Suess
Film Editor: Otto Ludwig

CAST: Ann Sheridan (Eleanor Johnson), Dennis O'Keefe (Danny Leggett), Robert Keith (Inspector Ferris), Frank Jenks (Detective Shaw), Ross Elliott (Frank Johnson), John Qualen (Mailbus), J. Farrell McDonald (Sea Captain), Thomas P. Dillon (Joe Gordon).
Location: San Francisco, California
Filming Completed: August 1, 1950
Released: Universal-International, November 29, 1950
Running Time: 77 minutes
[NOTE: Manuel Seff and Paul Yawitz filed a plagiarism suit against Fidelity Pictures, which was settled out of court. The plaintiffs claimed that *Woman on the Run* was based on their story "Pay The Piper."]

When artist Frank Johnson innocently witnesses a murder, he hides out of fear that the murderer will try to kill him, too. Johnson's wife, Eleanor, is asked to help the police find her husband. She is reluctant at first, because their marriage was shaky but soon realizes the extent of Frank's danger and agrees to assist Inspector Ferris. She begins her search aided by reporter Danny Leggett, who is physically attracted to her. Eleanor discovers that Leggett is the murderer and is using her as a guide to her husband. Once Leggett realizes her suspicions, she too is in danger; but Eleanor finds her husband, and the police arrive in time to arrest Leggett.

Woman on the Run is written and directed by Norman Foster (originally an actor in Orson Welles's Mercury Players who later codirected *Journey into Fear* and directed the unusual film noir set in England, *Kiss the Blood off My Hands*). He and photographer Hal Mohr exploit the San Francisco locations and its menacing nighttime streets. Ann Sheridan, as the typically frightened and distraught noir protagonist, is also menaced by Dennis O'Keefe as Leggett, cast against type in the role of the murderer. Against the archetypal narrative structure of Eleanor's search for her husband—a search conducted by one unschooled in the deceptive qualities of

the noir underworld—both O'Keefe and the locales momentarily constitute seemingly unthreatening and stable elements in the film; but with typical noir ambience, they are ultimately revealed to be the most deadly.

—B.P. & A.S.

WORLD FOR RANSOM (1954)

Director: Robert Aldrich
Producer: Robert Aldrich, Bernard Tabakin (Plaza Productions)
Associate Producer: A. E. Houghton, Jr.
Screenplay: Lindsay Hardy [Uncredited: Hugo Butler]
Director of Photography: Joseph Biroc
Sound: Jack Solomon
Music Score: Frank DeVol
Song: "Too Soon" by Walter Samuels
Art Director: William Glasgow
Set Decoration: Ted Offenbacher
Production Manager: Jake R. Berne
Assistant Director: Nate Slott
Film Editor: Michael Luciano

CAST: Dan Duryea (Mike Callahan), Gene Lockhart (Alexis Pederas), Patric Knowles (Julian March), Reginald Denny (Major Bone), Nigel Bruce (Governor Coutts), Marian Carr (Frennessey March), Douglas Dumbrille (Inspector McCollum), Keye Luke (Wong), Clarence Lung (Chan), Lou Nova (Guzik), Arthur Shields (Sean O'Connor).
Filming Completed: September 1, 1953
Released: Allied Artists, January 27, 1954
Running Time: 82 minutes

Mike Callahan is an Irish emigré and war veteran working as a private investigator in Singapore. He is summoned by a wartime lover named Frennessey to the nightclub where she works. There she confides that her husband, Julian March, may be engaged in some illegal activities and asks Callahan to disentangle him—if he can. Callahan discovers that a black marketeer named Alexis Pederas has recruited March for a scheme involving a renowned nuclear physicist, Sean O'Connor. While Callahan searches for further information, March, impersonating a major, kidnaps O'Connor at the airport. Pederas then sends a message to the British command that he is offering O'Connor to the highest bidder whether Russian, Chinese, or Western. A photographer/informant of Callahan's who had taken a picture of March and O'Connor driving through town comes to Callahan with the snapshot; but March, aware of the incident, alerts Pederas who has the man killed and incriminating material planted in Callahan's room. Inspector McCollum comes to question Callahan and discovers the false clue; but Callahan surprises him with a blow and escapes. After spending the night at Frennessey's, Callahan

Mike Callahan (Dan Duryea) prepares to destroy the enemy in World For Ransom.

plans to slip out of town and go to a deserted jungle village where O'Connor may be hidden. He is spotted by Major Bone of British Intelligence who, uncertain of Callahan's role, decides to follow at a distance. In the process, Bone loses immediate contact with a support force and finds himself alone with Callahan at the village. They ascertain that March and Pederas's men are indeed there with O'Connor and decide not to wait for help. Bone is wounded in the assault but Callahan succeeds in slipping into March's bunker and holding the captors at bay with two grenades. Since O'Connor is out of the room, Callahan reacts to March's threatening gesture by throwing both charges and ducking for cover. All are killed except Callahan and O'Connor.

Callahan returns to Frennessey after having failed to save her husband but hoping to take his place. She rejects him violently, explains that she never loved Callahan or his sexual advances, and suggests that March's platonic affection was what she wanted because men are physically repellent to her. As she loses control, Callahan leaves and returns to the streets of Singapore.

"You shouldn't play Galahad. You're way out of character." By saying that the detective is not Galahad, Julian March ironically confirms that Callahan is precisely the Galahad type—the disillusioned idealist turned hard-boiled hero. This apprehension of Callahan is additionally colored by the element of locale. The word "Singapore" stenciled over

the first black-and-white frame triggers associations with mystery and exoticism, with opium rings and knife-wielding assassins bringing sudden death, with all the clichés of the inscrutable and perilous Orient. From this typical film noir background of sleazy bars and wet, shiny streets, the thin, white-suited figure of Mike Callahan detaches itself. The opening conflict contained within this first sequence and first frame is a profoundly archetypal one: East (milieu) versus West (hero), Galahad (white-suited purity) versus the forces of darkness (the shadowy, low-key aspect of the city). Like heroes of noir fiction, Callahan is caught in a struggle to survive. For Aldrich this basic concept motivates and justifies an expressive exploration of the forces that threaten the hero: the confining structures—the trap—and the compelling factors that precipitate the entrapment.

The initial discovery of such an exploration in *World for Ransom* is of an underlying determinism. From the establishing long shot of the street banked with flashing neon the cut-in is to a medium close shot of the woman Mai Ling selling fortunes. The tout is to "take a chance"; but the talk of inherited luck, of a hereditary fate, seems to contradict the notion of chance. The ambiguity of the fortune teller's line is really a formula of words chosen for their come-on value and uttered by rote.

The audience can appreciate, after these introductory shots, that the preoccupied Callahan must and will "take a chance"; but their understanding of Callahan's position

317

remains nonspecific. They sense that some conflict is present but do not know the details. A clarifying medium shot follows, isolating Callahan against a dark building as he turns up an alleyway. Visually, the conflict has now been fully stated: high angle of the entire street (milieu), emergence of a figure from a background (hero), and finally situation of the hero in graphic opposition to milieu.

Callahan moves up the alley, goes through a doorway, and starts up a flight of stairs; the camera, as if under the power of a predestined pull, travels in behind him. As the angle narrows, the wedges of light on each side of the doorway disappear from the frame. The blank diagonal walls siding the stairwell focus the converging lines of perspective on a corridor at the top of the stairs. A figure steps out into the vanishing point. For a moment, the point-of-view of Callahan and the viewer merge, as they share the sudden perception of a dark form at the top of the steps. A reverse angle looking down at Callahan reveals another figure blocking the doorway to the alley. A trap has, literally, closed on him, a trap that the components of the shot imply hold him in its grasp halfway between top and bottom, between polarities.

Much of the delineation and manipulation of Callahan is, of course, still within the traditional noir conception of the private eye. The character's mocking self-appraisal ("Mike Callahan . . . [shaking his head] . . . Private Eye.") or insistent idealization of Frennessey March, the woman who rejects him ("You were the only one that was way out there on that hill . . . the only one that was straight from beginning to end") are not without irony or precedent. What most gives dimension to Callahan as a noir hero are the scenes with Frennessey; and the sequence-shot encounter between Callahan and Frennessey on the eve of the pursuit and combat in the jungle provides the best illustration of this effect. A low angle captures Callahan reclining on a divan with a small table fan behind to his right in frame center—a possible extension of an earlier fan motif, which can serve as metaphor for turmoil at the emotional center of the film itself. Frennessey is again "frenetic," walking nervously back and forth on the left, an action that continues as they discuss the coming day's endeavors. As she tries to bring Callahan around to her way of thinking, the camera cranes up, coming in close behind her and tilting down at him, underscoring her attempt at dominance. The scene ends in much the same way as the earlier sequence in her dressing room: Callahan stands up and the pent-up energy of the sustained take is concentrated into a close two-shot. With Frennessey's visual dominance reduced and Callahan's delivery of the line about her being "Way up there on that hill," the viewer may expect the tension built up in the staging to be released in a kiss; and it is. But the dissolve-away-from-kiss to the jungle exterior that follows represents—depending on how wary of Frennessey the viewer is—not just a time lapse for physical consummation but also a final, possibly fatal, enmeshment seen in visual overlay. The ultimate noir statement of *World for Ransom* derives from the narrative revelation that Frennessey has indeed been lying. Callahan survives the real world, specifi-

cally the combat in the jungle, by physically defeating March and his associates; but that fails to insulate him against emotional destruction when he is cursed and viciously slapped by Frennessey. How well he survives is an unanswered question, tinged with fallen idealism. All that Callahan is offered by way of consolation are a repetition of Mai Ling's words: "Take a chance, Mr. Callahan. Love is a white bird, yet you cannot buy her."

—A.S.

THE WRONG MAN (1956)

Director and Producer: Alfred Hitchcock (Warner Brothers)
Associate Producer: Herbert Coleman
Screenplay: Maxwell Anderson and Angus MacPhail; from "The True Story of Christopher Emmanuel Balestrero" by Maxwell Anderson
Director of Photography: Robert Burks
Sound: Earl Crain, Sr.
Music: Bernard Herrmann
Art Directors: Paul Sylbert, William L. Kuehl
Technical Director: Frank O'Connor (Police Magistrate to the District Attorney, Queens County, New York)
Assistant Director: Daniel J. McCauley
Film Editor: George Tomasini

CAST: Henry Fonda (Manny Balestrero), Vera Miles (Rose Balestrero), Anthony Quayle (O'Connor), Harold J. Stone (Lt. Bowers), Esther Minciotti (Manny's Mother), Charles Cooper (Detective Matthews), Nehemiah Persoff (Gene Conforti), Laurinda Barrett (Constance Willis), Norma Connolly (Betty Todd), Doreen Lang (Ann James), Frances Reid (Mrs. O'Connor), Lola D'Annunzio (Olga Conforti), Robert Essen (Gregory Balestrero), Kippy Campbell (Robert Balestrero), Dayton Lummis (Judge Groat), John Heldabrand (Tomasini), Richard Robbins (Daniell), John Vivyan (Detective Holman), Will Hare (McKaba), Werner Klemperer (Dr. Banay), Mel Dowd (Nurse), Peggy Webber (Miss Dennerly), Anna Karen (Miss Duffield). **BITS:** Michael Ann Barrett (Miss Daly), Alexander Lockwood (Emmerton), Emerson Treacy (Mr. Wendon), Bill Hudson (Police Lieutenant from the 110th Precinct), Marc May (Tomasini's Assistant), William Le Massena (Sang), Josef Draper, William Crane (Jurors), Leonard Capone (Court Clerk), Charles J. Guiotta, Thomas J. Murphy (Court Officers), Harold Berman (Court Stenographer), John Caler (Soldier), Silvio Minciotti (Mr. Balestrero), Barry Atwater (Mr. Bishop), Dino Terranova (Mr. Ferrero), Rossana San Marco (Mrs. Ferrero), Daniel Ocko (Felony Court Judge), Olga Fabian (Mrs. Mank), Otto Simanek (Mr. Mank), Dave Kelly (Policeman), Maurice Manson (District Attorney John Hall), John McKee, Gordon Clark (Police Attendants), Paul Bryar (Interrogation Officer), Sammy

Armaro, Allan Ray, John Truax (Suspects), Ray Bennett, Clarence Straight (Policemen), Don Turner (Detective), Penny Santon (Spanish Woman), Bonnie Franklin, Pat Morrow (Young Girls), Charles Aidman (Jail Medical Attendant), Richard Durham, Harry Stanton, Mike Keene, Frank Schofield, Chris Gampel, Maurice Wells (Department of Correction Guards), Helen Shields (Receptionist), Don McGovern (Waving Man), Cherry Hardy, Elizabeth Scott (Waving Women), Walter Kohler (Manny's Attorney, Felony Court), Spencer Davis (Prisoner's Lawyer), Ed Bryce (Court Officer), Henry Beckman (Prisoner), Maria Reid (Spanish Woman), Paul Carr (Young Man), Tuesday Weld, Barbara Karen (Giggly Girls), Dallas Midgette (Customer at Bickford's), Donald May (Arresting Patrolman), John C. Becher (Liquor Store Proprietor), Earl George (Delicatessen Proprietor), Mary Boylan (Curious Customer), Natalie Priest (Delicatessen Proprietor's Wife), Rhodelle Heller, Olive Stacey (Stork Club Customers), John Stephen (Man in Stork Club).

Location: New York, New York
Filming Completed: June 8, 1956
Released: Warner Brothers, December 23, 1956
Running Time: 105 minutes

Christopher Emmanuel Balestrero, a New York bass player, works nights at the Stork Club and comes home to his wife Rose and family in the early morning. He likes to chart the horses while riding the subway, perhaps because his family is never ahead financially; but he does not often go to the races and bet. Manny, as he is called, goes to turn in his wife's insurance policy for extra money and is wrongly recognized as a holdup man by one of the cashiers. Returning home, he is picked up by detectives who take him in for questioning and ask him to write a note like that used by the holdup man. The anxious Manny accidentally misspells a word in the same way as the note and soon, identified by employees of the insurance company, he is spending the night in jail. In the morning, he is freed on bail and retains a lawyer, O'Connor, who believes in his innocence. Manny and Rose attempt to establish his alibi; but they find that the witnesses are either missing or dead. Rose has a nervous breakdown and is placed in a mental hospital. The saddened Manny proceeds to trial; but a mistrial is declared, and he is faced with the prospect of going through the entire process again. He prays. At that very moment, the actual criminal attempts another robbery but is subdued by his would-be victims. One of the detectives who arrested Manny notices the resemblance, and Manny is cleared. He goes to the mental hospital to tell Rose that the nightmare is over; but for her, it is not finished. "That's fine for you," she declares, staring blankly into space.

Other directors make noir films that are often highly individualized manifestations of personal feelings; but Alfred Hitchcock, whose work is diverse in range and tone, makes films that seem as if they would exist independently of the traditions offered by any genre. His technique, remaining supple over the years, is simply a refinement of classical practices employed with unceasing resourcefulness. *The Wrong Man,* one of the bleakest films in the history of the cinema, betrays no cynicism and makes no recourse to facile melodramatics. This film's story of the near destruction of a man through a merciless quirk of fate, which becomes the actual destruction of his more fragile wife, describes a cruel and uncaring universe with a humanism found in few classical film noir. Here the characters do not choose to suffer like the crippled beings of other films in the cycle but are enmeshed against their will and because their limitations are turned against them by the caprices of circumstance. The quiet Manny journeys through his modern hell with a childlike awe; and this same innocence prevents him from ever knowing the inner hell of his wife, burning quietly until it blazes out of control. *The Wrong Man,* with its final tragic irony, becomes an unrelenting depiction of the desolation of existence.

Hitchcock's presentation uses subjective techniques for Manny; and the audience is encouraged to be disturbed as each shot darkens his nightmare. But the camera does not encourage identification with Rose, and the audience is as surprised as Manny is when he learns that his wife has wrongly assumed the burden of his guilt. Hitchcock's choices when determining the nature of each shot, visual and psychological, result in the possibility of feeling genuine compassion. He makes the film appear detached and restrained, even while touching the audience's fears, until the final subdued meeting of the broken-hearted Manny and the insane Rose, which brings forth the feeling of catharsis that Hitchcock has held in suspense.

—B.L.

YOU ONLY LIVE ONCE (1937)

Director: Fritz Lang
Producer: Walter Wanger (Walter Wanger Productions)
Screenplay: Gene Towne and Graham Baker
Director of Photography: Leon Shamroy
Music: Louis Alter, Paul Webster
Music Director: Alfred Newman
Song: "A Thousand Dreams of You" by Louis Alter and Paul Webster
Art Director: Alexander Toluboff
Assistant Director: Robert Lee
Film Editor: Daniel Mandell

CAST: Sylvia Sidney (Joan "Jo" Graham), Henry Fonda (Eddie Taylor), Barton MacLane (Stephen Whitney), Jean Dixon (Bonnie Graham), William Gargan (Father Dolan), Warren Hymer (Muggsy), Charles "Chic" Sale (Ethan), Margaret Hamilton (Hester), Guinn Williams (Rogers), Jerome Cowan (Dr. Hill), John Wray (Warden), Jonathan Hale (District Attorney), Ward Bond (Guard), Wade Boteller (Policeman), Henry Taylor (Kozderonas), Jean Stoddard (Stenographer), Ben Hall (Messenger), Walter De Palma (Man).
Released: United Artists, January 29, 1937
Running Time: 87 minutes

As Eddie Taylor is released from his third term in prison, he is greeted at the gate by his fiancée, Jo Graham. Eddie promises her that he is through with crime; he marries Jo, settles down, and takes a job as a truck driver. Yet after a local bank is robbed and an employee killed, Eddie is a prime suspect. Although innocent, he is arrested and convicted on circumstantial evidence and, in view of his past record, sentenced to death. On the date set for his execution, Eddie is sent a message that a gun has been hidden for him in the prison hospital. By slitting his wrists, he has himself admitted to the hospital, finds the gun, and, with the prison doctor as a hostage, demands his release. Both Eddie and the warden are unaware that the actual robber has been captured and that a pardon is being prepared for Eddie. When this word arrives and the warden announces it to him, Eddie assumes it is merely a ruse. He refuses to give up and impulsively shoots the chaplain who bars his way. Jo, who is pregnant, joins him in a waiting car. After their baby is born and given to Jo's sister, they drive for the border. At a roadblock, a flurry of gunfire forces them to abandon the car and flee on foot. A few yards from freedom, both are shot, Eddie falling last while he carries the already mortally wounded Jo in his arms.

As with the lynch mob victim, Joe Wheeler, in *Fury,* Lang's narrative focus in *You Only Live Once* is on the outrage of the unjustly punished. Compounding the melodrama in this production (made immediately after and in the same year as *Fury*) is the fact that its protagonist, Eddie Taylor, is not an average citizen but a "three-time loser." More significantly, where *Fury* concentrated to a great extent on the question of mob psychology and recruited such stereotypes as the gruffly authoritarian sheriff, politically motivated governor, and even righteously liberal district attorney (rather than the hapless Joe Wheeler) to probe that psychology, Lang does not elect to dramatize many of the possible parallel events in *You Only Live Once.* As the title suggests, the individual and his or her one life is the major concern.

Where Joe Wheeler's only significant narrative "act" was one of omission—failing to report his survival of the jailhouse fire—Eddie Taylor takes a far more active, if unwitting, part in the sequence of events that doom him. The result in *You Only Live Once* is not only a more sustained treatment of a character's alienation at the personal level than in *Fury,* which in turn is more typical of future film noir (both in general and of the sub-type of "fugitive couple" films in particular), but also a more diverse visual style than in his previous film. In the earlier picture, Lang relied on montage and an occasional moment of overt symbolism to support his basically apersonal plot. As *You Only Live Once* is a more subjective film so is its *mise-en-scène* keyed to the emotions of Eddie and Jo.

In the opening sequences, a series of elegiac details establish Eddie and Jo's romantic dependence on one another, culminating as they stand in the evening by the frog pond of a small motel where Eddie explains to Jo that the frogs mate for life and always die together. Even as they feel secure in themselves, the motel manager is inside searching through his collection of pulp detective magazines under the harsh glare of his desk lamp. When he finds several photos and a story on Eddie's criminal past, Lang underscores the irony with a cut to a frog jumping into the pond and diffracting Eddie's reflection in the water; then there is a cut to a dark, vaporous swamp where the truck that could prove Eddie innocent of a crime of which he is not yet even aware sinks into the quicksand. Lang's staging and cutting make the frog pond scene, which could have either ridiculed the rustic naïveté of his characters of awkwardly stressed their proletarian status, a simple, evocative metaphor for the entire narrative. In the trial sequence, the soft lighting and lyricism are replaced by high fill and oppressively harsh key lights. Lang even constructs a grim traveling shot that pulls back from a banner headline reading "Taylor Innocent" to reveal an alternate choice of "Taylor Guilty." Finally, for Eddie's escape, Lang fills the prison courtyard with fog, so that the searchlight beams reach out for him like white, spectral fingers; and the whole, nightmarish array of mists, massive walls, blurred lights, hazy figures, and loudspeaker voices becomes an extension of Eddie's frightened and disoriented state of mind. In this visual context, Eddie's murder of the priest becomes, if not pardonable, at least understandable as the desperate response to a prolonged assault not merely on his life but on his very conception of the world with its moral and physical realities of truth, justice, and love, an assault of the foundations of his sanity.

It cannot really be claimed that Eddie Taylor's consciousness as a character, of his existential being, is very high. At the same time, Lang's neo-Jansenism recurrently enmeshes his characters in a narrative web of deterministic complications from which, consciously or not, they must try to free themselves. For Eddie and Jo, as for numerous noir figures to follow, the only way to that freedom is through death. Despite the inappropriate, quasi-religious conceit—reworked from his earlier *Der Müde Tod*—of having the dead priest cry out, "Open the gates," in voice-over, Lang's final shot of his couple through the crosshairs of a police sniper's gunscope is an image that is both characteristically noir and surprisingly modern.

—A.S.

APPENDICES

Appendix A

Since the editorial position of this study has been that film noir is not merely a genre of American film but also a movement inspired and supported by a collective vision, it may seem arbitrary to exclude films with certain noir characteristics simply because they are genre pieces. On first examination such diverse genre productions as *Scarface, The Lodger, Murder He Says,* or *The Devil's Doorway* may all seem worthier of inclusion in the canon of film noir than many titles covered in the reference portion of this book. Aesthetically, the interest in these films, compared with many of our entries, is clearly greater. But aesthetic value judgments can no more be a criterion in this study than could box-office receipts or film industry awards. Nor can the fact that the directors of these films also may have directed one or more noir films, which bear an auteurish resemblance to their genre work, be any more of a consideration than the fact that the producing studios, cinematographers, or writers of these genre films also produced or worked on noir films.

The determining factors in excluding productions from the comedy, gangster, Western, and period genres are simple. The concept that the action of film noir must be grounded in a contemporary setting excludes Westerns and period films. The concept that film noir must have a narrative that is dramatically developed with an underlying seriousness and verisimilitude in exposition excludes comedies. The concept of a complex protagonist with an existential awareness of his or her situation excludes the gangster film. Clearly, the rigorous application of such determinants must exclude from full consideration many productions that do bear an important relationship to the noir movement and its particular vision. For obvious reasons, only a few of the most significant precursors of film noir or later productions that pointedly reflect the move-

ment's influence on current film-making could be included in the reference section. The purpose of these appendices is to cover at some length examples of various types of American films that, while predominantly genre pieces, do reflect to a greater or lesser degree the same narrative and visual preoccupations, the same style, as film noir.

1. The Gangster Film

The gangster film and film noir share several narrative and iconic characteristics, most obviously crime, violence, and the urban environment. At its emergence, during the close of the silent period in the late 1920s, the gangster genre of American films treated crime and the underworld in a romanticized and melodramatic fashion. Films such as *The Underworld* (1927), *The Racket* (1928), *Tenderloin* (1928), and *Dragnet* (1928) recreated the idealized milieu of the gangster: nightclubs and speakeasies nestled under dark buildings, a secret, subterranean world where nattily dressed gang bosses and their molls toasted their crimes and dishonest acts with illegal gin. It was a romantic vision of a very dark side of American society. The vicious and mindless brutality of the gangster was infrequently depicted and never stressed until *Scarface* (1932), which bore the apt subtitle "The Shame of a Nation." Initially the film gangster was a quasi-noble characterization, not unlike the cowboy of the Western film, who symbolized rugged individualism in an impersonal and ruthless world. The character analogies between cowboy and gangster and their respective genres do not apply to film noir; yet the milieu of film noir often coincides with that of the gangster film. This overlapping has sometimes obscured the two film cycles' differences.

The fundamental difference between the gangster film and film noir is that of narrative attitude. While the gangster film never lost its demented idealism: Ricco's struggle to "get to the top" in *Little Caesar* (1930); Tom's use of crime to pull himself out of the slums in *Public Enemy* (1931); the charismatic character portrayed by George Bancroft in films from *Underworld* to *Blood Money* (1932). The noir vision compelled its characters to contemplate their destruction. Harry Fabian's ruse to throw the blood money paid for his death at his girl friend in *Night and the City* (1950); Cody's death at "the top of the world" in *White Heat* (1949); the Swede's quiet acceptance of death at the hands of paid assassins in *The Killers* (1946). All distinctions between these two cycles of film extend from this simple construction. Characters populating film noir are either corrupt or morally ambiguous. The gangster has a sense of right and wrong. The gangster exercises his free will under the influence of a warped desire to better himself. In the earliest manifestations, the gangster was not a cause of corruption but often a simple-minded victim of it. The element of the femme fatale, so prevalent in film noir, had no place in the straightforward world of gangsters characterized by Ricco, Tom, or Duke Mantee in *The Petrified Forest* (1934).

Iconically there is an even wider rift between the two groups of film. The gangster film contains violence that is explosive, almost flamboyant, and graced with a staccato rhythm: machine guns blazing; wild bullet bursts from moving cars; bombs shattering storefronts. The noir film's use of violence is more controlled and ultimately more brutal. There is a ritualization of violence in the film noir that is unique: Bianco's shooting in *Kiss of Death*; Wallace Ford's death in a steam bath in *T-Men*; John Ireland perfuming his bullets in *Railroaded*; Alan Ladd's vicious beating in *The Glass Key*. The effect tends to deglamorize violence and direct attention to the concept of pain rather than cinematic action. Mood and tone engendered by such sequences are the ultimate differentiation of noir film and gangster film. The darkness that pervades the noir film, an ambience that links the low-key photography to the ultimate human condition, makes it truly the dark age of American cinema. This is not true of the gangster film. Some gangster antecedents skirt this darker mood. *Scarface* exemplifies the brutal and ironic character found in later film noir, which deal with claustrophobia, perverse sexuality, and entrapment. Most gangster films have an eventual restoration of order, a redemption, in a sense of social values. There is the simplest moral dilemma in the gangster film: good versus evil; and good always triumphs. To such a degree is this absolute, that many gangster films, such as *Dead End* (1937) and *Angels with Dirty Faces* (1938), acquired reputations for social consciousness. These films, where cleaning up the environment meant putting an end to crime, present an idealized point of view far removed from that of the noir underworld in which layer upon layer of corruption extended from petty criminals to the most powerful individuals in business and government. This explicit social viewpoint did not find its way into film noir until later in its cycle in films like *Knock on Any Door* (1949), *Crossfire* (1947), and *The Sound of Fury* (1950).

There are a number of gangster films produced during the 1930s that anticipate film noir in one or more of these areas. They possess an ambience that is removed from that of the common gangster film; yet there is a compromise in characterization or style that does not allow the noir elements to dominate. *Scarface* has already been mentioned. Probably the most unusual pre-noir films are those of Rowland Brown. His *Quick Millions* (1931) and *Blood Money* (1932) have a complex view of the underworld. There are the expected loyalties and rivalry among criminals; but the background of decadence and grotesque action exceeds that of the typical gangster film. In *Blood Money* Frances Dee's portrayal of a woman addicted to the sexual thrills associated with violence anticipates the noir psychology of films like *Gun Crazy*. *Gambling Ship* (1933) is another esoteric film; it deals with a high-class prostitute who wants to use a "john" to pull herself up out of the illegal environment of crime she is attached to. Unknown to her, her new lover is a kingpin of organized crime who is "lying low." They discover their true backgrounds and engage in a love-hate relationship through a major portion of the film.

Perhaps the best known gangster films—*Scarface, Little Caesar,* and *Public Enemy*—are also the most prototypical. Each anticipates the major iconic and narrative motifs of a genre that survives to this day. Each also anticipates certain elements later developed in film noir. The central figures of these films are not pre-noir characterizations. Their egomania and misogyny run counter to the sense of inferiority and obsessive sexuality common in film noir. The scene in which Tom Powers abuses a woman with a grapefruit remains a classic example of the gangster's sexual attitudes. The extremes represented by Ricco's open mistrust of all women and his latent homosexuality and Carmonte's incestuous desires effectively antedate some of the exaggerated character types that were to populate the background of the noir world. But only Tom in *Public Enemy,* with his climactic realization that "I ain't so tough," comes close to the existential anguish that plagues so many noir protagonists.

The pre-noir aspects of these films are more apparent in their visualization: the long, articulated moving camera that opens *Scarface;* the night location work for the gas station holdup early in *Little Caesar;* or the nocturnal shoot-out in the rain in *Public Enemy.* The brutality and irony evoked in the deaths of the gangsters—Ricco cut down behind a rural billboard; Tom dumped on his mother's doorstep; or, most explicit of all, the pan up to the flashing sign for "Cook's Tours" in *Scarface*—are tonal elements that were to be refined and elaborated in film noir. There were an estimated 50 productions in the gangster genre in the two years following *Little Caesar* and scores more before the ends of the decade. Some like Brown's films or certain Warner Bros. productions directed by William Keighley—*G-Men* (1935) and *Each Dawn I Die* (1939)—were to anticipate further the narrative and visual styles of film noir. *G-Men,* for instance, employs revenge as its principal plot motivation, balances expressionistic lighting with several scenes of graphic violence, and features many touches of bizarre humor, as when the main character skewers a fly with his fountain pen. Despite these elements, *G-Men*'s hero is not a noir figure. Simply to contrast the way in which he enacts revenge for a murdered comrade with the quasi-legal methods of Gagin in *Ride the Pink Horse* is sufficient to separate generically the characters and their respective films.

The distinction between a genre and a movement is the inevitable terminus of any comparison of the development of the gangster film and film noir. The gangster film, as a genre, has remained popular from its inception to the present. The noir cycle is time-bound, locked into the social and cultural values of the years before and after World War II. There are gangster films produced during the height of the noir period from *Dillinger* (1945) to *The Hoodlum* (1951) that are nothing more than genre pieces. There are also ostensible gangster films from those years that transcend the elements of gangsterism and become film noir: *White Heat, The Gangster, The Racket.* The reverse, of course, is not possible. No film noir can detach itself from the movement and become a simple genre piece, be it gangster film or any other. Still, because of the many motifs which they share with film noir, certain gangster films may bear a closer resemblance than any other genre pieces to the noir movement without fully embracing its style. Because of this unique relationship between the gangster genre and film noir, difficult questions of character motivation or narrative irony may be the only qualities separating a work in this genre from a similar noir film; and there is no easy answer to those who would dispute this study's classification of certain marginal films. However, marginal or not, the distinctions between films like *Scarface, Blood Money,* and *G-Men* and noir films must be made and, once made, must be applied as consistently as possible.

2. The Western

One of the most difficult genres to associate with film noir, both in terms of visual style and narrative, is the Western. Conceived with a different aesthetic in mind, even the most superficial examination of these individualistic film forms reveals a tremendous shift in environments and motivations. The Western with its wide vistas and natural exteriors can be the visual antithesis of film noir's cluttered urban skylines and slick, city streets. This contrast between the claustrophobic atmosphere of many noir films and the emphasis on open spaces in the Western coincides with the narrative separation inherent in these two forms. The Western, like the gangster film, was founded on simple moral conflicts—opposing good and evil; yet, in the same way that period films are occasionally able to transcend their locales or generic constructs to approach certain noir themes, the Western—which could also be considered as a period film—may also involve itself with the patterns and sensibilities of the film noir.

As early as 1940 the typically noir preoccupations with perverse sexuality and overt brutality were evident in certain Westerns. Howard Hughes's production of *The Outlaw* with its low-key photography by Gregg Toland (similar in tone to his work on Wyler's *The Westerner,* also in 1940) and the unusual love relationship between Billy the Kid (Jack Buetel), Pat Garrett (Thomas Mitchell), and Doc Holliday (Walter Huston) is atypical in genre construction. The screenplay by Jules Furthman, a regular contributor to film noir, is filled with double entendres and muted sexuality. After 1945 the brutalizing effects of World War II and the growing ambivalence toward corruption began to surface in most genres of American films, including the Western. By the end of the war, the Western hero, along with the private eye, had become one of the most durable figures in popular American culture. The detective, following the ground-breaking fiction of Hammett, Chandler, and others, was easily integrated into the noir cycle. But the chaotic and incongruous noir world was not readily associated with the character of the Westerner. The Western was versatile enough, however, to assimilate some of the tonality of the noir attitude.

My Darling Clementine (1946) is a John Ford film that focuses thematically on revenge and cynicism. The film's heroes are not above ignoble motives and prejudices. After their younger brother is ruthlessly murdered by a gang of rustlers, Wyatt Earp (Henry Fonda) and his brothers descend on the town of Tombstone, a virtually lawless community, where they encounter the criminal Clanton family. The introduction of Doc Holliday (Victor Mature), a fatalistic character who dresses all in black, is reminiscent of the noir narrative pattern. The final, ritualistic showdown is a set piece of low-key, somnambulistic violence. The brutality of the Clantons complements the coldness of Wyatt Earp and the doomed Doc Holliday and reinforces the noir iconography of Joe McDonald's camerawork and Mature's portrayal.

As with Victor Mature, many of the usual film noir actors began to appear in Westerns. Their presence, when combined with increasingly downbeat story lines, supported the influence of the noir sensibility in many of the Westerns produced in the late 1940s and early 1950s. The actor who carried his noir persona most fully into the Western genre was Robert Mitchum. His *Blood on the Moon* (1948) and *Pursued* (1947) are prime examples of a hybrid "noir Western." The first film, *Pursued,* is overtly Freudian in plot. The Mitchum character loses a coin flip with his stepbrother over who will serve the Union cause. After the Civil War he returns to his New Mexico hometown but is anxious and almost tormented by past events that he cannot quite remember. His dreams are full of reoccurring images of a mysterious, violent incident, which mars his relationship with his foster family. Eventually after he has killed his stepbrother in self defense and overcome the hatred of his stepsister, he learns the truth about the past incident that has threatened his sanity. Directed by Raoul Walsh from an original screenplay by Niven Busch, *Pursued* is the most stylistically noir of Westerns. The psychological elements combine with the isolation and insecurity of the central character to create a typically noir aura. The nightmares which, in flashback form, literally intrude into the narrative, become—as stylized by cinematographer James Wong

Howe—emblems of an uncertain predestination. This combination of visual usage and central character creates an underlying tone in *Pursued* that is not that of a Western but rather of a psychological melodrama.

Blood on the Moon (1948) is more conventionally Western in imagery. Adapted from a story by Luke Short, *Blood on the Moon,* like *Pursued,* exploits Mitchum's tough guy persona. In *Pursued,* this tough exterior pose was undermined by an amnesiac tension and a sense of paranoia, the latter reminiscent of Mitchum's role in *Out of the Past. Blood on the Moon* situates a similar character in a narrative of Western stereotypes. The use of these situations—cattle rustling, bush-whacking, etc.—results in an anomalous combination of plot and character. This may be the result of adapting material from writers like Luke Short. However, two other Westerns with noir overtones were also adapted from the writings of Short; and both isolate a noir character in an alien environment. The first of these adaptations, *Ramrod* (1947), centers on an archetype of the noir cycle: the femme fatale. Veronica Lake is cast as Connie Dickason, a predatory woman manipulating the men around her in order to achieve wealth and independence. Sex and violence are treated with objectivity, almost as part of the environment. There are several sequences in the noir style in *Ramrod.* The murder of one of the cowhands, caught alone after dark, recalls the threatening urban landscape of numerous noir films in terms of style and execution. The final rejection by Dave Nash (Joel McCrea) of Connie Dickason's sexual advances does suggest that the Western hero, supported by a misogynistic generic tradition, is less likely than a noir figure to be depicted as falling prey to sexual impulses. Andre DeToth's direction of *Ramrod* supports the noir characteristics of the plot with an aptly low-key visualization.

Station West (1948) is another Luke Short adaptation. In this production, the basic elements of a detective story have been transposed into a Western setting. An army intelligence officer (Dick Powell) becomes an undercover investigator in order to discover those responsible for hijacking gold shipments from a small mining community. Both the plot and the presence of Powell—the first actor to portray Philip Marlowe—underscore the aspects of crime in this film. The femme fatale is present in the guise of local saloon proprietress, played by Jane Greer. Several villains, most notably Raymond Burr and Steve Brodie, are also recruited from film noir. Other elements from the hard-boiled dialogue to the brutal, nocturnal fistfight in the muddied streets of town complete the link to the noir universe. The fight in particular, with its handheld camera-work and the portrayal of brutal rage by Dick Powell has a savage and chaotic undercurrent strongly reminiscent of the noir film. Even in a Western context, the RKO visual style, typified in Harry Wild's photography, is dark and foreboding almost to the point of cliché.

In the same year Paramount produced *Whispering Smith.* Alan Ladd had a similar part as Powell, a stoic railroad agent. Again, the tough-guy image is the most obvious example of the noir influence. Supported by the ambivalent villainy of Robert Preston—who played a similar role in *Blood on the Moon*—Ladd's character bears certain resemblances to a noir figure, however out of place in a Technicolor West. *Whispering Smith* may be partially evocative of the noir outlook, while demonstrating that characterization or, more specifically, an actor's screen persona alone cannot support that outlook.

William Wellman's *Yellow Sky* (1949) has a narrative line that might easily be followed in a noir film: a group of bank robbers who flee into a desert area to avoid a posse—compare *Storm Fear.* The story line of W. R. Burnett and Lamar Trotti develops in a claustrophobic atmosphere, colored by doublecrosses, muted violence, and sensuality. Even the landscape of hugh, rocky defiles has particular significance, for in the same way that contemporary criminals might conceal themselves in the protective under-brush of the urban jungle, these Western bandits lose themselves in the folds and creases of the rocks. The final gunfight takes place off-screen inside an abandoned saloon. The figurative suggestion—that violence survives and threatens even in a locus that civilization has abandoned is much more "modern" than the film's setting.

Wellman directed two other Westerns of unusual narrative outlook, *The Ox-Bow Incident* (1945) and *Track of the Cat* (1954), both adaptations of novels written by Walter Van Tilburg Clark. The first film with its ritualization and socially-conscious treatment of mob violence seems to anticipate the anti-McCarthyism of a later film like Nicholas Ray's *Johnny Guitar* (1954). Although made that same year, *The Track of the Cat* succeeds more fully in condensing a number of noir motifs and reflecting the waning influence of the noir cycle. Adapted by A. I. Bezzerides, the screen-writer of *Kiss Me Deadly,* the narrative focuses on the strained relationships in a family at a snowbound ranch terrorized by a black panther roaming the hills. The selfishness and monomania of the main characters is, like that of many in film noir, ultimately self-destructive. The imagery, particularly the use of color in the film in which black and white sets and costumes are photographed on color stock—muted and expressionistic in effect—under-scores the narrative abstraction of reality. The resultant dreamlike quality of *Track of the Cat,* a quality adapted from the noir style, reoriented the plot's sensationalism to create a sense of fatality and entrapment.

Another film that deals with claustrophobic terror is Henry Hathaway's *Rawhide* (1951). As in *The Dark Corner,* Hathaway creates an aura of intense fear and paranoia in *Rawhide.* Instead of William Bendix's "White Suit," menace is personified in *Rawhide* by character actor Jack Elam. The grotesque facial expressions of Elam are in the tradition of sinister noir personalities. The brutality of the protagonist's assault on their persecutors in the final confrontation in *Rawhide* is also in the noir style. When the Elam character is shot by the woman he has tormented, the moment is both cathartic and distasteful. As he squirms in a death dance, his convulsions become a parody of the sexual assault.

Possibly the most important film-maker to bring noir techniques to the Western is Anthony Mann. In films like *T-Men, Raw Deal, Desperate* and *Railroaded,* Mann helped to develop the semidocumentary, low-budget noir thriller. Yet these films merely laid the groundwork for the personal vision expressed in Mann's later and more consistent body of Westerns. From *Devil's Doorway* (1950) through *Man of the West* (1958), Anthony Mann directed 10 Westerns—six starring James Stewart—that carry over elements from his earlier noir work. *The Devil's Doorway* considers the problem of the Indian in adjusting socially to white majority and its bigotry. The nature of Lance Poole's (Robert Taylor) fatal rebellion against the encroachment of the white man is almost existential in its futility. Given a dynamic visualization by John Alton's cinematography, *Devil's Doorway* is an extremely cynical vision of the social prejudices that supported the westward expansion. The image of Poole framed against clouds of black smoke by a low-angle shot in a simple metaphor for the darkness overshadowing all of his race. In that context Poole's final, self-destructive stand is as much political and tribal as it is existential or purely personal. It is also, much in the same way as Ford's "cavalry trilogy" and *The Searchers,* a markedly individual vision of the Old West, colored by the cynicism of the noir cycle.

In *Winchester '73,* Mann is thematically closer to his earlier thrillers. In the noir manner *Winchester '73* uses a plot of pursuit and revenge to propel Lynn McAdam (James Stewart) across a Western landscape filled with threatening forces and populated by grotesque characters. Dan Duryea as Waco Johnny Dean is typical of the noir characterizations of broad-based recognition that Mann transposes. The nature of Waco Johnny Dean is like that of the swaggering, effete villains that Duryea portrayed in numerous noir films. Under such influences, *Winchester '73* colors its generic background so the final gunfight between McAdam and his brother is fully as ironic as any similar confrontation in film noir.

In his later films, Mann would often manipulate the environment to permit the fatalistic nature of his narrative to be echoed in the landscapes. There is a clear example of this expressionistic use of environment in *The Man from Laramie* (1955). Will Lockhart (James Stewart), after having just delivered a load of goods to a general store, is directed to a salt flat where he will supposedly be able to load free salt and not return home with empty wagons. But as he and his crew begin to load his rigs, a group of riders appear on the barren horizon. They claim that Lockhart and his men are trespassing and begin an orgy of destruction. After killing Lockhart's mules, burning his wagons, and humiliating him in front of his men, they simply ride off. No questions asked. No excuses accepted. This incident, already strongly nightmarish in tone, is supported by the empty landscape, a silent, ironic witness to the action. The entire sequence has an almost surreal quality—remote, highly emotional, and yet ultimately lifeless—more typical of film noir than the Western. In sequences like this, in the context of genre, Anthony Mann's noir sensibilities express

themselves most fully. The humiliations and subsequent reversals undergone by characters in *Man from Laramie, The Naked Spur* (1954), and *Man of the West* (1958), create an aura of uncertainty and bitterness perhaps more appropriate to the noir world than to the West. Mann's body of films represents, much in the same way as Budd Boetticher's oddly metaphysical Ranown cycle with Randolph Scott, a distinct interpretation of the American character.

The Westerns that reflected the influence of the noir series also represented a view of the West stripped of the heroics of such figures as Johnny Mack Brown, William S. Hart, and the Three Mesquiteers. There was a certain, perhaps false, sense of verisimilitude in many of these Westerns. Their black and white images were part of a visual iconography that underscore the dusty realities of the Southwest with its cheap, makeshift dwellings and relatively banal personalities. Most of these films must remain more deeply rooted in the Western, a genre tradition that precludes more than marginal participation in the noir movement. A number of oddities like Fritz Lang's neurotic *Rancho Notorious* (1952) and Ray's *Johnny Guitar* use flashback techniques and invoke the narrative concept of the dark past, undercutting genre expectations so fully that they are difficult to classify. More recently productions by directors like Sam Peckinpah and Arthur Penn have assimilated the patterns of films like *The Devil's Doorway* and *Pursued,* creating a new wave of psychological and cynical Westerns, which exist in a distorted, subjectified reality. Of these new Westerns, two films come closest to extending the earlier relationship to film noir: *Welcome to Hard Times* (1967, directed by Burt Kennedy) and *High Plains Drifter* (1973, directed by Clint Eastwood). Films like these sustain the noir-related method of dislocating the Western milieu to create a quasi-metaphysical background for narratives of vengeance, greed, and above all indifference.

3. The Period Film

The narrative elements in films that allow them to transcend genre typing, such qualities as chaos, alienation, and cynicism, are not unique to the rain-slicked, urban streets of film noir. The period film occasionally reflects these attitudes while replacing contemporary settings with a world solidly rooted in the past. These productions, whether typed as "Victorian," "atmosphere films," or "period melodramas," are the genre pieces that come closest to full participation in the noir cycle.

Initially, the period noir film was an offshoot of Victorian melodrama. John Brahm's *The Lodger* (1944) and Edgar G. Ulmer's *Bluebeard* (1944) are representative examples. *The Lodger* is based on Marie Belloc-Lowndes's novelized version of the "Jack the Ripper" murders committed in 1888 London. It was originally adapted by Alfred Hitchcock in 1926. The American version of *The Lodger* did not incorporate Hitchcock's "wrong man" theme. Rather, Laird Cregar, as the lodger of the title, was cast as a killer obsessed with beautiful women, whom he murdered out of a twisted sense of revenge for his brother and his betrayal by a ruinous woman. This character's exaggerated love for his brother and the fanatical purity of his memory lends an overtly aberrant quality to the film. The nature of Cregar's interpretation, which suggests sinister and violent passions locked up in a tormented mind, underscores the sexual alienation of the character. The imagery is nightmarish, filled with shots of the hulking lodger wandering through the dimly lit, fog-covered streets of Victorian London on his perverse mission of revenge.

Bluebeard is quite similar. John Carradine plays Gaston Morel, a puppeteer who kills women in order to preserve his artistic creativity but does so under a psychotic compulsion he cannot control. Ulmer's use of expressionistic techniques, which included oblique camera angles and surreal sets, are in contrast to Brahm's attention to detail in *The Lodger*. The death of Morel, at the film's conclusion, is treated as a psychological release for a character enmeshed by a frightening series of events he is unable to understand.

Most of the films of this genre had a quasi-romantic narrative accentuated by a dark and sinister atmosphere. To a certain extent, this may be traced to a European sensibility, latent in the work of directors like Siodmak, Ulmer, Brahm, and even Hitchcock. There is a common outlook, which stresses ironic instability and perverse, almost Byronic romanticism. In period films these directors could create an aura of dread and apprehension unencumbered by the conventions and attitudes that would become common in the postwar film noir. Douglas Sirk's *Lured*, for instance, simply inverts the narrative viewpoint of *The Lodger*, i.e. the central figure is a woman who agrees to act as bait for a psychotic killer. While such a procedure might seem commonplace in a contemporary plot, the period context makes it seem unusual and reinforces the sense of peril implicit in the situation.

John Brahm's success with his initial period production prompted another film utilizing the talents of both Laird Cregar and *Lodger* screenwriter Barre Lyndon. *Hangover Square* (1945) is Brahm's melodramatic vision of controlled chaos and romantic destruction. From a novel by Patrick Hamilton about a young composer, whose lapses of memory conceal the fact that he is a mentally disturbed murderer, Lyndon and Brahm produce a treatment of the mind of an artist unable to master his own sense of inadequacy. *Hangover Square* becomes a frenetic, almost explosive nightmare, which ends in the artist's transfigured death amid crumbling debris and enveloping flames. While not designed to be as suspenseful as the earlier *Lodger*, *Hangover Square* is a baroque set-piece—the type of film-making that parallels the noir sensibility.

A second unconventional period thriller, which was adapted from the writings of Patrick Hamilton, is George Cukor's *Gaslight* (1944). More concerned with paranoia and the loss of perception, *Gaslight* moves away from the eccentric passions in Brahm's films and concentrates on the psychological frustrations of a relationship in which a husband tries to convince his wife that she is insane. Cast

against type, Charles Boyer as the menacing husband is like many similar figures in the noir world, not driven by decadence or psychosis yet possessed of a strange, menacing quality typical of the noir vision. The claustrophobic Victorian house as photographed by Joseph Ruttenberg underscores the silent menace of Boyer's portrayal and provides an apt background for a depiction of greed and obsession.

Robert Siodmak's *The Suspect* (1945) also deals with Victorian maladjustment and murder but from the point-of-view of the killer rather than the victim. In *The Suspect* Charles Laughton is cast as a husband whose affection for a beautiful young employee eventually leads him to murder his domineering wife and an inquisitive neighbor. *The Suspect* deflates the image of eccentric or exotic period criminals by dealing with a middle class murderer acting out commonplace motivation. The Laughton character and the mental turmoil he experiences after his criminal act resemble the protagonists of Siodmak's major noir films.

Although Siodmak is typical of directors whose visual style is essentially the same for film noir and period film, the latter, as a genre, developed independently of conventional noir films. The trend that started in the early 1940s with *The Maltese Falcon, Stranger on the Third Floor,* and *I Wake Up Screaming* evolved quickly. Within three years the cycle had been refined with such films as *Murder My Sweet, Double Indemnity,* and *Woman in the Window* (1944). When such elements as the femme fatale and existential anguish began to take on more importance in film noir, the period genre began to incorporate them. The adoption of semidocumentary techniques and a postwar emphasis on films with a realistic impact caused the studio-based period films to decline. The productions that were set in previous eras reflected many of the same changing attitudes and sensibilities that would characterize noir film-making.

The initial period films in the noir style—*The Lodger, Gaslight, Bluebeard*—were not concerned with the decay and corruption depicted in the typical contemporary film noir. Rather these films concentrated on exploiting the mental conflicts and disturbances that isolated differing, insular personalities from the rest of their society. The nature of the disturbances displayed by actors like Cregar, Boyer, and Carradine appeared to be self-contained and ultimately painful. The manner in which Carradine's "bluebeard" is drawn helplessly toward murders; the ritualized washing of the lodger's blood-stained hands in the Thames; Boyer's monomaniacal persecution of his wife—all are an idealization of evil. Many period films reflect an aura of ever-present evil, balanced by narrative retribution and the restoration of order. The split between good and evil is well defined, creating a moral stability that many noir films work against.

The postwar period films began to approach the atmosphere of corruption and chaos inherent in the more prevalent urban noir films from a different perspective. The changes in the period film were at first subtle readjustments in characterization. The fatal quality of women like Brigid

O'Shaughnessy, Phyllis Dietrichson, and Ellen Berent, the qualities of the femme fatale, emerged as a fixture in the period noir film. Linda Darnell as Netta Longden in *Hangover Square* is a classic vision of the fatal woman. Her ability to exploit and dehumanize her lover and her ultimate destruction underscore a narrative situation devoid of pity or compassion. George Bone (Laird Cregar) burns his mistress atop a bonfire, a gesture that satisfies his misguided love. Her end is appropriate to a woman driven by greed and a sense of power, an opposite of earlier women in period films, for Netta Longden is a manipulator rather than an entrapped innocent. With the development and exploitation of this type of character, the period film acquired the bitter taste of sinister sexuality.

The femme fatale was the principal rather than supporting character in several period films. Joan Fontaine in the title role in Sam Wood's *Ivy* (1947) is perhaps the most clearly defined fatal woman in the period thrillers. Adapted from another Marie Belloc-Lowndes novel, *Ivy* is the story of a sophisticated murderess whose goals are simple: social gain, wealth, and status. Her methods are also simple: a suggestion of sexual favors complemented by a small dose of poison. As the film describes her, Ivy is a totally evil personality possessed by a consumptive corruption that evokes the noir mood. The reality of self-destruction, a common noir motif, attends the climax of *Ivy*. Pursued, with little hope of escape in sight, Ivy flutters about a decaying Victorian mansion like a trapped moth. Her eventual plunge down an empty elevator shaft is symbolically linked to her profound decadence. *Ivy* possesses a strong visual unity based on Sam Wood's deliberate direction. Russell Metty's low-key photography, and William Cameron Menzies's imaginative production design. The darkness of the film is reinforced by the images: Joan Fontaine can remain the perfect black-widow figure in her white dress and elaborate coiffure because the stylistic elements form an effective contrast to her mental state.

The machinations of Ethyl Barrymore's character in *Moss Rose* (1947) are similarly understated. Her sinister figure bent on manipulating an innocent young woman could easily be a noir character. Even the relationship between this character and her son develops as an exotic form of entrapment. Forced to live in an environment that is filled with images and relics from his childhood, the son resembles the classic, impotent noir hero. Immersed in a distorted past the character's inadequacies develop into a typically noir paranoia. The young woman's inevitable redemption is vitiated because someone she doesn't even like is responsible. *Moss Rose* is a film that adheres to the narrative scheme of film noir without compromising its period context.

So Evil My Love (1948) is a more "realistic" period film that deals with manipulation from a different perspective. In this film, it is an "homme fatale," played by Ray Milland, who eventually succeeds in turning a gentle woman, Olivia Sacret (Ann Todd), into a murderess. Her indoctrination into the criminal mentality is so complete that she even-tually lets another woman be accused of her crimes, while she turns her attentions toward destroying the man who betrayed her. Olivia Sacret realizes the potential for criminal behavior that lurks below the surface of many noir characters. Her swift rise from naive widow to socially elegant murderess is accomplished without the undercurrent of maladjustment that is typical of many noir characters.

Most of the postwar period films dealt with individual cases of decadence or malevolence. But the general aura of corruption, a common situation in the contemporary productions of the noir cycle, was rejected in these period narratives which stressed social stability. It wasn't until Anthony Mann, the director of such noir films as *T-Men*, *Raw Deal*, and *Border Incident*, turned to the genre that a period film finally acquired the consuming sense of fear and total helplessness that characterized the greater number of noir films. Mann's stunning period production, *The Black Book* (1949), extends the traits of decadence and violence to an entire society. Robespierre's reign of terror in revolutionary France provides a background of political assassinations, civic instability, and an authentic societal madness. From this Mann creates an artificial portrait of social cynicism and destruction untroubled by historical perspective.

The plot of *The Black Book* (also released as *Reign of Terror*) is that of a dime novel thriller. Charles D'Aubigny (Robert Cummings), a somewhat passive hero, is called upon to secure a small black book, which would expose Robespierre as a totally self-serving public official, who has ordered the death of members of the government opposed to his policies. D'Aubigny becomes, in effect, a private eye investigating a past full of sinister characters and dehumanizing situations. Throughout the film, D'Aubigny is hounded by agents and double agents; and the characters populating *The Black Book* are so confusing in their loyalties, that it becomes difficult to separate them. There is a feeling of menace in the film that is akin to the work of Anthony Mann in film noir. His graphic depiction of torture and pain, done with the minimum of actual onscreen violence, is unmistakably in the noir style. Charles McGraw, an actor in most of Mann's noir films, portrays a physically repellent henchman of Robespierre in *The Black Book*. His presence forges an iconographic link to the contemporary noir world, which although the character may be bulging out of his sloppy sergeant's uniform, does not seem out of place in a period setting. It is this figure who grimly applies torture to the film's heroine in a dark underground chamber; who is constantly forcing Robert Cummings into retreat; who typifies the noir characteristics of *The Black Book*. Richard Basehart as Robespierre is another example of a genre portrait of noir personality. As presented in this film, Robespierre is a seemingly dominant figure; his sense of power rests in his ability to control the confused citizens of France through treachery and prevarication. Because his failure ultimately derives from his overassessment of power, Robespierre is a victim, like so many noir characters, of his own devices. The megalomania that blinds him in regard to the changing political tide is analogous to Martin in *He Walked by Night,* also, as it happens, played by Richard Basehart. Impotence becomes as important a convention for the period film as it is with film noir.

A major contributing factor to the imagery in *The Black Book* is John Alton's photography. As Mann expressed it: ". . . maximum performance with the minimum means. The least shot had to contribute to the significance of the whole." Forced to work with a small budget, Alton created a portrait of 18th-century France from shadows and silhouettes. It is Alton's photography that, in the noir manner, gives *The Black Book,* the dark quality of a milieu mired in despair and turbulent with chaotic activity. The visual texture of Alton's work, enables Mann to develop the same figurative values in this genre piece as he does in his noir films.

Because the distinctions that define noir films can be extremely tenuous, there are many productions that border between the period genre and film noir. One of the most difficult films to classify is Robert Siodmak's *The Spiral Staircase* (1946). Even as an exercise in gothic suspense, *The Spiral Staircase* contains a unique vision of entrapment that derives from the noir universe. The mute servant who thinks she has witnessed a murder finds herself effectively trapped inside her own body. Unable to communicate adequately her fear and knowledge, she becomes a victim of paranoia. Her problems are compounded by her own fantasies, such as the film's mock marriage ceremony. Because she actually becomes the target of an aberrant killer preying on handicapped women, *The Spiral Staircase* creates a narrative irony as strong as any film noir. However, the film ultimately fulfills dreams rather than destroys them and undercuts the elements of paranoia and exoticism.

Night of the Hunter also goes beyond the "realism" of the noir world. It is a period film precise and absolute in its portrait of evil, yet preserving throughout a strong moral framework. The difference between good and evil is so highly contrasted in the character of Harry Powell—on whose knuckles are, on the right hand, tattooed "love," and on the left, "hate"—that this demented evangelist becomes evil personified and little more. Charles Laughton's adaptation of James Agee's script, is a classic example of "American gothic" filmmaking. Some of the ambience of film noir is present; but ultimately the nightmarish plot demands a sense of salvation because Harry Powell is too concrete a force of evil. Accordingly Rachel, the old woman who intercedes on behalf of the children, is an archetype of goodness. In this context, even the visual richness of Stanley Cortez's camerawork, ranging from expressionistic lighting and to stark imagery, draws *Night of the Hunter* away from the noir world. Violent, grotesque, nightmarish, decadent, and yet not hopeless, *The Night of the Hunter* employs the elements of noir film-making without exploring the existential core of the cycle.

Val Lewton produced several period films that exploited the noir style, most notably *Body Snatcher* (1945) and *Bedlam* (1946). Both films are visions of a past inhabited by grotesque characters; and both are strongly linked to traditions of perverse romanticism and gothic extravagance. *Bedlam,* with its portrait of institutionalized sadism, comes closest to the noir series. The narrative elements are present but the emphasis on their existential implications is not. Lewton as producer was most intent on recreating a past reality of terror and innocence. His world was balanced between extremes, but the final restoration of order perpetuates a Victorian attitude and does not reflect the noir sensibility. There is an oneirism in Lewton's films that further suggests the presence of the noir ambience, but ultimately Lewton channeled these influences of mood and tone to fit his own design.

Alfred Hitchcock's *Under Capricorn* (1949) falls into the same category, a creative force recruiting noir elements to a particularly well-defined, personal vision. Set in colonial Australia, *Under Capricorn* is a highly romanticized drama of manners. The haunted, distressed characterization of the heroine by Ingrid Bergman and Margaret Leighton's interpretation of the servant who afflicts her create an aura of chaos, which is controlled by Joseph Cotten's portrayal of the ex-convict husband. Hitchcock's use of color reinforces rather than dispels the dark atmosphere of the film but does not actually invoke the noir vision. Rather *Under Capricorn* remains Hitchcock's personal statement on period mores. In adapting the fin-de-siecle viewpoint of Oscar Wilde's original story, Albert Lewin's *The Picture of Dorian Gray* (1945) also uses elements of noir film-making. The fog-shrouded sequences at the waterfront tavern, to which Dorian Gray (Hurd Hatfield) goes to sample the illicit pleasures of the Victorian era, are stylistically noir. The character of Dorian Gray, himself, resembles the driven figures of numerous noir films.

The existential angst that imbued the noir universe after World War II was not readily imposed on the period genre or the particular narrative situations found in the past. Ultimately, the period film became a showcase for lavish sets and "classic" plots. By the early 1950s, with the noir cycle at its height, the period productions that shared the noir style had diminished. The virtues of films like Anthony Mann's *The Tall Target* (1951), based on a historical assassination attempt on Abraham Lincoln as embellished by writer Geoffrey Homes, were lost in the new stylistic dichotomy between period genre and noir movement. Still to a certain extent, the 1940s period film can be cited as an exception to the assertion that the noir vision was confined to the contemporary world. These films did create an atmosphere of chaos, complicated by a loss of perception and sense of meaninglessness, that rival film noir. But the period context insulates these elements, as well as perverse sexuality or character alienation, and mitigates the immediacy of their impact. These period melodramas are influenced by and perhaps influence themselves the coincidental emergence of film noir. But the requirements and expectations associated with genre prevent an audience from relating to them as it would to film noir. In that sense and varying with individual productions in the genre, the period film may be said to participate at once marginally and substantially in the noir cycle.

4. The Comedy Film

It may seem difficult to make substantial associations between comedy films and film noir. However, a simple examination of several recurring motifs found in many comedy films made during the 1940s reveals how the noir sensibility affected the major comedians and comedy directors. In the 1930s, aside from Nathanael West's decidedly bleak vision in novels like *Day of the Locust* and *Miss Lonelyhearts* with their cynical, almost determinstic outlook, Dashiell Hammett was offering his sole concession to Hollywood in the guise of "The Thin Man." This tonal divergence of a hard-boiled writer was concurrent with Hollywood's growing commitment to themes and characters that would ultimately lead to the noir cycle. W. C. Fields's crude, manipulatory humor; the Marx Brothers' anarchistic chaos; and Harold Lloyd's brand of thrill comedy had all demonstrated the willingness of American audiences to laugh at absurd adversity. These diverse elements combined to precipitate the noir vision's infiltration of comedy films in the 1940s.

As the comedies of the 1930s grew more sophisticated, writers like Preston Sturges and Billy Wilder found new directions to express their particularly bitter view of the world. By 1940 even the mood of Capra's films, initially defined by *It Happened One Night* and *Mr. Smith Goes to Washington,* began to change. His *Meet John Doe* (1941) exposes the hypocrisy of American society, and the ease with which a natural martyr such as Doe can be overwhelmed by the elements of corruption. Capra perceived the change in America's self-image but wasn't able to manipulate it. His inability to find a satisfactory conclusion—several were shot, none of which was deemed adequate by Capra, who envisioned Doe's death—reflects a shift in audience expectations that ultimately resolved itself in the cynicism of film noir.

Such an outlook developed at a time when the noir cycle was just beginning to take shape in films like *The Maltese Falcon* and *This Gun for Hire.* Although most comedies were slow to exploit this shift in attitude, a great many noir films contained a level of comic relief. *I Wake Up Screaming,* with its portrait of aberrant sexual adoration, is infested with the foolish posturings of Alan Mowbray and Allyn Joslyn. Lloyd Nolan, in a series of films based on the pulp detective Mike Shayne, played his hard-boiled role for laughs. Many "Falcon" films, including *The Falcon Takes Over* (1942), which adapted Raymond Chandler's *Farewell, My Lovely* into a comedy thriller, became semicomedies on film. These films blended the atmosphere and environment of the noir world with rough-talking, Runyonesque comedy.

One of the most elaborate screwball comedies of this period, *Whistling in the Dark* (1941), is also the most noir in tone. Red Skelton stars as a radio sleuth known as "The Fox." He becomes involved with a weird religious cult, headed by Conrad Veidt and dedicated to bilking old women out of their fortunes with the promise of everlasting tranquility. When the services of The Fox are needed by the cultists to create the perfect murder and appropriate a large inheritance, the plot of *Whistling in the Dark* expands to accommodate the subjects of death and torture. The complications are absurd, yet the film contains an aura of violence and paranoia, however unreal, that separates it from most comedy films of the period. As in Bob Hope's earlier horror-comedies *The Cat and the Canary* (1939) and *The Ghost Breakers* (1940), *Whistling in the Dark* deflates the phoney gothic melodrama and mysticism but not the evil characteristics of people who calmly plan murders.

Preston Sturges, beginning with *Sullivan's Travels* (1941), in which the protagonist is sent to a chain gang while his associates believe he has been killed by a train, extended the concept of cynical comedy influenced by film noir—compare *I Was a Fugitive from a Chain Gang.* The plot for his *Miracle at Morgan's Creek* (1944) involves a very downbeat portrait of American life during the war years. In the film a young woman's zeal for "kissing the boys goodbye" results in an unexpected pregnancy complicated by the lack of a husband. Trudy Kockenlocker (Betty Hutton), with a little help from her younger, "liberated" sister, convinces a lifelong acquaintance to serve as a proxy husband until her "real" spouse comes home. When she realizes that she is in love with this 4-F, Trudy's desire not to hurt him by her actions leads her to contemplate suicide. Eventually Norval Jones (Eddie Bracken) dons an archaic military uniform and impersonates her husband to make her expected child legal in the eyes of the law. Their plot collapses when Norval is arrested for moral turpitude and becomes a fugitive. When Trudy gives birth to sextuplets, both she and the assumed father, Norval, become national heroes; and the entire sordid affair is conveniently swept under the carpet.

Sturges's next film, *Hail the Conquering Hero* exposes the veneer of respectability glossing over small-town politics and reveals a nest of corruption and petty disputes rivaling any in the noir world. When a disenchanted veteran named Woodrow Truesmith (Eddie Bracken, again) is discharged for physical reasons and returns home, he concocts a story portraying him as a hero, so as not to disappoint his mother or tarnish the memory of his father, a genuine war hero. Woodrow is disconcerted when he receives a hero's welcome and is offered a berth as a candidate for local office. When he confesses to his mother that he has lied about his record as a soldier, the community does not ostracize him for his deception but salutes him for his honesty.

Although made during the war, Sturges was able to incorporate sentiments of meaninglessness and abject existentialism into both of these unusual comedies. Through the use of caustic dialogue, Sturges creates vivid portraits of losers forced to resort to absurd machinations to survive. The key to Sturges's outlook is his ability to manipulate this cast of losers beyond the limits of the rational. The sequence in which Norval returns to an empty and decaying house on Christmas Eve to search for his lost love is both a philosophical and visual incorporation of the noir tone into comedy. Like most noir characters, Sturges's heroes refuse to accept "fate" but rather attempt to overcome "obviously" insurmountable obstacles. They never really succeed, yet these personalities may manage to alter the direction of the initial conflicts so that, for a time, it seems as though problems are solved.

In a pattern opposed to Sturges's well-defined character studies, George Marshall and Frank Capra used a black situation to lampoon a genre in *Murder He Says* (1945) and *Arsenic and Old Lace* (1944) respectively. Both films are death-oriented; but whereas *Arsenic and Old Lace* follows the mercy killings of a couple of likable old women from the point-of-view of their sane nephew, *Murder He Says* is often a terribly realistic vision of an insurance salesman's encounter with a family of crazed killers. Although the moral stance of these films may be colored by caricature and satire, it is basic and well-defined, i.e. good triumphs. The absence of film noir's ambivalence, however, does not prevent these films from extending their thematic statements beyond the scope of the typical 1940s comedy. There is a distinct ambience in each film that suggests a darker-than-normal vision of the world. Both films exploit an element of grotesqueness. In *Arsenic and Old Lace* the weird characterizations of Raymond Massey and Peter Lorre as a couple of fugitive murderers who hide in the basement of a house of lunatics, are an exaggerated, iconographic link to the noir world. *Murder He Says* contains a pair of hulking, monstrous twins whose glee in performing acts of violence is an unquestionably perverse as it is comic. Both productions exist on the fringe of the noir world. *Arsenic and Old Lace,* like a psychological melodrama, combines the traits of repellent characters with the incomprehensible logic of irrational beings. *Murder He Says* more fully exploits the noir clichés of a threatening, alien locale and a desperate flight, all for comic effect.

There is very little to laugh at in noir films. As a result, the cycle invites parodies like *Wonder Man* (1945; starring Danny Kaye) or *My Favorite Brunette* (1947; starring Bob Hope). In *Wonder Man,* Kaye plays a dual role: a shy bookworm whose twin is a rude and tough-talking night-club entertainer. The latter's death is far from laughable, but it permits his return to earth as a ghost who haunts his uncooperative brother. The narrative plays off a familiar noir plot element—impersonation—against the criminal corruption inherent in the urban setting. *My Favorite Brunette* is a more straightforward parody of the hard-boiled detective film. An unsuspecting photographer, Hope, gets mixed up with a gang of criminals because his studio adjoins that of a private investigator (played by Alan Ladd who makes a trench-coated cameo appearance). The context of the thriller becomes the rationale for Hope's elaborate gags. His helplessness is a typically noir response to an underworld filled with vile characters and unexpected situations. An even more extreme example of a parody of hazardous situations is *The Secret Life of Walter Mitty* (1947). In this film the framing device used to give narrative

structure to James Thurber's short story depicts Mitty as an editorial assistant at a publishing house that exploits hard-boiled novels through cover art featuring sex and violence. In fantasy Mitty is attacked by a morose killer (Boris Karloff), who attempts to alter his sense of reality. The recurring motif of surreal, dream imagery and a femme fatale (played by Virginia Mayo) are unmistakable elements of the noir canon used for satire. Mitty's confusion, a clear loss of identity, brings the film even closer to the "Woolrich-esque" noir films of the period. Perhaps the most comprehensive parody of film noir is the work of the cycle's archetypal director, Robert Siodmak. His *Fly by Night* (1942) incorporates elements of the "wrong man" and fugitive couple themes in a narrative reminiscent of Hitchcock's *The 39 Steps* (1935). After a series of comic encounters punctuated by unusual escapes—for instance, the couple rides for a while in a new automobile loaded on a car carrier, which they leave by merely putting their vehicle in reverse and driving off—the protagonist, ironically *and* comically enough, feigns intense paranoia and has himself committed to an asylum, which is a front for an espionage ring.

With a slight alteration in comic reading, *Fly by Night* could easily be regarded as a light but basically serious thriller in the manner of *The 39 Steps* or *Saboteur* (also 1942; also by Hitchcock). What ultimately separates such films is the fine distinction between comedy and comic relief. Clearly, Hitchcock's comic relief can be among the blackest. For instance, there is the weekly get-together in *Shadow of a Doubt* in which two neighbors relieve the tedium of their commonplace lives by swapping recipes for the perfect murder. In contrast, Hitchcock's last outright comedy, *The Trouble with Harry* (1955), which centers on the discovery and disposal of a corpse in parody of his own *Rear Window* (1954), is neither as humorous nor as black as many of the ostensibly lighter moments in his thrillers.

For Chaplin, a character like the "Merry Widow" killer in *Shadow of a Doubt* is an apt subject for comic portrayal. His *Monsieur Verdoux* (1947), developed from an original story by Orson Welles, reflects much the same vision of American moral preoccupations as the noir cycle does. Chaplin's highly stylized depiction of a "bluebeard" killer—he is never seen actually murdering old women—combined with his ritualization of Verdoux's money-counting and other personal affectations lead the film away from morbid connotations and into cultural criticism. Chaplin's attempts, as Verdoux, to kill the character played by Martha Raye provide the film with its purest moments of black comedy. At the same time, when he extends the question of Verdoux's criminal motivation to an ethic that criticizes the capitalistic need for instability and the genocide that takes place in the name of social change, Chaplin's rhetoric derives from the noir vision. In *Verdoux* Chaplin alters completely his "usual" screen persona (i.e., the Tramp). His bluebeard is diabolical yet acutely sensitive; brazen yet inept; morbid yet dedicated to the well-being of his family. The result is a complex portrait, a man like a noir protagonist unable to overcome the existential pressures of a society that sometimes drives people to their own destruction.

In the same year as *Verdoux*, Preston Sturges directed two of his blackest comic visions of American society. The first, *The Sin of Harold Diddlebock* (1947), is distinguished by the return to the screen of Harold Lloyd. Sturges exploits Lloyd's stereotypical character both by incorporating footage from Lloyd's *The Freshman* (1925) and by debunking the middle-class values that Lloyd so perfectly typified. As a bookkeeper suddenly laid off after a quarter of a century, Lloyd plays the situation for comic discovery rather than bitterness. What Diddlebock discovers is a world devoid of compassion, a world in which money and power are everything, a world like that of film noir. The morose quality of the first third of this film does not mitigate the comedy. But it does create the emotionless image of a middle-aged man with no prospects, an image familiar to the noir series. Even though, through Sturges's absurdist turn of events, Diddlebock moves from a point of total debasement to one of power, the underlying, basically cynical assessment of American culture is not dispelled.

In *Unfaithfully Yours* (1948), Sturges makes much the same statement. When a symphony conductor (Rex Harrison) believes that his wife is having an affair, he concocts plans to do away with his wife while he conducts a concert. As each musical piece is played, the camera is slowly drawn into a huge close-up of the conductor's eye. From this point the film becomes an externalization of his elaborate and insane schemes to revenge the imagined infidelity. All the characters created by Sturges in this film are frantic and explosive; but Harrison, as he wanders around his apartment and considers the folly of infidelity, is a particularly acute parody of a driven man. *Unfaithfully Yours*, produced at 20th Century-Fox, is actually the comic embodiment of the noir spirit, both in visualization and narrative implication. Of all the films discussed that contain indications of the noir influence, none rivals *Unfaithfully Yours*, for as Sturges moved away from the intricate dialogue scenes that characterized his earlier films, he moved into the visual style of film noir. Each segment of the film ends morbidly; there is no comic compromise in these vignettes. They are almost noir set pieces. Because the audience knows that they are not real, the absurdity and grotesque complications of the grisly murders merely embellish the satire. But again the underlying effect and the underlying seriousness of Sturges's narrative statement remain unaltered.

Obviously, neither Sturges nor Anthony Mann nor John Brahm, no matter how cohesive their personal vision, could transform a genre piece into a film noir. What the work of such distinguished directors, writers, photographers, and actors both in and out of the noir cycle confirms, is not merely the pervasive impact of what may be termed the noir outlook on American culture but also the ability of film-makers to adapt elements of the noir style to other forms. The results, whether viewed as complex hybrids or simple stylistic graftings, are varied enough to enrich viewer appreciation and perhaps understanding of the noir cycle proper.

Appendix B

The purpose of this appendix is to establish a more detailed reference to the main text than that provided by the general index. The cross-indexing by chronology, production company, and individual film-maker groups titles according to particular areas of interest while graphically displaying the predominant years, studios, and personnel involved in film noir.

The criterion for inclusion in the lists of directors, writers, cinematographers, composers, and producers is participation in two or more productions in the noir cycle. The list of actors has been limited editorially to those who are most significant, based on the amount and the quality of their work in film noir.

1. Chronology of Film Noir
(titles are listed alphabetically within year of release followed by releasing companies)

1927
Underworld (Paramount-Famous Players-Lasky)

1928
The Racket (Paramount-Famous Players-Lasky)

1929
Thunderbolt (Paramount-Famous Players-Lasky)

1931
City Streets (Paramount)

1932
Beast of the City (MGM)
I Am a Fugitive from a Chain Gang (Warner Brothers)

1935
The Scoundrel (Paramount)

1936
Fury (MGM)

1937
You Only Live Once (United Artists)

1940
The Letter (Warner Bros-First National)
Stranger on the Third Floor (RKO)

1941
Among the Living (Paramount)
High Sierra (Warner Bros-First National)
The Maltese Falcon (Warner Bros)
The Shanghai Gesture (United Artists)

1942
The Glass Key (Paramount)
I Wake Up Screaming (20th Century-Fox)
Johnny Eager (MGM)
Street of Chance (Paramount)
This Gun for Hire (Paramount)

1943
Journey into Fear (RKO)
Shadow of a Doubt (Universal)

1944
Christmas Holiday (Universal)
Double Indemnity (Paramount)
Laura (20th Century-Fox)
The Mask of Dimitrios (Warner Bros)
Murder, My Sweet (RKO)
Phantom Lady (Universal)
When Strangers Marry (Monogram)

1945
Conflict (Warner Bros)
Cornered (RKO)
Danger Signal (Warner Bros)
Detour (Producers Releasing Corporation)
House on 92nd Street (20th Century-Fox)
Johnny Angel (RKO)
Lady on a Train (Universal)
Leave Her to Heaven (20th Century-Fox)
Mildred Pierce (Warner Bros)
Ministry of Fear (Paramount)
My Name Is Julia Ross (Columbia)
Scarlet Street (Universal)
Strange Illusion (Producers Releasing Corporation)
Uncle Harry (Universal)
The Woman in the Window (RKO)

1946
The Big Sleep (Warner Bros)
Black Angel (Universal)
The Blue Dahlia (Paramount)
The Chase (United Artists)
Crack-Up (RKO)
The Dark Corner (20th Century-Fox)
The Dark Mirror (Universal-International)
Deadline at Dawn (RKO)
Decoy (Monogram)
Fallen Angel (20th Century-Fox)
Fear (Monogram)
Gilda (Columbia)
The Killers (Universal)
Night Editor (Columbia)
Nobody Lives Forever (Warner Bros)
Nocturne (RKO)
Notorious (RKO)
The Postman Always Rings Twice (MGM)
So Dark the Night (Columbia)
Somewhere in the Night (20th Century-Fox)
The Strange Love of Martha Ivers (Paramount)

The Stranger (RKO)
Suspense (Monogram)
Undercurrent (MGM)

1947
Body and Soul (United Artists)
Born to Kill (RKO)
The Brasher Doubloon (20th Century-Fox)
Brute Force (Universal-International)
Calcutta (Paramount)
Crossfire (RKO)
Dark Passage (Warner Bros)
Dead Reckoning (Columbia)
Desperate (RKO)
Fall Guy (Monogram)
Fear (Monogram)
Fear in the Night (Paramount)
Framed (Columbia)
The Gangster (Allied Artists)
The Guilty (Monogram)
The High Wall (MGM)
Johnny O'Clock (Columbia)
Kiss of Death (20th Century-Fox)
Lady in the Lake (MGM)
The Locket (RKO)
Nightmare Alley (20th Century-Fox)
Nora Prentiss (Warner Bros)
Out of the Past (RKO)
Possessed (Warner Bros)
The Pretender (Republic)
Railroaded (Producers Releasing Corporation)
Ride the Pink Horse (Universal-International)
They Won't Believe Me (RKO)
The Unsuspected (Warner Bros)

1948
Behind Locked Doors (Eagle-Lion)
Berlin Express (RKO)
The Big Clock (Paramount)
Call Northside 777 (20th Century-Fox)
Canon City (Eagle-Lion)
Cry of the City (20th Century-Fox)
The Dark Past (Columbia)
A Double Life (Universal-International)
Force of Evil (MGM)
Hollow Triumph (Eagle-Lion)
I Walk Alone (Paramount)
I Wouldn't Be in Your Shoes (Monogram)
Key Largo (Warner Bros)
Kiss the Blood Off My Hands (Universal-International)
The Lady from Shanghai (Columbia)
The Naked City (Mark Hellinger)
Night Has a Thousand Eyes (Paramount)
The Pitfall (United Artists)
Raw Deal (Eagle-Lion)
Road House (20th Century Fox)
Sleep, My Love (United Artists)
Sorry, Wrong Number (Paramount)

The Street with No Name (20th Century Fox)
They Live By Night (RKO)
T-Men (Eagle-Lion)

1949
Abandoned (Universal-International)
The Accused (Paramount)
Act of Violence (MGM)
Beyond the Forest (Warner Bros)
Border Incident (MGM)
The Bribe (MGM)
Caught (MGM-Enterprise)
Chicago Deadline (Paramount)
Criss Cross (Universal-International)
The Crooked Way (United Artists)
Follow Me Quietly (RKO)
He Walked by Night (Paramount)
House of Strangers (20th Century-Fox)
Knock on Any Door (Columbia)
Manhandled (Paramount)
Moonrise (Republic)
The Reckless Moment (Columbia)
Scene of the Crime (MGM)
The Set-Up (RKO)
Thieves' Highway (20th Century-Fox)
Too Late for Tears (United Artists)
The Undercover Man (Columbia)
White Heat (Warner Bros)
The Window (RKO)

1950
Armored Car Robbery (RKO)
The Asphalt Jungle (MGM)
Between Midnight and Dawn (Columbia)
The Breaking Point (Warner Bros)
Caged (Warner Bros)
Convicted (Columbia)
The Damned Don't Cry (Warner Bros)
Dark City (Paramount)
Destination Murder (RKO)
D.O.A. (United Artists)
Edge of Doom (RKO)
The File on Thelma Jordon (Paramount)
Guilty Bystander (Film Classics)
Gun Crazy (United Artists)
In a Lonely Place (Columbia)
Kiss Tomorrow Goodbye (Warner Bros)
A Lady without Passport (MGM)
Mystery Street (MGM)
Night and the City (20th Century-Fox)
Panic in the Streets (20th Century-Fox)
Red Light (United Artists)
711 Ocean Drive (Columbia)
Shakedown (Universal-International)
Side Street (MGM)
The Sleeping City (Universal-International)
Southside 1-1000 (Allied Artists)
Sunset Boulevard (Paramount)

The Tattooed Stranger (RKO)
Tension (MGM)
Try and Get me (United Artists)
Union Station (Paramount)
Where Danger Lives (RKO)
Where the Sidewalk Ends (20th Century-Fox)
Woman on the Run (Universal-International)

1951
Appointment with Danger (Paramount)
The Big Carnival (Paramount)
The Big Night (United Artists)
Cause for Alarm (MGM)
Cry Danger (RKO)
Detective Story (Paramount)
The Enforcer (Warner Bros)
He Ran All the Way (United Artists)
His Kind of Woman (RKO)
House on Telegraph Hill (20th Century-Fox)
I Was a Communist for the F.B.I. (Warner Bros)
The Killer That Stalked New York (Columbia)
M (Columbia)
The Man Who Cheated Himself (20th Century-Fox)
The Mob (Columbia)
The People Against O'Hara (MGM)
The Prowler (United Artists)
The Second Woman (United Artists)
Strangers on a Train (Warner Bros)
The Strip (MGM)
Roadblock (RKO)
The Racket (RKO)
The Thirteenth Letter (20th Century-Fox)
The Unknown Man (MGM)

1952
Beware, My Lovely (RKO)
The Captive City (United Artists)
Clash by Night (RKO)
Kansas City Confidential (United Artists)
Loan Shark (Lippert)
Macao (RKO)
The Narrow Margin (RKO)
On Dangerous Ground (RKO)
Scandal Sheet (Columbia)
The Sniper (Columbia)
Sudden Fear (RKO)
Talk About a Stranger
The Thief (United Artists)
The Turning Point (Paramount)

1953
Angel Face (RKO)
The Big Heat (Columbia)
The Blue Gardenia (Warner Bros)
The City That Never Sleeps (Republic)
The Hitch-Hiker (RKO)
I, the Jury (United Artists)
Niagara (20th Century-Fox)
99 River Street (United Artists)

Pickup on South Street (20th Century-Fox)
Vicki (20th Century-Fox)

1954
Crime Wave (Warner Bros)
Drive a Crooked Road (Columbia)
Human Desire (Columbia)
The Long Wait (United Artists)
Loophole (Allied Artists)
The Other Woman (20th Century-Fox)
Private Hell 36 (Filmakers)
Pushover (Columbia)
Rogue Cop (MGM)
Shield for Murder (United Artists)
Suddenly (United Artists)
Witness to Murder (United Artists)
World for Ransom (Allied Artists)

1955
The Big Combo (Allied Artists)
The Big Knife (United Artists)
The Brothers Rico (Columbia)
Hell's Island (Paramount)
House of Bamboo (20th Century-Fox)
I Died a Thousand Times (Warner Bros)
Killer's Kiss (United Artists)
Kiss Me Deadly (United Artists)
Mr. Arkadin (M & A/Alexander)
Murder Is My Beat (Allied Artists)
New York Confidential (Warner Bros)
The Night Holds Terror (Columbia)

1956
Beyond a Reasonable Doubt (RKO)
The Harder They Fall (Columbia)
The Killer Is Loose (United Artists)
The Killing (United Artists)
Nightmare (United Artists)
Slightly Scarlet (RKO)
Storm Fear (United Artists)
While the City Sleeps (RKO)
The Wrong Man (Warner Bros)

1957
Baby Face Nelson (United Artists)
The Brothers Rico (Columbia)
The Burglar (Columbia)
Crime of Passion (United Artists)
The Garment Jungle (Columbia)
The Night Runner (Universal-International)
Nightfall (Columbia)
Plunder Road (20th Century-Fox)
Sweet Smell of Success (United Artists)
The Tattered Dress (Universal-International)

1958
The Lineup (Columbia)
Party Girl (MGM)
Touch of Evil (Universal-International)

1959
The Beat Generation (MGM)
The Crimson Kimono (Columbia)
Odds Against Tomorrow (United Artists)

1961
Blast of Silence (Universal-International)
Underworld U.S.A. (Columbia)

1962
Cape Fear (Universal-International)
Experiment in Terror (Columbia)
The Manchurian Candidate (United Artists)

1964
The Naked Kiss (Allied Artists)

1965
Brainstorm (Warner Bros)

1967
Point Blank (MGM)

1968
Madigan (Universal)
The Split (MGM)

1969
Marlowe (MGM)

1970
The Kremlin Letter (20th Century-Fox)

1971
Dirty Harry (Warner Bros)
The French Connection (20th Century-Fox)

1972
Hickey & Boggs (United Artists)

1973
The Friends of Eddie Coyle (Paramount)
The Long Goodbye (United Artists)

1974
Chinatown (Paramount)
The Outfit (MGM)

1975
Farewell, My Lovely (Avco-Embassy)
The French Connection II (20th Century-Fox)
Hustle (Paramount)
The Nickel Ride (20th Century-Fox)
Night Moves (Warner Bros)

1976
Taxi Driver (Columbia)

2. Directors

Aldrich, Robert
The Big Knife
The Garment Jungle (Uncredited Co-Dir)
Hustle
Kiss Me Deadly
World for Ransom

Allen, Lewis
Appointment with Danger
Chicago Deadline
Suddenly

Bernhardt, Curtis
Conflict
The High Wall

Berry, John
Caught (Uncredited Co-Dir)
He Ran All the Way
Tension

Boetticher, Budd
Behind Locked Doors
The Killer Is Loose

Brahm, John
The Brasher Doubloon
The Locket

Cromwell, John
Caged
Dead Reckoning
The Racket (1951)

Curtiz, Michael
The Breaking Point
Mildred Pierce
The Unsuspected

Dassin, Jules
Brute Force
The Naked City
Night and the City
Thieves' Highway

De Toth, Andre
Crime Wave
The Pitfall

Dieterle, William
The Accused
Dark City
The Turning Point

Dmytryk, Edward
Cornered

Crossfire
Murder, My Sweet
The Sniper

Douglas, Gordon
Between Midnight and Dawn
I Was a Communist for the F.B.I.
Kiss Tomorrow Goodbye

Farrow, John
The Big Clock
Calcutta
His Kind of Woman
Night Has a Thousand Eyes
Where Danger Lives

Fleischer, Richard
Armored Car Robbery
Follow Me Quietly
The Narrow Margin

Florey, Robert
The Crooked Way
Danger Signal

Foster, Norman
Kiss the Blood Off My Hands
Journey into Fear (Co-Dir)
Woman on the Run

Frankenheimer, John
The French Connection II
The Manchurian Candidate
52 Pick-up

Friedkin, William
The French Connection
To Live and Die in L.A.

Fuller, Samuel
The Crimson Kimono
House of Bamboo
The Naked Kiss
Pickup on South Street
Underworld U.S.A.

Garnett, Tay
Cause for Alarm
The Postman Always Rings Twice

Haskin, Byron
I Walk Alone
Too Late for Tears

Hathaway, Henry
Call Northside 777
The Dark Corner
Kiss of Death

House on 92nd Street
Niagara

Heisler, Stuart
Among the Living ·
The Glass Key
I Died a Thousand Times

Hitchcock, Alfred
Notorious
Shadow of a Doubt
Strangers on a Train
The Wrong Man

Horner, Harry
Beware, My Lovely
Vicki

Huston, John
The Asphalt Jungle
Key Largo
The Kremlin Letter

Ingster, Boris
Southside 1-1000
Stranger on the Third Floor

Karlson, Phil
The Brothers Ricco
Hell's Island
Kansas City Confidential
99 River Street
Scandal Sheet

Kubrick, Stanley
Killer's Kiss
The Killing

Lang, Fritz
Beyond a Reasonable Doubt
The Big Heat
The Blue Gardenia
Clash by Night
Fury
Human Desire
Ministry of Fear
Scarlet Street
Woman in the Window
You Only Live Once

Leroy, Mervyn
I Am a Fugitive from a Chain Gang
Johnny Eager

Lewis, Joseph H.
The Big Combo

Gun Crazy
A Lady Without Passport
My Name Is Julia Ross
So Dark the Night
Undercover Man

Losey, Joseph
The Big Night
M
The Prowler

Lupino, Ida
The Hitch-Hiker

Mankiewicz, Joseph L.
House of Strangers
Somewhere in the Night

Mann, Anthony
Border Incident
Desperate
He Walked by Night (Uncredited Co-Dir)
Railroaded
Raw Deal
Side Street
T-Men

Marin, Edwin L.
Johnny Angel
Nocturne

Maté, Rudolph
The Dark Past
D.O.A.
Union Station

Milestone, Lewis
The Racket (1928)
The Strange Love of Martha Ivers

Montgomery, Robert
The Lady in the Lake
Ride the Pink Horse

Negulesco, Jean
The Mask of Dimitrios
Nobody Lives Forever
Road House

Newman, Joseph M.
Abandoned
711 Ocean Drive

Ophuls, Max
Caught (Co-Dir)
The Reckless Moment

Parrish, Robert
Cry Danger
The Mob

Preminger, Otto
Angel Face
Fallen Angel
Laura
The Thirteenth Letter
Where the Sidewalk Ends

Quine, Richard
Drive a Crooked Mile
Pushover

Ray, Nicholas
In a Lonely Place
Knock on Any Door
Macao (Uncredited Co-Dir)
On Dangerous Ground
Party Girl
They Live by Night

Robson, Mark
Edge of Doom
The Harder They Fall

Rossen, Robert
Body and Soul
Johnny O'Clock

Rouse, Russell
New York Confidential
The Thief

Rowland, Roy
Rogue Cop
The Scene of the Crime
Witness to Murder

Sherman, Vincent
The Damned Don't Cry
The Garment Jungle (Co-Dir)
Nora Prentiss

Siegel, Don
Baby Face Nelson
Dirty Harry
The Line-Up
Madigan
Private Hell 36

Siodmak, Robert
Christmas Holiday
Criss Cross
Cry of the City

The Dark Mirror
The File on Thelma Jordon
The Killers
Phantom Lady
Uncle Harry

Sturges, John
Mystery Street
The People Against O'Hara

Tourneur, Jacques
Berlin Express
Nightfall
Out of the Past

Tuttle, Frank
Suspense
This Gun for Hire

Ulmer, Edgar G.
Detour
Murder Is My Beat
Strange Illusion

Von Sternberg, Josef
Macao (Co-Dir)
The Shanghai Gesture
Thunderbolt
Underworld

Walsh, Raoul
The Enforcer
High Sierra
White Heat

Welles, Orson
Journey into Fear (Uncredited Co-Dir)
The Lady from Shanghai
Mr. Arkadin
The Stranger
Touch of Evil

Wilder, Billy
The Big Carnival
Double Indemnity
Sunset Boulevard

Wise, Robert
Born to Kill
The Captive City
House on Telegraph Hill
Odds Against Tomorrow
The Set-Up

Wyler, William
Detective Story
The Letter

APPENDIX

3. Writers

(Key to abbreviations:

SS—*Screen story.* Usually a screen story is an unpublished and untitled story purchased by a producing studio or producer who then commissions a different writer to draft screenplay.

Scr—*Screenplay.*

Co-Scr—*Co-authorship of screenplay or contributing author.* No distinction has been made in this appendix between the many different types of writing contributions that are made during the film-making process. This may include adaptations of other materials into screenplay form, added scenes of dialogue, or complete rewriting of existing material with or without the consent and co-operation of the original screenwriter.

Co-Ss—Any contributions to the screen story before work is placed in screenplay form.)

Adams, Gerald Drayson
Armored Car Robbery (Co-Scr)
Between Midnight and Dawn (Co-Ss)
Dead Reckoning (Co-Ss)
His Kind of Woman (Ss)

Ambler, Eric
Journey into Fear (Based on his novel, same title)
The Mask of Dimitrios (Based on his novel, same title)

Anderson, Maxwell
Key Largo (Based on his play, same title)
The Wrong Man (Co-Scr, based on his article "The True Story of Christopher Emanuel Balestrero")

Anhalt, Edna and Edward
Panic in the Streets (Co-Ss)
The Sniper (Co-Ss)

Armstrong, Charlotte
Talk About a Stranger (Based on her short story "The Enemy")
The Unsuspected (Based on her novel, same title)

Babcock, Dwight V.
Loophole (Co-Ss)
So Dark the Night (Co-Scr)

Baker, Graham
Danger Signal (Co-Scr)
You Only Live Once (Co-Scr)

Bercovici, Leonardo
Dark City (Co-Scr)
Kiss the Blood Off My Hands (Co-Scr)

Bezzerides, A. I.
Kiss Me Deadly (Scr)
On Dangerous Ground (Scr & Co-Adapt)
Thieves' Highway (Scr)

Boehm, Sydney
The Big Heat (Scr)
The High Wall ((Co-Scr)
Mystery Street (Co-Scr)
Rogue Cop (Scr)
Side Street (Scr)
The Undercover Man (Scr)
Union Station (Scr)

Booth, Charles Gordon
Johnny Angel (Based on his novel, *Mr. Angel Comes Aboard*)
House of 92nd Street (Ss & Co-Scr)

Bowers, William
Abandoned (Co-Scr)
Convicted (Co-Scr)
Cry Danger (Scr)
The Mob (Scr)

Brackett, Charles
Niagara (Co-Scr)
Sunset Boulevard (Co-Scr)

Brackett, Leigh
The Big Sleep (Co-Scr)
The Long Goodbye (Scr)

Breen, Richard
Appointment with Danger (Co-Scr)
Niagara (Co-Scr)

Bricker, George
Loophole (Co-Ss)
Roadblock (Co-Scr)

Brooks, Richard
Brute Force (Co-Scr)
Crossfire (Based on his novel *The Brick Foxhole*)
Key Largo (Co-Scr)
Mystery Street (Co-Scr)

Brown, Harry
Kiss Tomorrow Goodbye (Scr)
The Sniper (Scr)

Brown, Rowland
Blood Money (Co-Scr)
Kansas City Confidential (Co-Ss)
Nocturne ((Co-Ss)

Burnett, W. R.
The Asphalt Jungle (Based on his novel, same title)
Beast of the City (Ss)
High Sierra (Co-Scr, based on his novel, same title)
I Died a Thousand Times (Scr, based on his novel *High Sierra*)
Nobody Lives Forever (Scr, based on his novel, same title)
The Racket (Co-Scr)
This Gun for Hire (Co-Scr)

Cady, Jerome
Cry Danger (Ss)
Call Northside 777 (Co-Scr)

Cain, James M.
Mildred Pierce (Based on his novel, same title)
The Postman Always Rings Twice (Based on his novel, same title)
Slightly Scarlet (Based on his novel, same title)
Double Indemnity (Based on his novel, same title)

Caspary, Vera
The Blue Gardenia (Based on her short story "Gardenia")
Laura (Based on her novel and play, same title)

Chandler, Raymond
The Big Sleep (Based on his novel, same title)
The Blue Dahlia (Scr)
The Brasher Doubloon (Based on his novel *The High Window*)
Double Indemnity (Co-Scr)
Farewell, My Lovely (Based on his novel, same title)
Lady in the Lake (Based on his novel, same title)
The Long Goodbye (Based on his novel, same title)
Marlowe (Based on his novel *The Little Sister*)
Murder, My Sweet (Based on his novel *Farewell, My Lovely*)
Strangers on a Train (Co-Scr)

Chodorov, Edward
Road House (Scr)
Undercurrent (Co-Scr)

Coffee, Lenore
Beyond the Forest (Scr)
Sudden Fear (Co-Scr)

Cole, Lester
Among the Living (Co-Ss & Co-Scr)
The High Wall (Co-Scr)

Commandini, Adele
Danger Signal (Co-Scr)
Strange Illusion (Scr)

Cooper, Dennis J.
Fear (Co-Scr)
When Strangers Marry (Co-Scr)

Cormack, Bartlett
Fury (Scr)
The Racket (1928 & 1951) (Based on his play, same title)

Dimsdale, Howard
A Lady Without Passport (Co-Scr)
Somewhere in the Night (Co-Scr)

Dinelli, Mel
Beware, My Lovely (Scr, based on his play *The Man*)
Cause for Alarm (Co-Scr)

The Reckless Moment (Co-Scr)
The Window (Scr)

Dratler, Jay
Call Northside 777 (Co-Scr)
The Dark Corner (Co-Scr)
Laura (Co-Scr)
Pitfall (Based on his novel, same title)

Duff, Warren
Appointment with Danger (Co-Scr)
Chicago Deadline (Scr)
The Turning Point (Scr)

Eisinger, Jo
Crime of Passion (Scr)
Gilda (Co-Scr)
Night and the City (Scr)
The Sleeping City (Scr)

Erskine, Chester
Angel Face (Ss)
Witness to Murder (Scr)

Essex, Harry
Desperate (Scr)
He Walked by Night (Co-Scr)
I, the Jury (Scr)
Kansas City Confidential (Co-Scr)
The Killer That Stalked New York (Scr)

Felton, Earl
Armored Car Robbery (Scr)
The Narrow Margin (Scr)

Fenton, Frank
His Kind of Woman (Co-Scr)
Nocturne (Co-Ss)

Fisher, Steve
City That Never Sleeps (Scr)
Dead Reckoning (Co-Scr)
I Wake Up Screaming (Based on his novel, same title)
I Wouldn't Be in Your Shoes (Scr)
Johnny Angel (Scr)
Lady in the Lake (Scr)
Roadblock (Co-Scr)
Vicki (Based on his novel *I Wake Up Screaming*)

Fort, Garrett
Among the Living (Co-Scr)
Street of Chance (Scr)

Frings, Ketti
Dark City (Co-Scr)
The Accused (Co-Scr)
The File on Thelma Jordon (Scr)

Fuchs, Daniel
Criss Cross (Scr)
The Gangster (Scr, based on his novel *Low Company*)
Hollow Triumph (Scr)
Panic in the Streets (Co-Scr)

Fuller, Sam
The Crimson Kimono (Scr)
House of Bamboo (Co-Scr)
The Naked Kiss (Scr)
Pickup on South Street (Scr)
Scandal Sheet (Based on his novel *The Dark Page*)
Underworld U.S.A. (Co-Scr)

Furthman, Charles
Thunderbolt (Co-Ss)
Underworld (Co-Scr)

Furthman, Jules
The Big Sleep (Co-Scr)
Nightmare Alley (Scr)
The Shanghai Gesture (Co-Scr)
Thunderbolt (Scr & Co-Ss)

Garret, Oliver H. P.
City Streets (Co-Scr)
Dead Reckoning (Co-Scr)

Goldsmith, Martin M.
Detour (Scr)
Hell's Island (Co-Ss)
The Narrow Margin (Co-Ss)
Shakedown (Co-Scr)

Goodis, David
The Burglar (Co-Scr)
Dark Passage (Based on his novel, same title)
Nightfall (Based on his novel, same title)

Gordon, James B.
See Kent, Robert E.

Greene, Clarence
D.O.A. (Co-Scr)
New York Confidential (Co-Scr)
The Thief (Scr)

Greene, Graham
Ministry of Fear (Based on his novel, same title)
This Gun for Hire (Based on his novel, same title)

Greene, Harold
Kansas City Confidential (Co-Ss)
Vicki (Co-Scr)

Gruber, Frank
Johnny Angel (Co-Scr)
The Mask of Dimitrios (Scr)

Hammett, Dashiell
City Streets (Ss)
The Glass Key (Based on his novel, same title)
The Maltese Falcon (Based on his novel, same title)

Hawkins, John and Ward
Crime Wave (Based on their short story "Criminal's Mark")
The Killer Is Loose (Based on their novelette, same title)

Hayes, Alfred
Clash by Night (Co-Scr)
Human Desire (Scr)

Hecht, Ben
Edge of Doom (Co-Scr)
Kiss of Death (Co-Scr)
Notorious (Scr)
Ride the Pink Horse (Co-Scr)
The Scoundrel (Co-Scr)
Underworld (Ss)
Where the Sidewalk Ends (Co-Scr)

Hemingway, Ernest
The Breaking Point (Based on his novel *To Have and Have Not*)
The Killers (Based on his short story, same title)

Higgins, John C.
Border Incident (Scr & Co-Ss)
He Walked by Night (Co-Scr)
Railroaded (Scr)
Raw Deal (Co-Scr)
Shield for Murder (Co-Scr)
T-Men (Scr)

Holland, Marty
Fallen Angel (Based on his novel, same title)
The File on Thelma Jordon (Ss)

Homes, Geoffrey
See Mainwaring, Daniel

Huggins, Roy
Pushover (Scr)
Too Late for Tears (Scr)

Hughes, Dorothy B.
In a Lonely Place (Based on her novel, same title)
Ride the Pink Horse (Based on her novel, same title)

Huston, John
The Asphalt Jungle (Co-Scr)
High Sierra (Co-Scr)
Key Largo (Co-Scr)
The Kremlin Letter (Co-Scr)
The Maltese Falcon (Scr)
The Stranger (Co-Scr)

Irish, William
See Woolrich, Cornell

Jacobs, Alexander
French Connection II (Co-Scr)
Point Blank (Co-Scr)

Johnson, Nunnally
The Dark Mirror (Scr)
The Woman in the Window (Scr)

Kamb, Karl
The Captive City (Co-Scr)
Pitfall (Scr)

Katcher, Leo
Between Midnight and Dawn (Co-Ss)
M (Co-Scr)
Party Girl (Ss)

Kellogg, Virginia
Caged (Co-Scr)
T-Men (Ss)
White Heat (Ss)

Kent, Robert E.
The Reckless Moment (Co-Scr)
Where the Sidewalk Ends (Co-Scr)

Kleiner, Harry
Fallen Angel (Scr)
The Garment Jungle (Scr)
House of Bamboo (Co-Scr)
The Street with No Name (Scr)

Koch, Howard
The Letter (Scr)
The Thirteenth Letter (Scr)

Kubrick, Stanley
Killer's Kiss (Scr)
The Killing (Scr)

Latimer, Jonathan
The Accused (Co-Scr)
The Big Clock (Scr)
The Glass Key (Scr)
Night Has a Thousand Eyes (Co-Scr)
Nocturne (Scr)
They Won't Believe Me (Scr)

Lederer, Charles
Kiss of Death (Co-Scr)
Ride the Pink Horse (Co-Scr)

Leonard, Jack
Hell's Island (Ss)
His Kind of Woman (Co-Scr)
The Narrow Margin (Co-Ss)

Ling, Eugene
Behind Locked Doors (Co-Scr)
Between Midnight and Dawn (Scr)
Loan Shark (Co-Scr)
Scandal Sheet (Co-Scr)

Lipsky, Eleazar
Kiss of Death (Ss)
The People Against O'Hara (Based on his novel, same title)

Lupino, Ida
The Hitch-Hiker (Co-Scr)
Private Hell 36 (Co-Scr)

Lyndon, Barre
The Accused (Co-Scr)
House on 92nd Street (Co-Scr)
Night Has a Thousand Eyes (Co-Scr)

McCoy, Horace
Kiss Tomorrow Goodbye (Based on his novel, same title)
The Turning Point (Ss)

MacDonald, Philip
The Dark Past (Co-Scr)
The Man Who Cheated Himself (Co-Scr)
Nora Prentiss (Uncredited Co-Scr)

MacDougall, Ranald
The Breaking Point (Scr)
Mildred Pierce (Scr)
Possessed (Co-Scr)
The Unsuspected (Scr)

McGivern, William P.
The Big Heat (Based on his novel, same title)
Odds Against Tomorrow (Based on his novel, same title)
Rogue Cop (Based on his novel, same title)
Shield for Murder (Based on his novel, same title)

Maddow, Ben
The Asphalt Jungle (Co-Scr)
Framed (Scr)
Kiss the Blood Off My Hands (Co-Scr)

Mahin, John Lee
Beast of the City (Scr)
Johnny Eager (Co-Scr)

Mainwaring, Daniel
Baby Face Nelson (Scr)
The Hitch-Hiker (Ss)
Out of the Past (Based on his novel "Build My Gallows High")
Roadblock (Co-Ss)

Maltz, Albert
The Naked City (Co-Scr)
This Gun for Hire (Co-Scr)

APPENDIX

Mankiewicz, Herman J.
Christmas Holiday (Scr)
Thunderbolt (Co-Scr)

Mankiewicz, Joseph L.
Somewhere in the Night (Co-Scr)
Thunderbolt (Co-Scr)

Mann, Anthony
Desperate (Co-Ss)
Follow Me Quietly (Co-Ss)

Marcus, Larry
Brainstorm (Ss)
Cause for Alarm (Ss)
Dark City (Scr)

Martin, Don
Destination Murder (Scr)
The Pretender (Scr)
Shakedown (Co-Ss)

Maugham, W. Somerset
Christmas Holiday (Based on his novel, same title)
The Letter (Based on his short story, same title)

Medford, Harold
Berlin Express (Scr)
The Damned Don't Cry (Co-Scr)
The Killer Is Loose (Scr)

Meltzer, Lewis
The Beat Generation (Co-Scr)
The Brothers Rico (Co-Scr)

Miller, Seton I.
Calcutta (Scr)
Convicted (Co-Scr)
The Man Who Cheated Himself (Ss & Co-Scr)
Ministry of Fear (Scr)

Monks, John, Jr.
House on 92nd Street (Co-Scr)
Knock on Any Door (Co-Scr)
The People Against O'Hara (Scr)

Murphy, Richard
Cry of the City (Scr)
Panic in the Streets (Co-Scr)

Odets, Clifford
The Big Knife (Based on his play, same title)
Clash by Night (Based on his play, same title)
Deadline at Dawn (Scr)
Sweet Smell of Success (Co-Scr)

Pagano, Jo
Try and Get Me (Scr, based on his novel *The Condemned*)

Partos, Frank
The House on Telegraph Hill (Co-Scr)
Stranger on the Third Floor (Scr)

Patrick, Jack
Framed (Ss)
The Strange Love of Martha Ivers (Ss)

Paxton, John
Cornered (Scr)
Crack-Up (Co-Scr)
Crossfire (Scr)
Murder, My Sweet (Scr)

Poe, James
The Big Knife (Scr)
Scandal Sheet (Co-Scr)

Polonsky, Abraham
Body and Soul (Scr)
Force of Evil (Co-Scr)
Madigan (Co-Scr)

Rackin, Martin
Desperate (Co-Scr)
The Enforcer (Scr)
Loan Shark (Co-Scr)

Rivkin, Allen
The Accused (Co-Scr)
Dead Reckoning (Co-Scr)
The Strip (Scr)
Tension (Scr)

Roberts, Marguerite
The Bribe (Scr)
Undercurrent (Co-Scr)

Rossen, Robert
Johnny O'Clock (Scr)
The Strange Love of Martha Ivers (Scr)

Rosten, Leo
The Dark Corner (Based on his short story, same title)
Sleep, My Love (Co-Scr, based on his novel, same title)
Where Danger Lives (Ss)

Rouse, Russell
D.O.A. (Co-Scr)
New York Confidential (Co-Scr)
The Thief (Co-Scr)

Rubin, Stanley
Decoy (Ss)
Macao (Co-Scr)

Samuels, Lesser
The Big Carnival (Co-Scr)
The Long Wait (Co-Scr)

Schnee, Charles
The Accused (Co-Scr)
I Walk Alone (Co-Scr)
Scene of the Crime (Scr)
They Live by Night (Scr)

Schoenfeld, Bernard C.
Caged (Co-Scr)
The Dark Corner (Co-Scr)
Macao (Co-Scr)
Phantom Lady (Scr)

Shane, Maxwell
Hell's Island (Scr)
Nightmare (Scr)

Silliphant, Sterling
The Lineup (Scr)
Marlowe (Scr)
Nightfall (Scr)

Smith, Robert
I Walk Alone (Co-Scr)
99 River Street (Scr)
The Second Woman (Co-Scr)
Sudden Fear (Scr)

Spigelgass, Leonard
The Accused (Co-Scr)
Mystery Street (Ss)

Spillane, Mickey
I, the Jury (Based on his novel, same title)
Kiss Me Deadly (Based on his novel, same title)
The Long Wait (Based on his novel, same title)

Stark, Richard
See Westlake, Donald E.

Taylor, Dwight
Conflict (Co-Scr)
I Wake Up Screaming (Scr)
Pickup on South Street (Ss)
Vicki (Co-Scr)

Tidyman, Ernest
The French Connection (Scr)

Townsend, Leo
Southside 1-1000 (Co-Scr)
Vicki (Co-Scr)

Trivas, Victor
The Stranger (Ss)
Where the Sidewalk Ends (Co-Scr)

Veiller, Anthony
The Killers (Scr)
The Stranger (Co-Scr)

Wald, Malvin
Behind Locked Doors (Co-Scr)
The Dark Past (Co-Scr)
The Naked City (Co-Scr)
The Undercover Man (Co-Scr)

Walker, Gertrude
The Damned Don't Cry (Based on her short story, same title)
Railroaded (Based on her short story, same title)

Walsh, Thomas
Pushover (Based on his serialized story "The Killer Wore a Badge" and his novel *The Night Watch*)
Union Station (Ss)

Weidman, Jerome
The Damned Don't Cry (Scr)
House of Strangers (Based on his novel *I'll Never Go There Again*)

Welles, Orson
Journey into Fear (Co-Scr)
The Lady from Shanghai (Scr)
Mr. Arkadin (Scr, based on his novel, same title)
The Stranger (Co-Scr)
Touch of Evil (Scr)

Westlake, Donald E.
The Outfit (Based on his novel, same title)
Point Blank (Based on his novel *The Hunter*)
The Split (Based on his novel *The Seventh*)

Wilburn, Crane
Canon City (Scr)
Crime Wave (Scr)
He Walked by Night (Ss & Co-Scr)
I Was a Communist for the F.B.I. (Scr)

Wilder, Billy
The Big Carnival (Co-Scr)
Double Indemnity (Co-Scr)
Sunset Boulevard (Co-Scr)

Woolrich, Cornell
Black Angel (Based on his novel, same title)
The Chase (Based on his novel *The Black Path of Fear*)
Deadline at Dawn (Based on his novel, same title)
Fall Guy (Based on his novel, same title)
The Guilty (Based on his short story "Two Men in a Furnished Room")

I Wouldn't Be in Your Shoes (Based on his novel, same title)
Night Has a Thousand Eyes (Based on his novel, same title)
Nightmare (Based on his novel, same title)
Phantom Lady (Based on his novel, same title)
Street of Chance (Based on his novel *The Black Curtain*)
The Boy Cried Murder (Based on his novel, same title)

Yordan, Philip
The Big Combo (Scr)
The Chase (Scr)
Detective Story (Co-Scr)
Edge of Doom (Co-Scr)
The Harder They Fall (Scr)
House of Strangers (Scr)
Suspense (Scr)
When Strangers Marry (Co-Scr)

Young, Collier
Act of Violence (Ss)
The Hitch-Hiker (Co-Scr)
Private Hell 36 (Co-Scr)

Zuckerman, George
Border Incident (Co-Ss)
99 River Street (Ss)
The Tattered Dress (Scr)

4. Directors of Photography
("C" indicates a color film)

Ahern, Lloyd
The Brasher Doubloon
Cry of the City

Alonzo, John
Chinatown (c)
Farewell My Lovely (c)

Alton, John
The Big Combo
Border Incident
Canon City
The Crooked Way
He Walked by Night
The Hollow Triumph
I, the Jury
Mystery Street
The People Against O'Hara
The Pretender
Raw Deal
Slightly Scarlet (c)
T-Men
Talk about a Stranger

Ballard, Lucien
Berlin Express
The House on Telegraph Hill
The Killer Is Loose
The Killing

Biroc, Joseph P.
Cry Danger
The Garment Jungle
Hustle (c)
The Killer That Stalked New York
Loan Shark
Nightmare
World for Ransom

Bredell, Woody
Christmas Holiday
The Killers
Lady on a Train
Phantom Lady
The Unsuspected

Brodine, Norbert
Beast of the City
House on 92nd Street
Kiss of Death
Somewhere in the Night
Thieves' Highway

Burks, Robert
Beyond the Forest
The Enforcer
Possessed (Special Effects)
Strangers on a Train
The Wrong Man

Daniels, William
Abandoned
Brute Force
Marlowe (c)
The Naked City

de Grasse, Robert
Born to Kill
The Crack-Up
Follow Me Quietly

Diskant, George E.
Between Midnight and Dawn
Beware My Lovely
Desperate
Kansas City Confidential
The Narrow Margin
On Dangerous Ground
The Racket (1951)
They Live by Night

APPENDIX

DuPar, Edwin
Beyond the Forest (Special Effects)
I Was a Communist for the F.B.I.

Edeson, Arthur
The Maltese Falcon
The Mask of Dimitrios
Nobody Lives Forever

Fitzgerald, Eddie
New York Confidential
The Other Woman

Freund, Karl
Key Largo
Undercurrent

Garmes, Lee
The Captive City
Caught
City Streets
The Detective Story
Nightmare Alley
The Scoundrel

Gaudio, Tony
High Sierra
The Letter
The Racket (1928)

Glennon, Bert
Crime Wave
Red Light
Underworld

Greenhalgh, Jack
Fear in the Night

Guffey, Burnett
The Brothers Rico
Convicted
Framed
The Harder They Fall
Human Desire
In a Lonely Place
Johnny O'Clock
Knock on Any Door
My Name Is Julia Ross
Night Editor (Co-Photog)
Nightfall
Private Hell 36
The Reckless Moment
Scandal Sheet
The Sniper
So Dark the Night
The Split
The Undercover Man

Guthrie, Carl E.
Caged
The Tattered Dress

Haller, Ernest
Mildred Pierce
Plunder Road

Harlan, Russell
Gun Crazy
The Man Who Cheated Himself
Southside 1-1000

Hickox, Sid
The Big Sleep
Dark Passage
White Heat

Howe, James Wong
Body and Soul
Danger Signal
He Ran All the Way
Nora Prentiss
The Sweet Smell of Success

Ivano, Paul
Black Angel
The Gangster
The Shanghai Gesture
Uncle Harry

Krasner, Milton
The Accused
The Dark Mirror
A Double Life
House of Strangers
Scarlet Street
The Set-Up
Vicki
The Woman in the Window

Lang, Charles B.
The Big Carnival
The Big Heat
Sudden Fear

LaShelle, Joseph
Crime of Passion
Fallen Angel
Laura
Road House
Storm Fear
The Thirteenth Letter
Where the Sidewalk Ends

347

APPENDIX

Laszlo, Ernest
The Big Knife
D.O.A.
Kiss Me Deadly
M
Manhandled
While the City Sleeps

Lathrop, Philip
Experiment in Terror
Point Blank (c)

Lawton, Charles, Jr.
Drive a Crooked Road
The Lady from Shanghai

Leavitt, Samuel
Brainstorm
Cape Fear
The Crimson Kimono
The Thief

Lindon, Lionel
The Blue Dahlia
Hell's Island (c)
The Manchurian Candidate
The Turning Point

McCord, Ted
The Breaking Point
The Damned Don't Cry
I Died a Thousand Times (c)

MacDonald, Joseph
Call Northside 777
The Dark Corner
House of Bamboo (c)
Niagara (c)
Panic in the Streets
Pickup on South Street
The Street with No Name

Mellor, William
Too Late for Tears
The Unknown Man

Metty, Russell
Kiss the Blood Off My Hands
Madigan (c)
Ride the Pink Horse
The Stranger
Touch of Evil

Milner, Victor
Dark City
The Strange Love of Martha Ivers

Mohr, Hal
Baby Face Nelson
The Big Night
The Line-Up
The Second Woman
Underworld U.S.A.
Woman on the Run

Musuraca, Nicholas
The Blue Gardenia
Clash by Night
Deadline at Dawn
The Hitchhiker
The Locket
Out of the Past
Roadblock
Stranger on the Third Floor
Where Danger Lives

Planer, Franz F.
The Chase
Criss Cross
The Long Wait
99 River Street
711 Ocean Drive

Polito, Sol
I Am a Fugitive from a Chain Gang
Sorry, Wrong Number

Roe, Guy
Armored Car Robbery
Behind Locked Doors
Railroaded
Try and Get Me

Roizman, Owen
The French Connection

Rose, Jackson J.
Destination Murder
Fear

Rosson, Harold
The Asphalt Jungle
Johnny Eager

Russell, John L.
The City That Never Sleeps
Moonrise

Ruttenberg, Joseph
The Bribe
Cause for Alarm
Fury
Side Street

Seitz, John F.
Appointment with Danger
The Big Clock
Calcutta
Chicago Deadline
Double Indemnity
The Night Has a Thousand Eyes
Rogue Cop
Sunset Boulevard
This Gun for Hire

Shamroy, Leon
Leave Her to Heaven (c)
You Only Live Once

Sharp, Henry
The Guilty
Ministry of Fear

Sparkuhl, Theodore
Among the Living
The Glass Key
Street of Chance

Steiner, William
The Tattooed Stranger
The Window

Stengler, Mack
Fall Guy
I Wouldn't Be in Your Shoes

Stradling, Harry
Angel Face
Edge of Doom
Tension

Struss, Karl
Journey into Fear
Suspense

Surtees, Bruce
Dirty Harry (c)
Night Moves (c)
The Outfit (c)

Surtees, Robert
Act of Violence
The Strip

Tannura, Philip
Night Editor (Co-Photog)
Strange Illusion

Tover, Leo
Dead Reckoning
I Walk Alone

Valentine, Joseph
Possessed
Shadow of a Doubt
Sleep, My Love

Vogel, Paul
The High Wall
Lady in the Lake
Lady without a Passport
Scene of the Crime

Walker, Joseph
The Dark Past
The Mob

Wild, Harry J.
Cornered
His Kind of Woman
Johnny Angel
Macao
Murder, My Sweet
Nocturne
The Pitfall
They Won't Believe Me

5. Composers

Amfitheatrof, Daniele
The Damned Don't Cry
House of Strangers
Human Desire
Suspense

Anthiel, George
In a Lonely Place
Knock on Any Door
The Sniper

Bakaleinikoff, Constantin
Angel Face
Born to Kill
The Racket (1951)
The Set-Up

Bakaleinikoff, Mischa
The Lineup
My Name Is Julia Ross
Night Editor

Bernstein, Elmer
Storm Fear
Sudden Fear
Sweet Smell of Success

APPENDIX

Buttolph, David
The Brasher Doubloon
Crime Wave
The Enforcer
House on 92nd Street
I Died a Thousand Times
Kiss of Death
Somewhere in the Night
Street of Chance
Talk about a Stranger

Butts, Dale
City That Never Sleeps
Too Late for Tears

Deutsch, Adolph
Danger Signal
High Sierra
The Maltese Falcon
The Mask of Dimitrios
Nobody Lives Forever

DeVol, Frank
The Big Knife
Hustle
Kiss Me Deadly
World for Ransom

Dragon, Carmen
Kiss Tomorrow Goodbye
People Against O'Hara

Duning, George
Between Midnight and Dawn
Brainstorm
The Brothers Rico
Convicted
The Dark Past
Johnny O'Clock
The Mob
Nightfall
Scandal Sheet
The Undercover Man

Dunlap, Paul
Crime of Passion
Cry Danger
Loophole
The Naked Kiss
Shield for Murder

Ellis, Don
The French Connection
The French Connection II

Erody, Leo
Detour
Strange Illusion

Forbes, Louis
The Crooked Way
Pitfall

Friedhofer, Hugo
The Big Carnival
Body and Soul
Edge of Doom
The Harder They Fall
So Dark the Night
Try and Get Me

Friedman, Irving
Behind Locked Doors
Canon City

Gershenson, Joseph
The Night Runner
Shakedown

Gertz, Irving
Destination Murder
Plunder Road

Gilbert, Herschel Burke
Beyond a Reasonable Doubt
Nightmare
The Thief
While the City Sleeps
Witness to Murder

Glasser, Albert
The Beat Generation (Co-Comp)
Murder Is My Beat

Grusin, Dave
The Friends of Eddie Coyle
The Nickel Ride

Harline, Leigh
Crack-Up
His Kind of Woman
House of Bamboo
Johnny Angel
Nocturne
Pickup on South Street
They Live by Night
Vicki

Herrmann, Bernard
Cape Fear
On Dangerous Ground
Taxi Driver
The Wrong Man

Hollander, Frederick
Berlin Express
Caught
Conflict

Kaper, Bronislau
Act of Violence
The High Wall
Johnny Eager
The Stranger

Kaplan, Sol
The Burglar
The Hollow Triumph
House on Telegraph Hill
Niagara
711 Ocean Drive

Kay, Edward J.
Fall Guy
I Wouldn't Be in Your Shoes

Lange, Arthur
99 River Street
The Woman in the Window
Woman on the Run (Co-Comp)

Mancini, Henry
Experiment in Terror
Touch of Evil

Michelet, Michel
The Chase
M

Mockridge, Cyril
The Dark Corner
I Wake Up Screaming
Nightmare Alley
Road House
Where the Sidewalk Ends

Murray, Lyn
The Big Night
The Prowler

Newman, Alfred
Cry of the City
Leave Her to Heaven
Panic in the Streets
Thieves' Highway

Newman, Emil
Cry Danger
99 River Street (Co-Comp)
Woman on the Run (Co-Comp)

Previn, André
Border Incident
Cause for Alarm
Scene of the Crime
Tension

Raab, Leonid
Follow Me Quietly
He Walked by Night

Raksin, David
The Big Combo
Fallen Angel
Force of Evil
A Lady without Passport
Laura
Suddenly

Rozsa, Miklos
The Asphalt Jungle
The Bribe
Brute Force
Criss Cross
Double Indemnity
A Double Life
The Killers
Kiss the Blood Off My Hands
Lady on a Train
The Naked City
The Strange Love of Martha Ivers

Salter, Hans J.
Christmas Holiday
The Killer That Stalked New York
Phantom Lady
The Reckless Moment
Scarlet Street
Uncle Harry

Sawtell, Paul
Born to Kill
Desperate
Kansas City Confidential
Raw Deal
Roadblock
Southside 1-1000
T-Men

Schrager, Rudy
The Guilty
Sleep, My Love

Skiles, Marlin
Dead Reckoning
Framed

Skinner, Frank
Black Angel
The Naked City
Ride the Pink Horse
The Sleeping City
The Tattered Dress

Steiner, Max
Beyond the Forest
The Big Sleep
Caged
Key Largo
The Letter
Mildred Pierce
White Heat

Stevens, Leith
Beware, My Lovely
The Garment Jungle
The Hitch-Hiker
Private Hell 36

Sukman, Harry
The Crimson Kimono
Underworld U.S.A.

Talbot, Irving
Hell's Island
The Turning Point
Union Station

Tiomkin, Dimitri
Angel Face
D.O.A.
The Dark Mirror
Guilty Bystander
Red Light
Shadow of a Doubt
Strangers on a Train
When Strangers Marry

Waxman, Franz
Dark City
Dark Passage
Fury
He Ran All the Way
I, the Jury
Night and the City
Nora Prentiss
Possessed
Sorry, Wrong Number
Sunset Boulevard
The Unsuspected

Webb, Roy
Armored Car Robbery
Clash by Night
Cornered
Crossfire
Journey into Fear
The Locket
Murder, My Sweet
Notorious
Out of the Past
They Won't Believe Me

Where Danger Lives
The Window

Young Victor
The Accused
Appointment with Danger
The Big Clock
The Blue Dahlia
Calcutta
Chicago Deadline
The File on Thelma Jordon
The Glass Key
Gun Crazy
I Walk Alone
Ministry of Fear
Night Has a Thousand Eyes

6. Producers

Aldrich, Robert
The Big Knife
Hustle
World for Ransom (Co-Prod)

Bassler, Robert
The Brasher Doubloon
The House on Telegraph Hill
Suddenly
Thieves' Highway

Berman, Pandro S.
The Bribe
Undercurrent

Bick, Jerry
The Long Goodbye
Farewell My Lovely (Exec-Prod)

Bischoff, Samuel
Macao (Exec-Prod)
The Pitfall

Blanke, Henry
Beyond the Forest
The Maltese Falcon
The Mask of Dimitrios

Bogeaus, Benedict
The Crooked Way
Slightly Scarlet

Bressler, Jerry
Abandoned
Convicted
The Mob

Chartoff, Robert
Point Blank
The Split

De Haven, Carter
The Kremlin Letter (Co-Prod)
The Outfit

De Dylva, B. G.
Double Indemnity (Exec-Prod)
The Glass Key (Exec-Prod)
Ministry of Fear (Exec-Prod)

Eagle, S. P.
See Spiegel, Sam

Engel, Samuel G.
Night and the City
The Street with No Name

Feld, Milton
Phantom Lady (Exec-Prod)
Uncle Harry (Exec-Prod)

Fellows, Robert
Appointment with Danger
Chicago Deadline

Foy, Bryan
Crime Wave
Hollow Triumph
I Was a Communist for the F.B.I.

Fromkess, Leon
Detour
The Naked Kiss (Exec-Prod)
Strange Illusion

Fuller, Samuel
The Crimson Kimono
The Naked Kiss
Underworld U.S.A.

Goldstein, Leonard
The Sleeping City
Vicki

Gottlieb, Alex
The Blue Gardenia
Macao

Granet, Bert
Berlin Express
The Locket

Gross, Jack J.
Crack-Up (Exec-Prod)
Johnny Angel

The Locket (Exec-Prod)
Nocturne (Exec-Prod)
They Won't Believe Me (Exec-Prod)

Harrison, Joan
Nocturne
Phantom Lady
Ride the Pink Horse
They Won't Believe Me
Uncle Harry

Hellinger, Mark
Brute Force
High Sierra
The Killers
The Naked City

Houseman, John
The Blue Dahlia
On Dangerous Ground
They Live by Night

Jackson, Felix
Christmas Holiday (Exec-Prod)
Lady on a Train

Jacobs, William
Conflict
Danger Signal
Nora Prentiss

Kane, Robert
Canon City
He Walked by Night

Kastner, Elliott
Farewell My Lovely (Exec-Prod)
The Long Goodbye (Exec-Prod)

Kaufman, Joe
Red Light (Assoc-Prod)
Sudden Fear

King, Frank and Maurice
The Gangster
Gun Crazy
Southside 1-1000
Suspense
When Strangers Marry

Kohlmar, Fred
The Dark Corner
The Glass Key
Kiss of Death

Kraike, Michael
Criss Cross
Desperate

Lord, Robert
The High Wall
In a Lonely Place
Knock on Any Door
The Letter (Assoc-Prod)

Miller, Seton I.
Calcutta
Ministry of Fear (Assoc-Prod)

Mirisch, Walter
Fall Guy
I Wouldn't Be in Your Shoes

Nebenzal, Seymour
The Chase
M

Parsons, Lindsley
Fear
Loophole

Pasternak, Joe
Party Girl
The Strip

Pine, William H.
Fear in the Night (Co-Prod)
Hell's Island (Co-Prod)
Manhandled (Co-Prod)
Nightmare (Co-Prod)

Popkin, Harry M.
D.O.A.
The Second Woman (Exec-Prod)
The Thief (Exec-Prod)

Preminger, Otto
Angel Face
Fallen Angel
Laura
The Thirteenth Letter
Where the Sidewalk Ends

Rachmil, Lewis J.
The Brothers Rico
Human Desire
Roadblock

Richmond, Ted
The Night Editor
Nightfall
Shakedown
So Dark the Night

Roberts, Bob
Body and Soul

Force of Evil
He Ran All the Way

Rogell, Sid
Born to Kill (Exec-Prod)
Deadline at Dawn (Exec-Prod)
Murder, My Sweet (Exec-Prod)

Rosenberg, Frank P.
Madigan
Where the Sidewalk Ends (Assoc-Prod)

Saville, Victor
I, the Jury
Kiss Me Deadly

Schary, Dore
Berlin Express (Exec-Prod)
Crossfire (Exec-Prod)
They Live by Night (Exec-Prod)

Schenck, Aubrey
Shield for Murder
T-Men

Schermer, Jules
Framed
Pickup on South Street
Pushover
Union Station

Schlom, Herbert
Armored Car Robbery
Born to Kill
Follow Me Quietly

Scott, Adrian
Cornered
Crossfire
Deadline at Dawn
Murder, My Sweet

Siegel, Sol C.
Among the Living
Cry of the City
House of Strangers
Panic in the Streets

Small, Edward
Kansas City Confidential
99 River Street
Raw Deal
Scandal Sheet
T-Men (Exec-Prod)

Sparks, Robert
His Kind of Woman
Out of the Past

Sperling, Milton
The Enforcer
I Wake Up Screaming

Spiegel, Sam
The Prowler
The Stranger

Stromberg, Hunt
Beast of the City
Between Midnight and Dawn
Too Late for Tears

Thomas, William C.
Fear in the Night (Co-Prod)
Hell's Island (Co-Prod)
Manhandled (Co-Prod)
Nightmare (Co-Prod)

Wald, Jerry
The Breaking Point
Caged
The Damned Don't Cry
Dark Passage
Key Largo
Mildred Pierce
Possessed

Wallis, Hal B.
The Accused
Dark City
High Sierra
The File on Thelma Jordon
I Am a Fugitive from a Chain Gang
I Walk Alone
The Letter
The Maltese Falcon
Sorry, Wrong Number
The Strange Love of Martha Ivers

Wanger, Walter
The Reckless Moment
Scarlet Street (Exec-Prod)
You Only Live Once

Warner, Jack L.
The Letter (Exec-Prod)
Nobody Lives Forever (Exec-Prod)
White Heat (Exec-Prod)

Waxman, Philip A.
The Big Night
Pushover (Assoc-Prod)

Wiesenthal, Sam
Cry Danger
The Kremlin Letter (Co-Prod)

Wright, William H.
Act of Violence
The People Against O'Hara

Young, Collier
Beware, My Lovely
The Hitch-Hiker
Private Hell 36

Zugsmith, Albert
The Beat Generation
The Tattered Dress
Touch of Evil

7. Actors and Actresses

Adler, Jay
The Big Combo
Crime of Passion
Cry Danger
The Long Wait
The Mob
Murder Is My Beat
99 River Street
Scandal Sheet
Sweet Smell of Success

Adler, Luther
Cornered
D.O.A.
House of Strangers
Kiss Tomorrow Goodbye
M

Alda, Robert
The Man I Love
Nora Prentiss

Ames, Leon
Angel Face
Lady in the Lake
The Postman Always Rings Twice
Scene of the Crime

Andrews, Dana
Beyond a Reasonable Doubt
Brainstorm
Edge of Doom
Fallen Angel
Laura
Where the Sidewalk Ends
While the City Sleeps

Astor, Mary
Act of Violence
The Maltese Falcon

APPENDIX

Bacall, Lauren
The Big Sleep
Dark Passage
Key Largo

Ball, Lucille
The Dark Corner

Bancroft, Anne
New York Confidential
Nightfall

Bancroft, George
Thunderbolt
Underworld

Barrymore, John, Jr.
The Big Night
While the City Sleeps

Basehart, Richard
He Walked by Night
House on Telegraph Hill
Tension

Begley, Ed
Convicted
Dark City
Odds Against Tomorrow
On Dangerous Ground
Sorry, Wrong Number
Street with No Name
The Turning Point

Bel Geddes, Barbara
Caught
Panic in the Streets

Bendix, William
The Blue Dahlia
Calcutta
The Dark Corner
Detective Story
The Glass Key

Bennett, Joan
Hollow Triumph
The Reckless Moment
Scarlet Street
The Woman in the Window

Bergman, Ingrid
Notorious

Bickford, Charles
Brute Force
Fallen Angel

Bissell, Whit
The Big Combo
The Brothers Rico
Convicted
Canon City
A Double Life
He Walked by Night
The Killer That Stalked New York
The Manchurian Candidate
Raw Deal
Side Street
Somewhere in the Night
The Turning Point

Blyth, Ann,
Brute Force
Mildred Pierce

Bogart, Humphrey
The Big Sleep
Conflict
Dark Passage
Dead Reckoning
The Enforcer
The Harder They Fall
High Sierra
In a Lonely Place
Key Largo
Knock on Any Door
The Maltese Falcon

Bond, Ward
Fury
Kiss Tomorrow Goodbye
The Maltese Falcon
On Dangerous Ground
You Only Live Once

Boone, Richard
The Big Knife
The Garment Jungle
The Kremlin Letter
Vicki

Borgnine, Ernest
Hustle
The Mob
The Split

Brand, Neville
D.O.A.
Kansas City Confidential
Kiss Tomorrow Goodbye
The Mob
The Turning Point
Where the Sidewalk Ends

Brasselle, Keefe
Railroaded

356

T-Men
The Unknown Man

Brennan, Walter
Fury
Nobody Lives Forever

Bridges, Lloyd
Moonrise
Try and Get Me

Brocco, Peter
The Breaking Point
His Kind of Woman
The Killer That Stalked New York
The Reckless Moment
Roadblock
Rogue Cop
Tension
The Undercover Man
Underworld U.S.A.

Brodie, Steve
Armored Car Robbery
Crossfire
Desperate
Kiss Tomorrow Goodbye
M
Out of the Past

Bronson, Charles
Crime Wave
The Mob
The People Against O'Hara

Burr, Raymond
Abandoned
The Blue Gardenia
Crime of Passion
Desperate
His Kind of Woman
M
Pitfall
Raw Deal
Red Light
Sleep, My Love

Cabot, Bruce
Fallen Angel
Fury

Cagney, James
Kiss Tomorrow Goodbye
White Heat

Calhern, Louis
Asphalt Jungle
Notorious

Carey, Timothy
Crime Wave
The Killing
The Outfit

Carlson, Richard
Behind Locked Doors
Try and Get Me

Carr, Marian
The Harder They Fall
Kiss Me Deadly
Nightmare
World for Ransom

Castle, Peggy
I, the Jury
The Long Wait
99 River Street

Chandler, Jeff
The Accused
Johnny O'Clock
The Tattered Dress

Charisse, Cyd
Party Girl
Tension

Cianelli, Eduardo
The Mask of Dimitrios
The People Against O'Hara
The Scoundrel

Clark, Dane
Moonrise

Clark, Fred
Cry of the City
Ride the Pink Horse
Sunset Boulevard
The Unsuspected
White Heat

Cobb, Lee J.
Call Northside 777
The Dark Past
The Garment Jungle
Johnny O'Clock
The Man Who Cheated Himself
Party Girl
Thieves' Highway

Cochran, Steve
The Beat Generation
The Damned Don't Cry
Private Hell 36
White Heat

APPENDIX

Conrad, William
Body and Soul
Cry Danger
The Killers
The Racket
Sorry, Wrong Number
Tension

Conte, Richard
The Big Combo
The Blue Gardenia
The Brothers Rico
Call Northside 777
Cry of the City
House of Strangers
New York Confidential
The Sleeping City
Thieves' Highway

Cook, Elisha, Jr.
Baby Face Nelson
The Big Sleep
Born to Kill
Fall Guy
The Gangster
I, the Jury
I Wake Up Screaming
The Killing
The Maltese Falcon
The Outfit
Phantom Lady
Plunder Road
Stranger on the Third Floor

Corey, Jeff
Brute Force
Canon City
Follow Me Quietly
The Gangster
The Killers
Somewhere in the Night

Corey, Wendell
The Accused
The Big Knife
The File on Thelma Jordon
I Walk Alone
The Killer Is Loose
Sorry, Wrong Number

Cortesa, Valentina
House on Telegraph Hill
Thieves' Highway

Cotten, Joseph
Beyond the Forest
Journey into Fear
The Killer Is Loose

Niagara
Shadow of a Doubt
Touch of Evil

Coulouris, George
Lady on a Train
Nobody Lives Forever
Sleep, My Love

Craig, James
A Lady Without Passport
Sidestreet
The Strip
While the City Sleeps

Crain, Jeanne
Leave Her to Heaven
The Tattered Dress
Vicki

Crawford, Broderick
Black Angel
Convicted
Human Desire
The Mob
New York Confidential
Scandal Sheet

Crawford, Joan
The Damned Don't Cry
Mildred Pierce
Possessed
Sudden Fear

Cregar, Laird
I Wake Up Screaming
This Gun for Hire

Cronyn, Hume
Brute Force
The Postman Always Rings Twice
Shadow of a Doubt

Cummings, Robert
The Accused
The Chase
Sleep, My Love

Cummins, Peggy
Gun Crazy

Curtis, Tony
Criss Cross
Sweet Smell of Success

Dahl, Arlene
Scene of the Crime
Slightly Scarlet

Dall, John
Gun Crazy
The Man Who Cheated Himself

Danton, Ray
The Beat Generation
Night Runner

Darnell, Linda
Fallen Angel
The Thirteenth Letter

Da Silva, Howard
The Blue Dahlia
Border Incident
M
They Live by Night

Davis, Bette
Beyond the Forest
The Letter

DeCarlo, Yvonne
Brute Force
Criss Cross
This Gun for Hire

DeCorsia, Ted
Baby Face Nelson
The Big Combo
Crime Wave
The Enforcer
The Killing
The Lady from Shanghai
The Naked City
Slightly Scarlet

DeFore, Don
Dark City
Southside 1-1000
Too Late for Tears

Dekker, Albert
Among the Living
Destination Murder
The Killers
Kiss Me Deadly
The Pretender
Suspense

Dennis, Nick
The Big Knife
Kiss Me Deadly

Derek, John
Knock on Any Door
Scandal Sheet

Dickinson, Angie
The Killers
Point Blank

Dietrich, Marlene
Touch of Evil

Donlevy, Brian
The Big Combo
The Glass Key
Kiss of Death
Shakedown

Dorn, Dolores
Underworld U.S.A.

Doucette, John
The Big Heat
The Breaking Point
Canon City
Convicted
Criss Cross
The Crooked Way
House of Bamboo
I Wouldn't Be in Your Shoes
New York Confidential
Ride the Pink Horse
Strangers on a Train

Douglas, Kirk
The Big Carnival
Detective Story
I Walk Alone
Out of the Past
Strange Love of Martha Ivers

Douglas, Paul
Clash by Night
Panic in the Streets

Duff, Howard
Brute Force
The Naked City
Private Hell 36
Shakedown
While the City Sleeps

Duryea, Dan
Black Angel
The Burglar
Criss Cross
Lady on a Train
Manhandled
Ministry of Fear
Scarlet Street
Storm Fear
Too Late for Tears
The Woman in the Window
World for Ransom

Edwards, Vince
The Killing
The Night Holds Terror
Rogue Cop

Elam, Jack
Baby Face Nelson
Kansas City Confidential
Kiss Me Deadly

Evans, Gene
Armored Car Robbery
Berlin Express
The Big Carnival
Criss Cross
The Long Wait

Fitzgerald, Barry
The Naked City
Union Station

Fitzgerald, Geraldine
Nobody Lives Forever
Uncle Harry

Fleming, Rhonda
Cry Danger
The Killer Is Loose
Out of the Past
Slightly Scarlet
While the City Sleeps

Flippen, Jay C.
Brute Force
The Killing
The People Against O'Hara
They Live by Night

Fonda, Henry
Madigan
The Wrong Man
You Only Live Once

Fontaine, Joan
Beyond a Reasonable Doubt
Kiss the Blood Off My Hands

Ford, Glenn
The Big Heat
Convicted
Experiment in Terror
Framed
Gilda
Human Desire
The Undercover Man

Ford, Wallace
Beast of the City

The Breaking Point
Crack-Up
Dead Reckoning
He Ran All the Way
The Set-Up
Shadow of a Doubt
T-Men

Foster, Preston
I Am a Fugitive from a Chain Gang

I, the Jury
Kansas City Confidential

Gardner, Ava
The Bribe
The Killers

Garfield, John
Body and Soul
The Breaking Point
Force of Evil
He Ran All the Way
Nobody Lives Forever
The Postman Always Rings Twice

Gomez, Thomas
Force of Evil
Johnny O'Clock
Key Largo
Macao
Phantom Lady
Ride the Pink Horse

Grahame, Gloria
The Big Heat
Crossfire
Human Desire
In a Lonely Place
Macao
Odds Against Tomorrow
Sudden Fear

Granger, Farley
Edge of Doom
Side Street
Strangers on a Train
They Live by Night

Grant, Cary
Notorious

Gray, Coleen
Kansas City Confidential
The Killing
Kiss of Death
Nightmare Alley
The Sleeping City

Greenstreet, Sydney
Conflict
The Maltese Falcon
The Mask of Dimitrios

Greer, Jane
Out of the Past
The Outfit
They Won't Believe Me

Hackman, Gene
The French Connection
The French Connection II
Night Moves
The Split

Hayden, Sterling
Asphalt Jungle
Crime of Passion
Crime Wave
The Killing
The Long Goodbye
Manhandled
Suddenly

Hayward, Susan
Among the Living
Deadline at Dawn
House of Strangers
They Won't Believe Me

Hayworth, Rita
Gilda
Lady from Shanghai

Heflin, Van
Act of Violence
Johnny Eager
Possessed
The Prowler
The Strange Loves of Martha Ivers

Helton, Percy
Criss Cross
The Crooked Way
Kiss Me Deadly
Thieves' Highway

Hendrix, Wanda
Nora Prentiss
Ride the Pink Horse

Hepburn, Katharine
Undercurrent

Heston, Charlton
Dark City
Touch of Evil

Hodiak, John
The Bribe
A Lady without Passport
The People Against O'Hara
Somewhere in the Night

Holden, William
The Dark Past
Sunset Boulevard
The Turning Point
Union Station

Huston, Walter
Beast of the City
The Maltese Falcon
The Shanghai Gesture

Ireland, John
Farewell, My Lovely
The Gangster
Party Girl
Railroaded
Raw Deal

Jaffe, Sam
The Accused
Asphalt Jungle

Jagger, Dean
Dark City
The Kremlin Letter
Private Hell 36
When Strangers Marry

Jones, Carolyn
Baby Face Nelson
The Big Heat
The Shield for Murder
The Turning Point

Kelly, Paul
Crossfire
Fear in the Night
The File on Thelma Jordon
Side Street

Kennedy, Arthur
Chicago Deadline
High Sierra
Too Late for Tears
The Window

Keyes, Evelyn
Johnny O'Clock
The Killer That Stalked New York
99 River Street
The Prowler

APPENDIX

Kiley, Richard
The Mob
Pickup on South Street
The Sniper

Ladd, Alan
Appointment with Danger
The Blue Dahlia
Calcutta
The Glass Key
This Gun for Hire

Lake, Veronica
The Blue Dahlia
The Glass Key
This Gun for Hire

Lambert, Jack
Border Incident
The Enforcer
The Killers
Kiss Me Deadly
99 River Street
The Unsuspected

Lancaster, Burt
Brute Force
Criss Cross
I Walk Alone
The Killers
Kiss the Blood Off My Hands
Sorry, Wrong Number
Sweet Smell of Success

Lanchester, Elsa
The Big Clock
Mystery Street

Laughton, Charles
The Big Clock
The Bribe

Leigh, Janet
Act of Violence
The Manchurian Candidate
Rogue Cop
Touch of Evil

Leonard, Sheldon
Decoy
Force of Evil
The Gangster
Somewhere in the Night
Street of Chance

Lockhart, Gene
House on 92nd Street

Leave Her to Heaven
Red Light
World for Ransom

Lorre, Peter
Black Angel
The Chase
The Maltese Falcon
The Mask of Dimitrios
Stranger on the Third Floor

Lovejoy, Frank
The Hitch-Hiker
I Was a Communist for the F.B.I.
In a Lonely Place
Try and Get Me

Lupino, Ida
Beware, My Lovely
The Big Knife
High Sierra
On Dangerous Ground
Private Hell 36
Road House
While the City Sleeps

McGraw, Charles
Armored Car Robbery
Berlin Express
Border Incident
Brute Force
The Gangster
His Kind of Woman
The Killers
Loophole
The Narrow Margin
Roadblock
Side Street
T-Men

MacLane, Barton
High Sierra
Kiss Tomorrow Goodbye
The Maltese Falcon
Red Light
You Only Live Once

MacMurray, Fred
Double Indemnity
Pushover

Macready, George
The Big Clock
Detective Story
Gilda
Knock on Any Door

A Lady without Passport
My Name Is Julia Ross

Malone, Dorothy
The Big Sleep
Convicted
The Killer That Stalked New York
Loophole
Private Hell 36
Pushover

Marshall, Herbert
Angel Face
Crack-Up
The High Wall
The Letter

Marvin, Lee
The Big Heat
I Died a Thousand Times
Point Blank

Mature, Victor
Cry of the City
I Wake Up Screaming
Kiss of Death
The Shanghai Gesture

Mayo, Virginia
Red Light
White Heat

Mazurki, Mike
Abandoned
Dark City
I Walk Alone
Murder, My Sweet
New York Confidential
Night and the City
Nightmare Alley
The Shanghai Gesture

Meeker, Ralph
Kiss Me Deadly

Meyer, Emile
Baby Face Nelson
The Big Night
The Line-Up
The Mob
The Outfit
The People Against O'Hara
The Shield for Murder
Sweet Smell of Success

Milland, Ray
The Big Clock
Ministry of Fear
The Thief

Mitchum, Robert
Angel Face
Cape Fear
Cross Fire
Farewell, My Lovely
The Friends of Eddie Coyle
His Kind of Woman
The Locket
Macao
Out of the Past
The Racket
Undercurrent
When Strangers Marry
Where Danger Lives

Monroe, Marilyn
Asphalt Jungle
Clash by Night
Niagara

Montgomery, George
The Brasher Doubloon

Montgomery, Robert
Lady in the Lake
Ride the Pink Horse

Morgan, Henry
Appointment with Danger
The Big Clock
Dark City
The Gangster
Moonrise
Red Light
Scandal Sheet
Somewhere in the Night

Nolan, Lloyd
House on 92nd Street
Lady in the Lake
Somewhere in the Night
Street with No Name

Novak, Kim
Pushover

O'Brien, Edmond
Between Midnight and Dawn
D.O.A.
A Double Life
The Hitch-Hiker
The Killers
711 Ocean Drive
The Shield for Murder
The Turning Point
White Heat

O'Donnell, Cathy
Detective Story
Side Street
They Live by Night

Palance, Jack
The Big Knife
I Died a Thousand Times
Panic in the Streets
Sudden Fear

Payne, John
The Crooked Way
Hell's Island
Kansas City Confidential
99 River Street
Slightly Scarlet

Peters, Jean
Niagara
Pickup on South Street
Vicki

Powell, Dick
Cornered
Cry Danger
Johnny O'Clock
Murder, My Sweet
Pitfall

Price, Vincent
The Bribe
His Kind of Woman
Laura
Leave Her to Heaven
While the City Sleeps

Raft, George
Johnny Angel
Loan Shark
Nocturne
Red Light
Rogue Cop

Raines, Ella
Brute Force
Phantom Lady
Uncle Harry

Rains, Claude
Notorious
The Unsuspected
Where Danger Lives

Robinson, Edward G.
Double Indemnity
House of Strangers
Key Largo
Night Has a Thousand Eyes

Nightmare
Scarlet Street
The Stranger
The Woman in the Window

Roman, Ruth
Beyond the Forest
Strangers on a Train
The Window

Rooney, Mickey
Baby Face Nelson
Beast of the City
Drive a Crooked Road
The Strip

Russell, Gail
Calcutta
Moonrise
Night Has a Thousand Eyes
The Tattered Dress

Russell, Jane
His Kind of Woman
Macao

Ryan, Robert
Act of Violence
Berlin Express
Beware, My Lovely
Caught
Clash by Night
Crossfire
House of Bamboo
Johnny O'Clock
Odds Against Tomorrow
On Dangerous Ground
Out of the Past
The Racket
The Set-Up

Sanders, George
The Kremlin Letter
Uncle Harry
While the City Sleeps
Witness to Murder

Scott, Lizabeth
Dark City
Dead Reckoning
I Walk Alone
Pitfall
The Racket
The Strange Love of Martha Ivers
Too Late for Tears

Scott, Zachary
Danger Signal

Guilty Bystander
The Mask of Dimitrios
Mildred Pierce

Sidney, Sylvia
City Streets
Fury
You Only Live Once

Sloane, Everett
The Big Knife
The Enforcer
Journey into Fear
The Lady from Shanghai

Stanwyck, Barbara
Clash by Night
Crime of Passion
Double Indemnity
The File on Thelma Jordon
Sorry, Wrong Number
The Strange Love of Martha Ivers
Witness to Murder

Steiger, Rod
The Big Knife
The Harder They Fall

Sterling, Jan
Appointment with Danger
The Big Carnival
Caged
The Harder They Fall
Mystery Street
Union Station

Stevens, Mark
Between Midnight and Dawn
The Dark Corner
The Street with No Name

Stewart, James
Call Northside 777

Stewart, Paul
Appointment with Danger
Edge of Doom
Johnny Eager
Kiss Me Deadly
Loan Shark
The Window

Stone, Milburn
Phantom Lady
Pickup on South Street
The Racket (1951)
Roadblock

Sullivan, Barry
Cause for Alarm
Framed
The Gangster
I Was a Communist for the F.B.I.
Loophole
Suspense
Tension
The Unknown Man

Tamiroff, Akim
The Gangster
Mr. Arkadin
Touch of Evil

Taylor, Robert
The Bribe
The High Wall
Johnny Eager
Party Girl
Rogue Cop
Undercurrent

Teal, Ray
Asphalt Jungle
The Big Carnival
Brute Force
Captive City
Convicted
Decoy
Edge of Doom
The High Wall
I Wouldn't Be in Your Shoes
Road House
Rogue Cop
Scene of the Crime
The Turning Point
Where Danger Lives

Tierney, Gene
Laura
Leave Her to Heaven
Night and the City
The Shanghai Gesture
Where the Sidewalk Ends

Toomey, Regis
Beyond the Forest
The Big Sleep
Cry Danger
The Guilty
I Wouldn't Be in Your Shoes
The People Against O'Hara
Phantom Lady
Strange Illusion

Totter, Audrey
The High Wall

Lady in the Lake
The Postman Always Rings Twice
The Set-Up
Tension
The Unsuspected

Trevor, Claire
Born to Kill
Crack-Up
Johnny Angel
Key Largo
Murder, My Sweet
Raw Deal
Street of Chance

Van Cleef, Lee
The Big Combo
Kansas City Confidential

Vickers, Martha
The Big Sleep
The Burglar

Webb, Clifton
The Dark Corner
Laura

Webb, Jack
Appointment with Danger
Dark City
He Walked by Night
Hollow Triumph
Sunset Boulevard

Welles, Orson
Journey into Fear
The Kremlin Letter
The Lady from Shanghai
Mr. Arkadin
The Stranger
Touch of Evil

Whitmore, James
Asphalt Jungle
Madigan
The Split
The Undercover Man

Widmark, Richard
Kiss of Death
Madigan
Night and the City
Panic in the Streets
Pickup on South Street
Road House
The Street with No Name

Wilde, Cornel
The Big Combo
High Sierra
Leave Her to Heaven
Road House
Storm Fear

Windsor, Marie
The City That Never Sleeps
Force of Evil
The Killing
The Narrow Margin
The Outfit
The Sniper

Winters, Shelley
The Big Knife
Cry of the City
A Double Life
The Gangster
He Ran All the Way
I Died a Thousand Times
Odds Against Tomorrow

Young, Loretta
The Accused
Cause for Alarm
The Stranger

Young, Robert
Crossfire
The Second Woman
They Won't Believe Me

8. Releasing Companies

Allied Artists
The Big Combo (1955)
The Gangster (1947)
Loophole (1954)
Murder Is My Beat (1955)
The Naked Kiss (1964)
Southside 1-1000 (1950)
World for Ransom (1954)

Avco-Embassy
Farewell, My Lovely (1975)

Columbia
Between Midnight and Dawn (1950)
The Big Heat (1953)
The Brothers Rico (1955)
The Burglar (1957)
Convicted (1950)
The Crimson Kimono (1959)
The Dark Past (1948)

Dead Reckoning (1947)
Drive a Crooked Road (1954)
Experiment in Terror (1962)
Framed (1947)
The Garment Jungle (1957)
Gilda (1946)
The Harder They Fall (1956)
Human Desire (1954)
In a Lonely Place (1950)
Johnny O'Clock (1946)
The Killer That Stalked New York (1951)
Knock on Any Door (1949)
The Lady from Shanghai (1948)
The Line-Up (1958)
M (1952)
The Mob (1951)
My Name Is Julia Ross (1945)
Night Editor (1946)
The Night Holds Terror (1955)
Nightfall (1957)
Pushover (1954)
The Reckless Moment (1949)
Scandal Sheet (1952)
711 Ocean Drive (1950)
The Sniper (1952)
So Dark the Night (1956)
Taxi Driver (1976)
The Undercover Man (1949)
Underworld U.S.A. (1961)

Eagle-Lion
Behind Locked Doors (1948)
Canon City (1948)
Hollow Triumph (1948)
Raw Deal (1948)
T-Men (1948)

Film Classics
Guilty Bystander (1950)

Lippert
Loan Shark (1952)

M & A Alexander
Mr. Arkadin (1955)

Metro-Goldwyn-Mayer
Act of Violence (1949)
The Asphalt Jungle (1950)
Beast of the City (1932)
The Beat Generation (1959)
Border Incident (1949)
The Bribe (1949)
Caught (1949)
Cause for Alarm (1951)
Force of Evil (1948)
Fury (1936)
The High Wall (1947)

Johnny Eager (1942)
Lady in the Lake (1947)
A Lady without Passport (1950)
Marlowe (1969)
Mystery Street (1950)
The Outfit (1974)
Party Girl (1958)
The People Against O'Hara (1951)
Point Blank (1967)
Rogue Cop (1954)
Scene of the Crime (1949)
Side Street (1949)
The Split (1968)
The Strip (1951)
Talk About a Stranger (1952)
Tension (1950)
The Undercover Man (1951)
Undercurrent (1946)
The Unknown Man (1951)

Monogram
Decoy (1946)
Fall Guy (1947)
Fear (1946)
The Guilty (1947)
I Wouldn't Be in Your Shoes (1948)
Suspense (1946)
When Strangers Marry (1944)

Paramount
The Accused (1949)
Among the Living (1941)
Appointment with Danger (1951)
The Big Carnival (1951)
The Big Clock (1948)
The Blue Dahlia (1946)
Calcutta (1947)
Chicago Deadline (1949)
City Streets (1931)
Dark City (1950)
Detective Story (1951)
Double Indemnity (1944)
Fear in the Night (1947)
The File on Thelma Jordon (1950)
The Friends of Eddie Coyle (1973)
The Glass Key (1942)
He Walked by Night (1949)
Hell's Island (1955)
Hustle (1975)
I Walk Alone (1948)
Manhandled (1949)
Ministry of Fear (1945)
Night Has a Thousand Eyes (1948)
The Racket (1928)
The Scoundrel (1935)
Sorry, Wrong Number (1948)
The Strange Love of Martha Ivers (1946)
Street of Chance (1942)

Sunset Boulevard (1950)
This Gun for Hire (1942)
Thunderbolt (1929)
The Turning Point (1952)
Underworld (1927)
Union Station (1950)

Producers Releasing Corporation (PRC)
Detour (1945)
Railroaded (1947)
Strange Illusion (1945)

RKO
Angel Face (1953)
Armored Car Robbery (1950)
Berlin Express (1948)
Beware, My Lovely (1952)
Beyond a Reasonable Doubt (1956)
Born to Kill (1947)
Clash by Night (1952)
Cornered (1945)
Crack-Up (1946)
Crossfire (1947)
Cry Danger (1951)
Deadline at Dawn (1946)
Desperate (1947)
Destination Murder (1950)
Edge of Doom (1950)
Follow Me Quietly (1949)
His Kind of Woman (1951)
The Hitch-Hiker (1953)
Johnny Angel (1945)
Journey into Fear (1943)
The Locket (1947)
Macao (1952)
Murder, My Sweet (1944)
The Narrow Margin (1952)
Nocturne (1946)
Notorious (1946)
On Dangerous Ground (1952)
Out of the Past (1947)
The Racket (1951)
Roadblock (1951)
The Set-Up (1949)
Slightly Scarlet (1956)
The Stranger (1946)
Stranger on the Third Floor (1940)
Sudden Fear (1952)
The Tattooed Stranger (1950)
They Live by Night (1949)
They Won't Believe Me (1947)
Where Danger Lives (1951)
While the City Sleeps (1956)
The Window (1949)
The Woman in the Window (1945)

Republic
City That Never Sleeps (1953)

Moonrise (1949)
The Pretender (1947)

20th Century-Fox
The Brasher Doubloon (1947)
Call Northside 777 (1948)
Cry of the City (1948)
The Dark Corner (1945)
Fallen Angel (1946)
The French Connection (1971)
The French Connection II (1975)
House of Bamboo (1955)
House of Strangers (1949)
House on 92nd Street (1945)
House on Telegraph Hill (1951)
I Wake Up Screaming (1942)
Kiss of Death (1947)
The Kremlin Letter (1970)
Laura (1944)
Leave Her to Heaven (1945)
The Man Who Cheated Himself (1951)
Niagara (1953)
The Nickel Ride (1975)
Night and the City (1950)
Nightmare Alley (1947)
The Other Woman (1954)
Panic in the Streets (1950)
Pickup on South Street (1953)
Plunder Road (1957)
Road House (1948)
Somewhere in the Night (1946)
The Street with No Name (1948)
Thieves' Highway (1949)
The Thirteenth Letter (1951)
Vicki (1953)
Where the Sidewalk Ends (1950)

United Artists
Baby Face Nelson (1957)
The Big Knife (1955)
The Big Night (1951)
Blood Money (1933)
Body and Soul (1947)
The Captive City (1952)
The Chase (1946)
Crime of Passion (1957)
Criss Cross (1949)
The Crooked Way (1949)
D.O.A. (1949)
Gun Crazy (1950)
He Ran All the Way (1951)
Hickey and Boggs (1972)
I, the Jury (1953)
Kansas City Confidential (1952)
The Killer Is Loose (1956)
Killer's Kiss (1955)
The Killing (1956)
Kiss Me Deadly (1955)

The Long Goodbye (1973)
The Long Wait (1954)
The Manchurian Candidate (1962)
Nightmare (1956)
99 River Street (1953)
Odds Against Tomorrow (1959)
The Outfit (1974)
Pitfall (1948)
The Prowler (1951)
Red Light (1950)
The Second Woman (1951)
The Shanghai Gesture (1941)
The Shield for Murder (1954)
Sleep, My Love (1948)
Storm Fear (1956)
Suddenly (1954)
Sweet Smell of Success (1957)
The Thief (1952)
Too Late for Tears (1949)
Try and Get Me (1950)
Witness to Murder (1954)
You Only Live Once (1937)

Universal
Abandoned (1949)
Black Angel (1946)
Blast of Silence (1961)
Brute Force (1947)
Cape Fear (1962)
Christmas Holiday (1944)
The Dark Mirror (1946)
A Double Life (1948)
The Killers (1946)
Kiss the Blood Off My Hands (1948)
Lady on a Train (1945)
Madigan (1968)
The Naked City (1948)
The Night Runner (1957)
Phantom Lady (1944)
Ride the Pink Horse (1947)
Scarlet Street (1945)
Shadow of a Doubt (1943)
Shakedown (1950)
The Sleeping City (1950)
The Tattered Dress (1957)
Touch of Evil (1958)
Uncle Harry (1945)
Woman on the Run (1950)

Warner Bros
Beyond the Forest (1949)
The Big Sleep (1946)
The Blue Gardenia (1953)
Brainstorm (1965)
The Breaking Point (1950)
Caged (1950)
Conflict (1945)
Crime Wave (1954)

The Damned Don't Cry (1950)
Danger Signal (1945)
Dark Passage (1947)
Dirty Harry (1971)
The Enforcer (1951)
High Sierra (1941)
I Am a Fugitive from a Chain Gang (1932)
I Died a Thousand Times (1955)
I Was a Communist for the F.B.I. (1951)
Key Largo (1948)
Kiss Tomorrow Goodbye (1950)
The Letter (1940)
The Maltese Falcon (1941)
The Mask of Dimitrios (1944)
Mildred Pierce (1945)
Mr. Arkadin (1955)
New York Confidential (1955)
Night Moves (1975)
Nobody Lives Forever (1946)
Nora Prentiss (1947)
Possessed (1947)
Strangers on a Train (1951)
The Unsuspected (1947)
White Heat (1949)
The Wrong Man (1956)

9. A Revised Note on Research Sources

Jack Shadoian observes in Dreams and Dead Ends that, "Films are often cavalierly dated." While no absolute consensus may exist, film historians generally try to date pictures by year of release. For American motion pictures that year is not determined by the date of completion nor by the copyright issue date but is "officially" set by the Academy of Motion Picture Arts and Sciences (AMPAS), so that a picture may not compete for Academy Awards in more than one year. Academy rules require a minimum run of seven days at a theater selling admission to the general public to qualify in a calendar year. In some cases, such as Gun Crazy (1949 or 1950) or They Live by Night (1948 or 1949), recutting and/or retitling by the distributor has split standard references over release year. In these instances, a year has been chosen and notes have been added to explain the dating process. Also clouding the issue with regard to classic period titles was the practice of "tradeshows," or special screenings to reviewers for trade periodicals and local (i.e Los Angeles) press, which has resulted in some anomalies. For example, a great many published works give 1944 as the release year for two of Fritz Lang's films, Ministry of Fear and Woman in the Window. Ministry of Fear was actually completed in 1943, Woman in the Window in 1944. Both pictures were reviewed in 1944; but the AMPAS dates are quite clear: January 1 and January 19, 1945 respectively. Unless and until film historians agree on some other method, 1945 is the date for both these films.

APPENDIX

The discrepancies over release year pale compared to those over running time. Alternate or abridged versions aside, the film industry's primary interest in running times has always been from a scheduling point-of-view. It was not uncommon for trade reviews of films of the classic period appearing in *Daily Variety* and *The Hollywood Reporter* on the same day to have differing running times and for both of those to differ from a press release or listing in *The Motion Picture Almanac* or *Production Encyclopedia*. Where available the most reliable indicators were moviola continuities or the prints themselves; but access to such archival materials for hundreds of titles was not feasible. Where discrepancies between sources were found, running times were determined by the preponderance of evidence. If information about alternate times seemed pertinent, it has been included; but in general it would be safest to assume, as have most video distributors, that all running times are approximate.

Perhaps the greatest source of error in all film books is the limited availability of the films themselves. Prior to 1978, the year before the first edition of this book appeared, none of the films discussed were available on videotape. This book was compiled from screenings of 16mm prints graciously provided by private collectors and memories of late night television viewings. While many can now be rented in tape format and more become available every year, unless the economics of video release change in the future, a significant number will never be. Some like the public domain *D.O.A.* have been released by several sources and print quality varies accordingly. In the case of *Kiss Me Deadly*, the video version like all of the 16mm prints is mysteriously without Scene 306, the final two shot of Hammer and Velda in the surf, which needless to say considerably distorts the narrative implications and affects the detailed commentaries of Jack Shadoian and J.P. Telotte. [The shot in question, of Velda and Hammer in the surf, is actually reproduced in Tom Hutchison's piece on *Kiss Me Deadly* in *Movies of the Fifties* (London: Orbis, 1982), p. 145.] Of those which are available on video and are listed below, most cannot be rented at smaller outlets but are mainly to be found in specialty or nostalgia stores. Fortunately many titles not for rent provide fodder for cable channels and may occasionally be seen there.

In research work for subsequent editions, particularly the filmography on additional classic period films, a frequently consulted source was *The Motion Picture Guide* (Cinebooks, Chicago, first published in 1983 with annual updates). While this is a very useful multivolume reference its prohibitive price means that it is not available in many libraries. We also feel compelled to note that much of the information on the noir titles seems quite similar to the contents of *Film Noir: An Encyclopedia Reference*. For more recent titles, the filmography is generally based on reviews in *Daily Variety* annuals. On occasion, credits and running times were taken directly from videotapes of the films. A final note: while most of the new films discussed in the Neo-Noir Section are available on videotape, as with the titles from the classic period, many are not. There are several paperback guides available to titles on video, which may be of assistance to those seeking such information.

10. Films of the Classic Period Available On Videotape

Accused, The
Asphalt Jungle
Berlin Express
Beware my Lovely
Beyond the Forest
Big Combo, The
Big Heat, The
Big Sleep, The
Body and Soul
Born to Kill

Cape Fear
Caught
Chase, The
Chinatown
City for Conquest
City that Never Sleeps
Clash by Night
Cornered
Crack-up
Criss Cross
Crossfire
Cry Danger

D.O.A.
Dark Corner, The
Dark Mirror, The
Dark Passage
Dark Past, The
Dark Waters
Dead Reckoning
Deadline at Dawn
Desperate
Detour
Devil Thumbs A Ride, The
Dirty Harry
Double Indemnity
Double Life

Enforcer, The
Experiment in Terror

Fallen Sparrow, The
Farewell, My Lovely
Female Jungle
Follow Me Quietly
Force of Evil
French Connection, The
French Connection II
Fury

Gangster, The
Gilda

Glass Key, The
Guest in the House
Gun Crazy

Harder They Fall, The
He Walked by Night
High Sierra
His Kind of Woman
House of Strangers
Hustle

I Am a Fugitive from a Chain Gang
I Died a Thousand Times
I, the Jury
I Wake Up Screaming
Impact
In A Lonely Place

Johnny Angel
Journey into Fear

Kansas City Confidential
Key Largo
Killer's Kiss
Killing, The
Kiss Before Dying, A
Kiss Me Deadly
Kiss of Death
Kiss Tomorrow Goodbye
Knock on Any Door

Lady from Shanghai, The
Lady in the Lake
Laura
Letter, The
Long Goodbye, The

Macao
Madigan
Maltese Falcon, The
Manchurian Candidate, The
Marlowe
Mildred Pierce
Mr. Arkadin
Moonrise
Murder, My Sweet

Narrow Margin, The
Niagara
Nightmoves
Nightfall
Nocturne
Notorious

On Dangerous Ground
Out of the Past

Panic in the Streets

Party Girl
Pick-up on South Street
Pitfall (Laser Disc only)
Place in the Sun, A
Plunder Road
Point Blank
Possessed
Postman Always Rings Twice, The
Private Hell 36

Quicksand

Racket, The (1951)
Railroaded
Red House, The
Rogue Cop

Scarlet Street
Second Woman, The
Secret Beyond the Door, The
Set-up, The
Shadow of A Doubt
Shanghai Gesture, The
Shock
Slightly Scarlet
Sorry, Wrong Number
Spellbound
Strange Illusion
Strange Love of Martha Ivers, The
Stranger, The
Stranger on the Third Floor
Strangers on a Train
Street with No Name
Suddenly
Sunset Boulevard
Suspicion
Sweet Smell of Success

T-Men
Taxi Driver
They Live by Night
They Won't Believe Me
This Gun for Hire
Threat, The
Tomorrow is Forever
Touch of Evil
Trap, The
Try and Get Me

Underworld U.S.A.
Union Station

Walk Softly, Stranger
While the City Sleeps
White Heat
Window, The
Wrong Man, The

You Only Live Once

APPENDIX

Appendix C. Other Studies of Film Noir

History is not usually what has happened. History is what some people have thought to be significant.

Idries Shah, *Reflections*

In the decade since the 1st Edition of this book, awareness of and interest in film noir has grown considerably among film historians and film producers alike. The result has been both a significant number of new films echoing the movies of the classic period, which are discussed in Appendix E, and an ever-enlarging bibliography of books and articles. As *Film Noir: An Encyclopedic Reference* was the first comprehensive survey to appear in the English language and as the definition of film noir from which it proceeded was narrowly drawn, subsequent studies have created their own boundaries for the noir movement, or genre, as some still consider it. Nonetheless, there is a common ground: a body of key films which all writers agree are part of the noir cycle. Those films, in turn, from roughly *Maltese Falcon* to *Touch of Evil* define a span of the "classic period."

The definition of film noir used in this work, treating it as a cycle which combines aspects of both movement (style) and genre (content), is quite similar to that of the seminal book-length work of the subject, Raymond Borde and Etienne Chaumeton's *Panorama du Film Noir Americain* first published in 1955. *Kiss Me Deadly* had not yet been released when this book first appeared, but in their postscript to a later edition, Borde and Chaumeton erect a poetic definition of the "classic period": 1955 . An era ends. Film noir had fulfilled its role, which was to create a specific malaise and to drive home a social criticism of the United States. Robert Aldrich gave this venture a fascinating and dusky conclusion: *Kiss Me Deadly*. It's the despairing reversal of the film which fourteen years earlier had opened the series, *Maltese Falcon*." (p. 277) It is in their introduction that Borde and Chaumeton type the "noir" phenomenon as a "series," which they define as "a group of films from one country, sharing common traits (style, atmosphere, subject...) palpable enough to mark them unmistakably and giving them, in the context of the times, an inimitable character. These series have a variable longevity, sometimes two years, sometimes ten." (p. 2) This sense of a close-ended cycle and their analogies to Russian Social Realism or German Expressionism, initially suggest that Borde and Chaumeton conceived of film noir as what English-language critics would term a movement; but Borde and Chaumeton also compare film noir to the American Western and gangster film, which are clearly genres, primarily defined by their subject matter and open-ended. In their later "postface" they do discuss "a rebirth around 1965" and ultimately extract from *Point Blank, Dirty Harry*, and other titles on their post-noir list the conclusion that the "noir series in the 70s is important in its reflection of an America beset by crime, torn between generations, and wondering if it should not take justice into its own hands." (p. 282)

In their first chapter, "Towards a Definition of Film Noir," the authors expound on Nino Frank and his concept of "criminal adventure." "It's the presence of crime which gives film noir its most constant characteristic." (p. 5) They distinguish film noir from such quasi-documentary crime films as Elia Kazan's *Boomerang* or the Louis de Rochement productions, *House on 92nd Street* and *Call Northside 777*. After discussing the preponderance of tired heroes, femme fatales, and "the theme of violence" (p. 10), Borde and Chaumeton refine their ground and conclude that ambiguity is the other key, the element "which creates a nightmarish atmosphere." (p. 13) Perhaps their most telling observation is when they note the manner in which the indirect narratives and the visual style of film noir "disorient the spectator" (p. 14), an effect often cited in *Film Noir: An Encyclopedic Reference* because it makes the viewer a participant in the sensation of the noir underworld.

In their subsequent chapter on "sources," Borde and Chaumeton consider not only the obvious influence of hard-boiled detective fiction but also the emergence of psychoanalysis in the 40s as a popular technique for treating nervous disorders. The core of the book, the actual survey of films, spans Chapters III through VI from "the first work," *Maltese Falcon* (p. 35) through "the end of the series." In fact, Borde and Chaumeton's work preceded the end of the series. Nonetheless, the original edition of *Panorama du Film Noir Americain* has the distinction of being not merely the first but also the most contemporaneous study of film noir. From this unique perspective, despite being colored by their position as "foreign correspondents" remarking on an American phenomenon, Borde and Chaumeton's survey cannot be dislodged as the benchmark for all subsequent work attempting to define the same subject.

Film noir was quickly accepted as a phenomenon in Europe. By 1962, George Sadoul was casually noting in his *Histoire du Cinema* that "one was able to rank the best and the worst in American film noir, which was a school, not merely a new stage of the 'Thriller,' the 'suspense film,' or the 'detective story'... Psychoanalysis was applied in a *film noir*... a childhood trauma became the cause of criminal behavior just as unemployment explained social unrest." (p. 353) Both the term and the concept were slower to be adopted by English-language critics. It is generally accepted that the first extended discussion of film noir in English appeared in the second chapter, "Black Cinema," of Charles Higham and Joel Greenberg's compendium *Hollywood in the Forties*. Beginning with an oft-cited paragraph describing dark wet streets and flashing neon signs that attempts to evoke the "ambience of *film noir*" (p. 19) the chapter is really just a broad overview of what Higham and Greenberg consider "a genre deeply rooted in the nineteenth century's vein of grim romanticism." (p. 19) After a few paragraphs listing directors (most notably the German-speaking expatriates), composers, and cinematographers, Higham and Greenberg group their titles auteurishly and consider films by Hitchcock, Siodmak, Lang, Preminger, Wilder et al. but limit themselves almost entirely to colorfully worded summaries of the films and characters with little analysis. Higham and Greenberg touch very briefly on a few themes such as the "fatal woman" or the underworld; but nothing approaching a definition of what is for them a genre emerges from their impressionistic essay, nothing to explain such offhanded value judgments as "this [*The Postman Always Rings Twice*] is the perfect *film noir*, harsh and heartless in its delineation of character" (p. 29) or "replete with impressive images of cruelty and destructiveness, this *chef d'oeuvre* [*Strange Love of Martha Ivers*] could not have been more persuasively directed." (p. 27) The last third of the essay diverges into period films "closely allied to the pure 'black' cinema… though not quite in the same category." (p. 31) Ultimately Higham and Greenberg are most notable in their omissions: *Maltese Falcon, This Gun for Hire, The Big Sleep* and other adaptations of Hammett, Chandler, and Greene are somewhat inexplicably in Chapter Three, "Melodrama." The fugitive couples of *Gun Crazy* and *They Live By Night* are "oddities" left for "some other book, some other time…" (p. 18) Of films unmentioned anywhere in the book, *Detour* or *D.O.A.* may be understandable but also entirely missing are *White Heat* and, amazingly, *Out of the Past*.

Higham and Greenberg notwithstanding, three years later in his 1971 monograph for the Museum of Modern Art, *Violent America*, Lawrence Alloway discusses many individual noir films and makes such observations as "the reading and decoding of *I Walk Alone* can best do done in terms of the context of related movies," (p. 12) without ever using the expression, *film noir*. Despite illustrations from *The Big Heat, Kiss Me Deadly, Pickup on South Street*, and *Touch of Evil*, the appendix/filmography is titled "The American Action Movie, 1946-1964."

"The essence of these *Serie Noire* pictures is a fascination with death . . . The utter moral ambivalence of these pictures is intended to arouse fear more than tension, and in this it is successful: it creates an atmosphere of nightmare, of existential oppression." Martin Schlappner's brief overview of the psychology of the noir protagonist written for the Jung Institute's 1967 collection, *Evil*, is one of the earliest overt associations of film noir *angst* with existentialism. That connection was also explored in Barbara Deming's *Running Away from Myself: A Dream Portrait of America Drawn from the Films of the Forties* which appeared the year after Hollywood in the Forties. While it, too, never uses the term "film noir," Deming's study goes much further than Higham and Greenberg in probing the movement's socio-psychological impeti. In her first chapter, Deming reproduces two pages of photographs of actors playing emotionally tortured characters, and indirectly constructs one of the earliest iconographies of noir protagonists. While Deming's analyses of the persons portrayed in the decade's motion pictures are primarily thematic, she presages many later assertions about film noir. When she writes about the conclusion of *The Chase* that "in a queer way this duplication of the very elements of his [the hero's] bad dream leaves us still entangled in that dream--intrudes

a note of, if not death again, than at the very least of unreality," (p. 109) Deming is reacting to the oneiric quality that emanates from the noir underworld. In Chapters entitled "Where Am I?," "Tough Boy," and "The Nihilists," Deming probes that underworld without giving it an appellation. "From the very start of the film, we move with the hero towards a known fatality." (p. 180fn) When she describes the viewer's experience of *Double Indemnity*, Deming sees the noir vision without naming it.

The first book-length study of film noir in English is Amir Karimi's doctoral dissertation completed in 1970 but not published until 1976. Karimi generally follows the lead of Borde and Chaumeton in focusing on "three [postwar] realistic genres, semi-documentary, gangster, and film noir." (p. 1) His second chapter is "A Working Definition." Karimi's orientation becomes bifocal as he breaks film noir in "two large categories: the variant forms of the private eye and the murder mystery." (p. 31) A few pages later, Karimi divides the cycle along another line in asserting that "there are two worlds in the film noir…the small world of middle-class greed and incest, the world which surrounds the characters of James Cain and others who write in this vein…and the world of Dashiell Hammett and Raymond Chandler." (p. 35) For Karimi "the world of the private eye" is central because he "is in an ambiguous position," (p. 37) the condition which was also the key for Borde and Chaumeton. Unlike them, Karimi does not really break down the cycle into component parts but establishes his own list of "sources" in a discursive section on origins, both literary from Gothic romance to "Black Mask" and cinematic from mysteries to horror films. Karimi concurs with Borde and Chaumeton and cites *Maltese Falcon* as the first film noir, beginning a pattern of conformance most later studies would follow. Again he continues with a long meandering essay, organized variously by source material (Chandler, Cain, etc.), themes ("the wrong man," returning veterans), settings (period films), and icons (supporting actors). The only consistent element is the use of the director's name as an identifying signature; but despite this auteurist context, Karimi does not explore directorial vision or any concept in detail. Borrowing the terms of Borde and Chaumeton, Karimi leaves open the issue of the end of the "film noir series." (p. 156) Finally after digressions to James Bond (anticipating Borde and Chaumeton's "postface") and *la politique des auteurs*, he does conclude almost in passing that "the artistic contribution of the American" film noir is more to a style rather than the creation of a new genre." (p. 161). Oddly, Karimi includes in his filmography listings of the complete films of more than a score of directors. As a brief, early study, it is not surprising that Karimi's text is mostly descriptive and generalized, essentially an indirect translation of many of Borde and Chaumeton's ideas put forth in the survey style of Higham and Greenberg. It is easy in hindsight to criticize the "meandering" and superficial aspects of this essay; but Karimi does make several interesting points in clearly separating Cain-like characters from the "nobler" private eyes of Chandler and at least touching on the issue of style (or movement) versus content (or genre) as it affects film noir.

Later in 1970, an article by Raymond Durgnat appeared in the British magazine *Cinema*. "Paint It Black: the Family Tree of Film Noir" is the first structural approach to film noir which clearly types it as something other than a genre. "The *film noir* is not a genre," writes Durgnat, "as the Western or gangster film is, and takes us into the realms of classification by motif and tone." (p. 49) From this unequivocal statement, Durgnat plods through dozens of titles in less than a score of pages using his family tree:

1. Crimes and Social Criticism
2. Gangsterism
3. On the Run
4. Private Eyes and Adventurers
5. Middle-class murder
6. Portraits and Doubles
7. Sexual Pathology
8. Psychopaths
9. Hostages to Fortune
10. Blacks and Reds
11. Guignol, Horror, Fantasy

Is his attempt to be comprehensive, Durgnat is at times necessarily simplistic. The problem with his family tree is that while its branches twist around and entangle themselves with each other, Durgnat has no time and perhaps no inclination in his brief essay to plot these intertwinings. At the center of the tree, in categories 4 and 5 is Karimi's dichotomy. At the extremes are films which Durgnat concedes are "clearly first cousins to film noir." (p. 56) What is most crucial in Durgnat's piece (and what *Film Comment* extracted) is the tree itself, for within its broad branches, all later discussions would be contained. For those who would narrow the focus of film noir, that tree is Durgnat's most dubious achievement. Perhaps more important, after noting in a nod to Borde and Chaumeton that "the French *film noir* precedes the American genre," (p. 49) is Durgnat's conclusion that the American cycle is not a genre at all.

Durgnat's article stripped of its many punning, tongue-in-cheek asides and regrouped by sub-categories was reprinted in 1974 in *Film Comment* (see below). It was two years earlier in that magazine that "Notes on Film Noir" by Paul Schrader, another seminal English-language article, had appeared. Adapted from program notes for a film noir retrospective at the first Los Angeles Film Exposition, Schrader's piece was for many American readers the first analysis of film noir and remains the most easily accessible overview. After acknowledging and embracing Durgnat's assertion that "film noir is not a genre...[but] defined by the more subtle qualities of tone and mood," (p. 8) Schrader supplants the "Family Tree" format with a more straightforward glance, first at the mediating influences on film noir and then, in a reversal of the usual order, its style and themes. After noting that film noir is "extremely unwieldy," Schrader hedges on a definition by falling back on a Pauline Kaelish approach and stressing the subjec-

tive: "Almost every critic has his own definition of *film noir*, and a personal list of film titles and dates to back it up.... Since *film noir* is defined by tone rather than genre, it is almost impossible to argue one critic's descriptive definition against another. How many *noir* elements does it take to make a *film noir*?" (p. 9) After this disclaimer and "at the risk of sounding like Arthur Knight," Schrader finally begins his analysis by isolating four latent causalities in American society and its film industry: (1) War and post-war disillusionment; (2) post-War realism; (3) the German influence; and (4) the hard-boiled tradition. In a paean to cinematographer John Alton, Schrader tries to resolve "seemingly contradictory elements...an uneasy, exhila-rating combination of realism and expressionism." (p. 10) Despite his familiarity with film noir and its literary influences from Dostoevski to Chandler, Schrader never makes the point that there is no inherent contradiction between realistic narrative and expressionistic style, never even considers the concept of an oneiric reality, of how dreamlike and nightmarish images can reflect a psychological truth as first touched on by Borde and Chaumeton. Even more puzzling are scattered remarks about the hard-boiled tradition. After crediting Chandler rather than Cain or Billy Wilder with the "unflinching *noir* vision," i.e. the underlying cynicism and hopelessness, of *Double Indemnity*, Schrader lumps the two somewhat antithetical novelists together into "the romantic *noir* tradition of MILDRED PIERCE and THE BIG SLEEP." Unquestionably Hollywood filmmakers could go counter to a novel's thrust and stress romanticism in Cain or cynicism in Chandler. Somehow for Schrader this effect was part of a parenthetical and unexplained process in which film noir became "post-hardboiled." Included in this category are films such as *Kiss Tomorrow Goodbye*, despite that fact that it was adapted from Horace McCoy.

The key to Schrader's article is the outline of film noir stylistics and themes. Both sections are sketchy, the latter deferring heavily to Durgnat but raising significant points from the visceral impact of odd angles and broken shadows to the character nostalgia and implicit future shock of many protagonists. Schrader segues from this to his own version of Borde and Chaumeton's progressive phases of film noir through the classic period, which for Schrader ends in 1953. Schrader is much more focused on a particular shift from the quasi-romanticism of the war period to the disillusionment and the overt discovery of underlying corruption following the War. He goes even further by typing the last phase as "a period of psychotic action and suicidal impulse." Finally Schrader considers the question of film noir and auteurism: "*Auteur* criticism is interested in how directors are different; *film noir* criticism is interested in what they have in common." (p. 13) Schrader's generalization assumes a contradiction that has vastly differing implications. For directors like Anthony Mann or Fritz Lang, all of whose work is imbued with noir "stylistics" and themes, there is no antagonism between the personal and noir world views. Again Schrader makes a note without carrying through on its premise. In the end, the difficulty with Schrader's piece, although less prevalent than in Durgnat and certainly than in Higham and Greenberg, is that impressionistic asides often obscure and sometimes derail the analysis of the noir phenomenon. In Schrader's defense, his "Notes" never claim to be definitive. When compared to Tom Flinn's coincident piece "Three Faces of Noir" for *The Velvet Light Trap*, a glib essay that in no way attempts to trace the limits of *film noir*, "Notes" is exhaustive.

In many ways of equal significance to the Durgnat and Schrader articles is Janey Place and Lowell Peterson's "Some Visual Motifs of *Film Noir*," which appeared in *Film Comment* in early 1974. (The piece is reprinted in the book *Movies and Methods*--see Bibliography.) An overview of the noir photographic style which makes extensive use of frame enlargements "Visual Motifs" is actually two separate pieces. In the text Place and Peterson discuss the relationship of what they call "anti-traditional elements," i.e. staging by directors and lighting by cinematographers that radically diverges from the studio norm. While some of the assumptions are a bit facile, e.g."shadows and darkness which carry connotations of the mysterious and the unknown" (p. 30), Place and Peterson are the first to attempt a systematic assessment of noir style. The second part of the piece ostensibly illustrates the first; but the stills and frame enlargements have particular annotations which permit them to stand alone as a statement on noir form. If there is a shortcoming in the essay, it is the sometimes limited or ineffective interaction between text and frames. For instance Place and Peterson's assertion that "the archetypal noir shot is probably the extreme high-angle long shot, an oppressive and fatalistic angle that looks down on the victim to make it look like a rat in a maze" (p. 32) may be a valid one; but the only illustrations that exemplify this, taken from *Night and The City* and *Kiss Me Deadly*, are neither extremely high nor long and draw there implications of entrapment or enmeshment from other graphic aspects of the shot. There is also a perceptive textual observation regarding shots that "track forward before a running man, at once involving the audience in the movement and excitement of the chase, recording the terror on the character's face and looking over his shoulder at the forces visible or not which are pursuing him." (p. 32) This might be evidenced by frames from *Night and the City* or Losey's *M*; but it is not supported by any shots in part two.

Two book-length genre studies of the early 70s briefly considered film noir. Colin McArthur's *Underworld U.S.A.* (1972) does not use the term "film noir" but describes movies which are "neither gangster films nor thrillers, but which are variously related by mood, iconography, or theme to both" (p. 8); he draws no clear demarcation between these two genres or film noir. Under the influence of early cine-structuralism, McArthur considers both the sociology and the iconography of genre but eventually subsumes both to auteurist values. Stuart Kaminsky's *American Film Genres* (1974) contains a chapter on film noir which attempts to distinguish its visual and moral atmosphere from that of one literary source, Hemingway. Later in 1974,

Alfred Appel's unusual study *Nabokov's Dark Cinema* dedicated a chapter to film noir. After beginning with the sociology of noir "masked as genre entertainment," Appel shifts to the German-speaking refugees: "Characteristic of their film noirs is the more refined and poetic *stimming* (mood) of the German cinema, with stylized, mannered lighting rather than bizarre sets." (p. 198) Appel also cites the visual impact of actual locations from *Double Indemnity* to *Touch of Evil* (although he mislocates Jerry's market in the former).

Appel was one of several contributors to a special issue of *Film Comment* featuring film noir at the end of 1974. As mentioned above a two-page synthesis of Durgnat's family tree opened the section, white on black with "Policiers" standing in for the original's "Portraits and Doubles." Despite the reiteration of Durgnat's dictum that noir is not a genre, the subsequent articles follow thematic lines from Stephen Farber's superficial and regressive "Violence and the Bitch Goddess" to Mitchell Cohen's "Villains and Victims" which asserts that "the manipulation of the actors who move through this murky environment should be considered a key factor in the genre's effectiveness." Cohen's piece and Paul Jensen's survey of films associated with Raymond Chandler, with a detailed side-bar on the 1946 adaptation of *The Big Sleep*, raise valid points but stay on established ground, a tendency that would constrain most articles through the end of the decade. Originally designed to be included in this issue but delayed until March, 1975 was Alain Silver's "*Kiss Me Deadly* Evidence of a Style." While retrograde in asserting that "the shot selection and lighting provide immediate keys to the genre type, to film noir," the second part of the piece, from an outline developed with Janey Place, explores how elements of style (in this case, of film noir) significantly alter, by enhancing or undercutting, all of the movie's surface dramatic and narrative values.

Larry Gross in a 1976 *Film Comment* piece postulates the demise of film noir because "the sense of irreversible moral decay" in which Durgnat's family tree is rooted "is no longer a relevant category." James Damico's 1978 "Film Noir: A Modest Proposal" in *Film Reader* notes the limitations of the genre model based on "plot structure and character type" used by Alloway and others but produces no alternative concepts other than a prototype heavily dependent on the femme fatale. Damico has frequently been cited as a viewpoint in opposition to Paul Schrader's because of his search for a narrative model; and yet both Durgnat's "family tree" and Schrader's "Notes" are genealogies of narrative first and foremost, and Damico's typification is synthesized from their overviews. Damico has good reason to decry Durgnat's diffusive and rambling categories, as later writers seeking a viable alternative to the tree have discovered. What Damico's "Modest Proposal" lacks is any substantive proposal, modest or otherwise.

Richard Dorfman's 1980 "Conspiracy City" searches for the source of noir paranoia in the socio-industrial context: "*film noir* is the clearest example of the self-reflexive practices of advanced European narrative ineluctably influencing the more intelligent filmmaker working within the Hollywood system." (p. 44) Paul Kerr's Winter 1979/80 article, "Out of What Past? Notes on the B *Film Noir*," attempts "to refocus...on one important, industrially-defined, fraction of the genre -- the B film noir" (p. 222) but views the cycle as a genre. Legitimate assertions these all may be, but not exactly ground-breaking. After spending several pages summarizing past assessments from Borde and Chaumeton to Damico's prototype, Kerr never produces more than a digest of observations. He raises interesting points such as low key lighting being used to mask low-budget sets or night shooting being used to get more set-ups into each production day but never develops the case for "technological determinism." His final remarks about television and color marking the end of the noir movement are, as far as film noir itself is concerned, largely irrelevant.

Of more interest are Jack Shadoian's 1977 book *Dreams and Dead Ends: the American Gangster/Crime Film* and the essay collection edited by E. Ann Kaplan for the BFI in 1978, *Women in Film Noir*. The former is primarily a study of the gangster/crime genre with only a secondary emphasis on film noir. In Shadoian's schematic, noir is only a classification within that genre. "The gangster/crime film is a genre like pornography and the horror film, held in contempt socially and intellectually not because it may corrupt and not because it is artistically inferior to other kinds of film but because it realizes our dreams, exposes our deepest psychic urges...The gangster is a paradigm of the American Dream." (pp. 1-2) This sociological approach to the genre permeates the remainder of the text. For example, when discussing the appearance of post-World War II noir, Shadoian cross-references films such as *The Killers* and *Criss Cross* to the disillusionment and disaffection at large in society during that period (Chapter Two). When surveying the 50s crime films in Chapter Five, he makes the standard correlation between movies like *Pickup On South Street*, *99 River Street*, *The Big Heat*, and *Kiss Me Deadly* to the sense of paranoia over the Bomb and McCarthy Hearings coupled with a widespread disenchantment with established order and rigidly enforced conformity.

Shadoian's book is divided into six chapters. In the first chapter the classic gangster film is described, with special emphasis on *Little Caesar* and *Public Enemy*. Again, he sets the films in a social context--the Great Depression--and presents their protagonists as symbols of the American Dream turned into a Nightmare of unrestrained capitalist greed. In Chapter Two he begins his analytical "descent into noir." Included is the now familiar sociology of its rise during World War II: war anxiety and disillusionment, a preponderance of German emigres working in Hollywood (bringing with them an Expressionist tone), and the popularity of hard-boiled fiction.

In Chapter Three, Shadoian traces the continually shifting terrain of noir. By analyzing three films, *Kiss of Death*, *Force of Evil*, and *Gun Crazy*, he suggests that filmmakers were trying to work through the pessimism of noir by af-

firming a humanistic position. In *Force of Evil*, particularly, the trajectory is upward from corruption through suffering to redemption. In Chapter Four, he delineates the influence of modernism on noir crime films: realistic narrative is undermined by extreme subjectification and an abstract patina. *D.O.A.* and *White Heat* are cited as particularly fine examples of this change in style. Their visuals are stark, eschewing the chiaroscuro of their predecessors, while the narrative itself hinges on the "disequilibrium" (p. 167) felt by the main characters, Bigelow in *D.O.A.* and Cody in *White Heat*.

In Chapter Five Shadoian posits the theory that at the end of the noir cycle in the 50s the films became increasingly violent and anti-conformist. His examples, *99 River Street*, *The Brothers Rico*, *Pickup on South Street*, and *Kiss Me Deadly*, move towards savage violence as a solution to the corruption of civilized society. "The gangster/crime genre shows us where we got to--the evil of civilization, which can be combated only by reverting to primitivity and savagery..." (p. 211) In the final chapter Shadoian superficially reviews what became of the crime/gangster films following the classic period. His centerpieces for this are *Point Blank*, *Bonnie and Clyde*, and the *Godfather* films.

Women in Film Noir is a series of articles from a predominantly feminist/semiological perspective. All the writers in the study recognize the crucial position of women in the noir iconography, particularly as opposed to mainstream American film where women are usually confined to safe stereotypes such as sexpot, wife, mother, girlfriend which relate in some way to the male protagonist. Film noir females dominate the discourse of many of the films; and rather than being adjuncts to the world of the hero, noir femme fatales disrupt that patriarchal world, even though they are often safely neutralized by the final scene. This disruption of the male discourse is the ground which this book explores.

In the framing essays, "A Contemporary Film Noir and Feminist Criticism" and "Feminism and *Klute*," Christine Gledhill centers on Klute as an example of how feminist criticism can be applied to the discussion of a film noir. According to Gledhill, although an argument can be made for this film as a critique of male hypocrisy and the bourgeois family, it can also be seen as a reaffirmation of the patriarchy's power as a male heroic character rescues a potentially disruptive female presence from herself. In the second essay by Sylvia Harvey, "Woman's Place: the Absent Family of Film Noir," the author explores the post-World War II noir films with an emphasis on the family. She analyzes their radical feminist potential, particularly as they present women--often, admittedly, femme fatales--" outside the strictures of the family. This implied attack on the sacred nuclear family is related to postwar disillusionment and the societal fear of newly liberated women in the workplace.

In "Women in Film Noir" Janey Place chooses the method of close visual analysis in grappling with the role of women in film noir. Using frame enlargements from films like *Double Indemnity*, *Gun Crazy*, *Gilda*, and *Lady from*

Shanghai, Place points out the visual dominance of women in the mise-en-scene of noir and how this corresponds to their thematic dominance within the story. "Duplicity in *Mildred Pierce*" by Pam Cook carries on the ideas of the other preceding authors by centering on one film, *Mildred Pierce.* Cook, however, qualifies the power of these women by demonstrating how, more often than not, the structure of the film leads the noir "heroine" to her own destruction or, alternately, reconfinement within the patriarchal system.

In "The Place of Women in Fritz Lang's *The Blue Gardenia*" E. Ann Kaplan tries to demonstrate how a surface male discourse on female duplicity and weakness brackets a female discourse by the heroine Nora buried within. This subverts the male point-of-view and exposes male repression. In "Resistance through Charisma: Rita Hayworth and *Gilda*" Richard Dyer also questions the mainstream reading of a film noir such as Gilda by presenting an alternate interpretation. By analyzing the power of Rita Hayworth's persona and performance, Dyer presents a version of the film which contradicts and at times overpowers the male protagonist's voice-over narration. In the penultimate essay, "*Double Indemnity*," by Claire Johnston, the author applies a psychoanalytic analysis to the noir classic *Double Indemnity.* She explores the female threat posed by Phyllis Dietrichson to the male order. And, in addition, she casts a Freudian light on the Neff/Keyes relationship.

Two book-length studies appeared in 1979. The first, Robert Porfirio's two volume dissertation for Yale University, "The Dark Age of American Film: A Study of the American *Film Noir*," remains one of the most thoroughly researched and meticulously considered studies of the noir cycle to date. In a 1976 *Sight and Sound* piece extracted from his larger work, Porfirio noted that "visual style rescued many an otherwise pedestrian film from oblivion." In the introduction to the dissertation, Porfirio struggles with the past definitions of film noir. Is it a genre, a sub-genre, a style, a movement, a cycle? He finally comes down on the side of a movement: "Although there are certain problems inherent in treating the film noir as a film movement, the advantages of such a conceptual model, I believe, far outweigh the disadvantages. For one thing it allows us to isolate the film noir as a distinct body (or cycle) of films according to certain formal standards..." (p. 12) In Chapters Two, Three, and Four, Porfirio retraces the now-familiar ground of film noir sources: German expressionism, hard-boiled fiction, etc. He does, however, add considerable detail in a section on the sociological-cultural-economic reasons for the creation of the basic American film genres in the 30s. He also discusses the influence of radical theater (Mercury Theater, Group Theater, Federal Theater, etc.) on film noir, a subject rarely visited in other studies.

Porfirio's working assumptions are detailed in Chapter Six on Narrative Structure: "Without invoking the polemical notion of a 'classically realist text' I think it is safe to assume that the American cinema played a prominent role in establishing the 'story' film as a global system. And if we consider the film noir from the standpoint of story content alone it becomes quite difficult to distinguish it from its predecessors among the crime films of the thirties, or for that matter, from contemporary varieties of crime films. This is why critics seeking to isolate the *film noir* as a genre direct their attention to such criteria as 'style' or 'atmosphere.' Fortunately for our purposes modern film criticism has borrowed from Russian formalism the distinction between 'story' (essentially 'what happens'-the spectator's ordered reconstruction of events) and 'plot' (essentially 'how it happens'-actual mode of presentation of events)." (p. 132) Porfirio's examination of the style/content interchanges of film noir anticipates the work of Richard Maltby and J.P. Telotte, while never "radicalizing" film noir or displacing it for the sake of observations about cultural influences. Porfirio also explores in depth the influence of *Citizen Kane,* listing "those aspects of CITIZEN KANE (both cinematic and extra-cinematic) which constitute an important part of the noir cycle's distinctive idiolect."

The most detailed and unique work in this study is the close analysis of the "texts" of film noir. The exegetical overview has two thrusts: a narrative dissection of the film plots themselves and visual and aural elements, the latter similar to Silver's *Kiss Me Deadly* piece. The second volume, which contains over two hundred and seventy-five illustrations (mostly frame enlargements) is not merely a supplement to the visual analysis but an exhaustive consideration of scores of metaphorical, expressionistic, semiotic, and dramatic implications in the images of film noir. To compare it to Place and Peterson's seminal article would be like comparing "The Kreutzer Sonata" to *War and Peace.* Also in Volume II are filmographies by Year, Studio, Director, etc. that were the basis for this book's Appendix B as well as a grouping of titles by "Thematic Category" and a list of "*Noire*d Films," which Porfirio views as outside of but clearly influenced by the movement. If there is any drawback to Porfirio's study (which certainly deserves to be more widely disseminated), it is his overuse of structuralist and semiotic terminology, which can even burden Volume II's disclaimer: "Although the terms presented here are usually associated with semiological criticism, my purpose in explicating them here is heuristic and not precisely semiotic.... [in order to avoid] the atomistic reduction of the Peircean triad (icon-index-symbol) which has haunted cine-semiology since at the least the publication of Peter Wollen's *Signs and Meaning in the Cinema.*"

Francois Guerif's *Le Film Noir Americain* is a profusely illustrated but somewhat diffuse study of the movement. After a brief homage to the pioneering work of Borde and Chaumeton, Guerif builds his own definition of film noir. "What is a film noir? The word 'black' implies a certain view of the world, a subjective vision, a pessimistic approach to things. The presence of crime does not necessarily make a movie 'noir.' It must also be realistic. Accordingly a film noir is both realistic and focused on a crime, that is to say, there is always a misdeed whether a simple scam or a series of murders." (p. 20) From this point, Guerif rambles through the entirety of the cycle using dozens of subheads rather than chapters and attempts to balance scholarly and populist approaches. The results are mixed. When he details the early "black" novel and realist films beginning with Griffith's *Broken Blossoms*, resonances of which he discovers in a David Goodis novel, Guerif can offer the reader unusual insights. More often than not, the jumble of quotes, photos, footnotes, and opinionated text is more cryptic than cogent. Guerif has two director filmographies (one apparently added for an undated second printing in the early 1980s) and a haphazard bibliography which includes many "The Films of"-type books on actor careers.

Of course, the third book on film noir completed in 1979 was *Film Noir An Encyclopedic Reference to the American Style*. It appeared late in the year and has been followed in the 1980s and early 90s by an outpouring of English-language book-length studies: two each in 1981 and 1984 and single volumes in 1988, 1989, 1991, and 1992. In addition, there were articles, theses, conference presentations, film noir festivals, television documentaries, catalogues and even a calendar. Writers at the trade periodicals, *Daily Variety* and the *Hollywood Reporter* added film noir to their reviewer's vocabulary, as did newspaper critics throughout the country.

Carlos Clarens' *Crime Movies* (1980) was, like the books by McArthur and Shadoian, primarily a study of the gangster *genre*. In Chapter Seven, "Shades of Noir," Clarens makes several unusual statements as he charts the familiar waters from France to Germany to hard-boiled fiction to documentary realism, for examples, "Film academics have employed the term *film noir* as a blanket definition for any movie without a happy ending, from *King Kong* to *Citizen Kane*: quite a large piece of fabric, and full of holes." (p. 194) Leaving aside the question of just where these "academics" might have promulgated their blanket definition, Clarens segues to visual style and analyses of *Murder. My Sweet* and *The Killers*. For the rest of the essay, Clarens skips randomly from *auteurist* to sociological to generic viewpoints, usually opting for the former. After discussing *Criss Cross*, he concludes that the director Robert Siodmak had "a Teutonic taste for the subtleties of sex-enslavement; he shared this quality with American directors like Joseph H. Lewis and Nicholas Ray, whose crime movies were as lyrical as his own." (p. 200) As in previous work, Clarens muddies his insights with glib extrapolations. What this essay lacks most of all is a structure. For other than associational transitions such as from director to director, theme to theme, or blacklisted filmmakers (Dassin and Garfield) to the House Un-American Activities Committee, there is no progression. Clarens discerns a multiplicity of sub-texts in *Night and the City* but merely concludes "before Dassin went symbol happy in *Night and the City*, the two modes of gangster *film noir*, the realistic and the allegorical, were nobly represented by Siodmak and Hathaway respectively." (p. 215) Whatever the "nobility" of their representation, Clarens' own rhetoric clouds his conclusion that Hathaway's less-conscious style did not interpose itself as forcefully as Siodmak on realistic

locations. Moreover, after dubbing *Cry of the City* an informal sequel to "the first major postwar gangster movie, *Kiss of Death*," Clarens disregards the opportunity to further contrast Siodmak's style with Hathaway's. Nor does Clarens ever reconsider one of his most interesting introductory remarks, that "no real life criminals were portrayed in American film from *Dillinger* in 1945 until *Baby Face Nelson* in 1957, roughly the heyday of the film noir." (p. 192) The chapter closes on another half-note, the exploitation of genre expectation in film noir, specifically in *The Big Combo*: "Alton could dispense with decor and define space with a pool of light, as in the scenes set in a fog-bound airfield. Yordan gave free rein to his invention, knowing that by then gangland was psychological terrain. Lewis could charge two-shots with such tension that he could dispense with the usual violence. Such chances paid off because the filmmakers were aware that genre could fill in the empty spaces." (p. 233) In a different and inappropriate context, Clarens makes much the same assumption about his readers.

Robert Ottoson's *A Reference Guide to the American Film Noir: 1940-1958* is immediately summed up by its title. Ottoson's introduction manages to recap criticial, sociological, and production history of film noir, with a twenty-word foray into art and opera, in just three pages. Ottoson's own viewpoint is largely subsumed by the nearly five-hundred citations from books, articles, and reviews; but he does affirm that "Film noir cannot be considered a genre. That might be the reason why it took decades after the origination of the term for English-language critics to deal with film noir. Critics usually agree about what constitutes a western, gangster, horror, or musical film, but film noir is a strange hybrid." (p. 2-3). While Ottoson may not probe too deeply into the nature of this "strange hybrid" he does annotate it and illustrate it with a score of photographs. Although the pure data contained in the 200 plus pages of filmography is quite abbreviated, featuring only director, script, and photographer credits and actors without character names, his two or three paragraphs of notes range broadly over the general subject. In combining plot summary, career sketches, quotes from contemporary reviews, filmmaker opinions, value judgments, and some occasional brief analysis, Ottoson's notes on a film such as *Reckless Moment* are typical. In paragraph one, there are comments on Max Ophuls, *Caught*, and his view of America. Paragraph two, Joan Bennett's work in other noir films, notably Fritz Lang's and a plot summary with a quote from an article. Paragraph three, two quasi-analytical citations and Ottoson's own comment: "The way Ophuls eschews typical noir lighting by resorting to mostly flat, brightly-lit scenes negates the ominous in favor of invoking the Harper family's environment. Yet he constantly employs Sirkian images of entrapment, by cluttering the foreground with objects--bar, furniture, columns--that separate the characters from the viewers." (p. 147) This is rather short shrift for a film as important to the noir cycle as *Reckless Moment*. On the other hand, it would seem to be, in Ottoson's determinedly egalitarian approach, about the same length as ninety percent of his other entries. Ottoson also has an appendix of forty-odd titles "presented in shortened form...because of their relative obscurity" that includes such mainstream films as *Blue Gardenia, 711 Ocean Drive,* and *Union Station.* Ottoson ends with a detailed bibliography and a complete index. While he does include a few films not covered in the book you are reading, Ottoson's study is basically just a condensed version of it.

The Dark Side of the Screen: Film Noir by Foster Hirsch is a comprehensive study of what the author calls "a full-fledged genre." He asserts that, "A genre, after all, is determined by conventions of narrative structure, characterizations, theme, and visual design, of just the sort noir offers in abundance." (p. 72) From this theoretical position Hirsch goes on to break film noir down into those very elements, chapter by chapter.

Hirsch's three character archetypes, the sleuth, the criminal, the middle-class victim, are effective refinements of Karimi's two forks in the noir path. *Scarlet Street*'s hero typifies the latter victim, while Phyllis Dietrichson and Walter Neff in *Double Indemnity* epitomize the criminal. Chandler's Marlowe and Hammett's Spade are Hirsch's obvious choices for sleuths, but Hirsch does include the less well-known detectives from the array of regular police and well-meaning amateurs who are ubiquitous in noir films. Hirsch also spends time detailing common patterns in narrative structures. He differentiates between the "stories told from the vantage of private eye" (p. 168), such as *The Big Sleep, The Maltese Falcon,* or *Kiss Me Deadly,* and those which tell the story from the criminal's or victim's perspective, such as *Double Indemnity, Woman in the Window, Out of the Past,* etc. According to this interpretation, the victim-criminal noir is much more emotional and neurotic while the sleuth film is cold and detached, in reflection of the personalities of the respective protagonists.

Hirsch also devotes a significant amount of space to the iconography of noir. He reiterates the importance of the visual facade by interpretation and illustrations to support his point. For example: "Objects, things, fragments of decor loom as large as places in the noir iconography. Clocks, mirrors, staircases, windows and bedposts create images of entrapment and anticipate moments of doom... exaggerated angles are a regular, expected element of noir visual style." (p. 89) In an attempt to be comprehensive, Hirsch dedicates a chapter each to the "noir director" and the "noir actor." In the latter are discussions of performances by players like Humphrey Bogart, Robert Mitchum, Joan Crawford, and Gloria Grahame. Hirsch sees them as "stylized" tour-de-forces which parallel the expressionist dimensions of the films themselves. In the "noir director" he centers on the careers of the most influential of the filmmakers--the Germanic quartet (Fritz Lang, Robert Siodmak, Billy Wilder, and Otto Preminger), Jules Dassin, Sam Fuller, Orson Welles, Alfred Hitchcock, Joseph H. Lewis, etc. While there is little new in any of this, *Dark Cinema* is an effective recapitulation.

The most valuable part of this book is the section on the literary and visual roots of noir. In tracing these roots Hirsch turns to the seminal work of naturalists like Theodore Dreiser and Frank Norris, early detective writers like Poe and Arthur Conan Doyle and finally to the standard list of hard-boiled writers: Cain, Hammett, Chandler, Horace McCoy, and Cornell Woolrich. Hirsch does overlook the progenitor of the sensationalist crime novel, Emile Zola. With works like *La Bête Humaine,* and *Thérese Raquin,* Zola set the pattern for both the naturalists and the hard-boiled writers who followed.

In his discussion of the visual roots, Hirsch intermixes analysis of German Expressionism in film and art with an insightful discussion of the influence on noir of painters like Edward Hopper and Reginald Marsh, a painter not usually associated with the movement. Hirsch ends by noting the residue of noir in films after the classic period from 1940 to 1958, singling out films like *Taxi Driver* and *Farewell, My Lovely* as particularly notable inheritors of the style. The book's most significant flaw is its truncated filmography, which even omits films that are mentioned in the text, such as *The Steel Trap* and *The Dividing Line.* In 1983 *The Velvet Light Trap* published a translation of French critic Marc Vernet's close inspection of six classic period films: *Maltese Falcon, Double Indemnity, The Big Sleep, The Lady from Shanghai, Out of the Past,* and *The Enforcer.* Vernet begins with the enigma, "the black hole," which progresses from Borde and Chaumeton's key concept of ambiguity to address the chaos that underlies the noir universe. Vernet's approach is both structural and semiological. Because film noir is resistant to a straightforward semiological deconstruction, Vernet quickly concedes that "the sense of disorder and reversal, however, is in every case relative." (p. 7) What Vernet never adequately considers is that each film noir is part of a body of films whose exterior associations create underlying meaning. Conclusions such as "a hero cannot be both strong and vulnerable, the woman good and evil" (p. 7) are part of a simplistic, structuro-semiological rush to judgment that is clearly at odds with the narrative position of film noir as a whole. Vernet's search for oppositions using the method of Propp or Levi-Strauss becomes a search through enclosed texts where "each functions perfectly within the context of its own system" ignores the critical context, the viewer expectations of film noir. As with any "genre" expectations film noir uses the context to create visual and narrative shorthand. Vernet falls back on the femme fatale--"the woman is made guilty and, despite her protestations, she is either abandoned or killed by the hero" (p. 88)--as the linchpin in his scheme of inversion and ignores the more fundamental, existential inversions of the noir underworld. Perhaps the real problem is that Vernet seeks designating structures in a cataclysmic movement, where a better guiding principle might have been Merleau-Ponty's observation that "the dialectic proper to the organism and the milieu can be interrupted by 'catastrophic' behavior."

Two more black-cloth bound, dust-jacketless studies (Ottoson's being the first of three) appeared in 1984. Of the three, Spencer Selby's *Dark City: the Film Noir* is by far the most useful, particularly his annotated filmography and appendices. Selby's introduction is as brief as Ottoson's and delineates his approach: (1) "detailed," film-by-film analysis of twenty-five notable films noirs...a detailed plot synopsis and an interpretive essay"; and (2) "an exhaustive filmography of nearly 500 noir films...the largest ever compiled." If there is a short-coming to Selby's work, it may be in this self-image of a "compiler" of facts or, as he puts it, "no attempt was made to fit the films to any preconceived or accepted notion of noir thematics. This tendency has been a major problem with previous material on film noir." (p. 3) Without further elucidation from Selby, one can only wonder why any author would approach any subject by disparaging the very concept of analysis, whether auteurist or sociological, iconographic or thematic, as "attempts by a zealous critic to derive them [connections]."

After effectively cutting the critical ground from beneath him, Selby proceeds with a chronologically based survey of twenty-five films, which the reader must assume--as Selby fails to assert it--were selected because they were milestones and/or prototypes of the noir phenomenon. From *Maltese Falcon* to *The Killing*, Selby merely repeats the process of summary and interpretation over and over. Although Appendix D is "Directors' Filmographies," Selby seems determined to make up for zealous auteurists of the past by discussing thematic viewpoints without reference to the authors of those viewpoints. Hence, three films directed by Robert Siodmak are discussed (*The Killers, Criss Cross, The File on Thelma Jordan*); but Siodmak is mentioned by name only once. Then, in a burst of overcompensation, the last essay mentions the Kubrick's name over a dozen times, something which might have been more appropriate in discussing *Detour*. One is not dragged to the brink of critical excess or an automatic subscription to Clarens' views on the lyricism of sex-enslavement by merely mentioning Nicholas Ray or Joseph H. Lewis; yet, astonishly, Selby analyzes *In a Lonely Place* and *The Big Combo* without doing so. Obviously, auteurism is not the issue here; but Selby's dogged insistence on ignoring the intentionality behind a film, whether social, personal, or purely phenomenological, is puzzling. Without any reference points, also puzzling are his choices of "notable" films. Conspicuously absent are *Murder, My Sweet, Dark Corner, Gun Crazy, Night and the City,* and even *Kiss Me Deadly*. If there are to be no films in the twenty-five directed by Robert Aldrich, Joseph Losey, or, most amazing of all, Anthony Mann, why include *Undercurrent, Dark City,* or, admirable thought it may be, *The Man I Love*. Not that Raoul Walsh is mentioned in the analysis, but would not *High Sierra* or *The Enforcer* been a more apt selection from his filmography? If Robert Siodmak directed 12% of the works considered, why chose *Thelma Jordan* over *Phantom Lady* or *Cry of the City*? In his own zeal to view "each film as a unique, creative entity," Selby frustrates the reader by ignoring all the implicit questions.

Despite all this, the heart of Selby's book, the 490 titles in his filmography, make it all but indispensable--the assumption being, of course, that the reader already owns

Film Noir: An Encyclopedic Reference--for the serious student of the noir cycle. This is not to say that these 490 films are the final word on the classic period. A comparison of just the "A" titles with a 1973 filmography by Selise Eiseman and William K. Everson or Robert Porfirio's listings reveals two PRC pictures, *Accomplice* and *Apology for Murder*, not included by Selby. All this really proves is how difficult if not impossible the certainty of "completeness" is in film history. Nonetheless, the breadth of Selby's research eclipses most other observers. Also interesting is Appendix A " Off-Genre and Other Films Noirs." Cross-referenced from Westerns and melodramas to "precursors" and "postnoirs" are another hundred titles. Curiously, Selby's obsessive chronologizing organizes the year-by-year list into monthly sub-sets, which is harder to read.

With the possible exception of Barry Gifford's intoxicated collection of essays, probably the most unusual and certainly the most overwrought study of film noir is Jon Tuska's *Dark Cinema: American Film Noir in Cultural Perspective.* Published in the same year as Selby and in the same "book noir" binding, Tuska's approach verges on that of the self-important, critical zealot whom Selby deemed so misguided. For Tuska, film noir "is a gasping for breath, a struggle to hang onto life. It is an essay in personal martyrdom, much in the sense of the highly personal speculations of Friedrich Nietzsche or Soren Kierkegaard, although their names would perhaps not be familiar to most people watching these films." (p. xx-xxi) Tuska supersedes the prose excesses of Clarens, the footnote count of Ottoson (530 versus 490), and the tangential thrusts of Karimi. After an introduction in which by a commodius vicus of recirculation he transforms his own recollection of George Raft's description of an emphysema attack into a definition of film noir that parallels the post-nihilist, post-phenomenological experience of the world, Tuska launches into a 15,000 word essay on Greek, Roman, and Elizabethan tragedy. While he does mix in two or three film titles and while it may be interesting to note that tragedy is derived from the Greek for goat or that "Seneca's work on India contained references to 60 rivers and 118 different races," (p. 29) whether most of these words are needed to put American film noir in cultural perspective is debatable. Tuska then produces twice as many words on a more pertinent but still excessively enumerated discussion of Gothic and hard-boiled writers. In the end Tuska's detailed summaries of work by Woolrich and Cain, heavily annotated with excerpts from other commentators, like his chapter on Tragedy, do reveal a foundation for noir themes and characters. The problem for the reader is that, when no stone is left unturned, a lot of detritus is uncovered as well.

When Tuska is not waxing quite so prolifically or condescendingly, there are passages of interest in *Dark Cinema*. If it is page 105 before Tuska gets to German Expressionism and if that Chapter begins with a thumbnail history of the Weimar Republic, it does finally introduce film history into the discourse. In the Chapter "*Film Noir* Canon," Tuskas reviews much of the previous writing on the subject, adopts the concept of "film noir, as a cinematic movement within the Hollywood system," but adds "I hold that a film noir cannot have a conventional happy ending and still be considered a *film noir*." (p. 152) In the text and most particularly in the chronology of titles from 1940 to 1950 that follows, Tuska tags each production as *film noir, film gris,* or melodrama. As the chapter wanders from title to title, Tuska continues to summarize narratives and cite other opinions but never fully defines his criteria other than melodramas have happy endings, *film gris* may or may not. The results are confusing. Tuska discusses *I Wake Up Screaming* at length as a seminal example. Cornell's suicide in that film is certainly not part of a "conventional happy ending," but it is dubbed melodrama. The equally seminal *Maltese Falcon* is *film gris*, but Bogart "getting the girl" in *Conflict* is noir. Perhaps the death of the hit-man in *This Gun for Hire* gives it a noir rating; but *The Reckless Moment* is melodrama? In fact, nine others of Selby's twenty-five notables are, according to Tuska, not noir; and two are not even listed in any category. Tuska takes pains to explain how the noir style transcends *Pick-up on South Street*'s happy ending. One might extrapolate that other exceptions where the moral protagonists triumph, such as *The Big Heat, Shadow of a Doubt, Desperate Hours, The Killer is Loose,* or *Blue Gardenia*, might prove the rule, if there were not so many of them. In the end, both Selby and Tuska might have been more mindful of Schrader's facetious question and less concerned about how many noir elements it takes to make a film noir.

Tuska's chronology of the classic period and "Subsequent Films Influenced by *Film Noir*," refers readers to this book or Ottoson's for more detail with the note that Ottoson's release years are "invariably correct." Given the unlikelihood that any reference book on film has ever been invariably correct, this is an odd aside. *Dark Cinema* itself instructs readers to find more information about *Film Noir: An Encyclopedic Reference* in its bibliography but fails to include it there. As regards release year, our original methodology is explained in Appendix C1, but in the twenty-one disparities between the first edition of this book and Ottoson's, his data was incorrect eighteen times. A fairer comparison would be between this book and Selby's, where in ten disparities the score was *Film Noir*, 6, *Dark City*, 3, with one draw (*They Live by Night*). (Seriously, this aside is an appropriate place to note that scores of corrections have been made to subsequent printings and new editions of this book but there are likely scores more undiscovered; and the editors have always appreciated input from readers in that regard.)

"What differentiates *film noir* from other psychological crime and social problem films of this period is that through the use of flashbacks, subjective camera and other visual and narrative analogues for his disturbed mental state, the controlling perception of *film noir* is that of the maladjusted protagonist, whose world we enter in the often forlorn hope that we will find a way to leave it. These movies are about maladjustment, but more that that, they are themselves maladjusted texts." (p. 68) In his 1984 arti-

cle, Richard Maltby" extends the "traditional" socio-historical reading of the classic noir period, i.e. noir malaise as a cultural reflection, to the text itself. Maltby posits several limitations for extrapolation of cultural truisms from film noir, before concluding with an extrapolation of his own: "As documents in cultural history, it is difficult to regard the postwar *films noirs* as documents of liberal existentialism. Their rhetoric of paranoia, however much their liberal critics psychoanalysed it, was more closely attached to an alternative political tendency...a new melodramatic politics of emotion." (p. 70)

Devil Thumbs a Ride and Other Unforgettable Films by Barry Gifford easily supersedes Appel as the quirkiest and most idiosyncratic study of film noir to date. In fact, one is hard-pressed to call it a "study." Written by novelist Barry Gifford it adopts the style of a hard-boiled thriller in prose and in attitude while surveying the author's list of favorite "unforgettable" movies.

Like many crime novels it is supremely subjective, avoiding all "academic flapdoodle" (p. 1) in favor of personal reminiscences. For example: on *Gun Crazy*, "My friend Steve Fagin thinks that *Gun Crazy* is the greatest American movie ever made. It was Fagin who made me watch it and I'm not sorry I did." (p. 65); on *The 400 Blows*, "I saw *The 400 Blows* with my mother in 1959, when I was 12 years old, the same as the film's protagonist..." (p. 59). Equally subjective and extravagant are his appraisals of actors like Timothy Carey and Lawrence Tierney: "Timothy Carey justifies the French intellectual's image of the typical American male," (p. 58) and "...but that mean look was still in his [Tierney's] eyes; that bad-to-the-bone, never-give-in visage. There is no daylight in that face." (p. 52) He is not even averse to throwing in bit of gossip such as his reference to the legendary rivalry between Lillian Gish and Bette Davis, quoting Davis: "...of course it's a lovely close-up. The bitch [Gish] invented close-ups." (p. 113)

Gifford's writing style is also carefully modeled on the dialogue of the films he discusses, so that the line between novel writing and film analysis virtually disappears. He is colloquial and hard-bitten, peppering his prose with slang. On *Detour*, "He [Tom Neal] can't live without her so he gives up his solid gig and suffers through the tortures of the road dreaming of that blonde pussy at the end of the trail." (p. 47) On *The Killing*, "Marie Windsor is, as always, the big breasted blonde who falls for the wrong guy. In this case she's married to a milquetoast track betting window teller, Elisha Cook, Jr., but has a man on the side, to whom she spills the beans about the robbery, and who throws a wrench in the works." (p. 91) Actually, Marie Windsor was almost always a brunette, but who can fault Gifford's enthusiasm.

Gifford's criteria for choosing these hundred plus films is (what a suprise!) never really delineated in the book. The only common denominator among these films seems to be a dark vision coupled with the author's unbridled admiration for the movie. Gifford's unrestrained style is what makes the book so engaging. What he lacks in

APPENDIX

analytical insight is overcompensated for as he mimics the flavor of film noir with his writing style. Whether he is feverishly praising favorites like *Tom Horn, Detour, Out of the Past, Mildred Pierce,* or the eponymous *Devil Thumbs a Ride* or lovingly criticizing the defects of *Suddenly* or *Road House,* Gifford maintains a close-up, personal point-of-view which can't help but entertain a reader who may have overdosed on academic flapdoodle.

Bruce Crowther's book *Film Noir: Reflections in a Dark Mirror* is at best a cursory survey, although it is profusely illustrated. After the now-familiar defining of terms, "Much less readily defined than either the musical or the western, the film noir category, while often centering on tales of cops and crooks and private eyes, usually reflects a darker world than that inhabited by such characters in other movies or even real life." (p. 7), Crowther turns to the equally familiar historical background of noir (disillusionment and paranoia growing out of WW II and the ensuing Cold War), its literary roots (crime fiction, the hard-boiled tradition), and the influence of the emigre directors like Lang, Siodmak, and Wilder. These are not observations which a book published in 1988 needs to belabor.

Although most of the material is not new, he does include two writers often given short shrift in other noir studies: Cornell Woolrich and W.R. Burnett. He briefly synopsizes their careers as well as discussing a number of the film adaptations of their works. On Cornell Woolrich, Crowther is more enthusiastic and succinct than Tuska: "More than most tough-guy writers, Cornell Woolrich helped establish the mood for film noir which attracted and inspired numerous filmmakers of the day, and his sour tales of depraved humanity foreshadow the work of many later writers who were able to expand the boundaries of tough-guy fiction in directions Woolrich could only hint at..." (p. 19)

Crowther also includes a particular appreciation of noir directors of photography; or as he puts it, "Recognition of the cinematographer is long overdue and comes much too late for many talented men who worked within Hollywood's studio system and were only rarely allowed to shine." (p. 61) Crowther devotes an entire chapter (Chapter Four -- "Technique: The Look of Noir") to the contributions of men like Gregg Toland, John Alton, Lee Garmes, Burnett Guffey, Milton Krasner, Nicholas Musuraca, James Wong Howe, and John Seitz. He even gives a bit of biographical information on these neglected contributors, while recounting their efforts to create the visual look of noir.

Crowther also tries to rescue character actors from their anonymity in noir films. The chapter called "Noir Performers: Minor Icons, Grotesques, and Other Supporting Players," looks at the careers of actors whose faces added so much to the mood of noir that they truly can be called icons. Elisha Cook, Jr., John Ireland, Charles McGraw, Laird Cregar, and Peter Lorre are a few of the figures in his gallery of expressionist performers. In addition, Crowther devotes a considerable amount of space to analyzing the impact of these actors on the individual films they

appeared in. Crowther concludes like so many authors by seeking the noir tradition in recent films but only finds it in the most obvious places: in the action/crime films of the 70s and 80s and in the neo-noir revival films like *Chinatown* and *Body Heat.* Crowther eschews a filmography; oddly his is the first bibliography to include Porfirio's dissertation but overlooks (Shadoian, Ottoson, Tuska) or misspells ("Shelby" for "Selby") others.

Both Dale Ewing's 1988 article and J.P. Telotte's 1989 book derive partly from the idea of a narrative model raised but largely unexplored by James Damico. Ewing surveys the earlier writing and remarks that "the fact that analysts have made generalizations about film noir from its stylistic content does not necessarily invalidate their conclusions; it only forces them to take into account basic objections to their method." (p. 68) What Ewing seems to overlook when he says that "After 1970, all film noir criticism seemed to spring from this central idea [style as content]." (p. 64) is that beginning with Borde and Chaumeton and certainly since *Women in Film Noir,* most studies including this one have accepted film noir as a cycle or series, whose classic period combined aspects of movement (form) and genre (content). The overemphasis on style in the early work of Durgnat and Schrader was heavily rhetorical and designed to counterbalance those who would make film noir into a genre. Liker Damico, Ewing does not credit Durgnat, Schrader et al for moving beyond their own rhetoric, beyond "motif and tone" (Durgnat) or "tone and mood" (Schrader) to film noir defined by both narrative and visual usage. Another summary of critical commentary on film noir which appeared in 1988 was Jack Nachbar's essay in *Film Genres.*

For J.P. Telotte, the narrative patterns of film noir are the central concern and the sub-title of his 1989 book, *Voices in the Dark.* Rather than concern himself, more than thirty years after Borde and Chaumeton, with what film noir is, Telotte simply sidesteps the issue and moves on: "Is noir, then, simply a cycle of films that flourished in the backwash of World War II and the early cold war days, borrowing its markings from a variety of established genres; or is it a genre in its own right, simply appearing, disappearing, and then reappearing in keeping with the usual principles of audience popularity and need?... It is an argument that finally has as much to do with criticism itself, especially with the varying ways that we define film genres, as with film noir itself, and thus one that we probably cannot fully resolve here." (p. 3) Like Damico and Ewing, Telotte assumes that Durgnat and Schrader headed up a phalanx of writers intent on defining rather than refining noir in terms of style. His statement on that--"The noir style, I would suggest, ultimately seems as curiously diverse as its subject matter, and equally inadequate for accurately defining the form." (p. 10)-- is inconsistent tautology. In treating diverse subject matter, what by definition is the formal nexus, if not style? As for exploration of that narrative nexus in English, does it not go back to Durgnat's "family tree"?

On the whole, despite the fact that it is somewhat, like

382

early Raymond Chandler novels, a compilation of previous short pieces, Telotte's is the first book-length study to isolate and satisfactorily explore this particular aspect of the noir cycle. By page 16, Telotte has fixed his ground and laid the cornerstone: "While classical film narrative usually tries to conceal its point of view--to cover over relativity-- these films reveal theirs, in in that revelation lies their true strength. For what impels them and forges their strongest appeal is an abiding desire to assert their own view of truth, their private vision as a rival and alternative to a public, supposedly objective one." This statement, except for its being in the form of a pathetic fallacy about the abiding desire of these films, is not a new one. How Telotte develops it is.

Telotte minutely explores both direct (*Lady in the Lake, Dark Passage*) and indirect (*Murder, My Sweet*) subjectivity and then turns to "semi-documentary style." Less clearly devised is Chapter Ten, which gives the impression of operating from an auteurist assumption (the films discussed are introduced as Edmund Goulding's *Nightmare Alley*, Nicholas Ray's *In A Lonely Place*, etc) but fails to explore that avenue. Surely after discussing *Double Indemnity* in Chapter Two and *The Big Carnival* here, Telotte must have considered probing further with *Sunset Boulevard* but does not. It is no coincidence that all of Wilder's noir protagonists perish. In his particular, cynical take on the noir universe, there is no possibility of redemption, an observation that would provide telling contrast with Telotte's overall conclusion.

The next chapter on "Robert Aldrich's *Kiss Me Deadly*" also provides an opportunity for comparison with other work by Aldrich or A.I Bezzerides (*On Dangerous Ground, Thieves' Highway*) that is not taken. Telotte's analysis is sound; but given a movie whose themes (Shadoian), style (Silver), and even aural signifiers (Porfirio) have been closely read before, one would expect Telotte to take a new slant and/or relate back to his central premise of narrative patterns more consistently than he does. Telotte's conclusion, that "in trying to articulate our personal and cultural anxieties, the film noir...offer[s] us a better sense of ourselves, or at least a clearer notion of who we are individually and collectively." (p. 222) suggests that the noir cycle is in itself a redemptive movement. Again while the concept of film as social catharsis is not new, Telotte's appraisal of such an effect is much more thorough than Maltby's "maladjusted text" or any other antecedent and a useful addition to the noir commentaries.

"Film noir has been valued by successive critics for its supposed challenges to or disruptions of the stylistic, narrative and generic norms of the classical system of filmmaking." (p. x). Frank Krutnik tantalizes the reader of *In A Lonely Street* (1991) with such assertions, with the suggestion that his study will rigorously examine valuations and suppositions and expose them for what they are. But within a few paragraphs, Krutnik is already buying into the first piece of half-baked critical pie: "This fascination with internal, subjectively generated criminal impulses has widely been recognized as a crucial characteristic of 1940s

film noir." (p. xii) Like other late-comers to the critical discourse on film noir, Krutnik would like to pick and choose from what has gone before or simply dodge the issue entirely: "Any attempt to construct distinctions within or between cycles and genres is inevitably contentious...in the case of film noir this difficulty is exacerbated in particular by the widespread trend towards generic combination which marks 1940s Hollywood cinema." (p. 25) In support of this latter point, Krutnik cites six examples, four of which are actually from the 1940s. Trends as widespread as this are rare indeed. After repeatedly implying that commentators since Borde and Chaumeton have taken great liberties in drawing assumptions about film noir from the cultural context without proper regard to its status as a post-constructed phenomenon, perhaps the most egregious of Krutnik's remarks is that "the studios deliberately encouraged their staff to experiment with new techniques which could be achieved by means of fixed equipment." (p. 21) This is post-constructed film history at its best. Having borne with Krutnik this far, the reader may be surprised to discover that the balance of his reassessment in Parts I and II echoes so much that has gone before. Hardboiled sources, popularity of psychoanalysis, postwar maladjustment, it almost seems as if Krutnik is trying to reconcile Maltby to Borde and Chaumeton. Mercifully, he never resembles Tuska, although there are some moments, for instance: "As text, one does not read *My Darling Clementine* as one reads *The Wild Bunch*, in spite of the fact that both are Westerns." (p. 11), when one wonders who Krutnik presumes his audience is.

Expecting that Part III will finally include the "judicious use of textual analysis" promised on the back cover, one is again surprised at what comes next: a neo-Freudian precis on masculine rites of passage. Retrograde as it may seem, decades after R.D. Laing's existential personalization of psychosis, *Out of the Past* becomes a case history of Oedipal transference. In discussing *The Killers*, Edmund O'Brien as Riordan becomes a phallic male opposed to a castrating femme fatale. Krutnik does spend some time discussing "mise-en-scene dominated by triangular compositions," even how foreground objects may be seen to separate or constrict characters in the frame. For the most part, Krutnik's focus remains generic and Freudian. While he may occasionally cite a film title preceded by a director's name in the possessive case, there is generally no comment on the metteur-en-scene, on the intentionally behind "triangular compositions" or other elements of style. The narrative and psychological analyses are designed to relate to three broad categories of "tough" thriller--investigative, suspense, and criminal-adventure--but there is considerable overlapping. Krutnik's most interesting observations are at the very end of the book, in a sub-section of Appendix 2, "the outlaw-couple film," where *Gun Crazy* and *Shockproof* are considered in detail. Krutnik's "filmography" is of titles and "hard-boiled" writers only, but it would have been quite useful to have a recap of the titles grouped by the categories which Krutnik has proposed for them. Also, in a book as heavily referential as this, a bibliography should be *de riguer*.

The most recently published books (both 1992) are focused on particular films: *Autopsy, An Element of Realism in Film Noir* by Carl Richardson which treats *Maltese Falcon, The Naked City,* and *Touch of Evil,* and *Double Indemnity* by Richard Schickel, one of the first studies in the BFI Classics series. The latter is a discursive look at the Wilder/Chandler adaptation of James M. Cain which operates from the perspective that "in the long history of literary adaptation, it is hard to think of a screenplay that more markedly improved on its source." (p. 53) Schickel's most interesting observations relate to Wilder's casting and cutting decisions, in particular the revised ending, all reinforcing the underlying assumption of a "classic" work. Richardson's analytical ambitions are quite different: "it is not success but failure that is of concern...the failure of film noir to assimilate an element of realism into its voluminous corps of films." (p. 2) In the introductory comments Richardson collapses Porfirio's four periods of the classic era into three and selects an example from each. Richardson's focus on "realism" leads him to sub-categorize each subsequent chapter. *Maltese Falcon* epitomizes the Studio Picture, *Naked City,* the location picture, and *Touch of Evil* is "In Limbo." Before dealing with the individual productions, Richardson makes several assertions that are unsubstantiated or inaccurate. "Film noir benefited from the disintegration of the studio system." (p. 11) Even if one accepts that the studio system did disintegrate during the classic period (which was hardly the case), the assumption that greater control by individual filmmakers somehow benefited film noir is entirely unsupported. Richardson relies heavily on Andre Bazin for his definition of "realism." In fact, the title and opening sentences of the book are almost a parodies of Bazin's introductory analogy to mummificaction in "The Ontology of the Photographic Image." But, contrary to what Richardson uses ellipses to suggest, Bazin does not actually equate aesthetic realism with "true realism" in that essay. The dichotomy which Bazin addressed is not as much aesthetic/psychological as it is Expressionist/Impressionist. What Bazin does say about the aesthetic/psychological split is that "the great artists, of course, have always been able to combine the two tendencies." Richardson also interprets Bazin as extolling "restraint." But nature is not restrained; and, if one considers the *last* sentence of Bazin's paragraph from which *Autopsy* cites only the *first*, nature is the key: "By the power of photography, the natural image of a world that we neither know nor can know, nature at last does more than imitate art: she imitates the artist." Of course, Bazin still allows for creative mediation: "The personality of the photographer enters into the proceedings *only* [italics ours] in his selection of the object to be photographed and by way of the purpose he has in mind." Given that there is no inherent antipathy between this position of Bazin's and the psychological figures whom Richardson markedly chooses not to cite and given a discursive survey of realism/naturalism from Von Stroheim to Flaherty and from Courbet to Zola, *Autopsy's* introduction fails, first, actually to define his point-of-view and, second, substantially to relate his observations to film noir.

Ultimately nothing in *Autopsy* has greater clarity or a newer take on the subject than J.P. Telotte's chapters on "Reality" and "Documentary Noir". Despite all this and such annoying fine points as citing Borde and Chaumeton in French without translation even in the footnotes, Richardson's chapters on the films, like Schickel's study of *Double Indemnity,* do contain a wealth of information gleaned from archival sources. Sometimes there is an over abundance. Does it really matter on which sound stages at Warner Bros. *Maltese Falcon* was shot? And why include three pages of item after item on the location arrangements for *Touch of Evil* in Venice, California, which compared with those of any motion picture or television program shot on location are remarkably ordinary? It would have been better to add a few words analyzing more pertinent details, such as the "rationing" of set budgets during World War II. There are also two recent (both 1990) unpublished studies. *Embattled Voices: the Narrator and the Woman in Film Noir and the Woman's Film* is a dissertation by Karen Hollinger. While it may not be clear from the complicated title, Hollinger's primary focus is the Narrator, whether male or female, particularly the first person narrator in film noir. In Chapters III and IV on the Detective Narrator and the Criminal/Victim Narrator, Hollinger's discussion are much more focused and effective than anything in Krutnik's work. In the comparisons of Chandler's first person novels and the film adaptations, Hollinger does fall prey to the tendency to get mired in the "unnatural" subjective camera of *Lady in the Lake;* but the observations on *Murder, My Sweet* and *The Big Sleep* compare favorably with Telotte's detailed consideration. In analyzing *Double Indemnity* as a "struggle to usurp patriarchal power" (p. 97) and suggesting that "the threat that tries the strength of the patriarchy is the figure of the femme fatale," (p. 104) Hollinger provides a significant addendum to the classic approach of Schickel and others. It is in treating concepts such as the narrative dislocation in *Laura,* that Hollinger's analysis itself lacks resolution. In the end, Hollinger does relate the dislocations and antiheroes of film noir to Bordwell et al and counters by observation their suggestion that film noir is a mere aberration in classical Hollywood narrative.

Todd Erickson's Master's thesis, *Evidence of Film Noir in Contemporary American Cinema,* has as its declared focus films outside the classic period. To establish background, Erickson's first two chapters are "overviews" of classic noir films and the previous literature. Erickson's novel assertion is that the contemporary films which follow the noir tradition themselves compel a definition of film noir as more than a movement. "More specifically, the accumulated critical writings of the 1970s and 1980s, coupled with the contemporary cinema's new cycle of noir-influenced crime films have provided a more favorable vantage point from which to contemplate the accurate definition of film noir. From this vantage point, I submit that the film noir can be understood not only as a movement, but also as a genre, which developed within, and emerged from, the movement itself." (p. 32) From this vantage also, Erickson's review of the noir tradition is more detached than any of the other commentators from Selby to Krutnik who have tried to evaluate their precursors. Erickson omits certain critics by design. If anything is overlooked, it is the possibility raised by Borde and Chaumeton and sketchily developed in their later postface of a noir series as a recurring cycle.

In essence, Erickson offers a critical compromise that is more forthright than Telotte or Tuska and resembles the combined narrative and stylistic considerations of Porfirio and Silver/Ward et al. Chapter Three, "Defining the Film Noir," elaborates sketchily on Erickson's general position, as if he were in haste to reach the contemporary cinema. Erickson's case for "neo-noir" is wide-ranging citing in turn social historians and rock lyricists, film reviewers and filmmakers, to demonstrate awareness of the noir phenomenon. Given Erickson's focus, what classic film noir was may be less important that what contemporary filmmakers perceive it to have been.

Three factors are isolated as affecting neo-noir: (1) improved color film stock (an implicit analog to improved black-and-white stock after World War II); (2) an ongoing public fascination with crime and criminals; and (3) an unprecedented awareness of film noir on the part of current directors and writers. Erickson adds that "color film has become a guarantee of realism to audiences, just as black-and-white was in the forties..." (p. 46) Ancillary to Point 2 are the new editions of hard-boiled writers and new work in that tradition by current novelists. The heart of the matter is the last point; and Erickson claims to have "conservatively counted at least 70 noir attempts that were released as theatrical features by the major and minor distributors during the 1980s." (p. 62) Unfortunately, Erickson fails to provide a complete list; but he does select eight examples from *Body Heat* (1981) to *Cop* (1988) for more detailed analysis. Erickson's concluding chapter is more of a recapitulation for formal, academic purposes, but he does include an extensive appendix of interviews with current filmmakers and a lengthy bibliography.

The amount of critical interest which film noir has attracted particularly in the last decade may suggest to some why, barely thirty years after the informal conclusion of the classic period, it still captures the attention of viewers. Perhaps the fascination of film noir for writers is both the diversity of its titles and the diversity of critical approaches which it tolerates or even encourages. What remains after any quest for anthropo-socio-econo-phenomeno-psycho-structuro-semio-critical insights is the work itself, the films that are or would be noir.

For many, the very concepts film history and criticism are ill-defined and uncertain, as their grappling with film noir quickly reaffirms. If Idries Shah's remark is taken into account, the same might be true of any history. If the books and articles on the matter clearly demonstrate anything, it may well be the validity of our assertion that film noir, which so often used ambivalence and ambiguity for dramatic effect, whose characters were so often obsessed, alienated, and self-destructive, and that followed twisted narrative roads into so many dark corners, still resists facile explanation. Perhaps in the truest sense, in the ironic or existential sense, film noir needs no explanation at all. Its real meaning is where it has always been, in the films themselves.

Appendix D

1. Additional Films from the Classic Period

Despite an attempt to be as comprehensive as possible in the 1st Edition, omissions proved unavoidable. In studying the noir cycle, one encounters two formidable hurdles: first, access to the original "texts" themselves; and secondly the sheer number of films produced by the American movie industry, especially in the low budget area where so many noir films originated. Before the advent of home video researchers were limited to archival holdings, 16mm prints, and television. Now, with the boom in the video market, many formerly unavailable titles are for rent at local video outlets.

As a consequence, in the intervening years since the 1st and 2nd editions of this book, movies which were overlooked in sifting through the mass of prospective titles have become available for review. Some were suggested to the editors and some were discovered in preparing this edition. All sufficiently reflect the elements of film noir, the icons, characters, and thematic preoccupations to merit discussion here.

Psychological Persecution: Who's Zooming Who?

> Permit me to observe that if this be madness, it is the sole raison d'etre of your profession, gentlemen.
>
> The Father,
> *Six Characters in Search of An Author*

Film Noir is so deeply rooted in the neurotic personality, whether it be that of the scarred protagonist or the ruthless villain, that it is not surprising that psychology should play a significant part in so many of the plots. Alfred Hitchcock's *Spellbound* (1945) is perhaps the bellwether for this type of film. It contains the central motif which would inform so many noir films, that of psychological persecution. An already neurotic individual portrayed by Gregory Peck is driven to insane behavior by a manipulative, power-hungry individual (Leo G. Carroll). Drawing on Peck's childhood guilt concerning his brother's death, Carroll plays a psychiatrist who exploits Peck's trauma to make him the "fall guy" in a murder he has committed in order to advance his career. The film also epitomizes Hollywood's burgeoning fascination with Freudianism. Dream sequences designed by artist Salvador Dali provide rather blatant and often simplistic clues not only to Peck's neuroses but also to the mystery of the film.

This theme of psychological persecution by one whose profession is to guide individuals out of neurotic disorder not into them dominates three other films: *The Scarf, Shock,* and *Whirlpool. The Scarf* (1951), directed by celebrated German expressionist filmmaker E.A. Dupont stars John

Ireland as an escapee from an institution for the criminally insane where he has been committed based on the evidence of psychiatrist Emlyn Williams. Wandering in an anguished daze, reminiscent of Emil Jannings' anomie in Dupont's 1925 *Variety*, Ireland discovers that the real murderer is Williams and so frees himself of the debilitating guilt. *Shock* (1946) with Vincent Price as the ruthless psychiatrist was roundly attacked on its release by psychiatric organizations for its "loathsome" portrayal of a mental health professional. Price's brutal exploitation of a female patient in order to hide the murder of his wife which she inadvertently witnessed is echoed in Otto Preminger's *Whirlpool* (1949). Again the victim is a woman. Jose Ferrer as a hypnotherapist involves kleptomaniacal Gene Tierney in a complex and ultimately implausible murder scheme. The portrait of the psychiatric profession this time is tempered by the presence of Richard Conte as the caring professional, Dr. Sutton.

In *Dark Waters* (1944), *The Secret Fury* (1950), and *The Man with My Face* (1951) the psychological persecutors not in medical costume become, respectively, greedy con-men, a lawyer, and an ingenious doppelganger. In *The Secret Fury* Claudette Colbert is driven insane by a lawyer bent on revenge. Although she is rescued when her fiance (Robert Ryan) uncovers the plot, her ordeal is no less tormenting. *Dark Waters* resembles *Spellbound, Whirlpool,* and *The Scarf* in that the exploiters are taking advantage of a psychogical dysfunction which is already present. Characters embodied by Peck in *Spellbound*, Tierney in *Whirlpool*, Ireland in *The Scarf*, and Merle Oberon in this film enter the scene already damaged. Their exploiters only utilize and aggravate the extant traumas and neuroses. *Dark Waters* opens with watery superimpositions and headlines proclaiming a naval disaster over the face of deeply troubled Merle Oberon. Having lost her parents in a Japanese attack on a passenger ship, she is receiving psychiatric care. In order to recuperate she goes to stay in the bayous with relatives. In a setting of fog, swamp water, and decaying mansions she becomes the victim of a plot by a con-man (Thomas Mitchell) to disinherit her. Her mental fragility and quasi-somnambulist state is effectively externalized by the bayou environment, as she seems to glide through a nightmare of persecution and illusion. In *The Man with My Face* an accountant (Barry Nelson) arrives home to find a duplicate of himself has taken over his life and identity in order to put into motion an elaborate million dollar swindle and in so doing shift the blame to Nelson. Nelson strives to regain his identity while convincing the police he is not the criminal.

Fritz Lang's *Secret Beyond the Door* (1948) presents an interesting twist on the psychological persecution theme. In this tale of a woman (Joan Bennett) who marries a man she hardly knows (Michael Redgrave), the psychological disturbance emanates from within the character himself, so that it is actually a case of self-persecution. Architect Redgrave, believing himself responsible for the death of his first wife, reconstructs the bedroom within which she died in exact detail while surrounding the room with famous murder chambers. In a dream sequence Redgrave acts as prosecutor and defendant in his own trial situated in a courtroom resurrected from Lang's UFA period and replete with elongated shadows and asymmetrical furnishings. In a typically naive, Freudian resolution, Redgrave comes to understand with Bennett's aid that he suffered a childhood trauma and that an Oedipal attachment to a mother who abandoned him created his hostility towards women. Without the subtleties of Lang's earlier *Woman in the Window* or *Scarlet Street*, *Secret Beyond the Door* shares the concept of "breakthrough" or curing a profound illness through remembering psychic shocks with *Spellbound* et al.

In *Bewitched* (1945) the theme of self-persecution is carried to its logical extreme. The protagonist (Phyllis Thaxter) exhibits a schizophrenia which leads her to murder and deception. When "Karen," the name she gives to the "evil" side of her nature, comes to dominate her, she is driven to murder her boyfriend on the eve of their wedding and then pathologically manipulate both her psychiatrist and her lawyer. In the end the only one who can convict Thaxter is herself, as she screams out her guilt to a shocked courtroom.

While *Fallen Sparrow,* made in 1943, is less Freudian than other noir films which share this theme, it is among the earliest delineations of psychological persecution. Being more political in nature, the film features John Garfield as a fear-ridden veteran of the Spanish Civil War who survived capture and torture by Franco's army. Back in the United States, he is pursued by Fascists searching for a symbolic item, a flag. Much like *The Maltese Falcon*'s statuette, this icon becomes the focus of the characters' psychic energies. Garfield, scarred physically and emotionally by his war experience, captures, as he does in better known performances in *Body and Soul* and *Force of Evil*, that noir sense of entrapment and alienation. As the Fascists try to take advantage of his frailty and play "mind games" in order to break his will, Garfield uses an existential resolve to avoid slipping into a psychological pit from which he might never emerge.

Femme Fatale, Fatally Drawn

> I'm not bad; I'm only drawn that way. Jessica Rabbit,
> *Who Framed Roger Rabbit?*

The issue of the female image in noir films has been and continues to be considered at length in other books and articles. While some commentators have interpreted the impressive array of femme fatales in noir as a reinforcement of negative female stereotypes--the black widow, the bitch goddess, the castrator--others have seen these archetypes as forces which threaten to upset the stable order of the patriarchal world established in these films.

Three films by director/writer/actor Hugo Haas particularly reinforce this interpretation: *Pickup* (1951), *Strange Fascination* (1952), and *Hit and Run* (1957). In all three films there is an older, well-established figure: a railroad employee about to retire with a sizable pension in the first; a successful concert pianist in the second; a junk yard proprietor in the third--all played by Haas. Each man has his safe and solid but lonely world disrupted by a callow, blonde temptress: Beverly Michaels in the first film; Cleo Moore in the second and third. Their arrival not unexpectedly wreaks havoc on the lives of the older men. In *Pickup* Haas is almost murdered by his scheming wife in collusion with her young lover, while in *Strange Fascination* the pianist mutilates his own hand in order to collect on an insurance policy so that he might satisfy Moore's everexpanding desires. At the end of both films the femme fatales survive relatively unscathed, in contrast to *Out of the Past, Double Indemnity,* and other noir films where they are annihilated as the patriarchy reasserts its social control. These women leave their victims lonely inhabitants of a world no longer secure. The railroad worker adopts a new dog and returns to his lonely abode; the pianist plays one-handed piano on skid row. In *Hit and Run* the voracious blonde showgirl does get her comeuppance, as she is tricked into admitting the murder of her husband to his twin brother, although her punishment is never clearly defined.

In *Quicksand* (1950) this female disruption of patriarchal order is exponentially worse. As the title of the film implies, the protagonist (Mickey Rooney) is dragged deeper and deeper into a nightmare world of crime and sex. In order to impress a woman (Jeanne Cagney as the archetypal trashy, blonde temptress), Rooney steals twenty dollars. This initial minor larceny expands to car theft, fraud, mugging, and finally "murder." As Rooney is drawn further and further into this pit, the bright daytime exteriors of the street and the garage where he works are replaced by the murky world of Peter Lorre's arcade, the fog-shrouded pier, and the crowded streets of downtown Los Angeles.

Three other films, *Impact* (1949), *Strange Triangle* (1946), and *The Las Vegas Story* (1952), also contain femme fatales with subversive potential, impersonated by Helen Walker in the first film, Signe Hasso in the second, and Jane Russell in the third. In *Impact* Helen Walker and her lover plan to murder her husband (Brian Donlevy) for his cash. The murder attempt goes predictably awry as Donlevy survives; but disillusioned, wounded, and now believed dead, a bitter Donlevy holes up in a small town where hard work and the love of a "good girl" (Ella Raines) restore his desire for life. Willing to forgive his wife he returns to the city only to be confronted with further devious manipulations on the part of his "black widow," who now charges him with the murder of her lover. In *Strange Triangle* Hasso, no shrinking violet, takes on two men. She destroys each through her greed and lasciviousness and leads one of the men to murder and madness. In *The Las Vegas Story,* Jane Russell also toys with the affection of two men, her husband (Vincent Price) and a former flame (Victor Mature). In seducing policeman Mature into aiding her compulsive gambler husband, Russell uses her robust figure to reprise her femme fatale role from *His Kind of Woman* (1951) with only a slight variation on the tortured love triangle.

Affair in Havana (1957) showcases a more ambiguous femme fatale. Initially the melancholic wife (Sara Shayne) of a crippled industrialist (Raymond Burr) elicits the audience's sympathy with her downcast gaze, demure appearance, and obvious solicitude towards her husband. As the film progresses her purity is stained by greed. She refuses to leave her husband because he will disinherit her. Slowly Burr begins to displace her as the sympathetic center. With his hulking presence strapped into a wheelchair, he impotently stares at his wife's half-naked body, forlornly watches 16mm footage taken by a detective of his wife and her lover (John Cassavetes), and broods over the boating accident caused by his wife which left him paralyzed. Even when he concocts his plan to force his wife to murder him, it is more the despairing act of a man tormented by his fate than a simple scheme for revenge. By this point in the film Shayne has been transformed into a full-blown femme fatale as she causes her husband's death and then blames a lovelorn ranchhand who believed he was protecting her from her husband.

Affair in Trinidad (1952) re-teams Rita Hayworth and Glenn Ford in a virtual remake of *Gilda* (1946). Hayworth, as tempestuous and sultry as ever, dances and sashays her way through the lives of several men, leaving some with temporary wounds, others with permanent damage. Her husband dies defending her. Alexander Scourby, the villainous spy, falls for her charms which leads to his ultimate unraveling. And, of course, Glenn Ford repeats the role of the suspicious self-tormenter who can never really accept Hayworth's unbridled sexuality, epitomized by her lascivious dances, and, consequently, alternates between all-consuming passion for and bitter distrust of this free spirit. As in *Gilda* Hayworth dominates the imagery of the film, refusing to be confined by the patriarchal world view of the film until the end. As in so many of her performances, she crystallizes what the male characters most feared in the femme fatale archetype.

Alienation and Despair—Is There "No Exit"?

> Sometimes I think we're all of us in our own private traps.
> Norman Bates,
> *Psycho*

The question of redemption plays a part in most noir narratives. In the existential trap which the "forces" around the noir characters have set, with or without their assistance, there often seems to be no way out. It can be a truly Sartrean hell, a murky vortex which spins its victims around for eternity, or there may a light at the end of the dark passage.

Five films that represent the pessimistic side of this equation are *The Long Night, One Way Street, The Money Trap, A Place in the Sun,* and *Night Without Sleep. The Long Night* (1947) is a remake of the proto-noir classic *Le Jour Se Leve* (1939, directed by Marcel Carne). In both versions the protagonist, played by Jean Gabin in the original and Henry Fonda in the American version, opens and closes the story trapped like an animal, barricading himself against the police while reflecting back on the events that led him down his one-way street. Haunted by his war experience and by his inability to provide his girlfriend with an escape from their drab, depressing life, he is driven alternately to depression and fury, which leads to his accidental murder of a con-man (Vincent Price) who threatened and seduced his girl. In the final scene Fonda battles it out with the police, only to be shot down in a chiaroscuro nightmare of shadows and slums.

On the other hand, despite its title, *One Way Street* (1950) at least explores the possibility of redemption as a runaway couple (Marta Toren and James Mason) attempt to start a new life in Mexico, the would be destination of so many noir fugitives. There Mason, a doctor, treats the villagers while Toren doffs her stylish city clothes for those of a *campesina*. Ultimately they are driven away from the pastoral countryside and back to the dark city by the lingering threat of their pursuer, Dan Duryea as a mob boss. There Mason meets his doom, ironically hit by a car after defeating his nemesis. As the epigraph at the beginning of the film declares: "In life and death there is no choice. Fate determines all"--as overt and prototypical a statement of the noir philosophy as any.

The Red House (1947) is remarkable not just for its pessimism but also for its perversity. Edward G. Robinson plays a man who has killed the woman he loves when she spurned him fifteen years earlier and then raised her daughter to become, it is implied, his future bride. Robinson is not only trapped by the deeds of his past, which are externalized by the mysterious red house where his first love lived and died, but by his physical infirmity. Dependent on a sister who was sacrificed her own life to care for him, he is unbalanced by the appearance of a man in his foster daughter's life. This quasi-incestuous conflict is resolved when, failing to kill his foster daughter and her lover, he commits suicide by driving his truck into the red house and literally joining his first love's remains in the swamp around it. At the end, there is a striking shot of his face, sinking out of frame, as he accepts his destiny.

Of the five films *The Money Trap* (1966) is the most recent and the bleakest. Visually it evokes a noir urban jungle of wet streets, ethnic slums littered with mutilated bodies and, above it all, naked greed. Glenn Ford and Ricardo Montalban are good cops who have had their fill of public abuse, vicious crimes, and financial woes. When presented with the opportunity to score a stash of cash, they succumb to temptation with predictable consequences. Montalban dies from a bullet wound, clutching the bag of money. Ford's ex-girlfriend, portrayed with iconographic irony by Rita Hayworth, is pushed from a multi-story building. Ford himself, wounded in a gun battle with drugdealer Joseph Cotten, stands bleeding as he stares disconsolately at his lighted pool, a symbol of the high life for which he is now dying. As the title of the movie says, money is the trap. The desire for more of it by those who already possess enough such as Ford, Montalban, Ford's avaricious wife, and the drug dealer-doctor counterbalances the genuine need of it by the underclass, sym-

bolized by the appearance several times of a melancholy Hispanic child whose mother was forced into prostitution by poverty and whose father was driven to crime by their plight. This is the force that drags both type of people into the chaotic noir underworld.

A Place in the Sun (1951) is one of the few noir films to draw on an actual work by the naturalist writers who were so influential on the tone and attitude of the movement. Fritz Lang's *Human Desire*, an adaptation of Zola's *La Bête Humaine*, is another. Theodore Dreiser's classic tale of literal and figurative entrapment, *An American Tragedy*, is a most apt vehicle for film noir. A fate whose machinations are fully as powerful but considerably less outlandish than Al Roberts' in *Detour* enmeshes *Place in the Sun's* young protagonist (Montgomery Clift) from the opening moments. As he claws his way up the social ladder and is impeded at every rung by his clinging girlfriend (Shelley Winters) and her unwanted pregnancy, the detached staging maintains an emotionless and deterministic perspective. His bungled murder of her is both a desperate and driven act. As dissolve follows dissolve, linking the events his life in a predestined chain, Clift is convicted of murder and sentenced to death. As he is set to be executed, the image of Elizabeth Taylor, the rich girl who symbolized the high life he so desperately sought, floats superimposed, advertising like those billboards earlier in the film the American Dream, which for him has abruptly turned acrid.

Night Without Sleep (1952) presents a truly unsympathetic protagonist in the person of an alcoholic, abusive, self-pitying composer (Gary Merrill). Merrill awakens one morning to discover that he may have killed his wife in a drunken stupor. In flashback he recreates the events in order to clear himself, only to find that indeed he was the murderer. He has created his own existential hell and then fallen directly into it.

On the side of redemption is a slightly longer list of films. Most notable are *City for Conquest*, *The Raging Tide*, and *Tomorrow Is Another Day*. In all three the protagonists are bruised and beaten by life, in the first film literally. James Cagney in *City for Conquest* (1940) is a tough New York kid who takes up prizefighting to support his struggling musician brother and to prove his worth to his girl. The constant beatings and the dirty sport's tricks, such as sand being rubbed into his eyes during one fight, precipitate his eventual blindness. Reduced to selling papers on a corner, he is nonetheless uplifted as he hears his brother conducting "Symphony of the City" on the radio. Now he knows his suffering has been for a purpose; his life has not been in vain. As he stares into the dark night, a light seems to surround his damaged eyes.

In *The Raging Tide* (1951) Richard Conte, a mobster on the run, also finds redemption. As in *One Way Street* it is in a pastoral setting, a seaside community where he finds work on a fishing boat, that a change of attitude begins. In the final scenes, he sacrifices his life for a boy of whom he has become fond, manifesting a spiritual regeneration. In both *City for Conquest* and *The Raging Tide*, the casting of the leads initially according to stereotype underscores the impact of the characters' transformation, as the final images of Cagney and Conte are far different from those in *White Heat* or *Cry of the City*.

The initial trajectory of *Tomorrow Is Another Day* (1951) is entirely bleak. Two alienated, embittered characters meet, become involved in the killing of a police officer with whom Roman had been involved, and end up on the lam. Steve Cochran is an awkward, boyish character who had his youth taken away by prison, while Ruth Roman is a tawdry, cynical taxi dancer. She lets Cochran believe that he is responsible for their dilemma but softens as the story progresses. As she removes the blonde dye from her hair and alters her wardrobe from flashy to subdued, her hard-bitten posture becomes a loving, even maternal attitude towards her man-child companion. When they end up hiding out as migrant workers, the rural setting, as in *The Raging Tide, One Way Street*, and *Impact* is again invoked as a locus of redemption, where they can dream of escaping their fate. Although the couple is betrayed by a woman friend whose husband has been seriously injured in a car crash, Cochran's character abandons his vow never to be taken alive and re-imprisoned. With the metamorphosis of both figures accomplished, the second chance comes when they learn that the "murdered" man is admitted that he was shot in self-defense before he died. The final image is of two figures in silhouette, on a mountain top, gazing hopefully at a rising sun.

The Female Jungle, Naked Alibi, Johnny Stool Pigeon, and *Warning Shot* revolve around the noir archetype of the detective-protagonist: cynical, disillusioned but ultimately on a quest for truth. That quest can lead to the solution of a crime and the punishment of the a villain as in *Naked Alibi* and *Johnny Stool Pigeon*, or it can take on a much darker psychological turn as in *The Female Jungle* (1955) and *Warning Shot* (1967). *Warning Shot* features David Janssen as a police detective obsessed by the death of a man whom he accidentally killed in the line of duty. The crux of the film is Janssen's struggle not merely to exonerate himself in the eyes of society but to clear his own conscience. *The Female Jungle* is directed by Bruno Ve Sota, the co-creator of the 1955 silent horror film, *Daughter of Horror*, who uses expository sequences in this film to underscore the sense of a personal quest. Lawrence Tierney portrays an alcoholic policeman who emerges from an all-night drinking spree to find that he may have murdered someone. Like that of Janssen, his odyssey across the sleazy, ill-lit back streets of Los Angeles is a journey of self-revelation common to noir narratives. As in *Night Without Sleep*, such a journey both to uncover the source of guilt, whether real or imagined and to expiate it. While ostensibly piecing together his movements on the night of the murder, the hero is actually reconstructing his own integrity. His discovery of the real killer, a neurotic artist played by the writer, Burt Kaiser, restores his sense of self and his faith in his own abilities.

Love's Lovely Counterfeit

> But all of a sudden she looked at me, and I felt a chill creep straight up my back and into the roots of my hair.
> Walter Huff,
> *Double Indemnity*

For the detective-protagonists, it is a fundamental sense of duty which overcomes disillusionment and drives the central figures. *In Tomorrow Is Forever, The Man I Love*, and *Shockproof*, it is love which encloses the protagonists in their existential dilemma. In *Tomorrow Is Forever* (1946) Orson Welles plays a man disfigured and crippled in the World War I. Psychologically unable to face his wife (Claudette Colbert), he fakes his own death and adopts a new identity; but fate, as usual, has other plans for him. Years later he is hired by a firm owned by his wife's new husband. Hidden by age, scars, and a beard, he suffers the torment of a man who must decide between the love he still feels for his wife and his sense of fairness which tells him not to disrupt her new life. Welles conveys that angst with a minimum of histrionics. His pained expression when he sees her and his debilitating limp express all that is needed. In the resolution he conveniently dies of a heart attack, exiting the scene with a minimum of embarrassment to his wife; but the impression left by the film is that this is not a natural death. Having feigned his death years earlier, the character is now compelled to actualize it both to insure her happiness and to end his mental anguish.

The Man I Love (1946) is not a typical postwar film noir. Although it presents self-sacrifice and love as potentially redemptive forces, it is closer in some respects to musical drama with the noir themes alternating between foreground and background. When the torch singer, Petey (Ida Lupino), falls for San Thomas, a disillusioned pianist (Bruce Bennett), the musical ironies are obvious. Like countless others, Bennett is also a cipher for postwar restlessness, and his unemotional performance suggests a certain self-consciousness in his enigmatic behavior, which gives the character a noir outlook and definition. In this context, San and his melancholy piano melodies are stylized manifestations of the same irrational, alienation that grips Petey's shellshocked brother-in-law. "San Thomas" is both a stage name and the doubting apostle, both symbolic of his anomie caused by his wife's betrayal and his inability to trust.

The milieus of the film, the dingy apartment Petey shares with her family and the beach bar where she meets San contrasting with the flashy nightclub and its patrons, represent the dual impulses of the main character. For Lupino as Petey is the true protagonist of the film and what disturbs her, more than the antipathy between these two environments through which she moves or her tenuous relationship with the impenetrable San, is the sense of imprecise but tangible malaise which those around her both experience and engender. The use of a heroine who takes charge of a situation is not common in film noir. Certainly Ella Raines in *Phantom Lady* and to some extent Lucille Ball in *The Dark Corner* are examples. Ida Lupino imbues Petey with an unusual self-reliance that also colors her work in *Road House* and *On Dangerous Ground.* The songs which she sings in *The Man I Love* capture her emotional vacillation from the idealism in the title song and "My Bill" to the hopelessness of "Why Was I Born?"

In *Shockproof* (1949) the ending is less ambiguous, if unrealistically upbeat. Cornel Wilde is Griff, a parole officer who falls for parolee Jenny (Patricia Knight). Hoping that he can redeem her through kindness and love, he finds himself instead caught up in her criminal underworld, including the "murder" of her ex-lover. In an ending quite similar to *Tomorrow Is Another Day*, working in the oil fields and thinking that they have been recognized by their neighbors, the fugitive couple turns themselves in only to discover that the supposed victim is still alive and has exonerated them. With the promise of a new life, Knight and Wilde face a more hopeful future together. Given that Wilde's character has violated the moral and ethical constraints of his profession because of an illicit and obsessive love, the ending is remarkably free of consequences for that behavior. Unlike Bill Clark (Steve Cochran) in *Tomorrow is Another Day*, who returns to migrant labor and will never recapture the years of his youth spent in prison, Wilde's parole officer takes up his old life.

The Dark Past

> Much too old. And too beat up around the edges. With a past. A black past.
> Ann Miller,
> *Build My Gallows High*

The Trap and *The Woman on Pier 13* are examples of discovering redemption in reliving the past and reaffirming both sexual and familial love. In *The Woman on Pier 13* (1949) Robert Ryan must face up to his violent history, which includes a murder, and purge himself of his guilt by defending his wife and brother-in-law. The web of past conflicts in *The Trap* (1959) is not quite as easy to untangle as in *The Woman on Pier 13*. Richard Widmark is a mob lawyer who is pressured to return to his hometown to help a client escape the country. In his journey homeward he encounters the same elements which formed his cynical and compromised character: a domineering father, a weak, treacherous brother, and a girlfriend who married that brother. In the stifling heat and dust, an atypical use of a high key environment to create a noir atmosphere, Widmark exorcizes his demons one by one. His father is killed trying to warn him of danger. His brother, for whose misdemeanor he had taken the blame, proves cowardly still and dies also as Widmark tries to redeem him. He regains his girl as well as his self-respect when he risks his own death to prevent the mob boss's escape.

The dialectic between urban and rural (or semi-rural small town) settings in film noir, with the open-country rural representing redemption and the city representing corruption, is finely delineated in *Walk Softly, Stranger* and *Cry of the Hunted*. Much like *The Raging Tide, One Way Street*, and *Impact* the protagonists of these films find escape from the chaos and crime of the urban jungle in a natural environment. In *Walk Softly, Stranger* (1950) Joseph Cotten is small-time con man who with a fateful coin flip heads back for his small hometown. Returning to live in the house in which he was raised and that is now a boarding house run by Spring Byington, he reacquaints himself with a girl from his past (Alida Valli), now crippled and embittered like him. Their first dialogues are examples of classic noir pessimism written by Frank Fenton who also penned *His Kind of Woman, Nocturne*, and *Out of the Past*. "We're failures," Cotten opines; Valli agrees. She cannot accept her confinement, just as he laments his wasted past. He does soon come to realize that only by cutting himself off from such symbols of the city as his mobster pursuers in black, only by exposing himself to the positive influence of the small town evoked by the benign Spring Byington, only by helping Valli accept her fate can he finally regain a degree of self-respect. In a final violent battle with his antagonists, Cotten emerges victorious, resolved to face prison for his former crimes. In the prison waiting room, Valli awaits him, a smile now on her face, an emblem of regeneration.

In *Cry of the Hunted* (1953) the two protagonists are figurative doppelgangers. Although, Vittorio Gassman is ostensibly the hunted and Barry Sullivan, the hunter, the two men are both hunted and haunted. Sullivan is a driven prison supervisor who empathizes with Gassman the convict but wants information about his crime. After an initial scene, in which Sullivan and Gassman wrestle each other to exhaustion and then sit sharing cigarettes like brothers, Sullivan refuses to persecute Gassman and prevents other cons from killing him. When Gassman manages to escape back to his home in the bayous, Sullivan follows and clearly goes beyond the call of duty, as both his subordinate and the local sheriff point out. In the nightmarish maze of the swamps Sullivan pursues his *fata morgana* Even his sleep is obsessive as he dreams of the escapee in homoerotic terms. Gassman, too, seems drawn to this pursuer, even to the point of rescuing Sullivan when he comes down with swamp fever and, consequently, exposing himself to recapture.

Maniacs and Mayhem

> We're on a merry-go-round none of us can get off until they push us off.
> Lily,
> *Cry Vengeance*

The most disruptive force in film noir is the maniac. Since the psychopath has no qualms about destroying the order of society, such a figure creates an atmosphere of violence and fear wherever he goes, as both versions of *Cape Fear* epitomize.

The first type of threat is to the middle class family and/or values. In films like *Guest in the House, A Kiss Before Dying*, and *The Devil Thumbs a Ride*, a sociopath focuses his or her psychoses on the centerpieces of bourgeois life: home, work, and family. In *Guest in the House* (1944) mental patient Anne Baxter, after moving into her psychiatrist's idyllic cottage for further treatment, fixates on his younger brother. While there she performs every trick which her sick mind can conjure up in order to split up the family and gain dominance over the younger brother. Gaining dominance and in the process disrupting the bourgeois family is also the key to the 1956 *A Kiss Before Dying*. Robert Wagner pursues one sister, causes her death when she becomes inconveniently pregnant, then pursues the other sister, all with the objective of reaching the father and his fortune. Although the family here is not idealized like the one in *Guest in the House*--the mother is missing and there is tremendous conflict--the effect is the same. The way in which each fall to their death, particularly Anne Baxter who is driven to suicide in *Guest in the House* when small birds are released inside her cottage, suggests the symbolic triumph of the social order.

The Devil Thumbs a Ride (1947) deals with the same subject matter but in a much more sardonic mode. Lawrence Tierney is a charming and conniving drifter who commits a deadly crime and hitches a ride with a young sales executive (Ted North) traveling back to his lovely wife and snug suburban home. Tierney's performance reeks of menace, as he plays a convoluted series of games to escape capture and coincidentally prevent North from attaining his objective. He offers a ride to couple of attractive women. He weaves a sob story of an abused and battered childhood. He incapacitates North's car. North acts out the role of a naif and is sucked into a whirlpool of deceit and murder. In both *Guest in the House* and *The Devil Thumbs A Ride*, the manipulators prey on the ingenuousness of their victims. Even at the end of the films, when the depth of their sociopathic behavior has been revealed, those same victims are slow to realize how profoundly their own underlying belief in an orderly and predictable world imperiled them.

Two films which are remarkable for their variations on this theme of family threat are *Make Haste To Live* (1954) and *Cry Vengeance* (1954). In *Make Haste To Live* the threat is from the protagonist's (Dorothy McGuire) husband (Stephen McNally) who has returned from prison after serving time for the "murder" of his wife. Although McGuire has hidden herself away in a small town in New Mexico with a new identity, McNally finds her. In a sequence as unsettling as either version of *Cape Fear*, his ominous presence is glimpsed in the first shots of the film. McGuire awakens from a troubled sleep and wanders the house while a shadow unseen by her watches from below. This invasion of her household soon extends to an invasion of her family life as McNally tries to reassert his position as father to his daughter (Mary Murphy), seducing her through blandishments and an affection which seems not entirely familial. The ambiguity of this film revolves around McNally's moral position. He is indeed the father of Murphy and has rights in that area. In addition he was sentenced to prison for a murder he never committed, of which his wife could have cleared him. Unlike the maniacs in *Kiss Before Dying* or *The Devil Thumbs a Ride* and even more than the poorly-represented rapist in *Cape*

Fear, McNally does act from a position of some moral righteousness.

If the character in *Make Haste To Live* can be seen as acting out of an understandable if not laudable desire for vengeance and vindication, Mark Stevens' position in *Cry Vengeance* is even more sympathetic. As an ex-cop who not only lost his child, his wife, and part of his face in a bombing but also served time on a frame-up, his compulsion to stalk and kill the one who framed him has the fearful symmetry of an Old Testament verse. In many respects *Cry Vengeance* is a sequel to *The Dark Corner* (1946). The oppressed, "all dead inside" detective whom Stevens incarnated in that earlier film is duplicated here with an added level of psychic suffering. *Cry Vengeance's* protagonist is literally and figuratively "eating himself up inside." He walks stoop-shouldered as if racked by body pains. He alternately chews on his lips and his nails. He rubs his scarred face compulsively. When questioned he answers with as few words as possible, as with the terse epithet: "I never forget." Compounding the moral ambiguity of the film, the ex-mobster whom he is stalking (Douglas Kennedy) is raising his daughter alone and has reformed his life entirely in a small town in Alaska. As his associate ruefully observes, given all the crimes of which they are guilty, to be stalked for one of which they are innocent seems crazy. When he approaches Kennedy's child and gives her a bullet for her father, Stevens, like the viewer, is both appalled and overwhelmed by his action. As close as he is to culminating his quest, the child's naive acceptance of his scarred face enervates his deadly resolve. Forced to realize that he has been reduced to the level of the maniac, who murdered his own family, Stevens abandons his resolve. When Kennedy is gunned down by the real killer, whom Stevens in turn dispatches, the issue of his reconstruction is left unresolved. He goes back to San Francisco, perhaps to return later, perhaps not.

No Man of Her Own (1950) is based on the Cornell Woolrich novel *I Married a Dead Man* and relates in flashback the tale of a pregnant moll (Barbara Stanwyck), so battered by life and a gangster boyfriend that she switches identity with a dead woman and finds solace in the arms of her loving, middle-class family. Secluded in a womb-like Victorian mansion, which in its chiaroscuro interiors seems to represent the refuge which she so desperately needs, Stanwyck keeps up the deception until her boyfriend returns to tear apart her reverie and thrust her back into the real world.

When society at large is threatened, the psychopaths presented tend to be of the most violent ilk, as if to justify social repression by exaggerating the threat. Edward G. Robinson as gangster Vincent Canelli in *Black Tuesday* (1954) exhibits a sadistic bent rivaled only by James Cagney in *White Heat*. The opening shot of the film sets the tone. Robinson paces his death row cell like an animal while a fellow prisoner sings a lament, only to be squelched by Robinson yelling, "Shut up!" and the main title appears. In the subsequent escape from prison, Canelli throws his former death-row mates to the pursuers, except for Manning, whose loot from a bank robbery Canelli covets. Cornered by the police in an abandoned warehouse, where he threatens to pass out the bodies of a dead hostages, Canelli's rage leads to one act of violence after another. Only the presence of Peter Graves as the self-destructive, guilt-ridden Manning, who finally puts an end to Robinson's reign of terror and then walks calmly into a barrage of police bullets, humanizes the film and softens the ending of this otherwise brutal tale.

Revenge is the uncomplicated motive of the maniacs in *Without Warning* (1952) and *The Threat* (1949). On their road to destruction, they choose to take along selected individuals. In *Without Warning* Adam Williams is a serial killer who searches out women who resemble the wife who deserted him. In *The Threat* Charles McGraw escapes from prison with the express purpose of finding and killing those responsible for his conviction.

One by one he ingeniously rounds up his victims and transports them to an abandoned shack in the Mojave desert. McGraw's character epitomizes the cold-blooded, methodical, almost intellectual maniac. Whether torturing one of his hostages with pliers or humiliating his ex-girlfriend (Virginia Grey), he seems almost invulnerable. Even the ostensible hero of the film (Michael O'Shea) cannot defeat this formidable presence, as McGraw pins him to the floor in the style of a crucifixion. Like the protagonist in both versions of *Cape Fear*, McGraw in smarter and more powerful than his victims. When he is finally defeated, it is by a woman spurned. For the first time he demonstates fear as he begs for his life, only to be answered by a volley of bullets.

The Strange Case of Alfred Hitchcock

> I moved a little deeper inward. My own reflection glided unexpectedly across a mirror I hadn't noticed and gave me a guilty little shock...
> Alberta,
> *The Black Angel*

It is sometimes difficult to view the films of directors who possess a strong personal vision which informs all their films in terms of any movement or cycle. Such films are often expressions of a particular mind-set, of specific neuroses or individual obsessions only partially colored by mediating influences. Alfred Hitchcock, with his intensely personal style and concerns, is such a case. Nonetheless, many of Hitchcock's films manifest enough qualities of film noir that they must be considered from that perspective. (*Strangers on a Train*, *The Wrong Man*, *Notorious*, and *Shadow of a Doubt* are already covered in the main text.)

Spellbound, as noted before, helped establish a pattern for the themes of psychological persecution and transference of guilt in noir films. *Suspicion* (1941), for most of its narrative, appears to share these motifs with *Spellbound*, but as the film concludes the persecutor (Cary Grant) turns out to have been misjudged.

Obsession is a classic noir character trait, which dominates much of Hitchcock's later work from *The Paradine*

Case to *Vertigo*. *The Paradine Case* (1948) traces the personal disintegration of a respected lawyer (Gregory Peck) as he defends an accused murderess (Alida Valli). His middle class life and home is gradually torn apart as he falls in love with Valli whom he believes is innocent. His investigation of her draws him into her black widow's web until she turns on him, revealing her guilt and accusing him of driving her lover to suicide. Peck ends the picture a broken man, disheveled, forlorn, and despairing.

Vertigo (1958) ends with an image very similar to *The Paradine Case*: a man on the edge but this time literally, as James Stewart leans from the church bell tower after his lover has just fallen to her death for a second time. Purely as a narrative, *Vertigo* falls neatly into the film noir mode. Not only is it ostensibly a detective film involved with surveillance and death, but the detective Scottie Ferguson (Stewart) is scarred by the death of a colleague for which he feels responsible for and is duped by a femme fatale (Kim Novak). The setting is initially urban San Francisco, but as with most Hitchcock films the landscape is broadly drawn and adds layers of meaning and complexity typical of film noir. The city is not really a jungle but more an externalization of Stewart's disturbed and distracted state as he glides somnambulistically through it in pursuit of his dream lover (Novak). Novak herself is not really a femme fatale. She is as much a victim of the man who has paid her to impersonate his wife and deceive Stewart as he is.

To some extent Hitchcock is continually externalizing character emotion in terms of landscape. He may alter the terrain itself by tilting the camera to accentuate the steepness of the hill on which Ferguson lives and suggest the mental brink on which he is precariously balanced. Other "extrapolated" values such as the twisted one-way street and the directional signs seen so often in the background are typical noir metaphors. In combining genuine locations with process shots or in the suffused look of the dream sequences, the landscape itself is diffracted, until it becomes, like Ferguson's description of a dream, "the fragments of a mirror."

The protagonist guilty by transference, also a noir staple, is preeminent in other Hitchcock films such as *I Confess, Rear Window,* and *Psycho*. In *I Confess* (1953) a murderer tells a priest (Montgomery Clift) of his crime to obtain sacramental absolution and in that confession imparts some of his guilt to him. When he refuses to break the seal of confession, society as represented by the police begins to believe the priest may be implicated, while the murderer himself forthrightly tells Clift that he does share in his guilt. The concept of original sin and that we are all tainted by each other's crimes informs both this film and *Rear Window* (1954). In that narrative, based on the same Cornell Woolrich story that inspired the earlier film noir, *The Window,* James Stewart is recuperating from a broken leg and using his sophisticated camera equipment to spy on his neighbors through his rear window. Although admonished by friends to end this invasion of privacy, he continues and eventually "witnesses" what he believes is a murder. As he tries to solve the case, he and his girlfriend are caught in the murderer's growing frenzy. When the guilty man discovers Stewart spying on him, he confronts him like one victimized and asks why he is persecuting him. Stewart has no adequate answer and, for his sins, is pushed out his own rear window, suffering a second broken leg. His guilt figuratively expiated, he returns to his apartment, both legs in casts and his chair facing safely away from the window.

Psycho (1960) is a film of maniacal horror which begins as an understated film noir. A woman (Janet Leigh) embezzles money in order to run away with her lover with whom she is having an adulterous affair. Midway through her escape and the film, as she stops to rest in an isolated motel, she begins to regret her deed and decides on restitution. When she is murdered during a symbolically cleansing shower, fate has stepped in the person of Norman Bates; and the film moves on to a more horrific plateau.

2. Additional Filmography of the Classic Period

Affair in Havana. (Allied Artists, 1957). Produced by Richard Goldstone. Directed by Laslo Benedek. Script by Burton Lane, Maurice Zimm, based on a story by Janet Green. Director of Photography, Alan Stensvold. Production Designer, Gabriel Scognamillo. Music, Ernest Gold. Editor, Stefan Arnsten. Starring John Cassavetes (Nick), Raymond Burr (Mallabee), Sara Shayne (Lorna), Lilia Lazo (Fina), Sergio Pena (Valdes), Celia Cruz (Singer). 71 minutes.

Affair in Trinidad. (Columbia/Beckworth, 1952). Produced by Vincent Sherman, Virginia Van Upp (uncredited). Directed by Vincent Sherman. Script by Oscar Saul, James Gunn, based on story by Virginia Van Upp and Berne Giller. Director of Photography, Joseph Walker. Production Designer, Walter Holscher. Music, George Duning. Editor, Viola Lawrence. Starring Rita Hayworth (Chris Emery), Glenn Ford (Steve Emery), Alexander Scourby (Max Fabian), Valerie Bettis (Veronica), Torin Thatcher (Inspector Smythe), Howard Wendell (Anderson), Juanita Moore (Dominique). 98 minutes.

Bewitched. (MGM, 1945). Produced by Jerry Bresler. Directed by Arch Oboler. Script by Arch Oboler. Director of Photography, Charles Salerno. Music, Bronislau Kaper. Editor, Harry Komer. Starring Phyllis Thaxter (Joan Alris Ellis), Edmund Gwenn (Dr. Bergson), Henry H. Daniels, Jr. (Bob Arnold), Addison Richards (John Ellis), Francis Pierlot (Dr. George Wilton), Gladys Blake (Glenda), Stephen McNally (Eric Russell). 65 minutes.

Black Tuesday. (United Artists, 1954). Produced by Robert Goldstein. Directed by Hugo Fregonese. Script by Sydney Boehm from his story. Director of Photography, Stanley Cortez. Music, Paul Dunlap. Editor, Robert Golden. Starring Edward G. Robinson (Vincent Canelli), Peter Graves (Peter Manning), Jean Parker (Hatti Combert), Milburn Stone (Father Slocum), Warren Stevens (Joey Stewart), Jack

Kelly (Frank Carson), Sylvia Findley (Ellen Norris). 80 minutes.

City for Conquest. (Warner Bros., 1941). Produced and Directed by Anatole Litvak. Script by John Wexley, based on the novel by Aben Kandel. Director of Photography, Sol Polito, James Wong Howe. Production Designer, Robert Haas. Music, Max Steiner. Editor, William Holmes. Starring James Cagney (Danny Kemp), Ann Sheridan (Peggy Nash), Frank Craven (Old Timer), Donald Crisp (Scotty McPherson), Arthur Kennedy (Eddie), Anthony Quinn (Murray Burns), George Tobias (Pinky). 105 minutes.

Cry of the Hunted. (MGM, 1953). Produced by William Grady. Directed by Joseph H. Lewis. Script by Jack Leonard. Director of Photography, Harry Lipstein. Music, Rudolph G. Kopp. Editor, Conrad A. Nervig. Starring Vittorio Gassman (Jory), Barry Sullivan (Lt. Tunner), William Conrad (Goodwin), Polly Bergen (Janet Tunner), Mary Zavian (Ella). 78 minutes.

Cry Vengeance. (Allied Artists, 1954). Produced by Lindsley Parsons. Directed by Mark Stevens. Script by Warren Douglas and George Bricker. Director of Photography, William Sickner. Production Designer, David Milton. Music, Paul Dunlap. Editor, Elmo Veron. Starring Mark Stevens (Vic), Martha Hyer (Peg), Skip Homeier (Roxey Davis), Joan Vohs (Lily), Douglas Kennedy (Tino Morelli/Al Carey), Don Haggerty (Lt. Ryan), Cheryl Callaway (Marie Morelli), John Doucette (Red Miller). 83 minutes.

Dark Waters. (United Artists, 1944). Produced by Benedict Bogeaus. Directed by Andre de Toth. Script by Joan Harrison and Marion Cockrell. Director of Photography, Archie Stout. Music, Miklos Rozsa. Editor, James Smith. Production Designer, Charles Odds. Starring Merle Oberon (Leslie Calvin), Franchot Tone (Dr. George Grover), Thomas Mitchell (Mr. Sidney), Fay Bainter (Aunt Emily), John Qualen (Uncle Norbert), Elisha Cook, Jr. (Cleeve), Rex Ingram (Jackson). 90 minutes.

The Devil Thumbs a Ride. (RKO, 1947). Produced by Herman Schlom. Directed by Felix Feist. Script by Felix Feist, based on the novel by Robert C. DuSoe. Director of Photography, J. Roy Hunt. Production Designer, Alberto D'Agostino, Charles F. Pyke. Music, Paul Sawtell. Editor, Robert Swink. Starring Lawrence Tierney (Steve), Ted North (Jimmy), Nan Leslie (Carol), Betty Lawford (Agnes), Andrew Tombes (Joe Brayden), Harry Shannon (Owens), Glenn Vernon (Jack). 63 minutes.

The Fallen Sparrow. (RKO, 1943). Produced by Robert Fellows. Directed by Richard Wallace. Script by Warren Duff, based on the novel by Dorothy B. Hughes. Production Designer, Van Nest Polglase. Director of Photography, Nicholas Musuraca. Music, Roy Webb. Editor, Robert Wise. Starring John Garfield (Kit), Maureen O'Hara (Toni Donne), Walter Slezak (Dr. Skass), Patricia Morison (Barby

Taviton), Martha O'Driscoll (Whitney Hamilton), Bruce Edwards (Abe Parker), John Banner (Anton). 94 minutes.

The Female Jungle. (AIP, 1955). Produced by Burt Kaiser. Directed by Bruno Ve Sota. Script by Kaiser and Ve Sota. Director of Photography, Elwood Bredell. Production Designer, Ben Roseman. Editor, Carl Pingitore. Starring Lawrence Tierney (Sgt. Stevens), John Carradine (Claude Almstead), Jayne Mansfield (Candy Price), Burt Kaiser (Alec Voe), Kathleen Crowley (Peggy Voe), James Kodl (Joe). 70 minutes.

Guest in the House. (United Artists, 1944). Produced by Hunt Stromberg. Directed by John Brahm. Script by Ketti Frings, from the play by Hagar Wilde and Dale Eunson. Director of Photography, Lee Garmes. Production Designer, Nicolai Remisoff. Music, Werner Janssen. Editor, Walter Hannemann. Starring Anne Baxter (Evelyn Heath), Ralph Bellamy (Douglas Proctor), Aline MacMahon (Aunt Martha), Ruth Warrick (Ann Proctor), Scott McKay (Dan Proctor), Marie McDonald (Miriam). 121 minutes.

Hit and Run. (United Artists, 1957). Produced, directed and written by Hugo Haas. Director of Photography, Walter Strenge. Production Designer, Rudi Feld. Music, Frank Steininger. Editor, Stefan Arnsten. Starring Cleo Moore (Julie), Hugo Haas (Gus), Vince Edwards (Frank), Dolores Reed (Miranda), Mari Lea (Anita), Pat Goldin (Undertaker). 85 minutes.

House of Numbers. (MGM, 1957). Produced by Charles Schnee. Directed by Russell Rouse. Script by Russell Rouse, Don Mankiewicz, based on the novel by Jack Finney. Director of Photography, George J. Folsey. Music, Andre Previn. Editor, John McSweeney, Jr. Starring Jack Palance (Bill Judlow/Arne Judlow), Barbara Lang (Ruth), Harold J. Stone (Henry Nova), Edward Platt (Warden). 90 minutes.

Impact. (United Artists, 1949). Produced by Leo C. Popkin. Directed by Arthur Lubin. Script by Dorothy Reid and Jay Dratler. Executive Producer, Harry Popkin. Director of Photography, Ernest Laszlo. Music, Michel Michelet. Editor, Arthur Nadel. Starring Brian Donlevy (Walter Williams, Ella Raines (Marsha Peters), Helen Walker (Irene Williams), Charles Coburn (Lt. Quincy), Anna May Wong (Su Lin), Mae Marsh (Mrs. Peters). 111 minutes.

Johnny Stool Pigeon. (Universal, 1949). Produced by Aaron Rosenberg. Directed by William Castle. Script by Robert L. Richards, based on a story by Henry Jordan. Director of Photography, Maury Gertsman. Production Designer, Bernard Herzbrun, Emrich Nicholson. Music, Milton Schwarzwald. Editor, Ted. J. Kent. Starring Howard Duff (George Morton), Shelley Winters (Terry), Dan Duryea (Johnny Evans), Tony Curtis (Joey Hyatt), John McIntire (Avery). 76 minutes.

A Kiss Before Dying. (United Artists, 1956). Produced by Robert Jacks. Directed by Gerd Oswald. Script by Lawrence Roman based on the novel by Ira Levin. Director of Photography, Lucien Ballard (Color). Production Designer, Addison Hehr. Music, Lionel Newman. Editor, George A. Gittens. Starring Robert Wagner (Bud Corliss), Jeffrey Hunter (Gordon Grant), Virginia Leith (Ellen Kingship), Joanne Woodward (Dorothy Kingship), Mary Astor (Mrs. Corliss), George Macready (Leo Kingship). 94 minutes.

The Las Vegas Story. (RKO, 1952). Produced by Robert Sparks. Directed by Robert Stevenson. Script by Earl Felton and Harry Essex, based on a story by Jay Dratler. Director of Photography, Harry J. Wild. Production Designer, Albert S. D'Agostino, Feild Gray. Music, Leigh Harline. Editor, George Shrader. Starring Jane Russell (Linda Rollins), Victor Mature (Dave Andrews), Vincent Price (Lloyd Rollins), Hoagy Carmichael (Happy), Brad Dexter (Thomas Hubler), Jay C. Flippen (Harris), Gordon Oliver (Drucker). 87 minutes.

The Long Night. (RKO, 1947). Produced and Directed by Anatole Litvak. Script by John Wexley, based on the story by Jacques Viot. Director of Photography, Sol Polito. Production Designer, Eugene Lourie. Music, Dimitri Tiomkin. Editor, Robert Swank. Starring Henry Fonda (Joe Adams), Barbara Bel Geddes (Jo Ann), Vincent Price (Maximilian), Ann Dvorak (Charlene), Howard Freeman (Sheriff), Moroni Olsen (Chief of Police), Elisha Cook, Jr. (Frank). 101 minutes.

Make Haste To Live. (Republic, 1954). Produced by Herbert J. Yates. Directed by William Seiter. Script by Warren Duff, based on the novel by the Gordons. Director of Photography, John L. Russell, Jr. Production Designer, Frank Hotaling. Music, Elmer Bernstein. Editor, Fred Allen. Starring Dorothy McGuire (Zena/Crystal), Stephen McNally (Steve Blackford), Mary Murphy (Randi), Edgar Buchanan (Sheriff), John Howard (Josh), Carolyn Jones (Mary Rose). 90 minutes.

The Man I Love. (Warner Bros., 1946). Produced by Arnold Albert. Directed by Raoul Walsh. Script by Catherine Turney and Jo Pagano, based on the novel Night Shift by Maritta Wolff. Director of Photography, Sid Hickox. Production Designer, Stanley Fleischer, Eddie Edwards. Music, Max Steiner. Editor, Owen Marks. Starring Ida Lupino (Petey Brown), Robert Alda (Nicky Toresca), Andrea King (Sally Otis), Bruce Bennett (Sam Thomas), Martha Vickers (Virginia Brown). 96 minutes.

The Man With My Face. (United Artists, 1951). Produced by Edward Gardner. Directed by Edward J. Montagne. Script by Samuel W. Taylor, T.J. McGowan, based on the novel by Taylor. Director of Photography, Fred Jackman, Jr. Music, Samuel G. Engel. Starring Barry Nelson (Chick Graham/Albert Rand), Lynn Ainley (Cora Graham), John

Harvey (Buster Cox), Carole Mathews (Mary Davis), Jim Boles (Meadows), Jack Warden (Walt). 86 minutes.

The Money Trap. (MGM, 1966). Produced by Max E. Youngstein, David Karr. Directed by Burt Kennedy. Script by Walter Bernstein based on the novel by Lionel White. Director of Photography, Paul C. Vogel. Production Designer, George W. Davis, Carl Anderson. Music, Hal Schaefer. Editor, John McSweeney. Starring Glenn Ford (Joe Baron), Elke Sommer (Lisa Baron), Rita Hayworth (Rosalie Kenny), Ricardo Montalban (Peter Delanos), Joseph Cotten (Dr. Horace Van Tilden), James Mitchum (Detective). 91 minutes.

The Naked Alibi. (Universal, 1954). Produced by Ross Hunter. Directed by Jerry Hopper. Script by Lawrence Roman from a story by J. Robert Bren and Gladys Atwater. Director of Photography, Russell Metty. Music, Joseph Gershenson. Editor, Al Clark. Starring Sterling Hayden (Joseph E. Conroy), Gloria Grahame (Marianna), Gene Barry (Al Willis), Marcia Henderson (Helen Willis), Casey Adams (Det. Lt. Parks), Billy Chapin (Petey), Chuck Connors (Capt. Kincaide). 85 minutes.

Night Without Sleep. (20th Century-Fox, 1952). Produced by Robert Bassler. Directed by Roy Baker. Script by Frank Partos, Elick Moll. Director of Photography, Lucien Ballard. Production Designer, Lyle Wheeler, Addison Hehr. Music, Cyril Mockridge. Editor, Nick DeMaggio. Starring Linda Darnell (Julie Bannon), Gary Merrill (Richard Morton), Hildegarde Neff (Lisa Muller), Joyce MacKenzie (Laura Harkness), June Vincent (Emily Morton), Donald Randolph (Dr. Clarke), Hugh Beaumont (John Harkness). 77 minutes.

No Man of Her Own. (Paramount, 1950). Produced by Richard Maibaum. Directed by Mitchell Leisen. Script by Sally Bensen, Catherine Turney, based on *I Married a Dead Man* by Cornell Woolrich. Director of Photography, Daniel L. Fapp. Production Designer, Hans Dreier, Henry Bumstead. Music, Hugo Friedhofer. Editor, Alma Macrorie. Starring Barbara Stanwyck (Helen Ferguson), John Lund (Bill Harkness), Jane Cowl (Mrs. Harkness), Phyllis Thaxter (Patrice Harkness), Lyle Bettger (Stephen Morley), Henry O'Neill (Mr. Harkness), Richard Denning (Hugh Harkness). 98 minutes.

One Way Street. (Universal, 1950). Produced by Leonard Goldstein. Directed by Hugo Fregonese. Script by Lawrence Kimble. Director of Photography, Maury Gertsman. Production Designer, Bernard Herzbaum. Music, Frank Skinner. Editor, Milton Carruth. Starring James Mason (Doc Matson), Marta Toren (Laura), Dan Duryea (Wheeler), William Conrad (Ollie), King Donovan (Grieder), Jack Elam (Arnie). 79 minutes.

Pickup. (Columbia, 1951). Produced and Directed by Hugo

Haas. Script by Hugo Haas, based on the novel *Watchman 47* by Joseph Kopta. Director of Photography, Paul Ivano. Music, Harold Byrns. Editor, Douglas W. Bagier. Starring Hugo Haas (Jan Horak), Beverly Michaels (Betty), Allan Nixon (Steve), Howland Chamberlin (Professor), Jo Carroll Dennison (Irma). 76 minutes.

A Place in the Sun. (Paramount, 1951) Produced and Directed by George Stevens. Script by Harry Brown and Michael Wilson, based on the novel *An American Tragedy* by Theodore Dreiser. Director of Photography, William C. Mellor. Music, Franz Waxman. Editor, William Hornbeck. Production Designer, Hans Dreier, Walter Tyler. Starring Montgomery Clift (George Eastman), Elizabeth Taylor (Angela Vickers), Shelley Winters (Alice Tripp), Anne Revere (Hannah Eastman), Shepperd Strudwick (Anthony Vickers), Frieda Inescort (Mrs. Vickers), Keefe Brasselle (Earl Eastman), Fred Clark (Bellows), Raymond Burr (Frank Marlowe). 122 minutes.

Quicksand. (United Artists, 1950). Produced by Mickey Rooney and Peter Lorre. Directed by Irving Pichel. Script by Robert Smith. Director of Photography, Lionel Lindon. Production Designer, Emil Newman. Music, Louis Gruenberg. Editor, Walter Thompson. Starring Mickey Rooney (Don Brady), Jeanne Cagney (Vera Novak), Barbara Bates (Helen), Peter Lorre (Nick), Taylor Holmes (Harvey). 79 minutes.

The Raging Tide. (Universal, 1951). Produced by Aaron Rosenberg. Directed by George Sherman. Script by Ernest K. Gann, from his novel *Fiddler's Green*. Director of Photography, Russell Metty. Production Designer, Bernard Herzbrun. Music, Frank Skinner. Editor, Ted J. Kent. Starring Shelley Winters (Connie Thatcher), Richard Conte (Bruno Felkin), Stephen McNally (Det. Lt. Kelsey), Charles Bickford (Hamil Linder), Alex Nicol (Carl Linder), John McIntire (Corky). 93 minutes.

The Red House. (United Artists, 1947). Produced by Sol Lesser. Directed by Delmer Daves. Script by Delmer Daves, based on the novel by George Agnew Chamberlain. Director of Photography, Bert Glennon. Production Designer, McClure Capps. Music, Miklos Rozsa. Editor, Merrill White. Starring Edward G. Robinson (Pete Morgan), Lon McCallister (Nath Storm), Allene Roberts (Meg Morgan), Judith Anderson (Ellen Morgan), Julie London (Tibby), Rory Calhoun (Teller). 100 minutes.

The Scarf. (United Artists, 1951). Produced by I.G. Goldsmith. Directed by E. A. Dupont. Script by E.A. Dupont from the novel *The Dungeon* by I.G. Goldsmith and Edwin Rolfe (Dupont). Director of Photography, Franz Planer. Production Designer, Rudolph Sternad. Music, Herschel Burke Gilbert. Editor, Joseph Gluck. Starring John Ireland (John Barrington), Mercedes McCambridge (Connie Carter), Emlyn Williams (David Dunbar), James Barton (Ezra

Thompson), Lloyd Gough (Dr. Gordon), Basil Ruysdael (Cyrus Barrington). 93 minutes.

Secret Beyond the Door. (Universal, 1948). Produced by Walter Wanger and Fritz Lang. Directed by Fritz Lang. Script by Sylvia Richards from a story by Rufus King. Director of Photography, Stanley Cortez. Production Designer, Max Parker. Music, Miklos Rozsa. Editor, Arthur Hilton. Starring Joan Bennett (Celia Lamphere), Michael Redgrave (Mark Lamphere), Barbara O'Neill (Miss Robey), Natalie Schaefer (Edith Potter), Paul Cavanaugh (Rick Barrett), Anne Revere (Caroline Lamphere). 98 minutes.

The Secret Fury. (RKO, 1950). Produced by Jack H. Skirball and Bruce Manning. Directed by Mel Ferrer. Script by Lionel Houser. Director of Photography, Leo Tover. Production Designer, Albert S. D'Agostino, Carroll Clark. Music, Roy Webb. Editor, Harry Marker. Starring Claudette Colbert (Ellen), Robert Ryan (David), Jane Cowl (Aunt Clara), Paul Kelly (Eric Lowell), Philip Ober (Kent), Elisabeth Risdon (Dr. Twining), Vivian Vance (Leah). 86 minutes.

Shock. (20th Century-Fox, 1946). Produced by Aubrey Schenck. Directed by Alfred Werker. Script by Eugene Ling, from a story by Albert DeMond. Director of Photography, Glen MacWilliams, Joe MacDonald. Production Designer, Lyle Wheeler, Boris Leven. Music, David Buttolph. Editor, Harmon Jones. Starring Vincent Price (Dr. Cross), Lynn Bari (Elaine Jordan), Frank Latimore (Lt. Paul Stewart), Anabel Shaw (Janet Stewart), Michael Dunne (Stevens), Reed Hadley (O'Neill). 70 minutes.

Shockproof. (Columbia, 1949). Produced by S. Sylvan Simon and Helen Deutsch. Directed by Douglas Sirk. Script by Helen Deutsch and Samuel Fuller. Director of Photography, Charles Lawton, Jr. Production Designer, Carl Anderson. Music, George Duning. Editor, Gene Havlick. Starring Cornel Wilde (Griff Marat), Patricia Knight (Jenny Marsh), Esther Miniciotti (Mrs. Marat), Howard St. John (Sam Brooks), Russell Collins (Fred Bauer), Charles Bates (Tommy Marat). 79 minutes.

Spellbound. (Selznick/United Artists, 1945). Produced by David O. Selznick. Directed by Alfred Hitchcock. Script by Ben Hecht and Angus MacPhail, based on the novel *The House of Dr. Edwardes* by Francis Beeding. Director of Photography, George Barnes. Production Designer, James Basevi. Music, Miklos Rozsa. Editor, Hal C. Kern, William Ziegler. Starring Ingrid Bergman (Dr. Constance Peterson), Gregory Peck (John "J.B." Ballantine), Jean Acker (Matron), Rhonda Fleming (Mary Carmichael), Leo G. Carroll (Dr. Murchison), Norman Lloyd (Garmes). 111 minutes.

Strange Fascination. (Columbia, 1952). Produced, Directed, and Written by Hugo Haas. Director of Photography, Paul Ivano. Production Designer, Rudi Feld. Music, Vaclav Divina, Jacob Gimpel. Editor, Merrill G. White. Starring

Cleo Moore (Margo), Hugo Haas (Paul Marvan), Mona Barrie (Diana), Rick Vallin (Carlo), Karen Sharpe (June), Marc Krah (Shiner). 80 minutes.

Suspicion. (RKO, 1941). Produced by Harry E. Edington. Directed by Alfred Hitchcock. Script by Samson Raphaelson, Joan Harrison, Alma Reville, based on the novel *Before the Fact* by Francis Iles. Director of Photography, Harry Stradling. Production Designer, Van Nest Polglase. Music, Franz Waxman. Editor, William Hamilton. Starring Cary Grant (Johnnie Aysgarth), Joan Fontaine (Lina McLaidlaw), Sir Cedric Hardwicke (General McLaidlaw), Nigel Bruce (Beaky Thwaite), Dame May Whitty (Mrs. McLaidlaw), Isabel Jeans (Mrs. Newsham). 99 minutes.

The Threat. (RKO, 1949). Produced by Hugh King. Directed by Felix Feist. Script by Hugh King and Dick Irving. Director of Photography, Harry Wild. Production Designer, Albert S. D'Agostino, Charles F. Pyke. Music, Paul Sawtell. Editor, Samuel E. Beetley. Starring Michael O'Shea (Williams), Virginia Grey (Carol), Charles McGraw (Kluger), Julie Bishop (Ann), Frank Conroy (Mac), Robert Shayne (Murphy). 66 minutes.

Tomorrow Is Another Day. (Warner Bros., 1951). Produced by Henry Blanke. Directed by Felix Feist. Script by Art Cohn, Guy Endore based on his story "Spring Kill." Director of Photography, Robert Burks. Production Designer, Charles H. Clarke. Music, Daniele Amphitheatrof. Editor, Alan Crosland, Jr. Starring Ruth Roman (Catherine), Steve Cochran (Bill Clark), Lurene Tuttle (Mrs. Dawson), Ray Teal (Mr.), Morris Ankrum (Wagner), John Kellogg (Monroe). 90 minutes.

Tomorrow Is Forever. (RKO, 1946). Produced by David Lewis. Directed by Irving Pichel. Script by Lenore Coffee, based on the novel by Gwen Bristow. Director of Photography, Joseph Valentine. Production Designer, Wiard B. Ihnen. Music, Max Steiner, Charles Tobias. Editor, Ernest Nims. Starring Claudette Colbert (Elizabeth MacDonald/Hamilton), Orson Welles (John MacDonald/Erich Kessler), George Brent (Larry Hamilton), Lucile Watson(Aunt Jessie), Richard Long (Drew), Natalie Wood (Margaret). 105 minutes.

The Trap. (Paramount, 1959). Produced by Norman Panama and Melvin Frank. Directed by Norman Panama. Script by Panama and Richard Alan Simmons. Director of Photography, Daniel Fapp. Music, Irvin Talbot. Editor, Everett Douglas. Starring Richard Widmark (Ralph Anderson), Lee J. Cobb (Victor Massonetti), Tina Louise (Linda Anderson), Earl Holliman (Tippy Anderson), Carl Benton Reid (Sheriff Anderson), Lorne Greene (Mr. Davis). 82 minutes.

Under the Gun. (Universal, 1951). Produced by Ralph Dietrich. Directed by Ted Tetzlaff. Script by George Zuckerman, based on a story by Daniel B. Ullman. Director of

Photography, Henry Freulich. Production Designer, Bernard Herzbrun, Edward L. Ilou. Music, Joseph Gershenson. Editor, Virgil Vogel. Starring Richard Conte (Bert Galvin), Audrey Totter (Ruth Williams), John McIntire (Langley), Sam Jaffe (Gower), Shepperd Strudwick (Milo Bragg). 84 minutes.

Walk Softly, Stranger. (RKO, 1950). Produced by Robert Sparks. Directed by Robert Stevenson. Script by Frank Fenton, based on a story by Manny Seff and Paul Yawitz. Director of Photography, Harry Wild. Production Designer, Albert S. D'Agostino, Alfred Herman. Music, Frederick Hollander. Editor, Frederic Knudtson. Starring Joseph Cotten (Chris Hale), Alida Valli (Elaine Corelli), Spring Byington (Mrs. Brentman), Paul Stewart (Whitey), Jack Paar (Ray Healey), John McIntire (Morgan). 81 minutes.

Warning Shot. (Paramount/Banner, 1967). Produced by Buzz Kulik, Bob Banner. Directed by Buzz Kulik. Script by Mann Rubin based on the novel *711 Officer Needs Help* by Whit Masterson. Director of Photography, Joe Biroc (Color). Production Designer, Hal Pereira, Roland Anderson. Music, Jerry Goldsmith. Editor, Archie Marshek. Starring David Janssen (Sgt. Tom Valens), Ed Begley (Capt. Roy Klodin), Keenan Wynn (Sgt. Ed Musso), Sam Wanamaker (Frank Sanderman), Lillian Gish (Alice Willows), Stefanie Powers (Liz Thayer), Eleanor Parker (Mrs. Doris Ruston). 100 minutes.

Whirlpool. (20th Century-Fox, 1949). Produced by Otto Preminger. Directed by Otto Preminger. Script by Lester Bartow [Ben Hecht] and Andrew Solt, based on the novel *Me Thinks the Lady* by Guy Endore. Director of Photography, Arthur Miller. Production Designer, Lyle R. Wheeler, Leland Fuller. Music, David Raksin. Editor, Louis R. Loeffler. Starring Gene Tierney (Ann Sutton), Richard Conte (Dr. William Sutton), Jose Ferrer (David Korvo), Charles Bickford (Lt. Colton), Barbara O'Neill (Theresa Randolph), Edward Franz (Martin Avery), Constance Collier (Tina Cosgrove). 97 minutes.

Without Warning. (United Artists, 1952). Produced by Arthur Gardner and Jules V. Levy. Directed by Arnold Laven. Script by Bill Raynor. Director of Photography, Joseph Biroc. Music, Herschel Burke. Editor, Arthur H. Nadel. Starring Adam Williams (Carl Martin), Meg Randall (Jane), Edward Binns (Pete), Harlan Warde (Don), John Maxwell (Fred Saunders). 75 minutes.

The Woman on Pier 13. (aka *I Married a Communist*). (RKO, 1949). Produced by Jack J. Gross. Directed by Robert Stevenson. Script by Charles Grayson and Robert Hardy Andrews from a story by George W. George and George Slavin. Director of Photography, Nicholas Musuraca. Production Designer, Albert S. D'Agostino, Walter E. Keller. Music, Leigh Harline. Editor, Roland Gross. Starring Laraine Day (Nan Collins), Robert Ryan (Brad Collins), John Agar (Don Lowry), Thomas Gomez (Vanning), Janis Carter (Christine), William Talman (Bailey). 73 minutes.

D3. Additional Directors of the Classic Period

Castle, William
Johnny Stool Pigeon
When Strangers Marry

Daves, Delmer
Dark Passage
Red House, The

Feist, Felix
Devil Thumbs A Ride, The
Man Who Cheated Himself, The
Threat, The
Tomorrow is Another Day

Fregonese, Hugo
Black Tuesday
One Way Street

Haas, Hugo
Hit and Run
Other Woman, The
Pickup
Strange Fascination

Litvak, Anatole
City for Conquest
Long Night, The
Sorry, Wrong Number

Montagne, Edward J.
Man with My Face, The
Tattooed Stranger, The

Oswald, Gerd
Crime of Passion
Kiss Before Dying, A

Pichel, Irving
Quicksand
They Won't Believe Me
Tomorrow is Forever

Sherman, George
Raging Tide, The
Sleeping City, The

Sirk, Douglas
Shockproof
Sleep, My Love

Stevenson, Robert
The Las Vegas Story
Walk Softly, Stranger
Woman on Pier 13, The

Tetzlaff, Ted
Under the Gun
Window, The

Wallace, Richard
Fallen Sparrow, The
Framed

Werker, Alfred
He Walked by Night
Shock

Appendix E

To realize the power of light and what it can do to the mind of the audience, visualize the following little scene:

The room is dark. A strong streak of light sneaks in from the hall under the door. The sound of steps is heard. The shadows of two feet divide the light streak. A brief silence follows. There is suspense in the air. Who is it? What is going to happen? Is he going to ring the bell? Or just insert a key and try to come in? Another heavier shadow appears and blocks the light entirely. A dim hissing sound is heard, and as the shadow leaves, we see in the dim light a paper slip onto the carpet. The steps are heard again... This time they leave. A strong light appears once more and illuminates the note on the floor. We read it as the steps fade out in the distance. "It is ten o'clock. Please turn off your radio. The Manager." JOHN ALTON,
Painting with Light

What is film noir? Not a genre. Producers and consumers both recognize a genre as a distinct entity; nobody set out to make or see a film noir in the sense that people deliberately chose to make a Western, a comedy, or a musical. Is film noir then a style? Critics have not succeeded in defining specifically noir visual techniques... or narrative structure. The problem resembles one in art history, that of defining "non-classical" styles. DAVID BORDWELL,
The Classical Hollywood Cinema

1. Neo-Noir

David Bordwell's assertions in a general reference work published in 1985 are in a sub-section called "The case of film noir." At first glance there seems to be little to dispute. As was delineated in Appendix C, critics have indeed disagreed over the nature of film noir. Whether it is called a series, style, genre, movement, cycle, or all of the above, everyone including Bordwell agrees that it is an observable phenomenon. Though not necessarily conforming in every detail--and when have critics ever done that?--they have defined the visual techniques and narrative structures of film noir in scores of books and articles.

Clearly Bordwell is correct in that no filmmakers of the classic period consciously decided to make "a film noir" just as Monet never opted for "an Impressionist painting" over a still life or a landscape. But film and its questions of style are not those of painting, or theater, or music, or literature, or a combination of all of these; and the problems of art history have limited relevance. The solution to the case of film noir, if one must be had, will never be found in hard-boiled fiction, German Expressionism, or postwar paranoia. The investigator must first look, as always, at the heart of the matter, at the films themselves. Bordwell's implication that filmmakers were unaware of working in a style, of being part of a movement, or of utilizing an iconography is highly disputable. John Alton called his sub-section, "The Power of Light," and published his extraordinary text on cinematography in 1949. What better demonstration could there be of his conscious understanding of that power than his work on *T-Men* or *The Big*

Combo or a dozen other classic noir films? Whether they had a name for it or not, whether they called their pictures thrillers or mysteries, actioners or mellers, it would be fairest to assume, particularly for those who did so again and again, that the filmmakers of the noir cycle were well aware of what type of motion picture they were creating.

As was observed in the introduction, while the noir cycle never formally concluded, the attempts to sustain its viewpoint were few in the 1960s and 1970s. Particularly near its end, however, the 1980s brought a significant resurgence of interest in the themes and protagonists that typified classic film noir. In just two and a half years, the 1990s so far have added dozens more to the fifty-odd titles of the preceding decade. If there is a most significant difference between then and now, it is in what motivates the creation of the films.

Also as was noted earlier, at the height of the movement individual noir films transcended personal and generic outlook to reflect cultural preoccupations. From the late 1970s to present, in a "Neo-Noir" period, many of the productions that recreate the noir mood, whether in remakes or new narratives, have been undertaken by filmmakers cognizant of a heritage and intent on placing their own interpretation on it. As the various interviews conducted by Todd Erickson and reproduced in his thesis (see Appendix B10) affirm, most of the filmmakers approach neo-noir with a conscious, expressive intent. David Mamet put it most succinctly regarding *House of Games*: "I am very well acquainted with the genre, both in print and on film, and I love it. I tried to be true."

If neo-noir is to some extent like its antecedent, America's stylized vision of itself, one might expect a cynicism made even harsher by forty more years of cold war, nuclear peril, fiscal uncertainty, and sexual revolution. While the emphasis may have shifted in recent months among these social realities, the outpouring of films has continued. The actual results remain mixed. One aspect of film noir which many filmmakers have chosen to underscore is its forlorn romanticism, the need to find love and honor in a new society that venerates only sex and money. Many others have followed alternative narrative paths blazed in the classic period, and as a result any overview such as this needs a new "family tree" to trace through the titles. Of course, as with Durgnat's original, many of the categories overlap and intersect, and many titles crossover several branches.

The Conscious Auteurs

One of the earliest and most stylized examples of conscious neo-noir is *The Driver* (1978). Walter Hill's main characters are so consciously archetypal that they do not even have names; they are simply the Driver, the Detective, and the Woman. The narrative is spare, alternating balletic interludes of high speed chases down dark, wet streets or in claustrophobic parking structures with terse, expository scenes. The Detective is so obsessed with catching the

Driver that he blackmails another criminal into setting him up. The woman known as the Player is so obsessed with gambling that she is unable to give the Driver any emotional support. While *their* motivations are reasonably clear, the Driver's never is. Being the "best wheel man in town" leaves him in the grip of some quasi-existential anguish. Like many classic noir figures, wandering through dark rooms, silhouetted or in sidelight, the Driver lives on the edge of an ill-defined underworld. Like the title figure in Melville's *Le Samourai* (1967) he lives by an unwritten code, but it seems mostly to burden him as relentlessly as Sisyphus' stone. When he finally violates its basic tenet ("Never carry a gun") in what could be either a liberating act or a hollow triumph, it merely completes the Driver's transformation into a cipher.

The viewer can accept a noir protagonist without a name but not one without an identity. Both as a film and as a character, *The Driver* takes the concept of action as being, creates dramatic conflict, then leaves it unresolved. Hill's later *48 Hrs.* (1982) comes closer to a genuine noir ambience. The two seemingly antithetical characters thrown together by circumstances--a rumpled, alienated detective and a glib well-dressed convict--create a stronger central irony than anything in *The Driver*. As in the Hill-scripted *Hickey and Boggs*, where one of the title characters observes that "It's not about anything anymore," the Detective in *48 Hrs.* has to wrestle with his lost idealism.

Hill's *Johnny Handsome* (1989) posits a small-time crook, betrayed by his associates, whose grotesque facial features are ameliorated by a prison doctor before his parole. The concept of an identity change harks back to *Dark Passage* and *The Hollow Triumph*, but the theme here is revenge. In the jewelry store robbery sequence, Hill immediately includes the violent action opening which typifies his work from *The Warriors* and *Streets of Fire* to *Extreme Prejudice* and *Red Heat*; but the other thrust is towards the mood of noir. The seamier *quartiers* of New Orleans, the setting of Hill's first picture, the period piece *Hard Times,* provide the dark, wet streets that are the stereotypical noir locus. But unlike *Hard Times* or *The Warriors*, where Hill successfully merged genre expectations and a dark visual style to create set pieces more reminiscent of the samurai film than noir, *Johnny Handsome* never finds its core narrative line. Bronson's character in *Hard Times* is more effectively a noir-cum-samurai protagonist than Mickey Rourke in *Johnny Handsome*. Certainly if there is a contemporary actor who could typify the neo-noir *angst*, Rourke or Sean Penn seem likely candidates; yet the portrayal here alternates between undercurrents of sensitivity and psychoses that are more baffling than ambiguous. As revenge ends in self-destruction, the potentially powerful irony is undercut by the commentary of Lt. Drones, the detective who has dogged Johnny's trail. From *Hickey and Boggs* on, in his action films Hill has been as or more conscious of the workings of genre expectations and the noir tradition as or than any other writer or director. He has repeatedly called *Johnny Handsome* a film noir; but perhaps what that film and certainly what *Another 48 Hrs.* (1990) demonstrate is

Ryan O'Neal in the title role of The Driver.

Matty Walker (Kathleen Turner) and Ned Racine (William Hurt) in Body Heat.

District Attorney Tom Krasny (Peter Coyote) and Teddy Barnes (Glenn Close) in Jagged Edge.

that mere consciousness does not always correlate with successful recreation of the sensation of film noir.

Body Heat (1981) is the earliest and perhaps best example of neo-noir films that directly confront the love/sex, honor/money dichotomies. A less-than-average lawyer gets involved with a rich man's wife and, despite clear warnings from both law-enforcement and criminal associates, develops a scheme to murder her husband. Lawrence Kasdan's script has as many twists and turns as the most complicated classic period narrative, but his male protagonist is emotionally closer to Steve Thompson in *Criss Cross* than Walter Neff in *Double Indemnity*. That leaves him vulnerable to the ultimate double-cross by an 80s femme fatale more cunning than most of her antecedents. Kasdan uses unexpected detail, such as the wind-chimes in the early conversation on the porch or the dancing prosecutor, to distract both viewer and protagonist from the sordidness of the underlying reality. Because the viewer co-experiences his betrayal, *Body Heat* evokes the noir sensibility much more powerfully than many of the films which followed it.

Two new examples of flaccidity are *Shattered* (1991) and *Final Analysis* (1992). It would be hard to imagine a greater pastiche of noir elements than *Shattered*: a nearly fatal car crash, a femme fatale (perhaps two), amnesia, an identity changed through plastic surgery, a quasi-amateur private detective (he also owns a pet shop), flashback truths and flashback lies, corrupt deals for public works, the list goes on and on. It would also be hard to imagine a poorer

result. As part of a small neo-contigent of German and Hungarian emigres in Hollywood, director Wolfgang Peterson and cinematographer Laszlo Kovacs must have more than a casual awareness of the tradition of Siodmak, Lang, de Toth, and Curtiz. Nonetheless the visualization full of dark corners and sinister landscapes is also full of slow-motion and opticals that make for a curious mixture. Given the narrative convolutions of *Shattered*, which are certainly not without antecedents in the classic period, what was needed was a compelling protagonist to create a through-line. On an expressive level Don Merrick is a lot more like Frank Bigelow in *D.O.A.*, trying to piece together a picture puzzle whose subject is unknown, than the amnesiac in *Somewhere in the Night* or Bogart in *Dark Passage*. Of course, while it may not be a surprise to many in the audience, Merrick does not even know plastic surgery has changed his identity until near the conclusion. Giving out bits and pieces of this information in flashcuts creates more confusion than suspense, for the protagonist and for the audience. Likewise a surfeit of red herrings creates too little tension and too much of a fishy smell.

Compared to *Shattered*, the self-consciousness of *Final Analysis* seems almost restrained. Neither director Phil Joanou nor director of photography Jordan Cronenweth are emigres; and Cronenweth is certainly one of the most remarkable of contemporary American cameramen whose style stresses source light and naturalistic effects. While it has distinctive plot twists of its own, *Final Analysis* is not a narrative pastiche, but more of a reverse of the earlier neo-noir *Jagged Edge* (1985). Given the noir sensibility of Joanou and Cronenweth's earlier collaboration on *State of Grace* (1991), the unsubtle echoes in *Final Analysis*, in particular the insistent allusions to *Vertigo*, that reduce it to cartoonish parody are somewhat unexpected. Despite the self-awareness of the psychiatrist protagonist who actually says, "I want to be surprised" and remarks on "existential angst," the story-line is simple: two sisters trap him into unwittingly assisting in murder. But *Final Analysis* is not *Vertigo*, and no amount of suffused sidelight coming off wood-paneled rooms, depth of field holding full face and silhouette in close two-shots, or tracking back into empty space from figures at the edge of a great height can underscore character emotion which is never developed. After watching Richard Gere hang precariously over an abyss, seeing Kim Basinger plunge to her matte-shot death, followed by an epilogue in which Uma Thurman seems to assume her dead sister's identity, one realizes not only that it would have been no better with James Stewart, Kim Novak, and Barbara Bel Geddes but also how thin the line between masterful and turgid can be.

The Hard-boiled School and Remakes

Against All Odds (1984) and *No Way Out* (1987), the remakes of *Out of the Past* and *The Big Clock* respectively, may have their plots dressed up with sports car chases or computers, but dramatically they are somewhat retrograde. Where the protagonists perished in *Out of the Past*, *Against All Odds* merely condemns them to a narrative limbo, apart but alive. And the cold-war plot revelation which concludes *No Way Out* is less novel than anticlimactic. Other remakes such as *The Big Sleep* (1978) and *The Postman Always Rings Twice* (1981) are even further off the mark. In the former, Robert Mitchum reprises Philip Marlowe; but the battered idealism that sustained *Farewell, My Lovely* has become mere indifference as the filmmakers inexplicably relocate Raymond Chandler's quintessential Angeleno from L.A. to London. In the latter Nicholson and Lange in the Garfield/Turner roles recapture the impulsive sexuality but little of the determinism of Cain's original or the 1947 adaptation. *Sharky's Machine* (1981) takes the central premise of *Laura* and little else. The detective's obsession with a high-priced call girl he thinks is dead is a small noir twist in a very tangled scenario.

Kiss Me A Killer (1991) is a Latino remake (without crediting Cain) of *The Postman Always Rings Twice*. In fact, the narrative borrows liberally from other types of films from Siegel's *Crime In the Streets* to Hitchcock's *I, Confess*; but the narrative centers on the Mexican-American wife of a white bar owner and a guitar-playing drifter named Tony who helps transform the place into a salsa hot spot. Like Visconti's 1942 *Ossessione*, this unsanctioned adaptation of Cain's novel emphasizes the loutish qualities of the husband and builds audience sympathy with the killers. There are also several interesting narrative inventions: the dream sequence in which Teresa imagines her husband mounted on the wall of the bar like a game fish and the

ending which has Tony killed by a former friend who resents being "set up" in the first attempt on the husband.

If Cain, Chandler, and other *Serie Noire* authors have not led to inspired filmmaking in the last decades, their narrative preoccupations have been borrowed quite liberally by writers of original scripts. Cain's motifs of doubt and trust underscore the plots of such diverse original scripts as *Jagged Edge*, *Still of the Night* (1982), and *The Morning After* (1986). Yet none is truly effective as film noir, none discovers the unstable undercurrent at the core of such similarly plotted films as *Beyond a Reasonable Doubt*, *In A Lonely Place*, and *Blue Gardenia* respectively. An auteurist explanation of this phenomenon might cite the passing of Fritz Lang and Nicholas Ray, each of whom directed a half dozen or more noir films. But the stylistic touches of Lang and Ray, the slow, ensnaring dolly moves or the disorienting cuts during panning shots, are used just as often by contemporary filmmakers. The most derivative direction, such as Brian de Palma's unabashed recapitulations of Hitchcock in *Dressed to Kill*, *Blow-out*, and *Body Double*, may slightly enrich or impoverish the basic material but cannot overwhelm it.

One writer whose novels have been adapted several times in neo-noir is Jim Thompson, whose only work in the classic period was dialogue credit for Stanley Kubrick on *The Killing*. In the past decade Thompson's "rediscovery" has led to adaptations of no less than five of his books, two by French filmmakers. The best known, thanks to Anjelica Huston's award-winning performance, is *The Grifters* (1990). While clearly meant to be faithful to Thompson's unrelentingly bleak vision, *The Grifters* presents its cast of "losers" straightforwardly and fails to capture Thompson's undercurrent of forlorn perseverance that mutates into classic existential despair. The 1976 film *The Killer Inside Me* lacked the chilling tone of Thompson's saga of a small-town psychopath who happens to be a cop, a novel which typified his leitmotif that "You can't hurt people who are already dead." Not even the combined efforts of Sam Peckinpah, Walter Hill, and Steve McQueen in *The Getaway* (1972) translated this aspect of Thompson to the screen. In the adaptors' hands, the novelist's usual assumptions about the sordidness of crime and its corrupting influence on the criminal's will, became instead a story of betrayal and redemption, of self-righteous violence and paranoiac romance. For Thompson, the ultimate irony of *The Getaway* is the very title, for as his Doc and Carol learn in Mexico what Lou Ford does in *The Killer Inside Me* that "I'll never be free as long as I live..." This is not to disparage *The Getaway*, but its alterations of the novel move it farther from rather than closer to films of the classic period like *Criss Cross* or *The Killing*. After two French adaptations of the early 1980s, *Serie Noire* (from *A Hell of a Woman*) and particularly Bertrand Tavernier's *Coup de Torchon* (from *Population 1280*), American filmmakers discovered Thompson again in the 90s.

Although released in 1990, as were *The Grifters* and *After Dark, My Sweet*, the independent *The Kill-Off* was the first of the recent adaptations. While it attempts to retain the

Myra Langtry (Annette Bening) squares off against Lilly Dillon (Angelica Huston, right) over Lily's son Roy (John Cusack) in The Grifters.

multiplicity of viewpoints used in the novel, cutting be-tween narrators each trapped in their what Thompson saw as personal hells, *The Kill-Off* suffers from its lack of budget, particularly in the uneven performances of its quasi-professional actors. As it happens, *The Grifters*, with its still modest but substantially larger budget has much the same problem. The characters in *The Grifters* are people whose business is deception, whose emotions are con-cealed to all but a few. John Cusack's laconic rendering of Roy does not catch the glib turns of the con-man, especially if compared to a performance like Joe Man-tegna's in *House of Games* or Anjelica Huston's in the same film.

Another contrast is Jason Patric's portrayal of "Collie" in *After Dark, My Sweet*. The credit sequence is an expres-sionistic rendering of the prize fight in which he kills his opponent. Midway through the titles, a sound-buffered jump cut takes the viewer to a tight close-up of him as he now is. *After Dark, My Sweet* is a first person film on several levels from the voiceover narration to the opticals and sound effects which intermittently externalize his troubled mental state. Employing these stylistic elements typical of the classic period permits all the narrative ten-sions to be effectively laid out within the first few minutes. A cut back from the close-up reveals the protagonist in a desert landscape coming out of an escarpment of large stones. As he shuffles across the highway, the narration ("I wonder where I'll be tomorrow...") rambles over shot. The key phrase is, "I couldn't walk away." As he enters the town, the sound of a train is heard and a sudden, sidewise camera move swings past him but holds the

figure in a 180 degree arc, fixes his body in the sun-bleached highway. It prevents him from walking out of the shot, figuratively holding him as firmly as his troubled memories grip his mind.

Like all Thompson's characters, Collie is slowly dying in his personal hell. When Fay, a femme fatale in sandals and a stray hat, picks him up, she treats him like a stray puppy, patting the car seat and saying, "Come on, now, there's a good boy" to entice him in. Her directness--she wants to call him Collie because he reminds her of a shaggy dog--is what makes her ambiguous, what sets her apart in a Thompsonesque milieu of con men and petty crooks. The desert itself, with its clean, brightly-lit vistas, is in constant contrast to the emotional darkness within. But it is through Patric's performance, full of tics, stumbl-ing, and false starts, that *After Dark, My Sweet* evokes the hopelessness of both Thompson and film noir more forcefully than *The Grifters*.

Whether from a position of ignorance or knowledge, the interaction of protagonist and viewer seems much more seldom to reveal the instability, the dark undercurrent that served as a thematic constant of the noir cycle. That "Fate or some mysterious force" that destroyed or endangered scores of characters like Frank Bigelow and Al Roberts in *Detour* is less often a factor in neo-noir. If the remake *DOA* (1988) illustrates anything, it is that the arbitrariness of death in an era of Yuppie values and AIDS can still matter. The remake is stylistically too self-conscious, not just in the black-and-white sequences which bracket college pro-fessor Dexter Cornell's (the new Frank Bigelow) flashback story of how he was killed, but in the diffused, desaturated color scenes as well. The key story point--that Cornell has been poisoned because he might recognize a novel, the student-author of whom has been killed by an another professor who wants to publish it as his own--is even more suggestive of ethical values gone totally awry.

Martin Scorsese's *Cape Fear* (1991) epitomizes the synthesis of a conscious auteur and the remaking of a picture from the classic period. Even more than the original, the new *Cape Fear* transforms Al Roberts' lament into a relentless litany. As the sense of helplessness grows in the family tormented by a vindicative ex-convict, the sense of menace is as palpable as in the original or *The Killer is Loose*. In another remake, *Desperate Hours* (1990), the posturing of the criminals never seems as threatening to the family as its own inner turmoil. In *Cape Fear* Scorsese unabashedly creates a preternatural figure with Robert De Niro's portrayal of Max Cady, a tattooed, vindictive, self-righteous brute, whose monomania becomes, for his victims, the pointed finger of the mysterious force.

Victims of Circumstance I— Love with an Improper Stranger

Even when Roberts' "mysterious force" does appear to be in play, the result can be quite different. The failure of a film like *Out of Bounds* (1986) to be anything more than a "kid noir" parody is the failure to exploit viewer expectations. The motivating plot element, picking up the wrong bag, is accomplished with a lot more verisimilitude than in *Too Late for Tears*; but little else is. Hunted by both a murderous pusher and the police, helped only by a Hollywood punkette, the fresh-from-the-farm protagonist perseveres where many a noir hero would have despaired or, at least, faltered. This melange of violence and teen-grit falls a bit short of the noir sensibility.

On the other hand, the popular success of a picture like *Fatal Attraction* (1987) is more dependent on the noir formula. Certainly its very title is in the same "boldface" used by so many classic period films. Despite that, it manipulates viewer expectations. More significantly, it manipulates them by drawing the viewer into the protagonist's point-of-view. The audience fails to discern the latent psychoses of Alex Forrest, fails to read any real menace in her slight lack of focus or an occasional nervous gesture, because Dan Gallagher does not see it. Alex Forrest is no femme fatale, luring the unwary hero down a deadly path of criminal activity or other degradation. Like the woman in *The Locket*, the veneer of normality is enhanced by her sexual vulnerability. From the protagonist's, and audience's, frame of reference, her behavior is more disturbing for its unexpectedness. Like many noir figures before him, Gallagher's inability to anticipate or respond is the real source of peril. Like Sam Bowden in *Cape Fear*, he finds that the very social order which he thought would protect him, only makes him and his family easier to assail.

Neo-noir has fatal men as well as women, although the cultural prejudices which helped create the femme fatale are still in play. Tim Whelan, the protagonist of *Masquerade*

Max Cady (Robert De Niro) awaits a secret rendezvous with the naive daughter of the family he is terrorizing in Cape Fear.

(1988), is a gigolo intent on seducing an heiress. Like Nick Blake in *Nobody Lives Forever*, the victim's naivete gives Whelan pause; but in the typical schematic of neo-noir, nothing can prevent his destruction. Despite its literally explosive conclusion which annihilates the protagonist, *Masquerade* is a flaccid reflection of the classic period, surprisingly so given the gritty ambience of Bob Swaim's French film, *La Balance*. Equally ineffective is the similarly plotted second adaptation of the Ira Levin novel *A Kiss Before Dying* (1991). In *Fatal Attraction*, *Masquerade*, and *A Kiss Before Dying*, in films as diverse as *Sea of Love*, *Mortal Passions*, *Paint It Black*, or *The Hot Spot*, what makes many of the figures in neo-noir into victims of circumstance is their proclivity for love with an improper stranger.

The Hot Spot (1990) is a reciprocal of *Strange Love of Martha Ivers* or what might have happened if Martha Ivers had accomplished her aims. The film's fatal woman, Dolly Harshaw, does manage to kill her husband and trap the protagonist in her black widow's web. Of course, Harry Madox, *The Hot Spot*'s protagonist, is a con-man, bank robber, and killer, who in the film's final words accepts his fate: "I found my level, and I'm living it." *The Hot Spot* is fully as self-conscious of the noir tradition as *Shattered* and *The Final Analysis*. If it succeeds where they fail, part of the reason is a directness which verges on parody. From the opening titles, revealing its "hero" among sand dunes under a blistering sky as a hawk screeches on the soundtrack, director Dennis Hopper uses the shorthand of iconic indicators like a wry commentary. The robbery, the extortions, the seductions are secondary elements in a plot that hinges on an allegorical triangle that seems descended from those of David Goodis. On the one hand is the lascivious, animalistic Dolly, repeatedly posed with her legs parted on a car seat or covered with shaving cream, linked in fatalistic side moves of the camera with a rearing polar bear, or, in the penultimate sequence, crawling on the floor counter posed with a stuffed cougar. On the other hand is Gloria, demure, virginal, blackmailed by Frank Sutton who has photographs of her in an apparently lesbian interlude. "That little gal's got you all stoked up," Sutton correctly observes to Harry; and what Don Johnson's performance suggests has Harry stoked up is the hint of sordidness in Gloria. It is the sights and sounds of the milieu where the buzz of a fly on Sutton's hand is like the stench of corruption, where Madox's black-finned Studebaker swoops down on Sutton's place like a bird of prey, that truly situate *The Hot Spot* and enclosed Harry Madox in a personal hell as fiery as any of Jim Thomspon's.

Variants of obsessive love are as commonplace in neo-noir as they were in the classic period. The difference between *Revenge* (1990) and *Cat Chaser* (1989) is one of tone. The latter has script work by Elmore Leonard from his own novel and in Peter Weller an actor who could blend the resignation of Sterling Hayden and the edginess of John Ireland while delivering lines such as "Sometimes you see somebody and you see yourself going down a road you could have gone." Ultimately while it may be the least violent of director Abel Ferrara's neo-noir credits, *Cat Chaser* is too caught up in the conditional mode and its impact diffracted through a supporting cast of losers and thugs. It is the aspects of irresistible compulsion and betrayal that make a less complex film like *Revenge* at least superficially truer to the noir tradition.

These sub-themes of betrayal and mistrust which were at play in *Out of the Past* and *Criss Cross* also find diverse new examples in *Klute* (1971), *The Last Embrace* (1976), *Sea of Love* (1989), *Kill Me Again* (1990), and *Deceived* (1991). The last of these is a pallid echo of *Suspicion*, using stray cats for shock cuts but less suspenseful than another Hitchcock-inspired (from *The 39 Steps*) Goldie Hawn vehicle, *Bird on a Wire*, which is essentially comic. Jonathan Demme's early *The Last Embrace* is an even greater melange, with its plotted maladies ranging from a simple nervous breakdown to psychopathic schizophrenia tied into arcane Judaica and a trip down Niagara Falls without a barrel.

The earliest of these, *Klute*, sets a pattern for plot and character development aspects of which are frequently echoed in neo-noir (see sections 6 and 8 below). Bree Daniel is the target of a deadly killer and a prostitute. Like Frank Bigelow, circumstances, not her line of work, have put her in jeopardy. The scenes which track Bree at work, at auditions, at her therapist's are part of a parallel schematic with John Klute, the small-town cop investigating

his friend's death, and Peter Cable, the killer trying to cover his tracks. The discussions about love and trust are direct reflections on themes from the classic period. From the costumes and characterizations down to sound effects and underscore, the style is expressive of the interplay of the noir underworld and "normal" society.

Also of interest in terms of narrative structure are *Sea of Love* and *Kill Me Again*. Both were sold to audiences as erotic thrillers but the key to each is not whether the female lead is a femme fatale as much as how the male detective (police and private respectively) perceives her. When the protagonist in *Sea of Love* finds himself fixated on a woman whom he suspects is a "lonely hearts" killer, there are two possible narrative resolutions: either she is or she is not. The conflict becomes an inner one fixed on his inability to trust his feelings. This is not uncommon and is often situated outside of a noir environment. With *Kill Me Again* as in *Criss Cross*, the question is not whether the object of the detective's attraction is capable of lying to him, for he knows she has done that repeatedly, but whether she will continue to do so. In the end, *Kill Me Again*'s Jack Andrews is neither Walter Neff nor Steve Thompson; but like other noir and neo-noir p.i.'s, from Sam Spade on, he is capable of hedging his bets.

Cops—Good, Bad, and All Dead Inside

The concept that "anyone can be killed" is central to *Best Seller* (1987). A hired killer named Cleve wants Dennis Meechum, a detective/novelist, to write his biography to expose his former employer, a noted philanthropist, because, like the syndicate figures in John Flynn's earlier *The Outfit* who "act like they own the world," he needs his comeuppance. The killer also asserts that he and the cop are a lot alike, a notion which the detective must resist. The same contention is made by a mass murderer to Graham, the detective in *Manhunter* (1986). For the latter protagonist, in particular, getting inside the criminal mind has had psychically damaging implications. For both men, the most alienating aspect of their job is the latent fear that they are indeed becoming like the criminals they track. Director Michael Mann, who brought a noir viewpoint to the small screen with *Miami Vice*, has his camera constantly gliding behind the title character in *Manhunter*, picking up disturbing resonances of fear and death. Graham is actually more disturbed by his visits to the imprisoned Dr. Lecter than his attempts at mind-melding with the "tooth fairy." In the scene of where he tells Lecter how he managed to capture him ("You had certain disadvantages." "What disadvantages?" "You're insane."), Graham fidgets nervously in the chair. When he feels the fabric of the victim's clothing in the evidence room and asks the absent killer out loud, "What is it you're becoming," Graham seems totally in control. From that scene, Mann cuts to the killer's home and a close-up of William Blake's watercolor of "The Red Dragon," the being with which the psychopath identifies.

For Meechum and Graham, being touched by the pollution and sordidness of the noir underworld is part of the job description. Unable to behave like the brutal cops in *The Detective Story* or *Where the Sidewalk Ends*, these more modern policeman suffer from a job-related, mental dysfunction that makes them feel more like the ex-con Galt in *The Dark Corner*, "all dead inside."

By its very title, *Murphy's Law* (1986) epitomizes the narrative counter-influences on neo-noir. When the viewer expects things to go wrong for the protagonist, they invariably do; but when the protagonist expects things to go wrong, the delicate balance of the noir universe is upset. What keeps many of the Charles Bronson pictures after *Death Wish* and the Clint Eastwood vehicles after *Dirty Harry* from evoking the noir sensibility is the grim miens of their stars, the lines in their faces that suggest they are beyond wondering about the vagaries of life. The antithesis of these portrayals would be Bruce Dern as the Detective in *The Driver*.

The distinction between police conscience and police corruption can be finely drawn in neo-noir. Clint Eastwood's slightly kinky detective in *Tightrope* (1984) cannot help but see a little of himself in the sexually frustrated killer he is stalking. Even as the implacable "Dirty Harry" Callahan in *Sudden Impact* (1983), he becomes so involved with a woman tracking a gang of murderous rapists that he lets her go at the film's conclusion. The federal agents in *To Live and Die in L.A.* (1986) get so caught up in the

underworld they are combing for a master criminal that they cross the line, as do the street cops in *King of New York* (1990). Even *Stakeout* (1987), which is seriocomic in depicting a detective's unforeseen affair with a woman he has under surveillance, is just slightly removed from the darker implications of the classic period's *Pushover*. Like *Someone to Watch over Me* (1987), which reduces the concept to soap opera, *Stakeout* does confront the issue of conflict of interest as a human failing with possibly fatal results.

Obviously none of these characters is a "bad cop" in the classic sense, accepting bribes like the title figure in *Rogue Cop* or killing for money as in *Shield for Murder*. The police figure in *The Big Easy* (1987) is on the take and happily so. As with the cliquish detectives in *Prince of the City* (1981), it's easier to be part of the game than to buck the system. Even after being caught, the character's remorse is more over the possibility of losing a job he's good at and a love interest who's a district attorney than from any sense of wrongdoing. Ironically, the character's easy virtue makes him all the more guilty when he discovers the extent of the corruption in his department. The string of corrupt cops featured in neo-noir is long and growing from *The Border* (1982) to *Black Rain*, *Q & A*, and *Internal Affairs* (all 1990) not to mention where such characters are less prominent, as in *Witness* (1985) or *Narrow Margin* (1990), but still central to the plot. Given the cross-cultural thrusts of *The Border*, *Black Rain*, and even *Q & A*, only *Internal*

American detectives Nick Conklin (Michael Douglas, left) and Charlie Vincent (Andy Garcia) surrounded by bikers in Osaka, Japan, in Black Rain.

Affairs is as focused on bad cops as *The Big Easy.*

What separates and sometimes redeems the rogue cops of neo-noir is their motivation. Of those involved in crime, the supporting characters in *The Border* or *Witness* are merely venal and either perish or are caught. The characters in *Q & A* and *Black Rain* are a bit more complicated. But neither the former who administers his own justice or the latter who rehabilitates some of his honor in Japan seem troubled by the fact of their imperfect behavior as by its consequences. Ultimately the protagonists in *The Border* and *Internal Affairs* are closer to the classic tradition. The former who accepts the corruption around him and almost falls prey to it because he needs money cannot accept the devaluation of human life which his working environment fosters. Unlike the title character in the earlier *Serpico* (1973), whose outrage at larcenous cops is met by institutionalized disregard, the investigator in *Internal Affairs* is charged to uncover bad cops. Consequently, *Internal Affairs* is even more overt in its treatment of corruption as latent in everyone; but the dark possibilities of transference of guilt which it raises are left unexplored at its end. Conversely, a picture such as *The Onion Field* (1979) initially makes transference a key note; however, the guilt which one cop feels after his partner's murder is quickly subsumed to the study of the criminal mentalities of the two killers, which is ultimately closer to the "true story" connotations of *In Cold Blood* than to neo-noir.

The cops of the classic period from *I Wake Up Screaming* to *Pushover* or even *Laura* who were compromised because of sexual obsessions are less common in neo-noir. Certainly *Sea of Love* might have taken that narrative direction but did not. There are sexual overtones in *Internal Affairs* and even *The Border*, but they are secondary considerations. Essentially the protagonists of both those films act out of idealism, compromised idealism, perhaps, but sufficiently intact to compel their outrage when they discover inhuman and murderous behavior. By 1992 idealism is in short supply. The protagonist of *Basic Instinct* (1992) is a cop whose cocaine addiction may have driven his wife to suicide, who has had an affair with his psychotherapist and is seduced by a murder suspect. Beneath the surface flashes of violence and sex, the potential alienation of *Basic Instinct*'s wayward cop is lost in a miasma of plot convolutions and quirky nostalgia, as in the casting of Dorothy Malone, a classic period icon, as a older psychopath. The similar themes of such modestly-budgeted efforts as *To Kill For* or *Criminal Intent* (both 1992) provide telling comparisons with *Basic Instinct*. The San Francisco detective in *To Kill For* is similarly seduced by a female suspect and the brutal cop in *Criminal Intent* is being investigated by internal affairs. While neither film succeeds where *Basic Instinct* fails in truly evoking a noir ambience, these failures are, at least from the viewpoint of time and money involved, much more modest. Even a true idealist, such as the deputy sheriff in *White Sands* (1992), who becomes enmeshed in an labyrinthine plot involving corrupt operatives from several federal agencies simply because

he is diligently investigating a murder, is extricated from the potential miasma of neo-noir alienation by some convenient plot twists. Dennis Hopper as Harry Niles, a "pissed off white cop who's been suspended," does embody some of that alienation in John Flynn's *Nails* (1992). His portrayal, despite snippets of personal philosophy such as "Cautious men die; the reckless survive," is ultimately more style than substance. Where Harry Niles is a self-professed relic, the character of John Hull makes *Deep Cover* (1992) the only recent release to put a new spin on the noir hero. Opening with an incident from the protagonist's childhood twenty years in the past (he sees his father gunned down while robbing a liquor store) and using voiceover narration throughout, *Deep Cover* incorporates many traditional noir elements with such newer optical devices as step printing, staggered zoom shots, and interlaced montages. This staccato imagery combined with a pulsing underscore and the main character's monotone narration create a kind of "rap noir," an emblem of 90s alienation entirely appropriate to an example of neo-noir focused on drugs, racism, and mixed loyalties. Even as titled angles externalize Hull's sense of disequilibrium, the surface irony remains that the street cop protagonist is more at home undercover than in uniform, that he is full of anti-authoritarian tendencies which lead the federal agent who recruits him to observe that "undercover all your faults will become virtues. You'll be star there, John." Compounding this is the perspective of first-person recollection, a commentary which reveals a deterministic overview: "I felt that it would be the biggest mistake of my life, and I was right." Through a series of violent and chaotic set pieces, that determinism drives the narrative towards a climactic moment when the protagonist must make a choice typical of the noir underworld, not just between good and evil, but between past and present, rich and poor, old allegiances and new. Clearly the undercover agent's criminal partner, though white and middle-class, is a mirror of his own "dark" side. Because it focuses more on the cop than the criminal than such films as *New Jack City* or *King of New York*, the viewer expects from the first what that choice will be. If there is a false note in the conclusion of *Deep Cover*, it is not the protagonist's survival as much as the reversal of his position with a system that has manipulated him from childhood.

Essentially the neo-noir cop begins with the Frank Sinatra pictures of the late 1960s, *The Detective* (1968) and *Lady in Cement* (1968). The iconic playing with type and exploiting both the professional and private personas of the actor-singer could not sustain those pictures nor the later *The First Deadly Sin* (1980). But they are significant in helping define a type, more effectively portrayed in *Madigan* or *Hickey and Boggs* but more directly delineated here, of the job-weary, burnt-out cases, plodding on because the alternative to enduring is expiring. That tradition is mirrored to an extent twenty years later in such Burt Reynolds' pictures as *Malone* (1988) and *Rent-A-Cop* (1988), iconography without substance.

Perhaps the most estranged for the least apparent reason

is the suicidal vice-cop in *Lethal Weapon* (1987). He is, as it happens, a Vietnam veteran who has lost a loved one. Like his G.I. counterparts back from World War II, he neither thinks nor acts normally: he is as likely to push a jumper off a roof as pull him back. Like Gagin in *Ride the Pink Horse*, the unforeseen association with his new partner's family brings him back from the brink. Unlike Gagin, or any classic noir protagonist, his catharsis is a torrent of violent action culminating in hand-to-hand combat on his partner's lawn. Given the restorative impact of *Lethal Weapon*'s narrative on the alienated protagonist, it is not surprising that *Lethal Weapon II* (1989) and *Lethal Weapon III* (1992) lack the nervous energy of the first picture.

More recent variations are *Cop* (1988), *Dead-Bang* (1989), *State of Grace* (1990), *Homicide* (1991), *Thunderheart* (1992), and, of course, *Deep Cover*. The first two are versions of the burnt-out case, investigators estranged from their families and bending the rules as they doggedly pursue leads and try to convince others of the connection in a string of crimes. *Cop*, in particular, dwells on the brutality that is both suffered and inflicted by its protagonist. Where Riggs in the conclusion of *Lethal Weapon* gave the taunting killer a duelist's chance, Hopkins in this picture has a different response to the jibes of the captured murderer. Having seen the victims' bodies and imagining a trial where pleas will be entered and facts distorted, Hopkins realizes that, while "I'm a cop and I've got to take you in," he is suspended from duty. He says as much to the suspect and then blows him away.

The latter two films, in particular, unflinchingly question many of the values in the standard cops and robbers or good guys versus bad approach of some many law enforcers. The undercover cop in *State of Grace* sent back to his old neighborhood to bring down the friends of his childhood has a far different experience than the detective in *Cry of the City*. As the distinction between good and evil is increasingly blurred, the warring factions do not merely murder in the coldblooded tradition of the 30s gangster film but rationalize it as well. As the hospital-endowing drug lord of *King of New York* remarks on his rapacious victims, "Those guys are dead because I didn't want to make money that way. I never killed anybody that didn't deserve it." As in *Deep Cover*, ethnic prejudice is also a key issue in both *State of Grace* and *Homicide*. While the guilt-ridden undercover officer in *State of Grace* may try to achieve catharsis by confronting his antagonists and opening fire, there is no simple method to expiate the convoluted betrayals in *Homicide*. The frustration and confusion which he experiences are not only disquieting but they short-circuit the kind of Hawksian professionalism in which he thought he found an identity. The film's ending in which he is blackmailed by those he thought were his new brothers and loses his partner as a consequence of his personal failure are no so much anti- as pre-Hawksian, the descent into self-loathing from which redemption may or may not be possible.

A similar theme, with a slightly more upbeat conclusion, is explored in *Thunderheart*. While the Native-American F.B.I. agent is not directly betrayed by the inhabitants of

Terry Noonan (Sean Penn) and Jackie Flannery (Gary Oldman) in State of Grace.

the reservation where he goes to investigate a murder, he does discover that many of them are not above selling out. In that sense, even through the melange of mysticism and identity crisis, the concept of betrayal is still in play. It remains to be seen whether *Thunderheart* and *The Dark Wind*, based on a series of novels by Tony Hillerman featuring a reservation policeman, fully constitute a sub-category of Native-American noir.

For all the police characters in neo-noir films, violence betokens both solution and problem, dispelling a physical threat but compounding a moral dilemma. Some protagonists as in *Best Seller* manage to resist the temptation of the quick fix; others, as in *To Live and Die in L.A.*, are consumed by it.

Serial Murder and Psychopaths—The Killer Inside Me

Perhaps the explicit threat of transference, of mentally trading places with the criminals they pursue, experienced by the detectives in *Best Seller* and *Manhunter*, is epitomized by the female investigator in *Black Widow* (1987). Like her male counterparts, she is warned about her "obsession," about her abnormal relationship with the woman she is pursuing. Other noir protagonists have established relationships with suspects--Fallon in *White Heat* and the undercover cops in *Street with No Name* and *House of Bamboo*--but they never forgot they were playing a role. In *Black Widow*, the protagonist's involvement, first with the suspected murderess and then with her fiance, violates all the usual rules. The scene in which she gives her adversary a black widow brooch clarifies the nature of the deadly duel in which the two women are consciously locked: a conflict not just of crime and law, of chaos and order, but, like Det. Diamond and Mr. Brown in *The Big Combo*, a conflict of sheer will as well.

Transference is also a factor in such diverse productions as *Mike's Murder* (1984), *52 Pick-up* (1986), and *At Close Range* (1986). Neither *52 Pick-up* nor *At Close Range* have much to recommend them as additions to the noir canon. In the former, twenty-five years after *Manchurian Candidate*, John Frankenheimer's adaptation of Elmore Leonard explores the intrusion the underworld of sex and drugs into the clean, well-lit lives of a small businessman and his politically-active wife. At first, the protagonist seems unable to deal with the coldblooded, anonymous extortionist who suddenly turns his world upside-down; but as he first tracks down his antagonist and then confronts him, the victim becomes the aggressor. At *Close Range* is most memorable for director of photography Juan Ruiz Anchia's hard-lit images. The plot, a criminal father's seduction of his sons into the life he and his own brothers live, never develops beyond its "based on a true story" pathos. Eventually, even the austere side-lit close-ups and dark frames cut by white light, visualizations in the noir tradition that subtly suggest the violence smouldering just below the surface, lose their impact, drowned by listless staging and an overused underscore.

The Bedroom Window is little more than a pastiche of Woolrich and Hitchcock. Not until the last third of its narrative, when the original victim returns to help clear the innocent protagonist does the production do more than simply borrow plot from a film like *Phantom Lady*, too late to create anything more than a superficial noir ambience. *Mike's Murder* is a bit more ambitious. Unlike the male figure in *52 Pick-up*, the woman's odyssey into the same subculture of sex and drugs in *Mike's Murder* is a voluntary one. After a series of bizarre encounters, like those of Van Stratten in *Mr. Arkadin*, what she discovers about herself as well as about her murdered friend is that the noir underworld is indeed still just beneath the surface, menacing those who probe too deeply. Moreover, in this film and *Black Widow*, Debra Winger takes on roles that are traditionally male and gives them a new perspective. While her characters have a situational resemblance to the Ella Raines' portrayal of a woman trying to clear the boss she secretly loves of murder in *Phantom Lady*, Winger's sexuality is more of a tool than a motivation. In *Betrayed* (1988) Winger plays an F.B.I. agent enamored of the white supremacist whose group she has infiltrated. The ending in which the undercover agent must accept that she has been intimate with a killer, and shoots him, is effectively a reversal of *Phantom Lady*.

Given its narrative pretexts and its source material, the sequel to *Manhunter*, *Silence of the Lambs* (1991) is remarkably asexual. In expanding the character of Hannibal Lecter, both novelist and filmmakers create a cipher for the all the psychopaths at large in the neo-noir underworld. What fascinates Lecter is the grim skull beneath the skin, the chaos beneath the surface order. As disquieting as he may appear strapped to a stretcher in a straightjacket and mask, his bare face is even more disturbing. His leering offer, "I'll help you catch him, Clarice," is more carnivorous that lubricious. "Hannibal the Cannibal," "The Tooth Fairy," "Buffalo Bill," all the epithets suggest a search for food not sex. Lecter and his ilk also represent the most fundamental assault on the ostensibly normal, ordered world which the protagonists inhabit. "Don't tell him anything personal," Crawford advises Clarice, "You don't want Hannibal Lecter inside your head." Since Lecter's price for information is being permitted inside her head, the final face to face meeting is both terrible and cathartic for Clarice. The visual style alternates tight, low-lit close-ups of Lecter with slow zooms into her face, externalizationing the process of his mind penetrating hers.

For the F.B.I. agent in a picture such as *Shoot to Kill* (1988), the psychopath, the victims, the alternate lifestyle of his back country guide are all secondary considerations, in a stereotypical and one-dimensional portrait of a law enforcer. For Clarice Starling, as it was for Will Graham, whose name and history are directly invoked in *Silence of the Lambs*, Lecter is frightening in and of himself and also as a symbol of the terrifying underworld that was integral to the classic noir narrative. Unlike Graham, Clarice is not an empath whom Lecter brings face to face with his own dark side. Lecter's probing of her past and her values never menaces her life and ultimately reinforces her own sanity.

During and just after the classic period encounters between cops and serial murderers were less frequent and more predictable: Dirty Harry shot him, tortured him, and shot him again at the end. Neo-noir has many variants that blur the distinction from the simplistic, blue-lit, low-budget *The Rain Killer* (1990), in which the F.B.I. man is the psychopath, to *Relentless* (1989), in which the killer's father was a policeman, to *Miami Blues* (1990), in which the criminal impersonates a cop. In a production like *The Rain Killer*, where the poor technical choices and poorer acting discredit the entire effort, the viewer is not encouraged to consider the elements of transference in the plot. *Miami Blues* actually focuses on that concept in opposing a killer who wants to try a normal domestic life in which murder and robbery are his nine-to-five job with a cop who might be happier on skid row.

Perhaps the ultimate and most unsettling example of the domestic serial killer is *White of the Eye* (1988). In confronting the question of the killer inside, Director Donald Cammell drags along often inappropriate effects from *Performance* and stages the killings as repellant ballets of death. A shot of a victim reflected in an extreme close-up of an eye may be a less than subtle statement of intent about recreating the killer's point-of-view; but without benefit of the killer's identity, the crimes are anonymously grotesque. For most of the narrative the viewer is encouraged to believe that the killer is actually an innocent victim, whose only "crime" is cheating on his wife. It is, in fact, the wife's point-of-view that is most severely manipulated; yet the ironic flashbacks and the encounter with her old boyfriend who has mysteriously returned to Arizona after a prison sentence create an aura less of vague apprehension or even dislocation than ennui. The final sequences where "all is revealed" have some chilling moments as the psychopath puts on his ritual costume and terrorizes his own wife and child, but nothing of that comes close to the effect of a single low-lit view of Lecter in his glass cage.

Victims of Circumstance II—Welcome to My Nightmare

Just as there were in the classic period, there are other types of victims of circumstance in neo-noir. Certainly Frank Bigelow and Al Roberts are paradigm of the extreme twists of fate, where the victim perishes. In neo-noir, the parallels are more often to pictures like *Nightfall* or *The Hitch-hiker*, where the protagonists manage to overcome the forces that menace them. Edmund O'Brien played the parts of Bigelow, Ray Collins in *The Hitch-hiker*, and Mal Granger in *711 Ocean Drive*. While all three characters share an iconic and narrative typing and react similarly to the perilous events that suddenly threaten them, the latter figure is lured into criminal activity by the prospect of being well paid for his technical skills. Like the couple in *Too Late for Tears*, he is typical of those who are wholly or partly responsible for their dilemmas. Analogs in neo-noir of those trying to seize an opportunity of easy money are the protagonists of *Atlantic City* (1981) or *Who'll Stop the Rain* (1978).

Dr. Hannibal Lector (Anthony Hopkins) in his cell in The Silence of the Lambs.

From *Hardcore* (1979) or *Eyewitness* (1981) to the self-conscious, almost "new age" tone of *Union City* (1980) or *Slam Dance* (1987), the linking principle is, exactly as it was with *The Hitch-hiker*, the lack of security and stability in everyday living, no matter how commonplace. Some of these figures, like the janitor in *Eyewitness* who pretends to know a killer's identity to prolong his association with a female reporter, do contribute to their problems. The cartoonist hero of *Slam Dance* is initially short-circuited by his own disbelief which seems an occupational hazard. Even the self-righteous father in *Hardcore* must ultimately accept that his own stern behavior towards his daughter makes him partly responsible for her disappearance. Perhaps the noir credo is that no one, not even the women in *Narrow Margin* or *Someone to Watch Over Me*, is entirely blameless on some moral or ethical level when fate points the finger. That is certainly the underlying concept that inspired the first script of *The Bodyguard* (199?), which mixed the disturbed psychology of repressed siblings with ecology, feminism, professionalism, et al. Because the title character's self-awareness never transcends the tenuous allusions to *Yojimbo* or *Star Wars* to become a "dark past," an atmosphere of alienation or obsession never materializes. As in *Someone to Watch Over Me*, the concept of not being able to do one's job and be emotionally involved with a "client" cannot generate or sustain a noir tone alone. Similarly the preternatural overtones of the motiveless killer in *The Hitcher* (1986), like the murderous gasoline truck in Steven Spielberg's television movie, *Duel* (1971) are not neo-noir.

Along those lines, *Paint It Black* (1989) is also typical. After an opening scene in which police investigate an art theft, the protagonist is introduced: a sculptor who believes that he is being misled by his agent/mistress. He has two unusual encounters: a woman swerves to avoid a pedestrian and hits his car. He finds an injured man in alley and helps him home. He begins an affair with the woman; and when the young man comes by to thank him, he confides in him about his problems. Shortly after he breaks into his agent's office to verify that he has been cheating him, she is killed by someone else. It turns out that the new girlfriend is the daughter of a well-known art agent and that the killer is the young man, who is sexually fixated on the sculptor and wants to represent his work. Fearful of being incriminated and under threat from the young man, he can tell no one.

Such a story-line might work if the actors and filmmakers were less conscious of its unwieldy convolutions; but in a post-De Palma era, it takes more than visual and musical homages to Hitchcock to bring off such a movie. *Paint It Black* is only one low-budget variant of the miscues of *Shattered* or *Final Analysis*. *Call Me* has a female protagonist who mistakes an obscene caller for her boyfriend which leads her to a seamy bar where she witnesses the murder of a pusher in drag in the ladies' room. Such a plot needs more than elements from *Sorry, Wrong Number* or *Experiment in Terror* for success. *P.I. Private Investigations* (1987) attains a measure of impact by holding down the sheer volume of unfavorable circumstances, for, as in the classic period, one mischance can prove more than perilous enough. *Red Rock West* (1992), written (as was *P.I. Private Investigations*) and directed (as was *Kill Me Again*) by John Dahl uses the same technique. A drifter from Texas arrives in a small Wyoming town and is mistaken by a bar owner for another man from Texas hired sight unseen to kill his wife. The drifter not only takes the money and goes to warn the wife, but calmly accepts another sum from her to kill the husband instead. Just when the mischance is about to turn into a unforeseen profit, his car breaks down just outside of town.

Bad Influence (1990) is a new twist on the darkly humorous *The Devil Thumbs a Ride*. Using Rob Lowe as the manipulator turned killer and extortionist exploits the same iconic values as *Masquerade* but allows for a different type of ironic realization. Here the seductive elements are connected to power rather than sex, and the misled hero finds himself ensnared by his previously unrealized desire to control his own life. *Mortal Thoughts* has a similar theme involving two women. In this instance, also, one character is so much a participant in the other's perspective that their experience becomes a shared nightmare, one so palpably

real that memories may become distorted and flashback recollections may lie. The living nightmares of *Bad Influence* and *Mortal Thoughts* recall the oneiric mode of classic film noir. Both end with their respective male and female protagonists waiting to tell the police what really happened.

If there is an archetypal situation for victims of circumstance in neo-noir, it might be as the target of an obsessive, possibly deadly stalker in the manner of either version of *Cape Fear*. *Lady Beware* (1987), *Fear City* (1984), *Out of the Dark* (1988), *Scissors, Intimate Stranger, Sleeping with the Enemy* (all 1991)--in all of these films as in *Klute* the victims are women. The particulars do vary. One is already a fearful neurotic set up by her psychiatrist (*Scissors*). Another is fleeing her abusive husband (*Sleeping with the Enemy*). Several work in telephone sex (*Intimate Stranger, Out of the Dark*) and, like Bree Daniel, might be likelier to encounter deadly sexual deviates. Another works as a window dresser (*Lady Beware*) but is similarly plagued. Some of these women try to flee; most, to confront their tormentors. Some perish, but most survive. The results are mixed, but most, concentrating on the idea of suspense rather than the sense of disruption, fail to evoke a noir sensibility.

Criminal Law incorporates diverse elements without having recourse to extensive narrative complication. The premise is direct: an aggressive attorney successfully defends a client who is accused of a brutal rape and murder. After the not guilty verdict, the attorney learns that the client actually committed the crime. The character's motivations are also direct. Not only must the attorney blame himself for leaving a dangerous psychopath at large, but he would still be ethically compromised if he used information acquired within the context of attorney/client privilege against him. A version of the same dilemma confronts the assistant district attorney in *Presumed Innocent* (1990), for as he investigates the murder of a colleague with whom he had an affair, he finds that much of the physical evidence could incriminate him. In this picture and the earlier *Frantic* (1988), Harrison Ford's portrayals capture the edge between panic confronting circumstances beyond one's control and resilience in fighting to regain it.

What separates the moral problem of these attorneys, initially at least, from those in *True Believer* or *Suspect*, from courtroom drama, is the profundity of their error. The defense attorneys in *True Believer* and *Suspect* are idealists at heart, whose discovery of corruption within the system does imperil them, but whose faith in that same system is ultimately redemptive, particularly in *True Believer*. The protagonist of *Criminal Law* is closer to Frank Bigelow in his determined resolve to put things right. When his client threatens another woman with whom the attorney is emotionally involved, the web of circumstances closes and creates a quandary as dark as Vanning's in *Nightfall*. Like other neo-noir victims caught in such a web, thrashing about is futile. Only those able to find assistance manage to escape.

Liebestraum (1991) takes its name from an old song and its dreamlike style is as insistently imposed as the droning underscore. As in *At Close Range* cinematographer Juan Ruiz Anchia's hard light knifes though the images, both real and dreamed, to create a tangible fatality. The plot, which brings a celebrated young architect to a small town to meet his birth mother who is dying of cancer, turns on a deadly lover's tryst in a 50s-style department store. That scene is staged or remembered--the first of many narrative uncertainties--in the movie's opening sequence. Because the point-of-view may be either omniscient or subjective, whether the events of the scenes are actual or imagined is always in question. It is in the protagonist's flashbacks, where shafts of light seem to pierce passing hopper cars, that the style and sensation of the first sequence most impinge on the present; but its tone hangs over the entire film and welcomes the viewer to his nightmare.

When the architect begins an affair with the photographer wife of a college friend who is dismantling the department store building, the line between dream and reality, past and present is further blurred. The audience can fully empathize with the chance remark of the cab driver who takes the architect to the college friend's party: "You mind if I ask you a question? I feel like I know you. You on TV or what?" Squirming inexplicably in the back seat as patches of white and red light cut in and out of the frame, the architect's reply can only be an ambiguous "what." Because the entire film is suffused with an hallucinatory languor, seeming at times to move in slow motion, it not only tests the limits of photographic reality but of what the viewer will tolerate. By the time, the end credits arrive and a young girl plays "liebestraum" on the piano in an unlikely homage to *Guest in the House*, some points have been clarified, but most have not. This leaves *Liebestraum* as much a neo-Jungian, plastic-fantastic voyage as neo-noir.

Laura Burney (Julia Roberts) and obsessed husband Martin (Patrick Bergin) in Sleeping With The Enemy.

Gangsters, Pushers, Pimps, And Con-Men

As in the classic period, neo-noir does occasionally feature protagonists who are professional criminals. While the pitilessness of such characters remains constant, the other aspects, their greed, their thirst for power, their code of behavior have taken new turns. As a genre, gangster films can stand alone, imbued with their own expectations and iconic values; but, as was discussed in Appendix A, crossovers and connections with film noir remain.

While Coppola's *Godfather* series have often been cited by other commentators on neo-noir, those pictures exemplify the evolution of the gangster genre. Although they share an evocation of period with other films, like *The Untouchables*, their focus on the inner workings of criminal syndicates is unwavering. On the other hand, unlike "pure" gangster pictures from *The Brotherhood* to *Scarface*, part of the *Godfather* saga's appeal, particularly in the first and final parts, is the sense that Michael Corleone's criminal career was to some extent forced on him by outside events.

Even though the *Godfather* films never fully cross over

into the noir mode, other period films like *Miller's Crossing* (1990) may. If anything, *Miller's Crossing* stresses the question of ethics to the point of exaggeration. The musings of Johnny Caspar--"You double-cross once, where does it all end"--are a bit incongruous from one who teaches his killers to put "one [bullet] in the brain." The real enigma of *Miller's Crossing* is Tom Reagan. A gangster without a gun, his odd traits from attachment to his hat to fixation on his boss's "twist" could easily relocate him into a Western or a noir milieu. Of his character traits, the narrative asserts only that he has no heart. There are stylistic elements of *Miller's Crossing* that recall the classic period. Dark rooms where harsh sidelight bisects the actors' faces create a mood. Sequences from the tableaux of a boy and a dog finding a body in an alley or the tommy-gun battle accompanied by the strains of "Danny Boy" to the tilted angles and demented screams when Caspar bludgeons his own lieutenant to death all reinforce the sense of chaos. In the end, for all the dramatic impact of its set-pieces or the stylistic evocation of the noir underworld, *Miller's Crossing* leaves the viewer, like its protagonist, leaning against a tree in the middle of nowhere.

There are few capers in neo-noir. The careful plan gone awry by mischance in *The Asphalt Jungle* or *The Killing* becomes a disintegration in psychoses and recrimination in *Dog Day Afternoon* (1974). The bank robbery planned by disaffected Vietnam vets in *Special Delivery* (1976) is so logistically complicated that it falls apart from sheer inertia. Only the recent *Reservoir Dogs* uses a caper in a classic way; but even that is merely as a hub for other explorations. The figures in *King of New York* and *New Jack City* (1990) are more representative of the neo-noir criminal. Both films also feature portraits of policemen, whose antagonisms are much more forthright than in *Cry of the City* or even *The Big Combo. New Jack City* has its own Mr. Brown, who like Frank White in *King of New York* imagines that he is a servant of his oppressed community. As he explains to the vice cop who infiltrates his gang, killing is part of business not personal, a sentiment which echoes Sollezzo's excuse in *The Godfather* even before it becomes the motto in *Diary of a Hitman.*

Both these characters, who seem to be named by their skin color, have a point-of-view, however twisted. That "philosophy" becomes a mocking reply to the cops who try to rebuke them. For those cops facing this scorn, the temptation to cross the line is intensified. The fact that the police in *King of New York* take the law into their own hands while those in *New Jack City* almost do but stop short is less significant that the blurring of distinctions between cop and crook, the reaffirmation of Cleve's point in *Best Seller.* As Frank White sardonically confesses, "My feelings are dead. I got no remorse." For Frank and Nino Brown, the universe is born of injustice and sustained by fury.

Stylistically, both films recruit cultural indicators such as hip-hop, whether creating an insistent, chaotic buzz on the soundtrack in *New Jack City* or the occasional litany of death as in Jimmy Jump's rap in *King of New York.* Abel Ferrara's staging in the latter film not only creates killing scenes that are at once graphic and surreal but constructs sequences that manifest an awareness of abstract terror. A sequence at a theater which begins "within" the play is a subtle metaphor compared to the meeting between White's envoy and a Chinese gang. They discuss their antagonisms and demands in a private theater where the Asians watch Murnau's *Nosferatu*, either not noticing or not caring about how much they resemble the grotesque images projected on the wall. Throughout the film, Ferrara's relentless use of close-ups holding the figures in tight hard-lit frames creates a sense of deterministic constriction.

The pimps and pushers in films as diverse as *The Killing of a Chinese Bookie* (1976), *Year of the Dragon*, and *Eight Million Ways to Die* (1986) are characters which could only be implied in the classic period when production codes made drug addiction and prostitution unfit subjects. In the ten years between John Cassavetes' *The Killing of Chinese Bookie* and Hal Ashby's *Eight Million Ways To Die*, the sense of honor among thieves eroded completely. By using brutish character actors like Morgan Woodward and Timothy Carey to portray the cheap hoodlums who hound nightclub owner Cosmo Vitelli to kill the bookie in lieu of paying a gambling debt, Cassavetes suggests that life is cheap because killers are inept and grotesque. In *Eight Million Ways to Die*, the slick, evil pimp and pusher por-

trayed by Andy Garcia kills and tortures because he likes to. Dennis Hopper's performance as drug lord in *Midnight Heat* (1992) is a smarmy stereotype but the only anchor in a muddled narrative.

Seeing "working girls" and "candy men" for what they are in neo-noir changes the impact and the tone, as the violence and the sordidness in the milieu froth on the surface rather than simmer below it, perhaps the outrage of the authority figures from *Cop* to *New Jack City* becomes understandable if not acceptable. Outside of the Thompson adaptations discussed earlier and a few other titles, there are not many pictures which assume the criminal's point-of-view. *Tequila Sunrise* (1988) attempts it through the guise of a love triangle and old friends on opposite sides of the law, a common motif in the gangster genre. Portraying the racketeer as sincere and the detective as manipulating may seem novel on paper, but the film is merely perplexing, especially its romantic ending. *Pacific Heights* (1990) features a con-man and gigolo who exploits his landlords through a complicated narrative that seems designed to create menacing situations no matter how contrived.

Thief (1981) is director Michael Mann's antecedent to *Manhunter.* Like *Miller's Crossing* or the *Godfather* films, its perspective is wholly within the criminal underworld. Like Hill's Driver, Mann's Thief is a nonviolent specialist, a safecracker. Unlike the Driver, he has a name, Frank, but only a first one. In the neo-noir underworld such nonviolence and no last name are not protection. As Frank's mentor nostalgically observes when he visits him in prison, there is no sense of honor anymore in the big house or outside. On a narrative level, *Thief* is about betrayal, Frank's betrayal by the cops who beat him, by the mob types who exploit and extort him, by a thieves' code which he trusted. In that sense, the destruction and death which he effectuates at the conclusion are an outraged response. Mann's stylized treatment of the events, as Frank systematically demolishes his links with underworld, also suggests a redemptive ritual in the classic noir tradition.

For the grifters and con artists in *House of Games* (1987), *The Horseplayer* (1991), or *Night and the City* (1992) redemption is not an issue. In the earlier film, the con itself is the ritual. As the female psychiatrist who believes she has stumbled into their world discovers, they are like the scorpion in Mr. Arkadin's parable, they cannot help but con, it's their nature. The lack of perception by a psychiatrist who has studied and written about compulsive behavior may lack verisimilitude; but in the enclosed world of marks and cheats which writer/director David Mamet creates, misperception is the key to making a buck. Caught up in that illicit milieu and its freedom from responsibility is a giddy experience for the protagonist. Her outrage at betrayal is both the fury of a woman scorned and of a child deprived of her secret playground, motives quite different from if not opposite of Frank's in *Thief.* In that sense, her real crime at the film's conclusion also becomes ritual reversal. It is a full and final initiation into the noir underworld which fascinates her and makes the premise of her new book, "Forgive Yourself," disturbingly ironic.

Detective Nick Peretti (Judd Nelson) and "Scotty" Appleton make an arrest in New Jack City.

Cosmo Vitelli (Ben Gazzara) is threatened in The Killing *of a Chinese Bookie.*

"Viewed from the proper angle, all our lives are a little bit sordid." The Horseplayer puts a new twist on *Scarlet Street*. An artist has his girlfriend pose as his sister and seduce subjects for his surrealistic paintings. The latest victim is a "horseplayer" and a creature of habit in a very insular world: he works in a "box," a liquor store freezer compartment restocking the shelves. Filled with oppressive close-ups, *The Horseplayer's* twisted relationships are full of overtly symbolic behavior, as when the artist draws a scar on the girl's face with a china marker, while telling her "You're like a mirror to me. I can see myself reflected so clearly."

Superficially *Night and the City* is a straightforward remake moved from postwar London to contemporary New York. Its protagonist, Harry Fabian, is still a cheap hustler, still trying to muscle in on the fight game and conning money from Helen Nasseros with a forged liquor license. The changes, the missing characters, the rougher language, are relatively minor; but the tone is different. Widmark's Harry Fabian never was more than a hustler, an American in a strange country trying to turn a buck.

De Niro's Fabian is an attorney who admits to chasing ambulances in his own neighborhood: "I never been out of New York practically. One time I was gonna move to L.A. I wanted to be a talent scout, but..." Where Widmark's character seemed trapped by circumstances of time and place and driven by a need to score big, De Niro's seems to be where he is by his own choice looking for an easy buck because it's easy. Both Fabians make the same play and meet the same fate; but in the remake, the ironies, like the scams, are mostly off the mark.

Two modestly-budgeted pictures confront the issue of criminal "professionalism" most directly, *Diary of a Hitman* and *Reservoir Dogs* (both 1992). Although he is killer for hire, the title character of *Diary of a Hitman* more closely resembles John Hull in *Deep Cover* than the dozens of analogs in other neo-noir films. Unlike *Deep Cover*, the real irony of *Diary of a Hitman* may be unconscious in casting an African-American actor in a part not necessarily written for one. Also unlike Larry Fishburne in *Deep Cover*, Forest Whitaker does not bring an iconic signature to *Hitman*, does not suggest (there's no other way to put it) a "black" noir persona. His character, Dekker, is a throwback and the film's narrative style follows suit. The story unfolds as a flashback, a message which Dekker is leaving on his "booking agent's" answering machine, and his voiceover narration is used heavily throughout.

Early on, Dekker confesses to being troubled by his work and maintaining the illusion that "it's not personal." He even consults a psychiatrist, to whom he confesses the killings as "bad dreams." Because *Hitman* ultimately becomes a performance piece for Whitaker and Sherilyn Fenn as his last victim, Jain, most of these echoes of classic noir are left unexplored. Dekker's key comment is "I was a pro. A pro is a pro, right?" The answer from Mr. Pink in *Reservoir Dogs* is "a psychopath ain't a professional." From the perspective of the classic noir style and narrative, *Reservoir Dogs* is pointedly aware of a relationship to that tradition.

As was noted, the plot of *Reservoir Dogs* derives from the caper film. An organizer brings a group of otherwise unrelated criminals together for one job and keeps their true identities from each other with "colorful" names. The botched robbery itself is never seen, only its aftermath as the survivors come to the rendezvous point and argue over what happened and what to do now. Flashbacks within flashbacks create narrative layers that are both "traditionally" noir and endistance the modern view from identification with the criminal protagonists. Equally endistancing are slow motion optical effects and moments of grisly, self-conscious humor. The psychopathic Mr. Blonde might well be alluding to *Point Blank* when he confesses to being "a big Lee Marvin fan"; but his character grimly transcends the violence of that type of picture when he cuts off the ear of a police hostage and talks to it. In the end, *Reservoir Dogs* is also about self-immolation, but not just because the characters shoot each other in an absurd, quasi-parody of a Mexican standoff. There is an also existential justice in the fact that what may be Mr. White's one redemptive quality, his sense of loyalty to the severely wounded Mr. Orange, is also his undoing. That personal connection to a cohort who is actually an undercover cop is both human and, in the noir scheme of things, appropriately deadly.

The New Age P.I. and De-Tech Noir

If the 70s were a transitional period for the attitudes of police protagonists, a resolution was always available through their criminal nemeses. The world-weary attitudes of the private investigators in *Hickey and Boggs* and *The Long Goodbye* needed a similar counterbalance. Actors like Steve McQueen or Clint Eastwood, playing skip tracers in *The Hunter* and *Pink Cadillac* respectively, rely on genre expectations of rugged individualism closer to the Western than to film noir. The comic aspects of De Niro in *Midnight Run* outweigh the noir sensibility, but that film's use of technological props are part of a new tradition that goes back to Coppola's *The Conversation* (1974).

Harper and *The Drowning Pool* where Paul Newman impersonates Ross MacDonald's "Lew Archer," whose name comes from Hammett and attitude from Chandler, are the last vestiges of the classic gumshoe, working with just his wits and luck through plots as tangled as *The Big Sleep* or *Lady in the Lake*. By the time of the 1982 remake of *I, the Jury*, the consummate cynicism of Mike Hammer is drowned in a sea of car chases, automatic weapons, and naked woman that have very little to do with either Spillane's original or film noir.

Warren Oates in *Chandler* (1971) says, "I'm a relic"; and the picture is littered with shoe shine stands, bars with pool tables in them, and incongruous old cars that seem leftover from *The Big Sleep*. Chandler's attitude towards women--his last words are "You'll do"--is especially regressive. Despite the train rides and cameo appearances by Gloria Grahame and Charles McGraw, Chandler's clipped dialogue and conscious nostalgia ("that's Chandler, as in Raymond") are also part of the crossover of old-time private eyes into a new age. In that same year, another title character, John Klute, took a remarkably different slant from his technical methods to his attitude towards the woman he was following. The process is a continuing one and could ultimately lead to "contemporary" versions of *Blade Runner* or *Total Recall* where Philip K. Dick's visions of a noir future become reality.

Klute's techniques include wiretaps, recordings, and slides of typewriter fonts. Harry Caul in *The Conversation* is a technical legend. He is also a loner who guards his privacy with a paranoiac fervor. Caul takes satisfaction in being the best but is troubled by the current job eavesdropping on a couple as they walk in a crowded square. As he mixes a version of their conversation together, Caul cannot help but think that they may somehow be in danger. When a rival tells a story at a party of how Caul once bugged a crooked union official, who assumed his accountant had betrayed him and had his family murdered, Caul realizes that he "can't let it happen again." After his master tapes are stolen, Caul decides to try and warn the couple.

Coppola's visualization is keyed to the technology. The spaces of the loft which house Caul's operation are compartmentalized by grilled enclosures, so that even at the party characters are constantly framed against electronic equipment and metal. Caul's bus ride back from his girlfriend's apartment, which he leaves abruptly because she asks too many personal questions, is a long side angle close-up with his silhouette framed against the studded white-painted wall and dark window of the bus, his face isolated against stark manufactured forms. It is only in his traditionally furnished apartment, playing his saxophone, that Caul lets down his guard and reveals his humanity. Unlike *Chandler* where the riffling piano underscore contributed another layer of heavy nostalgia, David Shire's clean, jazzy measures are a contrast, an element of irregular, nonmechanized expression. It is in the final sequence, when Caul discovers that things were the opposite of what they seemed, that his insular world collapses. The final pan as he sits playing the sax after tearing up the wall and floors of his apartment searching for a bug reveal a disturbing metaphor. For in divulging the industrial underpinnings behind the walls and under the floors, Caul himself has created an apparition of technical ruin that undermines his belief system, an imagistic analog to Lecter in or out of his straightjacket.

If *Blade Runner*'s dark vision of Los Angeles of the future, where aerocars navigate through smog belts and the steamy streets are reserved for the lowest castes of a new society, is, like the name of the disco in *The Terminator*, "tech noir," then *Dead Again* (1991) is "karmic noir." As in *Liebestraum*, *Dead Again*'s characters are more than casually affected by a past crime. The elaborate "past life" recollections, shot in black-and-white, are at once a plot device and a stylistic commentary on the classic noir style. If the flashbacks, trances, and other hocus-pocus are a bit forced, they continue, via stylistic dissertation, to function as a form deconstructing itself as relentlessly as Harry Caul

prying up floorboards with a crowbar. In this sense, *Dead Again*, like the earlier period films *The Two Jakes* (1990) and *Hammett* (1983), is both a throwback and look back, a film which can recreate but never reenter a period. It is not coincidental that while they may not be as forthrightly comic as the parody *Dead Men Don't Wear Plaid*, the former two have more than a few moments of tongue-in-cheek humor. Where *Hammett* plods through with an enforced nostalgia, the self-indulgence in *The Two Jakes* is more humorous, as when the double-breasted, fedoraed form of Jack Nicholson is catapulted across the frame in slow-motion, a truer relic of classic noir than all of the old cars in *Chandler*.

Neo-noir has produced other "throwbacks," but almost always with a twist. An early example is *Shaft* (1971), which features a tough-talking, New York City-based private detective reminiscent of Mike Hammer. Shaft is hired to rescue the daughter of a black mobster from Italian kidnappers in a straightforward narrative. A few years later, *Black Eye* (1974) sends its rogue detective, suspended for killing a drug pusher, down a crooked trail of Jesus freaks and sexual deviants while investigating the murder of a silent movie star. Other "blaxploitation" titles of the early 70s often turned on a revenge motif in films such as *Slaughter, Black Gunn* (both 1972), and *Coffy* (1973).

More recently, the main character who pieces together the puzzling clues in a string of killings in *The Rosary Murders* (1987) is a skilled amateur *and* also a priest. The title figure in *V.I. Warshawski* (1991) is a wisecracking, two-fisted, gun-toting private dick, who happens to be a woman. *The Last Boy Scout* (1991) features a down-on-his-luck, ex-secret service agent, who's a sucker for home and family. For all his cynical veneer, when the private detective in that film asks the de-facto partner of his last adventure to formalize their relationship, one might imagine that was how the title figures in *Hickey and Boggs* got together; and the cycle begins again.

Kid Noir

As progenitors of "kid noir," one could cite *The Window* or *Talk about a Stranger*, films with youthful protagonists whom the adults won't believe. That same concept is the core of *Night Visitor* (1989). With films like *Out of Bounds*, adolescents are featured, but the problems they face are those of adults.

Bad Boys (1983) is as much a gangster film as kid noir, with rival factions and racial antagonisms in the manner of *Miller's Crossing* or *State of Grace*. *Run* (1991) posits a victim of circumstance with a *39 Steps* plot who just happens to be a college student. What separates them in terms of noir sensibility are the emotions of the characters. Sean Penn's performance in *Bad Boys* is as much about the painful transition to adulthood as it is about the codes of behavior imposed by gangs and prisons. His anger and catharsis are more proximate temporally and emotionally to James Caan in *Thief* than Bobby Driscoll in *The Window*. Patrick Dempsey's portrayal of a victim of circumstance

Detective Joe Hallenbeck (Bruce Willis) is confronted by hired killer Milo (Taylor Negron) in The Last Boy Scout.

in *Run*, on the other hand, has little progression. His character is not so much matured by the experience as he is delivered from it.

Dangerously Close (1986), *Gleaming the Cube* (1988), *Prime Suspect* (1989), and *Out of the Rain* (1990) are several more recent films having a story-line where a young man, usually still in high school, investigates the death of a friend or loved one. *Dangerously Close* and *Gleaming the Cube* are a bit like Bill and Ted's Excellent Mystery; but they do use the fact of an adolescent hero as plot keys. Ultimately *Dangerously Close* drowns in its own incoherences that have nothing to do with kid noir. *Gleaming the Cube* in which a ne'er-do-well skateboarder refuses to believe that his Vietnamese-born, adopted brother committed suicide introduces many other issues, from racial tensions to the judgment of teenagers based on their appearance. All of these are brushed aside in the rush to a climactic action sequence of boys on skateboards chasing crooks in cars on the freeway.

The narrative structures of *Out of the Rain* and *Prime Suspect* are more traditional but equally listless. As in *Gleaming the Cube, Out of the Rain*'s protagonist refuses to believe his brother's suicide. In an ending that involves a merry-go-round rather than skateboards, the psychopathic killer is revealed. That it is the girl whom both brothers loved should be a poignant disclosure rather than merely predictable; but the protagonists of kid noir may seem as empty of feeling as the most hardened adults.

Prime Suspect begins on a chilling note with a pre-credit sequence of a little girl witnessing her mother's murder. But the music box motif that carries through on the soundtrack over the credits is the end of that point-of-view. Plot entanglements follow: the girl is killed as a teenager and her boyfriend, who witnesses the murder from the center of a small lake, is so traumatized that he loses his voice. He is put in an asylum, where a woman psychiatrist is pressured by a supervisor (who, of course, turns out to be the killer) to certify him fit for trial. The woman's boyfriend is the local sheriff, so when the young man whom she believes innocent overpowers a sadistic, bisexual orderly and escapes, her loyalties are divided. After another murder and false leads involving a violent, sociopathic cook, who is another of the woman's patients (?!), and the PCP-ingesting restaurant manager who singlehandedly decimates the sheriff's department before the boy intervenes, the real killer is finally revealed, stabbed with his own knife, and, when he gets up for more, pushed out a window. This is the short version of a storyline that might have worked for Woolrich, but not here.

From *Union City* to *Final Analysis* neo-noir has outrageous or derivative plots in abundance; and those may be part of its wry outlook. What neo-noir does not have is the permeating influence of being part of the classic tradition rather than merely alluding to or recalling it. From the perspective of the 90s, a film like *Night Visitor*, which is most notable for such outlandish scenes as Elliott Gould and Michael J. Pollard dueling with shotgun and chain saw in a basement, seems likelier to evoke the gothic excesses of *Whatever Happened to Baby Jane* than *Talk About a Stranger*.

Whether a film such as *Drugstore Cowboy* (1989) is kid noir or neo-noir is debatable. The pathetic crime spree of its drugged-out protagonists seems to owe more to Gorki than Cain. The death by overdose and the impact of that event on its main character is the stuff of television movies. The ending suggests that the tentacles of the noir underworld are a factor; and the film as a whole uses the youth of its characters to enhance not obviate dramatic irony. Kid noir is not yet a rich tradition, but in certain aspects of these films and others such as *Guncrazy* (1992), which is discussed later, it holds promise for the future.

Still Out for Revenge

In the nearly twenty years since *Death Wish* (1974) nothing has superseded it as the prototype of the revenge film. The fact that its sequels have turned Paul Kersey to into a comic book vigilante conforms with the general line which revenge movies have followed. The original *Death Wish* may not be that far removed from *The Big Heat* or *Underworld U.S.A.*. Unlike the figures in *The Big Heat* or *Underworld U.S.A.*, Kersey never found the actual street punks who killed his wife and raped his daughter and ultimately no longer cared. *Death Wish* brought the audience as forcefully into the revenge seeker's point-of-view as any film of the classic period and then, in its own self-aware use of prop newspaper headlines and magazine covers, mocked its own viewers for empathizing with that point-of-view. Long before *Death Wish V*, when keeping track of the body count was literally impossible, a different kind of mockery was in question.

In their postface to *Panorama du Film Noir*, Borde and Chaumeton perceived certain aspects of the classic noir figure in James Bond. If Bond's sardonic, world-weary, and increasingly mechanistic actions are spun off from the alienation of the noir hero, the newest incarnations are the seemingly invulnerable and usually vindictive martial arts protagonists. The pictures starring Chuck Norris and more recently Steven Seagal and Jean-Claude Van Damme often hinge on a character seeking revenge for the murder or maiming of a close relative or friend. It would be hard to equate Van Damme's smirk or Seagal's perpetual scowl in films with such interchangeable titles as *Marked for Death* or *Hard to Kill* with a mask of alienation even if there were some doubt about their ultimate triumph over scores of leering antagonists. In the most recent Seagal vehicle, *Out for Justice*, the search for his partner's killer leaves an trail of battered and dead men and women that is not easily tallied. More significantly, although it has the same director as *Best Seller* and *Rolling Thunder* and *Lock-up*, John Flynn, *Out for Justice* is a Seagal picture before all else and unambiguous about his inevitable conquest. In certain films, Chuck Norris comes closer to an evocation of a noir persona, as in *The Hero and the Terror*, which uses flashbacks to flirt with the sometimes psychic relationship

between detective and serial killer probed more deeply in *Manhunter*. Perhaps the ultimate expression of the vengeful and alienated "super-hero" is the Australian-made *The Punisher*, based on a comic-book character and appropriately cartoonish. The same principle of invincibility creates an "anti-noir" iconic typing is at work in mainstream films and prevents characters portrayed by Sylvester Stallone in *Cobra* or *Lock-Up* or Arnold Schwarzenegger in *Raw Deal* from becoming neo-noir. *Rolling Thunder* (1977) involves a returning veteran, more specifically a Vietnam-war POW. As in scenarist's Paul Schrader's *Taxi Driver*, the expressions of the protagonist's maladjustment alternate between rage and despair, most memorably when he shoves his arm into a garbage disposal. Major Ranes' experiences as a prisoner of war and the brutal assault he suffers on his return would seem to give him more cause for alienation than Travis Bickle; but in numbing himself to torture, Ranes has detached himself from feeling. Unlike Bickle, the brutal hunt for his assailants is more an expression of personal than social or existential outrage.

The low-budget pictures, *The Killing Time* (1987) and *Jezebel's Kiss* (1990), both feature youthful revenge seekers and might alternately be considered as kid noir. The key to both stories is revealed in flashback: they have returned to obtain reprisal for the death of a parent which they witnessed as children. As it happens both films are situated in small California coastal communities, and the deaths are tied to land swindles. *The Killing Time*'s protagonist murders and takes the place of the small town's new deputy sheriff and features a performance by Kiefer Sutherland that evokes Jim Thompson's Deputy Lou Ford. *Jezebel's Kiss* has a title character who rides into town on a Harley, and a lead performance that is best left undescribed.

Ms. 45 (1981), *Positive I.D.* (1987), *Alligator Eyes* (1991), and *The Hand that Rocks the Cradle* (1992) all feature women seeking revenge. Like *Jezebel's Kiss* the productions are mostly low-budget; but unlike it, all rely on performances to help carry them through the occasionally outlandish plot twist. As it happens, the most recent and costliest of these, *The Hand that Rocks the Cradle*, is the least interesting. There is a decidedly disturbing tone in a narrative which features a deadly nanny, trying to steal the family of a woman who accused her doctor-husband of improper sexual advances, which led to his suicide and her miscarriage. This victim of circumstance-cum-psychopath who could be pathetic is merely vindictive; and overhead shots of her thrashing around in a bathroom stall make her look silly not angst-ridden. At the other extreme is *Alligator Eyes*, which features a blind woman who also witnessed a parent's murder as a child, which is also recalled in flashback. Her interaction with the trio of vacationers that pick her up hitch-hiking is more eccentric than noir in mood.

Ms. 45 also features a disabled victim, a mute who is raped twice in the same afternoon and kills her second attacker with an iron. Afraid that her actions will be misunderstood, she decides to dismember the body and discard the parts throughout the city, a procedure which makes her understandably apprehensive, so she takes the gun with her. Her wordless descent into psychosis leads her to gun down a string of real and imagined rapists before being killed herself. Like *Alligator Eyes* and *Ms. 45*, *Positive I.D.* is shot in a gritty, quasi-documentary style atypical of neo-noir. What sustains a noir ambience is the heroine's monomaniacal plan to murder the man who brutally raped her, creating a bar-girl alter ego but abandoning both new identity and family after exacting retribution.

If women are freer in the context of neo-noir to join men in seeking revenge, they are still portrayed as more prone to psychological imbalance after being victimized. *Ms. 45*'s reaction is no more violent than that of Major Ranes or Paul Kersey, no more demented than Travis Bickle's. The real difference is her fate.

Women in Film Noir

Recent neo-noir examples of women fighting prejudice in assuming traditional male roles are *Blue Steel, Impulse,* and *Love Crimes*. Not coincidentally, all three films are directed by women, Katherine Bigelow, Sondra Locke, and Lizzie Borden respectively. Women directors are also responsible for *Lady Beware, Stripped to Kill* (1987), *The Kill Off, Body Chemistry, Rush* (all 1990), *Past Midnight,* and *Guncrazy* (both 1992). Although it might surprise die-hard chauvinists, it is not coincidental either that most of these titles deal with women in law enforcement.

The earliest, *Stripped to Kill*, is probably also the lowest in budget. On a narrative level it employs elements of the stalker and the relationship between the male and female detectives; but its main thrust is a common motif in later pictures: the undercover cop who gets caught up in the cover identity. When compared to *Impulse* or *Rush*, getting too involved in the role of exotic dancer may seem trivial next to that of prostitute or drug user; and stripping to earn a living may be seamy but is certainly not criminal. In fact, the very seaminess, triviality, and the momentary desire, which grips the female protagonist to be as good or better than the other dancers, enhance the dramatic irony; and when her partner tells her to come to her senses, it also reveals the depth of his own prejudice.

In *Blue Steel* the question of role ambiguity begins with the title sequence as an androgynous form puts on a police uniform. In its early stages, *Blue Steel* develops the issue of prejudice against women in male roles merely as ironic undercurrent, as the main character (Jamie Lee Curtis) faces the prejudice not only of her colleagues but of her own family. Eventually the woman protagonist's struggle with an obsessive killer becomes the narrative focus, and the film becomes a conventional, quasi-noir *policier*. That its heroine uses violence to overcome her nemesis is less liberating than constricting, a validation of the usual male technique. There is much more of a noir undertone in Bigelow's *Point Break*, where through what is almost a parody of male-bonding an undercover F.B.I. agent begins to identify with the zen-surfer philosophy of the bank robbers he is trying to convict and irreparably compromises himself from an ethical standpoint.

Impulse also features a female cop (Theresa Russell). Here harassment is more overt in that she must deal with the sexual advances of a superior officer, but the core premise is that the central character, who works undercover as a prostitute, gets caught up in the lifestyle. When a man who picks her up in an up-scale bar is murdered, she conceals the fact that she was present. The film could be viewed as a gender-switching variant on pictures where male cops stray from ethical behavior, from *Where the Sidewalk Ends* to *Point Break*; but as with *Blue Steel*, the plot twists draw the film back to a traditional line. Less traditional is Lily Fini Zanuck's *Rush* (1991). Ostensibly focused on the male protagonist, who has been undercover and using drugs for much longer, much of his ethical deterioration is seen from the point-of-view of his newly recruited female partner. Clearly her entry into the twilight lifestyle is full of ironic transference, admiration for her more experienced and "dedicated" partner which becomes love, sympathy for the petty criminals she helps entrap which frustrate attempts to help save them, sexual and maternal instincts twisted and turned awry often by a sense of professional obligations. *Rush* is not about good and bad cops, categories into which the detectives' supervisor and the chief of police fall respectively, nor even about good/bad cops, as much as about a young woman almost destroyed by a rash of sometimes macho, sometimes pathetic, seldom heroic male values. Stylistically long takes and a rock-derived driving underscore may occasionally suggest a sense of entrapment or compulsion but may also give a techno-pop patina that can trivialize the subject.

Most recent are *Love Crimes* (1992) and *Past Mightnight*. The latter resembles pictures from *Deceived* back to *Suspicion* in its main plot: a social worker relocating a parolee who committed a particularly brutal murder is intrigued by inconsistencies in the case file. Of course, the inevitable liaison develops and the equally inevitable questions about whether the man did commit the crime and will or will not murder her. Despite the performance of Natasha Richardson and Rutger Hauer, *Past Midnight*'s now all-too-familiar "suspense" style undercuts much of the would-be noir mood. *Love Crimes*' troubled production history, with scenes re-shot and performances altered in post-production, make for an aesthetic result that is uneven at best; but *Love Crimes* is probably the most iconoclastic statement from a women filmmaker using elements of neo-noir. In pop-critical jargon, Lizzie Borden takes a cinematic ax and gives her audience forty whacks. From the first scene, which frames the narrative and in which Johnson, a black, female police lieutenant, makes a statement about a woman prosecutor, the point is things would have gone differently "if she wasn't a woman." The androgyny of the prosecutor, Dana Greenway (Sean Young), from her name to her hair style, is both subtler and more significant than in *Blue Steel*. As in *Impulse*, the protagonist's first scene involves an undercover officer posing as a prostitute; but in this case, Greenway is using her friend Johnson to trap fellow officers preying on hookers.

Ultimately, the narrative is encumbered with numerous

complications, most notably from the flashback-within-flashbacks to Greenway's apparent abuse by a father who kills her mother. On one level the focus of *Love Crimes* is the transference relationship between Greenway and the man she is personally pursuing, a charlatan who poses as a photographer to seduce and abandon women. The revelations in flashcuts that he resembles her abusive father who also locked her in a closet as a child are timed to create visual irony but blur the issue of women fighting male stereotypes. It is that stereotyping which, on another level, the two female protagonists are actually confronting and which in the end they can only overcome by acting unethically and destroying evidence. The narrative ironies are multiform. When Greenway changes her hair and her clothes and abandons her masculine style to "go under-cover" posing as a schoolteacher on vacation, she is falling back on those stereotypes, perhaps more consciously than the protagonists of *Blue Steel* or *Impulse* but entrapped by them nonetheless. When "David Hanover" (whose real name is never revealed) holds her hostage, his mind game is to convince Greenway that he can set her free of her inhibitions. When circumstances impugn her behavior, even Johnson assumes that she may have succumbed to the strange allure of her antagonist. The gender of the sexual dynamics may differ but the issues become much the same as in *Manhunter* or *Point Break*, law enforcers encountering the surprisingly complex criminal mind and misled by the charm of the sociopath.

The final irony is that it is Greenway's surprising resistance to that charm of his which traps "Hanover," makes him unable to go back to seducing others until he has settled his score with her. In the climactic scene, the flashes of his camera strobe violate her more profoundly that any physical assault, triggering more flashbacks and pulsing through the frame like an externalization of her psychic spasms. It is that strobe, which keeps going even after he is struck down and drops the camera, which is isolated in a final close-up, and which triggers a white optical that blots out the frame, that is the mechanistic metaphor for the social strictures that hinder Greenway, Johnson, and all the other women "victims." In that context, Greenway's burning the polaroids that "Hanover" had taken while he held her hostage becomes less an act of destruction than one of liberation from her dark pasts, both distant and immediate.

The Fugitive Couple

Sexuality in the noir cycle figured most prominently in the narratives of fugitive couples, the *amour fou* of *Gun Crazy* or the entrapment of *Where Danger Lives*. Surprisingly, few neo-noir films have followed this lead; and those that have seem more homages than self-sustained narratives. At the top of this list are *Blood Simple* (1986) and *Wisdom* (1987). The former may be more than another cross of Woolrich and Hitchcock--certainly there are many derivative scenes--but it is still less than authentic film noir. There is a deterministic aura that hangs over films like

Liebestraum and *Blood Simple*, much of it created by the low-key photography and austere production design. In the case of *Blood Simple*, the characters' halfhearted flight is just one component in an unsuccessful attempt to substitute style for substance. *Wisdom* sets itself up as a conscious parable of modern youth; but the conclusion, revealing that the entire narrative is daydream, is more parody than parable. As such it falls with Terence Malick's quixotic *Badlands* (1974) somewhere between black comedy and noir film.

This is not to say that homage cannot evoke the noir ambience, as is the case with Francois Truffaut's couple in his adaptation of Woolrich, *Mississippi Mermaid* (1970) or even when the fugitive couple goes to the land of Oz in *Wild at Heart*. In a film like *No Mercy* (1986), the fugitives are thrown together by circumstance not passion. The noir mood in *No Mercy* derives as much from the cop-protagonist's desire to avenge his murdered partner, as from the love interest that develops later. In fact, the narrative begins in the tradition of *The Big Heat* or *Dirty Harry* only to shift focus in midstream to that of the fugitive couple. *Breathless* (1983) is an indirect homage, by way of Jean-Luc Godard's original, that works as *amour fou* if not necessarily as film noir. The level of self-consciousness in *Breathless* is even higher than in *Mississippi Mermaid*. Where Truffaut is content to recreate the suspenseful long take

Monica (Valerie Kaprisky) and Jesse (Richard Gere) in Breathless.

Anita (Drew Barrymore) and Howard (James Le Gros) in Tamra Davis's Guncrazy.

from the rear seat of the car first used in *Gun Crazy*, *Breathless* has its lovers embracing behind the flickering screen of a movie theater that is actually showing *Gun Crazy*. Richard Gere's kinetic portrayal is in some ways closer to Cagney's Cody Jarrett in *White Heat* than either Belmondo or John Dall. Although *Breathless* actually reverses the male/female roles of *Gun Crazy*, it reaffirms that even in the 90s certain men and women still combine explosively "like guns and ammunition."

The newest twist on the fugitive couple was 1991's *Thelma and Louise*, two women on the run. The narrative setup, in which Louise shoots a drunken rapist who attacks Thelma, is straightforward enough; but the rest of the picture moves from set piece to set piece without developing a point-of-view. Certainly there are overtones of liberation in the women's behavior, whether it is Louise coming to terms with the troubled relationships of her past, Thelma discovering orgasm, or both of them blowing up the tankers of a leering trucker. Ultimately guns are not empowerment, and the women's decision to never be taken alive is at once an extravagant homage to an inap-

propriate desperado tradition as it pointlessly romanticizes their fate. In the noir tradition, fugitives die because they must, because fate, mischoice, or the burden of their crimes compels it. Occasionally there is a redemptive context to death; in Thelma and Louise, there is a freeze frame emblematic of futility.

Guncrazy (1992) is not a remake, but a mixture of the fugitive couple and kid noir concepts. The script posits a high-school girl, living in a trailer with her mother's abusive boyfriend while mom turns tricks in Fresno, who becomes pen pals and eventually marries a young ex-con with a fascination for handguns. The film echoes classic period titles in both visual imagery reminiscent of Lewis' picture in scenes of the couple locked in a parody of embrace while they shoot at cans and bottles and also in its use of ingenuous dialogue in the manner of *They Live by Night*. Because the characters themselves, Howard and Anita, are much more like Ray's Bowie and Keechie than those in Robert Altman's aimless, direct remake, *Thieves Like Us*, they naively romanticize their sordid dilemma, epitomized when they break into a house and dress up for a candle-lit dinner. Their inadvertent, grisly killing spree often becomes darkly comic. In a sense, perhaps the strongest allusion and the blackest joke is in the implicit parallel to *Tomorrow Is Another Day* as the mocking Freudianism of the Howard's high-caliber impotence and idealization of Anita despite her numerous sexual experiences are the 90s equivalent of Steve Cochran's character having gone through puberty in prison and fixating on a taxi dancer. When Anita fulfills her promise to Howard, who purposely walks into a hail of police gunfire, and glances up from his body to flatly intone, "He made me do it," the emotional transaction is much closer to *They Live by Night* than the quirky neo-realism of Altman's much more recent remake. There is, in fact, a different kind of transference at work, more akin to the love of kidnapper and victim in Robert Aldrich's bleak period picture, *The Grissom Gang* (1971) based on the celebrated novel, *No Orchids for Miss Blandish*. In a sequence such as when Howard and Anita bury their first victims, the high school boys who have tormented her, shot in one take with the camera looking up from inside a shallow grave at their silhouettes against the sky and ending as the last shovelful of dirt covers the lens, both the narrative and the grimly humorous style most closely echo *Badlands*.

Neo-B

Guncrazy, like its namesake and many recent productions, is also a low-budget picture. In the classic period, film noir may have been disproportionately involved with productions done on limited means. The original *Gun Crazy* as well as *Kiss Me Deadly, D.O.A., Detour* and score of others were all made on limited budgets and shooting schedules, which seemed to mesh well with the spare, ill-lit locales that typified the noir underworld. In many ways, the resurgence of interest in the noir style by low-budget filmmakers represents a return to the roots of the cycle. The

"B-film" or "programmer," the less costly productions of the 40s and 50s from the major studios such as *Thieves' Highway* (Fox), *Scene of the Crime* (MGM), or *Black Angel* (Universal), whose second-tier actors, writers, and directors were featured on the bottom-half of double bills, has transformed itself into the limited release and made-for-video efforts of the 80s and 90s. While other than theatrical production is not directly considered in this study, the low-budget feature, made at a cost ranging from less than $500,000 to $3 or 4 million, is; and it cannot be financed based on U.S. theatrical prospects alone but must follow the dictates of the foreign, video, and cable markets. Not only do those markets still prize the "action" picture or "thriller," whose spare narratives translate more easily for non-English speaking audiences, but the violence and compulsive sexual behavior that has always been part of film noir are more "saleable" than ever. Since many productions of the classic period were criticized at the time for their violence and unsavory themes, this is just another aspect of neo-noir's return to its roots.

Many of the films already discussed from *Guncrazy* to *After Dark, My Sweet* have worked within the range of limited budget and successfully evoked the noir tradition. In fact, in the worst of neo-noir, the failing is seldom because of monetary restrictions. *Hit List* and *Relentless* (both 1989) are two interesting productions directed by William Lustig, which both feature obsessive cops and victims of circumstance. The setup in *Hit List* is prototypical: a dying cop wants to put away a racketeer and has a protected witness to use against him. A hit man sent to eliminate him literally goes to the wrong address and wreaks havoc on the inhabitants of the house across the street. The twist has the innocent victim recruiting the witness to help retrieve his kidnapped son. What imbalances the picture are the performances, with Rip Torn, Lance Henriksen, and Leo Rossi performing at one level and Jan-Michael Vincent and Charles Napier at another.

If *Hit List* turns on the concept of the wrong address, the modus operandi in *Relentless*, where the killer chooses his victims by opening a page at random from the telephone directory, is even more arbitrary. Although Judd Nelson's portrayal of the psychopath brought the picture much opprobrium, his manic interpretation works within the context much as did Richard Basehart's in *He Walked by Night*. The ironies of the displaced cop (Leo Rossi) trying to prove himself and the old veteran (Robert Loggia) dying because of his carelessness are reinforced by the iconographic context of prior work, particularly Loggia's in *Jagged Edge*. In this sense, *Relentless* maximizes the impact of its limited means. While the flashbacks to the killer's abused childhood at the hands of his police officer-father may seem an "antique" device, it economically fulfills a necessary narrative function.

Not only is such economy the key in "neo-B," it helps generate a higher percentage of films that are rooted in the noir tradition without overwhelming it like such high-budget efforts as *Shattered* or *Final Analysis*. In copying *Fatal Attraction*, *Body Chemistry* must circumvent the obstacles of short schedule and less celebrated actors; and it certainly had no budget to re-shoot endings after test screenings. Despite that, the result is both stark and affecting. Without the clutter of freight elevators or operatic arias, *Body Chemistry* focuses relentlessly on the central premise; and when the "hero" is gunned down it arrives literally and figuratively at a very different conclusion. *Mortal Passions* takes types from the James L. Cain mold. Its plot--which turns fraternal loyalty into betrayal, literally buries bodies in the back yard, and has a would-be femme fatale fall in love--recalls more than anything in its final sequence Cain's ending to *Double Indemnity*, the novella.

In *Genuine Risk*, *Delusion*, even *Femme Fatale*--the titles are remarkably unambiguous. Equally remarkable is how well these pictures succeed in the noir tradition. *Femme Fatale* is the most complicated, recalling elements of *The Locket* and *Chicago Deadline*, in which a man marries a woman who turn outs to be someone else or, more accurately, someone suffering from a multiple personality disorder. Like the reporter in *Chicago Deadline*, her husband pieces her other lives together through a succession of leads, while dodging some street hoodlums whom another of her personalities swindled.

Delusion is more derivative of Al Robert's "mysterious force" in *Detour* or *The Hitch-hiker*. Embittered over his long-time employer's sale of the company, George O'Brien has embezzled a million dollars and is driving to Las Vegas with the cash in his trunk. He stops to help a young couple, Patti and Chevy, in a car that has swerved of the road, and they abduct him. O'Brien does not realize that the young tough has not been planning to kill him and does not know about the money, until Chevy kills someone else. Now O'Brien is a witness; and they dump him in the desert. He survives; but by the time he tracks them down, Patti has found the money and is preparing to go off on her own.

Stylistically both of these films benefit from the isolated or seedy locales, which permit a spare and stark visualization in the manner of *Border Incident* or *On Dangerous Ground*. As in *After Dark, My Sweet* or *Kill Me Again*, the desert locations in *Delusion* permit an arrangement of figures in a landscape that create a sense of otherworldliness or mirage (the film's original title), of acting out a bad dream without having recourse to optical effects or mood lighting. At the victim's trailer site or in a rundown motel at the aptly named Death Valley Junction, the isolated environment underscores the narrative tension in the classic noir manner. The last shot literally drives away from O'Brien as he stands looking off from the wounded Chevy lying in the dusty driveway and continues down the road for the entirety of the end credits. When that shot cedes to Patti, back to working as a showgirl and singing "These Boots are Made for Walking," the final note is both sardonic and deterministic.

Genuine Risk has the deadliest of the femme fatales and is the most traditional in approach. It is also the most self-conscious, as locations, lighting style, and art direction constantly underscore the sordidness of the milieu. Even

Crime boss Paul Hellwart (Terrence Stamp) in Genuine Risk.

more overt is the script which features lines like "A race-track is like a woman…a man weathers so much banality in pursuit of the occasional orgasmic moment." What distinguishes *Genuine Risk* is the offhandedness of its violence, where people are beaten or die painfully, abruptly and without reason in stagings that capture the disturbing tone of videotapes of real events from surveillance cameras. It also has some wryness and novelty in its plot and casting, most notably Terence Stamp as a 60s British pop-star turned petty mobster. Although deceived by this mobster's wife, the "hero," a hapless petty criminal and compulsive gambler named Henry, survives while just about everyone else perishes and goes back to the track for another play.

The plots of these pictures, all budgeted at under a million dollars, take only what they can afford from the classic tradition; but that is a considerable amount. All have enough money for a femme fatale, a hired killer or two, a confused and entrapped hero, an employer ripped off, a shakedown. Two have flashbacks, two have gang bosses, one a psychiatrist. The locations vary from Los Angeles to Las Vegas, from Death Valley to Big Bear Lake, but two have mansions, two cheap motels, two isolated rural locales where killers take their proposed victims. Like its antecedent, neo-noir and neo-B in particular makes few if any extravagant demands in terms of production value.

Foreign Influences and the Future of Noir

From its inception, American film noir has influenced other film industries and other media. One could argue that the French adaptations of Jim Thompson novels in the 80s, which have already been mentioned, go back to the source without the mediating influence of film noir. The very title *Serie Noire* suggests otherwise. This is certainly true of Francois Truffaut's adaptations of hard-boiled writers, which besides *Mississippi Mermaid* include *Shoot the Piano Player* from David Goodis and another Woolrich, *The Bride Wore Black*. Like *La Balance*, there is also more original work in the noir mode: Louis Malle's *Ascenseur pour L'Echafaud* in 1957; Claude Chabrol's *This Man Must Die* (1969) and *The Butcher* (1970); *The Outside Man* (1973), shot in Los Angeles with an American supporting cast by Jacques Deray; Jean-Jacques Beineix's *The Moon in the Gutter* (1983 also from David Goodis); and Luc Besson's *La Femme Nikita* (1991).

In the early 70s, Mike Hodges' *Get Carter* (1971) and *Pulp* (1972) combined elements of the British gangster tradition with film noir, which is carried on in *The Long Good Friday* (1982) and *The Krays* (1991). Before working in America in neo-noir, British directors Stephen Frears and Mike Figgis made *The Hit* (1984) and *Stormy Monday* (1988) respectively. Of course, our personal favorite must be *The*

McGuffin (1985), not because Charles Dance plays a film critic involved in a *Rear Window*-like discovery but because he pulls a prop copy of the first edition of *Film Noir* from his bookshelf. Actually, our personal favorite among new foreign noir is the Australian picture *Dead Calm*, but one good plug deserves another.

From television to comic books, film noir has exerted and continues to exert its narrative and stylistic influence. It has been a while since *Dragnet, The Naked City, Johnny Staccato, The Fugitive, Run for Your Life,* and *Harry-O* were on network television, but movies-of-the-week and cable originals frequently explore the noir terrain. After *Fish Police*, can it be long before an angst-ridden Bart Simpson skateboards down his own mean streets?

In neo-noir, titles again tell the tale: the words "kill" or "dead" or "black" appear in a score of them. Characters are deceived, shattered, and sleeping with the enemy, presumably with one eye open. The impersonal aspect of urban sprawl is the visual motif in the main title sequences of *New Jack City, V.I. Warshawski,* and *Run*, which feature helicopter shots sweeping over New York, Chicago, and Boston respectively. Echoes of the classic period from its undercurrent of despair to its the dark visual style continue to manifest themselves in other types of films, in political thrillers from *Parallax View* and *Winter Kills* to *JFK*, in the surreal *Blue Velvet*, the docu-drama *Henry, Portrait of a Serial Killer*, or the big-budget, comic book *Batman*.

The last few years have seen the greatest resurgence of interest in the themes and styles of film noir since the "classic" period. Many of these motion pictures, but not all, would have met the criteria in our original selection process for the main body of this book. If film noir is no longer *the* American style, certainly no other movement has emerged to replace it. And, unless filmmakers discover another mirror to hold up to American society, none ever will.

2. Filmography of Neo-Noir

After Dark, My Sweet. (Avenue Pictures, 1990). Produced by Robert Redlin and Ric Kidney. Directed by James Foley. Script by Robert Redlin and James Foley, based on the novel by Jim Thompson. Director of Photography, Mark Plummer. Production Designer, David Brisbin. Music, Maurice Jarre. Editor, Howard Smith. Starring Jason Patric (Collie), Rachel Ward (Fay), Rocky Giordani (Bert), Bruce Dern (Uncle Bud), Thomas Wagner (Counterman), George Dickerson (Doc Goldman). 114 minutes.

Against All Odds. (Columbia, 1984). Produced by Taylor Hackford and William S. Gilmore. Directed by Taylor Hackford. Script by Eric Hughes, based on [uncredited] Daniel Mainwaring's novel, *Build My Gallows High*. Executive Producer, Jerry Bick. Director of Photography, Donald Thorin. Production Designer, Richard James Lawrence; Gene Rudolf, consultant. Music, Michel Colombier, Larry Carlton. Editors, Fredric Steinkamp, William S. Steinkamp. Starring Rachel Ward (Jessie Wyler), Jeff Bridges (Terry Brogan), James Woods (Jake Wise), Alex Karras (Hank Sully), Jane Greer (Mrs. Wyler), Richard Widmark (Ben Caxton), Dorian Harewood (Tommy), Swoosie Kurtz (Edie). 125 minutes.

Alligator Eyes. (Castle Hill, 1990). Produced by John Feldman and Ken Schwenker. Directed by John Feldman. Script by John Feldman. Director of Photography, Todd Crockett. Production Designer, Jeff Tandy. Music, Sheila Silver. Editor, John Feldman, Cynthia Rogers, Mike Frisino. Starring Annabelle Larsen (Pauline), Roger Kabler (Robbie), Mary McLain (Marjorie), Allen McCullogh (Lance). 95 minutes.

Another 48 Hours. (Lawrence Gordon/Paramount, 1990). Produced by Lawrence Gordon and Robert D. Wachs. Directed by Walter Hill. Script by John Fasano, Jeb Stuart, and Larry Gross. Director of Photography, Matthew F. Leonetti. Production Designer, Joseph C. Nemec, III. Music, James Horner. Editor, Freeman Davies, Carmel Davies, Donn Aron.Starring Eddie Murphy (Reggie Hammond), Nick Nolte (Jack Cates), Brion James (Ben Kehoe), Kevin Tighe (Blake Wilson), Ed O'Ross (Frank Cruise), David Anthony Marshall (Willie Hickok), Bernie Casey (Kirkland Smith). 95 minutes.

At Close Range. (Hemdale/Orion, 1986). Produced by Elliott Lewitt and Don Guest. Directed by James Foley. Script by Nicholas Kazan, based on a story by Kazan and Lewitt. Director of Photography, Juan Ruiz Anchia. Production Designer, Peter Jamison. Music, Patrick Leonard. Editor, Howard Smith. Starring Sean Penn (Brad Whitewood Jr.), Christopher Walken (Brad Sr.), Christopher Penn (Tommy), Mary Stuart Masterson (Terry), Millie Perkins (Julie), Eileen Ryan (Grandma), Tracey Walter (Patch). 115 minutes.

Atlantic City. (Paramount, 1981). Produced by Denis Heroux. Directed by Louis Malle. Script by John Guare. Director of Photography, Richard Ciupka. Production Designer, Anne Pritchard. Music, Michel Legrand. Editor, Suzanne Baron. Starring Burt Lancaster (Lou), Susan Sarandon (Sally), Kate Reid (Grace), Michel Piccoli (Joseph), Hollis McLaren (Chrissie), Robert Joy (Dave), Al Waxman (Alfie). 104 minutes.

Bad Boys. (EMI/Universal, 1983). Produced by Robert Solo. Directed by Richard Rosenthal. Script by Richard Dilello. Director of Photography, Bruce Surtees, Donald Thorin. Production Designer, J. Michael Riva. Music, Bill Conti. Editor, Anthony Gibbs. Starring Sean Penn (Mick), Reni Santoni (Ramon Herrera), Esai Morales (Paco), Jim Moody (Gene Daniels), Eric Gurry (Horowitz), Clancy Brown (Viking), Ally Sheedy (J.C.). 123 minutes.

Bad Influence. (Epic Prods., 1990). Produced by Steve Tisch. Directed by Curtis Hanson. Script by David Koepp. Director of Photography, Robert Elswit. Production Designer,

Ron Foreman. Music, Trevor Jones. Editor, Bonnie Koehler. Starring Rob Lowe (Alex), James Spader (Michael Boll), Tony Maggio (Patterson), Christian Clemenson (Pismo Boll), Lisa Zane (Claire). 110 minutes.

Basic Instinct. (Carolco/TriStar, 1992). Produced by Alan Marshall. Directed by Paul Verhoeven. Script by Joe Eszterhas and Gary Goldman. Executive Producer, Mario Kassar. Director of Photography, Jan De Bont. Production Designer, Terence Marsh. Music, Jerry Goldsmith. Editor, Frank J. Urioste. Starring Michael Douglas (Nick Curran), Sharon Stone (Catherine Tramell), George Dzunda (Gus Moran), Jeanne Tripplehorn (Dr. Beth Garner), Leilani Sarelle (Roxy), Dorothy Malone (Hazel Dobkins). 123 minutes.

The Bedroom Window. (De Laurentiis, 1987). Produced by Martha Schumacher. Direction and Script by Curtis Hanson, based on the novel, *The Witness,* by Anne Holden. Executive Producer, Robert Towne. Director of Photography, Gil Taylor. Production Designer, Ron Foreman. Music, Michael Shrieve and Patrick Gleeson. Editor, Scott Conrad. Starring Steve Guttenberg (Terry Lambert), Elizabeth McGovern (Denise), Isabelle Huppert (Sylvia), Paul Shenar (Collin), Carl Lumbly (Quirk), Wallace Shawn (Attorney), Brad Greenquist (Henderson). 112 minutes.

Best Seller. (Hemdale/Orion, 1987). Produced by Carter De Haven. Directed by John Flynn. Script by Larry Cohen and [uncredited] John Flynn. Director of Photography, Fred Murphy. Production Designer, Gene Rudolf. Music, John Ferguson. Editor, David Rosenbloom. Starring James Woods (Cleve), Brian Dennehy (Dennis Meechum), Victoria Tennant (Roberta), Allison Balson (Holly), Paul Shenar (Madlock). 95 minutes.

Betrayed. (MGM/UA, 1988). Produced by Irwin Winkler. Directed by Constantin Costa-Gavras. Script by Joe Eszterhas. Director of Photography, Patrick Blossier. Production Designer, Patrizia Von Brandenstein. Music, Bill Conti. Editor, Joelle Van Effenterre. Starring Debra Winger (Katie Philips/Cathy Weaver), Tom Berenger (Gary Simmons), John Heard (Michael Carnes), Betsey Blair (Gladys Simmons), John Mahoney (Shorty), Ted Levine (Wes), Jeffrey DeMunn (Flynn). 123 minutes.

The Big Easy. (Kings Road/Universal, 1987). Produced by Stephen Friedman. Directed by Jim McBride. Script by Daniel Petrie Jr. Director of Photography, Afonso Beato. Production Designer, Jeannine Claudia Oppewall. Music, Brad Fiedel. Editor, Mia Goldman. Starring Dennis Quaid (Remy McSwain), Ellen Barkin (Anne Osborne), Ned Beatty (Jack Kellom), John Goodman (Andre De Soto), Lisa Jane Persky (McCabe). 108 minutes.

The Big Sleep. (United Artists, 1978). Produced by Elliott Kastner and Michael Winner. Direction and Script by Michael Winner, based on the novel by Raymond Chand-

ler. Director of Photography, Robert Paynter. Music, Jerry Fielding. Editor, Freddie Wilson. Starring Robert Mitchum (Philip Marlowe), Sarah Miles (Charlotte), Oliver Reed (Eddie Mars), Richard Boone (Canino), Candy Clark (Camilla), Joan Collins (Agnes), James Stewart (Sherwood). 100 minutes.

Black Eye. (Warner Bros., 1974). Produced by Pat Rooney. Directed by Jack Arnold. Script by Mark Haggard and Jim Martin, based on the novel *Murder on the Wild Side* by Jeff Jacks. Director of Photography, Ralph Woolsey. Production Designers, Chuck Pierce, John Rozman. Music, Mort Garson. Editor, Gene Ruggiero. Starring Fred Williamson (Stone), Rosemary Forsyth (Miss Francis), Teresa Graves (Cynthia), Richard Anderson (Dole), Richard X. Slattery (Bowen). 98 minutes.

Black Rain. (Paramount, 1989). Produced by Stanely R. Jaffe, Sherry Lansing. Directed by Ridley Scott. Script by Craig Bolotin, Warren Lewis. Director of Photography, Jan De Bont. Production Designer, Norris Spencer. Music, Hans Zimmer. Editor, Tom Rolf. Starring Michael Douglas (Nick), Andy Garcia (Charlie), Ken Takakura (Masahiro), Kate Capshaw (Joyce), Yusaku Matsuda (Sato), Shigeru Koyama (Ohari). 125 minutes.

Black Widow. (20th Century-Fox, 1987). Produced by Harold Schneider. Directed by Bob Rafelson. Script by Ronald Bass. Director of Photography, Conrad Hall. Production Designer, Gene Callahan. Music, Michael Small. Editor, John Bloom. Starring Debra Winger (Alexandra), Theresa Russell (Catharine), Sami Frey (Paul), Dennis Hopper (Ben), Nicol Williamson (William), Terry O'Quinn (Bruce), James Hong (Shin), Diana Ladd (Etta). 103 minutes.

Blood Simple. (Circle Releasing/Skouras, 1984). Produced by Ethan Coen. Directed by Joel Coen. Script by Ethan Coen and Joel Coen. Executive Producer, Daniel Bacaner. Director of Photography, Barry Sonnenfeld. Production Designer, Jane Musky. Music, Caster Burwell. Editors, Roderick Jaynes and Don Wiegmann. Starring John Getz (Ray), Frances McDormand (Abby), Dan Hedaya (Julian), M. Emmet Walsh (Private Detective), Samm-Art Williams (Meurice). 96 minutes

Blue Desert. (Academy Entertainment, 1992). Produced by David Andrew Peters. Directed by Bradley Battersby. Script by Arthur Collis and Bradley Battersby. Executive Producers, Joel Soisson, Michael S. Murphey. Director of Photography, Paul Murphy. Production Designer, Michael T. Perry. Music, Joel Goldsmith. Editor, Debra Bard. Craig Sheffer (Randall Atkins), D.B. Sweeney (Steve Smith), Courteney Cox (Lisa Roberts). 93 minutes.

Blue Steel. (MGM, 1990). Produced by Edward R. Pressman and Oliver Stone. Directed by Kathryn Bigelow. Script by Kathryn Bigelow and Eric Red. Director of Photography,

Remy McSwain (Dennis Quaid, left) confers with his eccentric lawyer, Lamar Parmentel (Charles Ludlam, Jr.) in The Big Easy.

Amir Mokri. Production Designer, Toby Corbett. Music, Brad Fiedel. Editor, Lee Percy. Starring Jamie Lee Curtis (Megan Turner), Ron Silver (Eugene Hunt), Clancy Brown (Nick Mann), Elizabeth Pena (Tracy Perez), Louise Fletcher (Shirley Turner), Philip Bosco (Frank Turner), Kevin Dunn (Stanley Hoyt). 101 minutes.

Body Chemistry. (Concorde, 1990). Produced by Alida Camp. Directed by Kristine Peterson. Script by Jackson Barr. Director of Photography, Phedon Papamichael. Music, Terry Plumeri. Production Designer, Gary Randall. Editor, Nina Gilberti. Starring Marc Singer (Tom), Lisa Pescia (Claire), Mary Crosby (Marlee), David Kagen (Freddie), H. Bradley Barneson (Jason), Doreen Alderman (Kim). 85 minutes.

The Bodyguard. (Warner Bros., 1992). Produced by Lawrence Kasdan, Jim Wilson, and Kevin Costner. Directed by Mick Jackson. Script by Kasdan. Director of Photography, Andrew Dunn. Production Designer, Jeffrey Beecroft. Editor, Richard A. Harris. Starring Kevin Costner (Farmer), Whitney Houston (Rachel), Gary Kemp (Shelley), Bill Cobbs, Michele Lamar Richards.

Body Heat. (Ladd Co./Warner Bros., 1981). Produced by

Fred T. Gallo. Direction and Script by Lawrence Kasdan. Director of Photography, Richard H. Kline. Production Designer, Bill Kenney. Music, John Barry. Editor, Carol Littleton. Starring William Hurt (Ned Racine), Kathleen Turner (Matty Walker), Richard Crenna (Edmund Walker), Ted Danson (Peter Lowenstein), J.A. Preston (Oscar Grace), Mickey Rourke (Teddy Lewis). 118 minutes.

The Border. (Universal, 1982). Produced by Edgar Bronfman. Directed by Tony Richardson. Script by Deric Washburn, Walon Green, and David Freeman. Director of Photography, Ric Waite, Vilmos Zsigmond. Music, Ry Cooder. Editor, Robert K. Lambert. Production Designer, Toby Rafelson. Starring Jack Nicholson (Charlie), Harvey Keitel (Cat), Valerie Perrine (Marcy), Warren Oates (Red), Elpidia Carrillo (Maria), Shannon Wilcox (Savannah), Manuel Viescas (Juan). 109 minutes.

Breathless. (Orion, 1983). Produced by Martin Erlichman. Directed and Written by Jim McBride. Executive Producer, Keith Addis. Director of Photography, Richard H. Kline. Production Designer, Richard Sylbert. Music, Jack Nitzsche. Editor, Rob Estrin. Richard Gere (Jesse), Valerie Kaprisky (Monica), Art Metrano (Birnbaum), John P. Ryan (Parmental). 100 minutes.

Cape Fear. (Amblin/Cappa/Tribeca/Universal, 1991). Produced by Barbara De Fina. Directed by Martin Scorsese. Script by Wesley Strick, based on a screenplay by James R. Webb and *The Executioners* by John D. MacDonald. Director of Photography, Freddie Francis. Production Designer, Henry Bumstead. Music, Elmer Bernstein, Bernard Herrmann. Editor, Thelma Schoonmaker. Starring Robert De Niro (Max Cady), Nick Nolte (Sam Bowden), Jessica Lange (Leigh Bowden), Juliette Lewis (Danielle Bowden), Joe Don Baker (Claude Kersek), Robert Mitchum (Lt. Elgart), Gregory Peck (Lee Heller). 130 minutes.

Call Me. (Vestron, 1988). Produced by John Quill and Kenneth Martel. Directed by Sollace Mitchell. Script by Karyn Kay. Director of Photography, Zoltan David. Production Designer, Steve McCabe. Music, David Frank. Editor, Paul Fried. Starring Patricia Carbonneau (Anna), Steven McHattie (Jellybean), Boyd Gaines (Bill), Sam Freed (Alex), Patti D'Arbanville (Cori), Steve Buscemi (Switchblade). 93 minutes.

Cat Chaser. (Vestron, 1989). Produced by Peter Davis. Directed by Abel Ferrara. Script by Elmore Leonard, Jim Borrelli, and Alan Sharpe, based on Leonard's novel. Director of Photography, Anthony Richmond. Production Designer, Dan Leigh. Music, Chick Corea. Editor, Tim Kennedy. Starring Peter Weller (George Moran), Kelly McGillis (Mary de Boya), Charles Durning (Jiggs Scully), Frederic Forrest (Nolan Tyner), Tomas Milan (Andres de Boya), Juan Fernandez (Rafi). 90 minutes.

Chandler. (MGM, 1971). Produced by Michael S. Laughlin. Directed by Paul Magwood. Script by John Sacret Young, based on a story by Magwood. Director of Photography, Alan Stensvold. Music, George Romanus. Editor, Richard Harris. Starring Warren Oates (Chandler), Leslie Caron (Katherine), Alex Dreier (Carmady), Gloria Grahame (Selma), Scatman Crothers (Smoke), Royal Dano (Sal), Charles McGraw (Bernie Oakman). 85 minutes.

Criminal Intent. (Promark, 1992). Produced by Ashok Amritraj and Steve Beswick. Directed by Woth Ketter. Script by Michael Potts. Executive Producers, Carol M. Rossi, Barry Collier. Director of Photography, Doyle Smith. Music, Michael Linn. Editor, Kert Van Der Meulen. Starring Robert Davi (Walker), Joan Severance (Melissa), Jack Scalia (Yarnell), James Russo (Tanner). 103 minutes.

Criminal Law. (Hemdale/TriStar, 1989). Produced by Robert Maclean, Hilary Heath, and Ken Cord. Directed by Martin Campbell. Script by Mark Kasdan. Director of Photography, Philip Meheux. Production Designer, Curtis Schnell. Music, Jerry Goldsmith. Editor, Chris Wimble. Starring Gary Oldman (Ben Chase), Kevin Bacon (Martin Thiel), Karen Young (Ellen Faulkner), Joe Don Baker (Detective Mesel), Tess Harper (Detective Stillwell). 117 minutes.

The Conversation. (Paramount, 1974). Produced, written, and directed by Francis Ford Coppola. Co-producer, Fred Roos. Director of Photography, Bill Butler. Production Designer, Dean Tavoularis. Music, David Shire. Editors, Walter Murch, Richard Chew. Starring Gene Hackman (Harry Caul), John Cazale (Stan), Allen Garfield (Bernie Moran), Frederic Forrest (Mark), Cindy Williams (Ann), Teri Garr (Amy), Harrison Ford (Martin Stett), Michael Higgins (Paul). 113 minutes.

Cop. (Atlantic, 1988). Produced by James B. Harris and James Woods. Directed and Written by James B. Harris. Director of Photography, Steven Dubin. Production Designer, Gene Rudolf, Music, Michel Colombier. Editor, Anthony Spano. Starring James Woods (Lloyd Hopkins), Lesley Ann Warren (Kathleen McCarthy), Charles Durning (Dutch Peltz), Charles Haid (Delbert "Whitey" Haines), Raymond J. Barry (Capt. Gaffney). 110 minutes.

Dangerously Close. (Cannon, 1986). Produced by Harold Sobel. Directed by Albert Pyun. Script by Scott Fields, John Stockwell, and Marty Ross. Director of Photography, Walt Lloyd. Production Designer, Marcia Hinds. Music, Michael McCarty. Editor, Dennis O'Connor. Starring John Stockwell (Randy), J. Eddie Peck (Donny), Carey Lowell (Julie), Bradford Bancroft (Krooger), Don Michael Paul (Ripper). 92 minutes.

The Dark Wind. (New Line, 1992). Produced by Patrick Markey. Directed by Errol Morris. Executive Producers, Robert Redford, Bonni Lee. Script by Eric Bergren, Neal Jiminez, and Mark Horowitz, based on novels by Tony Hillerman. Director of Photography, Stefan Czapsky. Production Designer, Ted Bafaloukos. Music, Michel Colombier. Editor, Freeman Davies. Starring Lou Diamond Philips (Officer Jim Chee), Fred Ward (Lt. Joe Leaphorn), Gary Farmer (Albert "Cowboy" Dashee), John Karlen (Jake West), Lance Baker (Mr. Archer), Arlene Bowman (Edna), Jane Loranger (Gail Pauling). 109 minutes.

Dead Again. (Paramount/Mirage, 1991). Produced by Lindsay Doran, Charles H. Maguire, and Dennis Feldman. Directed by Kenneth Branagh. Script by Scott Frank. Director of Photography, Matthew Leonetti. Production Designer, Tim Harvey. Music, Patrick Doyle. Editor, Peter E. Berger. Starring Kenneth Branagh (Mike Church/Roman Strauss), Emma Thompson (Grace/Margaret Strauss), Andy Garcia (Gary Baker), Derek Jocobi (Franklyn Madson), Robin Williams (Dr. Carlisle), Hanna Schygulla (Inga). 111 minutes.

Dead-Bang. (Lorimar/Warner Bros., 1989). Produced by Steve Roth. Directed by John Frankenheimer. Script by Robert Foster. Director of Photography, Gerry Fisher. Production Designer, Ken Adam. Music, Gary Chang. Editor, Robert F. Shugrue. Starring Don Johnson (Jerry Beck), Penelope Ann Miller (Linda), William Forsythe (Arthur

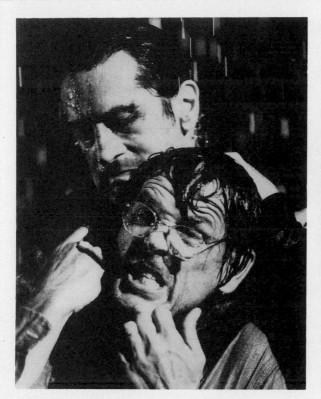 

Ex-convict Max Cady (Robert De Niro) exacts revenge on his former attorney Sam Bowden (Nick Nolte) in Martin Scorsese's 1991 remake of Cape Fear. *Leigh Bowden (Jessica Lange) comforts Danielle (Juliette Lewis).*

Kressler), Bob Balaban (Elliot Welby), Frank Military (Bobby Burns), Tate Donovan (John Burns). 105 minutes.

Death Wish. (De Laurentiis/Paramount, 1974). Produced by Hal Landers, Bobby Roberts, and Michael Winner. Director, Michael Winner. Script by Wendell Mayes, based on the novel by Brian Garfield. Director of Photography, Arthur J. Ornitz. Production Designer, Robert Gundlach. Music, Herbie Hancock. Editor, Bernard Gribble. Charles Bronson (Paul Kersey), Hope Lange (Joanna Kersey), Vincent Gardenia (Frank Ochoa), Steven Keats (Jack Toby), William Redfield (Sam Kreutzer), Stuart Margolin (Aimes Jainchill). 93 minutes.

Deceived. (Touchstone/Silver Screen Partners IV, 1991). Produced by Michael Finnell, Wendy Dozoretz, Ellen Collett. Directed by Damian Harris. Script by Donoghue and Derek Saunders. Director of Photography, Jack N. Green. Production Designer, Andrew McAlpine. Music, Thomas Newman. Editor, Neil Travis. Starring Goldie Hawn (Adrienne), John Heard (Jack), Robin Bartlett (Charlotte), Ashley Peldon (Mary), Tom Irwin (Harvey). 103 minutes.

Deep Cover. (New Line, 1992). Produced by Pierre David and Henry Bean. Directed by Bill Duke. Script by Michael Tolkin and Henry Bean. Executive Producer, David Streit. Director of Photography, Bojan Bazelli. Production Designer, Pam Warner, Music, Michael Colombier. Editor, John Carter. Starring Larry Fishburne (John Hull), Jeff Goldblum (David Jason), Victoria Dillard (Betty), Clarence Williams III (Taft). 112 minutes.

Delusion. (Cineville, 1991). Produced by Daniel Hassid. Directed by Carl Colpaert. Script by Carl Colpaert and Kurt Voss. Director of Photography, Geza Sinkovics. Production Designer, Ilkido Toth. Music, Barry Adamson. Editor, Mark Allan Kaplan. Starring Jim Metzler (George O'Brien), Jennifer Rubin (Patti), Kyle Secor (Chevy), Jerry Orbach (Larry). 100 minutes.

Desperate Hours. (DeLaurentiis/MGM, 1990). Produced by Dino De Laurentiis and Michael Cimino. Directed by Michael Cimino. Script by Lawrence Konner, Mark Rosenthal, Joseph Hayes, based on the novel by Joseph Hayes. Director of Photography, Doug Milsome. Production

Kelly Lynch portrays the modern femme fatale *opposite Mickey Rourke in* Desperate Hours.

Designer, Victoria Paul. Music, David Mansfield. Editor, Peter Hunt. Starring Mickey Rourke (Michael Bosworth), Anthony Hopkins (Tim Cornell), Lindsay Crouse (Chandler), Kelly Lynch (Nancy Brewers), Elias Koteas (Willy Bosworth), David Morse (Albert). 105 minutes.

The Detective. (20th Century-Fox, 1968). Produced by Aaron Rosenberg. Directed by Gordon Douglas. Script by Abby Mann based on the novel by Roderick Thorp. Director of Photography, Joe Biroc. Production Designer, Jack Martin Smith, William Creber. Music, Jerry Goldsmith. Editor, Robert Simpson. Starring Frank Sinatra (Joe Leland), Lee Remick (Karen Leland), Ralph Meeker (Lt. Curran), Jack Klugman (Dave Schoenstein), Horace McMahon (Farrell), Lloyd Bochner (Dr. Roberts). 114 minutes.

Diary of a Hitman. (Vision, 1992). Produced by Amin Q. Chaudhri. Directed by Roy London. Script by Kenneth Pressman, based on his play, "Insider's Price." Executive Producer, Mark Damon. Director of Photography, Yuri Sokol. Music, Michel Colombier. Editor, Brian Smedley-Ashton. Starring Forest Whitaker (Dekker), Sherilyn Fenn (Jain), Seymour Cassel (Koenig), Lewis Smith (Zidzyk), John Bedford-Lloyd (Dr. Jamison), Sharon Stone (Kiki), James Belushi (Shandy), Lois Chiles (Sheila), Wayne Crawford (Wallace), Jimmy Butler (Eddie). 91 minutes.

DOA. (Touchstone, 1988). Produced by Ian Sander and Laura Ziskin. Directed by Rocky Morton and Annabel Jankel. Script by Charles Edward Pogue. Director of Photography, Yuri Neyman. Production Designer, Richard Amend. Music, Chaz Jankel. Editor, Michael R. Miller. Starring Dennis Quaid (Dexter Cornell), Meg Ryan (Sydney Fuller), Charlotte Rampling (Mrs. Fitzwaring), Daniel Stein (Hal Petersham), Christoper Neame (Bernard). 96 minutes.

Dog Day Afternoon. (Warner Bros., 1975). Produced by Martin Bregman and Martin Elfand. Directed by Sidney Lumet. Script by Frank Pierson, based on the article by P.F. Kluge and Thomas Moore. Director of Photography, Victor J. Kemper. Production Designer, Charles Bailey. Editor, Dede Allen. Starring Al Pacino (Sonny), John Cazale (Sal), Charles Durning (Moretti), Chris Sarandon (Leon), Sully Boyar (Mulvaney), Penny Allen (Sylvia), James Broderick (Sheldon), Carol Kane (Jenny), Lance Henriksen (Murphy). 130 minutes.

The Driver. (20th Century-Fox/EMI, 1978). Produced by Lawrence Gordon. Directed and Written by Walter Hill. Director of Photography, Philip Lathrop. Production Designer, Harry Horner. Music, Michael Small. Editors, Tina Hirsch and Robert K. Lambert. Starring Ryan O'Neal (the Driver), Bruce Dern (the Detective), Isabelle Adjani (the Player), Ronee Blakely (the Connection), Matt Clark (Red Plainclothesman), Felice Orlandi (Gold Plainclothesman), Joseph Walsh (Glasses), Rudy Ramos (Teeth). 91 minutes.

The Drowning Pool. (Warner Bros., 1975). Produced by Lawrence Turman and David Foster. Directed by Stuart

Rosenberg. Script by Tracy Keenan Wynn and Lorenzo Semple, Jr., Walter Hill based on the novel by John D. MacDonald. Director of Photography, Gordon Willis. Production Designer, Paul Sylbert. Music, Michael Small. Editor, John Howard. Starring Paul Newman (Harper), Joanne Woodward (Iris Devereaux), Tony Franciosa (Det. Broussard), Murray Hamilton (Kilbourne), Gail Strickland (Mavis Kilbourne), Melanie Griffith (Schuyler Devereaux). 108 minutes.

Drugstore Cowboy. (Avenue, 1989). Produced by Nick Wecksley and Karen Murphy, Directed by Gus Van Sant, Jr. Script by Daniel Yost and Van Sant, based on the novel by James Fogle. Director of Photography, Robert Yeoman. Production Designer, David Brisbin. Music, Elliott Rosenthal. Editor, Curtiss Clayton. Starring Matt Dillon (Bob), Kelly Lynch (Dianne), James Le Gros (Rick), Heather Graham (Nadine), James Remar (Detective), William Burroughs (himself). 100 minutes.

Eight Million Ways To Die. (TriStar, 1986). Produced by Steve Roth. Directed by Hal Ashby [and Charles Mulvehill]. Script by Oliver Stone and David Lee Henry, based on the novels *A Stab in the Dark* and *Eight Million Ways To Die* by Lawrence Block. Director of Photography, Stephen H. Burum. Production Designer, Michael Haller. Music, James Newton Howard. Editor, Stuart Pappe, Robert Lawrence. Starring Jeff Bridges ((Scudder), Rosanna Arquette (Sarah), Alexandra Paul (Sunny), Randy Brooks (Chance), Andy Garcia (Angel Maldonado), Lisa Sloan (Linda Scudder), Christa Denton. (Laurie Scudder). 115 minutes.

Eyewitness. (20th Century-Fox, 1981). Produced and Directed by Peter Yates. Script by Steve Tesich. Director of Photography, Matthew F. Leonetti. Production Designer, Philip Rosenberg. Music, Stanley Silverman. Editor, Cynthia Scheider.Starring William Hurt (Darryl Deever), Sigourney Weaver (Tony Sokolow), Christopher Plummer (Joseph), James Woods (Aldo), Irene Worth (Mrs. Sokolow), Pamela Reed (Linda), Kenneth McMillan (Mr. Deever). 108 minutes.

Fatal Attraction. (Paramount, 1987). Produced by Stanley Jaffe and Sherry Lansing. Directed by Adrian Lyne. Script by James Dearden. Director of Photography, Howard Atherton. Production Designer, Mel Bourne. Music, Maurice Jarre. Editors, Michael Kahn and Peter Berger. Starring Michael Douglas (Dan Gallagher), Glenn Close (Alex Forrest), Anne Archer (Beth), Ellen Hamilton Latzen (Ellen), Stuart Pankin (Jimmy), Ellen Foley (Hildy), Fred Gwynne (Arthur). 119 minutes.

Fear City. (Zupnik/Curtis, 1984). Produced by Bruce Cohn Curtis and Jerry Tokosfsky. Directed by Abel Ferrara. Script by Nicholas St. John. Director of Photography, James Lemmo. Music, Dick Halligan. Editor, Jack Holmes, Anthony Redman. Starring Tom Berenger (Matt Rossi), Billy Dee Williams (Al Wheeler), Jack Scalia (Nicky Piacenza), Melanie Griffith (Loretta), Rossano Brazzi (Carmine), Rae Dawn Chong (Liela). 96 minutes.

Femme Fatale. (Republic/Gibraltar, 1991). Produced by Andrew Lane and Nancy Rae Stone. Directed by Andre Guttfreund. Script by Michael Ferris and John D. Brancato. Director of Photography, Joey Forsyte. Production Designer, Pam Warner. Music, Parmer Fuller. Editor, Richard Candib. Starring Colin Firth (Joe Prince), Lisa Zane (Elizabeth/Cynthia/Maura), Billy Zane (Elijah), Scott Wilson (Dr. Beaumont), Lisa Blount (Jenny), Suzanne Snyder (Andrea). 96 minutes.

52 Pick-up. (Cannon, 1986). Produced by Menahem Golan and Yoram Globus. Directed by John Frankenheimer. Script by Elmore Leonard and John Steppling, based on the novel by Leonard. Director of Photography, Jost Vacano. Production Designer, Philip Harrison. Music, Gary Chang. Editor, Robert F. Shugrue. Starring Roy Scheider (Harry Mitchell), Ann-Margret (Barbara Mitchell), Vanity (Doreen), John Glover (Raimy), Robert Trebor (Leo), Kelly Preston (Cini), Clarence Williams III (Bobby Shy). 114 minutes.

Final Analysis. (Warner Bros., 1992). Produced by Charles Roven, Paul Junger Witt, and Tony Thomas. Directed by Phil Joanou. Script by Wesley Strick, based on a story by Strick and Robert Berger. Executive Producers, Richard Gere and Maggie Wilde. Director of Photography, Jordan Cronenweth. Production Designer, Dean Tavoularis. Music, George Fenton. Editor, Thom Noble. Starring Richard Gere (Isaac Barr), Kim Basinger (Heather Evans), Uma Thurman (Diana Baylor), Eric Roberts (Jimmy Evans, Keith David (Det. Huggins), Paul Guilfoyle (Mike O'Brien). 124 minutes.

The First Deadly Sin. (Filmways, 1980). Produced by George Pappas and Mark Shanker. Directed by Brian G. Hutton. Script by Mann Rubin based the novel by Lawrence Sanders. Director of Photography, Jack Priestley. Production Designer, Woody MacKintosh. Music, Gordon Jenkins. Editor, Eric Albertson. Starring Frank Sinatra (Edward Delaney), Faye Dunaway (Barbara Delaney), David Dukes (Daniel Blank), George Coe (Dr. Bernardi), Brenda Vaccaro (Monica Gilbert), Martin Gabel (Christopher Langley). 112 minutes.

48 Hrs. (Paramount, 1982). Produced by Lawrence Gordon and Joel Silver. Directed by Walter Hill. Script by Roger Spottiswoode and Walter Hill & Larry Gross and Steven E. de Souza. Director of Photography, Ric Waite. Production Designer, John Vallen. Music, James Horner. Editors, Freeman Davies, Mark Warner, and Billy Weber. Starring Nick Nolte (Jack Cates), Eddie Murphy (Reggie Hammond), Annette O'Toole (Elaine), Frank McRae (Haden), James Remar (Ganz), David Patrick Kelly (Luther), Sonny Landham (Billy Bear). 96 minutes.

Frantic. (Warner Bros., 1988). Produced by Thom Mount. Directed by Roman Polanski. Script by Polanski and Gerard Brach. Director of Photography, Witold Sobocinski. Production Designer, Pierre Guffroy. Music, Ennio Morricone. Editor, Sam O'Steen. Starring Harrison Ford (Richard Walker), Emmanuelle Seigner (Michelle), Betty Buckley (Sondra Walker), John Mahoney (Williams), Jimmy Ray Weeks (Shaap), Yorgo Voyagis (Kidnapper). 120 minutes.

Genuine Risk. (IRS, 1990). Produced by Larry J. Rattner, Guy J. Louthan, William Ewart, and Kurt Voss. Directed by Kurt Voss. Director of Photography, Dean Lent. Production Designer, Elisabeth A. Scott. Music, Deborah Holland. Editor, Christopher Koefoed. Starring Terence Stamp (Hellwart), Peter Berg (Henry), Michelle Johnson (Girl), M.K. Harris (Cowboy Jack), Max Perlich (Chris), Teddy Wilson (Billy). 89 minutes.

Gleaming the Cube. (20th Century-Fox, 1989). Produced by Lawrence Turman and David Foster. Directed by Graeme Clifford. Script by Michael Tolkin. Director of Photography, Reed Smoot. Production Designer, John Muto. Music, Jay Ferguson. Editor, John Wright. Starring Christian Slater (Brian Kelly), Steven Bauer (Lucero), Richard Herd (Ed), Le Tuan (Col. Trac), Min Luong (Tina Trac), Art Chudabala (Vinh Kelly). 104 minutes.

The Grifters. (Scorsese/Miramax, 1990). Produced by Martin Scorsese, Robert A. Harris, James Painten, and Peggy Rajski. Directed by Stephen Frears. Script by Donald E. Westlake, based on the novel by Jim Thompson. Director of Photography, Oliver Stapleton. Production Designer, Dennis Gassner. Music, Elmer Bernstein. Editor, Nick Audsley. Starring Anjelica Huston (Lilly Dillon), John Cusack (Roy Dillon), Annette Benning (Myra Langtry), Jan Munroe (Guy at Bar), Pat Hingle (Bobo), Richard Holden (Cop). 119 minutes.

Guncrazy. (Zeta Entertainment/Overseas, 1992). Produced by Zane W. Levitt and Diane Firestone. Directed by Tamra Davis. Script by Matthew Bright. Director of Photography, Lisa Rinzler. Music, Ed Tomney. Editor, Kevin Tent. Starring Drew Barrymore (Anita), James Legros (Howard), Billy Drago (Hank), Rodney Harvey (Hank), Ione Skye (Joy), Michael Ironisde (Kincaid), Joe Dallesandro (Rooney). 96 minutes.

Hammett. (Orion/Warner Bros./Zoetrope, 1983). Produced by Fred Roos, Ronald Colby, and Don Guest. Directed by Wim Wenders. Script by Ross Thomas, Dennis O'Flaherty, and Thomas Pope. Director of Photography, Philip Lathrop, Joe Biroc. Production Designer, Eugene Lee, Dean Tavoularis. Music, John Barry. Editor, Barry Malkin, Marc Laub, Robert Q. Lovett, Randy Roberts. Starring Frederic Forrest (Hammett), Peter Boyle (Jimmy Ryan), Marilu Henner (Kit Conger), Roy Kinnear (Hagedorn), Lydia Lei (Crystal Ling). 97 minutes.

The Hand that Rocks the Cradle. (Buena Vista/Interscope, 1992). Produced by David Madden. Directed by Curtis Hanson. Script by Amanda Silver. Executive Producers, Ted Field, Rick Jaffa, and Robert W. Cort. Director of Photography, Robert Elswit. Production Designer, Edward Pisoni. Music, Graeme Revell. Editor, John F. Link. Starring Annabella Sciorra (Claire Bartel), Rebecca De Mornay (Peyton Flanders), Matt McCoy (Michael Bartel), Ernie Hudson (Solomon), Julianne Moore (Marlene), Madeline Zima (Emma), John de Lancie (Dr. Mott). 110 minutes.

Hardcore. (Columbia, 1979). Produced by Buzz Feitshans. Directed and Written by Paul Schrader. Director of Photography, Michael Chapman. Production Designer, Paul Sylbert. Music, Jack Nitzsche. Editor, Tom Rolf. Starring George C. Scott (Jake Van Dorn), Peter Boyle (Andy Mast), Season Hubley (Niki), Dick Sargent (Wes De Jong), Leonard Gaines (Ramada), David Nichols (Kurt), Gary Rand Graham (Tod). 105 minutes.

Harper. (Warner Bros., 1966). Produced by Elliott Kastner and Jerry Gershwin. Directed by Jack Smight. Script by William Goldman, based on the novel *The Moving Target* by Ross MacDonald. Director of Photography, Conrad Hall. Production Designer, Alfred Sweeney. Music, Johnny Mandel, Editor, Stefan Arnsten. Starring Paul Newman (Harper), Lauren Bacall (Mrs. Sampson), Julie Harris (Betty Fraley), Arthur Hill (Albert Graves), Janet Leigh (Susan Harper), Pamela Tiffen (Miranda Sampson), Robert Wagner (Alan Traggert), Robert Webber (Dwight Troy), Shelley Winters (Fay Estabrook), Harold Gould (Sheriff Spanner), Strother Martin (Claude). 121 minutes.

Hit List. (New Line, 1989). Produced by Paul Hertzberg and Jef Richard. Directed by William Lustig. Script by John Goff and Peter Brosnan. Director of Photography, James Lemmo. Production Designer, David Brian Miller. Music, Gary Shuyman. Editor, David Kern. Starring Jan-Michael Vincent (Jack Collins), Leo Rossi (Frank De Salvo), Lance Henriksen (Chris Calek), Charles Napier (Tom Mitchum), Rip Torn (Vic Luca), Jere Burns (Jared). 90 minutes.

Homicide. (Triumph/Cinehaus, 1991). Produced by Edward R. Pressman and Michael Hausman. Directed and Written by David Mamet. Director of Photography, Roger Deakins. Production Designer, Michael Merritt. Music, Alaric Jans. Editor, Barbara Tulliver. Starring Joe Mantegna (Bobby Gold), William H. Macy (Tim Sullivan), Natalija Nogulich (Chava), Ving Rhames (Randolph), Rebecca Pidgeon (Miss Klein), Vincent Guastaferro (Senna). 102 minutes.

Horseplayer. (Relentless, 1991). Produced by Larry Rattner. Directed by Kurt Voss. Script by Voss and Rattner. Director of Photography, Dean Lent. Production Designer, Steve Karman. Music, Gary Shuyman. Editor, John Rosenberg. Starring Brad Dourif (Bud), Sammi Davis (Randi), M.K. Harris (Matthew), Vic Tayback (George), Max Perlich. (Kid). 92 minutes.

Harry Madox (Don Johnson) in The Hot Spot.

The Hot Spot. (Film Now/Orion, 1990). Produced by Paul Lewis. Directed by Dennis Hopper. Script by Nona Tyson and Charles Williams, based on the novel *Hell Hath No Fury* by Charles Williams. Director of Photography, Ueli Steiger. Production Designer, Cary White. Music, Jack Nitzsche. Editor, Wende Phifer Mate. Starring Don Johnson (Harry Madox), Virginia Madsen (Dolly Harshaw), Jennifer Connelly (Gloria Harper), Charles Martin Smith (Lon Gulik), William Sadler (Frank Sutton), Jerry Hardin (George Harshaw). 128 minutes.

House of Games. (Filmhaus/Orion, 1987). Produced by Michael Hausman. Directed and Written by David Mamet. Director of Photography, Juan Ruiz Anchia. Production Designer, Michael Merritt. Music, Alaric Jans. Editor, Trudy Ship. Starring Lindsay Crouse (Margaret Ford), Joe Mantegna (Mike), Mike Nussbaum (Joey), Lilia Skala (Dr. Littauer), J.T. Walsh (Businessman), Willo Hausman (Girl with Book). 101 minutes.

I, the Jury. (20th century-Fox, 1982). Produced by Robert Solo. Directed by Richard T. Heffron. Script by Larry Cohen, based on the novel by Mickey Spillane. Director of Photography, Andrew Laszlo. Production Designer, Robert Gundlach. Music, Bill Conti. Editor, Garth Craven.

Starring Armand Assante (Mike Hammer), Barbera Carrera (Dr. Charlotte Bennett), Alan King (Charles Kalecki), Laurene Landon (Velda), Geoffrey Lewis (Joe Butler), Paul Sorvino (Det. Pat Chambers), Judson Scott (Kenricks). 109 minutes.

Impulse. (Warner Bros., 1990). Produced by Albert S. Ruddy and Andre Morgan. Directed by Sondra Locke. Script by John De Marco and Leigh Chapman. Director of Photography, Dean Semler. Production Designer, William A. Elliott. Music, Michel Colombier. Editor, John W. Wheeler. Starring Theresa Russell (Lottie), Jeff Fahey (Stan), George Dzundza (Lt. Joe Morgan), Alan Rosenberg (Charlie Katz), Nicholas Mele (Rossi), Eli Danker (Dimarjian). 109 minutes.

Internal Affairs. (Paramount, 1990). Produced by Frank Mancuso, Jr. Directed by Mike Figgis. Script by Henry Bean. Director of Photography, John A. Alonzo. Production Designer, Waldemar Kalinowski. Music, Mike Figgis, Anthony Marinelli, Brian Banks. Editor, Robert Estrin. Starring Richard Gere (Dennis Peck), Andy Garcia (Raymond Avilla), Nancy Travis (Kathleen Avilla), Laurie Metcalf (Amy Wallace), Richard Bradford (Grieb), William Baldwin (Van Stretch). 115 minutes.

Intimate Stranger. (SouthGate, 1991). Produced by Yoran Pelman and J.J. Lichauco Pelman. Directed by Allan Holzman. Script by Rob Fresco. Director of Photography, Ilan Rosenberg. Music, Jonathan Sheffer. Editor, Lorraine Salk. Starring Deborah Harry (Cory Wheeler), James Russo (Nick Ciccini), Tim Thomerson (Malcolm Henthoff), Paige French (Meg), Grace Zabriskie (D.P. Ashley). 94 minutes.

Jagged Edge. (Columbia/EMI, 1985). Produced by Martin Ransohoff. Directed by Richard Marquand. Script by Joe Eszterhas. Director of Photography, Matthew F. Leonetti. Production Designer, Gene Callahan. Music, John Barry. Editors, Sean Barton and Conrad Buff. Starring Glenn Close (Teddy Barnes), Jeff Bridges (Jack Forrester), Peter Coyote (Krasny), Robert Loggia (Sam Ransom), Leigh Taylor-Young (Virginia), John Dehner (Judge Carrigan). 108 minutes.

Jezebel's Kiss. (Shapiro Glickenhaus/Film Warriors, 1990). Produced by Eric F. Sheffer. Directed and Written by Harvey Keith. Director of Photography, Brian Reynolds. Production Designer, Alan Baron. Music, Mitchel Forman. Editor, Mort Fallick. Starring Katherine Barrese (Jezebel), Malcolm McDowell (Ben Faberson), Meredith Baxter-Birney (Virginia De Leo), Meg Foster (Amanda Faberson). 97 minutes.

Johnny Handsome. (Carolco/TriStar, 1989). Produced by Charles Koven. Directed by Walter Hill. Script by Ken Friedman, based on the novel by John Godey. Director of Photography, Matthew F. Leonetti. Production Designer, Gene Rudolf. Music, Ry Cooder. Editors, Freeman Davies, Carmel Davies, Donn Aron. Starring Mickey Rourke (John Sedley), Ellen Barkin (Sunny Boyd), Elizabeth McGovern (Donna McCarty), Forest Whitaker (Dr. Steven Resher), Lance Henriksen (Rafe Garrett), Morgan Freeman (Lt. A.Z. Drones), Scott Wilson (Mikey Chalmette). 94 minutes.

Kill Me Again. (MGM/Progaganda Films, 1990). Produced by David W. Warfield, Steve Golin, and Sigurjon Sighvatsson. Directed by John Dahl. Script by John Dahl and David Warfield. Director of Photography, Jacques Steyn. Production Designer, Michelle Minch. Music, William Olvis. Editor, Frank Jimenez, Jonathan Shaw, Eric Beason. Starring Val Kilmer (Jack Andrews), Joanne Whalley-Kilmer (Fay Forrester), Michael Madsen (Vince Miller), Jonathan Gries (Alan Swayzie), Michael Greene (Lt. Hendrix). 94 minutes.

The Kill-Off. (Filmworld International/Cabriolet, 1990). Produced by Lydia Dean Pilcher. Directed by Maggie Greenwald. Script by Maggie Greenwald, based on the novel by Jim Thompson. Director of Photography, Declan Quinn. Production Designer, Pamela Woodbridge. Music, Evan Lurie. Editor, James Y. Kwei. Starring Loretta Gross (Luane), Jackson Sims (Pete), Steve Monroe (Ralph), Cathy Haase (Danny Lee), Andrew Lee Barrett (Bobbie), Jorjan Fox (Myra). 91 minutes.

The Killer Inside Me. (Devi/Warner Brothers, 1976). Produced by Michael W. Leighton. Directed by Burt Kennedy. Script by Edward Mann and Robert Chamblee, based on the novel by Jim Thompson. Director of Photography, William A. Fraker. Music, Tim McIntire, John Rubinstein. Editor, Danford B. Greene, Aaron Stell. Starring Stacy Keach (Lou Ford), Susan Tyrell (Joyce Lakeland), Tisha Sterling (Amy Stanton), Keenan Wynn (Chester Conway), Charles McGraw (Howard Hendricks), John Dehner (Bob Maples). 99 minutes.

The Killing of a Chinese Bookie. (Faces, 1976). Produced by Al Ruben. Directed and Written by John Cassavetes. Director of Photography, Mike Ferris. Production Designer, Sam Shaw. Music, Bo Harwood. Editor, Tom Cornwell. Starring Ben Gazzara (Cosmo Vitelli), Timothy Carey (Flo), Azizi Johari (Rachel), Meade Roberts (Mr. Sophistication), Seymour Cassel (Mort Weil), Morgan Woodward (John the Boss), Alice Friedland (Sherry), Donna Gordon (Margo). 135 minutes.

The Killing Time. (New World, 1987). Produced by Peter Alrans and Robert L. Levy. Directed by Rick King. Script by Don Bohlinger, James Nathan Bruce, and Franklin Singer. Director of Photography, Paul H. Goldsmith. Music, Paul Chihara. Editor, Lorenzo De Stefano. Starring Beau Bridges (Sam Wayburn), Kiefer Sutherland (Brian), Joe Don Baker (Sheriff), Camelia Kath (Laura Winslow), Wayne Rogers (Jake Winslow). 96 minutes.

King of New York. (Seven Arts/New Line, 1990). Produced by Mary Kane. Directed by Abel Ferrara. Script by Nicholas St. John. Director of Photography, Bojan Bazelli. Production Designer, Alex Tavoularis. Music, Joe Delia. Editor, Anthony Redman. Starring Christopher Walken (Frank White), David Caruso (Dennis Caruso), Larry Fishburne (Jimmy Jump), Wesley Snipes (Flannagan), Janet Julian (Jennifer), Joey Chin (Larry Wong). 103 minutes.

A Kiss Before Dying. (Universal/Initial, 1991). Produced by Robert Lawrence. Directed by James Dearden. Script by Dearden, based on the novel by Ira Levin. Director of Photography, Mike Southon. Production Designer, Jim Clay. Music, Howard Shore. Editor, Michael Bradsell. Starring Matt Dillon (Jonathan Corliss), Sean Young (Ellen/Dory Carlsson), Max Von Sydow (Thor Carlsson), James Russo (Dan Corelli), Diane Ladd (Mrs. Corliss). 95 minutes.

Kiss Me a Killer. (Califilm, 1991). Produced by Catherine Cyran. Directed by Marcus DeLeon. Script by Christopher Wooden and Marcus DeLeon. Director of Photography, Nancy Schreiber. Production Designer, James R. Shumaker. Music, Nigel Holton. Editor, Glenn Garland. Starring Julie Carmen (Teresa), Robert Beltran (Tony), Guy Boyd (Jake), Ramon Franco (Ramon), Charles Boswell (Lt. Dennehy), Sam Vlahos (Father Dominquez). 92 minutes.

Klute. (Warner Bros, 1971). Produced and Directed by Alan J. Pakula. Script by Andy and Dave Lewis. Director of Photography, Gordon Willis. Production Designer, George Jenkins. Music, Michael Small. Editor, Carl Lerner. Starring Jane Fonda (Bree Daniel), Donald Sutherland (John Klute), Charles Cioffi (Peter Cable), Dorothy Tristan (Arlyn Page), Nathan George (Tresk), Roy Scheider (Frank), Rita Gam (Trina), Vivian Nathan (Psychiatrist). 114 minutes.

Lady Beware. (Scotti Bros./International Video Entertainment, 1987). Produced by Tony Scotti. Directed by Karen Arthur. Script by Susan Miller and Charles Zev Cohen. Production Designer, Tom Wells. Director of Photography, Tom Neuwirth. Music, Craig Safan. Editor, Roy Watts. Starring Diane Lane (Katya Yarno), Michael Woods (Jack Price), Cotter Smith (Mac Odell), Peter Nevargic (Lionel), Edward Penn (Thayer), Tyra Ferrell (Nan). 108 minutes.

Lady in Cement. (20th Century-Fox, 1968). Produced by Aaron Rosenberg. Directed by Gordon Douglas. Script by Marvin H. Albert and Jack Guss, based on the novel by Guss. Director of Photography, Joe Biroc. Production Designer, Leroy Deane. Music, Hugo Montenegro. Editor, Robert Simpson. Starring Frank Sinatra (Tony Rome), Raquel Welch (Kit Forrest), Richard Conte (Lt. Santini), Martin Gabel (Al Mungar), Lainie Kazan (Maria Baretti), Pat Henry (Rubin). 93 minutes.

The Last Boy Scout. (Geffen/Silver, 1991). Produced by Joel Silver, Michael Levy, and Steve Perry. Directed by Tony Scott. Script by Shane Black, based on a story by Black and Greg Hicks. Director of Photography, Ward Russell. Production Designer, Brian Morris. Music, Michael Kamen. Editor, Stuart Baird, Mark Goldblatt, Mark Helfrich. Starring Bruce Willis (Joe Hallenbeck), Damon Wayans (Jimmy Dix), Chelsea Field (Sarah Hallenbeck), Noble Willingham (Sheldon Marcone), Taylor Negron (Milo), Danielle Harris (Darian Hallenbeck). 101 minutes.

Last Embrace. (United Artists, 1979). Produced by Michael Taylor and Dan Wigatow. Directed by Jonathan Demme. Script by David Shaber, based on the novel *Thirteenth Man* by Murray Teigh Bloom. Director of Photography, Tak Fujimoto. Production Designer, James A. Taylor. Music, Miklos Rozsa. Editor, Barry Malkin. Starring Roy Sheider (Harry Hannan), Janet Margolin (Ellie Fabian), John Glover (Richard Peabody), Sam Levene (Sam Urdell), Charles Napier (Dave Quittle), Christopher Walken (Eckart). 103 minutes.

Lethal Weapon. (Warner Bros., 1987). Produced by Richard Donner and Joel Silver. Directed by Richard Donner. Script by Shane Black. Director of Photography, Stephen Goldblatt. Production Designer, J. Michael Riva. Music, Milt Kamen and Eric Clapton. Editor, Stuart Baird. Starring Mel Gibson (Riggs), Danny Glover (Murtaugh), Gary Busey (Joshua), Mitchell Ryan (General), Tom Atkins (Hunsaker),

Darlene Love (Trish), Traci Wolfe (Rianne), Jackie Swanson (Amanda). 110 minutes.

Lethal Weapon II. (Warner Bros., 1989). Produced by Richard Donner, Joel Silver, Steve Perry, and Jennie Lew-Tugend. Directed by Richard Donner. Script by Jeffrey Boam, based on a story by Shane Black and Warren Murphy. Director of Photography, Stephen Goldblatt. Production Designer, J. Michael Riva. Music, Michael Kamen, Eric Clapton, David Sanborn. Editor, Stuart Baird. Starring Mel Gibson (Martin Riggs), Danny Glover (Roger Murtaugh), Joe Pesci (Leo Getz), Joss Ackland (Arjen Rudd), Derrick O'Connor (Pieter Vorstedt), Patsy Kensit (Rika Van Den Haas). 114 minutes.

Lethal Weapon III. (Warner Bros., 1992). Produced by Richard Donner and Joel Silver. Directed by Richard Donner. Script by Jeffrey Boam, story by Boam and Robert Mark Kamen. Director of Photography, Jan De Bont. Production Designer, James Spencer. Music, Michael Kamen, Eric Clapton, and David Sanborn. Editor, Robert Brown, Battle Davis, Dallas Pruett. Starring Mel Gibson (Riggs), Danny Glover (Murtaugh), Renne Russo (Lane), Joe Pesci (Leo Getz), Stuart Wilson, Steve Kahan, Darlene Love (Trish), Traci Wolfe (Rianne), Damon Harris, Ebonie Smith. 115 minutes.

Liebestraum. (Pathe/MGM/Initial, 1991). Produced by Eric Fellner and Stephen Buck. Directed and Written by Mike Figgis. Director of Photography, Juan Ruiz Anchia. Production Designer, Waldemar Kalinowski. Music, Mike Figgis. Editor, Mark Hunter. Starring Kevin Anderson (Nick Kaminsky), Pamela Gidley (Jane Kessler), Bill Pullman (Paul Kessler), Kim Novak (Lillian Anderssen), Thomas Kopache (Dr. Parker), Catherine Hicks (Mary Parker). 102 minutes.

Love Crimes. (Millimeter/Sovereign, 1992). Produced by Lizzie Borden and Randy Langlais. Directed by Lizzie Borden. Script by Allan Moyle and Laurie Frank, based on a story by Moyle. Executive Producer, Forrest Murray. Director of Photography, Jack N. Green. Production Designer, Armin Ganz. Music, Graeme Revell. Editors, Nicholas C. Smith, Mike Jackson. Sean Young (Dana Greenway), Patrick Bergin ("David Hanover"), Arnetia Walker (Lt. Maria Johnson), James Read (Stanton Gray), Ron Orbach (Tully), Fern Dorsey (Colleen Dells), Tina Hightower (Anne Winslow), Donna Biscoe (Hanna). 85 minutes.

Malone. (Fuchs Prods./Orion, 1987). Produced by Leo L. Fuchs. Directed by Harley Cokliss. Script by Christopher Frank. Director of Photography, Gerald Hirschfeld. Production Designer, Graeme Murray. Music, David Newman. Editor, Todd Ramsay. Starring Burt Reynolds (Malone), Cliff Robertson (Delaney), Kenneth McMillan (Hawkins), Cynthia Gibb (Jo Barlow), Scott Wilson (Paul

Barlow), Lauren Hutton (Jamie), Phil Anglim (Harvey). 92 minutes.

Manhunter. (De Laurentiis, 1986). Produced by Richard Roth. Directed and Written by Michael Mann, based on the novel, *Red Dragon*, by Thomas Harris. Executive Producer, Bernard Williams. Director of Photography, Dante Spinotti. Production Designer, Mel Bourne. Music, The Reds and Michel Rubini. Editor, Dov Hoenig. Starring William L. Petersen (Will Graham), Kim Griest (Molly), Joan Allen (Reba), Brian Cox (Dr. Lecter), Dennis Farina (Crawford), Tom Noonan (Francis Dollarhyde). 118 minutes.

Masquerade. (MGM/UA, 1988). Produced by Michael I. Levy. Directed by Bob Swaim. Script by Dick Wolf. Director of Photography, David Watkin. Production Designer, John Kasarda.Music, John Barry. Editor, Scott Conrad. Starring Rob Lowe (Tim Whelan), Meg Tilly (Olivia Lawrence), Doug Savant (Mike McGill), Kim Cattrall (Brooke Morrison), John Glover (Tony Gateworth), Dana Delaney (Annie Briscoe). 91 minutes.

Miami Blues. (Orion/Tristes Tropiques, 1990). Produced by Jonathan Demme, Gary Goetzman, Kenneth Utt, and Ron Bozman. Directed and Written by George Armitage, based on the novel by Charles Willeford. Director of Photography, Tak Fujimoto. Production Designer, Maher Ahmad. Music, Gary Chang. Editor, Craig McKay. Starring Alec Baldwin (Frederick J. Frenger), Fred Ward (Sgt. Hoke Moseley), Jennifer Jason Leigh (Susie Waggoner), Charles Napier (Sgt. Bill Henderson), Martine Beswicke (Noira). 97 minutes.

Midnight Heat. (New Line, 1992). Produced by Kandace King and Lance King. Directed by John Nicolella. Script by Max Strom and John Allen Nelson. Director of Photography, Charles Rosher, Jr. Editor, Chris Koefoed. Starring Michael Pare (Eric), Adam Ant (Danny) Dennis Hopper (Carl), Daphne Ashbrook (Julie), Charlie Schlatter (David), Little Richard (Brandon), Tracy Tweed (Lena). 100 minutes.

Mike's Murder. (Ladd Co./Warner Bros., 1984). Written, Produced, and Directed by James Bridges. Executive Producer, Kim Kurumada. Director of Photography, Rey Villalobos. Production Designer, Peter Jamison. Music, John Barry. Editors, Jeff Gourson and Dede Allen. Starring Debra Winger (Betty), Mark Keyloun (Mike), Paul Winfield (Phillip), Darrell Larson (Pete), Brooke Alderson (Patty). 109 minutes.

Miller's Crossing. (20th Century-Fox, 1990). Produced by Ethan Coen. Directed by Joel Coen. Script by Joel and Ethan Coen. Executive Producer, Ben Barenholtz. Director of Photography, Barry Sonnenfeld. Production Designer, Dennis Gassner. Music, Carter Burwell. Editor, Michael R. Miller. Starring Gabriel Byrne (Tom Reagan), Marcia Gay Harden (Verna), John Turturro (Bernie Birnbaum), Jon

Polito (Johnny Caspar), J.E. Freeman (Eddie Dane), Albert Finney (Liam "Leo" O'Brien). 114 minutes.

The Morning After. (20th Century-Fox/Lorimar, 1986). Produced by Bruce Gilbert. Directed by Sidney Lumet. Script by James Hicks and [uncredited] Jay Presson Allen. Executive Producer, Faye Schwab. Director of Photography, Andrzej Bartkowiak. Production Designer, Albert Brenner. Music, Paul Chihara. Editor, Jack Goodman. Starring Jane Fonda (Alex Sternbergen), Jeff Bridges (Turner Kendall), Raul Julia (Joaquin Manero), Diane Salinger (Isabel), Richard Foronjy (Sgt. Greenbaum). 103 minutes.

Mortal Passions. (Gibraltar Releasing, 1990). Produced by Gwen Field. Directed by Andrew Lane. Script by Alan Moskowitz. Director of Photography, Christian Sebaldt. Production Designer, Tucker Johnston. Music, Parmer Fuller. Editor, Kimberly Ray. Starring Zach Galligan (Todd), Michael Bowen (Burke), Krista Errickson (Emily), Sheila Kelley (Adele), David Warner (Dr. Powers), Luca Bercovici (Darcy). 98 minutes.

Mortal Thoughts. (Columbia/New Visions/Polar, 1991). Produced by John Fiedler, Mark Tarlov, and Demi Moore. Directed by Alan Rudolph. Script by William Reilly and Claude Kerven. Director of Photography, Elliot Davis. Production Designer, Howard Cummings. Music, Mark Isham. Editor, Tom Walls. Starring Demi Moore (Cynthia Kellogg), Glenne Headly (Joyce Urbanski), Bruce Willis (James Urbanski), John Pankow (Arthur Kellogg), Harvey Keitel (Det. Woods), Billie Neal (Linda Nealon). 104 minutes.

Ms. 45. (Navaron/Rochelle, 1981). Produced and Directed by Abel Ferrara. Script by Nicholas St. John. Executive Producer, Rochelle Weisberg. Director of Photography, James Momel. Music, Joe Delia. Editor, Christopher Andrews. Starring Zoe Tamerlis (Thana), Steve Singer (Photographer), Jack Thibeau (Man in Bar), Peter Yellen (Second Rapist), Darlene Stuto (Laurie), Editta Sherman (Landlady). 84 minutes.

Murphy's Law. (Cannon, 1986). Produced by Pancho Kohner. Directed by J. Lee Thompson. Script by Gail Morgan Hickman. Director of Photography, Alex Phillips. Production Designer, William Cruise. Music, Marc Donahue, Valentine McCallum. Editor, Peter Lee Thompson. Starring Charles Bronson (Jack Murphy), Kathleen Wilhoite (Arabella McGee), Carrie Snodgress (Joan Freeman), Robert F. Lyons (Art Penny), Richard Romanus (Frank Vincenzo), Angel Tompkins (Jan). 100 minutes.

Nails. (Viacom, 1992). Produced by George W. Perkins. Directed by John Flynn. Script by Larry Ferguson and Roderick Taylor, from a story by Ferguson and Marvin Schwartz. Executive Producer, Dale Rosenbloom. Director of Photography, Mac Ahlberg. Production Designer, Victoria Paul. Music, Bill Conti. Editor, Michael N. Knue. Starring Dennis Hopper (Harry), Anne Archer (Mary), Tomas Milian (Herrera). 97 minutes.

Narrow Margin. (Carolco/TriStar, 1990). Produced by Jonathan A. Zimbert and Jerry Offsay. Directed and Written by Peter Hyams, based on the RKO film of the same title. Director of Photography, Peter Hyams. Production Designer, Joel Schiller. Music, Bruce Broughton. Editor, Beau Barthel-Blair. Starring Gene Hackman (Caulfield), Anne Archer (Hunnicut), James B. Sikking (Nelson), J.T. Walsh (Michael Tarlow), M. Emmet Walsh (Sgt. Dominick Benti), Susan Hogan (Kathryn Weller). 97 minutes.

New Jack City. (Warner Bros., 1991). Produced by Doug McHenry, George Jackson, and Preston L. Holmes. Directed by Mario Van Peebles. Script by Thomas Lee Wright and Barry Michael Cooper. Director of Photography, Francis Kenny. Production Designer, Charles C. Bennett. Editor, Steven Kemper. Starring Mario Van Peebles (Det. Stone), Judd Nelson (Det. Peretti), Ice-T (Scotty Appleton), Russell Wong (Det. Park), Wesley Snipes (Nino Brown). 97 minutes.

Night and the City. (20th Century-Fox/Penta Entertainment, 1992). Produced by Jane Rosenthal and Irwin Winkler. Directed by Irwin Winkler. Script by Richard Price, based on the novel by Gerald Kersh. Executive Producers, Harry Ufland and Mary Jane Ufland. Director of Photography, Tak Fujimoto. Production Designer, Peter Larkin. Music, James Newton Howard. Editor, David Brenner. Starring Robert De Niro (Harry Fabian), Jessica Lange (Helen Nasseros), Cliff Gorman (Phil Nasseros), Jack Warden (Al Grossman), Alan King (Boom Boom Grossman). 105 minutes.

Night Visitor. (MGM/UA 1989). Produced by Alain Silver. Directed by Rupert Hitzig. Script by Randal Viscovich. Executive Producers, Tom Broadbridge and Shelley E. Reid. Director of Photography, Peter Jensen. Production Designer, Jon Rothschild. Music, Parmer Fuller. Editor, Glenn Erickson. Starring Elliott Gould (Devereaux), Allen Garfield (Willard), Michael J. Pollard (Stanley), Shannon Tweed (Lisa Grace), Richard Roundtree (Captain Apollo Crane), Derek Rydall (Billy Colton), Brooke Bundy (Mrs. Colton), Teresa Vanderwoude (Kelly), Scott Fults (Sam Loomis). 93 minutes.

No Mercy. (TriStar, 1986). Produced by D. Constantine Conte. Directed by Richard Pearce. Script by Jim Carabatsos. Executive Producer, Michael Hausman. Director of Photography, Michel Brault. Production Designer, Patrizia Von Brandenstein. Music, Alan Silvestri. Editors, Jerry Greenberg and Bill Yahraus. Starring Richard Gere (Eddie Jillete), Kim Basinger (Michel Duval), Jeroen Krabbe (Losado), George Dzundza (Stemkowski), Gary Basabara (Joe), William Atherton (Deveneux), Ray Sharkey (Angles Ryan). 105 minutes.

No Way Out. (Orion, 1987). Produced by Laura Ziskin and Robert Garland. Directed by Roger Donaldson. Script by Robert Garland, based on the novel, *The Big Clock*, by Kenneth Fearing. Executive Producer, Mace Neufeld. Director of Photography, John Alcott. Production Designer, Dennis Washington. Music, Maurice Jarre. Editor, Neil Travis. Starring Kevin Costner (Tom Farrell), Gene Hackman (David Brice), Sean Young (Susan), Will Patton (Scott), Howard Duff (Duvall), George Dzundza (Sam), Jason Bernard (Donovan), Iman (Nina), Fred Dalton Thompson (Marshall). 116 minutes.

The Onion Field. (Avco Embassy, 1979). Produced by Walter Cobelnz. Directed by Harold Becker. Script by Joseph Wambaugh, based on his book. Director of Photography, Charles Rosher. Production Designer, Brian Eatwell. Music, Eumir Deodato. Editor, John W. Wheeler. Starring John Savage (Karl Hettinger), James Woods (Greg Powell), Franklin Seales (Jimmy Smith), Ted Danson (Ian Campbell), Ronny Cox (Pierce Brooks), David Huffman (Phil Halpin), Christopher Lloyd ("Jailhouse" Lawyer). 124 minutes.

Out of Bounds. (Columbia, 1986). Produced by Charles Fries and Mike Rosenfeld. Directed by Richard Tuggle. Script by Tony Kayden. Executive Producers, John Tarnoff and Ray Hartwick. Director of Photography, Bruce Surtees. Production Designer, Norman Newberry. Music, Stewart Copeland. Editor, Keny Beyda. Starring Anthony Michael Hall (Daryl Cage), Jenny Wright (Dizz), Jeff Kober (Roy Gaddis), Glynn Turman (Lt. Delgado), Raymond Barry (Hurley), Pepe Serna (Murano). 92 minutes.

Out of the Dark. (New Line/Cinetel, 1989). Produced by Zane W. Levitt. Directed by Michael Schroeder. Script by J. Greg DeFelice and Zane Levitt. Executive Producers, Paul Bartel, Paul Hertzberg. Director of Photography, Julio Macat. Production Designer, Robert Schulenberg. Music, Paul F. Antonelli. Editor, Mark Manos. Starring Tracey Walter (Detective), Cameron Dye (Kevin), Karen Black (Ruth), Bud Cort (Stringer), Lynn Danielson (Kristel), Paul Bartel (Clerk). 90 minutes.

Out of the Rain. (Acme Company/Live, 1990). Produced and Directed by Gary Winick. Script by Shem Bitterman, based on his play. Executive Producer, Mike Ross. Co-Producer, Rick Bowman. Director of Photography, Makoto Watanabe. Music, Cengiz Yaltkaya. Editor, Carole Kravetz. Starring Bridget Fonda (Jolene), Michael O'Keefe (Frank), John E. O'Keefe (Neff), John Seitz (Nat Reade), Georgine Hall (Tilly), Al Shannon (Drew), Michael Mantell (Warren), Mary Mara (Trisha), Kathleen Chalfont (Ruth). 88 minutes.

Pacific Heights. (Morgan Creek/20th Century-Fox, 1990). Produced by Scott Rudin, William Sackheim. Directed by John Schlesinger. Script by Daniel Pyne. Director of Photography, Amir Mokri. Production Designer, Neil Spisak. Music, Hans Zimmer. Editor, Steven Ramirez.

Starring Melanie Griffith (Patty Palmer), Matthew Modine (Drake Goodman), Michael Keaton (Carter Hayes), Mako (Toshio Watanabe), Nobu McCarthy (Mira Watanabe), Laurie Metcalf (Stephanie MacDonald), Tippi Hedren (Florence Peters). 103 minutes.

Paint It Black. (Vestron, 1989). Produced by Anne Kimmel and Mark Forstater. Directed by Tim Hunter [uncredited: Roger Holzberg]. Script by A.H. Zacharias [Tim Harris and Hershel Weingrod] and Michael Drexler. Executive Producers, William J. Quigley, Dan Ireland. Director of Photography, Mark Irwin. Production Designer, Steve Legler. Music, Jurgen Knieper. Editor, Michael J. Sheridan. Starring Rick Rossovich (Jonathan Dunbar), Sally Kirkland (Marion Easton), Julie Carmen (Gina), Martin Landau (Lambert), Doug Savant (Eric), Jason Bernard (Lt. Wilder), Joel Hershman (Valet). 101 minutes.

Past Midnight. (New Line, 1992). Produced by Lisa M. Hansen. Directed by Jan Eliasberg. Script by Frank Norwood and Quentin Tarantino. Executive Producer, Paul Hertzberg. Director of Photography, Robert Yoeman. Editor, Christopher Rouse. Starring Natasha Richardson (Laura Matthews), Rutger Hauer (Ben Jordan), Clancy Brown (Steve). 100 minutes.

P.I. Private Investigations, 1987 (Polygram/MGM-UA). Produced by Steven Golin and Sigurjon Sighvatsson. Directed by Nigel Dick. Script by John Dahl and David Warfield. Director of Photography, David Bridges. Production Designer, Piers Plowden. Music, Murray Munro. Editor, Scott Chestnut. Starring Clayton Rohner (Joey), Ray Sharkey (Ryan), Paul Le Mat (Lieutenant), Talia Balsam (Jenny), Antony Zerbe (Charles Bradley), Martin Balsam (Cliff). 91 minutes.

Point Break. (20th Century Fox/Largo, 1991). Produced by Peter Abrams, Robert L. Levy, Michael Rauch, and Rick King. Directed by Kathryn Bigelow. Script by W. Peter Iliff, based on a story by King and Iliff. Director of Photography, Donald Peterman. Production Designer, Peter Jamison. Music, Mark Isham. Editor, Howard Smith. Starring Patrick Swayze (Bodhi), Keanu Reeves (Johnny Utah), Gary Busey (Pappas), Lori Petty (Tyler), John McGinley (Beh Harp), James LeGros (Roach). 122 minutes.

Positive I.D. (Universal, 1987). Produced, directed, and written by Andy Anderson. Director of Photography, Paul Barton. Production Designer, David Keens. Music, Steven Jay Hoey. Editor, Andy Anderson, Robert J. Castaldo. Starring Stephanie Rascoe (Julie Kenner), John Davies (Don Kenner), Steve Fromholz (Lt. Roy Mercer), Laura Lane (Dana), Gail Cronauer (Melissa), Matthew Sachs (Mr. Tony), Stephen Jay Moey (Johnny). 96 minutes.

The Postman Always Rings Twice. (Paramount/Lorimar, 1981). Produced by Bob Rafelson and Charles Mulvehill. Directed by Bob Rafelson. Script by David Mamet, based on the novel by James M. Cain. Executive Producer, Andrew Braunberg. Director of Photography, Sven Nykvist. Production Designer, George Jenkins. Music, Michael Small. Editor, Graeme Clifford. Starring Jack Nicholson (Frank Chambers), Jessica Lang (Cora Papadakis), John Colicos (Nick Papadakis), Michael Lerner (Katz), John P. Ryan (Kennedy), Anjelica Huston (Madge), Christopher Lloyd (the Salesman). 125 minutes.

Presumed Innocent. (Warner Bros., 1990). Produced by Sydney Pollack and Mark Rosenberg. Directed by Alan J. Pakula. Script by Frank Pierson and Alan J. Pakula. Director of Photography, Gordon Willis. Production Designer, George Jenkins. Music, John Williams. Editor, Evan Lottman. Starring Harrison Ford (Rusty Saboch), Brian Dennehy (Raymond Horgan), Raul Julia (Sandy Stern), Bonnie Bedelia (Barbara Sabich), Paul Winfield (Judge Larren Lyttle), Greta Scacchi (Carolyn Polhemus), John Spencer (Detective Lipranzer). 126 minutes.

Prime Suspect. (SVS/Sony, 1989). Produced by Alain Silver and Patrick Regan. Directed by Mark Rutland. Script by Alex Josephs. Executive Producers, Tom Broadbridge and Shelley E. Reid. Director of Photography, Fernando Arguelles. Production Designer, Gary T. New. Music, Bruce Kimmel. Editor, Sergei Goncharoff. Starring Susan Strasberg (Dr. Warren), Robert F. Lyons (Hank Fallon), Tom Breznahan (Tod Jennings), Michael Parks (Nevins), Billy Drago (Cyril), Dana Plato (Diana), Frank Stallone (Chambers), Doug McClure (Dr. Brand), Mark Keyloun (Sgt. Blaze), Ken Wright (D.A.). 91 minutes.

Prince of the City. (Orion/Warner Bros., 1981). Produced by Burtt Harris. Directed by Sidney Lumet. Script by Jay Presson Allen and Sidney Lumet. Executive Producer, Jay Presson Allen. Director of Photography, Andrez Bartkowiak. Production Designer, Tony Walton. Music, Michael Chihara. Editor, John J. Fitzstephens. Starring Treat Williams (Danny Ciello), Jerry Orbach (Gus Levy), Richard Foronjy (Joe Marinaro), Norman Parker (Rick Cappolino), Lindsay Crouse (Carla). 167 minutes.

Q and A. (TriStar/Regency/Odyssey, 1990). Produced by Arnon Milchan and Burtt Harris. Directed by Sidney Lumet. Script by Sidney Lumet, based on the novel by Edwin Torres. Director of Photography, Andrzej Bartkowiak. Production Designer, Philip Rosenberg. Music, Ruben Blades. Editor, Richard Cirincione. Starring Nick Nolte (Mike Brennan), Timothy Hutton (Al Reilly), Armand Assante (Bobby Texador), Patrick O'Neal (Kevin Quinn), Jenny Lumet (Nancy Bosch), Lee Richardson (Leo Bloomenfeld). 134 minutes.

The Rain Killer. (Concorde/New Horizons, 1990) Produced by Rodman Flender. Director and Executive Producer, Ken Stein. Script by Ray Conneff. Director of Photography, Janusz Kaminsly. Production Designer, Gary Randall. Music, Terry Plumeri. Editor, Patrick Rand. Starring Ray

Sharkey (Capra), David Beecroft (Dalton), Tania Coleridge (Adele), Michael Chiklis (Reese), Bill La Vallee (Hacket), Woody Brown (Rosewall), Maria Ford (Satin), Larry Manley (Angel). 87 minutes.

Red Rock West. (Polygram/Propaganda, 1992). Produced by Joni Sighvatsson, Steve Golin. Directed by John Dahl. Script by John and Rick Dahl. Executive Producer, Michael Kuhn. Director of Photography, Marc Reshovsky. Production Designer, Rob Pierson. Editor, Scott Chesnut. Starring Nicholas Cage (Michael), Lara Flynn Boyle (Suzanne), Dennis Hopper (Lyle), J.T. Walsh (Wayne).

Relentless. (New Line, 1989). Produced by Howard Smith and Paul Hertzberg. Directed by William Lustig. Script by Jack T. Robinson (Phil Alden Robinson). Director of Photography, James Lemmo. Production Designer, Gene Abel. Music, Jack Chattawan. Editor, David Kern. Starring Judd Nelson (Buck), Robert Loggia (Bill Malloy), Leo Rossi (Sam Dietz), Meg Foster (Carol Foster), Patrick O' Brien (Todd Arthur). 93 minutes.

Rent-A-Cop. (Kings Road, 1988). Produced by Raymond Wagner. Directed by Jerry London. Script by Dennis Shryack and Michael Blodgett. Director of Photography, Giuseppe Rotunno. Production Designer, Tony Masters. Music, Jerry Goldsmith. Editor, Robert Lawrence. Starring Burt Reynolds (Church), Liza Minnelli (Della), James Remar (Dancer), Richard Masur (Roger), Dionne Warwick (Beth), Bernie Casey (Lemar), Robby Benson (Pitts). 95 minutes.

Reservoir Dogs. (Miramax, 1992). Produced by Lawrence Bender. Directed and Written by Quentin Tarantino. Executive Producers, Richard N. Gladstein, Ronna B. Wallace, Monte Hellman. Co-Producer, Harvey Keitel. Director of Photography, Andrzej Sekula. Production Designer, David Wasco. Music Supervisor, Karyn Rachtman. Editor, Sally Menke. Starring Harvey Keitel (Mr. White), Tim Roth (Mr. Orange/Freddy), Michael Madsen (Mr. Blonde), Chris Penn (Nice Guy Eddie), Steve Buscemi (Mr. Pink), Lawrence Tierney (Joe Cabot), Eddie Bunker (Mr. Blue), Quentin Tarantino (Mr. Brown). 99 minutes.

Revenge. (Columbia/Rastar/New World, 1990). Produced by Hunt Lowry and Stanley Rubin. Directed by Tony Scott. Script by Jim Harrison and Jeffrey Fiskin, based on the novella by Harrison. Director of Photography, Jeffrey Kimball. Production Designer, Michael Seymour, Benjamin Fernandez. Music, Jack Nitzsche. Editor, Chris Lebenzon. Starring Kevin Costner (Cochran), Anthony Quinn (Tibey), Madeleine Stowe (Miryea), Tomas Milan (Cesar), Joaquin Martinez (Mauro). 124 minutes.

Rolling Thunder. (AIP, 1977). Produced by Norman T. Herman. Directed by John Flynn. Script by Paul Schrader and Heywood Gould. Director of Photography, Jordan Croneweth. Production Designer, Steve Berger. Music,

Barry De Vorzon. Editor, Frank P. Keller. Starring William Devane (Major Charles Rane), Tommy Lee Jones (Johnny Voliden), Linda Haynes (Linda Forchet), Dabney Coleman (Maxwell), James Best (Texan), Cassie Yates (Candy). 99 minutes.

The Rosary Murders. (New Line, 1987). Directed by Fred Walton. Script by Elmore Leonard and Fred Walton, based on the novel by William X. Kienzle. Executive Producers, Robert G. Laurel and Michael R. Mahalick. Associate Producer, Chris Coles. Director of Photography, David Golia. Music, Bobby Laurel and Don Sebesky. Editor, Sam Vitale. Starring Donald Sutherland (Father Koesler), Charles Durning (Father Nabors), Belinda Bauer (Pat Lennon), Josef Sommer (Lt. Koznicki), James Murtaugh (Javison), Kathleen Tolan (Sister Ann), Anne Minot (Sister Mary Martyrs). 105 minutes.

Run. (Buena Vista, 1991). Produced by Raymond Wagner. Directed by Geoff Burrowes. Script by Dennis Shryack and Michael Blodgett. Director of Photography, Bruce Surtees. Production Designer, John Willett. Music, Phil Marshall. Editor, Jack Hofstra. Starring Patrick Dempsey (Charlie Farrow), Kelly Preston (Karen Landers), Ken Pogue (Halloran), Alan C. Peterson (Denny Halloran), Christopher Lawford (Martins). 91 minutes.

Rush. (Zanuck/MGM, 1991). Produced by Richard D. Zanuck. Directed by Lili Fini Zanuck. Script by Pete Dexter, based on the novel by Kim Wozencraft. Director of Photography, Kenneth MacMillan. Production Designer, Paul Sylbert. Music, Eric Clapton. Editor, Mark Warner. Starring Jason Patric (Raynor), Jennifer Jason Leigh (Kristen), Sam Elliott (Dodd), Max Perlich (Walker), Gregg Allman (Gaines), Tony Frank (Nettle). 145 minutes.

Scissors. (DDM Films, 1991). Produced by Mel Pearl, Don Levin, and Hal Polaire. Directed by Frank De Felitta. Script by De Felitta, based on a story by Joyce Selznick. Director of Photography, Tony Richmond. Production Designer, Craig Stearns. Editor, John Schreyer. Starring Sharon Stone (Angie), Steve Railsback (Alex/Cole), Ronny Cox (Dr. Carter), Michelle Phillips (Ann). 105 minutes.

Sea of Love. (Bregman/Universal, 1989). Produced by Martin Bregman and Louis A. Stroller. Directed by Harold Becker. Script by Richard Price. Director of Photography, Ronnie Taylor. Production Designer, John Jay Moore. Music, Trevor Jones. Editor, David Bretherton. Starring Al Pacino (Frank Keller), Ellen Barkin (Helen), John Goodman (Sherman), Michael Rooker (Terry), William Hickey (Frank, Sr.), Richard Jenkins (Gruber), Paul Calderon (Serafino). 113 minutes.

Serpico. (Paramount, 1973). Produced by Marton Bregman. Directed by Sidney Lumet. Script by Waldo Salt and Norman Wexler, based on the book by Peter Maas. Executive Producer, Dino De Laurentiis. Director of Photography,

Arthur J. Ornitz. Production Designer, Charles Bailey. Music, Mikis Theodorakis. Editors, Dede Allen, Richards Marks. Starring Al Pacino (Frank Serpico), John Randolph (Chief Green), Jack Kehoe (Tom Keough), Biff McGuire (Capt. McClain), Barbara Eda Young (Laurie), Cornelia Sharpe (Leslie), Tony Roberts (Bob Blair). 129 minutes.

Shaft. (MGM, 1971). Produced by Joel Freeman. Directed by Gordon Parks. Script by Ernest Tidyman and John D.F. Black, based on Tidyman's novel. Executive Producer, Sterling Silliphant. Director of Photography, Urs Furrer. Production Designer, Emmanuel Girard. Music, Isaac Hayes. Editor, Hugh A. Robertson. Starring Richard Roundtree (John Shaft), Moses Gunn (Bumpy Jonas), Victor Arnold (Charlie) Charles Cioffi (Lt. Vic Androzzi), Christopher St. John (Ben), Gwenn Mitchell (Elke), Lawrence Pressman (Tom). 98 minutes.

Sharky's Machine. (Orion/Warner Bros., 1981). Produced by Hank Moonjean. Directed by Burt Reynolds. Script by Gerald Di Pego, based on the novel by William Diehl. Director of Photography, William Fraker. Production Designer, Walter Scott Herndon. Music Supervision, Snuff Garrett. Editor, William Gordon. Starring Burt Reynolds (Sharky), Rachel Ward (Dominoe), Vittorio Gassman (Victor), Brian Keith (Papa), Charles Durning (Friscoe), Earl Holliman (Hotchkins), Bernie Casey (Arch), Richard Libertini (Nosh), Darryl Hickman (Smiley). 119 minutes.

Shattered. (MGM, 1991). Produced by Wolfgang Petersen, John Davis, and David Korda. Directed by Wolfgang Petersen. Script by Petersen, based on the novel by Richard Neely. Director of Photography, Laszlo Kovacs. Production Designer, Gregg Fonseca. Music, Alan Silvestri. Editor, Hannes Nikel. Glenn Farr. Starring Tom Berenger (Don Merrick), Bob Hoskins (Gus Klein), Greta Scacchi (Judith Merrick), Joanne Whalley-Kilmer (Jenny Scott), Corbin Bensen (Jeb Scott). 97 minutes.

Shoot To Kill. (Touchstone, 1988). Produced by Ron Silverman and Daniel Petrie, Jr. Directed by Roger Spottiswoode. Script by Harv Zimmel, Michael Burton, and Daniel Petrie, Jr. Director of Photography, Michael Chapman. Production Designer, Richard Sylbert. Music, John Scott. Editor, Garth Craven, George Bowers. Starring Sidney Poitier (Warren Stanton), Tom Berenger (Jonathan Knox), Kirstie Alley (Sarah), Clancy Brown (Steve), Richard Masur (Norman). 110 minutes.

The Silence of the Lambs. (Orion/Strong Heart, 1991). Produced by Edward Saxon, Kenneth Utt, and Ron Bozman. Directed by Jonathan Demme. Script by Ted Tally, based on the novel by Thomas Harris. Director of Photography, Tak Fujimoto. Production Designer, Kristi Zea. Music, Howard Shore. Editor, Craig McKay. Starring Jodie Foster (Clarice Starling), Anthony Hopkins (Dr. Hannibal Lecter), Scott Glenn (Jack Crawford), Ted Levine (Jame Gumb), Brooke Smith (Catherine Martin), Anthony Heald (Dr.

Frederick Chilton), Roger Corman, (FBI Director). 118 minutes.

Slamdance. (Island Pictures, 1987). Produced by Rubert Harvey and Barry Opper. Directed by Wayne Wang. Script by Don Opper. Director of Photography, Amir Mokri. Production Designer, Eugenio Zanetti. Music, Mitchell Froom. Editor, Lee Purcy, Sandy Nervig. Starring Tom Hulce (C.C. Drood), Adam Ant (Jim), Judith Barsi (Bean), Virginia Madsen (Yolanda), John Doe (Gilbert), Robert Beltran (Frank), Millie Perkins (Bobbie Nye). 99 minutes.

Sleeping with the Enemy. (20th Century-Fox, 1991). Produced by Leonard Goldberg. Directed by Joseph Ruben. Script by Ronald Bass, based on the novel by Nancy Price. Director of Photography, John W. Lindley. Production Designer, Doug Kramer. Music, Jerry Goldsmith. Editor, George Bowers. Starring Julia Roberts (Sara/Laura), Patrick Bergin (Martin), Kevin Anderson (Ben), Elizabeth Lawrence (Chloe), Kyle Secor (Fleishman). 98 minutes.

Someone To Watch over Me. (Columbia, 1987). Produced by Thierry de Ganay and Harold Schneider. Directed by Ridley Scott. Script by Howard Franklin. Director of Photography, Steven Poster. Production Designer, James D. Bissell. Music, Michael Kamen. Editor, Claire Simpson. Starring Tom Berenger (Mike Keegan), Mimi Rogers (Claire Gregory), Lorraine Bracco (Ellie Keegan), Jerry Orbach (Lt. Garber), John Rubinstein (Neil Steinhart), Andreas Katsulas (Joey Venza). 106 minutes.

Special Delivery. (BCP, 1976). Produced by Dick Berg. Directed by Paul Wendkos. Script by Don Gazzaniga and Gilbert Ralston, based on a story by Gazzaniga. Executive Producer, Charles A. Pratt. Director of Photography, Harry Stradling, Jr. Production Designer, Jack Poplin. Music, Lalo Schifrin. Editor, Houseley Stevenson. Starring Bo Svenson (Jack Murdock), Cybill Shepherd (Mary Jane), Michael C. Gwynne (Carl Graff), Vic Tayback (Wyatt), Robert Ito (Mr. Chu), John Quade (Barney), Gerrit Graham (Swivot), Jeff Goldblum (Snake). 99 minutes.

Stakeout. (Buena Vista, 1987). Produced by Jim Kouf and Cathleen Summer. Directed by John Badham. Script by Jim Kouf. Director of Photography, John Seale. Production Designer, Philip Harrison. Music, Arthur B. Rubinstein. Editors, Tom Rolf and Michael Ripps. Starring Richard Dreyfuss (Chris Lecce), Emilio Estevez (Bill Reimers), Madeleine Stowe (Maria), Aidan Quinn (Montgomery), Dan Luaria (Coldshank). 115 minutes.

State of Grace. (Orion/Cinehaus, 1990). Produced by Ned Dowd, Randy Ostrow, and Ron Rotholz. Directed by Phil Joanou. Script by Dennis McIntyre. Director of Photography, Jordan Cronenweth. Production Designer, Patrizia Von Brandenstein, Doug Kraner. Music, Ennio Morricone. Editor, Claire Simpson. Starring Sean Penn (Terry), Ed Harris (Frankie), Gary Oldman (Jackie), Robin Wright

(Kathleen), John Turturro (Nick), John C. Reilly (Stevie), R.D. Call (Nicholson), Burgess Meredith (Finn). 134 minutes.

Still of the Night. (MGM/UA, 1982). Produced by Arlene Donovan. Directed and Written by Robert Benton, based on a story by David Newman and Benton. Director of Photography, Nestor Almendros. Production Designer, Mel Bourne. Music, John Kandler. Editor, Jerry Greenberg. Starring Roy Scheider (Sam Rice), Meryl Streep (Brooke Reynolds), Jessica Tandy (Grace Rice), Joe Grifasi (Joseph Vitucci), Sara Botsford (Gail), Josef Sommer (George). 91 minutes.

Stripped to Kill. (Concorde Pictures, 1987). Produced by Andy Ruben. Directed by Katt Shea Ruben. Script by Andy and Katt Shea Ruben. Director of Photography, John Leblanc. Production Designer, Paul Raubertas. Music, John O'Kennedy. Editor, Zach Staenberg. Starring Kay Lenz (Cody/Sunny), Greg Evigan (Sgt. Heineman), Norman Fell (Club Owner), Tracy Crowder (Fanny), Athena Worthey (Zeena). 84 minutes.

Sudden Impact. (Warner Bros., 1983). Produced and Directed by Clint Eastwood. Script by Joseph C. Stinson, based on a story by Earl E. Smith and Charles Pierce. Executive Producer, Fritz Manes. Director of Photography, Bruce Surtees. Production Designer, Edward Carfagno. Music, Lalo Schifrin. Editor, Joel Cox. Starring Clint Eastwood (Harry Callahan), Sondra Locke (Jennifer), Pat Hingle (Chief Jennings), Bradford Dillman (Capt. Briggs), Audrie Nienan (Ray), Jack Thibeau (Kruger). 117 minutes.

Suspect. (TriStar, 1987). Produced by Daniel A. Sherkow. Directed by Peter Yates. Script by Eric Roth. Executive Producer, John Veitch. Director of Photography, Billy Williams. Production Designer, Stuart Wurtzel. Music, Michael Kamen. Editor, Ray Lovejoy. Starring Cher (Kathleen Riley), Dennis Quaid (Eddie Sanger), Liam Neeson (Carl Wayne Anderson), Joe Mantegna (Charlie Stella), John Mahoney (Judge Matthew Helms), Philip Bosco (Paul Grey), E. Katherine Kerr (Grace Comisky). 101 minutes.

Tequila Sunrise. (Warner Bros., 1988). Produced by Thom Mount. Directed and Written by Robert Towne. Director of Photography, Conrad Hall. Production Designer, Richard Sylbert. Music, Dave Grusin. Editor, Claire Simpson. Starring Mel Gibson (Dale McKussic), Michelle Pfeiffer (Jo Ann Vallenari), Kurt Russell (Frescia), Raul Julia (Commandante Escalante), J.T. Walsh (Maguire). 116 minutes.

Thelma and Louise. (Pathe/Percy Main, 1991). Produced by Ridley Scott, Mimi Polk, Callie Khouri, and Dean O'Brien. Directed by Ridley Scott. Script by Callie Khouri. Director of Photography, Adrian Biddle. Production Designer, Norris Spencer. Music, Hans Zimmer. Editor, Thom Noble. Starring Susan Sarandon (Louise), Geena Davis (Thelma), Harvey Keitel (Hal), Michael Madsen (Jimmy), Christopher

McDonald (Darryl), Brad Pitt (J.D.). 128 minutes.

Thief. (United Artists, 1981). Produced by Jerry Bruckheimer and Ronnie Caan. Directed by Michael Mann. Script by Michael Mann, based on the novel *The Home Invaders* by Frank Hohimer. Director of Photography, Donald Thorin. Production Designer, Mel Bourne. Music, Tangerine Dream. Editor, Dov Hoenig. Starring James Caan (Frank), Tuesday Weld (Jessie), Robert Prosty (Leo), Tom Signorelli (Attaglia), Dennis Farina (Carl), James Belushi (Barry), Willie Nelson (Doc). 122 minutes.

Thieves Like Us. (United Artists, 1974). Produced by Jerry Bick and George Litto. Directed by Robert Altman. Script by Calder Willingham, Joan Tewksbury, and Robert Altman, based on the novel by Edward Anderson. Director of Photography, Jean Boffety. Editor, Lou Lombardo. Starring Keith Carradine (Bowie), Shelley Duvall (Keechie), John Schuck (Chicamaw), Bert Remsem (T-Dub), Louise Fletcher (Mattie), Ann Latham (Lula), Tom Skerritt (Dee). 123 minutes.

Thunderheart. (Tri-Star, 1992). Produced by Robert DeNiro, Jane Rosenthal, John Fusco. Directed by Michael Apted. Script by John Fusco. Executive Producer, Michael Nozik. Director of Photography, Roger Deakins. Production Designer, Dan Bishop. Music, James Horner. Editor, Ian Crafford. Starring Val Kilmer (Ray Levol), Sam Sheppard (Frank Coutelle), Graham Greene (Walter Crow Horse), Fred Ward (Jack Milton), Sheile Tousey (Maggie Eagle Bear), Chief Ted Thin Elk (Granpa Sam Reaches), John Trudell (Jimmy Looks Twice). 118 minutes.

Tightrope. (Warner Bros., 1984). Produced by Clint Eastwood and Fritz Manes. Directed and Written by Richard Tuggle. Director of Photography, Bruce Surtees. Production Designer, Edward Carfagno. Music, Lennie Niehaus. Editor, Joel Cox. Starring Clint Eastwood (Wes Block), Genevieve Bujold (Beryl), Dan Hedaya (Molinari), Alison Eastwood (Amanda), Jennifer Beck (Penny), Marco St. John (Wolfe). 114 minutes.

To Kill For. (Moviestore, 1992). Produced by Stacy Codikow. Directed by John Dirlam. Script by George D. Putnam. Executive Producer, Mark Polan. Director of Photography, John Dirlam. Production Designer, Gary Lee Reed. Music, Stephen Allen and Bobby Crew. Editor, Rachel Igel. Starring Michael Madsen (Burden), Laura Johnson (Catherine Merrims), Richard Forojny. 93 minutes.

To Live and Die in L.A. (MGM/UA, 1985). Produced by Irving H. Levin. Directed by William Friedkin. Script by Friedkin and Gerald Petrivich, based on his novel. Executive Producer, Samuel Schulman. Director of Photography, Robby Muller. Production Designer, Lilly Kilvert. Music, Wang Chung. Editors, Bud Smith and Scott Smith. Starring William L. Petersen (Chance), Willem Dafoe (Masters), John Pankow (Vukovich), Debra Feuer (Bianca), Darlanne Fluegel (Ruth), John Turturro (Cody). 116 minutes.

The Two Jakes. (Paramount, 1990). Produced by Robert Evans, Harold Schneider. Directed by Jack Nicholson. Script by Robert Towne. Director of Photography, Vilmos Zsigmond. Production Designer, Jeremy Railton, Richard Sawyer. Music, Van Dyke Parks. Editor, Anne Goursaud. Starring Jack Nicholson (Jake Gittes), Harvey Keitel (Jake Berman), Meg Tilly (Kitty Berman), Madeleine Stowe (Lillian Bodine), Eli Wallach (Cotton Weinburger), Ruben Blades (Mickey Nice), Frederic Forrest (Newty). 137 minutes.

True Believer. (Columbia, 1989). Produced by Walter F. Parkes and Lawrence Lasker. Directed by Joseph Ruben. Script by Wesley Strick. Director of Photography, John W. Lindley. Production Designer, Lawrence Miller. Music, Brad Fiedel. Editor, George Bowers. Starring James Woods (Eddie Dodd), Robert Downey, Jr. (Roger Barron), Margaret Colin (Kitty Greer), Yuzio Okimoto (Shu Kai Kim), Kurtwood Smith (Robert Reynard), Tom Bower (Cecil Skell). 104 minutes.

Union City. (Kinesis, 1980). Produced by Graham Belin. Directed by Mark Reichert. Script by Reichert, based on the Cornell Woolrich story "The Corpse Next Door." Director of Photography, Edward Lachman. Production Designer, George Stavrinos. Music, Chris Stein. Editor, Lana Tokel, Eric Albertson, J. Michaels. Starring Dennis Lipscomb (Harlan), Deborah Harry (Lillian), Irina Maleeva (Contessa), Everett McGill (Larry Longacre), Pat Benatar (Jeanette), Sam McMurray (Young Vagrant). 87 minutes.

V.I. Warshawski. (Buena Vista/Hollywood Pictures/Silver Screen Partners IV, 1991). Produced by Jeffrey Luri and Doug Claybourne. Directed by Jeff Kanew. Script by Edward Taylor, David Aaron Cohen, and Nick Thiel, based on the novels of Sara Paretsky. Director of Photography, Jan Kiesser. Production Designer, Barbara Ling. Music, Randy Edelman. Editor, C. Timothy O'Meara, Debra Neil. Starring Kathleen Turner (V.I.), Jay O. Sanders (Murray), Charles Durning (Lt. Mallory), Angela Goethals (Kat Grafalk), Nancy Paul (Paige Grafalk). 89 minutes.

White of the Eye. (Paramount/Palisades Entertainment, 1988). Produced by Cassian Elwes and Brad Wyman. Directed by Donald Cammell. Script by Donald and China Cammell, based on the novel, Mrs. White, by Margaret Tracy. Executive Producer, Elliott Kastner. Directors of Photography, Alan Jones (Lighting Cameraman), Larry McConkey. Production Designer, Philip Thomas. Music, Nick Mason, Rick Fenn. Editor, Terry Rawlings. Starring David Keith (Paul White), Cathy Moriarty (Joan White), Alan Rosenberg (Mike DeSantos), Art Evans (Mendoza), Danielle Smith (Danielle), Alberta Watson (Anne Mason). 113 minutes.

White Sands. (Warner Bros., 1992). Produced by William Sackheim and Scott Rudin. Directed by Roger Donaldson. Script by Daniel Pyne. Director of Photography, Peter Menzies, Jr. Production Designer, John Graysmark. Music, Patrick O'Hearn. Editor, Nicholas Beauman. Starring Willem Dafoe (Ray Dolezal), Mickey Rourke (Gorman Lebbox), Mary Elizabeth Mastrantonio (Lae Bodine), Samuel L. Jackson (Greg Meeker), Mimi Rogers (Mrs. Dolezal), M. Emmet Walsh (Coroner). 101 minutes.

Who'll Stop the Rain. (United Artists, 1978). Produced by Herb Jaffe and Gabriel Katzka. Directed by Karel Reisz. Script by Judith Rascoe and Robert Stone, based on his novel *Dog Soldiers*. Director of Photography, Richard H. Kline. Music, Lawrence Rosenthal. Editor, John Bloom. Starring Nick Nolte (Ray), Tuesday Weld (Marge), Michael Moriarty (John), Anthony Zerbe (Antheil), Richard Masur (Danskin), Ray Sharkey (Smitty), Gail Strickland (Chairman). 125 minutes.

Witness. (Paramount, 1985). Produced by Edward S. Feldman and David Feldman. Directed by Peter Weir. Script by Earl W. Wallace and William Kelley. Director of Photography, John Seale. Production Designer, Stan Jolley. Music, Maurice Jarre. Editor, Thom Noble. Starring Harrison Ford (John Book), Kelly McGillis (Rachel), Josef Sommer (Schaeffer), Lukas Haas (Samuel), Jan Rubes (Eli Lapp), Danny Glover (McFee). 112 minutes.

Year of the Dragon. (MGM/UA, 1985). Produced by Dino De Laurentiis. Directed by Michael Cimino. Script by Oliver Stone and Michael Cimino, based on the novel by Robert Daley. Director of Photography, Alex Thomson. Production Designer, Wolf Kroger. Music, David Mansfield. Editor, Françoise Bonnot. Starring Mickey Rourke (Stanley White), John Lone (Joey Tal), Ariane (Tracey Tzu), Leonard Termo (Angelo Rizzo), Ray Barry (Bukowski), Caroline Kava (Connie). 136 minutes.

3. Chronology of Neo-Noir

1966
Harper (Warner Bros.)

1968
The Detective (20th Century-Fox)
Lady in Cement (20th Century-Fox)

1971
Chandler (MGM)
Klute (Warner Bros.)
Shaft (MGM)

1973
Serpico (Paramount)

1974
Black Eye (Warner Bros.)
Death Wish (Paramount)

The Conversation (Paramount)
Thieves Like Us (United Artists)

1975
Dog Day Afternoon (Warner Bros.)
The Drowning Pool (Warner Bros.)

1976
The Killer Inside Me (Warner Bros.)
The Killing of a Chinese Bookie (Faces)
Special Delivery (BCP)

1977
Rolling Thunder (AIP)

1978
The Big Sleep (United Artists)
The Driver (20th Century-Fox)
Who'll Stop the Rain (United Artists)

1979
Hardcore (Columbia)
The Last Embrace (United Artists)
The Onion Field (Avco Embassy)

1980
The First Deadly Sin (Filmways)
Union City (Kinesis)

1981
Atlantic City (Paramount)
Body Heat (Ladd Co./Warner Bros)
Eyewitness (20th Century-Fox)
Ms. 45 (Navaron/Rochelle)
The Postman Always Rings Twice (Paramount)
Prince of the City (Orion/Warner Bros.)
Sharky's Machine (Orion/Warner Bros)
Thief (United Artists)

1982
The Border (Universal)
48 Hrs. (Paramount)
I, the Jury
Still of the Night (MGM/UA)

1983
Bad Boys (EMI/Universal)
Breathless (Orion)
Hammett (Orion/Warner Bros.)
Sudden Impact (Warner Bros)

1984
Against All Odds (Columbia)
Blood Simple (Circle Releasing/Skouras)
Fear City (Zupnik/Curtis)
Mike's Murder (Ladd Co./Warner Bros.)
Tightrope (Warner Bros)

1985
Jagged Edge (Columbia)
To Live and Die in L.A. (MGM/UA)

Witness (Paramount)
Year of the Dragon (MGM/UA)

1986
At Close Range (Hemdale/Orion)
Dangerously Close (Cannon)
Eight Million Ways To Die (TriStar)
52 Pick-up (Cannon)
Manhunter (De Laurentiis)
The Morning After (20th Century-Fox/Lorimar)
Murphy's Law (Cannon)
No Mercy (TriStar)
Out of Bounds (Columbia)

1987
The Bedroom Window (De Laurentiis)
Best Seller (Hemdale/Orion)
The Big Easy (Kings Road/Universal)
Black Widow (20th Century-Fox)
Fatal Attraction (Paramount)
House of Games (Orion)
The Killing Time (New World)
Lady Beware (IVE)
Lethal Weapon (Warner Bros.)
Malone (Orion)
No Way Out (Orion)
P.I. Private Investigations (MGM/UA)
Positive I.D. (Universal)
Rosary Murders (New Line)
Slamdance (Island)
Someone To Watch Over Me (Columbia)
Stakeout (Buena Vista)
Stripped to Kill (Concorde)
Suspect (TriStar)

1988
Betrayed (MGM/UA)
Call Me (Vestron)
Cop (Atlantic)
DOA (Touchstone)
Frantic (Warner Bros.)
Masquerade (MGM/UA)
Rent-A-Cop (Kings Road)
Shoot to Kill (Touchstone)
Tequila Sunrise (Warner Bros.)
White of the Eye (Paramount)

1989
Black Rain (Paramount)
Criminal Law (Hemdale/TriStar)
Dead-Bang (Warner Bros.)
Gleaming the Cube (20th Century-Fox)
Hit List (New Line)
Johnny Handsome (TriStar)
Lethal Weapon II (Warner Bros.)
Night Visitor (MGM/UA)
Out of the Dark (New Line)
Paint It Black (Vestron)
Prime Suspect (SVS/Sony)

APPENDIX

Relentless (New Line)
Sea of Love (Universal)
True Believer (Columbia)

1990

After Dark, My Sweet (Avenue Pictures)
Alligator Eyes (Castle Hill)
Another 48 Hrs. (Paramount)
Bad Influence (Epic)
Blue Steel (MGM)
Body Chemistry (Concorde)
Cat Chaser (Vestron)
Desperate Hours (MGM)
Genuine Risk (IRS)
The Grifters (Miramax)
The Hot Spot (Orion)
Impulse (Warner Bros.)
Internal Affairs (Paramount)
Jezebel's Kiss (Shapiro/Glickenhaus)
Kill Me Again (MGM)
The Kill-Off (Filmworld)
King of New York (Seven Arts/New Line)
Miami Blues (Orion)
Miller's Crossing (20th Century-Fox)
Mortal Passions (Gibraltar)
Narrow Margin (TriStar)
New Jack City (Warner Bros.)
Out of the Rain (Acme Co./Live)
Pacific Heights (20th Century-Fox)
Presumed Innocent (Warner Bros.)
Q & A (TriStar)
The Rain Killer (Concorde/New Horizons)
Revenge (Columbia)
Sleeping with the Enemy (20th Century-Fox)
State of Grace (Orion)
The Two Jakes (Paramount)

1991

Cape Fear (Universal)
Dead Again (Paramount)
Deceived (Touchstone)
Delusion (Cineville)
Femme Fatale (Republic/Gibraltar)
Homicide (Triumph/Cinehaus)
The Horseplayer (Relentless/J&N)
Intimate Stranger (Southgate)
A Kiss Before Dying (Universal)
Kiss Me a Killer (Califilm)
The Last Boy Scout (Geffen)
Liebestraum (Pathe/MGM)
Mortal Thoughts (Columbia)
Point Break (20th Century-Fox)
Run (Buena Vista)
Rush (MGM)
Scissors (DDM Films)
Shattered (MGM)
Silence of the Lambs (Orion)
Thelma and Louise (Pathe)
V.I. Warchavsky (Buena Vista)

1992

Basic Instinct (Carolco/TriStar)
The Bodyguard (Warner Bros.)
Blue Dessert (Academy Entertainment)
Criminal Intent (Promark)
The Dark Wind (New Line
Deep Cover (New Line)
Diary of a Hitman (Vision)
Final Analysis (Warner Bros.)
Guncrazy (Overseas)
The Hand that Rocks the Cradle (Buena Vista)
Lethal Weapon III (Warner Bros.)
Love Crimes (Millimeter/Sovereign)
Midnight Heat (New Line)
Nails (Viacom)
Night and the City (20th Century-Fox)
Past Midnight (New Line)
Red Rock West (Polygram/Propaganda)
Reservoir Dogs (Miramax)
Thunderheart (TriStar)
To Kill For (Moviestore)
White Sands (Warner Bros.)

4. Directors of Neo-noir

Arnold, Jack
The Tattered Dress
Black Eye

Bigelow, Katherine
Blue Steel
Point Break

Coen, Joel
Blood Simple
Miller's Crossing

Dahl, John
Kill Me Again
Red Rock West

Demme, Jonathan
The Last Embrace
Silence of the Lambs

Donaldson, Roger
No Way Out
White Sands

Donner, Richard
Lethal Weapon
Lethal Weapon II
Lethal Weapon III

Douglas, Gordon
The Detective
Lady in Cement

Ferrera, Abel
Cat Chaser
Fear City

King of New York
Ms. 45

Figgis, Michael
Internal Affairs
Liebestraum

Flynn, John
Best Seller
Nails
The Outfit Rolling Thunder

Foley, James
After Dark, My Sweet
At Close Range

Hanson, Curtis
Bad Influence
The Bedroom Window
The Hand that Rocks the Cradle

Hill, Walter
Another 48 Hrs
The Driver
48 Hrs
Johnny Handsome

Joanou, Phil
Final Analysis
State of Grace

Kennedy, Burt
The Killer Inside Me
The Money Trap

Lumet, Sidney
Dog Day Afternoon
The Morning After
Q & A
Serpico

Lustig, William
Hit List
Relentless

Mamet, David
Homicide
House of Games

Mann, Michael
Manhunter
Thief

McBride, Jim
The Big Easy
Breathless

Pakula, Alan J.
Klute
Presumed Innocent

Rafelson, Bob
Black Widow
*The Postman Always Rings
    Twice*

Scorsese, Martin
Cape Fear
Taxi Driver

Scott, Ridley
Black Rain
Someone to Watch Over Me
Thelma and Louise

Scott, Tony
The Last Boy Scout
Revenge

Tuggle, Richard
Out of Bounds
Tightrope

Voss, Kurt
Genuine Risk
The Horseplayer

Wendkos, Paul
The Burglar
Special Delivery

Winner, Michael
The Big Sleep
Death Wish

Yates, Peter
Eyewitness
The Narrow Margin
Suspect

Afterword

In 1955, Raymond Borde and Etienne Chaumenton wrote in their Introduction to Panorama du Film Noir American: "It seems apparent to all that there has been a 'noir series' among the films produced in Hollywood. It is another matter to define its essential traits." More than a dozen books and scores of articles later, little seems to have changed. Nor are any of the books, dissertations, articles, etc. which doubtless will continue to appear likely to bring a new, clarifying light to bear.

In preparing this 3rd Edition, we reviewed the literature, considered dozens more films from the 40s and 50s, and assessed newer films as "neo-noir." We also spoke with other critics and with filmmakers responsible for both high and low-budget pictures and reconfirmed what Paul Schrader wrote more than twenty years ago that almost everyone "has his own definition of film noir, and a personal list of film titles and dates to back it up." There is still a consensus that the "classic period" produced a series of films which we now call "noir"; and there is a core group of titles which all observers would agree are part of that phenomenon. Beyond that, where are we?

As we have asserted several times in the essays which comprise this latest edition, with regard to what "film noir" and any successor may be, the surest indicator remains the motion pictures themselves. In creating this book, the aim has always been to make it an accessible work, both as a specific reference and as an overview. Given the number of original contributors and points-of-view, the imposition of an overriding methodology rather than a mere format would have been needlessly constraining. If there

are any underlying critical assumptions at work in this study, they relate variously to auteurism, genre expectation, or metaphorical expression through stylistic manipulation. Strictly speaking, while many of the contributors ascribed creative responsibility to the director, that actual person could just as easily be considered a cipher for the abstract, phenomenological "intentionality" that creates meaning in any artistic expression. In the process of assembling this book, it was readily apparent that, although film noir was not a genre, its creators were quick to recognize the viewer expectations that became associated with it and to exploit them. It was equally clear that, although film noir was not particularly conducive to the expression of a "world view" by individual auteurs, it was not antithetical to such expression either.

This book was originally conceived as a series of essays on aspects of film noir; but it is only in this 3rd Edition that a measure of that original design has been accomplished. In the introspective rhetoric that typifies much of neo-noir, filmmakers comment on filmmakers and work comments on work. The explications offered there, for better or for worse, are beyond "academic flapdoodle" but within the realm of criticism. Neo-noir both recalls and extrapolates on the classic period vividly demonstrating that film noir is both a specific event and an ongoing cycle. Whatever it is called, the "film noir" type of movie is as popular today as any style of film has ever been. Whether these films will ultimately lead down a new set of mean streets only to arrive at a similar destination remains to be seen, and for the next generation of critics to analyze.

SELECTED BIBLIOGRAPHY

The books and articles listed below are concerned with film noir as a general subject or with several individual noir films. Titles concerning films and film makers are not listed because they can be found by using book and periodical indexes such as the *Chicorel Index to Film Literature*, volume 22–22A, of an index series edited by Marietta Chicorel (New York: Chicorel Library Publishing, 1975) or the *Cinema Booklist* by George Rehrauer (Metuchen, N.J.: Scarecrow Press, 1972, with supplements published in 1977). Periodical indexes include the *Retrospective Index to Film Periodicals 1930–1971*, by Linda Batty (New York: R. R. Bowker, 1975): *The New Film Index 1930–1970*, by Richard Dyer MacCann and Edward S. Perry (New York: E. P. Dutton, 1975); *Index to Critical Film Reviews In British and American Film Periodicals*, by Stephen E. Bowles (New York: Burt Franklin and Co., 1974); *The Critical Index*, by John C. and Lana Gerlach (New York: Teachers College Press, 1974); the annual volumes of *International Index to Film Periodicals*, edited by Karen Jones of the Fédération Internationale des Archives du Film (New York: R. R. Bowker, 1972 et seq.); and the *Film Literature Index*, edited by Vincent Aceto, et al. (New York: R. R. Bowker, 1976 et seq.).

BOOKS

Alloway, Lawrence. *Violent America: The Movies 1946–1964*. New York: Museum of Modern Art, 1971. 95 pp., illus., filmography.

Appel, Alfred. *Nabokov's Dark Cinema* ["Dark Cinema," pp. 195–255]. New York: Oxford University Press, 1974. 324 pp., illus.

Borde, Raymonde, and Chaumeton, Etienne. *Panorama du Film Noir Américain (1941–1953)*. Paris: Editions de Minuit, 1955. 279 pp., plates, bibliography, filmography.

Cameron, Ian. *A Pictorial History of Crime Films*. London: Hamlyn, 1975. 221 pp., illus., index.

Cauliez, Armand-Jean. *Le Film Criminal et le Film Policier*. Paris: Editions du Cerf, 7eme Art series, 1956. 123 pp., illus.

Deming, Barbara. *Running Away From Myself: A Dream Portrait of America Drawn From the Films of the Forties*. N.Y.: Grossman Publishers, 1969, 210 pp., illus., filmography.

Gow, Gordon. *Hollywood in the Fifties*. Cranbury, N.J.: A. S. Barnes, 1971. 208 pp., illus., index.

Haskell, Molly. *From Reverence to Rape: The Treatment of Women in the Movies* ["The Forties," pp. 189–221]. New York: Holt, Rinehart & Winston, 1974. 338 pp., illus.

Higham, Charles, and Greenberg, Joel. *Hollywood in the Forties*. Cranbury, N.J.: A. S. Barnes, 1968. ["Black Cinema," pp. 19–36]. 192 pp., illus., index.

Kaminsky, Stuart. *American Film Genres* ["Literary Adapta-tion and Change; The Killers, Hemingway, Film Noir and the Terror of Daylight," pp. 43–59]. Dayton, Ohio: Pflaum Publishing Co., 1974. 232 pp., illus.

Karimi, Amir M. *Toward a Definition of the American Film Noir (1941–1949)*. New York: Arno Press, 1976, 255 pp., bibliography, filmography. [Originally presented as the author's thesis, University of Southern California, 1970.]

Lacassin, Francis. *Mythologie du Roman Policier*. Paris: Union Générale d'Editions, 1974. 2 Volumes, Collection 10/18.

McArthur, Colin. *Underworld USA*. Cinema One, no. 20. New York: Viking, 1972. 176 pp., illus., index.

McCarthy, Todd, and Flynn, Charles, editors. *Kings of the B's: Working Within the Hollywood System*. New York: E. P. Dutton, 1975. 561 pp., illus., filmographies, index.

Mandion, René. *Cinéma: Reflet du Monde, Tableau d'un Art Nouveau* ["Le Film Policier," pp. 139–145]. Paris: Paul Montel, 1944.

Mauriac, Claude. *L'Amour du Cinéma* ["La Dialectique du Gangster et du Flic," pp. 274–279]. Paris: Editions Albin Michel, 1954.

Nichols, Bill, editor. *Movies and Methods* [Place, J., and Peterson, L. S., "Some Visual Motifs of Film Noir," pp. 325–338, illus.]. Berkeley: University of California Press, 1976. 640 pp., illus.

Shadoian, Jack. *Dreams and Dead Ends, The American Gangster/Crime Film*. [Chapter 2, pp. 59–113: "Dark Transformations: The Descent into Noir."] Cambridge, Mass.: MIT Press, 1977, 366 pp., illus., bibliography.

Siclier, Jacques. *Le Mythe de la Femme dans la Cinema Americain* ["Misogynie des Films Noirs," pp. 77–89]. Paris: Editions du Cerf, 7eme Art series, 1956. 196 pp., illus.

Wolfenstein, Martha, and Leites, Nathan. *Movies: A Psychological Study* ["Killers and Victims," pp. 175–242]. New York: The Free Press, 1950.

Wood, Michael. *America in the Movies, or Santa Maria It Had Slipped My Mind* ["The Interpretation of Dreams," pp. 97–125]. New York: Basic Books, 1975. 206 pp., illus.

PERIODICAL ARTICLES

Appel, Alfred. "Fritz Lang's American Nightmare." *Film Comment* 10 no. 6 (1974), pp. 12–17, illus.

Baxter, John. "Something More Than Night." *Film Journal* 2 no. 4 (1975), pp. 4–9, illus.

Borde, Raymond, and Chaumeton, Etienne. "A Propos du Film Noir Americain." *Positif* 19 (1956), pp. 52–57, illus.

Borde, Raymond, and Chaumeton, Etienne. "Vingt Ans Apres, Le Film Noir des Annees 70." *Ecran* 32, January 1975, pp. 5–8, illus.

Buning, Meino. "Nein Zu Dr. No: Kriminalliterature und Kriminalfilm." *Filmstudio* 42 (1963), pp. 26–32, illus.

Chabrol, Claude. "Evolution du Film Policier." *Cahiers Du Cinema* 54 (1955), pp. 27–33, illus.

Chartier, Jean-Pierre. "Les Américains Aussi Font des Films Noirs." *Revue Du Cinema* 2 (1946), pp. 66–70.

Cieutat, Michel. "La Ville dans le Film Policier Américain." *Positif* 171–172 (1975), pp. 26–38, illus.

Cohen, Mitchell S. "Villains and Victims." *Film Comment* 10 no. 6 (1974), pp. 27–29, illus.

Dorémieux, Alain. "Le Film Policier." *Cinematographie Française* 30.1 (1965), pp. 10–15, 18–22, illus.

Dorfman, R. "D.O.A. and the Notion of Noir." *Movietone News* 48 (February, 1976), pp. 11–16, illus.

Durgnat, Raymond. "Paint It Black: The Family Tree of Film Noir." *Cinema* (U.K.) 6/7 (1970), pp. 49–56.

Durgnat, Raymond. 'The Family Tree of Film Noir." [Graph] *Film Comment* 10 no. 6 (1974), pp. 6–7.

Farber, Stephen. "Violence and the Bitch Goddess." *Film Comment* 10, no. 6 (1974), pp. 8–11, illus.

Ferrini, F. "Generi Classici del Cinema Americano." *Bianco & Nero* 35 (1974), pp. 32–39, illus.[Bibliography of foreign language articles.]

Fischer, Hans. "Amerikas Schwarze Serie: Entstehung und Geschichte." *Filmstudio* 42 (1964), pp. 36–45, illus.

Flinn, Tom. "*The Big Heat* and *The Big Combo*: Rogue Cops and Mink Coated Girls." *The Velvet Light Trap* 11 (1974), pp. 23–28, illus.

Flinn, Tom. "Three Faces of Film Noir." *The Velvet Light Trap* 5 (1972), pp. 11–5, illus.

Frank, Nino. "Un Nouveau Genre 'Policier': L'Adventure Criminelle." *L'Ecran Français* 61, no. 28.8 (1946), pp. 8–9, 14, illus.

Gregory, Charles. "Living Life Sideways." *Journal of Popular Film*, Vol. V, #3–4 (1976), pp. 289–311, illus.

Gross, Larry. "Film Apres Noir." *Film Comment* 12, no. 4 (1976), pp. 44–49, illus.

Guibbert, P. "Film Noir: Ou Film Policier. Good Bad Girls and Smart Tough Guys." *Cahiers de la Cinema* 20 (Summer, 1976), pp. 38–45, illus.

Henry, Clayton R., Jr. "Crime Films and Social Criticism." *Films in Review* 2 no. 5 (1951), pp. 31–34.

Houston, Penelope. "The Private Eye." *Sight and Sound* 26 no. 1 (1956), pp. 22–23, 55, illus.

Jameson, Richard T. "Son of Noir." *Film Comment* 10 no. (1974), pp. 30–33, illus.

Jensen, Paul. "Raymond Chandler and the World You Live In." *Film Comment* 10 no. 6 (1974), pp. 18–26, illus.

Jensen, Paul. "The Return of Dr. Caligari: Paranoia in Hollywood." *Film Comment* 7 no. 4 (1971), pp. 36–45, illus.

Kochenrath, Hans-Peter. "Der Gangster Film." *Filmstudio* 39 (1963), pp. 47–53, illus.

Legrand, Gérard. "Elixirs des Navets et Philtres sans Etignette." *L'Age Du Cinema* 4/5 (1951), pp. 17–20, illus.

Legrand, Gérard. "Reflections in a Dark Eye: Sur la "Saga" des "Privé." *Positif* 171/172 (1975), pp. 19–25, illus.

Lyons, Barry. "Fritz Lang and the Film Noir." *Mise-En-Scene* 1 (1972), pp. 11–15, illus.

Madden, David. "James M. Cain and the Movies of the Thirties and Forties." *Film Heritage* 2 no. 4 (1972), pp. 9–25, illus.

Miller, Don. "Films on TV." [Film Noir on Television.] *Films In Review* 12 no. 8 (1961) pp. 495–497, and 12 no. 9 (1961), pp. 561–563.

Miller, Don. "Private Eyes: From Sam Spade to J. J. Gittes." *Focus On Film* 22 (1975), pp. 15–35, illus.

Place, J. A., and Peterson, L. S. "Some Visual Motifs of Film Noir." *Film Comment* 10 no. 1 (1974), pp. 30–32, illus.

Porfirio, Robert G. "No Way Out: Existential Motifs in the Film Noir." *Sight and Sound* 45 no. 4 (1976), pp. 212–217, illus.

Schrader, Paul. "Notes On Film Noir." *Film Comment* 8 no. 1 (1972), pp. 8–13, illus.

Silver, Alain. "*Kiss Me Deadly*: Evidence of a Style." *Film Comment* 11 no. 2 (1975), pp. 24–30, illus.

Siodmak, Robert. "Hoodlums: The Myth." *Films and Filming* 5 no. 9 (1959), p. 10, illus.

Simsolo, N. "Notes Sur Le Film Noir." *Cinema* (Paris) 223 (July, 1977), pp. 23–30, illus.

Wead, George. "Towards a Definition of Filmnoia [sic]." *The Velvet Light Trap* 13 (1974), pp. 2–6, illus.

Whitehall, Richard. "Crime Inc.: A Three Part Dossier on the American Gangster Film." *Films and Filming* 10 no. 4 (1964), pp. 7–12, illus.

Whitehall, Richard. "Some Thoughts on Fifties Gangster Films." *The Velvet Light Trap* 11 (1974), pp. 17–19, illus.

Whitney, J. S. "A Filmography of Film Noir." *Journal of Popular Film*, Vol. V, #3–4 (1976), pp. 321–371, appendix, index.

Wilson, Richard. "Hoodlums: . . . Or the Reality." *Films and Filming* 5 no. 9 (1959), p. 10, illus.

Van Wert, William. "Philip Marlowe: Hardboiled to Softboiled to Poached." *Jump Cut* 3 (1974), pp. 10–13, illus., filmography.

Vesselo, Arthur. "Crime Over the World." *Sight and Sound* 6 no. 23 (1937), pp. 135–137, illus.

BIBLIOGRAPHY - 1979 TO 1991

Since the 1st Edition Bibliography was compiled, a significant number of other book-length general surveys of film noir have been published, five since the 2nd Edition in 1987, all of which are discussed in Appendix C. Of those volumes, the two by Robert Ottoson and Spencer Selby take the broadest view of what constitutes film noir and provide filmographic data and plot summaries on the greatest number of titles.

BOOKS

Clarens, Carlos. *Crime Movies*. New York: W.W. Norton, 1980. 351 pp., illus., bibliography, index.

SELECTED BIBLIOGRAPHY

Crowther, Bruce. *Film Noir: Reflections in a Dark Mirror*. London: Columbus Books, 1988. 192 pp., illus., bibliography, index.

Derry, Charles. *The Suspense Thriller*. Jefferson, North Carolina and London: McFarland and Co., 1988.

Erickson, Todd R. *Evidence of Film Noir in the Contemporary American Cinema*. Unpublished Master's Thesis, Brigham Young University, 1990. 198 pp., interviews, bibliography.

Gifford, Barry. *The Devil Thumbs A Ride & Other Unforgettable Films*. New York: Grove Press, 1988. 162 pp.

Guerif, Francois. *Le Film Noir Americain*. Paris: Henri Veyrier, 1979. 329 pp., illus., director filmographies, bibliography.

Hirsch, Foster. *The Dark Side of the Screen: Film Noir*. New York: A.S. Barnes, 1981. 229 pp., illus., index, bibliography, filmography (selected).

Hollinger, Karen Wallis. *Embattled Voices: the Narrator and the Woman in Film Noir and Women's Films*. Unpublished Doctoral Dissertation, University of Illinois, Chicago, 1990. 245 pp, bibliography, filmography (selected).

Kaplan, E. Ann, Editor. *Women in Film Noir*. London: British Film Institute, 1978. 129 pp., illus.

Krutnik, Frank. *In A Lonely Street, Film Noir, genre, masculinity*. London and New York: Routledge, 1991. 268 pp., index.

Luhr, William. *Raymond Chandler and Film*. New York: Frederick Ungar, 1982.

Ottoson, Robert. *A Reference Guide to the American Film Noir*. Metuchen, New Jersey: The Scarecrow Press, 1981. 285 pp., filmography, bibliography, index.

Porfirio, Robert. *The Dark Age of American Film: A Study of American Film Noir (1940-1960)*. Unpublished Doctoral Dissertation, Yale University, 1979. 526 pp., illus., filmographies, chronologies, bibliography.

Richardson, Carl. *Autopsy: An Element of Realism in American Film Noir*. Metuchen, New Jersey: The Scarecrow Press, 1992. 247 pp., illus., bibliography, index.

Rosow, Eugene. *Born to Lose, The Gangster Film in America*. New York: Oxford University Press, 1978. 422 pp., illus., index.

Schickel, Richard. *Double Indemnity*. London: BFI Publishing, 1992. 72 pp. illus., filmography, bibliography.

Selby, Spencer. *Dark City, the Film Noir*. Jefferson, North Carolina and London: McFarland and Co., 1984. 255 pp., illus., filmography, chronology, bibliography, index.

Straw, William O. *Problems in the Historiography of Cinema: the Case of Film Noir*. Unpublished Master's Thesis, McGill University, 1980.

Telotte, J.P. *Voices in the Dark, The Narrative Patterns of Film Noir*. Urbana and Chicago, University of Illinois Press, 1989. 248 pp., illus., filmography, bibliography, index.

Tuska, Jon. *Dark Cinema: American Film Noir in Cultural Perspective*. Westport, Connecticut: Greenwood Press, 1984. 305 pp., illus, chronology, bilbiography, index.

Werner, Paul. *Film Noir: Die Schattenspiele der ''Schwarzen Serie.''* Frankfurt: Fischer-Taschenbach, 1985.

PERIODICALS

Baxter, John. "Something More than Night." *Film Journal* 2 no. 4 (1975), pp. 4-11, illus.

Butler, Jeremy G. "Miami Vice: The Legacy of Film Noir." *Journal of Popular Film* 13 no. 3 (Autumn, 1985), pp. 127-138, illus.

Curtis, Terry Fox. "Hardboiled Hollywood - City Knights." *Film Comment* 20 no. 5 (October, 1984), pp. 29-49, illus., filmo.

Damico, James. "Film Noir: A Modest Proposal." *Film Reader* 3 (1978), pp. 48-57.

Dorfman, Richard. "Conspiracy City." *Journal of Popular Film and Television*, 7 No. 4 (1980), pp. 434-456, illus.

Ewing, Dale E., Jr. "Film Noir: Style and Content." *Journal of Popular Film and Television* 16 no. 2 (Summer, 1988), pp. 60-69.

House, Rebecca. "Night of the Soul: American Film Noir." *Studies in Popular Culture*, No 1 (1986), pp. 61-83.

Jenkins, S. "James M. Cain and Film Noir." *Screen No. 23* (1982), pp. 80-82. Kerr, Paul. "Out of What Past? Notes on the B film noir." *Screen Education*, Nos. 32-33 (Autumn/Winter, 1979-80), pp. 220-244.

Krutnik, Frank. "Desire, Transgression, and James M. Cain." *Screen No. 23* (1982), pp. 31-44, illus.

Maltby, Richard. "Film Noir: the Politics of the Maladjusted Text." *Journal of American Studies* 18 no. 1 (1984), pp. 49-71.

Nachbar, Jack. "Film Noir" in *Film Genres*. Wes D. Gehring, editor. Westport, Connecticut: Greenwood Press, 1988, pp. 64-84.

Polan, Dana. "Film Noir." *Journal of Film & Video* (Spring, 1985), pp. 75-83.

Porfirio, Robert G. "Whatever Happened to the Film Noir: The Postman Always Rings Twice (1946-1981)." *Literature/Film Quarterly* (No. 2, 1985).

Renov, Michael. "Raw Deal: the Woman in the Text." *Wide Angle* 6 no. 2 (1984), pp. 18-22.

Schiff, S. "Collector's Choice: Film Noir, a dozen gloomy movies on cassette that shine in a darkened living room." *American Film* (May, 1983), pp. 21-23.

Schlappner, Martin. "The Cinema" in *Evil*. Curatorium of the C.G. Jung Institute, editors. Evanston, Illinois: Northwestern University Press, 1967, pp. 139-145.

Tabrizian, M. "Correct Distance: Photo Texts on Film Noir." *Screen* No. 25 (1984), pp. 157-163, illus.

Telotte, J.P. "Talk and Trouble, Kiss Me Deadly's Deadly Discourse." *Journal of Popular Film* (No. 2, 1985), pp. 69-79, illus.

Vernet, Marc. "The Filmic Transition: on the Openings of Films Noirs." *Velvet Light Trap* 20 (Summer, 1983), pp. 2-9, illus.

Wegner, Hart. "From Expressionism to Film Noir: Otto Preminger's WHERE THE SIDEWALK ENDS." *Journal of Popular Film and Television* 13 no. 2 (Summer, 1985), pp. 59-65, illus.

INDEX

Both films and novels appear in italics. Novels are identified as such parenthetically. Production years appear only where needed to distinguish between films with the same title, for example: *The Glass Key* (1935) and *The Glass Key* (1942). Page numbers in italics indicate illustrations. Working titles appear in italics and are cross-indexed to the release titles. Pseudonyms are cross-indexed to actual names. Due to the amount of filmographic data contained in this volume, all major cast and technicians are included, but only the more prominent bit players are indexed. Whenever secondary materials have supported it, variant spellings in the credits are standardized. In other instances, spellings from primary sources have been reproduced as is.

INDEX